MARKETING, 8E

Book Activation Key

015

This key activates your online textbook.
Scratch off gray area above to see your book activation key. If the key is
already visible, then it has been used and is no longer valid. Contact us at
www.atomicdog.com or **800-310-5661 x6** to order your online textbook.

Marketing, 8e

MARKETING IN THE 21st CENTURY

Joel R. Evans
Hofstra University

Barry Berman
Hofstra University

Cincinnati, OH
www.atomicdogpublishing.com

ISBN 1-931442-07-X

Library of Congress Control Number: 2001093343

Printed in the United States of America by Atomic Dog Publishing, 1203 Main Street, Third floor,
Cincinnati, OH 45210.

10 9 8 7 6 5 4 3 2

To

Linda, Stacey, and Jennifer
Linda; Glenna, Paul, and Danielle; and Lisa and Ben

Brief Contents

Contents

Part 3 Consumer Analysis: Understanding and Responding to Diversity in the Marketplace 221

Part 6 Promotion Planning 509

Part 7 Price Planning 593

Part 8 Marketing Management 651

Appendixes

Indexes

Preface

In moving into the new millennium, *Marketing, 8e* has undergone a dramatic and exhilarating transformation into a state-of-the-art multimedia package. Our new subtitle, *Marketing in the 21st Century*, is not just a cute catchphrase. It is intended to signify that we are focused on the marketing concepts that will be essential for the future success of any organization or person, presented in a technologically advanced pedagogical format. We are proud to lead the principles of marketing textbook market into the realm of full reader interactivity—at a value price point.

Marketers in the 21st century, more than ever before, will need to understand and properly apply new communication technologies, especially on the World Wide Web. Although the media have widely reported on the difficulties associated with *E-commerce* (referring to online sales transactions), the potential uses of E-marketing (encompassing any marketing activities conducted through the Internet, from customer analysis to marketing-mix components) are enormous.

With this in mind, *Marketing, 8e* not only covers emerging topics in detail, it does so in an interactive, dynamic matter. Here's how: The book can be purchased in two ways: (1) in a four-color print format with access to a full-featured Web site or (2) as a subscription to the full-featured Web site. The print version has all of the elements that you expect: comprehensive topical coverage, a colorful design, a mix of 40 short and long cases, career material, etc. The Web site has the complete text, chapter by chapter, in a reader-enticing format. It contains 1,500 hotlinks to actual Web sites, distributed throughout the book; 120 short online video clips, 4 to 6 in every chapter; more than 100 animated in-chapter figures that visually display flowcharts, bar charts, and so on; a clickable glossary so the reader can immediately see the definitions of key terms; a list of "Web Sites You Can Use" in each chapter (which also appears in the printed version); hotlinks to a strategic marketing plan outline; an online Web exercise in each chapter; and a whole lot more!

These are fascinating times for all of us. During recent years, we have seen the true arrival of the PC age and the World Wide Web, the steady movement in the United States and many other nations around the globe to service- rather than production-driven economies, a growing understanding and interest in customer service and customer satisfaction, greater attention to consumer diversity in the marketplace, the emergence of free-market economies in Eastern Europe, business and government grappling with such ethical issues as the consumer's right to privacy, the impact of deregulation on society, and a host of other actions.

The years ahead promise to be even more intriguing, as the European Union adds more member countries; nations in the Americas make their markets more accessible to one another; other foreign opportunities grow; technological advances continue; and we try to cope with slow-growth economies in various parts of the globe. As we prepare for the coming decade and beyond, an appreciation of marketing (and its roles and activities) become critical.

We believe that a 21st century principles of marketing textbook must incorporate both traditional and contemporary aspects of marketing, carefully consider environmental factors, address the roles of marketing managers, and show the relevance of marketing for those who interact with or who are affected by marketing activities (such as consumers). We also believe such a textbook should describe marketing concepts to readers in a lively, comprehensive, and balanced way. As we indicate at the start of Chapter 1, marketing is "an exciting, fast-paced, and contemporary business discipline."

Although the basic components of marketing (such as consumer behavior, marketing research and information systems, and product, distribution, promotion, and price planning) form the foundation of any introductory-level marketing textbook, contemporary techniques and topics also need to be covered in depth. Among the contemporary topics that are examined in full-chapter length in *Marketing,, 8e* are developing and enacting strategic marketing plans; societal, ethical, and consumer issues; global marketing; marketing and the Web; organizational consumers (including manufacturers, wholesalers, retailers, government, and nonprofit organizations); goods versus services marketing (including nonprofit marketing); integrated marketing communications; and coordinating and analyzing the marketing plan. Environmental effects are noted throughout the book.

Marketing, 8e explains all major principles, defines key terms, integrates topics, and demonstrates how marketers make everyday and long-run decisions. Examples based on such diverse organizations as Amazon.com, BMW, British Airways, Coca-Cola, ESPN, General Electric, Kenmore, Lands' End, Metropolitan Life, Napster, Nestlé, Swatch, Toyota, United Parcel Service (UPS), Visa, Yahoo!, and Wrigley appear in each chapter. The examples build on the text materials, reveal the stimulating and dynamic nature of marketing, cover a wide variety of firms, and involve students in real-life applications of marketing.

A NEW TRADITION BEGINS WITH *MARKETING, 8E*

We are as dedicated today as in the first edition of *Marketing* to have **the** most contemporary principles of marketing text on the market. Thus, we have listened very carefully to the feedback from our colleagues, students, and our new Atomic Dog Publishing team. And we have acted on this feedback. The world is evolving and so are we. *Marketing, 8e* has some major changes, which can be divided into two categores: interactive learning and content.

Interactive Learning Brings *Marketing, 8e* to Life

During the time that we have worked on *Marketing, 8e*, we have been dazzled by the skills of Atomic Dog Publishing. We hope you will be, too. As was already noted, *Marketing, 8e* has a full-featured, highly interactive Web site. We believe this Web site will motivate students to learn about marketing principles in a way that encourages their participation in the learning process. **Our goal is to move the reader from passive learning to active learning.**

These are just some of the ways in which our Web site brings *Marketing, 8e* to life:

- The complete text is available online. Material may be accessed via concise, simple-to-follow sections. There is a drop-down screen in every chapter that enables the reader to easily move between topics in the chapter.

- There are animated figures in each chapter to illustrate key concepts. For example, in Chapter 1, the reader can see how marketing evolves, era by era; in Chapter 10, alternative consumer demand patterns actually break apart or move together; in Chapter 12, the goods/services continuum is easier to understand through its visual depiction; and in Chapter 22, sales analysis is enlivened.

- The figures are not only animated; they are also highly interactive. Through the use of "mouseovers" and "clickovers," the reader can access more information (such as definitions and examples) about the topics in the figures. This means that the online design of the figures is less cluttered and that instant self-testing is possible.

- All of the in-chapter key terms are linked to the glossary. With just a click, the definition of a term appears onscreen.

- Through a drop-down screen, the reader can do a key word search for any topic in the book from any chapter in the book.

- To further involve the reader, there are numerous short video clips, carefully selected and tied into the text.

- Each chapter has in-chapter study questions.

- At the end of each chapter, there is a full study guide for the chapter, complete with a series of self-review questions and their answers.

- A simple click connects the reader to one of the 1,500 hotlinks that are noted throughout the book. These links deal with a wide range of organizations and information. At the end of every chapter, online and in print, there is a section called "Web Sites You Can Use;" and there is a Web-based exercise.

- At the beginning of each part of the online book, there is a hotlink to the relevant section of a strategic marketing plan.

- There are 18 computer exercises (keyed to important marketing topics) that are available through an online download. In addition, there is a comprehensive computerized strategic planning exercise (keyed to Chapter 3).

Content Changes for the 21st Century

Here is a synopsis of the content changes we have made for *Marketing, 8e*. We hope you are pleased with them:

1. The book is shorter, without any dilution of coverage. There are now 22 chapters (rather than 23).

2. These substantive chapter changes have been made:

   a. Chapter 1 (Marketing Today)—The coverage of customer service and relationship marketing is enhanced.

   b. Chapter 2 (The Environment in Which Marketing Operates)—The discussion of corporate culture is expanded. Examples are more focused.

   c. Chapter 3 (Developing and Enacting Strategic Marketing Plans)—The section "Devising a Strategic Marketing Plan" has been greatly revised. There is a much more detailed strategic marketing plan online, with a new comprehensive computer exercise (which is explained in a Chapter 3 appendix).

   d. Chapter 4 (Information for Marketing Decisions)—There are now several hotlinks to firms that market commercial data bases, as well as examples of online marketing research.

e. Chapter 5 (Societal, Ethical, and Consumer Issues)—Throughout the chapter, there are hotlinks to organizations and government agencies involved with societal, ethical, and consumer issues.

f. Chapter 6 (Global Aspects of Marketing)—To provide more insights about the global marketplace, several online resources are noted and hotlinks to leading economic communities are provided.

g. Chapter 7 (Marketing and the Internet)—This **new chapter** demonstrates why the Internet is a valuable marketing tool, explores the multifaceted potential marketing roles for the Internet, shows how to develop an Internet marketing strategy, illustrates how the Internet is being utilized to enhance marketing strategies, considers the challenges of using the Internet in marketing, and forecasts the future of E-marketing.

h. Chapters 8–10 (Part 3: Consumer Analysis)—All examples and data are new or have been updated. The material on final consumer demographics, lifestyles, and decision making has been combined into one chapter (Chapter 8: Final Consumers) to create a smoother flow of information.

i. Chapters 11–13 (Part 4: Product Planning)—The material on branding and packaging has been integrated into Chapter 11 (Basic Concepts in Product Planning). The "Web Sites You Can Use" section in Chapter 12 (Goods Versus Services Planning) has hotlinks to dozens of diverse organizations that engage in service marketing. The discussion on the product life cycle has been moved to Chapter 13 (Conceiving, Developing, and Managing Products).

j. Chapters 14–16 (Part 5: Distribution Planning)—Chapter 14 (Value Chain Management and Logistics) now focuses more on the value chain, the value delivery chain, and logistics. In Chapters 15 (Wholesaling) and 16 (Retailing), the sections on recent trends have been completely revised.

k. Chapters 17–19 (Part 6: Promotion Planning)—Chapter 17 (Integrated Marketing Communications) has much greater coverage of integrated marketing communications, and introduces that topic early in the chapter. Chapters 18 (Advertising and Public Relations) and 19 (Personal Selling and Sales Promotion) have been thoroughly updated.

l. Chapters 20–21 (Part 7: Price Planning)—All data and examples are new or have been updated. Many hotlinks have been added.

m. Chapter 22 (Pulling It All Together: Integrating and Analyzing the Marketing Plan)—There is greater emphasis on the value of integrated marketing plans and enhanced coverage of benchmarking and customer satisfaction research.

3. All of the opening vignettes are new. The vignettes deal with major events that relate to the chapter at hand, such as valuing the customer's time, do-it-yourself research, college students and the Web, low-budget integrated marketing communications, and the value of economies of scale in marketing.

4. All in-chapter boxes are new. Two of the boxes have a similar theme as the prior edition of *Marketing*: "Ethical Issues in Marketing" and "Global Marketing in Action."

The theme of the third box is new: "Marketing and the Web." The boxes' thought-provoking nature has been retained.

a. The ethics boxes involve such subjects as "Big Business Does Not Have to Mean Bad Ethics," "Taking Advantage of Vulnerable Consumers for Diet Products," "Should There Be a 'Cocktail Hour' on Television?," and "Will Napster's New Business Model Succeed?"

b. The global boxes deal with such subjects as "When in Rome: Playing by Different Rules for Advertising to Children," "The Declining Reliance on English in Online Activities," "Innovation: Anywhere, Any Time," and "Paying the Price for Growing Too Fast in Global Markets."

c. The Web boxes cover such subjects as "Internet Sales May Be Taxing—Or Maybe Not!," "Measuring Web Site Effectiveness by Counting Eyeballs," "Doing a College Search without Leaving Home," and "Bargaining for a Vacation with an Internet Auction."

5. "Web Sites You Can Use" is a new, very reader-friendly, in-text feature. In every chapter, just before the summary, there is a listing of valuable Web sites for marketers. These chapter-related Web sites range from search engines to shopping venues to benchmarking practices.

6. All cases are new and divided by part. Among the organizations included in the 32 short cases are AT&T, Deere, Dial, Ikea, Kinko's, and Xerox. The 8 comprehensive cases deal with "Customer Research, Not Marketing Research," "The True Price of Penalties," "Transactional Segmentation to Slow Customer Defections," "Market-Driven Product Development," "Communicating for Better Channel Relationships," "Communications and Sports Marketing," "Value Measures in the Executive Suite," and "Creating Long-Term Marketing Health."

7. All data and examples are as current as possible.

8. The careers appendix (Appendix A) has been expanded and has a number of hotlinks.

9. The computer exercises, keyed to the text, have been revised and are included in Appendix C.

BUILDING ON THE STRONG FOUNDATION OF *MARKETING*

These **general features** have been retained from prior editions of *Marketing*:

- A lively easy-to-read writing style.
- A balanced treatment of topics (by size of firm, goods- and service-based firms, profit-oriented and nonprofit firms, final and organizational consumers, etc.).
- Comprehensive coverage of all important marketing concepts, including eleven chapters on the marketing mix (product, distribution, promotion, and price planning).
- A full-color design throughout the book, including lots of photos and figures. These illustrations are all keyed to the text, as well as visually attractive.
- Part openers that provide integrated overviews of the chapters in every part.

- Many definitions from the American Marketing Association's *Dictionary of Marketing Terms*.
- Early coverage of societal, ethical, and consumer issues, and global marketing (Chapters 5 and 6 respectively).
- Service marketing coverage in the section on product planning (Chapter 12).
- A mix of short and long cases, 40 in all (four short cases and one comprehensive case per part).
- An appendix on careers in marketing.
- An appendix on marketing mathematics.
- An appendix on computerized exercises that accompany the text. A computer symbol in the relevant chapters keys the exercises to the concepts involved.
- A detailed glossary.
- Separate company, name, and subject indexes.

These features have also been retained and are contained **in each chapter:**

- Chapter objectives that outline the major areas to be investigated.
- An opening vignette that introduces the material through a real-world situation.
- An introductory overview that sets the tone for the chapter.
- Thought-provoking boxed extracts on key marketing topics.
- Descriptive marginal notes (in the print version) that highlight major concepts.
- Boldface key terms that identify important definitions.
- Many flowcharts and current figures and tables that explain how marketing concepts operate and provide up-to-date information.
- Numerous footnotes to enable the reader to do further research.
- Chapter summaries keyed to chapter objectives. These summaries are followed by a listing of key terms, with text page references.
- End-of-chapter questions divided into separate "review" and "discussion" categories.

THE *MARKETING, 8E* PACKAGE

A complete package accompanies *Marketing, 8e*. For students, there are online computerized exercises, a study guide, numerous hotlinks to career information, current events, etc. For professors, there are lecture and resource materials, as well as testing materials. To aid the classroom learning experience, there are longer video clips and hundreds of PowerPoint slides.

HOW *MARKETING, 8E* IS ORGANIZED

Marketing, 8e is divided into eight parts. Part 1 presents marketing in a contemporary society, describes the environment within which it operates, presents strategic planning from a marketing perspective, and discusses marketing information systems and the marketing research process. Part 2 covers the broad scope of marketing: societal, ethical, and consumer issues; global marketing; and marketing and the Internet. Part 3 deals with marketing's central thrust: understanding final and organizational consumers in the diverse marketplace. It examines demographics, lifestyle factors, consumer decision making, target market strategies, and sales forecasting.

Part 4 encompasses product planning, branding and packaging, goods versus services marketing, the product life cycle, new products, and mature products. Part 5 deals with distribution planning, value chain management, logistics, wholesaling, and retailing. Part 6 examines integrated promotion planning, the channel of communication, advertising, public relations, personal selling, and sales promotion. Part 7 covers price planning, price strategies, and applications of pricing. Part 8 integrates marketing planning—including benchmarking and customer satisfaction measurement—and looks to the future.

Please note: we don't want you getting lost as you move between the Web and print formats, so we numbered the primary heads and subheads in each chapter the same. For example, the first primary head in Chapter 1 is labeled 1-1, the second primary head in this chapter is labeled 1-2, and so on. The subheads build from the designation of their corresponding primary head: 1-1a, 1-1b, etc.

The numbering system is designed to make moving between the online and print versions as seamless as possible. So if your instructor tells you to read the material in 2-3 and 2-4 for tomorrow's assignment, you'll know that the information appears in Chapter 2 of both the Web and print versions of the text, and you can then choose the best way for you to complete the assignment.

We are pleased that previous editions of *Marketing* were adopted at hundreds of colleges and universities nationwide and around the world. We hope *Marketing, 8e* is satisfying to continuing adopters and meets the needs of new ones. Thanks for your support and encouragement.

Please feel free to communicate with us. We welcome comments regarding any aspect of *Marketing, 8e* or its package: Joel R. Evans or Barry Berman, Department of Marketing and International Business, Hofstra University, Hempstead, N.Y., 11549. You can E-mail us at mktjre@hofstra.edu or mktbxb@hofstra.edu. We promise to reply to any correspondence we receive.

Joel R. Evans
Barry Berman
Hofstra University

A Brief Walk Through

MARKETING, 8e: *Marketing in the 21st Century*

In this walking tour, you will find an overview of several distinctive features of *Marketing in the 21st Century.* Through these features, we present the most complete coverage possible of the field of marketing—and do so in an interesting, interactive, and contemporary way.

It's all covered—from absolute product failure to yield management pricing.

Marketing in the 21st Century. introduces and integrates key marketing concepts, many of which have grown in importance in recent years, such as commercial data bases, integrated marketing communications, marketing and the Internet, strategic marketing plans, and value chain management.

4-2b Commercial Data Bases

Commercial data bases can provide useful ongoing information.

Because client companies need current, comprehensive, and relatively inexpensive information about the environment in which they operate, many specialized research firms offer ongoing **commercial data bases** with information on population traits, the business environment, economic forecasts, industry and individual companies' performance, and other items. Data bases may include newspaper and magazine articles, business and house-

We look at how commercial data bases enhance marketing decision making.

17-3 AN INTEGRATED APPROACH TO PROMOTION PLANNING

When a well-coordinated promotion plan is developed and applied, a firm uses **integrated marketing communications (IMC).** As defined by the American Association of Advertising Agencies (www.aaaa.org), IMC "recognizes the value of a comprehensive plan that evaluates the strategic roles of a variety of communication disciplines—advertising, public relations, personal selling, and sales promotion—and combines them to provide clarity, consistency, and maximum communication impact."[5] For example, Frito-Lay

The value of integrated marketing communications is an underlying theme in *Marketing.*

TABLE 7-1	Top 10 Countries' Internet Penetration of the Home Market, as of January 2001			
	Active Home Users	**Average Time Spent Per Month**	**Average Number of Sessions Per Month**	**Active Home Users as a Percentage of Total Population**
United States	101.4 million	9 hours, 58 min.	18	36
Japan	15.4 million	7 hours, 57 min.	16	12

The marketing potential of the Internet around the globe is discussed.

3-6a A Sample Outline for a Written Strategic Marketing Plan

What are the ingredients of a good strategic marketing plan? Here is a brief list:

* It should be integrated into an organization's overall business plan.
* It should affect the consideration of strategic choices.
* It should force a long-range view.
* It should make the resource allocation system visible.

We fully describe how to build a strategic marketing plan.

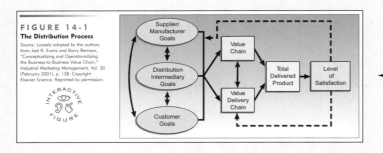

FIGURE 14-1
The Distribution Process
Source: Loosely adapted by the authors from Joel R. Evans and Barry Berman, "Conceptualizing and Operationalizing the Business-to-Business Value Chain," *Industrial Marketing Management,* Vol. 30 (February 2001), p. 138. Copyright Elsevier Science. Reprinted by permission.

The importance of the value chain and the value delivery chain are highlighted.

This highlights our extensive coverage of domestic and global marketing.

Sephora (www.sephora.com) is a retail concept intent on generating loyal customers: Founded in 1993, Sephora is the leading chain of perfume and cosmetics stores in France and the second biggest in Europe. It has stores in France, Luxembourg, Spain, Italy, Portugal, Poland, Germany, Great Britain, and Japan; and it is growing rapidly. Sephora

FIGURE 1-8

Sephora: Bringing Its Relationship Marketing Philosophy to Perfume and Cosmetics

Offering custom colors is one of the many tactics used by Sephora to generate repeat business and very loyal shoppers.

Source: Reprinted by permission of PricewaterhouseCoopers.

Because we believe marketing's vital role should be shown in varied situations, we have worked especially hard to present a balance of examples on domestic and international marketing, large and small firms, goods and services, and final consumers and organizational consumers.

Small firms, as well as large ones, are involved with marketing and strategic planning.

3-6b Moonstruck Chocolatier: A Strategic Marketing Plan by a Small Specialty Firm[28]

In 1992, Bill Simmons and his wife Deb decided to open Moonstruck Chocolatier in Portland, Oregon. Moonstruck opened for business in 1993 as a maker of truffles for the wholesale market. It sold to other retailers, including Neiman Marcus, Marshall Field, and Starbucks. The firm introduced it first retail store in 1996 and sales rose rapidly. Today, Moonstruck is a successful firm, specializing in chocolate-based products, with annual

Although a small company, Moonstruck Chocolatier has a detailed strategic marketing plan.

Chapter 12 ("Goods Versus Services Planning") integrates services marketing into product planning.

12-3a A Goods/Services Continuum

A *goods/services continuum* categorizes products along a scale from pure goods to pure services. With pure goods, the seller offers the consumer only physical goods without any accompanying services. With pure services, the seller offers the consumer only nongoods services without any accompanying physical goods. Between the two extremes, the seller would offer good/service combinations to the consumer.

With a goods/services continuum products are positioned from pure goods to pure services.

Both final and organizational consumers are important to marketers.

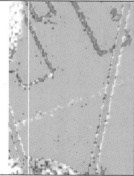

8 Final Consumers

This chapter is devoted to final consumer demographics, lifestyles, and decision making. We examine several specific demographics (objective and quantifiable characteristics that describe the population) for the United States and other countries around the globe. By studying final consumer lifestyles and decision making, we can learn about why and how consumers act as they do. Lifestyles encompass various social and psychological factors, many of which we note here. The decision process involves the steps as consumers move from stimulus to purchase or nonpurchase.

9 Organizational Consumers

Here, we focus on organizational consumers purchasing goods and services for further production, use in operations, or resale to other consumers. We look at how they differ from final consumers and at their individual characteristics, buying goals, buying structure, constraints on purchases, and decision process.

For *Marketing, 8e: Marketing in the 21st Century,* we have three all-new thought-provoking boxes in every chapter:

- "Ethical Issues in Marketing."
- "Global Marketing in Action."
- "Marketing and the Web."

Each box presents a real-life situation and asks the reader to be a decision maker and state a position or make suggestions.

ETHICAL Issues in Marketing

Chapter	Title
1	Goodyear: Trying to Capitalize on Bridgestone/Firestone's Public Relations Disaster
2	Yes, Deere, the EPA Can Be a Friend to Business (Sometimes, Anyway)
3	Making Sense of Confusing Company Earnings Reports
4	On the Internet, Is There Any Privacy Regarding Personal Information?
5	Big Business Does Not Have to Mean Bad Ethics
6	The Hybrid Eco-Car: The Japanese Take the Lead
7	At Online Auction Sites, Who Is Responsible for Fraud in Selling Bogus Goods?
8	Taking Advantage of Vulnerable Consumers for Diet Products
9	The Virtues of Assisting Minority-Operated Suppliers
10	In a Product Recall, Should All Customers Be Treated the Same?
11	What Is an SUV—And Why Does It Matter?
12	Cause Marketing: Profiting by Giving
13	Why Scotchgard Was Withdrawn as a Protector of Fabrics and Upholstery
14	The "People's Republic of Counterfeiting"
15	The Battle Between Property Owners and Their Hotel Operators
16	The Good Works of Starbucks
17	The Creativity of Big Tobacco
18	Should There Be a "Cocktail Hour" on Television?
19	The Controversy Behind Free Drug Samples
20	The Winners and Losers in Gray Markets
21	Hello, We Have a Cheaper Fare Online
22	Can a New Napster Business Model Succeed?

GLOBAL Marketing in Action

Chapter	Title
1	Wired in the U.S.A., Wireless in Europe
2	When in Rome: Playing by Different Rules for Advertising to Children
3	Sweden's Electrolux: The Quiet Giant
4	Nestlé's E-Revolution: From Information to Action
5	Overturning a Ban on Tobacco Advertising
6	Alibaba.com: An Asia-Based Worldwide Internet Trading Portal
7	The Declining Reliance on English in Online Activities
8	Marketing High-Tech Status Products in China
9	Show Me That You Want Me: How Foreign Countries Attract Businesses
10	The Gender Gap in E-Tailing Outside the United States
11	Generic Brands Come to Brazil
12	Virgin Air: Stormy Weather Ahead
13	Innovation: Anywhere, Any Time
14	Optimizing Supply Chains
15	Thailand's Siam Makro: A Wholesaling Powerhouse
16	Who Owns Dunkin' Donuts Anyway?
17	Promotion in India: New Strategies Come into Focus
18	U.S. Public Relations Blunders Overseas
19	Loyalty Programs Welcomed in South America
20	The Euro: An Underachieving New Currency
21	Is It Possible for Prices to Be Too Low?
22	Paying the Price for Growing Too Fast in Global Markets

MARKETING *and the Web*

Marketing in the 21st Century has 32 short cases (four per part) and 8 comprehensive part cases. These cases cover a wide range of companies and scenarios. All are new to this edition and extremely current.

PART 1 SHORT CASES
Case 1

It's Not Easy Being a Consumer [1-1]

Some market analysts believe that today is the best time for consumers. Their viewpoint is based on the increased amount of consumer choices due to the number of new products and to deregulation. In addition, the Web provides people with improved access to information, as well as an added form of competition.

The number of auto models has doubled since the 1970s. So have the number of cereals, book titles, and toothpastes. In telecommunications there are now hundreds of long-distance carriers, up from one in the 1970s and three major carriers in the 1980s. And while there were only 300 mutual funds in the 1970s, there are now more than 7,200. A frequently cited statistic is that there are now more mutual funds than individually listed stocks. Likewise, online shopping bots such as mySimon (www.mysimon.com), CNET (www.cnet.com), and Yahoo! Shopping (www.shopping.yahoo.) enable consumers to compare prices and offerings from their homes and offices. The Web also represents another marketing channel for manufacturers, wholesalers, and retailers.

A big ramification of increased choice is that the consumer now faces a much more complex shopping environment. Consumer decision making has also gotten more difficult due to the presence of whole categories of products that did not exist 10 to 20 years ago (such as personal computers, DVD players, CD burners, and high-definition TV). Thus, while increased choice is positive from a competitive perspective, it may generate confusion among customers.

What can marketers do to reduce confusion and simplify consumer choice? One strategy is for firms to facilitate the process by offering fewer alternatives. For example, it is easier for a consumer to evaluate and choose a vacuum cleaner at Sears when three models—"good," "better," and "best"—are offered than when consumers must choose among a dozen or so alternatives. This limited-choice strategy may also provide the retailer with higher inventory turnover, lower training expenses, and lower overall sales costs.

Another strategy is for companies to simplify pricing. Airfare pricing is clearly an area that needs attention! In addition to the confusion of numerous fare categories and conditions, the current large number of fares for the same flight requires considerable time for travel agents and reservations clerks to explain to customers. In the long-distance telephone market, Sprint is a good example of how a firm increased both revenues and profits when it switched to a single price per minute of long-distance service.

Firms can further simplify the choice process by focusing on those market segments where they have the greatest ability to add value. An example of a firm that uses this focused strategy is Charles Schwab. While Schwab's initial target customer was the "do-it-yourself" investor who was attracted by the low transaction costs, the company has since expanded its target market to include customers desiring a fuller range of financial services (such as a portfolio of mutual funds). This strategy made Schwab better able to offer different types of value propositions to different target groups of customers.

Lastly, companies need to examine the overall costs of the customer's total experience, not just the basic costs of the good or service. Included in the total-cost approach should be the costs of searching for the appropriate good or service. Thus, firms that provide easy access, or high levels of information, to consumers may have lower costs than the "lower basic price" marketers that do not provide such services.

Questions

1. Describe how this case illustrates the "value-based philosophy" aspect of the marketing concept.
2. What are the ramifications of "do-it-yourself" firms shifting basic marketing functions from the firms to their consumers?
3. If the large number of airfares causes consumer confusion, why do you think most airlines have so many fares?
4. Explain how a Web-based transaction can reduce a consumer's total cost.

Each of the eight parts in *Marketing* ends with four short cases on real companies.

PART 8 COMPREHENSIVE CASE

Creating Long-Term Marketing Health [pc-8]

Introduction

When financial results are not up to standard, marketing generally is viewed as a prescription drug to be taken in larger doses to help cure lackluster performance. The advice is to increase advertising and sales promotion, cut prices, expand distribution, and add more products aimed at smaller target markets. Dispensed in strong dosages, the medicine seldom works. Moreover, the marketers who have prescribed it have become more suspect. They've fostered the view that marketing is a "quick fix" to a firm's poor results, rather than convincing chief executive officers (CEOs) of marketing's long-term strategic role.

Marketing is viewed as a short-term fix because the metrics used are calibrated to measure short-term organizational outcomes or results. Like a thermometer measuring body temperature on a real-time basis, marketing is evaluated on daily, weekly, or monthly sales, market share, and profit margin. Economist John Maynard Keynes said, "We may plan for the long run but we eat in the short run." CEOs and chief marketing officers (CMOs) have jointly embraced marketing's central role in helping the organization eat in the short run. We feast on short-term gains of marketing expenditures today; however, we don't do things that invest in marketing's long-term contribution to the firm today, we won't eat tomorrow.

Marketing Health

A marketing organization is healthy when it can build and maintain exchange relationships with both customers and suppliers under conditions of competitive, technological, and economic turbulence. These unstable environments create stress for the organization, making it difficult to survive and prosper. During such times, it won't work to take more drugs because the weakened or faltering firm must have a reservoir of good health to survive and recover.

There are 10 indicators of marketing health that can be divided into three areas: potential, people, and performance. CMOs wanting to guide their organization's health must focus them on markets with long-term potential; recruit and retain people with the necessary knowledge, skills, and experience; and develop performance metrics that foster a long-term orientation.

Potential

Organizations with good long-term marketing health focus on future market potential. One such firm is Procter & Gamble Co. (www.pg.com), which continually focuses on both high-potential geographic and product markets. More than a quarter century ago,

it began to put a high priority on global expansion, and by 1993, international business represented more than half of total annual sales. Today, P&G employs more than 100,000 people in 140 nations. Although the firm had focused on North America and Western Europe, it now commits to obtaining new growth from emerging markets. Product innovation aimed at developing new brands and improving existing brands is a constant priority and essential to a strategy to double business over the next decade. This doesn't prevent P&G from pursuing acquisitions in attractive and high-potential markets, such as acquiring Tambrands and its market-leading tampon brand, Tampax.

Metric No. 1: Percent of sales from products introduced in the last three years; and percent of sales from markets (geographic or product) entered in the last three years. All products and markets have life cycles; they are born, and then they grow, mature, decline, and decay. Companies that don't recognize this continue to live off past product and market successes. Importantly, they're not staying fit by innovating and creating tomorrow's breadwinners. Consequently, once sales and profits begin to stagnate or decline, it's too late to recover. Drugs and marketing quick fixes won't work.

It is suggested that the CMO and CEO (possibly in conjunction with the chief financial officer) set specific goals for Metric No. 1. No matter whether the goal is 10 percent or 50 percent or for three or five years, it will communicate and send a clear signal throughout the organization that new product and market development are critical to future success. Because financial markets favor sales largely derived from new products, if a company succeeds in achieving its goals regarding this metric, it also will find that the financial markets will respond with increased firm valuation (see Metrics No. 7 and No. 8). This is because firm valuation is a function of expected future cash flows.

Metric No. 2: Percent growth projected over the next three years in size of target market(s). Another indicator of potential is in the growth of the firm's target market(s). The huge attention today on the over-65 age group stems from its projected growth and its specialized needs for many goods and services. As a former director of the U.S. Census Bureau said, "When firms fail to focus their marketing efforts toward the future, they may discover their markets do not have much of a future." If a firm focuses substantial marketing resources on yesterday's growth markets, then it's misallocating marketing resources.

Metric No. 3: Percent of sales over the last three years from new-wave marketing channels. Perhaps one of the most significant opportunity sources occurs in distribution channels. These channels respond to changes in how people would like to buy or secure goods and services. Although with the growth of E-commerce, we tend to view this as a recent phenomenon; it's not new. Department stores, supermarkets, category killers, membership stores, supercenters,

[pc-8] Adapted by the authors from Robert F. Lusch, "Creating Long-Term Marketing Health," *Marketing Management* (Spring 2000), pp. 18–22. Reprinted by permission of the American Marketing Association.

684

End-of-part cases integrate the material discussed in the group of chapters in particular parts of the text.

Our goal is to reinforce the principles in *Marketing in the 21st Century* in a useful and lively way. So, we've got all the in-text pedagogy you could want: part openers, chapter objectives, chapter vignettes, highlighted key terms and marginal notes, photos and line art, bottom-of-page footnotes, useful Web links, summaries linked to chapter objectives, review and discussion questions, appendixes, and more!

Chapter-opening vignettes engage students in marketing in a very reader-friendly manner. These vignettes cover diverse organizations and situations.

⟶

The fragmentation of the mass market and the rising importance of segmented media such as cable TV and special-interest magazines have led to greater use of market segmentation strategies by mainstream marketers. One newer segmentation strategy, called diversity marketing, focuses on pursuing customers on the basis of race and language preference.

Although it comprises only four percent of the U.S. population, the Asian-American market segment has been viewed as diversity's darlings. Not only is this market segment the fastest-growing population group according to census data, but also it is affluent and well educated. Of particular importance to marketers is the large spending by Asian-Americans on PCs, insurance, and international telephone calls.

One firm that has successfully appealed to Asian-Americans is the *New York Times*. Its campaign consisted of print ads, commercials, direct mail, and community events targeted directly at Asian-Americans. The campaign was so successful that the *Times* is expanding it from New York City to San Francisco, Oakland, and Silicon Valley in California.

For several reasons, reaching and appealing to this market segment is far from easy. One, marketers must fully understand the various cultural issues in dealing with Asian-Americans. For example, the number "4" may imply death and therefore would be a poor choice in a business telephone number. Two, there are significant differences among the ethnicities that comprise the Asian-American market. AT&T utilizes seven different languages to reach Asian-Americans, which increases the complexity and overall expense in reaching this segment. Three, vital marketing research data on the Asian-American market is often not available. Nielsen does not break out television viewership by Asian-Americans.

In an attempt to increase the information about Asian-Americans, the 2000 federal census, for the first time, was printed in four Asian languages (Chinese, Korean, Tagalog, and Vietnamese), in addition to English and Spanish. Census employees speaking each of these languages also staffed census telephone assistance centers. Some marketers feel the additional data will result in more ads being aimed at Asian-Americans by pharmaceutical firms, packaged food marketers, and health care providers.[1]

In this chapter, we will examine each step involved in planning a target market strategy and the related topic of sales forecasting. Ethnicity or race is only one of many possible bases of segmentation.

10-1 OVERVIEW

After gathering data on consumer traits, desires, and decision making, company and industry attributes, and environmental factors, a firm is ready to select the target market(s) to which it will appeal and for which it will develop a suitable strategy. The total *market* for a particular good or service consists of all the people and/or organizations who

*A **market** is all possible consumers for a good or service. Through **market segmentation**, it can be subdivided.*

[1]Stuart Elliott, "Marketers Study Nuances to Reach a Valued Audience," *New York Times on the Web* (March 6, 2000).

283

 **WEB SITES YOU CAN USE**

There are numerous Web sites that provide access to current and past advertisements. Many offer real-time video commercials. Here is a cross-section of sites where you can view or read ads [Please note: TV ads are best viewed through a high-speed connection. The download time may be lengthy with a telephone modem]:

AdCritic.com (www.adcritic.com)—TV commercials

Adeater (www.adeater.com)—Click on "Cinema library" to access thousands of TV commercials from around the world

Adflip (www.adflip.com)—Print ads

AdReview (www.adreview.com)—TV commercials

Advertising Council (www.adcouncil.org/fr_camp.html)—Multimedia public service announcements (PSAs)

USA TV Ads (www.usatvads.com)—TV commercials

In each chapter, there is a NEW feature entitled "Web Sites You Can Use."

⟵

About the Videos That Accompany
MARKETING, 8e: Marketing in the 21st Century

We have an extensive video supplement. There are 4 to 6 short video clips in each chapter of the online version of *Marketing in the 21st Century*. These clips are all tied to the text and reinforce major concepts. The print version shows video icons for these videos in each chapter.

In addition to the online in-chapter video clips, there are eight part videos that accompany *Marketing*. These videos are available to professors in a VCR format. They range from 6 to 9 minutes in length, based on marketing research that indicates a preference for videos of this length:

Part	*Video Title/Brief Summary*
1	**Marketing Research:** This video defines marketing research, applies marketing research to a study of the effectiveness of a Wendy's advertising campaign, and describes the research process.
2	**European Union:** This video explains the major economic implications of the European Union. Specific topics include the free movement of goods, common product standards, the opening of public procurement, and airline deregulation.
3	**Wholesale and Industrial Salesmanship:** This video focuses on the sales process. Major differences in selling consumer versus industrial products are noted. The role of competitive bidding in organizational marketing is also discussed.
4	**Product Planning:** This video distinguishes among convenience, shopping, specialty, and unsought products. The marketing implications of this classification system are reviewed.
5	**Franchising:** This video explores different types of franchising. Examples and trends are noted.
6	**Broadcast Media:** This video describes the planning and evaluation of TV advertising. Topics include the calculation of gross rating points, the characteristics of TV as an ad medium, and the appropriate use of cable and network TV.
7	**Markdown Planning:** This video explains the reasons for markdowns, the appropriate use of early markdowns and an automatic markdown policy, and the calculation of different types of markdowns.
8	**Relationship Marketing:** This video describes the use of relationship marketing principles by a small ladies' specialty clothing retailer, Harley Davidson, and Saturn autos.

About the Computer Supplements Accompanying MARKETING, 8e: Marketing in the 21st Century

As noted in the preface, *Marketing* has a series of computer exercises that may be downloaded from our Web site. These exercises are extremely user-friendly, are self-contained, and operate in the Windows environment. All directions are contained on computer screens and are self-prompting.

Computer-Based Marketing Exercises is designed to apply and reinforce specific individual concepts in *Marketing in the 21st Century*. The exercises are explained in Appendix C; and throughout *Marketing in the 21st Century*, a computer symbol signifies which concepts are related to the exercises:

1. Marketing Orientation
2. Boston Consulting Group Matrix
3. Questionnaire Analysis
4. Ethics in Action
5. Standardizing Marketing Plans
6. Vendor Analysis
7. Segmentation Analysis
8. Product Positioning
9. Services Strategy
10. Product Screening Checklist
11. Economic Order Quantity
12. Wholesaler Cost Analysis
13. Advertising Budget
14. Salesperson Deployment
15. Price Elasticity
16. Key Cost Concepts
17. Performance Ratios
18. Optimal Marketing Mix

There is also a detailed computer exercise, *StratMktPlan*, that encompasses all of the major elements of a strategic marketing plan. It is explained in a Chapter 3 appendix and linked to the part openers throughout *Marketing in the 21st Century*. This exercise may be downloaded separately from our Web site.

For professors who like to demonstrate how Excel may be applied in marketing situations, there is a special download at the Web site with a variety of simple Excel-based exercises.

Acknowledgments

Throughout our professional lives and during the period of time that the various editions of this book have been researched and written, a number of people have provided us with support, encouragement, and constructive criticism. We would like to publicly acknowledge and thank many of them.

In our years as graduate students, we benefited greatly from the knowledge transmitted from professors Conrad Berenson, Henry Eilbirt, and David Rachman, and colleagues Elaine Bernay, William Dillon, Stanley Garfunkel, Leslie Kanuk, Michael Laric, Kevin McCrohan, Leon Schiffman, and Elmer Waters. We learned a great deal at the American Marketing Association's annual consortium for doctoral students, the capstone of any marketing student's education.

At Hofstra University, colleagues Benny Barak, Emmanuel Erondu, Andrew Forman, Tony Gao, Neil Herndon, William James, Keun Lee, Anil Mathur, Charles McMellon, Rusty Mae Moore, James Neelankavil, Ralph Polimeni, Alexander Sharland, Elaine Sherman, Gladys Torres-Baumgarten, and Yong Zhang have provided the collegial environment needed for a book of this type.

We would especially like to thank the following colleagues who have reviewed *Marketing in the 21st Century* or previous editions of *Marketing* and *Principles of Marketing*. These reviewers have made many helpful comments that have contributed greatly to this book:

Wayne Alexander (Moorhead State University)
Rolph Anderson (Drexel University)
Julian Andorka (DePaul University)
Kenneth Anglin (Mankato State University)
Thomas Antonielli, Sr. (Strayer College)
Harold Babson (Columbus State Community College)
Ken Baker (University of New Mexico)
John Bates (Georgia Southern University)
Stephen Batory (Bloomsburg University)
Richard Behr (Broome Community College)
Kurt Beran (Oregon State University)
Wanda Blockhus (San Jose State University)
John Boos (Ohio Wesleyan University)
Jeff Bradford (Drake University)
Donald Bradley, III (University of Central Arkansas)
James Brock (Susquehanna University)
Harvey Bronstein (Oakland Community College)
Sharon Browning (Northwest Missouri State University)
John Bunnell (Broome Community College)
Jim Burrow (North Carolina State University)
Gul Butaney (Bentley College)
Stephen Calcich (Hampton University)
Robert Chapman (Orlando College)
Yusef Choudhry (University of Baltimore)
Gloria Cockerell (Collin County College)

Barbara Coe (University of North Texas)
Linda Jane Coleman (Salem State College)
Kenneth Crocker (Bowling Green State University)
James Cronin, Jr. (Cape Cod Community College)
John Cronin (Western Connecticut State University)
Richard Cummings (College of Lake County)
Benjamin Cutler (Bronx Community College)
Homer Dalbey (San Francisco State University)
Betty Diener (University of Massachusetts, Boston)
Peter Doukas (Westchester Community College)
Rebecca Elmore-Yalch (University of Washington)
Mort Ettinger (Salem State University)
Roland Eyears (Central Ohio Technical College)
Frank Falcetta (Middlesex Community College)
Lawrence Feick (University of Pittsburgh)
Benjamin Findley, Jr. (University of West Florida)
Frank Franzak (Virginia Commonwealth University)
Stanley Garfunkel (Queensborough Community College)
Betsy Gelb (University of Houston)
Donald Gordon (Illinois Central College)
Jill Grace (University of Southern California)
Harrison Grathwohl (California State University at Chico)
Blaine Greenfield (Bucks County Community College)
Thomas Greer (University of Maryland)
Charles Gulas (Wright State University)
Gregory Gundlach (University of Notre Dame)
Robert Gwinner (Arizona State University)
Rita Hall (Sullivan Junior College)
Robert Hammond (Lexington Community College)
G. E. Hannem (Mankato State University)

Nancy Hansen (University of New Hampshire)
William Harris, III (Quinnipiac University)
Douglas Hawes (University of Wyoming)
Jon Hawes (University of Akron)
Dean Headley (Wichita State University)
Allen Heffner (Lebanon Valley College)
Thomas Hickey (State University of New York at Oswego)
Nathan Himmelstein (Essex County College)
Patricia Hopkins (California State Polytechnic
    University at Pomona)
Jerry Ingram (Auburn University at Montgomery)
Laurence Jacobs (University of Hawaii)
Rajshekhar Javalgi (Cleveland State University)
Norma Johansen (Scottsdale Community College)
Edna Johnson (North Carolina Agricultural and Technical
    State University)
Paul Joice, Sr. (Walla Walla College)
Mary Joyce (Emerson College)
Albert Kagan (University of Northern Iowa)
Ruel Kahler (University of Cincinnati)
Bernard Katz (Oakton Community College)
J. Steven Kelly (DePaul University)
John Kerr (Florida State University)
Bettie King (Central Piedmont Community College)
Gail Kirby (Santa Clara University)
Charles Knapp (Waubonsee Community College)
John Krane (Community College of Denver)
R. Krishnan (University of Miami)
Darwin Krumrey (Kirkwood Community College)
J. Ford Laumer (Auburn University)
William Layden (Golden West College)
Marilyn Liebrenz-Himes (George Washington University)
Robert Listman (Valparaiso University)
James Littlefield (Virginia Polytechnic Institute and
    State University)
Yusen Liu (University of St. Thomas)
John Lloyd (Monroe Community College)
William Locander (University of South Florida)
Kenneth Lord (Niagra University)
Robert Lorentz (Florida Institute of Technology)
William Lovell (Cayuga Community College)
Keith Lucas (Ferris State College)
Jacob Manakkalathil (University of North Dakota)
Scott Marzluf (National College)
Michael Mayo (Kent State University)
Ken McCleary (Virginia Polytechnic Institute and
    State University)
Elaine McGivern (Bucknell University)

James McMillan (University of Tennessee)
H. Lee Meadow (Eastern Illinois University)
John Mentzer (University of Tennessee)
Jim Merrill (Indiana University)
James Meszaros (County College of Morris)
Ronald Michael (University of Kansas)
Ronald Michman (Shippensburg State University)
John Milewicz (Jacksonville State University)
Howard Mills (Ulster City Community College)
Edward Moore (State University of New York
    College at Plattsburgh)
Linda Morable (Richland College)
John Morgan (West Chester University)
Linda Morris (University of Idaho)
Ed Mosher (Laramie County Community College)
Carol Stewart Mueller (Nassau Community College)
Paul Murphy (John Carroll University)
Margaret Myers (Northern Kentucky University)
Donald Nagourney (New York Institute of Technology)
Peter Nye (Northeastern University)
Kenneth Papenfuss (Ricks College)
Dennis Pappas (Columbus State Community College)
Terry Paul (Ohio State University)
William Perttula (San Francisco State University)
Michael Peters (Boston College)
Ann Pipinski (Northeast Institute of Education)
Robert Pollero (Anne Arundel Community College)
Edward Popper (Bellarmine University)
William Qualls (University of Illinois)
S. R. Rao (Cleveland State University)
Lloyd Rinehart (Michigan State University)
Edward Riordan (Wayne State University)
David Roberts (Virginia Polytechnic Institute and
    State University)
Mary Lou Roberts (University of Massachusetts at Boston)
Scott Roberts (Old Dominion University)
Donald Robin (University of Southern Mississippi)
John Rogers (California Polytechnic State University at
    San Luis Obispo)
Randall Rose (University of South Carolina)
Barbara Rosenthal (Miami Dade Community College)
Thomas Rossi (Broome Community College)
Nancy Ryan-McClure (Texas Tech University)
Barbara Samuel (University of Scranton)
Peter Sanchez (Villanova University)
Alan Sawyer (University of Florida)
Robert Schaffer (California State Polytechnic
    University at Pomona)

Martin Schlissel (St. John's University)
Stanley Scott (University of Alaska at Anchorage)
Donald Self (Auburn University at Montgomery)
Mohamad Sepehri (Sheperd College)
Rajagopalan Sethuraman (Southern Methodist University)
Reshma Shah (University of Pittsburgh)
Richard Sielaff (University of Minnesota at Duluth)
M. Joseph Sirgy (Virginia Polytechnic Institute and
    State University)
Richard Skinner (Ashland University)
Michael Smith (Temple University)
Norman Smothers (California State University at Hayward)
Gregory Snere (Ellsworth Community College)
Michael Solomon (Auburn University)
Patricia Sorce (Rochester Institute of Technology)
A. Edward Spitz (Eastern Michigan University)
Thomas Stafford (Texas Women's University)
Gary Stanton (Erie Community College)
Margery Steinberg (University of Hartford)
Jeffrey Stoltman (Wayne State University)
Robert Swerdlow (Lamar University)
Richard Szecsy (St. Mary's University)
Donna Tillman (California State Polytechnic
    University at Pomona)

Ed Timmerman (Abilene Christian University)
Frank Titlow (St. Petersburg Junior College)
Charles Treas (University of Mississippi)
David Urban (Virginia Commonwealth University)
Anthony Urbaniak (Northern State University)
Richard Utecht (University of Texas at San Antonio)
William Vincent (Santa Barbara City College)
Gerald Waddle (Clemson University)
Donald Walli (Greenville Technical College)
John Walton (Miami University)
J. Donald Weinrauch (Tennessee Technological University)
Colleen Wheeler (St. Cloud University)
Mildred Whitted (St. Louis Community College at
    Forest Park)
Jack Wichert (Orange Coast College)
David Wills (Sussex County Community College)
George Winn (James Madison University)
Martin Wise (Harrisburg Area Community College)
Joyce Wood (Northern Virginia Community College)
Gene Wunder (Washburn University)
Richard Yalch (University of Washington)
Anthony Zahorik (Vanderbilt University)
William Ziegler (Seton Hall University)

To the many students at Hofstra who have reacted to the material in *Marketing in the 21st Century*, we owe a special thanks because they represent the true constituency of any textbook authors.

Our appreciation is extended to the fine people at Atomic Dog Publishing. We expressly thank (in alphabetical order) the outstanding team for *Marketing in the 21st Century*: Mark Beck, Tom Doran, Dave Hart, Dan Jones, Mary Melloy, Chris Morgan, Victoria Putman, Steven Ray, Steve Scoble, Mikka Weber, and Chad Williams as well as our publisher, Alex von Rosenberg.

We are pleased to recognize the contributions of Diane Schoenberg, our editorial associate; Linda Berman, for comprehensive indexes; Linda Evans, for editorial work; and Rashid Coates and Alok Mehta, our graduate research assistants. Our appreciation and thanks are extended to Chip Galloway for his continued outstanding work on the computer exercises, Mid Semple for the creative PowerPoint package that accompanies this book, and Michael Laric for the use of his Excel templates. We also thank the American Marketing Association, PricewaterhouseCoopers, and Retail Planning Associates for their cooperation and the right to reproduce case materials and photos.

To our families, this book is dedicated—out of respect, love, and appreciation.

Joel R. Evans
Barry Berman

About the Authors

Joel R. Evans, Ph.D., is the RMI Distinguished Professor of Business and Professor of Marketing and International Business at Hofstra University. Before joining Hofstra, he worked for a *Fortune 500* firm, owned a business, and taught at Baruch College and New York University. Dr. Evans is author or editor of numerous books and articles and is active in various professional associations. At Hofstra, he has received three Dean's Awards and the School of Business Faculty Distinguished Service Award. Dr. Evans has also been honored as Teacher of the Year by the Hofstra M.B.A. Association.

Barry Berman, Ph.D., is the Walter H. "Bud" Miller Distinguished Professor of Business and Professor of Marketing and International Business at Hofstra University. He also serves as the Director of Hofstra University's Executive Master of Business Administration program. Dr. Berman is author or editor of numerous books and articles and is active in various professional associations. At Hofstra, he has received two Dean's Awards. Dr. Berman has also been honored as Teacher of the Year by the Hofstra M.B.A. Association.

Joel R. Evans and Barry Berman are co-authors of several best-selling texts, including *Marketing, 8e: Marketing in the 21st Century* and *Retail Management: A Strategic Approach* (Prentice Hall). They have co-chaired numerous prestigious conferences, including the 1995 American Marketing Association Faculty Consortium on "Ethics and Social Responsibility in Marketing" and the 2000 Academy of Marketing Science/American Collegiate Retailing Association Triennial Retailing Conference. Each has a chapter in the most recent edition of Dartnell's *Marketing Manager's Handbook*. Drs. Evans and Berman have been consultants for such firms as Fortunoff, NCR, PepsiCo, and Simon Properties. Both regularly teach undergraduate and graduate marketing courses to a wide range of students.

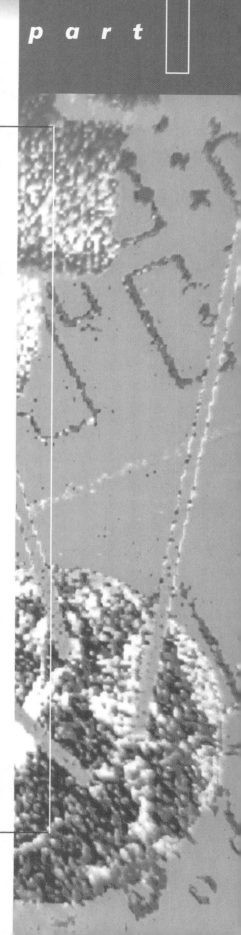

An Introduction to Marketing in the 21st Century

In Part 1, we begin our study of marketing and discuss concepts that form the basis for the rest of the text.

1 Marketing Today

Here, we show the dynamic nature of marketing, broadly define the term "marketing," and trace its evolution. We pay special attention to the marketing concept, a marketing philosophy, customer service, and customer satisfaction and relationship marketing. And we examine the importance of marketing, as well as marketing functions and performers.

2 The Environment in Which Marketing Operates

In this chapter, we look at the complex environment within which marketing functions, with an emphasis on both the factors that can be controlled and those that cannot be controlled by an organization and its marketers. We demonstrate that without adequate environmental analysis, a firm may function haphazardly or be shortsighted.

3 Developing and Enacting Strategic Marketing Plans

Here, we first distinguish between strategic business plans and strategic marketing plans, and describe the total quality approach to planning. Next, we look at different kinds of strategic plans and the relationships between marketing and other functional areas. We then present the steps in the strategic planning process. A sample outline for a strategic marketing plan is presented and the actual strategic marketing plan of a small firm is highlighted.

4 Information for Marketing Decisions

In this chapter, we explain why marketing decisions should be based on sound information. We explain the role and importance of the marketing information system, which coordinates marketing research, continuous monitoring, and data storage and provides the basis for decision making. We also describe the process for undertaking marketing research. We show that marketing research may involve surveys, observation, experiments, and/or simulation.

After reading Part 1, you should understand elements 1–5 of the strategic marketing plan outlined in Table 3-2 (pages 72–75).

Marketing Today

Chapter Objectives

1 To illustrate the exciting, dynamic, and influential nature of marketing

2 To define marketing and trace its evolution—with emphasis on the marketing concept, a marketing philosophy, customer service, and customer satisfaction and relationship marketing

3 To show the importance of marketing as a field of study

4 To describe the basic functions of marketing and those that perform these functions

Despite all the technology intended to speed up customer transactions and reduce waiting times, some businesses "just haven't learned." Think about how many times you have waited in a long line at an airport check-in station or spent 20 minutes on the phone to just reach a customer service representative.

According to some experts, even when businesses try to attach a value to a customer's wasted time, they often show a lack of critical insight. Take, for example, the cable TV industry that promised to pay consumers $20 if a technician shows up late for an appointment. When asked how the industry computed the $20 amount, a spokesperson for the National Cable Television Association said, "Well, it won't put us out too much, people are happy with it, and $20 is $20." Yet, the spokesperson also conceded that, when surveyed, consumers said they would be happier if a service was delivered on time than with $20.

Let's look at some winners and losers in the battle to save customers' time: airlines, online retailing, fast-food restaurants, and rental cars. These evaluations are from George Gilder, a technology expert.

- *Airlines*—The winner in this category is Virgin Atlantic (www.virgin-atlantic.com), which is known for its enabling first-class passengers to check-in from their chauffeur-driven cars. The loser is United Airlines (www.ual.com), which has had the most flight delays of any airline for the past 13 years.

- *Online Retailing*—Amazon.com (www.amazon.com) is known for its one-click shopping, as well as its fast processing of orders. In contrast, Value America went out of business, largely due to long delays in refunds and customer adjustments.

- *Fast-Food Restaurants*—Wendy's (www.wendys.com) scores highly because it can deliver a Big Bacon Classic within 2 1/2 minutes of an order. In contrast, Steak n Shake (www.steaknshake.com), takes almost 6 minutes for a steakburger. Some consumers have dubbed the chain "Wait and Wait."

- *Rental Cars*—Enterprise (www.enterprise.com) wins due to its customer pickup and excellent relations with repair shops. The loser is Alamo (www.goalamo.com), due to its long and slow lines.[1]

In this chapter, we will learn more about the importance of service quality. We will also explore the roles of marketing, see how marketing has evolved over the years, and look at its scope.

[1]Kelly Barron, "Hurry Up and Wait," *Forbes* (October 16, 2000), pp. 158–164.

1-1 OVERVIEW

Marketing is an exciting, fast-paced, and contemporary business discipline. We engage in marketing activities or are affected by them on a daily basis, both in our business-related roles and as consumers. Okay, but what exactly does "marketing" mean? Well, it is not just advertising or selling goods and services, although these are aspects of marketing. And it is not just what we do as supermarket shoppers every week, although this, too, is part of marketing.

As formally defined in the next section, "marketing" encompasses the activities involved in anticipating, managing, and satisfying demand via the exchange process. As such, marketing encompasses all facets of buyer/seller relationships. Specific marketing activities (all discussed later in this chapter) include environmental analysis and marketing research, broadening an organization's scope, consumer analysis, product planning, distribution planning, promotion planning, price planning, and marketing management.

In a less abstract way, here are two examples of real-world marketing—one from a business perspective and one from a consumer perspective:

Business perspective: Marie Jackson, a 1996 BBA with an accounting major and a CPA certification, has worked for a large accounting firm since graduating from college. She is now ready to open her own practice, but must make a number of decisions: Who should her clients be? What accounting services should she offer? Where should she open her office? How will she attract her clients? What fee schedule should she set? Is it ethical to try to attract clients that she worked with from her old firm? *Each of these questions entails a business-related marketing decision.*

Let's look at some of Marie Jackson's marketing options:

- *Clients*—Marie could target small or medium businesses, such nonprofit organizations as local libraries, and/or individuals (for personal tax and estate planning).

- *Accounting services*—Marie could be a full-service accountant for her clients or specialize in a particular accounting task (such as developing customized accounting software).

- *Office location*—Marie could open an office in a professional building, a small shopping center, or her home. She could also do client visits, thus making the choice of office location less important.

- *Attracting clients*—Marie must determine if she is from the "new" school—where it is acceptable to run ads in local newspapers, send out direct mail pieces to prospective clients, etc.—or from the "old" school—where most forms of promotion are viewed as being unprofessional.

- *Fee schedule*—Marie must rely on her own experience with her previous firm and look at what competitors are doing. Then, she could price similar to others or lower/higher than them (depending on her desired image and a realistic reading of the marketplace).

- *Ethics*—Marie must weigh the personal dilemma of "stealing" clients from her old firm against the difficulty of starting a business from scratch without any client base.

Consumer perspective: At the same time that Marie Jackson is making decisions about her new accounting practice, Albert Sampson is reappraising his status as an accounting client. He owns a small furniture repair store and has been a client of a mid-sized accounting firm for ten years. That firm has been responsible for Albert Sampson's store and personal accounts. Yet, he is now unhappy. He feels the accounting firm takes him for granted. But before switching accountants, these questions must be answered: What kind of firm should he select? What accounting services should he seek? Where should the accounting firm be located? How will he learn more about possible firms? What fees should he be willing to pay? Is it ethical to show prospective firms samples of the work from his present accountant? *Each of these questions addresses a consumer-related marketing decision.*

GLOBAL *Marketing in Action*

Wired in the U.S.A., Wireless in Europe

Although it may be hard for New Yorkers to believe, New York is a wireless phone underachiever. As measured by the percent of households with cell phones, Finland has the world's highest per-capita usage. According to a cultural affairs consul of Finland, "We Finns are enjoying ourselves because we are beginning to feel a little superior here. We are obviously more developed in regard to wireless."

Italy and Japan also have greater cell phone penetration than New York. Furthermore, in the United States, Atlanta, San Jose, Charlotte (North Carolina), Miami, and Chicago also have higher market penetration than New York. According to a senior analyst with one marketing research firm, "New York has some of the hardest square miles to provide service in the country," referring to the difficulty in picking up signals both outside and inside Manhattan due to the large number of skyscrapers and the accompanying amount of steel and brick. An additional problem is the high number of people who use cellular phones in New York relative to the number of connections. Lastly, while most of Europe has one wireless carrier, in the United States there are three carriers with incompatible digital technologies. It is not surprising to many New Yorkers that a recent study ranked New York last among 16 major cities for affordability and convenience of wireless services.

The uses of cellular phones are also more developed in countries such as Finland than in the United States. For example, Finnish consumers commonly pay for golf balls with their cellular phone. Golf balls can be ordered by dialing a specific number. The charges then appear on a monthly statement.

As marketing manager for a New York wireless telephone service, what can you do to expand operations?

Source: Based on material in Dean E. Murphy, "Two Continents, Disconnected," *New York Times on the Web* (December 14, 2000).

Let's look at some of Albert Sampson's marketing options:

- *Kind of firm*—Albert could select a small, medium, or large accounting firm. Given his current dissatisfaction, he would probably avoid medium and large firms.
- *Accounting services*—Albert could continue having his accountant perform all accounting tasks for him; or he could take on some of the tasks himself (such as maintaining ledger books and paying bills).
- *Office location*—Albert could look for an accountant that makes on-site visits (as his accountant does now) or seek a firm that has an office near to his store or residence.
- *Learning about firms*—Albert could ask prospective firms for references, check out accountants' credentials, interview candidates, and/or require firms to perform a sample task.
- *Fee schedule*—Albert knows he must get "fair" quotes, not "low ball" ones. He recognizes that you get what you pay for; and he wants better service.
- *Ethics*—Albert must determine whether he, as the client, has the right to show any old work to prospective firms—or whether there is a client/accountant relationship that he should not violate.

A marketing match? For "marketing" to operate properly, buyers and sellers need to find and satisfy each other (conduct exchanges). Do you think that Marie Jackson and Albert Sampson would make a good marketing match? We do—but only if their strategy (Marie) and expectations (Albert) are in sync.

As the preceding examples show, goods and service providers ("sellers") make marketing-related decisions like choosing who customers are, what goods and services to offer, where to sell these goods and services, the features to stress in ads, and the prices to charge. They also determine how to be ethical and socially responsible, and whether to sell products globally in addition to domestically. Marketing-related activities are not limited to industrial firms, large corporations, or people called "marketers." They are taken on by all types of companies and people.

As consumers ("buyers"), the marketing practices of goods and service providers impact on many of the choices made by our parents, spouses, other family members, friends and associates, and/or us. For virtually every good and service we purchase, the marketing process affects whom we patronize, the assortment of models and styles offered in the marketplace, where we shop, the availability of knowledgeable sales personnel, the prices we pay, and other factors. Marketing practices are in play when we are born (which doctor our parents select, the style of baby furniture they buy), while we grow (our parents' purchase of a domestic or foreign family car or minivan, our choice of a college), while we conduct our everyday lives (the use of a particular brand of toothpaste, the purchase of status-related items), and when we retire (our consideration of travel options, a change in living accommodations).

The formal study of marketing requires an understanding of its definition, evolution (including the marketing concept, a marketing philosophy, and customer service), importance and scope, and functions. These principles are discussed throughout Chapter 1.

1-2 MARKETING DEFINED

A broad, integrated definition of marketing forms the basis of this text:

> *Marketing* is the anticipation, management, and satisfaction of demand through the exchange process.

It involves goods, services, organizations, people, places, and ideas.

Anticipation of demand requires a firm to do consumer research on a regular basis so it can develop and introduce offerings desired by consumers. *Management of demand* includes stimulation, facilitation, and regulation tasks. Stimulation motivates consumers to want a firm's offerings due to attractive product designs, distinctive promotion, fair prices, and other strategies. Facilitation is the process whereby the firm makes it easy to buy its offering by having convenient locations, accepting credit cards, using well-informed salespeople, and implementing other strategies. Regulation is needed when there are peak demand periods rather than balanced demand throughout the year or when demand exceeds the supply of the offering. Then, the goal is to spread demand throughout the year or to demarket a good or service (reduce overall demand). *Satisfaction of demand* involves product availability, actual performance upon purchase, safety perceptions, after-sale service, and other factors. For consumers to be satisfied, goods, services, organizations, people, places, and ideas must fulfill their expectations. See Figure 1-1.

Marketing can be aimed at consumers or at publics. **Consumer demand** refers to the attributes and needs of final consumers, industrial consumers, wholesalers and retailers, government institutions, international markets, and nonprofit institutions. A firm may appeal to one or a combination of these. **Publics' demand** refers to the attributes and needs of employees, unions, stockholders, the general public, government agencies, consumer groups, and other internal and external forces that affect company operations.

The marketing process is not concluded until consumers and publics *exchange* their money, their promise to pay, or their support for the offering of a firm, institution, person, place, or idea. Exchanges must be done in a socially responsible way, with both the buyer

In some way, we are all involved with or affected by marketing.

Marketing *includes anticipating demand, managing demand, and satisfying demand.*

Demand *is affected by both* **consumers** *and* **publics.**

Exchange *completes the process.*

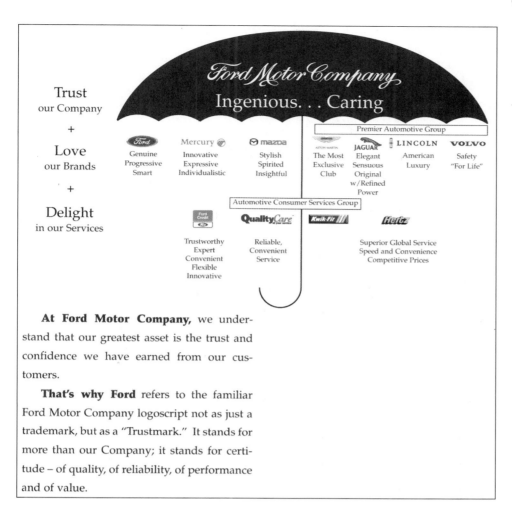

FIGURE 1-1
Ford's Customer-Focused Strategy

Source: Reprinted by permission.

and the seller being ethical and honest—and considering the impact on society and the environment.

A proper marketing definition should not be confined to economic goods and services. It should cover organizations (Big Brothers and Big Sisters), people (politicians), places (Hawaii), and ideas (the value of seat belts). See Figure 1-2. A consumer orientation must be central to any definition. And from a societal perspective, a firm needs to ask whether a good or service should be sold, besides whether it can be sold.

1-3 THE EVOLUTION OF MARKETING

Marketing's evolution in an industry, country, or region of the world may be viewed as a sequence of stages: barter era→production era→sales era→marketing department era→marketing company era. In some industries, nations, and regions, marketing practices have moved through each stage and involve a good consumer orientation and high efficiency; in others, marketing practices are still in infancy.

Marketing's origins can be traced to people's earliest use of the exchange process: the *barter era.* With barter, people trade one resource for another—like food for animal pelts. To accommodate exchanges, trading posts, traveling salespeople, general stores, and cities evolved along with a standardized monetary system. In the least developed nations of the world, barter is still widely practiced.

The modern system of marketing begins with the industrialization of an industry, country, or region. For the world's most developed nations, this occurred with the Industrial Revolution of the late 1800s. For developing nations, efforts to industrialize are

Marketing can be traced to the **barter era.**

F I G U R E   1 - 2
Marketing and U.S. Savings Bonds: Take Stock in America

Marketing is not only conducted by profit-driven firms but by nonprofit ones, such as the U.S. government, as well.

Source: Reprinted by permission.

now under way. Why is industrialization so important in marketing's evolution? Unless industrialization takes place, exchanges are limited since people do not have surplus items to trade. With the onset of mass production, better transportation, and more efficient technology, products can be made in greater volume and sold at lower prices. Improved mobility, densely populated cities, and specialization also let more people share in the exchange process: They can turn from self-sufficiency (such as making their own clothes) to purchases (such as buying clothes). In the initial stages of industrialization, output is limited and marketing is devoted to products' physical distribution. Because demand is high and competition is low, firms typically do not have to conduct consumer research, modify products, or otherwise adapt to consumer needs. The goal is to lift production to meet demand. This is the ***production era*** of marketing.

In the **production era,** *output increases to meet demand.*

The next stage takes place as companies expand production capabilities to keep up with consumer demand. At this point, many firms hire a sales force and some use advertising to sell their inventory. Yet, since competition is still rather low, when firms develop new products, consumer tastes or needs receive little consideration. The role of the sales force and advertising is to make consumer desires fit the features of the products offered. For example, a shoe manufacturer might make brown wingtip shoes and use ads and personal selling to persuade consumers to buy them. That firm would rarely determine consumer tastes before making shoes or adjust output to those tastes. This is the ***sales era*** of marketing. It still exists where competition is limited, such as in nations recently converting to free-market economies.

In the **sales era,** *firms sell products without first determining consumer desires.*

As competition grows, supply begins to exceed demand. Firms cannot prosper without marketing input. They create marketing departments to conduct consumer research and advise management on how to better design, distribute, promote, and price products. Unless firms react to consumer needs, competitors might better satisfy demand and leave the firms with surplus inventory and falling sales. Yet, although marketing departments share in decisions, they may be in a subordinate position to production, engineering, and sales departments. This is the ***marketing department era.*** It still exists where marketing has been embraced, but not as the driving force in an industry or company.

The **marketing department era** *occurs when research is used to determine consumer needs.*

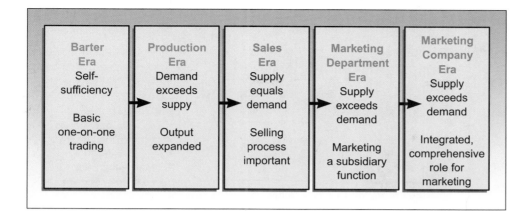

FIGURE 1-3
How Marketing Evolves

Over the past 45 years, firms in a growing number of industries, nations, and regions have recognized marketing's central role; marketing departments at those firms are now the equal of others. The firms make virtually all key decisions after thorough consumer analysis: Since competition is intense and sophisticated, consumers must be aggressively drawn and kept loyal to a firm's brands. Company efforts are well integrated and regularly reviewed. This is the **marketing company era.** Figure 1-3 indicates the key aspects of each era in marketing's evolution.

The marketing concept, a marketing philosophy, customer service, and customer satisfaction and relationship marketing are the linchpins of the marketing company era. They are examined here.

*The **marketing company era** integrates consumer research and analysis into all efforts.*

1-3a The Marketing Concept

As Figure 1-4 shows, the **marketing concept** is a consumer-oriented, market-driven, value-based, integrated, goal-oriented philosophy for a firm, institution, or person.[2] Here is an illustration of it in action:

*The **marketing concept** is consumer-oriented, market-driven, value-driven, integrated, and goal-oriented.*

> buy.com offers its more than 3 million customers a comprehensive selection of brand-name products in a broad range of categories including computer hardware and software, electronics, wireless products and services, books, music, DVDs, games, sporting goods, clearance products, a small business superstore, and more at everyday low prices. We offer more than 950,000 products identified as separate stock-keeping units, using a convenient, easy-to-use shopping interface that features extensive product information and multimedia presentations. buy.com is also the title sponsor of the BUY.COM GOLF TOUR. Our e-commerce portal, www.buy.com, links our twelve specialty stores and is designed to simplify the customer's online shopping experience. We also allow our customers to track packages online and access customer service representatives all day, every day. The company's virtual operating model allows for efficiency with one-stop shopping, broad selection, and a low-price guarantee. buy.com is a proud member of the new Internet coalition that brings merchants and the payment industry together to fight fraud. buy.com was named "Best of the Web" in the computer and electronics category by *Forbes* (Spring, 2000) and #1 on the Gomez Advisors Internet Computer Scorecard for the third time (Summer, 2000). buy.com, founded in June 1997, is located in Aliso Viejo, California.[3] [Its 2000 sales were about $750 million.]

[2]For a comprehensive analysis of the marketing concept and its applications, see Frederick E. Webster, Jr., "Defining the New Marketing Concept," *Marketing Management*, Vol. 2 (Number 2, 1994), pp. 23–31; Dave Webb, Cynthia Webster, and Areti Krepapa, "An Exploration of the Meanings and Outcomes of a Customer-Defined Market Orientation," *Journal of Business Research*, Vol. 48 (May 2000), pp. 101–112; and Graham Hooley, Tony Cox, John Fahy, David Shipley, Jozsef Beracs, Krzysztof Fonfara, and Boris Snoj, "Market Orientation in the Transition Economies of Central Europe: Tests of the Narver and Slater Market Orientation Scales," *Journal of Business Research*, Vol. 50 (November 2000), pp. 273–286.

[3]"Press Room," www.irconnect.com/buyxpr (January 19, 2001).

FIGURE 1-4

The Marketing Concept

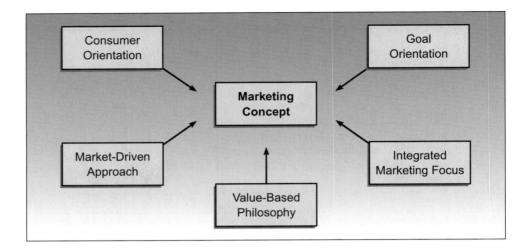

The marketing concept's five elements are crucial to the long-term success of a good, service, organization, person, place, or idea: A *consumer orientation* means examining consumer needs, not production capability, and devising a plan to satisfy them. Goods and services are seen as means to accomplish ends, not as the ends themselves. A *market-driven approach* means being aware of the structure of the marketplace, especially the attributes and strategies of competing firms. A *value-based philosophy* means offering goods and services that consumers perceive to have superior value relative to their costs and the offerings of competitors. With an *integrated marketing focus*, all the activities relating to goods and services are coordinated, including finance, production, engineering, inventory control, research and development, and marketing. A *goal-oriented firm* employs marketing to achieve both short- and long-term goals—which may be profit, funding to find a cure for a disease, increased tourism, election of a political candidate, a better company image, and so on. Marketing helps attain goals by orienting a firm toward pleasing consumers and offering desired goods, services, or ideas.

These are 15 things that managers can do to ensure that they adhere to the spirit of the marketing concept:

1. Create customer focus throughout the firm.
2. Listen to the customer.
3. Define and cultivate distinctive competences.
4. Define marketing as market intelligence.
5. Target customers precisely.
6. Manage for profitability, not sales volume.
7. Make customer value the guiding star.
8. Let the customer define quality.
9. Measure and manage customer expectations.
10. Build customer relationships and loyalty.
11. Define the business as a service business.
12. Commit to continuous improvement and innovation.
13. Manage the company culture along with strategy and structure.
14. Grow with partners and alliances.
15. Destroy marketing bureaucracy.[4]

[4]Frederick E. Webster, Jr., "Executing the New Marketing Concept," *Marketing Management*, Vol. 3 (Number 1, 1994), pp. 9–16.

ETHICAL Issues in Marketing

Goodyear: Trying to Capitalize on Bridgestone/ Firestone's Public Relations Disaster

After the highly-publicized Bridgestone/Firestone tire recall in 2000, other tire manufacturers and their dealers sought ways to exploit Firestone's problems in a manner that was not viewed as opportunistic by consumers. According to Chuck Sinclair, Goodyear's director of public relations, "This is not a way that anybody wants to get business. But, having said that, it's a business we're in." According to Sinclair, Goodyear has an obligation to consumers and to the retailers who sell its tires. Let's look at some of the ways that Goodyear has reacted to Bridgestone/Firestone's woes.

Goodyear purchased Web banner ads that would pop up whenever someone typed in "tire recall" at such Internet search engines as www.askjeeves.com and www.yahoo.com. Consumers wanting to know the latest information on the Bridgestone/Firestone recall were then instantly transported to a page listing Web site matches. Along the top of the one such page, this banner ad was placed: "Through bad weather, our all-terrain tires get you there safely— Goodyear." The ad also featured Goodyear's logo. Goodyear even added material on its own Web site that dealt specifically with the Bridgestone/Firestone recall. And to further emphasize Firestone's problems, Goodyear recently inserted a few seconds of footage of an SUV rolling over in one of its "Serious Freedom" television commercials.

According to Robert Falls, a public relations expert, no matter how discreetly Goodyear's efforts may be, its attempt to gain at Bridgestone/Firestone's expense is not risk-free: "Some might look at it as an opportunity to sell more, but the truth is, any time there is a crisis situation such as this one, it is a problem for an entire industry, not just one company."

What are the pros and cons of Goodyear's strategy in dealing with the Bridgestone/Firestone recall?

Source: Based on material in Mark Dodosh, "Firestone Woes Create Opportunity," *Advertising Age* (September 18, 2000), p. 105.

Although the marketing concept lets a firm analyze, maximize, and satisfy consumer demand, it is only a guide to planning. A firm must also consider its strengths and weaknesses in production, engineering, and finance. Marketing plans need to balance goals, customer needs, and resource capabilities. The impact of competition, government regulations, and other external forces must also be evaluated. These factors are discussed in Chapters 2 and 3.

1-3b Selling Versus Marketing Philosophies

Figure 1-5 highlights the differences in selling and marketing philosophies. The benefits of a marketing, rather than a sales, orientation are many. Marketing stresses consumer analysis and satisfaction, directs the resources of a firm to making the goods and services consumers want, and adapts to changes in consumer traits and needs. Under a marketing philosophy, selling is used to communicate with and understand consumers; consumer dissatisfaction leads to changes in policy, not a stronger or different sales pitch. Marketing looks for real differences in consumer tastes and devises offerings to satisfy them.

With a marketing orientation, selling helps to communicate with and understand consumers.

FIGURE 1-5
The Focus of Selling and Marketing Philosophies

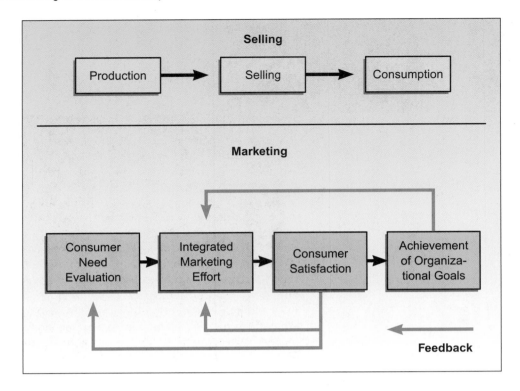

Marketing is geared to the long run, and marketing goals reflect overall company goals. Finally, marketing views customer needs broadly (such as heating) rather than narrowly (such as fuel oil).

As a case in point, consider Wahl Clipper Corporation (www.wahlclipper.com), which makes electric shavers, hair trimmers, and other personal care products. Its sales have grown at a double-digit percentage rate for years. Why? According to former company president Jack Wahl, "I realized the difference between sales and marketing. That's a big thing for a small company. Sales means simply presenting the product and collecting money. Marketing means stepping back and looking for the needs of the customer, and for the best way to get through to that user." In looking ahead to the 21st century, Wahl Clipper Corporation, now under the leadership of Jack's son Gregory, knows that "To maintain our leadership position in the personal care categories we serve, we must have vision. Vision to continually improve our existing products. Vision to bring new products to market which meet the wants and needs of consumers. Vision to stay ahead of our competitors in innovation. And vision to support our customers, the retailers, with sales and marketing programs that make it easy, fun, and profitable for them to sell more Wahl products. Leading with vision means constantly being alert to new opportunities. By sharing the vision, we can make tomorrow absolutely extraordinary."[5]

1-3c Customer Service

Customer service involves the identifiable, but rather intangible, activities undertaken by a seller in conjunction with the basic goods and/or services it offers.[6] In today's highly competitive marketplace, the level of customer service a firm provides can greatly affect its ability to attract and retain customers. Yet, firms often have to make customer service trade-offs. For instance, supermarkets must weigh the potential loss of business if waiting lines are too long versus the cost of opening additional lines.

Customer service *tends to be intangible, but quite meaningful, to many consumers.*

[5]Jerry Flint, "Father Says, 'Jump,'" *Forbes* (August 14, 1995), p. 144; and "More About Wahl," www.wahl.com/html/html/moreabout.html (January 26, 2001).

[6]Peter D. Bennett (Editor), *Dictionary of Marketing Terms*, Second Edition (Chicago: American Marketing Association, 1995), p. 73.

Unless a consumer is happy with *both* the basic good (such as a new auto) or service (such as an auto tune-up) offered by a seller *and* the quality of customer service (like polite, expert sales personnel and on-time appointments), he or she is unlikely to patronize the seller—certainly not in the long run. Imagine your reaction to this situation:

> When Tom Unger of New Haven started banking at First Union Corp. several years ago, he knew he wasn't at the top of the heap. But Unger didn't realize how dispensable he was until mysterious service charges started showing up on his account. He called the bank's toll-free number, only to reach a bored service representative who brushed him off. Then he wrote two letters, neither of which received a response. A First Union spokeswoman, Mary Eshet, says the bank doesn't discuss individual accounts but notes that customer service has been steadily improving. Not for Unger. He left: "They wouldn't even give me the courtesy of listening to my complaint."[7]

According to recent surveys, consumer perceptions about the overall level of customer service at U.S. businesses is declining. As one expert recently remarked (in an article titled "Customer Service Is an Oxymoron"), "Unfortunately, most giant corporations don't realize how powerfully harmful a bad reputation for service can be. Gone are the days in which the customer was always right, except perhaps for Stew Leonard's grocery chain (www.stewleonards.com) in Connecticut. Listed in the *Guinness Book of Records* as the store with the fastest-moving stock per square foot, the *New York Times* refers to it as the Disneyland of dairy stores, where employees dressed up as cows, chickens, and ducks stroll the aisles. The stores have two rules. Rule No. 1: The customer is always right. Rule 2: If the customer is ever wrong, read Rule No. 1." Why does customer service seem to be declining? The coordinator of the American Customer Satisfaction Index survey (http://acsi.asq.org) says, "It's too simplistic to say the customer is always right. The marketable company believes the *profitable* customer is always right. If the company can't generate a profit from that customer, the company is less likely to listen."[8]

This is how several firms are positively addressing the issue of customer service: Such companies as Ritz-Carlton, Kroger, Federal Express, and Avis are **empowering employees,** whereby workers are given broad leeway to satisfy customer requests. With empowerment, employees are encouraged and rewarded for showing initiative and imagination. They can "break the rules" if, in their judgment, customer requests should be honored: All Ritz-Carlton hotel (www.ritz-carlton.com) employees (including housekeepers) are trained to listen for customer complaints and to be familiar with possible solutions. At Kroger supermarkets (www.kroger.com), "We will satisfy consumer needs better than the best of our competitors. Operating procedures will reflect our belief that the organizational levels closest to the consumer are best positioned to respond to changing consumer needs." Similarly, Federal Express (www.fedex.com) drivers can help customers pack breakable items; and Avis (www.avis.com) airport rental agents can keep their counters open if flights are delayed.[9]

SAS (www.scandinavian.net), the Scandinavian airline, has ATM-like video stations outside many arrival gates for passengers to communicate feedback about good and bad customer service experiences. Caterpillar (www.caterpillar.com), the maker of heavy construction and agricultural equipment, monitors its customers' equipment remotely, by sending an electronic "warning" signal to its own service technicians, and indicating the parts and tools needed to make repairs. AT&T (www.att.com) has its call center employees enter customer data in real time. These data are then downloaded to marketing and operations departments, which adjust services to suit customer segments and modify

> *To offer better customer service, some firms are* **empowering employees.**

---

[7]Diane Brady, "Why Service Stinks," *Business Week* (October 23, 2000), p. 119.

[8]Timothy W. Maier, "Customer Service Is an Oxymoron," *Insight* (January 1, 2001), pp. 20–21.

[9]Marilyn Adams, "When Something Is Wrong, Those Who Care Make It Right," *USA Today* (September 12, 2000), p. E11; and company Web sites. See also Jean-Charles Chebat and Paul Kollias, "The Impact of Empowerment on Customer Contact Employees' Roles in Service Organizations," *Journal of Service Research*, Vol. 3 (August 2000), pp. 66–81.

processes to fix service failures.[10] PARKnSHOP (www.parknshop.com), the leading supermarket chain in Hong Kong with more than 180 stores and 8,500 employees, has a strong customer service approach—including a delivery policy that says: "With PARKnSHOP, you carry what's fresh. We deliver the rest. Free." See Figure 1-6.

1-3d Customer Satisfaction and Relationship Marketing

Firms cannot usually prosper without a high level of **customer satisfaction.**

As previously noted, **customer satisfaction** is a crucial element in successful marketing. It is the degree to which there is a match between a customer's expectations of a good or service and the actual performance of that good or service, including customer service.[11] As two experts say: "Successful firms know that the customer is the ultimate judge of the quality of a shopping experience. Consumers enjoy more choice than before—in stores, brands, and channels—and have access to an ever-increasing amount of information upon which to base their buying decisions. Capturing the purchasing power of these sophisticated consumers is a difficult and constant challenge."[12] Figure 1-7 shows eleven representative factors that affect overall customer satisfaction.

This is how daunting it can be to keep customers satisfied:

Customer satisfaction is doing what your customer expects—in a sense, being adequate. Most organizations provide adequate service. They do precisely what they say they are going to do—no less and, usually, no more. Unfortunately, people don't talk about adequate service. Instead, they tell anyone who will listen about really bad service or really delightful service. Customer delight goes beyond satisfaction. It ensures that each contact with your customers reinforces their belief that your organization is truly special, the best at what you do. It involves an element of the unexpected. Pleasant surprises are found in the small details of a customer interaction.

Some corporations learned this lesson long ago:
- A hotel opens the *TV Guide* to the correct day and time for each arriving guest.
- A car dealership delivers its new automobiles with the radio programmed to match the settings of those in the trade-in car, including preferred stations and sequencing of buttons.
- An airport shuttle service has complimentary coffee, cell phone, and newspaper for passengers.[13]

Through **relationship marketing,** *companies try to increase long-term customer loyalty.*

Companies with satisfied customers have a good opportunity to convert them into loyal customers, who purchase from those firms over an extended period. From a consumer-oriented perspective, when marketing activities are performed with the conscious intention of developing and managing long-term, trusting customer relations, **relationship marketing** is involved.[14] Why is this so important? According to one observer, it "is the new Holy Grail. All companies want it. We have all heard that it is three-five-ten times cheaper to retain an existing customer than to acquire a new one. Arguing for pro-relationship programs is like defending mom and apple pie. Customer retention rates are the critical element in lifetime value analysis, a preferred tool for avoiding shortsighted decisions."[15]

[10]Stephen W. Brown, "Practicing Best-in-Class Service Recovery," *Marketing Management* (Summer 2000), pp. 8–9.

[11]Bennett, *Dictionary of Marketing Terms*, p. 73. See also David M. Szymanski and David H. Henard, "Customer Satisfaction: A Meta-Analysis of the Empirical Evidence," *Journal of the Academy of Marketing Science*, Vol. 29 (January 2001), pp. 16–35; and Eugene W. Anderson and Vikas Mittal, "Strengthening the Satisfaction-Profit Chain," *Journal of Service Research*, Vol. 3 (November 2000), pp. 107–120.

[12]Theresa Williams and Mark J. Larson, "Preface," *Creating the Ideal Shopping Experience* (Bloomington, Indiana: Indiana University, 2000), p. 1.

[13]John Paul, "Are You Delighting Your Customers?" *Nonprofit World* (September-October 2000), pp. 34–35.

[14]Bennett, *Dictionary of Marketing Terms*, p. 242.

[15]Craig Douglas Henry, "Is Customer Loyalty a Pernicious Myth?" *Business Horizons*, Vol. 43 (July-August 2000), p. 13.

FIGURE 1-6

Customer Service: A Global Imperative

This PARKnSHOP approach demonstrates that customer service is vital anywhere in the world.

Source: Reprinted by permission of PricewaterhouseCoopers.

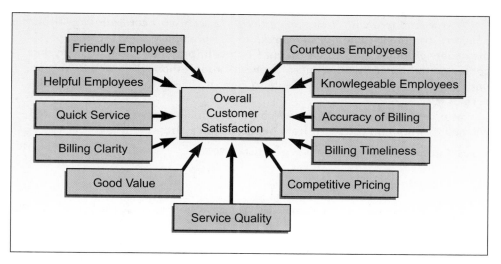

FIGURE 1-7

Factors That Affect Customer Satisfaction

Source: Steven Hokanson, "The Deeper You Analyze, the More You Satisfy Customers," *Marketing News* (January 2, 1995), p. 16. Reprinted by permission of the American Marketing Association.

Office Depot, the giant office-supplies-and-equipment chain, is one of many firms that has mastered relationship marketing, especially with its Web site (www.officedepot.com):

When a customer places an order online, the site confirms both Office Depot's inventory and the customer's credit card information. "When they finish the transaction, [customers] have complete confidence they're going to get the product the next business day," vice-president Beth Van Story says. "Who wants to hear eight hours later that their credit card didn't go through?" The Web site's ordering system is integrated with Office Depot's systems in San Francisco, so customers can use the site to review their purchasing history, including orders placed in other channels. That data helps customers create custom shopping lists, so they don't have to browse for items they order often. Customers can even create a special list that new employees can use to order everything they need.

Office Depot also develops separate Web sites for large accounts that spend more than $25,000 a year. These sites feature only the specific products the customer purchases and list its contracted prices. These customers typically have more complicated hierarchies for purchasing approvals,

MARKETING *and the Web*

At Sephora. com, Customer Relations Come Naturally

Smart Web-based marketers know the difference between building customer awareness and building loyalty. They understand the importance of regular, ongoing communications through E-mail newsletters, personal shopping assistants, and three-dimensional models (based upon customer body dimensions). Let's look at how Sephora.com (www.sephora.com) uses relationship marketing.

Sephora.com recognizes that many of its beauty products (from such manufacturers as Calvin Klein, Elizabeth Arden, and Nino Cerruti) can be purchased by consumers at multiple vendors. What distinguishes Sephora.com from other online retailers is the firm's attractive and comprehensive Web site. At Sephora.com, shoppers can browse or read a colorful magazine that is chock full of beauty secrets, peruse detailed product descriptions, get advice on shopping, and choose from nearly 100 brands of personal care products.

Besides these features, Sephora.com stresses high levels of customer service. For example, E-mail confirmations are sent immediately after orders are placed, there is no shipping charge on orders of $60 or more, products can be returned via the mail or at a Sephora store, and consumers can return products through the U.S. Postal Service without a shipping charge.

As the Sephora.com Web site notes, "We want to hear from you—your opinions, comments, and questions help us to continually offer the best possible beauty products and service. In our Contact Information pages you can find contact information for the entire Sephora organization. We want to you be happy with your purchase from Sephora.com. If there's a problem, we'll take care of it."

As a marketing manager for a Web-based retailer that features discounted cosmetics, what can you learn from Sephora.com's strategy?

Source: Based on material at www.spehora.com (July 9, 2001).

so Office Depot has a system to route purchasing data to appropriate employees of the customer's company.

Another feature, called Supplies QuickFind, helps users find products to fit equipment they already own. Customers use a series of pull-down menus to choose the type of supplies ("Copier Supplies"), manufacturer ("Xerox"), and model number ("5028"), and the site shows them the only product that fits their machine.[16]

Saturn, one of General Motors' auto divisions, is another leader in relationship marketing. It has won several awards in this area, due to its hassle-free, no-price-haggling sales process, such events as its annual Spring Hill Homecoming, and its customer-friendly Web site (www.saturnbp.com): "Ownership does have its advantages. In addition to great value and access to some of the best service in the business, there are a few added perks that we offer to you via the Saturn Owner Web site. You'll find special shopping opportunities exclusive to Saturn owners, like great travel deals from Carlson Travel Network and merchandise from Lands' End and Bite Shoes. You'll also find trip- and travel-planning assistance including maps, directions, and local attractions for your destination."

[16]Chad Kaydo, "Helping Customers Buy Online," *Sales and Marketing Management* (July 1999), p. 90.

Sephora (www.sephora.com) is a retail concept intent on generating loyal customers: Founded in 1993, Sephora is the leading chain of perfume and cosmetics stores in France and the second biggest in Europe. It has stores in France, Luxembourg, Spain, Italy, Portugal, Poland, Germany, Great Britain, and Japan; and it is growing rapidly. Sephora came to the United States in mid-1998 with its New York and Miami stores. There are now 50 U.S. stores. The key to Sephora's success is its unique "selling methodology," which emphasizes freedom, beauty, and pleasure: "When you enter Sephora, you meet the creative spirit driving the concept, a spirit that now offers you an entirely new way of shopping for beauty. *Freedom* comes to you in a hands-on, self-service shopping environment. Feel free to touch, smell, and experience each and every product. You are also free to choose the level of assistance you desire, from individual experience and reflection, to detailed expert advice. *Beauty* comes to you through a splendid international array of unique and luxurious beauty products. *Pleasure* comes through an environment designed to stimulate the senses—a blend of expert advice, personal freedom, and special service displays brings you the latest beauty tips and treatment breakthroughs."[17] See Figure 1-8.

There are many Web sites whose intent is to help client firms improve their level of customer satisfaction and relationship marketing. These are a few of them: Business Research Lab (www.busreslab.com/consult/custsat.htm), CustomerSat.com (www.customersat.com), Customer Value, Inc. (www.cval.com), and Triversity (www.triversity.com).

1-4 THE IMPORTANCE OF MARKETING

Here are several reasons why the field of marketing should be studied: Because marketing stimulates demand, a basic task for it is to generate consumer enthusiasm for goods and services. Worldwide, about $35 trillion of goods and services are produced annually, with the United States accounting for about $10 trillion of that sum.[18]

A large amount of each sales dollar goes to cover the costs related to such marketing activities as product development, packaging, distribution, advertising and personal selling, price marking, and administering consumer credit programs. Some estimates place the costs of marketing as high as 50 percent or more of sales in certain industries. Yet, it should not be assumed that the performance of some marketing tasks by consumers would automatically lead to lower prices. For example, could a small business really save money by having the owner fly to Detroit to buy a new truck directly from the maker rather than from a local dealer? Would a family be willing to buy clothing in bulk to reduce a retailer's transportation and storage costs?

Marketing stimulates consumers, costs a large part of sales, employs people, supports industries, affects all consumers, and plays a major role in our lives.

FIGURE 1-8

Sephora: Bringing Its Relationship Marketing Philosophy to Perfume and Cosmetics

Offering custom colors is one of the many tactics used by Sephora to generate repeat business and very loyal shoppers.

Source: Reprinted by permission of PricewaterhouseCoopers.

[17]"About Sephora," www.sephora.com/help/about_sephora.jhtml (February 12, 2001).
[18]"The World Economic Outlook Database," www.imf.org/external/pubs/ft/weo/2000/02/data/index.htm (February 1, 2001).

Tens of millions of people work in marketing-related jobs in the United States alone. They include those employed in the retailing, wholesaling, transportation, warehousing, and communications industries and those involved with marketing jobs for manufacturing, service, agricultural, mining, and other industries. Projections indicate future employment in marketing will remain strong.

Marketing activities also involve entire industries, such as advertising and marketing research. Total annual worldwide advertising expenditures approximate $500 billion. Many agencies, such as WPP Group (www.wpp.com) and Cordiant Communications Group (www.ccgww.com) of Great Britain, McCann-Erickson Worldwide (www.mccann.com) and BBDO Worldwide (www.bbdo.com) of the United States, and Dentsu (www.dentsu.com) of Japan have worldwide billings of several billion dollars each. Around $12 billion worldwide is spent yearly on various types of commercial marketing research. Firms such as A.C. Nielsen (www.acnielsen.com) and Information Resources Inc. (www.infores.com) of the United States, Taylor Nelson Sofres (www.tnsofres.com) of Great Britain, and GfK Group (www.gfk.com) of Germany each generate yearly worldwide revenues of more than $400 million dollars.

All people and organizations serve as consumers for various goods and services. By understanding the role of marketing, consumers can become better informed, more selective, and more efficient. Effective channels of communication with sellers can also be established and complaints resolved more easily and favorably. Consumer groups have a major impact on sellers.

Because resources are scarce, marketing programs and systems must function at their peak. Thus, by optimizing customer service, inventory movement, advertising expenditures, product assortments, and other areas of marketing, firms will better use resources. Some industries may even require demarketing (lowering the demand for goods and services). The latter often include energy consumption.

Marketing impacts strongly on people's beliefs and lifestyles. In fact, it has been criticized as fostering materialistic attitudes, fads, product obsolescence, a reliance on gadgets, status consciousness, and superficial product differences—and for wasting resources. Marketers reply that they merely address the desires of people and make the best goods and services they can at the prices people will pay.

Marketing has a role to play in our quality of life. For example, marketing personnel often encourage firms to make safer products, such as child-proof bottle caps. They create public service messages on energy conservation, AIDS prevention, driver safety, alcohol abuse, and other topics. They help new goods, ideas, and services—such as Razor scooters (www.razor-scooter.com), improved nutrition, and MSNBC (www.msnbc.com)—to be recognized and accepted by people and organizations.

Marketing awareness is invaluable for those in nonmarketing jobs.

A knowledge of marketing is extremely valuable for those not directly involved in a marketing job. For example, marketing decisions must be made by

- _Doctors_—What hours are most desirable to patients?
- _Lawyers_—How can new clients be attracted?
- _Management consultants_—Should fees be higher, lower, or the same as competitors' fees?
- _Financial analysts_—What investments should be recommended to clients?
- _Research and development personnel_—Is there demand for a potential "breakthrough" product?
- _Economists_—What impact will the economy have on how various industries market their offerings?
- _Statisticians_—How should firms react to predicted demographic shifts?
- _Teachers_—How can students become better consumers?
- _City planners_—How can businesses be persuaded to relocate to the city?
- _Nonprofit institutions_—How can donor contributions be raised?

Each profession and organization must address patient, client, consumer, student, taxpayer, or contributor needs. And more of them than before are doing marketing tasks such as research, advertising, and so on.

1-5 MARKETING FUNCTIONS AND PERFORMERS

There are eight basic *marketing functions:* environmental analysis and marketing research, broadening the scope of marketing, consumer analysis, product planning, distribution planning, promotion planning, price planning, and marketing management. They are shown in Figure 1-9, which also notes where they are discussed in the text.

    Here are brief descriptions of the functions:

Basic **marketing functions** *range from environmental analysis to marketing management.*

- *Environmental analysis and marketing research*—Monitoring and adapting to external factors that affect success or failure, such as the economy and competition; and collecting data to resolve specific marketing issues.
- *Broadening the scope of marketing*—Deciding on the emphasis on and approach to societal/ethical issues and global marketing, as well as the role of the Web in a marketing strategy.
- *Consumer analysis*—Examining and evaluating consumer characteristics, needs, and purchase processes; and selecting the group(s) of consumers at which to aim marketing efforts.
- Product planning (including goods, services, organizations, people, places, and ideas)—Developing and sustaining products, product assortments, product images, brands, packaging, and optional features; and deleting faltering products.
- *Distribution planning*—Forming logistical relations with distribution intermediaries, physical distribution, inventory management, warehousing, transportation, the allocation of goods and services, wholesaling, and retailing.
- *Promotion planning*—Communicating with customers, the general public, and others through some form of advertising, public relations, personal selling, and/or sales promotion.
- *Price planning*—Determining price levels and ranges, pricing techniques, terms of purchase, price adjustments, and the use of price as an active or passive factor.
- *Marketing management*—Planning, implementing, and controlling the marketing program (strategy) and individual marketing functions; appraising the risks and benefits in decision making; and focusing on total quality.

F I G U R E   1 - 9

The Basic Functions of Marketing

See Chapter 3   See Chapter 22

See Chapters 2 & 4 — Environmental analysis & marketing research

Marketing management

Price planning — See Chapters 20-21

See Chapters 5-7 — Broadening the scope of marketing

TOTAL MARKETING EFFORT

Promotion planning — See Chapters 17-19

Consumer analysis

Product planning

Distribution planning

See Chapters 8-10   See Chapters 11-13   See Chapters 14-16

Generally, a firm should first study its environment and gather relevant marketing information. The firm should determine how to act in a socially responsible and ethical manner, consider whether to be domestic and/or global, and decide on the proper use of the Web. At the same time, the firm should analyze potential customers to learn their needs and select the group(s) on which to focus. It should next plan product offerings, make distribution decisions, choose how to communicate with customers and others, and set proper prices. These four functions (in combination, known as the *marketing mix*) should be done in a coordinated manner, based on environmental, societal, and consumer analysis. Through marketing management, the firm's overall marketing program would be planned and carried out in an integrated manner, with fine-tuning as needed.

Although many marketing transactions require the performance of similar tasks, such as being ethical, analyzing consumers, and product, distribution, promotion, and price planning, they can be enacted in many ways, such as a manufacturer distributing via full-service retailers versus self-service ones, or a financial-services firm relying on telephone contacts by its sales force versus in-office visits to potential small-business clients by salespeople.

Marketing performers are the organizations or individuals that undertake one or more marketing functions. They include manufacturers and service providers, wholesalers, retailers, marketing specialists, and organizational and final consumers. As Figure 1-10 shows, each performer has a distinct role. While responsibility for marketing tasks can be shifted and shared in various ways, basic marketing functions usually must be done by one performer or another. They cannot be omitted in many situations.

Sometimes, one marketing performer decides to carry out all, or virtually all, marketing functions, such as Boeing analyzing the marketplace, acting ethically, operating domestically and globally, having a detailed Web site (www.boeing.com), seeking various types of customers, developing aerospace and related products, distributing products

> Usually at least one **marketing performer** *must undertake each basic marketing function.*

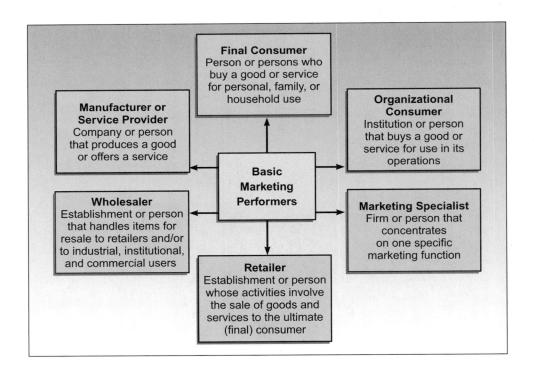

directly to customers, using its own sales force and placing ads in select media, and setting prices. Yet, for these reasons, one performer often does not undertake all marketing functions:

- Many firms do not have the financial resources to sell products directly to consumers. They need intermediaries to share in the distribution process.

- Marketing directly to customers may require goods and services producers to offer complementary products or sell the complementary products of other firms so distribution is carried out efficiently.

- A performer may be unable or unwilling to complete certain functions and may seek a marketing specialist to fulfill them.

- Many performers are too small to do certain functions efficiently.

- For many goods and services, established distribution methods are in force and it is difficult to set up other methods (such as bypassing independent soda distributors to sell directly to retail stores).

- Some consumers may want to buy in quantity, visit self-service outlets, and pay cash to save money.

1-6 FORMAT OF THE TEXT

This book has eight parts. The balance of Part 1 focuses on the marketing environment, developing marketing plans, and the information needed for marketing decisions. Part 2 covers the key topics related to the broadened scope of marketing: societal, ethical, and consumer issues; global marketing; and marketing and the Web. The discussion in Parts 1 and 2 sets the foundation for studying the specific components of marketing.

Part 3 deals with marketing's central orientation: understanding consumers. It looks at the demographics, social and psychological traits, and decision process of final consumers; organizational consumer attributes and decision making; and developing a target market and sales forecasting. Parts 4 to 7 discuss the marketing mix (product, distribution, promotion, and price planning) and the actions needed to carry out a marketing program in depth. Part 8 considers the marketing management implications of the topics raised throughout *Marketing in the 21st Century* and discusses how to integrate and analyze an overall marketing plan.

Numerous illustrations of actual marketing practices by a variety of organizations and individuals are woven into our discussions. And although such topics as marketing and society, global marketing, marketing and the Web, organizational consumers, and goods versus service marketing get separate chapter coverage to highlight certain points, applications in these areas are presented throughout the text.

WEB SITES YOU CAN USE

In every chapter of *Marketing in the 21st Century*, we present a variety of links to worthwhile Web sites related to that chapter.

An important tool for any Web "surfer" looking for information about a topic related to marketing is a search engine. This tool enables the user to generate a clickable list of Web links on virtually any subject imaginable, from advertising to zero-based budgeting. There are dozens of free search engines on the Web. Because each one has a slightly different method of searching, you should rely on multiple search engines if you want to do a comprehensive search of a subject. After experimenting with various search engines, many users settle on a few that they really like.

Here are some of the most popular and useful search engines. Visit them and see what they offer:

1st Headlines (www.1stheadlines.com)

Abuzz (www.abuzz.com)

About.com (www.about.com)

AltaVista (www.altavista.com)

Ask Jeeves! (www.askjeeves.com)

Askme (www.askme.com)

Auction Hawk (www.auctionhawk.com)

Britannica Internet Guide (www.britannica.com)

CNET Search (www.search.com)

Copernic (www.copernic.com)

Direct Hit (www.directhit.com)

Dogpile (www.dogpile.com)

Electric Library (www.elibrary.com)

Entreworld.org (www.entreworld.org)

EsearchCentral (www.esearchcentral.com)

Excite (www.excite.com)

ExpressFind (www.expressfind.com/)

Fast Search and Transfer (www.alltheweb.com)

Go.com (www.go.com)

Google (www.google.com)

HotBot (www.hotbot.com)

IcySpicy (www.icyspicy.com)

iWon (www.iwon.com)

Ixquick (www.ixquick.com)

Looksmart (www.looksmart.com)

Lycos (www.lycos.com)

Mamma (www.mamma.com)

NBCi (www.nbci.com)

Northern Light (www.northernlight.com)

Open Text (www.opentext.com)

Research-it! (www.itools.com/research-it)

The Big Hub (www.thebighub.com)

Webcrawler (www.webcrawler.com)

WorldPages (www.worldpages.com)

Yahoo! (www.yahoo.com)

SUMMARY

In every chapter in the text, the summary is linked to the objectives stated at the beginning of the chapter.

1. *To illustrate the exciting, dynamic, and influential nature of marketing* Marketing may be viewed from both business and consumer perspectives; and it influences us daily. As goods and service providers, we make such marketing-related decisions as choosing who customers are, what goods and services to offer, where to sell them, what to stress in promotion, what prices to charge, how to be ethical and responsible, and whether to operate globally. As consumers, the marketing process affects whom we patronize, choices in the marketplace, where we shop, the availability of sales personnel, the prices we pay, and other factors.

2. *To define marketing and trace its evolution—with emphasis on the marketing concept, a marketing philosophy, customer service, and customer satisfaction and relationship marketing* Marketing involves anticipating, managing, and satisfying demand via the exchange process. It includes goods, services, organizations, people, places, and ideas.

The evolution of marketing can be traced to people's earliest use of barter in the exchange process (the barter era); but, it has truly developed since the Industrial Revolution, as mass production and improved transportation have enabled more transactions to occur. For many firms, modern marketing has evolved via these eras: production, sales, marketing department, and marketing company. Yet, in developing nations, marketing is still in its early stages.

The marketing concept requires an organization or individual to be consumer-oriented, market-driven, and value-based; have an integrated effort; and be goal-oriented. A marketing philosophy means assessing and responding to consumer wants, to real differences in consumer tastes, and to long-run opportunities and threats, and to engage in coordinated decision making.

To prosper today, emphasis must be placed on customer service: the identifiable, rather intangible, acts performed by a seller in conjunction with the basic goods and/or services it offers. A number of firms now empower employees so as to improve the level of customer service. Customer satisfaction occurs when consumer expectations are met or exceeded; then, there are opportunities for firms to attract loyal customers by paying attention to relationship marketing.

3. *To show the importance of marketing as a field of study* Marketing is a crucial field for several reasons: it stimulates demand; marketing costs can be high; a large number of people work in marketing positions; it involves entire industries, such as advertising and marketing research; all organizations and people are consumers in some situations; it is necessary to use scarce resources efficiently; marketing impacts on people's beliefs and lifestyles; and marketing influences the quality of our lives. Some marketing knowledge is valuable to all of us, regardless of occupation.

4. *To describe the basic functions of marketing and those that perform these functions* The major marketing functions are environmental analysis and marketing research; broadening the scope of marketing; consumer analysis; product, distribution, promotion, and price planning; and marketing management. Responsibility for performing tasks can be shifted and shared among manufacturers and service providers, wholesalers, retailers, marketing specialists, and consumers. Due to costs, assortment requirements, specialized abilities, company size, established distribution methods, and consumer interests, one party usually does not perform all functions.

KEY TERMS

marketing (p. 6)
consumer demand (p. 6)
publics' demand (p. 6)
exchange (p. 6)
barter era (p. 7)
production era (p. 8)

sales era (p. 8)
marketing department era (p. 8)
marketing company era (p. 9)
marketing concept (p. 9)
customer service (p. 12)
empowering employees (p. 13)

customer satisfaction (p. 14)
relationship marketing (p. 14)
marketing functions (p. 19)
marketing performers (p. 20)

REVIEW QUESTIONS

1. Explain the
   a. Anticipation of demand.
   b. Management of demand.
   c. Satisfaction of demand.
   d. Exchange process.
2. Give an example of a good, service, organization, person, place, and idea that may be marketed.
3. Describe the five eras of marketing.

4. What are the five components of the marketing concept? Give an example of each component.
5. What is customer service? Why is it so important to any firm?
6. What is customer satisfaction? Why is it so important to any firm?
7. What are the basic functions performed by marketing?
8. Why do most consumers *not* buy products directly from manufacturers?

DISCUSSION QUESTIONS

1. a.   As Marie Jackson, CPA, what business-related marketing decisions would you make? Why?
    b.   As Albert Sampson, accounting client, what consumer-related marketing decisions would you make? Why?
    c.   Develop a plan for Marie Jackson to attract Albert Sampson as a client.

2. As the manager of an upscale health club, how would your customer services differ from those offered by a more price-oriented health club? Why?

3. Develop a seven-item questionnaire to assess the quality of a firm's customer satisfaction efforts.

4. What would a nonmarketing major learn by studying marketing? Give examples for three distinct majors (including at least two nonbusiness majors).

WEB EXERCISE

Visit the Web site of Zane's Cycles (www.zanescycles.com), a truly marketing-oriented small firm that has won many awards: "In the business where bicycles and accessories are pretty much the same, it's the people and policy of a company that make a difference. We know that it's your satisfaction with us that keeps us in business. That is why we, without reservation, guarantee that if for any reason, at any time, you are not completely satisfied with any item you purchased from us, we will gladly repair, replace, or refund your money." Discuss some of the tactics used by Zane's that make it so highly regarded.

Chapter 1 Appendix

Hints for Solving Cases

At the end of each part, from 1 through 8, there are four short cases (a total of 32) and one longer, more provocative case (a total of 8). All cases are intended to build on text discussions, improve your reasoning skills, and stimulate class discussions.

The cases in *Marketing in the 21st Century* describe actual marketing scenarios faced by a variety of organizations and people. The facts, situations, and people are all real. The questions following each case are designed to help you pinpoint major issues, foster your analysis, have you cite alternative courses of future action, and have you develop appropriate marketing strategies. The information necessary to answer the questions may be drawn from the case and the text chapter(s) to which the case relates.

These hints should be kept in mind when solving a case:

- Read (observe) all material carefully. Underline or take notes on important data and statements.
- List the key issues and company actions detailed in the case.
- Do not make unrealistic or unsupported assumptions.
- Read each question following the case. Be sure you understand the thrust of every question. Do not give similar answers for two distinct questions.

- Write up tentative answers in outline form. Cover as many aspects of each question as possible.
- Review relevant material in the appropriate chapter(s) of the text. In particular, look for information pertaining to the case questions.
- Expand your tentative answers, substantiating them with data from the case and the chapter(s).
- Reread the case and your notes to be sure you have not omitted any major concepts in your answers.
- Make sure your answers are clear and well written, and that you have considered their ramifications for the organization.
- Reread your solutions at least one day after developing your answers. This ensures a more objective review of your work.
- Make any necessary revisions.
- Be sure your answers are not a summary ("rehash") of the case, but that you have presented a real analysis and recommendations.

The Environment in Which Marketing Operates

2

Chapter Objectives

1 To examine the environment within which marketing decisions are made and marketing activities are undertaken

2 To differentiate between those elements controlled by a firm's top management and those controlled by marketing, and to enumerate the controllable elements of a marketing plan

3 To enumerate the uncontrollable environmental elements that can affect a marketing plan and study their potential ramifications

4 To explain why feedback about company performance and the uncontrollable aspects of its environment and the subsequent adaptation of the marketing plan are essential for a firm to attain its objectives

et's look at two firms' corporate culture: Disney (www.disney.com) and Main Street America Group (www.msagroup.com), a property/ casualty insurance company. As you will learn by reading this chapter, a corporate culture comprises shared values that are communicated and adhered to by employees. A firm's commitment to customer service is an example of a key value within a firm's corporate culture.

Disney's corporate culture is so consumer-oriented that many firms benchmark their own service levels against Disney's. Some send their employees and managers to Disney University for training. An important aspect of Disney's culture is reflected in the statement: "We make people happy." According to Disney, while Ford is in the motor vehicle business and Microsoft is in the software business, Disney's primary business is making people happy. Thus, all Disney employees are "in the show, not on the job," Disney employees wear costumes, not uniforms; and its employees are really cast members, not workers.

Main Street America Group's corporate culture is built around the statement, "I need to be able to trust you with my customers." Unlike many other insurance companies, it has no dedicated sales force; all of its policies are sold by independent agents. Thus, when an independent agent recommends an insurance carrier, he/she must be confident in that carrier's ability to deliver a high level of service. Main Street America Group also understands that independent agents have access to many competing insurers.

Like Disney, Main Street America Group puts its corporate culture in writing, has corporate culture workshops, makes sure that managers talk key values with their subordinates, and involves all employees in discussions of key values. Main Street America Group even realized that to satisfy its corporate culture goals, it had to redesign the way it handled claims so that the importance of agent and customer satisfaction was evident. According to the firm's chairman and chief executive officer, "I want my customer to feel your arm go around him (her) when he (she) has a claim." This is in contrast to some other insurers that have a strained relationship with their customers.[1]

In this chapter, we will study the complex environment in which marketing decisions are made. We will see that an organization's level of success (or failure) is related not only to its own efforts, but also to the external environment in which it operates and its ability to adapt to environmental changes.

2-1 OVERVIEW

The environment within which marketing decisions are made and enacted is depicted in Figure 2-1. The *marketing environment* consists of these five parts: controllable factors, uncontrollable factors, the organization's level of success or failure in reaching objectives, feedback, and adaptation.

The **marketing environment** *consists of controllable factors, uncontrollable factors, organizational performance, feedback, and adaptation.*

[1]John Guaspari, "We Make People Happy," *Across the Board* (April 2000), p. 53.

FIGURE 2-1

The Environment Within Which Marketing Operates

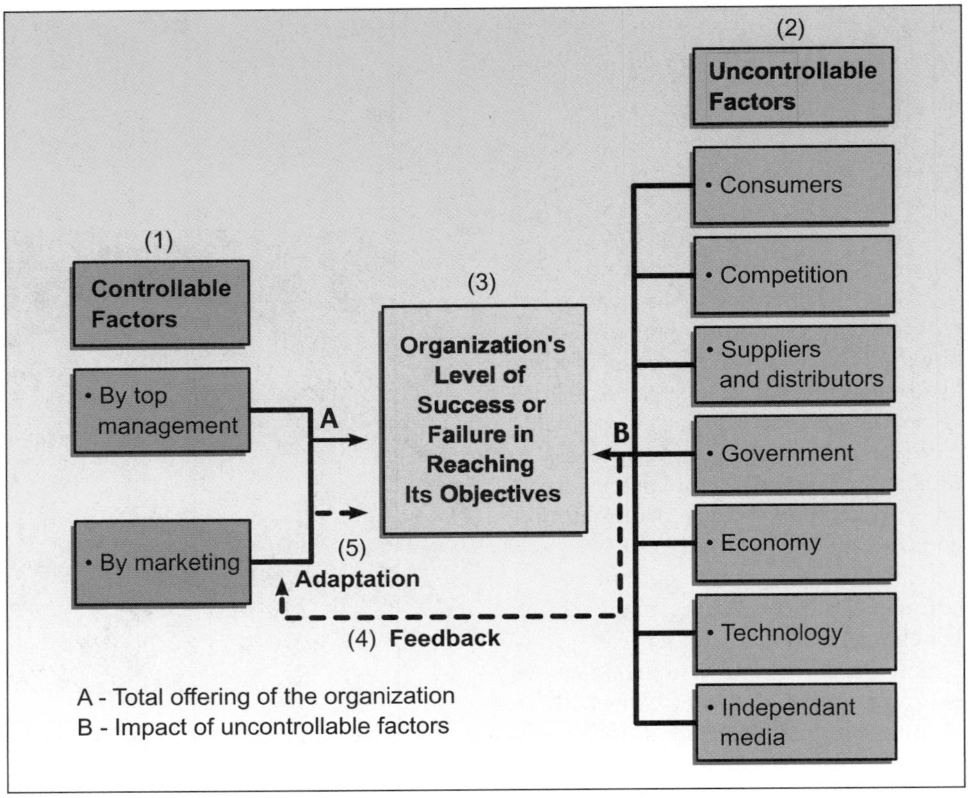

Figure content:

(1) **Controllable Factors**
- By top management
- By marketing

A — Total offering of the organization

(5) **Adaptation**

(4) **Feedback**

(3) **Organization's Level of Success or Failure in Reaching Its Objectives**

(2) **Uncontrollable Factors**
- Consumers
- Competition
- Suppliers and distributors
- Government
- Economy
- Technology
- Independant media

B — Impact of uncontrollable factors

Controllable factors are those directed by an organization and its marketers. First, several broad decisions are made by top management. Then, marketing managers make specific decisions based on the guidelines. In combination, these factors lead to an overall offering (A in Figure 2-1). The uncontrollable factors are beyond an organization's control, but they affect how well it does (B in Figure 2-1).

The interaction of controllable factors and uncontrollable factors determines an organization's level of success or failure in reaching its goals. Feedback occurs when a firm makes an effort to monitor uncontrollable factors and assess its strengths and weaknesses. Adaptation refers to the changes in a marketing plan that an organization makes to comply with the uncontrollable environment. If a firm is unwilling to consider the entire environment in a systematic manner, it increases the likelihood that it will have a lack of direction and not attain proper results.

Both the **macroenvironment** *and the* **microenvironment** *must be understood.*

When analyzing the environment, an organization should consider it from two perspectives: the macroenvironment and the microenvironment. The **macroenvironment** refers to the broad demographic, societal, economic, political, technological, and other forces that an organization faces. The **microenvironment** refers to the forces close to an organization that have a direct impact on its ability to serve customers, including distribution intermediaries, competitors, consumer markets, and the capabilities of the organization itself.[2] The Business Owner's Toolkit gives a good overview of the macroenvironment (www.toolkit.cch.com/text/P03_8023.asp).

Throughout this chapter, the various parts of Figure 2-1 are described and drawn together so the complex environment of marketing can be understood. In Chapter 3, the concept of strategic planning is presented. Such planning establishes a formal process for developing, implementing, and evaluating marketing programs in conjunction with the goals of top management.

[2]Peter D. Bennett (Editor), *Dictionary of Marketing Terms*, Second Edition (Chicago: American Marketing Association, 1995), pp. 159, 177.

ETHICAL *Issues in Marketing*

Yes, Deere, the EPA Can Be a Friend to Business (Sometimes, Anyway)

In what some analysts would call a classic role reversal, Deere & Co. (www.deere.com), a manufacturer of gasoline-powered lawn and garden tools, asked the Environmental Protection Agency (EPA) to enforce emissions guidelines two years ahead of the agency's announced schedule. Deere acknowledged that it had developed new technology for its hand-held lawn and garden tools which would provide considerably lower emissions than any competitive product.

Deere offered to license its new technology to such competitors as Sweden's AB Electrolux, but received no interest from them. According to an Electrolux spokesperson, "From what we know, we don't think it's able to start easily, idle properly, or provide acceptable performance at high speed. We believe the engine produces excess heat and can harm the operator and start fires."

Some critics of Deere's plan feel that hand-held lawn and garden tools contribute little to overall air pollution. For example, a report prepared for the Portable Power Equipment Manufacturers Association concluded that the devices made up a negligible part of the nation's total emissions: 0.8 percent of the volatile organic compounds, 0.6 percent of carbon monoxide, and a level of nitrogen oxide that was too low to measure.

Perhaps the real reason for Deere's seeking to speed up the regulatory process is that its newly-designed engines will add $20 to the cost of equipment, which generally now sell for between $59 and $99. Deere's vice-president for legal affairs said, "One reason we're after the EPA to tighten up is that we have to compete with the other engines. If we have to add on price, these units will sit on the shelf and gather dust."

As a marketing manager for Deere, develop a strategy for commercializing its low-emission engines.

Source: Based on material in Michael Fumento, "Hot Air," *Forbes* (March 20, 2000), p. 56.

2-2 CONTROLLABLE FACTORS

Controllable factors are internally directed by an organization and its marketers. Some of these factors are directed by top management; these are not controllable by marketers, who must develop plans to satisfy overall organizational goals. In situations involving small or medium-sized institutions, both broad policy and marketing decisions are often made by one person, usually the owner. Even in those cases, broad policies are typically set first and marketing plans adjust to them. Thus, a person could decide to open an office-supply store selling products to small businesses (broad policy) and stress convenient hours, a good selection of items, quantity discounts, and superior customer service (marketing plan).

The organization and its marketers can manage **controllable factors.**

2-2a Factors Directed by Top Management

Although top management is responsible for numerous decisions, five are of extreme importance to marketers: line of business, overall objectives, role of marketing, role of other business functions, and corporate culture. They have an impact on all aspects of marketing. Figure 2-2 shows the types of decisions in these areas.

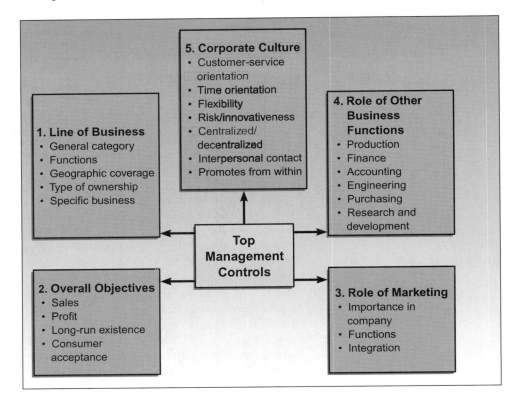

The **line of business** refers to the general goods/service category, functions, geographic coverage, type of ownership, and specific business of a firm. The general goods/service category is a broad definition of the industry in which a firm seeks to be involved. It may be energy, transportation, computing, or a number of others. The business functions outline a firm's position in the marketing system—from supplier to manufacturer to wholesaler to retailer—and the tasks it seeks to do. A firm may want to be in more than one position. Geographic coverage can be neighborhood, city, state, regional, national, or international. Ownership ranges from a sole proprietorship, partnership, or franchise to a multiunit corporation. The specific business is a narrow definition of the firm, its functions, and its operations, such as Lands' End and J. Crew (apparel direct marketers with long hours of service and a wide geographic reach).

A firm's **line of business** *refers to its business category.*

Overall objectives are the broad, measurable goals set by top management. A firm's success or failure may be determined by comparing objectives with actual performance. Usually, a combination of sales, profit, and other goals is stated by management for short-run (one year or less) and long-run (several years) periods. Most firms cite customer acceptance as a key goal with a strong effect on sales, profit, and long-run existence. The Business Owner's Toolkit gives a good synopsis of the considerations in goal setting (www.toolkit.cch.com/text/p01_0350.asp).

Top management determines the role of marketing by noting its importance, outlining its activities, and integrating it into a firm's overall operation. Marketing's importance is evident when marketing people have decision-making authority, the rank of the chief marketing officer is equal to that of other areas (usually vice-president), and proper resources are given. It is not considered important by a firm that gives marketing people advisory status, places marketing personnel in a subordinate position (like reporting to the production vice-president), equates marketing with sales, and withholds the funds needed for research, promotion, and other marketing tasks. The larger marketing's role, the greater the likelihood that a firm has an integrated marketing organization. The smaller its role, the greater the possibility that a firm undertakes marketing tasks on a project, crisis, or fragmented basis.

The roles of other business functions and their interrelationships with marketing need to be defined clearly to avoid overlaps, jealousy, and conflict. Production, finance, accounting, engineering, purchasing, and research and development departments each have different perspectives, orientations, and goals. This is discussed further in Chapter 3.

Top management strongly influences a firm's ***corporate culture:*** the shared values, norms, and practices communicated to and followed by those working for the firm. It may be described in terms of:

> **Corporate culture** *involves shared values, norms, and practices.*

- A *customer-service orientation*—Is the commitment to customer service clear to employees?

- A *time orientation*—Is a firm short- or long-run oriented?

- The *flexibility of the job environment*—Can employees deviate from rules? How formal are relations with subordinates? Is there a dress code?

- The *level of risk/innovation pursued*—Is risk taking fostered?

- The *use of a centralized/decentralized management structure*—How much input into decisions do middle managers have?

- The *level of interpersonal contact*—Do employees freely communicate with one another?

- The *use of promotions from within*—Are internal personnel given preference as positions open?

Kmart (www.bluelight.com) expects its employees to treat customers exceptionally well. See Figure 2-3. Metamorphics (http://www.competencysuite.com/demos.htm) is one of many firms that offers consulting services to enable clients to enhance their corporate cultures; and *Fortune* annually publishes a list of the best 100 companies to work for in the United States (www.fortune.com/fortune/bestcompanies).

FIGURE 2-3

Kmart: Communicating a Customer-Friendly Corporate Culture to Employees

Source: Reprinted by permission.

The company encourages its associates to always be respectful, fair and professional when working with one another and when serving all customers who shop at Kmart.

At its Web site (www.mutualofomaha.com), the Mutual of Omaha insurance company describes its corporate culture and the driving forces behind it:

> Mutual of Omaha has embraced a set of core values called "Values for Success." These 10 values form the foundation for a corporate culture that will help us realize our vision and achieve our goals. Our shared values set the standard for how we deal with customers and how we treat each other.
> - *Openness and Trust*—We encourage an open sharing of ideas and information, displaying a fundamental respect for each other, as well as our cultural diversity.
> - *Teamwork*—We work together to find solutions that carry positive results for others as well as ourselves, creating an environment that brings out the best in everyone.
> - *Accountability/Ownership*—We take ownership and accept accountability for achieving end results, and encourage and empower team members to do the same.
> - *Sense of Urgency*—We set priorities and handle all tasks and assignments in a timely manner.
> - *Honesty and Integrity*—We are honest and ethical with others, maintaining the highest standards of personal and professional conduct.
> - *Customer Focus*—We never lose sight of our customers, and constantly challenge ourselves to meet their requirements even better.
> - *Innovation and Risk*—We question the old ways of doing things and take prudent risks that can lead to innovative performance and process improvements.
> - *Caring/Attentive*—We take time to clear our minds to focus on the present moment, listening to our teammates and customers, and caring enough to hear their concerns.
> - *Leadership*—We provide direction, purpose, support, encouragement, and recognition to achieve our vision, meet our objectives, and live our values.
> - *Personal and Professional Growth*—We challenge ourselves and look for ways to be even more effective as a team and as individuals.[3]

After top management sets company guidelines, the marketing area begins to develop the factors under its control.

2-2b Factors Directed by Marketing

The major factors controlled by marketing personnel are the selection of a target market, marketing objectives, the marketing organization, the marketing mix, and assessment of the marketing plan. See Figure 2-4.

One of the most crucial marketing-related decisions involves selecting a **target market,** which is the particular group(s) of customers a firm proposes to serve, or whose needs it proposes to satisfy, with a particular marketing program. When selecting a target market, a company usually engages in some form of **market segmentation,** which involves subdividing a market into clear subsets of customers that act in the same way or that have comparable needs.[4] A company can choose a large target market or concentrate on a small one, or try to appeal to both with separate marketing programs for each. Generally, these questions must be addressed before devising a marketing approach: Who are our customers? What kinds of goods and services do they want? How can we attract them to our company? For some interesting insights on target markets, look at the Web site of Brock Henderson & Associates (www.iglou.com/bhenderson/target.htm).

At marketing-oriented firms, the choice of a target market impacts on all other marketing decisions. A book publisher appealing to the high school science market would have a different marketing approach than one appealing to the adult fiction market. The first firm would seek an image as a well-established publisher; specialize product offerings; make presentations to high school book-selection committees; sell in large quantities; offer durable books with many photos and line drawings that could be used for several

> A **target market** *is the customer group to which an organization appeals.* **Market segmentation** *is often used in choosing a target market.*

---

[3]Mutual of Omaha, "Our Vision and Values," www.mutualofomaha.com/about/values.html (February 5, 2001).

[4]Bennett, *Dictionary of Marketing Terms*, pp. 165–166.

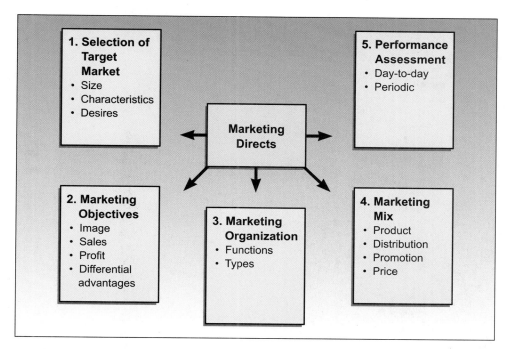

F I G U R E   2 - 4

**Factors Controlled
by Marketing**

years; and so on. The second firm would capitalize on well-known authors or publish books on hot topics to establish an image; have books on a variety of subjects; use newspaper ads and seek favorable reviews; distribute via bookstores; sell in small quantities (except if large chains are involved); de-emphasize durability, photos, and artwork and produce books as efficiently as possible; and so on.

Marketing objectives are more customer-oriented than those set by top management. Marketers are quite interested in the image consumers hold of a firm and its products. Sales goals reflect a concern for brand loyalty (repeat purchases), growth via new-product introductions, and appeal to unsatisfied market segments. Profit goals can be related to long-term customer loyalty. Most importantly, marketers seek to create ***differential advantages,*** the unique features in a firm's marketing program that cause consumers to patronize that firm and not its competitors. Without differential advantages, a firm would have a "me-too" philosophy and offer the consumer no reasons to select its offerings over competitors' products.

Differential advantages can be based on a distinct image, new products or features, product quality, customer service, low prices, availability, and other factors. Snapple (www.snapple.com) is known for offbeat flavors such as Cactus Tea and Diet Orange Carrot, Levi's Dockers (www.us.dockers.com) for a comfortable fit, Sony (www.sony.com) for high-tech audio/video products, Tiffany (www.tiffany.com) for high-quality jewelry, Nordstrom (www.nordstrom.com) for outstanding customer service, and Wal-Mart (www.walmart.com) for selection and prices. Figure 2-5 shows how Build-a-Bear Workshop lets customers make stuffed animals. The animals can even be built online (www2.buildabear.com/AboutUs; click on "Let's go shopping"): "Here in our online interactive workshop you and your children can choose, stuff, stitch, fluff, and dress your very own teddy bear. Your new teddy bear, shipped in our exclusive Cub Condo, will arrive in just 4–7 business days, just in time for a big hug from you!"

Differential advantages *consist of the firm's unique features that attract consumers.*

*A **marketing organization** may be functional, product-oriented, or market-oriented.*

A ***marketing organization*** is the structural arrangement that directs marketing functions. It outlines authority, responsibility, and the tasks to be done so that functions are assigned and coordinated. As illustrated in Figure 2-6, an organization may be functional, with jobs assigned in terms of buying, selling, promotion, distribution, and other tasks; product-oriented, with product managers for each product category and brand managers for each brand, in addition to functional categories; or market-oriented, with jobs assigned by geographic market and customer type, in addition to functional categories. A single firm may use a mixture of forms.

*The **marketing mix** consists of four elements: product, distribution, promotion, and price.*

A ***marketing mix*** is the specific combination of marketing elements used to achieve objectives and satisfy the target market. It encompasses decisions regarding four major variables: *Product* decisions involve determining what goods, services, organizations, people, places, and/or ideas to market; the number of items to sell and their quality; the innovativeness pursued; packaging; product features; warranties; when to drop existing offerings; and so on. *Distribution* decisions include determining whether to sell via intermediaries or directly to consumers, how many outlets to sell through, how to interact with other channel members, what terms to negotiate, the functions to assign to others, supplier choice, and so on. *Promotion* decisions include selecting a combination of tools (ads, public relations, personal selling, and sales promotion), whether to share promotions with others, the image to pursue, the level of personal service, media choice, message content, promotion timing, and so on. *Price* decisions include choosing overall price levels, the range of prices, the relation between price and quality, the emphasis to place on price, how to react to competitors, when to offer discounts, how prices are computed, what billing terms to use, and so on. A marketing mix is used by all firms, even farmers selling at roadside stands.

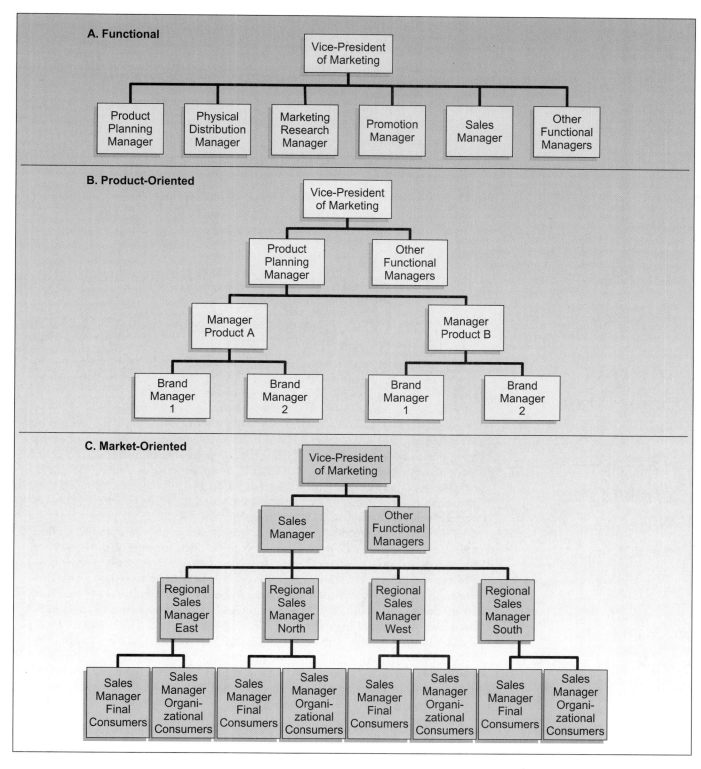

INTERACTIVE FIGURE

FIGURE 2-6

Illustrations of Marketing Organizations

When devising a marketing mix, these questions should all be considered:

- Is the target market precisely defined?
- Does the total marketing effort, as well as each element of the mix, meet the target market's needs?
- Are marketing mix elements consistent with one another?
- Do the elements add up to form a harmonious, integrated whole?
- Is each marketing mix element being given its best use?
- Does the marketing mix build on the firm's cultural and tangible strengths? Does the marketing mix imply a way to correct any weaknesses?
- Is a distinctive personality in the competitive marketplace created?
- Is the company protected from the most obvious competitive threats?[5]

MARKETING *and the Web*

Internet Sales May Be Taxing— Or Maybe Not!

In 1998, Congress passed the Internet Tax Freedom Act—a moratorium on new Internet taxes until October 2001. What this act did not resolve is whether taxes were due on Web sales before that date.

While many major online retailers (such as www.eddiebauer.com and www.radioshack.com) collect sales tax from shoppers in the 45 states that have a state sales tax (www.salestaxinstitute.com), many other merchants choose not to collect these taxes. Even though residents of states with a sales tax are legally obligated to pay a use tax if an online retailer doesn't collect it, very few consumers actually do so. And in 1992, the Supreme Court ruled that states cannot require a retailer to collect the sales tax from a customer unless it has a store or warehouse in his/her state.

In theory, online retailers with hundreds of stores throughout the United States (such as Barnes & Noble) are at a price disadvantage with those that have operations only in a single state (such as Amazon.com) due to their having to charge sales tax virtually everywhere. This puts them at a major cost disadvantage in areas with a high sales tax. To get around this problem, retailers such as Barnes & Noble and Wal-Mart have developed separate catalog subsidiaries to avoid sales tax collection.

According to some marketing analysts, Wal-Mart's tax-free strategy is "skating near the legal edge," since the retailer allows consumers who purchase goods tax-free through the Web to return their purchases to any of its retail stores. Interestingly, Wal-Mart is a co-founder of the E-Fairness Coalition, a group arguing that a tax-free Web gives an unfair advantage to Web-based merchants.

Should online purchases be taxed? Take both a consumer and traditional "bricks-and-mortar" retailer perspective.

Source: Based on material in Janet Novack, "E-Confusion: How Come You Pay Sales Taxes on Some Internet Purchases and Not on Others?" *Forbes* (February 28, 2000), p. 26.

[5]Benson P. Shapiro, "Rejuvenating the Marketing Mix," *Harvard Business Review*, Vol. 63 (September-October 1985), p. 34. See also Walter van Waterschoot and Christophe Van den Bulte, "The 4P Classification of the Marketing Mix Revisited," *Journal of Marketing*, Vol. 56 (October 1992), pp. 83–93; and Boonghee Yoo, Naveen Donthu, and Sungho Lee, "An Examination of Selected Marketing Mix Elements and Brand Equity," *Journal of the Academy of Marketing Science*, Vol. 28 (Spring 2000), pp. 195–211.

Olympus (www.olympus.com), a leading maker of cameras and other products, is an example of a firm applying the marketing mix concept well. It has distinct marketing mixes for different target markets. For beginners, it offers simple cameras with automatic focus and a built-in flash. The cameras are sold in all types of stores, such as discount and department stores. Ads appear on TV and in general magazines. The cameras typically retail for less than $100. For serious amateur photographers, Olympus has more advanced cameras with superior features and attachments. They are found in camera stores and finer department stores. Ads are in specialty magazines. The cameras sell for several hundred dollars. For professional photographers, Olympus has even more advanced cameras with top-of-the-line features and attachments. They are sold via select camera stores. Ads are in trade magazines. The cameras are costly (the E-10 is priced at about $2,000). In sum, Olympus markets the right products in the right stores, promotes them in the right media, and has the right prices for its various target markets.

The last, but extremely important, factor directed by marketers involves performance assessment: monitoring and evaluating overall and specific marketing effectiveness. Evaluations need to be done regularly, with both the external environment and internal company data being reviewed. In-depth analysis of performance should be completed at least once or twice each year. Strategy revisions need to be enacted when the external environment changes or the company encounters difficulties.

Performance assessment involves monitoring and evaluating marketing activities.

2-3 UNCONTROLLABLE FACTORS

Uncontrollable factors are the external elements affecting an organization's performance that cannot be fully directed by that organization and its marketers. A marketing plan, no matter how well conceived, may fail if uncontrollable factors have too adverse an impact. Thus, the external environment must be regularly observed and its effects considered in any marketing plan. Contingency plans relating to uncontrollable variables should also be a key part of a marketing plan. Uncontrollable factors that especially bear studying are consumers, competition, suppliers and distributors, government, the economy, technology, and independent media. See Figure 2-7.

Uncontrollable factors *influence an organization and its marketers but are not fully directed by them.*

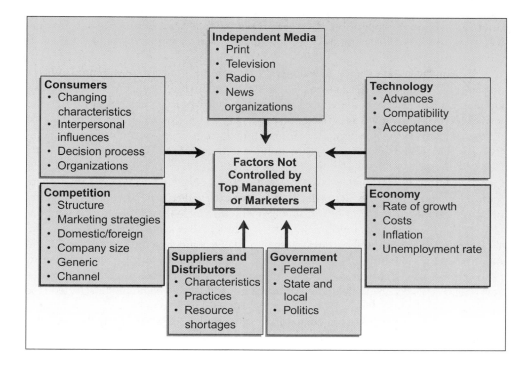

F I G U R E   2 - 7
Uncontrollable Factors

2-3a Consumers

Organizations need to understand consumer trends, interpersonal influences, the decision process, and consumer groups.

Although a firm has control over its selection of a target market, it cannot control the changing characteristics of its final or organizational consumers. A firm can react to, but not control, consumer trends related to age, income, marital status, occupation, race, education, place and type of residence, and the size of organizational customers. For example, health insurers must deal with the fact that many of their largest business customers are downsizing; thus, there are fewer employees to be insured there.

Interpersonal influences on consumer behavior need to be understood. People's purchases are affected by the corporate culture at their jobs as purchasing agents; their family, friends, and other social contacts; and the customs and taboos shaping culture and society. For instance, in some states, liquor sales are more regulated (as to outlets, prices, other goods that can be sold, and days open) than they are in others through state liquor boards (www.atf.treas.gov/alcohol/info/faq/subpages/lcb.htm).

Because people act differently in buying various types of goods and services, the consumer decision process—the steps people go through when buying products—affects the way that products are marketed. In the case of company cars, a purchasing agent carefully looks for information on a number of models, ranks several alternatives, selects a favorite, negotiates terms, and finally completes the purchase. On the other hand, with an inexpensive meal, a person looks at a watch, sees it is lunch time, and goes to a nearby fast-food outlet.

Consumer rights groups speak on behalf of consumers at public hearings, at stockholder meetings, and with the mass media. To avoid some negative consequences from active consumer groups, a firm must communicate with customers on relevant issues (such as a product recall), anticipate problems (such as order delays), respond to complaints (such as poor service), and be sure it has good community relations (such as sponsoring neighborhood projects). Consumers Union (www.consumersunion.org), which publishes *Consumer Reports*, is one of the largest consumer advocacy groups.

2-3b Competition

The competitive environment often affects a company's marketing efforts and its success in reaching a target market. Thus, a firm should assess its industry structure and examine competitors in terms of marketing strategies, domestic/foreign firms, size, generic competition, and channel competition. Each year, *Business Week* (www.businessweek.com) publishes an overview of the trends occurring in a number of industries. It also makes its forecasts available online.

Monopoly, oligopoly, monopolistic competition, *and* **pure competition** *are the main types of competitive structure.*

A company could operate under one of four possible competitive structures: With a **monopoly,** just one firm sells a given good or service and has a lot of control over its marketing plan. This occurs in the United States when a firm has a patent (exclusive rights to a sell a product it invented for a fixed number of years) or is a public utility, such as a local power company. In an **oligopoly,** a few firms—usually large ones—account for most industry sales and would like to engage in nonprice competition. The U.S. auto industry (www.activemedia-guide.com/motor_vehicle_industry.htm) is a good example of this. General Motors, Ford, DaimlerChrysler, Toyota, Honda, Nissan, and Volkswagen account for nearly 93 percent of U.S. auto sales. In **monopolistic competition,** there are several firms in an industry, each trying to offer a unique marketing mix—based on price or nonprice factors. It is the most common U.S. industry structure, followed by oligopoly. Service stations, beauty salons, stationery stores, garment makers, computer-clone makers, and furniture makers are some firms facing monopolistic competition. In **pure competition,** many firms sell virtually identical goods or services and they are unable to create differential advantages. This occurs rarely in the United States and is most common for selected food items and commodities (and happens if numerous small firms compete with each other).

After analyzing its industry's competitive structure, a firm should study the strategies of competitors. It should look at their target markets and marketing mixes, images, differential advantages, which markets are saturated and which are unfulfilled, and the extent to which consumers are content with the service and quality provided by competitors. See Figure 2-8. Hoover's Online (www.hoovers.com) is an excellent source of information on thousands of firms around the world. Brief company profiles are free.

FIGURE 2-8

REI: Succeeding in a Highly Competitive Marketplace

REI (www.rei.com) is a retailer of high-end gear, clothing, and footwear for camping, bicycling, climbing, paddling, and other outdoor activities. Although it competes with scores of other firms, from Sports Authority to North Face to L.L. Bean to Lone Arrow, REI stands out. Its stores are exciting (as this photo shows), it has strong guarantees, and its members can save money on the products carried.

Source: Reprinted by permission of PricewaterhouseCoopers.

Both domestic and foreign competition should be examined. For instance, in the United States, Merrill Lynch (www.ml.com) competes with Citigroup (www.citigroup.com), American Express (www.americanexpress.com), and others—besides traditional brokerage firms—for financial services business. Many U.S. and West European industries are mature; the amount of domestic competition there is rather stable. In some industries, competition is rising due to the popularity of innovations like notebook PCs. In others, domestic competition is intensifying as a result of government deregulation. For instance, there are 500 companies offering long-distance telephone service in the United States alone (www.active-media-guide.com/teleservices.htm).

Foreign competitors now play a major role in many industries. In the United States, foreign-based firms are capturing large market shares—33 percent for steel, 65 percent for clothing, 85 percent for shoes, and up to 98 percent for some consumer electronics. At the same time, competition in foreign markets is more intense for U.S.-based firms than before as rivals stress innovations, cost cutting, good distribution and promotion, and other factors. Nonetheless, U.S.-based firms remain globally dominant in such areas as aerospace, chemicals, information technology, pharmaceuticals, and food and beverages.[6]

Foreign competition is intensifying.

For many industries, there has been a trend toward larger firms because of mergers and acquisitions, as well as company sales growth. Over the last decade, mergers and acquisitions have involved: telecommunications firms such as Bell Atlantic, now Verizon (www.verizon.com), acquiring Nynex; food firms such as Nestlé (www.nestle.com) acquiring San Pellegrino water; pharmaceuticals firms such as Glaxo Wellcome and SmithKline Beecham merging to form GlaxoSmithKline (www.gsk.com); media firms such as AOL merging with Time Warner to form AOL Time Warner (www.aoltimewarner.com); consumer products firms such as Sony (www.sony.com) buying CBS Records; retailers such as McDonald's (www.mcdonalds.com) acquiring Boston Market; and numerous others.

[6]*U.S. Industry & Trade Outlook 2000* (New York: McGraw-Hill, 2000).

Internal sales growth has been great for such firms as Cisco Systems, Wal-Mart, Microsoft, Toyota, Dell, and Federal Express—each with annual sales of several billion dollars.

From a small-firm vantage point, personal service, a focus on underserved market segments, an entrepreneurial drive, and flexibility are differential advantages; cooperative ventures and franchising let such firms buy in bulk and operate more efficiently. To large firms, widespread distribution, economies of scale, well-known brands, mass-media ads, and low-to-moderate prices are competitive tactics.

Competition should be defined generically—as widely as possible.

Every firm should define competition in generic terms, meaning as broadly as possible. *Direct competitors* are similar to the firm as to the line of business and marketing approach. *Indirect competitors* are different from the firm, but still compete with it for customers. Both types should be accounted for in a marketing plan. For instance, a movie theater not only competes with other theaters—direct competitors; but with online entertainment (such as www.shockwave.com), video stores, TV and radio shows, video games, sporting events, amusement parks, bookstores, and schools—all indirect competitors. A theater owner should ask, "What can I do to compete with a variety of entertainment and recreation forms, in terms of movie selection, prices, hours, service, refreshments, and parking?"

A company should also study the competition from its channel members (resellers). Each party in the distribution process has different goals and would like to maximize its control over the marketing mix. Some wholesalers and retailers carry their own brands besides those of manufacturers.

2-3c Suppliers and Distributors

Many firms rely on their suppliers and distributors (wholesalers and retailers) to properly run their own businesses. Without their ongoing support, it would be hard, if not impossible, for a company to succeed.

Suppliers and distributors can have a dramatic impact on an organization.

Suppliers provide the goods and services that firms need to operate, as well as those that the firms resell to their customers. In general, a firm is most vulnerable when there are relatively few suppliers, specific goods and services are needed to run a business or satisfy customer demand, competitors would gain if the firm has a falling-out with a supplier, suppliers are better attuned to the desires of the marketplace, suppliers informally take care of maintenance and repair services, the turnaround time to switch suppliers is lengthy, and suppliers have exclusive access to scarce resources.

For firms unable to market products directly to consumers, distributors (wholesalers or retailers) are needed. In general, a firm is most vulnerable when there are relatively few distributors in an area, the distributors carry many brands, shelf space is tight, the firm is unknown in the marketplace, particular distributors account for a large part of the firm's revenues, distributors help finance the firm, distributors are better attuned to the marketplace, and competitors are waiting in the wings to stock the distributors.

These are among the supplier/distributor practices that a firm should regularly study: delivery time or requests, product availability, prices, flexibility in handling special requests, marketing support, consistency of treatment, returns policies, and other services. Unsatisfactory performance in one or more of these areas could have a lasting impact on a firm and its competence to enact marketing plans.

Regardless of suppliers' good intentions, a firm's ability to carry out its plans can be affected by the availability of scarce resources. Over the past 30 years, sporadic shortages and volatile price changes have occurred for many basic commodities, such as home heating oil, other petroleum-based products, plastics, synthetic fibers, aluminum, chrome, silver, tungsten, nickel, steel, glass, grain, fertilizer, cotton, and wool. And despite efforts at conservation, some raw materials, processed materials, and component parts may remain or become scarce over the next decade.

Resource shortages and/or rapid cost increases would require one of these three actions: (1) Substitute materials could be used to construct products, requiring more research and product testing. (2) Prices could be raised for products that cannot incorporate substitute materials. (3) Firms could abandon products if resources are unavailable and demarket others where demand is greater than can be satisfied.

2-3d Government

Worldwide, governmental bodies have a great impact on marketing practices by placing (or removing) restrictions on specified activities. Rulings can be on a regional, national, state, and/or local level. For example, in Europe, the European Union sets rules for its member nations.

In the United States, for more than 110 years, the Congress has enacted federal legislation affecting marketing practices, as highlighted in Table 2-1. This legislation can be divided into three groups: antitrust, discriminatory pricing, and unfair trade practices; consumer protection; and deregulation.

Laws in the first group protect smaller firms from anticompetitive acts by larger ones. These laws seek a "level playing field" for all by barring firms from using marketing practices that unfairly harm competitors. Laws in the second group help consumers deal with deceptive and unsafe business practices. These laws protect consumer rights and restrict certain marketing activities (like banning cigarette ads from TV and radio). Laws in the third group have deregulated various industries to create a more competitive marketplace. They allow firms greater flexibility in marketing plans. The Federal Trade Commission (FTC) is the major U.S. regulatory agency monitoring restraint of trade and enforcing rules against unfair competition and deceptive business practices (www.ftc.gov), such as the 30-day rule for direct marketing (www.ftc.gov/bcp/conline/pubs/buspubs/mailordr/index.htm).

In addition to federal regulation and agencies, each state and local government in the United States has its own legal environment. State and local laws may regulate where a firm is allowed to locate, the hours open, the types of items sold, if prices must be marked on every item sold, how goods must be labeled or dated, the amount of sales tax (www.salestaxinstitute.com), and so on. State and local governments may also provide incentives, such as small business assistance, for firms to operate there.

U.S. federal legislation involves interstate commerce. And each state and local government has its own regulations, as well.

TABLE 2-1 Key U.S. Legislation Affecting Marketers

Year	Legislation	Major Purpose
A. Antitrust, Discriminatory Pricing, and Unfair Trade Practices		
1890	Sherman Act	To eliminate monopolies
1914	Clayton Act	To ban anticompetitive acts
1914	FTC Act	To establish the Federal Trade Commission to enforce rules against restraints of trade
1936	Robinson-Patman Act	To prohibit price discrimination toward small distributors or retailers
1938	Wheeler-Lea Amendment	To amend the FTC Act to include more unfair or deceptive practices
1946	Lanham Trademark Act	To protect and regulate trademarks and brands
1976	Hart-Scott-Rodino Act	To require large firms to notify the government of their merger plans
1989	Trademark Revision Act	To revise the Lanham Trademark Act to include products not yet introduced on the market
1990	Antitrust Amendments Act	To raise the maximum penalties for price fixing
1994	International Antitrust Enforcement Assistance Act	To authorize the Federal Trade Commission and the Justice Department to enter into mutual assistance programs with foreign antitrust authorities
1995	Interstate Commerce Communication Termination Act	To require the Federal Trade Commission and the Justice Department to file periodic reports to assess and make recommendations concerning anticompetitive features of rate agreements among common carriers

continues

TABLE 2-1   Key U.S. Legislation Affecting Marketers *(continued)*

Year	Legislation	Major Purpose
B. Consumer Protection		
1906	Food and Drug Act	To ban adulterated and misbranded food and drugs, and form the
1906	Meat Inspection Act	the Food and Drug Administration (FDA)
1914	FTC Act	To establish a commission and provisions for protecting consumer
1938	Wheeler-Lea Amendment	rights
1939	Wool Products Labeling Act	To require wool, fur, and textile products to show contents and to
1951	Fur Products Labeling Act	prohibit dangerous flammables
1953	Flammable Fabrics Act	
1958	Textile Fiber Identification Act	
1958	Food Additives Amendment	To prohibit food additives causing cancer, require labels for
1960	Federal Hazardous Substances Labeling Act	hazardous household products, and require drug makers to demonstrate effectiveness and safety
1962	Kefauver-Harris Amendment	
1966	Fair Packaging and Labeling Act	To require honest package labeling and reduce package-size proliferation
1966	National Traffic and Motor Vehicle Safety Act	To set safety standards for autos and tires
1966	Child Protection Act	To ban hazardous products used by children, create standards for
1969	Child Toy Safety Act	child-resistant packages, and provide drug information
1970	Poison Prevention Labeling Act	
1972	Drug Listing Act	
1966	Cigarette Labeling Act	To require warnings on cigarette packages and ban radio and TV
1970	Public Health Smoking Act	cigarette ads
1967	Wholesome Meat Act	To mandate federal inspection standards
1968	Wholesome Poultry Act	
1968	Consumer Credit Protection Act	To have full disclosure of credit terms and regulate the use of credit
1970	Fair Credit Reporting Act	information
1970	Clean Air Act	To protect the environment
1972	Consumer Product Safety Act	To create the Consumer Product Safety Commission (CPSC) and set safety standards
1975	Magnuson-Moss Consumer Product Warranty Act	To regulate warranties and set disclosure requirements
1975	Consumer Goods Pricing Act	To disallow retail price maintenance
1980	Fair Debt Collection Practices Act	To eliminate the harassment of debtors and ban false statements to collect debts
1980	FTC Improvement Act	To reduce the power of the FTC to implement industrywide trade regulations
1990	Clean Air Act	To expand the 1970 Clean Air Act
1990	Children's Television Act	To reduce the amount of commercials during children's programs
1990	Nutrition Labeling and Education Act	To have the FDA develop a new system of food labeling
1991	Telephone Consumer Protection Act	To safeguard consumers against undesirable telemarketing practices
1992	Cable Television Consumer Protection and Competition Act	To better protect consumer rights with regard to cable television services

continues

Year	Legislation	Major Purpose
TABLE 2-1		**Key U.S. Legislation Affecting Marketers (continued)**
1996	Credit Repair Organizations Act	To prohibit misleading representations associated with credit repair services
1998	Children's Online Protection Act	To protect children's privacy by giving parents the tools to control what information is collected from their children online
1998	Telemarketing Fraud Protection Act	To strengthen penalties for telemarketing fraud
1999	Gramm-Leach-Bliley Act	To protect the privacy of consumers' personal financial information

C. *Industry Deregulation*

Over the last 25 years, a host of laws has been enacted to make the natural gas, airline, trucking, railroad, banking, electricity, telecommunications, and other industries more competitive.

GLOBAL *Marketing in Action*

When in Rome: Playing by Different Rules for Advertising to Children

Many European nations have more restrictive laws as to the use of promotions or advertising targeted to minors than the United States does. Let's look at some restrictions placed on marketing to children in Europe.

Italian TV programs with an adult orientation must display a symbol indicating that the programs are not suitable for children. In Britain, advertising codes specify that marketing to children should not encourage them to eat or drink at or near bedtime, to eat frequently throughout the day, or to replace main meals with snacks or candy. Sweden restricts all TV and radio advertising to children 12 and younger, and prohibits all direct marketing to children younger than 16. Austria has restrictions on the use of cartoon or comic characters and celebrities in child-oriented advertising.

Despite the presence of these and other laws throughout Europe, many Europeans still want more regulations and restrictions. Some consumer groups are concerned that children cannot distinguish between advertising and programming. Others feel that children lack judgment to separate puffery from reality. Belgian legislators are even considering a limit on the time that advertisers could run ads between St. Nicholas Day and Christmas. Many Belgians think that advertising starts too early and blurs the differences between each holiday. Some observers feel that it is possible that the European Union will set a unified set of restrictions for all of its member countries within the next three years.

Despite the stringent restrictions on advertising to children, only a few European countries restrict Web-based transactions. The lack of interest in regulating the Web in Europe may be due to the relatively slow rate of adoption of the Internet in Europe.

Should the U.S. adopt some of the restrictions on advertising to children that are popular in Europe?

Source: Based on material in Michael Plogell and Felix Hofer, "No-Nos in Europe," *Promo* (April 2000), pp. 23–26.

The political environment often affects legislation. Marketing issues such as these are typically discussed via the political process prior to laws being enacted (or not enacted): Should certain goods and services be stopped from advertising on TV? Should state governments become more active in handling consumer complaints? Both firms and consumer groups can have input into the process. The goal is to market their positions to government officials. A strength of the U.S. political system is its continuity, which lets organizations and individuals develop strategies for long periods of time.

Privatization is changing the number of businesses in foreign countries.

Outside the United States, one of the biggest legal and political challenges facing countries that now have free-market economies—after decades or more of government-controlled markets—is how to *privatize* organizations that were formerly run by the government: "Fluctuations in foreign exchange rates, inadequate domestic investments, and illogical pricing of stocks are among the most important obstacles to privatization. Misunderstanding, a lack of unified viewpoints among officials, fluctuations in stock prices, and rivalry between various state-run institutes and foundations with those in the private sector are other important impediments to the process."[7]

2-3e The Economy

The rate of growth in a nation's or region's economy can have a big impact on a firm's marketing efforts. A high growth rate means the economy is strong and the marketing potential large. Quite important to marketers are consumer perceptions—both in the business and final consumer sectors—regarding the economy. For instance, if people believe the economy will be favorable, they may increase spending; if they believe the economy will be poor, they may cut back. To measure consumer perceptions, the Conference Board (www.crc-conquest.org/consumer_confidence/index.htm) and the University of Michigan (http://athena.sea.isr.umich.edu), among others, do consumer confidence surveys to see if Americans are optimistic, pessimistic, or neutral about the economy. In uncertain times, many organizational consumers are interested in preserving their flexibility.

Economic growth is measured by the **Gross Domestic Product.**

A country's economic growth is reflected by changes in its **Gross Domestic Product (GDP),** which is the total annual value of goods and services produced in a country less net foreign investment. These are the estimated 2000 GDPs (in U.S. dollars and at purchasing parity) for ten selected nations: United States, $10 trillion; Japan, $3.0 trillion; Germany, $2.0 trillion; India, $1.9 trillion; France, $1.5 trillion; Italy, $1.2 trillion; Brazil, $1.1 billion; Mexico, $875 billion; Canada, $725 billion; and Thailand, $400 billion.[8] In recent years, the yearly growth in most of these nations has been three percent or so; and when certain industries, such as autos and housing, speed up or slow down, the effects are felt in other areas, such as insurance and home furnishings. The United States is expected to have real GDP growth averaging about 3 to 5 percent annually during the next few years.[9]

Several business costs—like raw materials, unionized labor wages, taxes, interest rates, and office (factory) rental—are generally beyond any firm's control. If costs rise by a large amount, marketing flexibility may be limited since a firm often cannot pass along all of the increase; it might have to cut back on marketing activities or accept lower profits. If costs are stable, marketers are better able to differentiate products and expand sales because their firms are more apt to invest in marketing activities.

Real income describes earnings adjusted for inflation. Both inflation and unemployment affect purchases.

From a marketing perspective, what happens to a consumer's real income is critical. While actual income is the amount earned by a consumer (or his/her family or household) in a given year, **real income** is the amount earned in a year adjusted by the rate of inflation.

---

[7]"Irani Minister Enumerates Obstacles to Privatization," *AsiaPulse News* (December 7, 2000), p. 0609.

[8]Estimated by the authors from the *World Factbook 2000* (Washington, D.C.: Central Intelligence Agency, 2000).

[9]For ongoing information about the U.S. economy, go to the Web site for the *Survey of Current Business:* www.bea.doc.gov/bea/pubs.htm.

For example, if a person's actual income goes up by 4 percent in a year (from $40,000 to $41,600) and the rate of inflation (which measures price changes for the same goods and services over time) is 4 percent for the year, real income remains constant [($41,600) − ($41,600/1.04) = $40,000]. If actual income increases exceed the inflation rate, real income rises and people can buy more goods and services. If actual income increases are less than the inflation rate, real income falls and people must buy fewer goods and services.

A high rate of unemployment can adversely affect many firms because people who are unemployed are likely to cut back on nonessentials wherever possible. Low unemployment often means substantial sales of large-ticket items, as consumers are better off, more optimistic, and more apt to spend earnings.

2-3f   Technology

Technology refers to developing and using machinery, products, and processes. Individual firms, especially smaller ones with limited capital, must usually adapt to technological advances (rather than control them).

Technology includes machinery, products, and processes.

Many firms depend on others to develop and perfect new technology, such as computer microchips; only then can they use the new technology in products, such as automated gasoline pumps at service stations, talking toys, or electronic sensors in smoke detectors for office buildings. With new technology, the inventor often secures patent protection, which excludes competitors from using that technology (unless the inventor licenses rights for a fee).

In several areas, companies have been unable to achieve practical technological breakthroughs. For example, no firm has been able to develop and market a cure for the common cold, a good-tasting nontobacco cigarette, a commercially acceptable electric car, or a truly effective and safe diet pill.

When new technology first emerges, it may be expensive and in short supply, both for firms using the technology in their products and for final consumers. The challenge is to mass produce and mass market the technology efficiently. In addition, some technological advances require employee training and consumer education before they can succeed. Thus, an emphasis on user-friendliness can speed up the acceptance of new technology.

Certain advances may not be compatible with goods and services already on the market or require retooling by firms wanting to use them in products or operations. Every time an auto maker introduces a significantly new car model, it must invest hundreds of millions of dollars to retool facilities. Each time a firm buys new computer equipment to supplement existing hardware, it must see if the new equipment is compatible. Can it run all the computer programs the firm uses and "talk" to its existing machines?

To flourish, technological advances must be accepted by each firm in the distribution process (manufacturer/service provider, wholesaler, retailer). Should any of the firms not use a new technology, its benefits may be lost. If small retailers do not use electronic scanning equipment, cashiers must ring up prices by hand even though packages are computer-coded by manufacturers. In 2000, *Time* magazine selected a list of the 20 most important technological developments of the 20th century, ranging from the automobile to the Internet (www.time.com/time100/builder/tech_supp/tech_supp.html).

2-3g   Independent Media

Independent media are communication vehicles not controlled by a firm; yet, they influence government, consumer, and publics' perceptions of that firm's products and overall image. Media can provide positive or negative coverage when a firm produces a new product, pollutes the air, mislabels products, contributes to charity, or otherwise performs a newsworthy activity. Coverage may be by print media, TV, radio, the Internet, and news organizations. To receive good coverage, a firm should willingly offer information to independent media and always try to get its position written or spoken about.

Independent media affect perceptions of products and company image.

Although the media's coverage of information about a firm or information released by a firm is uncontrollable, paid advertising is controllable by the firm. Ads may be rejected by the media; but, if they are accepted, they must be presented in the time interval and form stipulated by the firm.

2-4 ATTAINMENT OF OBJECTIVES, FEEDBACK, AND ADAPTATION

An organization's success or failure in reaching objectives depends on how well it directs its controllable factors and the impact of uncontrollable factors. As shown in Figure 2-1, it is the interaction of an organization's total offering and the uncontrollable environment that determines how it does.

Feedback *provides information that lets a firm* **adapt** *to its environment.*

To optimize marketing efforts and secure its long-run existence, a firm must get *feedback*—information about the uncontrollable environment, the organization's performance, and how well the marketing plan is received. Feedback is gained by measuring consumer satisfaction, looking at competitive trends, evaluating relationships with government agencies, studying the economy and potential resource shortages, monitoring the independent media, analyzing sales and profit trends, talking with suppliers and distributors, and utilizing other methods of acquiring and assessing information.

After evaluating feedback, a company—when necessary—needs to engage in *adaptation,* thereby fine-tuning its marketing plan to be responsive to the environment, while continuing to capitalize on differential advantages. The firm should look continually for new opportunities that fit its overall marketing plan and are attainable by it, and respond to potential threats by revising marketing policies.

For instance, many small optical shops are struggling due to the growth of such chains as LensCrafters (www.lenscrafters.com), Sterling Optical (www.sterlingoptical.com), Pearle Vision (www.pearlevision.com), and others. The latter advertise extensively, buy in quantity to get special deals, and offer fast service and good prices. To last in this environment, small optical shops use such adaptation strategies as this one by Eyetique (www.eyetique.com), an optical shop in Pittsburgh:

> At Eyetique, you get special attention, frames to fit your lifestyle and personality, a thorough examination, the right fit in contact lenses, the latest technology, help with your hearing, and the most outstanding service! We are committed to your complete satisfaction with all of the products and services we provide, from nonprescription sunglasses to hearing aids. Looking, seeing, and hearing your best. That is the goal of Eyetique, and that is why we provide the finest selection, quality, and service to all of our customers and patients.
>
> Eyetique Advantage is a corporate benefits program offered to a variety of Pittsburgh area employers, schools, and other organizations of 50 members or more. The plan provides special employee rates on vision and hearing examinations, eyewear, hearing aids, and more, with no cost or paperwork for the employer. Because of this, Eyetique Advantage is an extremely popular health-related benefit. For more information on how you can get the Eyetique Advantage, call 1-800-422-5320.
>
> Eyetique will now bring all of its exquisite service to you at your home or office. Just call Eyetique at 1-800-422-5320 and an optician will ask you a few questions about the style of eyewear you prefer. They can even fax a Personal Profile to you. After you have scheduled an appointment, one of Eyetique's talented opticians will come to you with a large selection of the world's most exciting eyewear. Relax as you select a frame you'll love in the comfort of your home or office. Experience the personal shopping experience, call us to schedule an appointment![10]

---

[10]"About Eyetique," www.eyetique.com/about.html (February 12, 2001).

In gearing up for the future, a firm must strive to avoid **marketing myopia**—a short-sighted, narrow-minded view of marketing and its environment. It is a "self-inflicted and avoidable harm caused to an organization due to a lack of attention to and poor implementation of marketing concepts and principles." These are some major warning signs:

> **Marketing myopia** *is an ineffective marketing approach.*

- *We-know syndrome*—This is an ongoing assumption that the correct answers are always known to crucial questions.

- *Me-tooism*—This occurs when goods and services are too similar to those of competitors and there is no competitive advantage.

- *Monopricis*—This occurs if a firm's primary (or only) marketing/competitive tool is changing prices.

- *Customerphobia*—This is the fear of having a close relationship with and really caring about consumers and their wants.

- *Fax-me complex*—This occurs when the firm is completely dominated by tasks that require immediate attention (crises).

- *Hypermentis*—This occurs when executives devote too much of their time to thinking, studying, and planning while they take little action.

- *Global idiosis*—This is the lack of ability or willingness to compete internationally.

- *If it works, don't fix it*—This occurs when business is very good; but, no one knows why and everyone is hesitant to make changes.

- *Interfunctionalphobia*—This is a lack of mutual understanding, integration, and cooperation among a firm's various functional areas.

- *Short-run fetish*—This occurs when decisions are too biased toward the short-run, thus sacrificing long-run performance.[11]

WEB SITES YOU CAN USE

The U.S. government has the most comprehensive collection of Web sites in the world. It makes available all sorts of information on a free or nominal fee basis. What a wealth of data! One general-access site (www.firstgov.gov) provides access to 27 million (and growing) government Web pages. Here are the addresses of several specialized U.S. government sites:

Bureau of Economic Analysis (www.bea.doc.gov)

Department of Commerce (www.doc.gov)

Department of Labor (www.dol.gov)

Fed World (www.fedworld.gov)

Federal Reserve Board (www.federalreserve.gov)

Fedstats (www.fedstats.gov)

International Trade Administration (www.ita.doc.gov)

Library of Congress (www.loc.gov)

Securities and Exchange Commission (www.sec.gov)

Small Business Administration (www.sba.gov)

---

[11]John H. Antil, "Are You Committing Marketcide?" *Journal of Services Marketing*, Vol. 6 (Spring 1992), pp. 45–53.

SUMMARY

1. *To examine the environment within which marketing decisions are made and marketing activities are undertaken* The marketing environment consists of controllable factors, uncontrollable factors, the organization's level of success or failure in reaching its objectives, feedback, and adaptation. The macroenvironment includes the broad societal and economic forces that a firm faces, while the microenvironment refers to the forces that more directly affect a firm's ability to serve its customers.

2. *To differentiate between those elements controlled by a firm's top management and those controlled by marketing, and to enumerate the controllable elements of a marketing plan* Controllable factors are the internal strategy elements directed by a firm and its marketers. Top management decides on the line of business, overall objectives, the role of marketing and other business functions, and the corporate culture. These decisions have an impact on all aspects of marketing.

The major factors directed by marketing personnel are the selection of a target market, which is the group(s) of customers a firm proposes to serve; marketing objectives, which are more customer-oriented than those set by top management; the marketing organization; the marketing mix, which is a specific combination of product, distribution, promotion, and price decisions; and performance assessment, which involves monitoring and evaluating marketing outcomes. It is important for marketing personnel to strive to create differential advantages—the unique features that cause consumers to patronize a firm and not its competitors.

3. *To enumerate the uncontrollable environmental elements that can affect a marketing plan and study their potential ramifications* Uncontrollable factors are the external elements affecting a company's performance that cannot be fully directed by the top management and marketers of a firm. Any marketing plan, no matter how well conceived, may fail if uncontrollable factors affect it too much.

Among the key uncontrollable variables are changing consumer traits, interpersonal influences on consumer behavior, the consumer decision process, and consumer groups; the competitive structure of the industry in which a firm operates (monopoly, oligopoly, monopolistic competition, or pure competition) and such competitor attributes as marketing strategies, country of origin, size, generic competition, and channel competition; suppliers and distributors, their traits and practices, and resource shortages; government legislation and the political environment; the rate of economic growth (as measured by the GDP and real income), the costs of doing business, and other economic factors; technology, which refers to the development and use of machinery, products, and processes; and independent media, the communication vehicles not controlled by the firm.

4. *To explain why feedback about company performance and the uncontrollable aspects of its environment and the subsequent adaptation of the marketing plan are essential for a firm to attain its objectives* A firm's level of success or failure in reaching its goals depends on how well it directs and implements its controllable factors and the impact of uncontrollable factors on the marketing plan. When enacting a marketing strategy, a firm should obtain feedback (information about both its overall and marketing performance and the uncontrollable environment) and adapt the strategy to be responsive to the surrounding environment while continuing to exploit its differential advantages. Marketing myopia, a shortsighted view of marketing and its environment, must be avoided.

KEY TERMS

marketing environment (p. 27)
macroenvironment (p. 28)
microenvironment (p. 28)
controllable factors (p. 29)
line of business (p. 30)
corporate culture (p. 31)
target market (p. 32)
market segmentation (p. 32)

differential advantages (p. 33)
marketing organization (p. 34)
marketing mix (p. 34)
uncontrollable factors (p. 37)
monopoly (p. 38)
oligopoly (p. 38)
monopolistic competition (p. 38)
pure competition (p. 38)

Gross Domestic Product (GDP) (p. 44)
real income (p. 44)
technology (p. 45)
independent media (p. 45)
feedback (p. 46)
adaptation (p. 46)
marketing myopia (p. 47)

REVIEW QUESTIONS

1. Explain the environment within which marketing operates.
2. Why are the factors controlled by top management usually considered uncontrollable by marketing personnel?
3. What criteria would you use to assess the role of marketing in a company?
4. Why should a firm select a target market before developing a specific marketing mix?
5. What is the most important marketing objective for an organization? Why?

6. Describe the four components of the marketing mix.
7. Why are suppliers an important uncontrollable factor for many companies?
8. What is the intent of each of these categories of federal legislation?
   a. Antitrust, discriminatory pricing, and unfair trade practices.
   b. Deregulation.
   c. Consumer protection.

DISCUSSION QUESTIONS

1. How does a firm's corporate culture influence the performance of its personnel? Relate your answer to a charter airline service that caters to corporate accounts.
2. What are the differential advantages for each of these? Explain your answers.
   a. Your college or university.
   b. 1-800 Flowers.com (www.800flowers.com).
   c. Discover Card (www.discovercard.com).
3. Distinguish between the marketing mixes used by Cadillac (www.cadillac.com) and Saturn (www.saturnbp.com), two car lines of General Motors.
4. Deregulation represents both opportunities and potential problems for companies. Offer several examples of both for the telecommunications industry.

WEB EXERCISE

As part of its Web site, MSNBC has a section that is devoted exclusively to current events in technology (www.msnbc.com/news/TECH_Front.asp?ta=y). Visit the site and discuss any two recent technological events in terms of their relevance for the marketing environment of an office supply chain.

3

Developing and Enacting Strategic Marketing Plans

C h a p t e r   O b j e c t i v e s

1 To define strategic planning and consider its importance for marketing

2 To describe the total quality approach to strategic planning and show its relevance to marketing

3 To look at the different kinds of strategic plans and the relationships between marketing and the other functional areas in an organization

4 To describe thoroughly each of the steps in the strategic planning process: defining organizational mission, establishing strategic business units, setting marketing objectives, performing situation analysis, developing marketing strategy, implementing tactics, and monitoring results

5 To show how a strategic marketing plan may be devised and applied

Thirty-year-old Todd Greene has invented a novel product. Now, he now needs to enhance and enact his marketing plan to take the product to the next level. Greene's product, known as HeadBlade, is a razor designed specifically for men who shave their heads. He named his firm the HeadBlade Company.

After two large grooming-product manufacturers rejected Greene's offer for a licensing or sales arrangement, he decided that it was time to sell his $15 product via the Web. To drum-up business, Greene posted messages on Web bulletin boards that catered to his target market: balding men, serious athletes, military men, and men who simply wanted to be appear to be different. During his first week of business, Greene generated $300 in sales revenues. Today, daily sales equal $3,000. HeadBlade is now sold in 16 retail stores, as well the firm's Web site (www.headblade.com).

To sustain and build his business, Greene must raise significant sums, far beyond the $150,000 in initial seed money. And that's not easy. The industry's market leader, Gillette, sells more than $3 billion worth of razors and blades *each year* and has a 70 percent share of the U.S. market. According to a consultant who helped Greene write his business plan, "The big guys are going to swat Todd away like a bug unless he's able to create a self-sustaining business. He's going to have to win, and win early to survive."

Until now, Greene has proven to be an adept businessperson. His product is also priced at a level which provides a very healthy gross margin of 65 percent. He has cut expenses and the need for start-up capital by working from home, hiring workers only on a temporary basis, and minimizing inventories by working closely with suppliers. He has also capitalized from free publicity in such magazines as *Sports Illustrated* and *Entertainment Weekly*.

Although Greene assumes that there's a potential market of 10 million consumers for his HeadBlade product, he acknowledges that there are no hard numbers to document this estimate. He is carefully weighing his options for financing the firm's expansion. These funds will be necessary for him to expand his product's distribution, as well as to generate brand awareness.[1]

In this chapter, we will consider strategic marketing plans and review each step in the strategic planning process. We will also examine strategic planning by both small and large firms.

3-1 OVERVIEW

As described in Chapter 2, the environment within which marketing operates includes a number of factors directed by top management and others directed by marketing. To coordinate these factors and provide guidance for decision making, it is helpful to deploy a formal strategic planning process. To marketers, such a process consists of two main components: a strategic business plan and a strategic marketing plan.

---

[1]Mike Hofman, "The Razor's Edge," *Inc.* (March 2000), pp. 86–87.

FIGURE 3-1
McDonald's: The Clear Strategic Vision of the Market Leader

Source: Reprinted by permission of McDonald's Corporation.

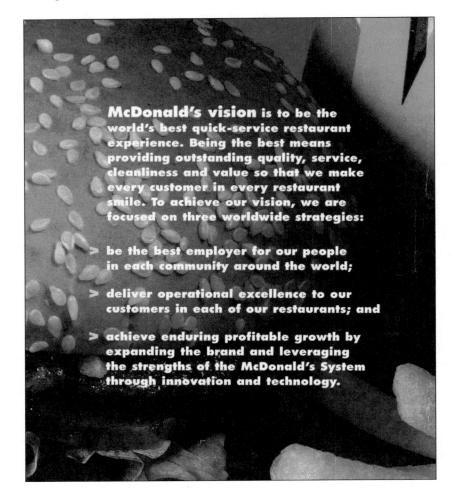

FIGURE 3-1
McDonald's: The Clear Strategic Vision of the Market Leader

Source: Reprinted by permission of McDonald's Corporation.

McDonald's vision is to be the world's best quick-service restaurant experience. Being the best means providing outstanding quality, service, cleanliness and value so that we make every customer in every restaurant smile. To achieve our vision, we are focused on three worldwide strategies:

> be the best employer for our people in each community around the world;

> deliver operational excellence to our customers in each of our restaurants; and

> achieve enduring profitable growth by expanding the brand and leveraging the strengths of the McDonald's System through innovation and technology.

Strategic planning involves both a **strategic business plan** *and a* **strategic marketing plan.**

A **strategic business plan** "describes the overall direction an organization will pursue within its chosen environment and guides the allocation of resources and effort. It also provides the logic that integrates the perspectives of functional departments and operating units, and points them all in the same direction." It has (1) an external orientation; (2) a process for formulating strategies; (3) methods for analyzing strategic situations and alternatives; and (4) a commitment to action.[2]

A **strategic marketing plan** outlines the marketing actions to undertake, why they are needed, who is responsible for carrying them out, when and where they will be completed, and how they will be coordinated. Thus, a marketing plan is carried out within the context of a firm's broader strategic plan.

Our discussion of strategic planning and marketing is presented early in this book for several reasons. One, strategic planning gives a firm direction and better enables it to understand the dimensions of marketing research, consumer analysis, and the marketing mix. It is a hierarchal process, moving from company guidelines to specific marketing decisions. Two, a strategic plan makes sure each division's goals are integrated with firmwide goals. Three, different functional areas are encouraged to coordinate efforts. Four, strategic planning forces a firm to assess its strengths and weaknesses and to consider environmental opportunities and threats. Five, the alternative actions or combinations of actions a firm can take are outlined. Six, a basis for allotting resources is set. Seven, the value of assessing performance can be seen. Figure 3-1 highlights how a firm can have a clear and directive strategic plan.

[2]Peter D. Bennett (Editor), *Dictionary of Marketing Terms*, Second Edition (Chicago: American Marketing Association, 1995), p. 276.

Marketing's role in strategic planning is indeed a crucial one:

The contribution to strategic planning and implementation begins with the analysis of market segments and an assessment of a firm's ability to satisfy customer needs. This includes analyzing demand trends, competition, and in industrial markets, competitive conditions. Marketing also plays a key role by working with top management to define business purpose in terms of customer-need satisfaction. In a market-oriented view of the strategic planning process, financial goals are seen as results and rewards, not the fundamental purpose of business.[3]

For example, mass merchandisers such as Wal-Mart (www.walmart.com) recognize that each element of their strategy must reflect a customer orientation. That is why Wal-Mart discount department stores employ sales personnel in product categories where customers want assistance.

In Chapter 3, we discuss a total quality approach to strategic planning, various kinds of strategic plans, relationships between marketing and other functional areas, and the strategic planning process—and show how strategic marketing plans may be outlined and applied. Chapter 22, which concludes the text, deals with how marketing plans are integrated and analyzed in a total quality framework.

A general planning Web site (www.businessplans.org/topic10.html) from Business Resource Software provides a good overview of planning issues from a small business perspective.

3-2 A TOTAL QUALITY APPROACH TO STRATEGIC PLANNING

When devising strategic plans, any firm—small or large, domestic or global, manufacturing or services driven—should adopt a total quality viewpoint. **Total quality** is a process- and output-related philosophy, whereby a firm strives to fully satisfy customers in an effective and efficient manner. To flourish, a total quality program needs a customer focus; top management commitment; an emphasis on continuous improvement; and support from employees, suppliers, and distribution intermediaries:

- *Process-related philosophy*—Total quality is based on all the activities that create, develop, market, and deliver a good or service for the customer. A firm gains a competitive advantage if it offers the same quality good or service at a lower cost or if it offers better quality than other companies.

- *Output-related philosophy*—Although process-related activities give a good or service its value, the consumer usually can only judge the total quality of the finished product that he or she purchases. Many consumers care about what they buy, rather than how it was made.

- *Customer satisfaction*—To the consumer, total quality refers to how well a good or service performs. Thus, customer service is a key element in a person's ultimate satisfaction, which is affected by the gap between that person's expectations of product performance and actual performance.

- *Effectiveness*—To a marketer, this involves how well various marketing activities (such as adding new product features) are received by consumers.

- *Efficiency*—To a marketer, this involves the costs of various marketing activities. A firm is efficient when it holds down costs, while offering consumers the appropriate level of quality.

- *Customer focus*—With a total quality viewpoint, a firm perceives the consumer as a partner and seeks input from that partner as it creates, develops, markets, and delivers a good or service.

- *Top management commitment*—Senior executives must be dedicated to making a total quality program work and to ensuring that corners are not cut in an attempt to be

[3]Frederick E. Webster, Jr., "The Rediscovery of the Marketing Concept," *Business Horizons,* Vol. 31 (May-June 1988), pp. 37–38.

more efficient. In the best firms, "total quality" becomes ingrained as part of the corporate culture.

- *Continuous improvement*—In most cases, today's total quality will become tomorrow's suboptimal quality; so, a firm must continuously improve its quality. A complacent firm will be hurt by the dynamics of the marketplace and fast-paced technological and global marketplace trends.

- *Employee support and involvement*—For a total quality program to work, employees must "buy into" it. Empowering employees not only gets them involved in the total quality process, but it also assures that customer problems are promptly addressed and resolved in the customer's favor.

- *Supplier and distributor support and involvement*—Due to their involvement in creating total quality, suppliers and resellers can greatly affect it. They too must "buy into" a firm's total quality efforts.

GLOBAL *Marketing in Action*

Sweden's Electrolux: the Quiet Giant

Even though Electrolux (www.electrolux.com), a Swedish-based firm with annual sales of more than $15 billion, owns such brands as Frigidaire, White Westinghouse, Eureka, and Kelvinator, most Americans associate the company with a vacuum cleaner brand that is not even affiliated with the firm. Unfortunately for Electrolux, during a good part of the 1990s, its brands did not do well in the United States and Europe. To rebuild the firm, Electrolux closed 23 factories, cut 11,000 jobs, and sold off its vending machine business in Europe. It then refocused itself as a supplier of white goods (major home appliances), floor-care products, outdoor appliances, and commercial heavy-duty appliances for restaurants and coin-operated laundries.

In the United States, Electrolux has also updated its products and rebuilt its relationships with major retailers such as Sears and Circuit City. Key to the U.S. strategy is Electrolux's plan to bring out a line of upscale appliances (including washers, refrigerators, freezers, and ranges) under the Electrolux brand. According to industry analysts, the luxury lines of appliances—with wood paneling or stainless steel exteriors, and features such as computer touch screens—are growing at 12 percent per year, double the growth rate of the overall appliance market.

There are rumors that Electrolux has considered acquiring the Maytag Corporation. Among the benefits of a Maytag acquisition to Electrolux are its new high-status lines of fast cook ranges and front-loading washers, and its established relationships with retailers such as Home Depot. Lastly, Maytag does only 5 percent of its business overseas. According to Electrolux's president, "I would prefer to grow organically, but sometimes you don't have the luxury. If we can find a good fit, we will pursue it."

As a marketing vice-president for Electrolux, evaluate Maytag as an acquisition candidate.

Source: Based on material in Mark Tatgle, "How Swede It is," Forbes (July 24, 2000). p. 56.

Figure 3-2 shows how a successful total quality program works. At the left are the participants in a total quality program, who together create total quality. There is an interchange among the parties and between the parties and the process. Through this process, a good's or service's effectiveness and efficiency are influenced; likewise, those factors are considered during the process. Total quality is the output of the process. The process and total quality itself are regularly improved. If a consumer feels a good or service has superior total quality, a purchase is made. When experience with a good or service is pleasing, customer satisfaction occurs. Since one effectiveness measure is customer satisfaction, there is an impact arrow. Finally, satisfaction is feedback that affects the consumer's future input into the process. The consumer's central focus is evident because the consumer appears three times: consumer input, consumer purchase, and customer satisfaction.

As the president and chief operating officer of the Ritz-Carlton hotel chain (www.ritzcarlton.com), the only two-time winner of the Malcolm Baldridge National Quality award in the service category, recently remarked, "To me, basic quality is understanding not just what the customer wants but truly understanding the customer and then creating processes—with the involvement of the employees connected with each process—to deliver that. And finally, quality means continuing to see how well you're doing and how to do it better, and then doing that, eventually bringing the processes to zero defects. Our standards and guidelines at Ritz-Carlton are determined by customer feedback—what the people who constitute our primary concern want. That's quality."[4]

For a total quality program to work, every party in the process must participate.

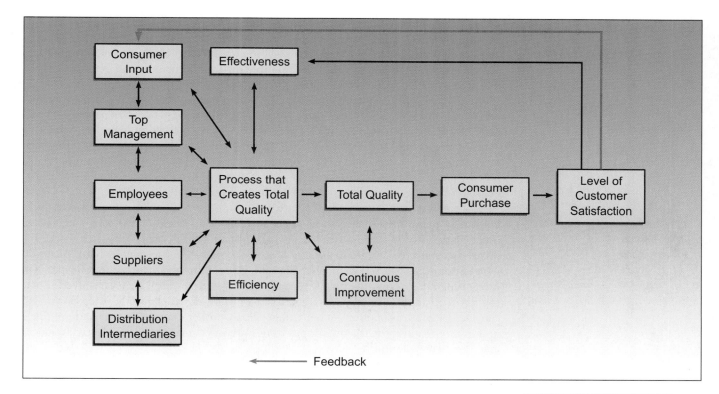

FIGURE 3-2

The Keys to a Successful Total Quality Program

[4]Robert Green, "Baldridge Award Winner Profile," www.qualitydigest.com/aug00/html/baldridge.html (August 2000).

Sometimes, the total quality process breaks down in a way that may be difficult to fix. For example, many firms have had glitches with their Web sites, including heavy traffic causing system overloads, poor inventory and shipping coordination, too long a time for replies to E-mail, and so forth. These problems require expensive and time-consuming solutions.

To learn more about the strategic aspects of total quality management (TQM), visit this ChamberBiz.com Web site (www.chamberbiz.com/bizcenter/P03_9000.cfm). It highlights the role of marketing in TQM.

3-3 KINDS OF STRATEGIC PLANS

Strategic plans can be categorized by their duration, scope, and method of development. They range from short run, specific, and department generated to long run, broad, and management generated.

Short-run plans are precise; long-run plans outline needs.

Plans may be short run (typically one year), moderate in length (two to five years), or long run (5 to 10 or even 15 years). Many firms rely on a combination: Short-run and moderate-length plans are more detailed and operational in nature than long-run plans.

At Japan's Canon (www.canon.com), the maker of cameras, machines, and optical products: "For 30 years from its foundation, Canon focused on expanding its business in the field of cameras. In the next 30 years, we used camera-related technologies as a base for diversification into new businesses. Throughout our history, we have developed our operations while remaining attentive to the needs of the times. Now, as we target the next stage of growth, we have set multimedia as the key factor that will let us contribute in a continually advancing network society. In line with the digitization and integration of products from input (scanners and cameras) to output devices (printers and displays), we are working aggressively to take a leading role in the information and communications industries, the key sectors of the future."[5]

Consumer-products firms often have plans for each line.

The scope of strategic plans also varies. There may be separate marketing plans for each of a firm's major products; a single, integrated marketing plan encompassing all products; or a broad business plan with a section devoted to marketing. Separate marketing plans by product line are often used by consumer-goods manufacturers; a single, integrated marketing plan is often employed by service firms; and a broad business plan is often utilized by industrial-goods manufacturers. A firm's diversity and the number of distinct market segments it seeks both have a strong influence here.[6]

Bottom-up plans foster employee input; top-down plans are set by top management.

Last, plans may be devised by a bottom-up, top-down, or combination approach. In bottom-up planning, input from salespeople, product managers, advertising people, and other marketing areas is used to set goals, budgets, forecasts, timetables, and marketing mixes. Bottom-up plans are realistic and good for morale. Yet, it may be hard to coordinate bottom-up plans and to include different assumptions about the same concept when integrating a companywide plan. Shortcomings of bottom-up plans are resolved in the top-down approach, whereby senior managers centrally direct planning. A top-down plan can use complex assumptions about competition or other external factors and provide a uniform direction for marketing. Input from lower-level managers is not actively sought and morale may diminish.

A combination of the two approaches could be used if senior executives set overall goals and policy, and marketing personnel form plans for carrying out marketing activities. As the chief executive of one firm once remarked: "You can't have a workable strategy forced down from the top. Empowering middle managers is a necessity. They manage

---

[5]"Excellent Global Corporation Plan," www.canon.com/about/excellent/index.html (February 7, 2001).

[6]For additional perspectives on the scope of strategic plans, see Robert S. Kaplan and David P. Norton, "Having Trouble with Your Strategy? Then Map It," *Harvard Business Review*, Vol. 78 (September-October 2000), pp. 167–176; and Kathleen M. Eisenhardt and Donald N. Sull, "Strategy as Simple Rules," *Harvard Business Review*, Vol. 79 (January 2001), pp. 106–116.

what we as a corporation want to accomplish. To make them think strategically comes from sharing the direction and from having a set of supportive organizational systems. So it's real work, not sermons, that makes us and our middle managers strategic thinkers."[7]

3-4 STRENGTHENING RELATIONSHIPS BETWEEN MARKETING AND OTHER FUNCTIONAL AREAS IN AN ORGANIZATION

An organization's strategic planning must accommodate the distinct needs of marketing and other functional areas. This is not always simple, due to the different orientations of each area, as shown in Table 3-1. Marketers may seek tailor-made products, flexible budgets, nonroutine transactions, many product versions, frequent purchases, customer-driven new products, employee compensation incentives, and aggressive actions against competitors. This may conflict with goals of other functional areas to seek mass production (production), stable budgets (finance), routinized transactions (accounting), limited models (engineering), infrequent orders (purchasing), technology-driven new products (research and development), fixed employee compensation (personnel), and passive actions against competitors (legal).

The perspectives of marketing and other functional areas need to be reconciled.

Top management's job is to make sure every functional area sees the need for a balanced view in company decision making and has input on decisions. While some degree of tension among departments is inevitable, conflict can be reduced by encouraging interfunctional contact; seeking personnel with both technical and marketing expertise; forming multifunctional task forces, committees, and management-development programs; and setting goals for each department that take other departments into account.[8]

TABLE 3-1 The Orientations of Different Functional Areas

Functional Area	Major Strategic Orientation
Marketing	To attract and retain a loyal group of consumers through a unique combination of product, distribution, promotion, and price factors
Production	To utilize full plant capacity, hold down per-unit production costs, and maximize quality control
Finance	To operate within established budgets, focus on profitable items, control customer credit, and minimize loan costs for the company
Accounting	To standardize reports, detail costs fully, and routinize transactions
Engineering	To develop and adhere to exact product specifications, limit models and options, and concentrate on quality improvements
Purchasing	To acquire items via large, uniform orders at low prices and maintain low inventories
Research and Development	To seek technological breakthroughs, improvements in product quality, and recognition for innovations
Personnel	To hire, motivate, supervise, and compensate employees in an efficient manner
Legal	To ensure that a strategy is defensible against challenges from the government, competitors, channel members, and consumers

---

[7]Manab Thakur and Luis Ma. R. Calingo, "Strategic Thinking Is Hip, But Does It Make a Difference?" *Business Horizons,* Vol. 35 (September-October 1992), p. 47.

[8]See Michael D. Hutt, Beth A. Walker, and Gary L. Frankwick, "Hurdle the Cross-Functional Barriers to Strategic Change," *Sloan Management Review,* Vol. 36 (Spring 1995), pp. 22–30; and "Special Issue: Marketing/Finance Interface," *Journal of Business Research,* Vol. 50 (November 2000).

ETHICAL *Issues in Marketing*

Making Sense
of Confusing
Company
Earnings
Reports

In recent years, investment managers have increasingly complained about how some firms boost their reported profits. When the U.S. economy slows down, oil prices rise, and the Euro is weak, these firms may resort to the ploys noted below as a way of keeping stock prices high. While sophisticated investors and market analysts can determine the impact of these ploys, many less sophisticated investors cannot.

Among the ploys used are highlighting earnings that do not include many normal expenses, paying compensation expenses with stock options, and boosting normal earnings by adding in investment income. Let's see how these techniques are being utilized:

- One way to build up profitability is to use EBITA (earnings before interest, taxes, depreciation, and amortization) as an alternative to net profits. A firm that manages Web sites recently announced that it reached a "milestone" when it achieved EBITA profitability. What the firm neglected to mention was that it lost 32 cents per share in that quarter!
- Current accounting guidelines do not require firms to list stock-options grants as an expense in the firm's calculation of earnings. According to one report, while Yahoo reported a 10-cent-a-share profit in 1999, after adjusting for stock option grants, it actually would have had a 50-cent-a-share loss.
- Firms such as Intel and Microsoft commonly make venture-capital investments in small firms as part of their research and development activities. When these firms go public, their market value often soars. Of Microsoft's fourth quarter 2000 earnings, nearly half came from such earnings.

As a marketing manager with stock options at a Web-based company, would you recommend that your firm's accountant adjust earnings using one of these techniques? Explain your answer.

Source: Based on material in Susan Scherreik, "What the Earnings Reports Don't Tell You," *Business Week* (October 16, 2000), pp. 201–204.

3-5 THE STRATEGIC PLANNING PROCESS

*The **strategic planning process** includes steps from defining a mission to monitoring results.*

The ***strategic planning process*** has seven interrelated steps: defining organizational mission, establishing strategic business units, setting marketing objectives, performing situation analysis, developing marketing strategy, implementing tactics, and monitoring results. Because the process encompasses both strategic business planning and strategic marketing planning, it should be conducted by a combination of senior company executives and marketers. It is depicted in Figure 3-3.

This process applies to small and large firms, consumer and industrial firms, goods- and services-based firms, domestic and international firms, and profit-oriented and non-profit-oriented institutions. Planning at each step in the process may differ by type of firm, but using a thorough strategic plan is beneficial for any company. The Business Owner's Toolkit site (www.toolkit.cch.com/tools/buspln_m.asp) shows sample strategic plans for three types of business: manufacturer, service provider, and retailer.

The steps in strategic planning are discussed in the following sections.

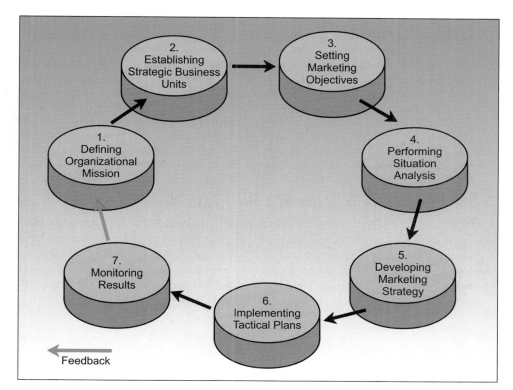

FIGURE 3-3

The Strategic Planning Process

3-5a Defining Organizational Mission

Organizational mission refers to a long-term commitment to a type of business and a place in the market. It "describes the scope of the firm and its dominant emphasis and values," based on that firm's history, current management preferences, resources, and distinctive competences, and on environmental factors.[9]

An organizational mission can be expressed in terms of the customer group(s) served, the goods and services offered, the functions performed, and/or the technologies utilized. It is more comprehensive than the line of business concept noted in Chapter 2. And it is considered implicitly whenever a firm seeks a new customer group or abandons an existing one, introduces a new product (good or service) category or deletes an old one, acquires another company or sells a business, engages in more marketing functions (a wholesaler opening retail stores) or in fewer marketing functions (a small innovative toy maker licensing its inventions to an outside company that produces, distributes, and promotes them), or shifts its technological focus (a phone manufacturer placing more emphasis on cellular phones). Organizations that diversify too much may not have a clear sense of direction.

Here are two diverse illustrations of a clear organizational mission:

Lands' End (www.landsend.com) is a leading direct merchant of traditionally styled, casual clothing for men, women and children, as well as soft luggage and products for the home. The company's products are offered through regular mailings of its primary and specialty catalogs and via the Internet. Lands' End is known for providing products of exceptional quality at prices representing honest value, enhanced by a commitment to excellence in customer service. We work directly with mills and manufacturers, eliminating middlemen. We pass the savings on to customers by offering them the best price possible. Our customers shop directly with us, from home or office, by phone or mail, by fax or Web. We ship directly to our customers, wherever in the world they may live. No driving to the mall, no running from store to store, no waiting in lines. It's our direct way of doing business, just like our logo says.[10]

A firm sets its direction in an **organizational mission.**

[9]Bennett, *Dictionary of Marketing Terms*, p. 67.

[10]"Lands' End Fact Sheet," www.landsend.com (February 11, 2001).

At the Coca-Cola Company (www2.coca-cola.com), our mission is to maximize share-owner value over time. To achieve this mission, we must create value for all the constituents we serve, including our consumers, our resellers, our bottlers, and our communities. The Company creates value by executing a comprehensive strategy guided by six key beliefs: (1) Consumer demand drives everything we do. (2) Brand Coca-Cola is the core of our business. (3) We will serve consumers a broad selection of the nonalcoholic ready-to-drink beverages they want to drink throughout the day. (4) We will be the best marketers in the world. (5) We will think and act locally. (6) We will lead as a model corporate citizen. The ultimate objectives of our strategy are to increase volume, expand our share of worldwide nonalcoholic ready-to-drink beverage sales, maximize our long-term cash flows, and create economic-value-added by improving economic profit.[11]

3-5b Establishing Strategic Business Units

Strategic business units (SBUs) *are separate operating units in an organization.*

After defining its mission, a firm can form strategic business units. Each **strategic business unit (SBU)** is a self-contained division, product line, or product department in an organization with a specific market focus and a manager with complete responsibility for integrating all functions into a strategy. An SBU may include all products with the same physical features or products bought for the same use by customers, depending on the mission of the organization. Each SBU has these general attributes:

- A specific target market.
- Its own senior marketing executive.
- Control over its resources.
- Its own marketing strategy.
- Clear-cut competitors.
- Distinct differential advantages.

The SBU concept lets firms identify the business units with the most earnings potential and allocate to them the resources needed for growth. For instance, at General Electric, every SBU must have a unique purpose, identifiable competitors, and all its major business functions (manufacturing, finance, and marketing) within the control of that SBU's manager. Units not performing up to expectations are constantly reviewed and, if necessary, consolidated with other units, sold, or closed down.

The proper number of SBUs depends on a firm's organizational mission, its resources, and the willingness of top management to delegate authority. A small or specialized firm can have as few as one SBU, a diversified one up to 100 or more. Thus, the WD-40 Company (www.wd40.com) has three SBUs: WD-40—a product line that cleans/degreases, penetrates to loosen up stuck parts, prevents corrosion, and is a light lubricant; 3-IN-ONE—a product line that enables users to lubricate tools, rollers, hinges, in-line skates, and wheels; and Lava—a product line with heavy-duty hand cleansers. General Electric (www.ge.com) has 23 SBUs—including aircraft engines, appliances, financial services, lighting, information services, medical services, NBC, plastics, and transportation systems. Johnson & Johnson (www.jnj.com) has more than 190 SBUs—"It is the world's most comprehensive and broadly-based manufacturer of health care products, as well as a provider of related services, for the consumer, pharmaceutical, and professional markets."[12] After careful consideration, PepsiCo (www.pepsico.com) spun off its restaurant SBUs—KFC, Pizza Hut, and Taco Bell—to concentrate on three businesses: carbonated beverages, snack foods, and noncarbonated beverages. See Figure 3-4. It recently bid to acquire Quaker Oats, with its Gatorade drinks and other food products.

---

[11]"Our Mission," www.thecoca-colacompany.com/tccc/index.html (February 11, 2001).

[12]"Background," www.jnj.com/who_is_jnj/who_is_jnj.html (February 11, 2001).

Product Portfolio. We have terrific products. Nine of our brands – Lay's, Doritos, Ruffles, Chee•tos, Pepsi, Diet Pepsi, Mountain Dew, 7UP, Mirinda – each sell over $1 billion a year at retail, making our portfolio very appealing to our customers.

F I G U R E   3 - 4

PepsiCo: Refashioning Its SBUs

In late 1997, PepsiCo decided to spin off its fast-food restaurants in order to get out of retailing. The company now devotes full attention to its food businesses.

Source: Reprinted by permission. © Pepsico.

3-5c Setting Marketing Objectives

A firm needs overall marketing objectives, as well as goals for each SBU. Objectives are often described in both quantitative terms (dollar sales, percentage profit growth, market share, etc.) and qualitative terms (image, level of innovativeness, industry leadership role, etc.).

For example, Paradigm Group (www.teamparadigm.com) is a 25-year-old, residential real-estate firm based in Florida that owns, develops, and manages multiunit housing. It has grown steadily and won a number of awards. Its goals for the future are very ambitious:

> Paradigm plans to expand outside Florida, become a force in the Southeast, and then establish a presence in the national real-estate market. In the past five years, Paradigm has grown at a compound rate in excess of 30 percent. Our business plan calls for us to exceed that growth through approximately 80 percent acquisitions and 20 percent new development.

> Another part of our strategic vision calls for taking customer service to a new level, unprecedented in the housing industry. We want to always pleasantly surprise, even astonish, our residents with our service, consistently *underpromising and overperforming*; if we tell a resident we'll take care of a problem the same day, we aim to get it done within the hour. As we do this, our customer service will be a marketing advantage, a difference that our residents see and feel on a daily basis. We are planning and creating systems that enable us to deliver this level of service

Marketing objectives may include quantitative and qualitative measures.

to customers, adding value to their lives as well as securing a competitive advantage for our company—occupancy levels that are always significantly above the market and service that lets us charge an appropriate premium.

We will know we have succeeded when our residents *urge* their friends to move into our communities, when our renewal rate is sky high, and when residents moving to another city ask if we manage a community there that they can move to.[13]

Small firms' goals are often less ambitious than those set by their larger counterparts, but they are no less important. The goals are necessary to focus the firm and to be able to monitor the level of success or failure. Without goals, how can a firm really measure its performance?

3-5d Performing Situation Analysis

Situation analysis *investigates a firm's strengths, weaknesses, opportunities, and threats.*

In *situation analysis,* also known as SWOT analysis, an organization identifies its internal strengths (S) and weaknesses (W), as well as external opportunities (O) and threats (T). Situation analysis seeks to answer: Where is a firm now? In what direction is it headed? Answers are derived by recognizing both company strengths and weaknesses relative to competitors, studying the environment for opportunities and threats, assessing the firm's ability to capitalize on opportunities and to minimize or avoid threats, and anticipating competitors' responses to company strategies. The Business Owner's Toolkit site (www.toolkit.cch.com/text/p03_8020.asp) provides an in-depth discussion of many of the factors to be reviewed during a situation analysis.

Situation analysis can, and should be, conducted at any point in a firm's life. Consider these examples:

Ignoring more than one billion potential customers isn't easy. Yet the thought crossed Dharmesh Shah's mind when he learned how expensive and complex cracking the China market would be. He wouldn't even have tried it if two things hadn't happened. First, Pyramid Digital Solutions Inc. (PDS), his $10-million software-design business based in Alabama (www.403bonline.com), received an additional $6 million in funding. Second, PDS was deemed a "partner" by $6-billion SunGard Data Systems, a monster in the PDS market of 401(k) plan software. Without SunGard's existing relationships, PDS wouldn't have had the wherewithal for an international debut, Shah says. SunGard hired PDS to write the software code for a system it sells to the Bank of China. PDS collects a quarterly check from SunGard, working in the background while the larger company handles the dirty work of legalities, currencies, and collection. Still, it's no free ride. PDS has paid $250,000 for private groups to lobby the Chinese government for business. In addition, PDS swallowed China's demand for discounted prices. The Bank of China "knows its value as a customer reference," observes Shah.[14]

What might Nike's customers want besides shoes and running apparel? When the company started asking that question a few years ago, it realized runners needed specialized sunglasses and watches. Then, it devised a speed-and-distance monitor that attaches the watch to the footwear; then a lightweight wearable MP3 music player. What Nike (www.nike.com) calls its equipment business is doing $400 million a year and growing fast. On a much larger, industrial scale, GE's Power Systems (www.gepower.com/en_us) business asked a similar question when it hit hard times several years ago and found that its customers—major electric utilities—were eager to buy a wide range of consulting and maintenance services. This was more than a good source of bonus revenue; margins on those services are considerably higher than on turbines and transformers, Power Systems' core products. This strategy is useful anytime, but a downturn often provides the motivation to make it happen. Do it now, and you'll come out of the slowdown like gangbusters.[15]

---

[13]"Growth & Goals," www.teamparadigm.com/corporate/goals.html (February 11, 2001).

[14]Ilan Mochari, "Selling Abroad without the Pain," *Inc.* (February 2001), p. 105.

[15]Ram Charan and Geoffrey Colvin, "Managing for the Slowdown," *Fortune* (February 5, 2001), pp. 81–82.

Here's what an accounting firm's SWOT analysis might look like: *Strengths*: experienced associates, prime location, reputation/image, income tax expertise. *Weaknesses*: seasonality, dependence on senior partner, limited funds. *Opportunities*: idle resources during off-season (offices, computers, employees), joint marketing arrangements with noncompeting firms, fee-based seminars, tax reform. *Threats*: learning required to be expert in new regulations, technology (enabling self-preparation), IRS policies that simplify tax returns, competition from newer types of firms (such as online tax preparers).[16]

Sometimes, situation analysis reveals weaknesses or threats that cannot be overcome, and a company opts to drop or sell a product line or division. Thus, in 1995, General Mills (www.generalmills.com) sold its restaurant division—comprised of the Red Lobster, Olive Garden, and China Coast chains. Why? Fifty-five percent of General Mills' food profits were used to fund the restaurant business; and the firm decided to focus instead on its leading food brands. This is the firm's focus today: "General Mills makes one of the U.S.' most popular cereal brands, Cheerios, as well as Wheaties and Chex. It is also a leader in flour (Gold Medal), baking mixes (Betty Crocker, Bisquick), dinner mixes (Hamburger Helper), grain snacks (Pop Secret, Chex Mix, Bugles), and fruit snacks (Fruit Roll-Ups). The company is number two in refrigerated yogurt (Yoplait and Colombo), behind Dannon. It also sells Betty Crocker cookbooks, licenses Betty Crocker housewares, and runs a food service unit. As the cereal wars eat profits, the company has sought power through acquisitions, including Diageo's Pillsbury unit."[17]

3-5e Developing Marketing Strategy

A marketing strategy outlines the way in which the marketing mix is used to attract and satisfy the target market(s) and achieve an organization's goals. Marketing-mix decisions center on product, distribution, promotion, and price plans. A separate strategy is necessary for each SBU in an organization; these strategies must be coordinated.

> *A good* **marketing strategy** *provides a framework for marketing activities.*

A marketing strategy should be explicit to provide proper guidance. It should take into account a firm's mission, resources, abilities, and standing in the marketplace; the status of the firm's industry and the product groups in it (such as light versus regular beer); domestic and global competitive forces; such environmental factors as the economy and population growth; and the best opportunities for growth—and the threats that could dampen it. For instance, IBM does a lot of image advertising as part of its overall marketing strategy in order to enhance its stature in the business community.

Four strategic planning approaches are presented next: product/market opportunity matrix, Boston Consulting Group matrix, General Electric business screen, and Porter generic strategy model.

The Product/Market Opportunity Matrix

The product/market opportunity matrix identifies four alternative marketing strategies to maintain and/or increase sales of business units and products: market penetration, market development, product development, and diversification.[18] See Figure 3-5. The choice of an alternative depends on the market saturation of an SBU or product and the firm's ability to introduce new products. Two or more alternatives may be combined.

> *The* **product/market opportunity matrix** *involves market penetration, market development, product development, and diversification options.*

Market penetration is effective when the market is growing or not yet saturated. A firm seeks to expand the sales of its present products in its present markets through more intensive distribution, aggressive promotion, and competitive pricing. Sales are increased by attracting nonusers and competitors' customers and raising the usage rate among current customers.

---

[16]"How to Develop a Strategic Business Plan," www.peoplestax.com/taxtools/plan1.htm (February 7, 2001).

[17]"General Mills, Inc.," www.hoovers.com/co/capsule/9/0,2163,10639,00.html (February 17, 2001).

[18]H. Igor Ansoff, "Strategies for Diversification," *Harvard Business Review*, Vol. 35 (September-October 1957), pp. 113–124. See also "Let the Product/Market Matrix Focus Your CVA Efforts," www.callcenterexchange.com/vsp_home.html (February 8, 2001).

FIGURE 3-5

The Product/Market Opportunity Matrix

Source: Adapted from H. Igor Ansoff, "Strategies for Diversification," *Harvard Business Review*, Vol. 35 (September-October 1957), pp. 113–124.

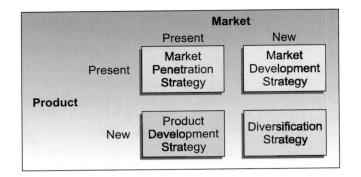

Market development is effective when a local or regional business looks to widen its market, new market segments are emerging due to changes in consumer lifestyles and demographics, and innovative uses are discovered for a mature product. A firm seeks greater sales of present products from new markets or new product uses. It can enter new territories, appeal to segments it is not yet satisfying, and reposition existing items. New distribution methods may be tried; promotion efforts are more descriptive.

Product development is effective when an SBU has a core of strong brands and a sizable consumer following. A firm develops new or modified products to appeal to present markets. It stresses new models, better quality, and other minor innovations closely related to entrenched products—and markets them to loyal customers. Traditional distribution methods are used; promotion stresses that the new product is made by a well-established firm.

Diversification is used so a firm does not become too dependent on one SBU or product line. The firm becomes involved with new products aimed at new markets. These products may be new to the industry or new only to the company. Distribution and promotion orientations are both different from those usually followed by the firm.

Here is how the product/market opportunity matrix can be applied to United Parcel Service—UPS (www.ups.com):

- *Market penetration*—UPS is the world's largest package-delivery firm. It advertises extensively on TV and in magazines. The current slogan is "Moving at the Speed of Business." It handles 1.8 million customers through its automatic daily pickup service.

- *Market development*—It is stepping up efforts around the world, where client use of delivery services tends to be much less than in the United States. In 1990, UPS International operated in 40 nations; now, it is in more than 200 countries and territories. The firm's Web site is accessible in 15 languages and dialects, and has dedicated content for 112 countries.

- *Product development*—It now offers more shipping choices than ever before, including BestFlight Same Day, Next Day Air Early A.M, Next Day Air, Next Day Air Saver, 2nd Day Air A.M., 2nd Day Air, 3 Day Select, Ground Next Day Air, and Worldwide Express services. See Figure 3-6.

- *Diversification*—While UPS' major focus is package delivery, it also runs such subsidiaries as UPS Worldwide Logistics (www.upslogistics.com/company)—which offers inventory management, facilities planning, site location, and other services; UPS Business Communications Services (www.upslogistics.com/services/call.html)—which offers support for call center services, E-commerce, quality measurement, and telecommunications consulting; and UPS Professional Services (www.ups-psi.com)—a global management consulting group that delivers strategic business solutions through innovative technologies, financial analysis, and logistics know-how.[19]

[19]"UPS Pressroom," http://pressroom.ups.com (March 1, 2001).

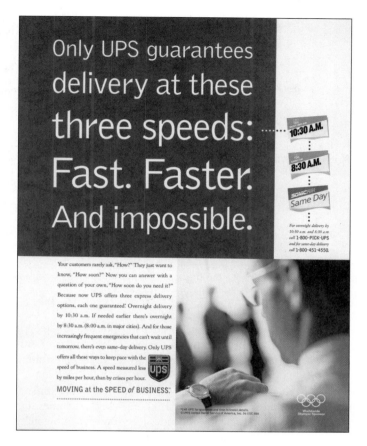

FIGURE 3-6
UPS: The Leader in Package Delivery

Source: Reprinted by permission. Photo by Michael McLoughlin.

The Boston Consulting Group Matrix

The *Boston Consulting Group matrix* lets a firm classify each SBU in terms of market share relative to key competitors and annual industry growth. A firm can see which SBUs are dominant compared to competitors and whether the industries in which it operates are growing, stable, or declining. The matrix highlights these SBUs: star, cash cow, question mark, and dog, as well as the strategies for them.[20] See Figure 3-7.

The assumption is that the higher an SBU's market share, the better its long-run marketplace position because of rather low per-unit costs and high profitability (www.bcg.com). This is due to economies of scale (larger firms can automate or standardize production, service tasks, distribution, promotion, and so on), experience (as operations are repeated, a firm becomes more effective), and better bargaining power. At the same time, the industry growth rate indicates a firm's need to invest. A high growth rate means a big investment will be needed to maintain or expand the firm's position in a growing market.

A *star* is a leading SBU (high market share) in an expanding industry (high growth). The main goal is to sustain differential advantages despite rising competition. It can generate substantial profits but needs financing to grow. Market share can be kept or increased by intensive advertising, product introductions, greater distribution, and/or price reductions. As industry growth slows, a star becomes a cash cow.

A *cash cow* is a leading SBU (high market share) in a mature or declining industry (low growth). It often has loyal customers, making it hard for competitors to woo them. Since sales are rather steady, without high costs for product development and the like, a

The **Boston Consulting Group matrix** *uses market share and industry growth to describe stars, cash cows, question marks, and dogs.*

---

[20]See *Perspectives on Experience* (Boston: Boston Consulting Group, 1972); and D. Sudharshan, *Marketing Strategy: Relationships, Offerings, Timing & Resource Allocation* (Englewood Cliffs, N.J.: Prentice Hall, 1995), pp. 244–253.

FIGURE 3-7
The Boston Consulting Group Matrix

Source: Adapted from Bruce D. Henderson, "The Experience Curve Reviewed: IV. The Growth Share Matrix of the Product Portfolio" (Boston: Boston Consulting Group, 1973). *Perspectives,* No. 135.

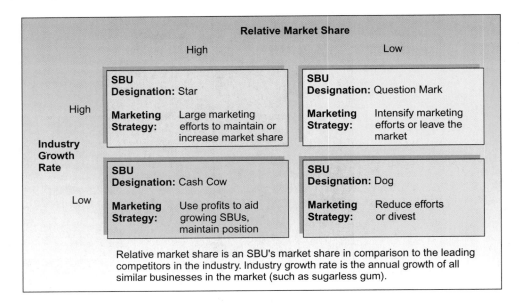

Relative market share is an SBU's market share in comparison to the leading competitors in the industry. Industry growth rate is the annual growth of all similar businesses in the market (such as sugarless gum).

cash cow produces more cash (profit) than needed to keep its market share. Profits support the growth of other company SBUs. Marketing is oriented to reminder ads, periodic price discounts, keeping up distribution channels, and offering new styles or options to encourage repurchases.

A *question mark* is an SBU that has had little impact (low market share) in an expanding industry (high growth). There is low consumer support, differential advantages are weak, and competitors are leaders. To improve, a big marketing investment is needed in the face of strong competition. A firm must decide whether to beef up promotion, add distributors, improve product attributes, and cut prices—or to abandon the market. The choice depends on whether a firm believes the SBU can compete successfully with more support and what that support will cost.

A *dog* is an SBU with limited sales (low market share) in a mature or declining industry (low growth). Despite time in the marketplace, it has a small customer following—and lags behind competitors in sales, image, and so on. A dog usually has cost disadvantages and few growth opportunities. A firm with such an SBU can appeal to a specialized market, harvest profits by cutting support, or exit the market.

Pall Corporation (www.pall.com), a maker of industrial fluid clarification equipment (which removes contaminants from liquids and gases), serves a diverse, global customer base with products that are used to purify raw materials, keep equipment running efficiently, ensure product quality, and clean up and minimize waste. The firm applies the principles suggested by the Boston Consulting Group matrix. It examines SBUs in terms of expected industry growth and market position, and then sets marketing strategies. Over the past decade, there has been a shift away from Aeropower—which now contributes 21 percent of overall Pall revenues (down from 30 percent)—and to Health Care, which now accounts for 53 percent of sales (up from 45 percent), and Fluid Processing, which now accounts for 26 percent of sales (up from 22 percent). The shift is due to a combination of declining aerospace sales, culling out unprofitable businesses, and building the Health Care and Fluid Processing businesses.[21]

The General Electric Business Screen

The *General Electric business screen* categorizes SBUs and products in terms of industry attractiveness and company business strengths. It uses more variables than the product/market opportunity matrix or the Boston Consulting Group matrix. Industry attractiveness factors include market size and growth, competition, technological

*The **General Electric business screen** measures industry attractiveness and company business strengths.*

[21]*Pall Corporation 2000 Annual Report.*

advances, and social/legal environment. Company business strengths embody differential advantages, market share, patent protection, marketing effectiveness, control over prices, and economies of scale. An SBU may have high, medium, or low industry attractiveness, as well as high, medium, or low business strengths; it would be positioned accordingly on the screen in Figure 3-8.[22]

SBUs in green are investment/growth areas. They are in strong industries and performing well. They are similar to stars in the Boston Consulting Group matrix. Full marketing resources are proper, and high profits are expected. Innovations, product-line extensions, product and image ads, distribution intensity, and solid price margins are pursued.

SBUs in yellow are selectivity/earnings areas. They are not positioned as well as investment/growth ones. An SBU may be strong in a weak industry (as a cash cow), okay in a somewhat attractive industry, or weak in an attractive industry (as a question mark). A firm wants to hold the earnings and strength of cash cows, and use marketing to maintain customer loyalty and distribution support. For question marks, a firm must decide whether to raise its marketing investment, focus on a specialized market niche, acquire another business in the industry, or trim product lines. The medium/medium SBU is an opportunity to appeal to underserved segments and to invest selectively in marketing.

SBUs in red represent harvest/divest areas. They are similar to dogs in the Boston Consulting Group matrix. A firm can minimize its marketing effort, concentrate on a few products rather than a product line, divest, or close down the SBU. Profits are harvested because investments are minimal.

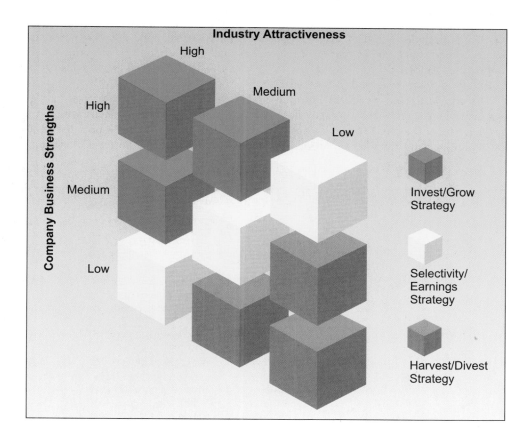

FIGURE 3-8

The General Electric Business Screen

Source: Maintaining Strategies for the Future Through Current Crises (Fairfield, Ct.: General Electric, 1975).

[22]See Derek F. Abell and John S. Hammond, *Strategic Market Planning* (Englewood Cliffs, N.J.: Prentice-Hall, 1979); and David A. Aaker, *Strategic Market Management*, Fifth Edition (New York: Wiley, 1999).

Bausch & Lomb (www.bausch.com) applies the fundamentals of the business screen. It is building its current eye care businesses, as well as pursuing new opportunities within the global eye care market: "The company is a leading maker of contact lenses and lens care solutions (including the ReNu and Boston brands). In addition to its eye care products, the firm also makes ophthalmic surgical equipment and prescription and over-the-counter medications. The company has expanded these operations through acquisitions and increased R&D funding. To focus on and strengthen its core business, Bausch & Lomb has sold its sunglasses division (including the Ray-Ban brand), its Miracle Ear hearing aid business, and its Charles River Laboratories animal research business."[23]

Visit the "GE at a Glance" section of the General Electric Web site (www.ge.com/news/podium_papers.html) to learn about the varied major contributions made by the firm that has given us the GE business screen.

The Porter Generic Strategy Model

The **Porter generic strategy model** identifies two key marketing planning concepts and the options available for each: competitive scope (broad or narrow target) and competitive advantage (lower cost or differentiation). The model pinpoints these basic strategies: cost leadership, differentiation, and focus.[24] See Figure 3-9.

With a *cost-leadership strategy,* an SBU aims at a broad market and offers goods or services in large quantities. Due to economies of scale, a firm can reduce per-unit costs and have low prices. This gives it higher profit margins than competitors, responds better to cost rises, and/or lures price-conscious consumers. Among those using cost leadership are UPS (www.ups.com), DuPont (www.dupont.com), and Wal-Mart (www.walmart.com).

In a *differentiation strategy,* an SBU aims at a large market by offering goods or services viewed as quite distinctive. The goods or services have a broad appeal, yet are perceived by consumers as unique by virtue of features, availability, reliability, etc.; price is less important. Among those using differentiation are Federal Express (www.fedex.com), Seiko (www.seiko.com), and Caterpillar Tractor (www.cat.com).

With a *focus strategy,* an SBU (which could be a small firm) seeks a narrow market segment via low prices or a unique offering. It can control costs by concentrating on a few key products aimed at specific consumers (cost focus) or by having a specialist reputation and serving a market unsatisfied by competitors (differentiation focus). Samsung

The **Porter generic strategy model** *distinguishes among cost leadership, differentiation, and focus strategies.*

FIGURE 3-9
The Porter Generic Strategy Model

Source: Tables developed by the authors based on concepts in Michael E. Porter, *Competitive Advantage: Creating and Sustaining Superior Performance* (New York: Free Press, 1985), pp. 11–16.

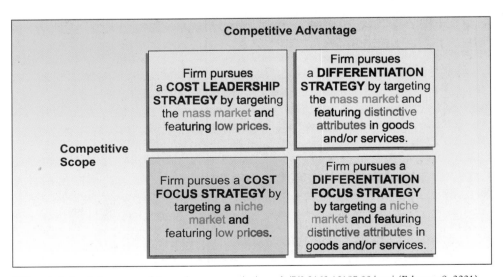

[23]"Bausch & Lomb Incorporated," www.hoovers.com/co/capsule/7/0,2163,10187,00.html (February 9, 2001).

[24]Michael E. Porter, *Competitive Advantage: Creating and Sustaining Superior Performance* (New York: Free Press, 1985), pp. 11–26; and Michael E. Porter, *Competitive Strategy: Techniques for Analyzing Industries and Competitors* (New York: Free Press, 1980), pp. 34–46. See also Chuck Profitt, "Competitive Strategy Through Differentiation," www.tsbj.com/editorial/02070803.htm (2000); and Chuck Profitt, "Competitive Strategy Through Focus," www.tsbj.com/editorial/02090903.htm (2000).

(www.samsung.com) is a low-cost South Korean maker of inexpensive consumer electronics, while the Baby Jogger Company (www.babyjogger.com) of Yakima, Washington, makes a line of strollers for those who like to jog with their babies and toddlers. A neighborhood hardware store typically provides a good combination of service, convenient location, and long hours; a local radio station may cater to an over-50 audience by playing mostly rock music from the 1960s and 1970s.

The Porter model shows that a small firm can profit by concentrating on one competitive niche, even though its total market share may be low. A firm does not have to be large to do well.

Evaluation of Strategic Planning Approaches

The strategic planning approaches just discussed are widely utilized—at least informally. Many firms assess alternative market opportunities; know which products are stars, cash cows, question marks, and dogs; recognize what factors affect performance; understand their industries; and realize they can target broad or narrow customer bases. Formally, strategic planning models are most apt to be used by larger firms; and the models are adapted to the needs of the specific firms employing them.

Strategic models have pros and cons, and should be only part of planning.

The approaches' major strengths are that they let a firm analyze all SBUs and products, study various strategies' effects, learn the opportunities to pursue and the threats to avoid, compute marketing and other resource needs, focus on meaningful differential advantages, compare performance with designated goals, and discover principles for improving. Competitors' actions and trends can also be studied.

The approaches' major weaknesses are that they may be hard to use (particularly by a small firm), may be too simplistic and omit key factors, are somewhat arbitrary in defining SBUs and evaluative criteria (like relative market share), may not be applicable to all firms and situations (a dog SBU may be profitable and generate cash), do not adequately account for environmental conditions (like the economy), may overvalue market share, and are often used by staff planners rather than line managers.

These techniques only aid planning. They do not replace the need for managers to engage in hands-on decisions by studying each situation and basing marketing strategies on the unique aspects of their industry, firm, and SBUs.

3-5f Implementing Tactical Plans

A *tactical plan* specifies the short-run actions (tactics) that a firm undertakes in implementing a given marketing strategy. At this stage, a strategy is operationalized. A tactical plan has three basic elements: specific tasks, a time frame, and resource allocation.

A marketing strategy is enacted via **tactical plans.**

The marketing mix (specific tasks) may range from a combination of high quality, high service, low distribution intensity, personal selling emphasis, and above-average prices to a combination of low quality, low service, high distribution intensity, advertising emphasis, and low prices. There would be a distinct marketing mix for each SBU, based on its target market and strategic emphasis. The individual mix elements must be coordinated for each SBU and conflicts among SBUs minimized.

Proper timing (time horizon) may mean being the first to introduce a product, bringing out a product when the market is most receptive, or quickly reacting to a competitor's strategy to catch it off guard. A firm must balance its desire to be an industry leader with clear-cut competitive advantages against its concern for the risk of being innovative. Marketing opportunities exist for limited periods of time, and the firm needs to act accordingly.

Marketing investments (resources) are order processing or order generating. Order-processing costs involve recording and handling orders, such as order entry, computer-data handling, and merchandise handling. The goal is to minimize those costs, subject to a given level of service. Order-generating costs, such as advertising and personal selling, produce revenues. Reducing them may be harmful to sales and profits. A firm should estimate sales at various levels of costs and for various combinations of marketing functions. Maximum profit rarely occurs at the lowest level of expenditure on order-generating costs.

Tactical decisions differ from strategic decisions in several key ways:

- They are less complex and more structured.
- They have a much shorter time horizon.
- They require a considerably lower resource commitment.
- They are enacted and adjusted more often.

At Frito-Lay (www.fritolay.com), tactical planning means prepping delivery people and retailers for product introductions, aggressively promoting products, maintaining profit margins—while not giving competitors opportunities to win market share by lower prices, and servicing retail accounts very well. Thus, when Frito-Lay worked on one project in salty snacks with a major Northeastern food chain, the chain "started with the notion that it could make more on its private-label snacks. What the chain found was that Frito-Lay products were accounting for 70 percent of [category] profits in 40 percent of the space and private label was [generating] 3 percent of profits in 20 percent of the space. As a result, the chain reversed course, killing its lower-tier private label line, although keeping its premium salty snacks store brand, and eliminating some small, underperforming regional brands. The retailer gave Frito-Lay more shelf space in the snack aisle. The bet paid off. Category growth, profits, and full-revenue snack sales were all up more than 10 percent at the chain following the move, and both its share of snack sales versus the competition and its profit margins rose. Frito-Lay saw sales jump 15 percent at the account."[25] On the other hand, small manufacturers may need to use outside food brokers to gain any access to food retailers. Even then, they may have a tough time getting chains as customers.

Performance is evaluated by **monitoring results.**

3-5g Monitoring Results

Monitoring results involves comparing the actual performance of a firm, business unit, or product against planned performance for a specified period. Actual performance data are then fed back into the strategic planning process. Budgets, timetables, sales and profit statistics, cost analyses, and image studies are just some measures that can be used to assess results.

When actual performance lags, corrective action is needed. For instance, "if implementation problems persist, it is not (in most instances) because employees mean to do the wrong thing. It is because they do not know the right thing to do. The first task in making strategy work is to identify the right behavior—which reduces costs, improves quality, pleases customers, and adds to profits."[26]

Some plans must be revised due to the impact of uncontrollable factors on sales and costs. Thus, many farsighted firms develop contingency plans to outline their responses in advance, should unfavorable conditions arise.

In Chapter 22, techniques for evaluating marketing effectiveness will be discussed. Those techniques are covered in Chapter 22, so the fundamental elements of marketing can be thoroughly explored first.

3-6 DEVISING A STRATEGIC MARKETING PLAN

Written documents aid strategic marketing planning and are useful for all sorts of firms.

Creating, implementing, and monitoring a strategic marketing plan best occur when a firm has a written plan. This encourages executives to carefully think out and coordinate each step in the planning process, better pinpoint problem areas, be consistent, tie the plan to goals and resources, measure performance, and send a clear message to employees and others.

---

[25]David Wellman, "The Direct Approach to the Bottom Line," *Supermarket Business* (August 1999), pp. 15–20.

[26]Steven J. Heyer and Reginald Van Lee, "Rewiring the Corporation," *Business Horizons*, Vol. 35 (May-June 1992), p. 21.

A sample outline for a written strategic plan and an application of strategic planning by a small firm are covered next.

3-6a A Sample Outline for a Written Strategic Marketing Plan

What are the ingredients of a good strategic marketing plan? Here is a brief list:

- It should be integrated into an organization's overall business plan.
- It should affect the consideration of strategic choices.
- It should force a long-range view.
- It should make the resource allocation system visible.
- It should provide methods to help strategic analysis and decision making.
- It should provide a basis for managing a firm or SBU strategically.
- It should provide a communication and coordination system both horizontally (between SBUs and departments) and vertically (from senior executives to front-line employees).
- It should help a firm and its SBUs cope with change.[27]

MARKETING *and the Web*

Can iWon's Marketing Plan Succeed in the Long Term?

The major difference between the net portal at iWon (www.iwon.com) and Yahoo! (www.yahoo.com) is that every time a consumer uses iWon to check the weather, surf the Web, or read the local news, he/she has a chance of winning a large sweepstakes prize. iWon acknowledges that it uses the same licensed search mechanism as some of its competitors. What sets iWon apart from the more established portals is its clever use of marketing, as well as the $26 million that iWon has given away in prizes to more than 1,000 people. According to Media Matrix, iWon is now the seventh-ranked portal with an average of 2.9 million daily visits.

It took iWon's founders less than 45 minutes to convince CBS to invest $30 million in the firm as a startup and to commit to spend $70 million in advertising over a four-year period. This was at a time when iWon had little more than a mock-up of a Web site and a 30-second commercial. Now, iWon has an agreement with Capital One Financial that gives its credit-card holders iWon sweepstakes points for each dollar charged. Sprint has agreed to match any iWon sweepstakes' winnings for its telephone customers. In February 2000, iWon raised an additional $100 million from investors.

Despite its initial success, there is some doubt about iWon's potential for overall long-term success. The Internet boom of early 2000 is clearly over, as witnessed by the recent number of Internet failures and the depressed prices of many Internet stocks. There is also some doubt as to whether iWon can turn a profit in an environment when many firms have reduced their Internet advertising.

Develop a marketing plan for iWon to become profitable, while increasing its business.

Source: Based on material in Nanette Byrnes, "Can iWon Keep Winning?" *Business Week* (October 9, 2000), pp. 192–193.

---

[27]Adapted by the authors from Aaker, *Strategic Market Management.*

Table 3-2 presents a sample outline for a written strategic marketing plan. This outline may be used by firms of any size or type. *[Please note: There is a comprehensive strategic marketing plan exercise accompanying this book. It is described in the appendix at the end of the chapter, beginning on page 81. If you are online, you may access the exercise by clicking on the special computer icon. In addition, at the beginning of each part of the text, there is a planning icon. Once you have finished that part, click on the icon at the part opener page to review the implications of what you have learned from a strategic marketing plan perspective.]*

TABLE 3-2

A Sample Outline for a Written Strategic Marketing Plan

Using as much detail as possible, please address each of these points for your organization:

1. Organizational Mission
   a. In 50 words or less, describe the current mission of your organization.
   b. In 50 words or less, describe how you would like your organizational mission to evolve over the next five years. The next ten years.
   c. How is the organizational mission communicated to employees?
2. Organizational Structure
   a. State and assess the current organizational structure of your organization.
   b. Does your organization have strategic business units? If yes, describe them. If no, why not?
   c. Does each major product or business unit in your organization have a marketing manager, proper resources, and clear competitors? Explain your answer.
3. Marketing Objectives
   a. Cite your organization's overall marketing goals for the next one, three, five, and ten years.
   b. Cite your organization's specific marketing goals by target market and product category for the next one, five, and ten years in terms of sales, market share, profit, image, and customer loyalty.
   c. What criteria will be used to determine whether goals have been fully, partially, or unsatisfactorily reached?
4. Situation Analysis
   a. Describe the present overall strengths, weaknesses, opportunities, and threats (SWOT) facing your organization.
   b. For each of the key products or businesses of your organization, describe the present strengths, weaknesses, opportunities, and threats.
   c. How do you expect the factors noted in your answers to (a) and (b) to change over the next five to ten years?
   d. How will your organization respond to the factors mentioned in the answers for (c)?
   e. Describe the methods your organization uses to acquire, distribute, and store the information necessary to make good marketing decisions.
5. Developing Marketing Strategy
   a. Compare your organization's overall strategy with those of leading competitors.
   b. Describe your organization's use of these strategic approaches: market penetration, market development, product development, and diversification.
   c. Categorize each of your organization's products or businesses as a star, cash cow, question mark, or dog. Explain your reasoning.
   d. For each product or business, which of these approaches is most appropriate: invest/grow, selectivity/earnings, or harvest/divest? Explain your reasoning.
   e. For each of your organization's products or businesses, which of these approaches is most appropriate: cost leadership, differentiation, cost focus, or differentiation focus? Explain your reasoning.
6. Societal, Ethical, and Consumer Issues
   a. What is your organization's view of its responsibilities regarding societal, ethical, and consumer issues?
   b. How are organizational policies developed with regard to societal, ethical, and consumer issues?

continues

Using as much detail as possible, please address each of these points for your organization:

   c. Discuss your organization's social responsibility approach in terms of the general public, employees, channel members, stockholders, and competitors.

   d. State your organization's code of ethics and how acceptable ethical practices are communicated to employees.

   e. Describe your organization's strategy for dealing with consumers' basic rights (information and education, safety, choice, and to be heard).

7. Global Marketing

   a. What is the role of global marketing in your organization's overall strategy?

   b. Describe the cultural, economic, political and legal, and technological environment in each major and potential foreign market that your organization faces.

   c. Describe your organization's strategy in terms of which and how many foreign markets your organization should enter.

   d. Develop an appropriate organizational format for each current and potential foreign market.

   e. State the extent to which your organization utilizes a standardized, nonstandardized, or glocal marketing approach in its foreign markets.

   f. Explain how your organization's marketing mix varies by foreign market.

8. Marketing and the Internet

   a. Does your organization use the Internet (Web) in its marketing strategy? If no, why not?

   b. If your organization uses the Web, does it engage in E-marketing rather than just in E-commerce? If no, why not?

   c. If your organization uses the Web, what are the marketing-related goals?

   d. If your organization uses the Web, is a systematic Internet marketing strategy applied?

9. Consumer Analysis and Target Market Strategy

   a. What are the demographic characteristics of the target market segments served or potentially served by your organization?

   b. What are the lifestyle and decision-making characteristics of the target market segments served or potentially served by your organization?

   c. Do you market to final consumers, organizational consumers, or both? How does this approach affect your overall marketing strategy?

   d. Describe the important consumer trends that could have a major effect on your organization.

   e. Explain the demand patterns that exist for your organization's products (homogeneous, clustered, or diffused).

   f. Describe your organization's choice of target market strategy (undifferentiated, differentiated, or concentrated marketing) and target market(s).

   g. Does your organization understand and utilize such concepts as derived demand, the heavy-usage segment, and benefit segmentation? Why or why not?

   h. State how your marketing mix(s) is (are) appropriate for the target market(s) chosen.

   i. What sales forecasting procedures are used by your organization? How are they related to your target market strategy?

10. Product Planning

   a. Describe your organization's products from the perspective of tangible, augmented, and generic product concepts.

   b. Are your organization's products viewed as convenience, shopping, or specialty products by consumers? How does this placement affect the marketing strategy?

   c. Discuss the rationale behind the width, depth, and consistency of your organization's product mix.

   d. Describe your organization's product management organization. Discuss your organization's competitive and company product positioning for each product/brand.

continues

TABLE 3-2	Using as much detail as possible, please address each of these points for your organization:
A Sample Outline for a Written Strategic Marketing Plan (*continued*)	

    e.   Describe your organization's use of corporate symbols and its branding strategy.

    f.   Outline your organization's overall packaging strategy.

    g.   What kinds of goods (durable and/or nondurable) and services (rented-goods, owned-goods, and/or nongoods) are sold by your organization? What are the ramifications of this for the marketing strategy?

    h.   How are your organization's products positioned along the goods/service continuum? What are the ramifications of this for the marketing strategy?

    i.   Describe your organization's new-product planning process.

    j.   In what product life-cycle stage is each of your organization's major product groupings?

    k.   How can your organization extend the life-cycle stage for those products now in the introduction, growth, and maturity life-cycle stages?

11. Distribution Planning

    a.   How are channel functions allocated among distribution intermediaries and your organization?

    b.   Explain how relationship marketing is used in your organization's channel of distribution.

    c.   State your organization's distribution approach with regard to channel length (direct or indirect) and channel width (exclusive, selective, or intensive distribution), and whether a dual distribution strategy is appropriate.

    d.   Present an approach for your organization's achieving and maintaining channel cooperation.

    e.   Describe your organization's overall logistics strategy (including transportation modes, inventory management, and foreign distribution).

    f.   Explain your organization's choice of wholesaler type and your choice of specific wholesalers.

    g.   Explain your organization's choice of retailer type and your choice of specific retailers.

    h.   How are wholesalers and retailers evaluated by your organization?

12. Promotion Planning

    a.   State your organization's broad promotion goals and the importance of each one.

    b.   Discuss your organization's overall promotion plan from the perspective of integrated marketing communications; and describe the roles of advertising, public relations, personal selling, and sales promotion at your organization.

    c.   Describe how your organization determines its overall promotional budget.

    d.   For each element of the promotional mix (advertising, public relations, personal selling, and sales promotion):

        ☐ Set specific goals.

        ☐ Assign responsibility.

        ☐ Establish a budget.

        ☐ Develop a strategy (such as themes/messages/selling techniques/ promotions, media choice, timing, cooperative efforts).

        ☐ Set criteria for assessing success or failure.

    e.   Describe how your organization's promotion efforts vary by target market and product.

    f.   At your organization, what is the role for new communications formats and technologies (such as the World Wide Web, electronic in-store point-of-purchase displays, and hand-held computers for salespeople)?

13. Price Planning

    a.   Explain your organization's overall pricing approach (price-based versus nonprice-based) and how you determine the "value" your organization provides to consumers.

    b.   Categorize your organization's target market(s) in terms of price sensitivity, and state how this affects the pricing strategy.

continues

Using as much detail as possible, please address each of these points for your organization:

c.   What is your organization's pricing philosophy for dealing with cost increases or decreases?

d.   What practices does your organization follow to ensure compliance with all government rules about pricing?

e.   Describe the role each channel member (including your organization) plays in setting prices.

f.   Explain the competitive pricing environment your organization faces.

g.   State your firm's specific pricing objectives.

h.   Describe your organization's price strategy with regard to its use of cost-based, demand-based, and/or competition-based pricing.

i.   When your organization implements a price strategy, which of these elements does it use: customary versus variable pricing, one-price versus flexible pricing, odd pricing, the price-quality association, leader pricing, multiple unit pricing, price lining, price bundling, geographic pricing, purchase terms, and price adjustments?

14. Integrating and Analyzing the Marketing Plan

   a.   Describe your organization's processes for integrating and analyzing its marketing plans.

   b.   Detail how the long-term, moderate-term, and short-term plans are compatible.

   c.   Explain how the elements of the marketing mix are coordinated.

   d.   Are ongoing marketing budgets sufficient? Does your organization differentiate between order-generating and order-processing costs? Explain your answers.

   e.   How do you expect competitors to react as you implement your organization's strategy?

   f.   Discuss how your organization utilizes benchmarking, customer satisfaction research, marketing cost analysis, sales analysis, and the marketing audit.

15. Revising the Marketing Plan

   a.   What contingency plans does your organization have in place if there are unexpected results?

   b.   Are marketing plans revised as conditions warrant? Explain your answer.

   c.   Is your organization reactive or proactive in its approach to revising marketing plans? Explain your answer.

Note: *Points 1–5 relate to Part 1 in the text.*
   Points 6–8 relate to Part 2 in the text.
   Point 9 relates to Part 3 in the text.
   Point 10 relates to Part 4 in the text.
   Point 11 relates to Part 5 in the text.
   Point 12 relates to Part 6 in the text.
   Point 13 relates to Part 7 in the text.
   Points 14–15 relate to Part 8 in the text.

3-6b   Moonstruck Chocolatier: A Strategic Marketing Plan by a Small Specialty Firm[28]

In 1992, Bill Simmons and his wife Deb decided to open Moonstruck Chocolatier in Portland, Oregon. Moonstruck opened for business in 1993 as a maker of truffles for the wholesale market. It sold to other retailers, including Neiman Marcus, Marshall Field, and Starbucks. The firm introduced it first retail store in 1996 and sales rose rapidly. Today, Moonstruck is a successful firm, specializing in chocolate-based products, with annual

Although a small compamy, Moonstruck Chocolatier has a detailed strategic marketing plan.

[28]The material in this section is based on Edward O. Welles, "The Next Starbucks," *Inc.* (January 2001), pp. 48–53; and Robert Goldfield, "Deal Aids Coffee, Chocolate Stores." *Business Journal—Portland* (October 29, 1999), p. 14.

sales of $2 million and high-powered goals for the future. Why? It has created, implemented, and monitored a solid strategic marketing plan. Let's look at the highlights of Moonstruck's plan.

Organizational Mission

Moonstruck has a clear sense of its mission: to bring the higher European standard for chocolate to the American marketplace and to create chocolate shops that serve as a meeting place in a busy, impersonal world. To do so, Moonstruck is "romancing" the cocoa bean and educating the customer, as Starbucks has done with coffee. Deb Simmons says, "We are not a chocolate store where you walk in and leave with a box of candy. We are about a chocolate experience. We want people to know what they're eating." The firm has retail stores, a direct sales operation (through 1-800-557-MOON), and a Web site.

Organizational Structure

Bill and Deb Simmons manage the business. Early on, through his business contacts, Bill Simmons was able to recruit a well-qualified board of directors. Initially, the board was divided over which direction to take the firm. "We had a couple of board members with bad experiences in retail. They were afraid of the investment in bricks and mortar," says Bill Simmons. On the other hand, board members advising against wholesaling were worried that the Moonstruck brand would never grow much by just wholesaling. At that juncture, Tony Roth purchased the exclusive rights to open Moonstruck stores in the Midwest; and his company acquired a 25 percent stake in Moonstruck Chocolatier. Roth came in as a strong supporter of a retail-dominant strategy: "Moonstruck could continue being a seasonal specialty business, but we needed to take the superior product and superior menu direct to the market."

Marketing Objectives

Moonstruck has grandiose goals. Its strategic plan calls for it to grow from half-a-dozen stores in early 2001 to 45 stores in Chicago, New York City, and Portland at year-end 2003, with sales of $26 million. According to *Inc.*, "Such a dizzying ascent may seem preposterous, considering where the company is today, but Moonstruck intends to hit those numbers and become a brand as well known as Starbucks. It plans to do that by copying the Starbucks model, substituting chocolate for coffee. And the parallels between what Moonstruck is setting out to do and what Starbucks has done are not inconsiderable."

Situation Analysis

Bill and Deb Simmons freely admit their strategic plan is based on that of Starbucks, the retail coffee giant. Thus, they did a comprehensive analysis of Starbucks' business model before opening Moonstruck. As reported in *Inc.*, this is what they found: "What really lit a fuse under Starbucks was not just its commitment to better beans but its move into retail—selling coffee by the cup. The stores were decorated with bins of coffee beans, photos of coffee trees, and shelves of gleaming coffee paraphernalia. Employees were trained to educate customers about what they were drinking and why it tasted good. For many, the experience was so engaging that Starbucks became a natural gathering place, and that made the brand familiar. 'The more we poked at the Starbucks model, the better it looked,' says Bill, who wondered what other commodity could command a cult following. The couple zeroed in on the cocoa bean, which had a romance and lore all its own."

Developing Marketing Strategy

The two strategic planning approaches with the most relevance for Moonstruck are the product/market opportunity matrix and the Porter generic strategy model. The firm is engaged in both a product development strategy (producing distinctive new chocolate products for current chocolate customers) and a market development strategy (seeking out those who have not thought of chocolate beverages as "must have" drinks). It is a great believer in a differentiation strategy (superior products at a premium price).

Societal, Ethical, and Consumer Issues

Moonstruck uses the highest-quality ingredients. It treats employees and customers courteously, honestly, and respectfully. The firm stands behind all of the products it makes and sells, and is socially responsible.

Global Marketing

Moonstruck searches the globe for the best cocoa beans, consistent with its organizational mission. It "selects chocolates prepared with cocoa beans from 'Les Grand Crus de Chocolat,' the choicest crops from the world's most exclusive plantations: South American Grand Cru—the most intensely flavored chocolate available; Caribbean Grand Cru—a fruity and harmonious couverture with a round, full-bodied taste on a background of dried fruits with a hint of fresh tobacco; and Indian Ocean Grand Cru—a unique and refreshing Criollo reminiscent of flowers and ripe red berries on a background of sweet almonds."

Marketing and Internet

Moonstruck has a colorful, animated Web site (www.moonstruckchocolate.com). The site describes the background of the company, the products it makes, and how to handle and store its chocolates. The site also lists the firm's retail locations and permits some online ordering. Moonstruck's slogan appears prominently on the home page: "Your expectations for chocolate will never be the same again."

Consumer Analysis and Target Market Strategy

Moonstruck appeals to customers who are interested in quality, uniqueness, assortment, and service—and are willing to pay for it. The firm has two market segments: final consumers (who buy for personal use and in small quantities) and corporate customers (who buy products as gifts and in larger quantities).

Product Planning

Moonstruck has greatly expanded its product line since the early days, adding products that complement each other well. As Inc. notes, "you can buy individual truffles, freshly handmade at the company's plant in Portland. You can buy all manner of coffee drinks. You can also buy all manner of chocolate drinks, hot and cold. Moonstruck mixes fresh, high-quality chocolate into exotic confections, combining it with ingredients like coffee, root beer, Earl Grey tea, vanilla, and fresh peppermint. Although it sells coffee, pastries, and ice cream, chocolate in varying forms yields two-thirds of sales."

Distribution Planning

Moonstruck's retail stores are changing, largely due to the influence of Tony Roth. The stores he has opened in Illinois bear little resemblance to the original store in Portland. They are several times larger; and each Roth store should generate three to four times the sales, with much higher profit margins. Roth's goal is to breathe life into the long-lost chocolate café of Europe.

Promotion Planning

Moonstruck uses in-store tastings and demonstrations to draw customers into impulse purchases. It also does some print advertising. But its biggest promotion effort revolves around the publicity it receives from newspaper and magazine stories about Moonstruck products. The reviews are trumpeted at the firm's Web site. Here's an example, from *Gift Basket Review:* "Exceptional—this is a Rolls Royce built like a truffle: airy, luxurious, and completely decadent."

Price Planning

Moonstruck has above-average prices, reflective of the quality and status accorded its products. About 60 percent of its revenues are from high-margin chocolate truffles and drinks. For example, one 10-piece truffle collection in a designer foil-wrapped crescent box retails for $33.00 and one 9-piece truffle collection in a standard box retails for $15.

Integrating and Analyzing the Plan

Moonstruck was fortunate that Tony Roth came aboard. As Bill Simmons recognized, "We needed a management catalyst. Tony has the conviction to go forward. He could visualize the concept in play. He's never afraid to run the numbers on an idea he likes." According to *Inc.*, what Simmons saw in Roth was a man whose discipline matched his energy. He remembers Tony Roth falling asleep over his laptop computer while writing insightful messages late into the night.

Revising the Marketing Plan

Until late 1999, Moonstruck owned a bakery in Portland. At that point, it sold off the bakery to focus better on its chocolate business and the marketing strategy for it. Investors in Moonstruck felt that the bakery had little synergy with the firm's core business. Bill Simmons agreed that they were right.

WEB SITES YOU CAN USE

A variety of Web sites provide step-by-step advice on strategic planning and many even have free, downloadable, easy-to-use templates. Here, we present a number of such sites, divided into two categories: strategic business plans and strategic marketing plans:

Strategic Business Plans

BizMove.com—*Developing a Successful Business Plan* (www.bizmove.com/small-business/business-plan.htm)

Bplans.com—*Develop Your Plan* (www.bplans.com/dp)

Business Owner's Toolkit—*Writing Your Business Plan* (www.toolkit.cch.com/text/p02_5001.asp)

Business Resource Software—*Writing a Business Plan* (www.planware.ie/resource/planware/bizplan.htm)

Center for Business Planning—*Business Planning Resources* (www.businessplans.org/plan.asp)

Entrepreneurial Edge—*How to Develop and Use a Business Plan* (http://edge.lowe.org) [Note: Once you are at this site, click on "Strategy" under "Find Your Edge." Then, click on "Business Plan" from the list of "Strategy Leadership Builders".]

Inc.—*Writing a Business Plan* (http://www.inc.com/advice/writing_a_business_plan)

Strategic Marketing Plans

BizMove.com—*Small Business Marketing* (www.bizmove.com/small-business/marketing.htm)

Bplans.com—*On Target: The Book on Marketing Plans* (www.bplans.com/ot/mp)

Business Resource Software—*Marketing Plan* (www.businessplans.org/Market.html)

ChamberBiz—*Building a Successful Marketing Plan* (www.chamberbiz.com/bizcenter/P03_8000.cfm)

Entrepreneurial Edge—*Marketing* (http://edge.lowe.org) [Note: Once you are at this site, click on "Customers" under "Find Your Edge." Then, click on "Marketing" from the list of "Customers Business Builders".]

Inc.—*Marketing & Advertising* (www.inc.com/advice/marketing_and_advertising)

Morebusinee.com—*Business & Marketing Plans* (www.morebusiness.com)

SUMMARY

1. *To define strategic planning and consider its importance for marketing* Strategic planning encompasses both strategic business plans and strategic marketing plans. Strategic business plans describe the overall direction firms will pursue within their chosen environment and guide the allocation of resources and effort. Strategic marketing plans outline what marketing actions to undertake, why those actions are needed, who is responsible for carrying them out, when and where they will be completed, and how they will be coordinated.

Strategic planning provides guidance via a hierarchal process, clarifies goals, encourages departmental cooperation, focuses on strengths and weaknesses (as well as opportunities and threats), examines alternatives, helps allocate resources, and points up the value of monitoring results.

2. *To describe the total quality approach to strategic planning and its relevance to marketing* A total quality approach should be used while devising and enacting business and marketing plans. With this approach, a firm adopts a process- and output-related philosophy, by which it strives to fully satisfy consumers in an effective and efficient manner. There is a customer focus; a top management commitment; emphasis on continuous improvement; and support and involvement from employees, suppliers, and channel members.

3. *To look at the different kinds of strategic plans and the relationships between marketing and the other functional areas in an organization* A firm's strategic plans may be short run, moderate in length, or long run. Strategic marketing plans may be for each major product, presented as one companywide marketing plan, or considered part of an overall business plan. A bottom-up, top-down, or combined management approach may be used.

The interests of marketing and the other key functional areas in a firm need to be accommodated in a strategic plan. Departmental conflict can be reduced by improving communications, employing personnel with broad backgrounds, establishing interdepartmental development programs, and blending departmental goals.

4. *To describe thoroughly each of the steps in the strategic planning process* First, a firm defines its organizational mission—the long-term commitment to a type of business and a place in the market. Second, it establishes strategic business units (SBUs), the self-contained divisions, product lines, or product departments with specific market focuses and separate managers. Third, quantitative and qualitative marketing objectives are set. Fourth, through situation analysis, a firm identifies its internal strengths and weaknesses, as well as external opportunities and threats.

Fifth, a firm develops a marketing strategy—to outline the way in which the marketing mix is used to attract and satisfy the target market(s) and accomplish organizational goals. Every SBU has its own marketing mix. The approaches to strategy planning include the product/market opportunity matrix, the Boston Consulting Group matrix, the General Electric business screen, and the Porter generic strategy model. They should be viewed as planning tools that aid decision making; they do not replace the need for executives to engage in hands-on planning for each situation.

Sixth, a firm uses tactical plans to specify the short-run actions necessary to implement a given marketing strategy. At this stage, specific tasks, a time horizon, and resource allocation are made operational. Seventh, a firm monitors results by comparing actual performance against planned performance; and this information is fed back into the strategic planning process. Adjustments in strategy are made as needed.

5. *To show how a strategic marketing plan may be devised and applied* Strategic marketing plans work best when they are integrated within the overall strategic business plan, and they are prepared systematically and comprehensively—as illustrated in Table 3-2. This is exemplified by Moonstruck Chocolatier, a small confectionary firm.

KEY TERMS

strategic business plan (p. 52)
strategic marketing plan (p. 52)
total quality (p. 53)
strategic planning process (p. 58)
organizational mission (p. 59)

strategic business unit (SBU) (p. 60)
situation analysis (p. 62)
marketing strategy (p. 63)
product/market opportunity matrix (p. 63)
Boston Consulting Group matrix (p. 65)

General Electric business screen (p. 66)
Porter generic strategy model (p. 68)
tactical plan (p. 69)
monitoring results (p. 70)

REVIEW QUESTIONS

1. Explain Figure 3-2, which deals with the total quality approach.
2. Distinguish between bottom-up and top-down strategic plans. What are the pros and cons of each?
3. Why are conflicts between marketing and other functional areas inevitable? How can these conflicts be reduced or avoided?
4. Under what circumstances should a company consider reappraising its organizational mission?

5. In situation analysis, what is the distinction between strengths and opportunities and between weaknesses and threats? How should a firm react to each of these factors?
6. Describe the General Electric business screen and the Porter generic strategy model.
7. Explain how tactical decisions differ from strategic decisions.
8. What are the ingredients of a good strategic marketing plan?

DISCUSSION QUESTIONS

1. Do you think your college or university is following a total quality approach? Why or why not? What total quality recommendations would you make for your school?

2. What issues should a small movie theater chain study during situation analysis? How could it react to them?

3. Give a current example of each of these strategic approaches: market development, product development, market penetration, and diversification. Evaluate the strategies.

4. Develop a rating scale to use in analyzing the industry attractiveness and company business strengths of a small stock brokerage firm, a medium-sized management consulting firm, or a large auto supplies manufacturer.

WEB EXERCISE

At the Business Resource Software Web site (www.businessinsight.org/bionline/bi00.asp), you may acquire feedback about the merit of a particular strategic marketing plan. Go to this site, read the overview statement, and click on the right arrow key toward the bottom of the screen to begin. Enter the requested information for a real or hypothetical company, screen by screen. Click the right arrow key at the top of each screen (after the overview) to move to the next planning topic. When you are finished, read the "Sample Analysis Results." Print out the analysis and explain what you have learned from it.

Chapter 3 Appendix

Strategic Marketing Plan Appendix

In Chapter 3, we presented a detailed sample outline for preparing a written strategic marketing plan (Table 3-2). Throughout *Marketing*, the part-opening pages refer to the specific sections of the sample plan that apply to each of the eight parts in the book.

To provide you with greater insights about strategic marketing plans, we have prepared the special computer exercise that is described in this appendix. It is called *StratMktPlan*. The *StratMktPlan* software is available on the online Resources page for this book. The Resources page may be accessed by clicking the online Resources link in your Backpack.

StratMktPlan is based on the sample outline in Chapter 3. From the sample outline, we have selected a cross-section of the questions for you to address. You will be assigned to a specific firm and gear your answers toward that company. Answers are typed directly into easy-to-use dropdown windows. The exercise questions are shown in Table 1.

By answering all of the *StratMktPlan* questions, you are preparing a comprehensive strategic marketing plan. Depending on the goals of your professor, different students or student teams can be assigned to competing companies in the same industry, or assigned to companies with totally different strategies and resources. One student or team can be assigned to a national firm selling mass appeal products, while another group is assigned to a local firm selling a product for a niche market.

You are encouraged to use secondary sources (including the Web) to devise a marketing plan when working on the *StratMktPlan* computer exercise. The SWOT analysis (strengths, weaknesses, opportunities, and threats) should include data derived from secondary sources.

There are two ways in which your professor can assign the *StratMktPlan* exercise: (1) You or a team of students can be requested to hand in *StratMktPlan* assignments one part at a time, with submissions spaced out over the term. (2) You or a team of students can be requested to work on *StratMktPlan* as a comprehensive course assignment, with one overall submission at the end of the semester.

Develop an integrated strategic marketing plan for the assigned company by addressing each of the questions below.

TABLE 1

StratMktPlan Exercise Outline

Organizational Mission
- In 50 words or less, describe the current mission of your organization.

Marketing Goals
- Cite your organization's overall marketing goals for the next one, three, five, and ten years.

Situation Analysis
- Describe the present overall strengths, weaknesses, opportunities, and threats (SWOT) facing your organization.

Developing Marketing Strategy
- Compare your organization's overall strategy with those of leading competitors.

Societal, Ethical, and Consumer Issues
- What is your organization's view of its responsibilities regarding societal, ethical, and consumer issues?

Global Marketing
- What is the role of global marketing in your organization's overall strategy?

Marketing and the Internet
- Does your organization use the Internet (Web) in its marketing strategy? If no, why not?

Consumer Analysis and Target Market
- What are the demographic characteristics of the target market segments served or potentially served by your organization?
- Do you market to final consumers, organizational consumers, or both? How does this approach affect your overall marketing strategy?
- Describe your organization's choice of target market strategy (undifferentiated, differentiated, or concentrated marketing) and target market(s).

continues

TABLE 1

**StratMktPlan Exercise
Outline (continued)**

> **Develop an integrated strategic marketing plan for the assigned company by addressing each of the questions below.**

Product Planning

- Describe your organization's products from the perspective of tangible, augmented, and generic product concepts.
- Discuss the rationale behind the width, depth, and consistency of your organization's product mix.

Distribution Planning

- Explain how relationship marketing is used in your organization's channel of distribution.
- State your organization's distribution approach with regard to channel length (direct or indirect) and channel width (exclusive, selective, or intensive distribution), and whether a dual distribution strategy is appropriate.

Promotion Planning

- State your organization's broad promotion goals and the importance of each one.
- Discuss your organization's overall promotional plan from the perspective of integrated marketing communications; and describe the roles for advertising, public relations, personal selling, and sales promotion at your organization.

Price Planning

- Explain your organization's overall pricing approach (price-based versus nonprice-based) and how you determine the "value" your organization provides to consumers.
- Categorize your organization's target market(s) in terms of price sensitivity, and state how this affects the pricing strategy.

Integrating and Organizing the Marketing Plan

- How do you expect competitors to react as you implement your organization's strategy?

Revising the Marketing Plan

- What contingency plans does your organization have in place if there are unexpected results?

We have included in the *StratMktPlan* computer exercise an illustration of a strategic marketing plan for COLLEGE TODAY BOOKSTORE, based on the questions in Table 1 in this appendix. COLLEGE TODAY BOOKSTORE is a private profit-oriented college store located within 1 mile of your campus. This retailer competes with the campus college store, as well as large retailers such as Staples and Office Max. Although the specific answers in this illustration may not be directly applicable to another company, the example should stimulate your thinking and give you a better idea of how to handle questions.

4

Information for Marketing Decisions

Although all online survey firms promise to deliver data quickly, there are vast differences in their approaches. Some firms have researchers who design polls based on client needs, while others provide do-it-yourself versions of surveys which must then be adapted by a client. Prices range from as low as $1,000 per survey to as high as $1,000 per question. Some analysts feel that users of online surveys need to use caution in analyzing data; others say inexpensive online research is suitable in many applications.

QuickTake.com (www.quicktake.com), a division of Greenfield Online (www.greenfield.com), is an online research provider that offers clients fast information. For a fee of $1,000, clients can write up a questionnaire, post it on the firm's Web site, and collect data from 250 respondents. QuickTake.com recruits its respondents through banner ads that promise them an entry in a sweepstakes with a $1,500 prize. The banner ads are placed by online advertising agencies and media buying firms. Consumers must complete the survey to be eligible for the drawing. Critics of QuickTake.com question the ability of clients to write a usable survey, as well as the representativeness of the respondents. Even QuickTake.com's general manager states that "We don't claim QuickTake.com to be qualitatively or quantitatively reliable." Instead, it's intended to validate ideas and to complement other studies.

At the other end of the cost spectrum is Harris Interactive (www.harrisinteractive.com). The firm's online research service costs $1,000 per question and collects data from 2,000 respondents within a 2-day period. Harris draws respondents from its existing panel, consisting of more than 6.6 million consumers. Harris selects respondents through a model that balances the respondents to reflect differences between online and typical respondents. For example, online respondents generally are more affluent and more educated than consumers who do not have Web access. As a test of its model, Harris sought to analyze voting behavior via online research. Harris was able to correctly project the winners in 95 percent of the elections for governor, a record similar to CNN's.[1]

In this chapter, we will look at the value of marketing information, explain the role of a marketing information system, and describe the marketing research process. We will also take another look at sampling methodologies and online surveys.

4-1 OVERVIEW

It is essential for a firm to have appropriate information before, while, and after making (and enacting) marketing decisions if strengths, weaknesses, opportunities, and threats are to be assessed accurately; actions are to be proper for a given marketing environment; and performance is to be maximized. See Figure 4-1.

Firms make better marketing decisions when they have good information.

---

[1]Kim Cross, "Stats to Go," *Business 2.0* (October 10, 2000), p. 284.

FIGURE 4-1
Taking a Proactive Approach to Marketing Information

A company's chances for success rise dramatically if it seeks out—and uses—in-depth marketing information.

Source: Reprinted by permission of Retail Planning Associates. Photography by Michael Houghton/STUDIOHIO.

*The **scientific method** requires objectivity, accuracy, and thoroughness.*

Good information enables marketers to

- Gain a competitive edge.
- Reduce financial and image risks.
- Determine consumer attitudes.
- Monitor the environment.
- Gather competitive intelligence.
- Coordinate strategy.
- Measure performance.
- Improve advertising credibility.
- Gain management support for decisions.
- Verify intuition.
- Improve effectiveness.

Relying on intuition, executive judgment, and past experience is not sufficient: "Marketing data represent an ever-growing puzzle waiting to be assembled—but if assembled, the data can help managers look ahead in terms of customer behavior and buying patterns and can help focus more effectively on critical marketing activities and, ultimately, higher profits."[2]

The *scientific method*—incorporating objectivity, accuracy, and thoroughness—should be followed when collecting and analyzing any marketing information. *Objectivity* means information is gathered in an open-minded way. Judgments are not reached until all data are collected and analyzed. *Accuracy* refers to the use of carefully constructed research tools. Each aspect of information gathering, such as the study format, the sample, interviewer training, and tabulations, are well planned and executed. *Thoroughness* deals with the comprehensive nature of information gathering. Mistaken conclusions may be reached if probing is not intense enough.

In this chapter, two vital aspects of marketing information are covered: marketing information systems and marketing research. A marketing information system guides all of a firm's marketing-related information efforts—and stores and disseminates data—on a continuous basis. Marketing research involves gathering and analyzing information on specific marketing issues.

[2]Keat Wilkins, "Increase Sales by More Effectively Using Data Routinely Generated Every Day," *National Petroleum News* (December 2000), p. 57.

4-2 MARKETING INFORMATION SYSTEMS

The collection of marketing information should not be a rare event that occurs only when data are needed on a specific marketing topic. If research is done this way, a firm faces these risks: Opportunities may be missed. There may be a lack of awareness of environmental changes and competitors' actions. It may not be possible to analyze data over several time periods. Marketing plans and decisions may not be properly reviewed. Data collection may be disjointed. Previous studies may not be stored in an easy-to-use format. Time lags may result if a new study is required. Actions may be reactionary rather than anticipatory. Thus, it is essential for any firm, regardless of its size or type, to devise and employ some form of marketing information system to aid decision making. See Figure 4-2.

A *marketing information system (MIS)* is "a set of procedures and methods designed to generate, analyze, disseminate, and store anticipated marketing decision information on a regular, continuous basis."[3] What this means is that a firm should

A **marketing information system** *regularly gathers, analyzes, disseminates, and stores data.*

- Purposefully amass data from internal company documents, existing external documents, and primary studies (when necessary).
- Analyze data and prepare suitable reports—in terms of the mission, strategy, and proposed tactics.
- Distribute the analyzed data to the right marketing decision makers in the firm. They will vary on the basis of the particular topics covered.
- Store data for future use and comparisons.
- Seek all relevant data that have either current or future marketing ramifications—not just data with specific short-term implications.
- Undertake data collection, analysis, distribution, and storage in an ongoing manner.

FIGURE 4-2

Marketing Information Systems: Now Affordable for Every Budget

With the advent of powerful, fast, and inexpensive PCs and computer networks, firms of any size can easily set up a marketing information system covering a wide range of topics. There are also numerous user-friendly software packages available to facilitate the process.

Source: Reprinted by permission of Retail Planning Associates. Photography by Michael Houghton/STUDIOHIO.

---

[3]Adapted by the authors from Robert A. Peterson, *Marketing Research*, Second Edition (Dallas: Business Publications, 1988), p. 31; and Peter D. Bennett (Editor), *Dictionary of Marketing Terms*, Second Edition (Chicago: American Marketing Association, 1995), p. 167.

GLOBAL *Marketing in Action*

Nestlé's E-Revolution: From Information to Action

Nestlé (www.nestle.com) is investing up to $1.8 billion from 2000 to 2003 to become a world-class Web-smart firm. The company wants to use the Web in such activities as buying, manufacturing, and marketing. Unlike smaller firms that have adopted Web technology, Nestlé has $50 billion in annual revenues from traditional sales and employs 230,000 people in 83 nations. According to a vice-president of one of its software suppliers, "This is about taking the world's largest elephant and making it dance."

Much of Nestlé's Web initiative concerns better linking the firm to its suppliers and retailers. It wants to use the Web to streamline its ordering, as well as to enable its U.S. retailers to order online. In addition, Nestlé wants all of its employees to be able to access information from Nestlé divisions in other countries.

Nestlé anticipates great savings from this Web initiative. For example, its order-processing costs for a Web order from a retailer are only 21 cents versus $2.35 from a phone or fax order. Nestlé also hopes that the high level of communication with retailers will let Nestlé more accurately schedule inventory. In the past, Nestlé had to use a "guesstimate" to determine how many candy bars it would sell during a major promotion. Web links with major supermarket chains have enabled the firm to reduce Nestlé's inventories by 15 percent, without having stockouts. In total, Nestlé estimates that such Web initiatives will reduce its current $3 billion worldwide logistics and administrative costs by as much as 20 percent.

What are the complexities of developing a Web-based marketing intelligence network for a large multinational corporation like Nestlé?

Source: Based on material in William Echikson, "Nestlé: An Elephant Dances," *Business Week* (December 11, 2000), pp. EB44–EB48.

Figure 4-3 shows how an information system can be used operationally, managerially, and strategically for several aspects of marketing.

Next, the components of a basic marketing information system, commercial data bases, data-base marketing, and examples of MIS in action are presented.

4-2a A Basic Marketing Information System

Figure 4-4 presents a basic marketing information system. It begins with a statement of company objectives, which provide broad guidelines. These goals are affected by environmental factors, such as competition, government, and the economy. Marketing plans involve the choice of a target market, marketing goals, the marketing organization, the marketing mix (product, distribution, promotion, and price decisions), and performance measurement.

After marketing plans are outlined, a firm's total marketing information needs can be specified and satisfied via a ***marketing intelligence network,*** which consists of continuous monitoring, marketing research, and data warehousing. ***Continuous monitoring*** is used to regularly study a firm's external and internal environment. It can entail subscribing to trade publications, observing news reports, getting constant feedback from employees and customers, attending industry meetings, watching competitors' actions (competitive intelligence), and compiling periodic company reports. ***Marketing research*** is used to obtain information on particular marketing issues (problems). Information may

A marketing intelligence network includes marketing research, continuous monitoring, and data warehousing.

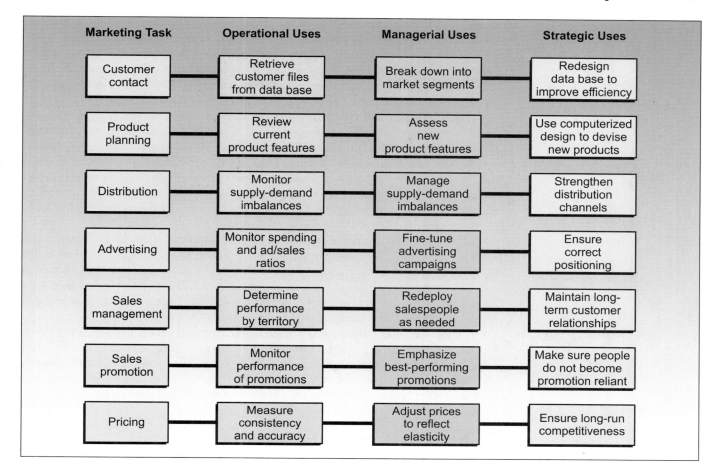

Marketing Task	Operational Uses	Managerial Uses	Strategic Uses
Customer contact	Retrieve customer files from data base	Break down into market segments	Redesign data base to improve efficiency
Product planning	Review current product features	Assess new product features	Use computerized design to devise new products
Distribution	Monitor supply-demand imbalances	Manage supply-demand imbalances	Strengthen distribution channels
Advertising	Monitor spending and ad/sales ratios	Fine-tune advertising campaigns	Ensure correct positioning
Sales management	Determine performance by territory	Redeploy salespeople as needed	Maintain long-term customer relationships
Sales promotion	Monitor performance of promotions	Emphasize best-performing promotions	Make sure people do not become promotion reliant
Pricing	Measure consistency and accuracy	Adjust prices to reflect elasticity	Ensure long-run competitiveness

FIGURE 4-3

How Marketing Information Can Be Utilized

Source: Adapted by the authors from Rajendra S. Sisodia, "Marketing Information and Decision Support Systems for Services," *Journal of Services Marketing,* Vol. 6 (Winter 1992), pp. 51–64.

Environment → Company Objectives

Company Objectives → Marketing Plans

Marketing Plans → Marketing Intelligence Network
• Marketing research
• Continuous monitoring
• Data storage

Marketing Intelligence Network → Implementing Marketing Plans

→ Implementation

← Feedback

FIGURE 4-4

A Basic Marketing Information System

be retrieved from storage (existing company data) or acquired by collecting external secondary data and/or primary data. ***Data warehousing*** involves retaining all types of relevant company records (such as sales, costs, personnel performance, etc.), as well as information collected through continuous monitoring and marketing research. These data aid decision making and are kept for future reference. Marketing research should be considered as just one part of an ongoing, integrated information system.

Depending on a firm's resources and the complexity of its information needs, a marketing intelligence network may or may not be fully computerized. Small firms can do well if their employees and managers read industry publications, attend trade shows, observe competitors, talk with suppliers and customers, track performance, and store the results of these efforts. In any event, information needs must be stated and regularly reviewed, data sources identified, personnel given information tasks, storage and retrieval facilities set up, and data routed to decision makers. The keys to a good MIS are consistency, completeness, and orderliness.

Marketing plans should be enacted based on information from the intelligence network. Thus, by continuous monitoring, a firm could learn that a competitor intends to cut prices by 7 percent during the next month. This would give the firm time to explore its own marketing options (e.g., switch to cheaper materials, place larger orders to get discounts, or ignore the cuts) and select one. If monitoring is not done, the firm might be caught by surprise and forced just to cut prices, without any other choice.

A basic MIS generally has many advantages: organized data collection, a broad perspective, the storage of important data, an avoidance of crises, coordinated marketing plans, speed in gathering enough data to make decisions, data amassed and kept over several time periods, and the ability to do cost-benefit analysis. Yet, forming an information system may not be easy. Initial time and labor costs may be high, and setting up a sophisticated system may be complex.

4-2b Commercial Data Bases

Commercial data bases can provide useful ongoing information.

Because client companies need current, comprehensive, and relatively inexpensive information about the environment in which they operate, many specialized research firms offer ongoing ***commercial data bases*** with information on population traits, the business environment, economic forecasts, industry and individual companies' performance, and other items. Data bases may include newspaper and magazine articles, business and household addresses culled from Yellow Pages and other sources, industry and company news releases, government reports, conference proceedings, indexes, patent records, and so on. The research firms sell access to their data bases to clients, usually for a relatively low fee.

Data bases are typically available in printed form; on computer disks, CD-ROMs, or tapes; and as online downloads from the Internet. There are commercial data-base firms that concentrate on tracking and clipping newspaper and magazine articles on an orderly basis; unlike with computerized data bases, these firms actually look for information on subjects specified by clients. They offer their services for a fee. The annual *Burwell World Directory of Information Brokers* (www.burwellinc.com/aboutBE.html) cites nearly 1,800 information brokers in the United States and about 45 other nations.

Firms such as InfoUSA (www.infousa.com/homesite) provide business and household addresses in CD-ROM, DVD, and download formats. InfoUSA gathers data from phone directories, annual reports, and government agencies; in addition, it makes 16 million calls per year to keep data bases current. For $59.95, a client can buy an annual CD-ROM or DVD subscription (updated quarterly) to a data base with 104 million businesses and households. InfoUSA has three million customers—from single-person firms to giant corporations. Other popular providers of commercial data bases are Donnelley Marketing (www.donnelleymarketing.com), Dun & Bradstreet (www.dnb.com), and Find/SVP (www.findsvp.com).

Many firms and libraries subscribe to one or more online data bases, whereby users are charged a fee. Among the best-known data-base services are ABI/Inform and ProQuest from Bell & Howell (www.infolearning.com), InfoTrac Web from Gale Group (www.infotrac-college.com/about), Dow Jones Interactive (http://www.djnr.com), and Lexis-Nexis (www.lexis-nexis.com) from Reed Elsevier. With these services, the user can do a search on a particular topic or firm, generate the names and abstracts of relevant articles or reports, and then print out the information. Full articles or reports may also be accessed and printed, sometimes for an additional fee.

4-2c Data-Base Marketing

In conjunction with their marketing information systems, growing numbers of firms are using data-base marketing to better identify target markets and more efficiently reach them. **Data-base marketing** is a computerized technique that compiles, sorts, and stores relevant information about customers and potential customers; uses that information to highlight opportunities and prioritize market segments; and enables the firm to profitably tailor marketing efforts for specific customers or customer groups. This process is shown in Figure 4-5.

Among the three steps in data-base marketing that are described in Figure 4-5, data mining is the most crucial step. **Data mining** is an in-depth, computerized search of available information to find profitable marketing opportunities that may otherwise be hidden. The goal is to pinpoint the most attractive customer segments, along with their unique attributes and needs.

Data-base marketing

creates a bank of information about individual customers (taken from orders, inquiries, external lists), uses it to analyze buying and inquiry patterns, and creates the ability to target goods and services more accurately to specific customers. It may be used to promote the benefits of brand loyalty to customers at risk from competition. It can fuel sales growth by identifying customers most apt to buy new goods and services. It can increase sales effectiveness. It can support low-cost alternatives to traditional sales methods. These include telemarketing and direct mail, which can be important in markets where margins are eroding.[4]

*Through **data-base marketing**, and careful **data mining**, companies can better reach and interact with customers.*

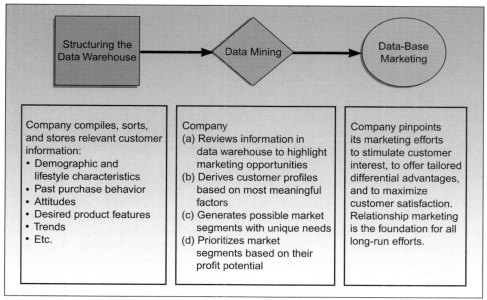

FIGURE 4-5

Applying Data-Base Marketing

[4]Robert Shaw and Merlin Stone, *Data-Base Marketing: Strategy & Implementation* (New York: Wiley, 1990), p. 4. See also Peter R. Peacock, "Data Mining in Marketing: Part 1," *Marketing Management* (Winter 1998), pp. 9–18; Mary Shacklett, "Data-Base Marketing," *Credit Union Magazine* (December 2000), pp. 4A–8A; and Alan Weber, "14 No-Fail Steps to Building a Data Base," *Target Marketing* (October 2000), pp. 153–163.

FIGURE 4-6

Using Data-Base Marketing to Foster Customer Relationships

Huntington Bancshares (www.huntington.com) has more than 600 offices in 11 states. Its data-base marketing strategy has pinpointed 10 consumer lifestyle segments, from student to retiree. It capitalizes on this data mining with its customer-oriented "My Huntington" program, whereby each customer can provide information that creates a free, customizable home page: "It is our goal to treat each customer as an individual."

Source: Reprinted by permission of Retail Planning Associates. Photography by Michael Houghton/STUDIOHIO.

Relationship marketing benefits from data-base marketing. A firm can identify those customers with whom it would most like to have long-term relationships, learn as much as possible about them (such as demographics, purchase behavior, and attitudes), tailor its marketing efforts toward them, and followup to learn the level of satisfaction. A firm might even compute a "lifetime value" for specific customers, based on their purchase history—and adjust marketing efforts accordingly. See Figure 4-6.

When setting up a data base, each actual or potential customer gets an identifying code. Then, contact information such as name, address, phone number, industry code (if a business customer), and demographic data (when appropriate), and marketing information such as source and date of contact(s) with firm, purchase history, product interests, and responses to offers are entered and updated for each customer. The information should be distributed to marketing decision makers in the firm and kept in the MIS, and company efforts should be coordinated so customers are not bombarded with mailings and there is a consistent image.

There are many consulting companies that help clients with data-base marketing. One is ePresence (www.epresence.com/asp/solutions), "an e-services company that provides highly personalized, integrated solutions to *Fortune 1000* clients, allowing them to maximize the value of each customer, business partner, and employee relationship. Leveraging expertise in customer-centric, Internet-based technologies, our consultants, partners, and methodologies help companies address new e-business models, expand business channels and drive growth."[5]

In practice, data-base marketing actually works like this:

[1] You may think you're just sending in a coupon, filling out a warranty card, or entering a sweepstakes. But to a marketer, you're also volunteering information about yourself—data that gets fed into a computer, where it's combined with more information from public records. [2] Using sophisticated statistical techniques, the computer merges different sets of data into a coherent, consolidated data base. Then, with powerful software, brand managers can "drill down" into the data to any level of detail they require. [3] The computer identifies a model consumer for a chosen product based on the common characteristics of high-volume users.

---

[5]"Company Overview," www.epresence.com/asp/about (February 17, 2001).

Next, clusters of consumers who share those characteristics—interests, incomes, and brand loyalties, for instance—can be identified as targets for marketing efforts. [4] The data can be used in many ways: to determine the values of coupons and who should get them; to develop new products and ensure that the appropriate consumers know about them; to tailor ad messages and aim them at the right audience. [5] Cash-register scanners provide reams of information about exactly what shoppers are buying at specific stores. Merged with the manufacturer's data, this intelligence helps to plan local promotional mailings, fine-tune shelf displays, and design store layouts. [6] The data base is continually updated with information collected from product-oriented clubs, responses to coupons, calls to 800 numbers, and sweepstakes entries, as well as with new lists from outside sources.[6]

4-2d MIS in Action

Worldwide, millions of organizations now use some form of MIS in their decision making, and the trend is expected to continue. In fact, as a result of computer networking, progressive firms (and divisions within the same firm) around the globe are transmitting and sharing their marketing information with each other quickly and inexpensively. According to recent studies, one-half of *Fortune 1000* companies and one-half of large retailers are actively engaged in data-base marketing.[7]

Information systems are being applied today in various settings.

Among the specific firms with superior marketing information systems are 3M, Marks & Spencer, and Louise's Trattoria. Each devotes considerable time and resources to its system. Here are examples of how they apply MIS.

3M (www.3m.com) makes such diverse products as advanced adhesives, reflective materials, dental and skin products, tapes, and insulating products. Among its best-known brands are Post-it Notes and Scotch tapes. It operates in more than 60 nations. To manage and market its products better, the firm recently introduced a $30 million online information system—complete with sales information, product descriptions, and customer records. Today, all senior executives get their information from the online data base: "3M doesn't have to ask its business customers what they buy. Customer accounts from 3M offices around the world can be summarized to give a quick-as-a-snap, global picture."[8]

Marks & Spencer (www.marks-and-spencer.co.uk), the British-based retailer, uses the information generated from customer credit cards to better tailor its marketing efforts. A short time ago, after studying its customer data base, the firm revamped its process for supplying products to stores: "By analyzing the demographics of customers, their lifestyles, working patterns, and shopping patterns, it identified different customer segments and where they shop. It then supplied merchandise accordingly."[9]

Louise's Trattoria (www.restaurantsatoz.com/intro/louise1.html) is a 13-unit chain of Italian restaurants, all in Los Angeles. By reviewing the information from computer-scanned customer receipts—that were electronically stored in the firm's data warehouse—Louise's learned that "customers were more interested in 'California Italian', as opposed to 'traditional Italian' foods, that they wanted more healthful menu items, and that the chain's patronage was skewed more female." Louise's then revised its strategy to reflect these factors.[10]

---

[6]Coopers & Lybrand Consulting, "Data-Base Marketing: How It Works," *Business Week* (September 5, 1994), pp. 56–57.

[7]"Data Entry," *American Demographics* (August 2000), p. 41; and "Retail I.T. 2000," *Chain Store Age* (October 2000), Section 2, p. 22.

[8]Darnell Little, "3M: Glued to the Web," *Business Week* (November 2, 2000), pp. EB64–EB70.

[9]"Dig Deeper into the Data-Base Goldmine," *Marketing* (January 11, 2001), p. 30.

[10]Alan J. Liddle, "Casual-Dining Chain's Mining of Customer Data Spurs Change, Management Indicates," *Nation's Restaurant Business* (October 30, 2000), p. 52.

4-3 MARKETING RESEARCH DEFINED

Marketing research involves systematically gathering, recording, and analyzing information about specific issues related to the marketing of goods, services, organizations, people, places, and ideas. It may be done by an outside party or by the firm itself. As indicated earlier, marketing research should be one component of a firm's overall marketing information efforts.

Several points about marketing research need to be emphasized. First, to be effective, it must not be conducted haphazardly. Second, it involves a sequence of tasks: data gathering, recording, and analysis. Third, data may be available from different sources: the firm itself, an impartial agency (such as the government), or a research specialist working for the firm. Fourth, it may be applied to any aspect of marketing that requires information to aid decision making. Fifth, research findings and their implications must be communicated to the proper decision maker(s) in the firm.

A firm's decision to use marketing research does not mean it must engage in expensive projects like test marketing and national consumer attitude surveys. It may get enough data by analyzing internal sales reports or from informal meetings with customer-service personnel. Marketing research does require an orderly approach and adherence to the scientific method.

For example, after many years of booming sales, the Hard Rock Cafe (www. hardrock.com) fell upon hard times in the late 1990s, as the excitement over theme restaurants diminished. As a result, the chain—with more than 100 outlets in 36 countries ("combining rock music sensibilities, memorabilia from top musical artists of the last 40 years, classic American food, and a commitment to widespread altruistic causes")—engaged in extensive marketing research. It examined company and industry data, studied the competitive environment, conducted consumer interviews, and brought in consultants for their insights. To revitalize itself, Hard Rock Cafe then introduced a chainwide facelift and nighttime concerts: "The redesign is one component of bringing Hard Rock into the 21st century with a music-centric strategy." The firm is also testing a new menu with higher-priced items such as a stuffed veal chop and a bacon-wrapped beef tenderloin.[11] See Figure 4-7.

FIGURE 4-7

Hard Rock Cafe: Balancing the Old and the New

The company's research showed that its customers are interested in a combination of entertainment memorabilia, a distinctive (updated) décor, good food, and continuous music. Its chainwide rock music memorabilia collection totals 63,000 pieces—valued at $32 million!

Source: Reprinted by permission of Retail Planning Associates. Photography by Michael Houghton/STUDIOHIO.

[11]Amy Zuber, "Hard Rock Debuts Latest Act: Chainwide Face-Lift, Nighttime Concerts," *Nation's Restaurant Business* (January 8, 2001), pp. 8, 64; and "A New Beat at the Hard Rock," *Business Week* (October 9, 2000), p. 166.

For each marketing issue studied, the amount and cost of research depend on the kinds of data needed to make informed decisions, the risk involved in making those decisions, the potential consequences of the decisions, the importance of the issue to the firm, the availability of existing data, the complexity of the data-gathering process for the issue, and other factors.

4-4 THE SCOPE OF MARKETING RESEARCH

Client companies annually spend about $12 billion worldwide (40 percent in the United States) for data gathered by marketing research firms. The top 25 research firms (nearly half of which are U.S.-based) account for $8 billion of that amount, with more than 1,000 firms responsible for the rest.[12] These amounts are in addition to research sponsored by government and other institutions and to internal research efforts of firms themselves—which also run to billions of dollars each year.

According to the American Marketing Association, these are the topical areas in which companies are most apt to engage in or sponsor research efforts: industry/market characteristics and trends, product satisfaction, market-share analyses, segmentation studies, brand awareness and preference, purchase intentions, and concept development and testing. On average, companies spend one percent of their revenues on marketing research.[13]

Five aspects of marketing research merit special discussion. These involve the rapid rise in customer satisfaction studies, the use of the Internet, the application of single-source data collection, ethical considerations, and the complexities of international marketing research.

Companies now participate in more customer satisfaction research than ever before, in keeping with the customer focus noted in Chapter 1. This form of research has more than doubled in recent years, with some firms doing their own studies and others hiring outside specialists. For instance, Whirlpool (www.whirlpool.com) sends its own surveys on appliance satisfaction to thousands of consumer households each year. It also pays hundreds of consumers per year to "fiddle" with computer-simulated products at its Usability Lab. Whirlpool's research also extends to its European, Latin American, and Asian marketplaces. On the other hand, Maritz Research (www.maritzresearch.com/index.html) generates worldwide revenues of several million dollars by doing customer satisfaction studies for clients. As one observer recently noted, "Competitors that are prospering in the new global economy recognize that measuring customer satisfaction is key. Only by doing so can they hold on to the customers they have and understand how to better attract new customers. Those that will be successful recognize that customer satisfaction is a critical strategic weapon that can bring increased market share and increased profits."[14]

Over the last few years, spending for online marketing research has grown quite rapidly—from $3.5 million in 1996 to $255 million in 2000. In fact, one of the largest marketing firms in the United States, NPD Group (www.npd.com), recently decided to shift its focus to Web-based research and away from "offline" research: "Welcome to the NPD Web site, and thank you for taking the time to visit us. As you browse our pages, you'll see that NPD is committed to harnessing the power of the Web to revolutionize our company—and our industry. We were among the first in our business to recognize the power of this new medium. We pioneered research on the Web, establishing the first online consumer panel. We also invented the groundbreaking Web measurement technology now

Global marketing research expenditures total several billion dollars each year.

---

[12]Jack Honomichl, "Honomichl Global Top 25," *Marketing News* (August 14, 2000), special section.

[13]Thomas C. Kinnear and Ann R. Root (Editors), *1994 Survey of Marketing Research* (Chicago: American Marketing Association, 1995).

[14]Kevin Cacioppo, "Measuring and Managing Customer Satisfaction," www.qualitydigest.com (September 2000).

marketed by our successful spin-off Media Metrix." Here are a few examples of how online marketing research is being employed:

- Many businesspeople start doing their research by checking out competitors' Web sites, using search engines, and accessing online annual reports and trade publications. Information is current, easy to obtain, and usually free.

- PlanetFeedback (www.planetfeedback.com) enables consumers to "send feedback to companies quickly and effortlessly. Learn more about how our site works by taking a quick tour, and tell us what you think by sending 'Feedback on Us.' Read about our commitment to consumer empowerment by reading our 'Consumer Manifesto.' Be sure to check out www.startup-tv.com, the video tale of how we began and where we're going!"[15]

Single-source data collection *is a result of high-tech advances.*

Due to technological advances, ***single-source data collection***—whereby research firms track the activities of individual consumer households from the programs they watch on TV to the products they purchase at stores—is now possible. For instance, via its BehaviorScan service, Information Resources Inc. (IRI) (www.infores.com) monitors the viewing habits and shopping behavior of thousands of households in various markets. Microcomputers are hooked to household TVs and note all programs and ads watched. Consumers shop in supermarkets and drugstores with scanning registers and present cashiers with special cards (resembling credit cards). Cashiers enter each consumer's identification code, which is electronically keyed to every item bought. Via computer analysis, viewing and shopping behavior are then matched with such information as age and income.

Because of the unethical practices of some firms, many potential respondents are "turned off" to participating in marketing research projects. In fact, a lot of Americans say they will not answer a survey. To turn the situation around, researchers need to avoid such practices as these:

- Unrealized promises of anonymity.

- False sponsor identification.

- Selling or fund raising under the guise of research.

- Misrepresenting research procedures.

- Observational studies without informed consent.

- Asking overly personal questions.

- Selling consumer demographic information for data-base use without consent.

- Misportraying research findings in ads and other communications.[16]

With more firms striving to expand their foreign endeavors, international marketing research is now more important. This can be quite challenging. For instance, the language used, respondent selection, and interviewer training are among the areas requiring special consideration. Consider this example.

---

[15]Betsy Spethmann, "What's the Buzz?" *Promo* (February 2001), pp.52–54; Stuart Elliott, "Advertising: The New World of Online Market-Research Exchanges," *New York Times on the Web* (December 19, 2000); and Dana James, "New Tricks for Old Dogs," *Marketing News* (January 15, 2001), p. 19.

[16]Gene R. Laczniak and Patrick E. Murphy, *Ethical Marketing Decisions: The Higher Road* (Needham Heights, Mass.: Allyn and Bacon, 1993), pp. 53–68. See also John R. Sparks and Shelby D. Hunt, "Marketing Researcher Ethical Sensitivity: Conceptualization, Measurement, and Exploratory Investigation," *Journal of Marketing*, Vol. 62 (April 1998) pp. 92–109.

ETHICAL *Issues in Marketing*

On the Internet, Is There Any Privacy Regarding Personal Information?

According to some observers, the "dark side" of E-commerce is the trail of personal information left whenever you visit a Web site. The same technology that remembers your name when you revisit a site or recommends a specific book based upon your last purchase may be used to violate your privacy.

One way that marketers collect data is through cookies, tiny blocks of text that Web-based firms store on your hard drive. Cookies generate privacy issues when they are used in conjunction with banner ads. Every time a consumer calls up a site through a banner ad, the advertising distributor is able to place a cookie on the consumer's hard drive. Over time, the distributor is able to generate a log of all sites that the consumer has visited. When a consumer indicates his or her name, credit card number, and phone number to place an order, the firm is able to link that information with the identifying number. At this point, firms are able to send targeted E-mails to those customers or to sell this information.

Although some consumers seek to defend themselves from these practices by blocking the use of cookies, some sites force them to enable cookies to use all of their features. Various software companies block or manage cookies by removing key information such as a consumer's IP address. Others, such as Privacy Net (www.privacy.net), enable consumers to analyze their Web connection by logging onto its Web site. Privacy Net shows consumers the types of information available to marketers, such as the kind of browser used, the type of monitor, and the consumer's IP address. Consumer groups are also seeking to protect personal information through new laws.

Develop an ethical code for Web-based marketers that deals with information privacy issues.

Source: Based on material in Don Clark, "Privacy: You Have No Secrets," *Wall Street Journal* (October 23, 2000), p. R32.

Firms deciding how to best market products to the hundreds of millions of people in Eastern Europe and Central Asia increasingly do marketing research there. Yet, designing and conducting research is hard. Some people have never been surveyed before. Communications systems, especially phone service, may be subpar by Western standards. Secondary data from government agencies and trade associations may be lacking. Thus, firms must be adaptable. When it did research there, Kodak (www.kodak.com) could not find relevant consumer data, a photography trade association, or pictures of local cameras for use in a questionnaire. So, to gather data on camera usage and preferences, Kodak took part in a multiclient survey devised by SRG International Ltd., a research firm. The survey was conducted in nine former Soviet republics; since each had its own language, nine questionnaire versions were prepared.

4-5 THE MARKETING RESEARCH PROCESS

The *marketing research process* consists of a series of activities: defining the issue or problem to be studied; examining secondary data (previously collected); generating primary data (new), if necessary; analyzing information; making recommendations; and implementing findings. InfoTech Marketing Consulting's Web site (www.infotechmarketing.net/research.htm) is a useful tool for learning more about the dimensions of this process.

*The **marketing research process** consists of steps from issue definition to implementation of findings.*

FIGURE 4-8

The Marketing Research Process

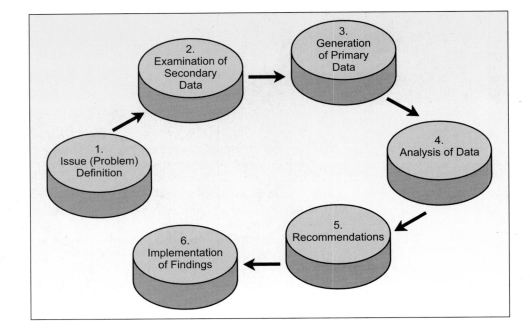

Figure 4-8 presents the complete process. Each step is completed in order. For example, secondary data are not examined until a firm states the issue or problem to be studied, and primary data are not generated until secondary data are thoroughly reviewed. The dashed line around primary data means these data do not always have to be generated. Many times, a firm can obtain enough information internally or from published sources to make a marketing decision without gathering new data. Only if secondary data are insufficient should a firm gather primary data. The research process is described next.

4-5a Issue (Problem) Definition

Research efforts are directed by the **issue definition.**

Exploratory research *looks at unclear topics;* **conclusive research** *is better defined.*

Issue (problem) definition is a statement of the topic to be looked into via marketing research. Without a focused definition, irrelevant and expensive data—which could confuse rather than illuminate—may be gathered. A good problem definition directs the research process to collect and analyze appropriate data for the purpose of decision making.

When a firm is uncertain about the precise topic to investigate or wants to informally study an issue, it uses exploratory research. The aim of *exploratory research* is to gain ideas and insights, and to break broad, vague problem statements into smaller, more precise statements.[17] Exploratory research, also called "qualitative research," may involve in-depth probing, small group discussions, and understanding underlying trends. Once an issue is clarified, conclusive research, also called "quantitative research," is used. *Conclusive research* is the structured collection and analysis of data pertaining to a specific issue or problem. It is more focused than exploratory research, and requires larger samples and more limited questions to provide quantitative data to make decisions. Table 4-1 contrasts the two forms of research.

4-5b Secondary Data

Secondary data have been previously gathered for purposes other than the current research.

Secondary data consist of information not collected for the issue or problem at hand but for some other purpose; this information is available within a firm or externally. Whether secondary data fully resolve an issue or problem or not, their low cost and rather fast accessibility mean that primary data should not be collected until a thorough secondary data search is done.

[17]Bennett, *Dictionary of Marketing Terms*, p. 103.

TABLE 4-1   Examples of Exploratory and Conclusive Research

Vague Research Topic	Exploratory Research	Precise Research Topic	Conclusive Research
1. Why are sales declining?	1. Discussions among key personnel to identify major cause	1. Why is the turnover of sales personnel so high?	1. Survey sales personnel and interview sales managers
2. Is advertising effective?	2. Discussions among key advertising personnel to define effectiveness	2. Do adults recall an advertisement the day after it appears?	2. Survey customers and noncustomers to gauge advertising recall
3. Will a price reduction increase revenues?	3. Discussions among key personnel to determine the level of a price reduction	3. Will a 10 percent price reduction have a significant impact on sales?	3. Run an in-store experiment to determine effects

Advantages and Disadvantages

Secondary data have these general advantages:

- Many types are inexpensive because primary data collection is not involved.
- Data assembly can be fast, especially for published or company materials.
- There may be several sources and perspectives available.
- A source (such as the government) may obtain data a firm could not get itself.
- There is high credibility for data assembled by independent sources.
- They are helpful when exploratory research is involved.

Secondary data also have these general disadvantages:

- Available data may not suit the current research purpose due to incompleteness and generalities.
- Information may be dated or obsolete.
- The methodology used in collecting the data (such as the sample size) may be unknown.
- All the findings of a research study may not be made public.
- Conflicting results may exist.
- Because many research projects are not repeated, the reliability of data may not be proven.

Sources

There are two major sources of secondary data: Internal secondary data are available within a firm. External secondary data are available outside a firm. Most companies use each source in some way.

A firm's records or past studies comprise internal secondary data.

Internal Secondary Data Before spending time and money searching for external secondary data or collecting primary data, the information inside a firm should be reviewed. Internal sources include budgets, sales figures, profit-and-loss statements, customer billings, inventory records, prior research reports, and written reports.

At the beginning of the business year, most firms set detailed budgets for the next 12 months. The budgets, based on sales forecasts, outline planned expenditures for every good and service during the year. By examining the sales of each division, product line, item, geographic area, salesperson, time of day, day of week, and so on, and comparing these sales with prior periods, performance can be measured. Through profit-and-loss statements, actual achievements can be measured against profit goals by department, salesperson, and product. Customer billings provide information on credit transactions, sales by region, peak selling seasons, sales volume, and sales by customer category. Inventory records show the levels of goods bought, manufactured, stored, shipped, and/or sold throughout the year.

Prior research reports, containing findings of past marketing research efforts, are often stored and retained for future use. When a report is used initially, it is primary data. Later reference to that report is secondary in nature because it is no longer employed for its basic purpose. Written reports (ongoing data stored by a firm) may be compiled by top management, marketing executives, sales personnel, and others. Among the information attainable from such reports are typical customer complaints.

Government and nongovernment sources make available external secondary data.

External Secondary Data If a research issue or problem is not resolved through internal secondary data, a firm should use external secondary data sources. There are government and nongovernment sources.

All levels of government distribute economic and business statistics. In addition, various U.S. government agencies publish pamphlets on such diverse topics as franchising and deceptive sales practices. These materials are usually distributed free of charge or sold for a nominal fee. The *Catalog of U.S. Government Publications* (www.access.gpo.gov/su_docs/locators/cgp) lists these items. In using government data, particularly census statistics, the research date must be noted. There may be a lag before government data are released.

There are three kinds of nongovernment secondary data: regular publications; books, monographs, and other nonregular publications; and commercial research houses. Regular publications contain articles on diverse aspects of marketing and are available in libraries or via subscriptions. Some are quite broad in scope (*Business Week*); others are more specialized (*Journal of Advertising*). Periodicals are published by conventional publishing companies, as well as by professional and trade associations. Here are the Web sites of 42 marketing-related publications:

- *Advertising Age* (www.adage.com)
- *American City Business Journals* (http://bizjournals.bcentral.com)
- *American Demographics* (www.demographics.com)
- *Business Week* (www.businessweek.com)
- *Chain Store Age* (www.chainstorage.com)
- *Consumer Reports* (www.consumerreports.org)
- *Demographic Research* (www.demographic-research.org)
- *Direct* (www.directmag.com)
- *DM News* (www.dmnews.com)
- *Drug Store News* (www.drugstorenews.com)
- *DSN Retailing Today* (www.dsnretailingtoday.com)
- *E-Commerce News* (www.internetnews.com/ec-news)
- *Entrepreneur Magazine* (www.entrepreneurmag.com)
- *FINWeb* (www.finweb.com)
- *Forbes* (www.forbes.com)

- *Fortune* (www.fortune.com)
- *Hoover's Online* (www.hoovers.com)
- *Inc.* (www.inc.com)
- *Journal of Consumer Marketing* (www.emeraldinsight.com/jcm.htm)
- *Journal of Marketing* (http://www.marketingpower.com/live/jump.php?Item_ID=1053)
- *Journal of Marketing Research* (http://www.marketingpower.com/live/jump.php?Item_ID=1054)
- *Journal of Markets & Morality* (www.acton.org/publicat/m_and_m)
- *Journal of Services Marketing* (www.emeraldinsight.com/jsm.htm)
- *London Times* (www.thetimes.co.uk)
- *Marketing News* (http://www.marketingpower.com/live/jump.php?Item_ID=1049)
- *Media Central* (www.mediacentral.com)
- *Newsweek International Business Resource Center* (www.newsweek-int.com)
- *New York Times* (www.nytimes.com)
- *Periodical Web Links* (www.the-dma.org/library/resourceperiodicals.shtml)
- *Point of Purchase Magazine* (www.popmag.com)
- *Progressive Grocer* (http://209.11.43.213/progressivegrocer/index.jsp)
- *Promo* (www.promomagazine.com)
- *Restaurant Business* (www.foodservicetoday.com/rb/index.shtml)
- *Sales & Marketing Management* (www.salesandmarketing.com)
- *Shopping Centers Today* (www.icsc.org/srch/sct/current/index.htm;)
- *Stores* (www.stores.org)
- *Supermarket Business* (http://209.11.43.214/supermarketbusiness/index.jsp)
- *Target Marketing* (www.targetonline.com)
- *USA Today* (www.usatoday.com)
- *Value Retail News* (www.valueretailnews.com)
- *Wall Street Journal* (www.wsj.com)
- *Women's Wear Daily* (www.wwd.com)

Books, monographs, and other nonrecurring literature are also published by conventional publishing companies, as well as by professional and trade associations. These materials deal with special topics in depth and are compiled on the basis of interest by the target audience.

Various commercial research houses conduct periodic and ongoing studies and make results available to many clients for a fee. The fee can be low or range into the tens of thousands of dollars, depending on the extent of the data. That kind of research is secondary when a firm purchasing the data acts as a subscriber and does not request specific studies pertaining only to itself; in this way, commercial houses provide a number of research services more inexpensively than if data are collected for a firm's sole use. Among the leaders are A.C. Nielsen (www.acnielsen.com), IMS Health (www.imshealth.com), Arbitron (www.arbitron.com), and Burke Marketing Research (www.burke.com/bmr).

An excellent online source of free marketing information on a variety of subjects is KnowThis.com's *Marketing Virtual Library* (www.knowthis.com).

4-5c Primary Data

Primary data consist of information gathered to address a specific issue or problem at hand. Such data are needed if secondary data are insufficient for a proper marketing decision to be made.

Primary data *relate to a specific marketing issue.*

Advantages and Disadvantages

Primary data have these general advantages:

- They are collected to fit the precise purpose of the current research topic.
- Information is current.
- The methodology of data collection is controlled and known by the firm.
- All findings are available to the firm, which can maintain their secrecy.
- There are no conflicting data from different sources.
- A study can be replicated (if desired).
- When secondary data do not resolve all questions, collecting and analyzing primary data are the only way to acquire information.

Primary data also have these general disadvantages:

- Collection may be time consuming.
- Costs may be high.
- Some types of information cannot be collected (e.g., Census data).
- The company's perspective may be limited.
- The firm may be incapable of collecting primary data.

Research Design

The **research design** *outlines data collection and analysis procedures.*

If a firm decides primary data are needed, it must devise a **research design**—which outlines the procedures for collecting and analyzing data. A research design includes the following decisions.

Internal or outside personnel can be used.

Who Collects the Data? A company can collect data itself or hire an outside research firm for a specific project. The advantages of an internal research department are the knowledge of company operations, total access to company personnel, ongoing assembly and storage of data, and high commitment. The disadvantages of an internal department are the continuous costs, narrow perspective, possible lack of expertise on the latest research techniques, and potentially excessive support for the views of top management. The strengths and weaknesses of an outside research firm are the opposite of those for an inside department.

What Information Should Be Collected? The kinds and amounts of data to be collected should be keyed to the issue (problem) formulated by the firm. Exploratory research requires different data collection than conclusive research.

Who or What Should Be Studied? First, the people or objects to be studied must be stated; they comprise the population. People studies generally involve customers, personnel, and/or distribution intermediaries. Object studies usually center on company and/or product performance.

Sampling the population saves time and money.

Second, the way in which people or objects are selected must be decided. Large and/or dispersed populations usually are examined by *sampling,* which requires the analysis of selected people or objects in the designated population, rather than all of them. It saves time and money; and when used properly, the accuracy and representativeness of sampling can be measured.

The approaches to sampling are probability and nonprobability. With a *probability (random) sample,* every member of the designated population has an equal or known probability of being chosen for analysis. For example, a researcher may select every fiftieth person in a phone directory. With a *nonprobability sample,* members of the population are chosen on the basis of convenience or judgment. For instance, an interviewer may select the first 100 dormitory students entering a college cafeteria. A probability sample is more accurate; but it is more costly and difficult than a nonprobability sample.

MARKETING *and the Web*

Online Surveys: Science or Art?

Instead of sending questionnaires through the mail in printed form or on disk, many companies now utilize Web-based surveying. With this format, respondents are asked specific questions at a Web site. One research firm estimates that as of 2004 between 25 and 33 percent of all marketing research dollars will be spent in an online format, up from about 10 percent at the beginning of 2001.

Hewlett-Packard, HP (www.hp.com) now uses a Web site maintained by Greenfield Online (www.greenfieldonline.com) to conduct marketing research surveys. According to one research analyst at HP, the all-electronic surveys save the firm both time and money, enable it to target specific respondents with instantaneous follow-ups, and allow product prototypes to be shown to respondents.

Some traditional research firms are concerned about the accuracy of Web surveys. Respondents to Web surveys tend to be more affluent, younger, more educated, and less apt to be minority members. Respondents may also answer multiple times. Lastly, respondents may actively seek out Web surveys.

Some online firms are trying to reduce biases. Knowledge Networks (www.knowledgenetworks.com) uses random-digit phone dialing to recruit panel members, and provides free Internet access and a WebTV unit to potential members who do not have Web access. As a result of the ensuing goodwill, Knowledge Networks gets a 70 percent to 95 percent response rate to its surveys. Harris Interactive uses a complex methodology (www.harrisinteractive.com/about/methodology.asp) to weight data to reflect the overall U.S. population. It also uses a high response rate to show that research is based on representative samples. Whereas in the past, phone polling used to get a 65 percent to 70 percent response rate, some researchers estimate that the response rate has now declined to as low as 15 percent for phone surveys.

Present a 5-step plan for ensuring the sampling accuracy of Web surveys.

Source: Based on material in Rebecca Buckman, "Market Research: A Matter of Opinion," *Wall Street Journal* (October 23, 2000), p. R46.

Third, the sample size studied must be set. Generally, a large sample will yield greater accuracy and will cost more than a small sample. There are methods for assessing sample size in terms of accuracy and costs, but a description of them is beyond the scope of this text.

One of the leading firms in client sampling support is Survey Sampling, Inc. (www.surveysampling.com).

What Technique of Data Collection Should Be Used? There are four basic primary-data collection methods: survey, observation, experiment, and simulation.

A *survey* gathers information from respondents by communicating with them. It can uncover data about attitudes, purchases, intentions, and consumer traits. Yet, it is subject to incorrect or biased answers. A questionnaire is used to record answers. A survey can be done in person or by phone or mail. At its Web site, Surveypro.com offers a series of free tutorials on how to design surveys (www.surveypro.com/tutorial) and dozens of sample surveys (www.surveypro.com/templates).

A **survey** *communicates in person, over the phone, or by mail.*

A nondisguised survey reveals its purpose, whereas a disguised one does not.

A *personal survey* is face-to-face and flexible, can elicit lengthy replies, and reduces ambiguity. It may be relatively expensive, however, and bias is possible because the interviewer may affect results by suggesting ideas to respondents or by creating a certain mood during the interview. A *phone survey* is fast and relatively inexpensive, especially with the growth of discount telephone services. Responses are usually brief, and nonresponse may be a problem. It must be verified that the desired respondent is the one contacted. Some people do not have a phone, or they have unlisted numbers. The latter problem is now overcome through computerized, random digit-dialing devices. A *mail survey* reaches dispersed respondents, has no interviewer bias, and is relatively inexpensive. Nonresponse, slowness of returns, and participation by incorrect respondents are the major problems. The technique chosen depends on the goals and needs of the specific research project.

A survey may be nondisguised or disguised. With a *nondisguised survey*, the respondent is told a study's real purpose; in a *disguised survey*, the person is not. The latter may be used to indirectly probe attitudes and avoid a person's answering what he or she thinks the interviewer wants to hear or read. The left side of Figure 4-9 is nondisguised and shows the true intent of a study on sports car attitudes and behavior. The right side shows how the survey can be disguised: By asking about sports car owners in general, a firm may get more honest answers than with questions directed right at the respondent. The intent of the disguised study is to uncover the respondent's actual reasons for buying a sports car.

Nondisguised	**Disguised**
1. Why are you buying a sports car?	1. Why do you think people buy sports cars?
_____	_____
_____	_____
_____	_____
2. What factors are you considering in the purchase of a sports car?	2. What factors do people consider in the purchase of a sports car?
_____	_____
_____	_____
_____	_____
3. Is status important to you in a sports car?	3. Are people who purchase sports cars status-conscious?
_____ Yes	_____ Yes
_____ No	_____ No
4. On the highway, I will drive my sports car	4. On the highway, sports car owners drive
_____ within the speed limit.	_____ within the speed limit.
_____ slightly over the speed limit.	_____ slightly over the speed limit.
_____ well over the speed limit.	_____ well over the speed limit.

FIGURE 4-9

Nondisguised and Disguised Surveys

INTERACTIVE FIGURE

A *semantic differential* is a list of bipolar (opposite) adjective scales. It is a survey technique with rating scales instead of, or in addition to, traditional questions. It may be disguised or nondisguised, depending on whether the respondent is told a study's true purpose. Each adjective in a semantic differential is rated on a bipolar scale, and average scores for all respondents are computed. An overall company or product profile is then devised. The profile may be compared with competitors' profiles and consumers' ideal ratings. Figure 4-10 shows a semantic differential.

Observation is a research method whereby present behavior or the results of past behavior are observed and noted. People are not questioned and cooperation is unnecessary. Interviewer and question bias are minimized. Observation often is used in actual situations. The major disadvantages are that attitudes cannot be determined and observers may misinterpret behavior.[18]

In disguised observation, a person is unaware he or she is being watched. A two-way mirror, hidden camera, or other device would be used. With nondisguised observation, a person knows he or she is being observed. Human observation is done by people; mechanical observation records behavior by electronic or other means, like a video camera taping in-store customer behavior or reactions to a sales presentation.

*A **semantic differential** uses bipolar adjectives.*

*In **observation,** behavior is viewed.*

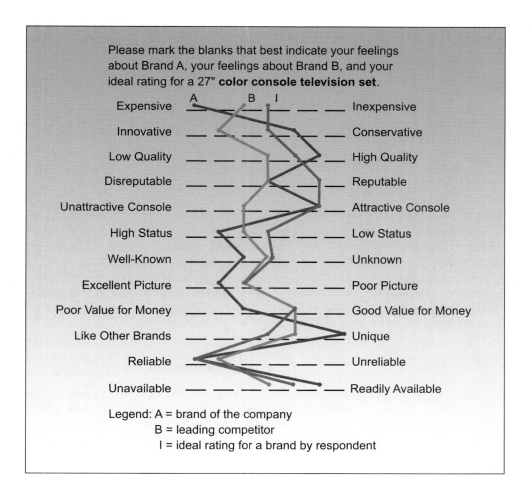

FIGURE 4-10

A Semantic Differential for a Color Television

---

[18]See Pui-Wing Tam, "That Nosy Shopper May Be a Handspring Executive," *Wall Street Journal* (November 29, 2000), pp. B1, B4; and Gerry Khermouch, "Consumers in the Mist," *Business Week* (February 26, 2001), pp. 92, 94.

*An **experiment** varies marketing factors under controlled conditions.*

An **experiment** is a type of research in which one or more factors are manipulated under controlled conditions. A factor may be any element of marketing from package design to advertising media. In an experiment, just the factor under study is varied; all other factors remain constant. For example, to evaluate a new package design for a product, a manufacturer could send new packages to five retail outlets and old packages to five similar outlets; all marketing factors other than packaging remain the same. After one month, sales of the new package at the test outlets are compared with sales of the old package at similar outlets. A survey or observation is used to determine the reactions to an experiment.

An experiment's key advantage is that it can show cause and effect—like a new package lifting sales. It is also methodically structured and enacted. Key disadvantages are the rather high costs, frequent use of contrived settings, and inability to control all factors in or affecting a marketing plan.

***Simulation** enables marketing factors to be analyzed via a computer model.*

Simulation is a computer-based method to test the potential effects of various marketing factors via a software program rather than real-world applications. A model of the controllable and uncontrollable factors facing the firm is first built. Different combinations of factors are then fed into a computer to see their possible impact on a marketing strategy. Simulation requires no consumer cooperation and can handle many interrelated factors. Yet, it may be complex and hard to use; does not measure actual attitudes, behavior, and intentions; and is subject to the accuracy of the assumptions made. For an online, interactive demonstration of a marketing simulation, visit Marketing Strategy & Planning's Web site (www.msandp.com/mspsim.html).

Table 4-2 shows the best uses for each kind of primary data collection.

How Much Will the Study Cost?   The overall and specific costs of a study must be outlined. Costs may include executive time, researcher time, support staff time, pre-testing, computer usage, respondent incentives (if any), interviewers, supplies, printing, postage or phone expenses, special equipment, and marketing expenses (such as ads).

Research costs range from personnel time to marketing expenses.

A study's expected costs should be compared with the expected benefits to be derived. Suppose a consumer survey costing $10,000 would let a firm improve the package design of a new product. With the changes suggested by research, the firm would lift its first-year profit by $30,000. Thus, the net increase due to research is $20,000 ($30,000 profit less $10,000 in costs).

How Will the Data Be Collected?   The people needed to collect the required data must be determined and the attributes, skills, and training of the data-collection force specified. Too often, this important phase is improperly planned, and data are collected by unqualified people.

Interviewers administer surveys, or respondents fill them out.

Data collection can be administered by research personnel or it can be self-administered. With *administered collection*, interviewers ask questions or observers note behavior; they record answers or behavior and explain questions (if asked) to respondents. With

TABLE 4-2 **The Best Uses of Primary Data-Collection Techniques**	**Technique**	**Most Appropriate Uses**
	1. Survey	When determining consumer or distribution intermediary attitudes and motivations toward marketing-mix factors; measuring purchase intentions; relating consumer traits to attitudes
	2. Observation	When examining actual responses to marketing factors under realistic conditions; interest in behavior and not in attitudes
	3. Experiment	When controlling the research environment is essential, and establishing a cause-and-effect relationship is important
	4. Simulation	When deriving and analyzing many interrelationships among variables

self-administered collection, respondents read questions and write their answers. There is a trade-off between control and interviewer probing (administered) versus privacy and limited interviewer bias (self-administered).

How Long Will the Data-Collection Period Be? The time frame within which data are collected must be stipulated, or else a study can drag on. Too long a time frame may lead to inconsistent responses and secrecy violations. Short time frames are easy to set for personal and phone surveys. Mail surveys, observation, and experiments often require much more time to implement; nonetheless, time limits must be defined.

When and Where Should Information Be Collected? The day and time of data collection must be set. It must also be decided if a study is done on or off a firm's premises. The desire for immediacy and convenience have to be weighed against the need to contact hard-to-reach respondents at the proper time.

Data Collection

After the research design is detailed, data are then collected. Those engaged in data collection must be properly supervised and follow directions exactly. Responses or observations must be entered correctly.

4-5d Data Analysis

In *data analysis,* the information on questionnaires or answer forms is first coded and tabulated and then analyzed. Coding is the process by which each completed data form is numbered and response categories are labeled. Tabulation is the calculation of summary data for each response category. Analysis is the evaluation of responses, usually by statistical techniques, as they pertain to the specific issue or problem under investigation. The relationship of coding, tabulation, and analysis is shown in Figure 4-11.

One Web-based firm that handles data analysis services is 1010data (http://www.1010data.com). Visit it for a "test drive."

Data analysis *consist of coding, tabulation, and analysis.*

4-5e Recommendations

Recommendations are suggestions for a firm's future actions that are based on marketing research findings. They are typically presented in written (sometimes oral) form to marketing decision makers. The report must be written for the audience that reads it. Thus, technical terminology must be defined. Figure 4-11 shows recommendations flowing from completed research.

After recommendations are made to the proper decision makers, the research report should be warehoused in the marketing intelligence network. It may be retrieved in the future, as needed. Sample research reports may be viewed at Envirosell's Web site (www.envirosell.com/enreport/report_1.html).

4-5f Implementation of Findings

A research report represents feedback for marketing managers, who are responsible for using findings. If they ignore the findings, research has little value. If they base decisions on the results, then marketing research has great value and the organization benefits in the short and long run.

Marketing managers are most apt to implement research findings if they have input into the research design, broad control over marketing decisions, and confidence that results are accurate. Figure 4-11 provides an illustration of how a firm could implement research findings.

FIGURE 4-11

Data Analysis, Recommendations, and Implementation of Findings for a Study on Coffee

1. Do you drink coffee?	☐ Yes	01	300
	☐ No	02	200
2. In general, how frequently do you drink coffee? (Check only one answer.)	☐ Two or more times per day	03	142
	☐ Once per day	04	84
	☐ Several times per week	05	42
	☐ Once or twice per week	06	20
	☐ One to three times per month	07	12
	☐ Never	08	200
3. During what time of day do you drink coffee? (Check all answers that apply.)	☐ Morning	09	270
	☐ Lunch time	10	165
	☐ Afternoon	11	100
	☐ Dinner time	12	150
	☐ Evening	13	205
	☐ None	14	200

Coding: Questionnaires numbered A001 to A500. Each response is labeled 01 to 14 (e.g., Morning is 09. Evening is 13.) Question 3 is a multiple-response question.

Tabulation: Total responses are shown above right.

Analysis: 60% drink coffee. About 28% drink coffee two or more times daily (representing 47% of all coffee drinkers); almost 25% of coffee drinkers (74 people) consume coffee less than once per day. 90% of coffee drinkers consume coffee in the morning; only one-third consume it in the afternoon.

Recommendations: The coffee industry and individual firms need to increase the advertising geared toward noncoffee drinkers, as well as infrequent coffee drinkers. Emphasis should also be placed on lifting coffee consumption during afternoon hours.

Implementation of findings: New, more aggressive advertising campaigns will be developed and the annual media budgets devoted to increasing overall coffee consumption will be expanded. One theme will stress coffee's value as an afternoon "pick-me-upper."

WEB SITES YOU CAN USE

There are a number of intriguing Web sites that a firm may visit when collecting the information necessary to make the proper marketing decisions. Here is a cross-section of general interest sites:

Askme.com (www.askme.com)—"Get answers to your questions from real people—for free! Join the over 10 million users who found answers at AskMe.com."

NewsDirectory.com (http://www.newsdirectory.com): "This free directory of newspapers, magazines, television stations, colleges, visitor bureaus, governmental agencies, and more can help you get to where you want to go, or find sites you didn't know about."

CyberAtlas (http://cyberatlas.internet.com): "This site provides readers with valuable statistics and Web marketing information, enabling them to understand their business environment and make more informed business decisions."

Fortune 500
(www.fortune.com/fortune500/index.html)—"Click on any company name to get a company snapshot." One thousand companies are listed.

How Stuff Works (www.howstuffworks.com)— "Have you ever wondered how the engine in your car works or what makes your refrigerator cold? Then How Stuff Works is the place for you!"

Information Please Almanac
(www.infoplease.com)—"All the knowledge you need." This is a comprehensive almanac site.

Internet Public Library Reference Center (www.ipl.org/ref)—"The Internet Public Library is the first public library of the Internet."

LibrarySpot (www.libraryspot.com)—"We created LibrarySpot.com to break through the information overload of the Web and bring the best library and reference sites together with insightful editorial in one user-friendly spot."

The Dismal Scientist (www.dismal.com)—"The Dismal Scientist covers over 65 economic releases from over 15 countries."

SUMMARY

1. *To show why marketing information is needed* Marketing information lets a firm accurately assess its strengths, weaknesses, opportunities, and threats; operate properly in the marketing environment; and maximize performance. Reliance on intuition, judgment, and experience are not sufficient. The scientific method requires objectivity, accuracy, and thoroughness in research projects.

2. *To explain the role and importance of marketing information systems* Collecting marketing information should not be viewed as an infrequent occurrence. Acting in that way can have negative ramifications, especially with regard to misreading the competition and other external factors that can affect a firm's performance.

A marketing information system (MIS) is a set of procedures to generate, analyze, disseminate, and store anticipated marketing decision information on a regular, continuous basis. It can aid a company operationally, managerially, and strategically.

3. *To examine a basic marketing information system, commercial data bases, data-base marketing, and examples of MIS in action* The key aspect of a basic MIS is the marketing intelligence network, which consists of continuous monitoring, marketing research, and data warehousing. The intelligence network is influenced by the environment, company goals, and marketing plans; and it affects the implementation of marketing plans. Marketing research should be considered as just one part of an ongoing, integrated information system. An MIS can be used by both small and large firms.

Specialized research firms offer valuable information via commercial data bases that contain data on the population, the business environment, the economy, industry and company performance, and other factors. Data bases are available in printed form; on computer diskettes, CD-ROMs, or tapes; and as online downloads from the Internet.

An increasing number of firms are looking to data-base marketing to improve their interactions with customers. Data-base marketing involves setting up an automated system to identify and characterize customers and prospects and then using quantifiable information to better reach them. The key is data mining, whereby firms seek out hidden opportunities related to specific customers.

Marketing information systems are being used by firms of every size and type.

4. *To define marketing research and its components and to look at its scope* Marketing research entails systematically gathering, recording, and analyzing data about specific issues related to the marketing of goods, services, organizations, people, places, and ideas. It may be done internally or externally.

Expenditures on marketing research run into the billions of dollars annually. Five aspects of research are noteworthy: customer satisfaction studies, the growth of Web-based research, single-source data collection, ethical considerations, and intricacies of international research.

5. *To describe the marketing research process* This process has a series of activities: defining the issue or problem to be studied, examining secondary data, generating primary data (when needed), analyzing data, making recommendations, and implementing findings. Many considerations and decisions are needed in each stage of the process.

Exploratory (qualitative) research is used to develop a clear definition of the study topic. Conclusive (quantitative) research looks at a specific issue in a structured manner. Secondary data—not gathered for the study at hand but for some other purpose—are available from internal and external (government, nongovernment, commercial) sources. Primary data—collected specifically for the purpose of the investigation at hand—are available through surveys, observation, experiments, and simulation. Primary data collection requires a research design: the framework for guiding data collection and analysis. Primary data are gathered only if secondary data are inadequate. Costs must be weighed against the benefits of research. The final stages of marketing research are data analysis—consisting of coding, tabulating, and analysis stages; recommendations—suggestions for future actions based on research findings; and the implementation of findings by management.

KEY TERMS

scientific method (p. 86)
marketing information system (MIS) (p. 87)
marketing intelligence network (p. 88)
continuous monitoring (p. 88)
data warehousing (p. 90)
commercial data bases (p. 90)
data-base marketing (p. 91)
data mining (p. 91)

marketing research (p. 94)
single-source data collection (p. 96)
marketing research process (p. 97)
issue (problem) definition (p. 98)
exploratory research (p. 98)
conclusive research (p. 98)
secondary data (p. 98)
primary data (p. 101)

research design (p. 102)
sampling (p. 102)
survey (p. 103)
semantic differential (p. 105)
observation (p. 105)
experiment (p. 106)
simulation (p. 106)
data analysis (p. 107)

REVIEW QUESTIONS

1. Why is marketing information necessary? What may result if managers rely exclusively on intuition?

2. What is the scientific method? Must it be used each time a firm does research? Explain your answer.

3. Describe the elements of a basic marketing information system.

4. Distinguish between commercial data bases and data-base marketing.

5. Differentiate between conclusive and exploratory research. Give an example of each.

6. When is primary data collection necessary?

7. Outline the steps in a research design.

8. Under what circumstances should a firm use surveys to collect data? Observation? Explain your answers.

DISCUSSION QUESTIONS

1. A jeweler wants to get information on the average amounts that U.S. consumers spend on gold jewelry, the incomes and occupations of gold jewelry consumers, the time of year when gold jewelry purchases are heaviest and lightest, sales of leading competitors, the criteria people use in choosing gold jewelry, and consumer satisfaction. Explain how the firm should set up and enact a marketing intelligence network. Include internal and external data sources in your answer.

2. Taco Bell is an internationally oriented fast-food chain. Juan's Tacos is an independent local fast-food restaurant. If both gather data about their respective competitors' marketing practices, how would your research design differ for each?

3. Develop a semantic differential to determine attitudes toward the tuition level of your college or university. Explain your choice of adjectives.

4. Comment on the ethics of disguised surveys. When would you recommend that they be used?

WEB EXERCISE

At its Web site, Surveypro.com (www.surveypro.com/tutorial) provides a number of tutorials regarding how to develop a good survey. Select any three tutorials and describe what you have learned from them.

PART 1 SHORT CASES
Case 1

It's Not Easy Being a Consumer [c1-1]

Some market analysts believe that today is the best time for consumers. Their viewpoint is based on the increased amount of consumer choices due to the number of new products and to deregulation. In addition, the Web provides people with improved access to information, as well as an added form of competition.

The number of auto models has doubled since the 1970s. So have the number of cereals, book titles, and toothpastes. In telecommunications there are now hundreds of long-distance carriers, up from one in the 1970s and three major carriers in the 1980s. And while there were only 300 mutual funds in the 1970s, there are now more than 7,000. A frequently cited statistic is that there are now more mutual funds than individually listed stocks. Likewise, online shopping bots such as mySimon (www.mysimon.com), CNET (www.cnet.com), and Yahoo! Shopping (www.shopping.yahoo) enable consumers to compare prices and offerings from their homes and offices. The Web also represents another marketing channel for manufacturers, wholesalers, and retailers.

A big ramification of increased choice is that the consumer now faces a much more complex shopping environment. Consumer decision making has also gotten more difficult due to the presence of whole categories of products that did not exist 10 to 20 years ago (such as personal computers, DVD players, CD burners, and high-definition TV). Thus, while increased choice is positive from a competitive perspective, it may generate confusion among customers.

What can marketers do to reduce confusion and simplify consumer choice? One strategy is for firms to facilitate the process by offering fewer alternatives. For example, it is easier for a consumer to evaluate and choose a vacuum cleaner at Sears when three models—"good," "better," and "best"—are offered than when consumers must choose among a dozen or so alternatives. This limited-choice strategy may also provide the retailer with higher inventory turnover, lower training expenses, and lower overall sales costs.

Another strategy is for companies to simplify pricing. Airfare pricing is clearly an area that needs attention! In addition to the confusion of numerous fare categories and conditions, the current large number of fares for the same flight requires considerable time for travel agents and reservations clerks to explain to customers. In the long-distance telephone market, Sprint is a good example of how a firm increased both revenues and profits when it switched to a single price per minute of long-distance service.

Firms can further simplify the choice process by focusing on those market segments where they have the greatest ability to add value. An example of a firm that uses this focused strategy is Charles Schwab. While Schwab's initial target customer was the "do-it-yourself" investor who was attracted by the low transaction costs, the company has since expanded its target market to include customers desiring a fuller range of financial services (such as a portfolio of mutual funds). This strategy made Schwab better able to offer different types of value propositions to different target groups of customers.

Lastly, companies need to examine the overall costs of the customer's total experience, not just the basic costs of the good or service. Included in the total-cost approach should be the costs of searching for the appropriate good or service. Thus, firms that provide easy access, or high levels of information, to consumers may have lower costs than the "lower basic price" marketers that do not provide such services.

Questions

1. Describe how this case illustrates the "value-based philosophy" aspect of the marketing concept.
2. What are the ramifications of "do-it-yourself" firms shifting basic marketing functions from the firms to their consumers?
3. If the large number of airfares causes consumer confusion, why do you think most airlines have so many fares?
4. Explain how a Web-based transaction can reduce a consumer's total cost.

[c1-1]The data in the case are drawn from Gordon A. Wyner, "The Customer's Watch," *Marketing Management* (Spring 2000), pp. 6–7.

Case 2

The Role of the FTC in a High-Tech World [c1-2]

The Federal Trade Commission (FTC) is the federal regulatory agency responsible for gathering information and recommending and enforcing legislation as to online privacy. In this role, the FTC has held public workshops, audited Web sites, made recommendations to Congress for additional legislation, and brought actions against firms that have violated its policies.

Between 1998 and 2000, the FTC brought actions against five Web sites that allegedly violated its privacy policies. These sites included a firm that focused on children, a financial Web site, and an online auction. In one action, the FTC issued a consent order to prevent a Web site from selling data that the firm claimed would be maintained anonymously. In a similar case, the FTC would not allow a Web-based company facing bankruptcy to sell its customer data base, since its privacy policy prohibited this practice.

While in the past, the FTC had recommended that self-regulation was the best means of controlling online privacy, the agency recently changed its position. The need for the change was based on the FTC's audit of a random sample of 335 Web sites that had 39,000 or more visitors each month and 91 of the busiest sites. The objective of the audit was to examine the extent to which these sites incorporated five principles of fair information practice: notice, choice, access, security, and enforcement:

- *Notice:* Regards how information is collected and used, and what third parties may receive this information.
- *Choice:* Gives consumers options as to how personal information may be used.
- *Access:* Allows consumers to access information about themselves and to correct errors.
- *Security:* Takes steps to ensure that information will be secure.
- *Enforcement:* Initiates an enforcement procedure to make sure the core principles of privacy protection are in place.

The FTC's report concluded that only about 20 percent of the sites in the random sample and 42 percent of the busiest sites had adopted principles for protecting consumer privacy.

As a result, the FTC recommended that Congress adopt legislation and that firms develop better consumer privacy policies. Both the proposed legislation and company privacy policy should incorporate these elements:

- *Notice:* Web sites should provide consumers with a clear statement as to what information the sites collect, how they collect it, and how they will use it.
- *Choice:* Web sites should allow consumers—not the companies operating the sites—to decide whether the personal information collected from them can be sold or traded to other firms.
- *Access:* Consumers should be able to easily view and assess any information about them to judge both accuracy and completeness and to contest inaccuracies.
- *Security:* Firms need to have policies in place to ensure that consumer information is safe and sound.
- *Enforcement:* Sanctions should be imposed on firms that do not comply with these regulations.

The FTC has also identified children as a special class of consumers that require additional protection.

Questions

1. What are the pros and cons of self-regulation versus legislation in controlling information privacy?
2. Develop a privacy policy for a Web site that sells business supplies to small and medium firms. Build the policy based on the five principles of fair information practice.
3. Develop a privacy policy for a Web site that sells model train equipment to teenage enthusiasts. Build the policy based on the five principles of fair information practice.
4. How should the privacy policy for the Web sites in Questions 2 and 3 differ due to their target market population? How should they be similar?

[c1-2]The data in the case are drawn from Donna Gillin, "The Federal Trade Commission and Internet Privacy," *Marketing Research* (Fall 2000), p. 39; and Susan Stellin, "Dot-Com Liquidations Put Consumer Data in Limbo," *New York Times on the Web* (December 4, 2000).

Case 3

AT&T's New Business Plan: Breaking Up, Again![c1-3]

Shortly after the chairman of AT&T (www.att.com) announced that the firm was going to be split into four independent units as of 2002, he was asked if anything would be lost because of the breakup. After considering the question, he responded, "I can't think of anything." One thing that competitors will realize is that as a consequence of the breakup, AT&T's market power will be greatly diminished.

Although many of the specific details of AT&T's plan have not been finalized, the firm intends to be split into separate cable, business services, consumer, and wireless units. Let's look at the competitive environment facing each of these entities.

AT&T's cable TV unit will be called AT&T Broadband. It will be the largest cable firm in the United States. It is believed by most industry analysts that this unit will remain a leader in delivering high-speed Internet access, despite city-by-city competition from the Bell companies. Many analysts also feel that in the local markets where it operates, the cable firm's core business—television service—will remain relatively safe. This is despite strong competition from such satellite firms as DirecTV and EchoStar. Since there are few places where cable companies actually compete with one another, not only is there is no direct competition; but cable operators also often engage in joint lobbying activities. There have been bids by such firms as Comcast to acquire this business.

In the business services arena, WorldCom will remain as AT&T's major competitor. Industry observers say that since its inception in the 1980s, WorldCom and its predecessor firms have been more focused on serving business customers than has AT&T. WorldCom has Unnet, the world's largest Internet carrier as a key customer and, unlike AT&T, has heavily invested in placing new fiber optic networks in Europe. Even though Sprint is another key competitor in the business services market, it cannot match the scale of either AT&T or WorldCom and has had less success in attracting very large businesses. The business services area may be the most profitable telecommunications sector.

The consumer unit will be dominated by AT&T's long-distance operation. AT&T is the clear market leader with year 2000 long-distance toll-service revenues of $40.2 billion. In comparison, MCI/WorldCom's revenues were $23.4 billion during this period; Sprint's were $9.7 billion. Nonetheless, AT&T's long distance operation is expected to have revenue declines of more than 10 percent due to increased competition from the Bells and lower prices. Both the Worldnet and Sprint consumer long-distance units face a similar economic environment. Sales and profits at AT&T's Worldnet Internet service provider operation (www.att.net), another part of this unit, are unlikely to compensate for the difficulties at its long-distance operation.

Wireless may be the strongest AT&T unit. Despite coverage problems in the New York City area, this unit services almost the entire United States and is experiencing rapid growth. In the third quarter of 2000 alone, the wireless unit added 750,000 customers. However, it does face such competitors as Sprint, Verizon, Nextel, VoiceStream, and a new joint venture of BellSouth and SBC called Cingular. As of the third quarter of 2000, AT&T had 12.6 million wireless subscribers, compared with 26.3 million at Verizon and 19.0 million at Cingular.

In the short-run, it is predicted that the consumer unit of AT&T will be the one that will continue to pay meaningful stock dividends, that the wireless and cable units will pay no dividends, and that the business unit will pay small dividends.

Questions

1. Describe the pros and cons of the voluntary AT&T breakup from a strategic planning perspective.
2. Apply the Boston Consulting Group matrix concept to each unit.
3. Apply the General Electric business screen to each unit.
4. What will be the strategic marketing planning ramifications of the breakup? How should they be handled?

[c1-3]The data in the case are drawn from Seth Schiesel, "The Devolved AT&T: Are 4 Parts More Promising Than One?" *New York Times on the Web* (October 27, 2000); and Seth Schiesel, "Sprint Still Aspires to Offer One-Stop Communications," *New York Times* (January 15, 2001), pp. C1, C6.

Case 4

Researching Auto Shoppers' Use of the Internet[c1-4]

According to the Greenfield Online (www.greenfieldonline.com) "Cruising for Cars on the Information Highway" study of car buyers, the Internet is the most preferred means of gathering information by both new and used vehicle shoppers:

- The Internet was a preferred source by 76 percent of the shoppers; in comparison, local dealerships were a preferred source of 70 percent of the shoppers.
- In citing other sources, friends and family were preferred by 53 percent of the shoppers, newspapers by 49 percent, and auto publications by 42 percent.
- Besides the Internet's being the most frequently cited source, 93 percent of car shoppers who went online felt that the Internet made the auto shopping experience easier. And 80 percent of this group felt that they could better negotiate prices based on the information they collected on the Web, regardless of where they actually made the purchase.

These findings were based on a study of 2,000 active car buyers who had shopped for a new or used vehicle over the previous 12 months. All of the respondents were Web proficient and most of them had close to two years of online experience.

Table 1 shows the percentage of online vehicle shoppers who have visited the top five auto-information Web sites. This table provides separate data for new and used car shoppers.

In total, according to Greenfield Online, the respondents visited 59 different auto-information Web sites. Although each Web site contained some unique information, the common information contained on independent sites such as www.autobytel.com and www.kelleybluebook.com included the list price and dealer cost for new cars, trade-in values for used cars, option availability for various models, new car specifications for various models, and test drive reports. Several sites also allowed shoppers to get price quotes for specific models from participating dealers. The manufacturer sites, such as www.ford.com and www.chevrolet.com, typically included car selection guides, dealer locations, photos of car interiors and exteriors, and a listing of special offers and rebates.

Although the survey's respondents clearly preferred to gather information online, most of those who bought a vehicle during the prior 12 months did so at a traditional "bricks-and-mortar" dealership. Among the reasons cited by consumers for not purchasing or leasing a vehicle online, 53 percent stated that they were uncomfortable with purchasing a car online, 41 percent felt that the purchase was too large to conduct online, and 32 percent preferred to use a salesperson. In contrast, when questioned about their plans for their next vehicle purchase or lease, 36 percent of the respondents said that they would either purchase or lease their next vehicle via the Web.

Questions

1. What are the overall pros and cons of the research study noted in the case?
2. In evaluating the results of the study reported in the case, what are the implications of the fact that all the respondents were Web proficient?
3. What are the marketing ramifications of Table 1 for a new car dealer? A used car dealer?
4. Describe how an individual auto maker could engage in data-base marketing, using the data in this case.

TABLE 1

The Percentage of Online Car Shoppers Who Have Visited Five Specific Auto-Information Web Sites

Site	% of New Vehicle Shoppers Visiting Site	% of Used Vehicle Shoppers Visiting Site
www.autobytel.com	37	33
www.kelleybluebook.com	32	36
www.ford.com	32	26
www.autotrader.com	23	38
www.chevrolet.com	22	22

[c1-4]The data in the case are drawn from "The Internet Puts Online Auto Shoppers in the Driver's Seat," *Greenfield Online* (November 2, 2000).

PART 1 COMPREHENSIVE CASE

Customer Research, Not Marketing Research[pc-1]

Introduction

For almost 20 years, U.S. businesses have been measuring the satisfaction of both their employees and their customers. Using the mail, phone, and now the Internet, they've sought feedback from customers to help direct their improvement efforts toward the issues their customers identify as most important. Their goal has been to increase their competitive position by being better attuned to customer and employee needs. The people and firms tapped to administer these surveys have come from the marketing and survey research disciplines. That choice seems quite logical since these people are trained in drawing statistically appropriate samples, writing questionnaires, interviewing, and analyzing and reporting of findings.

Focusing on the needed information, customer and employee satisfaction efforts have been approached by businesses as measurement initiatives. In fact, we believe that perspective is substantially shortsighted. Although assessing the "pulse" of the customer franchise or employee community is the driving motivation, chances are the customers or employees contacted might view the outreach as far more pervasive. This might be one of the only times a customer will be asked for his or her opinion, and this might be the employee's one opportunity to make suggestions or to offer a process improvement. The special regard in which customers or employees hold the survey means the researcher probably should conduct it somewhat differently than if he or she were contacting consumers at large. Measuring customer and employee satisfaction requires a very different philosophy, even a different mind-set from marketing research. We emphasize this distinction by describing such projects as customer research.

Customer research is not simply conducting marketing research among populations of customers. Traditional marketing research is focused on the efficient capture of valid and unbiased information. To do so, marketing researchers have relied on many of the tools developed in survey research. But they have mistakenly extended these tools and the ethical precepts of survey research to their projects conducted among customers and employees. There are substantial differences between consumers and customers, and this naïve extension threatens the survival of the customer and employee satisfaction industries. We'll share our philosophy of customer research and we offer some verbatim comments from customers we've interviewed to illustrate this perspective.

Data Capture

The most basic difference between consumers and customers—and one that drives much of research practice—is found in the objectives of the project. Traditionally, marketing researchers have approached consumers with only one purpose in mind: to collect information. They expect consumers they sample to respond

because they've been asked to do so (and in many cases have been paid for their time). A customer researcher realizes that the interview or questionnaire he or she is administering might be one of the few direct contacts customers ever have with the sponsoring firm. As such, the customer researcher recognizes that his or her effort can and should serve two goals: (1) to collect valuable information, and (2) to help strengthen whatever relationship exists with those customers selected for survey participation.

I was very pleased to be asked my opinion, I felt it was about time they talked to me, and I was eager to help their marketing effort.

If communication is recognized as an important goal of all customer research, the people conducting these projects must become sensitive to the multiple aspects of the survey process beyond simply asking questions and collecting data. The questionnaire's appearance or the verbal introduction to the interview can be quite revealing to customers. They can suggest the degree of esteem with which the firm holds them and provide valuable clues about the importance of the survey to both the firm and the customer.

And look at the way some of those questionnaires are printed— even the quality of the paper they're printed on. (It's like toilet paper.) What does that tell me about the importance they attach to the survey?

Clues describing the extent of the "relationship" the customer might have with the company are ever present throughout the survey process. A poorly printed questionnaire or unprofessional interviewers might suggest the organization doesn't regard the effort as important. The salutation used (a generic "Dear Valued Customer" compared to a personalized "Dear Mrs. Johnson") can indicate how well the company really knows its customers. It also might indicate the respect for and valuation of the customer. Similarly, asking basic questions such as "Which of our products do you own or use?" or "How long have you been our customer?"— while permissible in mass-market, marketing research surveys— can reveal a total lack of knowledge about customers as individuals when asked of them in a satisfaction survey.

Considering how long I've done business with them, I thought they should know me by name, not "Dear Customer." And by now, they should know which of their products I buy. But I seem to be only a number to them.

To avoid such problems, customer researchers require an intelligent "customer base" as the driver of their customer satisfaction research process. This data base can identify for the satisfaction measurement process: customers' names, what good(s) or service(s) they buy, where and when they last bought, and generally much more. This is the kind of information any of us might expect a company with which we spend considerable sums of money to know. As customers, we generally will allow an organization to know and maintain such information because we perceive it's in our best interests. It helps a company offer us more relevant goods and services at more appropriate times. But in this age of concern

[pc-1]Adapted by the authors from Douglas R. Pruden and Terry G. Vavra, "Customer Research, Not Marketing Research," *Marketing Research* (Summer 2000), pp. 14–19. Reprinted by permission of the American Marketing Association.

for personal privacy, the customer researcher knows he or she must honor the confidentiality of customers. Selling data bases containing proprietary information (for momentary incremental revenue) is not only foolish, it borders on the unethical.

I worry that these companies will sell my name to others I don't want that, but I would like a way to talk to companies I like.

Recognizing consumers' increasing distrust of business and their concerns for personal privacy, the customer researcher knows he or she must earn customers' trust. So information is requested a little bit at a time. And only the most relevant information should be requested.

And why would they need to know if I read the Bible? What does reading the Bible or cooking have to do with the new camera I just purchased?

As customer researchers prove the value to customers of their having shared information, they earn the customer's trust, and then can ask for more information. It should be kept at the individual customer level so future interactions and future surveys might be even more personalized.

Attitude Toward Survey Participants

Trained in the world of opinion polls and tracking studies, marketing researchers revere cooperative respondents—but only as sources of information. Unless a marketing researcher is assembling a panel for ongoing follow-up, he/she doesn't want or expect to hear from survey respondents again. Not ever.

That's because respondents for marketing and survey research are usually just a small sample of a virtually infinite pool of consumers who can be sampled and interviewed. Although they would be reluctant to admit it, marketing researchers generally consider individuals within their samples an expendable commodity. If one responding consumer is lost, another easily can replace him or her.

You fill one of those (satisfaction) questionnaires out, and do you ever hear from the company again? It's as if the questionnaire is sucked into a black hole in space never to be seen or heard from again!

But the customer researcher must recognize the importance of each and every respondent, knowing that as current customers they're a "precious" entity. Businesses turn their profits based on how long they retain customers and how much additional goods and services they're able to sell to current customers. Customer researchers understand they can't afford to jeopardize the relationship their firm has with its customers. Understanding the lifetime value of a retained customer, researchers know they're dealing not with just a group of consumers, but communicating with individuals who are the lifeblood of the firm sponsoring the survey.

I've been buying their product for years; don't they have any consideration for how much money I've given them?

Purpose

The end point of a traditional marketing research study is reached when the unbiased, clinically pure report is turned over to the client. Unfortunately, data often will have been "cleaned." (This might mean some respondents, whose scores fall significantly outside the scores of most respondents, might be purged from the data. Removing such "outliers" is a typical statistical process to make responses more internally coherent.) Mean responses will be calculated to summarize the general feelings of the customer body. Satisfaction drivers will be identified at the "total customer level."

The customer researcher is no less interested in producing compelling results. Yet, in addition to desiring to identify the needed companywide additions and changes, the customer researcher also recognizes the sovereignty and importance of the reported problems and concerns of each participating customer. It must be assumed that a primary motivation urging customers' participation in a satisfaction survey is the hope that their situation with the firm will be improved (by bringing current problems to light or by providing guidance for the development of more relevant goods and services in the future).

I think the reason they're conducting their survey is to give people like me a chance to tell them what they should be doing, I like knowing they're willing to listen to their customers!

Rather than eliminating respondents who voice extreme ratings—either negative or positive—the customer researcher examines them first, on a case-by-case basis. The goal is to see what can be done to rectify the problems of the dissatisfied, as well as how the delight of the satisfied can be acknowledged and ultimately leveraged. Good satisfaction programs will issue "red flag reports" on each highly dissatisfied customer. These reports alert operational people to attend to a customer immediately so as to turn an unfortunate experience around. Rare is the marketing research program with such processes.

The pain of dissatisfied customers is minimized even more when the data are aggregated, which "buries" distraught customers among the more satisfied. True, it may be reassuring to some company executives to note that fewer than 3% of all their customers are "extremely dissatisfied," but this aggregation of data almost indemnifies one from having any person-to-person responsibility for attempting to fix unpleasant situations. The traditional marketing research perspective almost never includes the resources or the authority to revisit dissatisfied customers to attempt to correct problems and resolve disputes. Part of why this is never done has to do with participants' identities.

Anonymity

Most traditional marketing research studies not only strive to protect the identity of every respondent, but also suffer from the belief that research should be conducted on a "blind basis," keeping the name of the study's sponsor a secret. While biases are introduced, we believe the customer researcher stands to gain more than he or she loses by openly identifying the sponsor of a survey. Without this open sponsorship, some aspects of the customer's purchase behavior that need to be probed could not be reasonably approached in the interview. It's also less easy for a company to increase customers' understanding of its commitment to customer service and satisfaction if it's not openly credited for the satisfaction initiative.

> We all worry these days about giving out personal information. I'm not sure I'd do it. It depends; if I knew how they'd use what I told them, and if I thought I could really trust them, then I might. I'd have to wait and see.

Identifying the survey's sponsor can prompt certain expectations on behalf of participating customers. They'll know the company is interested enough in their well being to monitor their satisfaction. But if they're at all dissatisfied, then they also probably will expect the conscientious company to solve the problems they've identified, and/or to fix or change inappropriate systems or behaviors. So if a customer responds, he or she is likely to believe some corrective action will occur.

Correctly executed customer research programs always will incorporate some form of acknowledgment for those who have participated. This may be as inexpensive as a mass-mailed "we received your response, thanks for your help" postcard, to a highly personalized letter addressing specific issues that a participating customer raised. The key is closing the loop. Without some acknowledgment, many will believe no one took the time to read their responses or to listen to their needs and suggestions.

> How much could it cost them to simply say, "We received your response, thanks for filling it out?"

Nowhere is acknowledgment more important than in the cases of both extremely dissatisfied and extremely satisfied customers. These groups are highly motivated, and they need a response. Dissatisfied customers want to know someone has heard their problem. They're asking for help. A response can begin the "healing process." Highly satisfied customers are motivated, too. They want to affiliate with a firm by expressing their pleasure in being a customer. A failure to respond to these customers' comments will dampen their ardor, possibly diminishing their willingness to advocate the company.

> I described my problem in detail and told them how important it was to me that they fix it. That was six months ago, I haven't heard from anybody at the company!

What about the vast majority of reasonably satisfied customers who express moderate satisfaction? Why should organizations bother responding to everyone? If customers take their time to answer questions, they should be thanked. This means customer researchers require far more sophisticated contact-management programs to execute projects. Customer researchers must not only know which customers have responded so they can acknowledge participation; they also should know the particular delights or problems of each participant. Questions, issues, and problems must be kept at the level of the individual customer. Otherwise, the sponsoring firm will not only have missed an opportunity to retain the customer, but by creating an unfulfilled expectation, might even intensify the customer's angst.

> I was so impressed! Two days after I mailed the questionnaire, someone actually called me! Imagine that, they'd actually read my questionnaire! They told me how to get the missing piece. They were so nice. I'd buy again from that company in an instant!

Sample Size

Traditional marketing research is very precise in establishing the sample. The goal is to capture enough responses to be statistically valid at the desired confidence level without being guilty of overkill and "squandering" a project's budget through costly samples of excessive size.

Viewing customer research as an opportunity to build a closer relationship, and as one of a limited number of opportunities to unearth customer questions, problems, and dissatisfactions, the customer researcher's goals are almost the opposite. A customer researcher tries to reach as many customers as possible within the budget. In a business-to-business customer satisfaction survey, that might mean contacting every customer at least once per year. In more mass-market industry, the best that can be done is to sample moderate-value customers while doing a complete census of the most valuable customers.

Knowing that there is much more at stake than just delivering a statistically sound report, the customer researcher welcomes the opportunity to extend the opportunity for a survey-facilitated "dialogue" with the company to as many current customers as is financially feasible.

Frequency

Most satisfaction studies conducted in a marketing research mindset are executed on an annual basis. Last year's survey form is resurrected (perhaps the attributes are reviewed and revised). It's administered, results tabulated, and they're compared with last year's aggregate results.

> I look forward to their survey, because I've seen positive changes from previous years' surveys. So I offer my ideas for how they can better serve me.

A customer satisfaction survey really should be used to understand and respond to the ever-changing needs and requirements of customers. This is an opportunity to detect systematic problems before they lead to customer defections. They also should offer a continuous reading of the impact of changes that have been made. Conducting the survey in a single wave, once a year, is probably too infrequent to satisfy either of these needs. Customer researchers are most likely to divide their customer base and conduct their survey on an ongoing (weekly, monthly, or quarterly) basis.

Respect For Participating Customers' Time

Marketing researchers' strategies for contacting respondents are oriented to maximizing completion rates, not the satisfaction levels of those interviewed. This means if Saturday evening produces the most interviews, then the fieldwork will be concentrated on Saturday evenings. Customer researchers face a harder goal. They must deliver reasonable cooperation rates, but they dare not impose on customers during inappropriate parts of the day or weekends.

Marketing researchers are resigned to offering incentives to help boost cooperation rates. But their incentives (a quarter, a one-dollar bill, or a lottery ticket) actually can be an embarrassment in a customer survey, especially if there is any possibility the incentive will be interpreted as "fair compensation" for the customer's effort in completing the survey. It's always appropriate to position an incentive as a "token of appreciation," establishing the fact that the customer's opinion is essentially priceless.

> And guess what they taped to the letter? A dollar! Can you imagine? A dollar, as If I should be thrilled to get a dollar! I folded it up and sent it back to them in the envelope they'd enclosed! All they would have had to have done was to ask me, but they thought they could buy me!

In the realm of customer research, an incentive stronger than money usually is the customer's hope of bettering the good or service he or she receives. But be prepared to improve the customer's situation as a result of survey findings, since such promises are likely to increase customers' expectations.

There's another opportunity for customer researchers that marketing researchers wouldn't be as free to use. Branded (logo) merchandise often is favored by customers who like a brand. Wearing a Motorola cap would be a desirable way for some customers to show their respect for the Motorola company. Sporting a Mercedes-Benz polo shirt gives Mercedes owners the opportunity to tell the world they drive a Mercedes. Such branded merchandise can be a very attractive incentive, stimulating cooperation. At the same time, this merchandise can function to strengthen the relationship bonds as well.

Summary

As marketing evolves to recognize the importance of relationships with customers and suppliers, it's time for marketing research professionals similarly to embrace the importance of relationships as we practice our skills. We need to modify our practices and beliefs to create an additional arm of research—customer research. Unless satisfaction measurement begins to assume a more personalized front with customers and employees and show how it can actually strengthen relationships with businesses, it may be doomed. While the marketing research discipline will continue to fill many information needs, customer and employee satisfaction measurement must be managed with the different mind-set of "customer research."

Questions

1. According to the authors of this case, do traditional marketing researchers practice the marketing concept? Explain your answer.
2. Besides using surveys, what are some other ways in which firms can measure customer satisfaction?
3. Most firms buy from suppliers and market through resellers. What criteria should they study to determine how satisfied these business partners are?
4. How can a company change the corporate culture of its researchers from viewing themselves as marketing researchers to viewing themselves as customer researchers?
5. What should be the relationship between marketing research and a total quality approach to strategic planning?
6. Show how you would integrate customer satisfaction research into a marketing information system.
7. Present a 7-item customer satisfaction questionnaire for use by a local restaurant. Describe how you would administer the survey.
8. Cite an instance in which you complained about a good or service and your problem was properly handled, and an instance in which you complained and your problem was not handled well. What principles can you draw from these two experiences?

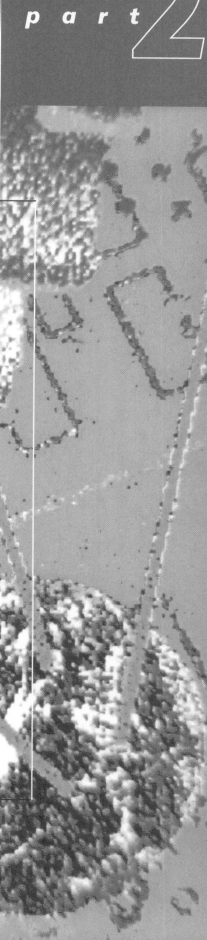

Broadening the Scope of Marketing

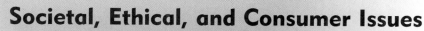

In Part 2, we present an expanded perspective of marketing—one that is necessary today.

5 Societal, Ethical, and Consumer Issues

In this chapter, we examine the interaction of marketing and society. We begin by exploring the concept of social responsibility and discussing the impact of company and consumer activities on natural resources, the landscape, environmental pollution, and planned obsolescence. Next, there is an in-depth discussion of ethics from several vantage points: business, consumer, global, and teachability. We then turn to consumerism and consider the basic rights of consumers: to information, to safety, to choice in product selection, and to be heard. We also note the current trends related to the role of consumerism.

6 Global Aspects of Marketing

Here, we place marketing into a global context—important for both domestic and international firms, as well as those large and small. First, we distinguish among domestic, international, and global marketing. Then, we see why international marketing takes place and how widespread it is. We assess cultural, economic, political and legal, and technological factors. We conclude by looking at the stages in the development of an international marketing strategy: company organization, market entry decisions, degree of standardization, and product, distribution, promotion, and price planning.

7 Marketing and the Internet

At this point, we look at the emergence of the Internet and its impact on marketing practices. We show why the Internet is a valuable tool in marketing and look at the many potential marketing roles for the Internet. Next, we cover how the Internet may be used to enhance a marketing strategy and present a number of examples. We end the chapter with a discussion of the challenges of using the Internet in marketing and a forecast about the future of E-marketing.

After reading Part 2, you should understand elements 6–8 of the strategic marketing plan outlined in Table 3-2 (pages 72–75).

5

Societal, Ethical, and Consumer Issues

C h a p t e r   O b j e c t i v e s

1 To consider the impact of marketing on society

2 To examine social responsibility and weigh its benefits and costs

3 To look into the role of ethics in marketing

4 To explore consumerism and describe the consumer bill of rights

5 To discuss the responses of manufacturers, retailers, and trade associations to consumerism and study the current role of consumerism

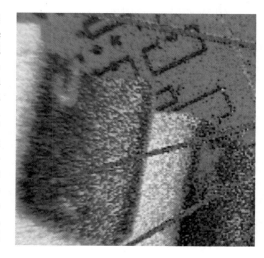

Soon after eBay (www.ebay.com) went public, founder Pierre Omidyar and his wife Pam decided to give away nearly all of their wealth. They vowed that by the year 2020, when Pierre will be 52, they will have given away all but 1 percent of their wealth. Although the value of the Omidyars' eBay stock had grown to $6.6 billion at its peak, they had a relatively simple lifestyle. For example, Pierre Omidyar drives a Volkswagen Cabriolet and much of their home has been furnished with goods from Target. Despite their wealth, Pierre Omidyar owns only four suits, all needed for business functions.

The Omidyars scoffed at the idea of establishing a traditional foundation to manage giving. To them, a traditional foundation would be viewed as inefficient and wasteful. In contrast to other foundations with elaborate facilities and large staffs, the Omidyar Foundation is staffed by only two full-time employees. Much of the bureaucratic work is done by consultants and the organizations that the Omidyars fund. Pierre Omidyar says, "When you create wealth in a short time, you think about philanthropy as you think about a business. You don't move from saying, 'How can we rationalize an industry?' to 'Where do I sign the big check?'" The foundation gave out $20 million in 2000.

The Omidyars want their philanthropic giving to represent a powerful agent for social change. In evaluating potential charities, they want to be sure the charities are run more like a business. Thus, they give preference to charities with clear business plans and benchmarks. The Omidyars also look for charities that can generate income streams to sustain their work, and want charities to be accountable for performance goals. Furthermore, since the needs of charities are greater than those of any donor's financial ability, the Omidyars want to give to charities with positive second-order effects, such as an educational foundation that is able to create jobs by attracting employers.

Among the foundation's primary grants are a $10 million contribution to Tufts University (for funding student and teacher projects in poor neighborhoods) and $10 million to the Community Foundation of Silicon Valley (for funding programs in education, urban renewal, and community arts).[1]

In this chapter, we will study several issues relating to the interaction of marketing with overall society, as well as with consumers. We will look again at business responses to social responsibility.

[1]Quentin Hall, "The Radical Philanthropist," *Forbes* (May 1, 2000), pp. 114–121.

5-1 OVERVIEW

Marketing can have both a positive and a negative impact on society.

Individually (at the company level) and collectively (at the industry level), the activities involved with marketing goods, services, organizations, people, places, and ideas can strongly impact on society. They have the potential for both positive and negative consequences, regarding such factors as these:

- The quality of life (standard of living).
- Natural resources, the landscape, and environmental pollution.
- Consumer expectations and satisfaction with goods, services, and so on.
- Consumer choice.
- Innovation.
- Product design and safety.
- Product durability.
- Product and distribution costs.
- Product availability.
- Communications with consumers.
- Final prices.
- Competition.
- Employment.
- Deceptive actions.

In the United States and many other highly industrialized nations, marketing practices have made a variety of goods and services available at rather low prices and via convenient locations. These include food products, transportation goods and services, telecommunications services, clothing, entertainment, books, insurance, banking and other financial services, audio and video equipment, furniture, and PCs.

At the same time, the lesser use of modern marketing practices in some parts of the world have often led to fewer product choices, higher prices, and less convenient shopping locations. For example,

> Most Americans have probably read or seen reports of the long-standing shortage of consumer goods available to the typical Russian shopper. The photos of empty shelves and long lines, the descriptions of surly shop attendants and depressing retail settings, provide a graphic picture of the Russian shopping experience. One woman provided a personal illustration of the difficulties faced by Russian shoppers. She said there was no butter available in her city of more than 1.5 million people for several years in the late 1980s and early 1990s. To provide for her family, she would stand in line at 6:00 A.M. to buy whole milk (the supply would always be sold out by 8:00), then churn it into butter. She said that stores remained open, but the shelves were often bare or stocked with empty cans just for the sake of appearance. We note that it was not simply luxuries, but the most basic consumer goods that were also lacking. Based on marketplace realities, Russian consumers have a word that is used at times in place of "buying" something. The word *dostats*, best interpreted as "to acquire with great difficulty," was used by another Russian consumer to describe his ability to "dostats" building materials for home repairs in only a few days. In sum, acquiring consumer goods in Russia remains a challenge and the retail environment provides a stark contrast to what we expect in America.[2]

Yet, even in the United States and other nations where marketing is quite advanced, marketing acts can create unrealistic consumer expectations, result in costly minor product design changes, and adversely affect the environment. Thus, people's perceptions of marketing are mixed, at best. Over the years, studies have shown that many people feel cheated in their purchases due to deception, the lack of proper information, high-pressure

[2]Mitch Griffin, Barry J. Babin, and Doan Modianos, "Shopping Values of Russian Consumers: The Impact of Habituation in a Developing Economy," *Journal Retailing*, Vol. 76 (Spring 2000), pp. 33–52.

sales pitches, and other tactics. Consumers may also believe they are being "ripped off" when prices are increased. And waiting on store lines and poor customer service are two more key areas of consumer unhappiness.

Firms need to realize that consumer displeasure is not always transmitted to them. People may just decide not to buy a product and privately complain to friends. Usually, only a small percentage of disgruntled consumers take time to voice complaints. The true level of dissatisfaction is hidden. However, few people who are displeased, but do not complain, buy a product again. In contrast, many who complain and have their complaints resolved do buy again:

> A Strategic Planning Institute study on customer complaints discovered that the average business does not receive complaints from 96 percent of its unhappy customers. At least nine out of ten of these people won't do business with the company again—they're gone forever. On the other hand, of the 4 percent of unhappy customers who launch a complaint, 7 of 10 will do business with the company again so long as their concern is handled properly, and a staggering 19 of 20 will do business with the company again if the grievance is dealt with swiftly. [3]

In this chapter, the discussion is broken into three broad areas: social responsibility—issues concerning the general public and the environment, employees, channel members, stockholders, and competitors; ethics—deciding upon and doing what is morally correct, with regard to society in general and individual consumers; and consumerism—focusing on the rights of consumers.

5-2 SOCIAL RESPONSIBILITY

Social responsibility is a concern for "the consequences of a person's or firm's acts as they might affect the interests of others."[4] Corporate social responsibility means weighing the impact of company actions and behaving in a way that balances short-term profit needs with long-term societal needs. This calls for firms to be accountable to society and for consumers to act responsibly—by disposing of trash properly, wearing seat belts, not driving after drinking, and not being abusive to salespeople. See Figure 5-1.

Social responsibility aids society. The socioecological view of marketing considers voluntary and involuntary consumers.

Will the discoverer's gender, race, sexual orientation, age or personal beliefs really matter?

FIGURE 5-1
Social Responsibility Involves ALL of Us

Source: Reprinted by permission.

---

[3]Kevin Lawrence, "How to Profit from Customer Complaints: Turning Problems into Opportunities," *Canadian Manager* (Fall 2000), p. 25.

[4]Peter D. Bennett (Editor), *Dictionary of Marketing Terms*, Second Edition (Chicago: American Marketing Association, 1995), p. 267.

From a marketing perspective, social responsibility also encompasses the *socioecological view of marketing.* According to this view, firms, their customers, and others should consider all the stages in a product's life span in developing, selling, purchasing, using, and disposing of that product. And the interests of everyone affected by a good's or service's use, including the involuntary consumers who must share the consequences of someone else's behavior, should be weighed. For example, how much of a scarce resource should a firm use in making a product? What should be the rights and responsibilities of smokers and nonsmokers (as involuntary consumers) to one another?

As one observer noted:

> In marketing, much debate has centered on the role and scope of marketing in society, and particularly marketing's role in the quality of life. A basic premise of societal marketing, as a philosophy guiding marketing efforts, is the creation of consumer satisfaction of particular consumer segments in society with the minimal social cost to society. In other words, marketers guide the development of goods and services that meet certain needs of consumer groups in a manner that may not tax other publics with pollution, product hazards, environmental clutter, energy depletion, etc.[5]

To respond to the socioecological view of marketing, many firms now use "design for disassembly" (DFD), whereby products are designed to be disassembled in a more environmentally friendly manner once they outlive their usefulness. With DFD, firms use fewer parts, less materials, and more snap-fits instead of screws, and recycle more materials. A pioneer DFD product was BMW's Z1 limited-production roadster. It had an all-plastic exterior that could be removed from the metal chassis in 20 minutes. All major "skin" components—doors, bumpers, and panels—were recyclable plastic. Among the current DFD products are Caterpillar (www.cat.com) tractors, Xerox (www.xerox.com) copiers, Kodak (www.kodak.com) cameras, Hewlett-Packard (www.hp.com) workstations, some BMW (www.bmw.com) autos, and IBM (www.ibm.com) PCs.[6]

There are times when social responsibility poses dilemmas for firms and/or their customers because popular goods and services may have potential adverse effects on consumer or societal well-being. Examples of items that offer such dilemmas are tobacco products, no-return beverage containers, food with high taste appeal but low nutritional content, crash diet plans, and liquor.

Until the 1960s, it was generally felt that marketing's role was limited to satisfying customers and generating profits. Such resources as air, water, and energy were seen as limitless. Responsibility to the general public was rarely considered. Many firms now realize they should be responsive to the general public and the environment, employees, channel members, stockholders, and competitors, as well as customers. Table 5-1 shows socially responsible marketing in these areas.

This is how Johnson & Johnson (www.jnj.com/who_is_jnj/cr_usa.html) views its societal role, as highlighted in Figure 5-2:

> We believe our first responsibility is to the doctors, nurses, and patients, to mothers and fathers and all others who use our products and services. In meeting their needs, everything we do must be of high quality. We must constantly strive to reduce our costs in order to maintain reasonable prices. Customers' orders must be serviced promptly and accurately. Our suppliers and distributors must have an opportunity to make a fair profit.

[5]M. Joseph Sirgy, "Can Business and Government Help Balance the Quality of Life of Workers and Consumers?" *Journal of Business Research*, Vol. 22 (June 1991), p. 332.

[6]Gene Bylinsky, "Manufacturing for Reuse," *Fortune* (February 6, 1995), pp. 102–112; and "Design-for-Recyclability," www.edf.org/programs/PPA/vlc/recyclability.html (February 19, 2001).

Regarding the General Public and the Environment

Community involvement

Contributions to nonprofit organizations

Hiring hard-core unemployed

Product recycling

Eliminating offensive signs and billboards

Properly disposing of waste materials

Using goods and services requiring low levels of environmental resources

Regarding Employees

Ample internal communications

Employee empowerment allowed

Employee training about social issues and appropriate responses to them

No reprisals against employees who uncover questionable company policies

Recognizing socially responsible employees

Regarding Channel Members

Honoring both verbal and written commitments

Fairly distributing scarce goods and services

Accepting reasonable requests by channel members

Encouraging channel members to act responsibly

No coercion of channel members

Cooperative programs addressed to the general public and the environment

Regarding Stockholders

Honest reporting and financial disclosure

Publicity about company activities

Stockholder participation in setting socially responsible policy

Explaining social issues affecting the company

Earning a responsible profit

Regarding Competitors

Adhering to high standards of performance

No illegal or unethical acts to hinder competitors

Cooperative programs for the general public and environment

No actions that would lead competitors to waste resources

TABLE 5-1

Illustrations of Socially Responsible Marketing Practices

We are responsible to our employees, the men and women who work with us throughout the world. Everyone must be considered as an individual. We must respect their dignity and recognize their merit. They must have a sense of security in their jobs. Compensation must be fair and adequate, and working conditions clean, orderly and safe. We must be mindful of ways to help our employees fulfull their family responsibilities. Employees must feel free to make suggestions and complaints. There must be equal opportunity for employment, development and advancement for those qualified. We must provide competent management, and their actions must be just and ethical.

FIGURE 5-2

Johnson & Johnson's Global Social Responsibility Credo

At Johnson & Johnson, "A shared system of values, known as *Our Credo,* serves as a guide for all who are part of the Johnson & Johnson Family of Companies. The Credo can be found in 36 languages, each expressing the responsibilities we have to our customers, employees, communities, and stockholders." All of the various language versions of the credo are at the company Web site (www.jnj.com).

Source: Reprinted by permission.

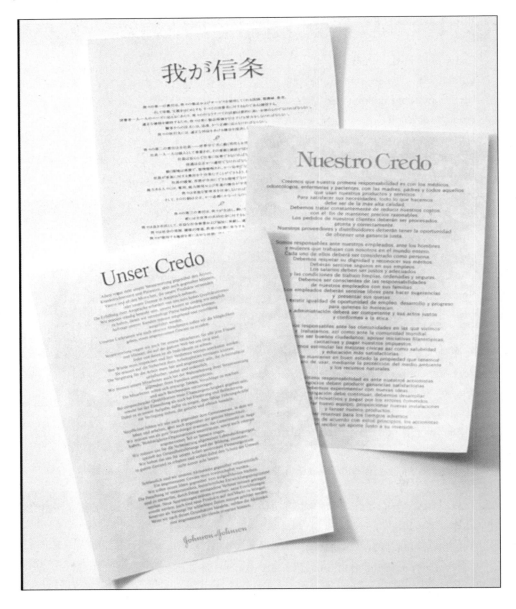

We are responsible to the communities in which we live and work and to the world community as well. We must be good citizens—support good works and charities and bear our fair share of taxes. We must encourage civic improvements and better health and education. We must maintain in good order the property we are privileged to use, protecting the environmet and natural resources.

Our final responsibility is to our stockholders. Business must make a sound profit. We must experiment with new ideas. Research must be carried on, innovative programs developed, and mistakes paid for. New equipment must be purchased, new facilities provided, and new products launched. Reserves must be created to provide for adverse times. When we operate according to these principles, the stockholders should realize a fair return.[7]

Company and consumer activities have a significant impact on natural resources, the landscape, pollution, and planned obsolescence. These areas are discussed next.

[7]"Our Credo," www.jnj.com/who_is_jnj/cr_usa.html (February 17, 2001).

GLOBAL *Marketing in Action*

Overturning a Ban on Tobacco Advertising

The European Court of Justice, Europe's highest court, recently sided with the German government and four British tobacco companies in overturning a law that would have phased out tobacco advertising among European Union member countries. The overturned law would have eliminated all tobacco ads in newspapers, magazines, and billboards as of 2006. In siding with the tobacco industry, the court ruled that since tobacco legislation is a health-related issue, it should be regulated by each member of the European Union separately. The ruling was based on a recommendation from the court's advocate general who said that the European Union did not have the legal standing to enact a ban.

Although this judgment was clearly a victory for tobacco manufacturers, some analysts believe that the industry's win will be short-lived, since individual members of the European Union are likely to develop similar bans that are applicable in their own countries. Some nations, such as Great Britain, are also considering introducing laws that would force tobacco manufacturers to reduce the tar content of cigarettes, as well as to require larger health warnings on cigarette packaging. According to a British-based anti-smoking group, more than a half million Europeans die each year due to tobacco-related illnesses.

In commenting on the court judgment, Great Britain's public health minister stated, "This ruling is a disappointment, but it will not deflect us from implementing our manifesto commitment to ban tobacco advertising." In response, an industry spokesperson said, "We urgently ask the minister to talk to us before framing any legislation so we can help them make sure that what they're proposing is workable."

Should Great Britain's public health minister work with the tobacco industry in drafting and enforcing tobacco-related legislation? Explain your answer.

Source: Based on material in Suzanne Kapner, "European Court Overturns Ban on Tobacco," *New York Times on the Web* (October 6, 2000).

5-2a Natural Resources

Today, we are aware that our global supply of natural resources is not unlimited. Both consumer behavior and marketing practices contribute to some resource shortages. Nonetheless, Americans annually discard 1,600 pounds of trash per person—including large amounts of paper, food, aluminum, plastic, tires, furniture, and clothing. Packaging is an especially big component of trash. How do other nations compare? The French discard 1,300 pounds per person, the Canadians 1,100 pounds, the British 1,060 pounds, the Germans 1,000 pounds, and the Japanese 840 pounds. In the less-industrialized Mexico, the amount is 660 pounds.[8] The U.S. Environmental Protection Agency (EPA) even has an entire Web site devoted to municipal solid waste (www.epa.gov/epaoswer).

[8]*Statistical Abstract of the United States 2000* (Washington, D.C.: U.S. Bureau of the Census, 2000).

FIGURE 5-3

Florida Power & Light: Stepping Up Recycling Efforts

Overall, FPL (www.fpl.com) has reduced its solid waste volume by 80 percent since 1991. The company recycles, refurbishes, or re-uses over 100 types of waste materials. In one year alone, the following was recycled, refurbished, or re-used: 2 million pounds of office paper and cardboard were recycled. 1.6 million pounds of waste porcelain and concrete were crushed and used in road bedding. 7.2 million pounds of scrap wood were mulched for landscaping. 13.9 million pounds of metals from transformer cores, miscellaneous hardware, scrap wire, and cable were reclaimed.

Source: Reprinted by permission.

Resource depletion can be slowed by reducing consumption, improving efficiency, limiting disposables, and lengthening products' lives.

Although Americans spend billions of dollars a year on garbage collection and disposal—and there are thousands of curbside recycling programs nationwide—only 27 percent of U.S. trash is actually recycled (up from 6 percent in 1960). The world's most ambitious formal recycling program is in Germany, where 80 percent of all packaging materials—from aluminum to paper—must be recycled.[9] See Figure 5-3.

Natural resource depletion can be reduced if the consumption of scarce materials is lessened and more efficient alternatives are chosen; fewer disposable items—such as cans, pens, and lighters—are bought; products are given longer life spans; and styles are changed less frequently. Convenient recycling and repair facilities, better trade-in arrangements, such common facilities as apartments (that share laundry rooms, etc.), and simpler packaging can also contribute to better resource use.

Progressive actions require cooperation among business, stockholders, government, employees, the general public, consumers, and others. They also involve changes in life-styles and corporate ingenuity: "This is perhaps the ultimate recycling system: a popcorn bag becomes a seat belt, a seat belt becomes a shirt, a shirt becomes a sheet of packaging film, the packaging film becomes a videotape, the videotape becomes an X-ray, and (after many more metamorphoses) may become a popcorn bag again."[10]

5-2b The Landscape

Garbage dumps and landfills, discarded beverage containers, and abandoned cars are examples of items marring the landscape.

In the United States, two-thirds of discarded materials are disposed of in dumps and landfills. But currently, many U.S. communities are not allowing new dumps and landfills, existing ones are closing for environmental reasons (there are now less than 2,400 landfills, down from 18,000 at their peak), and recycling efforts are being stepped up at existing dumps and landfills. In several areas of Europe and Japan, landfills are already at capacity—hence, a greater interest there in recycling and incineration.[11]

[9]"Basic Facts," www.epa.gov/epaoswer/non-hw/muncpl/facts.htm (February 20, 2001).

[10]*DuPont 1994 Annual Report.*

[11]"Basic Facts," www.epa.gov/epaoswer/non-hw/muncpl/facts.htm.

At one time, virtually all beverage containers were recycled. Then, no-return bottles and cans were developed; and littering at roadsides and other areas became a major problem. To reduce litter, several states and localities have laws requiring containers to have deposit fees that are refunded when consumers return empty containers. Many manufacturers and retailers feel the laws unfairly hold them responsible for container disposal, since littering is done by consumers—not them. Also, the labor and recycling costs associated with container returns have led to slightly higher beverage prices. Presently, container laws are just moderately effective; and consumers must be better educated as to the value of proper disposal.

Dumps and littering have become major factors in marring the landscape. Various communities have enacted rules to lessen them.

Cars are sometimes abandoned on streets, where they are then stripped of usable parts. One suggestion to cover the disposal of a car is to include an amount in its original price or in a transfer tax. For example, Maryland has a small fee on title transfers to aid in the removal of abandoned cars.

Other ways to reduce the marring of the landscape include limits or bans on billboards and roadside signs, fines for littering, and better trade-ins for autos and appliances. Neighborhood associations, merchant self-regulation, area planning and zoning, and consumer education can also improve appreciation for the landscape. This is a cooperative effort. A merchant cleanup patrol cannot overcome pedestrians who throw litter on the street rather than in waste baskets.

Here is what Nike has done to help:

Around the world, the firm famous for making shoes to wear on basketball courts is making courts out of shoes. And running tracks and playground mats, to boot. Nike's "Reuse a Shoe" program has recycled more than one million used and defective shoes. And not just Nikes—all sneakers are equal in the great polymer melting pot. Nike's shoes-to-court formula was first concocted, appropriately, in the Michael Jordan Building at Nike's Beaverton, Oregon, headquarters when its scientists wondered if there was a better, and cheaper, alternative to dumping old shoes and factory rejects in the world's landfills. Nike, which preaches environmental kindness, was spending some $300,000 a year on landfill and getting a bad conscience, too—some shoe materials take 100 years to break down.[12]

5-2c Environmental Pollution

Dangerous pollutants must be reduced and substitutes found. Environmental pollution can be generated by spray-can propellants, ocean dumping of industrial waste, lead from gas and paint, pesticides, sulfur oxide and other factory emissions, improper disposal of garbage, and other pollutants. Consider this:

Human pressures on the earth's natural systems have reached a point at which they are more likely to engender problems that we are less and less likely to anticipate. Dealing with this predicament is obviously going to require more than simply reacting as problems appear. Society needs a new ethic for managing its relationship with nature—one that emphasizes minimal interference in the lives of wild beings and in the broad natural processes that sustain all living things. Policy may need to be more a matter of creating not so much solutions per se as the conditions from which solutions can arise. In the face of the unexpected, our best hopes may lie in our collective imagination.[13]

Government and industry in the United States, Western Europe, and Japan spend a combined total of more than $300 billion annually on environmental protection. In addition, anti-pollution expenditures have gone up dramatically in several less-developed nations in Latin America, Asia, and Africa. The Environmental Protection Agency

Both government and business actions are needed to reduce dangerous environmental pollution.

[12]Roger Thurow, "Nike Makes Old Shoes Resurface as New Courts," *Wall Street Journal* (April 7, 1995), p. B12.
[13]Chris Bright and Dan Johnson, "Environmental Surprises: Planning for the Unexpected," *Futurist* (July-August 2000), p. 41.

(www.epa.gov) is the major U.S. government agency involved with pollution; a number of state agencies are also active in this area. Numerous other nations have their own government agencies to deal with the issue.

These are among the voluntary activities of companies and associations:

- New PCs, printers, monitors, and other devices automatically "power down" when not in use to reduce air pollution and conserve energy.
- The American Chemistry Council (www.cmahq.com) has been working with the EPA to keep hazardous compounds out of the environment.
- 3M (www.3m.com) devotes 15 percent of its overall research-and-development budget to projects involving environmental protection.
- Japan's Ebara Corporation (www.ebara.co.jp/en) uses its own technology to remove harmful sulphur dioxides and nitrogen oxides from power plants more efficiently.
- Several firms have joined to form the Global Environmental Management Initiative (www.gemi.org), with the goal of fostering an exchange of information about environmental protection programs.
- The Coalition for Environmentally Responsible Economies (www.ceres.org) is a nonprofit group of investors, public pension funds, foundations, unions, and environmental, religious, and public interest groups working with business to enhance corporate environmental responsibility worldwide.

5-2d Planned Obsolescence

Planned obsolescence is a marketing practice that capitalizes on short-run material wearout, style changes, and functional product changes.

In *material planned obsolescence*, firms choose materials and components that are subject to comparatively early breakage, wear, rot, or corrosion. For example, the makers of disposable lighters and razors use this form of planned obsolescence in a constructive manner by offering inexpensive, short-life, convenient products. However, there is growing resistance to material planned obsolescence because of its effects on natural resources and the landscape.

In *style planned obsolescence*, a firm makes minor changes to differentiate the new year's offering from the prior year's. Since some people are style-conscious, they will discard old items while they are still functional so as to acquire new ones with more status. This is common with fashion items and cars.

With *functional planned obsolescence*, a firm introduces new product features or improvements to generate consumer dissatisfaction with currently owned products. Sometimes, features or improvements may have been withheld from an earlier model to gain faster repurchases. A style change may accompany a functional one to raise consumer awareness of a "new" product. This form of planned obsolescence occurs most often with high-tech items such as computers.

Marketers reply to criticism thusly: Planned obsolescence is responsive to people's desires as to prices, styles, and features and is not coercive; without product turnover, people would be disenchanted by the lack of choices; consumers like disposable items and often discard them before they lose their effectiveness; firms use materials that hold down prices; competition requires firms to offer the best products possible and not hold back improvements; and, for such products as clothing, people desire continuous style changes.

A number of firms have enacted innovative strategies with regard to planned obsolescence. For example, Kodak (www.kodak.com) and Fuji (www.fujifilm.com) have programs for recycling their single-use disposable cameras, after people have the film developed. Canon (www.canon.com) has a factory in China that reconditions and refills used copier cartridges. SKF of Sweden (www.skf.com) is a worldwide bearings maker; to increase the life of its products, it has added more preventative maintenance services.

Planned obsolescence can involve materials, styles, and functions.

5-2e The Benefits and Costs of Social Responsibility

Socially responsible actions have both benefits and costs. Among the benefits are improved worker and public health, as reflected in fewer and less severe accidents, longer life spans, and less disease; cleaner air; better resource use; economic growth; a better business image; an educated public; government cooperation; an attractive, safe environment; an enhanced standard of living; and self-satisfaction for the firm. Many of these benefits cannot be quantified. Nonetheless, expectations are that the U.S. Clean Air Act and other nations' laws will ultimately save thousands and thousands of lives each year, protect food crops, reduce medical costs, and lead to clearer skies.

Although some social-responsibility expenditures are borne by a broad cross-section of firms and the general public (via taxes and higher product prices), the benefits of many environmental and other programs are enjoyed primarily by those living or working in affected areas. The costs of socially responsible actions can be high. For instance, U.S. environmental-protection spending is about 2 percent of the annual Gross Domestic Product. Various environmentally questionable products that are efficient have been greatly modified or removed from the marketplace, such as leaded gasoline. Because of various legal restrictions and fears of lawsuits, new-product planning tends to be more conservative; and resources are often allotted to prevention rather than invention. Furthermore, trade-offs have to be made in determining which programs are more deserving of funding. See Figure 5-4.

For socially responsible efforts to be effective, all parties must partake in the process—sharing benefits and costs. This means business, consumers, government, channel members, and others. The next several years promise to see the further emergence of **green marketing,** a form of socioecological marketing, whereby the goods and services sold, and the marketing practices involved in their sale, take into account environmental ramifications for society as a whole. To succeed in green marketing, firms must be sure to not mislead consumers or create unrealistic expectations about reformulated products' ability to be recycled, to not pollute, and so on.

Social responsibility has benefits as well as costs; these need to be balanced.

Green marketing *efforts will expand during this decade.*

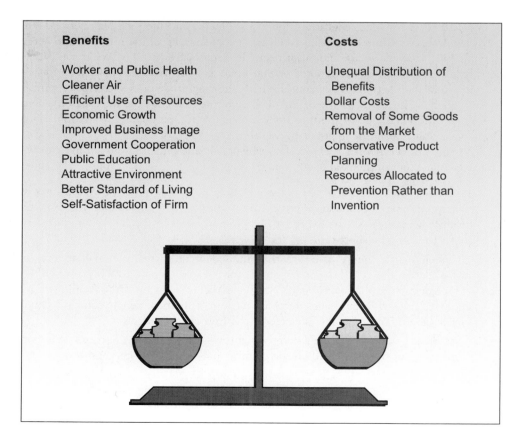

Benefits	Costs
Worker and Public Health	Unequal Distribution of Benefits
Cleaner Air	Dollar Costs
Efficient Use of Resources	Removal of Some Goods from the Market
Economic Growth	
Improved Business Image	Conservative Product Planning
Government Cooperation	Resources Allocated to Prevention Rather than Invention
Public Education	
Attractive Environment	
Better Standard of Living	
Self-Satisfaction of Firm	

FIGURE   5-4

The Benefits and Costs of Social Responsibility

FIGURE 5-5

A Framework for Ethical/Unethical Decision Making

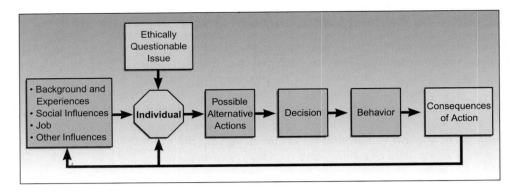

FIGURE 5-5

A Framework for Ethical/Unethical Decision Making

5-3 ETHICS

In any marketing situation, *ethical behavior* based on honest and proper conduct ("what is right" and "what is wrong") should be followed. This applies both to situations involving company actions that affect the general public, employees, channel members, stockholders, and/or competitors and to situations involving company dealings with consumers.

Figure 5-5 outlines a framework for ethical/unethical decision making. An individual is affected by his or her background and experiences, social influences, and the job. When an ethical dilemma occurs, these factors come into play (consciously or subconsciously). For each ethically questionable issue, the person considers alternative actions, makes a decision, and acts accordingly. He or she then faces the consequences, which impact upon future decisions. Figure 5-6 shows the ethics code of the American Marketing Association (http://www.marketingpower.com/live/jump.php?Item_ID=1175), marketing's leading professional group.

Of particular importance in the study of ethics are answers to these two questions: How do people determine whether an act is ethical or unethical? Why do they act ethically or unethically?[14] People *determine* (learn) whether given actions are ethical or not through their upbringing, education, job environment, and life-long experiences—and others' responses to their behavior. In addition, people may apply their own cognitive reasoning skills to decide what is morally acceptable. People *act* ethically or unethically based on their expectations of the rewards or punishments—financial, social, and so forth— flowing from their actions. They consider both the magnitude of the rewards or punishments (such as the size of a raise or the maximum fine that could be imposed on a company) and the likelihood of their occurrence (such as the probability of getting a large raise or having a large fine imposed on the firm).

Various ethical theories try to explain why people and organizations act in particular ways. Here are four of them, applied to marketing:

- *Egoism*—a theory asserting that individuals act exclusively in their own self-interest. Example: A product manager postpones investing in improvements for a mature product because he or she expects to be promoted within the next six months and wants to maximize short-term profits.

- *Utilitarianism*—a theory asserting that individual and organizational actions are proper only if they yield the greatest good for the most people (the highest net benefit). Example: A pharmaceutical company markets a Food and Drug Administration approved drug with some side effects as long as it helps more people combat a particular disease than the number affected by the (minor) side effect.

- *Duty-Based*—a theory asserting that the rightness of an action is not based on its consequences, but rather is based on the premise that certain actions are proper because

Ethical behavior involves honest and proper conduct.

Ethics theories range from egoism to virtue ethics.

[14]Shelby D. Hunt, "Foundations of the Hunt-Vitell Theory of Ethics," presented at the 1995 AMA Faculty Consortium on Ethics and Social Responsibility in Marketing" (Hempstead, N.Y.: Hofstra University).

Code of Ethics
Members of the American Marketing Association (AMA) are committed to ethical professional conduct. They have joined together in subscribing to this Code of Ethics embracing the following topics:

Responsibilities of the Marketer
Marketers must accept responsibility for the consequence of their activities and make every effort to ensure that their decisions, recommendations, and actions function to identify, serve, and satisfy all relevant publics: customers, organizations and society.

Marketers' professional conduct must be guided by:

1. The basic rule of professional ethics: not knowingly to do harm;
2. The adherence to all applicable laws and regulations;
3. The accurate representation of their education, training and experience; and
4. The active support, practice and promotion of this Code of Ethics.

Honesty and Fairness
Marketers shall uphold and advance the integrity, honor, and dignity of the marketing profession by:

1. Being honest in serving customers, clients, employees, suppliers, distributors and the public;
2. Not knowingly participating in conflict of interest without prior notice to all parties involved; and
3. Establishing equitable fee schedules including the payment or receipt of usual, customary and/or legal compensation or marketing exchanges.

Rights and Duties of Parties in the Marketing Exchange Process
Participants in the marketing exchange process should be able to expect that:

1. Products and services offered are safe and fit for their intended uses;
2. Communications about offered products and services are not deceptive;
3. All parties intend to discharge their obligations, financial and otherwise, in good faith; and
4. Appropriate internal methods exist for equitable adjustment and/or redress of grievances concerning purchases.

It is understood that the above would include, but is not limited to, the following responsiblities of the marketer:

In the area of product development and management,
• disclosure of all substantial risks associated with product or service usage;
• identification of any product component substitiution that might materially change the product or impact on the buyer's purchase decision;
• identification of extra-cost added features.

In the area of promotions,
• **avoidance of false and misleading advertising;**
• rejection of high pressure manipulation.
• avoidance of sales promotions that use deception or manipulation

In the area of distribution,
• not manipulating the availability of a product for purpose of exploitation;
• not using coercion in the marketing channel;
• not exerting undue influence over the reseller's choice to handle the product.

In the area of pricing,
• not engaging in price fixing;
• not practicing predatory pricing;
• disclosing the full price associated with any purchase.

In the area of marketing research,
• prohibiting selling or fund raising under the guise of conducting research;
• maintaining research integrity by avoiding misrepresentation and omission of pertinent research data;
• treating outside clients and suppliers fairly.

Organizational Relationships
Marketers should be aware of how their behavior may influence or impact on the behavior of others in organizational relationships. They should not demand, encourage or apply coercion to obtain unethical behavior in their relationships with others, such as employees, suppliers or customers:

1. Apply confidentiality and anonymity in professional relationships with regard to privileged information;
2. Meet their obligations and responsibilities in contracts and mutual agreements in a timely manner;
3. Avoid taking the work of others, in whole, or in part, and represent this work as their own or directly benefit from it without compensation or consent of the originator or owner;
4. Avoid manipulation to take advantage of situations to maximize personal welfare in a way that unfairly deprives or damages the organization of others.

Any AMA members found to be in violation of any provision of this Code of Ethics may have his or her Association membership suspended or revoked.

FIGURE 5-6

The American Marketing Association's Code of Ethics

Source: Reprinted by permission.

they stem from basic obligations. Example: A supermarket chain sets below-average prices in a low-income area even though this adversely affects company profits in that community.

• *Virtue Ethics*—a theory asserting that actions should be guided by an individual's or organization's seeking goodness and virtue ("living a good life"). Example: A virtuous firm is totally truthful in its ads, packaging, and selling efforts—and does not use manipulative appeals to persuade customers.[15]

Ethical issues in marketing can generally be divided into two categories: process-related and product-related.[16] **Process-related ethical issues** involve "the unethical use of marketing strategies or tactics." Examples include bait-and-switch advertising, price fixing, selling products overseas that have been found unsafe in the United States, and bribing purchasing agents of large customers. **Product-related ethical issues** involve "the ethical appropriateness of marketing certain products." For example, should tobacco products, sugar-coated cereals, and political candidates be marketed? More specifically, should cigarettes be sold? Should there be restrictions on their sales? Should cigarette ads be allowed? Should cigarette taxes be raised to dampen use? Should smoking be banned in offices, restaurants, and planes?

Marketers need to consider **process-related** *and* **product-related ethical issues.**

[15]Gene R. Laczniak and Patrick E. Murphy, *Ethical Marketing Decisions: The Higher Road* (Needham Heights, Mass.: Allyn & Bacon, 1993), pp. 28–42.

[16]Gene R. Laczniak, Robert F. Lusch, and William A. Strang, "Ethical Marketing: Perceptions of Economic Goods and Social Problems," *Journal of Macromarketing*, Vol. 1 (Spring 1981), p. 49.

The following comments sum up the intricacy of many ethical issues:

> Some employees may believe unethical activity is in the firm's best interest and is thus expected of them—or will at least be tolerated. Top management wants employees to be ethical and tells them so, but some people may not believe it, thinking instead that requests to be ethical are simply window dressing. Due to their loyalty to their firm, they engage in unethical conduct. Some employees act unethically because they may believe this conduct is in their self-interest. Those who want to get ahead sometimes seek ways to distinguish themselves by outperforming others. They may believe that unethical conduct is a way to improve their performance and is, thus, in their self-interest. Other employees may not always know they're doing something unethical. There certainly is a sense in which ethics is a matter of opinion—an art rather than a science. Where is the line between the sharp deal and the shady deal? Between profit maximization and social irresponsibility? Between clever advertising and fraud? These can sometimes be difficult questions for an employee to answer.[17]

Thus, to maintain the highest possible ethical conduct by employees, the senior executives in a firm must make a major commitment to ethics, communicate standards of conduct to every employee (perhaps via a written ethics code), reward ethical behavior, and discourage unethical behavior.

Next, ethics is examined from four vantage points: a business perspective, a consumer perspective, a global perspective, and the teachability of ethics.

5-3a A Business Perspective

Many companies have ethics codes; some have implicit standards.

Most of the firms listed in the U.S. *Fortune 500* have formal ethics codes. Some codes are general and, thus, like organizational mission statements; others are specific and operational. In contrast, French, British, and German firms are less apt to have formal codes; acceptable standards of behavior are more implied. The European Union has been working to clarify the latter situation.

One of the most complex aspects of business ethics is setting the boundaries as to what is ethical. To address this, the following scale was devised and tested with a variety of marketing personnel. The scale suggests that businesspeople make better decisions if they consider whether a marketing action (is):[18]

Fair — — — — — —	Unfair
Just — — — — — —	Unjust
Culturally Acceptable — — — — — —	Culturally Unacceptable
Violates an Unwritten Contract — — — — — —	Does Not Violate an Unwritten Contract
Traditionally Acceptable — — — — — —	Traditionally Unacceptable
Morally Right Violates an — — — — — —	Not Morally Right Does Not Violate
Violates an Unspoken Promise — — — — — —	Does Not Violate an Unspoken Promise
Acceptable to My Family — — — — — —	Unacceptable to My Family

---

[17]John Collins, "Why Bad Things Happen to Good Companies—And What Can Be Done," *Business Horizons*, Vol. 33 (November-December 1990), p. 18. See also Barry J. Babin, James S. Boles, and Donald P. Robin, "Representing the Perceived Ethical Work Climate Among Marketing Employees," *Journal of the Academy of Marketing Science*, Vol. 28 (Summer 2000), pp. 345–358; and Lawrence B. Chonko and Shelby D. Hunt, "Ethics and Marketing Management: A Retrospective and Prospective Commentary," *Journal of Business Research*, Vol. 50 (December 2000), pp. 235–244.

[18]R. Eric Reidenbach, Donald P. Robin, and Lyndon Dawson, "An Application and Extension of a Multidimensional Ethics Scale to Selected Marketing Practices and Marketing Groups," *Journal of the Academy of Marketing Science*, Vol. 19 (Spring 1991), p. 84.

ETHICAL *Issues in Marketing*

Big
Business
Does Not
Have to
Mean Bad
Ethics

Many large firms have not only enacted highly ethical guidelines, but they have also developed enforcement mechanisms to ensure that their employees are complying with these guidelines.

A growing number have installed corporate ethics officers, a job title unknown a decade or so ago. The Ethics Officer Association now has more than 700 members, up from 12 in 1992. As a vice-president at the Institute for Global Ethics (www.globalethics.org) says, "Instead of being a corporate policeman, ethics officers are becoming corporate coaches for ethical decision making."

Ethical issues are being discussed at higher managerial levels than before. According to a Conference Board study of 124 companies in 22 countries, the board of directors is now involved in 78 percent of ethical policies. As recently as 1987, board involvement took place in only 21 percent of ethical policies.

Here are some examples of positive ethical practices by major companies:

- Mattel developed a social audit that created 200 labor standards (such as length of breaks and the number of rest rooms) to ensure that none of its overseas plants were exploiting employees.
- Boeing requires all workers to take at least one hour of ethical training per year. At these sessions, employees are asked to respond to moral issues, such as whether to accept an outside supplier's offer of free base-ball tickets. (The correct answer is to refuse them.)
- Lockheed Martin created a special program to develop trust after an employee survey showed that more than one-half of workers said that they would not report misconduct due to fear of retaliation.

Under what conditions, should a supplier's offer of free baseball tickets be accepted? Rejected?

Source: Based on material in Amy Zipkin, "Management: Big Corporations Are Getting Religion on Ethics," *New York Times on the Web* (October 18, 2000).

Here are examples showing varying business responses to ethical issues:

- ***Cause-related marketing*** is a somewhat controversial practice where profit-oriented firms contribute specific amounts to given nonprofit organizations for each consumer purchase of certain goods and services during a special promotion (such as sponsorship of a sport for the Olympics). It has been used by such firms as American Express and MasterCard, and such nonprofits as the Red Cross. Advocates feel cause-related marketing stimulates direct and indirect contributions and benefits the images of both the profit-oriented firms and the nonprofit institutions involved in it. Critics say there is too much commercialism by nonprofit groups and implicit endorsements for sponsor products.

> **Cause-related marketing** *has good and bad points.*

- CEOs of large American firms overwhelmingly feel it is always wrong to use misleading advertising or labeling, sell goods and services that have poor safety, dump banned or flawed products in foreign markets, and cause environmental harm.

- Mary Kay Cosmetics was one of the first firms to halt product testing on animals. Its vice-chairman noted, "Our goal was to take the high ground. The decision meant putting a hold on new products for a while, which meant lost sales. Ethical decision making, by its very nature, is relative—what will be the effect of our decision on others? Is the decision right, not only for us, but also for society? Ethical corporate conduct is not easy and can be costly, but I believe ethics is good business."[19]

5-3b A Consumer Perspective

Consumers should act as ethically to businesses as they expect to be treated.

Just as business has a responsibility to act in an ethical and a societally oriented way, so do consumers. Their actions impact on businesses, other consumers, the general public, the environment, and so on. In marketing transactions, ethical standards can truly be maintained only if both sellers and buyers act in a mutually respectful, honest, fair, and responsible manner.

Yet, especially with regard to broad societal issues, consumers may find it hard to decide what is acceptable. Daniel Yankelovich (www.dyg.com), an expert in the area, says a society goes through seven stages to form a consensus on major issues (such as how to deal with health care):

1. People begin to become aware of an issue.
2. They develop a sense of urgency about it.
3. They start exploring choices for dealing with the issue.
4. There is resistance to costs and trade-offs—leading to wishful thinking.
5. The pros and cons of alternatives are weighed.
6. People take a stand intellectually.
7. A responsible judgment is made morally and emotionally.[20]

In terms of consumer perceptions about whether specific activities on their part are proper, consider the actions listed in Table 5-2. Which of them would you, *as a consumer*, deem to be ethically acceptable? Which would be ethically wrong? What should be the ramifications for consumers engaging in acts that are ethically unacceptable?

5-3c A Global Perspective

Ethical decisions can be complicated on an international level.

Ethical standards can be difficult to apply in a global setting due to several factors. First, different societies have their own views of acceptable behavior regarding interpersonal conduct, communications, and business practices. Second, there may be misunderstandings due to poor language translations. Third, in less-developed nations, there may be less concern for social and consumer issues than for improving the level of industrialization. Fourth, governments in some nations have questionable rules so as to protect domestic firms. Fifth, executives are usually more aware of ethical standards in their home nations than in foreign ones. Sixth, global ethical disputes may be hard to mediate. Under whose jurisdiction are disputes involving firms from separate nations?

---

[19]John Palmer, "We Are the Children," *Promo* (February 2001), pp. 55–65; Julie Edelson Halpert, "Dr Pepper Hospital? Perhaps, for a Price," *New York Times on the Web* (February 18, 2001); Gene R. Laczniak, Marvin W. Berkowitz, Russell G. Booker, and James P. Hale, "The Ethics of Business: Improving or Deteriorating?" *Business Horizons,* Vol. 38 (January-February 1995), p. 43; and Richard C. Bartlett, "Mary Kay's Foundation," *Journal of Business Strategy,* Vol. 16 (July-August 1995), p. 16.

[20]Daniel Yankelovich, "How Public Opinion Really Works," *Fortune* (October 5, 1992), p. 103.

As a consumer, how would you rate these actions in terms of their ethical appropriateness? Use a scale from 1–10, with 1 being fully ethical and 10 being fully unethical.

TABLE 5-2

Ethical Appropriateness of Selected Consumer Activities

Activities	Ratings
Changing price tags on merchandise in a retail store	_____
Drinking a can of soda in a supermarket without paying for it	_____
Using a long-distance telephone access code that does not belong to you	_____
Reporting a lost item as "stolen" to an insurance company in order to collect the money	_____
Inflating an insurance claim	_____
Giving misleading price information to a clerk for an unpriced item	_____
Getting too much change and not saying anything	_____
Observing someone shoplifting and ignoring it	_____
Stretching the truth on an income-tax return	_____
Joining a music club just to get some free CDs without any intention of buying	_____
Using computer software or games you did not buy	_____
Returning merchandise after wearing it and not liking it	_____
Repeating store visits to buy more merchandise that is available in limited quantity on a given shopping trip	_____
Exaggerating quality at a garage sale	_____
Selling a frequent flier ticket	_____
Being less than truthful on surveys	_____

Sources: Table devised by the authors using activities listed in James A. Muncy and Scott J. Vitell, "Consumer Ethics: An Investigation of the Ethical Beliefs of the Final Consumer," *Journal of Business Research*, Vol. 24 (June 1992), p. 303; and Sam Fullerton, David Taylor, and B. C. Ghosh, "A Cross-Cultural Examination of Attitudes Towards Aberrant Consumer Behavior in the Marketplace: Some Preliminary Results from the USA, New Zealand, and Singapore," *Marketing Intelligence & Planning*, Vol. 15 (April-May 1997), p. 211.

Here are some perspectives on the ethical challenges on a global level:

- "Ah, the good old days. Back 30, 20, even 10, years ago, companies could run their overseas business pretty much however they wanted. What happened in a land far away bore little consequence to the main operations. If a factory employed underage workers in poor countries, well, that's just the way things were done over there. Giving and accepting elaborate gifts? Part of the culture. And if your subsidiary didn't adhere to the same pollution control standards as its American counterparts, it was easily justified on the grounds that environmental laws overseas weren't as strict. But today, global business ethics has now become the ultimate dilemma for many U.S. businesses. 'The world is highly interconnected now, so American consumers increasingly know and care if a company is, say, dumping chemical waste in a river in China,' says Robert MacGregor, a leader of the Caux Round Table (www.cauxroundtable.org), a group of international business leaders aiming to focus attention on global corporate responsibility. 'Companies that are concerned with their reputations, and that's nearly all companies, recognize they have to focus on their global principles.' "[21]

- "No matter how many ethical mantras are repeated, no matter how many behavior guidelines are codified, they can't possibly cover the entire range of ethical behavior. As Motorola (www.motorola.com) has discovered, this situation is all the more complicated by globalization. Motorola has declared itself a company dedicated to 'Uncompromising Integrity'—with ethical values and standards an 'indispensable foundation' for the company's work, relationships, and business success. Yet at a time when almost half of Motorola's employees are non-American and more than half of its revenues come from non-American markets, this raises a vital question: How are the company's employees to remain faithful to Motorola's core ethical values, while at the same time respecting the values of the host cultures where it manufactures and markets its products?"[22]

- "Business ethics is an emerging field, depending strongly on economic factors, but also on political changes and a growing awareness of value conflicts and ethical and environmental demands. Because of its emerging character, it is difficult to capture the lasting features of business ethics and to foresee its likely developments. Each country and each region has its own 'business ethics' history; some, like the U.S. and Canada, are 'old-timers' (if 25 years can be called old) and some like China and South Africa are 'newcomers.' Of course, such an observation implies an understanding of business ethics and does not mean that ethical issues in particular regions did not exist and were not dealt with before. It means that different historical records matter a great deal; that, nonetheless, there are many opportunities to learn from each other, since we are not forced to reinvent the wheel again and again; and that the very conception of business ethics is important in international comparisons."[23]

- "Many foreign officials view public business dealings as profit-making opportunities and exploit them to supplement meager salaries, build personal fortunes, or recoup investments made to 'purchase' their positions. Some multinational firms have complied with questionable payments requests, hoping to trade payoffs and presents for favorable consideration by decision makers in order to win government or state enterprise contracts. The scale of international bribery has become immense; the World Bank estimates that five percent of exports to developing countries—$50 to $80 billion per year—goes to corrupt officials."[24]

Firms that market globally need to keep three points in mind: One, *core business values* provide the basis for worldwide ethics codes. They are company principles "that are so fundamental they will not be compromised" in any foreign markets. These include nonmaleficence (to not knowingly do harm), promise keeping, nondeception, and protection of societal and consumer rights. Two, *peripheral business values* are less important to the firm and may be adjusted to foreign markets. These relate to local customs in buyer-seller exchanges, selling practices, and so on. Three, if possible, *ethnocentrism*—perceiving other nations' moral standards in terms of one's own country—must be avoided.[25]

---

[21]Meryl Davids, "Ethics: Global Standards, Local Problems," *Journal of Business Strategy*, Vol. 20 (January-February 1999), p. 38.

[22]R.S. Moorthy, Robert C. Solomon, William J. Ellios, and Richard T. De George, "Friendship or Bribery?" *Across the Board* (January 1999), p. 43.

[23]Georges Enderle, "A Worldwide Survey of Business Ethics in the 1990s," *Journal of Business Ethics*, Vol. 16 (October 1997), pp. 1475–1476.

[24]Wayne Hamra, "Bribery in International Business Transactions and the OECD Convention: Benefits and Limitations," *Business Economics* (October 2000), p. 34.

[25]Gene R. Laczniak, "Observations Concerning International Marketing Ethics," presented at the 1995 AMA Faculty Consortium on Ethics and Social Responsibility in Marketing" (Hempstead, N.Y.: Hofstra University); and Laczniak and Murphy, *Ethical Marketing Decisions: The Higher Road,* p. 218.

5-3d The Teachability of Ethics

Given the impact of societal values, peer pressure, self-interests and personal ambitions (and fear of failure), and other factors on people's sense of ethically acceptable behavior, there has been considerable debate as to whether ethics can be taught—either in a classroom or business setting. Nonetheless, what can be transmitted to people are

Ethical concepts can be communicated.

- Clear ethics codes.
- Role models of ethical people.
- Wide-ranging examples of ethical and unethical behavior.
- Specified punishments if ethical behavior is not followed.
- The vigilance of professors and top management regarding such issues as cheating on tests, misleading customers, and other unethical practices.
- The notion that ethical actions will never put an employee in jeopardy (thus, a salesperson should not be penalized for losing a customer if he/she is unwilling to exaggerate the effectiveness of a product).

Consider this view of ethics and business students:

Business managers today confront unprecedented problems, issues, questions, and predicaments—the like of which earlier generations never knew. The techniques of the past are not only difficult to apply to today's demands, but they may simply be inadequate for, or irrelevant to, tomorrow's requirements; business students need to be prepared to deal creatively with the new and unforeseen, for they are rarely confronting the traditional and the predictable. Old ethical responses will have to be transformed in unexpected ways and interpreted with imagination. Business managers increasingly will have to concern themselves with encouraging new and maintaining existing supplies of such behavior in their organizations. Already many managers in leading internationalized businesses explicitly discuss the merits of other-regarding, and even the benefits of altruistic behavior among their employees, partners, collaborators, and colleagues. The teaching of business ethics, thus, is not likely to be a passing fad, but a long-term and important, though difficult, responsibility for colleges as well as for corporate businesses. The faculties of the former and the managers of the latter had better develop strategies and tactics that help them convince both students and employees that business ethics is an increasingly salient concern in the new, emerging environment of business, as well as in the rapidly changing corporate organization.[26]

For more ethics insights, visit Business Ethics Resources (www.ethics.ubc.ca/resources/business) and Ethics in Business: Advice (www.inc.com/advice/doing_business_ethically).

5-4 CONSUMERISM

Whereas social responsibility involves firms' interfaces with all of their publics, consumerism focuses on the relations of firms and their customers. **Consumerism** encompasses "the wide range of activities of government, business, and independent organizations that are designed to protect people from practices that infringe upon their rights as consumers."[27]

Consumerism *protects consumers from practices that infringe upon their rights.*

Consumer interests are most apt to be served in industrialized nations, where their rights are considered important, and governments and firms have the resources to address consumer issues. In less-developed nations and those now turning to free-market economies, consumer rights have not been as well honored due to fewer resources and to other commitments; the early stages of consumerism are just now emerging in many of these nations.

[26]James W Kuhn, "Emotion as Well as Reason: Getting Students Beyond 'Interpersonal Accountability'," *Journal of Business Ethics*, Vol. 17 (February 1998), pp. 297–299.
[27]Bennett, *Dictionary of Marketing Terms*, p. 62.

President Kennedy declared a **consumer bill of rights:** *to information, to safety, to choice, and to be heard.*

U.S. consumerism has evolved through four distinct eras, and is now in a fifth. The first era was in the 1900s and focused on the need for a banking system, product purity, postal rates, antitrust regulations, and product shortages. Emphasis was on business protection against unfair practices. The second era was from the 1930s to the 1950s. Issues were product safety, bank failures, labeling, misrepresentation, stock manipulation, deceptive ads, credit, and consumer refunds. Consumer groups, such as Consumers Union, and legislation grew. Issues were initiated but seldom resolved.

The third era began in the early 1960s and lasted to 1980. It dealt with all marketing areas and had a great impact. Ushering in this era was President Kennedy's **consumer bill of rights:** to information, to safety, to choice in product selection, and to be heard. These rights, cited in Figure 5-7, apply to people in any nation or economic system. Other events also contributed to the era's aggressiveness. Birth defects from the drug thalidomide occurred. Several books—on marketing's ability to influence people, dangers from unsafe autos, and funeral industry tactics—were published. Consumers became more unhappy with product performance, firms' complaint handling, and deceptive and unsafe acts; and they set higher—perhaps unrealistic—expectations. Product scarcity occurred for some items. Self-service shopping and more complex products caused uncertainty for some. The media publicized poor practices more often. Government intervention expanded; and the FTC (www.ftc.gov) extended its consumer activities.

The fourth era took place during the 1980s as consumerism entered a mature phase, due to the dramatic gains of the 1960s and 1970s—and an emphasis on business deregulation and self-regulation. Nationally, no major consumer laws were enacted and budgets of federal agencies concerned with consumer issues were cut. Yet, state and local governments became more active. In general, the federal government believed that most firms took consumer issues into account when devising and applying their marketing plans, and fewer firms did ignore consumer input or publicly confront consumer groups. Cooperation between business and consumers was better, and confrontations were less likely.

FIGURE 5-7
Consumers' Basic Rights

- To be informed and protected against fraudulent, deceitful, and misleading statements, advertisements, labels, etc.; and to be educated as to how to use financial resources wisely.

- To be protected against dangerous and unsafe products.

- To be able to choose from among several available goods and services.

- To be heard by government and business regarding unsatisfactory or disappointing practices.

Since 1990, the federal government has been somewhat more involved with consumer issues. Its goal is to balance consumer and business rights. Some national laws have been enacted and U.S. agencies have stepped up enforcement practices. At the same time, many state and local governments are keeping a high level of commitment. Unfair business tactics, product safety, and health issues are the areas with the most attention. Today, more firms address consumer issues and resolve complaints than before.

These key aspects of consumerism are examined next: consumer rights, the responses of business to consumer issues, and the current role of consumerism.

5-4a Consumer Rights

As noted, consumer rights fall into four categories: information and education, safety, choice, and the right to be heard. Each is discussed next.

Consumer Information and Education

The right to be informed includes protection against fraudulent, deceitful, or grossly misleading information, advertising, labeling, pricing, packaging, and so forth; and being given enough information to make good decisions. In the United States, there are many federal and state laws in this area.

The Magnuson-Moss Consumer Product Warranty Act (www.ftc.gov/bcp/conline/pubs/buspubs/ warranty/undermag.htm) is a major federal law. A *warranty* is an assurance to consumers that a product meets certain standards. An *express warranty* is explicitly stated, such as a printed form showing the minimum mileage for tires. An *implied warranty* does not have to be stated to be in effect; a product is assumed to be fit for use and packaged properly, and to conform to promises on the label. The Magnuson-Moss Act requires warranties to be properly stated and enforced. They must be available prior to purchases, so consumers may read them in advance. The FTC monitors product-accompanying information as to the warrantor's identity and location, exceptions in coverage, and how people may complain. A *full warranty* must cover all parts and labor for a given time. A *limited warranty* may have conditions and exceptions, and a provision for labor charges. Implied warranties may not be disclaimed.

> A **warranty** *assures consumers that a product will meet certain standards.*

Many states have laws about consumer information. For instance, cooling-off laws (allowing people to reconsider and, if they desire, cancel purchase commitments made in their homes with salespeople) are now in force in about 40 states. Unit-pricing laws that let people compare the prices of products coming in many sizes (such as small, medium, large, and economy), are likewise on a state-by-state basis. Government actions involving consumer information are also picking up internationally.

Unfortunately, the existence of good information does not mean consumers will use it in their decision making. At times, the information is ignored or misunderstood, especially by those needing it most (such as the poor); thus, consumer education is needed. Most state departments of education in the United States have consumer education staffs. Such states as Illinois, Oregon, Wisconsin, Florida, Kentucky, and Hawaii require public high school students to take a consumer education course. And hundreds of programs are conducted by all levels of government, as well as by private profit and nonprofit groups. The programs typically cover how to purchase goods and services; key features of credit agreements, contracts, and warranties; and consumer protection laws.

A very good online consumer information source is ConsumerAffairs.com (www.consumeraffairs.com).

MARKETING *and the Web*

The Debate Over Consumer Privacy Online

IBM is one of the many companies seeking to refine its target marketing efforts by online behavioral tracking. Through this technique, marketers seek to learn about consumer interests and preferences so they can specifically target banner ads, E-mails, and sales pitches to them.

Firms such as Vignette (www.vignette.com) and Net Perceptions (www.netperceptions.com) offer collaborative filtering services. Their software compiles information on the behavior of a large sample of consumers, places the data into segments, and then uses the preferences of some members of a segment to predict the buying behavior of other members of the same segment. By using a form of this technique, Net Peceptions has begun to suggest products to consumers that are unrelated to their original purchase, but were preferred by people with similar interests.

Since a big concern related to these practices is the issue of consumer privacy, online retailers have developed TRUSTe (www.truste.org), a self-policing organization. And TRUSTe's chief executive has threatened to pull certification on Web sites collecting data without disclosing this practice. Nonetheless, consumer activists are concerned. According to one analyst, "People might start to wonder whether E-commerce is worth the cost of having your whole life on file." When asked to comment on TRUSTe, the analyst noted: "Its credibility is in the gutter. This is like having McDonald's run the FDA."

A recent research study found that although 94 percent of consumers were concerned about the marketing practices of telemarketers, only 22 percent of them were concerned about online marketing practices. Despite the current high confidence, a consumer outcry could generate government regulation.

As a marketer of a niche product with an appeal to a very limited target market, assess the pros and cons of these filtering services to gather personal characteristics.

Source: Based on material in Michael Grebb, "Behavioral Science," *Business 2.0* (March 2000), pp. 112, 114.

Consumer Safety

There is concern over consumer safety because every year millions of people worldwide are hurt and thousands killed in incidents involving products other than motor vehicles. People also worry about having a safe shopping environment, one free from crime.

The yearly cost of product-related injuries is several billion dollars. Critics believe up to one-quarter of these injuries could be averted if companies made safer, better-designed products.

The Consumer Product Safety Commission, CPSC (www.cpsc.gov), is the federal U.S. agency with major responsibility for product safety. It has jurisdiction over 15,000 types of products—including TVs, bicycles, lamps, appliances, toys, sporting goods, ladders, furniture, housewares, and lawn mowers. It also regulates structural items in homes such as stairs, retaining walls, and electrical wiring. The major products outside the CPSC's authority are food, drugs, cosmetics, tobacco, motor vehicles, tires, firearms, boats, pesticides, and aircraft. Each of these is regulated by other agencies. The Environmental

Protection Agency (www.epa.gov) can recall autos not meeting emission standards; and the Food and Drug Administration (www.fda.gov) oversees food, drugs, cosmetics, medical devices, radiation emissions, and similar items.

The CPSC has extensive powers. It can

1. Develop voluntary standards with industry.
2. Issue and enforce mandatory standards, banning consumer products if no feasible standard would adequately protect the public.
3. Obtain the recall of products or arrange for their repair.
4. Conduct research on potential product hazards.
5. Inform and educate consumers through the media, state and local governments, and private organizations, and by responding to consumer inquiries.

When the CPSC finds a product hazard, it can issue an order for a firm to bring the product into conformity with the applicable safety rule or repair the defect, exchange the product for one meeting safety standards, or refund the purchase price. Firms found breaking safety rules can be fined; and executives can be personally fined and jailed for up to a year. ***Product recall,*** whereby the CPSC asks—orders, if need be—firms to recall and modify (or discontinue) unsafe products, is the primary enforcement tool. The CPSC has initiated many recalls, and a single recall may entail millions of units of a product. It has also banned such items as flammable contact adhesives, easily overturned refuse bins, asbestos-treated products, and Tris (a flame retardant in children's clothing that was linked to cancer).

The Consumer Product Safety Commission has several enforcement tools, including **product recall.**

The U.S. motor vehicle industry, overseen by the National Highway Traffic Safety Administration, NHTSA (www.nhtsa.gov), has had many vehicles recalled for safety reasons. Since 1980, there have been thousands of U.S. recalls (often voluntary actions under NHTSA prodding) involving millions of cars, trucks, and other vehicles (some of which have been recalled more than once). NHTSA even makes its vehicular testing data available at its Web site (www.nhtsa.dot.gov/cars/testing/comply).

Consumers also have the right to sue the maker or seller of an injurious product. A legal action on behalf of many affected consumers is known as a ***class-action suit.*** Each year in the United States, 20,000 consumer suits are filed in federal courts and 90,000 are filed in state courts; these include both individual and class-action suits.[28] Consumer suits are rarer outside the U.S. Yet, this too is changing:

A **class-action suit** *can be filed on behalf of many consumers.*

> Product liability, a concept practically unheard of here 20 years ago, has caught the attention of China's consumers—and they're applying it with a vengeance. For decades, the Chinese had little recourse when they were shocked, burned or dismembered by shoddy state-produced goods. Now they can sue. In the three years after China's consumer-rights laws took effect, liability lawsuits rose to more than half a million annually.[29]

A firm can reduce the negative effects of product recalls, as well as the possibility of costly class-action suits, by communicating properly when it learns a product is unsafe. This means voluntarily telling affected consumers, citing specific models that are unsafe, making fair adjustment offers (repair, replacement, or refund), and quickly and conveniently honoring those offers.[30]

---

[28]Paula Mergenhagen, "Product Liability: Who Sues," *American Demographics* (June 1995), pp. 48–54. See also Greg Winter, "Jury Awards Soar as Lawsuits Decline on Defective Goods," *New York Times on the Web* (January 30, 2001).

[29]Craig S. Smith, "Chinese Discover Product-Liability Suits," *Wall Street Journal* (November 13, 1997), p. B1.

[30]See Barry Berman, "Planning for the Inevitable Product Recall," *Business Horizons*, Vol. 42 (March–April 1999), pp. 69–78.

Consumer Choice

When consumers have several alternatives available to them, they are given the right to choose.

The right to choose means people have several products and brands from which to select. Figure 5-8 illustrates this. As noted earlier, the lack of goods and services (of any brand) is a key consumer concern in less-developed and newly free-market nations where demand often far outstrips the supply for such items as coffee, bread, jeans, shoes, cosmetics, and fresh meat.

The federal governments in many industrialized countries have taken various actions to enhance the already extensive consumer choices there:

- Patent rights have time bounds; then, all firms can use the patents.
- Noncompetitive business practices, like price fixing, are banned.
- Government agencies review proposed company mergers; in some cases, they have stopped mergers if they felt industry competition would be lessened.
- Restrictions requiring franchisees to purchase all products from their franchisers have been reduced.
- The media are monitored to ensure that ad space or time is available to both small and large firms.
- Imports are allowed to compete with domestic-made items.
- Various service industries have been deregulated to foster price competition and encourage new firms to enter the marketplace.

In the United States and many other highly industrialized nations, consumer choice for some product categories is so extensive that some experts wonder if there are too many options. For instance, according to a survey of 1,000 Western European consumers, "marketers are trying so hard to innovate that they are confusing consumers with too many new products and services, with one-third of consumers saying they are offered too much choice in goods and services. Only 10 percent of consumers said they had too little choice. The survey also revealed that there is a high level of confusion and cynicism among consumers about new products and how they are marketed. Some 91 percent of respondents agreed that manufacturers and service providers exaggerate the benefits and advantages of new products."[31]

Consumers' Right to Be Heard

There are various federal, state, and local agencies involved with consumers.

The right to be heard means people should be able to voice their opinions (sometimes as complaints) to business, government, and other parties. This gives consumers input into the decisions affecting them. To date, no overall U.S. consumer agency exists to represent

FIGURE 5-8

Alberston's: Facilitating the Consumer's Right to Choose

Source: Reprinted by permission of PricewaterhouseCoopers.

[31]Julia Day, "Consumers Spoilt for Choice," *Marketing Week* (December 16, 1999), pp. 26–27.

consumer interests, although several federal agencies regulate various business practices relating to consumers. Their addresses and phone numbers, as well as those of trade associations, are listed in the *Consumer's Action Handbook* from the Federal Consumer Information Center (www.pueblo.gsa.gov/crh/respref.htm). Most states and major cities have their own consumer affairs offices, as do many corporations. Each encourages consumer input.

There are also consumer groups representing the general public or specific consumer segments. They publicize consumer opinions and complaints, speak at government and industry hearings, and otherwise generate consumer input into the decision processes of government and industry. Because a single consumer rarely has a significant impact, consumer groups frequently become the individual's voice.

5-4b The Responses of Business to Consumer Issues

Over the last 40 years, in many nations, the business community has greatly increased its acceptance of the legitimacy and importance of consumer rights; many firms now have real commitments to address consumer issues in a positive manner. Nonetheless, a number of companies have raised reasonable questions about consumerism's impact on them. They particularly wonder why there isn't a *business bill of rights* to parallel the consumer's. Here are some of the questions that businesspeople raise:

Firms have become much more responsive to consumers, yet questions remain about the effects of consumerism on firms.

• Why do different states, municipalities, and nations have different laws regarding business practices? How can a national or global company be expected to comply with each of these laws?

• Don't some government rules cause unnecessary costs and time delays in new-product introductions that outweigh the benefits of these rules?

• Is it the job of business to ensure that consumers obey laws (such as not littering) and use products properly (such as wearing seat belts)?

• Isn't business self-regulation preferred over government regulation?

• Are multimillion-dollar jury awards to consumers getting out of hand?

Selected responses by manufacturers, retailers, and trade associations are discussed next.

Manufacturers

Numerous manufacturers have long-standing programs to handle consumer issues. In 1961, Maytag (www.maytag.com) introduced Red Carpet Service to improve its appliance repair service. Zenith (www.zenith.com) set up its customer relations department in 1968; Motorola (www.motorola.com) created an Office of Consumer Affairs in 1970; and RCA (www.rca.com) opened a consumer affairs office at the corporate level in 1972.

General Electric runs a GE Answer Center (www.geappliances.com/geac), which handles consumer phone inquiries 24 hours a day, 7 days a week. It processes millions of calls yearly—questions from potential consumers and do-it-yourselfers, complaints from unhappy customers, and suggestions as to improvements. At the Answer Center, GE can satisfy current customers and attract potential ones, gather data about demographics, and gain insights about its marketing strategy and possible new products.

In the area of product recalls, many firms are now doing better. For instance, LifeScan (www.lifescan.com), a Johnson & Johnson company, makes meters that diabetics use to monitor sugar levels. When one meter was found to be defective, LifeScan voluntarily recalled its entire product line and notified 600,000 customers within 24 hours. Because of how it handled the recall, LifeScan's market share has risen since that incident.

Many manufacturers have introduced new products or reformulated existing ones to better satisfy consumer concerns about a clean and safe environment for them and their children. One such firm is Clorox. See Figure 5-9.

Despite manufacturers' interest in consumer issues, there are still times when their performance could be better: "Many times, product design is severely deficient in the area of human interface, with insufficient attention paid to how people use—and learn to use—the things in their lives. PCs. Phone systems. Toys requiring assembly. Upscale autos. Even light switches. They all can cause havoc for a person who doesn't read what's in an accompanying 500-page manual, written in 'engineerese.'"[32]

Retailers

Various retailers have expressed a positive concern about consumer issues, some for several decades. J.C. Penney (www.jcpenney.com) first stated its consumer philosophy in 1913, and Macy's (www.macys.com) formed a Bureau of Standards to test merchandise in 1927. In the 1970s, the Giant Food (www.giantfood.com) supermarket chain devised its own consumer bill of rights (paralleling the one articulated by President Kennedy):

[32]Howard Schlossberg, "Design Disability," *Marketing Management* (Spring 1992), p. 6.

- Right to safety—no phosphates, certain pesticides removed, toys age labeled.
- Right to be informed—better labeling, readable dating of perishable items, and nutritional labeling.
- Right to choose—continued sale of cigarettes and food with additives.
- Right to be heard—consumer group meetings, in-house consumer advocate.
- Right to redress—money-back guarantee on all products.
- Right to service—availability of store services and employee attentiveness.

For more than a decade, Wal-Mart (www.walmart.com) has had in-store signs to inform consumers about environmentally safe products. It has also run newspaper ads encouraging suppliers to make more environmentally sound products. At 7-Eleven Japan (www.sej.co.jp), three times a week, top executives sample foods sold at the chain.

Retailers and consumer groups have opposing views involving **item price removal,** whereby prices are marked only on shelves or aisle signs and not on individual items. Numerous retailers, particularly supermarkets, want item price removal since electronic checkouts let them computer-scan prices through codes on packages. They say this reduces labor costs and that these reductions are passed on to consumers. Consumer groups believe the practice is deceptive and will make it harder for them to guard against misrings. Item price removal is banned in a number of states and local communities. Giant Food is a leading advocate of item price removal; it passes cost savings along to consumers.

With **item price removal,** *prices are displayed only on shelves or signs.*

Trade Associations

Trade associations represent groups of individual firms. Many have been quite responsive to consumer issues through such actions as coordinating and distributing safety-related research findings, setting up consumer education programs, planning product standards, and handling complaints.

The Major Appliance Consumer Action Program (MACAP) is an educational and complaint-handling program of the Association of Home Appliance Manufacturers (www.aham.org). The Bank Marketing Association (www.bmanet.org) has a Financial Advertising Code of Ethics (FACE) for members. The Direct Marketing Association (www.the-dma.org) sets industry guidelines and has a consumer action phone line. The National Retail Federation (www.nrf.com) has a Consumer Affairs Committee and offers information to the public. The Alliance Against Fraud in Telemarketing & Electronic Commerce (www.fraud.org/aaft/aaftinfo.htm) is dedicated to reducing fraudulent practices and consists of consumer groups, trade associations, labor unions, phone companies, federal and state agencies, and telemarketers.

The Better Business Bureau, BBB (www.bbb.com), is the largest and broadest business-run U.S. trade association involved with consumer issues. It publishes educational materials, handles complaints, supervises arbitration panels, makes available a Consumer Affairs Audit, outlines ethical behavior, publicizes unsatisfactory practices and the firms involved, and has nationwide offices. It supports self-regulation as a substitute to government regulation. Nationwide, the BBB handles hundreds of thousands of arbitration cases each year. These cases—many involving autos—are decided by impartial arbitrators. Rulings are usually binding on participating firms but not on consumers.

Trade associations may vigorously oppose potential government rules. For example, the Tobacco Institute (funded by tobacco firms) lobbied against further restrictions on tobacco sales, promotion, distribution, and use. Now, due to a civil legal settlement, its Web site (www.tobaccoinstitute.com) disseminates information. It "is designed to provide the public with access to documents produced by the Tobacco Institute in Attorney General reimbursement lawsuits and certain other specified civil actions, and to documents produced after October 23, 1998 through June 30, 2010 in smoking and health actions, and includes certain enhancements, all as provided for by paragraph IV of the Attorneys General Master Settlement Agreement (MSA)."

5-4c The Current Role of Consumerism

During the 1980s, there was much less U.S. federal government activity on consumer-related issues than during the 1960s and 1970s due to the quality of self-regulation, consumerism's success, increased conservatism by Congress and the American people, and the importance of other issues.

By 1980, many firms had become more responsive to consumer issues. Thus, there was less pressure for government or consumer groups to intervene. There was also a move to industry deregulation as a way of increasing competition, encouraging innovations, and stimulating lower prices. Consumerism activity was also less needed because of the successes of past actions. On all levels, government protection for consumers had improved dramatically since the early 1960s; and class-action suits won big settlements from firms, making it clear that unsafe practices were financially costly. Consumer groups and independent media publicized poor practices, so firms knew such activities would not go unnoticed. In the 1980s, many members of Congress and sectors of the American public became more conservative about the role of government in regulating business. They felt government had become too big, impeded business practices, and caused unneeded costs; thus, some government agency functions were limited and budgets cut. Consumerism issues were not as important as other factors, including unemployment, the rate of inflation, industrial productivity, and the negative international balance of trade.

After a decade of a "hands-off" approach, a growing number of government leaders, consumer activists, and business leaders in the United States felt that the balance between business and consumer rights had tipped a little too much in favor of business. Hence, there is now a somewhat more aggressive federal government posture toward consumer-related issues than in the 1980s; and states and localities are continuing to be heavily involved.

Here are some indications of the enhanced role of the U.S. government:

Federal U.S. consumerism efforts have picked up, after a relative lull in the 1980s.

- The U.S. Justice Department has vigorously pursued legal action against Microsoft, charging that the software giant has engaged in a number of anticompetitive actions that are harmful to consumers. To date, the government and Microsoft have both won key points in their court battles.

- In March 2000, the Federal Trade Commission and the Federal Communications Commission issued a joint policy statement (www.ftc.gov/opa/2000/03/ld.htm) to protect consumers from unfair and deceptive advertising of long-distance telephone services, including "10-10" numbers. The statement offered guidance to carriers to ensure that their advertising is truthful, complete, and nonmisleading.

- The FTC promotes its Bureau of Consumer Protection at its Web site (www.ftc.gov/bcp/bcp.htm).

- The Securities and Exchange Commission has a relatively new Office of Internet Enforcement, (OIE) (www.sec.gov/divisions/enforce/internetenforce.htm), that administers the Enforcement Division's Internet program. While "the Internet has brought significant benefits to investors—most notably, enhanced access to information and lower costs to execute trades, at the same time, unfortunately, the Internet has opened new avenues for fraud artists to attempt to swindle the investing public. To combat this online fraud, OIE identifies areas of surveillance, formulates investigative procedures, provides strategic and legal guidance to enforcement staff nationwide, conducts Internet investigations and prosecutions (a task it shares with the entire enforcement staff), performs training for Commission staff and outside agencies, and serves as a resource on Internet matters for the entire Commission."

Several states have also increased their activities. For example,

While Congress considers proposals for America's first federal rules on E-mail marketing, marketers must continue to maneuver within a confusing patchwork of state laws. Currently, 16 states have laws intended to reduce the volume of unsolicited computer messages (known as spam) and the marketing scams that rely on spam. The details of the laws and their attendant penalties (up to $100 per E-mail and $25,000 per day) differ widely from state to state, but experts note that most states' anti-spam laws do not deal with the specific content of an E-mail; fraudulent marketing is already illegal. The laws focus on whether E-mail is unsolicited, and reputable clients marketing reputable products can still run afoul of state laws if consumers did not choose to be on their mailing lists.[33]

In many nations outside the United States, government, industry, and consumer groups are stepping up efforts relating to consumer rights—as past efforts have often been lacking in foreign markets. Some nations are making real progress, while others have a long way to go. No other nation has gone through as many stages or passed as many laws to protect consumer rights as the United States. The worldwide challenge will be for government, business, and consumer groups to work together so the socioecological view of marketing, ethical behavior, consumer rights, and company rights are in balance.

WEB SITES YOU CAN USE

The Federal Consumer Information Center has made the complete 148-page **2001 Consumer Information Handbook** available online (www.pueblo.gsa.gov/crh/respref.htm). This handbook contains a lot of very useful consumer information, including the names, addresses, phone numbers, Web addresses, and E-mail addresses for thousands of consumer organizations, Better Business Bureaus, corporations, trade associations, state and local consumer protection offices, military consumer offices, and federal agencies.

SUMMARY

1. *To consider the impact of marketing on society* Marketing actions have the potential for both positive and negative consequences regarding such areas as the quality of life and consumer expectations. Various studies have shown that people's perceptions of marketing are mixed. Firms need to recognize that many dissatisfied consumers do not complain; they simply do not rebuy offending products.

2. *To examine social responsibility and weigh its benefits and costs* Social responsibility involves a concern for the consequences of a person's or firm's acts as they might affect the interests of others. It encompasses the socioecological view of marketing, which looks at all the stages of a product's life and includes both consumers and nonconsumers. Social responsibility can pose dilemmas when popular goods and services have potential adverse effects on consumer or societal well-being.

Consumers and marketing practices have led to some resource shortages. To stem that depletion, cooperative efforts among business, stockholders, government, employees, the public, consumers, and others are needed. Garbage dumps and landfills, discarded containers, and abandoned autos are marring the landscape. Thus, many areas have laws to rectify the situation. Dangerous pollutants

need to be removed and safe alternatives found to replace them; environmental pollution will be an issue for the foreseeable future. Planned obsolescence is a heavily criticized practice that encourages material wearout, style changes, and functional product changes. Marketers say it responds to consumer demand; critics say it increases resource shortages, is wasteful, and adds to pollution.

Socially responsible actions have such benefits as worker and public health, cleaner air, and a more efficient use of resources. They also have many costs, such as the unequal distribution of benefits, dollar expenditures, and conservative new-product planning. Benefits and costs need to be weighed. Green marketing will continue gaining popularity.

3. *To look into the role of ethics in marketing* Ethical behavior, based on honest and proper conduct, comes into play when people decide whether given actions are ethical or unethical and when they choose how to act. Egoism, utilitarianism, duty-based, and virtue ethics theories help explain behavior. Marketing ethics can be divided into two categories: process-related and product-related.

Ethics may be viewed from four vantage points: a business perspective, a consumer perspective, an international perspective, and teachability. A major difficulty of ethics in business relates to

[33]Steve Jarvis, "Caution Is Name of Spam-fighting Game," *Marketing News* (January 29, 2001), p 7.

setting boundaries for deciding what is ethical. For high ethical standards to be kept, both consumers and firms must engage in proper behavior. For various reasons, ethical standards in a global setting are especially complex. There has been a lot of debate as to whether ethics can be taught.

4. *To explore consumerism and describe the consumer bill of rights* Consumerism deals with the relations of firms and their consumers. It comprises the acts of government, business, and independent organizations that are designed to protect people from practices that infringe upon their rights as consumers.

U.S. consumerism has seen five eras: early 1900s, 1930s to 1950s, 1960s to 1980, 1980s, and 1990 to now. The third was the most important and began with President Kennedy's announcement of a consumer bill of rights—to information, to safety, to choice, and to be heard. The interest now is in balancing consumer and business rights—in the United States, as well as in other countries.

The right to be informed includes consumer protection against fraudulent, deceitful, grossly misleading, or incomplete information, advertising, labeling, pricing, packaging, or other practices. Consumer education involves teaching people to spend their money wisely.

The concern over the right to safety arises from the large numbers of people who are injured or killed in product-related accidents. The U.S. Consumer Product Safety Commission has the power to order recalls or modifications for a wide range of products; other agencies oversee such products as autos and pharmaceuticals.

The right to choose means consumers should have several products and brands from which to select. In the U.S., some observers wonder if there is too much choice.

The right to be heard means consumers should be able to voice their opinions to business, government, and other parties. Several government agencies and consumer groups provide this voice.

5. *To discuss the responses of manufacturers, retailers, and trade associations to consumerism and study the current role of consumerism* Many firms and associations are reacting well to consumer issues. A small number intentionally or unintentionally pursue unfair, misleading, or dangerous acts.

The decade of the 1990s witnessed more activism than in the 1980s and less than in the 1960s and 1970s. In the new millennium, government, business, and consumers will continue working together to resolve consumer issues.

KEY TERMS

social responsibility (p. 125)
socioecological view of marketing (p. 126)
planned obsolescence (p. 132)
green marketing (p. 133)
ethical behavior (p. 134)

process-related ethical issues (p. 135)
product-related ethical issues (p. 135)
cause-related marketing (p. 137)
consumerism (p. 141)
consumer bill of rights (p. 142)

warranty (p. 143)
product recall (p. 145)
class-action suit (p. 145)
item price removal (p. 149)

REVIEW QUESTIONS

1. Define the term *social responsibility*. What are the implications for marketers?
2. Describe the pros and cons of planned obsolescence as a marketing practice.
3. What is ethical behavior? Distinguish among the egoism, utilitarianism, duty-based, and virtue ethics theories.

4. Why is cause-related marketing a controversial practice?
5. Why are ethical standards of conduct particularly complex for international marketers?
6. How does consumerism differ from social responsibility?
7. Explain the consumer bill of rights.
8. Describe the current role of consumerism.

DISCUSSION QUESTIONS

1. From a company's perspective, why is hidden consumer dissatisfaction a particular problem? How would you go about making dissatisfaction less hidden?
2. Present a seven-point ethics guide for operating internationally.

3. How would you teach marketing ethics to a class of sophomore business majors? What topics would you discuss? Why?
4. As an executive for a leading toy manufacturer, how would you implement a product recall if you discover that one of your toys could easily be swallowed by children under age 3?

WEB EXERCISE

Ben & Jerry's, the specialty ice cream firm, is widely admired for its socially responsible practices. Go to these specific parts of its Web site: "Statement of Mission" (www.benjerry.com/mission.html), "Consumer Assistance" (www.benjerry.com/ca), and "Ben & Jerry's Foundation" (www.benjerry.com/foundation). Then, describe why the firm is rated so highly. What could other companies learn from Ben & Jerry's?

6

Global Aspects of Marketing

Chapter Objectives

1 To define domestic, international, and global marketing

2 To explain why international marketing takes place and study its scope

3 To explore the cultural, economic, political and legal, and technological environments facing international marketers

4 To analyze the stages in the development of an international marketing strategy

A widely publicized myth is that the U.S. economy is now totally service-based, due to the significant decline in U.S. manufacturing. In reality, manufacturing output is now at the highest level in U.S. history; and its share of the U.S. Gross Domestic product has held steady since 1977 at 17.1 percent.

Many people falsely attribute the decline in manufacturing to cutbacks in defense and to industrial restructuring in New England and Mid-Atlantic states. While both of these regions have lost thousands of manufacturing jobs, many manufacturing jobs were simply relocated to the Southeast.

Several other key economic measures confirm the robustness of the U.S. manufacturing sector. Between 1992 and 1999, the Federal Reserve Board's index of manufacturing output rose by 42 percent. Durable goods manufacturing was up by 73 percent, while the overall U.S. economy grew by 29 percent.

The United States accounts for about one of every eight dollars' worth of manufactured products in world trade. The value of goods produced by America's 380,000 manufacturing companies is also 50 percent more than the output in Japan, and 33 percent more than the combined manufacturing output of France, Germany, and Great Britain. Furthermore, 80 percent of U.S. exports are manufactured goods.

Several U.S. industries that some experts once felt in poor health, such as textiles and apparel, are now in excellent shape. For example, the U.S. exports $8 billion worth of apparel annually. Of that amount, $6.2 billion is pieces cut in the United States and then sent to the Caribbean and Mexico to be sewn. Skilled jobs, like pattern making and cutting, have been kept in the United States, with less-skilled jobs performed in other countries. The U.S. steel industry has also seen increased output due to the conversion to highly efficient plants. In 1982, it took more than 10 person-hours to make a ton of steel; newer mini-mills can perform this task in less than one hour.

According to one economist, "We are a nation that has specialized in high-skilled, higher-end products. So we are an exporter of civilian aircraft, space technology, and the like. And we will continue to expand those industries as we contract the lower-skilled ones."[1]

In this chapter, we will explore the environment facing international marketers, including data on U.S. imports and exports, and see how to develop an international marketing strategy.

6-1 OVERVIEW

International transactions generate trillions of dollars in yearly global sales. And virtually every nation engages in significant international business, whether it be the United States with $2.5 trillion in yearly exports and imports of goods and services, Namibia (in

Due to its impact, international marketing concepts should be understood by all types of firms.

[1]Philip Siekman, "The Big Myth About U.S. Manufacturing," *Fortune* (October 2, 2000), pp. 244BB–244NN.

southern Africa) with $3 billion in exports and imports, or Tonga (in the South Pacific) with $100 million in exports and imports. In many areas, the marketplace has a wide variety of foreign firms competing with domestic ones.

Whether a firm is small or large, operates solely in its home nation or both domestically and abroad, markets goods or services, and is profit- or nonprofit-driven, it needs to grasp key international marketing concepts and to devise a proper strategy. This means having a broadened marketing perspective. Thus,

> The idea that global business is the exclusive purview of large corporations must change. Too many smaller companies are missing opportunities for growth through exports. Promoting goods and services in larger international markets often results in profitable sales for those with the motivation, competency, and willingness to make use of help available from state and federal agencies. Despite increasing overseas opportunities, some businesses are not interested in exporting because they are comfortable in the domestic economy. This situation is dangerous because the global economy—with its accelerating pace of change and ever-newer information technology—brings competition from unexpected places. Small U.S. firms have a cultural disadvantage relative to most equivalent-sized firms elsewhere in the world. The immense size of the U.S. market has heretofore provided sufficient opportunity, with little need to learn other languages, other customs, or other ways of doing business. By contrast, European and Asian businesses have acquired the skills, networks, and support needed in the global marketplace, and have been involved in international business for a long time."[2]

By definition, **domestic marketing** encompasses a firm's efforts in its home country. **International marketing** involves marketing goods and services outside a firm's home country, whether in one or several markets. **Global marketing** is an advanced form of international marketing in which a firm addresses global customers, markets, and competition. It is used by both multinational and global firms.

A company may act domestically, internationally, or both; efforts vary widely. Here is the range of options that may be pursued:

- A **domestic firm** restricts its efforts to the home market. The firm believes its base market is both large enough and responsive enough to meet its sales and profit goals.

- An **exporting firm** is just embarking on sales expansion beyond the home borders. It recognizes that the home market is no longer adequate for it fully to meet revenue and profit goals. A firm typically uses exporting when it seeks to sell its traditional products in foreign markets, often via distribution and sales intermediaries. A relatively low percentage of business is outside the domestic market.

- An **international firm** goes beyond just exporting existing products. It makes modifications in those items for foreign markets or introduces new products there; the firm knows it must more aggressively cultivate foreign markets. There remains enough strength in the firm's domestic market for that market to remain the dominant one for the company.

- A **multinational firm** is a worldwide player. Although corporate headquarters are in the home nation, the domestic market often accounts for 50 percent or less of sales and profits—and the firm operates in dozens of nations or more. The business scope and opportunity search are broad geographically. Many leading U.S. players, like Boeing (www.boeing.com), Citicorp (www.citigroup.com), and McDonald's (www.mcdonalds.com), fall into this category; they market items around the world, but have a distinctly American business culture. See Figure 6-1.

- A **global firm** is also a worldwide player. Yet, because its domestic sales are low, it places even more reliance on foreign transactions. It has the greatest geographic business scope. Such firms have been more apt to emerge in smaller nations, where the firms have historically needed foreign markets to survive (in contrast to U.S. firms). The quintes-

Domestic marketing involves the home nation, **international marketing** *embraces foreign activities, and* **global marketing** *has a worldwide focus.*

A firm may be **domestic, exporting, international, multinational,** *or* **global.**

---

[2]Nadar H. Shooshtari and Jack Reece, "Global Business and the Smaller Company," *Montana Business Quarterly* (Summer 2000), p. 17.

FIGURE 6-1

McDonald's: A U.S.-Based Multinational Firm

About one-half of McDonald's sales are from outlets outside the United States. While it has restaurants in 120 different nations (such as the Shanghai unit shown here), it has a distinctly American corporate culture and image.

Source: Reprinted by permission of PricewaterhouseCoopers.

FIGURE 6-2

Ikea: A Truly Global Firm

Because of the small size of its domestic market (Sweden has a population of just 9 million), Ikea derives more than 90 percent of its sales from outside of Sweden. Therefore, it must think globally and seek expansion from foreign markets.

Source: Reprinted by permission of PricewaterhouseCoopers.

sential global firm is Sweden's Ikea furniture store chain (www.ikea.com/default.asp), which derives only 8 percent of total sales from its Swedish customers. It has stores in Europe, North America, Asia, Australia, and the Middle East, and purchases merchandise from suppliers in more than 50 nations. See Figure 6-2.

Now that we are in the 21st century, it is clear that more domestic firms will need to become exporters and then international in orientation. And multinational firms will need to become more global, thereby acting boundaryless and not dominated by a home-country-based corporate culture.

This chapter looks at why international marketing occurs, its scope, its environment, and the components of an international marketing strategy.

6-2 WHY INTERNATIONAL MARKETING TAKES PLACE

There are several reasons why countries and individual firms are engaging in greater international marketing efforts than ever before.[3] These are shown in Figure 6-3 and are discussed next.

Countries trade items in which they have a **comparative advantage.**

According to the concept of **comparative advantage,** each country has distinct strengths and weaknesses based on its natural resources, climate, technology, labor costs, and other factors. Therefore, nations can benefit by exporting the goods and services with which they have relative advantages and importing the ones with which they have relative disadvantages. Comparative advantages may generally be grouped into two categories: (a) those related to the physical environment of a country (such as natural resources and climate) and (b) those related to the socioeconomic development of a country (such as technological advances or low labor costs). Among the best U.S. comparative advantages are its agricultural productivity, the level of technological prowess, and service industry expertise.

The domestic economy and demographics affect international efforts.

Economic and demographic trends vary by country. A firm in a nation with weak domestic conditions (like high inflation) and/or a small or stagnant population base can stabilize or increase sales by marketing products in more favorable foreign markets. The U.S. market is attractive due to rather low inflation and unemployment rates, as well as the relative affluence. Developing and less-developed nations are potentially lucrative markets due to their population growth; more than 90 percent of world growth is there. Thus, Heinz (www.heinz.com) now targets developing and less-developed nations due to their population growth and nutrition needs. Its brands are established in Africa, China, and the Pacific Rim.

Home competition may lead to international efforts.

Competition in a firm's domestic market may become intense and lead to its expanding internationally, as these examples show:

- The U.S. optical-products marketplace is highly competitive. So, U.S.-based Bausch & Lomb (www.bausch.com) has increased its activities in regions with growth opportunities. Its non-U.S. revenues represent 47 percent of the firm's total; and it markets products in more than 100 nations.

- In Europe, Germany's Henkel (www.henkel.com) is a leading maker of detergents, cleansers, and personal-care items, as well as industrial chemicals. Yet, it faces intense European competition from Dutch-British Unilever (www.unilever.com) and America's Procter & Gamble (www.pg.com), among others. So, it has been pumping up efforts in Asia and Africa.

FIGURE 6-3
Why International Marketing Occurs

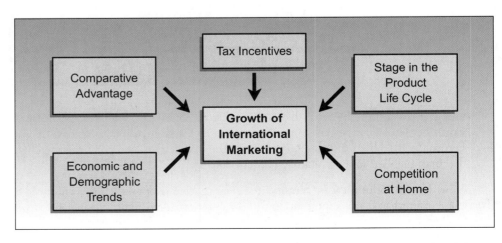

[3] See Jagdish N. Sheth, "From International to Integrated Marketing," *Journal of Business Research*, Vol. 51 (January 2001), pp. 5–9; and C. Samuel Craig and Susan P. Douglas, "Configural Advantage in Global Markets," *Journal of International Marketing*, Vol. 8 (Number 1, 2000), pp. 6–26.

Because products are often in different stages of their life cycles in different nations, exporting may be a way to prolong the cycles. For instance, the U.S. market for tobacco products has been falling, for health and social reasons. To stimulate cigarette sales, Philip Morris (www.pmintl.com) and R.J. Reynolds (www.rjrt.com) have turned more to foreign sales. The two firms have heightened their efforts in Eastern Europe—where cigarette smoking is popular and shortages of domestic tobacco products occur. International marketing can also be used to dispose of discontinued goods, seconds, and manufacturer remakes (products that have been repaired). These items can be sold abroad without spoiling the domestic market for full-price, first-quality items. However, firms must think carefully about selling unsafe products in foreign markets, a practice that can lead to ill will on the part of the governments there.

International marketing may extend the product life cycle or dispose of discontinued items.

There may be tax advantages with international marketing. Some countries entice new business from foreign firms by offering tax incentives in the form of low property, import, and income taxes for an initial period. In addition, multinational firms may adjust revenue reports so their largest profits are recorded in nations with the lowest tax rates.

6-3 THE SCOPE OF INTERNATIONAL MARKETING[4]

The world's leading export countries are the United States, Germany, Japan, France, and Great Britain. Together, they account for $3 trillion annually in goods and services exports (out of the more than $7 trillion in yearly world exports). In 2000, U.S. merchandise exports were $765 billion, an amount equaling 7.5 to 8 percent of the U.S. Gross Domestic Product and 12.5 percent of world merchandise exports. Services accounted for $305 billion in U.S. exports. Among the leading U.S. exports are capital goods, industrial supplies and materials, food grains, medical equipment, and scientific instruments, and such services as tourism, entertainment, engineering, accounting, insurance, and consulting. Although 70 percent of U.S. foreign business revenues are generated by large firms, 210,000 U.S. firms with less than 20 employees engage in some level of international marketing.

The United States is both the world's largest goods and services exporter and importer.

The United States is also the world's largest importer, followed by Germany, Japan, Great Britain, and France. In 2000, U.S. merchandise imports were about $1.215 trillion—one-sixth of total world merchandise imports. Service imports were an additional $225 billion. Leading U.S. imports are petroleum, motor vehicles, raw materials, and clothing.

Due to the high level of imports in 2000, the United States had a merchandise **trade deficit**—the amount by which the value of imports exceeds the value of exports—of $450 billion. This was far and away the greatest merchandise deficit in the world and set a U.S. record. On the other hand, U.S. services stayed strong, with a service **trade surplus**—the amount by which the value of exports exceeds the value of imports—of $80 billion in 2000. By a large amount, this was the greatest service surplus of any nation.

*The U.S. has had large merchandise **trade deficits** and large service **trade surpluses**.*

The U.S. merchandise trade deficit is due to a variety of factors:

- The attractive nature of the U.S. market. Per-capita consumption is high for most goods and services.

- The slow-growth economies in a number of other countries depressing consumer purchases there.

- Increased competition in foreign markets.

- U.S. dependence on foreign natural resources.

[4]The data cited in this section are from *U.S. Trade in Perspective* (Washington, D.C.: U.S. Department of Commerce, International Trade Administration, January 2001); *International Trade Statistics 2000* (France: World Trade Organization, 2000); Joseph Burns, "Tapping Overseas Markets Takes Expertise in Exporting," *Los Angeles Business Journal* (September 18, 2000), p. 45; and Helene Cooper, "Trade Deficit Shrinks to $32.99 Billion as Appetite for Imports May Be Easing," *Wall Street Journal* (February 22, 2001), p. A4.

- High U.S. labor costs.
- Trade restrictions in foreign markets.
- U.S. firms virtually exiting such markets as televisions and VCRs.
- Making products in the United States with imported parts and materials.
- The complacency of some U.S. firms in adapting their strategies to the needs of foreign markets.
- The rather poor image of U.S. products in the eyes of many Americans.
- The emphasis of many U.S. firms on profits over market share. In contrast, Japanese firms try to keep prices stable to maximize market share—even if they must reduce profit margins to do so.

Because U.S. merchandise trade deficits have been so high, American firms are improving their product quality, focusing on market niches, becoming more efficient, building overseas facilities, and engaging in other tactics to improve competitiveness. Some have called for tighter import controls and more access to restricted foreign markets; one outcome of their efforts is the Omnibus Trade & Competitiveness Act that requires the President to press for open foreign markets. The U.S. government has also negotiated with foreign governments to help matters. For example, Japan has agreed to amend some practices to improve its trade balance with the United States. Still, the United States has a trade deficit of more than $80 billion a year with Japan.

Despite the trade deficit, the United States is the dominant force globally. As one observer noted: "The deficit is not a product of declining U.S. exports, but of rising imports. American exports in 2000 jumped by 11.7 percent to top the $1 trillion mark for the first time in U.S. history—proof that foreign nations are not shutting their doors to U.S. goods. Imports, however, rose even more. The gap between exports and imports shows that Americans have more money to buy foreign goods than foreign consumers have to buy American goods—hardly cause for gloom and doom."[5]

6-4 THE ENVIRONMENT OF INTERNATIONAL MARKETING

Even though the marketing principles described in this book are applicable to international marketing strategies, there are often major environmental differences between domestic and foreign markets—and marketing practices may have to be adapted accordingly. Each market should be studied separately. Only then can a firm decide how much of its domestic marketing strategy can be used in foreign markets and what elements should be modified.

To gain insights about the global marketplace, useful resources such as these may be consulted:

- U.S. International Trade Administration (www.ita.doc.gov, 1-800-USA-TRADE).
- U.S. Census Bureau's International Programs Center (http://www.census.gov/ipc/www).
- World Trade Organization's "Resources" Web site (http://www.wto.org/english/res_e/res_e.htm).
- International Monetary Fund's "World Economic Outlook Data Base" (www.imf.org/external/map.htm).

The major cultural, economic, political and legal, and technological environments facing international marketers are discussed next. See Figure 6-4.

[5]"Trade Deficit's Real Meaning," *Detroit News* (February 22, 2001), p. 14.

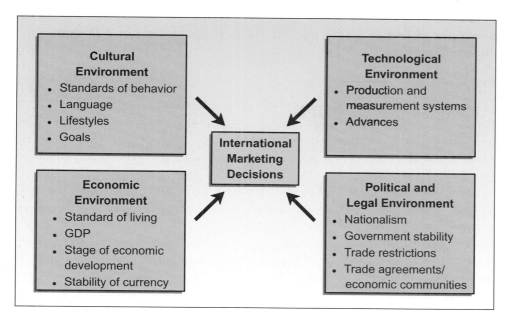

FIGURE 6-4
**The Environment Facing
International Marketers**

6-4a The Cultural Environment

International marketers need to be aware of each foreign market's cultural environment. A *culture* consists of a group of people sharing a distinctive heritage. It teaches behavior standards, language, lifestyles, and goals; is passed down from one generation to another; and is not easily changed. Almost every country has a different culture; continental differences exist as well. A firm unfamiliar with or insensitive to a foreign culture may try to market goods or services that are unacceptable to that culture. For example, beef and unisex products are rejected by some cultures.

Table 6-1 shows the errors a firm engaged in international marketing could commit due to a lack of awareness about foreign cultures. Sometimes, the firm is at fault since it operates out of a domestic home office and gets little local input. Other times, such as marketing in less-developed nations, information may be limited because a low level of population data exist and mail and phone service are poor. In either case, research—to determine hidden meanings, the ease of pronunciation of brand names and slogans, the rate of product consumption, and reasons for purchases and nonpurchases—may not be fully effective.

Cultural awareness can be improved by employing foreign personnel in key positions, hiring experienced marketing research specialists, locating offices in each country of operations, studying cultural differences, and responding to cultural changes. Table 6-2 shows several cultural opportunities.

Consider this critique regarding the way many Western firms act when dealing with foreign cultures:

> It is essential for people in business to understand cultural differences. Such understanding is not a matter of noting the "different ways" that "those" people have; it is about rooting out the reasons behind these differences. Yet, Westerners often fail to understand how culture affects the enterprise. Many Asians have mastered the comprehension of Western culture and have been highly successful in adapting to it; they have built on the knowledge conveyed to them by a variety of sources. In contrast, Westerners seldom have the patience to master an Asian language, let alone one of its cultures. Complex cultural environments require fluency not only in words, but more importantly in understanding what is not said—and this takes time, patience, and dedication. Westerners may argue that time is money and they cannot afford to learn everything it takes before even discussing a deal. In the long term, however, knowledge will pay off.[6]

*Inadequate information about foreign **cultures** is a common cause of errors.*

[6]Leo Dana, "Culture Is of the Essence in Asia," *Financial Times* (November 28, 2000), p.12.

Illustrations of Errors in International Marketing Because of a Lack of Cultural Awareness

In the Czech Republic, portable phones did poorly when first introduced because they were perceived as walkie-talkies.

Japanese cars had engine trouble in China, where drivers turn off their motors when stopped at red lights. Inasmuch as the air-conditioning in these cars kept going with the motors off, the engines malfunctioned.

At the Moscow Pizza Hut, consumers did not purchase the Moscva Seafood pizza, with sardines and salmon. "Russians have this thing. If its their own, it must be bad."

Pepsodent failed in Southeast Asia when it promised white teeth to a culture where black or yellow teeth are symbols of prestige.

In Quebec, a canned-fish manufacturer promoted a product by showing a woman dressed in shorts, golfing with her husband, and planning to serve canned fish for dinner. These activities violated cultural norms.

Maxwell House advertised itself as the "great American coffee" in Germany, although Germans have little respect for American coffee.

In Mexico, a U.S. airline meant to advertise that passengers could sit in comfortable leather seats; but the phrase used in its Spanish translation ("sentando en cuero") meant "sit naked."

African men were upset by a commercial for men's deodorant that showed a happy male being chased by women. They thought the deodorant would make them weak and overrun by women.

Source: Compiled by the authors from various publications.

TABLE 6-2

Illustrations of Cultural Opportunities for International Marketers

Globally, the greatest growth in ready-to-eat cereal sales is in Latin America, where there is new interest in convenience foods.

After one year of employment, in most European countries, people receive 20 to 25 days of vacation (compared to 10 days for Canadians and Americans). This means an emphasis on travel, summer homes, and leisure wear.

Japanese consumers are attracted by high-tech vending machines—such as those that play music, talk, dispense free products at random, and use splashy rotating signs.

Worldwide, consumers want the "American look" provided by Levi's jeans.

At Domino's outlets in Australia, the favorite pizzas are those with prawns and pineapple.

In China, the most popular color is red—indicating happiness. Black elicits a positive response because it denotes power and trustworthiness.

French Canadians drink more soda, beer, and wine than their English-speaking counterparts.

Nigerians believe "good beer only comes in green bottles."

British consumers insist on cake mixes that require adding fresh eggs, as Betty Crocker mixes do.

Source: Compiled by the authors from various publications.

A simple way to learn about a foreign culture is to visit Web-based search engines relating to specific countries or regions. For example, look at Multimania (www.multimania.fr)—France, Yahoo! UK & Ireland (www.uk.yahoo.com)—one of about two dozen country-based sites from Yahoo!, and Terra (www.terra.com)—Latin America. Most of these sites are in the languages of the nations they represent.

6-4b The Economic Environment

A nation's economic environment indicates its present and potential capacities for consuming goods and services. Measures of economic performance include the standard of living, the Gross Domestic Product (GDP), the stage of economic development, and the stability of the currency.

The *standard of living* refers to the average quantity and quality of goods and services that are owned and consumed in a given nation. United Nations (www.un.org) and Organization for Economic Cooperation & Development (www.oecd.org) data show that the United States has the highest standard of living of any major industrialized country. By examining a nation's per-capita ownership and consumption across a range of goods and services, a firm can estimate the standard of living there (regarding the average *quantity* of goods and services). Table 6-3 compares data for 11 diverse countries.

As noted in Chapter 2, the ***Gross Domestic Product (GDP)*** is the total value of goods and services produced in a country each year. Total and per-capita GDP are the most-used measures of a nation's wealth because they are regularly published and easy to calculate and compare with other nations. Yet, per-capita GDP may be misleading. The figures are means and not income distributions; a few wealthy citizens may boost per-capita GDP, although most of the population has low income. And due to price and product availability differences, incomes buy different standards of living in each nation. According to the World Bank (www.worldbank.org), a U.S. income of $30,000 yields the same standard of living as $16,500 in Poland, $13,700 in Mexico, $6,900 in India, $6,850 in China, and $4,950 in the Congo.

> *The quality of life in a nation is measured by its* **standard of living.**

> *The total value of goods and services produced in a nation is its* **Gross Domestic Product.**

TABLE 6-3   **Ownership and Consumption in Eleven Countries**

	PASSENGER CARS (per 100 People)	TV SETS (per 100 People)	RADIOS (per 100 People)	DAILY NEWSPAPER CIRCULATION (per 100 People)	TELEPHONE LINES (per 100 People)	ENERGY CONSUMPTION (Kilograms per Year per Person)
United States	77	81	212	21	64	8,040
Brazil	8	22	45	4	2	670
Canada	56	71	108	16	61	7,960
China	1	32	20	4	6	710
France	51	60	94	22	58	3,920
Great Britain	43	52	145	33	54	3,940
India	1.2	6	12	3	1	300
Italy	57	53	87	10	45	2,820
Japan	54	69	96	58	48	3,660
Nigeria	0.1	7	20	3	0.4	100
Russia	12	41	42	11	18	4,230

Source: "InfoNation," www.un.org/Pubs/CyberSchoolBus/infonation (February 23, 2001).

FIGURE 6-5
The Stages of Economic Development

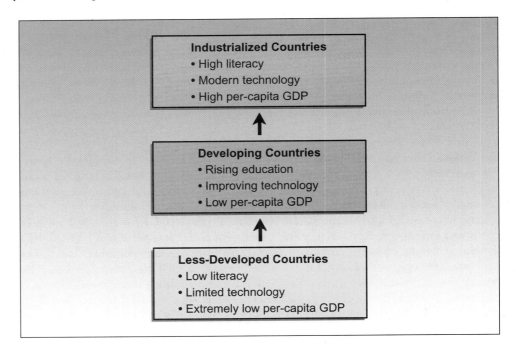

Countries can be classified as **industrialized, developing,** *and* **less developed.**

Marketing opportunities often can be highlighted by looking at a country's stage of economic growth. One way to classify growth is to divide nations into industrialized, developing, and less-developed groups.[7] See Figure 6-5.

Industrialized countries have high literacy, modern technology, and per-capita income of several thousand dollars. They can be placed into two main subgroups: established free-market economies and newly emerging free-market economies. The former include the United States, Canada, Japan, Australia, and nations in Western Europe; they have a large middle class, annual per-capita GDP of $15,000 and up, and plentiful goods and services to satisfy their needs. The latter include Russia and its former republics, as well as other Eastern European nations; while industrialized, they have a smaller middle class, annual per-capita GDP of $5,000 to $10,000, and insufficient goods and services to satisfy all their needs.

In **developing countries,** education and technology are rising, and per-capita GDP is about $3,000 to $8,000. Included are many Latin American and Southeast Asian nations. Although these countries are striving to build their industries, consumers are limited in what they can buy (due to the scarcity and relatively high prices of goods and services). They account for 20 percent of world population and almost one-third of its income.

Less-developed countries include a number of nations in Africa and Asia. Compared to other nations, literacy is lower and technology is more limited. Per-capita GDP is below $2,000 (sometimes less than $1,000). These nations have two-thirds of world population but less than 15 percent of world income. According to U.N. data, people in the most affluent one-fifth of the world have 65 times greater per-capita GDP than those in the bottom one-fifth.

The greatest marketing opportunities often occur in industrialized nations due to their higher incomes and standards of living. Yet, industrialized countries have slower rates of population growth, and sales of some product categories may have peaked. In contrast, developing and less-developed nations tend to have more rapidly expanding populations but now purchase few imports. There is long-run potential for international marketers in these nations. For example, Brazilians have only 81 cars per 1,000 population and Indians 12 per 1,000. The 1.3 billion people of China have 13 million cars—compared to 1.7 million cars in Denmark, a country with just 5.3 million people (0.4 percent of the Chinese population).

[7]Peter D. Bennett (Editor), *Dictionary of Marketing Terms,* Second Edition (Chicago: American Marketing Association, 1995), various pages.

MARKETING *and the Web*

The Educ.ar Initiative in Argentina

Through an innovative public-private initiative in Argentina, the federal Ministry of Education and privately held Educ.ar (www.educ.ar) have established a national student Internet portal. This portal is to be used to connect teachers and students in Argentina. The Ministry of Education wants to use the site to provide class listings, online registration, homework assignments and course materials, and student access to thousands of Web sites. Every student in Argentina will receive a separate E-mail address, as well as enough space on a server to create his/her own Web page. The goal of this joint initiative is to provide all Argentine students with online access within four years. Currently, fewer than 200,000 of Argentina's 10 million students have Internet access.

The Ministry of Education's partner is a newly-formed corporation, Educ.arS.A., whose responsibility will be to manage the portal on a day-to-day basis. While the ministry will control the site's content, Educ.arS.A. will be allowed to sell banner ads on the site. The income potential for Educ.arS.A. is significant since the site has the potential of reaching millions of students, teachers, and administrators. Educ.arS.A. plans to fulfill its capital needs through an initial public stock offering.

Besides the impact on education, the Educ.arS.A. partnership will have significant ramifications on Internet access and on Internet skills in Argentina. Currently, only about 3 percent of the Argentine population has Web access. This initiative is expected to increase access to at least 25 percent. In addition, it is expected to drastically increase the percentage of the population with computer skills. The head of Educ.arS.A. hopes that the increase in skills and rapid creation of jobs will lead to a more equitable distribution of income in Argentina and elsewhere.

What are the pros and cons of this initiative?

Source: Based on material in "Putting 10 Million Students Online in Argentina," *Business Week* (December 18, 2000), special advertising section.

Currency stability should also be considered in transactions because sales and profits could be affected if a foreign currency fluctuates widely relative to a firm's home currency. For example, during 2000, the value of the Greek drachma against the U.S. dollar fell from 305 to 365 drachmas per dollar—in January 2001, a Greek consumer had to spend 36,500 drachmas to buy a $100 U.S. good that cost 30,500 drachmas in January 2000. This decline in the drachma's value meant Greek goods became cheaper for U.S. consumers, while making it more expensive for Greek consumers to buy U.S. products.

Currency stability affects foreign sales and profit.

The currencies of both industrialized countries and developing and less-developed nations typically fluctuate—sometimes dramatically. As a rule, established free-market industrialized countries' currencies have been more stable than those of other nations.

6-4c The Political and Legal Environment

Every nation or region has a unique political and legal environment. Among the factors to consider are nationalism, government stability, trade restrictions, and trade agreements and economic communities. These factors can be complex, as the European Union has discovered.

Nationalism *involves a host country's attempts to promote its interests.*

Nationalism refers to a country's efforts to become self-reliant and raise its stature in the eyes of the world community. At times, a high degree of nationalism may lead to tight restrictions on foreign firms to foster the development of domestic industry at their expense. In the past, some nations even seized the assets of multinational firms, revoked their licenses to operate, prevented funds transfers from one currency to another, increased taxes, and/or unilaterally changed contract terms.

Government stability must be studied in terms of two elements: consistency of business policies and orderliness in installing leaders. Do government policies regarding taxes, company expansion, profits, and so on remain rather unchanged over time? Is there an orderly process for selecting and installing new government leaders? Firms will probably not function well unless both factors are positive. Thus, although several companies have made large investments in developing nations, others have stayed away from some less-developed and developing countries.

A firm can protect itself against the adverse effects of nationalism and political instability. Prior to entering a foreign market, it can measure the potential for domestic instability (riots, government purges), the political climate (stability of political parties, manner of choosing officials), and the economic climate (financial strength, government intervention)—and avoid nations deemed unsuitable. The PRS Group provides political risk assessment, and shows the most and least risky countries at its Web site (www.prsgroup.com/icrg/sampleissue.html). The U.S. government's Overseas Private Investment Corporation, OPIC (www.opic.gov), insures American investments in more than 140 developing and less-developed nations against such perils as asset takeovers and earnings inconvertibility; in addition, private underwriters insure foreign investments. Risks can also be reduced by using foreign partners, borrowing money from foreign governments or banks, and/or utilizing licensing, contract manufacturing, or management contracting (which are covered later in the chapter).

Another aspect of the international political and legal environment involves trade restrictions. The most common one is a **tariff,** which is a tax placed on imported products by a foreign government. The second major restriction is a **trade quota,** which sets limits on the amounts of products that can be imported into a country. The strictest form of trade quota is an **embargo,** which disallows entry of specified products into a country. The third major restriction involves **local content laws,** which require foreign-based firms to set up local plants and use locally made components. The goal of tariffs, trade quotas, and local content laws is to protect both the economies and domestic employment of the nations involved. Embargoes may also have political ramifications, such as the United States refusing to engage in any trade with Cuba. Here are examples:

Tariffs, trade quotas and embargoes, *and* **local content laws** *are forms of trade restrictions.*

* There are U.S. tariffs on imported clothing, ceramic tiles, rubber footwear, brooms, flowers, cement, computer screens, sugar, candy, trucks, and other items. They are administered by the U.S. Customs Service (www.customs.treas.gov/about/about.htm). The tariffs raise import prices relative to domestic items. At one of its Web sites (http://www.trade.gov/td/tic), the U.S. International Trade Administration cites specific tariffs by other countries and regions. At the site, click on "Tariff and Tax Information."

* Many European nations have had pacts with Japan that set voluntary quotas on certain goods exported by Japan to those nations. For instance, from 1993 to 1999, there was a quota on the number of Japanese cars sold in Europe.

* To stimulate domestic production, for nearly a decade, Brazil placed an embargo on most foreign computer products—thus banning their sales there.

* In Italy, food products cannot be called pasta unless they are made from durum wheat, which is the country's major kind of wheat.

Many barriers among nations have been reduced via trade agreements and economic communities. In 1948, 23 nations, including the United States, signed the General Agreement on Tariffs and Trade (GATT) to foster multilateral trade. By 1994, 115 nations participated in GATT. From its inception, GATT talks helped lower tariffs on manufactured goods. But member nations got bogged down because trade in services, agriculture, textiles, and investment and capital flows was not covered; and GATT let members belong to regional trade associations (economic communities) with fewer trade barriers among the nations involved in those associations than with those not involved.

On January 1, 1995, after eight years of difficult negotiations, GATT was replaced by the **World Trade Organization, WTO** (www.wto.org). About 140 nations have since joined the WTO, whose mission is to open up markets even further and promote a cooperative atmosphere around the globe:

> The WTO is the only international organization dealing with the global rules of trade between nations. Its main function is to ensure that trade flows as smoothly, predictably, and freely as possible. Decisions in the WTO are typically taken by consensus among all member countries and they are ratified by members' parliaments. Trade friction is channeled into the WTO's dispute settlement process where the focus is on interpreting agreements and commitments, and how to ensure that countries' trade policies conform with them. That way, the risk of disputes spilling over into political or military conflict is reduced. By lowering trade barriers, the WTO's system also breaks down other barriers between peoples and nations. At the heart of the system—known as the multilateral trading system—are the WTO's agreements, negotiated and signed by a large majority of the world's trading nations, and ratified by them. These agreements are the legal ground-rules for international commerce. Essentially, they are contracts, guaranteeing member nations important trade rights. They bind governments to keep trade policies within agreed limits to everybody's benefit.[8]

In contrast to the WTO, which promotes free trade around the world, each *economic community* promotes free trade among its member nations—but not necessarily with nonmember nations. As a result, the best interests of the WTO and economic communities may clash.

The two leading economic communities are the European Union (www.europa.eu.int) and the North American Free Trade community (www.mac.doc.gov/nafta/nafta2.htm). The *European Union (EU),* also called the Common Market, consists of Austria, Belgium, Denmark, Finland, France, Germany, Great Britain, Greece, Ireland, Italy, Luxembourg, the Netherlands, Portugal, Spain, and Sweden. Other European nations are expected to join the EU within the next few years. EU rules call for no trade restrictions among members; uniform tariffs with nonmembers; common product standards; and a free flow of people and capital. The aim is for members to have an open marketplace, such as exists among states in the United States. One of the EU's biggest challenges has been installing a common currency, the Euro, across all of the member countries. The combined GDP of EU nations is 110 percent that of the United States; the total population is 1.4 times that of the United States.

On January 1, 1994, the **North American Free Trade Agreement (NAFTA)** was enacted, creating an economic community that links the United States, Canada, and Mexico; it is helping to remove tariffs and other trade restrictions among the three countries. The NAFTA community and the EU are about the same size in both total GDP and total population (until the EU adds more members). There have been some very preliminary discussions about expanding NAFTA to include such emerging Latin American nations as Brazil and Chile, but it is quite unlikely that NAFTA will expand in the near future.

Other economic communities include the Andean Pact (www.comunidadandina.org), with 5 Latin American members; Association of South East Asian Nations (www.aseansec.org), with 10 members; Caribbean Common Market (www.caricom.org), with more than a dozen members; Central American Common Market (www.imf.org/external/np/sec/decdo/sieca.htm), with 5 members; Gulf Cooperation Council (www.imf.org/external/np/sec/decdo/gcc.htm), with 6 Arabic members; Economic Community of West African States (www.imf.org/external/np/sec/decdo/ecowas.htm), with 16 members; and Mercosur (www.mercosur.org), with 6 Latin American members.

The **World Trade Organization** *seeks to eliminate trade barriers*

The two leading **economic communities** *are formed by the* **European Union** *and the* **North American Free Trade Agreement.**

---

[8]"The WTO in Brief," www.wto.org/english/thewto_e/whatis_e/inbrief_e/inbr00_e.htm (March 1, 2001).

As many nations in Eastern Europe and elsewhere have moved to more open economies, they have become quite interested in hiking their participation in world trade. They are deregulating industries, encouraging foreign investment, and seeking trade agreements with free-market nations. In 1990, Eastern Europe's Council for Mutual Economic Assistance announced its own demise—members did not want to be hampered by a declining trading system. Since then, a number of Eastern European countries have expressed interest in eventually gaining entry into the European Union.

The International Monetary Fund gives descriptions of many other economic communities at its Web site (http://www.imf.org/external/np/sec/decdo/contents.htm).

6-4d The Technological Environment

Technological factors such as these affect international marketing:

International marketing may require adjustments in technology.

- Technology advances vary around the world. For example, outside the United States, cable TV is more limited. Even in Western Europe, only 35 percent of households have cable TV (compared to 70 percent in the United States).

- Foreign workers must often be trained to run equipment unfamiliar to them.

- Problems occur if equipment maintenance practices vary by nation or adverse physical conditions exist, such as high humidity, extreme hot or cold weather, or air pollution.

- Electricity and electrical power needs may vary by nation and require product modifications. For example, U.S. appliances work on 110 volts; European appliances work on 220 volts.

- Although the metric system is the one used in nations with 95 percent of the world's population, the United States still relies on ounces, pounds, inches, and feet. Thus, auto makers, beverage bottlers, and many other U.S. firms make items using metric standards—and then list U.S. and metric measures side-by-side on labels and packages. For the United States to convert to the metric system (which it has been trying to do since 1866, when Congress passed the first law on the metric system) the American consumer must be re-educated about measurement and learn meters, liters, and other metric standards; this process continues to be a slow one.

On the plus side, various technological advances are easing the growth of international marketing. They involve communications (TV satellites, the Internet, facsimile machines), transactions (automatic teller machines), order processing (computerization), and production (multiplant innovations).

6-5 DEVELOPING AN INTERNATIONAL MARKETING STRATEGY

The vital parts of an international marketing strategy are explored next: company organization, market entry decisions, the degree of standardization, and product, distribution, promotion, and price planning.

6-5a Company Organization

A firm has three organizational formats from which to choose: exporting, joint venture, and direct ownership. They are compared in Figure 6-6.

Exporting lets a firm reach international markets without foreign production.

With **exporting,** a firm reaches international markets by selling products made in its home country directly through its own sales force or indirectly via foreign merchants or agents. In direct selling, a firm situates its sales force in a home office or in foreign branch offices. This is best if customers are easy to locate, concentrated, or come to the seller. With indirect selling, a firm hires outside specialists to contact customers. The special-

ETHICAL *Issues in Marketing*

The Hybrid Eco-Car: The Japanese Take the Lead

The auto industry has launched its first "hybrid" cars, which are powered by both a gasoline engine and an electric motor. For example, Honda's Insight is a 65-mile-per-gallon, ultra-low-emissions vehicle. Not only does this car save consumers about $500 a year on gasoline as compared to the Honda Civic, but its engine also easily meets California's tough emissions standards. The Insight creates less than one-half of the carbon dioxide and other gases of such cars as the Toyota Corolla or Ford Focus. Toyota has a comparable vehicle called the Primus and plans to launch a hybrid minivan and SUV by 2002.

Ford, General Motors, and DaimlerChrysler are all working hard to catch up. For years, they fought the imposition of gas mileage regulations and California's stringent emissions standards. Observers feel that these manufacturers were less concerned about gas mileage regulations due to the popularity of their gas-guzzling SUVs and pickup trucks (which were not regulated as to gas consumption). Now Ford, for example, faces million of dollars in fines if it cannot comply with fuel economy standards.

In 2003, Ford plans to sell a hybrid version of its Escape SUV that would get 40 miles per gallon. Similarly, General Motors and DaimlerChrysler are working to develop hybrid versions of the Chevrolet Silverado and GMC Sierra pickups, and the Durango SUV, respectively.

Some market analysts think that Detroit is delaying the introduction of hybrid cars in the hope of receiving tax incentives from the federal government, while working hard to increase the efficiency of traditional gas engines during this time period. Critics of the delayed introduction plans say that the firms are missing a major opportunity.

What, if anything, should be done to speed up the efforts of Detroit-based manufacturers in terms of developing and introducing hybrid cars? Explain your answer.

Source: Based on material in David Welch and Lorraine Woellert, "The Eco-Car," *Business Week* (August 14, 2000) pp. 61–67.

ists may be based in the home or foreign nation. There are 2,000 specialized U.S. export management firms marketing products in foreign nations. Indirect selling is best if customers are hard to locate or dispersed, if a potential exporter has limited funds, and/or if local customs are unique.

An exporting structure requires minimal investment in foreign facilities. There is no foreign production by the firm. The exporter may modify packages, labels, or catalogs at its domestic facilities in response to foreign market needs. Exporting embodies the lowest level of commitment to international marketing. Most smaller firms that engage in international marketing rely on exporting. For example, Purafil Inc. (www.purafil.com) is a Georgia-based maker of equipment that removes corrosive, odorous, and toxic gases from commercial and industrial environments, as well as museums, libraries, and archives. It relies on local distributors to market its products around the globe; and foreign business now accounts for 60 percent of the firm's $26 million in annual revenues.[9]

[9]James Cox, "Small Business Find International Success," *USA Today* (June 30, 2000), p. 1B.

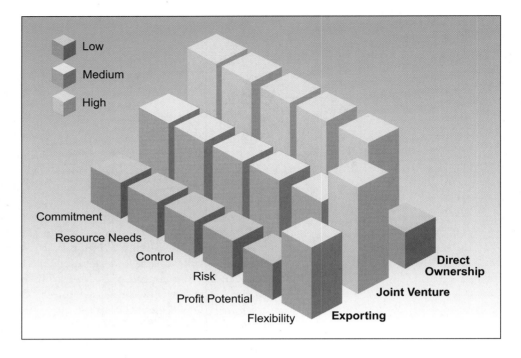

FIGURE 6-6
Alternate Company Organizations for International Marketing

Low

Medium

High

Commitment

Resource Needs

Control

Risk

Profit Potential

Flexibility

Exporting

Joint Venture

Direct Ownership

FIGURE 6-7

Goodyear and Sava: A Joint Venture

Goodyear (www.goodyear.com) has a joint venture with Slovenia's Sava that produces tires for local markets, as well as for Europe, Latin America, and Australia.

Source: Reprinted by permission of Goodyear.

A **joint venture** *can be based on licensing, contract manufacturing, management contracting, or joint ownership.*

With a *joint venture* (also known as a *strategic alliance*), a firm agrees to combine some aspect of its manufacturing or marketing efforts with those of a foreign company so as to share expertise, costs, and/or connections with key persons. As experts observe, "In this period of advanced technology and global markets, implementing strategies quickly is essential. Forming alliances is often the fastest, most effective method of reaching objectives. Yet, without the proper partner, a company should not undertake an alliance, even for the right reasons. Partners must be compatible and willing to trust one another."[10]

Here are examples of firms engaged in international joint ventures:

- Goodyear has a joint venture with Sava (www.sava.si/savauk/wellcome.htm) in Slovenia that is involved with making tires. See Figure 6-7.

[10]Bruce A. Walters, Steve Peters, and Gregory G. Dess, "Strategic Alliances and Joint Ventures: Making Them Work," *Business Horizons*, Vol. 37 (July-August 1994), p. 5.

- Airbus Industrie (www.airbus.com), a jet maker, is operated by two European aerospace firms: the European Aeronautic Defence and Space Company (arising from the merger of Airbus consortium "partners" Aerospatiale-Matra of France, DaimlerChrysler Aerospace of Germany, and CASA of Spain); and BAE Systems of Great Britain.

- Thailand's Charoen Pokphand (www.cpthailand.com) has a telecommunications venture with Verizon (United States) and an insurance venture with Allianz AG (Germany).

- Monsanto (United States) and PASA (www.baires.com/pasa) of Argentina are working together to make and market plastics.

A joint venture may lead to reduced costs and favorable trade terms from a foreign government if products are made locally and some degree of foreign ownership is set. Thus, joint ventures between Japanese and U.S. firms are growing because Japanese firms see them as lowering the possibility of U.S. trade restrictions. U.S. firms view the ventures as a means of opening the Japanese market and as a way of observing potential competitors.

A joint venture can involve licensing, contract manufacturing, management contracting, or joint ownership. *Licensing* gives a foreign firm the rights to a manufacturing process, trademark, patent, and/or trade secret in exchange for a commission, fee, or royalty. Coca-Cola (www2.coca_cola.com/about/whatwedo) and PepsiCo (www.pepsico.com/corp/overview.shtml) license products in some nations. In *contract manufacturing*, a firm agrees to have a foreign partner make its products locally. The firm markets the products itself and provides management expertise. This is common in book publishing. In management contracting, a firm acts as a consultant to foreign companies. Such hotel chains as Hilton International (www.hilton.com), Hyatt International (www.hyatt.com), and Sheraton (www.sheraton.com) use management contracting. With joint ownership, a firm produces and markets products in partnership with a foreign firm so as to reduce costs and spread risk. Sometimes, a foreign government may require joint ownership with local businesses as a condition for entry. In Canada, outsiders must use joint ownership with Canadian firms for new ventures.

With **direct ownership,** a firm owns production, marketing, and other facilities in one or more foreign nations without any partners. The firm has full control over its operations in those nations. Thus, Great Britain's Invensys (www.invensys.com) owns a factory in Belluno, Italy, that makes electromagnetic timers for washing machines. Sometimes, wholly owned subsidiaries may be established. In the United States, Stop & Shop, the supermarket chain, is a subsidiary of Royal Ahold (www.ahold.com) of the Netherlands. Similarly, foreign facilities of U.S.-based firms annually yield revenues of hundreds of billions of dollars.

> **Direct ownership** *involves total control of foreign operations and facilities by a firm.*

Under direct ownership, a firm has all the benefits and risks of owning a foreign business. There are potential labor savings, and marketing plans are more sensitive to local needs. Profit potential may be high, although costs may also be high. There is a possibility of nationalistic acts, and government restrictions are apt to be stricter. This is the riskiest organization form.

Companies often combine formats. For instance, a firm could use exporting in a country with a history of taking over the assets of foreign businesses and direct ownership in one with tax advantages for construction. McDonald's worldwide efforts (www.mcdonalds.com/countries) combine company-operated stores, franchisee-operated stores, and affiliate-operated stores (whereby McDonald's owns 50 percent or less of assets, with the rest owned by resident nationals). Company stores are largely in the United States, Canada, France, Great Britain, and Germany; franchisee outlets are mostly in the United States, Canada, France, Germany, and Australia; and affiliate restaurants are common in Latin America, Japan, and other Pacific nations.

6-5b Market Entry Decisions

There are a number of factors to consider in deciding which and how many foreign markets a firm should enter. Here are several of them:

Which Market(s) to Enter

- Are there cultural similarities between a foreign nation and a firm's home market? How vital is this?
- Are there language similarities between a foreign nation and a firm's home market? How vital is this?
- Is the standard of living in a foreign market consistent with what a firm would offer there?
- How large is a foreign market for the goods and services a firm would offer there? Is it growing? What is regional potential (e.g., Eastern Europe)?
- Is the technology in a foreign market appropriate for a firm to do business? Is the country's infrastructure appropriate?
- Are there enough skilled workers in a foreign country?
- Are the media in a foreign country adequate for a firm's marketing efforts?
- What is the level of competition in a foreign market?
- What government restrictions would a firm face in a foreign market? The economic communities?
- How stable are the currency and government in a foreign market?
- Is the overall business climate in a foreign country favorable to a firm?

How Many Markets to Enter

- What are the firm's available resources?
- How many foreign markets could a firm's personnel properly oversee and service?
- How diverse are multiple foreign markets? What is the geographic proximity?
- What are the marketing economies of scale from being regional or global?
- Are exporting arrangements possible? Are joint ventures?
- What are a firm's goals regarding its mix of domestic and foreign revenues?
- How extensive is competition in a firm's home market?

6-5c Standardizing Plans

A firm engaged in international marketing must determine the degree to which plans should be standardized. Both standardized and nonstandardized plans have benefits and limitations.

With a ***standardized (global) marketing approach,*** a firm uses a common marketing plan for all nations in which it operates—because it assumes worldwide markets are becoming more homogeneous due to better communications, more open country borders, the move to free-market economies, and other factors. This approach downplays differences among countries. There are marketing and production economies—product design, packaging, advertising, and other costs are spread over a large product base. A uniform image is presented, training foreign personnel is easier, and centralized control is applied. Yet, standardization is insensitive to individual market needs, and input from foreign personnel is limited:

The increase in global markets and global competition is attributed to many factors. The pressures in slow-growth home markets are driving companies to seek new markets. Converging customer tastes and requirements, the need to gain scale from world market development, shortening product life cycles, and expanding financial markets all have made globalization more necessary and feasible. Government changes, too, are encouraging increased global competition. Yet, regional conditions and tastes vary to the point where local customization is needed—often in products and usually in marketing—even within the United States. Many firms can support a business on a country or regional basis; they need not garner scale from cross-country or cross-region participation. Product development and production technologies, too, are providing flexibility to adjust products for local needs. Finally, as much as governments stimulate cross-border competition, they also restrict it.[11]

GLOBAL *Marketing in Action*

Alibaba.com: An Asia-Based Worldwide Internet Portal

In 1995, Jack Ma brought the commercial use of the Internet to China by offering to host Web pages for Chinese companies. His firm, Alibaba.com (www.alibaba.com), is now expanding by selling its services to importers and exporters throughout the world. Ma says that he has more than 200,000 registered members from 194 countries. The site is published in both Chinese (70 percent of members are Chinese), and English. It recently began a Korean site.

This is how Alibaba.com works. The firm does not charge for listing products; it hopes to earn money by providing such services as advertising, shipping, financing, and insurance. Of these services, it currently offers advertising services. Unlike competitors that focus on one industry, and others that have defined areas, Alibaba.com wants to apply to all product categories—and to have a global reach. Ma views his site as a worldwide bazaar, where sellers and buyers can meet, negotiate, and strike deals.

Since most of Alibaba.com's staff are Chinese and live in China, the firm's labor and operating costs are low. A Chinese computer engineer with three years of experience earns about $18,000 per year. In comparison, a similar engineer in Silicon Valley, California may earn $100,000.

Two main competitors are MeetChina.com (www.meetchina.com) and Industry-to-Industry, Inc. (www.i2.com). San Francisco-based MeetChina.com focuses on Chinese electronics. Boston-based Industry-to-Industry, Inc. focuses on chemicals, energy, retail goods, and engineering and construction.

According to *Forbes*, the costs of servicing world trade (such as phone bills, invoicing, sales calls, and travel) are about $470 billion per year. If Web sites such as Alibaba.com can reduce these costs by 20 percent, there's a significant profit potential in this industry.

Evaluate Alibaba.com's global marketing strategy.

Source: Based on material in Justin Doebele, "Fast as a Rabbit, Patient as a Turtle," *Forbes* (July 17, 2000), pp. 74–75.

---

[11]Marc C. Particelli, "A Global Arena," *Journal of Consumer Marketing*, Vol. 7 (Fall 1990), pp. 43–52. See also Jack Neff, "Rethinking Globalism," *Advertising Age* (October 9, 2000), pp. 1, 100.

With a *nonstandardized marketing approach,* a firm sees each nation or region as distinct, and requiring its own marketing plan. This strategy is sensitive to local needs and means grooming foreign managers, as decentralized control is undertaken. It works best if distinctive major foreign markets are involved and/or a firm has many product lines. For instance, although Italy's Luxottica Group (www.luxottica.it/english/home.html) has such "global" brands as Ray-Ban sunglasses (www.ray-ban.com), its strategy is tailored to individual markets. In Europe, Ray-Bans are flashier and pricier than in the United States. In Asia, the sunglasses are better suited to the Asian face—which tends to have a flatter bridge and higher cheekbones. As the company says, "From Hollywood to St. Tropez, from Soho to Tokyo, Ray-Ban is the world's best-selling brand of sunglasses. Setting the standard for excellence, Ray-Ban sunglasses consistently combine great styling with exceptional quality and comfort to deliver legendary sun performance. And as you would expect, Ray-Ban sunglasses offer 100% UV protection."

In recent years, more firms (such as Luxottica) have used a *glocal marketing approach*—which stands for *think global and act local.* Under this approach, combining standardized and nonstandardized efforts lets a firm attain production efficiencies, have a consistent image, have some home-office control, and still be sensitive and responsive to local needs. This is how U.S.-based GE (www.ge.com) applies a glocal approach to best address company and consumer needs:

> GE's Medical Systems department, run from Milwaukee, has two aspects to it—global products and local markets—and they need to be combined for the business to thrive. GE makes its machines in whichever place offers the right level of engineering talent and the best cost base—and that usually means the market where the demand for those machines is highest and the competition the toughest. For example, the most sophisticated machines are made in America, which also has the biggest demand for top-end medical equipment because it spends the most on health care. Japan is more midrange, with a preference for small, high-quality machines, and China is the center for production of the lower-tech end of products, such as CAT scanners. In all, GE Medical has eight factories in Asia, one each in Japan and Korea, and three each in India and China. All the factories sell both domestically and abroad. But the marketing and services need to have a local flair.[12]

When determining a marketing approach, a firm should evaluate whether differences among countries are sufficiently great to warrant changes in marketing plans, which elements of marketing can be standardized, whether the size of each foreign market could lead to profitable adaptation, and if modifications can be made on a regional rather than a country basis.

6-5d Product Planning

International product planning (including both goods and services) can be based on straight-extension, product-adaptation, backward-invention, and/or forward-invention strategies.

In a *straight extension* strategy, a firm makes and markets the same products for domestic and foreign sales. The firm is confident it can sell items abroad without modifying the products, the brand name, packaging, or ingredients. This simple approach capitalizes on economies of scale in production. Apple (www.apple.com) markets the same PCs in the United States and Mexico. Soda companies use straight extension in many (but not all) countries around the world. Beer makers also use straight extension, and imported beer often has a higher status than domestic beer. Yet, straight extension does not account for differences in customers, laws, customs, technology, and other factors.

With a *product adaptation* strategy, domestic products are modified to meet foreign language needs, taste preferences, climates, electrical requirements, laws, and/or other factors. It is assumed that new products are not needed and minor changes are sufficient. This is the most-used strategy in international marketing: Campbell Soup Company (www.campbellsoup.com) prints food packages in the languages of the nations in which

Straight extension, product adaptation, backward invention, and forward invention are basic methods of international product planning.

---

[12]Jim Rohwer, "GE Digs into Asia," *Fortune* (October 2, 2000), pp. 172, 174.

they are sold, as shown in Figure 6-8. Disneyland Paris (www.disneylandparis.com) features Mickey Mouse, Cinderella, and other U.S. Disney characters but also has food concessions and hotels that are adapted to European tastes; KFC (www.kfc.com) has grilled rice balls to go with its fried chicken wings in Japan; PepsiCo's Chee-tos cheese-flavored puff snack (www.fritolay.com/consumer.html) is cheeseless in China (with flavors such as buttered popcorn); gasoline formulations vary according to a nation's weather conditions; and appliances are modified to accommodate different voltage requirements.

With **backward invention,** a firm appeals to developing and less-developed nations by making products less complex than the ones it sells in its domestic market. This includes manual cash registers and nonelectric sewing machines for consumers in countries without widespread electricity and inexpensive washing machines for consumers in low-income countries. Whirlpool (www.whirlpool.com) affiliates build and sell an inexpensive "world washer" in Brazil, Mexico, and India. It is compact, is specially designed (so it does not tangle a sari), handles about one-half the capacity of a regular U.S. washer, and accommodates variations in component availability and local preferences.

In **forward invention,** a company develops new products for its international markets. This plan is riskier and more time-consuming and requires a higher investment than other strategies. It may also provide the firm with great profit potential and, sometimes, worldwide recognition for innovativeness. With 70 percent of its overall sales coming from foreign markets, U.S.-based Colgate-Palmolive (www.colgate.com) often engages in forward invention. For example, it has developed La Croix bleach for Europe and Protex antibacterial soap for Asia, Africa, and Latin America. See Figure 6-9.

FIGURE 6-8

Product Modification at Campbell Soup Company: Adapting to Local Markets

Campbell adjusts product ingredients and packaging to reflect cultural differences among countries.

Source: Reprinted by permission.

FIGURE 6-9

Forward Invention by Colgate-Palmolive

The firm has introduced a number of products especially made for its foreign markets, and not sold in its home base of the United States.

Source: Reprinted by permission.

6-5e Distribution Planning

Channel members and physical distribution methods depend on customs, availability, costs, and other factors.

International distribution planning encompasses the selection and use of resellers and products' physical movement. A firm may sell direct to customers or hire outside distribution specialists—depending on the traditional relationships in a country, the availability of appropriate resellers, differences in distribution practices from those in the home country, government restrictions, costs, and other factors. For example,

- Central cities in Europe often have more shopping ambience than central cities in the United States.
- In Brazil, PepsiCo markets soft drinks through the domestic Brahma beer and soda company because of Brahma's extensive distribution network.
- Amway sells its household products in Japan (www.amway.co.jp) via hundreds of thousands of local distributors (who are also customers); as in the United States, distributors earn commissions on sales.
- In the Philippines, Avon (www.avoncompany.com/world) uses a special system of branch outlets to service its representatives. See Figure 6-10.

Distribution often requires special planning: Processing marine insurance, government documents, and other papers may take time. Transportation modes may be inefficient. A nation may have limited docking facilities, poor highways, or few vehicles. Distribution by ship is slow and may be delayed. Stores may be much smaller than those in the United States. Inventory management must take into account warehousing availability and the costs of shipping in small amounts. In Russia, Ben & Jerry's initially had problems due to the lack of refrigerated trucks and freezers. So, it brought in Western trucks and freezers to store its ice cream. The firm learned that "Russia still lacks a distribution system that will deliver products to stores on time, consistently, and in good condition. To ensure quality, Ben & Jerry's and other firms are creating a soup-to-nuts distribution system. It's costly, but Ben & Jerry's hopes that by keeping quality high, it can win and keep fickle Russian consumers."[13]

FIGURE 6-10

Avon: Meeting Local Distribution Needs

For foreign markets where the distribution structure is underdeveloped, Avon uses a system of branches to help sales representatives receive products for delivery to customers. Avon has "branch supermarkets," like the one shown here, in the Philippines.

Source: Reprinted by permission.

[13]Neela Banerjee, "Ben & Jerry's Is Discovering That It's No Joke to Sell Ice Cream to Russians," *Wall Street Journal* (September 19, 1995), p. A18.

6-5f Promotion Planning

Promotion campaigns can be global, nonstandardized, or glocal. Figure 6-11 shows an example of a glocal ad.

Firms may use global promotion for image purposes: Coca-Cola's "Life tastes good" ads are used worldwide (sample a few of the ads at www.ltg.coca-cola.com), as are various IBM (www.ibm.com) ads that highlight its vast computing strengths. At Reebok, there is a new global campaign based on the slogan "Defy convention." The campaign includes many of the firm's athlete endorsers, such as Venus Williams (tennis), Allen Iverson (basketball), Jevon Kearse (football), and Julie Foudy (soccer). The firm says "'defy convention' celebrates individuals who have defied the odds; people who encounter difficulties and still succeed, despite those challenges. The program also celebrates the Reebok brand and the innovative, stylish products which defy convention." The campaign targets France, Germany, Italy, Japan, Spain, the United States, and Great Britain.[14]

Companies marketing in various European nations often find that some standardization is desirable due to overlapping readers, listeners, and viewers. For instance, German TV shows are received by a large percentage of Dutch households and *Paris Match* magazine has substantial readership in Belgium, Switzerland, Luxembourg, Germany, Italy, and Holland.

International promotion planning depends on the overlap of audiences and languages and the availability of media.

FIGURE 6-11
A Glocal Visa Ad

The Visa card, which appears in this ad, is a global symbol. The copy is adapted to the markets in which various ads appear. The ad depicted here appeared in French-speaking Europe.

Source: Reprinted by permission.

---

[14]Rebecca Flass, "Reebok Defies Convention with New Campaign," *Adweek* (January 22, 2001), p. 11.

There are also reasons for using nonstandardized promotion. Many countries have distinctions that are not addressed through a single promotion campaign. These differences include customs, language, the meaning of colors and symbols, and literacy rates. Media may be unavailable or inappropriate. In a number of nations, there are few TV sets, ads are restricted, and/or mailing lists are not current. National pride sometimes requires that individual promotions be used. Even within regions that have perceived similarities, such as Western Europe and Latin America, there are differences.

For instance, alcohol is banned in some Middle East nations. So, Heineken (www.heinekencorp.com) and others sell nonalcoholic beers there. Yet, even for nonalcoholic beer, ads are forbidden. The promotion emphasis is on store displays, special promotions, and contests.

Most firms end up utilizing glocal promotion plans:

Standardized strategies seem most apt if a product is utilitarian and the message is informational. Reasons for buying or using the good or service are rational—and less apt to vary by culture. Glue, batteries, and gasoline are such products. A standardized approach would also appear effective if a brand's identity and desirability are integrally linked to a specific national character. Coca-Cola and McDonald's are marketed as "quintessential American products;" Chanel is a "quintessential French product." Yet, it is generally more effective to *glocalize strategies* to local customs and cultures:

- Product usage often varies according to the culture. This applies to some foods, and beverages such as coffee and tea.
- For many products, benefits are more psychological than tangible, requiring an understanding of the psychologies of different cultures. Sweets, snacks, and clothing all have intangible benefits.
- When there is an emotional appeal, advertisers must recognize the vast differences in emotional expression that exist. Some societies are demonstrative and open; others are aloof or private.
- There are differences in humor even within a culture—not to mention differences among cultures. In addition, advertisers must consider a multicultural and flexible strategy or campaign if a brand is in different stages of development or of varying stature across different markets.
- A commercial for a mature market may not work well in a developing one.
- A commercial to support a brand's leadership in a market where it is number one may not have the characteristics to succeed in a market where it is number five.
- A commercial in a market where the product/brand is unique has quite a different task than a commercial where competition is intense.[15]

In recognition of the importance of international promotion planning, *Advertising Age* has added a new Web site, "AdAge Global" (www.adageglobal.com) with a lot of useful information.

6-5g Price Planning

Major decisions in international price planning involve standardization, levels, currency, and sales terms. **Dumping** *is disliked by host countries.*

The basic considerations in international price planning are whether prices should be standardized, the level at which prices are set, the currency in which prices are quoted, and terms of sale.

Standardization is hard unless a firm operates in an economic community, such as the EU. Taxes, tariffs, and currency exchange charges are among the costs a firm incurs internationally. For example, a car made in the United States might have to be priced at several thousand dollars higher when sold in Japan rather than sold in the United States, due to currency exchange fees, shipping costs, taxes, inspection fees, and so forth.

[15]McCollum Spielman Worldwide, "Global Advertising: Standardized or Multicultural?" *Topline* (Number 37, 1992), pp. 3–4.

"Homologation" alone (inspections and modifications needed to meet Japan's standards) could add $2,000 to $3,000 to the final selling price.

When setting a price level, a firm would consider such local factors as per-capita GDP. Thus, firms may try to hold down prices in developing and less-developed countries by marketing simpler product versions or employing less-expensive local labor. On the other hand, prices in such industrialized nations as France and Germany can reflect product quality and the added costs of international marketing.

Some firms set lower prices abroad to enhance their global presence and sales or to remove excess supply from their home markets and preserve the prices there. With **dumping,** a firm sells a product in a foreign nation at a price much lower than in its home market, below the cost of production, or both. In the United States and many other nations, duties may be levied on products "dumped" by foreign firms.[16]

If a firm sets prices on the basis of its home currency, the risk of a foreign currency devaluation is passed along to the buyer and there is better control. But this strategy also has limitations. Consumers may be confused or unable to convert a price into their own currency, or a foreign government may insist that prices be quoted in its currency. There are several online currency converter software programs that make calculations simple. Two such sites are Universal Currency Converter (www.xe.net/ucc) and FXConverter (www.oanda.com/converter/classic).

Finally, terms of sale need to be set. This involves such judgments as what fees or discounts channel intermediaries get for the tasks they perform, when ownership is transferred, what payment form is required, how much time customers have to pay bills, and what constitutes a proper refund policy.

WEB SITES YOU CAN USE

Among the many valuable Web sites pertaining to global marketing, two are especially noteworthy. The CIA World Factbook (www.odci.gov/cia/publications/factbook) is an annual publication that reports demographic and economic data on virtually every country in the world. The Center for International Business Education and Research (CIBER) at Michigan State University (www.ciber.bus.msu.edu) has a number of online resources.

[16]See "Monitoring Foreign Antidumping and Countervailing Duty Cases," www.ia.ita.doc.gov/foradcvd (March 7, 2001).

SUMMARY

1. *To define domestic, international, and global marketing* Domestic marketing covers a firm's efforts in its home country. International marketing involves goods and services sold outside a firm's home country. Global marketing engages a firm in operations in many nations. A company may be categorized as a domestic firm, exporting firm, international firm, multinational firm, or global firm. For any type of company (whether domestically or internationally oriented) to succeed in today's competitive marketplace, it must grasp key international marketing concepts and act appropriately.

2. *To explain why international marketing takes place and study its scope* International marketing occurs since nations want to exchange goods and services where they have comparative advantages for those with which they do not. Firms seek to minimize weak economic conditions and attract growing markets, avoid domestic competition, extend the product life cycle, and get tax breaks.

The United States is the world's largest exporter for both goods and services. Hundreds of thousands of U.S. firms engage in some level of international business. The United States is also the world's leading importer, with a huge merchandise trade deficit. In contrast, the United States has a trade surplus for services. There are several reasons for the merchandise trade deficit, ranging from the American market's allure to the emphasis of U.S. firms on profits over market share. Various actions are under way to reduce this deficit; and the United States is the dominant force worldwide.

3. *To explore the cultural, economic, political and legal, and technological environments facing international marketers* The cultural environment includes the behavior standards, language, lifestyles, and goals of a country's citizens. The economic environment incorporates a nation's standard of living, GDP, stage of development, and currency stability. The political and legal environment includes nationalism, government stability, trade rules, and trade agreements and economic communities like the World Trade Organization, European Union, and North American Free Trade group. The technological environment creates opportunities and problems, and varies by country.

4. *To analyze the stages in the development of an international marketing strategy* In developing a strategy, a firm may stress exporting, joint ventures, or direct ownership of operations. Each approach

has a different commitment, resource needs, control, risk, flexibility, and profit range.

When deciding on which and how many foreign markets to enter, a company should consider several factors. These include cultural and language similarities with the home market, the suitability of the standard of living, consumer demand, its own available resources, and so on.

A firm may use standardized (global), nonstandardized, or glocal marketing. Its decision would depend on the differences among the nations served, which marketing elements can be standardized, the size of each market, and the possibility of regional adaptation.

Product planning may extend existing products into foreign markets, modify them, produce simpler items for developing nations, or invent new products for foreign markets. Distribution planning looks at channel relations and sets a network for direct sales or channel intermediaries. Physical distribution features would also be analyzed. Promotion planning would stress global, mixed, or glocal campaigns. Price planning would outline whether prices should be standardized, the price level, the currency for price quotes, and terms of sale.

KEY TERMS

domestic marketing (p. 156)
international marketing (p. 156)
global marketing (p. 156)
domestic firm (p. 156)
exporting firm (p. 156)
international firm (p. 156)
multinational firm (p. 156)
global firm (p. 156)
comparative advantage (p. 158)
trade deficit (p. 159)
trade surplus (p. 159)
culture (p. 161)
standard of living (p. 163)
Gross Domestic Product (GDP) (p. 163)

industrialized countries (p. 164)
developing countries (p. 164)
less-developed countries (p. 164)
nationalism (p. 166)
tariff (p. 166)
trade quota (p. 166)
embargo (p. 166)
local content laws (p. 166)
World Trade Organization (WTO) (p. 167)
economic community (p. 167)
European Union (EC) (p. 167)
North American Free Trade Agreement
    (NAFTA) (p. 167)

exporting (p. 168)
joint venture (strategic alliance) (p. 170)
direct ownership (p. 171)
standardized (global) marketing approach (p. 172)
nonstandardized marketing approach (p. 174)
glocal marketing approach (p. 174)
straight extension (p. 174)
product adaptation (p. 174)
backward invention (p. 175)
forward invention (p. 175)
dumping (p. 179)

REVIEW QUESTIONS

1. Distinguish among domestic, international, and global marketing.

2. How can a firm improve its cultural awareness?

3. Differentiate among industrialized, developing, and less-developed countries.

4. If the value of the Kenyan shilling goes from 75 shillings per U.S. dollar to 85 shillings per U.S. dollar, will U.S. products be more or less expensive in Kenya? Why?

5. Define each of the following:
   a. Local content law.
   b. Tariff.
   c. Embargo.

6. What are the pros and cons of exporting versus joint ventures?

7. Why would a firm use a nonstandardized international marketing strategy? What are the potential disadvantages of this strategy?

8. Distinguish among these product-planning strategies: straight extension, product adaptation, backward invention, and forward invention. When should each be used?

DISCUSSION QUESTIONS

1. Cite three basic differences between marketing in the United States and in Mexico.
2. In China, there is 1 car per 100 people, compared with 77 per 100 people in the United States. What are the ramifications of this from a marketing perspective?
3. What are the advantages and disadvantages of a country's belonging to an economic community such as the European Union?
4. Develop a 10-question checklist by which a bank could determine which and how many foreign markets to enter.

WEB EXERCISE

Lands' End has separate Web sites for U.S. customers (www. landsend.com) and German customers (www.landsend.de). Comment on the similarities and differences between the two sites.

7

Marketing and the Internet

Chapter Objectives

1 To demonstrate why the Internet is a valuable marketing tool

2 To explore the multifaceted potential marketing roles for the Internet

3 To show how to develop an Internet marketing strategy

4 To illustrate how the Internet is being utilized to enhance marketing strategies

5 To consider the challenges of using the Internet in marketing and to forecast the future of E-marketing

According to John Graham, president of a marketing consulting firm, there are 16 principles that companies should review when considering whether and how to use the Internet. Here is a description of several of them:

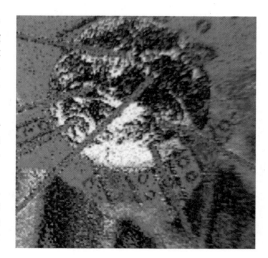

- *E-Commerce Is Not for Everyone*—A firm should not jump to the Web unless it has a valid and compelling reason.

- *The Web Does Not Stand Alone*—A variety of marketing strategies are needed to keep customers coming to a Web site, not just bookmarks or banner ads.

- *Traditional Marketing Channels Are Still Valid*—Direct mail, for example, is still very viable.

- *It's a Matter of Planning or Perish*—Even with the best research, everything does not go as planned. Therefore, contingency planning is needed.

- *Look at the Web as Research*—The Web is a reflection of what consumers do not like and what they want changed. It is excellent in transforming unpleasant and painful experiences (like car buying).

- *All That Counts Is the Customer*—Good Web-based firms know they must treat consumers as individuals who need to be understood.

- *Let's Get Outside Ourselves*—Greater attention should be paid to external forces of change. Firms must recognize that most breakthroughs are the result of looking outward at external trends.

- *If You See It, Don't Believe It*—E-commerce is not "right" for every firm.

- *Just Because It Works Doesn't Mean Its Right*—A firm could be vulnerable despite everything looking good.

- *It's 24/7 for Everyone*—The Web knows no place or time-based boundaries.

- *The Customer Is in Charge*—The more information that firms have on customers, the better the service levels they can provide.[1]

In this chapter we will explore the role of the Internet in a marketing setting. We will also look at how to develop an Internet marketing strategy and the challenges of using the Internet.

7-1 OVERVIEW

Before delving into our discussion of marketing and the Internet, let us define four basic terms.

The **Internet,** also known as "the Net," is a global electronic superhighway of computer networks—a network of networks in which users at one computer can get information from

The **Internet** is a global superhighway of computer networks. Through the **World Wide Web,** people work with easy-to-use Web addresses and pages.

[1]John R. Graham, "16 Ways to Keep a Business Online," *Interactive Marketing* (February 2000) pp. 56–64.

another computer (and sometimes talk directly to users at other computers). It is a public, cooperative, self-sustaining system accessible to hundreds of millions of people worldwide. The **World Wide Web (WWW),** also known as "the Web," comprises all of the resources and users on the Internet using the Hypertext Transfer Protocol (HTTP). It is a way of accessing the Internet, whereby people work with easy-to-use Web addresses and pages. Through the Web, users see words, colorful charts, pictures, and video, and hear audio.[2] Although the two terms have somewhat different meanings, they both relate to online activities—and they are both used interchangeably by the media and by companies. Thus, in this chapter (and book), both terms will have the same connotation: online actions.

E-marketing includes any marketing activity that is conducted through the Internet, from customer analysis to marketing-mix components. **E-commerce** refers to revenue-generating Internet transactions. E-marketing is the broader concept, and it does not necessarily have sales as the primary goal.

> **E-marketing** *involves any marketing activity on the Internet, while* **E-commerce** *is its revenue-generating component.*

By virtue of its rather low costs, its wide geographic reach, and the many marketing roles it can serve, the Internet should be a key part of *any* firm's marketing strategy—regardless of the firm's size or characteristics. The broadened scope of marketing in the decades ahead will require virtually every firm to have a Web presence, much as they now have a telephone, an answering machine, and other technological tools.

Since the Internet's inception as a commercially-viable business resource just a few years ago, its importance and value have been misperceived by many. At first, a number of experts talked of how Internet firms would soon overwhelm traditional retailers and drive them out of business. They predicted that by 2001 annual online retail sales in the United States alone would reach hundreds of billions of dollars. They were wrong: online retail sales are only a fraction of what was predicted. So, now, scores of experts are writing off the Internet as a short-lived fad; and they cite the high failure rate of "dot com" firms as evidence of the Internet's fall. Again, they are wrong about the Internet's impact.

These experts have not recognized how long a major new technology takes to permeate the marketplace. The majority of people in the world do not have a PC, "surf the Web," or shop online. Furthermore, a lot of people who own a PC, surf, and shop online still prefer shopping at stores due to the purchase immediacy, the hands-on buying experience, the social interaction with others, and so forth.

The true impact of the Internet, and the reason we are devoting a full chapter to this topic, relates to the multiple marketing tasks that can be undertaken, better and more efficiently—not to the level of sales revenues to be attained. This point underscores why the rush to judge the Internet as a declining fad is so wrong. Generating sales revenue is only one of a multitude of benefits that the Internet can achieve for a firm. Most of our focus is on E-marketing, not just on E-commerce.

In this chapter, we will cover these aspects of marketing and the Internet: why the Internet is such a valuable marketing tool, the multifaceted uses of the Internet, developing an Internet marketing strategy, applications of the Internet in marketing strategies, and the challenges and future of E-marketing.

7-2 WHY THE INTERNET IS A VALUABLE TOOL IN MARKETING

> *Web usage is rising rapidly worldwide.*

Hundreds of millions of people around the globe are surfing the Web. This signifies great E-marketing opportunities for firms. As Table 7-1 indicates, there are 175 million active home users in the top 10 nations alone; on average, they spend 7 to 8 hours monthly online and go online at least 12 times a month. Soon, the number of Internet users worldwide will reach 1 billion individuals. By 2005, it is predicted that three-quarters of all U.S. households will be online.[3]

People surf the Internet for a variety of reasons other than shopping. For instance, they seek out entertainment, financial, sports, and news sites. They do product research.

[2]"Look It Up," http://whatis.techtarget.com (March 9, 2001).
[3]"Global Internet Statistics," www.glreach.com/globstats/index.php3 (March 12, 2001).

 **Top 10 Countries' Internet Penetration of the Home Market, as of January 2001**

	Active Home Users	Average Time Spent Per Month	Average Number of Sessions Per Month	Active Home Users as a Percentage of Total Population
United States	101.4 million	9 hours, 58 min.	18	36
Japan	15.4 million	7 hours, 57 min.	16	12
Germany	12.8 million	8 hours, 16 min.	17	15
Great Britain	11.2 million	6 hours	12	19
Canada	9.0 million	10 hours, 48 min.	20	29
Italy	7.5 million	7 hours, 5 min.	13	13
Brazil	4.5 million	7 hours, 6 min.	12	3
France	5.6 million	6 hours, 32 min.	15	9
Australia	4.5 million	7 hours, 8 min.	12	24
Netherlands	3.9 million	7 hours, 8 min.	15	24

Sources: Compiled by the authors from *Nielsen//NetRatings*, www.nielsen-netratings.com (March 8, 2001); and U.S. Bureau of the Census, International Data Base.

They "talk" to one another (many via AOL Instant Messenger, www.aol.com/aim/home.html). They communicate with companies to register complaints and make suggestions. They send E-mails and greetings cards. The U.S. Postal Service (www.usps.com) handles 570 million pieces of mail per day; in contrast, there are 1.5 billion E-mail messages every day![4]

Companies (actually, their employees) also surf the Web for a variety of reasons other than shopping. For instance, they check out what competitors are doing. They read about industry trends and events. They communicate with their suppliers. They exchange data among offices anywhere in the world. They monitor inventory conditions. They survey customers and measure their satisfaction. They do very sophisticated analyses of customer data bases.

Procter & Gamble (www.pg.com), the consumer products giant, is a good illustration of how the Internet presents a variety of E-marketing opportunities beyond E-commerce:

P&G has never shied away from Web spending or innovating, since it went to the Net in the mid-1990s, experimenting first with pop-up ads for Scope mouthwash and Tide. The company also organized and hosted the first industry marketing forum on Internet advertising in 1998, inviting competitors and partners alike to its headquarters in Cincinnati. That group lives on simply as FAST, a coalition to discuss and develop interactive marketing and advertising.

Today, P&G operates about 70 user-friendly sites, often loaded with bells and whistles. The Web sites are only part of P&G's overall Internet strategy, of course, which includes extensive marketing partnerships with sites such as Bolt.com (www.bolt.com). It also includes a P&G venture capital incubator, Internet Venture Fund, to invest in promising Internet startups, including Plumtree Software (www.plumtreesoft.com) and Yet2.com (www.yet2.com). And it

[4]eMarketer, "Internet at a Glance," *Business 2.0* (February 6, 2001), p. 102; and Jupiter Research, "Internet at a Glance," *Business 2.0* (December 12, 2000), p. 282.

is involved in creating a global B-to-B marketplace online with fellow giants such as Unilever, Coca-Cola, and Nestlé called Transora (www.transora.com). The company has reaped value from its sites that can't be measured in dollars and cents. The sites build brand equity, for one; collect valuable data from consumers; and test the waters for direct sales to customers. The most important of those benefits right now is data collection. Ultimately, analysts doubt the company will launch any big selling effort that runs counter to its retail and channel partners. Its products are too readily available in grocery stores and drugstores, and direct sales are cost-intensive undertakings.[5]

Likewise, Ikea (www.ikea.com/default.asp) devotes a lot of attention to its Web site. It has colorful descriptions and photos of its home-furnishings product lines. There is a worldwide store locator. The firm explains its vision. But mostly, Ikea emphasizes in-store shopping as the way for consumers to get the most out of their home-furnishings shopping experience. The Swedish-based retailer has only recently added E-Commerce to its E-marketing efforts.

Next, let us examine two specific aspects of marketing and the Internet: the three phases of Internet use by companies and the benefits of using the Internet in marketing.

7-2a Bricks-and-Mortar, Clicks-Only, and Bricks-and-Clicks

E-marketing is evolving through the three phases highlighted in Figure 7-1. The phases are (1) bricks-and-mortar firms, (2) clicks-only firms, and (3) bricks-and-clicks firms.

Bricks-and-mortar firms are traditional companies that have not gotten involved with the Internet. Until a few years ago, this was very much the predominant business format, as these companies believed that the Internet provided too few benefits relative to the costs and complexity of being online. Now, bricks-and-mortar firms are likely to be small in size and scope.

> **Bricks-and-mortar firms** *are not involved with the Internet.* **Clicks-only firms** *do business just online.* **Bricks-and-clicks firms** *combine traditional and Internet formats.*

FIGURE 7-1
The Three Phases of Marketing and the Internet

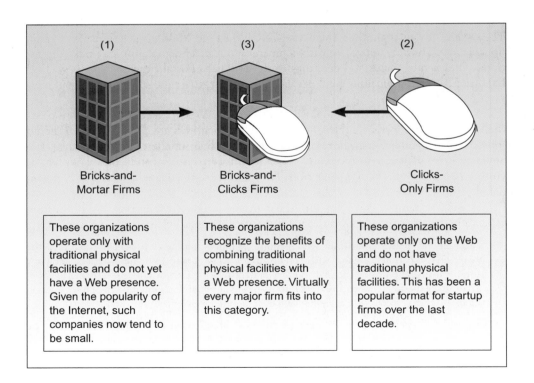

(1)	(3)	(2)
Bricks-and-Mortar Firms	Bricks-and-Clicks Firms	Clicks-Only Firms
These organizations operate only with traditional physical facilities and do not yet have a Web presence. Given the popularity of the Internet, such companies now tend to be small.	These organizations recognize the benefits of combining traditional physical facilities with a Web presence. Virtually every major firm fits into this category.	These organizations operate only on the Web and do not have traditional physical facilities. This has been a popular format for startup firms over the last decade.

[5]Beth Snyder Bulik, "Procter & Gamble's Great Web Experiment," *Business 2.0* (November 28, 2000), pp. 48–54.

In the 1990s, a number of innovative *clicks-only firms* entered the marketplace. These companies do business just online. They do not have traditional facilities. Many clicks-only firms have generated good revenues, but have had trouble turning a profit. They often expanded too fast and invested quite heavily in their infrastructures. There has been a major shakeup among clicks-only firms, with a number of once-popular ones going out of business. Still, there are now thousands and thousands of clicks-only firms.

Today, the trend is more toward *bricks-and-clicks firms* that operate in both a traditional setting and on the Internet. For example, virtually every large retailer (as well as a host of medium-size and small firms) has a substantial Web presence. The same is true of manufacturers, wholesalers, government organizations, nonprofit organizations, and others. The bricks-and-clicks approach enables companies to appeal to multiple market segments, maximize customer contact points, leverage the strengths of each form of business, and enter into new alliances.

Edmunds and Sharper Image are two examples of traditional firms that have actively moved into the bricks-and-clicks arena. See Figures 7-2 and 7-3. Edmunds (now Edmunds.com, www.edmunds.com) "was founded in 1966 for the purpose of publishing new and used vehicle guides to assist automotive buyers in making informed decisions. In 1994, Edmunds took advantage of the advent of the Internet by posting its vehicle data. The next year, Edmunds became the first company to establish a site on the World Wide Web on which consumers could obtain vehicle information at no cost, and in 2000, Edmunds became the first source for vehicle pricing information for

FIGURE 7-2

Edmunds.com: Where Smart Car Buyers Start

Source: Reprinted by permission.

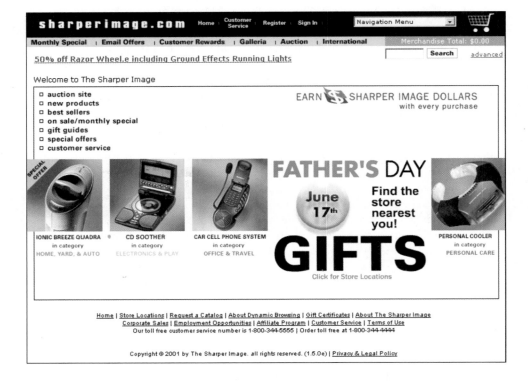

users of wireless Web-enabled devices." Sharper Image (www.sharperimage.com) "is a specialty retailer that is renowned as a leading source of new, innovative, high-quality products that make life easier and more enjoyable. The company operates about 100 stores throughout the United States and mails millions of catalogs each month. Products may also be purchased on the Internet via an online store. The company even has an online auction site where consumers can place bids to win Sharper Image products at lower prices; the auction site is accessed from the home page of the Web site."

Amazon.com (www.amazon.com) is one of the increasing number of formerly clicks-only firms that are now also operating traditional facilities or entering into alliances with partners that have traditional facilities. The company has alliances with Toys "R" Us (www.tru.com), Wal-Mart (www.walmart.com), and Walt Disney Stores (www.disney.com), among others.

7-2b The Benefits of a Company's Using the Internet in Marketing

The potential marketing benefits of the Internet range from communicability to sales revenues.

The Internet's value in marketing is best seen by reviewing the benefits that a company may receive by going online. Several of these benefits are shown in Figure 7-4 and described next.

Communicability—The Web makes it easy for a firm to communicate with every one of its constituencies: consumers, suppliers, resellers, employees, the media, government bodies, and others. As one observer noted, "The Internet allows you opportunities to talk to people on a continual, dialog basis in a way that we've never had before."[6]

Focus/tailored approach—The Web enables a company to focus on a specific target market and offer a marketing mix especially devised for that target market. For example, "With the Internet, you can keep track of purchase history—every single purchase

---

[6]Richard Lennox quote in Beth Snyder Bulik and Jennifer Gilbert, "Digital Marketing Hits the Mainstream," *Business 2.0* (March 20, 2001), p. 68.

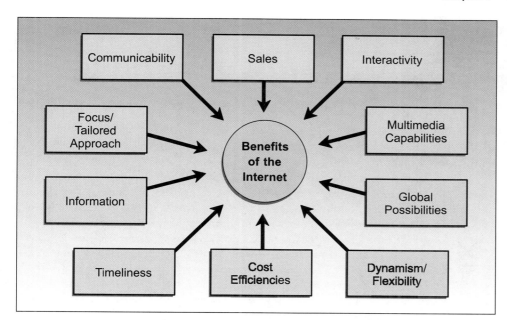

FIGURE 7-4
Company Benefits of Using the Internet in Marketing

a customer has ever made with you. The reason that's so important is because purchase history is probably one of the most predictive things in understanding what somebody is most inclined to buy in the future. The other thing the Internet is good for is targeted E-mails."[7]

Information—A firm can amass information about almost any facet of its business from free Web sites, as well as from fee-based ones. Both secondary data and primary data can be garnered via the Internet.

Timeliness—With the Internet, a company can operate in "real time," which means the ability to communicate, gather information, and so forth in a very contemporaneous manner. The time lags associated with other marketing tools are much shorter on the Web.

Cost efficiencies—There can be reduced costs from Internet usage. Postal costs decrease. Inventory costs can be lowered because there is more efficient communication between companies and their suppliers. Sales personnel can follow-up with clients in a more efficient manner. There are no shipping costs for items such as software that are sold via the Web and downloaded by customers.

Dynamism/flexibility—The Internet is a very dynamic and flexible medium, which lets a company rapidly adjust its marketing mix. For instance, if a firm sees that a particular product is not selling well, it can instantly change the advertising at its Web site or lower the price until consumer demand reaches a satisfactory level. Likewise, if a firm runs out of a popular item that it is selling, a reorder can be placed immediately through the Web.

Global possibilities—With the Internet, a company can effectively and inexpensively communicate with its various constituencies around the world, thereby increasing the reach of the firm's marketing strategy. The expensive part of operating a global E-commerce Web site is often the distribution costs that result from expanding into new geographic markets.

Multimedia capabilities—The Internet has large multimedia possibilities for marketers, especially as additional users convert to cable, DSL, or other fast connections. More company Web sites will soon be showing 3-D product pictures that can be rotated 360 degrees, streaming audio and video, photo galleries of product offerings,

GLOBAL *Marketing in Action*

The Declining Reliance on English in Online Activities

Just four years ago, the native language of 80 percent of all Web users was English. By 2004, it is estimated that only one-third of all Web users will be native English speakers.

The response to the declining importance of the English language is mixed. For example, a recent study showed that 55 percent of U.S.-based Web firms offer only an English language site. In contrast, some Web-based firms have begun to effectively communicate with multinational markets where English is not a dominant language. Examples include U.S.-based firms such as Yahoo! (www.yahoo.com)—with sites in a dozen or so languages; Amazon.com (www.amazon.com)—with sites in Japanese, French, and German; and eBay (www.ebay.com)—with sites in both German and French. Foreign-based firms are much more active in offering their sites in various languages because of the diversity of their audiences.

There is growing evidence that having sites in multiple languages represents an effective way to generate greater visits to the sites, as well as higher sales, by expanding a firm's geographic attractiveness. When GongShee.com (www.gongshee.com), an online retailer featuring Chinese foods, added Chinese-language descriptions for its products to its existing English-language copy, the firm's online sales increased by 700 percent.

In deciding whether to act more global, firms need to recognize that developing sites in multiple languages does not mean simply hiring translators. To be effective, sites must be able to handle different currencies, alphabet characters, and measurement systems. In addition, some languages read from right to left, and icons that are popular in the United States (such as mailboxes and shopping carts) may not be familiar to consumers in foreign countries.

Develop a checklist for a firm to use in developing a multiple-language Web site.

Source: Based on material in Roger O. Crockett, "Surfing in Tongues," *Business Week* (December 11, 2000), p. EB18.

---

and so forth. At Hard Rock Cafe, "We'll use the Web to create a forum for up-and-coming artists and to bring national bands that play our large concert venues into the smaller locations."[8]

Interactivity—Unlike traditional advertising, which is unidirectional (from company to audience), the Internet can be deployed in an interactive manner (from company to audience <u>and</u> from audience to company)—much like personal selling. Thus, a company can ask people to click on a section of its Web site that they would like to visit and then transport them to that particular section, where more user choices are made. For example, an airline site can gather data on the destination and date a person wants to travel to from his or her home area, and then display the alternative flights that fit the person's criteria.

Sales—For a clicks-only firm, the Internet represents the sole source of revenue. For a bricks-and-clicks firm, the Internet offers the potential for growing the business. As an

---

[8]Stefani Eads, "A New Beat at the Hard Rock," *Business Week* (October 9, 2000), p. 166E8.

example, in 1999, 25 percent of Southwest Airline's (www.southwest.com) reservations were made online. By 2004, the company expects 75 percent of its reservations to be made online. Also consider that among experienced Internet users (those who spend 18 hours a month online and who have been online for at least two years), one-fifth make 10 or more purchases via the Internet during any 90-day period.[9]

7-3 THE MULTIFACETED POTENTIAL MARKETING ROLES FOR THE INTERNET

After reviewing the company benefits of the Internet in marketing, it should be clear that the Web has the potential to serve multiple marketing roles. These are shown in Figure 7-5 and discussed next. Each firm must determine which roles to pursue and how to prioritize their importance.

Projecting an image—A firm can project an image at its Web site through the site's design (colors, graphics, etc.) and the content presented. Have you ever heard of Accenture (www.accenture.com), formerly known as Andersen Consulting? No? Well, you can learn a lot about the firm and the image it is striving to project by visiting its Web site. The site explains what Accenture is, what it does, the types of clients it serves, where it does business, and a whole lot more: "Clients are looking for more than 'advice.' Besides solid advice, they need total solutions. That's why Accenture has devised a comprehensive approach to consulting that moves clients forward at each level of their business, from high-level strategic planning to improved customer service to day-to-day operations."

Customer service—According to various surveys, many companies use the Internet to supplement their traditional customer service. At its Web site, Staples (www.staples.com), the office products chain, has a "Business Services" section—where it gives small business advice on topics ranging from how to select the proper copy machine to how to best plan a promotional mailing.

Channel relations—The Internet can help channel members to better understand one another, to coordinate their distribution strategies, to smooth over conflicts, and so forth. Two-year-old WineryExchange (www.wineryexchange.com) is "a neutral trading system

> *Depending on the company, the Internet can serve many roles besides generating sales.*

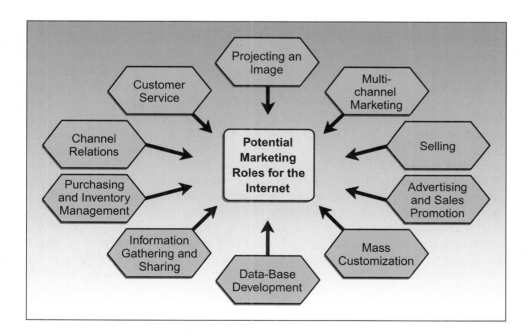

FIGURE 7-5

How the Internet May Be Utilized in Marketing

[9]Southwest Airlines, "Internet at a Glance," *Business 2.0* (February 20, 2001), p. 112; and Greenfield Online, "Experienced Users Shopping Online," *Business 2.0* (February 6, 2001), p. 98.

connecting wine growers, wineries, suppliers, and retailers. It offers access to goods and services for every link in the value chain—'from the dirt to the bottle.' WineryExchange also offers news, information, and analysis affecting the wine industry worldwide. By offering a single online destination for commercial wine transactions, we help our customers increase revenues, lower costs, and improve customer service."

Purchasing and inventory management—Company purchases and inventory management can be greatly facilitated through the Web. As *Fortune* recently noted, "Businesses are finding out that E-marketplaces do something even more important than locating a better price on materials. They save time. Before Sprint hooked up with the online auction site eBreviate (www.ebreviate.com) to speed procurement, parts of the process moved at the business-to-business equivalent of 28 Kbps. Sprint would issue a request for bids, often by mail, to a large number of suppliers. A paper trail then had to wind through its bureaucracy, which took as long as two months to select suppliers. Now, with online auctions, Sprint can whittle down an initial list of 120 suppliers to 10 or 20 in just hours."[10]

Information gathering and sharing—As previously noted, the Internet has considerable possibilities for providing marketing information. Procter & Gamble (P&G) "has marketed thousands of products over the years—but never its brains. Until now. For the first time, P&G will—for a price—open its treasure chest of marketing knowledge. The joint venture with Emmperative (http://www.emmperative.com) will offer for sale a good chunk of P&G's 160 years of marketing know-how. It's P&G's bid to cash in on its expertise as the world's top consumer-product marketer. The information will be available online to any company willing to pay the price—which could vary from thousands to millions of dollars. Initially, P&G will market this venture to the 2,000 largest global marketers. Later, it will be made available to smaller businesses. Among its earliest customers: Coca-Cola."[11]

Data-base development—As a result of the online interaction between a company and its suppliers and customers, extensive marketing data bases can be developed. Staples' Web site has one million registered users and more than 300,000 monthly repeat users, with purchase data on each one. Staples uses the data to determine "who bought what, and what do we market to them next?"[12]

Mass customization—An attractive feature of the Internet involves companies' ability to engage in **mass customization,** a process by which mass-market goods and services are individualized to satisfy a specific customer need, at a reasonable price. According to one systems design firm, "Based on the public's growing desire for product personalization, it is the ultimate combination of 'custom-made' and 'mass production.' E-commerce makes it possible for anyone to order a computer designed to his or her exact needs and specifications. Or compile music CDs containing any combination of songs. Or obtain customized home mortgages. Or design a one-of-a-kind friend of Barbie, complete with unique name, clothing, and personality. Unlike mass production, which produces some variety of an item in high volumes, mass customization is characterized by small volumes—in many cases, lot sizes of one. It is also characterized by competitive cost, timely deliveries, and a move away from centralized manufacturing to more distributed production. Mass customization not only benefits the consumer, it offers the manufacturer significant benefits as well: a high degree of product/service flexibility, reduced inventory risk, and a competitive edge in the marketplace."[13]

Advertising and sales promotion—Through the Internet, a company can promote its goods and services, along with its image. It can use banner ads at portal sites, be listed at search engines, and present multimedia messages and special sales promotions at its own Web site. Staples is very vigorous in its approach: It "has relationships with Yahoo! and

Through online **mass customization,** *a company can individualize mass-market goods and services to satisfy a specific customer need, at a fair price.*

[10]"Yank the Supply Chain," *Fortune Tech Guide* (Winter 2001), p. 153.

[11]Bruce Horovitz, "P&G Plans to Share Marketing Tips—For a Price," *USA Today* (January 24, 2001), p. B2.

[12]John Gaffney, "Pushing the Envelope," *Revolution* (March 2001), p. 42.

[13]Gerber Scientific, "What Is Mass Customization?" www.mass-customization.com (March 11, 2001).

FIGURE 7-6
Driving Global E-Commerce
The Internet is transforming the way people work, play, and shop. That is certainly true in Brazil, where Som Livre (assisted by Unisys) is the country's leading online music retailer. It has more than 50,000 Real Audio music files—from 150 recording labels—that customers can sample before buying.

Source: Reprinted by permission. Richard Bowditch, Photographer.

Lycos as the exclusive office-products provider for its shopping areas. The Staples affiliate network includes more than 1,000 sites, and it offers a sliding scale of 4 to 10 percent commissions on sales."[14]

Selling—Of course, generating sales is a key Internet marketing role for a number of firms. (We've listed it down here to re-emphasize that selling is only one role for the Internet.) When engaging in E-commerce, this should be kept in mind: "The task of creating a satisfying shopping experience online is different from the same task offline because an online shopper is both consumer and co-designer of the shopping experience. Clicking from site to site and page to page, online shoppers have more control over the time, the place, and the way in which they move through a merchandise offering than store shoppers. Thus, a site's role isn't simply to create the shopping experience. It is also to develop and share with the consumer the tools (such as product information, personalization options, navigational features, opinions of others, help guides, etc.) that can make a great shopping experience possible."[15] See Figure 7-6.

Multichannel marketing—Bricks-and-clicks firms engage in multichannel marketing, whereby they sell their products through more than one distribution format, in this case, the Internet and at least one other format. Staples has a Web site, more than 1,100 stores, an 800 number, and in-store video kiosks. It offers free next business-day shipping on orders of $50 and more.

7-4 DEVELOPING AN INTERNET MARKETING STRATEGY

To best utilize the Internet in marketing, a firm should adhere to a systematic process in preparing and enacting the proper strategy. Figure 7-7 presents the steps to be followed in this process. The six middle boxes in the flowchart relate to the basic components of an Internet marketing strategy. The four outside boxes are key influences in making strategic decisions. Let us explore each of these factors.

(1) Goal categories are set, drawn from the factors in Figure 7-5. Both quantitative and qualitative objectives should then be enumerated. According to one recent study, 67 percent of the responding companies want to use the Internet to attract new cus-

There are six basic steps in developing an Internet marketing strategy.

[14]Gaffney, "Pushing the Envelope," p. 42.

[15]Jackie Pollok, "The Online Shopping Experience," *Hot Topics* (Columbus, Ohio: PricewaterhouseCoopers, August 2000), p. 1.

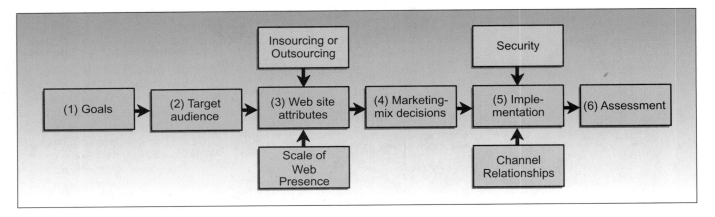

FIGURE 7-7

The Stages of an Internet Marketing Strategy

A company must decide between insourcing and outsourcing Web activities, and determine the scope of its Web presence.

tomers, 62 percent to build loyalty among existing customers, 58 percent to improve customer service, 48 percent to streamline business processes, 47 percent to grow market share, 45 percent to enhance communication among customers, and 41 percent to enhance communication among employees.[16]

(2) The target audience is identified and selected, and its desires studied. Here are some recent research findings about online users:

- Consumers around the world are more likely (80 percent) to shop online from home rather than while at work. In the United States and Canada, Web users are balanced between males and females; in India, 96 percent of users are men.[17]

- Six types of Internet consumers have been identified: newbie shoppers—first-time Web purchasers who are older than other online shoppers and start with small purchases; reluctant shoppers—who are motivated to buy but worried about security and privacy issues; frugal shoppers—those who actively search for the lowest prices; strategic shoppers—those who know what they want before going online and go to specific sites to shop; enthusiastic shoppers—those who like to shop; and convenience shoppers (the largest group)—those who buy online to save time.[18]

- As shown in Figure 7-8, people have numerous reasons for shopping online. Different target audiences place a different emphasis on these reasons. That is why consumer desires must be examined carefully before embarking on the specifics of an Internet marketing strategy.

(3) Web site attributes are determined. However, before getting into Web site details, the company must first decide whether to undertake all Web-related activities itself (insourcing) or to have specialized firms do some or all Web-related activities for it (outsourcing). Most companies outsource the technical development and maintenance of their Web sites; far fewer fully develop Web sites on their own.[19] Small firms often outsource the entire operation. MySite from Entrepreneur.com (www.entrepreneur.com) "will design your Web site, host it, and maintain it for only $29.95 a month." Second, the company must choose the scale of its Web presence, especially the importance of the Web site in its overall marketing strategy, the percent of the marketing budget to devote to the Web site, and how the Web site is to be implemented. How is the Web site to be used for customer service, channel relations, selling, and so forth? Are all of the company's product lines to be displayed at the Web site? Is the Web site to be a simple one or to have a full range of bells and whistles? How widely is the Web site to be promoted?

[16]"It's All About the Customer," *Sales & Marketing Management* (December 2000), p. 69.

[17]Debra Hazel, "Study: E-Shoppers Across World Strikingly Similar," *Shopping Centers Today* (January 2001), p. 16.

[18]Melinda Cuthbert, "All Buyers Not Alike," *Business 2.0* (December 26, 2000), pp. 134, 137.

[19]See "Ring It Up," *Fortune Tech Guide* (Winter 2001), pp. 192–195; and Carol Pickering, "Outsourcing the Store," *Business 2.0* (October 10, 2000), pp. 48–54.

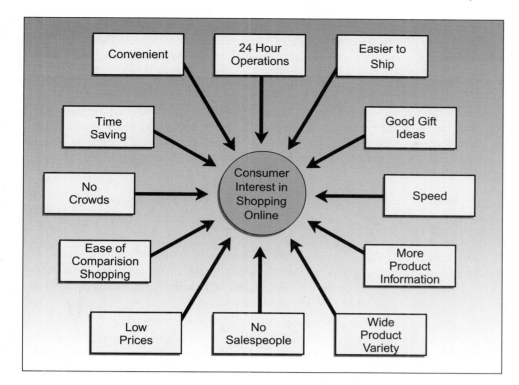

FIGURE 7-8

Why Consumers Purchase Online

It is critical for a Web site to be designed well.

After making decisions as to insourcing or outsourcing and the scale of the Web presence, Web site attributes are ascertained. Here are some factors to consider in designing a marketing-oriented Web site:

- *Web address*—The company can have its own Web address or be part of a Web community. It must carefully pick a name to use. There will soon be more confusion than before due to the addition of new domain suffixes: .info and .biz for general use, .pro for professionals, .name for personal sites, .museum for museums, .aero for the aerospace industry, and .coop for business cooperatives (as designated by ICANN, www.icann.com).

- *Home page*—The home page is the gateway to the firm. It projects an image, presents information, and routes viewers to other relevant company pages. It must be easy to navigate and laid out well.

- *Site content*—The content can include some or all of these topics: company background, company vision and philosophy, financial performance, product descriptions, where products are sold, community service involvement, customer service, an online shopping cart, career opportunities, press releases, and more.

- *Use of multimedia*—A site can be rather plain with mostly text and a few graphics, or it can involve the heavy use of photos, animations, audio clips, video clips, and so forth.

- Links—Web sites can have two types of links. Almost every company has <u>internal links</u>, whereby a person clicks on an icon on the home page and he or she is then transported to another section <u>within</u> the company's site. There may also be <u>external links</u>, whereby a person clicks on an icon on the home page and he or she is then sent to another Web site <u>outside</u> of the company's site, such as a trade association or a search engine. With the latter, the person may not return to the company site.

- *Shopping tools*—If a site engages in E-commerce, there must be a mechanism for directing shoppers through the purchase process, including a secure way of entering personal data. Amazon.com (www.amazon.com) is widely admired for the "1-Click" shopping format it offers to customers.

- *Electronic data interchange*—A Web site must be able to exchange pertinent information among company employees and between channel members. This is especially critical in E-commerce with regard to order shipping and inventory control.

- *Feedback*—Visitors must have a mechanism for communicating with the firm, and there must be a mechanism for the company to respond in a timely manner.

- *Trade-offs*—When designing a Web site, trade-offs must be weighed. For example, a Web site with a lot of graphics and photos may take a long time for users to download if they are using telephone modems to access the Internet. So, the question is: How many bells and whistles should a Web site have, given the limitations of them for some users?

(4) Internet-based marketing-mix decisions are made while developing the Web site; and they must be consistent (synergistic) with offline marketing decisions. These are some examples:

- *Product decisions*—Which products are cited at the Web site? Which products are featured at the Web site? Many firms do not list or describe all of the items in their product mix. Also, what should be the features of downloadable products (software, music, publications, etc.) that are sold online?

- *Distribution decisions*—If the company sells at its Web site, does it ship from one locale or from around the country (world)? How quickly can (should) products be delivered to customers? In 2000, it took an average of 6 days for customers to receive their orders, and only 36 percent of orders were received on time or early.[20]

- *Promotion decisions*—Which promotion mix should be used to reach the firm's Internet goals? There are many ways to promote a Web site and E-marketing efforts: ranging from banner ads to listing Web addresses in traditional ads to E-mail, and more. One of the most effective new online promotion tools is the **opt-in (permission-based) E-mail,** whereby Internet users agree to receive targeted E-mail from a firm. It is more effective than unsolicited E-mail, which turns off a lot of people. Each year, 40 billion opt-in E-mail messages are sent in the United States. Thus, "Marketers must make sure E-mails are targeted, of value to the customer, and integrated with their overall strategy. Only firms providing value will be able to maintain a dialogue with consumers."[21]

- *Pricing decisions*—A company engaging in E-commerce has two fundamental pricing decisions: How should online prices relate to those for offline businesses (including those of the firm itself)? How frequently should prices be changed to reflect market conditions? Because so many Internet shoppers are price-driven, online prices have tended to be lower than offline prices for the same products, and online transactions are often not subject to sales tax. Although the technology exists to adjust online pricing by the minute, firms must be careful not to confuse consumers or to get them upset if they visit a site and then return the next day to purchase, only to find that the price has risen.

Opt-in E-mail, *which is sent with the permission of the consumer, is good for both the company and the consumer.*

A Web site must be secure, protect privacy, and not be a threat to other channel members.

(5) At this point, the Internet marketing strategy is implemented. Again, there are two factors that affect the firm's ability to properly enact its strategy; this time, they are security and channel relationships. A vast number of Internet users are concerned about Web security, and they are hesitant to provide personal information for fear that "hackers" will obtain the data or that firms will resell the data. The security issue can be dealt with by offering a secure section of a Web site, protected by a well-known firm such as VeriSign (www.verisign.com) or beTrusted (www.betrusted.com), for entering personal data and credit-card information. The reselling issue can be handled by having a clear, user-friendly privacy policy that is accessible by clicking an icon at the firm's Web site.

[20]Accenture, "Shipping by Net Retailers," *Business 2.0* (March 6, 2001), p. 100.
[21]Evantheia Schibsted, "E-Mail Takes Center Stage," *Business 2.0* (December 26, 2000), pp. 64–69.

With regard to channel relationships, a move into E-commerce may place a company into conflict with its suppliers or resellers, which may view this action as a form of competition. So, the trade-offs have to be weighed.

Once the strategy is enacted, the firm must be sure that it runs smoothly. Thus, it must be alert to several possible breakdowns in the system, such as site crashes, out-of-stock conditions, a slow response to customer inquiries, incorrect prices, hacker invasions, and poor coordination with the offline strategy.

(6) The last step in an Internet marketing strategy is to assess performance and make necessary modifications. Assessment should be closely tied to the Web goals (step 1) that have been set in terms of image, customer service, sales, and so forth. These are some of the measures that can be utilized: daily Web site traffic, average length of the stay at the Web site, ratings on customer service surveys, sales revenues, the cost per transaction, repeat business, the number and type of system breakdowns per time period, and more. The value of banner ads placed at other sites must be also be judged for effectiveness.

MARKETING *and the Web*

Measuring Web Site Effectiveness by Counting Eyeballs

One of the many marketing research firms that help evaluate Web sites and provide recommendations to improve them is eyeTracking.com (www. eyetracking.com). While competitors often conduct Web usability studies through focus groups, one-to-one interviews, and automated software, eyeTracking. com uses an eye-tracking technique combined with sophisticated software.

eyeTracking.com provides test subjects with equipment that is strapped to their foreheads. This equipment tracks eye direction and measures the expansion and contraction of pupils. Participants are not asked any questions during the process since the firm believes questions would distract their attention.

A major advantage of eye-tracking methodology is that it minimizes interviewer and respondent biases. A significant drawback is that eye-tracking cannot explain *why* a subject may be unable to complete an online order. For example, the problem could be related to poor placement of a link or a cluttered design. To help provide such answers, eyeTracking.com offers clients the option of qualitative interviewing, whereby participants are interviewed after the eye-tracking experience for 20 to 30 minutes.

Four service levels are offered by eyeTracking.com, ranging in price from $8,000 to $18,500. The least expensive service includes only the eye-tracking study; the most expensive includes both qualitative testing and post-study analyses.

According to marketing analysts, firms that use eye-tracking should do so throughout the life of a site: from prototype stage through maturity. This enables them to develop benchmarks (such as how long specific material is viewed and the percentage of subjects who ultimately select the ordering location). Unfortunately, many companies use testing only when a site does not meet objectives.

Evaluate eyeTracking's methodology. What pros and cons does it offer? Explain your answer.

Source: Based on material in Tessa Romita, "The Eyes Have It," *Business 2.0* (November 14, 2000), p. 286.

Special attention should be paid to evaluating the quality of the Web site itself. These are among the factors that should be regularly reviewed from the Internet user's perspective:[22]

- Clarity of site's mission.
- Download time.
- Speed of site comprehension.
- Informational value.
- Ease of navigability.
- Use of graphics/multimedia.
- Interactivity.
- Currency.
- Security.
- Simplicity of purchasing.
- Printability of site pages.
- Creativity.

7-5 HOW THE INTERNET IS BEING APPLIED IN MARKETING STRATEGIES

We now present several examples of E-Marketing in action.

7-5a Consumer Analysis

Internet marketing is being applied in many ways.

As highlighted in Table 7-2, research shows that 27 percent of U.S. Internet users actually shop online, a higher percentage than in other nations. Shoppers worldwide are much more apt to buy books and music/CDs than any other product category. Online purchases as a percentage of total category sales (both offline and online) are growing rapidly in many categories. User activity is strongly influenced by age.

Internet stock brokers recognize that their least technologically-savvy clients are much less interested in real-time quotes, unlimited transaction history, profit-and-loss accounting, managing multiple accounts, and after-hours trading than the most technologically-savvy clients. Female car purchasers are more likely than male car purchasers to use the Internet for the purpose of avoiding high-pressure sales pitches.[23]

7-5b Product Planning

Companies are taking a variety of product planning approaches to the Internet, such as these two. Atomic Dog (www.atomicdog.com), the publisher of this text, is involved with Internet-driven texts and print versions of them. The online texts feature high-tech graphics, animations, interactivity, and other dynamic attributes not found in traditional paper-based books. At Pillsbury's Web site (www.pillsbury.com), people can download recipes which may require ingredients that the firm markets: "Things like pies do suggest

---

[22]See Joel R. Evans and Vanessa E. King, "Business-to-Business Marketing and the Worldwide Web: Planning, Managing, and Assessing Web Sites," *Industrial Marketing Management*, Vol. 28 (July 1999), pp. 343–358; and James Morris-Lee, "Assessing Web Site Effectiveness," *Direct Marketing* (July 2000), pp. 30–33.

[23]Todd Canfield, "Know Thy Customer," *Business 2.0* (October 24, 2000), p. 248; and Catherine Greenman, "Women Turn to Web to Avoid Sales Pressure," *New York Times on the Web* (January 5, 2001).

TABLE 7-2 Consumer Purchases Online

Country	Percent in 2000 of Internet Users Buying Online	Products Bought Online	Worldwide Percent in 2000 of Internet Users Buying Online
United States	27	Books	29
Japan	20	Music/CDs	20
Great Britain	18	Computer software	11
Germany	17	Apparel	10
South Korea	16	Food	10
Czech Republic	14	Computer hardware	9
Netherlands	12	Leisure travel	9
Australia	10	Electronics	6
		Toys and games	6

Products Bought Online	Percent of All 2001 U.S. Purchases in Category	Percent of All 2003 (est.) U.S. Purchases in Category	Attributes of U.S. Population	Percent in 2000
Air travel	12.5	15.4	Children 2 to 12 online	32
Apparel	1.4	3.7	Teens 13 to 18 online	46
Books	8.6	14.3	College students online	90
Computers (PCs)	28.9	40.4	Adults 35 to 50 online	47
Computer software	28.1	48.9	Adults 51 and up online	34
Consumer electronics	2.2	4.7	Male/female online ratio	50/50
Event tickets	4.7	12.5	Male/female online shopping ratio	52/48
Furniture	0.3	2.1	Online shoppers 65 and up share of all online shoppers	15
Groceries	0.4	1.5		
Hotel stays	6.5	9.8		
Music	9.2	14.0		
Toys	2.8	5.6		

Sources: Table compiled by the authors based on data from Taylor Nelson Sofres, "10% of Worldwide Net Users Buy Online," *BizReport,* www.bizreport.com/research/2000/08/20000801-1.htm (August 1, 2000); Jupiter Research, "Following the Money," *Wall Street Journal* (October 23, 2000), p. R4; eMarketer and BizRate.com, "Look Who's Spending Online," *Business 2.0* (December 26, 2000), pp. 126, 129; and "The Year of the Dot-Bomb," *Advertising Age* (December 18, 2000), p. 44.

using Pillsbury pie crust, but lots of the meal ideas don't even mention the brand. That gives us credibility with consumers."[24] More companies are also heeding this advice:

> On the Web, all goods are not equal. Products possess different attributes and different levels of the same attributes. One important dimension on which items differ is in the ability of consumers to ascertain the quality of products in cyberspace. On one end of the spectrum are commodity products, where quality can be clearly and contractually articulated and conveyed. Products such as oil, paper clips, and stock shares all fall under this category. On the other end of the continuum are products for which the perception of quality differs from consumer to consumer and product to product, such as produce, used cars, and works of art. Understanding how difficult it is for firms to convey quality, reliability, or consistency for certain classes of products over the Web enables businesspeople to think strategically about the long-term success of different types of E-commerce.[25]

7-5c Distribution Planning

On the one hand, there is Terry Precision Cycling (www.terrybicycles.com), a small manufacturer of bicycles and related products for women. The firm does relatively little E-commerce business at its Web site, and relies on independent bicycle shops around the country. On the other hand, there is J.C. Penney (www.jcpenney.com), the huge retail chain. While its stores generate well over $30 billion in sales each year, it is Penney's Web site that is providing the firm with its greatest sales growth. In 2000, online sales were $300 million. As of 2002, annual online sales are expected to hit $1 billion.

One of the most complex aspects of E-distribution involves business-to-business exchanges that connect sellers with potential buyers. For instance, in February 2000, several major auto makers established Covisint (www.covisint.com), with the ultimate goal of working online with 90,000 global suppliers—and saving $2,000 or more per vehicle. But more than a year later, only 20 suppliers had signed on.[26]

With the distribution problems that a number of online firms have faced, they are now more apt to outsource delivery to such industry powerhouses as UPS, which has a significant Internet logistical presence (www.ec.ups.com). See Figure 7-9.

7-5d Promotion Planning

With the demise of a number of prominent E-commerce firms, including Pets.com and eToys.com, Internet-driven firms have dramatically scaled back on their advertising efforts, particularly TV ads. These efforts proved too costly and too ineffective. Print and online ads remain popular. In-store kiosks have a role, as illustrated in Figure 7-10. And as mentioned earlier in the chapter, opt-in E-mail is rising rapidly in popularity.

For companies that are new to Web-based promotion planning, Wilson Internet Services has two excellent resources, entitled "The Web Marketing Checklist: 27 Ways to Promote Your Site" (www.wilsonweb.com/articles/checklist.htm) and "How to Attract Visitors to Your Web Site" (www.wilsonweb.com/articles/attract.htm).

7-5e Price Planning

According to Jupiter Research, 80 percent of Internet shoppers comparison shop before buying and 46 percent of Internet shoppers visit 3 to 5 sites before making a purchase. Some firms set their online prices similar to—or slightly below—their offline prices, and count on customer loyalty to their brands and the convenience of Web shopping to stimulate

---

[24]Helen Jones, "Attack of the Killer Not-Coms," *Revolution* (March 2001), p. 50.

[25]John M. de Figueiredo, "Sustainable Profitability in Electronic Commerce," *Sloan Management Review*, Vol. 41 (Summer 2000), p. 41.

[26]Martha Baer and Jeffrey Davis, "Some Assembly Required," *Business 2.0* (February 20, 2001), pp. 76–85.

FIGURE 7-9

Moving at the Speed of E-Logistics

UPS has established an E-logistics division to handle Internet transactions. It dominates the shipments of products purchased online.

Source: Reprinted by permission. Photo by John Huet.

FIGURE 7-10

A New Job for In-Store Kiosks

Federated Department Stores has been experimenting with how to best use in-store kiosks, which are part of the bricks-and-clicks integration envisioned by the firm. "Case in point: A shopper at a smaller suburban department store wants to purchase 12 place settings of fine china—a category the store displays, but does not stock in depth. She can examine the merchandise on display, then use a kiosk to order the merchandise with a swipe of her credit card. The customer's order is channeled to the nearest Federated distribution center with the china in stock, and shipped directly to her home within hours—freeing her to continue shopping the store."

Source: Reprinted by permission.

business. Other companies such as eBay (www.ebay.com) and Priceline.com (www.priceline.com) focus their appeal on people who like to price shop and get bargains.

Still other companies use the Internet to sell close-out merchandise at deep discounts:

> Retailers have always been ambivalent about close-out items. The racks of last season's worst sellers and returns are constant reminders of buying blunders, lost sales opportunities, and wasted space. Yet, these goods can be magnets for some customers who might come to the store for bargains but leave with a carload of full-price items. On the Web, close-outs cause no ambivalence. If close-out items belong to the E-tailer, E-mail is a cost-effective way to tell people about bargains and unload goods quickly. When merchants buy close-outs from manufacturers and distributors at a steep discount, they can use the goods not only to expand profit margins, but to lure existing customers back to the site.[27]

7-6 CURRENT CHALLENGES AND FUTURE PROSPECTS FOR E-MARKETING

In this section, we look at the challenges and future prospects for marketing and the Internet.

7-6a The Challenges of Using the Internet in Marketing

Some challenges that marketers face when employing the Internet are beyond their control (such as slow-speed modem connections and the complexity of multichannel marketing); others are self-inflicted (such as poor customer service and overly rapid expansion). Before turning to several specific challenges, both uncontrollable and self-inflicted, let us cite some general reasons why E-marketing can be so daunting:[28]

- The company's corporate culture may be resistant to change.
- Internet marketing may not capitalize on a company's core competencies.
- The proper roles for E-marketing may not be specified clearly enough—or be realistic in nature.
- Web users may be very demanding.
- The personal touch may be important to many customers.
- Channel partners may be alienated.
- Online and offline systems may be hard to integrate.
- It may be difficult to determine what Internet functions to insource and which to outsource.
- Investment costs and ongoing expenses may be underestimated.

Let us now review a number of specific challenges related to marketing and the Internet.

Consumer resistance to online shopping—Despite the rapid growth of online sales revenues, at present less than two percent of all retail sales revenues and less than five percent of all business-to-business sales revenues are from Internet transactions. Why? Final consumers still want personal contact, the immediacy of a store purchase, and the ability to touch products before buying. They also often find the online purchase process to be too cumbersome. In 2000, of every 100 potential consumers who visited a retail Web site, only 2 actually made a purchase. From a business-to-business perspective,

---

[27]Bob Tedeschi, "Close-Out Items a Reliable Source of Revenue for Online Retailers," *New York Times on the Web* (September 11, 2000).

[28]See Melinda Ligos, "Clicks & Misses," *Sales & Marketing Management* (June 2000), pp. 69–76; Rosabeth Moss Kanter, "You Are Here," *Inc.* (February 2001), pp. 85–90; and Rosabeth Moss Kanter, "The Ten Deadly Mistakes of Wanna-Dots," *Harvard Business Review*, Vol. 79 (January 2001), pp. 91–100.

"Most companies' existing suppliers are not yet on the Web, so purchasing agents see little reason to go there themselves. Moreover, purchasing managers are reluctant to learn how to use the various Intranet and Internet sites peddling everything from manufacturing supplies to printer cartridges, and they do not necessarily trust those sites to deliver critically important goods on time and at the right quality."[29]

Customer service—Web users often feel frustrated by what they perceive as inadequate customer service. According to a recent Jupiter Research survey of Internet shoppers, more than one-half of the respondents expected firms to respond to E-mail within six hours, but only 29 percent of firms met this goal. Delivery issues were the primary reason for online shoppers' contact with customer service reps. Besides many deliveries being delayed, one-third of customers who ordered items that were out of stock said they were not notified of a target delivery date. Overall, more than one-half of Internet shoppers were disappointed with the customer service. Furthermore, as one columnist noted, "These days, 'don't call us' seems to be the prevailing attitude among companies that do business online. Many companies require customers to fill out electronic forms to contact a representative, but rarely do they offer a phone number. And they tend to bury E-mail links—if they publish them at all—deep within their Web sites."[30] What all of this means is that companies must do better, some significantly better.

System breakdowns—Various system breakdowns have occurred and will continue to occur. Some are caused by companies' lack of attention to their sites, but most are due to the sheer complexity of E-marketing with regard to the number of parties involved in a typical Web site (from Internet service provider to content Web master), the amount of traffic on the Web, the number of links that firms have at their sites (which must be checked regularly to be sure they are not broken), the use of multimedia, and other factors. In addition, companies must constantly be vigilant and protect their Web sites against intrusions from hackers who may corrupt files, steal customer data, and otherwise be destructive.

Speed of site performance—Slow Internet connections are irritating to both users and companies that have Web sites. Users with dial-up connections (through modems that work via the telephone line)—still the dominant mode for home users—must wait to log on every time they dial-up, face periodic busy signals, and must endure long delays when photos or other multimedia tools are featured at the Web site. Some features, such as video clips, may not work at all with a dial-up connection. Firms are disappointed because they must scale down their sites so that downloads are not excessively slow for dial-up users. As mentioned before, with the advent of "always on" cable, DSL, and other high-speed connections, this challenge will not be as daunting in the years ahead as it is today. See Figure 7-11.

Internet connection costs—Although the promise of high-speed connections is great, the costs will have to come down for more users to hop on board. As of mid-2001, Optonline from Cablevision (www.optonline.com) charged $299 for a cable modem ($99 after a $200 rebate) and a monthly cable connection fee of $29.95 for those who also subscribed to its cable TV service and $39.95 for those who were not cable subscribers; and Verizon's DSL service (www.verizon.com/dsl) promoted a number of monthly pricing plans, including one for $39.95 (with a connect speed slower than with a cable modem) and one for $99.95 (with a connect speed comparable to a cable modem), and offered a free DSL modem. These services do not require the user to tie up a phone. For some consumers, even the dial-up services are too expensive. In mid-2001, the AOL (www.aol.com) standard monthly dial-up fee was raised to $23.90.

---

[29]Jupiter Communications, "Internet at a Glance," *Business 2.0* (November 28, 2000), p. 272; and Bob Tedeschi, "E-Commerce Report: Companies in No Hurry to Buy Over the Internet," *New York Times on the Web* (March 5, 2001).

[30]Valerie Seckler, "Web Lacking Customer Service," *Women's Wear Daily* (December 21, 2000), p. 2; and Susan Stellin, "New Economy: Online Companies' Customer Service Is Hardly a Priority," *New York Times on the Web* (February 19, 2001).

FIGURE 7-11

FIGURE 7-11

Faster Internet Connections Are Needed—And They Are Coming

AT&T (www.at.com/boundless) is one of an expanding group of companies offering faster connection speeds through cable, DSL, and other formats.

Source: Reprinted by permission.

Legal issues—Because the use of the Internet in business is so new, legal precedents often do not yet exist. The legal challenges facing E-marketing can be placed into two categories: company versus company and government activities. In the first category are disputes over copyrights, patents, and business practices. For example, a number of music companies have successfully sued Napster (www.napster.com) to require the firm to stop facilitating the free exchange of copyrighted materials, forcing Napster to change its business strategy. Amazon.com (www.amazon.com) has sued Barnes&Noble.com (www.bn.com) to prevent the latter from using a one-click shopping process, since Amazon.com has a patented process for this. The matter is still in the courts. With regard to government actions, among the most contentious issues are whether to tax items sold over the Internet (in the United States, sales tax is not required unless a firm has a physical presence in a state with a sales tax), whether children should be denied access to undesirable sites, whether there should be rules governing purchase terms and delivery dates, and whether and how to protect individuals' privacy.

Privacy issues—Internet users are willing to provide companies with personal information. However, they are concerned about <u>what</u> information is being requested at company Web sites and <u>how</u> that information is to be used. According to Cyber Dialogue (www.cyberdialogue.com), for Web sites in which they have an interest, 90 percent of people would be willing to provide an E-mail address, 87 percent their gender, 82 percent their name, 61 percent their ethnicity, 55 percent their address, 21 percent their employer, and 11 percent their credit-card number. However, people really do not want that information shared with other firms. Only 18 percent of people would be willing to have a company share their E-mail address, 27 percent their gender, 15 percent their name, 18 percent their ethnicity, 8 percent their address, 2 percent their employer, and 0 percent their credit-card number.[31]

[31]Cyber Dialogue, "Full Disclosure," *Promo* (October 2000), p. 43.

ETHICAL *Issues in Marketing*

At Online Auction Sites, Who Is Responsible for Fraud in Selling Bogus Goods?

A state judge recently ruled that eBay (www.ebay.com), the online auction firm, could not be held liable for the sale of bootlegged music that was sold on its Web site. The judge's ruling was based on a section of the Communications Decency Act, a federal law stating that an interactive computer service cannot be held legally responsible for material published on its network. This case represented the first time that the Communications Decency Act was applied to a Web site transaction.

The lawsuit was brought by a music buff who noticed that a seller was offering illegal recordings of live performances on eBay. He sued eBay through a state law that enables private citizens to file a complaint even if the complainant had no loss. The lawyer for the complainant argued that eBay played a major role in the sale of goods offered on its site, and that it was not merely providing a site for buyers to view goods. In his ruling, the judge concluded that eBay did not select the items to be sold, did not determine their minimum prices, did not inspect them, and never had the items in its possession.

This is a significant precedent for eBay, which has cited the Communications Decency Act as its defense in other pending cases. In one such case, seven buyers of forged copies of sports memorabilia said that eBay was negligent and violated state law by allowing such fraudulent sales to be conducted on its site.

Develop an ethical code of conduct for eBay relating to the sale of goods that could be fraudulent (such as music, computer software, fine art, and antiques).

Sources: Based on material in Lisa Guernsey, "eBay Not Liable for Goods That Are Illegal," *New York Times on the Web* (November 13, 2000); and Lisa Guernsey, "eBay Suit Refiled," *New York Times on the Web* (October 17, 2000).

Communicating without spam—As discussed earlier in the chapter, opt-in E-mail can be very successful. People respond well when they are asked if it is okay for a company to communicate with them and what kinds of information they would like to receive. What a growing number of Web users object to is the extensive use of *spam,* which is unsolicited and unwanted E-mail. "Be it an ad for a used PC or an urge to vote on a proposition, if you didn't ask for it, didn't sign up on a mailing list related to it, and didn't leave your E-mail address on a Web form asking for more information on it, it's spam."[32]

Clutter—Given the huge number of companies that are now online, there is a lot of clutter on the Web. It is becoming much tougher for any one company to be noticed and to stand out. For instance, in Chapter 1, we cited more than 40 search engines; and there are many others. They must work awfully hard to differentiate themselves. In general, this means that well-known firms will have an easier time attracting Web visitors and that all firms must keep up their promotion efforts.

Finding a workable business model—Few Internet-based firms have earned a profit because they have invested too much, expanded too fast, faced system breakdowns, and overestimated how quickly people would buy on the Web. They need a more realistic and focused business model. For example, although Webvan spent $1 billion during 1999-2000 to develop an online grocery business (which expanded to include electronics,

> *Internet users are really turned off by* **spam,** *unsolicited and unwanted E-mail.*

---

[32]"Stop Spam FAQ," www.mall-net.com/spamfaq.html (March 14, 2001). See also Stephen H. Wildstrom, "It's Time to Can the Spam," *Business Week* (March 12, 2001), p. 24.

toys, drugstore items, and other product lines), its 2000 sales were under $100 million and it suffered enormous losses. By mid-2001, it had lost a total of $800 million and decided to go out of business.

Expectations of free services—A particularly vexing challenge for companies that offer online services is how to generate revenues from them. As evidenced by all the free Web sites referenced in this book, there are thousands of sites that allow free access to valuable resources—including newspapers, magazines, encyclopedias, software, consulting advice, and a whole lot more. Thus, users often expect that these services will be free; and they will bypass sites that charge a fee. Attempts to generate revenues at these sites by having paid advertising have not proven to be very successful.

Integrating bricks-and-clicks operations—It is not simple for firms to integrate offline and online strategies. Some leading companies have misfired because of insufficient coordination, such as Toys "R" Us and Barnes & Noble, both of which did not allow in-store returns of online purchases when they began Internet selling. Today, they do. Due to the price-sensitive nature of Web shoppers, companies typically have lower prices online than offline. This may be disturbing to store shoppers who feel they should have the same opportunities for discounts. With store-based sales, on-premises inventory is preferred so that products are immediately available. Yet, with Web-based sales, central warehouses can be more efficient.

Global issues—Even though the Internet is a worldwide communications vehicle, cultural, language, currency, legal, and other differences among countries can impact on a firm seeking a global Internet strategy. Since global distribution tends to be complicated, there often is a need to outsource tasks.

7-6b The Future of E-Marketing

Here are some projections about the future of E-marketing:

As a major new technology, the Internet will have a bright future, with some stumbles along the way.

- The overall impact of the Internet on all parties will be enormous, but somewhat different than originally anticipated. The emphasis will be more on E-marketing (using the Internet to enhance marketing strategies) rather than on E-commerce (revenues from Internet transactions).

- Bricks-and-clicks firms will outperform bricks-and-mortar firms and clicks-only firms. Bricks-and-clicks firms that have a bricks-and-mortar background will do the best of all, due to their name recognition, their customer following, and their established physical presence.

- The growth of new high-speed transmission modes such as cable and DSL connection services will allow more multimedia capabilities to be incorporated into company Web sites, creating an exciting environment for browsing, entertainment, and shopping by users.

- Business-to-business E-commerce will far outstrip business-to-consumer E-commerce. According to eMarketer, by 2004, annual worldwide business-to-business online revenues will approach $2.8 trillion, while business-to-consumer revenues will be about $428 billion. See Figure 7-12.

North America

$48 bill. in b-to-c revenues, 2000

$198 bill. in b-to-c revenues, 2004 est.

$159 bill. in b-to-b revenues, 2000

$1.6 trill. in b-to-b revenues, 2004, est.

Europe

$8 bill. in b-to-c revenues, 2000

$183 bill. in b-to-c revenues, 2004 est.

$26 bill. in b-to-b revenues, 2000

$797 bill. in b-to-b revenues, 2004 est.

Asia

$3 bill. in b-to-c revenues, 2000

$38 bill. in b-to-c revenues, 2004 est.

$36 bill. in b-to-b revenues, 2000

$301 bill. in b-to-b revenues, 2004 est.

Latin America

$0.7 bill. in b-to-c revenues, 2000

$8 bill. in b-to-c revenues, 2004 est.

$3 bill. in b-to-b revenues, 2000

$58 bill. in b-to-b revenues, 2004 est.

Africa/ Middle East

$0.2 bill. in b-to-c revenues, 2000

$2 bill. in b-to-c revenues, 2004 est.

$2 bill. in b-to-b revenues, 2000

$18 bill. in b-to-b revenues, 2004 est.

Note: Marketing to final consumers is designated as b-to-c. Marketing to organizational (business) consumers is designated as b-b.

FIGURE 7-12
E-Commerce Around the World

Source: Figure developed by the authors based on data from eMarketer in *World Wide Web: E-Commerce Across the Globe* (Columbus, Ohio: ProicewaterhouseCoopers, January 2001), p. 2.

WEB SITES YOU CAN USE

Several companies conduct research related to the Internet and provide valuable marketing-related insights at their Web sites. These firms include

Business 2.0 magazine (www.business2.com)—Free site.

eMarketer (www.emarketer.com)—From the "Main Menu," click on "eStatNews" to obtain free news about the Internet.

Forrester Research (www.forrester.com)—Register as a guest to gain access to free sample reports.

Greenfield Online (www.greenfield.com)—Free site. Visit the company's "Newsroom."

Jupiter Research (www.jup.com)—Register as a guest to gain access to free sample reports.

SUMMARY

1. *To demonstrate why the Internet is a valuable marketing tool* The Internet is a global electronic superhighway of computer networks that is accessible to people worldwide. The World Wide Web is a way to access the Internet, whereby users see words, colorful charts, pictures, and video, and hear audio. In this chapter (and book), the terms are used interchangeably. E-marketing involves any marketing activity through the Internet. E-commerce refers to sales-generating Internet transactions. E-marketing is the broader concept, and it does not necessarily have sales as the primary goal.

Hundreds of millions of people around the globe are surfing the Web, a number that will soon reach 1 billion individuals. People surf the Internet for a variety of reasons other than shopping. For instance, they seek out entertainment, financial, sports, and news sites. They do product research. They "talk" to one another. They communicate with companies to register complaints and make suggestions. They send E-mails and greetings cards. Companies also surf the Web for a variety of reasons other than shopping. They check what competitors are doing. They read about industry trends and events. They communicate with suppliers. They exchange data among offices anywhere in the world. They monitor inventory. They survey customers. They analyze customer data bases.

E-marketing is evolving in three phases: (1) traditional bricks-and-mortar firms, (2) clicks-only Internet firms, and (3) bricks-and-clicks firms that combine the other two formats. Today, the trend is more toward bricks-and-clicks firms because they can appeal to multiple market segments, maximize customer contact points, leverage the strengths of each form of business, and enter into new alliances.

Companies can achieve various benefits from using the Internet in marketing. These include communicability, a focus/tailored approach, information, timeliness, cost efficiencies, dynamism/flexibility, global possibilities, multimedia capabilities, interactivity, and sales.

2. *To explore the multifaceted potential marketing roles for the Internet* The Web can serve multiple marketing roles. Each firm must determine which of these roles to pursue and how to prioritize their importance: projecting an image, customer service, channel relations, purchasing and inventory management, information gathering and sharing, data-base development, mass customization (a process by which mass-market goods and services are individualized to satisfy a specific customer need, at a reasonable price), advertising and sales promotion, selling, and multichannel marketing.

3. *To show how to develop an Internet marketing strategy* A firm should adhere to a systematic process in forming a proper strategy. The six steps in the process relate to the basic components of an Internet marketing strategy. There are also four outside influences in making strategic decisions.

(1) Goal categories are set. Both quantitative and qualitative objectives should then be enumerated. (2) The target audience is identified and selected, and its desires studied. (3) Web site attributes are determined. However, the company must first decide whether to undertake all Web-related activities itself (insourcing) or to have specialized firms perform some or all Web-related activities for it (outsourcing). Second, the company must choose the scale of its Web presence, especially the importance of the Web site in its overall marketing strategy, the percent of the marketing budget for

the Web site, and how the Web site is to be implemented. Then, Web site attributes (address name, home page, etc.) are ascertained.

(4) Internet-based marketing-mix decisions are made while developing the Web site, consistent with offline marketing decisions. (5) The strategy is implemented. Again, two factors affect a firm's ability to properly enact its strategy: security and channel relationships, and they must be dealt with well. Once the strategy is enacted, the firm must ensure that it runs smoothly. (6) The last step is to assess performance and make needed modifications.

4. *To illustrate how the Internet is being utilized to enhance marketing strategies* Many firms are actively using the Web in their consumer analysis, product planning, distribution planning, promotion planning, and price planning. Several examples are noted.

5. *To consider the challenges of using the Internet in marketing and to forecast the future of E-marketing* Some challenges are rather uncontrollable (such as slow-speed modems) and others are self-inflicted by companies. Attention must be paid to consumer shopping resistance, customer service, system breakdowns, site speed, connection costs, legal issues, privacy issues, spamless communications, clutter, a workable business model, expectations of free services, integrating bricks-and-clicks operations, and global issues.

In the future, Internet usage will continue growing, with E-marketing being even more essential. Bricks-and-clicks firms will succeed best. High-speed connections will lead to more multimedia-rich Web sites. Business-to-business E-commerce will greatly outstrip business-to-consumer E-commerce.

KEY TERMS

Internet (p. 183)
World Wide Web (WWW) (p. 184)
E-marketing (p. 184)
E-commerce (p. 184)

Bricks-and-mortar firms (p. 186)
Clicks-only firms (p. 187)
Bricks-and-clicks firms (p. 187)

Mass customization (p. 192)
Opt-in (permission-based) E-mail (p. 196)
Spam (p. 205)

REVIEW QUESTIONS

1. Distinguish between E-marketing and E-commerce.
2. Describe the three phases of E-marketing.
3. What cost efficiencies does the Internet offer for companies that use it properly?
4. What is mass customization? Give an example not mentioned in the chapter.
5. Discuss the six basic steps in developing an Internet marketing strategy.

6. Why is it important for a company to monitor the links, both internal and external, at its Web site?
7. Why is opt-in E-mail gaining in popularity by both companies and Internet users?
8. State four major challenges facing E-marketers.

DISCUSSION QUESTIONS

1. What can a firm learn by studying Tables 7-1 and 7-2?
2. Visit General Motors' (www.gm.com) Web site. Which of the marketing roles enumerated in this chapter do you think it is performing? Explain your answer.

3. Develop and explain a 5-item survey to use in assessing the design of a Web site.
4. What is your favorite Web site? Why?

WEB EXERCISE

WebReview.com (www.webreview.com) "is the largest and longest-standing weekly site dedicated to Web professionals. Published each Friday, our stance is about Web teams—ensuring that each member of a team gets what he or she needs to do their jobs quickly, efficiently, and with the best information and skills available." Visit the site and discuss what a professional marketer could learn from WebReview.com.

PART 2 SHORT CASES
Case 1

How Doctor Prescriptions Are Swayed[c2-1]

Of the $14 billion that pharmaceutical manufacturers spend to promote their products, about $12 billion is aimed at physicians and the small group of nurse practitioners and physicians' assistants who can prescribe some medications. To make sure that their marketing is effective, pharmaceutical manufacturers have compiled a data bank on these health care providers that is popularly called a "prescriber profile."

To add to and update these profiles, pharmaceutical marketers buy information from pharmacies, the federal government, and the American Medical Association (which generates $20 million by selling biographic information on each physician). According to a professor of pharmaceutical marketing, "The pharmaceutical industry has the best market research system of any industry in the world. They know more about their business than people who sell coffee or toilet paper or laundry detergent because they truly have a very small group of decision makers, most of whom are still physicians." While these profiles do not include the names of the patients and their dosage, they include other vital information as to the brands and types of drugs prescribed by each physician.

These profiles are used by pharmaceutical marketers to determine which doctors should be offered selected perks, ranging from prescription pads and pens to free lunches for the physician and his/her staff. Some doctors are even offered free all-expense-paid weekends at major resorts.

There are three broad ethical questions regarding these practices. One concerns how the prescriber profiles invade the privacy of the doctor-patient relationship. The second concerns how perks influence the drugs that physicians prescribe. The last involves the role of the American Medical Association in selling data.

As one expert in health privacy says, "As an extension of the doctor-patient relationship, doctors are entitled to privacy." This expert further states that the profiles are a "fundamental violation" of that privacy. Other industry observers are also quick to point out that the information is not collected directly from the doctors, pharmaceutical marketers do not ask the consent of doctors to collect the information, and, sometimes, doctors may be even unaware of the existence of such a data base.

The second ethical question relates to the extent to which the perks offered to a physician influence his or her behavior. For example, could a physician be induced to recommend a higher-priced drug instead of a low-cost generic due to the lure of a vacation? Could a physician conceivably recommend that a patient change brands or prescribe a one month's supply of a medication so that he/she would receive an incentive?

Lastly, should the American Medical Association, which is trying to discourage doctors from accepting perks, sell biographical information to pharmaceutical companies? The biographical data can enable a pharmaceutical sales rep to link a doctor to an old classmate or medical school professor who favors the firm's brand. Or drug firms can invite classmates to a peer meeting which is really nothing more than a pitch to sell a particular product.

Questions

1. Why do you think that the pharmaceutical industry spends most of its promotional dollars on doctors instead of patients?
2. Is the issue of perks influencing physician behavior a matter of social responsibility, consumerism, or both? Explain your answer.
3. Develop a 7-item code of ethics for a hospital relating to the receipt of perks by physicians on its medical staff.
4. Should the American Medical Association continue to sell the information noted in this case? Present arguments on both sides of the issue.

[c2-1]The data in the case are drawn from Sheryl Gay Stolberg and Jeff Gerth, "High-Tech Stealth Being Used To Sway Doctor Prescriptions," *New York Times on the Web* (November 16, 2000).

Case 2

Ikea in Moscow–Understanding the Bureauracy[c2-2]

Ikea (www.ikea.com), which is based in Sweden, has 160 stores in 30 countries and plans on adding 10 to 15 new stores each year. Its recent difficulties in setting up a store in Moscow bring to light the complexities of any firm's doing business in Russia. While the company has confronted problems like zoning opposition to its large stores in many nations, these problems are rather small when compared with those for its Moscow store.

Ikea managed to get just about everything right in planning and setting up its first Moscow store. The company even got the Russian government to change the way that duties (taxes) were levied on imported furniture. Previously, duties were based on the weight, not the value, of imported furniture. This method would have made duties so prohibitive that it would have been nearly impossible to sell Ikea's low-cost furniture in Russia.

Ikea's 300,000-square-foot Moscow store was very effective in reaching its planned target market. On opening day, it attracted a crowd of 37,000 shoppers; 265,000 people visited during the first two weeks of operation. Ikea was seen as a welcome relief for middle-class Russians who could not afford to pay the prices charged for home furnishings in the fancy shopping malls that had opened in Russia. About 30 percent of the consumers who visited the store in the first two weeks made a purchase. The low use of credit cards (accounting for about 3 percent) also indicated that Ikea was reaching its intended middle-class target market.

What Ikea could not imagine was the difficulties it would face in getting the Russian government to allow Ikea to complete a simple road overpass to reduce severe traffic congestion. Without the overpass, traffic can back up for miles as cars attempt to turn off the highway. Ikea agreed to build and fully pay for the $4.5-million overpass, and work on it began. Then, with the overpass being only two pillars short of completion, construction was halted by Moscow authorities who felt that these pillars would block the view of a famous World War II monument. The monument is on the spot where the German advance on Moscow was stopped by the Russian Army in 1941.

Some observers believe that Moscow's objections to the overpass were "pay back" for Ikea's decision to place its store 3 miles outside of the Moscow city limits. This deprived Moscow of tax revenues. One bargaining chip that Ikea considered was to negotiate the overpass issue based upon the promise to build a second store in Moscow.

According to Ikea's marketing manager for Russia, "The question here is, what is the law? We have a document from the region, telling us to build, and we are getting a decree from the city not to build. However we turn, we are illegal." If the overpass remains unfinished, it would stand "as another monument to a failure to come to terms with a major foreign investment in Russia," the marketing manager says.

Ikea's problems in Moscow could easily deter other foreign firms from making initial investments in or expanding in Russia. This case also highlights the fact that although the Russian economy is recovering from a deep slump, the Russian government still needs to reassess its laws and regulations relating to business conduct.

Questions

1. How could Ikea have better anticipated the overpass problem? Explain your answer.
2. What could other firms that are contemplating expansion into Russia learn from this case?
3. What are the pros and cons of negotiating the overpass as a condition of opening a second store in the Moscow area?
4. What are the pros and cons of Ikea's using a standardized marketing approach throughout the world?

[c2-2]The data in the case are drawn from Jonathan Fuerbringer, "A Miffed Moscow Means Headaches for Ikea," *New York Times* (April 9, 2000), p. BU4.

Case 3

Attracting Foreign Tourists to U.S. Malls[c2-3]

Taubman Centers (www.taubman.com) owns or manages more than 30 shopping centers throughout the United States, including the Biltmore Fashion Park in Phoenix, the Cherry Creek Shopping Center in Denver, and the Beverly Center in Los Angeles. Tenants in Taubman-owned centers have annual sales of about $3 billion.

The company considers eight of its centers to be major tourism attractions, due to the large number of international travelers who shop there. Taubman's research indicates that the foreign countries/areas accounting for the most visitors to its centers are Mexico, Canada, Great Britain, Latin America, and Germany. Taubman is aggressively courting international visitors to its major tourism centers through a number of marketing strategies:

- The marketing staff has attended trade shows throughout the world and sponsored press rooms at several trade shows.
- Taubman has developed relationships with tour groups that bring foreign tourists into the United States and hosted special fashion shows featuring clothing from tenants' stores. Tour groups represent an integral part of Taubman's international shopper strategy since overseas travelers are more apt to travel with a group than their American counterparts. This is particularly the case where English is not spoken by tourists or when foreign visitors feel safer traveling as a group.
- The firm has formed alliances with airlines, bus companies, tour operators, and hotels. In one promotion with Mexicana Airlines, passengers received a card entitling shoppers to receive gifts and discounts at six Taubman malls.

Taubman's director of communications says, "Travel agents and tour operators know that when someone's done one of their trips, they're looking to bring something back as a keepsake. So they asked, what else is there to do [in a mall]." In response to this type of question, the firm recently began a learning program for international travelers that features activities such as a cooking class at a Williams-Sonoma store and a behind-the-scenes tour of a popular restaurant.

To appeal to international tourists who shop at its Cherry Creek center in Denver in ski season, Taubman produced multilingual brochures. It also worked with travel and tour operators to feature the shopping center as a destination in a popular ski trip package tour. Cherry Creek is especially popular with foreign tourists since more than 27 languages are spoken among the center's overall employee base (counting both retailers' and Taubman's personnel).

Taubman has also worked with the U.S. Department of Commerce to produce *Shopping and Cultural/Heritage Tourism*, a book analyzing the characteristics of Japanese, British, German, and Brazilian consumers. The study, paid for by the government agency and Taubman Centers, found that Brazilian and German visitors are more likely to use credit cards, while Japanese visitors are more apt to use cash. Other findings are that Japanese visitors travel with large groups, often purchase a vacation package (that combines airfare, hotel, and other travel accommodations), and spend the least per trip of tourists from the four countries studied. Germans visit the most destinations, and Great Britain has the largest number of female travelers.

Questions

1. Evaluate Taubman's overall marketing strategy in attracting foreign shoppers.
2. Why would a shopping center developer care so much about attracting shoppers for its retailer tenants?
3. What are the pros and cons of attracting foreign versus domestic shoppers?
4. Design a program to attract foreign shoppers to a regional shopping center located close to your college/university.

[c2-3]The data in the case are drawn from Paula Lyon Andruss, "How Malls Tap Rich Vein of Foreign Tourists," *Marketing News* (December 4, 2000), pp. 6–7.

Case 4

Zagat and the World Wide Web[c2-4]

Since 1979, Tim and Nina Zagat have been publishing *Zagat Surveys*, which include listings and reviews of restaurants for cities and their surrounding areas. There are separate books for each major city. While Zagat will not disclose sales figures, each year, it sells 650,000 copies of the *New York City* edition alone.

With the *Zagat Surveys*, restaurants are reviewed by typical consumers, not gourmets or professional restaurant critics. Each *Survey* book rates restaurants on the basis of customer judgments of food, décor, service, and cost. Separate scores of 1 to 30 (the highest rating) are assigned to the food, décor, and service categories. The ratings classify restaurants from "poor to fair" to "extraordinary to perfection." Along with the numbered ratings, each restaurant gets a written summary review, which can be quite provocative. For example, an eatery can be described as a "major value," a "poor man's (woman's) steakhouse," or selling "tough and fatty meat."

Until recently, the Zagats did little to capitalize on their "Zagat" brand name. Promotion was mostly limited to word-of-mouth, and expansion into different areas was self-funded. According to Tim Zagat, "We've had constant calls from potential investors, but we weren't interested." Now, that has all changed! In 1999, after being overwhelmed by the popularity of their Tokyo guide that was launched on a wireless service, the Zagats decided to raise $31 million to fund expansion. They used these funds to triple their staff to 130 employees, to revamp their Web site (www.zagat.com), to expand their reach with partnerships that provide access to new media (such as NBCi Broadband, Ticketmaster Online, wireless providers, and Yahoo!), to develop new products (such as golfing and night-life publications), and to expand into 100 additional cities. The year 2000 marked the first time that the Zagats invested more in their business than they earned in profits. This is especially noteworthy since book sales were up by 70 percent over the previous year and its Web activity is soaring.

To help plan and implement its revamped strategy, the Zagats hired Amy McIntosh as the firm's first chief executive officer.

McIntosh was the former group president of Verizon Communications' Internet and Data Services Division. She also held senior positions at American Express. As McIntosh said, "I always thought there was an unexploited potential in this brand."

The Zagat Web site now rates 20,000 restaurants in the United States, London, Paris, Tokyo, Toronto, and Vancouver. Potential customers can search for a restaurant based on its name, neighborhood, cuisine, and cost. Although the Web site includes the same information as the books for the cities covered, the Web site also enables consumers to more easily search for restaurants tied to criteria such as food, décor, cost, and neighborhood.

The company's ambitious plans do carry some risks. While the Zagats believe that their Web site helps to increase the sales of its bound books, there is always the risk that the free Web site will take sales away from the print version. Furthermore, because the heart of each book is the consumer ratings of each restaurant, obtaining sufficient reviews from consumers on hundreds of restaurants in each of 100 new cities is not an easy task. Some analysts also question whether Tim and Nina Zagat will give sufficient freedom to professional managers. According to one observer, "It's like their baby." And lastly, there is strong direct competition for the firm's expanded services from travel guides, weekly magazines, and newspapers that typically evaluate travel, leisure, and entertainment facilities.

Questions

1. Evaluate Zagat's overall marketing strategy.
2. Evaluate Zagat's Web site (www.zagat.com).
3. How can Zagat better ensure that its Web site will not take sales away from the traditional book business?
4. What are the potential opportunities and difficulties in expanding reviews to foreign countries?

[c2-4]The data in the case are drawn from Diane Brady, "Zagats Zigs Over to the Net," *Business Week* (November 20, 2000), pp. 166–168.

PART 2 COMPREHENSIVE CASE

The True Price of Penalties[pc-2]

Introduction

More and more businesses are adopting consumer penalty policies. But instituting them can lead to consumer defections if used incorrectly. Consider the following scenario, which shows the complexity of a common consumer penalty—airline reticketing fees: "Thanks for nothing. I will never fly on your airline again. I'll also be sure to let all my friends know how badly you've treated me," Joe said to the airline customer service rep, slamming the phone down. He then turned to his wife and exclaimed, "I'm having an emergency wisdom tooth extraction tomorrow, and the airline won't let me change our flights without a $75 reticketing penalty fee on each of our four tickets. That's $300 extra we have to pay. You'd think they could cut me a break given the circumstances. The airline will probably sell our tickets to some last-minute traveler and make a lot of money with our seats while I'm stuck in the dentist's office."

His wife, Abbey, looked at him and said, "I understand that you're upset, but we've paid those fees before. Remember last year we decided to stay on in St. Thomas for a few extra days? You didn't seem too upset about paying the airline the penalty then." "Well, that was different," Joe rationalized. "I chose to pay the fee to get the benefit of the extra vacation days. This time I feel like the airline is adding insult to injury. I certainly didn't ask for this." "Joe," Abbey responded, "I don't think the airline cares why you change your flight plans. They have the expense and hassle of dealing with our late change regardless of the cause. Why, if they gave us a break, who knows where it would stop? People would be making up all kinds of sob stories to get the airlines to let them change their plans without paying the penalties."

Joe wasn't ready to agree. "I'd be willing to pay a little extra for a ticket I could change once with no penalty. Better yet, I'd be willing to pay a little extra for some insurance that would pay the penalty in this kind of situation. It seems like some airlines should come up with a program like that. I bet those airlines would take business away from others that charge the penalties."

Penalty Policy Trends

Joe's story illustrates a number of perspectives on airline reticketing fees—a common consumer penalty. A consumer penalty is defined as any extra fee paid by the consumer for violating the terms of the purchase agreement. In recent years, a wide variety of businesses have adopted consumer penalty policies. See Table 1 for examples of consumer penalties. Even the federal government charges a new type of fee. Individuals with EE Bonds are now penalized if they cash them before the five-year maturity.

Businesses impose consumer penalties for two reasons. They will allegedly (a) suffer an irrevocable revenue loss, and/or (b) incur significant added costs should customers be unable or unwilling to complete their purchase obligations. For the firm, these payments are part of doing business in a highly competitive marketplace. With profit margins increasingly coming under pressure, firms are looking to stem losses resulting from customers not meeting their obligations. However, consumer attitudes about the fairness of a penalty may depend on a number of issues and perceptions. Furthermore, the perceived fairness of a penalty may affect some consumers' willingness to patronize a business in the future.

Given the growing commercial trend in consumer penalty policies, we decided to assess the strategic options for both the companies that have penalty policies and those considering implementing them. This assessment required us to answer the following questions:

- What percentage of consumers have experience with penalties? How much have they paid?
- Do consumers think penalties are fair? What factors affect consumer perceptions of penalty fairness?
- Do consumer penalties work? Do they reduce the likelihood that buyers will cancel or try to change their purchase agreements?
- Do consumer penalties have negative effects on buyer behavior? Do they reduce the likelihood of future patronage or increase the incidence of negative word-of-mouth communications?
- Are consumers willing to either pay more or accept less quality in order to avoid the possibility of being assessed a penalty?

Consumer Study

We attempted to review current research and analysis related to these questions, but discovered that little had been published that could provide answers. According to one press analysis, restaurants have become aggressive in installing penalty policies because no-shows can range as high as 65 percent. Several years ago, 40 percent of one restaurant's patrons with Valentine's Day reservations failed to claim them. The next year, after the institution of potential penalties, only two small parties failed to show up. One restaurant owner estimates a potential loss of $2,000 per night if she were to abandon her penalty policy.

[pc-2]Adapted by the authors from Eugene H. Fram and Michael S. McCarthy, "The True Price of Penalties," *Marketing Management* (Fall 1999), pp. 48–56. Reprinted by permission of the American Marketing Association.

TABLE 1   **Common Consumer Penalties**

Airlines

- The penalty for changing reservations on discount tickets has been raised to $75.00 or more for most airlines.
- A lost ticket can result in traveler paying full price for a new ticket, with possible refund later, but usually with an administration penalty fee added.
- In 1996, some travel agents started charging an additional $10–$20 penalty for canceled tickets with values of less than $200.

Automobiles

- Early terminations of car leases have penalties associated with them. In some cases, deposits on canceled leases can be subject to penalties.
- Car owners in Great Britain pay penalties, administration fees, and commissions if they cancel an insurance policy early.

Banks

- Penalties are often associated with early withdrawal of a certificate of deposit.
- Some charge penalties for too many withdrawals in a month.
- Some have monthly penalties of $5–$10 if a client's balance falls below a minimum level.
- Banks can charge late fees, in addition to interest, for tardy payments.

Car Rentals

- Rental companies often have $25–$100 penalties for no-shows for specialty vehicles. Budget, National, and Dollar/Thrifty are experimenting with no-show fees on all rentals.

Cellular Phones

- Companies have cancellation penalties, often in the small print on the back of a contract, that can run as high as $525.

Cruises

- If a cruise is sailing, even if there are hurricane warnings, some cruise lines will assess penalties if a passenger cancels.
- Even trip cancellation insurance will not ensure a refund if the traveler has embarked on the trip.
- The Carnival Paradise will disembark passengers found smoking.

Restaurants

- Some now charge up to $50 per person for no-show parties.

Retail Stores

- Circuit City and Best Buy are leading others in charging a 15 percent restocking fee on some items.

Trains

- Amtrak has a $20 penalty for a returned ticket, and charges the same fee for changing a ticket.

Universities

- Many universities will give only a partial tuition refund if a student becomes ill after a course begins.

To better understand this marketing mystery, we did a primary consumer research study. We wanted not only to answer our questions, but also to develop a strategic framework to guide managers. We sent 1,000 questionnaires to members of an established national consumer group and got 714 usable replies. We weighted replies to yield a representative sample. The findings present interesting implications for managers either considering or administering consumer penalty programs.

Our most interesting conclusion was that consumers do not universally perceive penalties to be unfair. Another is that consumers are willing to accept responsibility for their own negligence in not completing the terms of a purchasing contract.

Just more than half of respondents indicated that they and/or their immediate family members had paid penalties in one or more of 13 categories in the last two-year period, with the average family paying penalties in two different categories. The 13 categories were later grouped into four major segments:

- About one-third of respondents reported paying penalties related to financial transactions such as late loan payments, early certificate of deposit withdrawals, or not carrying interest-generating balances on debit or credit cards.
- One-sixth reported penalties associated with canceled or changed reservations for hotel rooms or air, bus, and train travel.
- About one in 10 reported penalties involving merchandise, such as restocking fees or charges for refusing to accept ordered items.
- Smaller numbers (2 percent or less) reported penalties for late pickup at day-care centers, early termination of car leases/cellular phone agreements, and situations where college students had to unavoidably withdraw from classes (i.e., partial tuition refunds).

From a consumer perspective, these numbers indicate that people may be frustrated by the increase in penalties. Whereas bank penalties for early withdrawals or late payments long have been commonplace, penalties for early hotel departure or canceled car reservations are more recent in origin. In addition, some charges are increasing. Airline reticketing penalties increased to $75 in 1997 from $35 in 1995. More recently, some hotels have instituted penalties for "late check-in."

Fairness and Trade-Offs

Intuitively, one would expect consumers to universally oppose penalties and view them as being inherently unfair. We found, however, that a number of issues may influence perceptions of penalty fairness. One issue is whether the penalty is regarded by customers as "fair compensation for losses" or as a "method of business revenue enhancement." About 40 percent of respondents said that penalties are fair if they compensate a seller for a customer's failure to complete a purchase. About the same percentage took the opposite position, with a few responding that penalties transfer business risk to consumers. Nearly half of the respondents said that penalties are not fair when businesses make money from them.

Respondents who had experienced a penalty within the last two years were somewhat less likely to agree that penalties are fair compensation than those who had no recent penalty experience. Men were a little more likely to agree with the fair compensation argument. In addition, agreement was positively related to both household income and education level. About 22 percent of respondents without a high school diploma said that penalties are fair compensation, compared with nearly 50 percent of those with a bachelor degree. These results imply an effect of education on one's understanding of economic realities.

To confirm and better understand the quantitative data, we posed an open-ended question related to fairness to respondents. See Figure 1. Only 9 percent of the people who responded to this question find penalties to be a totally unfair practice. Customers know their obligations and that penalties will be imposed when they fail to meet them. However, the study also shows consumers expect some leniency in an emergency. The critical factor affecting perceptions of fairness is whether the consumer is assessed the penalty as a result of free choice, personal negligence, or unavoidable circumstances. When free choice was involved, almost half of respondents felt a penalty was fair. However, when asked if a penalty would be fair if a consumer missed a flight because of a broken leg, only 7 percent felt a charge was fair.

A similar pattern of results was obtained with a scenario involving a canceled hotel reservation. When a customer canceled after 6 P.M. on the day of arrival, two-thirds of respondents reported the penalty to be a satisfactory solution. However, when the cancellation was due to a family emergency, only 7 percent reported the penalty to be fair. Consumers feel penalties are much less acceptable if their problems are unavoidable. So, how does the firm efficiently separate legitimate claims from fraudulent ones?

Outcomes of a Penalty Policy

To assess whether penalties are apt to be effective in promoting consumer compliance, respondents were asked if the possibility of paying a penalty would make them more likely to go through with a transaction they might otherwise cancel. About 60 percent agreed that penalties are a factor.

Negative Outcomes of Penalties   The participants were asked to respond to three issues:

- Would the possibility of paying a penalty make it less likely they would buy a good or service? More than three-quarters, said "yes." Younger respondents and those with lower income were slightly less likely to buy a good or service carrying a penalty risk.
- Would participants patronize a firm in the future that had imposed a penalty on them? Nearly 60 percent said they would not. However, a greater proportion of older persons, as well as those in the $75,000 and up income group, would avoid buying from a penalizing firm.

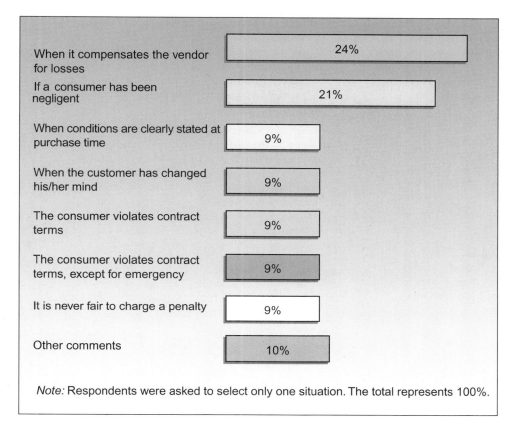

FIGURE 1

When Is It Most Fair to Charge a Penalty?

When it compensates the vendor for losses	24%
If a consumer has been negligent	21%
When conditions are clearly stated at purchase time	9%
When the customer has changed his/her mind	9%
The consumer violates contract terms	9%
The consumer violates contract terms, except for emergency	9%
It is never fair to charge a penalty	9%
Other comments	10%

Note: Respondents were asked to select only one situation. The total represents 100%.

- Finally, would respondents tell others if there were a penalty? A large majority of respondents—87 percent—said they would. Only 3 percent would be silent. The remainder did not render a reaction.

Some firms have observed that consumer predictions of how they would act in certain situations are not always indicative of their actual behavior. For example, a bargain price at a firm to which a customer had previously paid a penalty may be a motivation for another purchase. In the long run, however, there must be some damage to a firm's customer relations program, and the dollar value may be significant.

Consumer Trade-Offs   We were interested in determining whether consumers would trade price or quality to avoid paying a penalty. About 28 percent of respondents said they would accept reduced service, while 34 percent agreed they would pay more to avoid a penalty. More affluent households would be less inclined to trade price or quality, while older persons would be more inclined to do so. Clearly, increasing prices or decreasing product or service quality are not viable trade-off strategies for most consumers.

Implications for Managers

Experiencing a penalty is not an uncommon event. Furthermore, given the emergence of penalties in an increasing variety of transactions, the percentage of consumers being charged a penalty likely will rise in coming years. Two questions, therefore, arise regarding consumer reactions to penalty policies:

1. Does experiencing a penalty increase the likelihood that the consumer will comply with contract obligations? Only a little more than half of consumers who had experienced a penalty indicated that the possibility of paying a penalty would make them more likely to follow through on a transaction they otherwise would cancel. This has at least two implications. Firms assessing penalties primarily to promote contract compliance will need to continually examine the strategy to ensure its effectiveness. On the other hand, firms that impose penalties as a strategy to promote revenue enhancement should take solace from the study findings. It appears that a good number of consumers will continue to pay penalty fees. More important, they often will accept these fees as fair.

2. Will customers likely transfer their patronage to firms which don't have penalty policies? Our data indicate a substantial number of persons would transfer their patronage. However, many businesses operate in industries where penalties are the norm. Thus, a "maverick" firm which eliminates its penalty policy may have the potential to increase market share.

These findings open up three strategic options for firms with existing customer penalty policies:

1. Businesses that impose penalties because they suffer financial losses could self-insure against such losses by charging slightly more for their products. Significant customer communication would need to take place so that buyers understand the reason for the higher price. Communication must be creative since competitors will have lower prices, and many consumers simply will compare prices.
2. Businesses could offer customers the option of buying nominal insurance coverage that would pay any penalty imposed. This insurance is commonly offered in the cruise industry for about 5 percent of the total cost of a cruise.

Some European airlines offer passengers flying on promotional fares the option to buy insurance that would cover the cost of their tickets if travel plans change.
3. Businesses that would suffer negligible financial losses as a result of consumer noncompliance should be able to capture more market share by offering their goods and services penalty free.

Managing Consumer Perceptions of Penalty Fairness Although consumers are open to the idea that it is fair for sellers to impose penalties, we maintain that managers need to be aware of ways to manage customer perceptions of policy fairness. Our research indicates that consumer perceptions of penalty fairness are affected by a number of factors.

Figure 2 summarizes some of the factors businesses might need to manage in developing and implementing penalty programs. The positive and negative influences are, for the most part, derived from study findings. The bottom of the model presents the consequences of perceived penalty fairness.

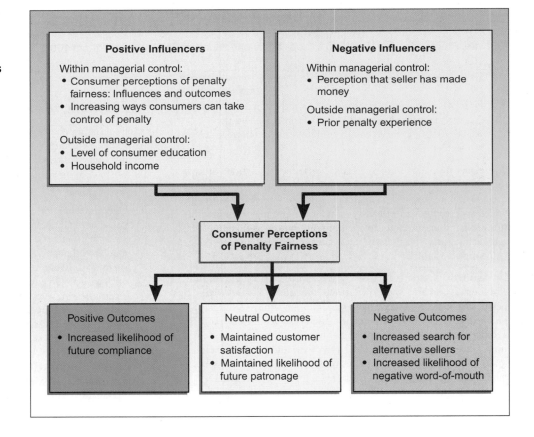

FIGURE 2
Consumer Perceptions of Penalty Fairness—Influences and Outcomes

Positive Influencers

Within managerial control:
- Consumer perceptions of penalty fairness: Influences and outcomes
- Increasing ways consumers can take control of penalty

Outside managerial control:
- Level of consumer education
- Household income

Negative Influencers

Within managerial control:
- Perception that seller has made money

Outside managerial control:
- Prior penalty experience

Consumer Perceptions of Penalty Fairness

Positive Outcomes
- Increased likelihood of future compliance

Neutral Outcomes
- Maintained customer satisfaction
- Maintained likelihood of future patronage

Negative Outcomes
- Increased search for alternative sellers
- Increased likelihood of negative word-of-mouth

Each influence merits managerial consideration, but the most important one is consumer control. Consumers feel penalties are fair when they are self-imposed or they believe the cause is within their control. Allowing the customer a maximum amount of control over the likelihood of facing a penalty will lead to the highest perceived level of fairness.

Increasing customer control can be facilitated in a number of ways. One is to disclose the possibility of a penalty and the conditions under which it will be imposed as clearly as possible from the outset. More than 80 percent of respondents believed that vendors don't make the proper effort to provide clarification. This could be due to vendor concerns about inserting negative discussion in the selling process. Another way to increase consumer control is to give the consumer the option to self-insure by paying a nominal charge. While this gives more risk-averse consumers the ability to reduce risk, it also allows others to "save" the premium. In either case, the consumer assumes control over the penalty risk.

Another important factor appears to be the need for consumers to conclude that a seller will suffer a financial loss as a result of the consumer's action and that the penalty is fair compensation for such a loss. If the consumer perceives the penalty is fair compensation for actual losses, the perception of penalty fairness should be higher. Again, this approach requires the seller to educate customers by providing clear and credible information about consequences to their businesses.

Strategic Conclusions

Strategically, the study shows a penalty policy will meet customer expectations provided that it is seen as fair. Few, if any, companies use all three guidelines in the operations of penalty policies:

- Customers feel they are justifiably reimbursing the seller for losses incurred, and the business is not making additional profit from the transaction.

- Customers are provided with some measure of control via the ability to insure against the imposition of a penalty and fully understand the associated risks.
- The seller is willing to forgo penalty charges which are caused by unavoidable human problems.

Questions

1. Describe the two possible reasons why a firm would have a consumer penalty policy.
2. Under what circumstances is it *ethical* for companies to charge consumer penalties? Explain your answer.
3. Under what circumstances is it *unethical* for companies to charge consumer penalties? Explain your answer.
4. Comment on the implications of Figure 2 for companies that charge consumer penalties.
5. Should a global firm have the same consumer penalty policy around the world? Why or why not?
6. What consumer penalties are Internet firms most likely to charge? Why?
7. Should a bricks-and-clicks retailer have separate consumer penalty policies for its store customers and its Internet customers? Explain your answer.

Consumer Analysis: Understanding and Responding to Diversity in the Marketplace

In Part 3, we see why consumer analysis is so essential and discuss consumer characteristics, needs, profiles, and decision making—and how firms can devise marketing plans responsive to today's diverse global marketplace.

8 Final Consumers

This chapter is devoted to final consumer demographics, lifestyles, and decision making. We examine several specific demographics (objective and quantifiable characteristics that describe the population) for the United States and other countries around the globe. By studying final consumer lifestyles and decision making, we can learn about why and how consumers act as they do. Lifestyles encompass various social and psychological factors, many of which we note here. The decision process involves the steps as consumers move from stimulus to purchase or nonpurchase.

9 Organizational Consumers

Here, we focus on organizational consumers purchasing goods and services for further production, use in operations, or resale to other consumers. We look at how they differ from final consumers and at their individual characteristics, buying goals, buying structure, constraints on purchases, and decision process.

10 Developing a Target Market Strategy

We are now ready to discuss how to plan a target market strategy. Consumer-demand patterns and segmentation bases are examined; and undifferentiated marketing, concentrated marketing, and differentiated marketing are explained and contrasted. The requirements for successful segmentation and the importance of positioning are also considered. We conclude with a discussion of sales forecasting.

After reading Part 3, you should understand element 9 of the strategic marketing plan outlined in Table 3-2 (pages 72–75).

Final Consumers

reenfield Online (www.greenfield.com) and YouthStream Media Networks (www.youthstream.com) recently conducted a joint survey which found that 31 percent of college students say they are Internet dependent, and 28 percent consider themselves to be "cybergeeks." While the average student spends three hours online every day, 20 percent of students spend four or more hours online on a daily basis.

College students represent an important market segment for Web-based firms. Even though most have discretionary spending power of less than $125 per month, 32 percent have discretionary budgets of more than $500 a month. About 90 percent of college students have access to personal computers.

The following summarized data are based on a study of 1,135 students drawn from an online research panel of 30,000 four-year college students. The data were collected in 2000:

- 81 percent of the students have made an online purchase, up from 51 percent in 1998. The most commonly purchased items are CDs (bought by 64 percent of the sample), clothing (42 percent), and concert, theater, and event tickets (32 percent).

- 25 percent of the students have bought textbooks on the Web. Amazon.com (www.amazon.com) and Varsitybooks.com (www.varsitybooks.com) are the two most widely used Web sites for textbooks. Students buy textbooks online because of low prices and vendors' guaranteed buy-back policies. Among the main reasons students do not buy textbooks on the Web are the inconvenience, shipping charges, poor selection, and high cost of returning the books.

- The most common locations for Web access are parents' home (65 percent), their own apartment/house (52 percent), library (48 percent), friends' PC (41 percent), and dorm room (40 percent).

- The most common student online activity is sending and receiving E-mail (used by 92 percent). Other common activities are surfing the Web (72 percent) and instant messaging (60 percent).[1]

In this chapter, we will explore a number of important consumer demographic and lifestyle trends, as well as how consumers make purchase decisions. This will enable us to better pinpoint market needs, reasons for purchases, changing lifestyles, and behavior patterns.

[1]Al Urbanski, "Campus Web-Watching," *Promo* (January 2000), pp. 19–21; and Greenfield Online, "The Internet Is 'Big Man on Campus,'" www.greenfield.com/pages/go_article.asp?aid=1343 (August 7, 2000).

8-1 OVERVIEW

As discussed in Chapters 1 and 2, the consumer is the central focus of marketing. To devise good marketing plans, it is essential to study consumer attributes and needs, lifestyles, and purchase processes, and then make proper marketing-mix decisions.

The scope of consumer analysis includes the study of *who* buys, *what* they buy, *why* they buy, *how* they make decisions to buy, *when* they buy, *where* they buy, and *how often* they buy.[2] For example, we might study a college student (who) buying textbooks (what) that are required for various classes (why). The student looks up the book list at the school store and decides whether to buy new or used books for each course (how). Just before the first week of classes (when), the student goes to the school store to buy the books (where). The student does this three times per year—fall, spring, and summer (how often).

An open-minded, consumer-oriented approach is imperative in today's diverse global marketplace so that a firm can identify and serve its target market, minimize dissatisfaction, and stay ahead of competitors. Why is this so important? "If we make customers feel that they are special and unique, we stand a better chance both of retaining their loyalty when they next make a buying decision and of gaining new business through word of mouth and recommendations."[3] See Figure 8-1.

In Chapters 8 to 10, the concepts needed to understand consumers in the United States and other nations, select target markets, and relate marketing strategy to consumer behavior are detailed. Chapter 8 examines final consumer demographics, lifestyles, and decision making. **Final consumers** buy goods and services for personal, family, or household use. Chapter 9 looks at **organizational consumers,** those buying goods and services for further

Final consumers buy for personal, family, or household use; *organizational consumers* buy for production, operations, or resale.

FIGURE 8-1

Creatively Appealing to the Consumer of Today

To address the needs of the growing number of time-pressed consumers, many Chevron gasoline stations feature a convenience store, a McDonald's, and an ATM, in addition to gasoline.

Source: Photo by Dennis Harding, Chevron Corporation. Reprinted by permission.

[2]Adapted from Leon G. Schiffman and Leslie Lazar Kanuk, *Consumer Behavior,* Seventh Edition (Upper Saddle River, N.J.: Prentice-Hall, 2000), p. 5.

[3]Ian Traynor, "Getting Intimate with Customers," www.tka.co.uk/magic/archive/featur11.htm (March 22, 2001).

production, usage in operating the organization, or resale to other consumers. Chapter 10 explains how to devise a target market strategy and use sales forecasts.

8-2 DEMOGRAPHICS DEFINED AND ENUMERATED[4]

Consumer demographics are objective and quantifiable population characteristics. They are rather easy to identify, collect, measure, and analyze—and show diversity around the globe. The demographics covered here are population size, gender, and age; location, housing, and mobility; income and expenditures; occupations and education; marital status; and ethnicity/race. After studying single factors, a firm can form a consumer demographic profile—a demographic composite of a consumer group. See Figure 8-2. By creating profiles, a firm can pinpoint both opportunities and potential problems.

> **Consumer demographics** *are easily identifiable and measurable.*

Several secondary sources offer data on demographics. For U.S. demographics, a key source is the *Census of Population*, a federal government research project with considerable national, state, and local data via printed reports, computer tapes, microfiche, CD-ROM, and online data bases. (The American FactFinder Web site, http://factfinder.census.gov/servlet/BasicFactsServlet, is especially useful.) Many marketing research firms and state data centers arrange *Census* data by ZIP code, make forecasts, and update data. Since complete *Census* data are gathered only once a decade, they must be supplemented by U.S. Bureau of the Census estimates (www.census.gov/population/www/estimates/popest.html) and statistics from chambers of commerce, public utilities, and others.

American Demographics (www.demographics.com) is a magazine dealing mostly with U.S. trends. The annual *Survey of Buying Power* (from *Sales & Marketing Management*, www.salesandmarketing.com) has current U.S. data by metropolitan area and state, including retail sales, income, and 5-year estimates. Other U.S. sources are *Editor & Publisher Market Guide* (www.editorandpublisher.com), *Rand McNally Commercial Atlas & Marketing Guide* (www.randmcnally.com), *Standard Rate & Data Service* (www.srds.com), local newspapers, and regional planning boards.

Three excellent sources for international demographics are the United Nations (www.un.org/english), Euromonitor (www.euromonitor.com), and the Organization for Economic Cooperation and Development (www.oecd.org). The U.N. publishes a

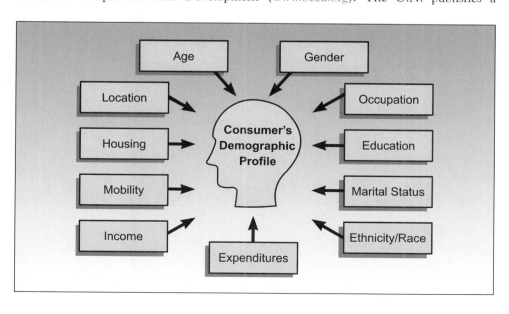

FIGURE 8-2

Factors Determining a Consumer's Demographic Profile

---

[4]Unless otherwise indicated, the data presented in this chapter are all from the U.S. Bureau of the Census (various publications); the U.S. Bureau of Labor Statistics; the United Nations (various publications); the Organization for Economic Cooperation and Development (various publications); the *CIA World Factbook 2000*; and authors' estimates and extrapolations.

Statistical Yearbook and a *Demographic Yearbook.* Euromonitor publishes *World Marketing Data and Statistics.* OECD issues demographic and economic reports on an ongoing basis. In highly industrialized nations, demographic data are pretty accurate since actual data are regularly collected. In less-developed and developing nations, demographic data are often based on estimates rather than actual data because such data are apt to be collected on an irregular basis.

Throughout the chapter, information is provided on both U.S. and worldwide demographics. A broad cross-section of country examples is provided to give a good sense of the diversity around the globe.

8-2a Population Size, Gender, and Age

The world population is expected to go from 6.15 billion in 2001 to 6.82 billion in 2010, an annual rise of 1.2 percent. Over the same period, the U.S. population will rise from 283 million to 300 million, an annual rise of less than 1 percent. The U.S. population will drop from 4.6 percent of world population in 2001 to 4.4 percent in 2010. Figure 8-3 shows world population by region for 2001 and 2010.

Newborns are less than 2 percent of the population (1.4 percent in the United States) in industrialized nations—compared with up to 4 percent or more in nations such as Afghanistan, the Congo, and Saudi Arabia. For the industrialized countries, a large proportion of the births are firstborns.

Worldwide, males and females comprise equal percentages of the population. Yet, in many industrialized nations, females are over one-half of the population—mostly due to differences in life expectancy. For newborn females, it is 83 years in Canada, 82 in Italy, 80 in the United States, and 73 in Russia; it is 76 years for newborn males in Canada, 76 in Italy, 74 in the United States, and 62 in Russia.

The populations in industrialized nations are older than in less-developed and developing nations. Today, the proportion of the population age 14 and under is 14 percent in Italy, 15 percent in Japan, 19 percent in Great Britain, 21 percent in the United States, 25 percent in China, 29 percent in Brazil, 34 percent in Mexico, and 44 percent in Nigeria.

FIGURE 8-3

The World's Population Distribution, 2001 and 2010

Source: U.S. Bureau of the Census, International Data Base.

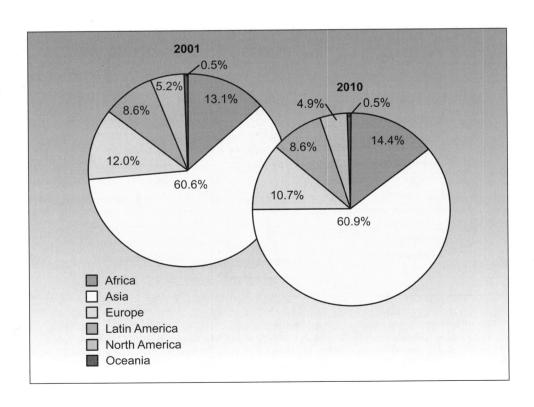

8-2b Location, Housing, and Mobility

During the 1900s, there was a major move of the world population to large urban areas and surrounding suburbs. As of 2001, 20 cities had at least 10 million residents each—led by Tokyo/Yokohama and Mexico City. Today, more than three-quarters of the U.S. population resides in urban areas and their suburbs. But, the level of urbanization varies greatly by country. In China, Pakistan, Laos, and Nepal, one-third or less of the population lives in urban areas.

The world is becoming more urban.

In many parts of the world, the majority of people own the homes in which they reside. Here are some examples: Bangladesh, Finland, Greece, New Zealand, Paraguay, Sri Lanka, and United States.

The worldwide mobility of the population is high; annually, millions of people emigrate from one nation to another and hundreds of millions move within their nations. During the last decade, roughly 10 million people have legally emigrated to the United States. Overall, about 10 percent of those living in the United States were born elsewhere. Among U.S. residents, 15 to 20 percent of all people move annually—60 percent within the same county, 80 percent within the same state, and 90 percent within the same region; only 10 percent of moves are to a new region or abroad. From 1990 to 2000, the most U.S. population growth was in Mountain, Pacific, South Atlantic, and Southwest areas.

8-2c Income and Expenditures

Consumer income and expenditure patterns are valuable demographic factors when properly studied. In examining them, these points should be kept in mind:

- Personal income is often stated as GDP per capita—the total value of goods and services produced in a nation divided by population size. This does not report what people really earn, and it inflates per-capita income if a small portion of the population is affluent. A better measure is median income—the income for those at the fiftieth percentile in a nation; it is a true midpoint. Yet, median incomes are rarely reported outside the United States.

- Personal income can be expressed as family, household, and per capita. Since families are larger than households and per-capita income is on an individual basis, these units are not directly comparable. Income can also be stated in pre-tax or after-tax terms, which are not directly comparable.

- Because prices differ by country, a comparison of average incomes that does not take purchasing power into effect will be inaccurate.

- Economic growth is cyclical. And at any given time, some countries will be performing well while others are struggling.

- Although the term "poverty" varies greatly by nation, more than 1 billion people in the world are characterized by malnutrition, illiteracy, and disease.

In 2000, the U.S. median household income was between $41,000 and $42,000—the highest level ever. Yet, even though the mean income for the top one-fifth of households was $130,000, and 40 percent of all households had incomes of $60,000 or more, the bottom one-fifth averaged just $18,000—and 12 percent of all households were at the poverty level. The United States has one of the greatest spreads between high-income and low-income households of any industrialized nation in the world. Furthermore, in terms of purchasing power, U.S. median household income has risen by only $5,000 since 1973.

The slow growth in real U.S. income (the amount after taking inflation into account) has occurred because the increases in household income have been virtually offset by increases in prices. The price increases have led to a higher *cost of living,* the total amount consumers annually pay for goods and services. Over the last three decades, the greatest price increases have been for medical care, auto insurance, and tobacco items; the smallest have been for phone services, apparel, and household furnishings.

*Changes in the **cost of living** are measured by a consumer price index.*

Many nations monitor their cost of living via a *consumer price index (CPI)*, which measures monthly and yearly price changes (the rate of inflation) for a broad range of consumer goods and services. Since 1983, the overall annual rise in the U.S. CPI has been less than 5 percent (except for 1990, when it rose by 5.5 percent). In 2000, the CPI rose by 4 percent or less in many countries around the world (about 3 percent in the United States).

Global consumption patterns have been shifting. In industrialized nations, the proportion of income that people spend on food, beverages, and tobacco has been declining. The percentage spent on medical care, personal business, and recreation has been rising. In less-developed and developing nations, the percentage of spending devoted to food remains high. Americans spend 16 percent of income on food, beverages, and tobacco; and 18 percent on medical care. In contrast, Pakistanis spend nearly one-half of their income on food, beverages, and tobacco; and about 5 to 6 percent on medical care.

Consumption reflects disposable income and discretionary income.

Disposable income is a person's, household's, or family's total after-tax income to be used for spending and/or savings. ***Discretionary income*** is what a person, household, or family has available to spend on luxuries after necessities are bought. Classifying some product categories as necessities or luxuries depends on a nation's standard of living. In the United States, autos and phones are generally considered necessities; in many less-developed countries, they are typically considered luxuries.

8-2d Occupations and Education

The work force in industrialized nations is still moving to white-collar and service jobs. In less-developed and developing nations, many jobs still involve manual work and are more often agriculture-based.

The total employed civilian U.S. labor force is 136 million people—compared with 65 million in Japan, 35 million in Germany, 27 million in Great Britain, 23 million in France, and 21 million in Italy. For the last 30 years, the percent of U.S. workers in service-related, technical, and clerical white-collar jobs has risen; the percent as managers, administrators, and sales workers has been constant; and the percent as nonskilled workers has dropped. Three million U.S. workers have an agriculture-related job.

Women are a large and growing percentage of the worldwide labor force.

Another change in the labor force around the world has been the increase in working women. Forty years ago, women comprised 32 percent of the total U.S. labor force. Today, the figure is 47 percent; and 60 percent of adult U.S. women are in the labor force. In Japan and Great Britain, one-half of adult women are in the labor force, while 55 percent of Sweden's adult women are in the labor force.

During 1960, 31 percent of all married U.S. women were employed. Now, 61 percent are in the labor force. The percent of married women with children under age 6 in the U.S. labor force has jumped from 19 percent in 1960 to 62 percent today. Similar rises have also occurred in other nations.

Unemployment rates, which reflect the percentage of adults in the total labor force not working, vary widely by nation. During 2000, the U.S. unemployment rate was 4 percent. In contrast, the rate for the 15 European Union nations averaged 8 percent. While the U.S. percentage was lower, it still meant millions of people without jobs. Some worldwide unemployment has been temporary, due to weak domestic and international economies. Other times, depending on the nation and industry, many job losses have been permanent. Unemployment is often accompanied by cutbacks in discretionary purchases.

Great strides are being made globally to upgrade educational attainment, but the level of education tends to be much higher in industrialized nations than in less-developed and developing ones. One measure of educational attainment is the literacy rate, the percentage of people in a country who can read and write. In industrialized nations such as the United States, this rate exceeds 95 percent. Here are the rates for some less-developed and developing nations: Bolivia, 83 percent; Chad, 48 percent; China, 82 percent; Ethiopia, 36 percent; Laos, 57 percent; and Saudi Arabia, 63 percent.

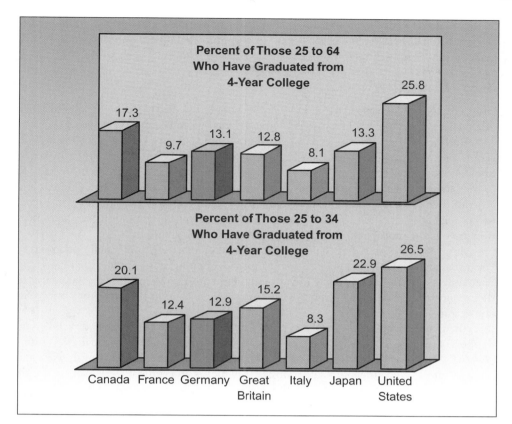

Percent of Those 25 to 64 Who Have Graduated from 4-Year College

17.3 9.7 13.1 12.8 8.1 13.3 25.8

Percent of Those 25 to 34 Who Have Graduated from 4-Year College

20.1 12.4 12.9 15.2 8.3 22.9 26.5

Canada France Germany Great Britain Italy Japan United States

FIGURE 8-4

Educational Attainment by Country

Note: These statistics are from 1996, the latest common date available.

Source: Organization for Economic Cooperation and Development 1996 data, as reported in *The Condition of Education 1999* (Washington, D.C.: U.S. Department of Education, 2000), Section V.

INTERACTIVE FIGURE

Another measure is the level of schooling completed; and compared to other large industrialized nations, the United States is the most educated. A higher percentage of U.S. adults has finished high school and college than those in Canada, France, Germany, Great Britain, Italy, or Japan. As of 2000, 84 percent of U.S. adults 25 years old and older were high school graduates, and one-quarter were college graduates. Of U.S. adults aged 25 to 34, 88 percent were high school graduates and 30 percent were college graduates. Figure 8-4 compares higher education in the United States with several other nations (based on 1996 data, the latest common data available).

The sharp increase in working women and higher educational attainment have generally contributed to the growing number of people in upper-income brackets; the rather high unemployment rate in some nations and industries, and slow-growth economies, have caused other families to have low incomes.

8-2e Marital Status

Marriage and family are powerful institutions worldwide, but in some nations, they are now less dominant. Although 2.3 million U.S. couples get married each year, only 53 percent of U.S. adults are married and living together (down from 76 percent in 1960); the percentage of married adults in many other nations is much higher. The median U.S. age at first marriage is 27 years for males and 25 years for females—up from 23 and 20 in 1960, as people wait to marry and have children. Thus, the average U.S. family size has gone from 3.7 members in 1960 to 3.1. The male and female ages at first marriage are much lower in less-developed and developing nations, and the average family is bigger there.

A *family* is a group of two or more persons residing together who are related by blood, marriage, or adoption. A **household** is a person or group of persons occupying a housing unit, whether related or unrelated. In many nations, average household size has been dropping. The U.S. average has gone from 3.3 in 1960 to 2.7 today—due to later marriages, more widows and widowers, a high divorce rate, many couples deciding to have

*A **family** has related persons residing together. A **household** has one or more persons who may not be related.*

fewer children, and the growth of single-person households. Of the 105 million U.S. households, just over one-quarter are one-person units. Family households are nearly 70 percent of U.S. households—down from 85 percent in 1960.

8-2f Ethnicity/Race

*Demographically, **ethnicity/race** is one measure of nations' diversity with regard to language, country of origin, or race.*

From a demographics perspective, ***ethnicity/race*** should be studied to determine the existence of diversity among and within nations in terms of language and country of origin or race.

Worldwide, there are more than 200 different languages spoken by at least 1 million people each—and 12 of those are spoken by at least 100 million people (including Mandarin, English, Hindi, and Spanish). Even within nations, there is often diversity as to the languages spoken. For example, Canada (English and French), Chad (French and Arabic), Peru (Spanish and Quechua), and the Philippines (Pilipino and English) have two official languages. One of the issues facing the European Community in its unification drive is the multiplicity of languages spoken in the 15 nations.

Most nations consist of people representing different ethnic and racial backgrounds. For instance, among those living in the Philippines are Malays, Chinese, Americans, and Spaniards. Sometimes, the people in various groups continue to speak in the languages of their countries of origin, even though they may have resided in their current nations for one or two generations.

The United States is comprised of people from virtually every ethnic and racial group in the world. The Bureau of the Census uses "Black or African-American," "White," "Asian," "Native Hawaiian and Other Pacific Islander," and "American Indian and Alaska Native" to delineate racial groups; "Hispanic" is an ethnic term, denoting people of any race.

The 2000 U.S. population was 75.1 percent White, 12.3 percent Black/African-American, 3.7 percent Asian/Native Hawaiian/Other Pacific Islander, and 0.9 percent American Indian/Alaska Native, with 5.6 percent defined as "Other Race" and 2.4 percent calling themselves as multiracial. Hispanics comprised 12.5 percent of the population. In the future, the U.S. population will become even more diverse, due to both higher birth rates and the immigration to the United States by Nonwhites. See Figure 8-5.

FIGURE 8-5
Marketing to a Diverse Marketplace

More and more companies, such as Sears (which is illustrated in this photo), recognize the changing face of the U.S. marketplace and are working hard to appeal to the increasingly diverse consumer population.

Source: Reprinted by permission of PricewaterhouseCoopers.

8-2g Uses of Demographic Data

As noted at the beginning of the chapter, after studying individual demographics, a firm can form demographic profiles to better focus its marketing efforts. Here are three examples.

The "millennial generation" consists of people born since 1982. In the United States, there are 70 million millennials. As a group, they will be better educated than any prior generation and be more technologically savvy. The group is also more diverse racially and ethnically. The spending power is high, with 13- to 17-year-olds alone accounting for $150 billion in U.S. consumer spending. Experts say that "there will be enormous rewards for companies who can figure out millennials a little earlier. Harry Potter books are a good example of something that reflects the generation in a totally unexpected way."[5]

Asian-Americans represent an appealing market for alert financial services firms. According to Datamonitor (www.datamonitor.com), "Asian-Americans possess the highest median U.S. income. They also are the best-educated group in the country and are one-and-a-half times more likely to have a bachelor's degree than Whites. Like other minorities, Asian-Americans have a younger and more rapidly growing population than do Whites. Given their economic status, Asian-Americans should be among the most sought-after customers. Yet, financial service firms routinely misrepresent themselves to this market, due to a failure to match their products to the preferences within different ethnic groups."[6]

Demographic profiles of nations, such Australia and Turkey, can be contrasted:

	Australia	*Turkey*
Gender ratio (male/female)	0.99/1.00	1.02/1.00
Annual population growth	1.0%	1.3%
Life expectancy	80 years	71 years
Population under 15 years of age	21%	29%
Urban population	85%	74%
Working women as part of total labor force	65%	31%
Literacy rate	100%	82%

Australia presents better marketing opportunities for firms targeting older, well-educated consumers, while Turkey presents better opportunities for firms marketing to children.[7]

8-2h Limitations of Demographics

In applying demographic data, these limitations should be noted: Information may be old; even in the United States, a full census is done once per 10 years and there are time lags before data are released. Data may be limited in some nations, especially less-developed and developing ones. Summary data may be too broad and hide opportunities and risks in small markets or specialized product categories. The psychological or social factors influencing people are not considered. The decision process used in purchasing is not explained. Demographics do not delve into the reasons why people make decisions.

Demographic data may be dated, unavailable, too general, require profile analysis, and not consider reasons for behavior.

[5]Bonnie Tsui, "Generation Next," *Advertising Age* (January 15, 2001), pp. 14, 16.
[6]Brian Angell, "Ethnic Population Is Too Big to Ignore," *U.S. Banker* (June 2000), p. 66.
[7]*CIA World Factbook 2000.*

ETHICAL Issues in Marketing

Taking Advantage of Vulnerable Consumers for Diet Products

Although virtually all weight-loss "cure alls" promising easy results with little exercise or dieting clearly do not work, there are always some unsuspecting consumers who are willing to try the latest weight-loss fad. And since fenfluramine, a prescription drug popularly known as fen-phen, was taken off the market due to serious health complications, the appetite of many dieters for a new miracle drug has increased. In the United States, sales of low-calorie foods and snacks have dropped 40 percent since 1996, while annual sales of diet pills and supplements have increased to about $800 million.

The market for diet pills and supplements is driven by both demand and supply factors. Demand is driven by the fact that more than one-half of all Americans are overweight, and 22 percent are overweight enough to be considered obese, according to the National Institutes of Health. At the same time, the supply of weight-loss products has increased due to less stringent laws relating to over-the-counter weight-loss products. Firms no longer have to submit data to the Food and Drug Administration (FDA) showing actual weight loss in clinical studies. The FDA also has insufficient resources to investigate the more than 25,000 dietary supplements currently on the market. Looser regulatory controls have been linked to least 17 deaths caused by consumer use of ephedra, an herbal stimulant.

The Federal Trade Commission (FTC) requires advertisers to have proof of their ad claims, but FTC investigations occur only after unsuspecting consumers have parted with their money and/or have had serious side effects.

As the new advertising manager for a small manufacturer of an untested diet supplement, how would you promote your product? Should there be a warning statement? Explain your answers.

Source: Based on material in Greg Winter, "Fraudulent Marketers Capitalize on Demand for Sweat-Free Diets," *New York Times on the Web* (October 29, 2000).

Here are some of the questions unanswered by demographic data:

- Why do consumers act as they do?
- Why do consumers with similar demographic characteristics act differently?
- To whom do consumers look for advice prior to purchasing?
- Under what situations do families (households) use joint decision making?
- Why does status play a large role in the purchase of some products and a small role in others?
- How do different motives affect consumer decisions?
- How does risk affect consumer decisions?
- Why do some consumers act as innovators and buy products before others?
- How important are purchase decisions to consumers?
- What process do consumers use when shopping for various products?
- How long will it take for consumers to reach purchase decisions?
- Why do consumers become brand loyal or regularly switch brands?

To answer these questions, more firms now go beyond demographics in studying final consumers. They use demographic data in conjunction with consumer lifestyle and decision-making analysis. A final consumer's *lifestyle* represents the way in which a person lives and spends time and money. It is based on the social and psychological factors that have been internalized by that person, as well as his or her demographic background.[8] These factors overlap and complement each other; they are not independent of one another. The consumer's decision process involves the steps a person uses in buying goods and services: stimulus, problem awareness, information search, evaluation of alternatives, purchase, and post-purchase behavior. Demographics, social factors, and psychological factors all affect the process.

Consumer **lifestyles** *describe how people live. In making purchases, people use a decision process with several stages.*

8-3 CONSUMER LIFESTYLES

The social and psychological characteristics that help form final consumer lifestyles are described next.

8-3a Social Characteristics of Consumers

The final consumer's social profile is based on a combination of culture, social class, social performance, reference groups, opinion leaders, family life cycle, and time expenditures (activities). See Figure 8-6.

As discussed in Chapter 6, a *culture* comprises a group of people who share a distinctive heritage, such as Americans or Canadians. People learn about socially proper behavior and beliefs via their culture. The American culture values achievement and success, activity, efficiency and practicality, progress, material comfort, individualism, freedom, external conformity, humanitarianism, youthfulness, and fitness and health.[9]

Roper Starch Worldwide (www.roper.com) recently did a cross-cultural study involving people around the globe. It asked them to state the importance of each of 60 "guiding principles":

> Some values exhibit polarizing trends from culture to culture, giving a great amount of insight to those countries and cultures. Respecting one's elders is the most important value in Vietnam, but ranks a low 46th in Germany. Faith is the single most important value in Indonesia, Egypt, and Saudi Arabia, but ranks nearly last in France. Friendship ranks first in Germany, but 26th in South Africa. Freedom rates second in Argentina, France, Italy, and

Each **culture** *transmits acceptable behavior and attitudes.* **Social class** *separates society into divisions.* **Social performance** *describes how people fulfill roles.*

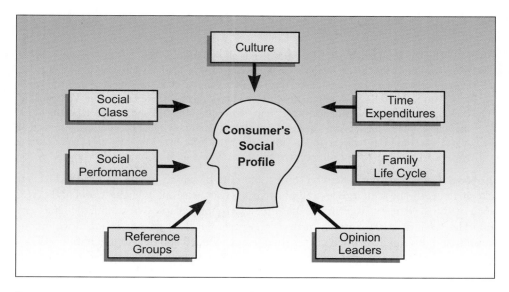

FIGURE 8-6

Factors Determining a Consumer's Social Profile

---

[8]Peter D. Bennett (Editor), *Dictionary of Marketing Terms*, Second Edition (Chicago: American Marketing Association, 1995), p. 154.

[9]Schiffman and Kanuk, *Consumer Behavior*, pp. 334–342.

TABLE 8-1   The Informal Social Class Structure in the United States

Class	Size	Characteristics
Upper Americans		
Upper-upper	0.5%	Social elite; inherited wealth; exclusive neighborhoods; summer homes; children attend best schools; money unimportant in purchases; secure in status; spending with good taste
Lower-upper	3.8%	Highest incomes; earned wealth; often business leaders and professionals; college educated; seek best for children; active socially; insecure; conspicuous consumption; money unimportant in purchases
Upper-middle	13.8%	Career-oriented; executives and professionals earning well over $60,000 yearly; status tied to occupations and earnings; most educated, but not from prestige schools; demanding of children; quality products purchased; attractive homes; socially involved; gracious living
Middle Americans		
Middle class	32.8%	Typical Americans; average-earning white-collar workers and the top group of blue-collar workers; many college educated; respectable; conscientious; try to do the right thing; home ownership sought; do-it-yourselfers; family focus
Working class	32.3%	Remaining white-collar workers and most blue-collar workers; working class lifestyles; some job monotony; job security sought more than advancement; usually high school education; close-knit families; brand loyal and interested in name brands; not status-oriented
Lower Americans		
Upper-lower	9.5%	Employed, mostly in unskilled or semiskilled jobs; poorly educated; low incomes; rather difficult to move up the social class ladder; protective against lower-lower class; standard of living at or just above poverty; live in affordable housing
Lower-lower	7.3%	Unemployed or most menial jobs; poorest income, education, and housing; the bottom layer; present-oriented; impulsive as shoppers; overpay; use credit

Sources: This table is adapted by the authors from Richard P. Coleman, "The Continuing Significance of Social Class in Marketing," *Journal of Consumer Research*, Vol. 10 (December 1983), pp. 265–280; Eugene Sivadas, George Mathew, and David J. Curry, "A Preliminary Examination of the Continued Significance of Social Class in Marketing," *Journal of Consumer Marketing*, Vol. 14 (Number 6, 1997), pp. 463–469; Roger D. Blackwell, Paul W. Miniard, and James F. Engel, *Consumer Behavior*, Ninth Edition (Fort Worth, TX: Harcourt, 2001), Chapter 11; and Leon Schiffman and Leslie Lazar Kanuk, *Consumer Behavior*, Seventh Edition (Upper Saddle River, NJ: Prentice Hall, 2000), Chapter 11.

Spain. In Communist China, where freedom is all but an irrelevant concept to many people, freedom is in 50th place. Knowledge appears to be of critical importance in India and Singapore, where it ranks second and third, respectively, but of less significance in Egypt where it is 34th. Stable relationships rate third in Japan and Great Britain, but 43rd in Venezuela. In Mexico and Russia, self-reliance is very important, ranking third and fourth respectively, but in Saudi Arabia, where people live under a monarchy and are ruled by strict religious beliefs, it is 33rd. Ambition ranks sixth for Egypt and seventh for Saudi Arabia, while Italy ranks it 55th. Looking good rates 13th in Egypt, but a low 54th place in China and Japan.[10]

Social class systems reflect a "status hierarchy by which groups and individuals are classified on the basis of esteem and prestige."[11] They exist all over the world and divide society into segments, informally or formally grouping those with similar values and lifestyles. Industrialized nations have a larger middle class, greater interchange among classes, and less rigidly defined classes than less-developed and developing nations. Social classes are based on income, occupation, education, and type of dwelling. Each class may represent a distinct target market. Table 8-1 shows the informal U.S. social class system.

[10]Roper Starch Worldwide, "Re-Mapping the World of Consumers," *American Demographics* (October 2000), special advertising section.

[11]Bennett, *Dictionary of Marketing Terms*, p. 265. See also Alison Stein Wellner, "The Money in the Middle," *American Demographics* (April 2000), pp. 56–64; and Paul Starobin and Olga Kravchenka, "Russia's Middle," *Business Week* (October 16, 2000), pp. 78–84.

Social performance refers to how a person carries out his or her roles as a worker, family member, citizen, and friend. A person may be an executive, have a happy family life, be active in the community, and have many friends. Or he or she may never go higher than assistant manager, be divorced, not partake in community affairs, and have few friends. Many combinations are possible.

A *reference group* is one that influences a person's thoughts or actions. For many goods and services, these groups have a large impact on purchases. Face-to-face reference groups, such as family and friends, have the most effect. Yet, other—more general—groups also affect behavior and may be cited in marketing products. Ads showing goods and services being used by college students, successful professionals, and pet owners often ask viewers to join the "group" and make similar purchases. By pinpointing reference groups that most sway consumers, firms can better aim their strategies.

Firms want to know which persons in reference groups are *opinion leaders.* These are people to whom other consumers turn for advice and information via face-to-face communication. They tend to be expert about a product category, socially accepted, long-standing members of the community, gregarious, active, and trusted; and they tend to seek approval from others. They normally have an impact over a narrow product range and are perceived as more believable than company-sponsored information.

> **Reference groups** *influence thoughts and behavior.* **Opinion leaders** *affect others through face-to-face contact.*

GLOBAL *Marketing in Action*

Marketing High-Tech Status Products in China

According to a phone store manager there, "Everybody in China wants to own a mobile phone. For men, it's like having a cigarette lighter. For women, it's like wearing an accessory." Cell phones are clearly viewed as a status symbol for a new generation of Chinese consumers. As the strategist for a wireless Web services firm says, "As a hip young professional (yuppie) in Shanghai, you're much more apt to be concerned about carrying around the latest phone than if you are from London or New York."

There are currently 65 million cell phone users in China, but the number of users is expected to grow to 105 million in 2002. As of that date, it is estimated that China will bypass the United States to become the largest market for cell phones in the world. The leading service provider there is China Mobile, with 40 million subscribers. Unlike in the United States, where wireless service providers typically sell phones at low rates to encourage usage, cell phone makers in China sell their phones with no incentives from service providers.

In contrast to many other goods and services, the Chinese market is at the forefront in both the design and marketing of cell phones. Chinese consumers are very technologically savvy in their purchase and use of cellular phones. Foreign cell phone makers, such as Motorola and Nokia, compete in China on the basis of state-of-the-art features like a built-in Chinese-English dictionary, wireless Web access, and fancy plastic covers. In contrast, local Chinese phone makers aim at the mass market through price. Whatever the origin, cell phones are marketed through displays in shopping malls and billboards.

How should Motorola market its cell phones in China?

Source: Based on material in Mark Landler, "Selling Status, and Cell Phones in China," *New York Times on the Web* (November 24, 2000).

*The **family life cycle** describes life stages, which often use **joint decision making**. The **household life cycle** includes family and nonfamily units.*

The *family life cycle* describes how a family evolves through various stages from bachelorhood to solitary retirement. At each stage, needs, experience, income, family composition, and the use of *joint decision making*—the process whereby two or more people have input into purchases—change. The number of people in life-cycle stages can be gotten from demographic data. Table 8-2 shows a traditional cycle and its marketing relevance. The stages apply to families in all nations—both industrialized and less-developed/developing, but the opportunities are most applicable for industrialized countries.

When using life-cycle analysis, the people who do not follow a traditional pattern because they do not marry, do not have children, become divorced, have families with two working spouses (even if there are very small children), and so on, should be noted. They are not adequately reflected in Table 8-2, but may represent good marketing opportunities. For that reason, the concept of the *household life cycle*—which incorporates the life stages of both family and nonfamily households—is taking on greater significance. Table 8-3 shows the current status of U.S. family and nonfamily households.

Time expenditures reflect the workweek, family care, and leisure.

Time expenditures refer to the activities in which a person participates and the time allocated to them. They include work, commuting, personal care, home maintenance, food preparation and consumption, child rearing, social interactions, reading, shopping, self-improvement, recreation, entertainment, vacations, and so on. While the average U.S. workweek for the primary job has stabilized at 35 to 40 hours, more people work at two jobs. Americans enjoy TV, phone calls, pleasure driving, walking, swimming, sightseeing, bicycling, spectator events, reading, and playing games and sports.

TABLE 8-2   The Traditional Family Life Cycle

Stage in Cycle	Characteristics	Marketing Opportunities
Bachelor, male or female	Independent; young; early in career, low earnings, low discretionary income	Clothing; auto; stereo; travel; restaurants; entertainment; status appeals
Newly married	Two incomes; relative independence; present- and future-oriented	Apartment furnishings; travel; clothing; durables; appeal to enjoyment and togetherness
Full nest I	Youngest child under 6; one to one-and-a-half incomes; limited independence; future-oriented	Goods and services for the child, home, and family; durability and safety; pharmaceuticals; day care: appeal to economy
Full nest II	Youngest child over 6, but dependent; one-and-a-half to two incomes; at least one spouse set in career; future-oriented	Savings; home; education; family vacations; child-oriented products; some luxuries; appeal to comfort and long-term enjoyment
Full nest III	Youngest child living at home, but but independent; highest income level; thoughts of future retirement	Education; expensive durables for children; replacement and improvement of parents' durables; appeal to comfort and luxury
Empty nest I	No children at home; independent; good income; thoughts of self and retirement	Vacation home; travel; clothing; entertainment; luxuries; appeal to self-gratification

continues

TABLE 8-2	The Traditional Family Life Cycle (*continued*)	
Empty nest II	Retirement; less income and expenses; present-oriented	Travel; recreation; new home; health-related items; less interest in luxuries; appeal to comfort at a low price
Sole survivor I	Only one spouse alive; actively employed; present-oriented; good income	Immersion in job and friends; interest in travel, clothing, health, and recreation areas; appeal to productive citizen
Sole survivor II	Only one spouse alive; retired; some feeling of futility; less income	Travel; recreation; pharmaceuticals; security; appeal to economy and and social activity

TABLE 8-3	The Current Status of U.S. Family and Nonfamily Households	
Household Status	**Percentage of All U.S. Households**	
Family Households	69	
Married couples, no children under age 18		29
Married couples, with children under age 18		25
Other types of families, no children under age 18		7
Other types of families, with children under age 18[a]		8
Single-Person Households[b]	26	
Age 24 and under		1
Age 25 to 44		8
Age 45 to 64		7
Age 65 and over		10
Other Nonfamily Households	5	
Unmarried couples, no children under age 18		2
Unmarried couples, with children under age 18		1
Other[c]		2
Total	100	100

[a]Includes one-parent families in which married couples are separated but not divorced, one-parent families headed by divorcees, one-parent families headed by widows and widowers, and one-parent families headed by never-married mothers and fathers.
[b]Includes people who have never married, as well as those who are widowed, separated, and divorced.
[c]Includes roommates.

Source: Computed by the authors from U.S. Bureau of the Census, *Current Population Reports*.

8-3b Psychological Characteristics of Consumers

The final consumer's psychological profile involves his or her personality, attitudes (opinions), class consciousness, motivation, perceived risk, innovativeness, and purchase importance. See Figure 8-7.

*A **personality** describes a person's composite internal, enduring psychological traits.*

A ***personality*** is the sum total of an individual's enduring internal psychological traits that make the person unique. Self-confidence, dominance, autonomy, sociability, defensiveness, adaptability, and emotional stability are selected personality traits. Personality has a strong impact on an individual's behavior. For example, a self-confident and sociable person often will not purchase the same goods and services as an inhibited and aloof person. It is necessary to remember that a personality is made up of many traits operating in association with one another.

***Attitudes** can be positive, negative, or neutral.*

Attitudes (opinions) are an individual's positive, neutral, or negative feelings about goods, services, firms, people, issues, and/or institutions. They are shaped by demographics, social factors, and other psychological traits. One marketing role is to foster favorable attitudes; given the intensive competition in many industries, a firm cannot normally succeed without positive consumer attitudes. When studying attitudes, two concepts should often be measured—the attitude itself and the purchase intention toward a firm's brand. For example: (1) Do you like brand A? Would you buy brand A in the future? (2) How does brand A compare with other brands? Would you buy brand A if it were priced higher than other brands?

***Class consciousness** is low for inner-directed persons and high for outer-directed ones.*

Class consciousness is the extent to which a person seeks social status. It helps determine the interest in social-class mobility, the use of reference groups, and the importance of prestige purchases. Inner-directed people want to please themselves and are often attracted by products that perform well functionally. They are not concerned with social mobility, rely on their own judgment, and do not value prestige items. Outer-directed people want to please others. Upward social mobility, reference group approval, and ownership of prestige items are sought. These people are often attracted by products with social visibility, well-known brands, and uniqueness. Functional performance may be less important.

***Motivation** is a drive-impelling action; it is caused by **motives**.*

Motivation involves the positive or negative needs, goals, and desires that impel a person to or away from certain actions, objects, or situations.[12] By identifying and appealing to people's ***motives***—the reasons for behavior—a firm can produce positive motivation. For example:

Motives	Marketing Actions That Motivate
Hunger reduction	Television and radio ads for fast-food restaurants
Safety	Smoke detector demonstrations in stores
Sociability	Perfume ads showing social success due to products
Achievement	Use of consumer endorsements in ads specifying how much knowledge can be gained from an encyclopedia
Economy	Newspaper coupons advertising sales
Social responsibility	Package labels that emphasize how easy it is to recycle products

Each person has distinct motives for purchases, and these change by situation and over time. Consumers often combine economic (price, durability) and emotional (social acceptance, self-esteem) motives when making purchases.

[12]Bennett, *Dictionary of Marketing Terms*, pp. 179–180.

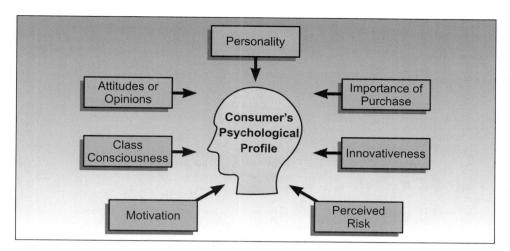

FIGURE 8-7

Factors Determining a Consumer's Psychological Profile

Perceived risk is the level of uncertainty a consumer believes exists as to the outcome of a purchase decision; this belief may or may not be correct. Perceived risk can be divided into six major types:

1. Functional—risk that a product will not perform adequately.
2. Physical—risk that a product will be harmful.
3. Financial—risk that a product will not be worth its cost.
4. Social—risk that a product will cause embarrassment before others.
5. Psychological—risk that one's ego will be bruised.
6. Time—risk that the time spent shopping will be wasted if a product does not perform as expected.[13]

Because high perceived risk can dampen customer motivation, firms must deal with it even if people have incorrect beliefs. Firms can lower perceived risk by giving more information, having a reputation for superior quality, offering money-back guarantees, avoiding controversial ingredients, and so on.

A person willing to try a new good or service that others perceive as risky exhibits *innovativeness.* An innovator is apt to be young and well educated, and to have above-average income for his or her social class. The person is also likely to be interested in change, achievement-oriented, open-minded, status-conscious, mobile, and venturesome. Firms need to identify and appeal to innovators when introducing a new good or service.

The *importance of a purchase* affects the time and effort a person spends shopping for a product—and the money allotted. An important purchase means careful decision making, high perceived risk, and often a large amount of money. An unimportant purchase means less decision time (an item may be avoided altogether) and low perceived risk, and it is probably inexpensive.

8-3c Selected Consumer Lifestyles

Many distinct consumer lifestyles will continue, including family values, voluntary simplicity, getting by, "me" generation, blurring of gender roles, poverty of time, and component lifestyles. Their marketing implications are shown in Table 8-4.

A *family values* lifestyle emphasizes marriage, children, and home life. It encourages people to focus on children and their education; family autos, vacations, and entertainment; and home-oriented products. Because the traditional family is becoming less representative of U.S. households, firms must be careful in targeting those who say they follow this lifestyle. They should also remember that a family values lifestyle remains the leading one in other nations. For instance, in Italy, less than one-half of women are in the labor force and the divorce rate is much lower than that of the United States.

Perceived risk *is the uncertainty felt by the consumer about a purchase.*

Innovativeness *is trying a new product others see as risky.*

The **importance of a purchase** *determines the time, effort, and money spent.*

In some households, family values have a great impact.

[13]Schiffman and Kanuk, *Consumer Behavior*, p. 153.

	Lifestyle Category	Marketing Opportunities in Appealing to the Lifestyle
TABLE 8-4 **Selected Marketing Opportunities of Consumer Lifestyles**	Family values	Family-oriented goods and services Educational devices and toys Traditional family events "Wholesome" entertainment
	Voluntary simplicity	Goods and services with quality, durability, and simplicity Environmentally safe products Energy-efficient products Discount-oriented retailing
	Getting by	Well-known brands and good buys ("value") Video rentals and other inexpensive entertainment Do-it-yourself projects such as "knock-down" furniture Inexpensive child care
	"Me" generation	Individuality in purchases Luxury goods and services Nutritional themes Exercise- and education-related goods and services.
	Blurring of gender roles	Unisex goods, services, and stores Couples-oriented advertising Child-care services Less male and female stereotyping
	Poverty of time	Internet and phone sales Service firms with accurate customer appointments Labor-saving devices One-stop shopping
	Component lifestyle	Situational purchases Less social class stereotyping Multiple advertising themes Market niching

Voluntary simplicity is based on self-reliance.

Voluntary simplicity is a lifestyle in which people have an ecological awareness, seek product durability, strive for self-reliance, and buy simple products. People with this lifestyle are cautious, conservative, and thrifty shoppers. They do not buy expensive cars and clothing, hold on to products for long periods, and rarely eat out or go on prepackaged vacations. They like going to a park or taking a vacation by car, are more concerned with product toughness than appearance, and believe in conservation. There is an attraction to rational appeals and no-frills retailing.

When economic circumstances are tough, some people emphasize getting by.

Getting by is a frugal lifestyle pursued by people because of economic circumstances. Those getting by seek product durability, self-reliance, and simple products. Unlike people with voluntary simplicity, they do so since they must. In less-developed and developing nations, most people have this lifestyle; a much smaller proportion do in industrialized nations. Getting-by consumers are attracted to well-known brands (to reduce perceived risk), do not try new products, rarely go out, and take few vacations. They seek bargains and patronize local stores. They rarely feel they have any significant discretionary income.

The "me" generation stresses self-fulfillment.

A *"me" generation* lifestyle stresses being good to oneself, self-fulfillment, and self-expression. It involves less pressure to conform, as well as greater diversity; there is also less interest in responsibilities and loyalties. Consumers with this lifestyle want to take care of themselves. They stress nutrition, exercise, and grooming. They buy expensive cars and apparel, and they visit full-service stores. These people are more concerned with product appearance than durability, and some place below-average value on conservation if it will have a negative effect on their lifestyle.

Since many women work, more men are assuming the once-traditional roles of their wives, and vice versa, thus *blurring gender* roles: "Men do more shopping and housework as women make them change. Knowing how men are changing, and how they aren't, is a key to targeting them. Meanwhile, more women are learning how to buy cars, program VCRs, and use power tools."[14] See Figure 8-8.

The prevalence of working women, the long distances between home and work, and the large number of people working at second jobs contribute to a *poverty-of-time* lifestyle in many households. For them, the quest for financial security means less free time. This lifestyle leads people to greater use of time-saving products. Included are convenience foods, quick-oil-change services, microwave ovens, fast-food restaurants, mail-order retailers, one-hour film processing, and professional lawn and household care.

Today, more people employ a *component lifestyle*, whereby their attitudes and behavior depend on particular situations rather than an overall lifestyle philosophy. People may take their children with them on vacation (family values), engage in trash recycling (voluntary simplicity), look for sales to save money (getting by), take exercise classes ("me" generation), share shopping chores (blurring gender roles), and eat out on busy nights (poverty of time). As the president of WSL Strategic Retail (www.wslstrategicretail.com) noted, grasping component lifestyles can be quite challenging for firms:

> Have you wondered what's going on with consumers? Why they are so full of contradictions? Why they will buy a $500 leather jacket at full price but wait for a $50 sweater to go on sale? Will buy a top-of-the-line sports utility vehicle then go to Costco to buy new tires? Will eagerly pay $3.50 for a cup of coffee but think $1.29 is too expensive for a hamburger? Will spend $2.00 for a strawberry-smelling bath soap but wait for a coupon to buy a $0.99 twin pack of toilet soap?[15]

Blurring gender roles involves men and women undertaking nontraditional duties.

A poverty of time exists when a quest for financial security means less free time.

With a component lifestyle, consumer attitudes and behavior vary by situation.

FIGURE 8-8
Blurring Gender Roles

More men and women are now engaging in nontraditional activities, such as shopping together at an Ace Hardware store.

Source: © Ace Hardware. Printed by permission.

[14]Diane Crispell, "The Brave New World of Men," *American Demographics* (January 1992), pp. 38, 43. See also Michelle Gillian Fisher, "A Latte with Your Lube?" *Sales & Marketing Management* (November 2000), p. 15.
[15]Wendy Liebmann, "How America Shops," *Vital Speeches of the Day* (July 15, 1998), p. 595.

8-3d Limitations of Lifestyle Analysis

Unlike demographics, many of the social and psychological aspects of final consumer lifestyles are difficult to measure, somewhat subjective, usually based on the self-reports of consumers, and sometimes hidden from view (to avoid embarrassment, protect privacy, convey an image, and other reasons). In addition, there are still some ongoing disputes over terminology, misuse of data, and reliability.

8-4 THE FINAL CONSUMER'S DECISION PROCESS

The **final consumer's decision process** *has many stages and various factors affect it.*

The *final consumer's decision process* is the way in which people gather and assess information and choose among alternative goods, services, organizations, people, places, and ideas. It consists of the process itself and factors affecting it. The process has six stages: stimulus, problem awareness, information search, evaluation of alternatives, purchase, and post-purchase behavior. Demographic, social, and psychological factors affect the process. Figure 8-9 shows the total decision-making process.

When a consumer buys a good or service, decides to vote for a political candidate or donate to a charity, and so on, he or she goes through a decision process. Sometimes, all six stages in the process are used; other times, only a few steps are utilized. For example, the purchase of an expensive stereo requires more decision making than the purchase of a new music video.

At *any* point in the decision process, a person may decide not to buy, vote, or donate—and, thereby, end the process. A good or service may turn out to be unneeded, unsatisfactory, or too expensive.

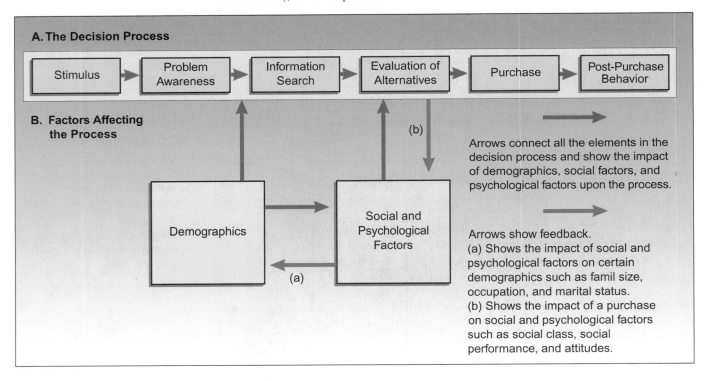

FIGURE 8-9

The Final Consumer's Decision Process

8-4a Stimulus

A *stimulus* is a cue (social, commercial, or noncommercial) or a drive (physical) meant to motivate a person to act.

A social cue occurs when someone talks with friends, family members, co-workers, and others. It is from an interpersonal source not affiliated with a seller. A commercial cue is a message sponsored by a seller to interest a person in a particular good, service, organization, person, place, or idea. Ads, personal selling, and sales promotions are commercial cues. They are less regarded than social cues because people know they are seller-controlled. A noncommercial cue is a message from an impartial source such as *Consumer Reports* (www.consumerreports.org) or the government. It has high believability because it is not affiliated with the seller. A physical drive occurs when a person's physical senses are affected. Thirst, hunger, and fear cause physical drives.

A person may be exposed to any or all of these stimuli. If sufficiently stimulated, he or she will go to the next step in the decision process. If not, the person will ignore the cue and delay or terminate the decision process for the given good, service, organization, person, place, or idea.

A **stimulus** *is a cue or drive intended to motivate a consumer.*

8-4b Problem Awareness

At the *problem awareness* stage, a consumer recognizes that the good, service, organization, person, place, or idea under consideration may solve a problem of shortage or unfulfilled desire.

Recognition of shortage occurs when a consumer realizes a repurchase is needed. A suit may wear out. A man or woman may run out of razor blades. An eye examination may be needed. A popular political candidate may be up for re-election. It may be time for a charity's annual fund-raising campaign. In each case, the consumer recognizes a need to repurchase.

Recognition of unfulfilled desire occurs when a consumer becomes aware of a good, service, organization, person, place, or idea that has not been bought before. Such an item may improve status, appearance, living conditions, or knowledge in a way not tried before (luxury car, cosmetic surgery, proposed zoning law, encyclopedia), or it may offer new performance features not previously available (laser surgery, tobacco-free cigarettes). Either way, a person is aroused by a desire to try something new.

Many consumers hesitate to act on unfulfilled desires due to greater risks. It is easier to replace a known product. Whether a consumer becomes aware of a problem of shortage or of unfulfilled desire, he or she will act only if the problem is perceived as worth solving.

Problem awareness *entails recognition of a shortage or an unfulfilled desire.*

8-4c Information Search

Next, an *information search* requires listing the alternatives that will solve the problem at hand and determining the characteristics of them.

A list of alternatives does not have to be written. It can be a group of items a consumer thinks about. With internal search, a person has experience in the area being considered and uses a memory search to list the choices. A person with minimal experience will do external search to list alternatives; this can involve commercial sources, noncommercial sources, and/or social sources. Often, once there is a list of choices, items (brands, companies, and so on) not on it do not receive further consideration.

The second phase of information search deals with the attributes of each alternative. This information can also be generated internally or externally, depending on the expertise of the consumer and the level of perceived risk. As risk increases, more information is sought. Once an information search is completed, it must be determined whether the shortage or unfulfilled desire can be satisfied by any alternative. If one or more choices are satisfactory, the consumer moves to the next step. The process is delayed or discontinued when no alternative provides satisfaction.

An **information search** *determines alternatives and their characteristics.*

The Internet has become a major source for consumer shopping information. Among the most useful sources are

- BotSpot (www.botspot.com)—"The spot for all [shopping] bots on the Net".
- CNET (www.cnet.com)—"The source for computers and technology".
- Epinions.com (www.epinions.com)—"Over one million reviews and comments".
- Gomez (www.gomez.com)—"Your guide to buying online".
- mySimon (www.mysimon.com)—"Compare products and prices from around the Web."
- StartSpot (www.shoppingspot.com)—"Product reviews, comparison shopping tools, and much more".
- Yahoo! Shopping (http://shopping.yahoo.com)—"Thousands of stores. Millions of products. All with one wallet."

MARKETING *and the Web*

SaveDaily.com: Shop Until You Drop, Then Save a Little

SaveDaily (www.savedaily.com) is an Internet-based investment firm. It offers a Web service that seeks to generate consumer loyalty by providing rebates based on purchases with selected online retailers. Unlike traditional rebates in which purchasers receive cash, SaveDaily's rebates are paid in the form of mutual fund shares.

The SaveDaily site offers clients two ways to invest. With the conventional format, individuals can invest their own funds. In the unconventional format, consumers earn retail credits of between 1 and 10 percent of their purchases from SaveDaily's 80 retail partners. These include such firms as J.C. Penney, Barnes & Noble, and Sharper Image. The retail credits are then invested in mutual funds managed by one of three firms. Like most mutual funds, investors are charged an annual fee of 1 percent of their assets.

According to advocates of this program, consumers can now save and invest significant sums of money without having to drastically change their buying habits. SaveDaily is an especially effective means of getting lower-income households to shop online, as well as to invest in mutual funds. This market segment has been mostly ignored by financial institutions due to the high costs of serving accounts with small balances.

Despite the merit of SaveDaily's service, it also faces a number of challenges. SaveDaily must obtain and retain a large number of merchants that are attractive to customers. A downturn in the stock market can negatively impact the program. Firms like AOL and Fidelity would be formidable competitors if they copy the concept.

Discuss the future prospects for SaveDaily. How would you market this site?

Source: Based on material in Andrea Adelson, "A New Lure for Loyal Shoppers: Buy a Little, Save a Little," *New York Times* (October 25, 2000), p. W34.

8-4d Evaluation of Alternatives

There is now enough information for a consumer to select one alternative from the list of choices. This is easy when one option is clearly the best across all attributes: A product with excellent quality and a low price will be a sure choice over an average-quality, expensive one. The choice is usually not that simple, and a consumer must carefully engage in an ***evaluation of alternatives*** before making a decision. If two or more alternatives seem attractive, a person needs to determine which criteria to evaluate and their relative importance. Alternatives would then be ranked and a choice made.

Decision criteria are the features a person deems relevant—such as price, style, quality, safety, durability, status, and warranty. A consumer sets standards for the features and forms an attitude on each alternative according to its ability to meet the standards. In addition, each criterion's importance is set because the multiple attributes of a given product are usually of varying weight. For example, a consumer may consider shoe prices to be more important than style and select inexpensive, nondistinctive shoes.

A consumer now ranks alternatives from most to least desirable and selects one. Ranking is sometimes hard because alternatives may have technical differences or be poorly labeled, new, or intangible (such as evaluating two political candidates). On these occasions, options may be ranked on the basis of brand name or price, which is used to indicate overall quality.

In situations where no alternative is satisfactory, a decision to delay or not make a purchase is made.

> **Evaluating alternatives** *consists of weighing features and selecting the most desired product.*

8-4e Purchase

After choosing the best alternative, a person is ready for the ***purchase act:*** an exchange of money, a promise to pay, or support in return for ownership of a specific good, the performance of a specific service, and so on. Three considerations remain: place of purchase, terms, and availability.

The place of purchase is picked the same way as a product. Choices are noted, attributes detailed, and a ranking done. The best locale is chosen. Although most items are bought at stores, some are bought at school, work, and home. *Purchase terms* involve the price and method of payment. Generally, a price is the amount (including interest, tax, and other fees) a person pays to gain the ownership or use of a good or service. It may also be a person's vote, time investment, and so on. The payment method is the way a price is paid (cash, short-term credit, or long-term credit). *Availability* refers to the timeliness with which a consumer receives a product that he or she buys. It depends on stock on hand (or service capacity) and delivery. Stock on hand (service capacity) relates to a seller's ability to provide a good or service when requested. For items requiring delivery, the period from when an order is placed by a consumer until it is received and the ease with which an item is transported to its place of use are crucial.

A consumer will purchase if these elements are acceptable. That is why companies such as AutoNation (www.autonation.com), highlighted in Figure 8-10, want to be perceived as consumer friendly. However, sometimes, dissatisfaction with any one of the elements may cause a person to delay or not buy, even though there is no problem with the good or service itself. Thus, if a store is closed or a salesperson is unfriendly, the consumer might not come back.

> The **purchase act** *means picking where to buy, agreeing to terms, and checking availability.*

8-4f Post-Purchase Behavior

Once a purchase is made, a person may engage in ***post-purchase behavior,*** via further purchases and/or re-evaluation. Many times, one purchase leads to others: A house purchase leads to the acquisition of fire insurance. A PC purchase leads to the acquisition of computer software. In addition, displaying complementary products near one another may encourage related purchases.

> **Post-purchase behavior** *often embodies further buying and/or re-evaluation.* **Cognitive dissonance** *can be reduced by proper consumer aftercare.*

A person may also re-evaluate a purchase after making it: Are expectations matched by performance? Satisfaction usually leads to a repurchase when a good or service wears out, a charity holds a fund-raising campaign, and so on, and leads to positive communication with other people interested in the same item. Dissatisfaction can lead to brand switching and negative communication. It is often due to *cognitive dissonance*—doubt that a correct decision has been made. A person may regret a purchase or wish another choice had been made. To overcome dissonance, a firm must realize the process does not end with a purchase. Follow-up calls, extended warranties, and ads aimed at purchasers can reassure people.

8-4g Factors Affecting the Final Consumer's Decision Process

Demographic, social, and psychological factors affect the way final consumers make choices and can help a firm understand how people use the decision process. For example, an affluent consumer would move through the process more quickly than a middle-income one due to less financial risk. An insecure consumer would spend more time making a decision than a secure one.

By knowing how these factors influence decisions, a firm can fine-tune its marketing strategies to cater to the target market and its purchase behavior, and answer these questions: Why do two or more people use the decision process in the same way? Why do two or more people use it differently?

8-4h Types of Decision Processes

Each time a person buys a good or service, donates to a charity, and so on, he or she uses the decision process. This may be done subconsciously, with the person not aware of using it. Some situations let a person move through the process quickly and de-emphasize or skip steps; others require a thorough use of each step. A consumer may use extended, limited, or routine decision-making—based on the search, level of experience, frequency of purchase, amount of perceived risk, and time pressure. See Figure 8-11.

Extended consumer decision making occurs when a person fully uses the decision process. Much effort is spent on information search and evaluation of alternatives for expensive, complex items with which a person has little or no experience. Purchases are made infrequently. Perceived risk is high, and the purchase is important. A person has time available to make a choice. Purchase delays often occur. Demographic, social, and

Final consumer decision making can be categorized as **extended, limited,** *or* **routine.**

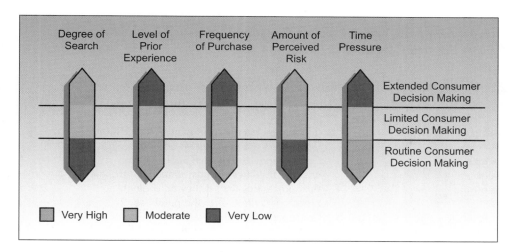

FIGURE 8-11

The Three Types of Final Consumer Decision Processes

psychological factors have their greatest impact. Extended decision making is often involved in picking a college, a house, a first car, or a location for a wedding.

Limited consumer decision making occurs when a person uses every step in the purchase process but does not spend a great deal of time on some of them. The person has previously bought a given good or service, but makes fresh decisions when it comes under current purchase consideration—due to the relative infrequency of purchase, the introduction of new models, or an interest in variety. Perceived risk is moderate, and a person is willing to spend some time shopping. The thoroughness with which the process is used depends on the amount of prior experience, the importance of the purchase, and the time pressure facing the consumer. Emphasis is on evaluating a list of known choices, although an information search may be done. Factors affecting the decision process have some impact. A second car, clothing, gifts, home furnishings, and an annual vacation typically need limited decision making.

Routine consumer decision making occurs when a person buys out of habit and skips steps in the process. He or she spends little time shopping and often rebuys the same brands (or those bought before). In this category are items with which a person has much experience. They are bought regularly, have little or no perceived risk, and are rather low in price. Once a person realizes a good or service is depleted, a repurchase is made. Time pressure is high. Information search, evaluation, and post-purchase behavior are normally omitted, as long as a person is satisfied. Impulse purchases, where consumers have not thought of particular items until seeing displays for them, are common. Factors affecting the process have little impact because problem awareness usually leads to a purchase. Examples of items routinely purchased are the daily paper, a haircut by a regular stylist, and weekly grocery items.

There are several differences between consumers in industrialized nations and those in less-developed and developing ones. In general, consumers in less-developed and developing countries

- Are exposed to fewer commercial and noncommercial cues.
- Have access to less information.
- Have fewer goods and services from which to choose.
- Are more apt to buy a second choice if the first one is not available.
- Have fewer places of purchase and may have to wait on long lines.
- Are more apt to find that stores are out of stock.
- Have less purchase experience for many kinds of goods and services.
- Are less educated and have lower incomes.
- Are more apt to rebuy items with which they are only moderately satisfied (due to a lack of choices).

TABLE 8-5 High-Involvement View of Active Consumers Versus Low-Involvement View of Passive Consumers

Traditional High-Involvement View of Active Consumers	Newer Low-Involvement View of Passive Consumers
1. Consumers are information processors.	1. Consumers learn information at random.
2. Consumers are information seekers.	2. Consumers are information gatherers.
3. Consumers are an active audience for ads and the effect of ads on them is *weak*.	3. Consumers are a passive audience for ads and the effect of ads on them is *strong*.
4. Consumers evaluate brands before buying.	4. Consumers buy first. If they do evaluate brands, it is done after the purchase.
5. Consumers seek to maximize satisfaction. They compare brands to see which provide the most *benefits* and buy based on detailed comparisons.	5. Consumers seek an acceptable level of satisfaction. They choose the brand least apt to have *problems* and buy based on few factors. Familiarity is key.
6. Lifestyle characteristics are related to consumer behavior because the product is closely tied to a consumer's identity and belief system.	6. Lifestyle characteristics are not related to consumer behavior because the product is not closely tied to a consumer's identity and belief system.
7. Reference groups influence behavior because of the product's importance to group norms.	7. Reference groups have little effect on behavior because the product is unlikely to be related to group norms.

Source: Henry Assael, *Consumer Behavior and Marketing Action,* Sixth Edition (Cincinnati: South-Western, 1998), p. 155. Reprinted by permission.

Because many consumers—in both industrialized nations and less-developed nations—want to reduce shopping time, the use of complex decision making, and risk, most purchases are made by routine or limited decision making. Consumers often employ low-involvement purchasing and/or brand loyalty.

Low-involvement purchasing *occurs with unimportant products.*

With **low-involvement purchasing,** a consumer minimizes the time and effort expended in both making decisions about and shopping for those goods and services he or she views as unimportant. Included are "those situations where the consumer simply does not care and is not concerned about brands or choices and makes the decision in the most cognitively miserly manner possible. Most likely, low involvement is situation-based, and the degree of importance and involvement may vary with the individual and with the situation."[16] In these situations, consumers feel little perceived risk, are passive about getting information, act fast, and may assess products after (rather than before) buying.

Firms can adapt to low-involvement purchasing by using repetitive ads to create awareness and familiarity, stressing the practical nature of goods and services, having informed salespeople, setting low prices, using attractive in-store displays, selling in all types of outlets, and offering coupons and free samples. Table 8-5 compares the traditional high-involvement view of consumer behavior with the newer low-involvement view.

Brand loyalty *involves consistent repurchases and preferences for specific brands.*

After a consumer tries one or more brands of a good or service, **brand loyalty**—the consistent repurchase of and preference toward a particular brand—may take place. With it, a person can reduce time, thought, and risk whenever buying a given good or service. Brand loyalty can occur for simple items such as gasoline (due to low-involvement purchasing) and for complex items such as autos (to minimize the perceived risk of switching brands).

[16]Bennett, *Dictionary of Marketing Terms,* p. 157.

According to America's Research Group (www.americasresearchgroup.com), at least 40 percent of U.S. adults say they are "very loyal" or "loyal" to brands in these categories: autos, bath soap, coffee, gasoline, hair products, insurance, major appliances, mayonnaise, soft drinks, and TVs. On the other hand, 30 percent or less are "very loyal" or "loyal" to jewelry, phone equipment, and sports equipment.[17]

How can firms generate and sustain customer loyalty? Here's the way Gateway (www.gateway.com), the computer and information services company, addresses this issue:

> Providing the best value in the industry is no mystery: we deliver better products, at better prices, with better service than anyone else out there. We've streamlined our base PC configurations to bolster customer satisfaction in our "rock-solid" configurations. We're teaching customers to get the most out of technology, supporting them in the way they find most convenient. A critical element to the value of a Gateway PC purchase to our customers is the support they receive after the sale. That's why we're driving to do all that we can to resolve any customer issue on first contact. Additionally, we're enhancing our portfolio of tools and services used to support our customer: new online and in-store testing tools, leading-edge training for our support representatives, and greater capabilities for in-store servicing. We can even diagnose and repair computers across the Internet, saving our customers the time and energy of having to bring a PC in for servicing. In the end, we're doing all that we can to reach the highest customer satisfaction level with our customers.[18]

8-4i Marketing Applications of the Final Consumer's Decision Process

Over the years, the final consumer's decision process has been studied and applied in many settings, as these illustrations indicate:

- When acquiring travel information for a leisure trip, 59 percent of all U.S. travelers consult friends and relatives; 47 percent, a travel agent; 42 percent, the Internet; and 16 percent, travel magazines. Those thinking about a cruise are much more likely to use a travel agent (81 percent), while those traveling internationally are more apt to use the Internet (55 percent) and read travel magazines (37 percent).[19]

- From 1996 to 2000, U.S. consumers doubled the number of stores they visited on their weekly shopping trip: "In 2000, consumers shopped 2.9 outlets in a week, in 1998 2.4, and in 1996 1.4. However, they are not making more shopping trips; they are shopping more stores on each trip. The increase in shopping is also driven by the level of shopping confidence and experience exhibited by female shoppers who willingly, eagerly, shop everywhere from bricks-and-mortar retailers to clicks-and-mortar retailers to catalogs, from kiosks, at sporting events, even from street vendors."[20]

- Nearly a third of Chinese consumers are "enthusiastic shoppers," who enjoy shopping and like to price bargain. They prepare complete shopping lists before shopping, consult with friends and neighbors prior to making major purchases, and are often innovators and opinion leaders. About 15 percent of Chinese consumers are "passive shoppers," who consider shopping to be a necessary burden. They are casual shoppers, do not prepare detailed lists before shopping, and do not like price bargaining. They are conservative in their purchase of new products.[21]

[17]"Complete Listing of 50 Brand Products for Loyalty Study," www.americasresearchgroup.com/50products.html (March 23, 2001).

[18]"Corporate Backgrounder," www.gateway.com/about/spotnews/backgrounder.shtml (March 27, 2001).

[19]American Society of Travel Agents, "Independent Research," *American Demographics* (March 2000), p. 52.

[20]Wendy Liebmann, "How America Shops," *Vital Speeches of the Day* (October 1, 2000), p. 753.

[21]Zhengyuan Wang, C. P. Rao, and Angela D'Auria, "Measuring Chinese Personal Values and Shopping Behavior: An Empirical Comparison of the Rokeach Value Survey and Perceived Attribute Importance" in Brian T. Engelland and Alan J. Bush (Editors), *Marketing: Advances in Theory and Thought* (Evansville, Ind.: Southern Marketing Association, 1994), pp. 378–381.

- For several reasons, "substantial time often elapses between the time people recognize the need for a product and the time they actually purchase it." People may believe they do not have enough time to devote to the decision. They may feel shopping is an unpleasant experience. They may experience perceived risk. They may need advice from others; and it is not readily available. They may not know how to gather adequate information about products and their attributes. They may expect prices to fall. They may expect improved products to be introduced later."[22]

- Satisfied consumers discuss their experiences with far fewer people than dissatisfied ones. As one insurance expert says, "Word of mouth has always been a powerful force, but never before could it be used so quickly, nor spread so widely as in this age of the digital nervous system. Unfortunately, negative news seems to spread more readily than positive news. Researchers have calculated that one offended person can repeat the story of his or her negative experience to as many as 13 people before either the offended person tires of telling it or runs out of people interested in hearing him or her rant and rave. On the other hand, a person with a positive experience will tell only five people."[23]

8-4j Limitations of the Final Consumer's Decision Process

The limitations of the final consumer's decision process for marketers lie in the hidden (unexpressed) nature of many elements of the process; the consumer's subconscious performance of the process or a number of its components; the impact of demographic, social, and psychological factors on the process; and the differences in decision making among consumers in different countries.

WEB SITES YOU CAN USE

One of the best features of the Web is that it gives us access to so much varied information. Thus, there are Web sites devoted to virtually every consumer lifestyle topic imaginable. Just type in a lifestyle topic in your favorite search engine, and away you go. Here is a tiny sampling of the Web sites devoted to mainstream consumer lifestyle topics:

American Association of Retired People (www.aarp.org)—Provides tips for people ages 50 and older.

Diabetic Lifestyle (www.diabetic-lifestyle.com)— Geared toward people with diabetes.

Excel International Sports (www.excelsports.net)— Offers custom-designed vacation trips to sporting events in Europe.

F.U.N. Place (www.thefunplace.com)—Devoted, in a colorful way, to parenting.

Technocopia (www.technocopia.com)—Looks at lifestyle issues associated with technology.

[22]Eric A. Greenleaf and Donald R. Lehmann, "Reasons for Substantial Delay in Consumer Decision Making," *Journal of Consumer Research,* Vol. 22 (September 1995), pp. 186–199.
[23]Jim Cecil, "The Vengeance Factor," *Rough Notes* (January 2001), p. 44.

SUMMARY

1. *To show the importance and scope of consumer analysis* By analyzing consumers, a firm is better able to determine the most appropriate audience to which to appeal and the combination of marketing factors that will satisfy this audience. This is a critical task given the diversity in today's global marketplace. The scope of consumer analysis includes who, what, why, how, when, where, and how often. Chapter 8 examines final consumers, while Chapters 9 and 10 cover organizational consumers, developing a target market strategy, and sales forecasting.

2. *To define and enumerate important consumer demographics for the U.S. population and other countries* Consumer demographics are objective and quantifiable population statistics. They include population size, gender, and age; population location, housing, and mobility; population income and expenditures; population occupations and education; population marital status; and population ethnicity/race. Profiles can be derived.

The world has 6.15 billion people, rising by 1.2 percent annually. The U.S. has 283 million people, increasing by less than one percent each year. In many nations, a large proportion of births involves firstborns. Worldwide, the number of men and women is roughly equal. However, women generally live longer than men; and the average age of populations in industrialized nations is higher than in less-developed and developing countries.

The level of urbanization does vary by country, with more than three-quarters of the U.S. population living in urban and suburban areas. In many countries, the majority of people own the home in which they live. Each year, millions of people emigrate from one country to another and hundreds of millions move within their countries.

The 2000 U.S. median household income was between $41,000 and $42,000. Many nations measure their cost of living and rate of inflation via a consumer price index. There are differences in consumption patterns between people in industrialized nations and ones in less-developed and developing countries. When assessing consumption patterns, the distinction between disposable-income spending and discretionary-income expenditures should be kept in mind.

In industrialized nations, the labor force is continuing its movement to white-collar and service occupations; many more jobs in less-developed and developing nations still entail manual work and are agriculture-based. Throughout the world, women comprise a significant part of the labor force. Unemployment varies widely among nations, based on economies and industry shifts. Globally, education has improved in recent decades.

Marriage and family are strong institutions, although less dominant than before for some nations. A family consists of relatives living together. A household consists of a person or persons related or not, occupying a housing unit. In many nations, both family and household size have declined, due to the growth in single-person households and other factors.

Demographically, ethnicity/race is important as it pertains to the diversity of people among and within nations. Most countries have populations representing different ethnic and racial groups.

3. *To show why consumer demographic analysis is not sufficient in planning marketing strategies* These limitations of demographics are noted: data may be obsolete; data may be unavailable for some nations; there may be hidden trends or implications; and demographics do not explain the factors affecting behavior, consumer decision making, and motivation.

Because demographic data do not answer such questions as why consumers act as they do, why demographically similar consumers act differently, how motives and risks affect decisions, and how long it takes people to reach purchase decisions, many firms now analyze the social and psychological aspects of final consumer lifestyles, as well as the way in which consumers make decisions—in conjunction with demographics.

4. *To define and describe consumer lifestyles and their characteristics, examine selected lifestyles, and consider the limitations of lifestyle analysis* A final consumer's lifestyle is the way in which a person lives and spends time and money. It is a function of the social and psychological factors internalized by that person, along with his or her demographic background. Consumer social profiles are made up of several elements, including culture, social class, social performance, reference groups, opinion leaders, the family life cycle, and time expenditures. Psychological profiles are based on a combination of personality, attitudes (opinions), the level of class consciousness, motivation, perceived risk, innovativeness, and purchase importance.

Seven lifestyle types are expected to continue, with their popularity often differing by country: family values, voluntary simplicity, getting by, the "me" generation stresses, blurring gender roles, poverty of time, and component lifestyles.

Many lifestyle concepts are hard to measure, rather subjective, based on consumer self-reports, and sometimes hidden from view. There are disputes over terms, misuse of data, and reliability.

5. *To define and describe the final consumer's decision process and consider the limitations of final consumer decision-making analysis* The decision process is the way by which people collect and analyze information and make choices among alternatives. It consists of the process itself and the factors affecting it (demographic, social, and psychological). It can be delayed or terminated by a consumer at any point.

The process has six steps: stimulus, problem awareness, information search, evaluation of alternatives, purchase, and post-purchase behavior. There are three types of process: extended, limited, and routine. The way people make decisions varies widely between industrialized nations and less-developed and developing nations. Consumers often reduce shopping time, thought, and risk via low-involvement purchasing and brand loyalty.

The limitations of the decision process for marketers lie in the unexpressed nature of many parts of the process; the subconscious nature of many consumer actions; the impact of demographic, social, and psychological factors; and the intercountry differences in consumer decision making.

KEY TERMS

final consumers (p. 224)
organizational consumers (p. 224)
consumer demographics (p. 225)
cost of living (p. 227)
disposable income (p. 228)
discretionary income (p. 228)
family (p. 229)
household (p. 229)
ethnicity/race (p. 230)
lifestyle (p. 233)
culture (p. 233)
social class (p. 234)
social performance (p. 235)
reference group (p. 235)

opinion leaders (p. 235)
family life cycle (p. 236)
joint decision making (p. 236)
household life cycle (p. 236)
time expenditures (p. 236)
personality (p. 238)
attitudes (opinions) (p. 238)
class consciousness (p. 238)
motivation (p. 238)
motives (p. 238)
perceived risk (p. 239)
innovativeness (p. 239)
importance of a purchase (p. 239)

final consumer's decision process (p. 242)
stimulus (p. 243)
problem awareness (p. 243)
information search (p. 243)
evaluation of alternatives (p. 245)
purchase act (p. 245)
post-purchase behavior (p. 245)
cognitive dissonance (p. 246)
extended consumer decision making (p. 246)
limited consumer decision making (p. 247)
routine consumer decision making (p. 247)
low-involvement purchasing (p. 248)
brand loyalty (p. 248)

REVIEW QUESTIONS

1. How does the use of consumer demographics aid marketing decision making?
2. Cite several reasons why it is difficult to contrast personal income data by country.
3. Why are demographic data alone frequently insufficient for marketing decisions?
4. Distinguish between the traditional family life cycle and the household life cycle.

5. Distinguish between actual risk and perceived risk. How may a firm reduce each type of perceived risk for a new arthritis pain reliever?
6. Compare the voluntary lifestyle with the getting-by life-style.
7. What could cause a consumer to *not* make a purchase even when he or she really likes a product?
8. Define low-involvement purchasing and explain its use by consumers. Give an example.

DISCUSSION QUESTIONS

1. Develop a demographic profile of the people residing in your census tract, using the *Census of Population*. What are the marketing overtones of this profile?
2. American culture emphasizes achievement and success, activity, efficiency and practicality, progress, material comfort, individualism, freedom, external conformity, humanitarianism, youthfulness, and fitness and health. What are the implications of this for firms marketing the following goods and services?
  a. Bicycles.
  b. Tanning salons.
  c. Adult education.
  d. Vacation travel.

3. A large apparel manufacturer has hired you as a marketing consultant. It is particularly interested in learning more about the concept of a component lifestyle and developing an appropriate strategy.
  a. Explain the relevance of the component lifestyle concept for the apparel industry.
  b. Suggest various ways in which the apparel manufacturer can appeal to component lifestyles.
4. How may Bose (www.bose.com), the maker of pricey audio equipment, reduce both perceived risk *and* cognitive dissonance through its marketing efforts?

WEB EXERCISE

Visit the site of the Keirsey personality test (www.advisorteam.com/user/ktsintro.asp) and answer the questions. What can a person learn about himself or herself from this site? Do you agree with the profile generated about you from the online survey? Explain your answer.

Organizational Consumers

NonStop Solutions (www.nonstop.com) is a software provider that analyzes sales patterns, inventory holding costs, and shipping costs to aid retailers in determining how much inventory they need to have on hand. The firm might suggest, for example, large order quantities of paper towels at one time due to the high freight costs in relation to their value. On the other hand, it might suggest that a pharmacy order no more than needed to meet its weekly demand for a costly prescription drug since the drug has low shipping costs but high inventory holding costs.

NonStop software is based on research by a professor of business and engineering at Stanford University who is a supply-chain management expert. NonStop has about 60 clients and annual revenues of $25 million. In late 2000, it received $50 million in funding from a variety of venture capitalists.

As compared with supply-chain management software firms that seek to sell data to manufacturers, NonStop focuses on wholesalers and retailers. Thus, it markets demand-chain management software. NonStop software is particularly useful for these intermediaries because it can deal with thousands of suppliers. In developing its marketing strategy, NonStop first targeted drugstores and then progressed to such segments as auto-parts sellers, grocers, and other specialty retailers.

According to the director of planning and allocation at Bombay Company, a furniture and home furnishing accessories retail chain that is a NonStop client, "A lot of retailers are getting caught up on the emotional side of the business and we want to bring that into balance with some mathematics." Other clients such as O'Reilly Automotive, a seller of car parts, have found that NonStop's software enabled O'Reilly to free up capital by reducing inventory requirements.

One potential problem for NonStop is that the firm's target markets do not have as much money to spend on software as manufacturers do. To get around this problem, NonStop allows its wholesale and retail clients to pay for software through a monthly subscription rather than by a single payment.[1]

In this chapter, we will study much more than the characteristics and behavior of organizational consumers. We will also discuss the different types of organizational consumers (including wholesalers and retailers), their buying objectives, buying structure, and purchase constraints.

9-1 OVERVIEW

As defined in Chapter 8, organizational consumers purchase goods and services for further production, use in operations, or resale to others. In contrast, final consumers buy for personal, family, or household use. Organizational consumers are manufacturers, wholesalers, retailers, and government and other nonprofit institutions. When firms deal with organizational consumers, they engage in *industrial marketing,* as shown in these examples.

Firms involved with organizational consumers use **industrial marketing.**

[1]Lisa Bransten, "NonStop Makes Science Out of Stocking Stores," *Wall Street Journal* (October 5, 2000), p. 58.

Purchasing executives around the world spend trillions of dollars annually for the goods and services their companies require. According to one estimate, "On average, manufacturers shell out 55 cents of each dollar of revenues on goods and services, from raw materials to overnight mail. By contrast, labor seldom exceeds 6 percent of sales, overhead 3 percent."[2]

The Principal Financial Group, PFG (www.principal.com), is a leader in insurance for business clients, with a customer base of 44,000 companies. PFG offers retirement plans (including investment management, employee education, enrollment, comprehensive consulting services, government reporting, compliance testing, and asset allocation); group life and health insurance; business protection plans (in case an owner or key employee dies, becomes disabled, retires, or leaves the client); and employee benefit plans (to help recruit, reward, and retain key employees).[3] See Figure 9-1.

FIGURE 9-1

Principal Financial Group: A Leader in Insurance for Businesses

Source: Reprinted by permission.

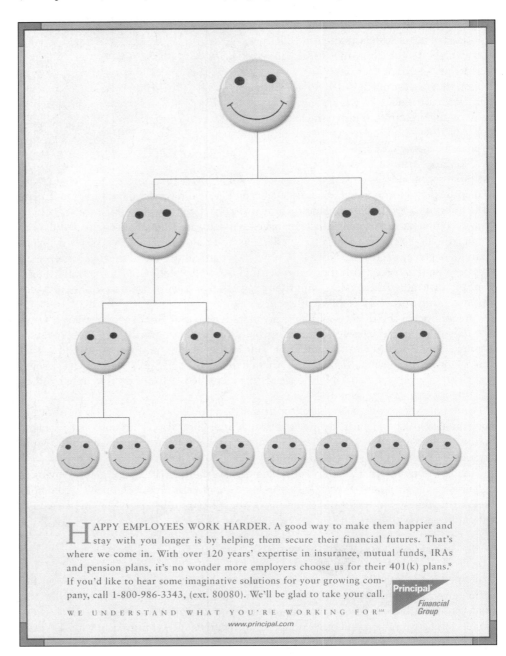

[2]Shawn Tully, "Purchasing's New Muscle," *Fortune* (February 20, 1995), pp. 75–76.
[3]"For Businesses," www.principal.com/biz.htm (March 26, 2001).

For a long time, Polaroid (www.polaroid.com) earned its reputation, and considerable profits, by making and marketing self-developing cameras for final consumers. But, in recent years, due to the popularity of digital cameras, inexpensive 35-mm cameras, and the growth of one-hour photo labs, Polaroid has placed more emphasis on products for organizational consumers (www.polaroidwork.com), including digital scanners, medical imaging systems, photo ID systems, and security systems. Organizational consumers now account for one-half of the firm's revenues.[4]

American Greetings (www.americangreetings.com) makes cards and other personal-communications products. It is the second-largest firm in the field, behind Hallmark, and markets products in more than 70 nations. Although its products are ultimately sold to final consumers, American Greetings must first get support from organizational consumers—the thousands of retailers (encompassing 112,000 stores around the world) that stock its cards and related items. Accordingly, American Greetings provides research on greeting-cards customers to its retailers, devises and sets up in-store displays, helps computerize transactions, runs special promotions to draw consumers to retail stores, and so on.[5]

Accenture (www.accenture.com), formerly a division of Andersen Worldwide, has annual revenues of $9 billion and 35,000 consultants in 50 nations: "Covering issues from strategy to solutions engineering and operations, our service lines let us quickly assemble whatever specific expertise, marketplace knowledge, and intellectual capital our clients in any industry require to redefine and lead their markets. The result: whether a new company is seeking advice, expertise, and capital or a *Fortune 500* organization is looking to create or refine its new economy strategy—or somewhere in between—Accenture has the capabilities to help companies create their future."[6]

Fluid Management (www.fluidman.com) is the worldwide leading maker of mixing and tinting equipment for the paint, coatings, and ink industries. It also markets specialized equipment and engineered systems to other industries, such as food, chemicals, and cosmetics. The firm's products increase the accuracy and efficiency of tinting and mixing paints, inks, and other fluids.[7] See Figure 9-2.

Two emerging trends in industrial marketing merit special attention: the growth of the Internet in business-to-business marketing and the rise in outsourcing. As we discussed in Chapter 7, the use of the Internet in business-to-business marketing is having a significant impact on the way companies deal with their suppliers. It is fostering closer relationships, better communications, quicker transaction times, cost efficiencies, barter exchanges (especially among smaller firms), and greater flexibility. Nonetheless:

> The B2B market is still in its infancy, and its structure and players remain in rapid flux. Despite breathless press coverage, very little is known about how business-to-business commerce will evolve on the Internet. The high level of uncertainty is causing widespread anxiety among executives—and for good reason. Whether as buyers, sellers, or both, all companies have substantial stakes in the business-to-business marketplace. Their supply chains, their product and marketing strategies, their processes and operations—even their business models—will be shaped by the way B2B relationships are formed and transactions are carried out. Yet, even the most basic questions remain difficult for firms to answer: Which exchanges should we participate in? Should we form a trading consortium with our competitors? Should we demand that our suppliers go online? What software should we invest in? Executives understand that the wrong choices could have dire consequences, but they also know that in the fast-paced world of the Internet they need to act soon or they'll be left behind.[8]

[4]Ginger Conlon, "Polaroid Sharpens Its Image," *Sales & Marketing Management* (October 2000), p. 31.

[5]"Investor Relations," www.corporate-ir.net/ireye/ir_site.zhtml?ticker=AM&script=2100 (March 27, 2001).

[6]"Bringing Innovations to Improve the Way the World Works and Lives," www.accenture.com/xd/xd.asp?it=enWeb&xd=aboutus\capabilities\our_capabilities.xml (March 27, 2001).

[7]"About FM," www.fluidman.com/about_fm.html (March 29, 2001).

[8]Richard Wise and David Morrison, "Beyond the Exchange: The Future of B2B," *Harvard Business Review,* Vol. 78 (November-December 2000), p. 88.

FIGURE 9-2
Fluid Management's TintMaster

For retailers such as Ace Hardware, "When you're being flooded with large custom paint orders and need to get that long string of tint tasks completed quickly, Fluid Management's TintMaster gets the job done right the first time, every time."

Source: Reprinted by permission.

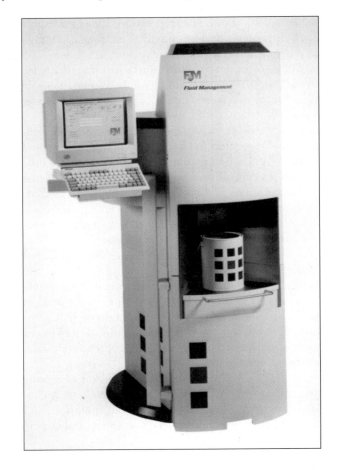

---

*With **outsourcing,** client firms farm out nonessential functions.*

Outsourcing occurs when one company provides services for another company that could also be or usually have been done in-house by the client firm.[9] According to Dun & Bradstreet (www.dnb.com), global outsourcing now accounts for $200 billion in annual revenues; and it is gaining momentum as companies look to "farm out" to third parties some of the functions that they consider to be nonessential. Among firms that outsource, the functions most commonly contracted out are information technology, transportation management, media management, human resources (employee leasing), and finance.[10] For further information on the topic of outsourcing, visit the Outsourcing Center (www.outsourcing-center.com).

In this chapter, organizational consumers are distinguished from final consumers and a global perspective is provided. The various types of organizational consumers are described. Key factors in organizational consumer behavior are presented. The organizational consumer's decision process is outlined. Marketing implications are offered.

9-2 THE CHARACTERISTICS OF ORGANIZATIONAL CONSUMERS

In undertaking industrial marketing, a firm must recognize that organizational consumers differ from final consumers in several key ways. As shown in Table 9-1, differences are due to the nature of purchases and the nature of the market. A firm must also see that organizational consumer characteristics vary by nation.

---

[9]"Outsourcing," http://whatis.techtarget.com/WhatIs_Definition_Page/0,4152,212731,00.html (March 29, 2001).

[10]Marq R. Ozanne, "Managing Strategic Alliances for the Virtual Enterprise," www.fortune-sections.com/outsourcing (March 31, 2001).

ETHICAL Issues in Marketing

The Virtues of Assisting Minority-Operated Suppliers

In an effort to increase the financial and marketing strength of its minority-owned suppliers, Procter & Gamble (P&G), has helped some of these suppliers merge together. For example, P&G played a major role in the merger plans of two packaging firms that were owned by African-Americans: Film Fabricators Inc. and Johnson-Bryce Corporation. To help facilitate the merger, P&G assured the newly-combined firm of a three-year $100 million contract to wrap its Pampers brand of disposable diapers. P&G also promised to help link the new firm with other corporate customers. According to the chairman and chief executive of the combined company, "With consumer products getting larger and competing on a global basis, the concern was that we would not be able to have a major role on our own. Now, we will be able to compete with anybody, anywhere."

The combined firm will also reap rewards for P&G. The company knows that the merger will lead to more efficiencies due to greater bargaining with its suppliers and economies of scale due to the increased size. P&G also feels that its assistance will be recognized by minority customers. A recent study by a major marketing research firm found that 87 percent of African-Americans were more likely to purchase products from companies that contribute to the minority community through charitable contributions or business activity. According to one P&G marketing and business development director, "In the 1970s and 1980s, firms did this to be seen as good corporate citizens. Today, it's a business imperative." P&G now does $548 million yearly in business with minority-owned suppliers, up from $85 million in 1989.

As a product manager for Pampers, how would you publicize your supplier relationships? Is a community backlash possible? Explain your answer.

Source: Based on material in Greg Winter, "P&G Helps Minority-Run Companies," *New York Times on the Web* (October 30, 2000).

TABLE 9-1   Major Differences Between Organizational and Final Consumers

Differences in Purchases

Organizational consumers

1. buy for further production, use in operations, or resale to others. Final consumers buy only for personal, family, or household use.
2. commonly purchase installations, raw materials, and semifinished materials. Final consumers rarely purchase these goods.
3. often buy on the basis of specifications and technical data. Final consumers frequently buy based on description, fashion, and style.
4. utilize multiple-buying and team-based decisions more often than final consumers.
5. are more apt to apply formal value and vendor analysis.
6. more commonly lease equipment.
7. more frequently employ competitive bidding and negotiation.

Differences in the Market

Organizational consumers

1. derive their demand from that of final consumers.
2. have demand states that are more subject to cyclical fluctuations than final consumer demand.
3. are fewer in number and more geographically concentrated than final consumers.
4. often employ buying specialists.
5. require a shorter distribution channel than do final consumers.
6. may require special relationships with sellers.
7. are more likely than final consumers to be able to make goods and undertake services as alternatives to purchasing them.

9-2a Differences from Final Consumers Due to the Nature of Purchases

Organizational and final consumers vary in how they use goods and services and in the items bought. Organizational consumers buy capital equipment, raw materials, semi-finished goods, and other products for use in further production or operations or for resale to others. Final consumers usually buy finished items (and are not involved with million-dollar purchases) for personal, family, or household use. Thus, organizational consumers are more apt to use specifications, multiple-buying decisions, value and vendor analysis, leased equipment, and competitive bidding and negotiation than are final consumers.

Many organizational consumers rely on product specifications in purchase decisions and do not consider alternatives unless they meet minimum standards, such as engineering and architectural guidelines, purity, horsepower, voltage, type of construction, and construction materials. Final consumers more often purchase on the basis of description, style, and color.

Multiple-buying responsibility *may be shared by two or more employees.*

Organizational consumers often use **multiple-buying responsibility,** whereby two or more employees formally participate in complex or expensive purchase decisions. A decision to buy computerized cash registers may involve input from computer personnel, marketing personnel, the operations manager, a systems consultant, and the controller. The firm's president might make the final choice about system characteristics and the supplier. Although final consumers use multiple-buying responsibility (joint decision making), they employ it less frequently and less formally.

Value analysis *reduces costs; vendor analysis rates suppliers.*

A lot of organizational consumers use value analysis and vendor analysis. In **value analysis,** organizational consumers thoroughly compare the costs and benefits of alternative materials, components, designs, or processes so as to reduce the cost/benefit ratio of purchases. They seek to answer such questions as: What is the purpose of each good or service under purchase consideration? What are the short-run and long-run costs of each alternative? Is a purchase necessary? Are there substitute goods or services that could perform more efficiently? How long will a good or service last before it must be replaced? Can uniform standards be set to ease reordering? In **vendor analysis,** organizational consumers thoroughly assess the strengths and weaknesses of current or new suppliers in terms of quality, customer service, reliability, and price.[11] Satisfaction with current vendors often means customer loyalty. Figures 9-3 and 9-4 illustrate value analysis and vendor analysis.

FIGURE 9-3

Value Analysis by a Purchaser of an Electric Pump

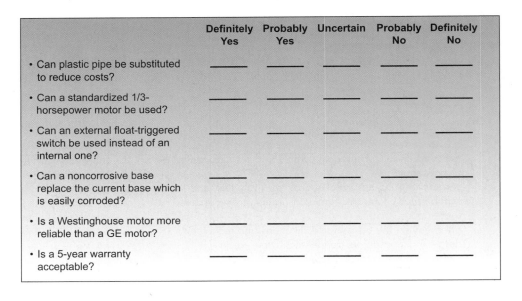

	Definitely Yes	Probably Yes	Uncertain	Probably No	Definitely No
• Can plastic pipe be substituted to reduce costs?	___	___	___	___	___
• Can a standardized 1/3-horsepower motor be used?	___	___	___	___	___
• Can an external float-triggered switch be used instead of an internal one?	___	___	___	___	___
• Can a noncorrosive base replace the current base which is easily corroded?	___	___	___	___	___
• Is a Westinghouse motor more reliable than a GE motor?	___	___	___	___	___
• Is a 5-year warranty acceptable?	___	___	___	___	___

[11]Peter D. Bennett (Editor), *Dictionary of Marketing Terms,* Second Edition (Chicago: American Marketing Association, 1995), pp. 297–299.

	Superior	Average	Inferior
• Speed of normal delivery	_____	_____	_____
• Speed of rush delivery	_____	_____	_____
• Distinctiveness of merchandise	_____	_____	_____
• Availability of styles and colors in all sizes	_____	_____	_____
• Handling of defective merchandise	_____	_____	_____
• Percent of merchandise defective	_____	_____	_____
• Ability for organizational consumer to make a profit when reselling merchandise	_____	_____	_____
• Purchase terms	_____	_____	_____

FIGURE 9-4

Vendor Analysis of a Sweater Supplier by a Purchaser

Organizational consumers of all sizes frequently lease major equipment. Each year, according to the Equipment Leasing Association (www.elaonline.org), U.S. firms spend $250 billion in leasing equipment (measured by the original cost of the equipment). Commonly leased equipment includes aircraft, computers, office machinery, and trucks and trailers. The worldwide use of commercial leasing is rising rapidly. Final consumers are less involved with leasing; it is most common in apartment and auto leasing.

Organizational consumers often use competitive bidding and negotiation. In *competitive bidding,* two or more sellers submit independent price quotes for specific goods and/or services to a buyer, which chooses the best offer. In *negotiation,* a buyer uses bargaining ability and order size to get sellers' best possible prices. Bidding and negotiation most often apply to complex, custom-made goods and services.

*In **competitive bidding,** sellers submit price bids; in **negotiation,** the buyer bargains to set prices.*

9-2b Differences from Final Consumers Due to the Nature of the Market

Derived demand occurs for organizational consumers because the quantity of the items they purchase is often based on the anticipated level of demand by their subsequent customers for specific goods and services. For example, the demand for the precision rivets used in cruise ships is derived from the demand for new cruise ships, which ultimately is derived from the demand for cruises. Firms know that unless demand is generated at the end-user level, distribution pipelines become clogged and resellers will not buy fresh goods and services. Organizational consumers' price sensitivity depends on end-user demand. If end users are willing to pay higher prices, organizational consumers will not object to increases. If end-user demand is low, organizational consumers will reduce purchases, even if prices to them are lowered. Figure 9-5 illustrates derived demand for major household appliances.

*Organizational consumers **derive demand** from their own customers. With the **accelerator principle,** final consumer demand impacts on many organizational consumers.*

The demand of organizational consumers tends to be more volatile than that of final consumers. A small change in the final demand for highly processed goods and services can yield a large change in organizational consumers' demand. This is a due to the *accelerator principle,* whereby final consumer demand affects many layers of organizational consumers. For example, a drop in auto demand by final consumers reduces dealer demand for cars, auto maker demand for steel, and steel maker demand for iron ore. In addition, capital purchases by organizational consumers are highly influenced by the economy.

There are fewer organizational consumers than final consumers. In the United States, there are about 400,000 manufacturing establishments, 525,000 wholesaling establishments (including manufacturer-owned facilities), and 2.5 million retailing establishments (including small family businesses), as compared with 105 million final consumer households. In some industries, large organizational consumers dominate, and their size and importance give them bargaining power in dealing with sellers.

Organizational consumers tend to be large and geographically concentrated.

FIGURE 9-5

Derived Demand for Major Appliances

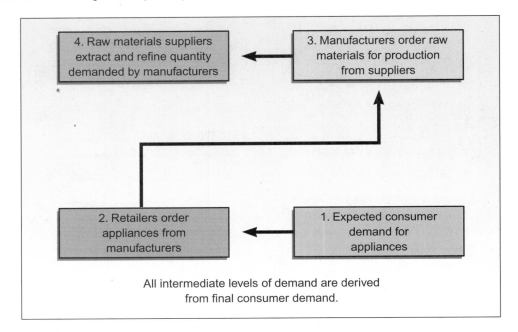

All intermediate levels of demand are derived
from final consumer demand.

Organizational consumers tend to be geographically concentrated. For instance, eight states (California, New York, Texas, Illinois, Pennsylvania, Ohio, Michigan, and Florida) contain about half of the nation's manufacturing plants. Some industries (such as steel, petroleum, rubber, auto, and tobacco) are even more geographically concentrated.

Due to their size and the types of purchases, many organizational consumers use buying specialists. These people often have technical backgrounds and are trained in supplier analysis and negotiating. Their full-time jobs are to purchase goods and services and analyze purchases. Expertise is high.

Inasmuch as many organizational consumers are large and geographically concentrated, purchase complex and custom-made goods and services, and use buying specialists, distribution channels tend to be shorter than those for final consumers. For example, a laser-printer maker would deal directly with a firm buying 100 printers; a salesperson would call on its purchasing agent. A company marketing printers to final consumers would distribute them via retail stores and expect final consumers to visit those stores.

Organizational consumers may require special relationships. They may expect to be consulted while new products are devised; want extra customer services, such as extended warranties, liberal returns, and free credit; and want close communications with vendors. That is why vendors like Micro Warehouse (www.warehouse.com) devote much attention to their sales force and customer relations. See Figure 9-6.

Systems selling and reciprocity are two specific tactics used in industrial marketing. In *systems selling,* a combination of goods and services is provided to a buyer by one vendor. This gives a buyer one firm with which to negotiate and consistency among various parts and components. For example, Hewlett-Packard (www.hp.com) uses systems selling for printers, personal computers, and servicing.

Reciprocity is a procedure by which organizational consumers select suppliers that agree to purchase goods and services, as well as sell them. In the United States, the Justice Department and the FTC monitor reciprocity due to its potential lessening of competition. However, in international marketing efforts, sellers may sometimes be required to enter into reciprocal agreements—known as "countertrade." Worldwide, countertrade accounts for 8 to 10 percent of business transactions between countries; and 600,000 companies participate in it.[12] The American Countertrade Association (www.countertrade.org) promotes trade and commerce between companies and their foreign customers who engage in countertrade as a form of doing business.

Systems selling *offers single-*
Systems selling *offers single-*

In **reciprocity,** *suppliers purchase as well as sell.*

[12]Bob Meyer, "The Original Meaning of Trade Meets the Future in Barter," *World Trade* (January 2000), pp. 46–50.

"*Our strength in the commercial marketplace is built on our team of dedicated Account Managers.*"

Mike Skolozdra, *Group Sales Director*

FIGURE 9-6
The Value of Commercial Accounts for Micro Warehouse
At Micro Warehouse (www.warehouse.com/ corporateAdvantage), "we know what businesses need and we're dedicated to providing the computer product solutions and services that work for you. Our easy-to-use online ordering and account reporting features put the power in your hands."

Source: Printed by permission.

Last, organizational consumers may produce goods and services themselves if they find purchase terms, the way they are treated, or available choices unacceptable. They may sometimes suggest to suppliers that they will make their own goods or perform services so as to improve bargaining positions.

9-2c A Global Perspective

As with final consumers, many dissimilarities exist among organizational consumers around the world, and sellers must understand and respond to them. In this section, these topics are discussed: attitudes toward foreign firms as suppliers, the effects of culture on negotiating styles and decision making, the impact of a nation's stage of economic development, the need for an adaptation strategy, and the opportunities available due to new technology.

Foreign organizational consumers must be carefully studied.

Firms doing business in foreign markets need to know how organizational consumers in those markets perceive the goods and services of firms from different countries. The attitudes of purchasing agents in foreign nations to U.S. products are often quite positive with regard to high-technology items, professional services, and industrial machinery. Likewise, many U.S. firms believe the product quality and/or prices for some foreign goods and services are better than those of American suppliers. That is why Ortho Biotech (www.thebody.com/ortho/ortho.html), a Johnson & Johnson subsidiary, has bought water-purification equipment from Finland and Limited Inc. (www.limited.com) buys clothing from Hong Kong, Taiwan, and other countries.

Nations' cultures have a large impact on the way their organizational consumers negotiate and reach decisions. Here is an illustration:

> The Chinese believe that one should build the relationship and, if successful, transactions will follow. Westerners build transactions and, if they are successful, a relationship will follow. This difference underlies many negotiating failures. In China, negotiating responses may be riddled with contradictions. Westerners will see illogical behavior, evasion, deviousness perhaps, where none may be intended. Disentangling these communications supplies much of the challenge that is China. The deadline-driven, transcontinental executive may find it hard to slow down to the pace required to share "a loaf of bread, a jug of wine, and Tao," but marketing in China requires the patient building of relationships. Not that China is slow. The pace can simultaneously be fast and slow. Those involved in negotiations know how long they can drag when the Chinese side is consulting internally or has other reasons for delay, and yet how swiftly they move on other occasions.[13]

The stage of economic development in foreign countries affects the types of goods and services bought by organizational consumers there. Many less-developed and developing nations do not yet have the infrastructure (electricity, roads, transportation systems, skilled workers) to properly use state-of-the-art machinery and equipment. In addition, such machinery and equipment may be too expensive for customers in those markets to afford. On the other hand, there is substantial long-term growth potential in those nations due to the scarcity of industrial goods and services there. Firms marketing to less-developed and developing nations need to be patient and flexible in dealing with organizational consumers.

When marketing goods and services to organizational consumers in foreign markets, firms have to consider how much to adapt their strategies to address the unique characteristics and needs of those customers. Because large organizational consumers can account for a significant part of any firm's overall revenues, selling firms are often quite willing to be responsive to customers' desires—by hiring personnel who fluently speak the language of the foreign markets, utilizing the most appropriate negotiating styles, and adapting product features and customer service as requested. In general, it is more likely that selling firms will engage in meaningful adaptation of their marketing efforts if a potential customer order is big, the good or service being marketed is complex, and the business cultures and stage of economic development in their domestic and foreign markets are dissimilar.

With the new technology now available, there are more opportunities to market to foreign organizational consumers than ever before. The Internet, E-mail, fax machines, satellite TV, and video conferencing all facilitate buyer-seller communications—and tear down the barriers caused by weak technological infrastructures, differences in time zones, and other factors.

9-3 TYPES OF ORGANIZATIONAL CONSUMERS

In devising a marketing plan aimed at organizational consumers, these attributes should be researched: areas of specialization, size and resources, location, and goods and services purchased. As shown in Figure 9-7, organizational consumers can be placed into five broad major categories: manufacturers, wholesalers, retailers, government, and nonprofit.

[13]Tim Ambler, "Reflections in China: Re-Orienting Images of Marketing," *Marketing Management* (Summer 1995), pp. 24, 25–26.

Show Me That You Want Me: How Foreign Countries Attract Businesses

When Costa Rica sought to attract Intel Corporation to build a plant, it devised an incentive package for the semiconductor manufacturer consisting of no income taxes for the first eight years, followed by four years at one-half the tax rate; duty-free imports of raw materials; and full freedom to move capital in and out of the country. That was only for starters! To further satisfy Intel, Costa Rica's government arranged to have the number of international flights increased, built an electric power substation near the Intel plant, and significantly reduced Intel's electric costs. The Costa Rican plant now employs 2,000 people.

When Advanced Micro Devices (AMD) considered locating a plant in Dresden, Germany, it very much liked that another microchip manufacturer was already located there, the presence of qualified labor, and that there were two universities in the area with strong computer science programs. On the other hand, AMD saw that Germany had a 40 percent corporate tax rate and that a large portion of the work force was used to communism (from earlier days in East Germany). To attract AMD, Germany gave the firm $370 million in cash and subsidies. The firm's plant currently employs 1,150 people.

According to analysts, while incentives are an important lure to attract a high-tech manufacturing facility, they are not the most important element. For example, areas with high-tech talent due to closeness to world-class research institutions do not need to offer tax incentives. That is what happened in Cambridge, England, which did not need incentives to attract an $80 million Microsoft research lab. However, analysts recognize that countries without distinctive attributes have to offer large financial incentives to induce firms to locate there.

What are the pros and cons to a country of attracting employers with financial incentives?

Source: Based on material in Chen May Lee, "Let's Make a Deal," *Wall Street Journal* (September 25, 2000), p. R10.

GLOBAL *Marketing in Action*

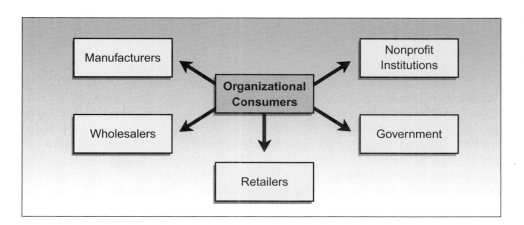

FIGURE 9-7
Types of Organizational Consumers

The **North American Industry Classification System (NAICS)** *provides information on U.S., Canadian, and Mexican organizational consumers.*

The **North American Industry Classification System, NAICS** (www.census.gov/epcd/www/naics.html), may be used to derive information about most organizational consumers. The NAICS, which is being phased in to replace the outdated Standard Industrial Classification (SIC), was introduced in 1999 and will be used by all federal agencies that report industry data by 2004. The NAICS is the official classification system for the United States, Canada, and Mexico (the members of NAFTA). It assigns organizations to 20 industrial classifications:

- Agriculture, forestry, fishing, and hunting
- Mining
- Utilities
- Construction
- Manufacturing
- Wholesale trade
- Retail trade
- Transportation and warehousing
- Information
- Finance and insurance
- Real estate and rental and leasing
- Professional, scientific, and technical services
- Management of companies and enterprises
- Administrative and support and waste management and remediation services
- Educational services
- Health care and social assistance
- Arts, entertainment, and recreation
- Accommodation and food services
- Other services (except public administration)
- Public administration

Within these groups, there are 1,350 more specific industry classifications, such as farm machinery and equipment manufacturing.

U.S. data by industry code are available from various government and commercial publications. The *U.S. Industry & Trade Outlook* (www.ita.doc.gov/td/industry/otea/outlook) and the *Annual Survey of Manufactures* (www.census.gov/prod/www/abs/industry.html) are U.S. government reports with data on hundreds of industries. *Standard & Poor's Industry Surveys* (www.standardpoor.com) and *D&B Reference Book of American Business* (www.dnb.com) also provide data by industry code and/or geographic area. Data on government institutions are available on a local, state, and federal level from the *Census of Governments* (www.census.gov/econ/www/go0100.html).

Although the NAICS is a North American classification system, considerable data on industrial activity and companies in other nations are available in the context of industry codes. The U.S. Department of Commerce's *U.S. Foreign Trade Highlights* (www.ita.doc.gov/td/industry/otea/usfth) has information on a number of international industries. Dun & Bradstreet's *Principal International Businesses Directory* lists 52,000 firms outside the United States.

With **end-use analysis,** *a seller studies sales made in different industries.*

End-use analysis is one way in which NAICS data can be employed. With it, a seller determines the proportion of sales made to organizational consumers in different industries. Table 9-2 shows end-use analysis for a glue manufacturer (in this case, the seller). First, the firm learns the current relative importance of various categories of customers—(section A of Table 9-2). It then applies end-use analysis to make an overall sales forecast by estimating the expected growth of each customer category in its area—(section B of Table 9-2).

Next, several characteristics of manufacturers, wholesalers, retailers, government, and nonprofit organizations as consumers are described.

9-3a Manufacturers as Consumers

Manufacturers produce products for resale to other consumers. The North American Industry Classification System lists 3 major two-digit industry groups in manufacturing. Each may be divided into 3-digit groups, 4-digit groups, 5-digit groups, and 6-digit groups.

Manufacturers *make items for resale to others.*

TABLE 9-2   End-Use Analysis for a Regional Glue Manufacturer

(A) Simple End-Use Analysis

NAICS Code	Industry Classification of Customers	Current Total Sales (in Percent)[a]
321	Wood product manufacturing	25
337	Furniture and related products manufacturing	20
323	Printing and related support activities	17
326	Plastics and related rubber products manufacturing	15
316	Leather and allied product manufacturing	10
339	Miscellaneous manufacturing	13
	Total	100

(B) Applying End-Use Analysis to Sales Forecasting

NAICS Code	Industry Classification of Customers	Current Total Sales (in Percent)	Estimated Annual Percentage Growth Rate of Industry[b]	Overall Sales Growth Percentage for a Glue Manufacturer[c]
321	Wood product manufacturing	25	+1.8	+0.45
337	Furniture and related product manufacturing	20	+3.2	+0.64
323	Printing and related support activities	17	+1.9	+0.32
326	Plastics and rubber products manufacturing	15	+3.0	+0.45
316	Leather and allied product manufacturing	10	−2.0	−0.20
339	Miscellaneous manufacturing	13	+2.0	+0.26
	Total estimated sales increase			+1.92

[a]Firm examines its sales receipts and categorizes them by NAICS group.
[b]Firm estimates growth rate of each category of customer (in its geographic area) on the basis of trade association and government data.
[c]Firm multiplies percent of current sales in each NAICS group by expected growth rate in each industry to derive its expected sales for the coming year. It expects sales to rise by 1.92 percent during the next year.

Thus, NAICS 33 is a manufacturing classification; 333 refers to machinery manufacturing; 3331 refers to agricultural, construction, and mining machinery manufacturing; 33311 refers to agricultural implement manufacturing; and 333112 refers to farm machinery and equipment manufacturing. Table 9-3 shows the 21 three-digit groups.

In the United States, one-third of manufacturers have 20 or more workers. The annual costs of their materials are $2.2 trillion. Their expenditures for plant and equipment (from trucks to generator sets) are hundreds of billions of dollars each year. They annually use trillions of BTUs of energy. Annual net sales (including shipments between firms in the same industry category) are $4.5 trillion, with the largest 500 industrial firms accounting for 60 percent of the total.

By knowing where different industries are located, a firm can concentrate efforts and not worry about covering dispersed markets. Because manufacturers' purchasing decisions tend to be made centrally at headquarters or at divisional offices, the seller must identify the location of the proper decision makers.

As consumers, manufacturers buy a variety of goods and services, including land, capital equipment, machinery, raw materials, component parts, trade publications, accounting services, supplies, insurance, advertising, and delivery services. For example, Boeing (www.boeing.com) has long- and short-term contracts with suppliers that total several billion dollars; and it buys equipment, raw materials, component parts, finished materials, and services from thousands of subcontractors and other businesses.

TABLE 9-3 **U.S. Manufacturing Industries**	**NAICS Code**	**Industry Name**
	31, 32, 33	Manufacturing
	311	Food manufacturing
	312	Beverage and tobacco product manufacturing
	313	Textile mills
	314	Textile product mills
	315	Apparel manufacturing
	316	Leather and allied product manufacturing
	321	Wood product manufacturing
	322	Paper manufacturing
	323	Printing and related support activities
	324	Petroleum and coal products manufacturing
	325	Chemical manufacturing
	326	Plastics and rubber products manufacturing
	327	Nonmetallic mineral product manufacturing
	331	Primary metal manufacturing
	332	Fabricated metal product manufacturing
	333	Machinery manufacturing
	334	Computer and electronic product manufacturing
	335	Electrical equipment, appliance, and component manufacturing
	336	Transportation equipment manufacturing
	337	Furniture and related product manufacturing
	339	Miscellaneous manufacturing

Source: "North American Industry Classification System (NAICS)—United States," www.census.gov/epcd/www/naics.html (March 30, 2001).

9-3b Wholesalers as Consumers

Wholesalers buy or handle merchandise and its subsequent resale to organizational users, retailers, and other wholesalers. They do not sell significant volume to final users but are involved when services are marketed to organizational consumers. Table 9-4 lists the major industry groups in wholesaling, as well as transportation industries and business services. Chapter 16 has a broad discussion of wholesaling.

U.S. wholesalers are most prominent in California, New York, Texas, Florida, Illinois, Pennsylvania, Ohio, and New Jersey. Annual wholesaling and related sales (excluding manufacturer wholesaling) are $3 trillion. Sales are largest for groceries and related products; motor vehicles and related parts and supplies; machinery, equipment, and supplies; professional and commercial equipment and supplies; electrical goods; petroleum products; and farm-product raw materials.

As consumers, wholesalers buy or handle many goods and services, including warehouse facilities, trucks, finished products, insurance, refrigeration and other equipment, trade publications, accounting services, supplies, and spare parts. A major task in dealing with wholesalers is getting them to carry the selling firm's product line for further resale, thereby placing items into the distribution system. For new sellers or those with new products, gaining cooperation may be difficult. Even well-established manufacturers may have problems with their wholesalers because of the competitive nature of the marketplace, wholesalers' perceptions that they are not being serviced properly, or wholesalers' lack of faith in the manufacturers' products.

Wholesalers *buy or handle merchandise and its resale to nonfinal consumers.*

NAICS Code	Industry Name
42	Wholesale trade
421	Wholesale trade, durable goods
422	Wholesale trade, nondurable goods
423	Merchant wholesalers, durable goods
424	Merchant wholesalers, nondurable goods
425	Wholesale electronic markets and agents and brokers
48, 49	Transportation and warehousing
481	Air transportation
482	Rail transportation
483	Water transportation
484	Truck transportation
486	Pipeline transportation
488	Support for transportation
491	Postal service
492	Couriers and messengers
54	Professional, scientific, and technical services
541	Professional, scientific, and technical services

TABLE 9-4

U.S. Wholesaling and Related Industries

Source: "North American Industry Classification System (NAICS)—United States," www.census.gov/epcd/www/naics.html (March 30, 2001); and "2002 NAICS United States Structure," www.census.gov/epcd/naics02/t102to97.pdf (March 30, 2001).

9-3c Retailers as Consumers

Retailers *sell to the final consumer.*

Retailers buy or handle goods and services for sale (resale) to the final (ultimate) consumer. They usually obtain goods and services from both manufacturers and wholesalers. Table 9-5 lists the major industry groups in retailing, as well as several related service businesses that cater to final consumers. Chapter 17 has a broad discussion of retailing.

TABLE 9-5

U.S. Retailing and Retailed Industries

NAICS Code	Industry Name
44, 45	Retail trade
441	Motor vehicle and parts dealers
442	Furniture and home furnishings stores
443	Electronics and appliance stores
444	Building materials and garden equipment and supplies dealers
445	Food and beverage stores
446	Health and personal care stores
447	Gasoline stations
448	Clothing and clothing accessories stores
451	Sporting good, hobby, book, and music stores
452	General merchandise store
453	Miscellaneous store retailers
454	Nonstore retailers
52	Finance and insurance
522	Credit intermediation and related activities
523	Securities, commodity contracts, and other financial investments
524	Insurance carriers and related activities
53	Real estate and rental and leasing
531	Real estate
532	Rental and leasing services
71	Arts, entertainment, and recreation
711	Performing arts, spectator sports, and related industries
712	Museums, historical sites, and similar institutions
713	Amusements, gambling, and recreational industries
72	Accommodation and food services
721	Accommodations
722	Food service, and drinking places
81	Other service, except public administration
811	Repair and maintenance
812	Personal and laundry services

Source: "North American Industry Classification System (NAICS)—United States," www.census. gov/epcd/www/naics.html (March 30, 2001); and "2002 NAICS United States Structure," www. census.gov/epcd/naics02/t102to97.pdf (March 30, 2001).

Annual U.S. retail sales (both store and nonstore) for firms in NAICS codes 44 and 45 exceed $3.5 trillion. Chains operate a quarter of all stores, accounting for 60 percent of total retail sales. About 600,000 retail stores are operated by franchisees. A large amount of retailing involves auto dealers, food stores, general merchandise stores, eating and drinking places, gas stations, furniture and home furnishings stores, and apparel stores.

As consumers, retailers buy or handle a variety of goods and services, including store locations, facilities, interior design, advertising, resale items, insurance, and trucks. Unlike wholesalers, they are usually concerned about both product resale and the composition of their physical facilities (stores). This is because final consumers usually shop at stores, whereas wholesalers frequently call on customers. Thus, retailers often buy fixtures, displays, and services to decorate and redecorate stores.

Getting retailers to stock new items or continue handling current ones can be difficult because store and catalog space is limited and retailers have their own goals. Many retail chains have evolved into large and powerful customers, not just "shelf stockers." Some are so powerful that they may even charge *slotting fees* just to carry manufacturers' products in their stores. For instance,

> Scott Hannah, chairman and CEO of Pacific Valley Foods (www.pacificvalleyfoods.com), and his son John, vice-president of the company, are breaking a de facto code of silence about slotting fees, which few manufacturers dare discuss openly for fear of offending retailers and losing business as a result. The fees—collected by retailers to offset the expense of putting new products onto the shelf and to put a damper on poorly-researched new product introductions—can run as high as $50,000 per product in a large chain. Critics say slotting has destroyed many small food processors, stymied product innovation, and severely restricted product selection in the frozen aisle for consumers.[14]

Retailers (wholesalers) sometimes insist that suppliers make items under the retailers' (wholesalers') names. For private-label manufacturers, the continued orders of these customers are essential. If a large retailer (wholesaler) stops doing business with a private-label manufacturer, that firm has to establish its own identity with consumers. It may even go out of business due to the lack of recognition.

9-3d Government as Consumer

Government consumes goods and services in performing its duties and responsibilities. Federal (1), state (50), and local (88,000) units together account for the greatest volume of purchases of any consumer group in the United States—with all branches spending $2 trillion (excluding employee wages) on goods and services each year. The federal government accounts for one-half of that spending. The biggest budget shares (including employee wages) go for operations, capital outlays, military services, postal services, education, highways, public welfare, health care, police, fire protection, sanitation, and natural resources. Data on all levels of U.S. government expenditures are compiled by the Census Bureau (www.census.gov/govs/www/index.html). Table 9-6 shows the major NAICS codes for government.

Governmental consumers buy a wide range of goods and services, including food, military equipment, office buildings, subway cars, office supplies, clothing, and vehicles. Some purchases involve standard products offered to traditional consumers; others, such as highways, are specially made for a government customer. Although many big firms (such as Boeing and Lockheed Martin) derive major percentages of their sales from government contracts, small sellers now account for several billion dollars in federal purchases. In fact, one-quarter of federal agency purchase contracts are with small firms.

Some small firms are unaccustomed to the bureaucracy, barriers, political sensitivities, and financial constraints of selling to government consumers. To aid them, the federal Government Service Administration uses regional Small Business Centers (http://hydra.gsa.gov/oed/region.htm) to issue directories, reference data, and technical reports on contracts and contracting procedures, bidding documents, and specifications.

> **Government** *purchases and uses a variety of routine and complex products.*

[14]Richard Merli, "Slotting Just About Killed Us," *Frozen Food Age* (April 2000), p. 1.

TABLE 9-6

U.S. Federal, State, and Local Government (Public Administration)

NAICS Code	Industry Name
92	Public administration
921	Executive, legislative, and other general government support
922	Justice, public order, and safety activities
923	Administration of human resource programs
924	Administration of environmental quality programs
925	Administration of housing programs, urban planning, and community development
926	Administration of economic programs
927	Space research and technology
928	National security and international affairs

Source: "North American Industry Classification System (NAICS)—United States," www.census. gov/epcd/www/naics.html (March 30, 2001).

9-3e Nonprofit Institutions as Consumers

Nonprofit institutions function in the public interest.

Nonprofit institutions act in the public interest or to foster a cause and do not seek financial profits. Public hospitals, museums, most universities, civic organizations, and parks are nonprofit institutions. They buy goods and services in order to run their organizations and also buy items for resale to generate additional revenues to offset costs. There are many national and international nonprofit institutions, such as the American Cancer Society (www.cancer.org), the Boy Scouts (www.bsa.scouting.org) and Girl Scouts (www.gsusa.org), and the International Committee of the Red Cross (www.icrc.org/eng). Hospitals, museums, and universities, due to fixed sites, tend to be local nonprofit institutions.

There are no separate NAICS codes for nonprofit- versus profit-oriented firms. Yet, firms in these SIC categories are often nonprofit: 61 (educational services); 62 (health care and social assistance); 712 (museums and similar institutions); and 813 (organizations and associations).

9-4 KEY FACTORS IN ORGANIZATIONAL CONSUMER BEHAVIOR

Organizational consumer behavior depends on buying objectives, buying structure, and purchase constraints.

9-4a Buying Objectives

Organizational buying objectives relate to availability, reliability, consistency, delivery, price, and service.

Organizational consumers have several distinct goals in purchasing goods and services. Generally, these organizational buying objectives are important: availability of items, reliability of sellers, consistency of quality, delivery, price, and customer service. See Figure 9-8.

Availability means a buyer can obtain items as needed. An organizational consumer's production or resales may be inhibited if products are unavailable at the proper times. *Seller reliability* is based on the fairness in allotting items in high demand, nonadversarial relationships, honesty in reporting bills and shipping orders, and reputation. *Consistency of quality* refers to buyers' interest in purchasing items of proper quality on a regular basis. Thus, drill bits should have the same hardness each time they are bought. *Delivery goals* include minimizing the time from ordering to receiving items, minimizing the order size required by the supplier, having the seller responsible for shipments, minimizing costs, and adhering to an

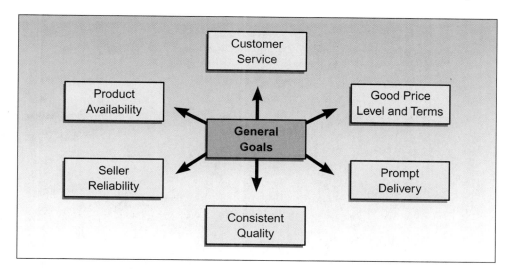

FIGURE 9-8
Goals of Organizational Consumers

agreed-on schedule. *Price considerations* involve purchase prices and the flexibility of payment terms. *Customer service* entails the seller's satisfying special requests, having a staff ready to field questions, promptly addressing problems, and having an ongoing dialogue. For example, Hewlett-Packard is committed to satisfying its small (www.hp.com/sbso) and large (www.hp.com/solutions1/corporatebusiness) business customers, as well as its government customers (http://government.hp.com/gov). See Figure 9-9.

Industrial marketers must recognize that price is only one of several considerations for organizational consumers. It may be lower in importance than availability, quality, service, and other factors:

> Cutting purchasing costs has surprisingly little to do with browbeating suppliers. Purchasers at firms like AT&T (www.att.com) and DaimlerChrysler (www.daimlerchrysler.com) aim to reduce the total cost—not just the price—of each part or service they buy. They form enduring partnerships with suppliers that let them chip away at key costs year after year. Purchasing companies are also packing once-fragmented purchases of goods and services into company-wide contracts for each.[15]

With regard to more specific goals, manufacturers are concerned about quality standards for raw materials, component parts, and equipment. Some like dealing with many suppliers to protect against shortages, foster price and service competition, and be exposed to new products. Others have been reducing the number of suppliers from which they buy to foster better relationships, cut ordering inefficiencies, and have more clout with each supplier.

Wholesalers and retailers consider further saleability (their customers' demand) to be the highest priority. If possible, they seek buying arrangements whereby the number of distribution intermediaries that can carry goods and services in a geographic area is limited. They also seek manufacturers' advertising, transportation, and warehousing support.

Government consumers frequently set exact specifications for some products they buy; as large-volume buyers, they can secure them. Government consumers may sometimes consider the economic conditions in the geographic areas of potential sellers. Contracts may be awarded to the firms with the higher unemployment in their surrounding communities.

Nonprofit consumers stress price, availability, and reliability. They may seek special terms in recognition of their nonprofit status.

Saleability and exclusivity are keys for wholesalers and retailers.

---

[15]Shawn Tully, "Purchasing's New Muscle," *Fortune* (February 20, 1995) p. 76.

FIGURE 9-9

Hewlett-Packard: Striving to Meet Buyers' Objectives

HP really tries to work with its business and government accounts. As this ad for an always-on, high-end computer server states, "You can pay less when you use less, or buy more when you need more. By adjusting capacity with a simple phone call, you pay only for what you use."

Source: Reprinted by permission.

If you're not at capacity, don't pay for capacity.

With the new hp superdome, you can pay less when you use less, or buy more when you need more.

By adjusting capacity with a simple phone call, you pay only for what you use—not unlike how you pay for electricity.

You can run IA-64, you can run multiple operating systems, and because comprehensive service is included,

you can run your business instead of your server. hp.com/superdome

9-4b Buying Structure

The buying structure refers to the formality and specialization used in the purchase process. It depends on the organization's size, resources, diversity, and format. The structure is apt to be formal (separate department) for a large, corporate, resourceful, diversified, and departmentalized organization. It will be less formal for a small, independently owned, financially limited, focused, and general organization.[16]

The organization's buying structure depends on its attributes.

[16]See Jim Kerstetter, "A Fruitful Relationship," *Business Week* (November 20, 2000), pp. EB93–EB96; and Michelle Cioci, "Marketing to Small Businesses," *Sales & Marketing Management* (December 2000), pp. 94–100.

Large manufacturers normally have specialized purchasing agents who work with the firms' engineers or production department. Large wholesalers tend to have a single purchasing department or a general manager in charge of operations. Large retailers tend to be quite specialized and have buyers for each narrow product category. Small manufacturers, wholesalers, and retailers often have their buying functions completed by the owner-operator.

Each government unit (federal, state, and local) typically has a purchasing department. The General Services Administration, GSA (www.gsa.gov), is the federal office responsible for centralized procurement and coordination of purchases. Each federal unit may buy via the GSA's Bureau of Federal Supply or directly from suppliers; either way, it must adhere to printed rules. In a nonprofit organization, there is often one purchasing department or a member of the operations staff performs buying functions.

9-4c Constraints on Purchases

For manufacturers, wholesalers, and retailers, derived demand is the major constraint on purchase behavior. Without the demand of consumers, production halts and sales drop as the backward chain of demand comes into play (final consumers→ retailers→wholesalers→manufacturers).

Manufacturers also are constrained by the availability of raw materials and their ability to pay for big-ticket items. Wholesalers and retailers are limited by the funds available to make purchases, as well as by the level of risk they are willing to take. In this case, risk refers to the probability that wholesalers or retailers can sell the products they buy in a reasonable time and at a satisfactory profit. Products like fashion clothing have higher risks than such staple items as vitamins and disposable diapers.

Government consumers are constrained by the budgeting process. Approval for categories of purchases must normally be secured well in advance, and deviations must be explained. Budgets must be certified by legislative bodies. For many nonprofit consumers, cash flow (the timing of the money they have coming in versus the money they spend) is the major concern.

Derived demand is the key constraint on organizational purchases.

9-5 THE ORGANIZATIONAL CONSUMER'S DECISION PROCESS

Organizational consumers use a decision-making procedure in much the same way as final consumers. Figure 9-10 shows the *organizational consumer's decision process,* with its four components: expectations, buying process, conflict resolution, and situational factors.[17]

*An **organizational consumer's decision process** is like that of a final consumer.*

9-5a Expectations

Purchasing agents, engineers, and users bring a set of organizational consumer expectations to any buying situation: "These expectations refer to the perceived potential of alternative suppliers and brands to satisfy a number of explicit and implicit objectives."[18]

For purchases to be made, buyers must have positive expectations on such supplier attributes as product availability and quality, vendor reliability, delivery time, price, and customer service. Expectations are based on the backgrounds of those participating in the buying process, the information received, perceptions, and satisfaction with past purchases.

Expectations are based on buyers' backgrounds, information, perceptions, and experience.

9-5b Buying Process

In the buying process, a decision as to whether to consider making a purchase is initiated, information gathered, alternative suppliers rated, and conflicts among different

[17]The material in this section is drawn from Jagdish N. Sheth, "A Model of Industrial Buyer Behavior," *Journal of Marketing,* Vol. 37 (October 1973), pp. 50–56. See also John F. Tanner, Jr., "Organizational Buying Theories: A Bridge to Relationships Theory," *Industrial Marketing Management,* Vol. 28 (May 1999), pp. 245–255.

[18]Sheth, "A Model of Industrial Buyer Behavior," p. 52.

FIGURE 9-10

The Organizational Consumer's Decision Process

Source: Adapted from Jagish N. Sheth, "A Model of Industrial Buyer Behavior," *Journal of Marketing* Vol. 37 (October 1973), p.51. Reprinted by permission of the American Marketing Association.

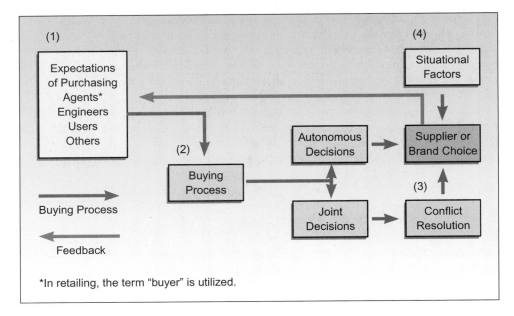

*In retailing, the term "buyer" is utilized.

Autonomous or joint decision making is based on product and company buying factors.

buyer representatives resolved. The process is similar to the final consumer buying process. Because of the Internet, information gathering—at Web sites such as Grainger.com (www.grainger.com), Thomas Register (www.thomasregister.com), and smarterwork (http://www.smarterwork.com)—has been simplified for many buyers.

The buying process may involve autonomous (independent) or joint decisions based on product and company factors. *Product-specific buying factors* include perceived risk, purchase frequency, and time pressure. Autonomous decisions occur mostly with low perceived risk, routine products, and high time pressure. Joint ones are more likely with high perceived risk, seldom-bought products, and low time pressure. *Company-specific buying factors* are a firm's basic orientation, size, and level of decision-making centralization. Autonomous decisions most often occur with a high technology or production orientation, small organization, and high centralization. Joint ones are more likely with a low technology or production orientation, large organization, and little centralization in decision making.

As noted earlier, competitive bidding is often used with organizational consumers: potential sellers specify in writing all terms of a purchase in addition to product attributes; the buyer then selects the best bid. With *open bidding*, proposals can be seen by competing sellers. With *closed bidding*, contract terms are kept secret and sellers are asked to make their best presentation in their first bids. Bidding is used in government purchases to avoid charges of unfair negotiations, and government bids tend to be closed.

9-5c Conflict Resolution

Problem solving, persuasion, bargaining, and politicking lead to **conflict resolution.**

Joint decision making may lead to conflicts due to the diverse backgrounds and perspectives of purchasing agents, engineers, and users. **Conflict resolution** is then needed to make a decision. Four methods of resolution are possible: problem solving, persuasion, bargaining, and politicking.

Problem solving occurs if purchasing team members decide to acquire further information before making a decision. This is the best procedure. *Persuasion* takes place when each team member presents reasons why a given supplier or brand should be picked. In theory, the most logical presentation should be chosen. Yet, the most dynamic (or powerful) person may persuade others to follow his/her lead.

MARKETING *and the Web*

Using the Internet with B-to-B Trade Shows

Of the 1,700 companies that had exhibits at a recent trade show for the semiconductor industry, 100 of them sought pre-show attention by having Web sites that offered viewers a preview of their exhibits. One of these firms was Rippey Corporation, a maker of high-tech cleaning products. Rippey's preview Web site included 360-degree views of its manufacturing operations, as well as three-dimensional product shots. As the firm's sales manager said, "Our customers are all over the world, so this type of technology is very compelling to them."

By allowing attendees to examine a firm's offerings prior to a trade show, the chances increase that they will stop at that firm's booth. Web site previews also enable trade show attendees to better plan their show schedules. In 1997, only 22 percent of attendees used the Web to plan their trade show schedule. As of 2000, the Web was consulted by 60 percent of attendees. Web sites let vendors collect key data on each prospect. At Web trade shows run by itradefair.com (www.itradefair.com), an exhibitor can track all prospects as they go through the site. This allows the exhibitor to determine each client's specific needs. Typically, trade show organizers keep Web sites up for a month or longer before and after the show.

According to Rippey's sales manager, Internet trade shows will not replace conventional booth-oriented trade shows: "The whole premise of a trade show environment is to get people face to face. The Web is effective as a means of attracting visitors to your booth location."

Develop specific goals for the use of a pre-show Web site for a manufacturer of industrial drill bits.

Source: Based on material in Mark McMaster, "On(line) With the Show," *Sales & Marketing Management* (November 2000), p. 111.

Under *bargaining*, team members agree to support each other in different situations, with less attention paid to the merits of a purchase. One member may select the supplier of the current item; in return, another member would choose a vendor the next time. The last, and least desired, method of conflict resolution is *politicking*. With it, team members try to persuade outside parties and superiors to back their positions, and seek to win at power plays.

9-5d Situational Factors

A number of **situational factors** can interrupt the decision process and the actual selection of a supplier or brand. These include "temporary economic conditions such as price controls, recession, or foreign trade; internal strikes, walkouts, machine breakdowns, and other production-related events; organizational changes such as merger or acquisition; and ad hoc changes in the marketplace, such as promotional efforts, new-product introduction, price changes, and so on, in the supplier industries."[19]

Situational factors *affect organizational consumer decisions.*

[19]Ibid., p. 56.

9-5e Purchase and Feedback

After the decision process is completed and situational factors are taken into account, a purchase is made (or the process terminated) and a product is used or experienced. The level of satisfaction with a purchase is then fed back to a purchasing agent or team, and the data are stored for future use.

To keep customers satisfied and ensure continued purchases, regular service and follow-up calls by sellers are essential: "Consultative selling—in which reps demonstrate not just a product's technical features, but how it can solve a business problem and save money—isn't a new idea. Yet, experts estimate that only 20 percent of American companies have adopted the idea. Why? Sales trainer Paul Goldner, president of Sales & Performance Group (www.redhotsales.com), says companies may be hesitant to invest in the training and support staffs needed to make value-based selling successful. Add to that a price-based culture, and Goldner says reps find it easier to underbid competitors than to learn enough about their clients to solve their problems." [20]

9-5f Types of Purchases

*Organizational buyers use a **new-task process** for unique items, **modified rebuys** for infrequent purchases, and **straight rebuys** for regular purchases.*

A **new-task purchase process** is needed for expensive products an organizational consumer has not bought before. A lot of decision making is undertaken, and perceived risk is high. This is similar to extended decision making for a final consumer. A **modified-rebuy purchase process** is employed for medium-priced products an organizational consumer has bought infrequently before. Moderate decision making is needed. This is similar to limited decision making for a final consumer. A **straight-rebuy purchase process** is used for inexpensive items bought regularly. Reordering, not decision making, is applied because perceived risk is very low. This is like a routine purchase for a final consumer.

9-6 MARKETING IMPLICATIONS

There are many similarities, as well as differences, between organizational and final consumers.

Although organizational and final consumers have substantial differences (as mentioned earlier), they also have similarities. Both

- Can be described demographically; statistical and descriptive data can be gathered and analyzed.
- Have different categories of buyers, each with separate needs and requirements.
- Can be defined by using social and psychological factors, like operating style, buying structure, purchase use, expectations, perceived risk, and conflict resolution.
- Use a decision process, employ joint decision making, and face various kinds of purchase situations.

This means that industrial marketers must have plans reflecting the similarities, as well as the differences, between organizational and final consumers. In their roles as sellers, manufacturers and wholesalers may also need two marketing plans—for intermediate buyers and for final consumers.

Finally, it must be recognized that purchasing agents or buyers have personal goals, as well as organizational goals. They seek status, approval, promotions, bonuses, and other rewards. And as noted in Figure 9-10, they bring distinct expectations to each buying situation, just as final consumers do.

---

[20]Betsy Cummings, "'Listen Don't Talk,' Selling a Solution, Not a Simple Fix, Through Consultative Sales," *Sales & Marketing Management* (March 2001), p. 65.

One leading consultant offers these suggestions for industrial marketers:

- *Understand how your customers run their business.*
- *Show how your good or service fits into your customer's business.*
- *Make sure the benefits you sell stay current.*
- *Know how customers buy, and fit your selling to their buying process.*
- *When selling, reach everyone on the customer's side involved in the buying decision.*
- *Communicate to each decider the message that will address his or her chief concerns.*
- *Be the person or firm with whom your customers prefer to have a relationship.*
- *Be sure everything is consistent with your chosen level of quality, service, price, and performance.*
- *Understand your competitors' strengths and weaknesses.*
- *Strive to dominate your niche.*
- *Train your people in each aspect of your business and that of your customers.*
- *Have a distribution system that meets your needs and those of your customers.*
- *Seek new markets and new applications for your existing products.*
- *Enhance your products with customer service.*
- *Have your goals clearly in mind.*[21]

WEB SITES YOU CAN USE

There are many Web sites devoted exclusively to industrial marketing. One of the best such sites is *BtoBonline.com* (www.netb2b.com), which calls itself "the magazine for marketing and E-commerce strategists." It covers a wide range of topics and has many special sections, including the "NetMarketing 200" (www.netb2b.com/netMarketing200/index.html)—which cites the 200 best business-to-business Web sites by category—and a "Directory of Portals" (www.netb2b.com/portalDirectory/index.html).

[21]F. Michael Hruby, "17 Tips (Not Just) for Industrial Marketers," *Sales & Marketing Management* (May 1990), pp. 68–76.

SUMMARY

1. *To introduce the concept of industrial marketing*   When firms market goods and services to manufacturers, wholesalers, retailers, and government and other nonprofit institutions, industrial marketing is used.

2. *To differentiate between organizational consumers and final consumers and look at organizational consumers from a global perspective*   Organizational consumers buy goods and services for further production, use in operations, or resale to others; they buy installations, raw materials, and semifinished materials. They often buy based on specifications, use joint decision making, apply formal value and vendor analysis, lease equipment, and use bidding and negotiation. Their demand is generally derived from that of their consumers and can be cyclical. They are fewer in number and more geographically concentrated. They may employ buying specialists, expect sellers to visit them, require special relationships, and make goods and undertake services rather than buy them.

There are distinctions among organizational consumers around the globe.

3. *To describe the different types of organizational consumers and their buying objectives, buying structure, and purchase constraints*   Organizational consumers may be classified by area of specialization, size and resources, location, and goods and services purchased. Major organizational consumers are manufacturers, wholesalers, retailers, government, and nonprofit. The North American Industry Classification System provides much data on organizational consumers in the United States, Canada, and Mexico.

These consumers have general buying goals, such as product availability, seller reliability, consistent quality, prompt delivery, good prices, and superior customer service. They also have more spe-

cific goals, depending on the type of firm involved. An organization's buying structure refers to its level of formality and specialization in the purchase process. Derived demand, availability, further saleability, and resources are the leading purchase constraints.

4. *To explain the organizational consumer's decision process*   It includes buyer expectations, the buying process, conflict resolution, and situational factors. Of prime importance is whether an organization uses joint decision making and, if so, how. Some form of bidding may be employed with organizational consumers (most often with government).

If conflicts arise in joint decisions, problem solving, persuasion, bargaining, or politicking is used to arrive at a resolution. Situational factors can intervene between decision making and a purchase. They include strikes, economic conditions, and organizational changes.

New task, modified rebuy, and straight rebuy are the different purchase situations facing organizational consumers.

5. *To consider the marketing implications of appealing to organizational consumers*   Organizational consumers and final consumers have many similarities and differences. Industrial marketers must understand them and adapt marketing plans accordingly. Dual marketing campaigns may be necessary for manufacturers and wholesalers that sell to intermediate buyers and have their products resold to final consumers.

Purchasing agents and buyers have personal goals, such as status, promotions, and bonuses; these may have a large impact on decision making.

Industrial marketers can do many things to enhance their chances for success. A number of them are outlined in this chapter.

KEY TERMS

industrial marketing (p. 255)
outsourcing (p. 258)
multiple-buying responsibility (p. 260)
value analysis (p. 260)
vendor analysis (p. 260)
competitive bidding (p. 261)
negotiation (p. 261)
derived demand (p. 261)
accelerator principle (p. 261)

systems selling (p. 262)
reciprocity (p. 262)
North American Industry Classification
   System (NAICS) (p. 266)
end-use analysis (p. 266)
manufacturers (p. 267)
wholesalers (p. 269)
retailers (p. 270)
government (p. 271)

nonprofit institutions (p. 272)
organizational consumer's decision
   process (p. 275)
conflict resolution (p. 276)
situational factors (p. 277)
new-task purchase process (p. 278)
modified-rebuy purchase process (p. 278)
straight-rebuy purchase process (p. 278)

REVIEW QUESTIONS

1. Describe five of the most important differences between organizational and final consumers.
2. Distinguish between vendor analysis and value analysis.
3. How is the North American Industry Classification System a useful marketing tool?
4. What are the most important general organizational consumer-buying objectives?
5. For manufacturers, wholesalers, and retailers, what is the major constraint on their purchase behavior? Why?

6. How do product-specific and company-specific buying factors affect the use of autonomous or joint decision making?
7. Which is the worst form of conflict resolution? The best? Explain your answers.
8. Cite several suggestions that industrial marketers should keep in mind when developing and enacting their strategies.

DISCUSSION QUESTIONS

1. As a university's purchasing agent, what criteria would you use for competitive bidding in the purchase of a new telephone system?

2. A packaging firm knows its current sales are allocated as follows: 15 percent to animal food manufacturers (NAICS code 3111), 20 percent to sugar and confectionery products manufacturers (NAICS code 3113), 30 percent to dairy products manufacturers (NAICS code 3115), 25 percent to bakeries (NAICS code 3118), and 10 percent to other food manufacturers (SIC code 3119). The firm expects next year's industry sales growth in these categories to be as follows:

3111, 5 percent; 3113, 4 percent; 3115, 1 percent; 3118, 0 percent; and 3119, 7 percent. According to end-use analysis, by how much should the packaging firm's sales increase next year? Explain your answer.

3. Describe a consumer electronics manufacturer's decision process with regard to what transportation firm to use to ship its products to retailers. Does this process entail a new task, modified rebuy, or straight rebuy? Explain your answer.

4. "It must be understood that organizational purchasing agents or buyers have personal as well as company goals." Comment on this statement.

WEB EXERCISE

What could a firm involved in business-to-business marketing learn from the U.S. Office of Trade and Economic Analysis' Web site (www.ita.doc.gov/td/industry/otea)? Cite at least five major topics in your answer.

10

Developing a Target Market Strategy

1 To describe the process for planning a target market strategy

2 To examine alternative demand patterns and segmentation bases for both final and organizational consumers

3 To explain and contrast undifferentiated marketing (mass marketing), concentrated marketing, and differentiated marketing (multiple segmentation)

4 To show the importance of positioning in developing a marketing strategy

5 To discuss sales forecasting and its role in target marketing

The fragmentation of the mass market and the rising importance of segmented media such as cable TV and special-interest magazines have led to greater use of market segmentation strategies by mainstream marketers. One newer segmentation strategy, called diversity marketing, focuses on pursuing customers on the basis of race and language preference.

Although it comprises only four percent of the U.S. population, the Asian-American market segment has been viewed as diversity's darlings. Not only is this market segment the fastest-growing population group according to census data, but also it is affluent and well educated. Of particular importance to marketers is the large spending by Asian-Americans on PCs, insurance, and international telephone calls.

One firm that has successfully appealed to Asian-Americans is the *New York Times*. Its campaign consisted of print ads, commercials, direct mail, and community events targeted directly at Asian-Americans. The campaign was so successful that the *Times* is expanding it from New York City to San Francisco, Oakland, and Silicon Valley in California.

For several reasons, reaching and appealing to this market segment is far from easy. One, marketers must fully understand the various cultural issues in dealing with Asian-Americans. For example, the number "4" may imply death and therefore would be a poor choice in a business telephone number. Two, there are significant differences among the ethnicities that comprise the Asian-American market. AT&T utilizes seven different languages to reach Asian-Americans, which increases the complexity and overall expense in reaching this segment. Three, vital marketing research data on the Asian-American market is often not available. Nielsen does not break out television viewership by Asian-Americans.

In an attempt to increase the information about Asian-Americans, the 2000 federal census, for the first time, was printed in four Asian languages (Chinese, Korean, Tagalog, and Vietnamese), in addition to English and Spanish. Census employees speaking each of these languages also staffed census telephone assistance centers. Some marketers feel the additional data will result in more ads being aimed at Asian-Americans by pharmaceutical firms, packaged food marketers, and health care providers.[1]

In this chapter, we will examine each step involved in planning a target market strategy and the related topic of sales forecasting. Ethnicity or race is only one of many possible bases of segmentation.

10-1 OVERVIEW

After gathering data on consumer traits, desires, and decision making, company and industry attributes, and environmental factors, a firm is ready to select the target market(s) to which it will appeal and for which it will develop a suitable strategy. The total *market* for a particular good or service consists of all the people and/or organizations who

*A **market** is all possible consumers for a good or service. Through **market segmentation,** it can be subdivided.*

[1]Stuart Elliott, "Marketers Study Nuances to Reach a Valued Audience," *New York Times on the Web* (March 6, 2000).

FIGURE 10-1

The Steps in Planning a Target Market Strategy

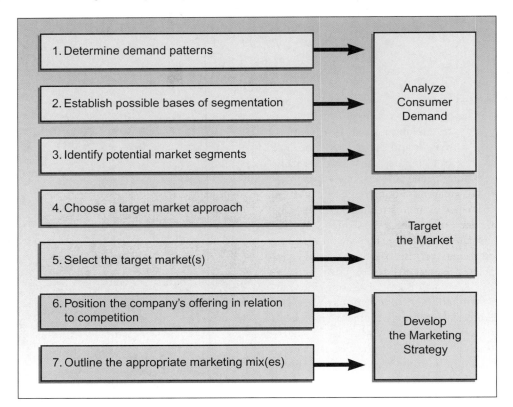

1. Determine demand patterns

2. Establish possible bases of segmentation

3. Identify potential market segments

→ Analyze Consumer Demand

4. Choose a target market approach

5. Select the target market(s)

→ Target the Market

6. Position the company's offering in relation to competition

7. Outline the appropriate marketing mix(es)

→ Develop the Marketing Strategy

In a **target market strategy,** *a firm first studies demand.*

Targeting approaches are **undifferentiated, concentrated,** *and* **differentiated marketing.**

The marketing strategy is developed with an emphasis on **product differentiation.**

desire (or potentially desire) that good or service, have sufficient resources to make purchases, and are willing and able to buy. Firms often use **market segmentation**—dividing the market into distinct subsets of customers that behave in the same way or have similar needs. Each subset could possibly be a target market, such as a specialty apparel store catering to young adult women shopping for mid-priced casual clothing.

Developing a **target market strategy** consists of three general phases: analyzing consumer demand, targeting the market, and developing the marketing strategy. This comprises the seven specific steps shown in Figure 10-1 and described in Chapter 10. First, a firm determines the demand patterns for a given good or service, establishes bases of segmentation, and identifies potential market segments. For example, do prospective consumers have similar or dissimilar needs and desires? What consumer characteristics, desires, and behavior types can be best used to describe market segments?

Second, a firm chooses the target market approach and selects its target market(s). It can use **undifferentiated marketing (mass marketing)**—targeting the whole market with a single basic marketing strategy intended to have mass appeal; **concentrated marketing**—targeting one well-defined market segment with one tailored marketing strategy; or **differentiated marketing (multiple segmentation)**—targeting two or more well-defined market segments with a marketing strategy tailored to each segment.[2]

Third, a firm positions its offering relative to competitors and outlines the proper marketing mix(es). Of particular importance here is attaining **product differentiation,** whereby the consumer perceives a product's physical or nonphysical characteristics, including price, as differing from competitors. When differentiation is favorable, it yields a competitive advantage. A firm may be able to achieve a key differential advantage by simply emphasizing how its offering satisfies existing consumer desires and needs better than competitors do. However, sometimes, demand patterns may have to be modified for consumers to perceive a firm's product differentiation as worthwhile. Thus, Tylenol (www.tylenol.com) is promoted as an alternative to aspirin for persons who cannot take

[2]Peter D. Bennett (Editor), *Dictionary of Marketing Terms,* Second Edition (Chicago: American Marketing Association, 1995), p. 166.

aspirin (appealing to existing consumer needs), whereas Dove (www.dovespa.com) is marketed as a nonsoap bar cleanser with moisturizing qualities (modifying consumer perceptions of soap's role). If targeted consumers do not believe that moisturizing is a meaningful product attribute, then they will probably not buy Dove—no matter how much better a job of moisturizing it does compared to competing soaps. Because Dove is an industry leader in sales, moisturizing is clearly a desirable attribute.

In this chapter, the steps in a target market strategy are detailed as they pertain to final and organizational consumers. Sales forecasting and its role in target marketing are also examined.

10-2 ANALYZING CONSUMER DEMAND

The initial phase in planning a target market strategy (analyzing consumer demand) has three steps: determining demand patterns, establishing possible bases of segmentation, and identifying potential market segments. DSS Research has a good synopsis on understanding market segmentation at its Web site (www.dssresearch.com/library/Segment/understanding.asp).

10-2a Determining Demand Patterns

A firm must first determine the **demand patterns**—which indicate the uniformity or diversity of consumer needs and desires for particular categories of goods and services—it faces in the marketplace. A firm would face one of the three alternative demand patterns shown in Figure 10-2 and described here for each good or service category it markets.

With **homogeneous demand,** consumers have rather uniform needs and desires for a good or service category. A firm's marketing tasks are straightforward: to identify and satisfy the basic needs of consumers in a superior way. For instance, business customers in the express mail-delivery market are most interested in rapid, reliable delivery and reasonable prices. UPS (www.ups.com) appeals to customers by convincing them it is better than competitors in these areas. As competition picks up, firms may try to modify consumer demand so new product features become desirable and homogeneous demand turns to clustered demand, with only one or a few firms marketing the new features.

With **clustered demand,** consumer needs and desires for a good or service category can be divided into two or more clusters (segments), each having distinct purchase criteria. A firm's marketing efforts must be geared toward identifying and satisfying the needs and desires of a particular cluster (or clusters) in a superior way. For example, in the golf equipment market, people can be grouped by their interest in performance and price.

> **Demand patterns** *show if consumer desires are similar for a good or service. People may have* **homogeneous, clustered,** *or* **diffused demand.**

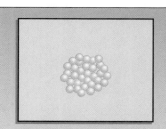 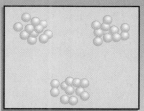 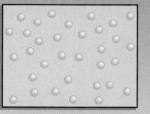

Homogeneous Demand	**Clustered Demand**	**Diffused Demand**
Consumers have relatively similar needs and desires for a good or service category	Consumer needs and desires can be grouped into two or more indentifiable clusters (segments), eash with it own set of purchase criteria.	Consumer needs and desires are so diverse that no clear clusters (segments) can be identified.

FIGURE 10-2

Alternative Consumer Demand Patterns for a Good or Service Category

INTERACTIVE FIGURE

Thus, the Sable Palm Golf Club in Florida offers name brand clubs such as Hogan for around $500 and its own private brand, American Golf Classic, for around $200—with each line appealing to a particular cluster of consumer needs and desires. Clustered demand is the most prevalent demand pattern.

With ***diffused demand,*** consumer needs and desires for a good or service category are so diverse that clear clusters (segments) cannot be identified. Marketing efforts are complex since product features are harder to communicate and more product versions may be offered. For example, consumers have diverse preferences for lipstick colors; even the same person may desire several colors to use on different occasions or to avoid boredom. Thus, cosmetics firms offer an array of lipstick colors. It would be nearly impossible for them to succeed with one color or a handful of colors. To make marketing strategies more efficient, firms generally try to modify diffused demand so clusters of at least moderate size appear.

Firms today often try to perform a balancing act with regard to consumer demand patterns. Just as the world marketplace is now getting closer due to more open borders and enhanced communications, there is also more information available on the diversity of the marketplace through customer data bases, point-of-sale scanning in stores, and other emerging data-collection techniques. On the one hand, some firms are looking for demand patterns that let them standardize (perhaps even globalize) their marketing mixes as much as possible—to maximize efficiency, generate a well-known image, and use mass media. On the other hand, some firms are searching for demand patterns that let them pinpoint more specific market segments—to better address consumer needs. The growth of Web sites such as www.epresence.com and www.reflect.com is indicative of companies' interest in addressing individual consumer needs.

10-2b Establishing Possible Bases of Segmentation

Next, a firm studies possible bases for segmenting the market for each product or product line. See Table 10-1. It must decide which of these segmentation bases are most relevant for its particular situation.

TABLE 10-1 **Possible Bases of Segmentation**

Bases	Examples of Possible Segments
Geographic Demographics	
Population (people or organizations)	
Location	North, South, East, West; domestic, global
Size	Small, medium, large
Density	Urban, suburban, rural
Transportation network	Mass transit, vehicular, pedestrian
Climate	Warm, cold
Type of commerce	Tourist, local worker, resident; NAICS codes
Retail establishments	Downtown shopping district, shopping mall
Media	Local, regional, national, global
Competition	Underdeveloped, saturated
Growth pattern	Stable, negative, positive
Legislation	Stringent, lax
Cost of living/operations	Low, moderate, high

continues

TABLE 10-1	Possible Bases of Segmentation (*continued*)
Bases	**Examples of Possible Segments**

Personal Demographics

A. Final Consumers

Age	Child, young adult, adult, older adult
Gender	Male, female
Education	Less than high school, high school, college
Mobility	Same residence for 2 years, moved in last 2 years
Income	Low, middle, high
Occupation	Blue-collar, white-collar, professional
Marital status	Single, married, divorced, widowed
Household size	1, 2, 3, 4, 5, 6, or more
Ethnicity or race	European, American; Black, White

B. Organizational Consumers

Industry designation	NAICS codes; end-use analysis
Product use	Further production, use in operations, resale to others
Institutional designation	Manufacturer, wholesaler, retailer, government, nonprofit
Company size	Small, medium, large
Industry growth pattern	Slow, moderate, high
Company growth pattern	Slow, moderate, high
Age of company	New, 5 years old, 10 years old or more
Language used	English, French, Japanese

Consumer Lifestyles

Social class (final consumers)	Lower-lower to upper-upper
Family life cycle (final consumers)	Bachelor to solitary survivor
Buying structure	Informal to formal, autonomous to joint
Usage rate	Light, medium, heavy
Usage experience	None, some, extensive
Brand loyalty	None, some, total
Personality	Introverted-extroverted, persuasible-nonpersuasible
Attitudes	Neutral, positive, negative
Class consciousness	Inner-directed, outer-directed
Motives	Benefit segmentation
Perceived risk	Low, moderate, high
Innovativeness	Innovator, laggard
Opinion leadership	None, some, a lot
Importance of purchase	Little, a great deal

Geographic Demographics

Geographic demographics are basic identifiable characteristics of towns, cities, states, regions, and countries. A firm may use one or a combination of the geographic demographics cited in Table 10-1 to describe its final or organizational consumers.

Geographic demographics *describe towns, cities, states, regions, and countries.*

Because a segmentation strategy can be geared to geographic differences, it is useful to know such facts as these: Brazilian, German, Korean, and Chinese consumers are more apt to buy books and magazines online. Per-capita chocolate consumption in Western

GLOBAL Marketing in Action

The Gender Gap in E-Tailing Outside the United States

In visits to the mall, female shoppers outnumber males by a significant margin. However, a recent global survey conducted by London-based Healey & Baker (www.healey-baker.com) found that male E-shoppers vastly outnumber female shoppers. This is especially true in Europe and Asia. While 65 percent of all Web shoppers worldwide are male, the proportion of males rises to 77 percent among Asian Web shoppers and 75 percent among European Web shoppers. In contrast, in the United States, males account for about one-half of Web shoppers. The proportion of male shoppers is also higher among older consumers. Male shoppers, for example, account for 71 percent of Web shoppers over 65.

According to Healey & Baker's head of retail research and consulting, "I think a lot of it does come down to time and convenience." The large proportion of male shoppers is due to the lack of time or inclination of male shoppers to shop at traditional stores. The large proportion of online male shoppers in Asia and Europe may also be due to the small number of Web retailers in both Japan and Europe. Consumers in these areas are also very much concerned about credit card security. More than one-half of Web shoppers are worried about payment security for Web purchases.

Furthermore, the large proportion of male Web shoppers in Europe and Asia is due to the types of products sold online in these regions. For example, food and groceries are bought online by 13 percent of European Web shoppers as compared to 5 percent of United States shoppers and 10 percent of Asian shoppers. On the other hand, 29 percent of Europeans purchase electrical goods online.

How can European and Asian Web-based retailers increase the presence of female shoppers?

Source: Based on material in "E-Tail Study: Male Shoppers Outnumber Female," *Shopping Centers Today* (December 2000), p. 74.

Europe is several times that in the United States; and per-capita consumption of bottled water in Italy is many times that in the United States. Germans want laundry detergents that are gentle on rivers, and will pay more for them; Greeks want small packages to keep down the cost per store visit. Canada and Mexico account for more than one-half of steel-mill products exported by U.S. firms.

Among U.S. urban areas, annual per household food and beverage sales are 10 percent higher in Denver than in Chicago; per household dining out revenues are 50 percent higher in San Jose, California, than the national average; per household furniture and appliance sales are 20 percent less in New Orleans than in St. Louis; and per household health and personal care sales are twice as high in Miami as in Atlanta.[3]

Figure 10-3 indicates the population size, urbanization, and per capita GDP ranking of the ten most populated nations of the world. Figure 10-4 shows a demographic map of the United States.

[3]"2000 Survey of Buying Power," *Sales & Marketing Management* (September 2000), various pages.

	Projected 2001 Population	2001 Urbanization Percentage[a]	2001 Top Ten GDP Ranking Per Capita
China	1.3 billion	32	5
India	1.0 billion	28	8
United States	283 million	77	1
Indonesia	228 million	40	6
Brazil	175 million	81	3
Russia	146 million	77	4
Pakistan	145 million	37	7
Bangladesh	131 million	24	9
Japan	127 million	79	2
Nigeria	125 million	43	10

[a]% of population living in urban areas.

FIGURE 10-3

Comparing the Ten Most Populated Countries in the World, 2001

Source: Compiled by the authors from the U.S. Bureau of the Census, International Data Base.

Personal Demographics

Personal demographics are basic identifiable characteristics of individual final consumers and organizational consumers, and groups of final consumers and organizational consumers. They are often used as a segmentation base because groups of people or organizations with similar demographics may have similar needs and desires that are distinct from those with different backgrounds. Personal demographics may be viewed singly or in combinations.

Personal demographics *describe people and organizations. They should be used in studying final and organizational consumers.*

FIGURE 10-4

A Demographic Map of the United States, 2000

Sources: Compiled by the authors from U.S. Bureau of the Census and U.S. Bureau of Economic Analysis data.

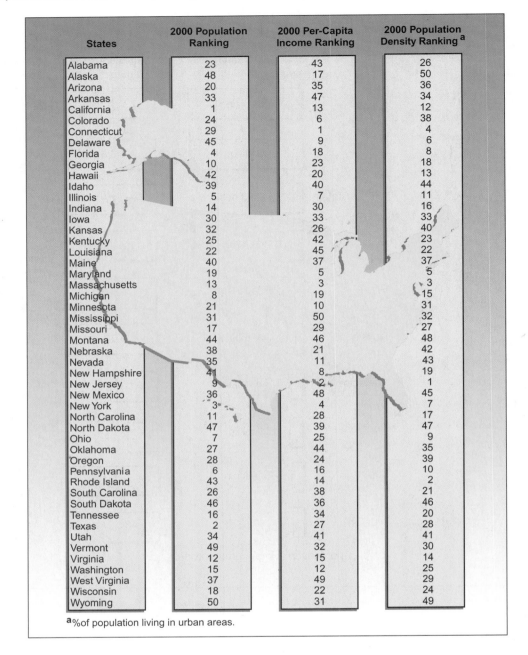

States	2000 Population Ranking	2000 Per-Capita Income Ranking	2000 Population Density Ranking[a]
Alabama	23	43	26
Alaska	48	17	50
Arizona	20	35	36
Arkansas	33	47	34
California	1	13	12
Colorado	24	6	38
Connecticut	29	1	4
Delaware	45	9	6
Florida	4	18	8
Georgia	10	23	18
Hawaii	42	20	13
Idaho	39	40	44
Illinois	5	7	11
Indiana	14	30	16
Iowa	30	33	33
Kansas	32	26	40
Kentucky	25	42	23
Louisiana	22	45	22
Maine	40	37	37
Maryland	19	5	5
Massachusetts	13	3	3
Michigan	8	19	15
Minnesota	21	10	31
Mississippi	31	50	32
Missouri	17	29	27
Montana	44	46	48
Nebraska	38	21	42
Nevada	35	11	43
New Hampshire	41	8	19
New Jersey	9	2	1
New Mexico	36	48	45
New York	3	4	7
North Carolina	11	28	17
North Dakota	47	39	47
Ohio	7	25	9
Oklahoma	27	44	35
Oregon	28	24	39
Pennsylvania	6	16	10
Rhode Island	43	14	2
South Carolina	26	38	21
South Dakota	46	36	46
Tennessee	16	34	20
Texas	2	27	28
Utah	34	41	41
Vermont	49	32	30
Virginia	12	15	14
Washington	15	12	25
West Virginia	37	49	29
Wisconsin	18	22	24
Wyoming	50	31	49

[a]% of population living in urban areas.

Final Consumers   As noted in Table 10-1, several personal demographics for final consumers may be used in planning a segmentation strategy.

Applications of personal demographic segmentation are plentiful, as these examples indicate: In the United States and other western nations, Clairol and many other companies are now placing greater emphasis on wooing consumers in the early stages of middle age. This group is quite large and particularly interested in slowing the aging process. Procter & Gamble has set up a special Web site for teenage girls sponsored by its Tampax and Always feminine care products (www.beinggirl.com). Godiva Chocolatier (www.godiva.com) has separate Valentine's Day promotions aimed at men and women; in the past, all ads were oriented at gift-giving by men. Nike (www.nike.com) and Reebok

FIGURE 10-5

The Booming Women's Market for Athletic Shoes

By expanding their product offerings, retailers such as Athlete's Foot are in tune with the growing demand by women for athletic shoes.

Source: Reprinted by permission of PricewaterhouseCoopers.

(www.reebok.com) are both devoting greater advertising to women's sports shoes and apparel. Why? Women annually spend more than $6 billion on athletic shoes—more than men spend![4] See Figure 10-5.

Dollar General (www.dollargeneral.com), a discount "neighborhood" store chain, attracts value-conscious consumers with low prices; many items are $10 or less. It locates in smaller communities, sells many irregulars and factory overruns, and has few employees per store. In contrast, American Express attracts upper-income consumers with its platinum card (http://www.americanexpress.com/platinum). Those consumers pay an annual fee of $300 and charge tens of thousands of dollars per year; in return, they get special services (such as a worldwide valet service to help them shop, plan trips, etc.) and a high credit line.

Bank of America (www.bankofamerica.com) recently launched a series of ethnic advertising campaigns to communicate its corporate brand promise: "to make banking work in ways it never has before." While the basic message is the same in both the general market and multicultural campaigns, the content of the ads is tailored for the African-American, Asian, and Hispanic markets. The ads for the Asian and Hispanic markets are in various languages, including Vietnamese, Korean, Chinese, and Spanish. "Instead of simply reproducing or translating our general ads, we worked with our ethnic advertising agencies to develop material that would address the unique characteristics and financial needs of each market," said Barbara Desoer, director of marketing for Bank of America.[5]

---

[4]Louise Lee, "Nike Tries to Get in Touch with Its Feminine Side," *Business Week* (October 30, 2000), p. 139.

[5]"Bank of America Launches New Ethnic Advertising Campaigns," (March 16, 2000), company press release.

Organizational Consumers   Table 10-1 also shows several personal demographics for organizational consumers that may be used in planning a segmentation strategy.

The easiest way to segment organizational consumers is by their industry designation. As an illustration, if a firm studies the U.S. information services and data processing services industry (NAICS code 514), it would learn it comprises 15,000 U.S. businesses, with a total of 350,000 employees, and that it generates tens of billions of dollars in annual revenues. Among the business segments in this industry are music archives, reference libraries, computer leasing bureaus, online information access services, Internet service providers (ISPs), and a whole lot more.[6]

To access potential organizational consumers by institutional type, some sellers rely on trade directories—like the *Blue Book of Building & Construction* (www.thebluebook.com) with 800,000 U.S. construction firms, *Hoover's MasterList of Major International Companies* with 1,600 businesses, *ABC Europ Production* with 410,000 European manufacturers in 40 countries (www.abconline.de), and *Scott's Directories* with 100,000 Canadian manufacturers and service firms (www.scottsinfo.com). Mailing lists of organizational consumers may also be bought. InfoUSA's business lists have information on 12 million U.S. manufacturers, wholesalers, retailers, professional service businesses, membership organizations, and others (www.infousa.com).

Organizational consumers may be divided into small, medium, and large categories. Some firms prosper by marketing goods and services to smaller customers, while others focus on medium and/or large accounts. For example, Brother (www.brother.com) has a line of inexpensive fax machines for small business customers that cost a few hundred dollars or less, while Pitney Bowes markets more expensive fax machines that can handle 1,200 pages of text, collate pages, and store 1,000 phone numbers (www.pitneybowes. com). Blackbourn, a major manufacturer of plastic packaging for audio and video products, has a primary market of large *Fortune 500* companies but also sells to small businesses.

Industry growth patterns may indicate a firm's future potential in marketing to businesses in those industries and provide a good segmentation base. The International Trade Administration of the U.S. Department of Commerce (www.ita.doc.gov) cites electronic information services, health services, semiconductors, and surgical and medical instruments as fast-growth industries. Paper industries machinery, personal leather goods, farm machinery, and newspapers are low-growth industries.

Consumer Lifestyles

Lifestyles are the ways in which people live and spend time and money, and many lifestyle factors can be applied to both final and organizational consumers. Table 10-1 lists several lifestyle segmentation bases; except where indicated, these factors are relevant when segmenting either final or organizational consumer markets.

Final consumer and organizational consumer segments each can be described on the basis of lifestyle factors.

Applications of lifestyle segmentation are abundant, as these examples show: Final consumers may be segmented by social class and stage in the family life cycle. The posh Four Seasons hotel chain (www.fourseasons.com) appeals to upper-middle-class and upper-class guests with luxurious accommodations, while the Hampton Inn chain (www.hampton-inn.com) appeals to middle-class and lower-middle-class consumers with low rates and limited services (such as no restaurant). Tiffany, Bloomingdale's, Williams-Sonoma, Crate and Barrel, and many other retailers offer online wedding registry services for prospective brides and grooms (www.weddingchannel.com). To attract families with children, some Club Med resorts (www.clubmed.com) have day camps.

*A **heavy-usage segment** has a rather large share of sales.*

Final and organizational consumer market segments may be based on their usage rate, the amount of a product they consume. People or organizations can use very little, some, or a great deal. A ***heavy-usage segment*** (at times known as the ***heavy half***) is a consumer group that accounts for a large proportion of a good's or service's sales relative to the size of the market. For instance, women buy 85 percent of all greeting cards. Heavy yogurt

---

[6]*U.S. Industrial Outlook 2000* (Washington, D.C.: U.S. Department of Commerce, 2000).

FIGURE 10-6
Applying Benefit Segmentation to Children's Toothpaste
Colgate and Oral-B realize that, as with adult toothpaste users, children are attracted to products that offer particular benefits—especially good-tasting flavors and packaging with their favorite characters.

Source: Reprinted by permission of PricewaterhouseCoopers.

consumers eat nearly double the amount as average yogurt consumers. On a per-capita basis, the Swiss drink 30 times more iced tea than the French or Portuguese. The roughly 150 tire manufacturing facilities in the United States use about one-half of all general-purpose synthetic rubber. Manufacturers, wholesalers, and retailers account for over 90 percent of all U.S. equipment leasing, while government and nonprofit organizations make less than 10 percent of equipment leases. Sometimes, a heavy-usage segment may be attractive because of the volume it consumes; other times, the competition for consumers in that segment may make other opportunities more attractive.[7]

Consumer motives may be used to establish benefit segments. ***Benefit segmentation*** is a procedure for grouping people into segments on the basis of the different benefits sought from a product. It was first popularized in the late 1960s when Russell Haley divided the toothpaste market into four segments: sensory—people wanting flavor and product appearance; sociable—people wanting brighter teeth; worrier—people wanting decay prevention; and independent—people wanting low prices. Since then, benefit segmentation has been applied in many final and organizational consumer settings.[8] Figure 10-6 shows how benefit segmentation may be used to market children's toothpaste.

> **Benefit segmentation** *groups consumers based on their reasons for using products.*

Blending Demographic and Lifestyle Factors

It is generally advisable to use a mix of demographic and lifestyle factors to set up possible bases of segmentation. A better analysis then takes place. Two broad classification systems are the ***VALS (Values and Lifestyles) program,*** which divides final consumers into lifestyle categories; and the ***Social Styles model,*** which divides the personnel representing organizational consumers into lifestyle categories.

> **VALS** *and the* **Social Styles model** *describe market segments in terms of a broad range of factors.*

In the United States, the current VALS 2 typology (future.sri.com/vals), shown in Figure 10-7, explains why and how people make purchases, and places them into segments based on self-orientation and resources. Principle-oriented people are guided by their beliefs; status-oriented people are influenced by others; and action-oriented people are

[7]Brian Wansink and Sea Bum Park, "Methods and Measures That Profile Heavy Users," *Journal of Advertising Research*, Vol. 40 (July-August 2000), pp. 61–72; Gerri Hirshey, "Happy [ ] Day to You," *New York Times Magazine* (July 2, 1995), p. 27; Henry Assael and David F. Poltrack, "Can Demographic Profiles of Heavy Users Serve as a Surrogate for Purchase Behavior in Selecting TV Programs?" *Journal of Advertising Research*, Vol. 34 (January-February 1994), pp. 11–17; "Brewing Up a Storm," *Advertising Age* (May 15, 1995), p. I–3; *Statistical Abstract of the United States 2000*, various pages; and *U.S. Industrial Outlook 2000*, various pages.

[8]Russell I. Haley, "Benefit Segmentation: A Decision-Oriented Research Tool," *Journal of Marketing*, Vol. 32 (July 1968), pp. 30–35; Russell I. Haley, "Benefit Segments: Backwards and Forwards," *Journal of Advertising Research*, Vol. 24 (February-March 1984), pp. 19–25; P. J. O'Connor and Gary L. Sullivan, "Market Segmentation: A Comparison of Benefits/Attributes Desired and Brand Preference," *Psychology & Marketing*, Vol. 12 (October 1995), pp. 613–635; and a special issue of *Journal of Segmentation in Marketing*, Vol. 8 (Number 10, 1999), focusing solely on this topic and applications of it.

guided by a desire for activity, variety, and risk taking. People's resources include their education, income, self-confidence, health, eagerness to buy, intelligence, and energy level; and resources rise from youth to middle age and fall with old age. Here are descriptions of the basic VALS 2 segments (in terms of adult characteristics):

- *Actualizers*—Greatest resources. Successful, sophisticated. Can indulge in any self-orientation. Have a taste for the finer things. 8 percent of population. 95 percent with at least some college. Median age of 43.

- *Fulfilleds*—Principle-oriented, abundant resources. Mature, satisfied, comfortable, and reflective. Mostly professional and well educated. As consumers, concerned with functionality, value, and durability. 11 percent of population. 81 percent with at least some college. Median age of 48.

- *Believers*—Principle-oriented, lower resources. Follow routines organized around homes, families, and social or religious organizations. Want American products and known brands. Resources sufficient for needs. 16 percent of population. 6 percent with at least some college. Median age of 58.

- *Achievers*—Status-oriented, second highest resources. Committed to jobs and families and satisfied with them. Like to be in control. Favor established products that demonstrate their success to peers. 13 percent of population. 77 percent with at least some college. Median age of 36.

- *Strivers*—Status-oriented, lower resources. Values similar to achievers but fewer resources. Unsure of themselves. Concerned about approval from others. Most-desired goods and services generally beyond reach. 13 percent of population. 23 percent with at least some college. Median age 34.

- *Experiencers*—Action-oriented, aquiring resources. Young, enthusiastic, and rebellious. Seek variety and excitement. Spend much of income on clothing, fast food, music, movies, and videos. 12 percent of population. 41 percent with at least some college. Median age 26.

- *Makers*—Action-oriented, lower resources. Live in a traditional context of family, work, and physical recreation. Unimpressed by possessions. Like do-it-yourself projects. 13 percent of population. 24 percent with at least some college. Median age 30.

FIGURE 10-7
The VALS 2 Network

Source: Reprinted by permission of SRI Consulting Business Intelligence, Menlo Park, CA.

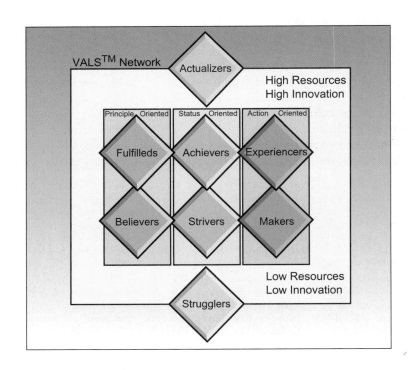

- *Strugglers*—Lowest resources (too few to include in any self-orientation). Chronically poor, ill-educated, older, and low in skills. Concerned about health, safety, and security. Brand loyal and cautious. 14 percent of population. 3 percent with at least some college. Median age 61.[9]

GeoVALS is a high-tech way to use the U.S. VALS 2 model. Through it, the eight VALS 2 market segments can be broken down by metropolitan area, city, and ZIP Code.

The VALS system is so popular that it is also utilized in Japan, and tailored to people there (http://future.sri.com/VALS/JVALS.shtml). For example, ryoshiki ("socially intelligent") innovators are career-oriented, middle-aged innovators; ryoshiki adapters are shy and look to ryoshiki innovators; tradition adapters are young and affluent; and low pragmatic are attitudinally negative and oriented to inexpensive products.

According to the Social Styles model as developed by Wilson Learning (www. wilsonlearning.com), shown in Figure 10-8, social styles affect how people react to various stimuli on and off the job. The model studies two traits—assertiveness and responsiveness—and divides organizational personnel into four social style types: analyticals, drivers, amiables, and expressives. Assertiveness is the degree to which a person states views with assurance, confidence, and force, and the extent to which he or she tries to direct others' actions. Responsiveness is the extent to which a person is affected by appeals, influence, or stimulation and how feelings, emotions, or impressions are shown to others.

Analyticals are detail people who are low in assertiveness and responsiveness. *Expressives* are more intuitive than analyticals; they are high in assertiveness and responsiveness. *Drivers* like to make fast decisions and get right to the point; they are low in responsiveness and high in assertiveness. *Amiables* believe strongly in relationship marketing; they are low in assertiveness and high in responsiveness. [10]

The Social Styles model has been used to classify personnel in such industries as banking, computers and precision instruments, chemicals, pharmaceuticals, telecommunications, aerospace, utilities, and industrial and farm equipment. In all cases, the analyticals segment is the largest.

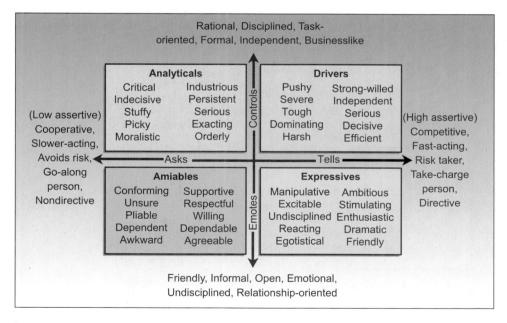

FIGURE 10-8

The Social Styles Model for Organizational Consumers

Source: Wilson Learning Corporation and Tracom Corporation. Reprinted by permission of Crain Communications Inc., from Tom Eisenhart, "How to Really Excite Your Prospects," *Business Marketing* (July 1988).

---

[9]SRI International, Menlo Park, California.

[10]Tom Eisenhart, "How to Really Excite Your Prospects," *Business Marketing* (July 1988), pp. 44–45 ff.; Raymond E. Taylor, Lorraine A. Krajewksi, and John R. Darling, "Social Style Application to Enhance Direct Mail Response," *Journal of Direct Marketing*, Vol. 7 (Autumn 1993), pp. 42–53; and Diana Sibberson, "For One-on-One Presentations, Know the 4 Personality Types," *Presentations* (December 1998), p. 12.

10-2c Identifying Potential Market Segments

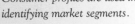

Consumer profiles are used in identifying market segments.

After establishing possible segmentation bases, a firm is ready to construct specific consumer profiles that identify potential market segments for the firm by aggregating consumers with similar traits and needs and separating them from those with different traits and needs. Here are some examples.

A supermarket can segment female and male shoppers in terms of their in-store behavior. In general, on each visit, women spend more time shopping, buy more items, are more apt to bring children, and more often use a shopping list than men; and they are equally apt to shop in the evening.

A gas station can divide its potential customers into five lifestyle market segments (based on extensive research by Mobil—www.mobil.com): Road Warriors—they drive 25,000 to 50,000 miles per year and buy premium gas with a credit card; True Blues—they are loyal to a brand and sometimes to a particular station; Generation F3—they want fuel and food, and they want it fast; Homebodies—they take a lot of trips around town to transport children and do errands, and use whatever gas station is on the way; and price shoppers—they are not loyal to a brand or a station and rarely buy premium.[11]

A photocopier manufacturer could group the office-copier market into benefit segments, such as: basic copying (satisfied via simple, inexpensive machines that make up to 99 black and white copies of a single page at a time); extensive copying (satisfied via mid-priced machines that make up to 100 or more one- or two-sided copies of multiple pages and then collate them); and desktop publishing (satisfied via expensive, sophisticated machines that make high-quality color copies in big quantities).

10-3 TARGETING THE MARKET

The second phase in planning a target market strategy (targeting the market) consists of choosing the proper approach and selecting the target market(s).

10-3a Choosing a Target Market Approach

A firm now selects undifferentiated marketing, concentrated marketing, or differentiated marketing. These options are shown in Figure 10-9 and Table 10-2, and discussed next.

FIGURE 10-9

Contrasting Target Market Approaches

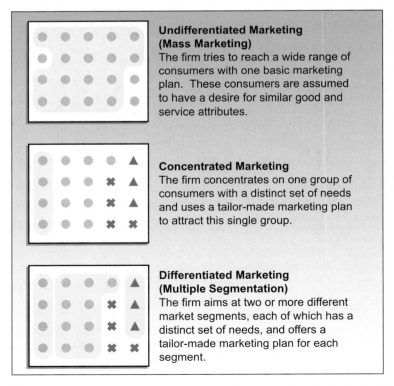

Undifferentiated Marketing (Mass Marketing)
The firm tries to reach a wide range of consumers with one basic marketing plan. These consumers are assumed to have a desire for similar good and service attributes.

Concentrated Marketing
The firm concentrates on one group of consumers with a distinct set of needs and uses a tailor-made marketing plan to attract this single group.

Differentiated Marketing (Multiple Segmentation)
The firm aims at two or more different market segments, each of which has a distinct set of needs, and offers a tailor-made marketing plan for each segment.

[11]Robert Kaplan, "The Masters Forum," www.mastersforum.com/archives/kaplan/Kaplan_Precis.htm (July 13, 1999).

TABLE 10-2 Contrasting Target Market Approaches

Strategic Factors	Approaches		
	Undifferentiated Marketing	Concentrated Marketing	Differentiated Marketing
Target market	Broad range of consumers	One well-defined consumer group	Two or more well-defined consumer groups
Product	Limited number of products under one brand for many types of consumers	One brand tailored to one consumer group	Distinct brand or version for each consumer group
Distribution	All possible outlets	All suitable outlets	All suitable outlets— differs by segment
Promotion	Mass media	All suitable media	All suitable media— differs by segment
Price	One "popular" price range	One price range tailored to the consumer group	Distinct price range for each consumer group
Strategy emphasis	Appeal to a large number of consumers via a uniform, broad-based marketing program	Appeal to one specific consumer group via a highly specialized, but uniform, marketing program	Appeal to two or more distinct market segments via different marketing plans catering to each segment

Undifferentiated Marketing (Mass Marketing)

An undifferentiated marketing (mass marketing) approach aims at a large, broad consumer market via one basic marketing plan. With this approach, a firm believes consumers have very similar desires regarding product attributes or opts to ignore differences among segments. An early practitioner of mass marketing was Henry Ford, who sold one standard car at a reasonable price to many people. The original Model T had no options and came only in black.

Mass marketing was popular when large-scale production started, but the number of firms using a pure undifferentiated marketing approach has declined a lot in recent years. Among the factors behind the drop are that competition has grown, consumer demand may be stimulated by appealing to specific segments, improved marketing research can better pinpoint different segments' desires, and total production and marketing costs can be reduced by segmentation.

Before engaging in undifferentiated marketing, a firm must weigh several factors. High total resources are needed to mass produce, mass distribute, and mass advertise. Yet, there may be per-unit production and marketing savings because a limited product line is offered and different brand names are not employed. These savings may allow low competitive prices.

A major goal of undifferentiated marketing is to maximize sales—that is, a firm tries to sell as many units as possible. Regional, national, and/or international goals are set. Diversification is not undertaken.

For successful mass marketing, a large group of consumers must have a desire for the same product attributes (homogeneous demand) so that a firm can use one basic marketing program. Or, demand must be so diffused that it is not worthwhile for a firm to aim marketing plans at specific segments; the firm would try to make demand more homogeneous. In undifferentiated marketing, different consumer groups are not identified and

With undifferentiated marketing, a firm appeals to a broad range of consumers with one basic marketing plan.

sought. For example, suppose all consumers buy Morton's salt for its freshness, quality, storability, availability, and fair price. Mass marketing is then proper. If various consumers want attractive decanters, low-sodium content, larger crystals, and smaller-sized packages (as they now do), Morton could not appeal to all consumers with one basic marketing mix (www.mortonsalt.com).

In undifferentiated marketing, a firm sells via all possible outlets. Some resellers may be displeased if a brand is sold at nearby locations and insist on carrying additional brands to fill out their product lines. It may be hard to persuade them not to carry competing brands. The shelf space a firm gets is based on its brand's popularity and the promotion support it provides.

An undifferentiated marketing strategy should take both total and long-run profits into account. Firms sometimes may be too involved with revenues and lose sight of profits. For example, for several years, A&P's sales rose as it competed with Safeway for leadership in U.S. supermarket sales. A&P incurred large losses during that period. Only when it began to close some unprofitable stores and stop pursuing sales at any cost did it regain profitability (www.aptea.com).

A firm and/or its products can ensure a consistent, well-known image with a mass-marketing approach. Consumers have only one image when thinking of a firm (or a brand), and it is retained for a number of years. Think of Wal-Mart and Kmart, discount department store chains that have a broad customer following.

TV Guide magazine (www.tvguide.com/magazine) is an example of undifferentiated marketing in action. It includes program listings, descriptions, and reviews, as well as current events and articles on personalities, shows, and the industry. Each week, 11 million copies are sold (about one-half of its peak more than a decade ago). It is advertised on TV and in newspapers and stores. It is inexpensive and available at a number of stores and newsstands. Many sales are via subscription. The product itself, the magazine, is the same throughout the United States—except for some differences in program listings (but not in program descriptions, articles, and features) by community. To be more competitive, *TV Guide* includes cable TV listings and VCR-Plus codes (for easy taping), and it has moved all feature stories to the front of the magazine. *TV Guide* is recognized as the standard in the field. Consumers of varying backgrounds and lifestyles buy it for the completeness of listings and the interesting stories.

Concentrated Marketing

Via concentrated marketing, a firm appeals to one segment with a tailored marketing plan.

A concentrated-marketing approach enables a firm to aim at a narrow, specific consumer segment with one specialized marketing plan catering to the needs of that segment. This is proper to consider if demand is clustered or if diffused demand can be clustered by offering a unique marketing mix.

Concentrated marketing has become more popular, especially for smaller firms. A firm does not have to mass produce, mass distribute, or mass advertise. It can succeed with limited resources and abilities by focusing efforts. This method does not usually maximize sales; the goal is efficiency—attracting a large part of one segment at controlled costs. The firm wants recognition as a specialist and does not diversify.

If concentrated marketing is used, a firm must do better than competitors in tailoring a strategy for its segment. Areas of competitor strength should be avoided and weaknesses exploited. For instance, a new vendor selling standard office stationery would have a harder time distinguishing itself from competitors than a new vendor that provides customers with free recycling services for the office stationery it sells.

*To avoid the **majority fallacy**, a company can enter a smaller, but untapped, segment.*

When there are two or more attractive market segments from which a firm may choose, it should select the one with the greatest opportunity—while being alert to these two factors: One, the largest segment may not be the best option, due to heavy competition or high consumer satisfaction with competitor offerings. A firm entering this segment may regret it due to the **majority fallacy,** which causes some firms to fail if they go after

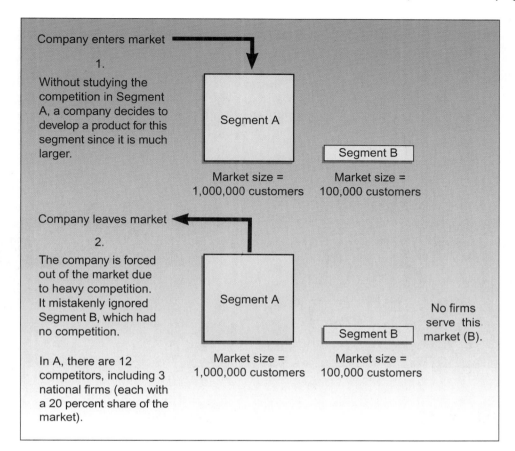

FIGURE 10-10

How the Majority Fallacy Occurs

the largest market segment, because competition is intense. See Figure 10-10. Two, a potentially profitable segment may be one ignored by other firms. As an example, Perdue (www.perdue.com) is very successful in the poultry business, due to its being the first chicken processor to see a market segment desiring superior quality, an identifiable brand name, and a guarantee—and having a willingness to pay premium prices. Previously, chicken was sold as an unbranded commodity.

Concentrated marketing can let a firm maximize per-unit profits, but not total profits, since only one segment is sought. It also allows a firm with low resources to vie effectively for specialized markets. There are many local and regional firms that profitably compete in their own markets with national and international companies but that do not have the finances to compete on a larger scale. However, minor shifts in population or consumer tastes can sharply affect a firm engaging in concentrated marketing.

By carving out a distinct niche via concentrated marketing, a firm may foster a high degree of brand loyalty for a current offering and also be able to develop a product line under a popular name. As long as the firm stays within its perceived area of expertise, the image of one product will rub off on another: Even though it makes several car models, Porsche (www.porsche.com) aims only at the upscale segment of the market—people interested in styling, handling, acceleration, and, of course, status. Whole Foods Market (www.wholefoodsmarket.com) offers products only for consumers interested in natural ingredients. See Figure 10-11.

FIGURE 10-11

Concentrated Marketing in Action

Founded in 1980 as one small store in Austin, Texas, Whole Foods Market is the world's largest retailer of natural and organic foods and related products, with 120 stores in 22 states and the District of Columbia. The company is very mission-driven: "We're highly selective about what we sell, dedicated to stringent quality goals, and committed to sustainable agriculture."

Source: Reprinted by permission of PricewaterhouseCoopers.

In differentiated marketing, two or more marketing plans are tailored to two or more consumer segments.

Differentiated Marketing (Multiple Segmentation)

Differentiated marketing (multiple segmentation) enables a firm to appeal to two or more distinct market segments, with a different marketing plan for each. It combines the best aspects of undifferentiated marketing and concentrated marketing: A broad range of consumers may be sought and efforts focus on satisfying identifiable consumer segments. Differentiated marketing is appropriate to consider if there are two or more significant demand clusters, or if diffused demand can be clustered into two or more segments and satisfied by offering unique marketing mixes to each one.

Some firms appeal to each segment in the market and achieve the same market coverage as with mass marketing. Kyocera Mita (www.kyoceramita.com) markets copiers ranging from simple and inexpensive to sophisticated and expensive, thus separately appealing to small and large businesses. Other firms appeal to two or more, but not all, segments. Thus, Marriott International (www.marriott.com) operates Marriott Hotels and Resorts, Fairfield Inn, Courtyard Hotels, Marriott Suites, Residence Inns, Renaissance Hotels and Resorts, and other hotel chains. It aims at several—but not all—hospitality segments. Switzerland's Swatch Group (www.swatchgroup.com) markets Swatch watches for teens and young adults, Hamilton watches for adults lured by classic styles, and upscale Blancpain, Omega, and Tissot brands. Microsoft has software for both home users and businesses. See Figure 10-12. Kapers for Kids markets a curriculum with fun and educational activities programs that are designed for use in several settings: family child-care homes, child-care centers, pre-schools, or the home. Its programs are geared to 3- to 5-year-olds.

Firms may use both mass marketing and concentrated marketing in their multiple segmentation strategies. They could have one or more major brands aimed at a wide range of consumers (the mass market) and secondary brands for specific segments. Time Inc. publishes *Time* and *People* for very broad audiences and *Fortune* and *Sports Illustrated for Kids* for more specialized segments.

FIGURE 10-12
Differentiated Marketing in Action

Microsoft has complete lines of software targeted separately at final consumers (for home use) and organizational consumers (for business use).

Source: Reprinted by permission of Retail Planning Associates, Photography by Michael Houghton/STUDIOHIO.

Multiple segmentation requires thorough analysis. Resources and abilities must be able to produce and market two or more different sizes, brands, or product lines. This can be costly, as with high-tech products. However, if a firm sells similar products under its own and retailer brands, added costs are low.

Differentiated marketing lets a firm reach many goals. It can maximize sales: Procter & Gamble (www.pg.com) is the world leader in laundry products with such brands as Tide, Bold, Dreft, Cheer, Gain, Era, Ivory Snow, and Ariel. Boeing (www.boeing.com) leads in the global commercial aircraft business—offering planes with different sizes and configurations (including the 737, 747, 757, 767, and 777). Recognition as a specialist can continue if the firm has separate brands for items aimed at separate segments or has a narrow product line: Whirlpool has a clear image under its own label (www.whirlpool.com); few people know it also makes products for Sears under the latter's Kenmore brand (www.kenmore.com). Multiple segmentation lets a firm diversify and minimize risks because all emphasis is not placed on one segment: Honda's motorcycles and small engines (for lawn mowers and outboard motors) provide an excellent hedge against a drop in the sales of its cars (www.honda.com).

Differentiated marketing does not mean a firm has to enter segments where competition is intense and face the majority fallacy. Its goals, strengths, and weaknesses must be weighed against competitors'. A firm should target only segments it can handle. The majority fallacy can work in reverse. If a firm enters a segment before a competitor, it may prevent the latter from successfully entering that segment.

Although differentiated marketing requires the existence of at least two consumer segments (with distinct desires by each), the more potential segments that exist, the better the opportunity for multiple segmentation. Firms that start with concentrated marketing often turn to multiple segmentation and pursue other segments after they become established in one segment.

ETHICAL Issues in Marketing

In a Product Recall, Should All Customers Be Treated the Same?

Should a firm be allowed to have varying safety standards in a situation where the risk of a fire hazard is significant? When General Electric discovered that a defective air-drying switch was a fire hazard, it ordered a recall program for the affected dishwashers. What set its recall program apart from almost all others was the way in which different classes of customers were treated.

Under General Electric's original recall program, only property managers were offered a rewiring kit and a set of instructions to repair the dishwashers at risk. Final consumers were only offered a rebate toward the purchase of a new General Electric dishwasher; they were not offered the rewiring option.

Critics of GE's plan said that since the same chance of a fire existed on units sold to both final and organizational consumers, each class of customers should be treated equally. Yet, under the original recall program, only 89,000 dishwashers in single-family homes were replaced, while 540,000 dishwashers in managed properties were rewired. Critics also found fault with General Electric's attempt to get homeowners to buy a new model appliance, instead of encouraging them to repair an unsafe unit.

General Electric defended its unequal treatment on these grounds: Since the units were 10 to 16 years old at the time of the recall, it was much easier to locate owners of managed properties than single-family homeowners who might have moved. It also assumed that property managers were better able to make the rewiring modification than homeowners.

After several months of negotiation, General Electric finally agreed to offer free repairs by a trained G.E. technician to all consumers owning the affected dishwasher (http://geappliances.com/plcy/recall.htm).

Comment on General Electric's original recall program based on ethical grounds.

Source: Based on material in Rosalie Radomsky, "G.E. Offers Repairs on Defective Dishwashers," *New York Times on the Web* (December 14, 2000).

Wholesalers and retailers usually find differentiated marketing by their suppliers to be attractive. It lets them reach multiple segments, offers some exclusivity, allows orders to be placed with fewer suppliers, and may enable them to carry their own private brands. For the selling firm, several benefits exist. Items can be placed with competing resellers under different brands. Space is given to display various sizes, packages, and/or brands. Price differentials among brands can be kept. Competitors may be discouraged from entering a channel. Overall, differentiated marketing places the seller in a good bargaining position.

Multiple segmentation can be quite profitable because total profits should rise as a firm increases the number of segments it services. Per-unit profits should also be high if a firm does a good job of enacting a unique marketing plan for each segment. Consumers in each segment would then be willing to pay a premium price for the tailor-made offering.

When a firm serves diverse segments, although risks from a decline in any one segment are lessened, extra costs may be incurred by making product variations, selling in more channels, and promoting more brands. The firm must weigh the revenues gained from selling to multiple segments against the costs.

A company must be careful to maintain product distinctiveness for each market segment and guard its overall image. Many consumers still perceive various General Motors' divisions as having "look-alike" cars. And IBM's image has been affected by its past weak performance in the home PC segment.

10-3b Selecting the Target Market(s)

At this point, a firm has these decisions to make: Which segment(s) offer the best opportunities? How many segments should it pursue? In assessing market segments, a firm should review goals and strengths, competition, segment size and growth potential, distribution requirements, necessary expenditures, profit potential, company image, ability to create and sustain differential advantages, and other factors.

A company now chooses which and how many segments to target.

Based on the approach chosen, a firm would decide whether to pursue one or more segments (or the mass market). Due to the high costs of entering the office PC market and the existence of well-defined demand clusters, it is most likely that a firm new to that industry would start with concentrated marketing. On the other hand, a new sweater maker could easily use differentiated marketing to target boys, girls, men, and women. Pep Boys (www.pepboys.com), the auto repair and parts giant, aims to serve two distinct segments: do-it-yourselfers and professional mechanics. It estimates the size of the U.S. do-it-yourself segment at $25 billion per year, while the professional segment is $50 billion.

Requirements for Successful Segmentation

For concentrated marketing or differentiated marketing plans to succeed, the selected market segment(s) have to meet five criteria:

Effectiveness requires segments that are distinct, homogeneous, measurable, large enough, and reachable.

1. There must be *differences* among consumers, or mass marketing would be an appropriate strategy.
2. Within each segment, there must be enough consumer *similarities* to develop an appropriate marketing plan for that segment.
3. A firm must be able to *measure* consumer attributes and needs in order to form groups. This may be hard for some lifestyle attributes.
4. A segment must be *large enough* to produce sales and cover costs.
5. The members of a segment must be *reachable* in an efficient way. For example, young women can be reached via *Teen* magazine. It is efficient since males and older women do not read the magazine.

Limitations of Segmentation

Segmentation is often a consumer-oriented, efficient, and profitable marketing technique; but it should not be abused. Firms can fall into one or more of these traps—which they should try to avoid. They may

The shortcomings of segmentation need to be considered.

- Appeal to segments that are too small.
- Misread consumer similarities and differences.
- Become cost inefficient.
- Spin off too many imitations of their original products or brands.
- Become short-run instead of long-run oriented.
- Be unable to use certain media (due to the small size of individual segments).
- Compete in too many segments.
- Confuse people.
- Become locked into a declining segment.
- Be too slow to seek innovative possibilities for new products.

10-4 DEVELOPING THE MARKETING STRATEGY

The third phase in planning a target market strategy (developing the marketing strategy) includes these steps: positioning the firm's offering relative to competitors and outlining appropriate marketing mix(es).

10-4a Positioning the Company's Offering in Relation to Competition

A good or service must be carefully positioned against competitors.

Once a firm selects its target market(s), it must identify the attributes and image of each competitor and select a position for its own offering.

For example, a firm considering entry into the office PC market could describe the key strengths of some of the major competitors as follows:

- IBM—Reliability, service, range of software applications, product variety.
- Apple—Ease of use, graphics, desktop publishing, innovativeness.
- Compaq—Innovativeness, construction, monitor quality, competitive pricing.
- Dell—Made-to-order products, range of accessories carried, direct marketing experience.

MARKETING *and the Web*

Doing a College Search without Leaving Home

Before the advent of the World Wide Web, college students and their parents faced a daunting task in their search for a college. The process often meant relying on the recommendations of guidance counselors and older siblings, and trips to local libraries to pore over college bulletins.

Now, by using the Web, prospective students can easily plug in locational preferences, expected tuition costs, the desired size of the student body, and other factors, and generate a list of colleges that meet their criteria. Sites such as www.embark.com and www.petersons.com/ugrad even let students view college ratings based upon specific criteria, and then send E-mail requests to the schools for additional information. Many colleges also maintain Web sites that feature virtual tours of their campus and facilities, and enable prospective students to engage in E-mail chats with faculty and students.

Although the Web sites are free and offer prospective students large volumes of information in a convenient format, they have their detractors. In some cases, the sites are free because of on-site advertising. Other sites make money by selling students' names and addresses to such retailers as banks, long-distance phone companies, and bookstores. And unless a student is very specific as to his or her requirements, the online programs will generate a list of hundreds of colleges.

According to Cris Maloney, an executive with an online college search service, "The tools have changed but the process hasn't changed. Simply learning that a college enrolls, say 15,000 students, offers a botany major, and features a low teacher-to-student ratio is not enough."

As a marketing consultant to a small liberal arts college, what types of information should the school offer on its Web site?

Source: Based on material in Lisa Guernsey, "The College Search Game," *New York Times on the Web* (September 2, 2000).

In positioning itself against these competitors, the firm would need to present a combination of customer benefits that are not being offered by them and that are desirable by a target market. Customers must be persuaded that there are clear reasons for buying the new firm's computers. It is not a good idea for the firm to go head on against such big, well-known competitors.

As one alternative, the firm could focus on small businesses that have not yet bought a computer and that need a personal touch during both the purchase process and the initial use of the product. It could thus market fully configured PC systems, featuring IBM clones that are installed by the seller (complete with software libraries and customized programs), in-office training of employees, and a single price for a total system. The positioning emphasis would be "to provide the best ongoing, personalized customer service possible to an underdeveloped market segment, small-business owners."

A fuller discussion of product positioning appears in Chapter 11.

10-4b Outlining the Appropriate Marketing Mix(es)

The last step in the target-marketing process is for a firm to outline a marketing-mix plan for each customer group sought. Marketing decisions relate to product, distribution, promotion, and price factors.

The marketing mix must be attractive to the target market.

Here is a logical marketing-mix plan for a firm newly entering the office PC market and concentrating on small-business owners:

- Product—Good-quality, Pentium-based IBM clone with expansion capability; very user friendly, with a simple keyboard layout; high-resolution color monitor; high-speed CD-ROM\DVD player and suitable speakers; 60-gigabyte hard drive; basic software library; customized software; and more.

- Distribution—Direct calls and installations at customers' places of business; follow-up service calls.

- Promotion—Focus on personal selling and direct mail; hands-on, on-site training; customer referrals.

- Price—Average to above average; customers presented with nonprice reasons to buy; positioning linked to high value for the price; price of computer, software, and service bundled together.

10-5 SALES FORECASTING

As a firm plans a target market strategy, it should forecast its short-run and long-run sales to the chosen market. A *sales forecast* outlines expected company sales for a specific good or service to a specific consumer group over a specific period of time under a specific marketing program. By accurately projecting sales, a firm can better set a marketing budget, allot resources, measure success, analyze sales productivity, monitor the environment and competition, and modify marketing efforts.[12]

A sales forecast predicts company sales over a specified period.

A firm should first study industry forecasts; they can strongly affect any company's sales. Next, sales potential outlines the upper limit for the firm, based on marketing and production capacity. A sales forecast then enumerates a firm's realistic sales. The forecast is also based on the expected environment and company performance. Figure 10-13 shows this sales forecasting process.

A sales forecast should take into account demographics (such as per-capita income), the economy (such as the inflation rate), the competitive environment (such as promotion levels), current and prior sales, and other factors. When devising a forecast, precision

[12]See Paul A. Herbig, John Milewicz, and James E. Golden, "The Do's and Don'ts of Sales Forecasting," *Industrial Marketing Management*, Vol. 22 (February 1993), pp. 49–57; John B. Mahaffie, "Why Forecasts Fail," *American Demographics* (March 1995), pp. 34–40; Gary S. Lynn, Steven P. Schnaars, and Richard B. Skov, "Survey of New Product Forecasting Practices in Industrial High Technology and Low Technology Businesses," *Industrial Marketing Management*, Vol. 28 (November 1999), pp. 565–571.

FIGURE 10-13

Developing a Sales Forecast

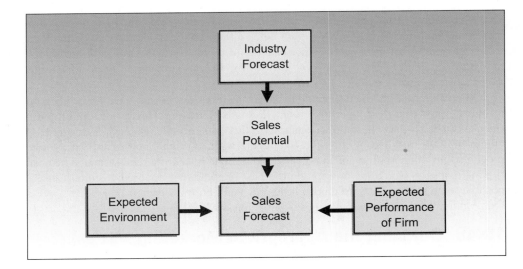

is required. A forecast should break sales down by good or service (model 123), consumer group (adult female), time period (July through September), and type of marketing plan (intensive advertising).

10-5a Data Sources

A firm can consult several external secondary sources to obtain some of the data needed for a forecast. Government agencies provide data on global, national, regional, and local demographic trends; past sales by industry and product; and the economy. Trade associations publish statistics and often have libraries. General and specialized media, such as *Business Week* and *Ward's Automotive Reports*, do forecasts.

A firm can also get data from present and future customers, executives, salespeople, research studies and market tests, and internal records. These data often center on company, not industry, predictions.

10-5b Methods of Sales Forecasting

Sales forecasting methods range from simple to sophisticated. Among the simple ones are trend analysis, market share analysis, jury of executive (expert) opinion, sales force surveys, and consumer surveys. Among the more complex ones are the chain-ratio technique, market buildup method, and statistical analyses. Table 10-3 illustrates each. By combining two or more techniques, a firm can have a better forecast and minimize the weaknesses in any one method.

With simple trend analysis, a firm forecasts sales on the basis of recent or current performance. For example, if sales have risen an average of 10 percent annually over the last five years, it will forecast next year's sales to be 10 percent higher than the present year's. Although the technique is easy to use, the problems are that sales fluctuations, changing consumer tastes, changing competition, the economy, and market saturation are not considered. A firm's growth may be affected by these factors.

Market share analysis is similar to simple trend analysis, except that a company assumes that its share of industry sales will be constant. However, all firms in an industry do not progress at the same rate. Market-share analysis has the same weaknesses as simple trend analysis, but uses more industry data—and it would let an aggressive or declining firm adjust its forecast and marketing efforts.

A ***jury of executive (expert) opinion*** is used if the management of a firm or other well-informed persons meet, discuss the future, and set sales estimates based on the group's experience and interaction. By itself, this method relies too much on informal analysis. In conjunction with other methods, it is effective because it enables experts to directly interpret and respond to concrete data. Because management lays out goals, sets priorities, and guides a firm's destiny, its input is crucial.

A **jury of executive (expert) opinion** *has informed people estimate sales.*

TABLE 10-3	**Applying Sales Forecasting Techniques**	
Technique	**Illustration**	**Selected Potential Shortcomings**
Simple trend analysis	This year's sales = $2 million; company trend is 5% growth per year; sales forecast = $2,100,000.	Industry decline not considered.
Market share analysis	Current market share = 18%; company seeks stable market share; industry forecast = $10,000,000; company sales forecast = $1,800,000.	New competitors and greater marketing by current ones not considered.
Jury of executive opinion	Three executives see strong growth and three see limited growth; they agree on a 6% rise on this year's sales of $11 million; sales forecast = $11,660,000.	Change in consumer attitudes not uncovered.
Jury of expert opinion	Groups of wholesalers, retailers, and suppliers meet. Each group makes a forecast; top management utilizes each forecast in forming one projection.	Different beliefs by groups about industry growth.
Sales force survey	Sales personnel report a competitor's price drop of 10% will cause company sales to decline 3% from this year's $7 million; sales forecast = $6,790,000.	Sales force unaware a competitor's price cut will be temporary.
Consumer survey	85% of current customers indicate they will repurchase next year and spend an average of $1,000 with the firm; 3% of competitors' customers indicate they will buy from the firm next year and spend an average of $800; sales forecast = $460,000.	Consumer intentions possibly not reflecting real behavior.
Chain-ratio method	Unit sales forecast for introductory marketing text = (number of students) × (% annually enrolled in marketing) × (% buying a new book) × (expected market share) = (10,000,000) × (0.07) × (0.87) × (0.11) = 66,990.	Inaccurate estimate of enrollment in introductory marketing course made.
Market buildup method	Total sales forecast = region 1 forecast + region 2 forecast + region 3 forecast = $2,000,000 + $7,000,000 + $13,000,000 = $22,000,000.	Incorrect assumption that areas will behave similarly in future.
Test marketing	Total sales forecast = (sales in test market A + sales in test market B) × (25) = ($1,000,000 + $1,200,000) × (25) = $55,000,000.	Test areas not representative of all locations.
Detailed statistical analyses	Simulation, complex trend analysis, regression, and correlation.	Lack of understanding by management; all factors not quantifiable.

The employees most in touch with consumers and the environment are sales personnel. A sales force survey allows a firm to obtain input in a structured way. Salespeople are often able to pinpoint trends, strengths and weaknesses in a firm's offering, competitive strategies, customer resistance, and the traits of heavy users. They can break sales forecasts down by product, customer type, and area. However, they can have a limited perspective, offer biased replies, and misinterpret consumer desires.

Many marketers feel the best indicators of future sales are consumer attitudes. By conducting a consumer survey, a firm can obtain information on purchase intentions, future expectations, consumption rates, brand switching, time between purchases, and reasons for purchases. Yet, consumers may not reply to surveys and may act differently from what they say.

In the **chain-ratio method,** a firm starts with general market information and then computes a series of more specific information. These combined data yield a sales forecast. For instance, a maker of women's casual shoes can first look at a trade association report to learn the industry sales estimate for shoes, the percentage of sales from women's shoes, and the percentage of women's shoe sales from casual shoes. It would then project its own sales of casual women's shoes to its target market. This method is only as accurate as the data plugged in for each market factor. It is useful since it gets management to think through a forecast and obtain different information.

With the **chain-ratio method,** *general data are broken down. The* **market buildup method** *adds segment data.*

Opposite to the chain-ratio method is the ***market buildup method*** by which a firm gathers data from small, separate market segments and aggregates them. For example, this method lets a firm operating in four urban areas devise a forecast by first estimating sales in each area and then adding them. A firm must note that consumer tastes, competition, population growth, and media do differ by area. Equal-size segments may present dissimilar opportunities; they should not be lumped together without careful study.

Test marketing is a form of market buildup analysis where a firm projects a new product's sales based on short-run, geographically limited tests. With it, a company usually introduces a new product into one or a few markets for a short time and enacts a full marketing campaign there. Overall sales are forecast from test market sales. Yet, test areas may not be representative of all locales; and test-market enthusiasm may not carry into national distribution. Test marketing is discussed more in Chapter 13.

There are many detailed statistical methods for sales forecasting. Simulation lets a firm enter market data into a computer model and forecast under varying conditions and marketing plans. In complex trend analysis, the firm includes past sales fluctuations, cyclical factors (such as economic conditions), and other factors when looking at sales trends. Regression and correlation techniques explore mathematical links between future sales and market factors, such as annual income or derived demand. These methods rely on good data and the ability to use them well. Further discussion is beyond the scope of our text.

10-5c   Additional Considerations

The method and accuracy of sales forecasting depend a lot on the newness of a firm's offering. A forecast for a continuing good or service could be based on trend analysis, market share analysis, executive (expert) opinion, and sales force surveys. Barring major alterations in the economy, industry, competition, or consumer tastes, the forecast should be relatively accurate.

A forecast for a continuing product should be the most accurate.

A forecast for an item new to the firm but continuing in the industry could be based on trade data, executive (expert) opinion, sales force and consumer surveys, and test marketing. The first year's forecast should be somewhat accurate, the ensuing years more so. It is hard to project first-year sales precisely since consumer interest and competition may be tough to gauge.

A forecast for a good or service new to both the firm and the industry should rely on sales force and consumer surveys, test marketing, executive (expert) opinion, and simulation. The forecast for the early years may be highly inaccurate since the speed of consumer acceptance cannot be closely estimated. Later forecasts will be more accurate. While an initial forecast may be imprecise, it is still needed for setting marketing plans, budgeting, monitoring the environment and competition, and measuring success.

Sales penetration shows whether a firm has reached its potential. **Diminishing returns** *may result if it seeks nonconsumers.*

A firm must consider ***sales penetration***—the degree to which a firm is meeting its sales potential—in forecasting sales. It is expressed as:

$$\text{Sales penetration} = \text{Actual sales/Sales potential}$$

A firm with high sales penetration needs to realize that ***diminishing returns*** may occur if it seeks to convert remaining nonconsumers because the costs of attracting them may outweigh revenues. Other products or segments may offer better potential. Table 10-4 illustrates sales penetration and diminishing returns.

A firm must remember that factors may change and cause a wrong forecast, unless revised. These include economic conditions, industry conditions, company performance, competition, and consumer tastes.

TABLE 10-4   Illustrating Sales Penetration and Diminishing Returns

Year 1	Year 2
Sales potential = $1,000,000	Sales potential = $1,000,000
Actual sales = $600,000 (60,000 units)	Actual sales = $700,000 (70,000 units)
Selling price = $10/unit	Selling price = $10/unit
Total marketing costs = $100,000	Total marketing costs = $150,000
Total production costs (at $8/unit) = $480,000	Total production costs (at $8/unit) = $560,000
Sales penetration = $\dfrac{\$600,000}{\$1,000,000}$ = 60%	Sales penetration = $\dfrac{\$700,000}{\$1,000,000}$ = 70%
Total profit = $600,000 – ($100,000 + $480,000) = $20,000	Total profit = $700,000 – ($150,000 + $560,000) = –$10,000

In year 1, sales penetration is 60% and the firm earns a $20,000 profit. In year 2, the firm raises marketing expenditures to increase sales penetration to 70%; as a result, it suffers diminishing returns—the additional $100,000 in actual sales is more than offset by a $130,000 rise in total costs (from $580,000 in year 1 to $710,000 in year 2).

WEB SITES YOU CAN USE

There are many valuable Web sites related to target marketing. Let us highlight five of them:

Easy Analytics (www.easidemographics.com/reports/easi_free_reports.phtml) makes available a number of free demographic and lifestyle reports by ZIP Code. This enables firms to study consumer backgrounds in different communities.

Claritas is a leader in lifestyle segmentation through its PRIZM and MicroVision programs, which it markets to business clients. At its Web site, Claritas discusses market segmentation (www.claritas.com/index.html) and enables visitors to try out its PRIZM and MicroVision programs (www.fallschurch.claritas.com/YAWYL).

The Yankelovich MindBase Monitor (secure.yankelovich.com/solutions/mindbase.asp) identifies eight major consumer groups based on attitudes and motivations. The groups are broken down into 32 distinct segments, which enable client firms to create high-impact marketing programs and develop high-value customer relationships. The segments are described at its Web site.

Given the popularity of the World Wide Web, companies are quite interested in the characteristics of Web users. The **GVU WWW User Survey** is a large-scale project that regularly conducts user surveys and reports the results online (www.gvu.gatech.edu/user_surveys).

Target Marketing has an online version of its magazine (www.targetonline.com) devoted to this topic from the perspective of direct marketing.

SUMMARY

1. *To describe the process for planning a target market strategy*   After collecting information on consumers and the environment, a firm can pick the target market(s) to which to appeal. A potential market has people with similar needs, enough resources, and a willingness and ability to buy.

Developing a target market strategy consists of three general phases, comprising seven specific steps: analyzing consumer demand—determining demand patterns (1), establishing bases of segmentation (2), and identifying potential market segments (3); targeting the market—choosing a target market approach (4) and selecting the target market(s) (5); and developing the marketing strategy—positioning the company's offering relative to competitors (6) and outlining the appropriate marketing mix(es) (7). Of particular importance is product differentiation, whereby a product offering is perceived by the consumer to differ from its competition on any physical or nonphysical product characteristic, including price.

2. *To examine alternative demand patterns and segmentation bases for both final and organizational consumers*   Demand patterns indicate the uniformity or diversity of consumer needs and desires for particular categories of goods and services. With homogeneous demand, consumers have relatively uniform needs and desires. With clustered demand, consumer needs and desires can be classified into two or more identifiable clusters (segments), with each having distinct purchase requirements. With diffused demand, consumer needs and desires are so diverse that clear clusters cannot be identified.

The possible bases for segmenting the market can be placed into three categories: geographic demographics—basic identifiable traits of towns, cities, states, regions, and countries; personal demographics—basic identifiable traits of individual final consumers and organizational consumers and groups of final consumers and organizational consumers; and lifestyles—patterns in which people (final consumers and those representing organizational consumers) live and spend time and money. It is generally advisable to use a combination of demographic and lifestyle factors to form possible segmentation bases. Although the distinctions between final and organizational consumers should be kept in mind, the three broad segmentation bases could be used in both cases.

After establishing possible segmentation bases, a firm is ready to develop consumer profiles, which identify potential market segments by aggregating consumers with similar characteristics and needs.

3. *To explain and contrast undifferentiated marketing (mass marketing), concentrated marketing, and differentiated marketing (multiple segmentation)*   Undifferentiated marketing aims at a large, broad consumer market via one basic marketing plan. In concentrated marketing, a firm aims at a narrow, specific consumer group via one, specialized marketing plan catering to the needs of that segment. Under differentiated marketing, a firm appeals to two or more distinct market segments, with a different marketing plan for each. When segmenting, a firm must understand the majority fallacy: the largest segment may not offer the best opportunity; it often has the most competitors.

In selecting its target market(s), a firm should consider its goals and strengths, competition, segment size and growth potential, distribution needs, required expenditures, profit potential, company image, and its ability to develop and sustain a differential advantage.

Successful segmentation requires differences among and similarities within segments, measurable consumer traits and needs, large enough segments, and efficiency in reaching segments. It should not be abused by appealing to overly small groups, using marketing inefficiently, placing too much emphasis on imitations of original company products or brands, confusing consumers, and so on.

4. *To show the importance of positioning in developing a marketing strategy*   In positioning its offering against competitors, a firm needs to present a combination of customer benefits that are not being provided by others and that are desirable by a target market. Customers must be persuaded that there are clear reasons for buying the firm's products rather than those of its competitors.

The last step in the target marketing process is for a firm to develop a marketing mix for each customer group to which it wants to appeal.

5. *To discuss sales forecasting and its role in target marketing*   Short- and long-run sales should be forecast in developing a target market strategy. This helps a firm compute budgets, allocate resources, measure success, analyze productivity, monitor the environment and competition, and adjust marketing plans. A sales forecast describes the expected company sales of a specific good or service to a specific consumer group over a specific time period under a specific marketing program.

A firm can obtain sales-forecasting data from a variety of internal and external sources. Forecasting methods range from simple trend analysis to detailed statistical analyses. The best results are obtained when methods and forecasts are combined. A sales forecast should consider the newness of a firm's offering, sales penetration, diminishing returns, and the changing nature of many factors.

KEY TERMS

market (p. 283)
market segmentation (p. 284)
target market strategy (p. 284)
undifferentiated marketing
    (mass marketing) (p. 284)
concentrated marketing (p. 284)
differentiated marketing (multiple
    segmentation) (p. 284)
product differentiation (p. 284)

demand patterns (p. 285)
homogeneous demand (p. 285)
clustered demand (p. 285)
diffused demand (p. 286)
geographic demographics (p. 288)
personal demographics (p. 289)
heavy-usage segment (heavy half) (p. 292)
benefit segmentation (p. 293)
VALS (Values and Lifestyles)
    program (p. 293)

Social Styles model (p. 293)
majority fallacy (p. 298)
sales forecast (p. 305)
jury of executive (expert) opinion (p. 306)
chain-ratio method (p. 307)
market buildup method (p. 308)
sales penetration (p. 308)
diminishing returns (p. 308)

REVIEW QUESTIONS

1. Distinguish between the terms "market" and "market segmentation."
2. Explain this comment: "Sometimes a firm can achieve a key differential advantage by simply emphasizing how its offering satisfies existing consumer desires and needs better than its competitors do. Sometimes demand patterns must be modified for consumers to perceive a firm's product differentiation as worthwhile."
3. Differentiate among homogeneous, clustered, and diffused consumer demand. What are the marketing implications?

4. Describe five personal demographics pertaining to organizational consumers.
5. What is the majority fallacy? How may a firm avoid it?
6. Cite the five key requirements for successful segmentation.
7. Why is sales forecasting important when developing a target market strategy?
8. Why are long-run sales forecasts for new products more accurate than short-run forecasts?

DISCUSSION QUESTIONS

1. How could a global financial services company apply geographic demographic segmentation?
2. Develop a personal-demographic profile of the students in your marketing class. For what goods and services would the class be a good market segment? A poor segment?

3. Describe several potential benefit segments for a firm marketing office furniture to business clients.
4. A firm has a sales potential of $5,000,000 and attains actual sales of $3,400,000. What does this signify? What should the firm do next?

WEB EXERCISE

Take an online survey to see what your own lifestyle segment is (http://future.sri.com/vals/surveynew.shtml). Discuss the results. What are the strengths and weaknesses of such an online survey?

PART 3 SHORT CASES

Case 1

Understanding How Leisure Travelers Make Decisions[c3-1]

In the late 1990s, the typical fee paid to travel agents by airlines was reduced from 10 percent of the ticketed price (with no cap) to 5 percent (with a cap of $50 per roundtrip ticket). Some analysts estimate that the savings to airlines was $5.2 billion per year, since agents booked 80 percent of all flights.

Today, 63 percent of travelers still use a travel agent at least some of the time, despite the number of airlines that have Web sites and the popularity of such travel sites as Travelocity (www.travelocity.com) that operate 24 hours per day/7 days per week. Agents have been able to keep their customers by utilizing sophisticated data bases to record shopper demographic and lifestyle factors and to then market appropriate trips to each individual. Thus, a last-minute cruise special may be marketed to a budget-oriented vacation traveler who likes a "rest and sun" type of vacation.

Travel agents have also been able to maximize revenues by better understanding the demographics of leisure travelers who use travel agents and the types of trips they book through agents. A market research study by Yesawich, Pepperdine & Brown/

Yankelovich Partners found this demographic profile for leisure travelers who use travel agents: 54 percent are male, 46 percent are female; 22 percent earn less than $30,000 per year, 25 percent earn between $30,000 and $50,000 per year, and 53 percent earn more than $50,000 per year. In terms of age, 31 percent of leisure travelers who use travel agents are 24 to 35 years old, 36 percent are 36 to 54 years old, and 33 percent are 55 and older. Furthermore, 56 percent of travel agent clients are married, 30 percent are single, and 14 percent are divorced, widowed, or separated.

Table 1 shows that travel agent clients take more trips in each category than nonclients: 4.8 leisure trips per year versus 3.5 trips. Table 2 examines the sources of information used by travelers when planning five types of trips: all travel, car travel, air travel, international travel, and cruises. Travel agents were used by the greatest percent of travelers for cruises (81 percent), international travel (70 percent), and air travel (68 percent). Travel agents were the second most widely used source for all travel (47 percent), and the fourth most widely used source for car travel (42 percent).

TABLE 1 Differences in Travel-Related Behavior Between Travel Agent Users and Nonusers

	Travel Agent Users	Travel Agent Nonusers
Total number of leisure trips taken per year	4.8	3.5
Number of short getaways	2.0	1.2
Number of long vacations	1.2	0.9
Number of trips to visit family	1.6	1.3

Source: ASTA Consumer Travel Purchase Report.

[c3-1]The data in the case are drawn from Stacy H. Small, "Fly Me to the Moon," *American Demographics* (March 2000), pp. 50–52.

TABLE 2 Percent of Travelers Who Consult Various Sources When Planning a Trip

	All Travelers	Car Travelers	Air Travelers	International Travelers	Cruise Travelers
Friends/relatives	59%	61%	51%	50%	58%
Travel agent	47	42	68	70	81
The Internet or online services	42	44	45	55	44
Hotel toll-free numbers	42	44	47	45	54
Airline toll-free numbers	27	29	45	46	44
Car rental toll-free numbers	19	18	34	20	8
Travel magazines	16	17	17	37	25
Newspaper travel ads	15	16	22	16	10

Source: ASTA Consumer Travel Purchase Report.

Questions

1. What information should a travel agent include in a final consumer data base to better serve customers?
2. What information should a travel agent include in an organizational consumer data base to better serve customers?
3. Develop a marketing strategy for travel agents based upon the demographic profile of leisure travelers who use travel agents.
4. Evaluate the marketing implications for travel agents of the data in Tables 1 and 2.

Case 2

Kinko's Goes Full Blast After the B-to-B Marketplace[c3-2]

Kinko's (www.kinkos.com), the 24-hour photocopy chain, needs little introduction to bleary-eyed college students who have worked late into the night completing term papers. Now, the chain is training its sights on large corporate customers that seek to outsource their printing and copying needs. Kinko's has already been successful in attracting smaller business clients, but this market segment generates too little repeat business. Kinko's management recognized that its new target market emphasis would necessitate a drastic change in its overall marketing strategy.

According to Mark Little, Kinko's vice-president of operations services, "Our salespeople used to be just order takers, because they were just an extension of the retail branches. We needed to turn them into solution salespeople who could have substantive discussions with companies to find out what they need and how we can help, rather than just take orders."

Within the first nine months, the commercial sales team exceeded its ambitious goals by 10 percent. It has succeeded in attracting such large customers as IBM, Hewlett-Packard, and Disney. Little predicts that this group will soon account for 30 percent of Kinko's total revenues. A major factor leading to the positive results of the commercial sales team is Kinko's use of relationship marketing with key accounts.

Kinko's relationship with PeopleSoft, a large software provider, is so strong that Kinko's sales representatives attend internal planning meetings of PeopleSoft's human resources department. PeopleSoft's vice-president of education services says, "Kinko's came in and sat down with us to have a long conversation about how it could help speed up the things we do. It has provided us with many options of services and became almost like a hired consultant for how we print and get our information to our employees." It took Kinko's three years before PeopleSoft entrusted Kinko's with its work.

Other vital components of the target-marketing plan were Kinko's information kits, training, and a revision of salesperson compensation plans:

- Kinko's realized that it had to provide its salespeople with kits that contained examples of each of the goods and services that Kinko's markets. As Bill Doolittle, Kinko's vice-

president of sales says, "We felt like if we gave them nice materials that clearly explained all our offerings, then they'd have that much more ammunition to throw at potential customers." In addition, Kinko's developed a new Intranet site that showed the sales process, customer case studies, frequently asked questions about any industry, and a worksheet for new hires that outlined tasks in their first 12 weeks on the job.

- Extensive sales training was provided to both existing and new sales personnel. Kinko's held a four-day meeting of all sales and operations personnel. The 900 participants were divided into six-person teams (comprised of field sales, sales management, operations, and even executive officers). Each team had the task of developing a presentation for a fictitious customer based upon a seven-step process: assess, plan, propose, close, fulfill, support, and expand. The company's 55 regional managers met with each of their salespeople at least monthly to coach them on this process. Training supplements were based on a "best practices model" that explained the strategies and tactics of the best-performing salespeople.

- Kinko's enacted a new compensation plan that now rewards everyone in the company if the firm meets specific company-wide objectives relating to incremental revenues, long-term relationships with customers, and customer service.

Questions

1. State several differences between the needs of students and organizational consumers at Kinko's.
2. How should Kinko's marketing approach differ for small and large organizational consumers? Why?
3. Show how Kinko's can utilize the North American Industry Classification System (NAICS).
4. Assess Kinko's overall target marketing strategy. How would you improve it?

[c3-2]The data in the case are drawn from Andy Cohen, "Copy Cats," *Sales & Marketing Management* (August 2000), pp. 49–58.

Case 3

Targeting Hispanics in Middle America^{c3-3}

Through its Wholesale Food Outlet (WFO) located in Omaha, Nash Finch (www.nashfinch.com) is seeking to appeal to the recent Mexican arrivals in the Upper Midwest. In recent years, the Hispanic population—which has always been an important market segment in the Southwest, Florida, and the Northeast—has expanded into the Midwest. For example, the Hispanic population in Omaha has doubled in the past 10 years. Nash Finch views the Omaha store as a laboratory for developing a competitive strategy with the greatest appeal to this growing target market. The firm's work on this store has been far from easy. According to Art Keeney, vice-president of corporate retail stores at Nash Finch, "In our Omaha store we've already reset some sections two or three times—like cooking oil."

Among the store's strategies in attracting Hispanics are the emphasis on imported groceries from Mexico, warehouse club multipacks, Hispanic-oriented perishables, and bilingual signage and check-cashing services. Although WFO stocks about 40 percent less merchandise than a traditional Nash Finch supermarket, a much larger percent of its goods consists of Hispanic specialties like canned hominy, jalapeno peppers, plantains, and pickled cactus. A basic merchandising feature of the WFO store is its Wall of Values, which stresses such staples as corn meal, shortening, and Ramen noodles. The items featured on the Wall of Values changes weekly, based on seasonality; but more Hispanic-oriented items are stocked during the beginning of the month when Hispanics tend to do their heaviest grocery shopping.

As a customer enters the store, large signs in both English and Spanish promote WFO's low prices. To further stress the low prices, all items are sold at cost. At the register, an additional 10 percent is added to cover WFO's expenses and profits. And to improve customer service, WFO utilizes postage-paid mail-in comment cards that are available in Spanish, English, and bilingual versions.

Other parts of WFO's strategy represent a radical departure from that in Nash Finch's traditional stores. The store has a thriving food stamp business, with food stamps representing as much as one-third of the store's total business during the first two weeks of a month. This drops to 20 percent of the store's total business during the last two weeks of the month. The Hispanic-American business is also much more cash-driven than a traditional store, where much of sales is completed by credit card. And while larger packs of meat are offered at the start of the month, these are much less frequent during the end of the month.

As Art Keeney notes, "Hispanics have not been served as well as they should have in the Upper Midwest. This is a heck of an opportunity for us. These are very loyal shoppers who are big on cooking from scratch, and not as restaurant-driven as the general population. They are like the typical supermarket customer 20 years ago."

As evidence of the success of the store in attracting its clientele, the WFO store was formerly part of the Hinky Dinky chain. As a Hinky Dinky unit, the store had a weekly sales volume of $70,000. Now, in the slowest week of the month, WFO does double that volume.

Nash Finch is seeking to open additional WFO stores in cities with an extensive Hispanic population nearby. At the Omaha store, more than 60 percent of its shoppers are Hispanic and 90 percent of them live within a mile and a half of the store.

Questions

1. From a market segmentation perspective, comment on Nash Finch's development of WFO as a prototype store.
2. What are the pros and cons of Nash Finch's choice of the Hispanic market as a target market?
3. What other target marketing opportunities should Nash Finch investigate?
4. How could Nash Finch prepare a 5-year sales forecast for its WFO store?

---

^{c3-3}The data in the case are drawn from Richard Turcsik, "Mexican of Omaha," *Progressive Grocer* (September 2000), pp. 38–44.

Case 4

Segmenting the Global Youth Market[c3-4]

This case highlights the results of "The New World Teen Study," conducted by Elissa Moses. The findings are based on interviews with more than 27,000 teenagers in 44 countries. Moses is the senior vice-president of global consumer and market intelligence for Royal Philips Electronics (www.philips.com). The full results of the study are contained in a book entitled *The $100 Billion Allowance: Accessing the Global Teen Market*.

Moses has identified six value segments, based on what high school students rate as the principles most important to them. For each value segment, she has uncovered what the teenagers enjoy, what worries them the most, what their attitudes are, and what they own, wear, and do. Moses feels that this segmentation basis provides an opportunity for firms to determine what products teenagers most desire, how advertising affects them, and what brands will be most successful.

According to Moses, values are established during the teenage years and may not measurably change over the course of a lifetime. Thus, a firm that is aware of a teen's value segment has a good chance of keeping the teenage customer over the course of his or her life. Among the values that Moses has studied are: relationships with family, accomplishing as much as possible, having as much fun as possible, relationships with friends, making the world a better place, being accepted as an individual, upholding time-honored customs and traditions, and never being bored.

"The New World Teen Study" classified teens into six distinct value clusters (note: not all teens fit into these groups). Much of the differences in the segments is due to the extent to which each group is inner- (me) versus other- (we) directed and conformist versus nonconformist. Here are the clusters and their characteristics:

- *Segment 1: Thrills and Chills* (18 percent of teenage population)—Teens in this segment come from affluent or middle-class parents, live mostly in developed countries, and have a significant allowance. They love to dine at restaurants and dance, and do not mind buying expensive items.
- *Segment 2: Resigned* (14 percent of teenage population)—Teens in this group have very low expectations about their future. They often come from blue-collar homes or from

countries with strong welfare assistance. This group scores low on such activities as going to the movies, attending cultural events, or even visiting relatives.

- *Segment 3: World Savers* (12 percent of teenage population)—These teens engage in activities relating to the environment and humanism. In general, this group consists of class leaders. Grades and higher education are important.
- *Segment 4: Quiet Achievers* (15 percent of teenage population)—Teens in this group are the least rebellious. They have strong family ties, and their major concern is not living up to their parents' expectations.
- *Segment 5: Bootstrappers* (14 percent of teenage population)—The main goal of these teens is achievement; but this extends far beyond grades. For example, they seek out class offices. They are well behaved, respectful, and have little desire to rebel.
- *Segment 6: Upholders* (16 percent of teenage population)—These teens are the most childlike of the segments. They live sheltered lives. Males seek positions similar to their fathers; females have little desire for a career.

Questions

1. Evaluate the six value segments based upon the requirements for successful segmentation list in Chapter 10.
2. Which two teen groups appear to be the most similar? How can a marketer seek to appeal to these groups with a common advertising campaign?
3. Which two teen groups appear to be the most dissimilar? What are the marketing implications of this?
4. As a maker of digital cameras, develop a marketing plan for appealing to the "thrills and chills" market segment. Develop a marketing plan for appealing to the "world savers" market segment.

[c3-4] The data in the case are drawn from "The Six Value Segments of Global Youth," *Brandweek* (May 22, 2000), pp. 38–50.

PART 3 COMPREHENSIVE CASE

Transactional Segmentation to Slow Customer Defections[pc-3]

Introduction

Can a business firm identify potentially defecting customers weeks or even months before they actually defect? A new process of identifying defecting customers uses changes in customer transaction patterns as a basis for segmentation. The basic concept of segmentation is to market to groups of individuals who are similar in some characteristic or characteristics. Transactional segmentation challenges this notion and promotes the concept of marketing to individuals rather than groups. Transactional segmentation uses a firm's internal data to determine changes in the individual consumer's transaction patterns in order to develop a personal marketing strategy to market directly back to that customer. The difficulties present in transactional segmentation modeling include: (1) The transactional pattern is multidimensional. (2) The customer units have differing transaction rates. (3) Modeling expertise is a necessity.

Setting the Stage

Just a few years ago, a large North American bank was facing a problem. It was losing 20 percent of its customers each year. This was not a new problem. The bank had faced this same problem year after year, but had always been successful in soliciting enough new customers to fill the void. Finally, however, three factors compelled this bank to turn this situation around.

First, high customer defection was a problem of the entire banking industry. A study from *Banker's Monthly* reported a medium-sized (70-branch) bank in a northeastern city losing 20 percent of its customers each year. This is very consistent with an article published in *Harvard Business Review* that stated other bank industry sources reporting 15 to 20 percent defection rates. With such highly mobile customers, and with higher competition and more marketing dollars spent to solicit these new customers, the bank's market share position was threatened.

Second, there were indications that increases and decreases in revenues and profits did not necessarily go hand-in-hand. The *HBR* article stated that a 5 percent improvement in customer retention could result in an 85 percent increase in bank profits. The Council on Financial Competition reported similar findings. More recent studies by the Council on Financial Competition, as reported in *HBR*, showed a 27 percent increase in profit resulting from a 5 percent increase in bank customer retention. There was potential, therefore, to increase profits greatly by identifying and properly servicing defecting customers.

Third, more and more marketing literature was focusing on the advantages of placing greater emphasis on defensive strategy (designed to retain existing customers) than on offensive strategy (designed to attract new customers). Strategies to attract new customers are a tough sell. They would likely require the bank to take some customers away from existing banks. If the market were stagnant, all new customers would have to be taken away from competitors—an occurrence that the competitors would not sit back and watch without reaction. In addition, a large percentage of the customers that are targets of this solicitation may be very happy with their existing relationship and, thus, have little predisposition to change sources of supply. On the other hand, a defensive strategy is designed to keep existing customers who are already familiar with the firm and products. A good percentage of this group will already feel positively toward the firm. Defensive strategy, therefore, should be more efficient and effective in meeting its goal than offensive strategy. It costs much more to get a new customer than to keep an old customer.

Solving Through Segmentation

The bank approached the problem as would most marketers, by assessing which segment to target. Who were the defecting customers? What characteristics did these customers hold in common?

The bank first grouped customers by income level and marketed to the segments with the highest rate of defection. The defection problem did not improve. The bank then segmented customers based on age, family size, and housing characteristics. Still, no improvement in customer defection rates. The bank tried life-cycle segmentation with no improvement. It did statistical studies to identify the characteristics of the defecting customers. Again, improvements in defection rates did not result.

Solving Through Transactions

Given the lack of results from focusing on traditional segmentation criteria, the bank tried a different approach. It pulled the previous year's transaction records for 500 customers who had defected. It also pulled the previous year's transaction records for 500 customers who had not left the bank. Then, the analysis began. The bank looked at number of transactions, frequency of transactions, average balance, and increases and decreases. It looked at transactions in checking accounts, saving accounts, certificates of deposit, home mortgages, and credit cards. It looked at the transactions separately and in combination with one another. It looked for differences between the defection and the nondefection groups.

What was concluded from all this transactional analysis was this. Customers form a pattern in their transactions. Those who stay true to their existing patterns are the customers who are likely to stay as bank customers. Customers who deviate from their established patterns are much more apt to defect from the bank. These customers must be identified (flagged) and targeted for marketing attention.

[pc-3]Adapted by the authors from Michael M. Pearson and Guy H. Gessner, "Transactional Segmentation to Slow Customer Defections," *Marketing Management* (Summer 1999), pp. 16–23. Reprinted by permission of the American Marketing Association.

The bank did just this. Each month, it ran through the transactional records of each customer and matched this against the transactional pattern for this customer over the previous year. When a difference between current transaction activity and a previous transactional pattern was detected, the computer would flag the customer. It then spit the name out to a branch manager or customer service person who would direct some marketing attention to that customer, such as a direct-mail piece, questionnaire, or phone call. This approach worked. The rate of customer defection decreased and everyone was happy.

It was not a fairy tale, but a real bank with a problem faced by many firms—actual customer defection. In this instance, ordinary market segmentation did not identify the target group well enough to improve the bank's defection rate. A new technique, transactional segmentation, was used to identify the customer upon whom marketing effort should be focused. This technique could be interesting to you.

The Changing Customer

A simple analogy might clarify transactional segmentation. If you decided to close out one of your bank credit cards, how would your transaction behavior change in the months before you actually notified your Visa or MasterCard provider? Your behavior might be to significantly reduce the activity on that card to get the balance to zero. Your transactional pattern would have changed. Another customer might increase activity on this card to be able to take advantage of the promotional incentives provided by many service providers to switch existing balances onto a new card. Again, the customer's transactional pattern would have changed. In either case, once the customer comes to the bank to close an account, it is too late for the banker to save that account. The mind of the customer is already set. To save that customer, the bank must identify defecting customers before they defect. If the bank can identify these customers beforehand, there is a window of opportunity to market to that individual customer and save the account.

Transactional Segmentation

The basic concept of segmentation is to market to groups of individuals who are similar in some characteristic or characteristics. While the characteristic(s) held in common might change the method of segmentation a firm might choose, firms still tend to think in terms of marketing to groups. Transactional segmentation challenges this and promotes the concept of marketing to individuals rather than groups.

Transactional segmentation uses a firm's internal data to determine changes in individual consumer transaction patterns to develop a personal marketing strategy to market directly back to that customer. Transactional segmentation puts several requirements on a firm's internal records:

- *Customers must be identified.* Many firms lose a tremendous source of potential information when they don't identify their consumers. While department stores with their own credit cards and a local video rental store with its membership card can identify their customers, can other retailers such as grocery stores, drugstores, discount stores, or restaurants say the same? (When a retailer gives the collection function to the bank cards, it also gives up its ability to identify its customer and match that customer with his or her transactions.)

- *Data must be stored by customer and transaction.* Just knowing your customer is not enough. You must be able to store all the relevant purchase data of that customer transaction. Can supermarkets, convenience stores, drugstores, discount stores, or restaurants say that they even know the names of their customers, let alone what they purchased and when? Certainly, there are retailers that keep records by customer. The local Blockbuster can tell you what videos you have rented over the last month. Department stores with their own credit cards can tell you what you bought at what date and in what branch. The distinguishing point is that the customer record must be more than a total of the customer's transactions. Data must be stored by transaction to see what other items were bought during that same transaction and when the transaction occurred.

- *The accounts must be householded.* In the banking industry, it is difficult to determine the status of a customer without looking at their checking account, savings account, certificates of deposit, home loans, and credit-card activity. All the accounts of the household unit must be combined together to form a single record so as to understand the economic behavior of this unit. While banks and other firms claim they have this kind of control over their data, this is often times not so. These firms have not in the past had reason to retrieve this information for decision making.

Transaction Modeling

The outline for constructing a transactional segmentation model is quite straightforward. First, you have to construct a standard transactional pattern. Second, you have to plot the consumer's actual transactions to see if this behavior deviates significantly from the standard. Once a significant deviation is detected, this customer is flagged for direct marketing action.

Retail bank customers show surprising regularity in their transaction patterns. When the pattern holds, the customer tends to remain with the existing bank. If the person breaks significantly from the existing pattern, the relationship is showing instability and the customer is showing an indication of leaving.

Difficulties in Transaction Modeling While the concept of transactional segmentation and customer flagging might be conceptually simple, the difficulties present in transactional segmentation modeling can be formidable:

- *The transactional pattern is multidimensional.* A customer may have a checking account, a savings account, a certificate of deposit, a money market account, a MasterCard or Visa card, and a home or auto loan. Constructing a pattern based upon several or all of these factors can be a task for some higher level statistical techniques.

- *Customer units have differing transaction rates.* Even if patterns appear to be the same, they may differ greatly in the number of transactions per period of time. Does the fact that a customer gets a weekly, biweekly, or monthly check really change the nature of the pattern? Does the fact that one customer writes 100 checks during a period, while another writes 10, change the pattern? Also, do differences mean we must use an absolute number change or a percentage change to decide whether a deviation from the existing pattern is enough to flag the customer as one who is leaving the bank?

- *The amount of data that need to be stored can be massive.* Transaction data are needed to construct transactional models. What transaction did the customer make at this time? It is not enough to keep cash register totals for the customer, bank, or store. To construct a transactional pattern, the model builder will want to look at many variables over a reasonable time period. Some variables might not help differentiate between customers who are defecting and those who are not. The problem is that we don't know what variables are the key until after the model is built. Also, for the purpose of continual improvement, we must maintain our collection of this data to fine tune our model in the future.

- *Modeling expertise is a necessity.* Transactional segmentation is not just a process of observation. It is the construction of a transaction pattern from individual transaction records. It is a matter then of comparing individual transaction patterns with ordinary ones to find significant changes that might predict future behavior. This is not easy because different variables are made available by each bank or firm. Besides, the quality of the information sources is inconsistent. To handle the vast amount of varying data of varying quality requires creativity in modeling. Without the availability of data, the computer, and the variety of modeling techniques, transactional segmentation would not be possible.

- *Marketing must be directed back to the individual.* Given these difficulties, it is understandable that statistical methods have been the method of choice for banks doing customer flagging and companies doing flagging analysis for banks. However, these methods take a more mass-market approach than is required by transactional segmentation. In transactional seg-

mentation, once the defecting consumer is identified, this account is automatically and individually entered into a direct marketing process to save the consumer. Characteristics of defecting customers are determined, and a marketing program is developed for a target market that matches these characteristics. Transactional segmentation is a one-to-one process where the bank deals with its customer on a direct and individual basis. When a business-to-business manager might be dealing with 100 customers, individual marketing programs can developed to save the few flagged customers. Retail bankers and retailers, however, would be overwhelmed by this many individual decisions. Direct marketing programs must be predetermined and put into action automatically and immediately.

The Customer Retention System

What makes the customer retention problem so difficult is that when new customers show up at the bank to close their accounts, there is almost no chance of saving this customer. This makes it strategically necessary to identify or flag these customers with enough lead time to successfully direct market them to remain with the bank (defensive strategy).

Even if you can identify defecting customers and with some degree of accuracy, you will have to manage your customer retention system. This includes the following steps:

- *Balancing the accuracy of the model.* This first step is used to decide what type of error to permit in a customer retention system. Is it better to flag too many customers, or is it better to flag too few? As you loosen the model to increase the probability of flagging the defecting customer, you also increase the probability of misidentifying continuing customers as defectors. If you tighten the model, you would accidentally identify far fewer continuing customers, but you would miss some defectors.

- *Valuing your customers.* What is the worth of this particular customer? While we would like to satisfy all customers, some are more valuable than others. This is especially evident when we balance the wasted cost of trying to salvage a non-defecting customer against the lost profits that a defecting customer who was not contacted would have brought in over the life of the account. This necessitates analyzing what we call the "value of customer retention."

- *Working customer defection flagging into your direct marketing program.* Once detected, time is of the essence to save a defecting customer. There is a window of opportunity for action. If we wait too long to remedy the problem, it will be too late. Dissatisfaction will be too deeply set to change the attitudes of this customer. Because timing is so critical and the window of opportunity for each customer is different, the marketing necessity is that we contact this potentially defecting customer directly and individually. The computer can be modeled to flag the defecting customer, and it can be programmed to select and address the proper marketing response. Interrupting the computer model for human input (selecting, sorting, addressing), when these items can be decided within the model, can add time to the process, causing us to miss our window of opportunity for saving this customer.

- *Developing a monitoring process.* If there is a need for speed in reaching the consumer, the same need exists in determining whether the process is working. Since contact is made with the individual customer, monitoring must be done for that person. Again this requires modeling. Has the direct marketing action led to a reaction? Has the transaction pattern changed? Was this an effective use of marketing dollars? Is it worth another direct marketing shot? All of these actions take place within a strategic window. There is no time to build an inventory of intended marketing actions. Not only must marketing be tied to the defection detection model, so must monitoring be tied to the model.

Applications

Transactional segmentation is presently used in many areas both inside and outside of the banking industry. Bank credit cards are monitored by transaction, size, frequency, and type of purchase. Of course, you are familiar with the purchase authorization that a retailer must go through to get the amount of your purchase approved. Have you had your credit card rejected because of too much activity while on a business trip? Have you been contacted by your bank card provider questioning the purchase of antiques on your card when you have no transaction history of buying antiques? These are examples of segmentation by transaction. These are not speculations into the future, but present applications.

Several applications of transactional segmentation are evident when we look at the direct marketing practices of several industries. Gamblers, who have transactions monitored through a casino-issued player card, are offered free rooms in Las Vegas if they have one type of transaction pattern and free airfare if they have another. Airline travel cards offer one mailing to customers with profitable transaction patterns and another to those whose patterns are not as profitable. Consumer-goods, specialty-catalog customers are marketed to differently, based upon transaction patterns. Even in the grocery store, you now get your own special coupons based upon your transactions (a peanut butter coupon if you purchase jelly or heartburn products if you buy hot sauce).

Applications for transactional segmentation are not limited to the banking industry or simply to detect customer defections. They are limited less by technology than by our marketing imaginations.

Implications

As applications of transactional segmentation increase, it is likely that several issues will be debated:

- We will have to respect and address the privacy issue. The thought of marketers keeping track of records for video rentals or library usage sounds sinister. Even with the best intentions and safeguards, there will be undoubtedly be attacks on the industry by consumer groups, media, legislators, and regulators.
- With an increase in transactional segmentation, we will face a shift in emphasis for marketing research. Working with improved internal records, we may not have to go as often to questionnaires or focus groups to ask about intended consumer behavior. One customer said that it was disturbing to her that the bank knew more about her intended behavior (changing to a new bank) than she did.
- A third implication is the importance of speed that is required when dealing with transactional segmentation. There is only a brief window of opportunity. When dealing with this open window, we need computer detection models and a computer-based direct marketing system.

Finally, transactional segmentation requires a one-to-one marketing orientation that forces us to rethink our basic marketing philosophy. We must no longer think of segments as groups of individuals, each with a common characteristic or characteristics. We must think of changes in the transaction pattern of one customer and market directly to that individual customer.

Questions

1. What demographic data about individual consumers are companies most likely to have in their data bases? How would you apply these data in transactional segmentation?
2. Present a 5-point plan for a stock broker to institute demographically-driven transactional segmentation.
3. What consumer lifestyle factors should be studied when applying transactional segmentation? Why?
4. Is the concept of a component lifestyle a help or a hindrance to transactional segmentation? Discuss your answer.
5. Is it easier to use transactional segmentation with final consumers or organizational consumers? Explain your answer.
6. State which demand pattern (Figure 10-2) best lends itself to transactional segmentation.
7. Under what circumstances would transactional segmentation *not* be a good marketing approach?
8. As a consumer, would you accept the trade-offs mentioned in this case and embrace transactional segmentation? Why or why not?

Product Planning

To practice the marketing concept, a firm needs a systematic marketing plan. This plan centers on the four elements of the marketing mix: product, distribution, promotion, and price. We present these elements in Parts 4 to 7, with Part 4 concentrating on product planning.

11 Basic Concepts in Product Planning

Here, we define tangible, augmented, and generic products and distinguish among different types of consumer and industrial products (both goods and services). We look at product mix strategies, product management organizations, and product positioning in detail. The roles of branding and packaging in product planning are also covered. The chapter concludes with a look at the global dimensions of product planning.

12 Goods Versus Services Planning

In this chapter, we look at the scope of goods and services, and introduce a goods/services continuum. We review goods and services classification systems. Then, we study the special considerations in the marketing of services. We also see that service marketing has lagged behind goods marketing and why this is changing. At this point, our discussion turns to nonprofit marketing and its distinction from profit-oriented marketing. We examine how nonprofits can be classified and the role of nonprofit marketing in the economy.

13 Conceiving, Developing, and Managing Products

To conclude Part 4, we look at products from their inception to their deletion. We present the concept of the product life cycle. Then, we discuss types of new products, reasons for new-product failures, and the new-product planning process. We explain the growth of products in terms of the adoption and diffusion processes, and note several methods for extending the lives of mature products. We also offer product deletion strategies.

After reading Part 4, you should understand element 10 of the strategic marketing plan outlined in Table 3-2 (pages 72–75).

11

Basic Concepts in Product Planning

Chapter Objectives

1 To define product planning and differentiate among tangible, augmented, and generic products

2 To examine the various types of products, product mixes, and product management organization forms from which a firm may select

3 To discuss product positioning and its usefulness for marketers

4 To study branding and packaging, and their roles in product planning

5 To look at the global dimensions of product planning

Some marketing analysts say that it is difficult for firms with a very narrow product line to succeed due to the lack of related-item selling opportunities and the high marketing costs (based on their inability to allocate advertising and distribution expenses among multiple products). An exception to this rule is the Roto Zip Tool Corporation (www.rotozip.com) with its Spiral Saw. Currently, this one-product, privately-held company has annual sales of $120 million.

Like many innovations, Spiral Saw grew out of the founder's frustration in using traditional tools. Robert Kopras was upset that existing tools could not easily cut rectangular holes for electrical outlet boxes. So, he developed a tool that combined elements of an electric drill and a jig saw. After Kopras was unable to sell or license his tool to major tool companies, including Black & Decker, he decided to develop and patent it on his own. Eventually, the Spiral Saw was modified so that it could cut through Plexiglas, tile, aluminum, and marble. Attachments were later added so that the Spiral Saw could file down nails and even blow away sawdust. To protect the saw against potential competition, Roto Zip owns all of the patents that enable a bit to cut in a linear mode.

The Spiral Saw's major break came after Home Depot agreed to market the tool. Now, Home Depot carries the saw in every one of its more than 1,000 stores. As the retailer's global product merchandiser notes, "It's one of the top-selling tools in our tool center. I think Roto Zip's future is so bright because Bob [Kopras] is a user as well as a thinker, and he knows what people are looking for." Kopras was also quite successful in selling the Spiral Saw on the QVC television network. Although QVC may not be a consistent channel for any firm, $2.3 million of Spiral Saws have been sold through QVC on a single day.

Roto Zip recently bought a small British manufacturer of such tools as precision drills and mini-table saws. These products are to be marketed under the Roto Zip brand name and sold in the same retail outlets in the Unites States as the Spiral Saw. Robert Zopras hopes these new products will enable Roto Zip to expand its sales through mass merchants like Wal-Mart.[1]

In this chapter, we will look at several product planning decisions that a firm must make, including the choice of the depth and width of a product line.

11-1 OVERVIEW

Product planning is systematic decision making relating to all aspects of the development and management of a firm's products, including branding and packaging. Each *product* consists of a bundle of attributes (features, functions, benefits, and uses) capable of exchange or use, usually a mix of tangible and intangible forms. Thus, "a product may be

Product planning *means devising and managing* **products** *that satisfy consumers.*

[1]Kemp Powers, "Entrepreneurs: Upward Spiral," *Forbes* (August 7, 2000), pp. 104–106.

an idea, a physical entity, or a service, or any combination of the three. It exists for the purpose of exchange in satisfying individual and organizational objectives."[2]

A well-structured product plan lets a company pinpoint opportunities, develop appropriate marketing programs, coordinate a mix of products, maintain successful products as long as possible, reappraise faltering products, and delete undesirable products. A firm should define products in three distinct ways: tangible, augmented, and generic. By considering all three definitions, consumer needs, competitive offerings, and distinctive product attributes can be better identified. This is illustrated in Figure 11-1.

A *tangible product* is a basic physical entity, service, or idea; it has precise specifications and is sold under a given description or model number. Windows Me software (www.microsoft.com/windowsme), a Caterpillar diesel engine (www.cat.com/products), a seven-day Caribbean cruise on the Adventure of the Seas ship (www.rccl.com), and a proposal to cut state income taxes by 3.5 percent are examples of tangible products. Color, style, size, weight, durability, quality of construction, price, and efficiency in use are some tangible product features.

An *augmented product* includes not only the tangible elements of a product, but also the accompanying cluster of image and service features. For example, one political candidate may receive more votes than another because of charisma (augmented product), despite identical platform issues (tangible product). Rolex watches (www.rolex.com) are popular chiefly due to the image of luxury and status they convey. At Cummins Engine (www.cummins.com), offering augmented products means helping customers to succeed, not just selling them quality engines. Cummins uses a value-added package of products, information systems, and support services to enhance customer performance.

A *generic product* focuses on what a product means to the customer, not the seller. It is the broadest definition and is consistent with the marketing concept: "In the factory we make cosmetics, and in the drugstore we sell hope" (Charles Revson, founder of Revlon, www.revlon.com). "We know our customers come to us to buy more than bearings and steel. They come to us looking for solutions" (Timken Company, www.timken.com).

> *A tangible product has precise specifications; an augmented product includes image and service features; and a generic product centers on consumer benefits.*

FIGURE 11-1

Illustrating the Three Product Definitions

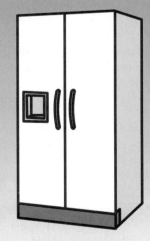

Tangible Product
- Color
- Design
- Quality
- Size
- Weight
- Features
- Materials used in construction
- Efficiency in use
- Power source
- Brand name

Augmented Product
- Image of product and brand
- Status of product and brand
- Guarantee/warranty
- Delivery
- Installation
- Repair facilities
- Instructions and technical advice
- Credit
- Return policy
- Follow-up service

Generic Product
- Stores, preserves, cools, and otherwise helps to satisfy home food-consumption needs

[2]Peter D. Bennett (Editor), *Dictionary of Marketing Terms*, Second Edition (Chicago: American Marketing Association, 1995), p. 219.

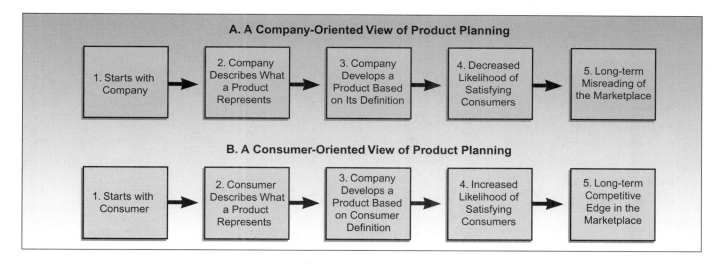

When applying the generic product concept, two points should be kept in mind.[3] First, because a generic product is a consumer view of what a product represents, a firm should learn what the product means to the consumer before further planning—as shown in Figure 11-2. Second, inasmuch as people in various nations may perceive the same product (such as a car) in different generic terms (such as basic transportation versus comfortable driving), a firm should consider the impact of this on a global strategy.

Chapter 11 provides an overview of product planning. It examines the areas in which a firm makes decisions: product type(s), product mix, product management organization, and product positioning. It also examines branding and packaging, and notes considerations for international marketers. Chapter 12 covers planning for goods versus services. Chapter 13 presents a discussion of how to manage products over their lives, from finding new product ideas to deleting faltering products.

11-2 TYPES OF PRODUCTS

The initial product-planning decision is choosing the type(s) of products to offer. Products can be categorized as goods or services and as consumer or industrial. Categorization is important because it focuses on the differences in the characteristics of products and the resulting marketing implications.

11-2a Fundamental Distinctions Between Goods and Services

Goods marketing entails the sale of physical products—such as furniture, heavy machinery, food, and stationery. *Service marketing* encompasses the rental of goods, servicing goods owned by consumers, and personal services—such as vehicle rentals, house painting, and accounting services.

Four attributes generally distinguish services from goods: intangibility, perishability, inseparability from the service provider, and variability in quality. Their impact is greatest for personal services—which are usually more intangible, more perishable, more dependent on the skills of the service provider (inseparability), and have more quality variations than rented- or owned-goods services.

The sales of goods and services are frequently connected. For instance, a computer manufacturer may provide—for an extra fee—extended warranties, customer training, insurance, and financing. In goods marketing, goods dominate the overall offering and services augment them. In service marketing, services dominate the overall offering and goods augment them.

FIGURE 11-2

Applying the Generic Product Concept

Source: Adapted by the authors from Leon G. Schiffman and Elaine Sherman, "Value Orientations of New-Age Elderly: The Coming of an Ageless Market," *Journal of Business Research*, Vol. 22 (March 1991), p. 193.

Goods marketing *relates to selling physical products.* **Service marketing** *includes rented-goods services, owned-goods services, and nongoods services.*

---

[3]See Daniel Doster and Eric Roegner, "Setting Pace with Solutions," *Marketing Management* (Spring 2000), pp. 51–54.

TABLE 11-1 Characteristics of Consumer Products

Consumer Characteristics	Type of Product		
	Convenience	**Shopping**	**Specialty**
Knowledge prior to purchase	High	Low	High
Effort expended to acquire product	Minimal	Moderate to high	As much as needed
Willingness to accept substitutes	High	Moderate	None
Frequency of purchase	High	Moderate or low	Varies
Information search	Low	High	Low
Major desire	Availability without effort	Comparison shopping to determine best choice	Brand loyalty regardless of price and availability
Examples	(a) Staple: cereal (b) Impulse: candy (c) Emergency: tire repair	(a) Attribute-based: name-brand clothes (b) Price-based: budget hotel	Hellmann's mayonnaise

The distinctions between goods and services planning are more fully discussed in Chapter 12.

11-2b Consumer Products

Consumer products *are final-consumer goods and services that may be categorized as convenience products, shopping products, and specialty products.*

Consumer products are goods and services destined for the final consumer for personal, family, or household use. The purpose of a good or service designates it as a consumer product. For example, a calculator, dinner at a restaurant, phone service, and an electric pencil sharpener are consumer products only if bought for personal, family, or household use. Consumer products may be classed as convenience, shopping, and specialty products—based on shoppers' awareness of alternative products and their characteristics prior to a shopping trip and the degree of search people will undertake. Thus, placing a product into one of these categories depends on shopper behavior. See Table 11-1.

Convenience products are those bought with a minimum of effort because a consumer has knowledge of product attributes prior to shopping and/or is pressed for time. The person does not want to search for much information and will accept a substitute, such as Libby's (www.senecafoods.com/website/products/Branded/libby.cfm) instead of Green Giant (www.greengiant.com) corn, rather than visit more than one store. Marketing tasks center on distribution at all available outlets, convenient store locations and hours, the use of mass advertising and in-store displays, well-designed store layouts, and self-service to minimize purchase time. Resellers often carry many brands.

Convenience products include staples, impulse products, and emergency products. Staples are low-priced and routinely purchased on a regular basis, such as detergent and cereal. Impulse products are items or brands a person does not plan to buy on a specific store trip, such as candy or a lottery ticket. About two-thirds of consumer brand decisions at supermarkets are made in the stores.[4] Emergency products are bought out of urgent need, such as an umbrella in a rainstorm and aspirin for a headache.

[4]Jennifer Lach, "Meet You in Aisle Three," *American Demographics* (April 1999), pp. 41–42.

Shopping products are those for which people feel they lack information about product alternatives and their attributes (or prices), and thus, must acquire more knowledge to make a purchase decision. People exert effort since these products are bought infrequently, are expensive, or require comparisons. The marketing emphasis is on full assortments (many colors, sizes, and options), the availability of sales personnel, the communication of competitive advantages, informative ads, well-known brands (or stores), distributor enthusiasm, and customer warranties and follow-up service to reduce perceived risk. Shopping centers and downtown business districts ease shopping behavior by having many adjacent stores.

Shopping products may be attribute- or price-based. With attribute-based products, consumers get information on features, performance, and other factors. The items with the best combination of attributes are bought. Sony electronics (www.sony.com) and Tommy Hilfiger clothes (www.tommy.com) are marketed as attribute-based shopping products. With price-based products, people feel the choices are rather similar and shop for low prices. Budget hotels and low-end electronics are marketed in this way.

Specialty products are particular brands, companies, and persons to which consumers are loyal. People are fully aware of these products and their attributes prior to making a purchase decision. They make a significant effort to acquire the brand desired and will pay an above-average price. They will not buy if their choice is unavailable: Substitutes are not acceptable. The marketing emphasis is on maintaining the attributes that make products unique to their loyal patrons, reminder ads, proper distribution (Hellmann's (www.hellmanns.com) mayonnaise and *Business Week* (www.businessweek.com) require different distribution to loyal customers: supermarkets versus home subscriptions), brand extension to related products (such as Hellmann's tartar sauce), product improvements, customer contact (such as opt-in E-mail from the Hilton HHonors program, www.hhonors.com), and monitoring reseller performance.

This classification is excellent for segmentation because many people may view the same products differently. For example, Tylenol pain reliever (www.tylenol.com) is a convenience product for some people (who will buy another brand if Tylenol is unavailable), a shopping product for others (who read ingredient labels), and a specialty product for others (who insist on Tylenol). Johnson & Johnson, maker of Tylenol, understands how Tylenol fits into the various categories and markets accordingly.

11-2c Industrial Products

Industrial products are goods and services purchased for use in the production of other goods or services, in the operation of a business, or for resale to other consumers. Customers are manufacturers, wholesalers, retailers, government entities, and other non-profit organizations.

Products may be grouped by the level of decision making in a purchase, costs, consumption rapidity, the role in production, and the change in form. Since industrial-products sellers often visit customers, stores are often not involved. Installations, accessory equipment, raw materials, component materials, fabricated parts, business supplies, and business services are types of industrial products. See Table 11-2.

Installations and *accessory equipment* are capital goods. They are used in the production process and do not become part of the final product. Installations are nonportable, involve considerable decision making (usually by upper-level executives), are expensive, last many years, and do not change form. Key marketing tasks are direct selling to the purchaser, negotiations on features and terms, having complementary services such as maintenance and repair, tailoring products to buyers' desires, and offering technical expertise and team selling (whereby various salespeople have different expertise). Examples are buildings, assembly lines, major equipment, large machine tools, and printing presses.

Industrial products *are organizational consumer goods and services that may be classified as installations, accessory equipment, raw materials, component materials, fabricated parts, industrial supplies, and industrial services.*

TABLE 11-2   Characteristics of Industrial Products

Characteristics	Type of Product						
	Installations	Accessory Equipment	Raw Materials	Component Materials	Fabricated Parts	Supplies	Services
Degree of consumer decision making	High	Moderate	Low	Low	Low	Very low	Low to high
Per-unit costs	High	Moderate	Low	Low	Low	Very low	Low to moderate
Rapidity of consumption	Very low	Low	High	High	High	High	Low to high
Item becomes part of final product	No	No	Sometimes	Yes	Yes	No	Sometimes
Item undergoes changes in form	No	No	Yes	Yes	No	No	Sometimes
Major consumer desire	Long-term facilities	Modern equipment	Continuous, low-cost, graded materials	Continuous, low-cost, specified materials	Continuous, low-cost, fabricated materials	Continuous, low-cost efficient supplies	Efficient, expert services
Examples	Production plant	Forklift truck	Coal	Steel	Thermostat	Light bulb	Machinery repair, accounting

Accessory equipment consists of movable goods that require moderate decision making, are less costly than installations, last many years, and do not become part of the final product or change form. The key marketing tasks are tying sales to those of installations; providing various choices in price, size, and capacity; having a strong distribution channel or sales force; stressing durability and efficiency; and having maintenance and technical support. Examples are drill presses, trucks, vans, and lathes.

Raw materials, *component materials*, and *fabricated parts* are used up in production or become part of final products. They are expense items. They require limited decision making, have low unit costs, and are rapidly consumed. Raw materials are unprocessed primary materials—such as minerals, coal, and crops. Component materials are semi-manufactured goods that undergo changes in form—such as steel, textiles, and basic chemicals. Fabricated parts are placed in products without changes in form—such as electric motors, thermostats, and microprocessors. Marketing tasks for materials and parts are to ensure consistent quality, continuity in shipments, and prompt delivery; pursue reorders; have fair prices; seek long-term contracts; use assertive distributors or sales personnel; and meet buyer specifications.

Industrial supplies are convenience goods used in a firm's daily operation. They can be maintenance supplies, such as light bulbs, cleaning materials, and paint; repair supplies, such as rivets, nuts, and bolts; or operating supplies, such as stationery, pens, and business cards. They require little decision making, are very low cost on a per-unit basis, are rapidly consumed, and do not become part of the finished product. Marketing emphasis is on availability, promptness, and ease of ordering.

Industrial services are maintenance and repair services, and business advisory services. Maintenance and repair services (janitorial services and machinery repair) usually involve little decision making, are rather inexpensive, and are consumed quickly. They may become part of a final product (keeping for-sale equipment in good working condition) or involve a change in form (janitorial services converting a dirty office into a clean one). The key marketing thrust is on consistent, efficient service at a reasonable price. Business advisory services (accounting and legal services) may involve a moderate to high level of decision making when first bought. Ongoing costs tend to be low to moderate, while benefits may be long-lasting. These services do not become part of the final product. The major marketing task is to have an image of expertise and convey reasons for clients to use the service.

11-3 ELEMENTS OF A PRODUCT MIX

After determining the type(s) of products to offer, a firm needs to outline the variety and assortment of those products. A **product item** is a specific model, brand, or size of a product that a company sells, such as a college principles of marketing course, a GMC Yukon XL sports utility vehicle (www.gmc.com), or the Sony CDRW33 CD Recorder (http://bpgprod.sel.sony.com). Usually a firm sells a group of closely related product items as part of a **product line.** In each product line, the items have some common characteristics, customers, and/or uses; they may also share technologies, distribution channels, prices, related services, and so on.[5] Avon (www.avoncompany.com/about/ourproducts) markets lipstick, eye makeup, and other cosmetics. Deere & Company (www.deere.com) makes several different tractor models. Atomic Dog (www.atomicdog.com) publishes various college textbooks on aspects of business and economics. Many local lawn-service firms offer mowing, landscaping, and tree-trimming services.

> A **product item** is a specific model; a **product line** has related items; a **product mix** is all a firm's lines.

A **product mix** consists of all the different product lines a firm offers. Heinz (www.heinz.com) markets ketchup, tuna fish, low-calorie foods, frozen french fries, soup, pet food, and other food products in more than 200 nations around the globe. Metropolitan Life Insurance Company (www.metlife.com) operates North America's largest life insurer (MetLife), and concentrates on insurance and related services. Tyco International (www.tycoint.com) is a global manufacturer with four product lines: telecommunications and electronics, fire and security, healthcare and specialty products, and flow control.

A product mix can be described in terms of its width, depth, and consistency. The *width of a product mix* is based on the number of different product lines a company offers. A wide mix lets a firm diversify products, appeal to different consumer needs, and encourage one-stop shopping. A narrow mix requires lower resource investments and does not call for expertise in different product categories.

The *depth of a product mix* is based on the number of product items within each product line. A deep mix can satisfy the needs of several consumer segments for the same product, maximize shelf-space, discourage competitors, cover a range of prices, and sustain dealer support. A shallow mix imposes lower costs for inventory, product alterations, and order processing; and there are no overlapping product items.

The *consistency of a product mix* is based on the relationship among product lines in terms of their sharing a common end-use, distribution outlets, consumer group(s), and price range. A consistent mix is generally easier to manage than an inconsistent one. It lets a firm focus on marketing and production expertise, create a strong image, and generate good distribution relations. Excessive consistency may leave a firm vulnerable to environmental threats, sales fluctuations, or less growth potential since emphasis is on a limited product assortment. Figure 11-3 shows product mix alternatives in terms of width and depth. Figure 11-4 highlights Colgate-Palmolive's product mix.

[5]Bennett, *Dictionary of Marketing Terms*, p. 222.

FIGURE 11-3
Product Mix Alternatives

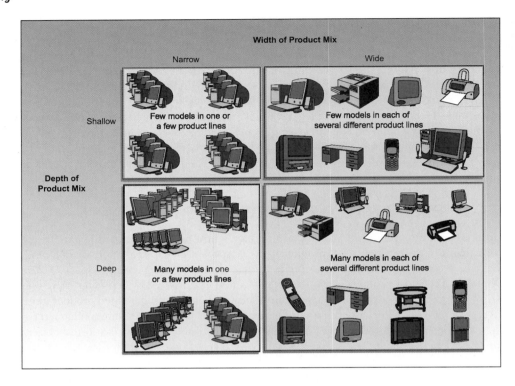

FIGURE 11-4
Colgate-Palmolive's Wide and Deep Product Mix

The company markets items in five product categories: oral care, personal care, household care, fabric care, and pet nutrition. Many of its well-known brands are displayed here.

Source: Reprinted by permission.

Product-mix decisions can have positive and negative effects, as these examples demonstrate:

- Wrigley (www.wrigley.com) concentrates on chewing gum and does not market even closely related items such as hard candies: "Our parent firm and its international associated companies make only one consumer product—quality chewing gum. In the United States, brands are Wrigley's Spearmint, Doublemint, Juicy Fruit, Big Red, Winterfresh, Eclipse sugar free gum, Extra sugar free gum, and Freedent nonstick gum. There are some other brands marketed outside the United States, such as P.K., Orbit, Excel, and Airwaves." Wrigley is so successful that it dominates the market with a 50 percent share of the U.S. gum market and annual total sales of $2.2 billion. It does business in 140 nations.[6]

- Canada's Bombardier Corporation (www.bombardier.com) is booming due to its diversification strategy. The firm began in the 1960s as the maker of Ski-Doo snowmobiles. It now makes aircraft for commuter airlines and corporate air fleets, railroad and subway cars, and Sea-Doo personal watercraft—as well as Ski-Doo snowmobiles: Its "mission is to be the leader in all the markets in which it operates." Annual revenues are nearly $10 billion today.[7]

- ConAgra Foods (www.conagra.com)—a firm with such brands as Armour meats, Butterball turkey, Jiffy Pop popcorn, and Wesson Oil—recently "underwent a major restructuring. Dubbed 'Operation Overdrive,' the program was designed to address problems the food goliath faced with its tangle of 10 operating units, roughly 68 retail brands, 45 foodservice brands, and a slew of food ingredients and agricultural products. The makeover included a financial restructuring, revamping sourcing strategies and production lines, and selling nonessential units such as a barge company and a wool company. The changes cleared the way for a focused mission heretofore inconceivable: to become America's favorite food company. The process by which ConAgra plans to achieve that mission includes the ability to create, re-create, and sharpen the promise of each of its brands."[8]

11-4 PRODUCT MANAGEMENT ORGANIZATIONS

A firm may select from among these organizational forms of product management: marketing manager, product manager, product planning committee, new-product manager, and venture team.[9] See Table 11-3.

Under a **marketing manager system,** an executive is responsible for overseeing a wide range of marketing functions (such as research, target marketing, planning existing and new products, distribution, promotion, pricing, and customer service) and for coordinating with other departments that do marketing-related activities (such as warehousing, order filling, shipping, credit, and purchasing). It works well for firms with a line of similar products or one dominant product line and for smaller firms that want centralized control of marketing tasks. It may be less successful if there are several product lines that require different marketing mixes—unless there are category marketing managers, each responsible for a broad product line. Pepsi-Cola North America (www.pepsico.com), Purex (www.purex.com), and Levi Strauss (www.levi.com) are among the firms that employed a marketing manager system at some point.

With a **product (brand) manager system,** there is a level of middle managers, each of whom is responsible for planning, coordinating, and monitoring a single product (brand) or a small group of products (brands). Managers handle both new and existing products and are involved with all marketing activities related to their product or product group. The

One person is directly in charge of a host of marketing tasks, including product planning, with a **marketing manager system.**

Middle managers handle new and existing products in a category in **the product (brand) manager system.**

[6]"Wm. Wrigley Jr. Co.," www.hoovers.com/co/capsule/8/0,2163,11648,00.html (April 6, 2001).

[7]"Bombardier Corporation," www.hoovers.com/co/capsule/1/0,2163,42381,00.html (April 6, 2001).

[8]Stephanie Thompson, "ConAgra Cooks Up Stronger Identity," *Advertising Age* (November 6, 2000), p. 42.

[9]The definitions in this section are drawn from Bennett, *Dictionary of Marketing Terms*, various pages.

| TABLE 11-3 | **Comparing Product Management Organizations** | | |

| | Characteristics | | |
Organization	**Staffing**	**Ideal Use**	**Permanency**
Marketing manager system	Key functional areas of marketing report directly to a senior marketer with a lot of authority.	A company makes one product line, has a dominant line, or uses broad category marketing managers.	The system is ongoing.
Product (brand) manager system	There is a layer of middle managers, with each focusing on a single product or a group of related products.	A company makes many distinct products, each requiring expertise.	The system is ongoing.
Product planning committee	Senior executives from various functional areas participate.	The committee should supplement another product organization.	The committee meets irregularly.
New-product manager system	Separate middle managers focus on new products and existing products.	A company makes several existing new products; and substantial time, resources, and expertise are needed for new products.	The system is ongoing, but new products are shifted to product managers after introduction.
Venture team	An independent group of company specialists guides all phases of a new product's development.	A company wants to create vastly different products than those currently offered, and needs an autonomous structure to aid development.	The team disbands after a new product is introduced, with responsibility going to a product manager.

*A **product planning committee** has top executives involved part-time.*

system lets all products or brands get adequate attention. It works well if there are many distinct products or brands, each needing marketing attention. It also has two potential weaknesses: lack of authority for the product manager and inadequate attention to new products. Procter & Gamble (www.pg.com), Nabisco (www.nabiscoworld.com), and Black & Decker (www.blackanddecker.com) are among the firms that have used product managers.

A ***product planning committee*** is staffed by high-level executives from various functional areas in a firm, such as marketing, production, engineering, finance, and research and development. It handles product approval, evaluation, and development on a part-time basis. Once a product is introduced, the committee usually turns to other opportunities and gives the item over to a product manager. This system lets management have input into decisions; but the committee meets irregularly and passes projects on to line managers. It is best as a supplement to other methods, and is used by many large and small firms.

*A **new-product manager system** has separate middle managers for new and existing products.*

A ***new-product manager system*** has product managers supervise existing products and new-product managers develop new ones. It ensures the time, resources, enthusiasm, and expertise for new-product planning. Once a product is introduced, it is given to the product manager who oversees existing products of that line (or brand). The system can be costly, incur conflicts, and cause discontinuity when an item is introduced. Kraft Foods (www.kraftfoods.com), General Electric (www.ge.com), and Johnson & Johnson (www.jnj.com) are among the firms that have used new-product managers.

A *venture team* is a small, independent department in a firm that has a broad range of specialists—drawn from that firm's marketing, finance, engineering, and other functional departments—who are involved with a specific new product's entire development process. Team members work on a full-time basis and act in a relatively autonomous manner. The team disbands when its new product is introduced, and the product is then managed within the firm's regular management structure. With a venture team, there are proper resources, a flexible environment, expertise, and continuity in new-product planning. It is valuable if a firm wants to be more far-sighted, reach out for truly new ideas, and foster creativity. It is also expensive to form and operate. Xerox (www.xerox.com), Polaroid (www.polaroid.com), Monsanto (www.monsanto.com), and 3M (www.3m.com) are among the firms that have used venture teams.

The correct organization depends on the diversity of a firm's offerings, the number of new products introduced, the level of innovativeness, company resources, management expertise, and other factors. A combination organization may be highly desirable; among larger firms, this is particularly common.

> A **venture team** *is an autonomous new-product department.*

11-5 PRODUCT POSITIONING

Critical to a firm's product-planning efforts is how the items in its product mix are perceived in the marketplace. The firm must work quite hard to make sure that each of its products is perceived as providing some combination of unique features (product differentiation) and that these features are desired by the target market (thereby converting product differentiation to a differential advantage).

When a product is new, a company must clearly communicate its attributes: What is it? What does it do? How is it better than the competition? Who should buy it? The goal is to have consumers perceive product attributes as the firm intends. When a product has an established niche in the market, a firm must regularly reinforce the image and communicate the reasons for its success. Once consumer perceptions are formed, they may be hard to alter. And it may also be tough later to change a product's niche in the market (for instance, from low price, low quality to high price, high quality).

Through *product positioning,* a firm can map each of its products in terms of consumer perceptions and desires, competition, other company products, and environmental changes. Consumer perceptions are the images of products, both a firm's and competitors', in people's minds. Consumer desires refer to the attributes that people would most like products to have—their *ideal points.* If a group of people has a distinctive "ideal" for a product category, that group is a potential market segment. A firm will do well if its products' attributes are perceived by consumers as being close to their ideal.

> **Product positioning** *maps out consumer perceptions of product attributes.* **Ideal points** *show the most preferred attributes.*

Competitive product positioning refers to people's perceptions of a firm relative to competitors. The goal is for the firm's products to be viewed as "more ideal" than those of competitors. *Company product positioning* shows a firm how consumers perceive that firm's different brands (items) within the same product line and the relationship of those brands (items) to each other. The goal is for each of the firm's brands to be positioned near an ideal point, yet not clustered near one another in the consumer's mind—the brands should appeal to different ideal points (market segments). A firm must monitor the environmental changes that may alter the way its products are perceived. Such changes could include new technology, changing consumer life-styles, new offerings by competitors, and negative publicity.

What Is an SUV— And Why Does It Matter?

According to newly-passed legislation, the federal government must come up with a new system to rank the risks of turnover in sport utilities. This new system will be based on road tests, unlike the previous test that was based on a mathematical formula. According to a senior vice-president at the Insurance Institute for Highway Safety, "This should give consumers pause, because they often think they're buying a car" when they purchase an SUV.

Based on the National Highway Traffic Safety Administration's proposed rollover score standards, popular SUVs, like recent-model Ford Explorers, Jeep Grand Cherokees, Chevrolet Suburbans, and Chevrolet Blazers would have only received 2 stars on a 5-star rating scale. Many of these SUVs meet lower safety standards because they are legally considered to be trucks, not cars. And many of these vehicles are specially modified four-wheel drive pickup trucks with 5-passenger bodies bolted onto a truck frame.

The new legislation comes at a time when SUVs are enjoying high popularity, outselling pickup trucks for the first time. Some analysts predict that SUVs will soon become the second-largest vehicle segment in the United States, just behind midsize cars.

To overcome customer resistance and to keep up sales, some car manufacturers have begun to market hybrid SUVs that have car designs. Others have developed stability control systems that use computer technology to help bring a spinning SUV back under control. As a group vice-president at Ford says, "We recognize that the sustained growth of SUVs depends on us addressing perceived environmental and safety disadvantages."

As a consumer affairs manager at Ford (www.ford.com), how would you address the ethical aspects of SUVs really being trucks, not cars as many consumers believe?

Source: Based on material in Joseph White and Jeffrey Ball, "Auto Makers' Definition of SUV Is Rapidly Changing," *Wall Street Journal* (October 13, 2000), p. B4.

Product positioning is illustrated in Figure 11-5, which depicts the U.S. auto marketplace in terms of the consumer desires regarding two key attributes: price and size. In this figure, there are nine ideal points (target markets)—I1 to I9, each associated with a specific type of car. Here is a brief description:

- *I1—full-size luxury cars.* Large cars typically priced at $40,000 and up. Cadillac Deville (www.cadillac.com/deville), Lincoln Continental (www.lincolnvehicles.com), and Infiniti Q45 (www.infiniti.com) are in this grouping.

- *I2—full-size cars.* Large cars typically priced at $20,000 to $30,000. Chevrolet Impala (www.chevrolet.com/impala), Buick Regal (www.buick.com/regal), and Mercury Grand Marquis (www.mercuryvehicles.com/vehicles/grandmarquis) are in this category.

- *I3—full-size economy cars.* Large cars typically priced at less than $20,000. There are currently no significant brands in this category selling in the United States.

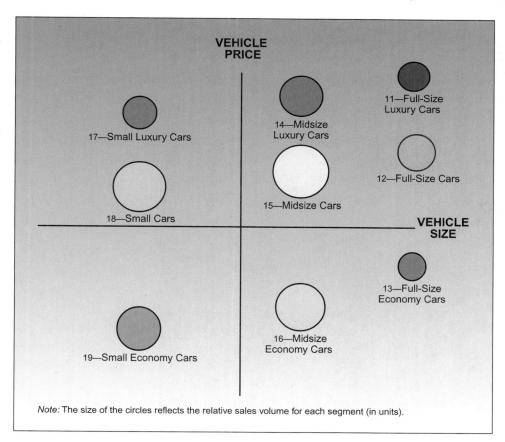

VEHICLE
PRICE

17—Small Luxury Cars

14—Midsize
Luxury Cars

11—Full-Size
Luxury Cars

18—Small Cars

15—Midsize Cars

12—Full-Size Cars

VEHICLE
SIZE

13—Full-Size
Economy Cars

19—Small Economy Cars

16—Midsize
Economy Cars

Note: The size of the circles reflects the relative sales volume for each segment (in units).

FIGURE 11-5

Product Positioning and the Auto Industry

Source: Figure developed by the authors based on data from www.wardsauto.com (April 27, 2001).

INTERACTIVE FIGURE

- *I4—midsize luxury cars.* Midsize cars typically priced at $30,000 and up. BMW 3 Series sedans (www.bmw.com/bmwe/products/automobiles/3er/sedan), Lexus ES 300 (www.lexus.com/showroom/model/es.html), and Cadillac Seville (www.cadillac.com/seville) are positioned here.

- *I5—midsize cars.* Midsize cars typically priced from $18,000 to $27,000. Toyota Camry (www.toyota.com/shop/vehicles/camry), Pontiac Grand Am GT sedan (www.pontiac.com/grandam), and Volkswagen Passat (www.volkswagen.com) fit here.

- *I6—midsize economy cars.* Midsize cars typically priced at less than $17,000. Hyundai Sonata (www.hyundaiusa.com), Saturn SL (www.saturnbp.com/sl), and Kia Sephia (www.kia.com/sephia) are in this grouping.

- *I7—small luxury cars.* Small cars typically priced at $30,000 and up. Cadillac Catera (www.cadillac.com/catera), BMW Z3 (www.bmw.com/bmwe/products/automobiles/z3), and Porsche Boxter (www.us.porsche.com/english/boxster) are in this category.

- *I8—small cars.* Small cars typically priced between $15,000 and $22,000. Volkswagen New Beetle (www.vw.com/newbeetle), Chevrolet Cavalier (www.chevrolet.com/cavalier), and Dodge Neon (www.4adodge.com/neon) are positioned here.

- *I9—small economy cars.* Small cars typically priced at less than $15,000. Hyundai Accent (www.hyundaiusa.com), Saturn SC1 coupe (www.saturnbp.com/sc1), and Kia Spectra (www.kia.com/spectra) are grouped here.

An examination of competitive product positioning reveals that there are competing products in each market niche except for I3 (full-size economy cars). In some instances, the marketplace is saturated. Nonetheless, the companies in the industry have generally done a good job in addressing the needs of the various consumer segments and in differentiating the products offered to each segment.

From an analysis of company product positioning, it is clear that General Motors (www.gm.com) serves eight of the identified market segments. The Cadillac Deville, Chevrolet Impala, Buick Regal, Cadillac Seville, Pontiac Grand Am GT sedan, Saturn SL, Cadillac Catera, Chevrolet Cavalier, and Saturn SC1 coupe are all marketed by General Motors. However, it must continue to differentiate carefully among its various brands to avoid confusion and a "fuzzy" perception by consumers.

By undertaking product-positioning analysis, a company can learn a great deal and plan its marketing efforts accordingly, as these two examples show:

- "Meet the Soft Scrub family (www.clorox.com/products/ssgrp.html), where the number one priority is solving the toughest cleaning problems without harming surfaces. You can count on Soft Scrub cleansers to remove tough stains in the bathroom and kitchen, on sinks, tubs, stovetops, appliances, and counters. It is tough on kitchen grease, bathroom soil, mildew stains, and soap scum. *Soft Scrub Regular* is a mild abrasive and versatile multipurpose cleanser that gently cleans tough dirt in the bathroom and kitchen. *Soft Scrub with Clorox Bleach* is a tough stain remover with a new antibacterial formula. It removes greasy dirt, mold and mildew, and soap scum and kills 99.9 percent of household germs. Use it on tubs and tiles, sinks and stove tops, toilets and countertops. *Soft Scrub with Lemon* cuts tough grease without harsh scratching. It uses real lemon every time you clean your kitchen. *Soft Scrub Gel* gives you the power of Clorox bleach in a versatile, easy-to-rinse formula. The penetrating gel removes tough stains and rinses clean."[10] See Figure 11-6.

[10]"Meet the Soft Scrub Family," www.clorox.com/products/ssgrp.html (April 9, 2001).

- Michelin (www.michelin.com) is renowned for the quality of its tires and a concern for consumer safety: "For more than a century, Michelin has remained loyal to the dual aim of its founders: product quality and quality of service to the customer." The company's positioning is reinforced by its popular Michelin Man icon (also known as Bibendum), which was recognized in a 2000 competition sponsored the *Financial Times* (www.ft.com). "This was a great achievement for a genuine star, born in France a little more than 100 years ago, and a well-earned recognition for the Group's 130,000 employees worldwide. For, if Bibendum is so well-known and loved, he also owes it to the performance, safety, and enjoyment provided by Michelin's tires and other products. As human like as ever, Bibendum has constantly evolved to suit the times. He still keeps the same friendly, jovial attitude, welcoming and eager to please."[11] See Figure 11-7.

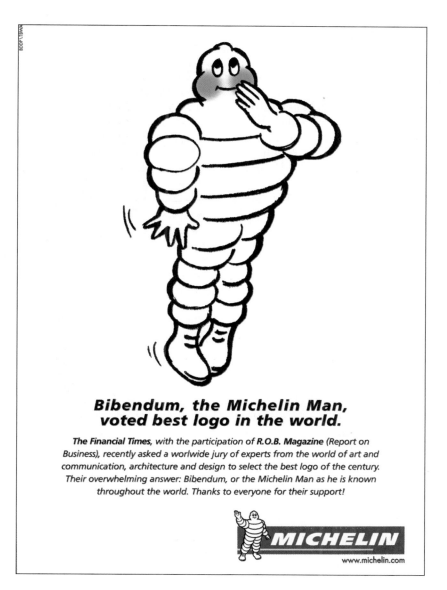

FIGURE 11-7
The Positioning Power of the Michelin Man

Source: Reprinted by permission of the Michelin Group.

[11]"Michelin History," http://michelinsh.webmichelin.com/groupe/about/eng/p113.htm (April 16, 2001).

11-6 BRANDING

Brands identify a firm's products.

Another key aspect of product planning is branding, the way a firm researches, develops, and implements its brands. A *brand* is a name, term, design, symbol, or any other feature that identifies the goods and services of a seller or group of sellers. There are four types of brand designation:

Branding involves **brand names, brand marks, trade characters,** *and* **trademarks.**

1. A *brand name* is a word, letter (number), group of words, or letters (numbers) that can be spoken. Examples are Magnavox, Windows 2000, and Lipton Cup-a-Soup.
2. A *brand mark* is a symbol, design, or distinctive coloring or lettering that cannot be spoken. Examples are Lexus' stylized L crest, Ralston Purina's checkerboard, and Prudential's rock.
3. A *trade character* is a brand mark that is personified. Examples are Qantas Airlines' koala bear, McDonald's Ronald McDonald, and the Pillsbury Doughboy.
4. A *trademark* is a brand name, brand mark, or trade character or combination thereof that is given legal protection. When used, a registered trademark is followed by ®, such as Scotch Brand® tape.

Brand names, brand marks, and trade characters do not offer legal protection against use by competitors, unless registered as trademarks (which all of the preceding examples have been). Trademarks ensure exclusivity for their owners or those securing permission, and provide legal remedies against firms using "confusingly similar" names, designs, or symbols. They are discussed more fully later in the chapter.

Worldwide, there are millions of brand names in circulation. Each year, the top hundred U.S. advertisers spend more than $80 billion advertising their brands. Permanent media expenditures (such as company logos, stationery, brochures, business forms and cards, and vehicular and building signs) for brands are another large marketing cost.

A key goal of firms is to develop brand loyalty, which allows them to maximize sales and maintain a strong brand image. As one expert noted: "If a *product* is something that is produced to function and exist in reality, then a *brand* has meaning beyond functionality and exists in people' minds. Part art, part science, a brand is the difference between a bottle of soda and a bottle of Coke, the intangible yet visceral impact of a person's subjective experience with the product—the personal memories and cultural associations that orbit around it." [12]

Some brands do so well that they gain "power" status—they are well known and highly esteemed. According to one study of 2,500 brands, the world's ten most valuable brands are (in order) Coca-Cola, Microsoft Windows, IBM, Intel, Nokia, General Electric, Ford, Disney, McDonald's, and AT&T. Brand rankings do differ by region. In Great Britain, six of the top ten brands are domestic; the other four are from the United States—McDonald's, Kellogg's Corn Flakes, Coca-Cola, and Nike. [13] The use of popular brands can also speed up public acceptance and gain reseller cooperation for new products.

Gaining and maintaining brand recognition is often a top priority for all kinds of firms. As an example, the four leading U.S. TV networks (ABC, CBS, Fox, and NBC) "are facing increasing competition and are very conscious of the need to get their brands out there. As more choices are given to consumers, networks have to make sure their viewers understand who they are and what they offer. That can mean anything from a logo subtly popping up in the corner of the viewer's TV screen to a major cross-promotion with some big-name packaged goods marketers." [14]

---

[12] Noah Hawley, "Brand Defined," *Business 2.0* (June 27, 2000), p. 131.

[13] Interbrand, "The World's Most Valuable Brands," *Business 2.0* (November 28, 2000), p. 155; and WPP Group's Millard Brown unit, "How Brands Stack Up," *Advertising Age* (October 5, 1998), p. 66.

[14] Cyndee Miller, "Stay Tuned for TV Networks as Brands," *Marketing News* (October 9, 1995), pp. 1, 10.

In recent years, a branding concept that more concretely recognizes brands' worth has emerged. It is known as **brand equity** and measures the "the amount of additional income expected from a branded product over and above what might be expected from an identical, but unbranded product."[15] As one research company noted:

> There are many different definitions of brand equity, but they do have several factors in common: *Monetary Value*. Grocery stores frequently sell unbranded versions of name-brand products. The branded and unbranded products are made by the same companies, but they carry a generic brand or store brand label like Kroger's or Albertson's. Store brands sell for much less than name-brand counterparts, even when the contents are identical. This price differential is the monetary value of a brand name. *Intangible*. Nike has created many intangible benefits for its products by associating them with star athletes. Children and adults want to wear Nike products to feel some association with these athletes. It is not the physical features that drive demand for Nike products, but the marketing image that has been created. Buyers will pay high price premiums over lesser-known brands which may offer the same, or better, product quality and features. *Perceived Quality*. Mercedes and BMW have established their brands as synonymous with high-quality, luxurious autos. Years of marketing, image building, brand nurturing, and quality manufacturing have led consumers to assume a high level of quality in everything these firms produce. Consumers are likely to perceive Mercedes and BMW as providing superior quality to other brands, even when such a perception is unwarranted. [16]

Brand equity represents a brand's worth.

These reasons summarize why branding is important:

- Product identification is eased. A customer can order a product by name instead of description.

- Customers are assured that a good or service has a certain level of quality and that they will obtain comparable quality if the same brand is reordered.

- The firm responsible for the product is known. Unbranded items cannot be as directly identified.

- Price comparisons are reduced when customers perceive distinct brands. This is most likely if special attributes are linked to different brands.

- A firm can advertise (position) its products and associate each brand and its characteristics in the buyer's mind. This aids the consumer in forming a *brand image*, which is the perception a person has of a particular brand.

- Branding helps segment markets by creating tailored images. By using two or more brands, multiple market segments can be attracted.

- For socially-visible goods and services, a product's prestige is enhanced via a strong brand name.

- People feel less risk when buying a brand with which they are familiar and for which they have a favorable attitude. This is why brand loyalty occurs.

- Cooperation from resellers is greater for well-known brands. A strong brand also may let its producer exert more control in the distribution channel.

- A brand may help sell an entire line of products, such as Kellogg cereals.

- A brand may help enter a new product category, like Reese's peanut butter.

- "Ultimately, the power of a brand lies in the minds of consumers, in what they have experienced and learned about the brand over time. Consumer knowledge is really at the heart of brand equity." [17]

Branding creates identities, assures quality, and performs other functions. Brand images are perceptions that consumers have of particular brands.

There are four branding decisions a firm must undertake as to corporate symbols, the branding philosophy, choosing a brand name, and using trademarks. See Figure 11-8.

---

[15]"Understanding Brand Equity," www.dssresearch.com/library/BrandEquity/understanding.asp (April 9, 2001).
[16]Ibid.
[17]Kevin Lane Keller, "The Brand Report Card," *Harvard Business Review,* Vol. 78 (January–February 2000), p. 157.

FIGURE 11-8
Branding Decisions

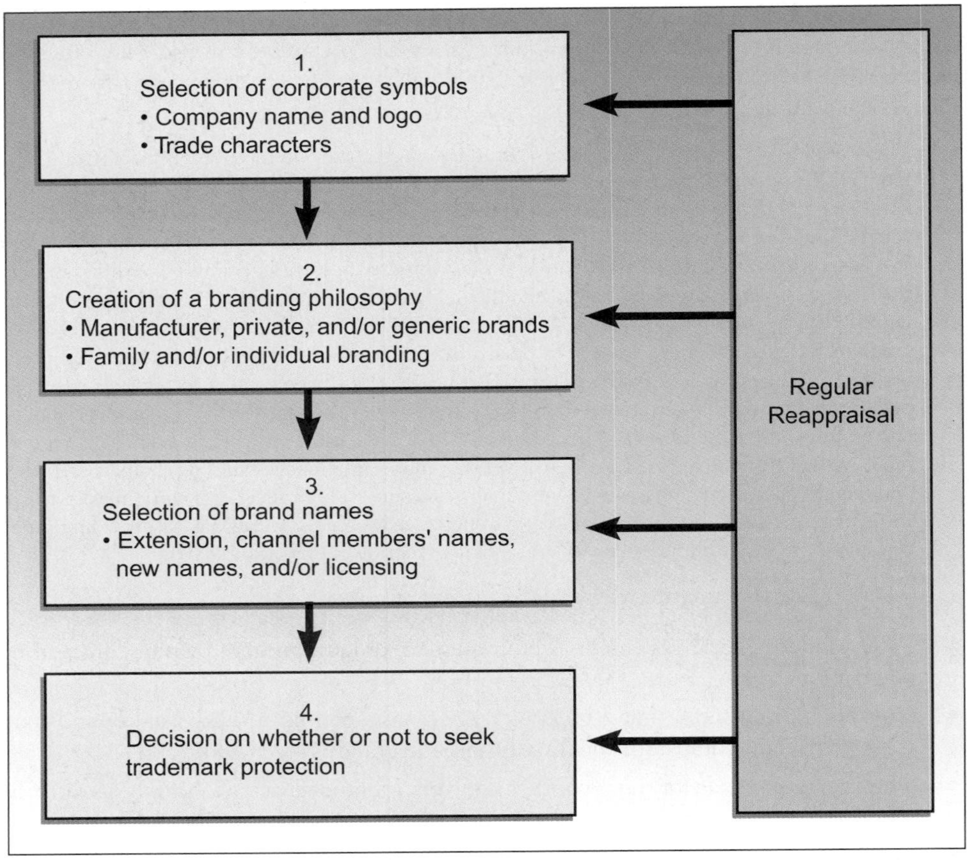

```
┌─────────────────────────────┐        ┌──────────┐
│ 1.                          │◄───────│          │
│ Selection of corporate      │        │          │
│ symbols                     │        │          │
│ • Company name and logo     │        │          │
│ • Trade characters          │        │          │
└─────────────────────────────┘        │          │
            │                          │          │
            ▼                          │          │
┌─────────────────────────────┐        │          │
│ 2.                          │◄───────│          │
│ Creation of a branding      │        │          │
│ philosophy                  │        │ Regular  │
│ • Manufacturer, private,    │        │ Reappraisal│
│   and/or generic brands     │        │          │
│ • Family and/or individual  │        │          │
│   branding                  │        │          │
└─────────────────────────────┘        │          │
            │                          │          │
            ▼                          │          │
┌─────────────────────────────┐        │          │
│ 3.                          │◄───────│          │
│ Selection of brand names    │        │          │
│ • Extension, channel        │        │          │
│   members' names,           │        │          │
│   new names, and/or         │        │          │
│   licensing                 │        │          │
└─────────────────────────────┘        │          │
            │                          │          │
            ▼                          │          │
┌─────────────────────────────┐        │          │
│ 4.                          │◄───────│          │
│ Decision on whether or not  │        │          │
│ to seek trademark protection│        │          │
└─────────────────────────────┘        └──────────┘
```

11-6a Corporate Symbols

Corporate symbols help establish a companywide image.

Corporate symbols are a firm's name (and/or divisional names), logos, and trade characters. They are key parts of the overall image. When a firm begins a business; merges with another company; reduces or expands product lines; seeks new geographic markets; or finds its name to be unwieldy, nondistinctive, or confusing, it should assess and possibly change its symbols. Here are examples of each situation.

PeopleSoft (www.peoplesoft.com) is a leading producer of software and services for collaborative enterprises. Its software enables organizations to optimize interactions with customers, employees, and suppliers to create more loyal, collaborative, and profitable relationships. When the firm was founded, it looked for a company name that would reflect its business orientation. "'The overall theory was that we build software for people to use,' says Heidi Melin, vice-president in marketing. 'SoftPeople doesn't work; Software for People is too long, so we came up with PeopleSoft.' Great. And those capital letters? 'We felt it was unique, and more visually entertaining. But there was no bigger intent behind it.'"[18]

Due to mergers, Burroughs and Sperry are now Unisys (www.unisys.com), Switzerland's UBS and the United States' PaineWebber are now UBS PaineWebber (www.ubspainewebber.com), and AOL and Time Warner are now AOL Time Warner (www.aoltimewarner.com).

Because the nature of its business changed, International Harvester is now Navistar International (www.navistar.com), after selling its farm equipment business, and General

[18]David A Gaffen, "Creative Names Mean Everything," www.thestreet.com/comment/easymoney/906101.html (March 25, 2000).

Shoe Corporation is Genesco (www.genesco.com), a diversified retailer. When Andersen Consulting was spun off from Andersen Worldwide, it changed its name to Accenture (www.accenture.com).

As it expanded into new market areas, Allegheny Airlines was renamed US Air (www.usair.com); the old name suggested a small regional airline. The Exxon (www.exxon.com) name was developed because the firm's regional brands, including Esso and Humble, could not be used nationwide, and other brands had unfortunate foreign connotations (for example, Enco means "stalled car" in Japanese).

The National Railroad Passenger Corporation was an unwieldy name; it became Amtrak (www.amtrak.com). Federal Express now promotes the FedEx name (www.fedex.com), since it is easier to say. United Telecommunications converted its nondistinctive name to Sprint (www.sprint.com), in recognition of its leading brand. The upscale Holiday Inn Crowne Plaza hotels were changed to the Crowne Plaza (www.sixcontinentshotels.com/crowneplaza) to avoid confusion with the middle-class Holiday Inn name.

Developing and maintaining corporate symbols are not easy. When Nissan (www.nissandriven.com) changed the name of its U.S. car division from Datsun to Nissan (to have a global brand), sales fell, despite a major ad campaign. It took years for the Nissan name to reach the level of awareness that Datsun had attained. Along the way, Nissan had clashes with dealers not wanting the name change.

11-6b Branding Philosophy

In preparing a brand strategy, a firm needs to determine its branding philosophy. This outlines the use of manufacturer, private, and/or generic brands, as well as the use of family and/or individual branding.

Manufacturer, Private, and Generic Brands[19]

Manufacturer brands use the names of their makers. They generate the vast majority of U.S. revenues for most product categories, including 85 percent of food, all autos, 75 percent of major appliances, and more than 80 percent of gasoline. They appeal to a wide range of people who desire good quality, routine purchases, status, convenience, and low risk of poor product performance. The brands are often well known and trusted because quality control is strictly maintained. They are identifiable and present distinctive images. Producers may have a number of product alternatives under their brands.

> **Manufacturer brands** *are well known and heavily promoted.*

Manufacturers have better channel control over their own brands, which may be sold through many competing intermediaries. Yet, individual resellers can have lower investments if the brands' pre-sold nature makes turnover high—and if manufacturers spend large sums promoting their brands and sponsor cooperative ads with resellers (so costs are shared). Prices are the highest of the three brands, with the bulk going to the manufacturer (which also has the greatest profit). The marketing goal is to attract and retain loyal consumers for these brands, and for their makers to direct the marketing effort for the brands.

Private (dealer) brands use names designated by their resellers, usually wholesalers or retailers—including service providers. They account for sizable U.S. revenues in many categories, such as 50 percent of shoes, one-third of tires, 14 percent of food items, and one-quarter of major appliances. Unit market shares are higher. Private brands account for 20 percent of unit sales in supermarkets. Firms such as The Limited, Inc. (www.limited.com) and McDonald's (www.mcdonalds.com) derive most revenues from their own brands. Private-brand foods are more popular in Europe than in the United States.

> **Private (dealer) brands** *enable channel members to get loyal customers.*

[19]See Roper Starch, "Store Brands and National Brands Share Space in the Shopping Cart," www.roper.com/Newsroom/content/news60.htm (April 6, 2001); Kusum L. Ailawadi, Scott A. Neslin, and Karen Gedenk, "Pursuing the Value-Conscious Consumer: Store Brands Versus National Brand Promotions," *Journal of Marketing,* Vol. 65 (January 2001), pp. 71–89; and John A. Quelch and David Harding, "Brands Versus Private Labels," *Harvard Business Review,* Vol. 74 (January-February 1996), pp. 99–109.

They generate 30 percent of revenues in British food stores and one-quarter in French and German ones.

Private brands appeal to price-conscious people who buy them if they feel the brands offer good quality at a lower price. They accept some risk as to quality, but reseller loyalty causes the people to see the brands as reliable. Private brands often have similar quality to manufacturer brands, with less emphasis on packaging. At times, they are made to dealer specifications. Assortments are smaller and the brands are unknown to people not shopping with a given reseller. Resellers have more exclusive rights for these brands, and are more responsible for distribution and larger purchases. Inventory turnover may be lower than for manufacturer brands; and promotion and pricing are the reseller's job. Due to lower per-unit packaging and promotion costs, resellers can sell private brands at lower prices and still have better per-unit profits (due to their higher share of the selling price). The marketing goal is to attract people who become loyal to the reseller and for that firm to exert control over marketing. Large resellers advertise their brands widely. Some private brands, such as Sears' Kenmore brand (www.kenmore.com), are as popular as manufacturer brands; and firms like Sherwin-Williams (www.sherwin-williams.com) are both manufacturers and retailers. Even the discounter Costco (www.costco.com), which features manufacturer brands, has a very popular private brand known as Kirkland. See Figure 11-9.

Generic brands emphasize the names of the products themselves and not manufacturer or reseller names. They started in the drug industry as low-cost alternatives to expensive manufacturer brands. Today, generics have expanded into cigarettes, batteries, motor oil, and other products. Forty-two percent of U.S. prescriptions are filled with generics; but, due to their low prices, this is only 8 percent of prescription-drug revenues. Although 85 percent of U.S. supermarkets stock generics, they account for less than 1 percent of supermarket revenues. Generics appeal to price-conscious, careful shoppers, who perceive them as being a very good value, are sometimes willing to accept lower quality, and often purchase for large families or large organizations.

> **Generic brands** *are low-priced items with little advertising.*

FIGURE 11-9
Kirkland from Costco: Private Branding Enhances Store Loyalty

Source: Reprinted by permission of PricewaterhouseCoopers.

GLOBAL *Marketing in Action*

Generic Brands Come to Brazil

After a long period when brand-name drugs dominated the Brazilian market, generic medicines are now starting to take off there. Among the firms seeking to capitalize on the increased popularity of generics are BioTeva (a joint venture of Teva, an Israeli firm that is the world's largest generic drug manufacturer, and Laboratórios Biosintética, www.biosintetica.com.br, a local pharmaceutical manufacturer) and EMS-Sigma Pharma, www.ems.com.br (which has a joint venture with Aphotex, a Canadian generic pharmaceutical manufacturer).

Brazil's first generic drugs appeared at the beginning of 2000 after the Brazilian Congress passed legislation allowing pharmaceutical manufacturers to make generic equivalents for all drugs that had been marketed in Brazil prior to 1996. As of November 2000, there were about 70 generic products available to Brazilians—with 190 generic drugs approved for sale.

The Brazilian Ministry of Health expects sales of generics to reach $2 billion in 2005, up from $150 million in 2000. Brazil is one of the largest consumers of medicines (behind the United States, Japan, Germany, and France), even though half of its population cannot afford brand name prescription drugs.

Generic drug sales already account for about 3 percent of sales at the third largest drugstore chain in Brazil, and some industry analysts predict that the overall market share for generics will increase to 30 percent over the next five years. The commercial director of one drugstore chain says, "It is a trend that is irreversible. Our policy is to push generics." The president of EMS-Sigma Pharma adds, "It is the customer who will notice the cheaper product and go to the doctor and ask about generics."

As the marketing director of a Brazilian-based generic manufacturer, develop a marketing strategy to increase sales of generic drugs there.

Source: Based on material in Jennifer L. Rich, "Explosion of Generics About to Occur in Brazil." *New York Times on the Web* (November 23, 2000).

Generics are seldom advertised and receive poor shelf locations; consumers must search out these brands. Prices are less than other brands by 10 to 50 percent, due to quality, packaging, assortment, distribution, and promotion economies. The major marketing goal is to offer low-priced, lower-quality items to consumers interested in price savings. Table 11-4 compares the three types of brands.

Many companies—including service firms—use a ***mixed-brand strategy,*** thereby selling both manufacturer and private brands (and maybe generic brands). This benefits manufacturers and resellers: There is control over the brand bearing each seller's name. Exclusive rights to a brand can be gained. Multiple segments may be targeted. Brand and dealer loyalty are fostered, shelf locations coordinated, cooperation in the distribution channel improved, and assortments raised. Production is stabilized and excess capacity used. Sales are maximized and profits fairly shared. Planning is better. In Japan, Kodak (www.kodak.com) markets its own brand of film and COOP private-brand film (for the 2,500-store Japanese Consumer Cooperative Union, www.co-op.or.jp/jccu/English_here). It is trying to make a dent in Fuji's large percent share of the Japanese market. Kodak does not market private-brand film in the United States.

> A **mixed-brand strategy** *combines brand types.*

TABLE 11-4 — Manufacturer, Private, and Generic Brands

Characteristic	Manufacturer Brand	Private Brand	Generic Brand
Target market	Risk avoider, quality conscious, brand loyal, status conscious, quick shopper	Price conscious, comparison shopper, quality conscious, moderate risk taker, dealer loyal	Price conscious, careful shopper, willing to accept lower quality, large family or organization
Product	Well known, trusted, best quality control, clearly identifiable, deep product line	Same overall quality as manufacturer, less emphasis on packaging, less assortment, not known to nonshoppers of the dealer	Usually less overall quality than manufacturer, little emphasis on packaging, very limited assortment, not well known
Distribution	Often sold at many competing dealers	Usually only available from a particular dealer in the area	Varies
Promotion	Manufacturer-sponsored ads, cooperative ads	Dealer-sponsored ads	Few ads, secondary shelf space
Price	Highest, usually suggested by manufacturer	Moderate, usually controlled by dealer	Lowest, usually controlled by dealer
Marketing focus	To generate brand loyalty and manufacturer control	To generate dealer loyalty and control	To offer a low-priced, lesser-quality item to those desiring it

*In the **battle of the brands,** the three brand types compete.*

Manufacturer, private, and generic brands also repeatedly engage in a **battle of the brands,** in which each strives to gain a greater share of the consumer's dollar, control over marketing strategy, consumer loyalty, product distinctiveness, maximum shelf space and locations, and a large share of profits. In recent years, this battle has intensified.

Family and Multiple Branding

Family (blanket) branding *uses a single name for many products.*

In *family (blanket) branding,* one name is used for two or more individual products. Many firms selling industrial goods and services such as Boeing (www.boeing.com) and Airborne Express (www.airborne.com), as well as those selling consumer services such as Teléfonos de México (www.telmex.com.mx), use some form of family branding for all or most of their products. Other companies employ a family brand for each category of products. For example, Sears has Kenmore appliances (www.kenmore.com) and Craftsman tools (www.craftsman.com). Family branding can be applied to both manufacturer and private brands, and to both domestic and international (global) brands.

Family branding is best for specialized firms or ones with narrow product lines. Companies capitalize on a uniform, well-known image and promote a name regularly—keeping promotion costs down. The major disadvantages are that differentiated marketing opportunities may be low (if only one brand is used to target all customers), company image may be adversely affected if vastly different products (such as men's and women's cologne) carry one name, and innovativeness may not be projected to consumers.

Brand extension *gains quick acceptance.*

Brand extension, whereby an established name is applied to new products, is an effective use of family branding. Quick customer acceptance may be gained since people are familiar with existing products having the same name, a favorable brand image can be carried over to a new product, and the risk of a failure is less. Brand extension may have a negative effect if people do not see some link between the original product and a new one. Most new products now use some form of brand extension.

These are situations in which brand extension could be effective:

- Same product in a different form—example, Jell-O Pudding Pops.
- Distinctive taste/ingredient/component in a new item—example, Arm & Hammer detergent.
- New companion product—example, Colgate Plus toothbrush.
- Same customer franchise for a new product (a different product offered to the same target market)—example, Visa traveler's checks aimed at Visa credit-card customers.
- Expertise conveyed to new product—example, Canon laser-jet printers.
- Benefit/attribute/feature conveyed to new product—example, Ivory shampoo (connoting mildness).
- Designer image/status conveyed to new item—example, Pierre Cardin sunglasses.[20]

With *individual (multiple) branding,* separate brands are used for different items or product lines sold by a firm. For example, in Procter & Gamble's (www.pg.com) wide and deep North American product mix are eight brands of laundry detergent: Bold, Cheer, Dreft, Era, Febreze, Gain, Ivory, and Tide. This enables Procter & Gamble to dominate the business with more than a 50 percent share of the market.

> **Individual (multiple) branding** *uses distinct brands.*

Individual branding enables a firm to create multiple product positions (separate brand images), attract various market segments, increase sales and marketing control, and offer both premium and low-priced brands. It also lets manufacturers secure greater shelf space in retail stores. However, each brand requires a promotion budget, and there is no positive brand image rub-off. Economies from mass production may be lessened. New products may not benefit from an established identity. And there may be some cannibalization among company brands. Consumer products firms are more likely than industrial products firms to engage in individual branding.

To gain the benefits of family and individual branding, many firms combine the two. A firm could have a flagship brand and other secondary brands: One-third of Heinz's products (www.heinz.com) use the Heinz name; the rest have names like StarKist and Ore-Ida. A family brand could be used with individual brands: At Honda, upscale Acura (www.acura.com) and mainstream Honda (www.honda.com) are the two auto lines. The Honda line includes the Honda Accord, Honda Civic, and Honda Prelude. It has an overall image and targets a specific market. New models gain from the Honda name, and there is a relationship among models. Individual brands are used with each model to highlight differences.

11-6c Choosing a Brand Name

There are several potential sources when a firm chooses brand names:

1. Under brand extension, an existing name is used with a new product (*Sports Illustrated for Kids,* www.sikids.com).

2. For a private brand, the reseller specifies the name (St. John's Bay—an apparel brand of J.C. Penney, www.jcpenney.com).

3. If a new name is sought, these alternatives are available:
   a. Initials (HBO, www.hbo.com).
   b. Invented name (Kleenex, www.kleenex.com).
   c. Numbers (Century 21, www.century21.com).
   d. Mythological character (Samsonite luggage, www.samsonite.com).

> *Brand sources range from existing names to* **licensing agreements** *and* **co-branding.**

---

[20]Edward M. Tauber, "Brand Leverage: Strategy for Growth in a Cost-Controlled World," *Journal of Advertising Research,* Vol. 28 (August–September 1988), pp. 26–30. See also David A. Aaker and Erich Joachimsthaler, "The Brand Relationship Spectrum: The Key to Brand Architecture Challenge," *California Management Review,* Vol. 42 (Summer 2000), pp. 8–23.

    e.   Personal name (Heineken, www.heineken.com).

    f.   Geographical name (Air France, www.airfrance.com).

    g.   Dictionary word (Scope mouthwash, www.scope-mouthwash.com).

    h.   Foreign word (Nestlé, www.nestle.com).

    i.   Combination of words, initials, numbers, etc. (Head & Shoulders shampoo, www.headandshoulders.com).

4. With a *licensing agreement,* a company pays a fee to use a name or logo whose trademark rights are held by another firm. Due to the high consumer recognition of many popular trademarks, sales for a product may be raised by paying a royalty fee to use one. Examples of names used in licensing are Coca-Cola, Dallas Cowboys, and George Foreman. Salton Inc. sells $200 million worth of George Foreman grills (www.salton-maxim.com/salton/grill) each year. Overall, licensing generates a total of $80 billion in U.S. retail sales alone each year.

5. In *co-branding,* two or more brand names are used with the same product to gain from the brand images of each. Typically, a company uses one of its own brand names in conjunction with another firm's—often, via a licensing agreement. For instance, there are the GM MasterCard (www.gmcard.com), the Lorus Mickey Mouse watches (www.iwearlorus.com), and the special edition RugRats Kraft Macaroni & Cheese (www.kraftfoods.com/thecheesiest). See Figure 11-10.

A good brand name has several attributes, depending on the situation: It suggests something about a product's use or attributes (Cleanwipes moist cleansing tissues, www.benchtm.com/pc/pc-prescribe-cleanwipes.htm). It is easy to spell and remember and is pronounceable in only one way (Bic, www.bicworld.com). It can be applied to a whole line of products (Deere tractors, www.deere.com). It is capable of legal protection from use by others (Perrier, www.perrierusa.com). It has a pleasant or at least neutral meaning internationally (Onvia—the business-to-business marketplace, www.onvia.com). It conveys a differential advantage (Pert Plus, www.pertplus.com).

As firms expand globally, branding takes on special significance. Regardless of whether brands are "global" or tailored to particular markets, their meanings must not have negative connotations or violate cultural taboos. To make sure that this does not happen, such specialized firms as Namestormers (www.namestormers.com) can devise names for clients that are acceptable around the world. But outside of the leading power brands, which firms may want to make into global brands, brands often must reflect the cultural and societal diversity in the way products are positioned and used in different nations.

FIGURE 11-10

Co-Branding for Macaroni and Cheese

Source: Reprinted by permission of PricewaterhouseCoopers.

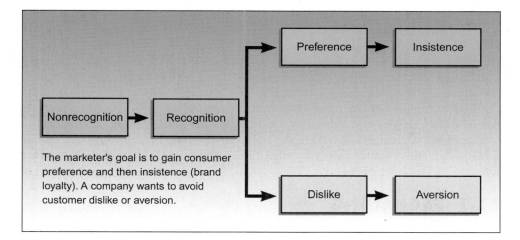

FIGURE 11-11
The Consumer's Brand Decision Process

The **consumer's brand decision process** *moves from nonrecognition to insistence (or aversion).*

When branding, a firm should plan for the stages in the ***consumer's brand decision process,*** as shown in Figure 11-11. For a new brand, a consumer begins with nonrecognition of the name; the seller must make the person aware of it. He or she then moves to recognition, where the brand and its attributes are known; the seller stresses persuasion. Next, the person develops a preference (or dislike) for a brand and buys it (or opts not to buy); the seller's task is to gain brand loyalty. Last, some people show a brand insistence (or aversion) and become loyal (or never buy); the seller's role is to maintain loyalty. Often times, people form preferences toward several brands but do not buy or insist upon one brand exclusively.

By using brand extension, a new product would begin at the recognition, preference, or insistence stage of the brand decision process because of the carryover effect of the established name. However, consumers who dislike the existing product line would be unlikely to try a new product under the same name, but they might try another company product under a different brand.

11-6d The Use of Trademarks

Finally, a firm must decide whether to seek trademark protection. In the United States, it would do so under either the federal Lanham Act (updated by the Trademark Law Revision Act) or state law. A trademark gives a firm the exclusive use of a word, name, symbol, combination of letters or numbers, or other devices—such as distinctive packaging—to identify the goods and services of that firm and distinguish them from others for as long as they are marketed. Both trademarks (for goods) and service marks (for services) are covered by trademark law; and there are 150,000 U.S. filings each year through the U.S. Patent and Trademark Office (www.uspto.gov/web/menu/tm.html).

Trademarks are voluntary and require registration and implementation procedures that can be time-consuming and expensive (challenging a competitor may mean high legal fees and years in court). A global firm must register trademarks in every nation in which it operates; even then, trademark rights may not be enforceable. To be legally protected, a trademark must have a distinct meaning that does not describe an entire product category, be used in interstate commerce (for federal protection), not be confusingly similar to other trademarks, and not imply attributes a product does not have. A surname by itself cannot be registered because any person can generally do business under his or her name; it can be registered if used to describe a specific business (such as McDonald's restaurants). The U.S. Supreme Court has ruled that the color of a product can gain trademark protection, as long as it achieves "secondary meaning," whereby the color distinguishes a particular brand and indicates its "source."

When brands become too popular or descriptive of a product category, they risk becoming public property and losing trademark protection. Brands working hard to remain exclusive trademarks include L'eggs (www.leggs.com), Rollerblade (www.rollerblade.com), Formica (www.formica.com), and Teflon (www.dupont.com/teflon). Former trademarks now considered generic—thus, public property—are cellophane, aspirin, shredded wheat, cola, linoleum, and lite beer.

DuPont has used careful research to retain a trademark for Teflon. Company surveys have showed that most people identify Teflon as a brand name. On the other hand, the U.S. Supreme Court ruled that *Monopoly* was a generic term that could be used by any game maker; and a federal court ruled that Miller could not trademark the single word Lite for its lower-calorie beer.

11-7 PACKAGING

*A **package** involves decisions as to a product's physical container, label, and inserts.*

Packaging is the part of product planning where a firm researches, designs, and produces package(s). A ***package*** is a container used to protect, promote, transport, and/or identify a product. It may consist of a product's physical container, an outer label, and/or inserts. The physical container may be a cardboard, metal, plastic, or wooden box; a cellophane, waxpaper, or cloth wrapper; a glass, aluminum, or plastic jar or can; a paper bag; styrofoam; some other material; or a combination of these. Products may have more than one container: Cereal is individually packaged in small boxes, with inner waxpaper wrapping, and shipped in large corrugated boxes; watches are usually covered with cloth linings and shipped in plastic boxes. The label indicates a product's brand name, the company logo, ingredients, promotional messages, inventory codes, and/or instructions for use. Inserts are (1) instructions and safety information placed in drug, toy, and other packages or (2) coupons, prizes, or recipe booklets. They are used as appropriate.

About 10 percent of a typical product's final selling price goes for its packaging. The amount is higher for such products as cosmetics (as much as 40 percent or more). The complete package redesign of a major product might cost millions of dollars for machinery and production. Packaging decisions must serve both resellers and consumers. Plans are often made in conjunction with production, logistics, and legal personnel. Errors in packaging can be costly.

Package redesign may occur when a firm's current packaging receives a poor response from channel members and customers or becomes too expensive; the firm seeks a new market segment, reformulates a product, or changes or updates its product positioning; or new technology is available. For instance,

> When Beverly Seckinger and Lee Buford started their gourmet cheese snack company, they always carried tins to sales calls to the Ritz-Carlton, Saks, and Neiman-Marcus. As annual sales reached $2 million, the partners heard complaints about their somewhat stark packages and hired a design firm. They needed a softer look, a color scheme to match stores' other gift items, and a picture of the product on the package to cultivate product identity. They got all that. The new packaging also included an 800 number through which callers could find local retailers that carried the products. Seckinger-Lee spent $250,000—about 12 percent of sales—on the packaging process. Previously, the firm spent only 5 percent of revenues on sales and marketing yearly. But the new look paid off. At the Fancy Food trade shows in Atlanta and New York City, the firm booked 50 percent more orders than at the prior year's shows. A buyer from Macy's decided to put the product in the New York store after almost 10 years of courting, citing the new packaging as the reason.[21] [Today, Seckinger-Lee is a prominent part of the Byrd Cookie Company (www.byrdcookiecompany.com).]

The functions of packaging, factors considered when making packaging decisions, and criticisms of packaging are described next.

[21]Sarah Schafer, "When It's Time for a Makeover," *Inc.* (December 1995), p. 118.

11-7a Basic Packaging Functions

The basic *packaging functions* are containment and protection, usage, communication, segmentation, channel cooperation, and new-product planning:

- *Containment and protection*—Packaging enables liquid, granular, and other divisible products to be contained in a given quantity and form. It protects a product while it is shipped, stored, and handled.

- *Usage*—Packaging lets a product be easily used and re-stored. It may even be reusable after a product is depleted. Packaging must also be safe for all, from a young child to a senior.

- *Communication*—Packaging communicates a brand image, provides ingredients and directions, and displays the product. It is a major promotion tool.

- *Segmentation*—Packaging can be tailor-made for a specific market group. If a firm offers two or more package shapes, sizes, colors, or designs, it may employ differentiated marketing.

- *Channel cooperation*—Packaging can address wholesaler and retailer needs with regard to shipping, storing, promotion, and so on.

- *New-product planning*—New packaging can be a key innovation for a firm and stimulate sales.

11-7b Factors Considered in Packaging Decisions

Several factors must be weighed in making packaging decisions.

Because package design affects the image a firm seeks for its products, the color, shape, and material all influence consumer perceptions. Thus, "After 115 years, Listerine Antiseptic changed from glass to plastic in its most popular bottle sizes, as well as redesigned the classic barbell-shaped package that signified amber mouthwash—and 'medicine-y' taste to generations of consumers. The product inside is the same. We wanted to modernize it from the package in your grandmother's medicine cabinet."[22]

In family packaging, a firm uses a common element on each package in a product line. It parallels family branding. Campbell (www.campbellsoup.com) has virtually identical packages for its traditional soups, distinguished only by flavor or content identification. American Home Products (www.ahp.com), maker of Advil and Anacin pain medicine, does not use family packaging with these brands; they have distinct packages to lure different segments.

A global firm must decide if a standardized package can be used worldwide (with only a language change on the label). Standardization boosts global recognition. Thus, Coke and Pepsi have standard packages when possible. Yet, some colors, symbols, and shapes have negative meanings in some nations. For example, white can mean purity or mourning, two vastly different images. As shown in Figure 11-12, Tide detergent (www.tide.com) has different packaging in Shanghai, China, than in the United States.

Package costs must be considered on both a total and per-unit basis. As noted earlier, total costs can run into the millions of dollars, and per-unit costs can go as high as 40 percent or more of a product's price—depending on the purpose and extent of packaging.

A firm has many packaging materials from which to select, such as paperboard, plastic, metal, glass, styrofoam, and cellophane. In the choice, trade-offs are probably needed: Cellophane allows products to be attractively displayed, but it is highly susceptible to tearing; paperboard is relatively inexpensive, but it is hard to open. A firm must also decide how innovative it wants its packaging to be. Aseptic packaging (for milk and juice boxes) allows beverages to be stored in special boxes without refrigeration. They are more popular in Europe than in the United States. Figure 11-13 displays some of the innovative packaging from Sonoco (www.sonoco.com).

---

[22]Glenn Collins, "New Looks for 2 Staples of the Medicine Cabinet," *New York Times* (July 19, 1994), p. D4.

FIGURE 11-12
Nonstandardized Packaging for Tide

Tide packaging adapts to the markets in which it is sold. In Shanghai, China, it is sold in tough plastic bags and labeled in Chinese.

Source: Reprinted by permission of PricewaterhouseCoopers.

FIGURE 11-13
Innovative Packaging from Sonoco

Sonoco's consumer packaging operations are known around the world for innovative packaging solutions. These products include composite canisters, plastic tennis ball containers, capseals, plastic and fiber caulk cartridges, carry-out plastic bags for supermarkets and high-volume retail stores, plastic produce roll bags, agricultural film, pressure-sensitive labels, promotional coupons, screen process printing for vending machine graphics, screen printing for fleet graphics, flexible packaging, specialty folding cartons, coasters, and glass covers.

Source: Reprinted by permission.

What size(s), color(s), and shape(s) are used?

There is a wide range of package features from which to choose, depending on the product. These features include pour spouts, hinged lids, screw-on tops, pop-tops, see-through bags, tuck- or seal-end cartons, carry handles, product testers (for items like batteries), and freshness dating. They may provide a firm with a differential advantage.

A firm has to select the specific sizes, colors, and shapes of its packages. In picking a package size, shelf life (how long a product stays fresh), convenience, tradition, and competition must be considered. In the food industry, new and larger sizes have captured high sales. The choice of package color depends on the image sought. Mello Yello (www.2.coca-cola.com/about/whatwedo/brands_melloyello.html), a citrus soft drink by Coca-Cola, has a label with bright orange and green lettering on a lemon-yellow background. Package shape also affects a product's image. Hanes created a mystique for L'eggs pantyhose (www.leggs.com) via the egg-shaped package. The number of packages used with any one product depends on competition and the firm's use of differentiated marketing. By selling small, medium, and large sizes, a firm may ensure maximum shelf space, appeal to different consumers, and make it difficult and expensive for a new company to gain channel access.

The placement, content, size, and prominence of the label must be set. Both company and brand names (if appropriate) need to appear on the label. The existence of package inserts and other useful information (some required by law) should be noted on the label. Sometimes, a redesigned label may be confusing to customers and hurt a product's sales.

Multiple packaging couples two or more product items in one container. It may involve the same product (such as razor blades) or combine different ones (such as a first-aid kit). The goal is to increase usage (hoarding may be a problem), get people to buy an assortment of items, or have people try a new item (such as a new toothpaste packaged with an established toothbrush brand). Many multiple packs, like cereal, are versatile—they can be sold as shipped or broken into single units.

Individually wrapping portions of a divisible product may offer a competitive advantage. It may also be costly. Kraft (www.kraftfoods.com) has done well with its individually wrapped cheese slices. Alka-Seltzer (www.alka-seltzer.com) sells tablets in individually wrapped tin-foil containers, as well as in a bottle without wrapping.

Should items be individually wrapped?

For certain items (such as shirts, magazines, watches, and candy), some resellers may want pre-printed prices. They then have the option of charging those prices or adhering their own labels. Other resellers prefer only a space for the price on the package and insert their own price labels automatically. Because of the growing use of computer technology by resellers in monitoring their inventory levels, more of them are insisting on pre-marked inventory codes on packages. The National Retail Federation (www.nrf.com) endorses the Universal Product Code (www.uc-council.org) as the voluntary vendor marking standard in the United States.

With the ***Universal Product Code (UPC),*** manufacturers pre-mark items with a series of thick and thin vertical lines. Price and inventory data bar codes are represented by these lines, which appear on outer package labels but are not readable by employees and customers. Lines are "read" by computerized scanning equipment at the checkout counter; the cashier does not have to ring up a transaction manually and inventory data are instantly transmitted to the main computer of the retailer (or manufacturer). In the UPC system, human-readable prices must still be marked, either by the manufacturer or the reseller.

Should a package have a pre-printed price and use the **Universal Product Code (UPC)?**

Last, a firm must be sure the package design fits in with the rest of its marketing mix. A well-known perfume may be extravagantly packaged, distributed in select stores, advertised in upscale magazines, and sold at a high price. In contrast, a firm making perfumes that imitate leading brands has more basic packages, distributes in discount stores, does not advertise, and uses low prices. The two brands may cost an identical amount to make, but the imitator would spend only a fraction as much on packaging.

How does the package interrelate with other marketing variables?

At its Web site, ChamberBiz (www.chamberbiz.com) has a very good discussion about package design, including its relationship with brand positioning, the use of graphics, and reflecting target market values. In the tool bar at the left of the screen, go to "Expand Your Business" and click on "Sales/Marketing." Then, scroll down to "Packaging and pricing your product."

11-7c Criticisms of Packaging

The packaging practices of some industries and firms have been heavily criticized and regulated due to their impact (or potential impact) on the environment and scarce resources, the high expenditures on packaging, questions about the honesty of labels and the confusion caused by inconsistent designations of package sizes (such as large, family, super), and critics' perceptions of inadequate package safety.

Packaging is faulted for waste, misleading labels, etc.

Yet, consumers—as well as business—must bear part of the responsibility for the negative results of packaging. Throwaway bottles (highly preferred by consumers) use almost three times the energy of returnable ones. Shoplifting annually adds to packaging costs because firms must add security tags and otherwise alter packages.

In planning their packaging programs, firms need to weigh the short-term and long-term benefits and costs of providing environmentally safer ("green"), less confusing, and more tamper-resistant packages. Generally, firms are responding quite positively to the criticisms raised here. These issues were examined further in Chapter 5.

MARKETING *and the Web*

New Uses for Bar Codes

Even though the UPC bar code on packages has long been used by retailers to capture point-of-sale data, Web firms such as BarPoint.com (www.barpoint.com) have expanded the use of the bar code to include information for consumers. For example, consumers with Verizon cellular phones can now click on the BarPoint.com icon and then key in a music CD's bar code. The bar code information, unique to each CD, enables a consumer to secure additional information such as other CDs by the same artist, short reviews of CDs, and price quotes from online stores.

This is how BarPoint.com works:

Users can access BarPoint's product information data base, as well as product information from our Mobile Merchant partners, from a desktop Web site or from wireless devices such as cellular phones, personal digital assistants, and interactive pagers. By partnering with such industry leaders as Symbol Technologies, AT&T Wireless, Cingular, Sprint, Verizon, Nextel, Palm, and more, BarPoint has ensured its service is device-agnostic, making valuable information available on all mobile devices. Shoppers can then make educated decisions when they need to most — at the point of purchase. BarPoint's search is simple: just enter or scan in a unique identifier such as UPC, SKU, or Catalog #, etc., and targeted results make it the ideal search technology for all hand-held devices.

Source: Based on material at www.barpoint.com (July 12, 2002).

11-8 THE GLOBAL DIMENSIONS OF PRODUCT PLANNING

Several factors should be considered with international product planning.

When a product plan is being devised, such points as these should be kept in mind with regard to international marketing:

- Although a firm may offer the same products in countries around the globe, these products can have distinct generic meanings in different countries.
- In developing and less-developed countries, product "frills" are often less important than in industrialized countries.
- Due to their intangibility, perishability, inseparability, and variability, the international marketing efforts for services are often more complex than those on behalf of goods.
- The concept of convenience, shopping, and specialty products is less valid in markets where distribution is limited or consumers have few choices.
- Installations and accessory equipment may be hard to ship overseas.
- Marketing all of the items in a wide and/or deep product mix may not be appropriate or economically feasible on a global basis.
- The diversity of international markets may necessitate a decentralized product management organization, with some executives permanently assigned to foreign countries.

- For many products, there are differences in product positioning and consumer ideal points by country or region. Simple positioning messages travel better than more complicated ones.

- Some products are in different stages of their life cycles in developing and less-developed countries than in industrialized countries.

- Expectations about goods/services combinations (discussed in the next chapter) may differ by nation.

- A product modification or minor innovation in a home market may be a major innovation internationally, necessitating different marketing approaches.

- The characteristics of the market segments—innovators, early adopters, early majority, late majority, and laggards—in the diffusion process (covered in Chapter 13) often differ by country.

- Even though global branding and packaging may be desirable, various nations may have special needs or requirements.

WEB SITES YOU CAN USE

There are a number of Web sites that provide expert advice on how to properly position company products and brands in the consumer's mind. Here is a sampling of them:

"Positioning" from About.com
(www.marketing.about.com/cs/positioning)

"Position Your Product" from It's Only Marketing
(www.onlymarketing.com/position.htm)

"Brand Positioning" from Strategic Marketing and Research Techniques (www.s-m-a-r-t.com/Exp_brandpos.htm)

SUMMARY

1. *To define product planning and differentiate among tangible, augmented, and generic products* Product planning allows a firm to pinpoint opportunities, develop marketing programs, coordinate a product mix, maintain successful products, reappraise faltering ones, and delete undesirable products.

A tangible product is a basic physical entity, service, or idea with precise specifications that is offered under a given description or model. An augmented product includes tangible elements and the accompanying image and service features. A generic product focuses on the benefits a buyer desires; this concept looks at what a product means to the consumer rather than the seller.

2. *To examine the various types of products, product mixes, and product management organization forms from which a firm may select* Goods marketing entails physical products. Service marketing includes goods rental, servicing consumer-owned goods, and personal services. Goods and services often differ in intangibility, perishability, inseparability from the provider, and variability in quality.

Consumer products can be classified as convenience, shopping, and specialty items – on the basis of consumer awareness of alter-

natives prior to the shopping trip and the degree of search and time spent shopping. Industrial products are installations, accessory equipment, raw materials, component materials, fabricated parts, business supplies, and business services. They are distinguished on the basis of decision making, costs, consumption, the role in production, and the change in form.

A product item is a model, brand, or size of a product sold by a firm. A product line is a group of closely related items sold by a firm. A product mix consists of all the different product lines a firm offers. Width, depth, and consistency of a product mix are important.

A firm may choose from or combine several product management structures, including marketing manager system, product (brand) manager, product planning committee, new-product manager system, and venture team. Each has particular strengths and best uses.

3. *To discuss product positioning and its usefulness for marketers* A firm must ensure that each of its products is perceived as providing some combination of unique features and that they are desired by the target market. In product positioning, a firm can map its offerings with regard to consumer perceptions, consumer desires, competition, its own products in the same line, and the changing environment. Competitive positioning, company positioning, and consumers' ideal points are key.

4. *To study branding and packaging, and their roles in product planning* Branding is the procedure a firm follows in planning and marketing its brand(s). A brand is a name, term, design, or symbol (or a combination) that identifies a good or service. A brand name is a word, letter (number), or group of words or letters (numbers) that can be spoken. A brand mark is a symbol, design, or distinctive coloring or lettering. A trade character is a personified brand mark. A trademark is a brand name, brand mark, or trade character given legal protection.

There are millions of brand names in circulation worldwide. Ad spending on them is many billions of dollars annually. Through strong brands, brand loyalty can be secured. Popular brands also speed up the acceptance of new products. Gaining and keeping brand recognition is a top priority, as are the development of brand equity and a brand image. Branding benefits all parties: manufacturers, distribution intermediaries, and consumers.

Four primary decisions are necessary in branding. First, corporate symbols are determined and, if applicable, revised. Second, a branding philosophy is set, which includes the proper use of manufacturer, private, and/or generic brands, as well as family and/or individual branding. At this stage, a mixed-brand strategy, the bat-

tle of the brands, and brand extension (a popular approach) are also assessed. Third, a brand name is chosen from one of several sources, including brand extension from existing names, private brands, licensing a name from another firm, and co-branding. With a new brand, the consumer's brand decision process moves from non-recognition to recognition to preference (dislike) to insistence (aversion). Fourth, the use of trademarks is evaluated and planned.

Packaging is the procedure a firm follows in planning and marketing product package(s). A package has a physical container, label, and/or inserts. Ten percent of a typical product's final selling price goes for packaging. There are six basic packaging functions: containment and protection, usage, communication, market segmentation, channel cooperation, and new-product planning.

Packaging decisions involve image; family packaging; standardization; package costs; packaging materials and innovativeness; package features; package size, color, and shape; the label and package inserts; multiple packaging; individual wrapping; pre-printed prices and inventory codes (such as the UPC); and integration with the marketing plan. Packaging has been criticized on the basis of environmental, safety, and other issues.

5. *To look at the global dimensions of product planning* If a firm intends to market products internationally, it should be kept in mind the distinctive generic meanings of products in different nations and the complexity of marketing services in foreign markets.

KEY TERMS

product planning (p. 323)
product (p. 323)
goods marketing (p. 325)
service marketing (p. 325)
consumer products (p. 326)
industrial products (p. 327)
product item (p. 329)
product line (p. 329)
product mix (p. 329)
marketing manager system (p. 331)
product (brand) manager system (p. 331)
product planning committee (p. 332)
new-product manager system (p. 332)

venture team (p. 333)
product positioning (p. 333)
ideal points (p. 333)
brand (p. 338)
brand name (p. 338)
brand mark (p. 338)
trade character (p. 338)
trademark (p. 338)
brand equity (p. 339)
corporate symbols (p. 340)
manufacturer brands (p. 341)
private (dealer) brands (p. 341)
generic brands (p. 342)

mixed-brand strategy (p. 343)
battle of the brands (p. 344)
family (blanket) branding (p. 344)
brand extension (p. 344)
individual (multiple) branding (p. 345)
licensing agreement (p. 346)
co-branding (p. 346)
consumer's brand decision process (p. 347)
package (p. 348)
packaging functions (p. 349)
Universal Product Code (UPC) (p. 351)

REVIEW QUESTIONS

1. Why is it so important to understand the concept of a generic product?
2. Distinguish between a consumer product and an industrial product.
3. How can the same product be a convenience, shopping, *and* specialty product? What does this mean to marketers?
4. Under what circumstances is a product manager system appropriate? A new-product manager system?

5. What is the role of product positioning for a new product? A continuing product?
6. Why do manufacturer brands have such a large percentage of sales in so many product categories? Will private and generic brands eventually displace manufacturer brands? Explain your answer.
7. What are the three components of a package?
8. Describe the six major functions of packaging. Give an example of each.

DISCUSSION QUESTIONS

1. For each of the following, describe the tangible, augmented, and generic product:
   a. A review course for the Graduate Management Aptitude Test (GMAT).
   b. A high-definition television.
   c. Highway paving materials.
2. What product positioning would you recommend for a small firm that makes, installs, and services home security systems? Explain your answer.
3. Present two successful and two unsuccessful examples of brand extension. Discuss why brand extension worked or did not work in these cases.
4. Evaluate the recent package redesigns of three products. Base your analysis on several specific concepts covered in this chapter.

WEB EXERCISE

The Product Development & Management Association (PDMA) is the leading trade association in product management. Visit the PDMA Web site (www.pdma.org) and then answer these questions:

(1) What is the PDMA and what are its goals? (2) What can a reader learn from *Visions* magazine? Give a couple of specific examples. (3) What other useful information is at the PDMA Web site?

12

Goods Versus Services Planning

1 To examine the scope of goods and services, and explain how goods and services may be categorized

2 To discuss the special considerations in the marketing of services

3 To look at the use of marketing by goods versus services firms and provide illustrations of service marketing

4 To distinguish between nonprofit and profit-oriented marketing

5 To describe a classification system for nonprofit marketing, the role of nonprofit marketing in the economy, and applications of nonprofit marketing

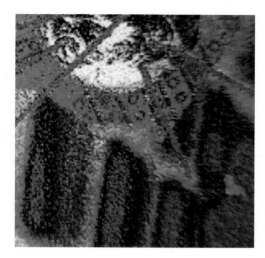

Business is booming for many high-tech consultants who make house calls to resolve computer software or hardware problems. According to Media Metrix (www.mediametrix.com), a marketing research firm, 60 million homes in the United States now have a computer. And as the number of computer users grows, so does the number of program crashes, computer viruses, and lost data.

Users of in-home service providers find them especially useful due to their "bag of tricks" in getting systems back to life, their fast service, and their convenience. As John Greenleaf, the founder of a computer consulting firm says, "Most of our work is crisis management." One of the more unusual calls that Greenleaf received was from a client whose computer monitor had gone blank. After going through a number of obvious questions with the client, such as "Is the computer plugged in? Is the monitor turned off?", Greenleaf offered to visit the client's home. "I have to admit, it wasn't all that hard taking the money [for a one-hour service call] after I plugged the computer back in."

Hal Kooistra says that his job involves equal parts sleuthing and psychology: "First you play 20 questions, being careful to keep the questions unaccusing while you gather information." Then, little by little, he may discover that after spilling a little water on the computer, his client turned the computer on. As a consequence, the client short-circuited everything.

Some computer technicians divide their customers into three groups: obsessive-compulsives, overeager, and lost generation. The *obsessive-compulsives* tend to be overly cautious about making even small cosmetic changes to their computers. As a result, technicians have to be especially meticulous about memorizing how the shortcuts and files were arranged. *Overeager* types want the latest technology even though they may not need it or know how to work it. They often want new software and hardware installed as soon as it is marketed. The *lost generation* typically consists of executives over 50 who exhibit varying degrees of technophobia. For example, the lost generation user would have no idea what the message "Abort program" means or what to do.[1]

In this chapter, we will study key concepts pertaining to the marketing of services. We will focus on the differences and similarities between goods and services marketing.

12-1 OVERVIEW

When devising and enacting product plans, a firm must fully comprehend the distinctions between goods and services—beyond the brief coverage in Chapter 11. Although the planning process is the same for goods and services, their differences need to be reflected by the decisions made in the process.

---

[1]Leah Rosch, "Computer Consultants Who Make House Calls," *New York Times On the Web* (December 21, 2000).

Chapter 12 covers the scope of goods and services, a goods/services continuum, goods and services classifications, special considerations in service marketing, and the use of marketing by goods and services firms. Also included is information on nonprofit marketing because most nonprofits (such as colleges, health facilities, and libraries) are involved with services.

12-2 THE SCOPE OF GOODS AND SERVICES

Goods marketing *involves the sale of* **durable** *and* **nondurable goods.**

Goods marketing entails the sale of physical products. **Durable goods** are physical products that are used over an extended period of time, such as furniture and heavy machinery. **Nondurable goods** are physical products made from materials other than metals, hard plastics, and wood; they are rather quickly consumed or worn out; or they become dated, unfashionable, or otherwise unpopular. Examples are food and office supplies.

Service marketing *covers* **rented-goods, owned-goods,** *and* **nongoods services.**

Service marketing includes the rental of goods, the alteration or maintenance/repair of goods owned by consumers, and personal services. **Rented-goods services** involve the leasing of goods (such as autos, hotel rooms, office buildings, and tuxedos) for a specified period of time. **Owned-goods services** involve alterations or maintenance/repairs of goods owned by consumers. These services include house painting, clothing alterations, lawn care, equipment maintenance, and machinery repair. **Nongoods services** involve personal service on the part of the seller, such as accounting, legal, consulting, and tutoring services; they do not involve goods.

Overall, the value of manufacturers' shipments of U.S.-made nondurable goods exceeds that of durable goods. The leading durable products are transportation equipment, electronic and electrical equipment, machinery, and fabricated metal products. Among U.S. final consumers, nondurables comprise nearly three-quarters of all goods purchases—led by food products. Because nondurables are bought more often and consumed more quickly, sales are more influenced by ads and sales promotions.

In industrialized nations, services account for a substantial share—generally well over one-half—of the Gross Domestic Product. In developing and less-developed nations, services account for a lower share of the GDP; goods production (including agricultural items and extracted resources) is more dominant. Yet, even there, the role of services is growing rapidly.

Service marketing is huge in industrialized nations, with the United States being the world leader.

The United States is the world's leading service economy: Services account for $6 billion in annual output—roughly 60 percent of the GDP. As noted in Chapter 6, on a global level, the United States is by far the leading service exporter. Three-fifths of U.S. service spending is by final consumers; the rest is by businesses, government, and other nonprofits. Among the leading U.S. service industries are housing and household operations, medical care, personal services, transportation services, and repair services. Three-quarters of the U.S. labor force are in service jobs. Among the other nations with at least one-half of their labor forces in service jobs are Australia, Canada, France, Great Britain, Japan, and Germany.[2]

These reasons have been cited for the worldwide growth of final consumer services: the rising living standard of the population; the complex goods that require specialized installation and repair; the lack of consumer technical skills; the high purchase prices of items that can be rented rather than bought; and the greater need for health care, child care, and educational services. In the industrial sector, here are some of the services experiencing the greatest growth: business services, computer repair and training, and equipment leasing.

The **hidden service sector** *refers to services offered by goods-oriented firms.*

The scope of services is sometimes underestimated since services may be lumped with goods in assigning revenues. The **hidden service sector** encompasses the delivery, installation, maintenance, training, repair, and other services provided by firms that emphasize

---

[2]Bureau of Economic Analysis, U.S. Commerce Department; and *Statistical Abstract of the United States 2000* (Washington, D.C.: U.S. Department of Commerce, 2000), various pages.

goods sales. For instance, although IBM is a manufacturer, its Global Services Consulting division (www.ibm.com/services) now accounts for almost 40 percent of the firm's revenues: "Customers want more than just parts—they want solutions. That's something we recognized long ago." IBM's consulting clients have included Abercrombie & Fitch, AOL, Amway, AT&T, British Airways, and a whole lot more. "Today, IBM is better than rivals at linking hardware sales to lucrative services. It generates more than $4 in software and services for every $1 in big hardware sales."[3]

12-3 CATEGORIZING GOODS AND SERVICES

Goods and services can be categorized in two ways. They can be located on a goods/services continuum; and they can be placed into separate classification systems.

12-3a A Goods/Services Continuum

A *goods/services continuum* categorizes products along a scale from pure goods to pure services. With pure goods, the seller offers the consumer only physical goods without any accompanying services. With pure services, the seller offers the consumer only nongoods services without any accompanying physical goods. Between the two extremes, the seller would offer good/service combinations to the consumer.

Figure 12-1 shows a goods/services continuum with four different examples. In each one, a pure good is depicted on the far left and a pure service is depicted on the

*With a **goods/services continuum**, products are positioned from pure goods to pure services.*

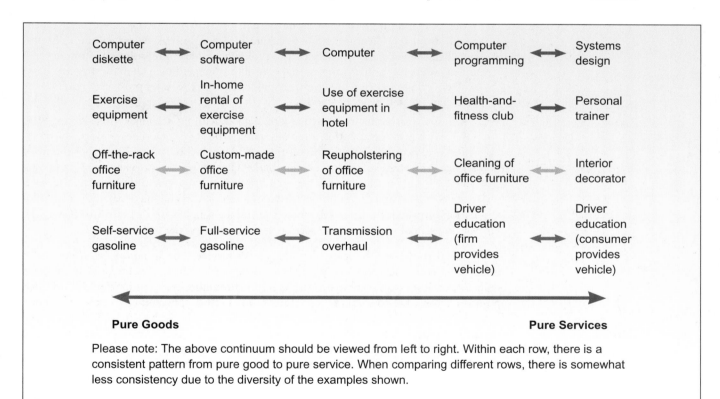

Please note: The above continuum should be viewed from left to right. Within each row, there is a consistent pattern from pure good to pure service. When comparing different rows, there is somewhat less consistency due to the diversity of the examples shown.

FIGURE 12-1

Illustrating the Goods/Services Continuum

---

[3]David Rocks, "IBM's Hottest Product Isn't a Product," *Business Week* (October 2, 2000), pp. 118, 120.

far right. Moving from left to right, within each example, the combined good/service offerings become more service-oriented. Here is the reasoning behind the continuum examples in Figure 12-1:

- A computer disk is usually sold as a pure good—a product free from defects. With most computer software, there is a telephone hotline for questions. A PC is typically configured by the seller, pre-loaded with software, and accompanied by on-site service. Computer programming involves labor-intensive service on a physical good. Systems design entails professional consultation as to a client's information system needs; the seller offers a pure service and does not sell or service goods.

- When a consumer buys such exercise equipment as a stationary bicycle, he or she obtains ownership of a pure good. If a person rents a stationary bicycle for the home, that individual obtains the use of a physical product. When a person uses a stationary bicycle at a hotel, he or she obtains the use of a physical product and the related facilities. If a person joins a health-and-fitness club, he or she not only gets to use the physical facilities but also can participate in exercise classes under the direction of various instructors. When a person hires a personal trainer, he or she is acquiring the pure service of an expert teacher in exercise and motivation.

- Off-the-rack office furniture may be marketed as a pure good—with the buyer responsible for delivery and set up. Custom-made office furniture is made on the basis of buyer specifications and buyer/seller consultations; delivery and set-up are included. Furniture reupholstering involves labor-intensive service on a physical good; the seller is marketing a service along with a physical good (the fabric used in the reupholstering). Cleaning office furniture is a labor-intensive service on a physical good; the seller markets a service (the value of the cleaning solution is minor). An interior decorator offers professional consultation regarding a client's office furniture, wall coverings, flooring materials, layout, and so on; the seller provides a pure service and does not sell or service goods.

- Self-service gasoline is marketed as a pure good, with no accompanying service. With full-service gasoline, a station attendant pumps the gas—sometimes washing the windshield and performing other minor tasks. A transmission overhaul is a labor-intensive service on a physical good; the seller markets both a physical product (new parts) and service. In driver education, where the driving school provides the vehicle, the seller teaches a potential driver how to drive in a school car; the major offering is the education provided. In driver ed, where the trainee supplies his or her own vehicle, the driving school markets a pure service; it is not offering the use of a vehicle.

Several things can be learned from a goods/services continuum. First, it applies to both final consumer and organizational consumer products. Second, most products embody goods/services combinations; the selling firm must keep this in mind. Third, each position along the continuum represents a marketing opportunity. Fourth, the bond between a goods provider and its customers becomes closer as the firm moves away from marketing pure goods. Fifth, a firm must decide if it is to be perceived as goods- or services-oriented. See Figure 12-2.

Whether goods- or services-oriented, a firm must specify which are core services and which are peripheral—and the level of peripheral services to offer. **Core services** are the basic services that firms provide to their customers to be competitive. At Casio (www.casio.com), they include prompt delivery, credit, advertising support, and returns handling for the retailers that carry its watches in 150 nations around the globe. At Federal Express (www.fedex.com), they involve taking phone orders, picking up packages, tracking them, shipping them overnight, and delivering them the next morning or afternoon.

Peripheral services are supplementary (extra) services that firms provide to customers. Casio's peripheral services are extended credit and advice on how to set up displays

By adding **peripheral services** *to their* **core services,** *firms can create a competitive advantage.*

FIGURE 12-2

A Goods *and* Services Strategy

Canada's Bell Mobility (www.bellmobility.com) has successfully positioned itself midway along the goods/services continuum. It markets such goods as cellular phones and pagers, accompanied by cellular telephone and paging services.

Source: Reprinted by permission of Retail Planning Associates. Photography by Michael Houghton/STUDIOHIO.

for retailers, and a toll-free phone number for consumer inquiries. Federal Express' peripheral services include shipping advice for customers, address labels and packaging materials, and tracing packages in transit. Although these services may increase a firm's costs, require added employee skills, and be time-consuming, they may also help a company create and sustain a competitive advantage.

12-3b Goods and Services Classification Systems

Figure 12-3 shows a detailed, seven-way classification system for goods. It is useful in demonstrating the diversity of goods marketing.

In selecting a market segment, a goods seller should remember that final and organizational consumers have similarities and differences. The same good may be offered to each segment. The major distinctions between segments are the reasons for purchases, the amount bought, and the features desired.

Goods may be classified as to market, durability, value added, goals, regulation, distribution channel, and customer contact.

Durable goods firms have a particular challenge. On the one hand, they want to stress the defect-free, long-running nature of their products. On the other hand, inasmuch as they need to generate repeat sales from current customers, they continually try to add unique features and enhance the performance of new models—and then convince people to buy again while the goods they own are still functional. For nondurable goods firms, the key task is to engender brand loyalty, so consumers rebuy the same brands.

High value-added goods are those where manufacturers convert raw materials or components into distinctive products. The more value firms add to the goods they sell, the better the chance for a goods-based differential advantage. Low value-added goods are those where manufacturers do little to enhance the raw materials or components they extract or buy. These firms often must compete on price since their goods may be seen as commodities. Superior customer service can be a major differential advantage and enable marketers of low value-added goods to avoid commodity status.

For the most part, goods-oriented firms are profit-oriented. Sometimes, as noted in Figure 12-3, goods are marketed by nonprofit organizations—usually as a way of generating revenue to support the organizations' activities. Nonprofit marketing is discussed in depth later in this chapter.

FIGURE 12-3

A Classification System for Goods

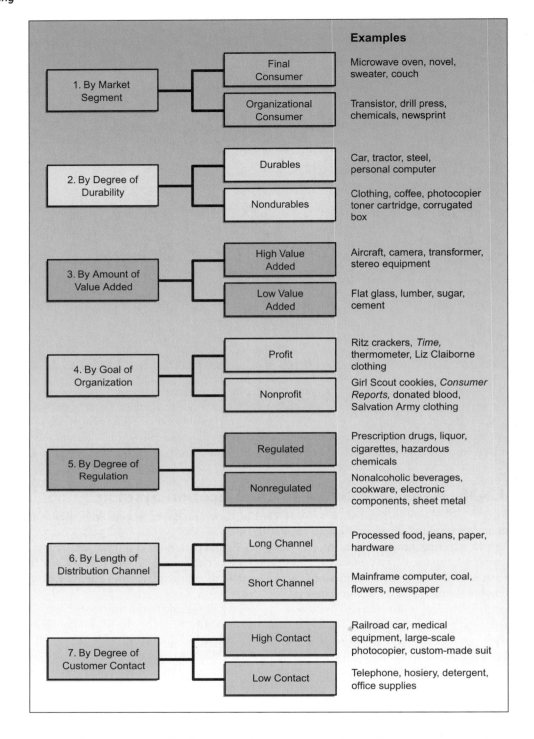

Goods may be grouped by the extent of government regulation. Some items, such as those related to the health and safety of people and the environment, are highly regulated. Others, generally those not requiring special health and safety rules, are subject to less regulation.

Distribution channel length refers to the number of intermediaries between goods producers and consumers. Final consumer goods tend to have more intermediaries than organizational consumer ones due to the size and importance of the latter. Furthermore, goods that are complex, expensive, bulky, and perishable are more apt to have shorter channels.

Goods may be classified by the degree of customer contact between sellers and buyers. Contact is greater for sophisticated equipment, items requiring some training, and custom-made goods. In these instances, proper employee training is needed. Low customer contact is required for goods that consumers are able to buy and use with little assistance from sellers.

A good would normally be classified on a combination of the factors in Figure 12-3. *Time* magazine (www.time.com) appeals to final consumers, is nondurable, has high value added, is profit-oriented, faces few regulations, is sold at newsstands and through home delivery, and has low customer contact.

Figure 12-4 displays a detailed, seven-way classification system for services. It is helpful in showing the diversity of service marketing.

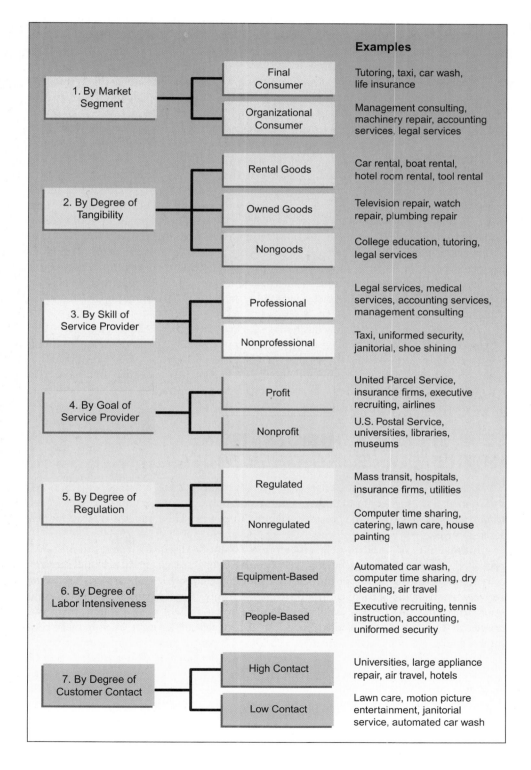

Examples

		Examples
1. By Market Segment	Final Consumer	Tutoring, taxi, car wash, life insurance
	Organizational Consumer	Management consulting, machinery repair, accounting services, legal services
2. By Degree of Tangibility	Rental Goods	Car rental, boat rental, hotel room rental, tool rental
	Owned Goods	Television repair, watch repair, plumbing repair
	Nongoods	College education, tutoring, legal services
3. By Skill of Service Provider	Professional	Legal services, medical services, accounting services, management consulting
	Nonprofessional	Taxi, uniformed security, janitorial, shoe shining
4. By Goal of Service Provider	Profit	United Parcel Service, insurance firms, executive recruiting, airlines
	Nonprofit	U.S. Postal Service, universities, libraries, museums
5. By Degree of Regulation	Regulated	Mass transit, hospitals, insurance firms, utilities
	Nonregulated	Computer time sharing, catering, lawn care, house painting
6. By Degree of Labor Intensiveness	Equipment-Based	Automated car wash, computer time sharing, dry cleaning, air travel
	People-Based	Executive recruiting, tennis instruction, accounting, uniformed security
7. By Degree of Customer Contact	High Contact	Universities, large appliance repair, air travel, hotels
	Low Contact	Lawn care, motion picture entertainment, janitorial service, automated car wash

FIGURE 12-4

A Classification System for Services

INTERACTIVE FIGURE

Services may be classified as to market, tangibility, skill, goals, regulation, labor intensity, and customer contact.

As with goods, final and organizational consumers have similarities and differences, so the same basic service may be offered to each segment. Both groups can counter high prices or poor service by doing some tasks themselves. The major differences between the segments are the reasons for the service, the quantity of service required, and the complexity of the service performed.

In general, the less tangible a service, the less service marketing resembles goods marketing. For nongoods services, performance can be judged only after the service is completed, and consistency is hard to maintain. Rentals and owned-goods services involve physical goods and may be marketed in a manner somewhat similar to goods.

Services may be offered by persons of varying skills. For those requiring high skill levels, customers are quite selective in picking a provider. That is why professionals often gain customer loyalty. For services requiring low levels of skill, the range of acceptable substitutes is usually much greater.

Service firms may be profit- or nonprofit-oriented. Nonprofit service marketing may be undertaken by government or private organizations. The major distinctions between profit- and nonprofit-oriented marketing are noted later in this chapter.

Services may be classed by level of government regulation. Some firms, like insurance companies, are highly regulated. Others, such as caterers and house painters, are subject to limited regulation.

The traditional view of services has been that they are done by one person for another. Yet, this view is too narrow. Services differ in labor intensity—such as automated versus teller-oriented bank services. Labor intensity rises if skilled personnel are used and/or services must be done at a customer's home or business. Also, do-it-yourself consumers may undertake some services—for example, home repair.

Services may be grouped by their degree of customer contact. If contact is high, training personnel in interpersonal skills is essential, in addition to the technical schooling needed to perform a service properly. Such personnel as appliance repairpeople and car mechanics may be the only contact a person has with a firm. If contact is low, technical skills are most essential.

A service would typically be classified on a combination of the factors in Figure 12-4. A firm tutoring students for college board exams appeals to final consumers, has an intangible service, requires skill by the service provider, is profit-oriented, is not regulated, has many trainers, and has high customer contact. A company may also operate in more than one part of a category (this also applies to goods marketers): A CPA may have both final and organizational consumer clients.

12-4 SPECIAL CONSIDERATIONS IN THE MARKETING OF SERVICES

*Services differ from goods in terms of **intangibility, perishability, inseparability,** and **variability.***

Services have four attributes that typically distinguish them from goods (as noted in Chapter 11): higher intangibility, greater perishability, inseparability of the service from the service provider, and greater variability in quality. Their effect is greatest for personal services.

Intangibility of services means they often cannot be displayed, transported, stored, packaged, or inspected before buying. This occurs for repair services and personal services; only the benefits derived from the service experience can be described. ***Perishability of services*** means many of them cannot be stored for future sale. If a painter who needs eight hours to paint a single house is idle on Monday, he or she will not be able to paint two houses on Tuesday; Monday's idle time is lost. A service supplier must try to manage consumers so there is consistent demand for various parts of the week, month, and/or year.

Inseparability of services means a service provider and his or her services may be inseparable. When this occurs, the service provider is virtually indispensable, and customer contact is often an integral part of the service experience. The quality of machinery repair depends on a mechanic's skill and the quality of legal services depends on a lawyer's ability. *Variability in service quality*—differing service performance from one purchase occasion to another—often occurs even if services are completed by the same person. This may be due to a firm's difficulty in problem diagnosis (for repairs), customer inability to verbalize service needs, and the lack of standardization and mass production for many services.

In planning its marketing strategy, a service firm needs to consider how intangible its offering is, how perishable its services are, how inseparable performance is from specific service providers, and the potential variability of service quality. Its goal would be to prepare and enact a marketing strategy that lets consumers perceive its offering in a more tangible manner, makes its services less perishable, encourages consumers to seek it out but enables multiple employees to be viewed as competent, and makes service performance as efficient and consistent as possible.

Service intangibility can make positioning harder. Unlike goods positioning, which stresses tangible factors and consumer analysis (such as touching and tasting) prior to a purchase, much service positioning must rely on performance promises (such as how well a truck handles after a tune-up), which can only be measured once a purchase is made. But, there are ways to use positioning to help consumers perceive a service more tangibly. A firm can

> *Service intangibility makes positioning decisions more complex.*

- Associate an intangible service with tangible objects better understood by the customer. Figure 12-5 shows how the Cleveland Browns football team (www.clevelandbrowns.com) does this.

- Focus on the relationship between the company and its customers. It can sell the competence, skill, and concern of employees.

- Popularize the company name.

- Offer tangible benefits, such as Northwest Airlines' (www.nwa.com) promoting specific reasons for people to fly with it. See Figure 12-6.

- Achieve a unique product position, such as 24-hour, on-site service for office equipment repair.[4]

FIGURE 12-5

How the Cleveland Browns Use Tangible Objects to Create Service Tangibility

Source: Reprinted by permission of Retail Planning Associates. Photography by Michael Houghton/STUDIOHIO.

[4]Gordon H. G. McDougall and Douglas W. Snetsinger, "The Intangibility of Services: Measurement and Competitive Perspectives," *Journal of Services Marketing,* Vol. 4 (Fall 1990), pp. 27–40. See also Charlene Pleger Bebko, "Service Intangibility and Its Impact on Consumer Expectations of Service Quality," *Journal of Services Marketing,* Vol. 14 (Number 1, 2000), pp. 9–26.

Service intangibility may be magnified if only a small portion of the service is seen by the consumer. For example, in-shop repairs are normally not viewed by consumers. Although a repairperson may spend two hours on a fax machine and insert two parts priced at $35, when the consumer sees a bill for $145, he or she may not realize the service time involved. Thus, a firm must explain how much time is needed for each aspect of service—and the tasks performed—to make the service more tangible to customers.

Due to service perishability, a firm must match demand and supply patterns as well as it can. It might have to alter the timing of consumer demand and/or exert better control over the supply of its service offering. It should try to avoid situations in which excess demand goes unsatisfied and cases in which excess capacity causes unproductive resource use. To better match demand with supply, a firm can

Services often cannot be stored for later sale, so demand must be matched with supply.

- Market similar services to segments having different demand patterns.
- Market new services with different demand patterns from existing services.
- Market new services that complement existing ones.
- Market service "extras" during nonpeak periods.
- Market new services not affected by existing capacity constraints.
- Train personnel to perform multiple tasks.
- Hire part-time employees during peak periods.
- Educate consumers to use services during nonpeak periods.
- Offer incentives and price reductions in nonpeak periods.[5]

[5]Leonard L. Berry, A. Parasuraman, and Valarie A. Zeithaml, "Synchronizing Demand and Supply in Service Businesses," *Business,* Vol. 34 (October-December 1984), pp. 36–37; James L. Heskett, W. Earl Sasser, Jr., and Christopher W. L. Hart, *Service Breakthroughs* (New York: Free Press, 1990), pp. 135–158; and Donald J. Shemwell, Jr. and J. Joseph Cronin, Jr., "Services Marketing Strategies for Coping with Demand/Supply Imbalances," *Journal of Services Marketing,* Vol. 8 (Number 4, 1994), pp. 14–24.

GLOBAL *Marketing in Action*

Virgin Air: Stormy Weather Ahead

Shortly after Australia's government changed its laws to allow foreign-ownership of air carriers, Great Britain's Sir Richard Branson announced plans for a new airline, Virgin Blue (www.virginblue.com.au), to begin operations there. The plan was to reduce prices through lower costs by using smaller planes, nonunion labor, and electronic ticketing. Virgin Blue's entry into the Australian market was highlighted by a publicized party that featured dancing and celebrities, including Sir Branson. Public confidence for Virgin Blue was so high that investors reduced the stock value of Qantas (www.qantas.com), a major Australian competitor, by 20 percent even before the new airline was launched.

Unfortunately for Virgin Blue, its Australian launch did not go as planned. Its launch date had to be postponed for several weeks due to the airline's failure to meet some regulations. This delay caused Virgin Blue to refund monies to 1,500 passengers. Competitors also met and even beat Virgin Blue's low fares. On the Sydney to Brisbane route, for example, prices dropped from $108 to $18. Even Quantas decided to sell about one-third of its seats within the Australian market at one-half the regular fare. High oil prices and a weak Australian dollar also hurt Virgin Blue's profitability.

Some marketing analysts say that Virgin Blue was at a competitive disadvantage with other airlines because its Australian fleet had only five 162-passenger planes. The small fleet gave leisure travelers less choice; it also made the airline less desirable to higher-fare paying business travelers who require flexibility in scheduling. To remedy this, Virgin Blue plans to add 10 new planes and several additional routes within the next two years. Virgin Blue also hopes that the heightened discount environment will result in an 8 percent overall increase in Australian air travel.

What should Virgin Blue do next? Why?

Source: Based on material in Becky Gaylord, "Virgin Is in for a Bumpy Ride," *Business Week* (October 30, 2000), p. 175.

The existence of a close service provider/consumer relationship makes employee interpersonal skills important. The work force must be trained to interact well with people in such diverse situations as selling and performing services, handling payments, and delivering repaired goods. Generally, more personal involvement, personal contact, and customer input are needed to market services than to market goods. Thus, employee empowerment can be quite beneficial. Those who participate in the marketing of complex services often act as relationship managers. Enterprise Rent-A-Car (www.enterprise.com) picks up customers who cannot make it to an Enterprise location—and brings cars to people who are stranded: "You've no doubt seen our ads . . . the ones featuring the wrapped car and that well-known slogan: 'Pick Enterprise. We'll pick you up.' Even if you are familiar with our advertising campaign, you may not realize that Enterprise Rent-A-Car is the largest car rental company in North America. We have more than a half million vehicles in our rental and leasing fleet, more than 38,000 employees and over 4,000 locations in the U.S., Canada, Germany, the United Kingdom, and Ireland."[6]

Interpersonal skills are crucial for service businesses.

[6]"About Enterprise Rent-A-Car," www.enterprise.com/car_rental/about (April 14, 2001).

In planning a service provider/consumer relationship, this should also be kept in mind: Customers of personal service firms often become loyal to a particular employee rather than the firm. If that person leaves the firm, he or she may take some customers with him or her. That is why it is important for a firm to show its customers that multiple employees are equally capable of providing excellent service.

By their nature, many services have the potential for great variability in quality. It is hard for lawn care firms to mow lawns exactly the same way each week, for consultants to make sales forecasts for clients that are always accurate, and for each airline flight to arrive on time. But what service firms can do is strive to make their performance as efficient and consistent as possible. Service reliability can also be improved by setting high-level standards and by tying employee pay and promotions to performance.

One solution to the issue of high costs (inefficiency) and low reliability (performance variability) is the **industrialization of services** by using hard, soft, and hybrid technologies.[7] *Hard technologies* substitute machinery for people, such as utilizing electronic financial transactions instead of human bank tellers. See Figure 12-7. Hard technologies are not as readily applied to services requiring extensive personal skill and contact—such as medical, legal, and hairstyling services. *Soft technologies* substitute pre-planned systems for individual services. For example, travel agents sell pre-packaged vacation tours to standardize transportation, accommodations, food, and sightseeing. *Hybrid technologies* combine both hard and soft technologies. Examples include muffler repair and quick-oil-change shops.

*The **industrialization of services** can lower inefficiency and excessive variability via hard technologies, soft technologies, or hybrid technologies.*

This is how the Internet may be used to address the need for closer student-teacher relationships by industrializing service activities:

> Cries of "the dog ate my homework" among northeast Florida students are about to end. Quadrant Technology, a developer of educational networks, has launched a service to bring parents, teachers, and students together on the Web. SmartKidZone.com (www.smartkidzone. com) lets teachers post homework assignments on the secure Web site. Parents can review assignments around the clock with or without their kids through the SmartKidZone Network. The network also offers students and teachers free E-mail and other resources. It includes a direct link to the Florida Department of Education data base that includes its curriculum for kindergarten through grade 12.[8]

FIGURE 12-7
Automated Teller Machines: Substituting Technology for People

At hundreds of thousands of locations around the world, automated teller machines (ATMs) enable people to access their accounts and process transactions without personal contact and at any time of day or night. While many like this approach, others still want the human touch.

Source: Reprinted by permission of PricewaterhouseCoopers.

---

[7]Theodore Levitt, *The Marketing Imagination* (New York: Free Press, 1983), pp. 50–71; and James S. Hensel, "Service Quality Improvement and Control: A Customer-Based Approach," *Journal of Business Research*, Vol. 20 (January 1990), pp. 43–54.

[8]"Quadrant Technology Service Connects Teachers and Parents," *Orlando Business Journal* (September 22, 2000), p. 51.

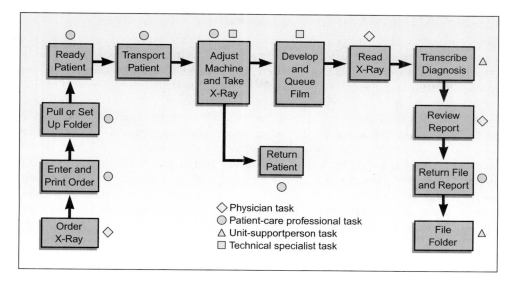

FIGURE 12-8

A Service Blueprint for an X-Ray

This service blueprint depicts the thirteen steps involved in a typical hospital's X-ray process. The steps can be completed in under one hour and they require multiple employees. Without such a blueprint, the X-ray process would probably be less systematic, more time-consuming, and less efficient.

Source: Stephen H. Baum, "Making Your Service Blueprint Pay Off!" *Journal of Services Marketing,* Vol. 4 (Summer 1990), p. 49. Reprinted by permission of MCB University Press.

*A **service blueprint** enhances productivity.* **Service gaps** *must be reduced.*

To industrialize their services better, many firms use a ***service blueprint***—a visual portrayal of the service process: "It displays each subprocess (or step) in the service system, linking the various steps in the sequence in which they appear. A service blueprint is essentially a detailed map or flowchart of the service process."[9] Figure 12-8 shows how a blueprint can be used in administering an X-ray to a patient.

While planning their marketing strategies, it is also important for firms to understand service quality from a customer perspective. They must try to minimize any possible ***service gap***—the difference between customer expectations and actual service performance. Consumer expectations regarding service companies cover these 10 areas:

- Tangibles—facilities, equipment, personnel, communication materials.
- Reliability—ability to perform a desired service dependably and accurately.
- Responsiveness—willingness to provide prompt service and assist customers.
- Competence—possession of the necessary skills and knowledge.
- Courtesy—respect, politeness, and friendliness of personnel.
- Credibility—honesty, trustiness, and believability of service performers.
- Security—freedom from risk, doubt, or danger.
- Access—ease of contact.
- Communication—keeping customers informed in a clear manner and listening to comments.
- Understanding the customer—knowing the customer's needs.[10]

12-5 THE USE OF MARKETING BY GOODS AND SERVICES FIRMS

Goods and services firms have differed in their use of marketing, but service firms are now better adapting to their special circumstances than in the past.

---

[9]Valarie A. Zeithaml, A. Parasuraman, and Leonard L. Berry, *Delivering Quality Service* (New York: Free Press, 1990), p. 158. See also Paul Harsin and Ray W. Wilson, *Process Mastering: How to Establish and Document the Best Known Way to Do a Job* (Portland: Productivity Press, 1998).

[10]Zeithaml, Parasuraman, and Berry, *Delivering Quality Service,* pp. 18–22. See also "Service Quality Measurement," www.imt.za/qrater/q-rater.html (February 2, 2001); and Michael A. McCollough, Leonard L. Berry, and Manjit S. Yadav, "An Empirical Investigation of Customer Satisfaction After Service Failure and Recover," *Journal of Service Research,* Vol. 3 (November 2000), pp. 121–137.

12-5a A Transition in the Marketing of Services

Service firms have tended to lag behind manufacturers in the use of marketing for several reasons. One, many service firms are so small that marketing specialists cannot be afforded. Two, because manufacturers often have a larger geographic market, they can more efficiently advertise. Three, a lot of service firms are staffed by people with technical expertise in their fields but limited marketing experience. Four, strict licensing provisions sometimes limit competition among service firms and the need for marketing; in most industries, manufacturers have faced intense competition for years. Five, consumers have held some service professionals, such as doctors and lawyers, in such high esteem that marketing has not been needed. Six, in the past, some professional associations banned ads by members; this was changed by court rulings that now permit it. Seven, there are still service professionals who dislike marketing, do not understand it, or question the use of marketing practices, such as advertising, in their fields. Finally, many manufacturers have only recently set up services as profit centers.

MARKETING *and the Web*

Online Ratings of Health Care Professionals

Web sites such as DoctorQuality.Com (www.doctorquality.com), BestDoctors.com (www.bestdoctors.com), and HealthGrades.com, (www.healthgrades.com) rate physicians, hospitals, health plans, and health care organizations based on information from the physicians themselves, government agencies, health-care watchdog organizations, and even patients.

While these sites seem more objective than asking a friend about his or her doctor or health plan, some experts remain skeptical. For example, physicians generally do not include negative information and peer ratings can be based more on a doctor's publications than his or her ability as a surgeon. Even third-party sources can be misleading, since a high mortality rate can be due to a doctor's taking on high-risk patients.

Let's take a brief look at the special services offered by these sites. DoctorQuality.Com enables patients to review both physicians and hospitals based on specialty, patient satisfaction scores, and board certification. It offers no grades, but a "best practice" stamp is given to selected physicians and hospitals. The rating is based on the firm's assessment of publicly-available data, as well as online customer satisfaction surveys. BestDoctors.Com narrows its list to the top 4 percent of specialists voted "the best" by other doctors in the same specialty. Prospective patients are also given the names of specialists within a radius of 3 to 300 miles from their ZIP Codes. HealthGrades.com uses a five-star system to rate more than 5,000 hospitals and 400 health plans. Hospitals are evaluated based on Medicare files, and health plans are judged based on data from the National Committee for Quality Assurance. Prospective patients can use HealthGrades.com to search for a physician based on specialty, gender preference, location, years in practice, and hospital affiliation.

How would you market these online rating services?

Source: Based on material in Kim Cross, "Stayin' Alive: Doctor Check-Up," *Business2.0* (November 14, 2000), pp. 254–259.

In recent years, the marketing of services has risen, due to a better understanding of customer service in gaining and retaining consumers, worldwide service opportunities, deregulation in many service industries, competition among service providers, consumer interest in renting/leasing rather than buying, the aggressive marketing of services by firms that once focused on manufacturing, the advent of high-technology services (such as video conferencing), the growth of do-it-yourselfers due to high service costs, and the number of service professionals with formal business training.

Service firms' use of marketing practices is expected to continue increasing in the future.

12-5b Illustrations of Service Marketing

This section examines the use of marketing by hotels, auto repair and servicing firms, and lawyers. The examples represent rented-goods services, owned-goods services, and non-goods services. They differ by the degree of tangibility, the service provider skill, the degree of labor intensiveness, and the level of customer contact. But, in all three instances, the use of marketing practices is expanding.

Hotels may target one or more market segments: business travelers, through tourists (who stay one night), regular tourists (who stay two or more nights), extended-stay residents (who stay up to several months or longer), and conventioneers. Each requires different services. The business traveler wants efficient service, a desk in the room, and convenient meeting rooms. A through tourist wants a convenient location, low prices, and quick food service. A regular tourist wants a nice room, recreational facilities, and sightseeing assistance. An extended-stay resident wants an in-room kitchen and other apartmentlike amenities. Conventioneers want large meeting rooms, pre-planned sightseeing, fax machines, computer access, and hospitality suites.

To attract and keep customers, hotels are upgrading, adding new services, opening units in emerging markets around the world, and improving marketing efforts. Elaborate, distinctive lobby areas and immaculate grounds are popular with resort hotels. First-run movies that can be viewed in the room, frequent-stay bonus plans, and special promotions are offered. For example, Starwood Hotels & Resorts Worldwide, the parent company of Sheraton, Westin, Four Points, St. Regis, and other hotel chains, has a huge global frequent-stay program (https://www.preferredguest.com/member/member_benefits.jhtml), with millions of members.

Hotel marketing efforts now rely more on research, publicity, TV ads, well-conceived slogans, personal attention for consumers, focused product positioning, and better employee training. The Professional Institute of Tourism, in partnership with the Educational Institute of the American Hotel & Motel Association, offers professional certificates (www.hospitalitytraining.net/pdit/tourism4RDM.html) for workers who complete courses in any of five key operational departments: rooms management, food and beverage management, marketing and hospitality management, accounting and financial management, and human resource management. Each specialization includes five departmental-specific courses plus a course on supervision in the hospitality industry.

Hotels are even trying to resolve consumer complaints more effectively. For instance, business travelers are quite concerned about overbooking, long waiting lines, late check-in times, and unresponsive or discourteous staffs. In response, many hotels arrange for alternative accommodations if they are overbooked, have computerized check-ins, offer express checkout (with bills placed under room doors or mailed to guests' businesses or homes), serve free drinks and provide baggage handling if check-in times are late, and give workers more flexibility. Hyatt Hotels (www.hyatt.com) recently eliminated black-out dates for customers to use their frequent-stay rewards and reduced the amount of points to earn rewards. As one expert noted, "You better do something to give the consumer a sense that there's something special about your brand."[11]

Repair and servicing firms operate in a variety of product categories, including motor vehicles, computers, TVs and appliances, industrial equipment, watches and jewelry, and a host of others. These firms fix malfunctioning products, replace broken parts, and provide maintenance. Let us highlight the auto repair and servicing industry.

[11]Dan Hanover, "Rooms for Improvement," *Promo* (October 2000), pp. 103–106.

Auto repairs and servicing are carried out at manufacturer-owned or sponsored dealers and independent service centers.[12] New-car dealers generate most of their profits from parts and servicing. In total, $125 billion is spent annually on U.S. auto repairs and servicing (including parts and labor), one-third at new-car dealers and two-thirds at independents. General Motors cars can be repaired and serviced through its Mr. Goodwrench program (www.gmgoodwrench.com), available at approved GM dealerships; independent repair and maintenance shops; tire, muffler, and battery outlets; mass merchants (such as Sears); and service stations. Independents handle many makes and models. Among the largest independents are Pep Boys (www.pepboys.com), general service; Jiffy Lube, (www.jiffylube.com), oil and lubricating fluids; Midas (www.midas.com), mufflers; and Aamco (www.aamco.com), transmissions.

How has the auto repair and servicing business changed? According to one industry spokesperson, "The old type of gas station with the dirty rags and cigar-smoking mechanic no longer exists. We have evolved due to the technology needed to service, repair, and diagnose modern-day vehicles. It has forced shops to upgrade their tools and equipment. Where it may have cost several thousand dollars in the past, now it can cost several hundred thousand dollars."[13] In addition, the Internet is having a major impact:

> The key to fixing a car is having the right information, and AutoZone is out in front of this customer service gold mine. Through its Web site (www.autozone.com), the firm shows customers how to fix nearly every conceivable automotive problem for their specific vehicles. If a customer drives a 1974 Volkswagen Beetle and needs to know how to replace the starter, what the spark plug gap should be, and what the firing order is, he or she can go to autozone.com and locate this information. By entering a few basic facts about their vehicles, people can research reams of specific information. The Web site also offers customized maintenance schedules, recall alerts, and a number of additional personalized tools designed to keep customers informed about their vehicles.[14]

About 25 years ago, the U.S. Supreme Court ruled that lawyers could not be barred from advertising their services. Since then, legal services advertising has risen significantly and many marketing innovations have been enacted. Overall, lawyers spend about 5 percent of revenues on marketing—up from 1 percent a few years ago. And today, all U.S. professionals are able to advertise their services.

The American Bar Association (www.abanet.org) says that more than 60 percent of its members engage in some form of advertising. Industry experts estimate that 20 to 30 percent of new clients now choose attorneys on the basis of the latter's marketing efforts; the rest rely on personal referrals. Thus, many attorneys advertise in the Yellow Pages (which annually accounts for nearly $1 billion in ads) and have printed brochures. Some advertise in newspapers and magazines; and certain ones use TV and radio ads. Various law firms send out newsletters, employ public relations firms, and have sessions where partners and associates practice selling services to clients. Many firms hire jury consultants to advise them on the characteristics to look for in potential jurors. In 2001, San Francisco-based Brobek, Phleger & Harrison (www.brobeck.com) even ran a $3.5 million ad campaign on CNN.[15]

Law clinics and franchised law firms have grown. They concentrate on rather routine legal services. They have large legal staffs, convenient locations (such as in shopping centers), standardized fees and services ($100 or so for a simple will), and plain fixtures. The largest franchised firms have hundreds of attorneys, cover a wide geographic area, advertise heavily, and set fees in advance and in writing.

---

[12]Bureau of Economic Analysis, U.S. Commerce Department.

[13]Fanglan Du, Paula Mergenhagen, and Marlene Lee, "The Future of Services," *American Demographics* (November 1995), p. 35.

[14]Jerry Colley, "Auto Zone's Service Obsession," *Business Perspectives* (Summer 2000), p. 10.

[15]Don Milazzo, "Attorneys Fine-Tune Ad Pitches," *Birmingham Business Journal* (September 20, 1999), p. 21; "Attorneys Find Success in Radio, Television Advertising," *Memphis Business Journal* (September 8, 2000), p. 9; Jennifer Fulkerson, "When Lawyers Advertise," *American Demographics* (June 1995), pp. 54–55; and "CNN Gets First National Spots for Law Firm," *Mediaweek* (January 22, 2001), p. 55

Legal-services marketing has been met with resistance from a number of attorneys. They criticize some advertising for stressing price at the expense of quality and mass-marketing techniques as eliminating personal counseling. They feel the public's confidence in the profession is falling, information in ads may be inaccurate, and overly high consumer expectations are created. A great many lawyers still do not advertise in mass media; they rely totally on referrals.

12-6 NONPROFIT MARKETING

Nonprofit marketing is conducted by organizations and individuals that operate in the public interest or that foster a cause and do not seek financial profits. It may involve organizations (charities, unions, trade associations), people (political candidates), places (resorts, convention centers, industrial sites), and ideas ("stop smoking"), as well as goods and services.

Nonprofit marketing serves the public interest and does not seek financial profits.

Although nonprofit organizations conduct exchanges, they do not have to be in the form of dollars for goods and services. Politicians request votes in exchange for promises of better government services. The U.S. Postal Service (www.usps.com) wants greater use of ZIP Codes in exchange for improved service and fewer rate hikes. The American Red Cross (www.redcross.org) seeks funds to help victims of all kinds of disasters.

Prices charged by nonprofit organizations often have no relation to the cost or value of their services. The Girl Scouts of the USA (www.girlscouts.org) sells cookies to raise funds; only a small part of the price actually goes for the cookies. In contrast, the price of a chest X-ray at an overseas health clinic may be below cost or free.

Due to its unique attributes, marketing by nonprofit organizations rates a thorough discussion from a product-planning perspective. It is important that nonprofit organizations address the following:

> A recent study suggests that few nonprofit organizations have incorporated a comprehensive approach to marketing. While many nonprofits perform one or more marketing functions, few have embraced a marketing approach to operations. The picture that emerges from the survey is of people in charge of many marketing tasks, but whose marketing responsibilities are secondary to other priorities. It is a picture of organizations that have added marketing tasks, but envision marketing in narrow terms. A majority of those performing marketing now came into their jobs without formal training. While low salary structures are a problem in attracting top talent, the larger problem may be nonprofit leaders who do not appreciate marketing as a comprehensive process and are not fully committed to incorporating the marketing approach into their marketing strategies.[16]

Next, nonprofit marketing is examined in terms of a comparison with profit-oriented marketing, a classification system, and its extent in the economy. Three detailed examples are also presented.

12-6a Nonprofit Versus Profit-Oriented Marketing

There are a number of marketing similarities between nonprofit and profit-oriented firms. In today's uncertain and competitive arena, nonprofit organizations must apply appropriate marketing concepts and strategies if they are to generate adequate support—financial and otherwise.

Nonprofit marketing has both similarities with and distinctions from profit-oriented marketing.

With both nonprofit and profit-oriented organizations, people usually can choose among competing entities; the benefits provided by competitors differ; consumer segments may have distinct reasons for their choices; people are lured by the most desirable product positioning; and they are either satisfied or dissatisfied with performance. Figure 12-9 shows how a political candidate could seek various voter segments via a well-conceived marketing mix and careful product positioning (party platform, past record, and personal traits). This approach is like the one a profit-oriented firm would use.

---

[16]Don Akchin, "Nonprofit Marketing: Just How Far Has It Come?" *Nonprofit World* (January–February 2001), p. 33.

FIGURE 12-9

The Political Marketing Process

Source: Adapted by the authors from Phillip B. Niffenegger. "Strategies for Success from the Political Marketers," *Journal of Consumer Marketing*, Vol. 6 (Winter 1989), p. 46. Reprinted by permission of MCB University Press.

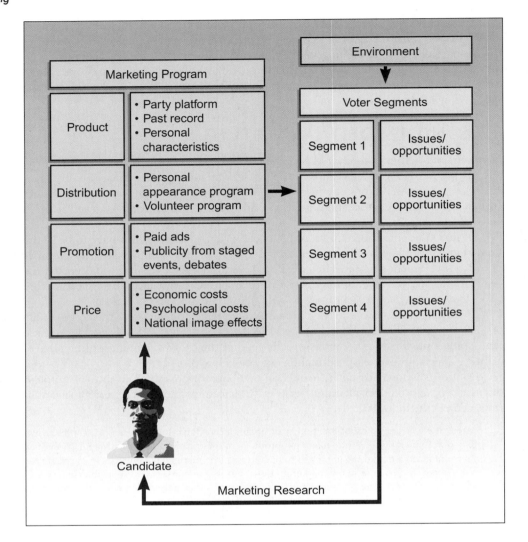

Doesn't this message from the president of the Dallas Symphony Orchestra sound like the approach a profit-oriented firm would take?

I welcome to you www.DallasSymphony.com, the Web site of the Dallas Symphony Orchestra. It is our intention for this site to include all the information you may need about the orchestra in an easily accessible format. I hope you will take advantage of this Web site often and we welcome your comments and suggestions to help us continually improve and expand its features. I encourage you to subscribe to SymphonEmail so that you will be certain to receive advance notice of exciting new features and events on a regular basis. For more information about this service and to subscribe, click on the SymphonyEmail link on the right side of this page. You will find information in the Music Makers section on our conductors and guest artists, and it is our goal to eventually profile every musician in the orchestra. Our online services will allow you to purchase tickets to all of our events. The Dallas Symphony Orchestra presents over 200 performances each year. We are confident this Web site will enhance your ability to access our concerts and services.[17]

There are also some basic differences in marketing between nonprofit and profit-oriented organizations. They are highlighted in Table 12-1 and described in the following paragraphs.

---

[17]Eugene Bonelli, "About Us," http://2001.dallassymphony.com/about.asp (April 3, 2001).

TABLE 12-1	**The Basic Differences Between Nonprofit and Profit-Oriented Marketing**
Nonprofit Marketing	**Profit-Oriented Marketing**
1. Nonprofit marketing is concerned with organizations, people, places, and ideas, as well as goods and services.	1. Profit-oriented marketing is largely concerned with goods and services.
2. Exchanges may be nonmonetary or monetary.	2. Exchanges are generally monetary.
3. Objectives are more complex because success or failure cannot be measured strictly in financial terms.	3. Objectives are typically stated in terms of sales, profits, and recovery of cash.
4. The benefits of nonprofit services are often not related to consumer payments.	4. The benefits of profit-oriented marketing are usually related to consumer payments.
5. Nonprofit organizations may be expected or required to serve economically unfeasible market segments.	5. Profit-oriented organizations seek to serve only those market segments that are profitable.
6. Nonprofit organizations typically have two key target markets: clients and donors.	6. Profit-oriented organizations typically have one key target market: clients.

ETHICAL Issues in Marketing

Cause Marketing: Profiting by Giving

A growing number of Web firms are using "cause marketing" as a means of increasing public awareness for their companies. In cause marketing, firms develop advertising campaigns that benefit both the firms and charities. According to a study by Roper Starch Worldwide, close to two-thirds of Americans feel that cause marketing should be a standard business practice. About the same percentage also say that they would switch brands or retailers based on their association with a good cause, other things being equal. Let's see how two Web firms have successfully used cause marketing.

Zeal Media (www.zeal.com) runs a service in which Web surfers rate and receive ratings of specific Web sites. Under its "Share Your Zeal" campaign, the firm donates money to a nonprofit group each time a user submits a review (2 cents), provides a directory listing (20 cents), or refers a new member ($5.00). Users can have their donation sent to any nonprofit organization registered with the Internal Revenue Service. Zeal Media reports that a recent cause marketing campaign generated 5,800 new members.

Dan's Chocolates (www.danschocolates.com) wanted to persuade shoppers that its fresh chocolate, shipped directly to consumers within 7 days of manufacture, tastes much better than traditional chocolate that could sit on a store's shelf for weeks. With its "Great Chocolate Challenge," the firm offered the first 10,000 visitors to its Web site a 6-piece chocolate sampler for a $1 donation to charity. While Dan's Chocolates' costs for the campaign were $3 million (including advertising), the program led to a fourfold order increase. Furthermore, almost 10 percent of first-time buyers became repeat customers.

As a marketing manager, what are the advantages and disadvantages of cause marketing from an ethical perspective?

Source: Based on material in Joanne R. Halperin, "All for the Cause," *Business 2.0* (October 24, 2000), pp. 106–113.

Nonprofit marketing is broad in scope and frequently involved with **social marketing.**

Nonprofit marketing includes organizations, people, places, and ideas, as well as goods and services. It is more apt to be involved with social programs and ideas than is profit-oriented marketing. Examples are AIDS prevention, recycling, highway safety, family planning, and conservation. Using marketing to gain the acceptability of social ideas is referred to as **social marketing.** Two Web sites devoted to social marketing are "A Short Course in Social Marketing" (www.foundation.novartis.com/social_marketing.htm) and the Social Marketing Institute (www.social-marketing.org).

The nonprofit exchange process can include nonmonetary and monetary transactions. Nonmonetary transactions can be votes, volunteers' time, blood donations, and so forth. Monetary transactions can be donations, magazine subscriptions, tuition, and so on. Some nonprofit marketing does not generate revenues in daily exchanges, relying instead on infrequent fund-raising efforts. A successful marketing campaign may even lose money if services or goods are provided at less than cost. Operating budgets must be big enough to serve the number of anticipated clients, so none are poorly treated or turned away.

Goals may be complex because success or failure cannot be measured just in financial terms. A nonprofit organization might have this combination of goals: raise $250,000 from government grants, increase client usage, find a cure for a disease, change public attitudes, and raise $750,000 from private donors. Goals must include the number of clients to be served, the amount of service to be rendered, and the quality of service to be provided.

Consumer benefits may not be related to their payments.

The benefits of nonprofit organizations may not be allotted on the basis of consumer payments. Only a small portion of the population contracts a disease, requires humanitarian services, visits a museum, uses a public library, or goes to a health clinic in a given year; yet, the general public pays to find cures, support fellow citizens, or otherwise assist nonprofit organizations. Many times, those who would benefit most from a nonprofit organization's activities may be the ones least apt to seek or use them. This occurs for libraries, health clinics, remedial programs, and others. With profit-oriented organizations, benefits are usually distributed equitably, based on consumers' direct payments in exchange for goods or services.

Nonprofit organizations may be expected, or required, to serve markets that profit-oriented firms find uneconomical. For example, the U.S. Postal Service must have rural post offices, and Amtrak must offer passenger rail service over some sparsely populated areas. This may give profit-oriented firms an edge; they can concentrate on the most lucrative market segments.

Nonprofit organizations must satisfy **clients** *and* **donors.**

Profit-oriented firms have one major target market—clients (customers)—to whom they offer goods and services and from whom they receive payment; a typical nonprofit organization has two: *clients*—to whom it offers membership, elected officials, locations, ideas, goods, and services—and *donors*—from whom it receives resources (which may be time from volunteers or money from foundations and individuals). There may be little overlap between clients and donors.

Private nonprofit organizations have been granted many legal advantages. These include tax-deductible contributions, exemptions from most sales and real-estate taxes, and reduced postal rates. Profit-oriented firms often feel they are harmed competitively by these legal provisions.

12-6b Classifying Nonprofit Marketing

The classification of nonprofit marketing may be based on tangibility, structure, goal, and constituency.

Nonprofit organizations may be classified in terms of tangibility, structure, goals, and constituency. This is shown in Figure 12-10. An organization would be classed by a combination of factors. For example, postage stamps for collectors are tangible, distributed by the federal government, intended to reduce the Postal Service's deficit, and aimed at the general public.

Nonprofit marketing involves organizations, people, places, ideas, goods, and services. Organizations include foundations, universities, religious institutions, and government; people include politicians and volunteers; places include resorts and industrial centers; ideas include family planning and patriotism; goods include postage stamps and professional journals; and services include medical care and education.

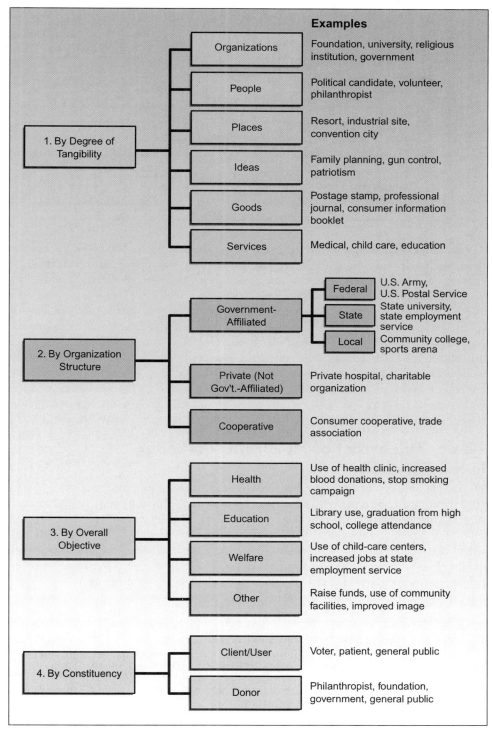

FIGURE 12-10

A Classification System for Nonprofit Marketing

Nonprofit organizations may have a government-affiliated, private, or cooperative structure. The federal government markets military service to recruits, postal services, and other goods and services; state governments market universities and employment services; local governments market colleges, libraries, and sports arenas. Government marketing is also used to increase voter registration, secure bond approval, and gain passage of school budgets. Private organizations market hospitals, charities, social services, and other goods and services. They also use marketing to increase membership and donations. Cooperative organizations (such as the Better Business Bureau, www.bbb.org) aid consumers and/or businesses; success depends on their securing a large membership base and efficiently doing functions.

	Clients Desire →	Convenient services
		Inexpensive services
		Access to services
		Tangible benefits

	Donors Desire →	Accountablity on the part of the organization
		Recognition of their contributions
		Efficient operations
		High success rates

Overall nonprofit marketing goals may be divided into health (increase the number of nonsmokers), education (increase usage of the local library), welfare (list more job openings at a state employment office), and other (increase membership in the Boy Scouts) components.

Nonprofit organizations usually require the support of both clients/users and donors. Clients/users are interested in the direct benefits they get by participating in an organization, such as their improved health, education, or welfare. Donors are concerned about the efficiency of operations, success rates, the availability of goods and services, and the recognition of their contributions. For each constituency, an organization must pinpoint its target market. For example, the League of Women Voters (www.lwv.org) might focus on unregistered voters during an enrollment drive and seek funds from corporate foundations. Figure 12-11 shows some of the differing interests between clients and donors.

12-6c The Extent of Nonprofit Marketing in the Economy

There are millions of nonprofit organizations in the world.

Worldwide, millions of organizations and people engage in nonprofit marketing. There are 1.1 million U.S. nonprofit organizations (24,000 of which are national or international in scope) with 8 million paid employees. They annually generate revenues of more than $1.3 trillion and receive $190 billion in private contributions, 85 percent from individual donors. On average, Americans allocate 2 percent of their incomes to nonprofit groups. The U.S. mass media provide billions of dollars in free advertising space for public-service messages. Half of U.S. adults do some form of volunteer work.[18]

This further demonstrates the scope of nonprofit marketing:

- The American Foundation for Aids Research (amfAR) is just one of the thousands of nonprofit organizations that operates an Internet site (www.amfar.org). Its site describes the organization, encourages online contributions, and provides a treatment directory.

- Many countries use tourism boards to market foreign travel to those nations. India's Ministry of Tourism (www.tourindia.com) actively promotes visits to that country. The British Tourist Authority (www.visitbritain.com) works with airlines, hotels, and credit-card firms to create and publicize special offers. The German Tourist Board (www.germany-tourism.de) distributes brochures describing lower-priced accommodations and has an elaborate Web site.

- In 2000, candidates for the U.S. Congress spent more than $1 billion on their election campaigns. Expenditures were for TV and radio ads, campaign staffs, public appearances, travel, campaign buttons and bumper stickers, public relations, direct mail, and fund-raising events.

---

[18]"Giving USA Charts," www.aafrc.org/trust/charts.html (May 1, 2001); and authors' estimates.

12-6d Illustrations of Nonprofit Marketing

This section looks at marketing by the U.S. Postal Service (USPS), colleges and universities, and the United Way. The activities differ due to the level of tangibility, structure, objectives, and constituencies.

The U.S. Postal Service (www.usps.com) is an independent federal agency with 800,000 employees and yearly revenues of $65 billion. It delivers 200 billion pieces of mail annually (46 percent of the world's mail) and has 38,000 post offices.[19] Competition is intense, and it must deliver all mail—no matter how uneconomical. The Postal Service often runs an annual deficit, and all rate increases must be approved by its Board of Governors.

To protect itself against competitors and stimulate consumer demand, the Postal Service has enacted a strong marketing program—comprising a mix of continuing and new offerings and extensive advertising. With Express Mail, packages and letters are delivered overnight; the items can be dropped at special boxes or picked up for a small fee (to eliminate waiting lines). Priority Mail is an inexpensive service, with two- to three-day delivery anywhere in the United States. ZIP + 4 is an improved ZIP-Code service that offers cost savings for both the Postal Service and its business customers, but it has not been used by customers as much as the Postal Service desires. In 2001, the Postal Service entered into an agreement with Federal Express for the latter to use its planes to ship USPS Express and Priority Mail.[20]

The Postal Service does hundreds of millions of dollars of business in commemorative stamps each year. It has featured celebrities such as Elvis Presley, sports heroes such as Jackie Robinson, and social marketing causes such as breast cancer awareness. Many post offices now sell hand-held scales, padded envelopes for packages, air mail markers, and devices to adhere stamps to envelopes. Self-service stamp vending machines are in shopping centers. Some post offices are "postal stores"—with interior space divided into two sections, one for specialized postal services and one for retail sales. The retail part of the stores carries stamps, envelopes, packing material, posters, T-shirts, coffee mugs, pen-and-pencil sets, and earrings. The Postal Service's annual ad budget exceeds $140 million, with large sums going to Express Mail and Priority Mail, direct-mail ads for business accounts, and commemorative stamps.

Colleges and universities know that population trends in many industrialized nations (such as smaller households and a relatively low birth rate) have affected their enrollment pools, especially with the number of 18- to 24-year-olds falling in some areas. For example, from 1977 to 1991, the number of U.S. high school graduates fell steadily and did not begin to go up again until 1992. Overall U.S. college enrollment has risen only slightly since then. Thus, new markets are being targeted and marketing strategies are being used by more educational institutions than ever before.

Many schools actively seek nontraditional students: Today, 43 percent of U.S. college students attend part-time; and 41 percent of college students are at least 25 years old. In addition, about 20 million people are now in adult higher-education programs at U.S. colleges, universities, and private firms.[21] The adult market needs convenient sites and classes not infringing on work hours. At New York University, the School of Continuing and Professional Studies (www.scps.nyu.edu) offers more than 2,000 courses to 60,000 students per year.

Traditional students are also being sought vigorously. Schools often spend hundreds of dollars—or more—on recruitment efforts for each new student who enrolls. Many buy direct-mailing lists of prospective students from the Educational Testing Service (www.ets.org), which administers college board examinations. A number of colleges distribute recruiting films or videocassettes, costing tens of thousands of dollars (and up) to produce, to high schools. And the vast majority of schools have a significant presence on the Web.

[19]"Postal Facts," http://new.usps.com/cgi-bin/uspsbv/scripts/content.jsp?D=23842 (April 2000); L. Scott Tillett, "Neither Snow Nor Rain Nor the Web," *InternetWeek* (September 4, 2000), p. 11; and Ira Carnahan, "Return to Sender," *Forbes* (February 5, 2001), p. 76.

[20]"FedEx Makes Deal to Haul Some Mail," *New York Times on the Web* (January 11, 2001).

[21]National Center for Education Statistics, "Projections of Education Statistics to 2000," http://nces.ed.gov/pubs2000/projections/chapter2.html#H1 (August 2000).

HOFSTRA UNIVERSITY

DEGREES OF EXCELLENCE

More than 120

graduate programs.

HOFSTRA UNIVERSITY
WE TEACH SUCCESS
Hempstead, NY 11549
1-800-HOFSTRA
www.hofstra.edu

The heightened use of marketing is not limited to poor- or average-quality schools. For example, New York's Hofstra University runs a regional full-color ad campaign, using the theme "We Teach Success." See Figure 12-12. Bryn Mawr, Duke, Harvard, and Stanford are among the nearly 1,000 colleges and universities that let prospective students submit applications via the Internet based on CollegeLink (www.collegelink.com) software, which enables applicants to enter standardized data just once and then add the customized information for each college. Miami University in Ohio participates in "virtual" college fairs: "It's an ideal application of Internet technology, targeted to those students who don't have the wherewithal to get to traditional fairs."[22]

The United Way of America (http://national.unitedway.org), with its 1,900 affiliated local organizations and annual fund-raising of $4 billion, is one of the leading nonprofit organizations in the world. It supports such groups as Boys & Girls Clubs of America (www.bgca.org), centers for children with learning disabilities, immigration centers, and mental health and drug rehabilitation programs. Most United Way donations come from deductions made from worker paychecks. In contrast, the Salvation Army USA (www.salvationarmyusa.org) receives most donations from nonworkplace sources. It gets $1 billion in yearly contributions, and earns hundreds of millions of dollars more from sales at its stores.[23]

---

[22]Rebecca S. Weiner, "Virtual College Fairs for Students," *New York Times on the Web* (October 3, 2000).

[23]"United Way of America," www.hoovers.com/co/capsule/4/0,2163,40484,00.html (April 10, 2001); and "Salvation Army USA," www.hoovers.com/co/capsule/8/0,2163,40408,00.html (April 10, 2001).

For years, the United Way has had an outstanding marketing orientation. It is well known for its long-run association with the National Football League (NFL) and the touching ads that appear during each NFL game. Employees in affiliated chapters are trained in marketing. Periodic conferences are held, such as a yearly marketing and advertising conference. Affiliated chapters present United Way videos, films, and slide-show programs to potential contributors and volunteers. The United Way even published a book, *Competitive Marketing,* so other charitable groups could learn from it.

WEB SITES YOU CAN USE

Service firms cover a very broad spectrum of businesses. Here is a sampling of them—from insurance to PC-based phone calls:

Aetna (www.aetna.com)

H&R Block (www.hrblock.com)

Blockbuster Entertainment (www.blockbuster.com)

Century 21 Real Estate (www.century21.com)

Choice Hotels International (www.hotelchoice.com)

Club Med (www.clubmed.com)

Cort Furniture Rental (www.cort1.com)

Jenny Craig (www.jennycraig.com)

Discovery Channel (www.discovery.com)

E* Trade (www.etrade.com)

ESPN (www.espn.com)

FTD (www.ftd.com)

Hertz (www.hertz.com)

Hilton (www.hilton.com)

Holiday Inn (www.sixcontinentshotels.com/ holiday-inn)

Jazzercise (www.jazzercise.com)

Kinko's (www.kinkos.com)

Knott's Berry Farm (www.knotts.com)

Madison Square Garden (www.thegarden.com)

MapQuest (www.mapquest.com)

Marriott (www.marriott.com)

MasterCard (www.mastercard.com)

Prudential (www.prudential.com)

Renters Choice (www.renterschoice.com)

Schwab (www.charlesschwab.com)

Sheraton (www.starwood.com/sheraton)

Sir Speedy (www.sirspeedy.com)

Supercuts (www.supercuts.com)

Thrifty Car Rental (www.thrifty.com)

Ticketmaster.com (www.ticketmaster.com)

Travelocity (www.travelocity.com)

Universal Studios (www.universalstudios.com)

Vindigo (www.vindigo.com)

Visa (www.visa.com)

visitalk.com (www.visitalk.com)

SUMMARY

1. *To examine the scope of goods and services, and explain how goods and services may be categorized*   Goods marketing encompasses the sales of durable and nondurable physical products; service marketing involves goods rental, goods alteration and maintenance/ repair, and personal services. In the United States, the revenues from nondurable goods are higher than those from durable goods— and final consumers spend several times as much on nondurables as on durables. Services account for a very large share of the GDP in industrialized nations, a smaller share in developing and less-developed nations. The United States has the world's largest service economy. Both final consumer and business services have seen significant growth in recent years. The scope of services is sometimes underestimated due to the hidden service sector.

With a goods/services continuum, products can be positioned from pure goods to goods/services combinations to pure services. Much can be learned by studying the continuum, including its use for final and organizational consumer products, the presence of unique marketing opportunities, and the changing relationship between sellers and buyers as pure goods become goods/services combinations. Both goods- and services-oriented firms need to identify core and peripheral services.

Goods can be classed by market, product durability, value added, company goal, regulation, channel length, and customer contact. Services can be classed by market, tangibility, service provider skill, service provider goals, regulation, labor intensiveness, and customer contact. A firm would be categorized on the basis of a combination of these factors.

2. *To discuss the special considerations in the marketing of services*   Services are generally less tangible, more perishable, less separable from their provider, and more variable in quality than goods that are sold. The effect of these factors is greatest for personal services. Service firms need to enact strategies that enable consumers to perceive their offerings more tangibly, make their offerings less perishable, encourage consumers to seek them out but enable multiple employees to be viewed as competent, and make performance as efficient and consistent as possible. Such approaches as the industrialization of services, the service blueprint, and gap analysis enable service firms to better devise and implement marketing plans by improving their performance.

3. *To look at the use of marketing by goods versus services firms and provide illustrations of service marketing*   Many service firms have lagged behind manufacturers in the use of marketing because of their small size, the larger geographic coverage of goods-oriented companies, their technical emphasis, less competition and the lack of need for marketing, the high esteem of consumers for certain service providers, past bans on advertising, a dislike of marketing by some service professionals, and the reluctance of some manufacturers to view services as profit centers. Yet, for a number of reasons, this has been changing; and the marketing of services is now expanding greatly.

The marketing practices of hotels, repair and servicing firms, and lawyers are highlighted.

4. *To distinguish between nonprofit and profit-oriented marketing*   Nonprofit marketing is conducted by organizations and people operating for the public good or to foster a cause and not for financial profits. It is both similar to and different from profit-oriented marketing. These are some differences: Nonprofit marketing is more apt to involve organizations, people, places, and ideas. Nonprofit exchanges do not have to involve money, and goals can be hard to formulate. The benefits of nonprofit firms may be distributed unequally, and economically unfeasible segments may have to be served. Two target markets must be satisfied by nonprofit organizations: clients and donors.

5. *To describe a classification system for nonprofit marketing, the role of nonprofit marketing in the economy, and applications of nonprofit marketing*   Nonprofit organizations can be classed on the basis of tangibility, organization structure, objectives, and constituency. A nonprofit organization would be categorized by a combination of these factors.

Worldwide, there are millions of organizations and people engaged in nonprofit marketing. There are 1.1 million nonprofit organizations in the United States, generating $1.3 trillion in annual revenues (including contributions). Their marketing efforts have increased greatly in a very short time. They play a key role in the U.S. economy. The marketing practices of the U.S. Postal Service, colleges and universities, and the United Way are highlighted.

KEY TERMS

goods marketing (p. 358)
durable goods (p. 358)
nondurable goods (p. 358)
service marketing (p. 358)
rented-goods services (p. 358)
owned-goods services (p. 358)
nongoods services (p. 358)
hidden service sector (p. 358)

goods/services continuum (p. 359)
core services (p. 360)
peripheral services (p. 360)
intangibility of services (p. 364)
perishability of services (p. 364)
inseparability of services (p. 364)
variability in service quality (p. 365)

industrialization of services (p. 368)
service blueprint (p. 369)
service gap (p. 369)
nonprofit marketing (p. 373)
social marketing (p. 376)
clients (p. 376)
donors (p. 376)

REVIEW QUESTIONS

1. Differentiate among rented-goods services, owned-goods services, and nongoods services.

2. What is a goods/services continuum? Why should firms be aware of this concept?

3. Distinguish between core and peripheral services. What is the marketing role of each?

4. How can a service be positioned more tangibly?

5. Describe how hard, soft, and hybrid technologies may be used to industrialize services.

6. What are some of the similarities and differences involved in the marketing efforts used by nonprofit and profit-oriented organizations?

7. Discuss the factors that may be used to classify nonprofit marketing.

8. How do the goals of clients and donors differ?

DISCUSSION QUESTIONS

1. Present a goods/services continuum related to higher education. Discuss the implications of this continuum for a firm interested in developing a marketing plan in the higher education field.
2. Give several ways that an airline can match demand and supply on days following holidays.
3. Draw and discuss a service blueprint for an insurance broker dealing with health insurance for families.
4. Discuss several innovative fund-raising programs that could be used by the Multiple Sclerosis Foundation (www.msfacts.org).

WEB EXERCISE

"ServiceMagic (www.servicemagic.com) was founded in December 1998 to meet the needs of both consumers and service professionals interacting in the local service communities. We've created a service that does more than just connect local service professionals to consumers. It matches the ideal consumer with the ideal local service professional. As a result, consumers get their job done right and service professionals get the right jobs that help their businesses grow." Visit ServiceMagic's Web site and evaluate its business approach.

13

Conceiving, Developing, and Managing Products

Chapter Objectives

1 To study how products are created and managed, with an emphasis on the product life cycle

2 To detail the importance of new products and describe why new products fail

3 To present the stages in the new-product planning process

4 To analyze the growth and maturity of products, including the adoption process, the diffusion process, and extension strategies

5 To examine product deletion decisions and strategies

A patent provides legal protection to inventors; and there is a complex process involved to gain patent protection through the United States Patent and Trademark Office (www.uspto.gov).

An important initial step in filing a patent application is to establish that an inventor's application is the first for a given technology. Thus, an inventor is required to go through existing patents that are applicable to the new invention, even if a particular patent expired years ago. In the past, the patent search was undertaken by the inventor or a patent agent visiting government patent depository libraries and going through applications stored in a variety of media (including computers, microfiche, and paper).

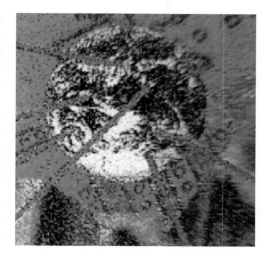

To facilitate patent search, the Patent and Trademark Office has added patent archives covering the years from 1790 through 1976 to its online data base. Previously, this data base was limited to the period from 1977 on, since only it was converted to digital format. Access to the data base is free and it can be searched via patent number, inventor, issue date, or key words and phrases that describe the invention.

Patent applications can also be now made via the Web. Software for writing and filing applications is available at the Patent and Trademark Office's Web site. The software has been designed not only to properly calculate the required filing fees, but also to compress, encrypt, and transmit the application. The software can even scan the application to make sure that an error does not delay or jeopardize proper filing. Inventors can track the progress of their patent application through a secure communications link.

Because secrecy is important with any patent application, inventors filing for a patent via electronic media receive a certificate that encrypts the application at the inventor's home or office computer and maintains the protection at the agency's electronic mailroom. The director of systems development and maintenance at the Patent and Trademark Office says that only the agency can decrypt a transmission. All of this work is done "in an area that is never accessible to the public." To further safeguard patent applications, the agency uses monitors on the network to look for intrusions. The agency is confident that electronically-filed patent applications are more secure than paper-filed ones.[1]

Next, we will study how new products are developed, the factors causing rapid or slow growth for new products, how to manage mature products, and what to do when existing products falter.

13-1 OVERVIEW

In this chapter, the conception and development of new products, the management of growing and mature products through their life cycle, and the termination of undesirable products are discussed.

Product planning involves new and existing products.

[1] Sabra Chartland, "Patents: Web Helps Ease Patent Process," *New York Times on the Web* (November 13, 2000).

While any product combines tangible and intangible features to satisfy consumer needs, a *new product* involves a modification of an existing product or an innovation the consumer perceives as meaningful. To succeed, a new product must have desirable attributes, be unique, and have its features communicated to consumers. Marketing support is necessary.

Modifications are alterations in or extensions of a firm's existing products and include new models, styles, colors, features, and brands. *Minor innovations* are items not previously marketed by a firm that have been marketed by others (like the Hewlett-Packard personal computer). *Major innovations* are items not previously sold by any firm (like the first cellular telephone). If a firm works with major innovations, the costs, risks, and time required for profitability all rise. Overall, most new products are modifications; few are major innovations.

> *New products may be modifications, minor innovations, or major innovations.*

New products may be conceived of and developed by a company itself or purchased from another firm. With the latter, a company may buy a firm, buy a specific product, or sign a licensing agreement (whereby it pays an inventor a royalty fee based on sales). Acquisitions may reduce risks and time demands, but they rely on outsiders for innovations and may require large investments.

Early in a product's life, there is usually strong sales growth, as more people purchase and repurchase. This is an exciting time; and if a product is popular, it can last for quite a while. Next, the market becomes more saturated and competition intensifies. At that point, a firm can maintain high sales by adding features that provide convenience and durability, using new materials in construction, offering a range of models, stressing new packaging, and/or adding customer services. It can also reposition a product, enter untapped geographic markets, demonstrate new uses, offer new brands, set lower prices, use new media, and/or appeal to new segments. For many products, at some point down the road, firms must decide whether those items have outlived their usefulness and should be dropped.

13-2 THE PRODUCT LIFE CYCLE

> *The product life cycle describes each stage in a product's life.*

The *product life cycle* is a concept that attempts to describe a product's sales, competitors, profits, customers, and marketing emphasis from its beginning until it is removed from the market.[2]

From a product-planning perspective, there is interest in the product life cycle for several reasons. One, some product lives are shorter than ever. Two, new products often require high marketing and other investments. Three, an understanding of the concept lets a firm anticipate changes in consumer tastes, competition, and support from resellers and adjust its marketing plan accordingly. Four, the concept enables a firm to consider the product mix it should offer; many firms seek a *balanced product portfolio,* whereby a combination of new, growing, and mature products is maintained.

> *Companies often desire a balanced product portfolio.*

The life-cycle concept can be applied to a product class (watches), a product form (quartz watches), and a brand (Seiko quartz watches). Product forms generally follow the traditional life cycle more faithfully than product classes or brands.

> *Product life cycles may be traditional, boom, fad, extended fad, seasonal, revival, or bust.*

Product life cycles may vary a lot, both in length of time and shape. See Figure 13-1. A *traditional* cycle has distinct periods of introduction, growth, maturity, and decline. A *boom*, or *classic*, cycle describes a very popular product that sells well for a long time. A *fad* cycle represents a product with quick popularity and a sudden decline. An *extended fad* is like a fad, but residual sales continue at a lower level than earlier sales. A *seasonal*, or *fashion*, cycle results if a product sells well in nonconsecutive periods. With a *revival*, or *nostalgia*, cycle, a seemingly obsolete product achieves new popularity. A *bust cycle* occurs for a product that fails.

---

[2]For a good overview article, see David R. Rink, Dianne M. Roden, and Harold W. Fox, "Financial Management and Planning with the Product Life Cycle Concept," *Business Horizons*, Vol. 42 (September–October 1999), pp. 65–72.

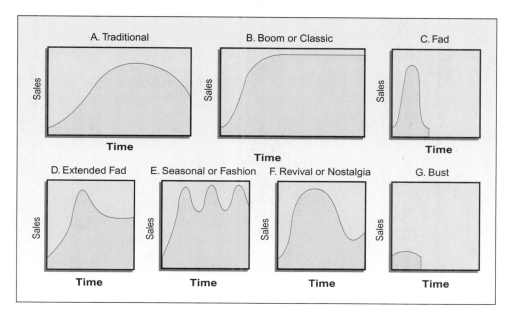

13-2a Stages of the Traditional Product Life Cycle

The stages and characteristics of the traditional product life cycle are shown in Figure 13-2 and Table 13-1, which both refer to total industry performance during the cycle. The performance of an individual firm may vary from that of the industry, depending on its specific goals, resources, marketing plans, location, competitive environment, level of success, and stage of entry.

During the ***introduction stage of the product life cycle,*** a new product is introduced to the marketplace and the goal is to generate customer interest. The rate of sales growth depends on a product's newness, as well as its desirability. Generally, a product modification gains sales faster than a major innovation. Only one or two firms have entered the market, and competition is minimal. There are losses due to high production and marketing costs; and cash flow is poor. Initial customers are innovators who are willing to take risks, can afford to take them, and like the status of buying first. Because one or two firms dominate and costs are high, only one or a few basic product models are sold. For a routine item like a new cereal, distribution is extensive. For a luxury item like a new boat, distribution is limited. Promotion must be informative, and samples may be desirable. Depending on the product and choice of target market, a firm may start with a high status price or low mass-market price.

In the ***growth stage of the product life cycle,*** a new product gains wider consumer acceptance, and the marketing goal is to expand distribution and the range of available product alternatives. Industry sales increase rapidly as a few more firms enter a highly profitable market that has substantial potential. Total and unit profits are high because an affluent (resourceful) mass market buys distinctive products from a limited group of firms and is willing to pay for them. To accommodate the growing market, modified versions of basic models are offered, distribution is expanded, persuasive mass advertising is utilized, and a range of prices is available.

During the ***maturity stage of the product life cycle,*** a product's sales growth levels off and firms try to maintain a differential advantage (such as a lower price, improved features, or extended warranty) for as long as possible. Industry sales stabilize as the market becomes saturated and many firms enter to appeal to the still sizable demand. Competition is at its highest. Thus, total industry and unit profits drop since discounting is popular. The average-income mass market makes purchases. A full product line is available at many outlets (or by many distributors) and at many prices. Promotion is very competitive.

In **introduction,** *the goal is to establish a consumer market.*

During **growth,** *firms enlarge the market and offer alternatives.*

In **maturity,** *companies work hard to sustain a differential advantage.*

FIGURE 13-2

The Traditional Product Life Cycle

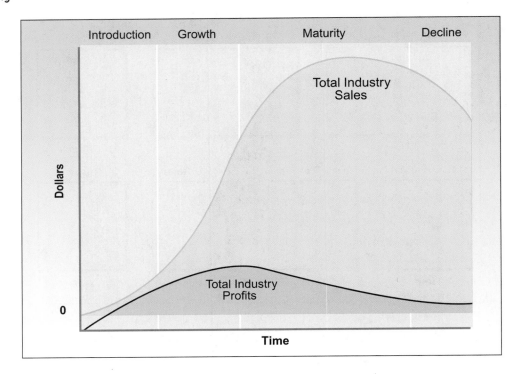

TABLE 13-1   The Characteristics of the Traditional Product Life Cycle

	Stage in Life Cycle			
Characteristics	**Introduction**	**Growth**	**Maturity**	**Decline**
Marketing goal	Attract innovators and opinion leaders to new product	Expand distribution and product line	Maintain differential advantage as long as possible	(a) Cut back, (b) revive, or (c) terminate
Industry sales	Increasing	Rapidly increasing	Stable	Decreasing
Competition	None or small	Some	Substantial	Limited
Industry profits	Negative	Increasing	Decreasing	Decreasing
Customers	Innovators	Resourceful mass market	Mass market	Laggards
Product mix	One or a few basic models	Expanding line	Full product line	Best-sellers
Distribution	Depends on product	Rising number of outlets/distributors	Greatest number of outlets/distributors	Decreasing number of outlets/distributors
Promotion	Informative	Persuasive	Competitive	Informative
Pricing	Depends on product	Greater range of prices	Full line of prices	Selected prices

At the ***decline stage of the product life cycle,*** a product's sales fall as substitutes enter the market or consumers lose interest. Firms have three options. They can cut back on marketing, thus reducing the number of product items they make, the outlets they sell through, and the promotion used; they can revive a product by repositioning, repackaging, or otherwise remarketing it; or they can drop the product. As industry sales decline, many firms exit the market since customers are fewer and as a group they have less money to spend. The product mix keys on best-sellers, selected outlets (distributors) and prices, and promotion stressing—informatively—availability and price.

*In **decline,** firms reduce marketing, revive a product, or drop it.*

The bulky, electric-powered portable calculator is an example of a product form that moved through the life cycle. It went from an exclusive, expensive item to a widespread, moderately priced item to a mass-marketed, inexpensive item to an obsolete item. Today, earlier versions of the calculator have been replaced by technologically advanced forms—such as credit-card sized, solar-powered calculators.

13-2b Evaluating the Product Life-Cycle Concept

The product life cycle provides a good framework for product planning; but, it has not proven very useful for forecasting. In using the product life-cycle concept, these key points should be kept in mind:

1. The stages, time span, and shape of a cycle (such as flat, erratic, or sharply inclined) vary by product.

2. Such external factors as the economy, inflation, and consumer life-styles may shorten or lengthen a product's life cycle.

3. A firm may do better or worse than the industry "average" at any stage in the cycle. An industry's being in the growth stage for a product does not mean success for every firm in the market, nor does its being in the decline stage for a product mean lower sales for every firm.

4. A firm may not only be able to manage a product life cycle, it may also be able to extend it or reverse a decline. Effective marketing may lure a new market segment, find a new product use, or foster better reseller support.

5. Many firms may engage in a ***self-fulfilling prophecy,*** whereby they predict falling sales and then ensure this by reducing or removing marketing support. See Figure 13-3. With proper marketing, some products might not fail.

*A **self-fulfilling prophecy** may occur when a firm reduces marketing.*

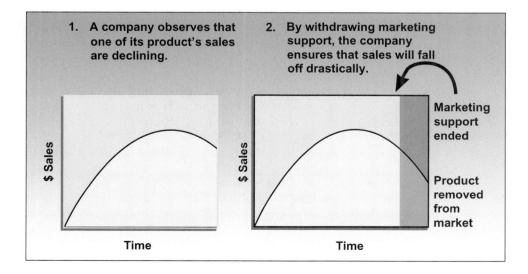

1. **A company observes that one of its product's sales are declining.**

2. **By withdrawing marketing support, the company ensures that sales will fall off drastically.**

Marketing support ended

Product removed from market

$ Sales — Time

$ Sales — Time

FIGURE 13-3
A Self-Fulfilling Prophecy

13-3 THE IMPORTANCE OF NEW PRODUCTS

A firm's product policy should be future-oriented and recognize that products, no matter how successful, tend to be mortal—they usually cannot sustain peak sales and profits indefinitely: "Who survives in today's highly competitive environment? The innovators. They don't just have new designs. They passionately pursue new ways to serve their customers."[3] So, product line additions and replacements should be constantly planned and a balanced product portfolio pursued—by both small and large firms.

New products offer differential advantages.

Introducing new products is important for several reasons. Desirable differential advantages can be attained. The Venus shaver from Gillette (www.gillettevenus.com) is a product especially designed for women, unlike Sensor for Women and other men's shaving products adapted for women. Gillette spent three years and $300 million to develop Venus, and introduced it simultaneously in 29 nations during early 2001. The product has three blades, a pivoting head, and aloe strips for comfort.[4] Matsucom markets the world's smallest computer. As the firm says at it Web site (www.onhandpc.com): "The onHand PC provides you with all the popular features of palm-type devices at a fraction of the size. With onHand PC you can view your to-do list, add appointments to the calendar, look up an address, balance your checkbook, or simply relax and play games. Oh yes, you can also use it to tell time. No more fumbling around trying to get to your Pilot. Always accessible, always onHand."

New products lead to sales growth or stability.

New products may be needed for continued growth. That is why ESPN (www.espn.com) has a new and growing restaurant chain, known as ESPN Zone, that is capitalizing on the cable network's strong brand loyalty among viewers. ESPN Zone was named as one of 2001's "Hot Concepts" by *Nation's Restaurant News*. The chain has outlets in Chicago, New York, Atlanta, Washington, D.C., Anaheim, Las Vegas, and Denver; and it has more on the way. Each restaurant features a large number of TVs, a customer-participation sports area, and more.[5] See Figure 13-4. For firms with cyclical or seasonal sales, new products can stabilize revenues and costs. Dow Chemical (www.dow.com) manufactures medical-testing equipment, and other rather stable product categories, to reduce its dependence on cyclical chemicals. Black & Decker (www.blackanddecker.com) has cut back on lawn-care items and looks for new opportunities in less seasonal products, such as power tools for the home.

New products can take time.

Planning for growth must take into account the total time it takes to move from the idea stage to commercialization. For instance, in 2001, Boeing (www.boeing.com/news/feature/concept) announced that it would develop a new long-range plane, tentatively named the "Sonic Cruiser," with the goal of introducing it in 2007 or 2008. The 200- to 300-seat plane will fly at up to Mach 0.95 or faster, saving one hour per 3,000 miles flown. As Boeing's executive vice-president of sales and marketing says, nothing in the plane besides its efficiency will be very different: "There is no other plane around at the moment that can travel 9,000 miles nonstop except for this one. However, it is still under development. The Sonic Cruiser is a result of Boeing's analysis on the need for a plane to fly from point to point. You can't fly often if you have a bigger aircraft. The demand now is for smaller airplanes and not the bigger ones."[6]

New products can increase profits and control.

New products can lead to larger profits and give a company better control over a marketing strategy. For example, new models of luxury cars such as Lincoln (www.lincolnvehicles.com) and Lexus (www.lexus.com) are often quite popular. When they are, the

---

[3]Amy Cortese, "Masters of Innovation," *Business Week 50* (Spring 2001), p. 159.

[4]Betsy Spethmann, "Venus Rising," *Promo* (April 2001), pp.52–61.

[5]"Nation's Restaurant News Names 2001 Hot Concepts! Winners," *Nation's Restaurant News* (March 12, 2001), pp. 6, 97.

[6]"Boeing Expects to Market New Sonic Cruiser Model in 2007 or 2008," *AsiaPulse News* (April 10, 2001), p. 0368; and "Boeing Focuses Commercial Airplane's Long-Range Product Strategy," www.boeing.com/news/releases/2001/q1/news_release_010329a.html (March 29, 2001).

FIGURE 13-4
**ESPSN Zone: A New
Restaurant Chain that
Offers Much More
Than Food**

Source: Reprinted by permission of
PricewaterhouseCoopers.

cars sell at or close to the "sticker" price, with dealers earning gross profits of up to $10,000 or more on each car sold. Because there are fewer luxury dealers relative to ones selling lower-priced cars, they do not use much price discounting and have firm command over their marketing efforts.

Risk may be lessened through diversity.

To limit risk, many firms seek to reduce dependence on one product or product line. That is why many movie theaters converted to multiplexes, so their revenues are not tied to any one film's performance. Hewlett-Packard (www.hp.com) makes electronic components and test equipment, medical electronic equipment, and analytical instrumentation—besides its core computing and printing products; and it regularly adds new products. Turtle Wax (www.turtlewax.com), the world's leader in car-care products, now makes glass cleaners, leather cleaners, carpet cleaners, and upholstery cleaners.

New products may improve distribution.

Firms may improve the efficiency of their established distribution systems by placing new products in them. They can then spread advertising, sales, and distribution costs among several products, gain dealer support, and discourage others from entering the market. Manufacturers like AT&T (www.att.com), Unilever (www.unilever.com), and Revlon (www.revlon.com) can place new products in many outlets quickly. Service firms such as the Royal Bank of Canada (www.royalbank.com) also can efficiently add new products (financial services) into their distribution networks.

Technology can be exploited.

Firms often seek technological breakthroughs. Makers of computer storage devices, such as Western Digital (www.westerndigital.com), are constantly introducing newer, faster, better versions of their products—at lower prices. In 2000, a Western Digital 15-gigabyte hard drive sold for $200. By 2001, the firm's newer 30-gigabyte drives were selling for $115. Japan's Toshiba (www.toshiba.com), one of the world's largest office equipment firms, has a new high-speed digital copier that prints up to 80 pages a minute and can store paper at 24 locations. The machine has the ability to print 440,000 copies per month. See Figure 13-5. General Electric even shows video clips of some of its major breakthroughs at the company Web site (www.ge.com/corporate/innovation).

Waste materials can be used.

Sometimes, firms want to find uses for waste materials from existing products—to aid productivity or be responsive to recycling: "Electric utilities are spinning gold out of gunk they once spewed in the air. To comply with the 1970 Clean Air Act, companies have been 'scrubbing' the smoke coming out of their stacks to remove sulfur and fly ash, then

FIGURE 13-5

Capitalizing on New Technology

Source: Reprinted by permission.

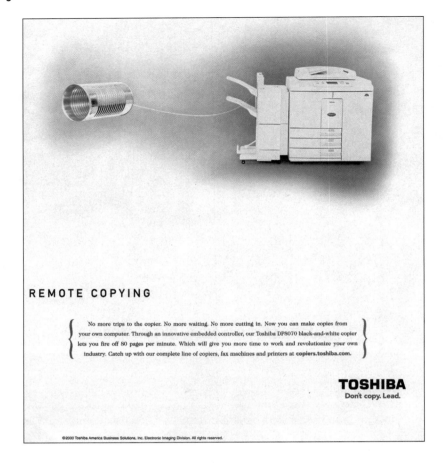

dumping the wastes into landfills. Now, they are finding farmers and construction companies will buy the stuff. Near Oak Ridge, Tennessee, a unit of Caraustar Industries (www.caraustar.com) built a factory to make wallboard out of sulfur residue produced at the Tennessee Valley Authority power plant next door. Farmers buy sulfur residue— 'scrubber sludge'—since it improves soil and boost crop yields. 'Wherever you put that stuff, it just greens up.' By selling what it calls 'coal byproducts,' the TVA (www.tva.gov) makes from $6 million to $10 million a year."[7]

New products respond to consumer needs.

Companies may bring out new products to respond to changing consumer demographics and life-styles. Single-serving pre-packaged foods are aimed at smaller households. Kodak (www.kodak.com) and Fuji (www.fujifilm.com) have introduced a full line of single-use disposable cameras that appeal to people interested in convenience. Microsoft (www.microsoft.com/products/hardware/keyboard) offers computer keyboards that are easier on the wrist. The Hain Celestial Group (www.hain-celestial.com) markets foods that appeal to consumers interested in natural, specialty, organic, and snack foods under brand names sold as "better-for-you" products.

Government mandates are addressed.

New products may be devised in response to government mandates. To address growing concerns about battery disposal (and the carcinogenic properties of nickel cadmium batteries), battery makers (led by Rayovac) have introduced rechargeable batteries that can be recharged up to 25 times or more. Rayovac (www.rayovac.com) even hired Michael Jordan as a celebrity endorser of its Renewal batteries. Although sales of rechargeable batteries are still rather low, they are expected to rise.

[7]John J. Fialka, "Once a Pollutant, 'Scrubber Sludge' Finds a Market," *Wall Street Journal* (October 5, 1998), pp. B1–B2.

GLOBAL *Marketing in Action*

Innovation: Anywhere, Any Time

As a professor of planning at the University of California at Berkeley says, "There's innovative capability all around the world now, even in places that were formerly peripheral. Anyone with a baseline of education can play. Innovation is being democratized." There are many examples of some peripheral places that have jumped to the cutting edge of innovation. Look at Finland's cellular company Nokia (www.nokia.com), the birth of instant messaging in Israel, Ireland's place as the world center for computer animation, and France's role in smart card technology.

According to one theory, new communication technologies, as well as the rising standards in technical literacy, are leveling the playing field. "This democratization of innovation gives disadvantaged nations a chance," says a leading German researcher.

An illustration of this process can be seen in the Philippines, one of Asia's poorest nations, which is now home to some world-class computer programmers. Both European and Asian Web designers are outsourcing their work to the Philippines. The popularity of the Web, the country's high literacy rate, and the willingness of Filipinos to adopt new technologies account for much of the high-tech success there. Surprisingly, the Philippine government has done little to foster the growth of technology.

Many countries use the Philippines for their high-tech projects. Bechtel (www.bechtel.com), an engineering firm, sends blueprints to the Philippines at night and has them placed on computers the next morning. America Online (www.aol.com) is building a worldwide service center in the Philippines that will house 800 engineers and software personnel who will answer E-mails from U.S.-based AOL users.

What are the pros and cons of producing goods and services in places like the Philippines?

Source: Based on material in G. Pascal Zachary and Robert Frank, "High-Tech Hopes," *Wall Street Journal* (September 25, 2000), p. R4.

Good long-run new-product planning requires systematic research and development, matching the requirements of new-product opportunities with company abilities, emphasizing consumer desires, properly spending time and money, and defensive—as well as offensive—planning. A firm must accept that some new products may fail; a progressive firm will take risks: "Innovation is a risky business, and failure is commonplace. Rewarding success is easy, but rewarding intelligent failure is more important. Don't judge people strictly by results; try to judge them by the quality of their efforts. People should take intelligent business risks without also risking their compensation or their careers."[8] There has been some criticism about the negative effects of many U.S. firms' short-run, bottom-line orientation on their level of innovativeness (and willingness to take risks).

[8]"How Can Big Companies Keep the Entrepreneurial Spirit Alive?" *Harvard Business Review*, Vol. 73 (November-December 1995), p. 190.

13-4 WHY NEW PRODUCTS FAIL

Despite better product-planning practices today than ever before, the failure rate for new products is quite high. According to various consulting firms, 35 percent *or more* of all new industrial and consumer products fail.[9] The marketplace can be quite tough on new products.

Product failure can be defined in both absolute and relative terms. **Absolute product failure** occurs if a firm is unable to regain its production and marketing costs. It incurs a financial loss. **Relative product failure** occurs if a firm makes a profit on an item but that product does not reach profit goals and/or adversely affects a firm's image. In computing profits and losses, the impact of the new product on the sales of other company items must be measured.

Even firms with good new-product records have had failures along the way. These include "light" pizza (Pizza Hut), Noxema Skin Fitness (Procter & Gamble), Crystal Pepsi (PepsiCo), Bic perfume, McLean Deluxe (McDonald's), Surge (Coca-Cola), Telaction interactive cable-TV shopping service (J.C. Penney), Premier smokeless cigarettes (R.J. Reynolds), and *The Legend of Bagger Vance* (the movie starring Matt Damon and Will Smith).

Numerous factors may cause new-product failure:

*   *Lack of a strong enough differential advantage:* "Entrepreneur and food developer Jeno Paulucci failed in his frozen pizza venture because he offered customers something they were not willing to pay for. His frozen pizza line, called Jeno's, was great tasting and offered customers a chance to customize their pizza as it came with a package of toppings. This customization, however, proved the product's undoing as cost-conscious customers were not willing to pay for the large number of toppings, some of which were going to waste."[10]

*   *Poor planning:* "Publishers one, authors nothing. In mid-2000, the horror writer Stephen King struck a blow for author independence, electing to forgo the help of a publisher and sell a new serial novel directly to his readers in digital form over the Internet. Titled *The Plant*, the novel tells the story of a predatory vine that terrorizes a small paperback house, and, as book publishers strain to discern the future of digital publishing, it spooked them in more ways than one. But attention and sales have steadily faded, and in November 2000, King decided to call it quits. He had issued installments of *The Plant* under a novel honor-system plan, asking readers voluntarily to pay $1 for each chapter downloaded and pledging to keep writing only if at least 75 percent of readers complied. 'If you pay, the story rolls. If you don't, the story folds.' And few readers were paying."[11]

*   *Poor timing.* Anheuser-Busch's LA beer failure was due to poor timing. LA beer was positioned as having half the alcohol of regular beer and was supported by marketing dollars. But, soon after it came out, nonalcohol beers arrived. The market became bifurcated; customers wanted either regular beer or beer with no alcohol, not a halfway beverage. LA beer was dropped as Anheuser-Busch turned to O'Doul's—its premium nonalcohol beer. As of 2001, according to the brand's Web site (www.odouls.com), "O'Doul's family of beer is the number one-selling brand in the category with more than 40 percent share of the U.S. nonalcohol category, according to Information Resources, Inc. (IRI)". Yet, in Europe, even nonalcohol beer flopped: "People don't feel the pressure to be seen drinking beer anymore. Now, there's a wider range of adult soft drinks available, and it's socially acceptable to drink a soft drink."[12]

---

[9]See Eric Berggren and Thomas Nacher, "Why Good Ideas Go Bust," *Management Review*, Vol. 89 (February 2000), pp. 32–36; and Tony Ulwick and John Eisenhauer, "Predicting the Success or Failure of a New Product Concept," http://ftp.channel1.com/users/acooper/Event_Center/I@WS/I@WS_paper3.html (April 12, 2001).

[10]Robert M. McMath, "Missing His Grab for a Piece of the Pie," *Across the Board* (February 1999), p. 12.

[11]David D. Kirkpatrick, "A Stephen King Online Horror Tale Turns Into a Mini-Disaster," *New York Times* (November 29, 2000), p. C1.

[12]Tara Parker-Pope, "Brewers Dismayed as Drinkers Decide That Suds Are a Dud Without Alcohol," *Wall Street Journal* (July 6, 1995), p. A5C.

(margin note) With **absolute product failure**, *costs are not regained. With* **relative product failure**, *goals are not met.*

(margin note) Leading to failure are lack of an advantage, poor planning and timing, and excess enthusiasm.

- *Excessive enthusiasm by the sponsor.* "Conde Nast's decision in June 2000 to fold its 3-year-old *Women's Sports & Fitness* magazine set off a debate within the industry about the future of multi-interest sports publications aimed at women. *Women's Sports & Fitness* editor Lucy Danziger says that covering a broad range of interests was not the problem. She argues that while women may be interested in sports and fitness, they're not yet conditioned the way men are to subscribe or stop at a newsstand for such magazines. 'I don't think there is a huge market for women's sports magazines right now.' Danziger says her magazine, with about 550,000 circulation, folded because it could not reach its promised ad base of 1 million fast enough. It left its subscribers to go to Conde Nast's all health-focused and more successful magazine, *Self.*"[13]

13-5 NEW-PRODUCT PLANNING

The ***new-product planning process*** has a series of steps from idea generation to commercialization. A firm generates ideas, evaluates them, weeds out poor ones, gets consumer feedback, devises the product, tests it, and brings it to market. An idea can be terminated at any time; costs rise as the process goes on. The process could be used by any firm, and applies to goods and services. See Figure 13-6. In the United States alone, Marketing Intelligence Service (www.marketingintel.com) reports that 32,000 new products are introduced into supermarkets every year.

During new-product planning, a firm needs to endeavor to balance such competing goals as these:

- A systematic process should be followed; however, there must be flexibility to adapt to each unique opportunity.

- The process should be thorough, yet not unduly slow down introductions.

- True innovations should be pursued, yet fiscal constraints must be considered.

- An early reading of consumer acceptance should be sought, but the firm must not give away too much information to potential competitors.

- There should be an interest in short-run profitability, but not at the expense of long-run growth.[14]

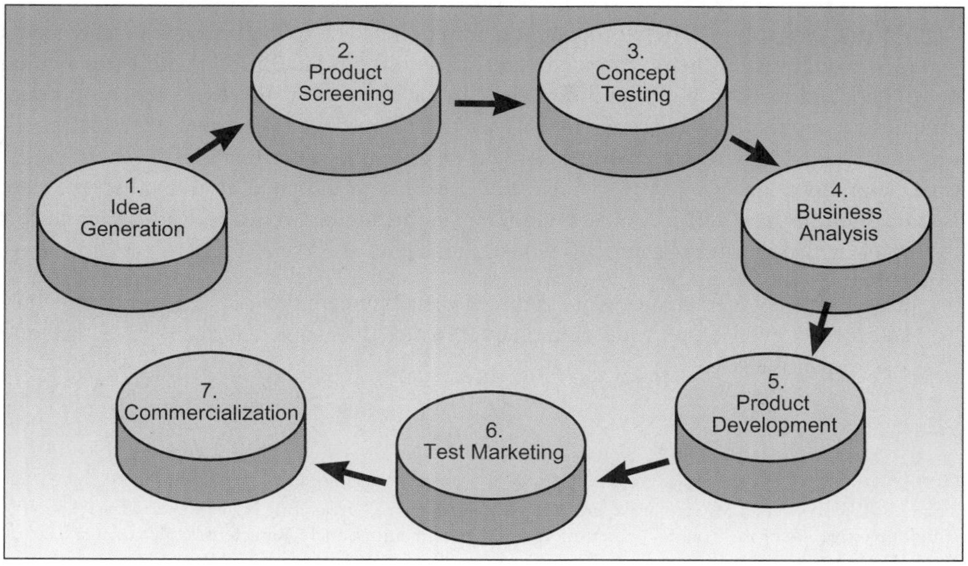

> The ***new-product planning process*** *moves from ideas to commercialization.*

FIGURE 13-6

The New-Product Planning Process

The New-Product Planning Process:
1. Idea Generation
2. Product Screening
3. Concept Testing
4. Business Analysis
5. Product Development
6. Test Marketing
7. Commercialization

[13]Keith L. Alexander, "'Women's Sports' Folds as Niche Gets Redefined," *USA Today* (July 3, 2000), p. B8.

[14]See Avan R. Jassawalla and Hemant C. Sashittal, "Strategies of Effective New Product Team Leaders," *California Management Review*, Vol. 42 (Winter 2000), pp. 34–51; and Gary Hamel, "Reinvent Your Company," *Fortune* (June 12, 2000), pp. 99–118.

Many companies do all the new-product planning activities themselves. Others outsource various tasks. There are a number of consulting firms that specialize in this area, such as Brand Farm (www.brandfarm.com), Cheskin (www.cheskin.com), Ideo (www.ideo.com), and Tality (www.tality.com).

13-5a Idea Generation

Idea generation *is the search for opportunities.*

Idea generation is a continuous, systematic search for new product opportunities. It involves new-idea sources and ways to generate ideas.

Sources of ideas may be employees, channel members, competitors, outside inventors, customers, government, and others. *Market-oriented sources* identify opportunities based on consumer needs and wants; laboratory research is used to satisfy them. Light beer, many ice cream flavors, and easy-to-open soda cans have evolved from market-oriented sources. *Laboratory-oriented sources* identify opportunities based on pure research (which seeks to gain knowledge and indirectly leads to specific new-product ideas) or applied research (which uses existing scientific techniques to develop new-product ideas). Penicillin, anti-freeze, and synthetic fibers have evolved from laboratory sources.

Methods for generating ideas include brainstorming (small-group sessions to come up with a variety of ideas), analyzing current products, reading trade publications, visiting suppliers and dealers, and doing surveys.[15] An open perspective is key: different people should be consulted; many ideas should be offered; and ideas should not be criticized, no matter how offbeat:

> Think of the *worst* possible idea you can for a new soup. How about one with rocks in it? Or a soup made of green slime? Terrible ideas, right? Maybe not. Thinking about a soup with rocks in it could inspire you to invent a new, extra-chunky brand. Thinking about green slime could lead you to create a new $100-million line of "Slime Soups" for young boys who like everything that's "gross."[16]

13-5b Product Screening

Product screening *weeds out undesirable ideas.*

Once a firm spots potential products, it must screen them. In **product screening,** poor, unsuitable, or otherwise unattractive ideas are weeded out from further consideration. Today, many firms use a new-product screening checklist for preliminary analysis. In it, they list the attributes deemed most important and rate each idea on those attributes. The checklist is standardized and allows ideas to be compared.

Figure 13-7 shows a new-product screening checklist with three major categories: general characteristics, marketing characteristics, and production characteristics (which can be applied to both goods and services). In each category, there are several product attributes to assess. They are scored from 1 (outstanding) to 10 (very poor) for each product idea. In addition, the attributes would be weighted because they vary in their impact on new-product success. For every idea, the checklist would yield an overall score. Here is an example of how a firm could develop overall ratings for two ideas. Remember, in this example, the best rating is 1 (so, 3 is worse than 2):

1. Idea A gets an average rating of 2.5 on general characteristics, 2.9 on marketing characteristics, and 1.4 on production characteristics. Idea B gets ratings of 2.8, 1.4, and 1.8, respectively.

---

[15]See Lisa C. Troy, David M. Szymanski, and P. Rajan Varadarajan, "Generating New Product Ideas: An Initial Investigation of the Role of Market Information and Organizational Characteristics," *Journal of the Academy of Marketing Science,* Vol. 29 (Winter 2001), pp. 89–101; W. Chan Kim and Renée Mauborgne, "Knowing a Winning Business Idea When You See One," *Harvard Business Review,* Vol. 78 (September-October 2000), pp. 129–138; and Michael Michalko, "Four Steps Toward Creative Thinking," *Futurist* (May-June 2000), pp. 18–21.

[16]Bryan W. Mattimore, "Eureka! How to Invent a New Product," *Futurist* (March–April 1995), p. 34.

General Characteristics of New Product	Rating
Profit potential	_____
Existing competition	_____
Potential competition	_____
Size of market	_____
Level of investment	_____
Patentability	_____
Level of risk	_____
Marketing Characteristics of New Product	
Fit with marketing capabilities	_____
Effect on existing products (brands)	_____
Appeal to current consumer markets	_____
Potential length of product life cycle	_____
Existence of differential advantage	_____
Impact on image	_____
Resistance to seasonal factors	_____
Production Characteristics of New Product	
Fit with production capabilities	_____
Length of time to commercialization	_____
Ease of production	_____
Availability of labor and material resources	_____
Ability to produce at competitive prices	_____

FIGURE 13-7

A New-Product Screening Checklist

2. The firm assigns an importance weight of 4 to general characteristics, 5 to marketing characteristics, and 3 to production characteristics. The best overall rating is 12 $[(1 \times 4) + (1 \times 5) + (1 \times 3)]$. The poorest possible average rating is 120 $[(10 \times 4) + (10 \times 5) + (10 \times 3)]$.

3. Idea A gets an overall rating of 28.7 $[(2.5 \times 4) + (2.9 \times 5) + (1.4 \times 3)]$. B gets an overall rating of 23.6 $[(2.8 \times 4) + (1.4 \times 5) + (1.8 \times 3)]$.

4. Idea B's overall rating is better than A's due to its better marketing evaluation (the characteristics judged most important by the firm).

In screening, patentability must often be determined. A **patent** grants an inventor of a useful product or process exclusive selling rights for a fixed period. An invention may be patented if it is a "useful, novel, and nonobvious process, machine, manufacture, or composition of matter" and not patented by anyone else. Separate applications are needed for protection in foreign markets. Many nations have simplified matters via patent cooperation treaties; however, some do not honor such treaties. Today, in the United States and the other members of the World Trade Organization, patents last for 20 years from the date that applications are filed. Until mid-1995, U.S. patents were 17 years from the date they were granted. Each year, the U.S. Patent and Trademark Office (www.uspto.gov) receives 325,000 patent applications and grants 170,000 patents. About 45 percent of U.S. patents involve foreign firms; in contrast, one-sixth percent of Japanese patents are held by foreigners.

A firm should answer these kinds of patent questions in screening: Can the proposed new product be patented? Are competitive items patented? When do competitors' patents expire? Are patents on competing items available under a licensing agreement? Would the company be free of patent liability (infringement) if it introduces the proposed new product?

A **patent** *gives exclusive selling rights to an inventor.*

13-5c Concept Testing

Next, a firm needs consumer feedback about the new-product ideas that pass through screening. *Concept testing* presents the consumer with a proposed product and measures attitudes and intentions at an early stage of the new-product planning process.

Concept testing is a quick, inexpensive way to assess consumer enthusiasm. It asks potential consumers to react to a picture, written statement, or oral product description. This lets a firm learn initial attitudes prior to costly, time-consuming product development. Heinz (www.heinz.com), Kodak (www.kodak.com), Sony (www.sony.com), and Sunbeam (www.sunbeam.com) are among those using concept testing. Figure 13-8 shows a brief concept test for a proposed fee-based online music service.

Concept testing generally asks consumers these types of questions:

- Is the idea easy to understand?
- Would this product meet a real need?
- Do you see distinct benefits for this product over those on the market?
- Do you find the claims about this product believable?
- Would you buy the product?
- How much would you pay for it?
- Would you replace your current brand with this new product?
- What improvements can you suggest in various attributes of the concept?
- How frequently would you buy the product?
- Who would use the product?[17]

13-5d Business Analysis

At this point, a firm does business analysis for the new-product concepts that are deemed attractive. *Business analysis* involves the detailed review, projection, and evaluation of such factors as consumer demand, production costs, marketing costs, break-even points, competition, capital investments, and profitability for each proposed new product. It is much more detailed than product screening.

Here are some of the considerations at this planning stage:

Criteria	Selected Considerations
Demand projections	Short- and long-run sales potential; speed of sales growth; price/sales relationship; seasonality; rate of repurchases
Production cost projections	Total and per-unit costs; startup versus continuing costs; estimates of raw materials and other costs; economies of scale; break-even points
Marketing cost projections	Product planning (patent search, product development, testing); promotion; distribution; marketing research; break-even points
Competitive projections	Short-run and long-run market shares of company and competitors; competitors' strengths and weaknesses; potential competitors; likely strategies by competitors in response to firm
Capital investment projections	Need for new equipment and facilities versus use of existing facilities and resources
Profitability projections	Time to recoup initial costs; short- and long-run total and per-unit profits; reseller needs; control over price; return on investment; risk

[17]Adapted from Philip Kotler, *Marketing Management: Analysis, Planning, Implementation, and Control,* Millennium Edition (Upper Saddle River, N.J.: Prentice-Hall, 2000), p. 339.

A leading music company is considering the introduction of a new online music service. The company would make its whole catalog of 10,000 recorded songs available under two different subscription plans. With plan 1, customers would pay a monthly fee of $10.00 for up to 50 downloads per month. With plan 2, customers would pay a fee of 30 cents for each song that is downloaded. All songs would have the same fee.

1. React to the overall concept described above.

2. What do you like most about the proposed concept? Why?

3. What do you like least about the proposed concept? Why?

4. What suggestions do you have for improving the proposed concept?

5. What else would you like to know about the proposed concept?

6. How likely would you be to participate in the proposed music service?

Very likely ⎯⎯ ⎯⎯ ⎯⎯ ⎯⎯ ⎯⎯ Very unlikely

Why? ⎯⎯⎯⎯⎯⎯⎯⎯⎯⎯⎯⎯⎯⎯⎯⎯⎯⎯

FIGURE 13-8

A Brief Concept Test for a Proposed New Online Music Service

Because the next step is expensive and time-consuming product development, critical use of business analysis is essential to eliminate marginal items. For an online demonstration of business analysis, go to Business Resource Software's Quick Insight Web site (www.businessplansoftware.org/qidemo/qidemo.asp) and click on the arrow key that appears in the upper right portion of the screen. Keep clicking until you have finished the demonstration.

13-5e Product Development

In *product development,* an idea for a new product is converted into a tangible form and a basic marketing strategy is identified. Depending on the product involved, this planning stage encompasses product construction, packaging, branding, product positioning, and consumer attitude and usage testing.

Product development *focuses on devising an actual product and a broad marketing strategy.*

Product construction decisions include the type and quality of materials comprising the product, the method of production, production time, production capacity, the assortment to be offered, and the time needed to move from development to commercialization. Packaging decisions include the materials used, the functions performed, and alternative sizes and colors. Branding decisions include the choice of a name, trademark protection, and the image sought. Product positioning involves selecting a target market and positioning the new good or service against competitors and other company offerings. Consumer testing studies perceptions of and satisfaction with the new product.

Product-development costs may be relatively low with a modification. However, an innovation may be costly (up to several million dollars or more), time-consuming (up to four years for a new car), and complex. This is true of services, as well as goods. The construction of the new Beau Rivage luxury hotel and casino (www.beaurivageresort.com) in Biloxi, Mississippi, cost $680 million and took six years: "A picture-perfect site on a 15-mile strip of beach welcomes attendees to the property, and the promise of a superb destination is planted. A 60-foot tall formal garden atrium beckons, with meticulously kept flora that is regularly replaced to reflect and celebrate the seasons. All 1,780 guest rooms boast custom furnishings and Italian marble floors and surfaces, and feature a work desk with data port, three phones, separate vanity, deluxe bedding, triple sheeting, and bath amenities, while many feature superb views of the Gulf."[18]

Some companies are especially creative in their product development:

> LeapFrog Enterprises (www.leapfrog.com) has turned the educational toy business into a rigorous exercise in product development. It routinely spends 18 months and $250,000 to develop a new product, pushing it through a battery of experts and skeptics. Only one in ten of the concepts proposed make it to the retailers' shelves.
>
> The process begins with a conversational free-for-all among a select thirty of LeapFrog's employees. Next, founder and president, Michael Wood and his vice-president of product development, Fisher-Price veteran Eric Shuler, run the selected concepts by an educational advisory board—mostly professors of education and childhood development—which sometimes puts the kibosh on ideas. For those that survive, Shuler makes sketches and presents them to 24 mothers in eight different groups. "This is where we learn the most. No one has better insight into what a child likes to play with. The moms kill nearly 50% of the toys at the sketch stage," says Wood.[19]

13-5f Test Marketing

Test marketing involves placing a fully developed new product (a good or service) in one or more selected areas and observing its actual performance under a proposed marketing plan. The purpose is to evaluate the product and planned marketing efforts in a real setting prior to a full-scale introduction. Rather than just study intentions, test marketing lets a firm monitor actual consumer behavior, competitor reactions, and reseller interest. After testing, the firm could decide to go ahead, modify the product and then go ahead, modify the marketing plan and then go ahead, or drop the product. AT&T (www.att.com), John Hancock Funds (www.johnhancock.com/funds), Home Depot (www.homedepot.com), Levi Strauss (www.levistrauss.com), McDonald's (www.mcdonalds.com), and Procter & Gamble (www.pg.com) are among the companies that use test marketing. Consumer products firms are more apt to engage in test marketing than industrial products firms, which often do intensive product-use testing with key customers.

Test marketing requires several decisions: when to test, where to test, how long to test, what test information to acquire, and how to apply test results. Figure 13-9 shows the criteria in making choices.

Although test marketing has often been beneficial, some firms now question its effectiveness and downplay or skip this stage in new-product planning. Dissatisfaction arises from test marketing's costs, the time delays before full introduction, the information being

Test marketing *occurs in selected areas and observes real performance.*

[18]Becky Neamy, "Beau Rivage: 'Beautiful Shore' and So Much More," *Successful Meetings* (February 2001), p. 21.
[19]Mary Ellen Egan, "Anything But Child's Play," *Forbes* (May 28, 2001), p. 66.

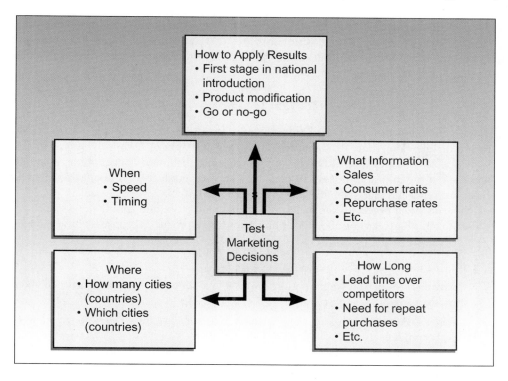

FIGURE 13-9
Test Marketing Decisions

provided to competitors, the inability to predict national (global) results based on limited test-market areas, and the impact of such external factors as the economy and competition on test results. Test marketing can even allow nontesting competitors to catch up with an innovative firm by the time a product is ready for a full rollout.

Sometimes, consumer panels are used to simulate test market conditions—even online. For example, as stated at its Web site, GlobalTestMarket.com (www.globaltestmarket.com) "is a global consumer research service sponsored by Global Market Insite (GMI)—the worldwide technology leader in multi-country online consumer research. GMI is also the sponsor of ConsumerInsite.com, a business-to-business site where clients can design and manage online research. Consumer research is conducted through GlobalTestMarket.com, as well as by research partners located around the world who have agreed to use the GMI standard for online surveying. In addition, this site provides online retailing of development-stage products via online test markets."

13-5g Commercialization

At this point, a firm is ready to introduce a new product to its full target market. This involves *commercialization* and corresponds to the introductory stage of the product life cycle. During commercialization, the firm enacts a total marketing plan and works toward production capacity. Among the factors to be considered are the speed of acceptance by consumers and distribution intermediaries, the intensity of distribution (how many outlets), production capabilities, the promotion mix, prices, competition, the time until profitability, and commercialization costs.

Commercialization may require large outlays and a long-term commitment. Manufacturers often spend millions of dollars for a typical national rollout in U.S. supermarkets—nearly half on consumer promotion and the rest on product costs, marketing research, and promotions for supermarkets. Yet, commercialization costs can go much higher. When the Venus shaver for women was introduced, it had a $150 million marketing budget—for TV and print ads, a Web site, contests, in-store promotions, and other activities. Look at how sophisticated and detailed the Web site (www.venus.com) is.

Commercializing a new product sometimes must overcome consumer and reseller reluctance because of ineffective prior company offerings. This occurred with Texas Instruments (www.ti.com) in the business computer market, after it bowed out of the

Commercialization *involves a major marketing commitment.*

home computer market. And many resellers were upset with the usually reliable Sony in 2000 when it was able to ship only 500,000 units of the Sony Playstation 2 (www.us.playstation.com) during the new product's North America debut, rather than the one million that had been promised.

13-6 GROWING PRODUCTS

Once a product is commercialized, the goal is for consumer acceptance and company sales to rise rapidly. Sometimes, this occurs; other times, it may take a while. The growth rate and total sales of new products rely on two consumer behavior concepts: the adoption process and the diffusion process. In managing growing products, a firm must understand these concepts and plan its marketing efforts accordingly.

*The **adoption process** explains the new-product purchase behavior of individual consumers.*

The ***adoption process*** is the mental and behavioral procedure an individual consumer goes through when learning about and purchasing a new product. It consists of these stages:

1. *Knowledge*—A person (organization) learns of a product's existence and gains some understanding of how it functions.

2. *Persuasion*—A person (organization) forms a favorable or unfavorable attitude about a product.

3. *Decision*—A person (organization) engages in actions leading to a choice to adopt or reject a product.

4. *Implementation*—A person (organization) uses a product.

5. *Confirmation*—A person (organization) seeks reinforcement and may reverse a decision if exposed to conflicting messages.[20]

The speed of adoption depends on consumer traits, the product, and the firm's marketing effort. It is faster if people have high discretionary income and are willing to try new offerings; the product has low perceived risk; the product has an advantage over others on the market; the product is a modification, not an innovation; the product is compatible with current life-styles or ways of operating a business; product attributes can be easily communicated; product importance is low; the product can be tested before a purchase; the product is consumed quickly; the product is easy to use; mass advertising and distribution are used; and the marketing mix adjusts as the person (organization) moves through the adoption process.

*The **diffusion process** describes when different segments are likely to purchase.*

The ***diffusion process*** describes the manner in which different members of the target market often accept and purchase a product. It spans the time from product introduction through market saturation and affects the total sales level of a product as it moves through the life cycle:

1. *Innovators* are the first to try a new product. They are venturesome, willing to accept risk, socially aggressive, communicative, and worldly. It must be learned which innovators are opinion leaders—those who influence others. This group is about 2.5 percent of the market.

2. *Early adopters* are the next to buy a new product. They enjoy the prestige, leadership, and respect that early purchases bring—and tend to be opinion leaders. They adopt new ideas but use discretion. This group is about 13.5 percent of the market.

3. The *early majority* is the initial part of the mass market to buy. They have status among peers and are outgoing, communicative, and attentive to information. The group is about 34 percent of the market.

4. The *late majority* is the second part of the mass market to buy. They are less cosmopolitan and responsive to change, and include people (firms) with lower economic and social status, those past middle age (or set in their jobs), and skeptics. This group is about 34 percent of the market.

[20]Everett M. Rogers, *Diffusion of Innovations*, Fourth Edition (New York: Free Press, 1995), Chapter 5.

MARKETING *and the Web*

Photo-Sharing Web Sites Revolutionize Picture Taking

Ofoto (www.ofoto.com) is one of the photo-sharing Web sites that not only develops film but also scans and posts pictures online. The service can work with either digital photos that are uploaded by consumers free-of-charge or traditional film negatives that are scanned by the Web-based business for free. In addition, such services typically let consumers store the equivalent of photo albums on their Web site free-of-charge. Consumers who want a reprint of a photo just click on their favorite photo and then enter their credit card numbers.

Unlike traditional photo processors that charge fees for developing both good and bad shots, the Web firms plan to make their money by charging customers—and their families and friends—for prints, picture frames, and coffee mugs of their favorite pictures. There are not only no costs for developing, but also most of the photo-sharing Web sites even provide postage-paid mailer envelopes to send film for processing.

The various photo-sharing Web sites have different features. Some enable users to lighten or darken images to correct lighting. Others allow users to improve their pictures through cropping, changing colors, and adjusting contrast. Some sites let users change the photo background and even customize each photo with a title, caption, and descriptive text.

One problem with these services is their relative slow speed and high cost. According to one report, processing and uploading time can take more than one week. The cost of reprints also average about 50 cents each, as compared to 30 cents for a traditional processing service.

How should a traditional film processor react to the new Web services? Explain your answer.

Source: Based on material in Larry Armstrong, "To Develop Your Vacation Pictures, Just Click," *Business Week* (August 28, 2000), pp. 258–259.

---

5. *Laggards* purchase last, if at all. They are price-conscious, suspicious of change, low in income and status, tradition bound, and conservative. They do not adopt a product until it reaches maturity. Some sellers ignore them since it can be hard to market a product to laggards. Thus, concentrated marketing may do well by focusing on products for laggards. This group is about 16 percent of the market.[21]

Growth for a major innovation often starts slowly because there is an extended adoption process and the early majority may be hesitant to buy. Sales may then rise quickly. For minor innovations or product modifications, growth is much faster right from the start.

The first high-definition television (HDTV) sets—a major innovation—were marketed in 1996; yet, by 2001, fewer than 1 percent of U.S. households had an HDTV set. And during 2000, only 625,000 of the 30 million TV sets purchased were HDTV sets. Consumers were hesitant to buy due to the high initial prices (several thousand dollars), the complexities of HDTV technology, the lack of programming in the HDTV format, and skepticism about how much better HDTV viewing was from regular viewing. Nonetheless, sales are expected to skyrocket within the next five years because of much

---

[21]Ibid, Chapter 7.

FIGURE 13-10
Waiting for Consumers to Want Their HDTV

Retail chains such as The Wiz (www.thewiz.com) are anxiously waiting for the sales of HDTV sets to take off. In anticipation of strong sales, The Wiz is allocating a lot of selling space and promotion resources to this major innovation.

Source: Reprinted by permission of Retail Planning Associates. Photography by Michael Houghton/STUDIOHIO.

Proper marketing can let mature products maintain high sales.

lower prices and a Federal Communications Commission ruling known as "digital must-carry," whereby cable TV operators will be required to offer HDTV reception as of 2006. [22] See Figure 13-10.

These products are among those now in the growth stage of the product life cycle, and represent good opportunities for firms: CD "burners," regional and national cellular phone services, upscale sports utility vehicles, men's hair-coloring products, generic drugs, all-in-one office machines (phone, fax, copier, printer), online financial services, adult education, noncarbonated beverages, and business-to-business video conferencing.

13-7 MATURE PRODUCTS

Products are in the maturity stage of the life cycle when they reach the late majority and laggard markets. Goals turn from growth to maintenance. Because new products are so costly and risky, more firms are placing marketing emphasis on mature products with steady sales and profits, and minimal risk.

When managing mature products, a firm should study the size, attributes, and needs of the current market; untapped market segments; competition; the potential for product modifications; the likelihood of new company products replacing mature ones; profit margins; the marketing effort for each sale; reseller attitudes; the promotion mix; the impact of specific products on the product line; each product's effect on company image; the remaining years for the products; and the management effort needed.

[22]"Video Industry Sales Scorecard," www.twice.com/html/statistics.html (April 12, 2001); Jill Carroll, "FCC Deals a Setback to Broadcasters in Ruling on HDTV and Cable Firms," *Wall Street Journal* (January 22, 2001), p. B8; and Alex Romanelli, "HDTV: What Is Going Wrong?" *Electronic News* (January 1, 2001), p. 41.

There are many possible benefits if a firm has a popular brand in a mature product category. First, the life cycle may be extended almost indefinitely. Budweiser beer (www.budweiser.com), Coke Classic soda (http:www2.coca-cola.com/about/ whatwedo/brands_coca-cola.html), Goodyear tires (www.goodyeartires.com), Ivory soap (www.ivory.com), Lipton tea (www.liptont.com), Maxwell House coffee (www.kraftfoods.com/maxwellhouse/mh_index.html), Life Savers candy (www. candystand.com/home.htm), and Sherwin-Williams paints (www.sherwin-williams.com) are among the leaders in their product categories; each brand is well over 75 years old. Second, a mature brand has a loyal customer base and a stable, profitable position in the market. Third, the likelihood of future low demand is greatly reduced; this is a real risk for new products. Fourth, a firm's overall image is enhanced. This may allow the firm to extend a popular name to other products. Fifth, there is more control over marketing efforts and more precision in sales forecasting. Sixth, mature products can be used as cash cows to support spending on new products. However, some marketing support must be continued if a mature product is to remain popular.

Successful products can stay in maturity for long periods, as the following illustrate:

- Although the paper clip was invented in 1899 by Norwegian Johan Vaaler, today it is more popular than ever due to its ease of use, flexible applications, and large customer following: "The paper clip is one of the simplest workplace tools; but it is also one of the most versatile. What other office instrument can be used as an after-lunch dental aid, emergency manicure device, eyeglass screw replacement kit, and magic apparatus?" It seems that, after more than 100 years, there is still nothing to match a paper clip. Twenty billion are sold yearly.[23]

- Chlorine is a chemical produced by the electrolysis of brine. It is used to process organic chemicals and in the production of pulp, paper, and other industrial goods. In industrialized nations, chlorine is a mature product—with stable sales in the United States and negative sales growth in Canada, Japan, and Europe. Sales are growing in Asia, Latin America, Africa, and the Middle East. Thus, chlorine producers' marketing efforts are now quite aggressive in developing and less-developed nations.

- "Whether clothes are lean or loose, short or long, there's a common thread running through much of today's fashion: Lycra (www.lycra.com)—DuPont's trademark for spandex fiber that started out in the 1950s as a substitute for rubber in girdles." After sales stagnated for a while, the fiber gained attention in the 1980s with the advent of cycling pants and leggings, and technological advances that let Lycra fibers be used in sheer hosiery. Lycra is now "in everything from long, willowy cotton and linen sheaths by Liz Claiborne's Lizsport to crewneck bodysuits from Anne Klein II and tank dresses from designer Donna Karan's DKNY division." In certain parts of Europe, the Lycra name has a consumer recognition rate of 98 percent; and expansion in Latin America and the Far East are under way. To ensure the continued success of Lycra, DuPont has steadily invested in it, developing ways to make the most effective practical use of its endlessly versatile properties: "This allows us to offer an increasingly broad choice of garments that make us feel good and look great.[24]

- Since the 1930s, Hormel Foods (www.hormel.com) has marketed canned chili. To keep the line as the best-selling chili in the United States, the company regularly introduces new versions—including ones that are fat-free and that have less sodium. Its online digital recipe book gives dozens of ways to use chili in casseroles, dips, sandwiches, pizza, and a lot more. See Figure 13-11.

Popular mature brands offer several benefits for companies.

[23]"The Sublime Paper Clip: A Design Classic," http://www3.autodesk.com/adsk/item/0,,325044-123112,00. html (April 14, 2001).

[24]Pat Sloan, "Lycra Stretches Fashion Appeal," *Advertising Age* (November 2, 1992), pp. 3, 36; and "The Lycra Difference," www.lycra.com/Lycra/home.html (May 4, 2001).

FIGURE 13-11
FIGURE 13-11
Hormel Chili: The Leader for 70 Years

Source: Reprinted by permission.

FIGURE 13-12
V8: Proud to Be Part of the Latest Health Craze—Again

Source: Reprinted by permission.

- Campbell's V8 juice (www.v8juice.com) has also been around for several decades. After a lull, Campbell has rejuvenated the brand through an updated marketing campaign that promotes V8 as "a full serving of vegetables," "a good source of potassium," "made with antioxidant rich tomatoes," "excellent source of antioxidants," and "50 calories per serving." See Figure 13-12.

There are many options available for extending the mature stage of the product life cycle. Table 13-2 shows seven strategies and examples of each.

TABLE 13-2	Selected Strategies for Extending the Mature Stage of the Product Life Cycle
Strategy	**Examples**
1. Develop new uses for products	Jell-O used in garden salads WD-40 used in the maintenance of kitchen appliances
2. Develop new product features and refinements	Zoom lenses for 35mm cameras Battery-powered televisions
3. Increase the market	American Express accounts for small businesses International editions of major magazines
4. Find new classes of consumers for present products	Nylon carpeting for institutional markets Johnson & Johnson's baby shampoo used by adults
5. Find new classes of consumers for modified products	Industrial power tools altered for do-it-yourself market Inexpensive copy machines for home offices
6. Increase product usage among current users	Multiple packages for soda and beer Discounts given for increased long-distance phone calls
7. Change marketing strategy	Greeting cards sold in supermarkets Office furniture promoted via mail-order catalogs

Not all mature products can be revived or extended. Consumer needs may disappear, as when frozen juice replaced juice squeezers. Life-style changes may lead to less interest in products, such as teller services in banks. Better and more convenient products may be devised, such as CD players to replace record players. The market may be saturated and marketing efforts may be unable to garner enough sales to justify time and costs, which is why Japan's NEC has a diminished role in consumer electronics.

13-8 PRODUCT DELETION

Products should be deleted if they offer limited sales and profit potential, reflect poorly on the firm, tie up resources that could be used for other opportunities, involve lots of management time, create reseller dissatisfaction due to low turnover, and divert attention from long-term goals.

However, there are many points to weigh before deleting a product: As a product matures, it blends in with existing items and becomes part of the total product line (mix). Customers and distribution intermediaries may be hurt if an item is dropped. A firm may not want competitors to have the only product for customers. Poor sales and profits may be only temporary. The marketing strategy, not the product, may cause the poor results. Thus, in-depth analysis should be used with faltering products.[25]

Low-profit or rapidly declining products are often dropped or de-emphasized:

* With its last issue in April 2001, *McCall's,* the 125-year-old women's magazine, moved into history. As a senior vice-president for Zenith Media said, "A reputation can only carry you so far. When there are so many choices, a reputation of yesteryear doesn't hold water." The magazine's circulation had fallen from a peak of 8.5 million in the late 1960s to 4 million at the time of its demise. Nothing clicked with its readers the way *McCall's* did in the 1960s. "It lost its way." To replace *McCall's,* the publisher introduced *Rosie: The Magazine,* targeted at "a younger, more educated, and upscale set of women. We've done everything we could with a great American history to succeed, and it didn't work. So we've made this decision to launch *Rosie.* American women are ready for something new."[26]

Products need to be deleted if they have consistently poor sales, tie up resources, and cannot be revived.

During deletion, customer and distributor needs must be considered.

[25]See George J. Avlonitis, Susan J. Hart, and Nikolaos X. Tzokas, "An Analysis of Product Deletion Scenarios," *Journal of Product Innovation Management,* Vol. 17 (January 2000), pp. 41–56.

[26]Heather Holliday, "How McCall's Lost Its Way," *Advertising Age* (March 12, 2001), p. 24.

ETHICAL Issues in Marketing

Why Scotchgard Was Withdrawn as a Protector of Fabrics and Upholstery

In late 1997, 3M (www.3m.com) found that tiny traces of its chemical perfluoroctane sulfonate (PFOS) were present in blood samples drawn from people throughout the United States. 3M was concerned since it made most of the world's supply of this chemical. While 3M did not know the exact source of the PFOS contamination, and the firm insisted that there was no evidence of a health risk to humans, the firm decided to phase out its products containing any PFOS as of May 16, 2000.

This decision meant that 3M would no longer produce its Scotchgard fabric protector product, as 3M did not have a replacement chemical for PFOS. In addition to its loss of Scotchgard's annual sales of $500 million, 3M had a restructuring cost of $200 million associated with discontinuing Scotchgard.

The action to abandon this successful product was noteworthy since it was voluntary. According to an Environmental Protection Agency administrator, "3M deserves credit for identifying this problem and coming forward voluntarily." A scientist with the National Resources Defense Council noted, "It took guts. Most firms, when faced with government nudging, go into anger, denial, and the rest of that stuff. What we are accustomed to seeing is decades-long arguments about whether a chemical is really toxic."

Since May 2000's announcement that 3M would phase out production of the PFOS used in some Scotchgard protection products, "the research labs at 3M have been busier than usual. A new Scotchgard treatment for carpet has already been provided to carpet manufacturers to replace previous formulations. New aerosol products for in-home use are being introduced to replace Scotchgard protector in a can. New formulations of cleaner-applied home and office treatments for carpet and upholstery have been tested and are being manufactured. 3M laboratories are working with our customers to identify and develop new products to meet the needs of the apparel, textile, and home furnishings markets."

As a 3M executive, what marketing activities would you take next?

Source: Based on material in Joseph Weber, "3M's Big Cleanup," *Business Week* (June 5, 2000), pp. 96–98; and "Scotchgard Breaking News," www.mmm.com/carpet/news.html (April 2, 2001).

- In late 2000, General Motors announced that it would phase out the 103-year-old Oldsmobile division (www.oldsmobile.com) within the next few years: "It turns out it was your father's Oldsmobile after all. The decision to phase out Oldsmobile illustrates how difficult it can be to resurrect a brand—even one with a century of history—once it has fallen out of favor. The drastic move follows more than a decade during which advertising failed to provide potential customers with a convincing reason to buy—despite a major modernization. Under mounting pressure, Oldsmobile hired a new ad director in a last-ditch effort to energize the brand. But attempts to remake the image of one of America's oldest car lines actually go back decades. In the 1960s, well aware that its very name gave the car a dated image, GM began calling it the 'Youngmobile' in a long-running ad campaign. In 1988, the firm switched its advertising tagline to 'It's Not Your Father's Oldsmobile.' Still, a fuddy-duddy image dogged the brand, keeping it from attracting younger buyers. But Oldsmobile's slide wasn't entirely the fault of ineffective advertising. Muddled product strategy was as big—or bigger—a culprit."[27]

- "If business is a jungle, then the rise and fall of the typewriter is a demonstration of evolution, of the little creature that could. When Smith Corona filed for bankruptcy in 1995, one of the final signals in the triumph of PCs and software over the typewriter [originally patented in 1868] was at hand."[28]

In discontinuing a product, a firm must decide about replacement parts, the notification time for customers and resellers, and the honoring of warranties/guarantees. A company planning to delete its line of office telephones, for example, must resolve these questions: (1) Replacement parts—Who will make them? How long will they be made? (2) Notification time—How soon before the actual deletion will an announcement be made? Will distributors be alerted early enough so they can line up other suppliers? (3) Warranties—How will warranties be honored? After they expire, how will repairs be done?

WEB SITES YOU CAN USE

These are just a few of the many helpful Web sites dealing with various aspects of product management:

Idea Site for Business
(www.ideasiteforbusiness.com)

Inventing.com
(www.inventing.com)

National Inventors Hall of Fame
(www.invent.org)

"Product Development"
(www.infotechmarketing.net/productdevelopment.htm)

"Product Development Strategies"
(www.tka.co.uk/magic/archive/featur13.htm)

ProductNews.com (www.productnews.com)

Ready 2 Launch
(www.ready2launch.com)

[27]Vanessa O'Connell and Joe White, "After Decades of Brand Bodywork, GM Parks Oldsmobile—For Good," *Wall Street Journal* (December 13, 2000), pp. B1, B4.
[28]Francis X. Clines, "An Ode to the Typewriter," *New York Times* (July 10, 1995), p. D5.

SUMMARY

1. *To study how products are created and managed, with an emphasis on the product life cycle* Product management creates and oversees products over their lives. New products are modifications or innovations that consumers see as substantive. Modifications are improvements to existing products. Minor innovations have not been previously sold by the firm but have been sold by others. Major innovations have not been previously sold by anyone.

The product life cycle seeks to describe a product's sales, competitors, profits, customers, and marketing emphasis from inception until removal from the market. Many firms desire a balanced product portfolio, with products in various stages of the cycle. The product life cycle has several derivations, from traditional to fad to bust. The traditional cycle consists of four stages: introduction, growth, maturity, and decline. During each stage, the marketing goal, industry sales, competition, industry profits, customers, and marketing mix change. While the life cycle is useful in planning, it should not be a forecasting tool.

2. *To detail the importance of new products and describe why new products fail* New products are important because they may foster differential advantages, sustain sales growth, require a lot of time for development, generate large profits, enable a firm to diversify, make distribution more efficient, lead to technological breakthroughs, allow waste products to be used, respond to changing consumers, and address government mandates.

If a firm has a financial loss, a product is an absolute failure. If it has a profit but does not attain its goals, a product is a relative failure. Failures occur due to such factors as a lack of a significant differential advantage, poor planning, poor timing, and excessive enthusiasm by the product sponsor.

3. *To present the stages in the new-product planning process* New-product planning involves a comprehensive, seven-step process. During idea generation, new opportunities are sought. In product screening, unattractive ideas are weeded out via a new-product screening checklist. At concept testing, the consumer reacts to a proposed idea. Business analysis requires a detailed evaluation of demand, costs, competition, investments, and profits. Product development converts an idea into a tangible form and outlines a marketing strategy. Test marketing, a much-debated technique, involves placing a product for sale in selected areas and observing performance under actual conditions. Commercialization is the sale of a product to the full target market. A new product can be terminated or modified at any point in the process.

4. *To analyze the growth and maturity of products, including the adoption process, the diffusion process, and extension strategies* Once a new product is commercialized, the firm's goal is for consumer acceptance and company sales to rise as rapidly as possible. However, the growth rate and level for a new product are dependent on the adoption process—which describes how a single consumer learns about and purchases a product—and the diffusion process—which describes how different members of the target market learn about and purchase a product. These processes are faster for certain consumers, products, and marketing strategies.

When products mature, goals turn from growth to maintenance. Mature products can provide stable sales and profits and loyal consumers. They do not require the risks and costs of new products. There are several factors to consider and alternative strategies from which to choose when planning to sustain mature products. It may not be possible to retain aging products if consumer needs disappear, life-styles change, new products make them obsolete, or the market becomes too saturated.

5. *To examine product deletion decisions and strategies* At some point, a firm may have to determine whether to continue a faltering product. Deletion may be hard because of the interrelation of products, the impact on customers and resellers, and other factors. It should be done in a structured manner; and replacement parts, notification time, and warranties should all be considered in a deletion plan.

KEY TERMS

new product (p. 386)
modifications (p. 386)
minor innovations (p. 386)
major innovations (p. 386)
product life cycle (p. 386)
balanced product portfolio (p. 386)
introduction stage of the product
   life cycle (p. 387)
growth stage of the product life cycle (p. 387)

maturity stage of the product life cycle
   (p. 387)
decline stage of the product life cycle (p. 389)
self-fulfilling prophecy (p. 389)
absolute product failure (p. 394)
relative product failure (p. 394)
new-product planning process (p. 395)
idea generation (p. 396)
product screening (p. 396)

patent (p. 397)
concept testing (p. 398)
business analysis (p. 398)
product development (p. 399)
test marketing (p. 400)
commercialization (p. 401)
adoption process (p. 402)
diffusion process (p. 402)

REVIEW QUESTIONS

1. Distinguish among a product modification, a minor innovation, and a major innovation. Present an example of each for a hospital.
2. Explain the basic premise of the product life cycle. What is the value of this concept?
3. Give four reasons why new products are important to a company.
4. How does product screening differ from business analysis?
5. What are the pros and cons of test marketing?
6. How can a firm speed a product's growth?
7. Cite five ways in which a firm could extend the mature stage of the product life cycle. Provide an example of each.
8. Why is a product deletion decision so difficult?

DISCUSSION QUESTIONS

1. Comment on the following statement: "We never worry about relative product failures because we make a profit on them. We only worry about absolute product failures."
2. Develop a 10-item new-product screening checklist for an online college textbook developer. How would you weight each item?
3. Differentiate between the commercialization strategies for a product modification and a major innovation. Relate your answers to the adoption process and the diffusion process.
4. Select a product that has been in existence for 20 or more years and explain why it has been successful for so long.

WEB EXERCISE

The CCH Business Owner's Toolkit (www.toolkit.cch.com) offers a lot of useful advice on new product development. Visit the site and type "new product" in the search box. Then, read at least three articles and comment on what you learned.

PART 4 SHORT CASES

Case 1

Positioning a Service Firm in a Competitive Industry[c4-1]

U-Save Auto Rental of America (www.usave.net) is the nation's number 2 ranking off-airport, neighborhood car rental firm. With about 12,000 cars and 400 locations, U-Save is well behind Enterprise Rent-A-Car (www.enterprise.com) in both locations and sales. For example, while Enterprise has about 60 percent of this market, U-Save is aiming for 25 percent. According to Tom McDonnell, U-Save's chief executive officer and president, "Our core strategy is to be No. 2. We see it as a real competitive advantage, and we'll never sacrifice profitability just to get market share." In a country where "winning isn't everything, it's the only thing," to quote the legendary football coach Vince Lombardi, it may seem surprising that an executive would tout the virtues of being second in an industry. Yet many industry experts and business school professors see a distinct benefit in being number 2. As a professor at George Washington's School of Business says, "It's much less risky. You get less competitive attention, and you can operate in the shadows while No. 1 takes the heat."

Marketing analysts suggest that these are the strategies that a number 2 firm in any industry needs to follow to be profitable:

- Coast on a large competitor's research, if possible.
- Let the number 1 firm stimulate demand. Then be ready to fill it.
- Appeal to a different market segment. Do not compete head-on with the market leader.

Let us look at how U-Save follows these rules by comparing its overall strategy to Enterprise.

Enterprise employs a large group of staff specialists to locate and evaluate prospective locations. Its location decisions are based on modeling techniques that predict whether a community needs an additional location. Enterprise then evaluates particular sites in that community based on vehicular traffic at key times during the day. In comparison, U-Save does little marketing research and merely locates near an Enterprise location. McDonnell says, "I tell our people to locate as close as possible to an Enterprise store—directly across the street, if possible. Enterprise has done a lot of good work picking a site, and we can benefit from it." A second benefit of following Enterprise to a location, McDonnell believes, is that it is able to trade on Enterprise's spending "a lot of time and effort educating the consumer that you don't have to go to the airport to rent a car."

U-Save focuses on a somewhat different target market than Enterprise. Although both Enterprise and U-Save offer low-cost rentals, provide pick-up services for renters, and cater to residents whose cars are being repaired, they focus their promotion on distinct groups. Enterprise places much of its marketing budget on making wholesale deals with auto insurers and body shops, while U-Save seeks to attract car rentals by individuals. For example, U-Save trains franchisees to sell to final consumers through religious and social affiliations.

U-Save also chooses not to compete on the basis of price. McDonnell states that "In our markets, Enterprise determines the pricing, and our pricing is usually slightly higher. People think competitors have to be cheaper, buy we can't afford that. We charge a little more, but aim to make it up by offering more service."

Questions

1. Comment on the pros and cons of being second in a market.
2. Apply the concept of product positioning to both U-Save Auto Rental and Enterprise Rent-A-Car.
3. How can U-Save use the goods/services continuum in defining its business?
4. Describe how U-Save can overcome service intangibility, perishability, inseparability, and variability in quality.

[c4-1]The data in the case are drawn from Robert McGarvey, "We're (Not) Number 1," *Entrepreneur* (January 2001), pp. 80–83; and Minda Zetlin, "After You . . . ," *Management Review* (March 1999), pp. 32–34.

Case 2

Should Salespeople Be Included in Product Development?[c4-2]

A research study by an innovation management consulting firm recently found that nearly one-half of the leading marketing firms do not formally include salespeople in their new-product planning. Furthermore, even when a salesperson is included as part of the process, he/she typically is assigned a minor role.

The most common reasons why salespeople are not included in the product development process are:

- Many companies are concerned that getting salespeople involved in product planning will take away from sales productivity.
- Sales personnel are too often seen as adding value only at the end of the new-product planning process (during the promotion planning phase).
- Firms do not understand how to select, motivate, and compensate salespeople for their involvement in new-product planning activities.
- Salespeople are often seen as having strong personalities. Some executives feel that they can dominate a product planning team and not get along well with other team members who are viewed as more process-driven and analytical.

The authors of the study say that there are several distinct benefits to including salespeople in the product planning process: consumer input, channel knowledge, competitive insights, and the sales buy-in:

- *Consumer Input:* Although a salesperson's views should never be used in place of consumer research, salespeople can augment traditional marketing research activities such as consumer surveys and focus groups. According to a principal at the IBM Global Consulting Group (www.ibm.com/services), "Because we are a 'service,' our salespeople are inextricably linked to the experience and the experience *is* the product. Sales function involvement in product development for a service firm is very important because their interaction with an end customer is often part of the offering itself."
- *Channel Knowledge:* As a former brand manager at Quaker Oats says, "Participation of the salesperson can prevent the team from making big mistakes at the shelf or the trade. For example, one consumer products marketer created a product

that did not fit on the shelves of a major distributor. This error could have been prevented if a salesperson was involved in the product planning process."

- *Competitive Insights:* A product manager for a household consumer products marketer offers this insight: "Salespeople are plugged into the rumor-mill with a good idea of what else is coming down the pipeline from other vendors, therefore providing insight as to whether what you are planning to launch is truly innovative. The earlier they get involved, the better."
- *Sales Buy-In:* If salespeople are involved in a new product's development, they will be more likely to aggressively support it in the field.

There are two basic ways to get salespeople involved with new-product planning. With full-time job rotation, high-performance salespeople are brought back to a firm's main office for rotations of six months to one year for work on important projects. Not only do these rotations provide sales personnel insights into key projects, but they also give participants the experience that is applicable for their career progression within the company. To encourage top-performing salespeople to accept this assignment, it may be necessary to pay them at their most recent compensation level. The second alternative—part-time job rotation—would be to have sales personnel spend between one-fifth and one-half of their time in new-product planning responsibilities. Under this approach, a firm would have to reduce the salesperson's current account management responsibilities.

Questions

1. Evaluate the use of sales managers versus salespeople on a new-product planning team.
2. Outline five potential pitfalls of the use of salespeople as part of the new-product planning process.
3. Is a firm's best-performing salesperson necessarily the best choice to use on a new-product planning team? Explain your answer.
4. What are the pros and cons of the use of full-time versus part-time job rotation?

[c4-2]The data in the case are drawn from Steve McDougal and Jeff Smith, "Wake Up Your Product Development," *Marketing Management* (Spring 1999), pp. 25–30.

Case 3

Innovating in Latin America—Not Just the USA[c4-3]

Although auto manufacturing has taken place in Latin America for years, until recently, high tariffs have forced manufacturers to both manufacture and sell locally. Now with import barriers having fallen, a car manufacturer can supply consumers from several countries from a single plant. This lets the manufacturer achieve needed economies of scale. So far, car manufacturers have centralized production in Mexico, Brazil, and, to a lesser degree, Argentina. These Latin American car operations target the local population, as well as the export market. Sales opportunities in Latin America are strong, since the ratio of people to cars on the road in Latin America is 9 to 1, versus 2 to 1 in developed countries.

In contrast to auto manufacturing in the United States, workers in Latin America are more willing to undergo months of intensive training in the hope of entering the region's growing middle class. Manufacturers are willing to invest in training in the hopes of higher-quality cars. Because wages in Latin America are low, manufacturers can invest in an unusual amount of training. In Mexico, an assembly line worker earns $2.10 to $2.60 per hour, as compared with $21 per hour in the United States and $19 per hour in Germany. Volkswagen (www.vw.com/worldwide), for example, trains new employees for three years; and each year it sends 100 Brazilian engineers to Germany to watch the production processes there.

Latin American workers have been actively involved as participants in experiments. In Brazil and Mexico, manufacturers have tested the use of such innovative production processes as modular assembly and lean manufacturing. Both of these processes significantly reduce the time needed to build a car.

At one of Volkswagen's Brazilian plants, most assembly work on trucks is being performed by parts suppliers—not by company workers. A large portion of Brazil's car-making capacity uses modular assembly. At a General Motors (www.gm.com) facility, 16 suppliers deliver pre-assembled modules to GM workers, who bolt assemblies together to build a subcompact car. This plant uses 60 percent fewer parts and 40 percent fewer components than generally needed for a car that is made by traditional methods. The manufacturing cost is reduced by 15 percent. The facility has an annual production rate of 100 cars per worker, more than some top-of-the-line European facilities.

Auto makers have begun exporting some of the state-of-the-art manufacturing methods that were perfected in their Mexican and Brazilian facilities to the United States and Germany, as new plants there are built or as older ones are renovated. As General Motors' president of Latin America, Africa, and Mideast regional operations notes, "We're building a book of knowledge about production systems, policies, and best practices from our experiences around the world."

Auto makers have also become more willing to have Latin American engineers collaborate with their European counterparts. For example, Fiat (www.fiat.com) used a team of 160 Brazilian mechanical engineers, along with their Italian engineering counterparts, to design the Fiat Palio subcompact car. The Brazilian engineers were instrumental in developing special shock absorbers and custom-designed dust filters that were necessary due to Brazil's rough road conditions and dust-prone environment. These innovations are featured in Palios that are sold worldwide.

Questions

1. Discuss the pros and cons of actively involving suppliers in the development of new car models.
2. Describe the advantages and disadvantages of using inter-country engineering teams to develop a "world car."
3. What marketing research would you do before introducing the new car features developed in Brazil into vehicles exported to the United States?
4. What could firms in other industries learn from this case?

[c4-3]The data in the case are drawn from Geri Smith, Jonathan Wheatley, and Jeff Green, "Car Power," *Business Week* (October 23, 2000), pp. 71–82.

Case 4

Why Are Consumers "Dial"ing Out? [c4-4]

At the time when the board of directors of Dial Corporation (www.dialcorp.com) appointed Herbert Baum as chief executive officer, it was the most troubled period in the firm's then 52-year history. Dial's quarterly earnings had dropped by 68 percent compared to the same time period one year earlier. The firm's stock price was also about 35 percent of the value from one year earlier. Dial Corporation not only markets the well-known Dial brand soap products; it also markets Purex detergent, Armour canned meats, Renuzit air fresheners, and a number of specialty lotions and bath products.

Baum, who previously had been chief executive at Campbell Soup Company (www.campbellsoup.com) and then at Quaker State (www.quakerstate.com), inherited several major problems at Dial. The firm's last chief executive officer, Malcolm Joziff, had acquired a number of businesses, launched new products that Dial could not profitably market, and enacted poor strategies.

Among his biggest blunders, according to some marketing analysts, was to use price promotions to load retailers with inventory on Dial products, especially Dial bar soap. This strategy not only hurt future sales and profits, but also resulted in retailers refusing to stock a new version of Dial soap. Retailers simply wanted to sell the old inventory before buying additional stock. Dial loaded up stores with Armour Star Vienna Sausage and then raised prices expecting that consumers would stockpile canned meat to prepare for a Y2K panic. Since there was no Y2K panic, and competitors did not raise their prices, retailer shelves were overflowing with Armour meat cans.

Two recent acquisitions, Sarah Michaels and Freeman Cosmetics—which produce scented lotions, bath gels, and aromatherapy oils mostly in gift packages—also did not work out well. Although on the surface these products seemed like an extension of Dial's soap business, the company was unable to predict inventory demand since these goods were largely sold as gifts.

Additionally, Purex Advantage (a new formulation of Purex that is more effective on stain removal) has not done well. Marketing analysts say that consumers were confused by the poorly defined advantages offered by the more costly Purex Advantage. Baum felt the product should have been renamed, stating "When Volkswagen bought Rolls-Royce, they didn't call it Volkswagen Advanced."

Some industry observers question whether Baum will be able to effectively compete against Procter & Gamble (www.pg.com) and Colgate-Palmolive (www.colgate.com) for both retail shelf space and consumer sales. These observers are quick to cite Dial's declining gross profit margins (which have fallen by 2 percent) and the firm's hundreds of millions of dollars in long-term debt. As one expert notes, "When you have that much debt, it exacerbates your mistakes and limits your choices." Another analyst says that slotting fees (payments to supermarket chains to get retail space) in the New York metropolitan market alone can cost as much as $25 million a year, up from $5 million a few years ago. Competitors such as Procter & Gamble have leverage with retailers to bring these costs down, Dial does not possess this competitive strength.

In his first year at Dial Corporation, Baum reorganized the company into five business units; the manager of each unit is now responsible for managing the unit's own inventory and profit-and-loss performance. Executive compensation will be based on profitability. Underperforming brands will be sold. Baum also began work on a "marketing makeover for Purex."

Questions

1. Evaluate Herbert Baum's product strategy.
2. Can the same Dial product be a convenience good to one consumer, a shopping good to another, and a specialty good to a third consumer? Explain your answer and its marketing implications.
3. How can Dial Corporation increase the sales of its mature products?
4. What criteria would you use to decide which Dial Corporation brands to sell off or eliminate? Explain your reasoning.

[c4-4]The data in the case are drawn from Arlene Weintraub and Christopher Palmeri, "Wish Everyone Used Dial? Dial Does," *Business Week* (September 25, 2000), pp. 132–134.

PART 4 COMPREHENSIVE CASE

Market-Driven Product Development[pc4]

Introduction

Today's markets do not allow many mistakes. Goods and services have to meet customer needs to be successful and extract premium prices from the market. Therefore, product development must be driven primarily by customer needs rather than by technological possibilities. This case describes how a target-costing pricing approach can help develop superior products while fully extracting the maximum prices from the market and positively affecting the bottom line.

Background

Porsche AG (www.porsche.com) stopped developing the Porsche 989 when it learned the cost would be 30 percent higher than the price that could be gained in the market. Spalding's (www.spalding.com) pump baseball glove was a great idea, but the $100 price soon ended its market chances. When Mercedes-Benz (www.mercedes-benz.com) introduced its new S-class, sales felt short of goals. Analysis revealed that the gap between customer demands and the features offered was too high to reach the established price.

Take the new Volkswagen Beetle (www.newbeetle.com). In Germany, the new Beetle is not a huge success, primarily as a result of the steep price tag that overestimated the value German consumers put on the car. Yet, when Volkswagen launched the vehicle in the United States, orders flooded in, resulting in consumers waiting nine months for a car. The value U.S. customers placed on owning a new Beetle, coupled with nostalgia, was clearly underestimated, and one could make the assumption that a $500 or $1,000 higher price might not have affected sales much but would have significantly increased profits.

These illustrations show the traditional inside-out approach for product development and pricing, which can be described by these characteristics:

- The process is driven by what the engineers have developed, rather than by what the market demands.
- Prices are set on a cost-plus basis, with the target margin added to the final cost of the product.
- The final cost of the product cannot be established until the final product is ready to be launched.
- The customer's voice is heard late, if at all, helping only to fine-tune the nearly finished product.
- Cooperation between departments is low. Engineers develop products; marketers try to sell them.

The result of this traditional approach is an array of over-engineered products that do not match customer requirements and that are priced incorrectly, giving away huge profit or sales potential. Many companies, even entire industries, have run into problems with this inside-out approach.

An example of success based on identifying customer needs is the Swatch Group (www.swatch.com). Before it entered the market and turned watches into a fashion item, the Swiss watch industry was nearly wiped out by the Japanese. The Swiss produced high-quality, high-precision time-measuring instruments that were more jewelry than watch. Prices were far above what people would pay, as many customers just wanted a reliable watch at a decent price. Swatch realized this and reinvented its watches.

Foreign markets often want different products. Many firms learn this when successful products in their home markets flop elsewhere. A leading European maker of air-conditioning systems developed a new system which ran noiselessly. While a success in Europe, the product initially flopped in the United States because Americans prefer that their air-conditioning systems hum.

What Target Costing Is About

These examples are proof that an inside-out approach often leads product development away from market demand, resulting in improperly designed products and ineffective pricing. With an outside-in approach, the product is developed according to what the market wants and at the highest price it will accept.

Figure 1 shows the general concept of target pricing and target costing. The horizontal axis describes the performance or technical level of a product attribute. While the value to the customer increases with performance, it does so at a decreasing rate. The value curve becomes flatter as we move farther to the right. The value is reflected in customer willingness to pay for this specific feature. The willingness to pay is the maximum price a customer will pay for a specific product or feature at a certain performance level. The higher the perceived value of a product or feature, the more the customer is willing to pay. Yet, the added willingness to pay for an improvement decreases just as the marginal value decreases.

The cost curve becomes steeper as technical performance increases. To improve performance already at a high level is more expensive per unit than improving it from a low level. The goal is to determine the technical performance level for each attribute that maximizes the difference between value and cost. The goal is not to maximize performance (that costs too much), but to optimize it at the target cost. In Figure 1, if performance is at level B, it should be increased, as the added cost is more than offset by the added customer value and willingness to pay. If performance is at level A, it should be reduced. The marginal costs of offering higher performance are more than the marginal willingness to pay by customers.

[pc4]Adapted by the authors from Stephan A. Butscher and Michael Laker, "Market-Driven Product Development," *Marketing Management* (Summer 2000), pp. 48–53. Reprinted by permission of the American Marketing Association.

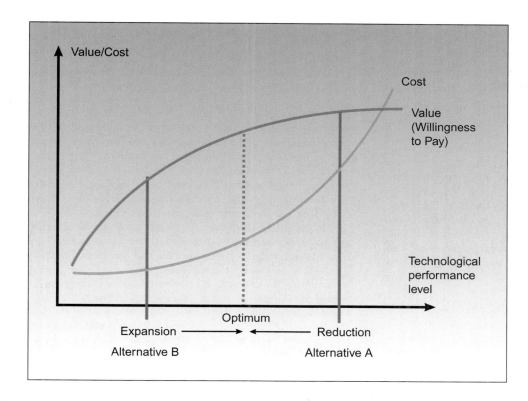

FIGURE 1

The Concept of Target Costing/Pricing

Value/Cost

Cost

Value
(Willingness
to Pay)

Technological
performance
level

Expansion ⟶ Optimum ⟵ Reduction

Alternative B   Alternative A

Traditional cost-plus calculations give way to a more market-oriented, price-minus calculation. The amount customers will pay for a product that fulfills their requirements is determined first. Based on the data, the highest acceptable price is calculated, and the target margin is deducted from that price. The result is the maximum cost allowable for this product. "How much will the product cost?" is replaced with "How much can the product cost?" The idea is to position products within the market's acceptable price range and within the manufacturer's acceptable cost range to reach target margins. This could mean that the decision might be not to launch the product if target cost cannot be reached. An example of this target-costing approach is the $999 personal computer. The price was set to conquer new segments. Manufacturers try to maximize product performance for that price, taking into account their target margin.

Case Study: JUMP

Let us discuss the example of a new basketball sneaker from JUMP that had several advanced features and a modified cushioning technology. The cost of the sneaker was $40. Adding the target margin of $40 would result in a price to the dealer of $80. Adding the

dealer's margin of $40 on top of that would lead to a market price of $120, which would put this sneaker in the upper-price range with the most expensive models from Adidas, Nike, and Reebok. Expected sales in this price category were thin.

Before introducing the product, JUMP decided to re-evaluate the new shoe using the target-costing approach. It discovered that the target segments preferred a less elaborate shoe. The maximum acceptable price for such a shoe was $99, just under the $100 price step, which positioned the JUMP sneaker at a slight price premium to most other basketball sneakers priced in the $70-to-$90 range. The new features of the JUMP sneaker justified this price premium. Deducting the dealer margin led to a price to the dealer of $66. Deducting the firm's target margin resulted in a target cost for the sneaker of $33, $7 lower than planned. Based on the data, JUMP slashed the cost to $33 by slightly redesigning the sneaker to lower production costs and by optimizing transportation from the Asian production plant to distribution centers globally. It launched the sneaker nine months after the original target date, and it was a success. Yet, had JUMP used target costing earlier in the development phase, it would not only have saved a lot of money, but also could have introduced the shoe during the

Olympic Games in Atlanta. Advertising during the televised basketball competition could have raised the sneaker's popularity and sales even more.

Early Implementation Needed

The earlier that specific targets are defined both for cost and product features, the better. Modifications to the product in the initial stages of development mean greater flexibility and a lower cost. The cost of product modifications increase strongly as the concept becomes more concrete. The target cost, as well as the product concept, should be scrutinized and adjusted during each successive product planning phase.

Implementing this approach requires changes in the interaction of the departments involved. Research and development cannot independently develop a product, hand it over to sales and marketing, and then report results to the finance department. Only an integrated product development team, with members representing different departments, customers, and suppliers, can be truly market-oriented.

The Target-Costing Concept

Target costing has six main steps. A condition that absolutely must be fulfilled for this approach is the determination of target dimensions like cost and product design. Detailed and accurate work is necessary.

Step 1: Defining Target Segments

The first step is to define the market segments to be targeted. Not every segment assigns the same value to the same features, nor do all people demonstrate the same willingness to pay for these features. A printing firm that prints primarily advertising flyers for local retailers will look for a printing machine with high output and standard print quality. A firm specializing in company brochures, annual reports, and other quality print items will sacrifice speed for quality.

Aside from variations in value or demand structure, market segments also can have different potential for revenue and profit, making them more or less attractive. This can be due to the higher prices they're willing to pay for a product compared with other segments, or the result of additional features or services with higher margins that can be offered to them. To maximize sales and profit, the right segments must be selected. Focusing on specific segments is an efficient use of limited resources. Target costing can help identify the segments valuing the technical features of a product most and consequently having the highest willingness to pay and—if those segments are not too small—the highest profit potential.

Step 2: Identifying Competitive Advantages and Disadvantages

The design of the new product should be based on competitive advantages and disadvantages, both for the product it will replace and for competitive products in the market. Competitive advantages and disadvantages are best identified using the matrix of competitive advantages.

First, all product factors relevant for the target segment's buying decision must be listed. In the case of a car, factors such as brand, price, driving comfort, engine power, and safety would apply. Second, potential customers from the target segments are asked to rate how important each factor is for them. The more important a factor is, the more benefits a customer will get from its high performance. Finally, potential customers evaluate how they perceive the performance of existing products (the manufacturer's and competitors' products). The relative performance is calculated by comparing the product's performance factor by factor with that of the strongest competitor on that particular factor.

Importance and relative performance then are summarized in the matrix of competitive advantages. Figure 2 shows an example from the auto industry. The matrix has four quadrants. Factors in quadrant I are strategic competitive disadvantages, as they're important for the customer. But the manufacturer's performance is weaker than that of its strongest competitor. It's crucial that these factors be improved, as they have a significant negative effect on the competitive position. In our example, the car maker should give priority to improving engine power and rethink the design/style of the car.

Factors in quadrant II are strategic competitive advantages. The product is better than all competitors' products on these factors, which are drivers of product success and must be kept to remain competitive. If a product does not have strategic competitive advantages, it cannot survive in the marketplace. Looking at the example from the auto industry, we see that the car in question has strategic competitive advantages on quality, safety, and brand. If one looks at these advantages and links them to the disadvantage on price, lowering the car's price probably is not the right action to take. Although a lower price would improve the car's value, the combination of higher price, higher quality, and greater safety, along with a strong brand name, creates very consistent positioning. The decision depends largely on the price structure of the market and customer willingness to pay for superior performances, which will be analyzed in a later step.

Quadrant III has factors of lower importance on which the product performs better than competitors. Because the factors have less importance in the buying decision, a superior performance is not necessary. Instead, a lower performance would be sufficient (quadrant IV). But, it must be made certain that changes in factor importance are observed. Thus, increasing importance (say, on gas mileage) is met with better performance so the actual movement of a factor's position in the matrix is diagonal. Factors in quadrant III are areas from which resources can be pulled out to invest in factors from quadrant I and quadrant II.

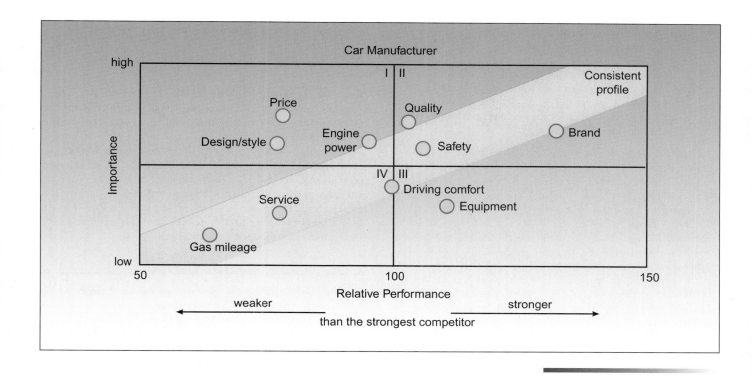

FIGURE 2

A Matrix of Competitive
Advantages

A product's ideal positioning would be to offer superior performance on important factors, and lower relative performance on factors of less importance, as shown by the "consistent profile" bar in Figure 2.

Step 3: Positioning the New Product within the Target Segments

Positioning the new product must be viewed in the context of the company's overall strategy. A firm positioned in the high-quality segments of a market could not introduce a low-quality product without sacrificing the clear positioning or value of its brand. Conflicting positioning was the primary reason for the failure of General Motors' Opel Senator in the German car market in the 1980s. It was positioned as a high-end luxury car against BMW and Mercedes, although Opel itself was positioned in the middle segment. Many firms use a two-brand product strategy in such situations (such as Panasonic and Quasar).

Positioning also can influence the target segments' willingness to pay to a certain extent. Many examples (say, in the fashion industry) show the effort to position a product at the upper end of the scale through marketing that results in target segments' higher willingness to pay for the product than had it been positioned in the middle of the market. It is necessary that product features have benefits that can be communicated in different ways. An example is the American trend of wearing outdoor clothing as leisure clothing. Initially, hiking boots were positioned to provide outdoor protection. Now, they are positioned as "in" products, even in an urban environment.

Step 4: Fine-Tuning Product Design and Pricing

In Step 2, competitive advantages and disadvantages were identified to establish what improvements in product design are needed. To fine-tune design and pricing, customer preferences, the perceived value of product features, and the willingness to pay must be measured. Questions to be answered in this step are:

- What overall value do the existing product and competitors' products deliver; what's the value of individual product features; and how can this value be expressed in quantitative terms?

- What is this value in monetary terms?
- Which improvements would increase the product value most?
- What is the willingness to pay for these improvements?
- What is the willingness to pay for specific product features or components?
- What is the optimal price for the complete product and for individual product components?

Questioning customers directly ("How much would you pay for another 20 horsepower?") often does not yield good results. Indirect questioning and realistic decision situations may be more reliable.

The more benefits a customer gets from using a product, the higher the perceived value of the product and the greater its chances of being selected over competing products. The value of a product is composed of the sum of the values of its features. The higher a feature's value, the more willing people are to pay for it and the product itself. An example from the machine tool industry shows a big difference between U.S. and Asian consumers' willingness to pay for different features. Americans would be willing to pay $6,585 for a change to automatic from manual machine setup, while Asians would pay only $1,975. This is mostly due to lower labor costs. An option is to sell different product versions in the two regions.

Step 5: Market Simulations

A price-response function can be generated for a new product with the help of a market-simulation model that combines information from the previous steps, so the product design can be tested in its expected market environment. Typically, decision-support models determine the value of a product in relation to the value of all products in the market. They estimate market shares and preferences based on this relation. The decision-support model produces market shares for different product or price scenarios.

Data can be accumulated into a price response function, which shows market shares and sales at different price levels. Total sales revenue can be calculated by multiplying the units sold with the price.

Step 6: Determining Target Costs

The maximum allowable cost is calculated by subtracting the target margin from the optimal price. The total cost amount is distributed among the different product components and features according to their contribution to the product's overall value. The more value a feature contributes, the higher the budget or target cost allowed for it. The objective is to invest the available resources in those areas that will create the most customer value. Product features that have costs above the target level are dropped, unless they are essential to the product's functionality or are a must in the market (such as seat belts in a car).

Questions

1. Describe and comment upon the application of target-costing pricing in product planning.
2. Explain what a firm could learn from studying Figure 1.
3. What is the relationship between target-costing pricing and product positioning?
4. Discuss what a firm could learn from studying Figure 2.
5. Is target-costing pricing a useful practice for service firms? Why or why not?
6. Cite a new product that you believe has done a poor job of target-costing pricing. Explain why.
7. Cite a mature product that you believe has done a superior job of target-costing pricing. Explain why.
8. What are the implications of this case for products in the decline phase of the product life cycle?

Distribution Planning

Part 5 deals with distribution, the second major element of the marketing mix.

14 Value Chain Management and Logistics

Here, we broadly study the value chain and value delivery chain, which encompass all of the activities and parties that create and deliver a given level of customer value. This requires careful distribution planning with regard to the physical movement and transfer of ownership of a product from producer to consumer. We explore the functions of distribution, types of channels, supplier/distribution intermediary contracts, channel cooperation and conflict, the industrial channel, and international distribution. We also look at logistics, in particular at transportation and inventory management issues.

15 Wholesaling

In this chapter, we examine wholesaling, which entails buying and/or handling goods and services and their subsequent resale to organizational users, retailers, and/or other wholesalers. We show the impact of wholesaling on the economy, its functions, and its relationships with suppliers and customers. We describe the major types of company-owned and independent wholesalers and note recent trends in wholesaling.

16 Retailing

Here, we concentrate on retailing, which consists of those business activities involved with the sale of goods and services to the final consumer. We show the impact of retailing on the economy, its functions in distribution, and its relationship with suppliers. We categorize retailers by ownership, store strategy mix, and nonstore operations. We also describe several retail planning considerations and note recent trends in retailing.

After reading Part 5, you should understand element 11 of the strategic marketing plan outlined in Table 3-2 (pages 72–75).

14

Value Chain Management and Logistics

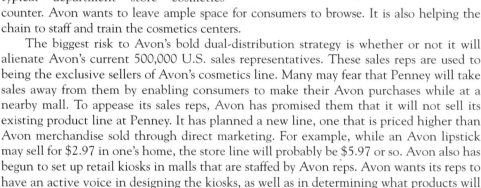

For its first 115 years, Avon (www.avon.com) never sold its products in U.S. stores. Then in 2000, the firm recognized that it had to respond to a changing environment with more working women and consumers reluctant to open their door to strangers. After months of negotiations, Avon decided to sell its cosmetics line through 75 J.C. Penney (www.jcpenney.com) stores beginning in September 2001. The potential for Avon to expand its business is great since Penney has nearly 1,100 stores.

The Avon units at these stores resemble a combination of a mini-salon and a typical department store cosmetics counter. Avon wants to leave ample space for consumers to browse. It is also helping the chain to staff and train the cosmetics centers.

The biggest risk to Avon's bold dual-distribution strategy is whether or not it will alienate Avon's current 500,000 U.S. sales representatives. These sales reps are used to being the exclusive sellers of Avon's cosmetics line. Many may fear that Penney will take sales away from them by enabling consumers to make their Avon purchases while at a nearby mall. To appease its sales reps, Avon has promised them that it will not sell its existing product line at Penney. It has planned a new line, one that is priced higher than Avon merchandise sold through direct marketing. For example, while an Avon lipstick may sell for $2.97 in one's home, the store line will probably be $5.97 or so. Avon also has begun to set up retail kiosks in malls that are staffed by Avon reps. Avon wants its reps to have an active voice in designing the kiosks, as well as in determining what products will be stocked there.

Avon's chief executive officer, Andrea Jung, says the firm chose Penney due to the potential to expand distribution. There was some speculation that Avon wanted to sign an agreement with Target stores due to its younger, trendier customer base and exclusive products. Furthermore, Sears backed out of an Avon agreement when the chain decided to exit the cosmetics business. There is some concern among industry observers about the dowdy image of Penney customers and Avon has little experience selling, distributing, and promoting its products through large department stores in the United States.[1]

In this chapter, we will learn about the decisions made in distribution planning and the activities involved in logistics, including dual channels of distribution and channel conflict.

14-1 OVERVIEW

In recent years, the distribution process has witnessed a dramatic transformation, one that is expected to continue in the future. Consider the following:

> Andrew Berger, a partner at the Accenture consulting firm (www.accenture.com), says he remembers visiting a Ford factory in the 1960s. "It made the steel, pressed the steel itself, and did everything itself until the car left the factory." Today, Ford is a consumer auto brand,

---

[1] Emily Nelson and Ann Zimmerman, "Avon Goes Store to Store," *Wall Street Journal* (September 18, 2000), pp. B1, B4; and Lorrie Grant, "Sears Tosses Out Cosmetics Counter," *USA Today* (July 1, 2001), p. B2.

responsible for only parts of the manufacturing process, and its partners include General Motors, a fact that would once have been inconceivable. Berger envisages the old-fashioned concept of the supply chain, which was largely internal, being replaced by value chains in which multiple companies join together to provide the most competitive source of supply for a product. As Charles Finley, another Accenture partner, says: "The value chain embraces all your customer's customers and your supplier's suppliers."

Each participating company must add value to its part of the supply process; otherwise, in the new, highly visible, and borderless world, somebody else will take its place. This helps focus companies and makes them ask the right questions. What is our real advantage? And who are the best firms in our network that we would like to partner with to create the best value for the customer? The creation of value networks is due to customer-focused thinking, from the marketing department to supply-chain management. Increasingly, customers are offered and expected to dictate the channel they will use, the exact product they want to buy, and how and when they want it to be delivered. The Web is a catalyst because of the connectivity it provides and the opportunities it creates, from collaborative working to whole new virtual functions, such as transport exchanges. The challenge for companies is to identify the areas where they can add value, find the best partners, and develop the capability to share information with those partners. They must collectively understand the market segments they address and find ways to balance activity with reward.[2]

This chapter presents an in-depth look at the value chain and the value delivery chain, distribution planning, and logistics. Chapter 15 covers wholesaling. Chapter 16 discusses retailing.

14-2 THE ROLE OF THE VALUE CHAIN AND THE VALUE DELIVERY CHAIN IN THE DISTRIBUTION PROCESS[3]

Figure 14-1 depicts the four stages of the distribution process: goals, value chain and value delivery chain, total delivered product, and level of satisfaction. Here are the key points to draw from Figure 14-1:

The distribution process consists of four stages, from setting goals to the level of satisfaction for each party in the process.

- The goals of the various parties are considered as inputs to the value chain and value delivery chain.
- The value chain and value delivery chain are parallel processes.

FIGURE 14-1
The Distribution Process

Source: Loosely adapted by the authors from Joel R. Evans and Barry Berman, "Conceptualizing and Operationalizing the Business-to-Business Value Chain," *Industrial Marketing Management*, Vol. 30 (February 2001), p. 138. Copyright Elsevier Science. Reprinted by permission.

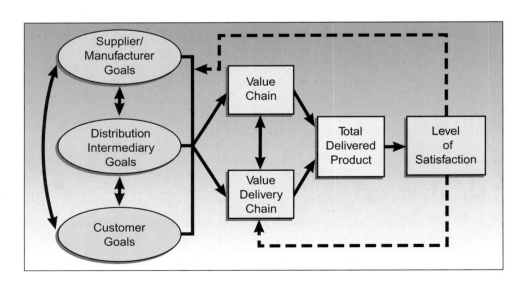

[2]"Driving the Value Chain from the Customer," *Management Today* (January 2001), p. 10.

[3]The material in this section is loosely adapted by the authors from Joel R. Evans and Barry Berman, "Conceptualizing and Operationalizing the Business-to-Business Value Chain," *Industrial Marketing Management*, Vol. 30 (February 2001), p. 135–148. Copyright Elsevier Science. Reprinted by permission.

- The total delivered product is the *actual* result of the value chain and value delivery chain.
- Satisfaction is based on the *perceived* value received from the value chain and value delivery chain.
- Feedback regarding service gaps and breakdowns must be handled systematically in the process.

Let us now discuss the stages in the distribution process.

14-2a Goals

The distribution process may be viewed from multiple perspectives; and the goals represented by these perspectives must be in sync for the distribution process to succeed in the long run. In many channels, there are three basic participants: suppliers/manufacturers, distribution intermediaries, and customers. Before enacting a distribution strategy, the goals of each party must be determined, exchanged, and reconciled. These goals then set the direction for the value chain and value delivery chain. As enumerated in Table 14-1, the three parties typically have distinct distribution goals.

 **Selected Distribution Goals by Party**

Party	Distribution Goals
Suppliers/Manufacturers	To gain access to the distribution channel
	To ensure that all distribution functions are performed by one party or another
	To hold down distribution and inventory costs
	To foster relationship marketing with distribution intermediaries and customers
	To obtain feedback from distribution intermediaries and customers
	To have some control over the distribution strategy
	To optimize production runs and achieve economies of scale
	To secure some exclusivity with distribution intermediaries
	To resist the payment of slotting allowances (the fees charged by some distribution intermediaries to secure shelf space)
	To receive a fair share of profits
Distribution Intermediaries	To have on-time deliveries and quick turnaround time for orders
	To ensure that all distribution functions are performed by one party or another
	To service multiple suppliers/manufacturers in order to present a choice for customers
	To meet customer needs
	To foster relationship marketing with manufacturers/suppliers and customers
	To obtain feedback from distribution manufacturers/suppliers and customers
	To have some control over the distribution strategy
	To be as efficient as possible in shipping and inventory management
	To secure some exclusivity with suppliers/manufacturers
	To receive a fair share of profits
Customers	To have an assortment of products from which to choose
	To have a variety of resellers from which to choose
	To purchase in small quantities
	To shop at convenient locations
	To find items in-stock, including those on sale
	To have a number of payment options
	To be able to easily return products that are unsatisfactory
	To be treated in a respectful manner
	To have enough information to make informed decisions
	To pay fair prices

14-2b Value Chain and Value Delivery Chain

*The **value chain** consists of activities that design, produce, market, deliver, and service a product for customers. The **value delivery chain** includes all the parties in a value chain.*

There are two components to a value chain: the value chain itself and the value delivery chain. A ***value chain*** represents the series of business activities that are performed to design, produce, market, deliver, and service a product for customers.[4] These are some value chain activities that are often performed: order fulfillment, product development, research and development, quality control, cost management, information interchange, facilities management, customer service, order fulfillment, procurement, product commercialization, and returns (reverse logistics). The value chain is task-based.

A ***value delivery chain*** encompasses all of the parties who engage in value chain activities. It is performer-based and involves three factors: the specific parties in a given value chain, their relationships, and the activities undertaken by each party. The effectiveness of the value chain is greatly affected by the caliber of the value delivery chain. Value is added by each participant, and differentiation is enhanced by the delivery chain, since each party adds something to the mix. A delivery chain is only as strong as its weakest link. If a supplier has quality control problems, this adversely impacts the manufacturer. If a manufacturer is late with shipments, this adversely affects the wholesaler. If the wholesaler does not keep its facilities well maintained, this adversely impacts the supplier and manufacturer. Win-win-win is a delivery chain goal. For the value delivery chain to work properly, the supplier/manufacturer, distribution intermediary, and customer must each feel its needs are properly satisfied. Firms must do everything possible to avoid value delivery chain breakdowns.

As an example, in a value chain for fresh-cut flowers, these are some of the activities that must be performed: growing and harvesting the flowers, selecting the best flowers and storing them as they await shipment, shipping the flowers to resellers, displaying and preserving the flowers in florists' shops, wrapping flowers for customers, delivering customer orders when requested, and providing instructions for extending the life of the flowers. Through the value delivery chain, the supplier undertakes certain tasks and outsources others, such as using a local delivery firm to ship flowers throughout the city in which it operates and selling at florists rather than at an on-site shop. The consumer is responsible for keeping the flowers in water and making sure they are not in direct sunlight.

14-2c Total Delivered Product

*The **total delivered product** is the bundle of product attributes that are actually provided to consumers, and depends on how well distribution functions are done.*

The ***total delivered product*** comprises the bundle of tangible and intangible product attributes that are actually provided to consumers through a value chain and its related value delivery chain. From a distribution perspective, the total delivered product reflects how well the activities in the distribution process are performed. For example: Is the product shipped on time? Does it arrive intact without breaking or spoiling? Are store shelves fully stocked? Is the product properly price-marked? Is the return policy clearly stated and reasonable? Is the waiting time to make a purchase short enough? In the case of the fresh-cut flowers, the total delivered product is greatly affected by on-time delivery, the refrigeration of delivery vehicles, the use of proper shipping containers, and other distribution activities.

The Web is a very promising tool for marketers to enhance the total delivered product, sometimes by adding value and other times by reducing costs. Through the Web, firms can access competitive intelligence, better communicate with one another, provide faster customer service, facilitate inventory planning, process orders, and reach channel members around the world. See Figure 14-2.

---

[4]Peter D. Bennett (Editor), *Dictionary of Marketing Terms*, Second Edition (Chicago: American Marketing Association, 1995), p. 298. See also Jim Webb and Chas Gile, "Reversing the Value Chain," *Journal of Business Strategy*, Vol. 22 (March–April 2001), pp. 13–17.

FIGURE 14-2

The *Total* Delivered Product: Making Customer Returns Simple

A vital part of the value chain and value delivery chain is the customer's ability to easily return a defective or unwanted product. UPS' E-Returns service does just that for its client firms and their customers.

Source: Reprinted by permission. Photo by Dennis Blachut.

14-2d Level of Satisfaction

The final stage in Figure 14-1 is the level of satisfaction with the distribution process, whereby the satisfaction of each party is determined and related to its goals. In cases where the total delivered product is below expectations, gaps exist. These may be due to poor performance, high prices, low profits, channel conflicts, and other factors. Value gaps become integrated with future goals (as indicated by the top feedback arrow). For instances where there are breakdowns in the delivery chain, such breakdowns must be resolved by the parties in the value delivery chain (as indicated by the bottom feedback arrow). Return policies must be clear. One reason why breakdowns may occur is that "at least one of the parties has unrealistic expectations relating to the structure or outcomes of the relationship."[5]

[5]Douglas M. Lambert, Margaret A. Emmelhainz, and John T. Gardner, "Building Successful Logistics Partnerships," *Journal of Business Logistics*, Vol. 20 (Number 1, 1999), pp. 165–181.

ETHICAL Issues in Marketing

The "People's Republic of Counterfeiting"

Chinese officials estimate that the level of counterfeiting activity in China is a $16 billion per year business. By most estimates, China produces more counterfeit items than any other nation—including beer, soap, toilets, and even cars. For example, Procter & Gamble (www.pg.com) estimates that about 25 percent of the goods bearing its name in China are fake, and Nike (www.nike.com) estimates that the volume of counterfeit Nike products approaches the volume of its legitimate business in China.

At the Liangfeng Food Group factory, for example, a chocolate is produced that looks just like that produced by Italy's Ferrero Rocher (www.rocherusa.com). And even though Ferrero Rocher refused a joint-venture offer from Liangfeng, the Chinese firm still produces its chocolate under the Jin Sha brand, a brand Ferrero Rocher uses in other Asian markets. Production of the Chinese brand cannot be stopped by Ferrero Rocher because the Chinese government does not consider it to be a counterfeit.

Many of the counterfeit goods are distributed through 1,000 wholesale markets that are run by the Administration of Industry and Commerce (AIC), a government agency responsible for overseeing all commercial development in China. AIC branches build the wholesale markets and collect management fees and rent from vendors. Yiwu, China's largest wholesale market, is a $3 billion per year enterprise. The heart of Yiwu is a shopping arcade specializing in consumer products such as batteries, watches, and shampoo (bearing names such as Duracell, Colgate, and Gillette). Surrounding this area are streets specializing in different products. According to one estimate, 80 percent of the consumer goods sold at Yiwu are fakes; so closing down the market would cripple the city's economy.

As a U.S. marketer of private-label sneakers, would you continue to buy sneakers from a supplier in China that also makes fake Nike sneakers?

Source: Based on material in Richard Behar, "Beijing's Phony War on Fakes," *Fortune* (October 30, 2000), pp. 189–208.

14-3 DISTRIBUTION PLANNING

Distribution planning *involves movement and ownership in a* **channel of distribution.** *It consists of* **channel members.**

Distribution intermediaries *often have a channel role.*

Distribution arrangements vary widely.

Distribution planning is systematic decision making regarding the physical movement of goods and services from producer to consumer, as well as the related transfer of ownership (or rental) of them. It encompasses such diverse functions as transportation, inventory management, and customer transactions.

Functions are carried out via a **channel of distribution,** which is comprised of all the organizations or people involved in the distribution process. Those organizations or people are known as **channel members** and may include manufacturers, service providers, wholesalers, retailers, marketing specialists, and/or consumers. When the term **distribution intermediaries** is used, it refers to wholesalers, retailers, and marketing specialists (such as transportation firms) that act as facilitators (links) between manufacturers/service providers and consumers.

A channel of distribution can be simple or complex. It can be based on a handshake between a small manufacturer and a local reseller or require detailed written contracts among numerous parties. Some firms seek widespread distribution and need independent wholesalers and/or retailers to carry their merchandise and improve cash flow. Others want direct customer contact and do not use independent resellers. Industrial channels usually have more direct contact between manufacturers/service providers and customers than final consumer channels. International channels also have special needs.

The importance of distribution planning, the tasks performed in the distribution process, the criteria to consider in picking a distribution channel, supplier/distribution intermediary contracts, channel cooperation and conflict, the industrial channel, and international distribution are discussed next.

14-3a The Importance of Distribution Planning

Distribution decisions have a great impact on a company's marketing efforts. Because intermediaries can perform a host of functions, a firm's marketing plan will differ if it sells direct rather than via intermediaries; and a decision to sell in stores rather than through the mail or the World Wide Web requires a different marketing orientation and tasks.

The choice of distribution channel is one of the most critical decisions a firm makes. Close ties with intermediaries and/or customers may take time to develop; if there are existing bonds among channel members, it may be hard for a new firm to enter. Once alliances are achieved, suitable new products can be put into distribution more easily. Channel members need to act in a coordinated way. Strong resellers enhance manufacturers' marketing abilities. Consumers like to buy products the same way over time.

Today, more firms recognize the value of good relationships throughout the distribution channel. Thus, many companies now engage in relationship marketing, whereby they seek to develop and maintain continuous long-term ties with suppliers, distribution intermediaries, and customers. These firms ensure a more consistent flow of goods and services from suppliers, encourage intermediaries to act more as partners than adversaries, and increase the likelihood of customer loyalty. They improve employee morale by empowering them to respond positively to reasonable requests from suppliers, intermediaries, and customers. They get earlier and better data on new products and the best strategies for continuing ones. They lower operating and marketing costs, thus improving efficiency. With relationship marketing, it is "traumatic to leave someone you believe is responsive to your needs. We don't change doctors, lawyers, or accountants at the drop of a hat. Firms want similar relationships with suppliers, distribution intermediaries, and customers so they won't leave every time they get a better offer."[6] See Figure 14-3.

In relationship marketing, firms seek ongoing ties with suppliers, intermediaries, and customers.

FIGURE 14-3

Relationship Marketing: The Costco Way

To maintain excellent, long-term relationships with its customers, Costco (www.costco.com) offers one-hour photo developing, discounted long-distance phone service, equipment leasing, small business loans, credit-card processing for small businesses, and a lot more.

Source: Reprinted by permission of PricewaterhouseCoopers.

[6]Aimee L. Stern, "Courting Consumer Loyalty with the Feel-Good Bond," *New York Times* (January 17, 1993), Section 3, p. 10. For further information on relationship marketing, see Carolyn Y. Nicholson, Larry D. Compeau, and Rajesh Sethi, "The Role of Interpersonal Liking in Building Trust in Long-Term Channel Relationships," *Journal of the Academy of Marketing Science*, Vol. 29 (Winter 2001), pp. 3–15; Alfred Wong, "Integrating Supplier Satisfaction with Customer Satisfaction," *Total Quality Management*, Vol. 11 (July 2000), pp. S427–S432; and Joseph P. Cannon and Christian Homburg, "Buyer-Supplier Relationships and Customer Firm Costs," *Journal of Marketing*, Vol. 65 (January 2001), pp. 15–28.

This is how effective relationship marketing in a distribution channel may be achieved:

- Relationship marketing should be conducted as a continuous and systematic process that incorporates both buyer and seller needs.
- Relationship marketing needs top management support; and its principles should permeate a firm's corporate culture.
- At a minimum, relationship marketing means understanding consumer expectations, building service partnerships, empowering employees, and total quality management.
- Suppliers, intermediaries, and customers should be surveyed—by category—to determine the aspects of relationship marketing to be emphasized for them.
- Although increased profitability is a desirable result from relationship marketing, other important measures of success are customer satisfaction, customer loyalty, and product quality.
- Both positive and negative feedback (going far beyond just passively receiving customer complaints) can provide meaningful information.
- Sellers need to communicate to their customers that relationship marketing involves responsibilities, as well as benefits, for both parties.
- There should be mutually agreeable (by buyer and seller) contingency plans if anything goes awry.[7]

Costs, as well as profits, are affected by the selection of a distribution channel. A firm doing all functions must pay for them itself; in return, it reaps all profits. A firm using intermediaries reduces per-unit distribution costs; it also reduces per-unit profits because those resellers receive their share. With intermediaries, a firm's total profits would rise if there are far higher sales than it could attain itself.

Distribution formats are long-standing in some industries. For example, in the beverage and food industry, manufacturers often sell through wholesalers that then deal with retailers. Auto makers sell through franchised dealers. Mail-order firms line up suppliers, print catalogs, and sell to consumers. So, firms must frequently conform to the channel patterns in their industries.

A firm's market coverage is often influenced by the location and number, market penetration, image, product selection, services, and marketing plans of the wholesalers, retailers, and/or marketing specialists with which it deals. In weighing options, a firm should note that the more intermediaries it uses, the less customer contact it has and the lower its control over marketing.

These examples show the scope of distribution planning:

- Sherwin-Williams (www.sherwin-williams.com) distributes its paints via 2,500 company-owned stores and through independent paint stores, mass merchandisers, and wholesale distributors. It also has a direct sales force for certain industrial markets, and employs distributors in 40 nations.[8]
- Shoppers Advantage is a member-based shopping service that operates exclusively through the Web (www.shoppersadvantage.com): "What is Shoppers Advantage? We're the one-stop shopping site where members and nonmembers can browse eight diverse superstores to find more than hundreds of thousands of name brand products at deep discounts every day. Members enjoy extra benefits including free extended warranties, cash back on qualifying purchases and a low-price guarantee."[9]

---

[7]Joel R. Evans and Richard L. Laskin, "The Relationship Marketing Process: A Conceptualization and Application," *Industrial Marketing Management*, Vol. 23 (December 1994), p. 451.

[8]*Sherwin-Williams Co. 2000 Annual Report.*

[9]"About Us," www.shoppersadvantage.com (April 23, 2001).

- Century 21 (www.century21.com) is the world's largest residential real-estate broker. It has a network of 6,300 franchisee-owned and -operated offices in nearly 30 countries and territories.

- Singer Company (www.singerco.com) "is a global retailer of not just sewing products, but a wide range of consumer products for the home. Singer remains the leading manufacturer and marketer of sewing machines worldwide. The distribution network spans more than 150 countries, including developed, developing, and emerging economies, and consists of 1,500 retail stores operated by the company and its affiliates, and approximately 58,200 outlets operated by independent dealers and mass merchants, as well as more than 18,000 door-to-door salespeople."[10]

14-3b Channel Functions and the Role of Distribution Intermediaries

For most goods and services, the *channel functions* shown in Figure 14-4 and described here must be done. They must be completed somewhere in a distribution channel and responsibility for them assigned.

Distribution intermediaries can play a vital role in marketing research. Due to their closeness to the market, they generally have good insights into the characteristics and needs of customers.

In buying products, intermediaries sometimes pay as items are received; other times, they accept items on consignment and do not pay until after sales are made. Purchase terms for intermediaries may range from net cash (payment due at once) to net 60 days (payment not due for 60 days) or more. If intermediaries do not pay until after resale, manufacturers risk poor cash flow, high product returns, obsolescence and spoilage, multiple transactions with intermediaries, and potentially low customer sales.

Manufacturers and service firms often take care of national (international) ads in assigning promotion roles. Wholesalers may coordinate regional promotions among retailers, and motivate and train retail salespeople. Many retailers undertake local ads, personal selling, and events.

Intermediaries can perform **channel functions** *and reduce costs, provide expertise, open markets, and lower risks.*

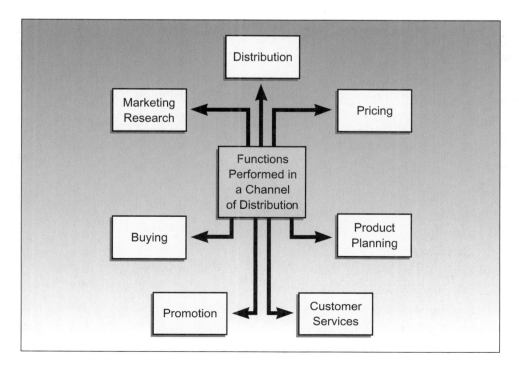

FIGURE 14-4
Channel Functions

[10]"Our Corporation," www.singerco.com/corporate/corporate.html (March 28, 2001).

Customer services include delivery, credit, in-office and in-home purchases, training, warranties, and return privileges. Again, these services can be offered by one channel member or a combination of them.

Distribution intermediaries can contribute to product planning in several ways. They often provide advice on new and existing products. Test marketing requires their cooperation. And intermediaries can be helpful in positioning products against competitors and suggesting which products to drop.

Wholesalers and retailers often have strong input into pricing decisions. They state their required markups and then price-mark products or specify how they should be marked. Court rulings limit manufacturers' ability to control final prices. Intermediaries thus have great flexibility in setting them.

Distribution incorporates three major factors: transportation, inventory management, and customer contact. Goods must be shipped from a manufacturer to consumers; intermediaries often do this. Because production capabilities and customer demand often differ, inventory levels must be properly managed (and items may require storage in a warehouse before being sold). Consumer transactions may require a store or other seller location, long hours of operation, and store fixtures (such as dressing rooms).

Manufacturers typically like to make a limited variety of items in large quantities and have as few transactions as possible to sell their entire output. However, consumers tend to want a variety of brands, colors, sizes, and qualities from which to select—and opt to buy a small amount at a time. Manufacturers might also prefer to sell products from a factory, have 9-to-5 hours and spartan fixtures, and use a limited sales force. Yet, organizational consumers may want salespeople to visit them and final consumers may want to shop at nearby locales and visit attractive, well-staffed stores on weekends and evenings.

*The **sorting process** coordinates manufacturer and consumer goals.*

To resolve these differences, intermediaries can be used in the **sorting process,** which consists of four distribution functions: accumulation, allocation, sorting, and assorting. *Accumulation* is collecting small shipments from several firms so shipping costs are lower. *Allocation* is apportioning items to various consumer markets. *Sorting* is separating products into grades, colors, and so forth. *Assorting* is offering a broad range of products so the consumer has many choices.

14-3c Selecting a Channel of Distribution

In choosing a distribution channel, several key factors must be considered:

Channel choice depends on consumers, the company, the product, competition, existing channels, and legalities.

- *The consumer.*
  Characteristics—number, concentration, average purchase size.
  Needs—shopping locations and hours, assortment, sales help, credit.
  Segments—size, purchase behavior.
- *The company.*
  Goals—control, sales, profit, timing.
  Resources—level, flexibility, service needs.
  Expertise—functions, specialization, efficiency.
  Experience—distribution methods, channel relationships.
- *The product.*
  Value—price per unit.
  Complexity—technical nature.
  Perishability—shelf life, frequency of shipments.
  Bulk—weight per unit, divisibility.

- *The competition.*

  Characteristics—number, concentration, assortment, customers.

  Tactics—distribution methods, channel relationships.

- *Distribution channels.*

  Alternatives—direct, indirect.

  Characteristics—number of intermediaries, functions performed, tradition.

  Availability—exclusive arrangements, territorial restrictions.

- *Legalities*—current laws, pending laws.

While assessing the preceding factors, a firm would decide about the type of channel, contractual arrangements or administered channels, channel length and width, channel intensity, and dual channels.

There are two basic types of channels: direct and indirect. A ***direct channel of distribution*** involves the movement of goods and services from producer to consumers without the use of independent intermediaries. An ***indirect channel of distribution*** involves the movement of goods and services from producer to independent intermediaries to consumers. Figure 14-5 shows the transactions necessary for the sale of 200,000 men's umbrellas under direct and indirect channels. Figure 14-6 shows the most common indirect channels for final consumer and organizational consumer products.

In a **direct channel** *one firm performs all tasks. An* **indirect channel** *has multiple firms.*

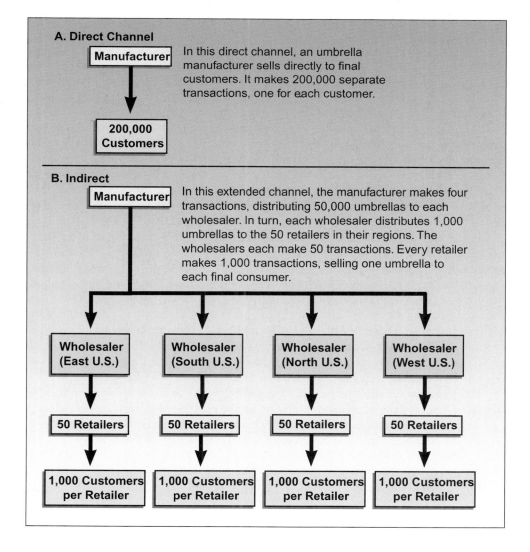

FIGURE 14-5
Transactions in a Direct Versus an Indirect Channel

A. Direct Channel

Manufacturer → 200,000 Customers

In this direct channel, an umbrella manufacturer sells directly to final customers. It makes 200,000 separate transactions, one for each customer.

B. Indirect

Manufacturer

In this extended channel, the manufacturer makes four transactions, distributing 50,000 umbrellas to each wholesaler. In turn, each wholesaler distributes 1,000 umbrellas to the 50 retailers in their regions. The wholesalers each make 50 transactions. Every retailer makes 1,000 transactions, selling one umbrella to each final consumer.

Wholesaler (East U.S.)	Wholesaler (South U.S.)	Wholesaler (North U.S.)	Wholesaler (West U.S.)
50 Retailers	50 Retailers	50 Retailers	50 Retailers
1,000 Customers per Retailer	1,000 Customers per Retailer	1,000 Customers per Retailer	1,000 Customers per Retailer

**Typical Indirect Channels
of Distribution**

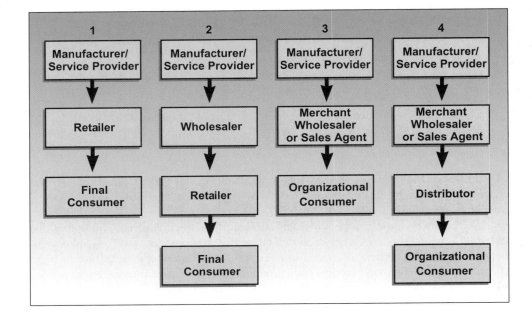

If a manufacturer or service provider sells to consumers at company-owned outlets (for example, Exxon-owned gas stations), this is a direct channel. In an indirect channel, a manufacturer may use several layers of independent wholesalers (for example, regional, state, and local) and sell at different kinds of retailers (such as discount, department, and specialty stores). A direct channel is most used by firms that want control over their entire marketing efforts, desire close customer contact, and have limited markets. An indirect channel is most used by firms that want to enlarge their markets, raise sales, give up distribution functions and costs, and will surrender some channel control and customer contact.

Because an indirect channel has independent members, a way is needed to plan and assign marketing responsibilities. With a *contractual channel arrangement*, all the terms regarding distribution tasks, prices, and other factors are stated in writing for each member. A manufacturer and a retailer could sign an agreement citing promotion support, delivery and payment dates, and product handling, marking, and displays. In an *administered channel arrangement*, the dominant firm in the distribution process plans the marketing program and itemizes and coordinates each member's duties. Depending on their relative strength, a manufacturer/service provider, wholesaler, or retailer could be a channel leader. Accordingly, a manufacturer with a strong brand could set its image, price range, and selling method.

Channel length refers to the levels of independent members along a distribution channel. In Figure 14-5, *A* is a short channel and *B* is a long channel. Sometimes, a firm shortens its channel by acquiring a company at another stage, such as a manufacturer merging with a wholesaler. This may let the firm be more self-sufficient, ensure supply, control channel members, lower distribution costs, and coordinate timing throughout the channel. Critics of the practice believe it limits competition, fosters inefficiency, and does not result in lower consumer prices.

Channel width refers to the number of independent members at any stage of distribution. In a narrow channel, a manufacturer or service provider sells via few wholesalers or retailers; in a wide channel, it sells via many. If a firm wants to enhance its position at its stage of the channel, it may buy other companies like itself, such as one janitorial services firm buying another. This lets a firm increase its size and share of the market, improve bargaining power with other channel members, and utilize mass promotion and distribution techniques more efficiently.

Channel length describes the levels of independents. Channel width refers to the independents at one level.

In selecting a distribution channel, a firm must decide on the intensity of its coverage. Under *exclusive distribution,* a firm severely limits the number of resellers utilized in a geographic area, perhaps having only one or two within a specific shopping location. It seeks a prestige image, channel control, and high profit margins and accepts lower total sales than in another type of distribution. With *selective distribution,* a firm employs a moderate number of resellers. It tries to combine some channel control and a solid image with good sales volume and profits. A firm uses a large number of resellers in *intensive distribution.* Its goals are to have wide market coverage, channel acceptance, and high total sales and profits. Per-unit profits are low. It is a strategy aimed at the most consumers. See Table 14-2.

Exclusive, selective, *and* **intensive distribution** *depend on goals, sellers, customers, and marketing.*

TABLE 14-2   **Intensity of Channel Coverage**

Attributes	Exclusive Distribution	Selective Distribution	Intensive Distribution
Objectives	Prestige image, channel control and loyalty, price stability and high profit margins	Moderate market coverage, solid image, some channel control and loyalty, good sales and profits	Widespread market coverage, channel acceptance, high volume sales and total profits
Resellers	Few in number, well-established, reputable firms (outlets)	Moderate in number, well-established, better firms (outlets)	Many in number, all types of firms (outlets)
Customers	Final consumers: fewer in number, trend setters, willing to travel to store, brand loyal Organizational consumers: focus on major accounts, service expected from manufacturer	Final consumers: moderate in number, brand conscious, somewhat willing to travel to store Organizational consumers: focus on many types of accounts, service expected from manufacturer or intermediary	Final consumers: many in number, convenience-oriented Organizational consumers: focus on all types of accounts, service expected from intermediary
Marketing emphasis	Final consumers: personal selling, pleasant shopping conditions, good service Organizational consumers: availability, regular communications, superior service	Final consumers: promotional mix, pleasant shopping conditions, good service Organizational consumers: availability, regular communications, superior service	Final consumers: mass advertising, nearby location, items in stock Organizational consumers: availability, regular communications, superior service
Major weakness	Limited sales potential	May be difficult to carve out a niche	Limited channel control
Examples	Autos, designer clothes, capital equipment, complex services	Furniture, clothing, mechanics' tools, industrialized services	Household products, groceries, office supplies, routine services

FIGURE 14-7

New Forms of Multichannel Distribution at REI

REI has marketed its products through stores for years. Today, it also uses in-store computerized kiosks and a Web site (www.rei.com) to sell its products.

Source: Reprinted by permission of PricewaterhouseCoopers.

A **dual channel (multichannel distribution)** *lets a firm reach different segments or diversify.*

Distribution contracts cover prices, sale conditions, territories, commitments, timing, and termination.

Some additional factors are noteworthy in selecting a channel. First, a firm may use a **dual channel of distribution** (also known as **multichannel distribution**), whereby it appeals to different market segments or diversifies business by selling through two or more separate channels. At our book Web site, you can see a four-slide hot link to a slide show presentation on multichannel distribution that was prepared by Linda Hyde of PricewaterhouseCoopers (www.pwcris.com). This presentation is reprinted by permission of PricewaterhouseCoopers.

A company could use selective distribution for a prestige brand of watches and intensive distribution for a discount brand, or use both direct and indirect channels (such as an insurance firm selling group health insurance directly to large businesses and individual life insurance indirectly to final consumers via independent agents). Second, a firm may go from exclusive to selective to intensive distribution as a product passes through its life cycle. Yet, it would be hard to go from intensive to selective to exclusive distribution. For example, designer jeans rapidly moved from prestige stores to better stores to all types of outlets. This process would not have worked in reverse. Third, a firm may distribute products in a new way and achieve great success. See Figure 14-7.

At its Web site, ChamberBiz (www.chamberbiz.com/bizcenter/P03_6000.cfm) gives some excellent advice for "Choosing Distribution Methods."

14-3d Supplier/Distribution Intermediary Contracts

Distribution contracts focus on price policies, conditions of sale, territorial rights, the services/responsibility mix, and contract length and conditions of termination. The highlights of a contract follow.

Price policies largely deal with the discounts given to intermediaries for their functions, quantity purchases, and cash payments, and with commission rates. Functional discounts are deductions from list prices for performing storage, shipping, and other jobs. Quantity discounts are deductions for volume purchases. Cash discounts are deductions for early payment. Some intermediaries get paid commissions.

Conditions of sale cover price and quality guarantees, payment and shipping terms, reimbursement for unsaleable items, and returns. A guarantee against a price decline protects one intermediary from paying a high price for an item that is then offered to others at a lower price; if prices are reduced, the original buyer receives a rebate so its costs are like those of competitors. Otherwise, it could not meet the competitors' resale prices. Suppliers sometimes use full-line forcing and require intermediaries to carry an entire product line. This is legal if they are not prevented from also buying items from other suppliers.

Territorial rights outline the geographic areas (such as greater Paris) in which resellers may operate and/or the target markets (such as small business accounts) they may contact. Sometimes, they have exclusive territories, as with McDonald's (www.mcdonalds.com) franchisees; in others, many firms gain territorial rights for the same areas, as with retailers selling Sharp (www.sharp-usa.com) calculators.

The *services/responsibility mix* describes the role of each channel member. It outlines such factors as who delivers products, stores inventory, trains salespeople, writes ad copy, and sets up displays; and it sets performance standards. If included, a hold-harmless clause specifies that manufacturers or service providers—not resellers—are liable in lawsuits arising from poor design or negligence in production.

Contract length and conditions of termination protect an intermediary against a manufacturer or service provider prematurely bypassing it after a territory has been built up. The manufacturer or service provider is shielded by limiting contract duration and stating the factors leading to termination.

Some firms rely on verbal agreements. However, without a written contract, there is a danger that there will be misunderstandings as to goals, compensation, tasks performed, and the length of the agreement. A constraint of a written contract may be its inflexibility under changing market conditions.

14-3e Channel Cooperation and Conflict

All firms in a distribution channel have similar general goals: profitability, access to goods and services, efficient distribution, and customer loyalty. Yet, the way these and other goals are achieved often leads to differing views, even if the parties engage in relationship marketing. For example: How are profits allocated along a channel? How can manufacturers sell products via many competing resellers and expect the resellers not to carry other brands? Which party coordinates channel decisions? To whom are consumers loyal—manufacturers/service providers, wholesalers, or retailers?

Channel member goals need to be balanced.

There are natural differences among the firms in a distribution channel by virtue of their channel positions, the tasks performed, and the desire of each firm to optimize its profits and control its strategy. A successful channel maximizes cooperation and minimizes conflict. In the past, manufacturers dominated channels since they had the best market coverage and recognition; resellers were small and local. Now, with the growth of large national (and global) distribution intermediaries, the volume accounted for by them, and the popularity of private brands, the balance of power has shifted more to resellers. Table 14-3 cites causes of channel conflict. Table 14-4 shows how channel cooperation can reduce these conflicts.

If conflicts are not resolved cooperatively, confrontations may occur. A manufacturer or service provider may then ship late, refuse to deal with certain resellers, limit financing, withdraw promotional support, or use other tactics. Similarly, a reseller may make late payments, give poor shelf space, refuse to carry items, return many products, and apply other tactics. A channel cannot function well in a confrontational framework. Here is an example of channel conflict:

> As the market share of department stores continues to be pressured by specialty stores, mid-market chains, and mass discounters, national brands are faced with a tough choice. Do they stick it out in the department store or do they risk upsetting their retail partners by moving the brand into other channels? It's a tough problem as exemplified by a decision in 2000 by Linda Wachner, chairwoman of Warnaco, to sell Calvin Klein innerwear to J.C. Penney (www.jcpenney.com). Wachner said she made the decision in part to make up for the loss of now-defunct department store customers like Uptons and T. Eaton's of Canada. But department stores can levy a heavy toll on brands that arouse their ire by adding new customers. Dillard's (www.dillards.com) dropped Calvin Klein innerwear after Wachner sold it to Penney's, and May Co. (www.mayco.com) stopped buying Cluett American Group's Arrow brand after it took on Kohl's (www.kohls.com) as a customer.[11]

---

[11]Thomas Cunningham, "Negotiating Channel Conflict; Gold Toe, Levi's, and Hanes Among Brands That Retail in Multiple Channels," *Daily News Record* (August 21, 2000), p. 40.

TABLE 14-3 Potential Causes of Channel Conflict

Factor	Manufacturer's/Service Provider's Goal	Distribution Intermediary's Goal
Pricing	To establish final price consistent with product image	To establish final price consistent with the intermediary's image
Purchase terms	To ensure prompt, accurate payments and minimize discounts	To defer payments as long as possible and secure discounts
Shelf space	To obtain plentiful shelf space with good visibility so as to maximize brand sales	To allocate shelf space among multiple brands so as to maximize total product sales
Exclusivity	To hold down the number of competing brands each intermediary stocks while selling via many intermediaries	To hold down the number of competing intermediaries carrying the same brands while selling different brands itself
Delivery	To receive adequate notice before deliveries are required	To obtain quick service
Advertising support	To secure ad support from intermediaries	To secure ad support from manufacturers/service providers
Profitability	To have adequate profit margins	To have adequate profit margins
Continuity	To receive orders on a regular basis	To receive shipments on a regular basis
Order size	To maximize order size	To have order size conform with consumer demand to minimize inventory investment
Assortment	To offer a limited variety	To secure a full variety
Risk	To have intermediaries assume risks	To have manufacturers/service providers assume risks
Branding	To sell products under the manufacturer's/service provider's name	To sell products under private brands as well as manufacturers'/service providers' brands
Channel access	To distribute products wherever desired by the manufacturer/service provider	To carry only those items desired by intermediaries
Importance of account	To not allow any one intermediary to dominate	To not allow any one manufacturer/service provider to dominate
Consumer loyalty	To have consumers loyal to the manufacturer/service provider	To have consumers loyal to the intermediary
Channel control	To make key channel decisions	To make key channel decisions

*In a **pushing strategy,** there is cooperation. With **pulling,** a firm generates demand before channel support.*

A thriving existing manufacturer or service provider can often secure reseller support and enthusiasm when introducing new products and continuing popular ones. This occurs because resellers know the manufacturer's or service provider's past track record, the promotion support to be provided, and the reliability in future deliveries. Thus, a *pushing strategy* is used, whereby the various firms in a distribution channel cooperate in marketing a product. With this approach, a manufacturer or service provider uses relationship marketing.

As a rule, it is harder for a new manufacturer or service provider to break into an existing channel. Resellers are unfamiliar with the firm, not able to gauge its sales potential, and wonder about its support and future deliveries. So, a new firm often needs a *pulling strategy,* whereby it first stimulates consumer demand and then gains dealer support. This means heavy promotion spending, fully paid by the manufacturer or service provider; the firm may have to offer guarantees of minimum sales or profits to resellers—and make up shortfalls. Figure 14-8 contrasts pushing and pulling strategies.

TABLE 14-4

Methods of Channel Cooperation

Factor	Manufacturer's/Service Provider's Actions	Distribution Intermediary's Actions
New-product introduction	Thorough testing, adequate promotional support	Good shelf location and space, enthusiasm for product, assistance in test marketing
Delivery	Prompt filling of orders, adherence to scheduled dates	Proper time allowed for delivery, shipments immediately checked for accuracy
Marketing research	Data provided to resellers	Data provided to manufacturers/ service providers
Pricing	Prices to intermediaries let them gain reasonable profits, intermediary flexibility encouraged	Infrequent sales from regular prices, maintaining proper image
Promotion	Training reseller's salespeople, sales force incentives, developing appropriate ad campaign, cooperative ad programs	Attractive store displays, knowledgeable salespeople, participation in cooperative programs
Financing	Liberal financial terms	Adherence to financial terms
Product quality	Product guarantees	Proper installation and servicing of products for customers
Channel control	Shared and specified decision making	Shared and specified decision making

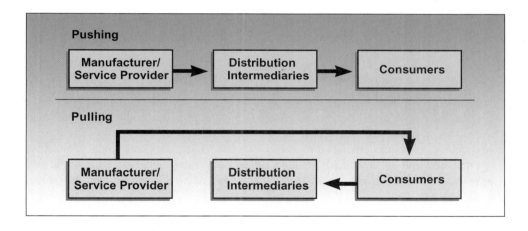

FIGURE 14-8
Pushing Versus Pulling Strategies

In today's competitive environment, with so many new domestic and foreign products being introduced each year, even market-leading firms must sometimes use pulling strategies. They need to convince resellers that demand exists for their products, before the resellers agree to tie up shelf space.

14-3f The Industrial Channel of Distribution

The distribution channel for industrial products differs from consumer products in these significant ways:

- Retailers are typically not utilized.
- Direct channels are more readily employed.

An industrial channel has unique characteristics.

- Transactions are fewer and orders are larger.
- Specification selling is more prevalent.
- Intermediaries are more knowledgeable.
- Team selling (two or more salespeople) may be necessary.
- Distinct intermediaries specialize in industrial products.
- Leasing, rather than selling, is more likely.
- Customer information needs are more technical.
- Activities like shipping and warehousing may be shared.

Industrial Distribution magazine (www.manufacturing.net/ind) is a good source for further information on this topic. Be sure to take a look at the online version of the *Supply Chain Yearbook*, available at the Web site.

14-3g International Distribution Planning

International distribution requires particular planning.

When devising an international distribution plan, a number of factors should be kept in mind. Here are several of them.

Channel length often depends on a nation's stage of economic development and consumer patterns. Less-developed and developing nations tend to use shorter, more direct channels than industrialized ones. They have many small firms marketing goods and services to nearby consumers, and the more limited transportation and communications networks foster local shopping. At the same time, cultural norms in nations—both developing and industrialized—affect expected interactions between sellers and consumers. For instance, in Japan, people treasure personal attention when making purchases, especially of expensive products. Unlike American shoppers, Japanese consumers are not used to buying by phone.

Distribution practices and formats vary by nation, as these examples show:

- Great Britain has the largest retail chains in Europe. The other nations have more independent retailers; but, with the opening of European borders, the growth of chains will speed up in the future.
- Some Mexican supermarkets shut off electricity overnight to hold down costs. Thus, items such as dairy products have a shorter shelf life and must be more frequently delivered than in the United States.
- Large Japanese firms often set up *keiretsus*. A vertical keiretsu is an integrated network of suppliers, manufacturers, and resellers. A horizontal keiretsu typically consists of a money-center bank, an insurance company, a trust banking company, a trading company, and several major manufacturers. U.S. firms have some channels that resemble vertical keiretsus, but they do not have networks that emulate horizontal keiretsus.[12]
- Although it has four times as many people as the United States, India has roughly the same number of retail establishments, and just one-quarter of them are in metropolitan areas. The leading retailers are the popular neighborhood grocery and general stores that offer very low prices.

If a firm enters a foreign market for the first time, it must resolve various questions: Should products be made domestically and shipped to the foreign market or made in the foreign market? If products are made domestically, what form of transportation is best?

---

[12]See George Ming-Hong Lai, "Knowing Who You Are Doing Business with in Japan: A Managerial View of Keiretsu and Keiretsu Business Groups," *Columbia Journal of World Business*, Vol. 34 (Winter 1999), pp. 423–448.

What kind of distribution intermediaries should be used? Which specific intermediaries should be used? The U.S. Department of Commerce runs a Commercial Service division (www.usatrade.gov) to assist small firms seeking advice on international distribution. That division has 105 Export Assistance Centers throughout the United States, as well as 160 international offices in 82 countries—which together represent more than 96 percent of the world market for exports. Together with Unz & Company (www.unzco.com), the U.S. Department of Commerce has prepared an online manual that includes the "Methods/Channels" to use when developing an export strategy (www.unzco.com/basicguide/c4.html).

Legal requirements for distribution differ by country—some have strict laws as to hours, methods of operation, and sites. In France, there are severe limits on Sunday retail hours. In Germany, there are strict limits on store size and Sunday hours. Many nations have complex procedures for foreign firms to distribute there. Thus, firms interested in standardized (global) distribution may be stymied.

What causes a company to be more or less satisfied with its international distribution channel? According to one study, the better a firm's domestic channel performs relative to its international channel, the lower its satisfaction with the international channel. The more experience a firm has in foreign markets, the greater its satisfaction with its existing international channel. A firm is more satisfied with an existing international channel if it feels it has the ability to change channels. It has less satisfaction with its existing international channel if environmental uncertainty is high. A firm is less satisfied if it is difficult to monitor the behavior of channel members.[13]

14-4 LOGISTICS

Logistics (also known as *physical distribution*) encompasses the broad range of activities concerned with efficiently delivering raw materials, parts, semifinished items, and finished products to designated places, at designated times, and in proper condition. It may be undertaken by any member of a channel, from producer to consumer.

Logistics involves such functions as customer service, shipping, warehousing, inventory control, private trucking-fleet operations, packaging, receiving, materials handling, and plant, warehouse, and store location planning. The logistics activities involved in a typical *order cycle*—the period of time that spans a customer's placing an order and its receipt—are illustrated in Figure 14-9.

> **Logistics (physical distribution)** *involves the location, timing, and condition of deliveries. An order cycle covers many activities.*

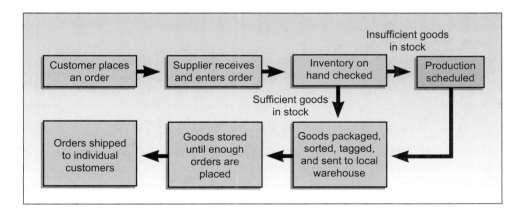

FIGURE 14-9

Selected Physical Distribution Activities Involved in a Typical Order Cycle

---

[13]Saul Klein and Victor J. Roth, "Satisfaction with International Marketing Channels," *Journal of the Academy of Marketing Science*, Vol. 21 (Winter 1993), pp. 39–44.

14-4a The Importance of Logistics

Logistics is important for a number of reasons: its costs, the value of customer service, and its relationship with other functional areas.

Costs

Cost control is a major goal.

Logistics costs amount to 10 to 12 percent of the U.S. GDP, with transportation (freight) accounting for more than one-half of that total. To contain costs, firms have been working hard to improve efficiency. Today, logistics tasks are completed faster, more accurately, and with fewer people than 25 years ago. Due to computerization and improved transportation, firms have reduced their inventory levels by tens of billions of dollars, thus saving on warehousing and interest expenses.

Distribution costs vary widely by industry and company type. At individual firms, total logistics costs depend on such factors as the nature of the business, the geographic area covered, the tasks done by other channel members, and the weight/value ratio of the items involved. For example, while many retailers spend 2 to 3 percent of their revenues on transportation from vendors and receiving, marking, storing, and distributing goods; petroleum refiners spend almost one-quarter of their sales just on inbound and outbound transportation. And whenever the U.S. Postal Service (www.usps.com) raises rates, shipping costs are dramatically affected for all kinds of firms.

Firms must identify the symptoms of poor distribution systems and strive to be more efficient. Up to one-fifth of the perishable items carried by U.S. grocers, like fish and dairy items, are lost to spoilage due to breakdowns in shipping or too much time on store shelves. To reduce losses, many grocers now insist on smaller, more frequent deliveries and have upgraded their storage facilities. And many firms engaged in E-commerce are still finding their way:

> Pity the poor logistics manager. No one really cares how a can of peas gets from Buffalo, New York, to Austin, Texas. Or what it takes to get that bright red sweater to your doorstep. As long as the grocery shelves are stocked and the clothes from the mail-order catalog arrive a few days later, we never give a second thought to how the goods are delivered. Until now. Buying online has spoiled customers. Go to a Web site, click on that book or CD, and two days later the doorbell rings. There's no room for delays or misplaced orders. Just ask Toys "R" Us (http://inc.toysrus.com). The Federal Trade Commission fined it $350,000 because of a breakdown in its order and delivery systems. The Web site mistakenly informed customers that things were on the way when they were really out of stock. Now, the firm is counting on Amazon.com (www.amazon.com) to handle its fulfillment tasks.[14]

Table 14-5 shows several cost ramifications of poor distribution.

Customer Service

A major concern in planning a firm's logistics program is the level of customer service it should provide. Decisions involve delivery frequency, speed, and consistency; the use of emergency shipments; whether to accept small orders; warehousing; coordinating assortments; whether to provide order progress reports (and when to do so online); the return policy (known as *reverse logistics*); and other factors. Weak performance may lose customers.

Accordingly, distribution standards—clear and measurable goals as to service levels in logistics—must be devised. Examples are filling 90 percent of orders from existing inventory, responding to customer requests for order information within two hours, filling orders with 99 percent accuracy, and limiting goods damaged in transit to 1 percent or less.

[14]Faith Keenan, "Logistics Gets a Little Respect," *Business Week* (November 20, 2000), pp. EB113–EB114.

Symptom	Cost Ramifications
1. Slow-turning and/or too-high inventory	Excessive capital is tied up in inventory. The firm has high insurance costs, interest expenses, and high risks of pilferage and product obsolescence. Merchandise may be stale.
2. Inefficient customer service	Costs are high relative to the value of shipments; warehouses are poorly situated; inventory levels are not tied to customer demand.
3. A large number of interwarehouse shipments	Merchandise transfers raise physical distribution cost because items must be handled and verified at each warehouse.
4. Frequent use of emergency shipments	Extra charges add significantly to physical distribution costs.
5. Peripheral hauls and/or limited backhauling	The firm uses its own trucking facilities; but many hauls are too spread out and trucks may only be full one way.
6. A large number of small orders	Small orders often are unprofitable. Many distribution costs are fixed.
7. Excessive number of returns	The firm incurs high handling costs and may lose disgruntled customers.

TABLE 14-5

Selected Symptoms and Cost Ramifications of a Poor Physical Distribution System

One way to set the proper customer service level is the **total-cost approach,** whereby the distribution service level with the lowest total costs—including freight (shipping), warehousing, and lost business—is the best service level. Figure 14-10 illustrates the total-cost approach. An ideal system seeks a balance between low expenditures on distribution and high opportunities for sales. Seldom will that be at the lowest level of distribution spending; lost sales would be too great.

By offering superior customer service, a firm may establish a significant competitive advantage. The opposite is also true: "As an owner of several Gateway computers, Phil Kirschner had been pleased with the technical support. He found that when he had problems, they were usually related to software, and that he could get the help he needed over the phone. But when he bought a new Gateway computer and heard churning and clicking noises the first time he turned it on, he called technical support right away. He had

*The **total-cost approach** considers both costs and opportunities.*

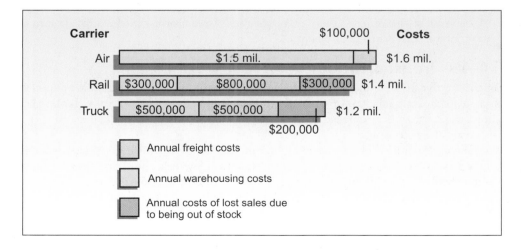

FIGURE 14-10

An Illustration of the Total-Cost Approach in Distribution

purchased a three-year on-site warranty for $99, so he assumed that someone would come to his house to fix the problem. Instead, Kirschner spent several hours over five days on the phone with tech support. Each time he called, he was told to test and reformat his hard drive and reinstall the drivers: 'I had to call eight times. All of the problems I was having were in part related to the hard drive, but they weren't willing to go on site.' At one point, Kirschner held the phone to the computer so the technician could hear the churning sounds from the hard drive. This persuaded the technician to send someone. Three days later a repairperson arrived at his house with a new hard drive."[15]

Logistics and Other Functional Areas

Logistics must be coordinated with other areas.

There is an interaction between logistics and every aspect of marketing, as well as other functional areas in the firm, as the following indicate.

Product variations in color, size, features, quality, and style impose a burden on a firm's distribution facilities. Greater variety means lower volume per item, which increases unit shipping and warehousing costs. Stocking a broader range of replacement parts also becomes necessary.

Logistics planning is related to the overall channel strategy. A firm seeking extensive distribution needs dispersed warehouses. One involved with perishables must be sure that most of a product's selling life is not spent in transit.

Because promotion campaigns are often planned well in advance, it is essential that distribution to resellers be done at the proper times to ensure ample stocks of goods. Resellers may get consumer complaints for not having sufficient quantities of the items they advertise, although the manufacturer is really at fault. Some new products fail or lag behind sales projections due to poor initial distribution. As noted in Chapter 13, during 2000–01, this occurred with the Sony Playstation 2 (www.us.playstation.com) when the firm ran out of merchandise due to a parts shortage.

Logistics also plays a key part in pricing. A firm with fast, reliable delivery and an ample supply of replacement parts—that ships small orders and provides emergency shipments—may be able to charge higher prices than one providing less service.

A logistics strategy is linked with production and finance functions. High freight costs inspire firms to put plants closer to markets. Low average inventories in stock allow firms to reduce finance charges. Warehouse receipts may be used as collateral for loans.

Overall, there are many decisions to be made and coordinated in planning a logistics strategy: the transportation form(s) used, inventory levels and warehouse form(s), and the number and sites of plants, warehouses, and shopping facilities. A strategy may be simple: A firm has one plant, focuses on one geographic market, and ships to resellers or customers without the use of decentralized warehouses. On the other hand, a strategy may include multiple plants, assembly and/or warehouse locations in each market, thousands of customer locations, and several transportation forms.

The rest of this chapter looks at two central aspects of a logistics strategy: transportation and inventory management.

14-4b Transportation

Transportation is rated on speed, availability, dependability, capability, frequency, losses, and cost. There are five major **transportation forms:** *railroads, motor carriers, waterways, pipelines, and airways.*

There are five basic *transportation forms* for shipping products, parts, raw materials, and so forth: railroads, motor carriers, waterways, pipelines, and airways. Table 14-6 shows the share of U.S. mileage and revenue for each. Table 14-7 ranks them on seven operating characteristics.

The deregulation of U.S. transportation industries has expanded the competition in and among these industries. Deregulation generally allows transportation firms to have greater flexibility in entering markets, expanding businesses, products carried, price setting, and functions performed. It also means more choice for those shipping. Each transportation form and three transport services are studied next.

[15]Catherine Greenman, "On-Site Service: Lots of Talk to Get Some Action," *New York Times on the Web* (April 12, 2001).

Transportation Form	Share of Ton Miles Shipped	Share of Shipping Revenue
Railroads	38%	7%
Motor carriers	28	81
Waterways	15	5
Pipelines	19	2
Airways	less than 0.5	5

TABLE 14-6

The Share of U.S. Shipping Mileage and Revenue by Transportation Form

Sources: Adapted by the authors from *Statistical Abstract of the United States 2000* (Washington, D.C.: U.S. Department of Commerce, 2000).

Railroads

Railroads usually carry heavy, bulky items that are low in value (relative to weight) over long distances. They ship items too heavy for trucks. Despite their position in ton miles shipped, railroads have had problems. Fixed costs are high due to facility investments. Shippers face railroad car shortages in high-demand months for agricultural goods. Some tracks and railroad cars are in need of repair. Trucks are faster, more flexible, and packed more easily. In response, railroads are relying on new shipping techniques, operating flexibility, and mergers to improve efficiency. See Figure 14-11.

Motor Carriers

Motor carriers predominantly transport small shipments over short distances. They handle about 80 percent of U.S. shipments weighing less than 500 or 1,000 pounds. Seventy percent of all motor carriers are used for local deliveries and two-thirds of total truck miles are local. For these reasons, motor carriers account for a huge share of shipping revenue. Motor carriers are more flexible than rail since they can pick up packages at a factory or warehouse and deliver them to the customer's door. They often supplement rail, air, and other forms that cannot deliver direct to customers. In addition, trucks are faster than rail for short distances. Like railroads, the trucking industry has been deregulated since 1980.

TABLE 14-7   **The Relative Operating Characteristics of Five Transportation Forms**

Operating Characteristics	Ranking by Transportation Form[a]				
	Railroads	Motor Carriers	Waterways	Pipelines	Airways
Delivery speed	3	2	5	4	1
Number of locations served	2	1	4	5	3
On-time dependability[b]	3	2	4	1	5
Range of products carried	1	2	3	5	4
Frequency of shipments	4	2	5	1	3
Losses and damages	5	4	2	1	3
Cost per ton mile	3	4	1	2	5

[a]1 = highest ranking.
[b]Relative variation from anticipated delivery time.
Sources: Adapted by the authors from Donald J. Bowersox and David J. Closs, *Logistical Management: The Integrated Supply Chain Process* (New York: McGraw-Hill, 1996); Ronald H. Ballou, *Business Logistics Management: Planning and Control*, Fourth Edition (Upper Saddle River, N.J.: Prentice Hall, 1999); and James R. Stock and Douglas Lambert, *Strategic Logistics Management*, Fourth Edition (New York: McGraw-Hill, 2001).

FIGURE 14-11

The Story of Union Pacific Railroad

Union Pacific (www.uprr.com) operates 38,654 miles of track and owns or leases 157,000 freight cars. It is one of the largest railroads in North America, operating in the western two-thirds of the U.S. The system serves 23 states, linking every major West Coast and Gulf Coast port. It also serves four major gateways to the east: Chicago, St. Louis, Memphis, and New Orleans. Union Pacific is the primary rail connection between the U.S. and Mexico. It interchanges traffic with the Canadian rail system. The firm has one of the most diversified commodity mixes in the industry, including chemicals, coal, food and food products, forest products, grain and grain products, intermodal, metals and minerals, and automobiles and parts.

Source: Reprinted by permission of Union Pacific Museum Collection.

Waterways

In the United States, *waterways* involve the movement of goods on barges via inland rivers and on tankers and general-merchandise freighters through the Great Lakes, intercoastal shipping, and the St. Lawrence Seaway. They are used primarily for transporting low-value, high-bulk freight (such as coal, iron ore, gravel, grain, and cement). Waterways are slow and may be closed by ice in winter, but rates are quite low. Various improvements in vessel design have occurred over the last several years. For example, many "supervessels" now operate on the Great Lakes and other waterways. They can each carry up to 60,000 gross tons or more of iron-bearing rock (or similar heavy materials) in one trip. Their conveyor systems are twice as efficient as the ones on older boats. Navigation is computer controlled.

Pipelines

Within *pipelines*, there is continuous movement and there are no interruptions, inventories (except those held by a carrier), and intermediate storage sites. Handling and labor costs are minimized. Although pipelines are very reliable, only certain commodities can be moved through them. In the past, emphasis was on gas and petroleum-based products. Pipelines have now been modified to accept coal and wood chips, which are sent as semiliquids. Still, the lack of flexibility limits their potential. Some pipelines are enormous. The Trans-Alaska Highway pipeline is 48 inches in diameter and 800 miles long. It carries 25 percent of all the U.S. crude oil produced. It can discharge up to 2 million barrels daily. Oil is loaded from the pipeline to supervessels and then sent by water to the lower 48 states.

Airways

Airways are the fastest, most expensive transportation form. High-value, perishable, and emergency goods dominate air shipments. Although air transit is costly, it may lower other costs, such as the need for outlying or even regional warehouses. The costs of packing, unpacking, and preparing goods for shipping are lower than for other transportation forms. Airfreight has been deregulated since the late 1970s. So, many firms have stepped up their air cargo operations. Some now use wide-bodied jets for large containers. Modern communications and sorting equipment have also been added to airfreight operations. Firms specializing in air shipments stress speedy, guaranteed service at acceptable prices.

MARKETING *and the Web*

How the Internet Is Transforming Long-Haul Logistics

While car manufacturers have begun to talk about placing Internet connections into cars, large-rig truckers are already using the Web to improve their business, as well as the quality of life for drivers.

U.S. Xpress (www.usxpress.com) has a Web site that enables customers to place orders, track freight shipments, and confirm deliveries. In 1999, about 10 percent of the firm's revenues were booked through its Web site. It expects to conduct 80 percent of its business on the Web as of 2005. An important part of U.S. Xpress' site is the customer's capability to determine if a delivery is running late and then to explore options to get the goods on time. For example, Leiner Health Products (www.leiner.com), a vitamin maker, can determine the availability and costs of using a team of drivers to get goods that are part of a major promotion delivered on time. According to Leiner's transportation manager, the U.S. Xpress Web site is "an early-warning system that helps us get our shipments back on track."

Trucking companies are also starting Web sites as a means of generating cost efficiencies that can be shared with customers. Transplace (www.transplace.com) uses the bargaining power of six large motor carriers and more than 600 smaller carriers to negotiate joint purchases of tires and other equipment, as well as to find loads on empty trips. Transplace has about 200 truckload customers, mostly manufacturers and retailers, and arranges about $1 billion a year in freight business. The firm's chairman says, "It's not about price itself. Truck companies already operate at the break-even point. It's about efficiency and utilization of the assets so both truck and customers can mutually benefit."

As a traffic manager for a long-haul carrier, what criteria would you use to select a Web-enhanced service firm such as those described above? Explain your answer.

Source: Based on material in Daniel Machalaba, "Trucking: Rig and Roll," *Wall Street Journal* (October 23, 2000), p. R51.

Transportation Services

Transportation service companies are marketing specialists that chiefly handle the shipments of small and moderate-sized packages. Some pick up at the sender's office and deliver direct to the addressee. Others require packages to be brought to a service company outlet. The major kinds of transportation service firms are government parcel post, private parcel, and express.

These transportation service companies ship packages: government parcel post, private parcel, and express.

Parcel post from the U.S. Postal Service (www.usps.com) operates out of post offices and has rates based on postal zones, of which there are eight in the United States. Parcel post can be insured and it can be sent COD (collect on delivery). Regular service is completed in a few days. Special handling (at an extra cost) can expedite shipments. Express mail is available for next-day service from a post office to most addressees.

Private parcel services specialize in small-package delivery, usually less than 50 pounds. Most shipments go from businesses to their customers. Regular service generally takes two to three days. More expensive next-day service is also available from many carriers. The largest firm is United Parcel Service (www.ups.com), a multibillion-dollar, global company that dominates the Internet delivery business.

Specialized express companies, such as Federal Express (www.fedex.com) and Emery Worldwide (www.emeryworldwide.com), typically provide guaranteed delivery of small packages for the next day. The average express delivery is less than 10 pounds.

Coordinating Transportation

Because a single shipment may involve a combination of transportation forms, a practice known as *intermodal shipping,* coordination is needed. A firm can enhance its ability to coordinate shipments via containerization and freight forwarding.

> **Containerization** *and* **freight forwarding** *simplify intermodal shipping.*

With **containerization,** goods are placed in sturdy containers that can be loaded on trains, trucks, ships, or planes. The marked containers are sealed until delivered, thereby reducing damage and pilferage. Their progress and destination are monitored. The containers are mobile warehouses that can be moved from manufacturing plants to receiving docks, where they remain until the contents are needed.

In **freight forwarding,** specialized firms (freight forwarders) collect small shipments (usually less than 500 pounds each) from several companies. They pick up merchandise at each shipper's place of business and arrange for delivery at buyers' doors. Freight forwarders prosper because less than carload (lcl) shipping rates are sharply higher than carload (cl) rates. They also provide traffic management services, such as selecting the best transportation form at the most reasonable rate. The online *Directory of Freight Forwarding Services* (www.forwarders.com) has a good listing of freight forwarders by name.

The Legal Status of Transportation Firms

> *Carriers are classified as* **common, contract, exempt** *or* **private.**

Transportation firms are categorized as common, contract, exempt, and/or private carriers. **Common carriers** must transport the goods of any company (or individual) interested in their services; they cannot refuse shipments unless their rules are broken (such as packing requirements). Common carriers provide service on a fixed, publicized schedule between designated points. Fees are published. All railroads and petroleum pipelines and some air, motor vehicle, and water transporters are common carriers.

Contract carriers provide transportation services to one or more shippers, based on individual agreements. Contract carriers do not have to maintain set routes or schedules and may negotiate rates. Many motor vehicle, inland waterway, and airfreight firms are contract carriers. Firms can operate as both common and contract carriers, depending on their services.

Exempt carriers are excused from legal regulations and must only comply with safety rules. They are specified by law. Some commodities moved by water and most agricultural goods are exempt from many legal restrictions.

Private carriers are firms with their own transportation facilities. They are subject to safety rules. In the United States, there are more than 100,000 private carriers.

14-4c Inventory Management

> **Inventory management** *deals with the flow and allocation of products.*

The intent of **inventory management** is to provide a continuous flow of goods and to match the quantity of goods kept in inventory as closely as possible with customer demand. When production or consumption is seasonal or erratic, this can be particularly difficult.

Inventory management has broad implications: A manufacturer or service firm cannot afford to run out of a crucial part that could halt its business. Yet, inventory on hand should not be too large since the costs of storing raw materials, parts, and/or finished products can be substantial. If models change yearly, as with autos, large inventories can adversely affect new-product sales or rentals. Excessive stock may also lead to stale goods, cause a firm to mark down prices, and tie up funds. That is why a pulling strategy by a manufacturer may be hard for a reseller to react to quickly.

> **Just-in-time (JIT)** *and* **quick response (QR) inventory systems** *monitor inventory levels.*

To improve their inventory management, a lot of companies are now applying either or both of two complementary concepts: a just-in-time inventory system and electronic data interchange. With a **just-in-time (JIT) inventory system,** a purchasing firm reduces the amount of inventory it keeps on hand by ordering more often and in lower quantity. This means better planning and information on the part of the purchaser, geographically closer sellers, improved buyer-seller relationships, and better production and distribution facilities. To retailers, a JIT system is known as a *quick response (QR) inventory system*—a cooperative effort between retailers and suppliers to reduce retail inventory while providing a merchandise supply that more closely addresses the actual buying patterns of consumers.[16]

JIT and QR systems are being used by virtually all auto makers, Hewlett-Packard (www.hp.com), Canon (www.canon.com), DuPont (www.dupont.com), Ryder System (www.ryder.com), Whirlpool (www.whirlpool.com), The Limited (www.limited.com), Levi Strauss (www.levistrauss.com), Wal-Mart (www.walmart.com), J.C. Penney (www.jcpenney.com), Motorola (www.motorola.com), General Electric (www.ge.com), Boeing (www.boeing.com), Deere & Company (www.deere.com), Black & Decker (www.blackanddecker.com), and many other large and small firms. For example, when a Camry (www.toyota.com/shop/vehicles/camry) lands at Toyota's Kentucky paint shop, a seat order—color, fabric, and type (bench or bucket)—is sent by computer to a nearby Johnson Controls (www.johnsoncontrols.com) factory. Just hours later, the seat can be installed in the Camry. Johnson Controls provides similar service for a dozen other auto makers.

Through **electronic data interchange (EDI),** suppliers and their manufacturers/service providers, wholesalers, and/or retailers exchange data via computer linkups. This lets firms maximize revenues, reduce markdowns, and lower inventory-carrying costs by speeding the flow of data and products. For EDI to work well, each firm in a distribution channel must use the Universal Product Code (UPC) and electronically exchange data. Although all major food makers use the UPC, some makers of general merchandise do not. However, the number of general merchandise manufacturers using the UPC on their products has been rising, and more will begin using the UPC in the near future. To learn more about EDI, visit the IBM Web site (www.ibm.com) and type "EDI" in the search box.

> *With* **electronic data interchange (EDI),** *computers are used to exchange information between suppliers and their customers.*

Four specific aspects of inventory management are examined next: stock turnover, when to reorder, how much to reorder, and warehousing.

Stock Turnover

Stock turnover—the number of times during a stated period (usually one year) that average inventory on hand is sold—shows the relationship between a firm's sales and the inventory level it maintains. It is calculated in units or dollars (in selling price or at cost):

> **Stock turnover** *shows the ratio between sales and average inventory.*

$$\text{Annual rate of stock turnover} = \frac{\text{Number of units sold during year}}{\text{Average inventory on hand (in units)}}$$

or

$$= \frac{\text{Net yearly sales}}{\text{Average inventory on hand (valued in sales dollars)}}$$

or

$$= \frac{\text{Cost of goods sold}}{\text{Average inventory on hand (valued at cost)}}$$

---

[16]See Frederick H. Abernathy, John T. Dunlop, Janice H. Hammond, and David Weil, "Control Your Inventory in a World of Lean Retailing," *Harvard Business Review*, Vol. 78 (November–December 2000), pp. 169–176; Dale D. Achabal, Shelby H. McIntyre, Stephen A. Smith, and Kirthi Kalanam, "A Decision Support System for Vendor Managed Inventory," *Journal of Retailing*, Vol. 76 (Winter 2000), pp. 430–454; Matthew B. Myers, Patricia J. Daugherty, and Chad W. Autry, "The Effectiveness of Automatic Inventory Replenishment in Supply Chain Operations: Antecedents and Outcomes," *Journal of Retailing*, Vol. 76 (Winter 2000), pp. 455–481; and Philip Siekman, "New Victories in the Supply-Chain Revolution," *Fortune* (October 30, 2000), pp. T208[C]–T208[HH].

GLOBAL Marketing in Action

Optimizing Supply Chains

Some distribution experts believe that British supermarket chains can "teach Americans a thing or two" about supply chain management. For example, British supermarkets are now using smaller temperature-controlled trucks to fit down narrow streets, computer-assisted traffic-tracking systems to avoid traffic jams, and railroads to bypass traffic.

Because British retailers have more channel power than the manufacturers from which they buy, the retailers have been able to develop and implement continuous replenishment systems. Unlike many U.S. supermarkets which buy on price and then store goods until they are needed, "about 80 percent of the total stock in the British supermarket system is actually on the shelf."

Tesco (www.tesco.com), a major British supermarket chain, has begun releasing real-time scanner data to suppliers on a store level through the Tesco Internet Exchange. This enables suppliers to optimize the amount of inventory and the timing of their deliveries. Tesco currently operates with about six days of total stock in its entire system, yet still maintains 98 percent in-stock availability.

Safeway UK (www.safeway.co.uk) is now using a stock-ordering system that allows orders to be placed continuously throughout the day, instead of at the close of business. With the exception of newspapers and magazines, everything is scanned and ordered based on sales activity. To further reduce the chance of a stockout, Safeway UK has devised a stock-tracking system that measures hourly sales. For example, if one of 9 customers purchases bananas and the system detects that bananas have not been purchased for 45 transactions, the chain realizes it lost 9 sales due to either stockouts or poor quality.

What supply chain management lessons can a U.S.-based supermarket learn from its British counterparts?

Source: Based on material in Richard Turcsik, "Novel Ideas," *Progressive Grocer* (August 2000), pp. 32–44.

For example, in retailing, average annual stock turnover ranges from less than 3 in jewelry stores to more than 40 in gasoline service stations.

High stock turnover has many advantages: inventory investments are productive, items are fresh, losses from style changes are reduced, and inventory costs (such as insurance, breakage, warehousing, and credit) are lower. Turnover can be improved by reducing assortments, dropping slow-selling items, keeping only small amounts of some items, and buying from suppliers that deliver on time. On the other hand, too high a turnover may have adverse effects: small purchases may cause a loss of volume discounts, low assortment may reduce sales volume if consumers do not have enough choice or related items are not carried, discounts may be needed to lift sales, and chances of running out of stock go up if average inventory size is low. Figure 14-12 shows how people can act should a firm run out of stock.

Knowing when to reorder helps protect against stockouts while minimizing inventory investments.

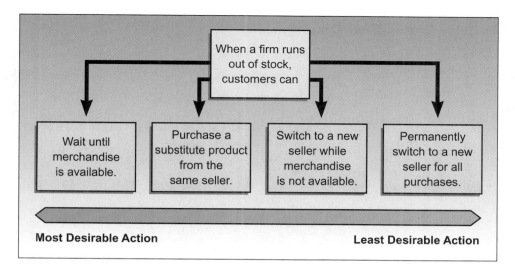

FIGURE 14-12
What Happens When a Firm Has Stock Shortages

When to Reorder Inventory

By having a specified **reorder point** for each of its products (or raw materials or parts), a firm sets the inventory levels at which to place new orders. A reorder point depends on order lead time, the usage rate, and safety stock. *Order lead time* is the period from the date of an order until the date items are ready to sell or use (received, checked, and altered, if needed). *Usage rate* is the average unit sales (for a reseller) or the rate at which a product is used in production (for a manufacturer). *Safety stock* is extra inventory to guard against being out of stock due to unexpectedly high demand or production and delivery delays.

The reorder point formula is

Reorder point = (Order lead time × Usage rate) + (Safety stock)

For instance, a wholesaler that needs four days for its purchase orders to be placed and received, sells 10 items per day, and wants to have 10 extra items on hand in case of a supplier's delivery delay of one day, has a reorder point of 50 [(4 × 10) + (10)]. Without safety stock, the firm would lose 10 sales if it orders when inventory is 40 items and the items are received in 5 days.

*The **reorder point** is based on lead time, usage, and safety stock.*

How Much to Reorder

A firm must decide on its *order size*—the right amount of products, parts, and so on, to buy at one time. Order size depends on volume discounts, the firm's resources, the stock turnover rate, the costs of processing each order, and the costs of holding goods in inventory. If a firm places large orders, quantity discounts are usually available, a large part of its finances are tied up in inventory, its stock turnover rate is relatively low, per-order processing costs are low, and inventory costs are generally high. The firm is also less apt to run out of goods. The opposite is true for small orders.

Many firms seek to balance order-processing costs (filling out forms, computer time, and product handling) and inventory-holding costs (warehouse expenses, interest charges, insurance, deterioration, and theft). Processing costs per unit fall as orders get bigger, but inventory costs rise. The *economic order quantity (EOQ)* is the order volume corresponding to the lowest sum of order-processing and inventory-holding costs. Table 14-8 shows three ways to compute EOQ for a firm that has an annual demand of 3,000 units for a product; the cost of each unit is $1; order-processing costs are $3 per order; and inventory-holding costs equal 20 percent of each item's cost. As shown in the table, the economic order quantity is 300 units. Thus, the firm should place orders of 300 units and have 10 orders per year.

Economic order quantity (EOQ) *balances ordering and inventory costs.*

TABLE 14-8 Computing an Economic Order Quantity

A.

Order Quantity (Units)	Average Inventory Maintained (Units)[a]	Annual Inventory-Holding Costs[b]	Annual Order-Processing Costs[c]	Annual Total Costs
100	50	$10	$90	$100
200	100	20	45	65
EOQ → 300	150	30	30	60
400	200	40	24	64
500	250	50	18	68

B.

C.

$$EOQ = \sqrt{\frac{2DS}{IC}} = \sqrt{\frac{2(3,000)(\$3)}{0.20(\$1)}} = 300$$

where EOQ = Order quantity (units)

D = Annual demand (units)

S = Costs to place an order ($)

I = Annual holding costs (as a % of unit costs)

C = Unit cost of an item ($)

[a]The average inventory on hand = 1/2 × Order quantity.

[b]Inventory-holding costs = Annual holding costs as a percent of unit cost × Unit cost × Average inventory.

[c]Order-processing costs = Number of annual orders × Costs to place an order. Number of orders = Annual demand/Order quantity.

Warehousing

Warehousing *involves storing and dispatching goods.*

Warehousing involves the physical facilities used to store, identify, and sort goods in expectation of their sale and transfer within a distribution channel. Warehouses can be used to store goods, prepare goods for shipment, coordinate shipments, send orders, and aid in product recalls.

Private warehouses are owned and operated by firms that store and distribute their own products. They are most likely to be used by those with stable inventory levels and long-run plans to serve the same geographic areas.

Public warehouses provide storage and related distribution services to any interested firm or individual on a rental basis. They are used by small firms without the resources or desire to have their own facilities, larger firms that need more storage space (if their own warehouses are full), or any size of firm entering a new area. They offer shipping economies by allowing carload shipments to be made to warehouses in local markets; then short-distance, smaller shipments are made to customers. Firms can also reduce their investments in facilities and maximize flexibility by using public warehouses. If products must be recalled, these warehouses can be used as collection points, where items are separated, disposed of, and/or salvaged. There are thousands of public warehouses in the United States.

Public warehouses can accommodate both bonded warehousing and field warehousing. In bonded warehousing, imported or taxable goods are stored and can be released for sale only after applicable taxes are paid. This enables firms to postpone tax payments until they are ready to make deliveries to customers. Cigarettes and liquor are often stored in bonded warehouses. In field warehousing, a receipt is issued by a public warehouse for goods stored in a private warehouse or in transit to consumers. The goods are put in a special area, and the field warehouser is responsible for them. A firm may use field warehousing because a warehouse receipt serves as collateral for a loan.

The most high-tech type of distribution center is quite automated and uses computer technology to replace people with machinery. Both private and public warehouses are now much more automated than in the past.[17]

WEB SITES YOU CAN USE

These Web sites offer a lot of information pertaining to the value chain and distribution planning:

BetterManagement.com
(www.bettermanagement.com)

IndustryWeek's Value Chain
(www.iwvaluechain.com)

Logistics Online (www.logisticsonline.com)

Supply Chain Management Review
(www.manufacturing.net/scm)

Supply Chain Management Articles
(www.bpubs.com/Management_
Science/Supply_Chain_Management)

[17]See Connie Robbins Gentry, "Moving Boxes Is Child's Play," *Chain Store Age* (February 2001), pp. 90, 92; Terry Hennessy, "Wiring the Produce Patch," *Progressive Grocer* (September 2000), pp. 79–86; and James Aaron Cooke, "Re-Inventing the Public Warehouse," *Logistics Management and Distribution Report* (May 2000), pp. 44–50.

SUMMARY

1. *To discuss the role of the value chain and the value delivery chain in the distribution process* The distribution process has four stages: goals, value chain and value delivery chain, total delivered product, and level of satisfaction.

In many channels, there are three participants: suppliers/manufacturers, distribution intermediaries, and customers. The goals of each must be determined, exchanged, and reconciled.

There are two components to a value chain: the value chain itself and the value delivery chain. A value chain represents the series of business activities that are performed to design, produce, market, deliver, and service a product for customers. A value delivery chain encompasses all of the parties who engage in value chain activities. It is performer-based and involves three factors: the specific parties in a given value chain, their relationships, and the activities undertaken by each party. A delivery chain is only as strong as its weakest link. Win-win-win is a delivery chain goal.

The total delivered product comprises the tangible and intangible product attributes that are actually provided to consumers. From a distribution perspective, the total delivered product reflects how well the activities in the distribution process are performed. The Web is a promising tool to enhance the total delivered product, sometimes by adding value and other times by reducing costs.

The final stage is the level of satisfaction with the distribution process, whereby the satisfaction of each party is determined and related to its goals.

2. *To explore distribution planning and review its importance, distribution functions, the factors used in selecting a distribution channel, and the different types of distribution channels* Distribution planning is systematic decision making as to the physical movement of goods and services from producer to consumer, as well as the related transfer of ownership (or rental). A channel of distribution consists of the organizations or people—known as channel members or distribution intermediaries—involved in the distribution process.

Distribution decisions often affect a firm's marketing plans. For many firms, the choice of a distribution channel is one of the most important decisions they make. More companies now realize the value of relationship marketing and work for long-term relations with suppliers, intermediaries, and customers. Both costs and profits are affected by the channel chosen. Firms may have to conform to existing channel patterns; and their markets' size and nature are also affected by the channel used.

No matter who does them, channel functions include research, buying, promotion, customer services, product planning, pricing, and distribution. Intermediaries can play a key role by doing various tasks and resolving differences in manufacturer and consumer goals via the sorting process.

In selecting a method of distribution, these factors must be considered: the consumer, the company, the product, the competition, the distribution channels themselves, and legal requirements.

A direct channel requires that one party do all distribution tasks; in an indirect channel, tasks are done by multiple parties. In comparing methods, a firm must weigh its costs and abilities against control and total sales. An indirect channel may use a contractual or an administered agreement. A long channel has many levels of independents; a wide one has many firms at any stage. A channel may be exclusive, selective, or intensive, based on goals, resellers, customers, and marketing. A dual channel (multichannel distribution) lets a company operate via two or more distribution methods.

3. *To consider the nature of distribution intermediary contracts, cooperation and conflict in a channel of distribution, the special aspects of a distribution channel for industrial products, and international distribution* In supplier/distribution intermediary contracts, price policies, sale conditions, territorial rights, the services/ responsibility mix, and contract length and termination conditions are specified.

Cooperation and conflict may occur in a channel. Conflicts must be settled fairly; confrontation can cause hostility and negative acts by all parties. Frequently, a pushing strategy—based on channel cooperation—can be used by established firms. A pulling strategy—based on proving that demand exists prior to gaining intermediary support or acceptance—must be used by many new companies.

An industrial channel normally does not use retailers; it is more direct, entails larger orders and fewer transactions, requires specification selling and knowing resellers, uses team selling and special intermediaries, includes more leasing, provides more technical data, and embraces shared activities.

Channel length depends on a nation's stage of economic development and consumer behavior. Distribution practices and structures differ by nation. International decisions must be made as to shipping and intermediaries. Each country has distinct legal provisions pertaining to distribution.

4. *To examine logistics and demonstrate its importance* Logistics (physical distribution) involves efficiently delivering products to designated places, at designated times, and in proper condition. It may be undertaken by any member of a channel, from producer to consumer.

There are various reasons for studying logistics: its costs, the value of customer service, and its relationship with other functional areas in a firm. With the total-cost approach, the service level with the lowest total cost (including freight, warehousing, and lost business) is the best one. In a logistics strategy, choices are made as to transportation, inventory levels, warehousing, and facility locations.

5. *To discuss transportation alternatives and inventory management issues* Railroads usually carry bulky goods for long distances. Motor carriers dominate small shipments over short distances. Waterways ship low-value freight. Pipelines provide ongoing movement of liquids, gases, and semiliquids. Airways offer fast, costly shipping of perishables and high-value items. Transportation specialists mostly handle small and medium-sized packages. Coordination can be improved by containerization and freight forwarding. There are common, contract, exempt, and private carriers.

Inventory management needs to provide a continuous flow of goods and match the stock kept in inventory as closely as possible with demand. In a just-in-time (JIT) or quick response (QR) system, the purchasing firm reduces the stock on hand by ordering more often and in lower quantity. With electronic data interchange (EDI), channel members exchange information via computer linkages.

The interplay between a firm's sales and the inventory level it keeps is expressed by stock turnover. A reorder point shows the inventory level when goods must be reordered. The economic order quantity (EOQ) is the optimal amount of goods to order based on order-processing and inventory-holding costs. Warehousing decisions include selecting a private or public warehouse and examining the availability of public warehouse services.

KEY TERMS

value chain (p. 426)
value delivery chain (p. 426)
total delivered product (p. 426)
distribution planning (p.428)
channel of distribution (p. 428)
channel members (p. 428)
distribution intermediaries (p. 428)
channel functions (p. 431)
sorting process (p. 432)
direct channel of distribution (p. 433)
indirect channel of distribution (p. 433)
exclusive distribution (p. 435)

selective distribution (p. 435)
intensive distribution (p. 435)
dual channel of distribution (multichannel
  distribution) (p. 436)
pushing strategy (p. 438)
pulling strategy (p. 438)
logistics (physical distribution) (p. 441)
total-cost approach (p. 443)
transportation forms (p. 444)
containerization (p. 448)
freight forwarding (p. 448)
common carriers (p. 448)

contract carriers (p. 448)
exempt carriers (p. 448)
private carriers (p. 448)
inventory management (p. 448)
just-in-time (JIT) inventory system (p. 448)
quick response (QR) inventory
  system (p. 449)
electronic data interchange (EDI) (p. 449)
stock turnover (p. 449)
reorder point (p. 451)
economic order quantity (EOQ) (p. 451)
warehousing (p. 452)

REVIEW QUESTIONS

1. Distinguish between the terms *value chain* and *value delivery chain*.
2. Explain the sorting process. Provide an example in your answer.
3. Which factors influence the selection of a distribution channel?
4. Under what circumstances should a company engage in direct distribution? Indirect distribution?
5. Explain how a product could move from exclusive to selective to intensive distribution.

6. Compare motor carrier and waterway deliveries on the basis of the total-cost approach.
7. The average stock turnover rate in jewelry stores is less than 3. What does this mean? How could a jewelry store raise its turnover rate?
8. Two wholesalers sell identical merchandise. Yet, one plans a safety stock equal to 20 percent of expected sales, while the other plans no safety stock. Comment on this difference.

DISCUSSION QUESTIONS

1. What distribution decisions would a new firm that rents vans to small furniture retailers have to make?
2. Devise distribution channels for the sale of music CDs, pianos, and women's apparel. Explain your choices.

3. Present a checklist that a firm could use in making international distribution decisions on a country-by-country basis.
4. Develop a list of distribution standards for a firm delivering fresh flowers to florists.

WEB EXERCISE

At Kohl Packing (www.kohlpacking.com), "Our business started by custom packing sales kits and samples for direct marketing. Now we offer a full range of services to accommodate even the most complex direct marketing or sales effort, whether it's a full-scale outbound effort or fulfillment on demand." Visit the company's Web site and evaluate its service offering.

15

Wholesaling

1 To define wholesaling and show its importance

2 To describe the three broad categories of wholesaling (manufacturer/service provider wholesaling, merchant wholesaling, and agents and brokers) and the specific types of firms within each category

3 To examine recent trends in wholesaling

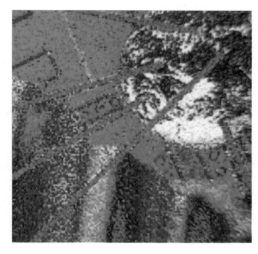

Some marketing experts believe that wholesalers may become an endangered species. At one end of the distribution channel, wholesalers must contend with the increased power of large retailers that can force manufacturers to bypass wholesalers and sell directly to them. At the other end, manufacturers can now easily bypass both wholesalers and retailers by selling directly to final users through Web transactions. United Stationers (www.unitedstationers.com) is the largest U.S. office products wholesaler. Let's see how it is flourishing despite a significant decline in the number of small office supply retailers

United Stationers allows all of its customers to tap into its inventory of more than 35,000 products from more than 500 manufacturers. As Branford Roos, the owner of a small office supply store says, "I order something by 4 P.M., and it gets here the next day. I'm in the boonies. That's fantastic." Roos can ask United Stationers to pack an order with his return label and then ship the order directly to Roos' customer: "It looks like I warehoused it and sent it, but I never touched it." United's order-filling accuracy is so high (99.8 percent) that retailers do not have to concern themselves with shipping errors.

United works hard to make its retail customers stronger. Its drop-shipping capability, for example, enables small retailers to increase their selection of goods while reducing their inventories. United Stationers has even helped 550 office supply store customers establish their own Web sites by using the wholesaler's catalog and training services. And unlike other wholesalers, United protects its current retail customers by refusing to sell to final customers at its own Web site.

United recognizes that the competitive landscape of the office supply business has changed with the increased popularity of such superstores as Staples and Office Depot. While these stores buy their fast-selling goods directly from manufacturers, they purchase goods that they stock in smaller quantities from wholesalers like United Stationers. For example, United Stationers sells 60 percent of superstores' products but this amounts to less than 10 percent of their sales. As superstores increase their offerings to provide a one-stop shopping appeal to customers, United Stationer's sales will continue to grow.[1]

In this chapter, we will further look at wholesalers' relationships with suppliers and customers. We will also study the different types of firms that perform wholesaling activities and the strategies they use.

15-1 OVERVIEW

Wholesaling encompasses the buying and/or handling of goods and services and their subsequent resale to organizational users, retailers, and/or other wholesalers—but not the sale of significant volume to final consumers. It assumes many functions in a distribution channel, particularly those in the sorting process.

Wholesaling *is the buying/ handling of products and their resale to organizational buyers.*

[1]Ashlea Eberling, "Paper Tiger," *Forbes* (February 21, 2000), pp. 71, 74.

Manufacturers and service providers sometimes act as their own wholesalers; other times, independent firms are employed. Independents may or may not take title to or possession of products, depending on the type of wholesaling. Some independents have limited tasks; others do a wide range of functions.

Industrial, commercial, and government institutions are wholesalers' leading customers, followed closely by retailers. Sales from one wholesaler to another also represent a significant proportion of wholesaling activity. The following show the diversity of transactions considered as wholesaling:

- Sales of goods and services to manufacturers, service providers, oil refiners, railroads, public utilities, and government departments.
- Sales of office or laboratory equipment, supplies, and services to professionals such doctors, chiropractors, and dentists.
- Sales of materials and services to builders of offices and homes.
- Sales to grocery stores, restaurants, hotels, apparel stores, stationery stores, and all other retailers.
- Manufacturer/service provider sales to wholesalers, and wholesaler sales to other wholesalers.

In this chapter, the importance of wholesaling, the different types of wholesaling, and recent trends in wholesaling are all discussed in depth.

15-2 THE IMPORTANCE OF WHOLESALING

Wholesaling is a significant aspect of distribution because of its impact on the economy, its functions in the distribution channel, and its relationships with suppliers and customers.

15-2a Wholesaling's Impact on the Economy

Wholesale sales are high; and wholesalers greatly affect final prices.

In the United States, there are about 525,000 wholesale establishments with total annual sales exceeding $4.5 trillion (including manufacturers with wholesale facilities); yet, although wholesale revenues are higher than those in retailing, there are more than five times as many retail establishments as wholesale.[2] According to the National Association of Wholesaler-Distributors (www.naw.org), U.S. wholesalers generate almost one-fifth of their total revenues from foreign markets, nearly double the amount of a decade ago.

Revenues are high since wholesaling involves any purchases by organizational consumers. Some products also move through multiple levels of wholesalers (e.g., regional, then local); an item can be sold two or three times at the wholesale level. There are far more retailers because they serve individual, dispersed final consumers; wholesalers handle fewer, larger, more concentrated customers.

From a cost perspective, wholesalers have a great impact on prices. Table 15-1 shows the percent of wholesale selling prices that go to selected wholesalers to cover their operating expenses and pre-tax profits. For example, 31.5 percent of the price that a hardware wholesaler charges its retailers covers that wholesaler's operating and other expenses (28.4 percent) and pre-tax profit (3.1 percent). Operating costs include inventory charges, sales force salaries, advertising, and rent.

Wholesaler costs and profits depend on inventory turnover, the dollar value of products, the functions performed, efficiency, and competition.

---

[2]*Statistical Abstract of the United States 2000* (Washington, D.C.: U.S. Department of Commerce, 2000).

TABLE 15-1   Selected Performance Data for U.S. Wholesalers by Product Category[a]

Product Category of Wholesaler	Gross Profit (As % of Sales)[b]	Operating Expenses (As % of Sales)	All Other Expenses (As % of Sales)	Profit Before Taxes (As % of Sales)
Books, periodicals, and newspapers	35.6	33.1	0.5	2.0
Construction materials	27.1	23.2	0.3	3.7
Chemicals and allied products	28.8	25.1	0.8	2.8
Drugs, drug proprietaries, and and druggists' supplies	31.3	27.2	0.1	4.1
Electronic parts and equipment	30.2	26.6	0.3	3.3
Fish and seafoods	14.3	12.4	0.1	1.9
Flowers, nursery stock, and and florists' supplies	35.4	31.1	1.0	3.3
General line groceries	18.3	16.3	0.4	1.6
Hardware	31.5	28.1	0.3	3.1
Jewelry, watches, precious stones, and precious metals	27.0	24.4	0.3	2.3
Photographic equipment and supplies	29.5	25.7	0.5	3.3
Wine and distilled alcoholic beverages	26.6	21.3	0.6	4.7

[a] In interpreting these data, RMA cautions that the Studies be regarded only as a general guideline and not as an absolute industry norm. This is due to limited samples within categories, the categorization of firms by their primary North American Industry Classification System (NAICS) number only, and different methods of operations by firms within the same industry. For these reasons, RMA recommends that the figures be used only as general guidelines in addition to other methods of financial analysis.

[b] Total costs of wholesaling, which include expenses and profit. There are some rounding errors.

Source: Adapted by the authors from *RMA Annual Statement Studies 2000–2001* (Philadelphia: Risk Management Association, 2000). © Risk Management Association. Reprinted by permission. All rights reserved. No part of this table may be reproduced or utilized in any form or by any means, electronic and mechanical, including photocopying, recording, or by any information storage and retrieval system without permission in writing from Risk Management Association.

15-2b The Functions of Wholesalers

With regard to functions performed, wholesalers can

Wholesalers do tasks ranging from distribution to risk taking.

- Enable manufacturers and service providers to distribute locally without making customer contacts.

- Provide a trained sales force.

- Provide marketing and research support for manufacturers, service providers, and retail or institutional consumers.

- Gather assortments for customers and let them make fewer transactions.

- Purchase large quantities, thus reducing total physical distribution costs.

- Provide warehousing and delivery facilities.

- Offer financing for manufacturers and service providers (by paying for products when they are shipped, not when they are sold) and retail or institutional consumers (by granting credit).

- Handle financial records.
- Process returns and make adjustments for defective merchandise.
- Take risks by being responsible for theft, deterioration, and obsolescence of inventory.

Wholesalers that take title to and possession of products usually perform several or all of these tasks. Agents and brokers that facilitate sales, but do not take title or possession, have more limited duties.

Independent wholesalers vary by industry. Most consumer products, food items, replacement parts, and office supplies are sold by independents. Yet, for heavy equipment, mainframe computers, gasoline, and temporary employment, manufacturers and service providers may bypass independent resellers.

Without independent wholesalers, organizational consumers have to develop supplier contacts, deal with a number of suppliers and coordinate shipments, do more distribution functions, stock greater quantities, and place more emphasis on an internal purchasing agent or department. Many small retailers and other firms might be avoided as customers because they might not be profitably reached by a manufacturer or service provider, and they might not be able to buy necessary items elsewhere.

MARKETING *and the Web*

Retail Exchange. com: A Nearly 100-Year-Old Wholesaler Turns to the Internet

According to *Ziff Davis Smart Business for the New Economy*, "Gordon Brothers, which specializes in liquidating defunct retailers and sometimes assuming ownership in extreme cases, has worked with major retailers since 1903 and more recently has modified its business to deal with distressed companies. The firm has a strong E-business strategy and began its push to take advantage of the Internet in the late 1990s." The firm recently created two new businesses: RetailExchange.com (www.retailexchange.com) and SmartBargains.com (www.smartbargains.com). The sites are business-to-business exchanges for retailers and manufacturers so they can conceal their identities to reduce brand dilution.

RetailExchange.com, launched on Valentine's Day 2000, is the brainchild of Gordon Brothers' great-grandson Kenneth Frieze (a Wharton MBA). Frieze "envisioned a marketplace matching fragmented consumer-goods manufacturers, distributors called jobbers, and retailers to sell large-lot consumer merchandise overstocks. With the consolidation environment, fussy retail buyers with increasing power had started pushing back inventory and canceling orders with manufacturers, creating a flood of goods with nowhere to go. While manufacturers and distributors got squeezed, retailers looking for overstock goods wanted a place for off-price deals. RetailExchange.com wouldn't warehouse any inventory itself. Rather, it would match new and infrequent trading partners, charging 5 percent on a completed transaction."

By July 2001, RetailExchange.com had signed up more than 7,500 members representing 6,000 businesses. One-third of the members were buyers; one-third were sellers; and the rest did both.

Assess RetailExchange.com's wholesale strategy from the perspective of a seller of excess inventory.

Source: Based on material in Maria Atanasov, "Keep the Excess Moving," *Ziff Davis Smart Business for the New Economy* (July 1, 2001), p. 72.

An illustration of wholesaling's value is the U.S. auto parts industry, in which there used to be thousands of firms making a wide range of products and marketing them via a multitude of sales organizations. At that time, customers (mostly specialty stores and service stations) faced constant interruptions by salespeople, and manufacturers' sales costs were high. A better system exists today with the organized use of a much smaller number of independent distributors.

15-2c Wholesalers' Relationships with Suppliers and Customers

Independent wholesalers are often very much "in the middle," not fully knowing whether their allegiance should be to manufacturers/service providers or their own customers. These comments show the dilemma many wholesalers face: "The challenge is to find ways individually, and as an industry, to show our customers and manufacturers exactly where and how we do and can add value. Our roles and performance are in a state of flux. The new theory is to cut out the wholesaler to reduce costs."[3]

Wholesalers have obligations to both suppliers and customers.

Many wholesalers feel they get scant support from manufacturers/service providers. They desire training, technical assistance, product literature, and advertising. They dislike it when vendors alter territories, add new distributors to cover an existing geographic area, or decide to change to a direct channel and do wholesale tasks themselves. Wholesalers want manufacturers/service providers to sell to them and not through them. *Selling to the wholesaler* means a distributor is viewed as a customer to be researched and satisfied. *Selling through the wholesaler* means retailers or consumers are objects of manufacturers'/service providers' interest and wholesalers are less important. See Figure 15-1.

To remedy the situation, this is what wholesalers need to do:

Wholesalers must expand their value-added services, improve productivity, expand geographically, enlarge existing lines, diversify into new product lines, and develop new markets. Historically, wholesalers were known for the products and brands they carried and the basic

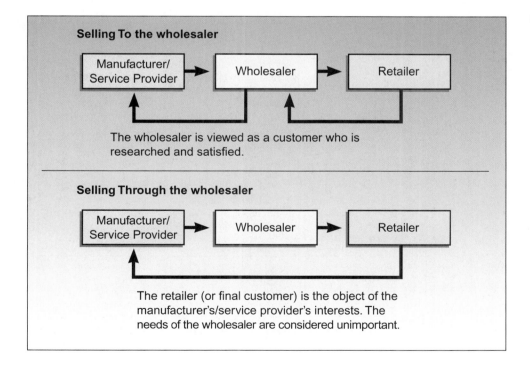

FIGURE 15-1
Selling TO versus Selling THROUGH the Wholesaler

[3]R. Craig MacClaren, "Squeezed Brokers Position for Value-Added Services," *Promo* (February 1995), p. 36; and Stephen Bennett, "Working the Middle Ground," *Progressive Grocer* (August 1995), p. 147.

services they provided. Yet, this traditional competitive edge has been blunted by a similarity of quality among brands and wholesalers' tendency to expand geographically and by product line until the market is saturated, creating a surplus of intermediary firms that look alike. In addition, the basic services offered by wholesalers—in-stock inventory, small-order handling, credit terms, and product training for their employees and customers—are no longer sufficient. In response, wholesalers are offering more value-added services such as free delivery, relabeling, repackaging, and applying bar codes. They must adopt an aggressive program to improve and expand value-added services by anticipating the needs of the customer, and using technologies now available to improve productivity, reliability, and service quality. Much of this can be done by enacting bar coding and a system of electronic data interaction to assure next-day delivery, product lot tracking, and comprehensive inventory controls.[4]

15-3 TYPES OF WHOLESALING

The three broad categories of wholesaling are outlined in Figure 15-2: manufacturer/service provider wholesaling, merchant wholesaling, and agents and brokers. Table 15-2 contains detailed descriptions of every type of independent wholesaler and shows their functions and special features.

FIGURE 15-2
The Broad Categories of Wholesaling

Factors	Manufacturer/Service Provider Wholesaling	Merchant Wholesaling	Agents and Brokers
Control/ Functions	• The manufacturer/ service provider controls wholesaling and performs all functions.	• The wholesaler controls wholesaling and performs many or all functions.	• The manufacturer/ service provider and wholesaler each have some control and perform some functions.
Ownership	• The manufacturer/ service provider owns products until they are bought by retailers or other organizational consumers.	• The wholesaler buys products from the manufacturer/service provider and resells them.	• The manufacturer/ service provider owns the products and pays the wholesaler a fee/commission.
Cash Flow	• The manufacturer/ service provider does not receive payment until the retailer or other customer buys products.	• The manufacturer/ service provider is paid when the wholesaler purchases products.	• The manufacturer/ service provider does not receive payment until products are sold.
Best Use(s)	• The manufacturer/ service provider deals with a small group of large and geographically concentrated customers; rapid expansion is not a goal.	• The manufacturer/ service provider has a large product line that is sold through many small and geographically dispersed customers; expansion is a goal.	• The manufacturer/ service provider is small, has little marketing expertise, and is relatively unknown to potential customers; expansion is a goal.

[4]"Wholesaling Industry," www.activemedia-guide.com/wholesaling_industry.htm (January 2000).

TABLE 15-2   **Characteristics of Independent Wholesalers**

Wholesaler Type	Provides Credit	Stores and Delivers	Takes Title	Provides Merchandising and Promotion Assistance	Provides Personal Sales Force	Performs Research and Planning	Special Features
I. Merchant wholesaler							
A. Full service							
1. General merchandise	Yes	Yes	Yes	Yes	Yes	Yes	Carries nearly all items a customer usually needs
2. Specialty merchandise	Yes	Yes	Yes	Yes	Yes	Yes	Specializes in a narrow product range, extensive assortment
3. Rack jobber	Yes	Yes	Yes	Yes	Yes	Yes	Furnishes racks and shelves, consignment sales
4. Franchise	Yes	Yes	Yes	Yes	Yes	Yes	Use of common business format, extensive management services
5. Cooperative							
a. Producer-owned	Yes	Yes	Yes	Yes	Yes	Yes	Farmer controlled, profits divided among members
b. Retailer-owned	Yes	Yes	Yes	Yes	Yes	Yes	Wholesaler owned by several retailers
B. Limited service							
1. Cash and carry	No	Stores, no delivery	Yes	No	No	No	No outside sales force, wholesale store for business needs
2. Drop shipper	Yes	Delivers, no storage	Yes	No	Yes	Sometimes	Ships items without physically handling them
3. Truck/wagon	Rarely	Yes	Yes	Yes	Yes	Sometimes	Sales and delivery on same call
4. Mail order	Sometimes	Yes	Yes	No	No	Sometimes	Catalogs used as sole promotion tool
II. Agents and brokers							
A. Agents							
1. Manufacturers' (service providers')	No	Sometimes	No	Yes	Yes	Sometimes	Sells selected items for several firms
2. Selling	Sometimes	Yes	No	Yes	Yes	Yes	Markets all the items of a firm
3. Commission (factor) merchants	Sometimes	Yes	No	No	Yes	Yes	Handles items on a consignment basis
B. Brokers							
1. Food	No	Sometimes	No	Yes	Yes	Yes	Brings together buyers and sellers
2. Stock	Sometimes	Sometimes	No	Yes	Yes	Yes	Brings together buyers and sellers

15-3a Manufacturer/Service Provider Wholesaling

In **manufacturer/service provider wholesaling,** *a firm has its own sales or branch offices.*

In **manufacturer/service provider wholesaling,** a producer does all wholesaling functions itself. This occurs if a firm feels it is best able to reach retailers or other organizational customers by doing wholesaling tasks itself. The format accounts for 31 percent of U.S. wholesale revenues and 6 percent of establishments. Manufacturer/service provider wholesalers include General Motors (www.gm.com), IBM (www.ibm.com), Pitney Bowes (www.pitneybowes.com), Frito-Lay (www.frito.com), Hanes (www.hanes.com), Prudential (www.prudential.com), and Citigroup (www.citigroup.com).

Wholesale activities by a manufacturer or service provider may be done at sales offices and/or branch offices. A *sales office* is located at a firm's production facilities or close to the market. No inventory is kept there. In contrast, a *branch office* has facilities for warehousing products, as well as for selling them.

Manufacturer/service provider wholesaling is most likely if independent intermediaries are unavailable, existing intermediaries are unacceptable to the manufacturer or service provider, the manufacturer or service provider wants control over marketing, customers are few in number and each is a key account, customers desire personal service from the producer, customers are near the firm or clustered, computerized ordering links a firm with customers, and/or laws (particularly in foreign markets) limit arrangements with independent resellers.

For instance, because it wants to maintain close contact with its retailers and control its marketing strategy, manufacturer wholesaling is a must for Frito-Lay. But, it sure is complex: "Distributing 9 billion bags of snacks a year creates quite a delivery crunch. With net sales exceeding $11 billion annually, Frito-Lay (a PepsiCo division) is the undisputed leader in the salty snack industry. Doritos, Ruffles, and dozens of other well-known Frito-Lay brands command half the U.S. snack chip market. Approximately 14,000 Frito-Lay sales and delivery personnel connect 200 distribution centers to hundreds of thousands of retailers. Each delivery generates a proof of delivery receipt, to the tune of 120,000 daily."[5]

15-3b Merchant Wholesaling

Merchant wholesalers *buy products and are* **full** *or* **limited service.**

Merchant wholesalers buy, take title, and take possession of products for further resale. This is the largest U.S. wholesaler type in sales (57 percent of the total) and establishments (83 percent of the total).

As an example, Sysco (www.sysco.com) is a merchant wholesaler that buys and handles 150,000 products from 3,000 producers of food and related products from around the world. It carries fresh and frozen meats, seafood, poultry, fruits and vegetables, bakery products, canned and dry foods, paper and disposable products, sanitation items, dairy foods, beverages, kitchen and tabletop equipment, and medical and surgical supplies. The firm operates throughout the contiguous United States and Alaska, and in parts of Canada. Sysco has 122 distribution facilities, and it serves more than 356,000 restaurants, hotels, schools, hospitals, retirement homes, and other locations.[6] See Figure 15-3.

Full-service merchant wholesalers perform a full range of distribution tasks. They provide credit, store and deliver products, offer merchandising and promotion assistance, have a personal sales force, offer research and planning support, pass along information to suppliers and customers, and give installation and repair services. They are prevalent for grocery products, pharmaceuticals, hardware, plumbing equipment, tobacco, alcoholic beverages, and television program syndication.

Limited-service merchant wholesalers do not perform all the functions of full-service merchant wholesalers. They may not provide credit, merchandising assistance, or marketing research data. They are popular for construction materials, coal, lumber, perishables, equipment rentals, and specialty foods.

[5]"HighView at Frito-Lay," www.htech.com/fritopoda.htm (April 25, 2001).
[6]"Investor Relations," www.sysco.com/customer/ir.html (April 26, 2001).

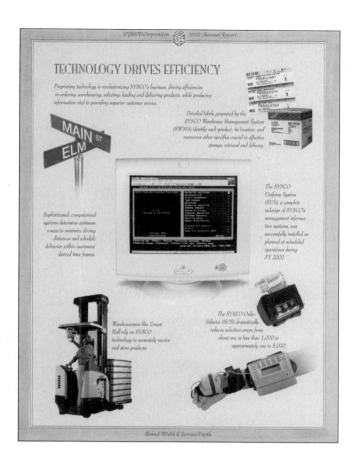

FIGURE 15-3
Sysco: A Leader in Merchant Wholesaling
Source: Reprinted by permission.

On average, full-service merchant wholesalers require more compensation than limited-service ones because they perform greater functions.

Full-Service Merchant Wholesalers

Full-service merchant wholesalers can be divided into general merchandise, specialty merchandise, rack jobber, franchise, and cooperative types.

General-merchandise (full-line) wholesalers carry a wide product assortment—nearly all the items needed by their customers. Some general-merchandise hardware, drug, and clothing wholesalers stock many product lines, but not much depth in any one line. They seek to sell their retailers or other organizational customers all or most of their products and foster strong loyalty and exclusivity.

General-merchandise wholesalers *sell a range of items.*

Specialty-merchandise (limited-line) wholesalers concentrate on a rather narrow product range and have an extensive selection in that range. They offer many sizes, colors, and models—and provide functions similar to other full-service merchant wholesalers. They are popular for health foods, seafood, retail store displays, frozen foods, and video rentals.

Specialty-merchandise wholesalers *sell a narrow line.*

Rack jobbers furnish the racks or shelves on which products are displayed. They own the products on the racks, selling them on a consignment basis—so their clients pay after goods are resold. Unsold items are taken back. Jobbers set up displays, refill shelves, price-mark goods, maintain inventory records, and compute the amount due from their customers. Heavily advertised, branded merchandise that is sold on a self-service basis is most often handled. Included are magazines, health and beauty aids, cosmetics, drugs, hand tools, toys, housewares, and stationery.

Rack jobbers *set up displays and are paid after sales.*

In *franchise wholesaling,* independent retailers affiliate with an existing wholesaler to use a standardized storefront design, business format, name, and purchase system. Suppliers often produce goods and services according to specifications set by a franchise

With **franchise wholesaling,** *retailers join with a wholesaler.*

wholesaler. This form of wholesaling is used for hardware, auto parts, and groceries. Franchise wholesalers include Independent Grocers Alliance (IGA, www.iga.com) and Franklin Stores (http://www2.benfranklinstores.com/index.asp).

Producers or retailers can set up **wholesale cooperatives.**

Wholesale cooperatives are owned by member firms to economize functions and provide broad support. Producer-owned cooperatives are popular in farming. They market, transport, and process farm products—as well as make and distribute farm supplies. These cooperatives often sell to stores under their own names, such as Farmland (www.farmland.com), Land O'Lakes (www.landolakes.com), Ocean Spray (www.oceanspray.com), Sunkist (www.sunkist.com), and Welch's (www.welchs.com). With retailer-owned cooperatives, independent retailers form associations that purchase, lease, or build wholesale facilities. The cooperatives take title to merchandise, handle cooperative ads, and negotiate with suppliers. They are used by hardware and grocery stores. Ace Hardware (www.acehardware.com) "is a cooperative of more than 5,100 independent retail stores. Ace is committed to providing low upfront costs on merchandise purchases by dealers from strategically located Ace hardware retail support centers or through other programs. Dealers are supported by over 65,000 brand name and Ace brand items, an advertising program, retail support systems, and headquarters and field staff personnel." See Figure 15-4.

FIGURE 15-4

Ace Hardware: The Power of a Cooperative for Small Retailers

Independent market research indicates that eight out of every 10 American consumers know Ace as the "Helpful Hardware Place."

Source: Reprinted by permission of Ace Hardware, © 2001.

Limited-Service Merchant Wholesalers

Limited-service merchant wholesalers can be divided into cash-and-carry, drop shipper, truck/wagon, and mail-order types.

In *cash-and-carry wholesaling,* small-business people drive to wholesalers, order products, and take them back to a store or business. These wholesalers offer no credit or delivery, no merchandising and promotion help, no outside sales force, and no research or planning assistance. They are good for fill-in items, have low prices, and allow immediate product use. They are used for construction materials, electrical supplies, office supplies, auto supplies, hardware products, and groceries.

Drop shippers (desk jobbers) buy goods from manufacturers or suppliers and arrange for their shipment to retailers or industrial users. They have legal ownership, but do not take physical possession of products and have no storage facilities. They purchase items, leave them at manufacturers' plants, contact customers by phone, set up and coordinate carload shipments from manufacturers directly to customers, and are responsible for items that cannot be sold. Trade credit, a personal sales force, and some research and planning are provided; merchandising and promotion support are not. Drop shippers are often used for coal, coke, and building materials. These goods have high freight costs, in relation to their value, because of their weight. Thus, direct shipments from suppliers to customers are needed.

Truck/wagon wholesalers generally have a regular sales route, offer items from a truck or wagon, and deliver goods when they are sold. These wholesalers provide merchandising and promotion support; however, they are considered limited service because they usually do not extend credit and offer little research and planning help. Operating costs are high due to the services performed and low average sales. These wholesalers often deal with goods requiring special handling or with perishables such as bakery products, tobacco, meat, candy, potato chips, and dairy products.

Mail-order wholesalers use catalogs, instead of a personal sales force, to promote products and communicate with customers. They may provide credit but do not generally give merchandising and promotion support. They store and deliver goods, and offer some research and planning assistance. These wholesalers are found with jewelry, cosmetics, auto parts, specialty food product lines, business supplies, and small office equipment.

15-3c Agents and Brokers

Agents and *brokers* perform various wholesale tasks, but do not take title to products. Unlike merchant wholesalers, which make profits on the sales of products they own, they work for commissions or fees as payment for their services. They account for 12 percent of wholesale sales and 11 percent of wholesale establishments. The main difference between agents and brokers is that agents are apt to be used on a permanent basis, while brokers are often temporary.

Agents and brokers enable a manufacturer or service provider to expand sales volume despite limited resources. Their selling costs are a pre-determined percent of sales; and they have trained salespeople. There are manufacturers'/service providers' agents, selling agents, and commission (factor) merchants.

Manufacturers'/service providers' agents work for several manufacturers/service providers and carry noncompetitive, complementary products in exclusive territories. By selling noncompetitive items, they eliminate conflict-of-interest situations. By selling complementary items, they stock a fairly complete line of products for their market areas. They do not offer credit but may store and deliver products and give limited research and planning aid. Merchandising and promotional support are provided. These agents may enhance the sales efforts of clients, help introduce new products, enter dispersed markets, and handle items with low average sales. They may carry only some of a firm's products; a manufacturer/service provider may hire many agents. Larger firms may hire a separate one for each product line. Agents have little say on marketing and pricing. They earn commissions of 5 percent to 10 percent of sales, and are popular for auto products, iron, steel, footwear, textiles, and commercial real-estate and insurance. The Manufacturers' Agents National Association (www.manaonline.org) is an organization with 22,000 manufacturers' reps.

In **cash-and-carry wholesaling,** *the customer drives to a wholesaler.*

Drop shippers (desk jobbers) *buy goods, but do not take possession.*

Truck/wagon wholesalers *offer products on a sales route.*

Mail-order wholesalers *sell through catalogs.*

Agents *and* **brokers** *do not take title to products.*

Manufacturers'/service providers' agents *work for many firms, selling noncompeting items.*

ETHICAL Issues in Marketing

The Battle Between Property Owners and Their Hotel Operators

To better understand the conflict between property owners and hotel operators, it is important to know who runs the hotels. Often, investors (such as insurance companies and pension funds) buy or build hotel facilities and hire hotel management companies to run the hotels for 20 to 25 years. Operators typically receive a fee of 1 percent to 3 percent of sales plus an incentive for meeting earnings or growth goals.

Recently, the partnership between Sheraton and John Hancock Financial Services ended for a Sheraton hotel located in Washington D.C. Hancock sued Sheraton claiming that the latter accepted kickbacks from suppliers. A Federal court jury agreed and awarded Hancock $50 million in damages. According to Hancock, Sheraton told suppliers of sheets, towels, and soap to add an average of 7 percent to the negotiated price and to return these monies to Sheraton. Since the kickbacks were not included in Sheraton's financial statements, they also inflated expenses.

While Sheraton admitted that it had participated in this purchasing program, it claimed that the 7 percent fee covered its administrative costs. It also asserted that bulk purchasing deals and fees were a standard policy followed in the hotel industry. Witnesses at the trial estimated that the 7 percent pricing adjustment resulted in Sheraton receiving an additional $32 million between 1992 and 1997.

Some industry analysts believe that the Hancock legal victory will lead to additional suits against hotel management companies. In one suit against Hyatt, the real-estate owners claimed that the hotel chain obtained "secret kickbacks" from vendors and "actively attempted to mislead" the real-estate owners for more than 10 years.

As the general manager of a hotel managed by a major chain, what would you do differently than the Sheraton in Washington, D.C. (while still generating a profit for your management company)?

Source: Based on material in Michael Freedman, "Lodging Complaints," *Forbes* (September 18, 2000), pp. 58, 60.

Selling agents *market all the products of a manufacturer or service provider.*

Selling agents are responsible for marketing the entire output of a manufacturer/ service provider under a contractual agreement. They become the marketing department for their clients and can negotiate price and other conditions of sale, such as credit and delivery. They do all wholesale tasks except taking title. While a firm may use several manufacturers'/service providers' agents, it may hire only one sales agent. These agents are more apt to work for small firms than large ones. They are common for textile manufacturing, canned foods, metals, home furnishings, apparel, lumber, and metal products. Since they do more tasks, they often get higher commissions than manufacturers'/service providers' representatives.

Commission (factor) merchants *assemble goods from local markets.*

Commission (factor) merchants receive goods on consignment, accumulate them from local markets, and arrange for their sale in a central location. They may offer credit; they do store and deliver goods, provide a sales force, and offer research and planning help. They normally do not assist in merchandising and promotion, but can negotiate prices with buyers—provided the prices are not below sellers' stated minimums. They may act in an auction setting; commissions vary. These wholesalers are used for agricultural and seafood products, furniture, and art.

Brokers are common in food and financial services. They are well informed about market conditions, terms of sale, sources of credit, price setting, potential buyers and sellers, and the art of negotiating. They do not take title and usually are not allowed to complete a transaction without approval.

Food brokers introduce buyers and sellers of food and related general-merchandise items to one another and bring them together to complete a sale. They operate in specific locales and work for a limited number of food producers. Their sales staff calls on chain-store buyers, store managers, and purchasing agents. They work closely with ad agencies. They often represent the seller, who pays a commission. They do not actually provide credit but may store and deliver. Commissions are 3 percent to 5 percent of sales. Cebco (www.cebco.com) and Dadant and Company (www.dadantco.com) are examples of food brokers with active Web sites.

Commercial stock brokers are licensed sales representatives who advise business clients, take orders, and then acquire stocks and/or bonds for the clients. They may aid firms selling stocks or bonds, represent either buyers or sellers (with both paying commissions), and offer some credit. While they operate in particular areas, they usually sell stocks and bonds of firms from around the United States—even around the world. They do a lot of business over the phone and may help publicize new stock or bond offerings. Commissions average 1 percent to 10 percent of sales, based on volume and stock prices.

> **Food brokers** *and* **commercial stock brokers** *unite buyers and sellers, as well as conclude sales.*

15-4 RECENT TRENDS IN WHOLESALING

During the last 20 years, wholesaling has changed dramatically, with independent wholesalers striving to protect their place in the channel. Among the key trends are those related to the evolving wholesaler mix, productivity, customer service, international opportunities, and target markets.

Since the early 1980s, the proportion of total sales volume contributed by manufacturer wholesaling, merchant wholesaling, and agents and brokers has stayed rather steady. However, manufacturer wholesalers now operate far fewer establishments (due to the consolidation of facilities) and merchant wholesalers operate many more (to provide better customer service). Overall, 250,000 companies currently engage in some form of U.S. wholesaling, down from 364,000 companies in 1987. Today, the average annual sales for the 31,000 U.S. manufacturer wholesaling establishments are $45 million—compared with $5.9 million for the 436,000 merchant wholesaling establishments and $9.3 million for the 58,000 agent/broker establishments. The 50 largest manufacturer wholesalers account for 53 percent of sales in that category; the 50 biggest merchant wholesalers account for 16 percent of sales in that category; and the 50 biggest agents/brokers account for 28 percent of category sales. The trend toward bigger firms is expected to continue well into the future.[7]

> *Firms are becoming larger and more cost-conscious.*

The Internet is also having a major impact on the wholesaler mix: "The biggest negative influence on wholesalers and the wholesaling industry may be the growth of the Web, which enables sellers and buyers to bypass wholesalers and interface directly with each other. This new medium has played a major factor in products such as books, CDs, and airline tickets."[8] Yet, some wholesalers are flourishing on the Web. They understand how to use it to their advantage.

Wholesalers are constantly looking for productivity gains to benefit their customers and themselves, and protect their position in the marketplace. As highlighted in Figure 15-5, consider the approach of United Stationers (www.unitedstationers.com):

> Our goal is to be the world-class, leading distributor of business and other products, serving land and Web resellers. We expect to reach it by making fulfillment excellence our central operating strategy: getting the right products to the right customers in the right package at the

[7]Updated estimates by the authors based on the *1997 Census of Wholesale Trade* (Washington, D.C.: U.S. Department of Commerce, 2000).

[8]"Wholesaling Industry."

GLOBAL *Marketing in Action*

Thailand's Siam Makro: A Wholesaling Powerhouse

Siam Makro PCL, Thailand's largest wholesaler, recently installed an Internet-based system to provide its more than 1,000 suppliers with real-time inventory data, as well as automated payments. According to Makro's buying director, by using computer and Internet access, suppliers can see inventory status on a store-by-store basis, daily sales volume, and how the supplier's products compare with competitive products. Information pertaining to the status of inventory purchase orders, payments, and promotions are also visible to suppliers. To ensure confidentiality, each supplier has its own user name and password. There are also security systems that monitor access to the Web site.

The president of Siam Makro says that the aim of the system is to "take costs out of the supply chain" through improved procurement and payments. Even though only 6 percent of its suppliers have thus far implemented electronic data interchange (EDI), Makro will continue to support EDI to those suppliers wanting to use it. Siam Makro's analysis indicates that "the minimum investment for a basic EDI system is 2.5 million baht ($58,725 in U.S. dollars) to 5 million baht ($117,450) whereas suppliers need to invest less than 100,000 baht ($2,349) to be part of the new B2B commerce."

The Web-based system has been tested between Siam Makro and five key suppliers: Unilever, Colgate-Palmolive, Philips, Dumex, and Nestlé. Siam Makro expects the majority of its suppliers to be linked to this system as of 2003.

As a large supplier, how would you benefit from Siam Makro's new system? What are the potential risks of participating? Explain your answer.

Source: Based on material in "Makro Calls Online Initiative a First: Suppliers Can Track Sales and Inventories," *Bangkok Post* (June 23, 2000).

right time—and tracking this process each step of the way. United already has a rock-solid operating platform that includes an extensive distribution network with 39 regional distribution centers handling general office products, 28 distribution centers dedicated to serving the janitorial and sanitation industry, 6 distribution centers that serve computer supply resellers, 3 distribution centers that serve Canada, and other facilities. This allows United to reach nearly every reseller or consumer in the U.S. within 24 hours.[9]

Wholesalers are emphasizing customer service and looking to international markets.

Wholesalers know customer service is very important in securing a competitive advantage, developing client loyalty, and attaining acceptable profit margins. Here is what two firms are doing:

- Kimberly-Clark (www.kimberly-clark.com) often acts as a manufacturer wholesaler: "For customers such as Costco (www.costco.com), it goes out of its way through a vendor-managed inventory system, whereby Kimberly-Clark oversees and pays for everything involved with managing Costco's inventory except the actual shelf-stockers in store aisles. For Costco, the benefits of such close cooperation are equally clear. Costco saves money not only on staffing in its inventory department, but also on storage. Before Kimberly-Clark began managing Costco's inventory, the retailer would keep an average of a month's supply of Kimberly-Clark products in its warehouses.

[9]"Company Profile," www.unitedstationers.com/profile/overview.html (April 26, 2001).

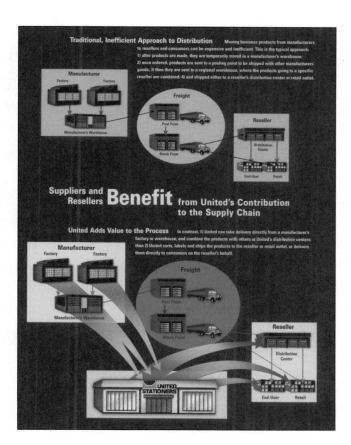

FIGURE 15-5
United Stationers: How a Wholesaler Helps Its Customers Be More Productive

Source: Reprinted by permission.

Now, because Kimberly-Clark has proven it can replenish supplies more efficiently, Costco needs to keep only a two-week supply. Kimberly-Clark manages inventory in Costco stores everywhere but the Northeast. It recently sent analysts to Costco headquarters in Issaquah, Washington, to push for a possible next stage: expanding to the Northeast and collaborating on forecasts, not just recorded sales."[10]

- At W.W. Grainger (www.grainger.com), a merchant wholesaler of maintenance, repair, and operating supplies, "We go above and beyond by offering valuable services to our customers as standard policy. We offer the breadth of products you need for one-stop shopping. Order by phone, fax, at your local branch, with your Grainger account manager, or on Grainger.com. We'll work with you to find the best way to get your order delivered as quickly as possible. Our Product Support Team is available to help with product selection, application assistance, installation, troubleshooting, performance data, maintenance, and general technical guidance."[11]

More U.S. wholesalers are turning to foreign markets for growth, but many are not necessarily moving quickly enough. According to Food Distributors International (www.fdi.org),

It's a rare distributor who can afford to kiss off more than 5 billion potential new customers, but that's what the firm is doing if it doesn't export products to other nations. Few distributors are taking advantage of the opportunity. "Only 2 percent of wholesale consumer products firms with 5 or more employees are involved in exporting," says Ellen Welby of the U.S. Department of Agriculture. "The number is 5 percent for industry as a whole. This is a great opportunity for the food industry." Those who have gone to the trouble of becoming exporters say it's worth it. Jack Todd, general manager of international business at Houston-based Grocers Supply

[10]Emily Nelson and Ann Zimmerman, "Minding the Store: Kimberly-Clark Keeps Costco in Diapers, Absorbing Costs Itself," *Wall Street Journal* (September 7, 2000), p. A1.

[11]"Family of Services," www.grainger.com/Grainger/static.jsp?page=fos_ordering.html (May 1, 2001).

FIGURE 15-6

Supervalu: From Merchant Wholesaling to Retailing

Supervalu is one of the leading food wholesalers in the United States. It provides distribution services to about 6,100 stores of all sizes and formats—including regional and national chain supermarkets, corporate owned and licensed retail locations, mass merchandisers, and E-tailers. It has also become the 10th largest U.S. supermarket chain with more than 1,100 outlets in 38 states. Among the retail stores it operates are Cub Foods, Save-A-Lot, Farm Fresh, Shop 'n Save (shown here), and Shoppers Food Warehouse.

Source: Reprinted by permission.

Target market strategies are more complex.

(http://gscapps.grocerybiz.com), says the company exports virtually all of the 25,000 items it carries, including perishables. Its overseas markets are concentrated in Central and South America, the Mideast, and the Indian subcontinent. California-based Unified Western Grocers (http://kpl.multi-ad.com/clients/unified) saw its international sales jump almost 30 percent in one year despite economic distress in many parts of the world. It exports thousands of products to Asia, Latin America, West Africa and Europe.[12]

In large numbers, wholesalers are diversifying the markets they serve or the products they carry: Farm and garden machinery wholesalers now sell to florists, hardware dealers, and garden supply stores. Plumbing wholesalers have added industrial accounts, contractors, and builders. Grocery wholesalers deal with hotels, airlines, hospitals, schools, and restaurants. Large food wholesalers such as Supervalu (www.supervalu.com) have moved more actively into retailing. See Figure 15-6.

[12]Carole Edwards, "Scouring the Earth for Customers," www.fdi.org/intl/fdmear.html (May 1, 2001).

WEB SITES YOU CAN USE

: Here are a variety of useful Web sites related to wholesaling:

Annual Wholesale Trade Survey (www.census.gov/svsd/www/whltable.html)

Food Distributors International (www.fdi.org)

Healthcare Distribution Management Association (www.healthcaredistribution.wegov2.com)

International Wholesale Furniture Association (www.iwfa.net)

WholesaleCentral.com (www.wholesalecentral.com)

Wholesale Source Magazine (www.wsmag.com)

Wholesaling Industry Profile (www.activemedia-guide.com/wholesaling_industry.htm)

SUMMARY

1. *To define wholesaling and show its importance* Wholesaling involves the buying and/or handling of goods and services and their resale to organizational users, retailers, and/or other wholesalers—but not the sale of significant volume to final consumers. In the United States, about 525,000 wholesale establishments distribute $4.5 trillion in goods and services annually.

Wholesale functions encompass distribution, personal selling, marketing and research assistance, gathering assortments, cost reductions, warehousing, financing, returns, and risk taking. These functions may be assumed by manufacturers/service providers or shared with independent wholesalers. The latter are sometimes in a precarious position because they are located between manufacturers/service providers and customers and must determine their responsibilities to each.

2. *To describe the three broad categories of wholesaling (manufacturer/service provider wholesaling, merchant wholesaling, and agents and brokers) and the specific types of firms within each category* In manufacturer/service provider wholesaling, a producer undertakes all wholesaling functions itself. This form of wholesaling can be done by sales or branch offices. The sales office has no inventory.

Merchant wholesalers buy, take title, and possess products for further resale. Full-service merchant wholesalers gather product assortments, provide trade credit, store and deliver products, offer merchandising and promotion assistance, provide a personal sales force, offer research and planning support, and complete other functions as well. These wholesalers fall into general merchandise, specialty merchandise, rack jobber, franchise, and cooperative types. Limited-service merchant wholesalers take title to products but do not provide all wholesale functions. These wholesalers are divided into cash-and-carry, drop shipper, truck/wagon, and mail-order types.

Agents and brokers provide various wholesale tasks, such as negotiating purchases and expediting sales, but do not take title. They are paid commissions or fees. Agents are used on a more permanent basis than brokers. Types of agents are manufacturers'/service providers' agents, selling agents, and commission (factor) merchants. Food brokers and commercial stock brokers are two key players in wholesale brokerage.

3. *To examine recent trends in wholesaling* The nature of wholesaling has changed over the last several years. Trends involve the evolving wholesaler mix, productivity, customer service, international openings, and target markets.

KEY TERMS

wholesaling (p. 457)
manufacturer/service provider
   wholesaling (p. 464)
merchant wholesalers (p. 464)
full-service merchant wholesalers (p. 464)
limited-service merchant
   wholesalers (p. 464)
general-merchandise (full-line)
   wholesalers (p. 465)

specialty-merchandise (limited-line)
   wholesalers (p. 465)
rack jobbers (p. 465)
franchise wholesaling (p. 465)
wholesale cooperatives (p. 466)
cash-and-carry wholesaling (p. 467)
drop shippers (desk jobbers) (p. 467)
truck/wagon wholesalers (p. 467)
mail-order wholesalers (p. 467)

agents (p. 467)
brokers (p. 467)
manufacturers'/service providers'
   agents (p. 467)
selling agents (p. 468)
commission (factor) merchants (p. 468)
food brokers (p. 469)
commercial stock brokers (p. 469)

REVIEW QUESTIONS

1. Differentiate between selling to a wholesaler and selling through a wholesaler.
2. Under what circumstances should a manufacturer or service provider undertake wholesaling?
3. Distinguish between a manufacturer's/service provider's branch office and a manufacturer's/service provider's sales office.
4. Which wholesaling functions are performed by merchant wholesalers? Which are performed by agents and brokers?

5. Distinguish between limited-service merchant wholesalers and full-service merchant wholesalers.
6. What are the unique features of cash-and-carry and truck/wagon merchant wholesalers?
7. Why are drop shippers frequently used for coal, coke, and building materials?
8. How do manufacturers'/service providers' agents and selling agents differ?

DISCUSSION QUESTIONS

1. "Wholesalers are very much in the middle, often not fully knowing whether their first allegiance should be to the manufacturer/service provider or the customer." Comment on this statement. Can they rectify this situation? Why or why not?

2. The marketing vice-president of Visa International (www.visa.com) has asked you to outline a support program to improve relations with the retailers that accept its cards. Prepare this outline.

3. Develop a short checklist that Sony Electronics (www.sel.sony.com) could use in determining whether to use merchant wholesalers or agents/brokers in different countries around the world.

4. Discuss how and why a perfume manufacturer would use a combination of manufacturer/service provider wholesaling, merchant wholesaling, and agents/brokers.

WEB EXERCISE

According to *Intergreet*, "Since 1997, we have been the Internet's premier provider of wholesale quality greeting cards. We carry a wide selection of designs, with a constant expansion of the diversity we pride ourselves on supplying. We cater to both large and small retailers, businesses, churches, and distributors. Our combination of high quality products at discounted prices will be a winner for you. So whether you are just starting out or are a 'multinational,' we have exactly the right program for you." As the owner of a small stationery store, what are the pros and cons of your buying cards from Intergreet?

16

Retailing

Chapter Objectives

1 To define retailing and show its importance

2 To discuss the different types of retailers, in terms of ownership, store strategy mix, and nonstore operations

3 To explore five major aspects of retail planning: store location, atmosphere, scrambled merchandising, the wheel of retailing, and technological advances

4 To examine recent trends in retailing

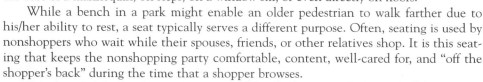

Paco Underhill, the chief executive of a leading marketing consulting firm (www.envirosell.com), feels that one of the most overlooked elements of store interior design is seating: "In most stores throughout the world, sales would instantly increase by the addition of one chair. I would remove a display if it meant creating space for a chair. I'd rip out a fixture. I'd kill a mannequin. A chair says, 'we care.'"

One way to determine if the number of chairs in a retail store is sufficient is simply to observe the number of shoppers who improvise in their seating. For instance, it may be common to see shoppers sitting on the base of a mannequin, on steps, on a window sill, or even directly on floors.

While a bench in a park might enable an older pedestrian to walk farther due to his/her ability to rest, a seat typically serves a different purpose. Often, seating is used by nonshoppers who wait while their spouses, friends, or other relatives shop. It is this seating that keeps the nonshopping party comfortable, content, well-cared for, and "off the shopper's back" during the time that a shopper browses.

Retailers that attract large percentages of female shoppers who come with male companions need to pay particular attention to the availability of seating for these males. Catering to this group with seating and other amenities could easily result in female shoppers spending more time.

Here are some suggestions to make male shoppers more comfortable in these stores:

- Seating should be placed alongside the ladies' dressing rooms. This allows males to more easily view how a particular clothing selection looks on their female counterparts.

- A selection of reading material appropriate for a male audience (such as sports, auto, and home improvement magazines) should be placed alongside seating areas.

- Coffee, cookies, and miniature pastries could be placed in an area away from clothing. This enables males to snack in an area where clothing will not be damaged.

- More seating may be needed on weekends and evenings than in daytime weekday hours.[1]

In Chapter 16, many aspects of the field of retailing are covered in depth.

16-1 OVERVIEW

Retailing encompasses the business activities involved with the sale of goods and services to the final consumer for personal, family, or household use. It is the final stage in a channel of distribution. Manufacturers, importers, and wholesalers act as retailers when they sell directly to the final consumer.

Retailing, *the last channel stage, entails selling to final consumers.*

---

[1]Paco Underhill, "You Are Where You Sit," *Across the Board* (June 2000), p. 9.

The average retail sale per shopping trip is small, less than $100 for U.S. department stores and specialty stores. Convenience stores, such as 7-Eleven (www.7-eleven.com), have average sales of just a few dollars (not including gasoline). U.S. chain supermarkets average less than $30 per customer transaction. Accordingly, retailers try to increase their sales volume by using one-stop shopping appeals, broadening merchandise and service assortments, increasing customer shopping frequency, and encouraging more family members to go shopping. Inventory controls, automated merchandise handling, and electronic cash registers enable retailers to reduce their transaction costs.

Despite the low average size of customer transactions, about one-half of sales for such retailers as department stores involve some form of customer credit. This means these retailers must pay a percentage of each transaction to a bank or other credit-card service company or absorb the costs of their own credit programs—in return for increased sales. Sears (www.sears.com) and J.C. Penney (www.jcpenney.com) each have millions of holders of their own credit cards, who spend billions of dollars with them every year.

Whereas salespeople regularly visit organizational consumers to initiate and conclude transactions, most final consumers patronize stores. This makes the location of the store, product assortment, store hours, store fixtures, sales personnel, delivery, customer service, and other factors critical tools in drawing customers to the store. See Figure 16-1.

Final consumers make many unplanned purchases. In contrast, those that buy for resale or use in production (or operating a business) are more systematic in their purchasing. Therefore, retailers need to place impulse items in high-traffic locations, organize store layout, train sales personnel in suggestion selling, place related items next to each other, and sponsor special events to stimulate consumers.

In this chapter, the importance of retailing, the various types of retailers, considerations in retail planning, and recent trends in retailing are all discussed in detail.

FIGURE 16-1

The Body Shop: An Appealing Global Retailer

The Body Shop International (www.the-body-shop.com) "is a values-driven, high-quality skin and hair care retailer operating in 49 countries with more than 1,700 outlets spanning 24 languages and 12 time zones. Famous for creating a niche market sector for naturally-inspired skin and hair care products, The Body Shop introduced a generation of consumers to the benefits of a wide range of best-sellers from Vitamin E Moisture Cream to Tea Tree Oil to Banana Nourishing Shampoo to Aloe Vera Body Lotion. The Body Shop has always believed that business is primarily about human relationships. We believe that the more we listen to our stakeholders and involve them in decision making, the better our business will run."

Source: Reprinted by permission of PricewaterhouseCoopers.

16-2 THE IMPORTANCE OF RETAILING

Retailing is a significant aspect of distribution because of its impact on the economy, its functions in the distribution channel, and its relationships with suppliers.

16-2a Retailing's Impact on the Economy

Retail sales and employment are considerable. Annual U.S. retail store sales are $3.5 trillion, an amount that does not include most vending machine, direct selling, and direct marketing revenues or many services. The world's top 100 retailers (38 from the United States) generate $1.8 trillion in total annual revenues and include firms from 17 nations. The largest retailer on the planet, by far, is U.S.-based Wal-Mart (www.walmart.com)— with total annual domestic and foreign sales of $200 billion, 4,200 stores, and multiple store formats (such as Wal-Mart and Sam's Clubs).[2]

Retailing embodies high annual sales, employment, and costs.

According to the Bureau of Labor Statistics, 23 million people are employed in 2.8 million U.S. retail establishments. Wal-Mart's work force alone is more than 1.2 million people (nearly 1 million in the United States). Industrywide and around the globe, a wide range of retailing career opportunities is available, including store management, merchandising, and owning one's own retail business.[3]

From a cost perspective, retailing is a significant field. On average, 30 to 35 cents of every dollar a consumer spends in a traditional U.S. department or specialty store goes to it as compensation for the functions it performs. The corresponding figure is 26 cents for a supermarket. This compensation—known as gross margin—is for rent, taxes, fuel, advertising, management, personnel, and other retail costs, as well as profits. One of the reasons for Wal-Mart's success is that its operating costs are so low (16 percent of sales) compared to other firms. For instance, Sears' (www.sears.com) operating costs are 28 percent of sales and Federated Department Stores' (www.federated-fds.com) are 32 percent.[4]

Although comprehensive retail data are not available on a global basis, these statistics indicate the magnitude of retailing around the world: China has 12 million retail stores; Brazil and Japan each have 1.5 million; South Korea and Spain each have 500,000. France's Carrefour (www.carrefour.com/en) operates 9,000 stores in 27 countries, the Netherlands' Royal Ahold (www.ahold.com) has 8,500 stores in 25 countries, and U.S.-based Wal-Mart has 1,000 stores in a dozen nations outside its home market.[5]

Current retail data may be found at the U.S. Bureau of the Census' "Retail & Wholesale Trade" Web site (www.census.gov/econ/www/retmenu.html).

16-2b Retailing Functions in Distribution

As highlighted in Figure 16-2, retailers generally perform four distinct functions. They

Retailers undertake four key functions.

- Engage in the sorting process by assembling an assortment of goods and services from a variety of suppliers and offering them for sale. Width and depth of assortment depend on the retailer's strategy.

- Provide information to consumers via ads, displays and signs, and sales personnel. And marketing research support (feedback) is given to other channel members.

- Store products, mark prices, place items on the selling floor, and otherwise handle products. Retailers usually pay for items before selling them to final consumers.

- Facilitate and complete transactions by having appropriate locations and hours, credit policies, and other services (like delivery).

---

[2] "2000 Retail Sales," *Monthly Retail Trade Survey* (Washington, D.C.: U.S. Bureau of the Census, April 2001); "Global Power of Retailing 2000," *Stores* (October 2000), Section 2; and *Wal-Mart 2000 Annual Report.*

[3] A discussion of careers in retailing can be found in Barry Berman and Joel R. Evans, *Retail Management: A Strategic Approach*, Eighth Edition (Upper Saddle River, New Jersey: Prentice Hall, 2001), Appendix A.

[4] *2000 Retail Yearbook* (Columbus, Ohio: PricewaterhouseCoopers, 2000).

[5] Data estimated by the authors, based on several sources.

ETHICAL Issues in Marketing

The Good Works of Starbucks

Business for Social Responsibility is a nonprofit association that defines corporate social responsibility "as operating a business in a manner that meets or exceeds the ethical, legal, commercial, and public expectations that society has of business. It goes beyond the standard measures of corporate citizenship—philanthropic activities and community commitment—and includes everything the company does." Among retailers, Starbucks Coffee (www. starbucks.com), Home Depot (www.homedepot.com), and Ben & Jerry's (www. benandjerrys.com) are frequently cited for their good works. Let's look at Starbucks, which has committed itself to providing a great work environment, contributing to the environment and community, and recognizing profitability as essential to its success.

Starbucks has been praised for a policy of providing benefits to both part-time and full-time workers. Part-time employees are eligible to participate in the firm's pension and stock purchase program.

The firm is trying to reduce its environmental impact by such strategies and tactics as composting coffee grounds, using recyclable napkins and cups, and recycling with its burlap bag program. Starbucks also has a program that honors volunteer activity by its employees. With this program, Starbucks matches the hours an associate volunteers with dollars to the same organization.

On the supplier level, Starbucks has several programs to improve the standard of living in the developing countries where its coffee is grown, harvested, and processed. Recently, it announced plans to purchase coffee beans from farmers at above-market prices: The new program "gives us an additional opportunity to have a meaningful impact on the working and living conditions faced by many who grow, harvest, and process coffee throughout the world."

How can a small floral shop store emulate some of Starbucks' good works?

Source: Based on material in Marianne Wilson, "More Than Just Causes," *Chain Store Age* (August 2000), pp. 37–40.

FIGURE 16-2
Key Retailing Functions

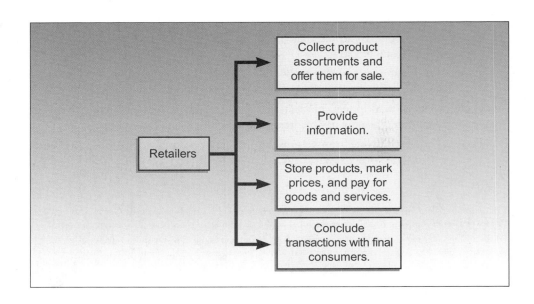

16-2c The Relationship of Retailers and Suppliers

Retailers deal with two broad supplier categories: those selling goods or services for use by the retailers and those selling goods or services that are resold by the retailers. Examples of goods and services purchased by retailers for their use are store fixtures, computer equipment, management consulting, and insurance. Resale purchases depend on the lines sold by the retailer.

Suppliers must have knowledge of their retailers' goals, strategies, and methods of business operation to sell and service accounts effectively. Retailers and their suppliers may have divergent viewpoints, which must be reconciled. Here is an example:

> Whether Wal-Mart's demands cross the line from the obsessive to the crushing is a subject of hot debate among suppliers. But Wal-Mart's purchasing power is so great that none of its trading partners are willing to go on the record saying negative things about it. Still, it is not hard to find firms whose bottom lines have been wounded by the retailer. In the 1990s, Rubbermaid was the leading brand-name maker of common kitchenware and household items like laundry baskets. But when the price for the main component in its products, resin, more than tripled between 1994 and 1996, Wal-Mart balked at paying higher prices. When Rubbermaid insisted, Wal-Mart relegated the firm's items to undesirable shelf space and used its market power to promote a Rubbermaid rival, Sterilite, which made lower-priced nonresin products. Profit margins fell at Rubbermaid, and it has since been bought by another household goods giant, Newell.[6]

16-3 TYPES OF RETAILERS[7]

Retailers can be categorized by ownership, store strategy mix, and nonstore operations. See Figure 16-3. The categories overlap; that is, a firm can be correctly placed in more than one grouping. For example, 7-Eleven is a chain, a franchise, and a convenience store. The study of retailers by group provides data on their traits and orientation, and the impact of environmental factors.

16-3a By Ownership

An *independent retailer* operates only one outlet and offers personal service, a convenient location, and close customer contact. Almost 80 percent of U.S. retail establishments (including those staffed by the owners and their families)—and a higher amount in some foreign nations—are run by independents, including many dry cleaners, beauty salons, furniture stores, gas stations, and neighborhood stores. This large number is due to the ease of entry because various kinds of retailing require low investments and little technical knowledge. So,

*An **independent retailer** has one store, while a **retail chain** has multiple outlets.*

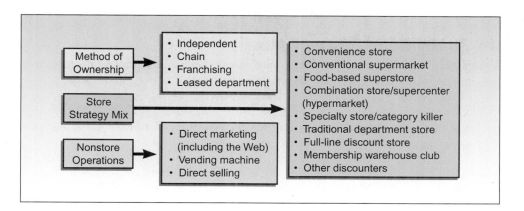

FIGURE 16-3

Categorizing Retailers

---

[6]Leslie Kaufman, "As Biggest Business, Wal-Mart Propels Changes Elsewhere," *New York Times* (October 22, 2000), Business section.

[7]Unless otherwise indicated, the statistics in these subsections are the authors' current projections, based on data from *Annual Retail Trade Survey* (Washington, D.C.: U.S. Bureau of the Census); "State of the Industry," *Chain Store Age* (August 2000), Section Two; *Stores; Progressive Grocer; Discount Store News; Direct Marketing; 2000 Vending Times Census of the Industry;* and *2000 Retail Yearbook.*

competition is plentiful. Numerous firms do not succeed due to the ease of entry, poor management skills, and inadequate resources. The U.S. Small Business Administration says that one-third of new retailers do not last one full year and two-thirds do not make it past three years. Nearly 40 percent of U.S. retail store sales are accounted for by independents.

A *retail chain* involves common ownership of multiple outlets. It usually has central purchasing and decision making. Although independents have simple organizations, chains tend to rely on specialization, standardization, and elaborate control systems. Chains can serve a large, dispersed target market and have a well-known company name. They operate one-fifth of U.S. retail outlets, but account for more than 60 percent of all retail store sales. About 40 U.S. chains have 1,000 or more units; and the largest 100 chains generate one-third of U.S. store sales. Chains are common for department stores, supermarkets, and fast-food outlets, among others. Examples are Home Depot (www.homedepot.com), Kroger (www.kroger.com), and Dillard's (www.dillards.com).

Retail franchising is a contractual arrangement between a franchisor (a manufacturer, wholesaler, or service sponsor) and a retail franchisee, which allows the latter to run a certain form of business under an established name and according to specific rules. It is a form of chain retailing that lets a small businessperson benefit from the experience, buying abilities, and name of a large multiunit retailer. The franchisee often gets training and engages in cooperative buying and advertising. The franchisor benefits from franchise fees and royalties, faster payments, strict operating controls, consistency among outlets, and motivated owner-operators. Franchises annually account for $1 trillion in U.S. retail sales at 600,000 outlets. Two-fifths of U.S. franchisors have stores in foreign markets, a growing number. Franchising is popular for auto dealers, gas stations, fast-food chains, hotels and motels, service firms, and convenience-foods stores. Examples are Chevrolet dealers (www.chevrolet.com/gmnav/dealers/index.htm), Pizza Hut (www.pizzahut.com), and H&R Block (www.hrblock.com).

A *leased department* is a section of a retail store rented to an outside party. The lessee operates a department—under the store's rules—and pays a percentage of sales as rent. Lessors gain from the reduced risk and inventory investment, expertise of lessees, lucrative lease terms, increased store traffic, and appeal to one-stop shopping. Lessees gain from the location in established stores, lessors' name awareness, overall store traffic, the customers attracted to stores, and the services (such as ads) that lessors provide. Leased departments are popular for beauty salons, jewelry, photo studios, shoes and shoe repairs, and cosmetics. In U.S. department stores, they generate $15 billion in annual sales. Meldisco (www.meldisco.com) leases shoe departments in 2,500 stores (mostly Kmarts).

Table 16-1 compares the retail ownership forms.

Retail franchising *uses an established name and operates under certain rules.*

A leased department *is one rented to an outside party.*

16-3b By Store Strategy Mix

Firms can be classed by the store strategy mix they undertake. A typical *retail store strategy mix* consists of an integrated combination of hours, location, assortment, service, advertising, prices, and other factors retailers employ. Store strategy mixes vary widely, as the following indicate.

A *convenience store* is usually a well-situated, food-oriented store with long hours and a limited number of items. In the United States, these stores have annual sales of $100 billion, excluding gasoline, and account for 7 to 8 percent of all grocery sales. Annual per-store sales are a fraction of those at a conventional supermarket. Consumers use a convenience store for fill-in merchandise, often at off-hours. Gasoline, milk, groceries, papers, soda, cigarettes, beer, and fast food are popular. 7-Eleven (www.7-eleven.com), Circle K (www.circlek.com), and Speedway SuperAmerica (www.speedway.com) operate such stores.

A retail store strategy mix *combines the hours, products, etc., offered.*

A convenience store *stresses fill-in items.*

GLOBAL Marketing in Action

Who Owns Dunkin' Donuts Anyway?

Allied Domecq (www.allieddomecqplc.com), a British-based spirits vendor (with such brands as Kahlua, Courvoisier, and Beefeater) has a fast-food franchise division with annual sales that exceed $500 million. The fast-food division consists of Dunkin' Donuts (www.dunkindonuts.com), Baskin-Robbins (www.baskinrobbins.com), and Togo's (www.togos.com), a 325-unit California-based sandwich chain.

Even though Dunkin' Donuts is a 50-year-old chain, it shows strong signs of vitality. In the past three years, it has opened 400 stores and successfully repositioned itself. Coffee now comprises 45 percent of its total sales, and bagels (which were added in 1996) now comprise 8 percent of sales. In 1997, Dunkin' Donuts added a Coffee Coolatta, a coffee-based slush that resembles Starbucks' Frappuccino. This product currently accounts for 6 percent of sales.

Baskin-Robbins is also in the process of repositioning itself through new store exteriors and interiors, the addition of exciting flavors like Kahula Blast, and its first national TV advertising campaign in four years. In the past, Baskin-Robbins charged its franchises high prices for ice cream. Franchisees now purchase ice cream at competitive prices, but pay a 5.9 percent royalty fee on their sales. The new system enables Baskin-Robbins franchisees to price ice cream more competitively; it also provides more money for cooperative advertising. Baskin-Robbins expects to increase same-store sales by 5 percent.

Because Dunkin' Donuts does most of its business at breakfast, Togo's is primarily a lunch business, and Baskin-Robbins is busiest in the evenings, the franchisor is now selling the concept of placing all three brands in one location. For double the normal franchise fee, a franchise operator can greatly expand sales with only a slightly larger retail location and staff.

As a potential franchisee, what are the pros and cons of purchasing a single store with Dunkin' Donuts, Togo's, and Baskin-Robbins in one location?

Source: Based on material in Leigh Gallagher, "Making Dough," *Forbes* (August 21, 2000), p. 82.

A *conventional supermarket* is a departmentalized food store with minimum annual sales of $2 million; it emphasizes a wide range of food and related products—general merchandise sales are limited. It originated 75 years ago, when food retailers realized a large-scale operation would let them combine volume sales, self-service, low prices, impulse buying, and one-stop grocery shopping. The car and refrigerator aided the supermarket's success by lowering travel costs and adding to perishables' life spans. These stores account for 43 percent of total U.S. supermarket sales (which exceed $375 billion) and nearly two-thirds of outlets. Kroger (www.kroger.com), Albertson's (www.albertsons.com), and Safeway (www.safeway.com) are among the large chains with conventional supermarkets.

A *food-based superstore* is a diversified supermarket that sells a broad range of food and nonfood items. The latter account for 20 to 25 percent of sales. This store usually has greeting cards, floral products, VCR tapes, garden supplies, some apparel, wine, film developing, and small appliances—besides a full line of supermarket items. While a conventional U.S. supermarket has 15,000 to 20,000 square feet of space and annual sales of

A **conventional supermarket** *is a large, self-service food store.*

A **food-based superstore** *stocks food and other products for one-stop shoppers.*

TABLE 16-1   Key Characteristics of Retail Ownership Forms

Ownership Form	Distinguishing Features	Characteristics	
		Major Advantages	Major Disadvantages
Independent	Operates one outlet, easy entry	Personal service, convenient location, customer contact	Much competition, poor management skills, limited resources
Retail chain	Common ownership of multiple units	Central purchasing, strong management, specialization of tasks, larger market	Inflexibility, high investment costs, less entrepreneurial
Retail franchising	Contractual arrangement between central management (franchisor) and independent businesspersons (franchisees) to operate a specified form of business	To franchisor: investments from franchisees, faster growth, entrepreneurial spirit of franchisees To franchisee: established name, training, experience of franchisor, cooperative ads	To franchisor: some loss of control, franchisees not employees, harder to maintain uniformity To franchisee: strict rules, limited decision-making ability, payments to store
Leased department	Space in a store leased to an outside operator	To lessor: expertise of lessee, little risk, diversification To lessee: lower investment in store fixtures, customer traffic, store image	To lessor: some loss of control, poor performance reflects on store To lessee: strict rules, limited decision-making ability, payments to store

$8 million, a food-based superstore has 25,000 to 50,000 square feet and $17 million in sales. About 7,500 superstores account for one-third of U.S. supermarket sales. Several factors have caused many conventional supermarkets to switch to superstores: consumer interest in one-stop shopping, the leveling of food sales due to competition from fast-food stores and restaurants, and higher profits on general merchandise. For large chains, the superstore is the preferred format.

A **combination store** unites food/grocery and general merchandise sales in one facility, with general merchandise providing 25 to 40 percent or more of sales. It goes further than a food-based superstore in appealing to one-stop shoppers and occupies 30,000 to 100,000 square feet or more. It lets a retailer operate efficiently, expand the number of people drawn to a store, raise impulse purchases and the size of the average transaction, sell both high-turnover/low-profit food items and lower-turnover/high-profit general merchandise, and offer fair prices. A **supercenter** (known as a **hypermarket** in Europe) is a combination store that integrates an economy supermarket with a discount department store, with at least 40 percent of sales from nonfood items. It is 75,000 to 150,000 square feet in size or larger and carries 50,000 or more items. Among the firms with combination stores are Wal-Mart (www.walmartstores.com), Fred Meyer (www.fredmeyer.com), and France's Carrefour (www.carrefour.com/en). See Figure 16-4.

A **specialty store** concentrates on one product line, such as stereo equipment or hair-care services. Consumers like these stores since they are not faced with racks of unrelated products, do not have to search in several departments, are apt to find informed salespeople, can select from tailored assortments, and may avoid crowding. Specialty stores are quite successful with apparel, appliances, toys, electronics, furniture, personal care products, and personal services. The total annual sales of the 20 largest U.S. specialty store chains are $125 billion annually. They include Circuit City (www.circuitcity.com), Gap (www.gap.com), Radio Shack (www.radioshack.com), and AutoZone (www.autozone.com).

A **combination store** *offers a large assortment of general merchandise, as well as food. One type is a* **supercenter (hypermarket).**

A **specialty store** *emphasizes one kind of product, with a* **category killer** *store being a large version.*

FIGURE 16-4
Carrefour: A Giant in European Hypermarkets
Through its chain of hypermarkets and other formats, France's Carrefour has become the world's second-largest retailer.

Source: Reprinted by permission of PricewaterhouseCoopers.

A *category killer* is an especially large specialty store. It features an enormous selection in its product category and relatively low prices, and consumers are drawn from wide geographic areas. Blockbuster (http://www.blockbuster.com), Sports Authority (www.sportsauthority.com), Sam Goody (www.samgoody.com), and Foot Locker (www.footlocker.com) are among the specialty chains largely based on the category-killer store concept. See Figure 16-5.

A department store employs at least 50 people and usually sells a general line of apparel for the family, household linens and textile products, and some mix of furniture, home furnishings, appliances, and consumer electronics. It is organized into functional areas for buying, promotion, service, and control. There are two types: the traditional department store and the full-line discount store.

A *traditional department store* has a great assortment of goods and services, provides many customer services, is a fashion leader, and often serves as an anchor store in a shopping district or shopping center. Prices are average to above average. It has high name recognition and uses all forms of media in ads. In recent years, traditional department stores have set up more boutiques, theme displays, and designer departments to compete with other firms. They face intense competition from specialty stores and discounters. Annual U.S. sales, including mail order, are $100 billion. Traditional department store chains include Marshall Field's (www.marshallfields.com), Macy's (www.macys.com), and Bloomingdale's (www.bloomingdales.com).

> A **traditional department store** *is a fashion leader with many customer services.*

FIGURE 16-5
Foot Locker: A Dominant Specialty Store Chain

Foot Locker is America's number one store for athletic footwear and apparel, annually accounting for $3 billion in U.S. sales alone. With more than 3,700 stores worldwide (most of which are category killers with their large assortments), Foot Locker is a global chain.

Source: Reprinted by permission of Venator Group.

A full-line discount store has self-service and popular brands.

A *full-line discount store* is a department store with lower prices, a broad product assortment, a lower-rent location, more emphasis on self-service, brand-name merchandise, wide aisles, shopping carts, and more goods displayed on the sales floor. U.S. full-line discounters (including supercenters) annually sell more than $200 billion in goods and services. They are among the largest retailers of apparel, housewares, electronics, health and beauty aids, auto supplies, toys, sporting goods, photographic products, and jewelry. Wal-Mart (www.walmart.com), Kmart (www.bluelight.com), and Target Stores (www.targetstores.com) account for three-quarters of U.S. full-line discount store sales. See Figure 16-6.

A membership warehouse club offers deep discounts to its member customers.

With a *membership warehouse club,* final consumers and businesses pay small yearly dues for the right to shop in a huge, austere warehouse. Products are often displayed in their original boxes, large sizes are stocked, and some product lines vary by time period (since clubs purchase overruns and one-of-a-kind items that cannot always be replaced). Consumers buy items at deep discounts. For a decade, this format, whose annual sales skyrocketed from $2.5 billion in 1985 to $25 billion (excluding sales to business customers) in 2000, was one of the fastest-growing form of U.S. retailing. Lately, growth has slowed due to marketplace saturation and overexpansion. The two leading chains are Sam's Club (www.samsclub.com) and Costco (www.costco.com).

Other forms of low-price retailing have also been growing. Among them are warehouse-style food stores, off-price specialty chains, discount drugstore chains, and factory outlet stores. These retailers hold prices down by carrying mostly fast-selling items, using plain fixtures, locating at inexpensive sites, using few ads, and offering less service. They attract price-sensitive consumers. Examples are Marshalls, an off-price apparel chain (www.marshallsonline.com), and Tanger Outlets (www.tangeroutlet.com), which operates shopping centers featuring manfacturers' outlet stores in 20 states.

Table 16-2 shows the differences between discount store and traditional department store strategies.

16-3c By Nonstore Operations

With *nonstore retailing,* a firm uses a strategy mix that is not store-based to reach consumers and complete transactions. It does not involve conventional store facilities.

Nonstore retailing is nontraditional.

Direct marketing occurs when a consumer is first exposed to a good or service by a nonpersonal medium (such as direct mail, TV, radio, magazine, newspaper, or PC) and then orders by mail, phone, or PC. More than one-half of U.S. households buy this way each year—mostly due to convenience. The popularity of manufacturer brands and the private brands of direct marketers (and consumer confidence in them), the number of working women, and the belief that direct marketing is a good way to shop are fueling its growth: "Direct marketing is unique in that it is a marketing method that lets consumers gather information about goods

In direct marketing, a seller first communicates with consumers via nonpersonal media.

Discount Store Strategy	Department Store Strategy
1. Less expensive rental location—lower level of pedestrian traffic. (Note: Some discount stores are using more expensive locations.)	1. More expensive rental location in shopping center or district—higher level of pedestrian traffic.
2. Simpler fixtures, linoleum floor, central dressing room, fewer interior and window displays.	2. More elaborate fixtures, carpeted floor, individual dressing rooms, many interior and exterior displays.
3. Promotional emphasis on price. Some discounters do not advertise brand names, but say "famous brands."	3. Promotional emphasis on full service, quality brands, and store image.
4. Fewer alterations, limited phone orders, delivery, and gift wrapping; less availability of credit.	4. Many alterations included in prices, phone orders accepted, and home delivery at little or no fee; credit widely available.
5. More reliance on self-service, plain displays with piles of merchandise; most merchandise visible.	5. Extensive sales assistance, attractive merchandise displays, a lot of storage in back room.
6. Emphasis on branded products; selection may not be complete (not all models and colors). Some discounters feature "seconds," remove labels from goods if asked by manufacturers, and stock low-price, little-known items.	6. Emphasis on a full selection of branded and privately branded first-quality products; does not stock closeouts, discontinued lines, or seconds.
7. Year-round use of low prices.	7. Sales limited to end-of-season clearance and special events.

TABLE 16-2

Comparing Retail Strategy Mixes: A Discount Store Versus a Traditional Department Store

and services, make educated buying decisions, and acquire the necessities and pleasures of life when and where we decide to do so—even from our kitchen tables at 3 A.M."[8]

For retailers, direct marketing offers lower operating costs, coverage of a wide geographic area, and new market segments. Direct marketing is used by specialized firms, as well as store-based retailers that apply it to supplement their regular business. Among the most popular direct-marketing items are books, tapes and CDs, clothing, magazines, insurance, home accessories, and sports equipment. Yearly U.S. retail sales are about $200 billion. Spiegel (www.spiegel.com), L.L. Bean (www.llbean.com), J.C. Penney (www.jcpenney.com), and QVC (www.qvc.com) are direct marketers.

Globally, the United States, Europe, and Japan account for more than 90 percent of the world's mail order business. The United States alone is responsible for almost one-half of the total.[9] According to *Stores* magazine, these are the 10 leading Internet retailers, in the order of their annual revenues:

- eBay (www.ebay.com)
- Amazon.com (www.amazon.com)
- Dell (www.dell.com)
- buy.com (www.buy.com)
- Egghead.com (www.egghead.com)
- Gateway (www.gateway.com)
- Quixtar (www.quixtar.com)
- uBid (www.ubid.com)
- Barnes & Noble (www.bn.com)
- Cyberian Outpost (www.outpost.com)[10]

[8]"Consumers: A Helpful Guide," www.the-dma.org/consumers (April 30, 2001).

[9]See Jennifer Derryberry, "Europe Hails Snail Mail," *Sales & Marketing Management* (September 2000), pp. 118, 120.

[10]"Top 100 Internet Retailers," *Stores* (September 2000).

A **vending machine** uses coin- or card-operated machinery to dispense goods (such as beverages) or services (such as life insurance policies at airports). It eliminates the need for salespeople, allows 24-hour sales, and can be placed outside rather than inside a store. Its sales are concentrated on a few products—various beverages and food items yield 85 percent of the U.S. total. Machines may need intensive servicing due to breakdowns, stock-outs, and vandalism. Improved technology lets vending machines make change for bills, "talk" to consumers, use video screens to show products, brew coffee, and so on. Yearly U.S. sales are $37 billion.

Direct selling involves personal contact with consumers in their homes (and other nonstore locations) and phone solicitations initiated by the retailer. Cosmetics, vacuum cleaners, encyclopedias, household services (like carpet cleaning), dairy products, and newspapers are sometimes marketed via direct selling. In a cold canvass, a salesperson calls people or knocks on doors to find customers. With referrals, past buyers recommend friends to the salesperson. In the party method, one consumer acts as host and invites people to a sales demonstration in his or her home (or other nonstore site). To some consumers, direct selling has a poor image. In addition, sales force turnover is high and many people are not home during the day. To increase business, salespeople for firms such as Avon now target working women via office presentations during breaks and lunch hours. Direct selling has yearly U.S. revenues of $25 billion; and the Worldwide Federation of Direct Selling Associations (www.wfdsa.org) estimates global sales at $85 billion.[11] Avon (www.avon.com), Mary Kay (www.marykay.com), Tupperware (www.tupperware.com), and Amway (www.amway.com) are leading direct selling organizations.

16-4   CONSIDERATIONS IN RETAIL PLANNING

There are many factors for retailers to weigh in devising marketing plans—and for manufacturers, service providers, and wholesalers to keep in mind. Five key factors are store location, atmosphere, scrambled merchandising, the wheel of retailing, and technological advances.

16-4a   Store Location

Store location is meaningful because it helps determine the customer mix and competition faced. Once selected, it is also inflexible. The basic forms of store location are the isolated store, the unplanned business district, and the planned shopping center.

An **isolated store** is a freestanding retail outlet located on a highway or street. There are no adjacent stores with which the firm competes, but there are also no stores to help draw shoppers. Customers may hesitate to travel to an isolated store unless it has a good product assortment and an established image. This site may be used by discount stores due to low rent and supplier desires for them to be far enough away from stores selling goods and services at full prices. Some Kmart (www.kmart.com) and 7-Eleven (www.7-eleven.com) stores are isolated.

An **unplanned business district** exists where multiple stores are located close to one another without prior planning as to the number and composition of stores. The four unplanned sites are central business district, secondary business district, neighborhood business district, and string.

A *central business district* (CBD) is the hub of retailing in a city and is often called "downtown." It has the most commercial, employment, cultural, entertainment, and shopping facilities in a city—with at least one major department store and a broad grouping of specialty and convenience stores. CBDs have had some problems with crowding, a lack of parking, older buildings, limited pedestrian traffic when offices close, nonstandardized store hours, crime, and other elements. Yet, in many urban areas, CBD sales remain strong. Among the tactics being used to strengthen CBDs are modernizing store-

[11]"International Statistical Survey: Worldwide Direct Sales Data," www.wfdsa.org/statsurvey.stm (March 16, 2001).

fronts, improving transportation, closing streets to vehicles, developing strong merchant associations, planting trees to make areas more attractive, and integrating the commercial and residential environment.

A *secondary business district (SBD)* is a shopping area bounded by the intersection of two major streets. Cities tend to have several SBDs, each with at least one branch department store, a variety store, and/or some larger specialty stores, as well as several smaller shops. Compared to a CBD, an SBD has less assortment and a smaller trading area (the geographic area from which customers are drawn), and sells more convenience-oriented items.

A *neighborhood business district (NBD)* satisfies the convenience-shopping and service needs of a neighborhood. It has a number of small stores, with the major retailer being a supermarket, a large drugstore, or a variety store. An NBD is located on the major street in a residential area.

A *string* is ordinarily composed of a group of stores with similar or compatible product lines that situate along a street or highway. Because this location is unplanned, various store combinations are possible. Car dealers, antique stores, and clothing stores are retailers often locating in strings.

A **planned shopping center** has centrally owned or managed facilities; it is planned and operated as an entity, ringed by parking, and based on balanced tenancy. With *balanced tenancy*, the number and composition of stores are related to overall shopper needs—stores complement each other in the variety and quality of their offerings. Thus, a center may limit the products a store carries. Planned centers account for 40 percent of total U.S. store sales; unplanned business districts and isolated stores generate the rest. There are regional, community, and neighborhood centers.

A *regional shopping center* sells mostly shopping goods to a geographically dispersed market. It has at least one or two department stores and up to a 100 or more smaller stores. People will drive up to a half hour to reach such a center. As with CBDs, some regional centers (especially those built a while ago) need renovation. Enhancements include adding new retailers, enclosing more malls, erecting new store directories, redesigning storefronts, adding trees and plants, and replacing concrete in parking lots. The largest regional center in the United States is Minnesota's Mall of America (www.mallofamerica.com).

A *community shopping center* has a branch department store and/or a large specialty store as its major retailer, with several smaller stores. It sells both convenience- and shopping-oriented items. A *neighborhood shopping center* sells mostly convenience-oriented goods and services. It has a supermarket and/or drugstore, and a few smaller stores.

As we discussed in Chapter 7, one of the biggest challenges facing retailers is moving to a bricks-and-clicks strategy, whereby firms operate both traditional stores and Web sites. Consider the case of Coldwater Creek (www.coldwatercreek.com):

> A good example of a retailer moving into multichannel formats is Coldwater Creek, the catalog and E-commerce retailer of upscale women's fashion and accessories. The company has recently embarked on an aggressive campaign to open 80 stores: "We went on a search to find a national representative that could identify the best real-estate opportunities for our brand. We chose to outsource our real-estate functions to the Staubach Company because it met our criteria and because we felt the way it motivates its people through incentives would give us a competitive edge. Also, we felt Staubach had the right talent in local markets to handle our needs." Outsourcing real estate "absolutely" let Coldwater Creek open stores faster than if the process had been managed internally.[12]

16-4b Atmosphere

Atmosphere (also known as *atmospherics*) is the sum total of the physical attributes of a retailer, whether in a store or a nonstore format, that are used to develop an image and draw customers. It affects the target market attracted, the customer's shopping mood and time spent with the retailer, impulse purchases, and retailer positioning; and is related to

A **planned shopping center** *is centrally planned and has balanced tenancy.*

Atmosphere (atmospherics) *consists of a retailer's exterior, general interior, layout, and displays.*

[12]"Power Brokers," *Chain Store Age* (November 2000), p. 167.

the strategy chosen.[13] As was shown in Table 16-2, a discount store would have simple fixtures, linoleum floors, and crowded displays. A full-service store would have elaborate fixtures, carpeted floors, and attractive displays.

There are four basic components of a retailer's atmosphere:

- Exterior—elements such as the storefront, the marquee, entrances, display windows, store visibility, store design, the surrounding area, and traffic. For a Web retailer, the exterior is the home page.

- General interior—elements such as flooring, colors, scents, lighting, fixtures, wall textures, temperature, aisle width, vertical transportation, personnel, cash registers, and overall cleanliness. For a Web retailer, the use of colors and descriptive text are quite important, as are the links to product departments.

- Store layout—elements such as the floor space allotted for customers, selling, and storage; product groupings; and department locations. For a Web retailer, this involves the physical layout of each Web page, as well as the way that the customer accesses pages with specific products; and the shopping process must also be clear.

- Interior (point-of-sale) displays—elements such as merchandise cases and racks, mobiles, in-store ads, posters, and mannequins. For a Web retailer, product displays can reflect the choices offered and even rotate items for 360-degree views.

Nordstrom, the upscale fashion department store chain, uses a variety of elements to present the most-pleasing atmosphere possible to shoppers:

> The Chicago Nordstrom features light marble flooring throughout, with carpeting and hardwood flooring accents in selling areas. An open, central escalator area is topped by clerestory windows. A second major entrance to the store is at Grand and Wabash Avenues, where a two-story atrium and escalator lead up to the main floor. As shoppers enter the main floor from the mall entrance, there is a massive women's shoe department to the left, taking almost half of the first floor. That department, plus men's and children's shoe departments, offers customers more than 150,000 pairs of shoes. To the right, past an espresso bar, is the cosmetics area. The new parfumerie is housed in an alcove of the department, set off by pink velvet curtains, with perfumes, bottles, and artisan pieces for the vanity displayed on lighted glass shelving.[14]

Figure 16-7 shows a typical Nordstrom store exterior.

FIGURE 16-7

Nordstrom: A Class Act

As the firm says at its Web site: (http://store.nordstrom.com) "Today, Nordstrom has grown from one downtown Seattle shoe store into a nationwide fashion specialty chain with renowned services, generous size ranges, and a selection of the finest apparel, shoes, and accessories for the entire family. Yet, even as the company accomplishes its 100th anniversary, the Nordstrom philosophy is no different than the one set by John Nordstrom at the turn of the last century: Exceptional service, selection, quality, and value."

Source: Reprinted by permission of PricewaterhouseCoopers.

[13]For a more in-depth discussion of atmosphere, see "Special Issue: Retail Atmospherics," *Journal of Business Research,* Vol. 49 (August 2000).

[14]Nancy Brumback, "Big Store, Big Shoulders; Nordstrom Anchors a Huge New Shopping Complex on Chicago's Biggest Retail Corridor," *Woman's Wear Daily* (October 3, 2000), p. 36S.

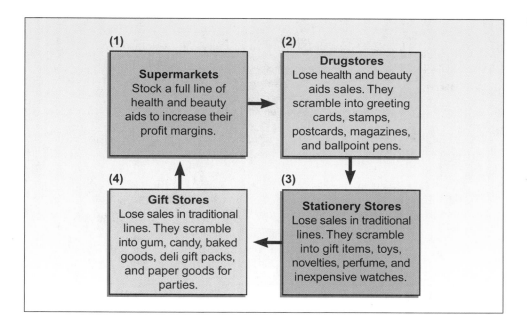

FIGURE 16-8
The Self-Perpetuating Nature of Scrambled Merchandising

16-4c Scrambled Merchandising

Scrambled merchandising occurs if a retailer adds goods and services that are unrelated to each other and the firm's original business. Examples are supermarkets adding video rentals, department stores offering theater ticket services, restaurants carrying newspapers, and car washes stocking postcards.

There are several reasons for the popularity of scrambled merchandising: Retailers seek to convert their stores to one-stop shopping centers. Scrambled merchandise is often fast selling, generates store traffic, and yields high profit margins. Impulse purchasing is increased. Different target markets can be attracted. And the effects of seasonality and competition may be lessened.

On the other hand, scrambled merchandising can spread quickly and cause competition among unrelated firms. For instance, when supermarkets branch into nonfood personal-care items, drugstore sales fall. This forces the drugstores to scramble into stationery and other product lines, which has a subsequent impact on specialty store sales. The situation is illustrated in Figure 16-8.

There are limits to how far a firm should go with scrambled merchandising, especially if adding unrelated items would reduce buying, selling, and service effectiveness. Furthermore, stock turnover might be low for certain product lines should a retailer enter too many diverse product categories. Finally, due to scrambled merchandising, a firm's image may become fuzzy to consumers.

16-4d The Wheel of Retailing

The *wheel of retailing* describes how low-end (discount) strategies can evolve into high-end (full service, high price) strategies and thus provide opportunities for new firms to enter as discounters. According to the wheel, retail innovators often first appear as low-price operators with low profit-margin requirements and low costs. As time passes, the innovators look to increase their sales and customer base. They upgrade product offerings, facilities, and services and turn into more traditional retailers. They may expand the sales force, move to better sites, and usher in delivery, credit, and alterations. The improvements lead to higher costs, which in turn cause higher prices. This creates openings for a new generation of retailers to emerge by appealing to the price-conscious shoppers who are left behind as existing firms move along the wheel. Figure 16-9 shows the wheel in action.

In **scrambled merchandising,** *a retailer adds items to obtain one-stop shopping, higher profit margins, and impulse purchases.*

The **wheel of retailing** *shows how strategies change, leaving opportunities for new firms.*

FIGURE 16-9
The Wheel of Retailing in Action

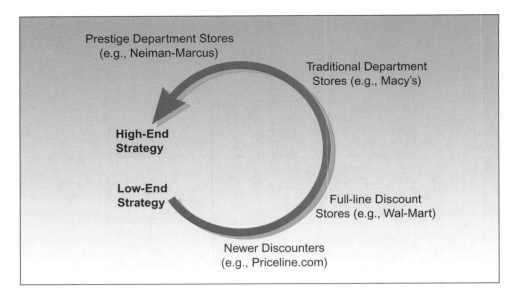

Prestige Department Stores (e.g., Neiman-Marcus)

Traditional Department Stores (e.g., Macy's)

High-End Strategy

Low-End Strategy

Full-line Discount Stores (e.g., Wal-Mart)

Newer Discounters (e.g., Priceline.com)

There are some limitations in applying the wheel-of-retailing theory too literally, these two in particular: many retailers do not follow the pattern suggested and trying to move along the wheel may cause a firm to lose its loyal customers. The best use of the wheel is in understanding that there can be distinct low-end, medium, and high-end strategies pursued by retailers.

16-4e Technological Advances

Technological advances range from computerized-checkout systems to enhanced operating efficiency.

Over the last several years, a number of technological advances related to retailing have emerged. The most dramatic involve checkout systems, video kiosks, atmospherics, computer-aided site selection, electronic banking, and enhanced operating efficiency.

Many retailers use a computerized-checkout (electronic point-of-sale) system, whereby a cashier manually rings up a sale or passes an item over or past an optical scanner; a computerized register instantly records and displays a sale. The customer gets a receipt, and inventory data are stored in the computer's memory bank. Such a system reduces checkout time, employee training, misrings, and the need for price marking on all products. It also generates a current listing of the merchandise in stock without taking a physical inventory, improves inventory control, reduces spoilage, and aids ordering. Some retailers are also experimenting with self-scanning, which enables consumers to bypass cashiers: "Wal-Mart's latest version of the Neighborhood Market has taken the convenience concept to the extreme once again, this time adding self-checkout service. At the newest store in the Dallas suburb of Mesquite, half of the checkouts are self-service, so customers can scan their own groceries and pay by machine with cash, debit, or credit cards. Other amenities, such as a drive-through pharmacy, have become standards in the test format Wal-Mart positions as a convenient neighborhood alternative to its larger supercenters."[15]

Video kiosks let retailers efficiently, conveniently, and promptly present information, receive orders, and process transactions—in a store or nonstore location, such as a university's student center: "Borders (www.borders.com) is among those retailers furthest along the kiosk path. When I entered a Borders in San Diego, I used a kiosk's Title Sleuth site on the store's Intranet. I typed in a title I figured Borders might not carry, but it popped right up on Title Sleuth, along with instructions to walk to the information desk to special-order it. 'There are three million items at Borders, but each store can only carry about 200,000 at a time. With the kiosks, our customers have access to everything.' Still,

[15]Debbie Howell, "Neighborhood Market Redefines Convenience," *DSN Retailing Today* (February 5, 2001), pp. 5, 87.

200,000 is a lot of items, and Borders stores are huge. The Borders kiosk in the Mission Valley store in San Diego provided store maps pinpointing where to find the item entered into the Sleuth search. With its new kiosks, customers will be able to swipe a credit card into a kiosk to pay for special orders or stocked items, then have the gifts shipped anywhere. This not only helps buyers but cuts the store's labor costs."[16]

Modern technology enables retailers to enhance their atmospherics by using electronic point-of-purchase displays with frequently updated scrolling messages, electronic coupons, and video monitors with programming or sales presentations. Sports Authority has ceiling-mounted TVs in some of its stores to encourage shoppers to stay longer: "We've built our own TV network geared to customers who are already in the store, with money in their pockets, in the mood to buy." The company has several goals: "To entertain shoppers, to keep them in the stores, to help them choose products, and to offer vendors an opportunity to showcase products."[17]

The availability of inexpensive computerized site-selection software is so prevalent that retailers of any size and type can now use it. For as little as $500 or less, a retailer can buy geographic information systems software that graphically depicts population characteristics, location attributes, roadways, and so on—for numerous potential or existing store sites. Vendors include Caliper (www.caliper.com), Claritas (www.claritas.com), ESRI (www.esri.com), and Tetrad Computer Applications (www.tetrad.com). They make their software available through downloads from the Internet or by CD-ROM disk.

Electronic banking involves the use of automatic teller machines (ATMs) and the instant processing of purchases. It provides central record keeping and lets customers conduct transactions 24 hours a day, seven days a week at many bank and nonbank locations (such as supermarkets). Deposits, withdrawals, and other banking and retailing functions can be done. There are 260,000 ATMs in U.S. banks, shopping centers, stores, airports, and other sites. Each year, Americans engage in trillions of ATM transactions.[18] To allow customers to make financial transactions over wider geographic areas, many banks have formed ATM networks. There are numerous local and regional networks, as well as national (global) ones.

As electronic banking spreads, more firms will encourage *debit transactions*; when purchases are made, the amount is immediately charged against buyer accounts. There is no delayed billing without an interest charge. A debit-card system differs from credit-card policy, in which consumers are sent bills and then remit payment. Debit cards will receive wide acceptance as a substitute for checks.

> *With debit transactions, payments are immediately deducted from customers' accounts.*

Technological advances are also leading to greater retailer efficiency by

- Increasing the use of self-service operations by firms marketing gasoline, air line tickets, and rental cars, and for hotel registrations and payment.
- Linking manufacturers, warehouses, and transportation firms.
- Producing antishoplifting tags that are attached to merchandise and set off an alarm if not properly removed by employees.
- Automating energy-control systems to monitor store temperature carefully and reduce fuel costs.
- Computerizing order entry in restaurants.

16-5 RECENT TRENDS IN RETAILING

Retailing is in a great state of flux, as firms strive to defend or expand their positions in the fast-changing marketplace. Many consumers no longer want to spend as much time shopping as they once did, various retail sectors have become saturated, a number of large

> *This is a tough period for many retailers, due to consumer life-styles, competition, and other factors.*

[16]Brian Alexander, "The Kiosk, Where Brick Meets Click," *New York Times* (December 13, 2000), p. H18.
[17]"Screen Test," *Chain Store Age* (October 2000), p. 76.
[18]Ivan Schneider, "The New Game in Town," *Bank Systems & Technology* (March 2001), pp. 26–32.

retailers are operating under heavy debt (typically caused by leveraged buyouts or overexpansion), and some retailers—after running frequent sales—have found it difficult to maintain "regular prices." This is where we're at:

> Successful retailers know that the customer is the ultimate judge of the quality of a shopping experience. Everyday, shoppers decide which merchant is doing the best job serving their needs. Consumers enjoy more choice than ever before—in stores, brands, and channels—and have access to an ever-increasing amount of information upon which to base their buying decisions. Capturing the purchasing power of these sophisticated consumers is a hard and constant challenge for retailers.[19]

To succeed in the long run, retailers must respond properly to the trends they face. Among the most prominent are those relating to consumer demographics and life-styles, competitive forces, operating costs, the labor force, and foreign opportunities. Here is how various retailers are dealing with them.

The aging U.S. population, geographic population shifts, and the saturation of many markets have resulted in innovative retailing strategies. For example, besides having a Web catalog, Wardrobe Wagon (www.wardrobewagon.com) uses "traveling clothing stores" to visit publicly funded nursing homes for the elderly in 16 states. Bloomingdale's (www.bloomingdales.com) has stores in Florida, California, Virginia, Illinois, and Minnesota to reduce the emphasis on its Northeast base. Nontraditional locations, which have been underserved, are being used—Baskin-Robbins (www.baskinrobbins.com) has outlets in U.S. Navy exchanges, and Godiva (www.godiva.com) has stores at various airports. See Figure 16-10.

Retailers are adapting to the shopping needs and time constraints of working women and dual-earner households, and the increased consumer interest in quality and customer service. They are stocking such laborsaving products as ready-to-eat foods and pre-loaded PCs; lengthening store hours and opening additional days; expanding catalog and phone sales efforts; re-emphasizing personal selling; pre-wrapping gift items to eliminate waiting lines; setting up comprehensive specialty boutiques to minimize the number of departments a consumer must visit; including special services, such as fashion coordinators; marketing high-quality private brands; and using more attractive displays.

Retailing's intense competition has led to a wide range of company responses. These are two illustrations: Service Merchandise (www.servicemerchandise.com) can no longer compete as a retail catalog showroom (a store category that has disappeared), with consumers shopping from catalogs and virtually all merchandise kept off the selling floor: "Until a recent revamping, the troubled firm was the nation's leading catalog-showroom retailer—a dubious distinction, considering the format peaked in the mid-1980s amid the rise of Wal-Mart and others. It is repositioning itself as a smaller, self-service retailer spe-

FIGURE 16-10
The Boom in Airport Retailing

According to *Airport Retail news*, commercial airports now have an average of 50 retail shops and concession stands (for food and related items).

Source: Reprinted by permission of PricewaterhouseCoopers.

[19]Theresa Williams and Mark J. Larson, "Preface," *Creating the Ideal Shopping Experience: What Consumers Want in the Physical and Virtual Store* (Bloomington, Indiana: Indiana University, 2000), p. 1.

cializing in jewelry and housewares, and exiting consumer electronics, sporting goods, toys, and indoor furniture. After closing about one-third of its locations, the firm has about 220 stores in 31 states. Customers can also place orders by mail, phone, or on the Internet." Pier 1 (www.pier1.com), the home furnishings and accessories chain, is quicker to freshen its product mix. Nearly one-half of its merchandise (imported from 50 nations) is new at any given time: "Our ever-changing collections are presented in a sensory environment that encourages customers to have fun shopping for their homes."[20]

Because of the level of competition in many sectors of retailing, the price sensitivity of a large segment of consumers, and their general interest in improving efficiency (and profit margins), retailers are more concerned with cost control than ever before. For instance, several fast-food companies now use a format whereby different outlets occupy the same building (as food courts have done for years in shopping malls). This format lets common costs, and some employees, be shared. Most small hardware stores belong to buying cooperatives to secure quantity discounts and "buy smarter." Many supermarkets have expanded bulk selling, by which consumers select items such as candy and dried fruit from open displays. A number of mail-order firms are better targeting customers and containing their catalog costs. Furthermore, the use of self-service in retailing has steadily increased.

Some U.S. retailers have trouble attracting and retaining a quality labor force. According to surveys, retailers rank the labor shortage as one of the most crucial issues for them to address. Among the reasons why the shortage exists are that the number of interested young people has declined; full-time career opportunities in other industries have attracted a number of part-time retail workers; many retail workers are inexperienced and have overly high job expectations, leading to employee dissatisfaction and turnover; hours can be long and irregular; some people do not like the pressure of interacting with customers on a regular basis; and the pay in other industries has been relatively higher.

Among the actions of retailers to resolve the labor shortage are recruiting more at high schools and colleges, hiring retired persons, offering child-care for working mothers, raising starting salaries (sometimes to double the minimum wage), rotating employees among tasks to lessen boredom, rewarding good performance with bonuses, and encouraging the best workers to pursue full-time retailing careers.

For retailers with the proper resources and management prowess, there are numerous retailing opportunities in foreign markets. These are a few examples:

Foreign opportunities are plentiful.

- Toys "R" Us (www.tru.com) has stores in 27 countries, accounting for more than one-quarter of total company revenues. It does well in foreign markets because of the wide merchandise selection in its stores, especially compared to local retailers.

- "Direct marketing is in its infancy in Russia. In the future, and based on what has been accomplished so far, we expect to witness a commercial environment intertwined with direct marketing applications. That process is certain to become more important and a more integrated function in the new Russian economy. This is especially true in view of the large distances and great span of the country, requiring the vital communication function that direct marketing can provide."[21]

- U.S.-based Starbucks (www.starbucks.com) opened its first foreign shop in Tokyo in August 1996. It now operates 500 stores in 20 foreign countries: "Coffee is a universal beverage, so we don't have to create an appetite for the basic product. But we do have to get customers to try our coffee." [22]

- McDonald's (www.mcdonalds.com) has built hundreds of restaurants in Central Europe, an underserved area for fast-food outlets. It is also expanding rapidly in Latin America and Asia.

[20]"Service Merchandise Company, Inc.," www.hoovers.com/co/capsule/2/0,2163,11342,00.html (May 3, 2001); and "About Us," www.pier1.com/corporateInfo/mission.asp? (May 3, 2001).

[21]Mark D. Mariska, "Direct Marketing in Russia," *Direct Marketing* (January 1995), p. 41.

[22]"Starbucks Brews the Coffee Experience Worldwide," *Stores* (October 2000), p. G19.

MARKETING *and the Web*

E-tailing and Customer Service

Nearly 8 percent of abandoned online shopping carts (representing billions of dollars in sales) could be salvaged with effective customer service. This is an enormous problem for Web retailing. As a Lands' End senior vice-president says, "If there's a train wreck, it's going to be around customer service."

Poor service is not the only thing that upsets Web shoppers. For example, Toysrus.com (www.toyrus.com) and macys.com (www.macys.com) ran into difficulties when they allowed customers to continue to place orders for items that were clearly out-of-stock. This prompted the Federal Trade Commission to fine these two companies and five other E-tailers a combined $1.5 million.

Research shows that more than 90 percent of satisfied consumers say they'll visit a site again, and 87 percent will recommend it to others. As a result, some retailers are redesigning both their site and their computer systems to avoid problems. Upscale retailer, eLUXURY.com (www.eluxury.com) has invested $2 million on new software that scans its warehouse every seven minutes to update its inventory records. In this way, it can assure customers that a product is in stock.

Other E-tailers have increased the level of customer service support for Web shoppers. Nordstrom (http://store.nordstrom.com) uses a cyber assistant that enables its service representative to literally take control of a customer's browser and lead that person to the optimal product. 1-800-Flowers.com (www.1800flowers.com) increases its service staff during peak periods to direct customers to the best flower arrangement.

Extra customer services are not unique to high-end retailers. Discounter Kmart's BlueLight.com (www.bluelight.com) lets customers return Web purchases directly to the nearest Kmart for full credit.

As a customer service manager for BlueLight.com, develop a customer service policy.

Source: Based on material in Jeanette Brown, "Service, Please," *Business Week* (October 23, 2000), pp. EB48, EB50.

 **WEB SITES YOU CAN USE**

There are trade associations covering almost every aspect of retailing. Most have detailed Web sites. Here is a sampling of them:

Direct Marketing Association (www.the-dma.org)

Direct Selling Association (www.dsa.org)

International Association of Department Stores (www.iads.org)

International Franchise Association (www.franchise.org)

International Mass Retail Association (www.imra.org)

National Association of Convenience Stores (www.cstorecentral.com)

National Automatic Merchandising Association (www.vending.org)

National Retail Federation (www.nrf.com)

SUMMARY

1. *To define retailing and show its importance*   Retailing encompasses the business activities involved with the sale of goods and services to the final consumer for personal, family, or household use. It is the final stage in a distribution channel. Average retail sales are small, yet use of credit is widespread. Final consumers generally visit a store to make a purchase, and they also make many unplanned purchases.

Retailing affects the economy due its total sales and the number of people employed. Retailers provide various functions, including gathering a product assortment, providing information, handling merchandise, and completing transactions. Retailers deal with suppliers that sell products the retailers use in operating their businesses as well as suppliers selling items the retailers will resell.

2. *To discuss the different types of retailers, in terms of ownership, store strategy mix, and nonstore operations*   Retailers may be classified in several ways. Basic ownership formats are independent, a retailer operating only one outlet; chain, a retailer operating two or more outlets; franchise, a contractual arrangement between a franchisor and a franchisee to conduct a certain business; and leased department—a department in a store that is leased to an outside party. The ease of entry into retailing fosters competition and results in many new firms failing.

Different strategy mixes are used by convenience stores, well-situated, food-oriented retailers; conventional supermarkets, departmentalized food stores with minimum annual sales of $2 million; food-based superstores, diversified supermarkets that sell a broad range of food and nonfood items; combination stores (including supercenters/hypermarkets), outlets that go further than food-based superstores in carrying both food and general merchandise; specialty stores (including category killers), outlets that concentrate on one merchandise or service line; traditional department stores, outlets that have a great assortment, provide customer services, are fashion leaders, often dominate surrounding stores, and have average to above-average prices; full-line discount stores, department stores with a low-price, moderate-service orientation; membership warehouse clubs, stores that offer very low prices in austere settings; and other discounters.

Nonstore retailing occurs when a firm uses a strategy mix that is not store-based. Direct marketing occurs when consumers are exposed to goods and services through nonpersonal media and then order via mail, phone, or the PC. It is now a large part of retailing. Vending machines use coin- or card-operated machinery to dispense goods and services. Direct selling involves both personal contact with consumers in their homes (or other places) and phone solicitations initiated by retailers.

3. *To explore five major aspects of retail planning: store location, atmosphere, scrambled merchandising, the wheel of retailing, and technological advances*   A firm may select from three forms of location: an isolated store, a freestanding outlet on a highway or street; an unplanned business district, in which two or more stores locate close to one another without prior planning as to their number and composition; and a planned shopping center, which is centrally managed, as well as planned and operated as an entity. Only planned centers utilize balanced tenancy.

Atmosphere is the sum total of a retailer's physical characteristics that help develop an image and attract customers. It depends on the exterior, general interior, layout, and interior displays.

Scrambled merchandising occurs when a retailer adds products unrelated to its original business. The goals are to encourage customer one-stop shopping, increase sales of high-profit items and impulse purchases, attract different target markets, and balance sales throughout the year.

The wheel of retailing explains low-end and high-end strategies and how they emerge. As low-cost, low-price innovators move along the wheel, they leave opportunities for newer, more cost-conscious firms to enter the market.

Several technological advances have emerged. These include electronic checkout systems, video kiosks, atmospherics, computer-aided site selection, electronic banking, and enhanced operating efficiency.

4. *To examine recent trends in retailing*   The nature of retailing has changed dramatically in recent years. Among the key trends retailers are adapting to are those relating to consumer demographics and life-styles, competitive forces, operating costs, the labor force, and global opportunities.

KEY TERMS

retailing (p. 477)
independent retailer (p. 481)
retail chain (p. 482)
retail franchising (p. 482)
leased department (p. 482)
retail store strategy mix (p. 482)
convenience store (p. 482)
conventional supermarket (p. 483)
food-based superstore (p. 483)

combination store (p. 484)
supercenter (hypermarket) (p. 484)
specialty store (p. 484)
category killer (p. 485)
traditional department store (p. 485)
full-line discount store (p. 486)
membership warehouse club (p. 486)
nonstore retailing (p. 486)
direct marketing (p. 486)

vending machine (p. 488)
direct selling (p. 488)
isolated store (p. 488)
unplanned business district (p. 488)
planned shopping center (p. 489)
atmosphere (atmospherics) (p. 489)
scrambled merchandising (p. 491)
wheel of retailing (p. 491)

REVIEW QUESTIONS

1. Describe the four basic functions performed by retailers.
2. What are the disadvantages of an independent retailer in competing with retail chains?
3. What are the benefits of retail franchising to the franchisee? To the franchisor?
4. Compare the strategies of full-line discount stores and membership warehouse clubs.
5. Distinguish between direct marketing and direct selling. Which has greater sales? Why?

6. What are the pros and cons of scrambled merchandising?
7. Explain the wheel of retailing from the perspective of the battle between traditional department stores and full-line discount stores for market share.
8. Differentiate between credit cards and debit cards. What is the benefit of debit cards to retailers?

DISCUSSION QUESTIONS

1. As a prospective franchisee for a Dunkin' Donuts outlet (www.dunkindonuts.com), what criteria would you use in deciding whether Dunkin' Donuts is right for you? What criteria do you think Dunkin' Donuts should use in assessing potential franchisees? Explain the differences in your answers to these two questions.

2. Develop a discount-store strategy for a jewelry store. How would the strategy differ from that for an upscale jewelry store?
3. Select a planned shopping center near your college or university and evaluate it.
4. How can an online retailer create a good shopping atmosphere for its customers?

WEB EXERCISE

Wal-Mart is by far the world's leading store-based retailer. Visit the firm's Web site (www.walmart.com) and evaluate it. Compare Wal-Mart's Web site with that of one other retailer of your choosing.

PART 5 SHORT CASES

Case 1

Lands' End: Offering Clients a B-to-B Supply Channel Online[c5-1]

Most consumers identify Lands' End (www.landsend.com) with traditionally-styled casual apparel, the firm also has a successful Corporate Sales division that offers customized logo merchandise for employee uniforms. Some analysts even believe that the Corporate Sales division, with revenues of approximately $140 million is its most profitable division. Lands' End's sales in 2000 totaled $1.3 billion.

Lands' End's Corporate Sales customers can choose from three types of online stores: a Corporate Web site for small and mid-sized companies, customized Intranet sites for *Fortune* 1000 companies (called Online Custom Stores), and online procurement for Lands' End's largest customers. Lands' End's first business-to-business site was through its Online Custom Stores configuration. Lands' End has developed 12 Online Custom Stores for firms such as Saturn, BellSouth Wireless Services, and Radio Shack, and plans many more.

Through the Online Custom Stores site, corporate customers can easily upload their corporate logos to Lands' End in minutes. Formerly, this was a very time-consuming process. And with Lands' End's Logo SnapShot feature, these customers can readily see what an item actually looks like in alternate logo and color combinations. According to the general manager of a Saturn dealership, "With the print catalog, you weren't sure what the end product was going to look like because you were looking at other corporations' logos. Now, I'm less likely to return something." The Online Custom Stores site also prevents an employee from ordering merchandise in a font or style that was not approved by his/her firm's corporate office.

During 1998, Lands' End developed an Intranet Web site for Carolina Power & Light (CPL) so that CPL employees could place and then track individual or bulk orders for Lands' End customized apparel customized with the utility's logo. As Lands' End's director of Internet development noted, "The whole reason we built the site was because they requested it. In a lot of cases, customers are saying, 'Give me an online store, or don't do business with me.'"

In January 2000, Lands' End initiated the Corporate Web site for small and mid-sized businesses which lets these firms use several of the features that are available to its largest customers on its specialized Online Custom Stores site. For example, while the Logo SnapShot feature is available on the Corporate Web site, the content is not specifically tailored to each customer. Corporate customers can access this Web site through Land's End's traditional consumer site. To ease ordering, this site contains many of the features of Lands' End's traditional final consumer Web site.

In March 2000, Lands' End initiated an online procurement system in which corporate buyers can purchase Lands' End's custom products through CommerceOne Inc. (www.commerceone.com) and Ariba (www.ariba.com). The firm did this because "Some of our largest customers say they don't want to go to 100 different sites to order from 100 different vendors. [They] are increasingly interested in doing business with online procurement companies and we want to be where our customers are."

Questions

1. Evaluate Lands' End's overall online business-to-business distribution strategy. What other factors should be considered that are not described in this case?
2. Go to the Lands' End Web site (www.landsend.com) and click on "Corporate Sales." Comment on the approach used by Lands' End.
3. From an organizational consumer's perspective, what are the pros and cons of dealing with Lands' End through an online store versus a catalog or telephone sales representative?
4. From Lands' End's perspective, what are the pros and cons of selling customized apparel items to organizational consumers from an online store versus a catalog or telephone sales representative?

[c5-1]The data in the case are drawn from Dana James, "Custom Goods Nice Means for Lands' End," *Marketing News* (August 14, 2000), pp. 5–6.

Case 2

Oh, Deere: A Dealer Channel Under Stress[c5-2]

Many Deere dealers acknowledge that Deere (www.deere.com) makes the best machines a farmer could buy and that Deere is committed to its dealer network. Nonetheless, a significant amount of dissatisfaction and conflict exists among Deere's dealers. In general, farm equipment sales have been weak in recent years due to low prices on agricultural commodities that left farmers with little profits to spend on heavy equipment such as tractors and combines.

One farm equipment dealer whose family has owned its dealership since 1946 sums up the situation this way: "We had a profitable business for a long time, and nobody questioned Deere. But there's no profitability anymore, and there's a lot of dissatisfaction out here." In that dealer's 28-year association with Deere, profit margins have dropped from 20 percent to about 6 percent.

Although there are some signs of a recovery, there is increased concern by many Deere dealers over the farm equipment manufacturer's setting market share goals that the dealers view as unrealistic. What has also angered the dealers is the manufacturer's policy of establishing so many dealerships that they must aggressively compete against one another, as well as Deere's selling used equipment over the Internet and new equipment through mass merchandisers in competition with the dealers.

To meet its corporate sales objectives, Deere wants each of its dealers to have a 10 to 30 percent market share in its area. To meet these goals, dealers frequently sell farm equipment in an adjacent dealers' territories and or agree to cut prices to make sales. While imposing these market share goals, Deere has expanded its number of dealers. According to one observer, a dealer ideally should have a 35-mile radius free from other Deere dealers. But, Deere only provides a 9-mile radius per dealer. Thus, there may be 48 Deere dealers in a state which should have only 9 dealers. In comparison with leading competitor Caterpillar (www.caterpillar.com), which has fewer than 70 dealers on a nationwide basis, Deere has more than 1,600 farm equipment dealers.

The large number of dealers also means that if Deere develops a "hot-selling product," a dealer may not be able to obtain its ordered quantity. For example, Deere recently developed a specialty mower designed for golf courses. Deere's sales target for the wide-area mower was for 1,500 units. When a Detroit-area dealer that markets Deere products to golf courses throughout Michigan ordered 40 such mowers, Deere refused the order. Deere said it wanted to provide sufficient quantities for all of its dealers.

Dealers have also been angry that Deere wants them to service lawn tractors that are sold through such mass merchandisers as Home Depot. One Detroit dealer remarked, "We're fighting a battle against Home Depot, and it looks like we're handing them the guns and ammunition." In retort to this complaint, Deere argues that this repair service will lead to increased sales by its traditional dealers.

Lastly, dealers are concerned about Web-based dealers like DirectAg.com (www.directag.com) that have negotiated with suppliers like Deere to sell a portion of its used farm equipment when it goes off lease.

Questions

1. Comment on the conflicting goals of Deere and its dealers.
2. Is channel conflict between Deere and its dealers inevitable? Explain your answer.
3. How can Deere attempt to resolve this conflict?
4. What would you do as a Deere dealer to increase your power in the channel relative to Deere?

[c5-2]The data in the case are drawn from Brandon Copple, "Plowed Under," *Forbes* (February 21, 2000), p. 59.

Case 3

The Changing Tides of Music Distribution[c5-3]

The year 2000 was a frustrating one for the major record labels as they sought to develop alternative distribution channels to Napster (www.napster.com), and other "free" digital music offerings. As EMI's senior vice-president of new media said, "We have to make buying music easier than stealing music." The Big Five music labels—BMG Entertainment (www.bmg.com), EMI Recorded Music (http://www.emigroup.com/rmusic), Sony Music Entertainment (www.sonymusic.com), Universal Music Group (www.umusic.com), and Warner Music Group (www.wmg.com)—have finally acknowledged that the proper role of the Web is not just selling, but also distribution (downloading music).

Distributing music via the Web presents a number of challenges. Since some consumers have not paid for downloaded music for two years, the major labels recognize that they will have to give away full music tracks as samples. And because music stores account for close to $40 billion in sales of recorded music versus less than $3 billion on the Web, it will be necessary to keep the leading store-based retailers such as Sam Goody (www.samgoody.com) and Virgin Megastores (www.virginmega.com) happy.

Let's look at the new distribution strategies that are under way by the Big Five music labels:

- BMG Entertainment surprised most marketing analysts when it announced that it would drop its lawsuit against Napster if Napster established a membership-based service. As of now, Napster has not been successful in doing so. Some industry experts have been critical of BMG Entertainment's strategy of developing marketing relationships with Yahoo! and Lycos and in investing in ARTISTdirect (www.artistdirect.com) and Riffage.com (which went out of business in December 2000). These experts say this represents too small a level of commitment to alternative distribution channels. BMG has also developed a BMG Visa card with which consumers get discounts on music based on overall credit-card purchases.

- According to some industry observers, EMI Recorded Music lags behind the other major labels in its digital technology. EMI owned just under one-half of Musicmaker.com, a custom CD site that went out of business in early 2001. It has also invested in Liquid Audio (www.liquidaudio.com), which has digitized EMI's music catalog. One novel program has been EMI's contract with Nokia that provides Nokia with the rights to use EMI's music in its custom ring tones. Some analysts feel that this may lead to EMI's being able to sell and transmit entire tracks of music through cellular phones.

- Sony Music Entertainment has what some marketing analysts call "synergy," due to its being a marketer of portable digital players. In addition, Sony recently formed 550 Digital Media Ventures (www.550digitalmediaventures.com) to fund, operate, and acquire digital media companies, thereby giving Sony greater access to a wide range of digital technologies. Sony has also invested in PacketVideo (www.packetvideo.com), which offers real-time video over wireless phone networks.

- Universal Music Group owns the world's largest music collection, including works by Aerosmith, Reba McEntire, and Sting. The French telecommunications company, Vivendi, announced its plans to purchase Seagram, Universal Music Group's parent company, as well as Canal+, a subcription television company. The firm created by this merger would give Universal access to broadband, as well as wireless Internet, capability throughout Europe. In addition, Universal plans to launch a music download subscription service. It owns GetMusic (www.getmusic.com), an online seller of CDs.

- Warner Music Group's strategy is largely based on the merger with AOL. Market analysts see some major opportunities for Warner Music Group to market its music products directly to AOL's base of 24 million subscribers. Time Warner's Road Runner broadband service will also greatly reduce the time required to download musical selections.

Questions

1. Explain how the Internet has blurred the distinction between suppliers and retailers. What are the distribution channel implications of this?
2. Comment on the Internet distribution strategies of the Big Five music companies.
3. How should a major music chain such as Sam Goody or Virgin Megastores respond to the new distribution technologies?
4. What else would you recommend that the Big Five do in music distribution? Why?

[c5-3]The data in the case are drawn from Mike Drummond, "Big Music Fights Back," *Business 2.0* (December 12, 2000), pp. 154–165.

Case 4

Can Home Depot Keep Growing?^{c5-4}

As a retailer Home Depot (www.homedepot.com) is certainly a formidable player. In fiscal 2001, the home improvement chain earned $2.6 billion in profits (up 11 percent from fiscal 2000) and generated revenues of $46 billion (up 19 percent from fiscal 2000). In 2000, Home Depot became the nation's second-largest retailer after Wal-Mart, displacing Sears, Roebuck from its number two position.

Arthur Blank, Home Depot's cofounder and former chief executive, says that the firm takes nothing for granted: "We're in the relationship business, not the transaction business. People can buy this merchandise somewhere else. The challenge is always remembering to walk in the customer's footsteps, not your own." Thus, customers, not managers, are responsible for suggesting 70 percent of Home Depot's items, such as pre-cut Venetian blinds, tool rentals, Christmas trees, and even large appliances.

The customer orientation of the firm means that managers (including senior executives) spend considerable time "cruising the aisles." Bernard Marcus, the firm's other co-founder and its chairman of the board, still goes to stores unannounced and asks a tool salesperson to "Tell me what your best-selling hammer is." According to the firm's executive vice-president for merchandising, "If it isn't obvious from the display, then we're not giving the customer what they want."

Even though Home Depot is good to its customers, it is known to play tough on its suppliers because of its strong bargaining power. When it announced that it would sell General Electric washer-dryers and refrigerators in its stores in 2001, it planned to only stock 60 percent of the appliance line. GE would ship the other 40 percent directly to consumers. Some retail analysts predict that Home Depot will soon become GE's second-largest customer, after Sears. Home Depot also recently sent a letter to all of its suppliers alerting them it may "be hesitant" to conduct business with anyone that sell goods directly to consumers via the Web. Lastly, Home Depot does not like suppliers that ask for a price increase. Some of Home Depot's top suppliers, say they can "count on the fingers" how often they've been given price increases over the past three years.

Home Depot has also used its bargaining power and market clout to change established distribution channel relationships. To get Deere mowers in its stores, for example, it sold them under the Scotts brand (www.deere.com/cce/scotts). Deere dealers are clearly unhappy about this arrangement, but they legally cannot stop it since the Deere name is not on the product. The Scotts brand mower sells for more than $250 less than the comparable Deere brand machine.

Perhaps the most critical question facing Home Depot is how it can maintain its current growth rate. The firm's four-year growth plan calls for Home Depot opening 900 additional stores in the United States and Canada. Although the chain had an existing-store growth rate in the low teens in the early 1990s, over the past few years, the growth rate has slowed to 7 percent per year. Overseas markets also represent a growth opportunity. Home Depot's staff feels there is a potential for 40 to 50 stores in Argentina alone. The chain currently has 4 stores in Chile and 2 in Argentina.

Blank states that Home Depot has only a 9 percent share of the $400 billion North American market (comprised of purchases by do-it-yourselfers, building tradespeople, and property managers). He is also quick to point out that by adding product categories and installation services, the average Home Depot needs only 30,000 consumers to support a store, down from 154,000 people in 1990.

Questions

1. What must Home Depot do to balance its strong bargaining power with a harmonious relationship with suppliers?
2. Is Home Depot a category killer? Explain your answer and its implications.
3. Is Home Depot vulnerable in terms of the wheel of retailing and scrambled merchandising? Explain your answer and its implications.
4. Evaluate Home Depot's growth strategy.

c5-4The data in the case are drawn from Bruce Upbin, "Profit in a Big Orange," *Forbes* (January 24, 2000), pp. 122–127.

PART 5 COMPREHENSIVE CASE

Communicating for Better Channel Relationships[pc-5]

Introduction

In today's volatile business environment, coordinating efforts between manufacturers and dealers continues to be potentially troublesome, yet rewarding. Channel relationships are difficult to manage, given the very different goals and objectives of dealers and manufacturers. In addition, with the advent of the Internet and data-base marketing, changes in the go-to-market landscape mean manufacturers and dealers (not to mention customers) have more choices. Finally, consolidation in many industries means that larger firms—both manufacturers and dealers—are able to exert more control over relationships with partners, and smaller players are left struggling to have a voice in the market.

In light of these monumental changes, several critical issues arise: How can channel relationships be managed to emphasize shared interests and common goals? How can manufacturers increase the likelihood that dealers comply with their programs and policies? Under what conditions will dealers feel satisfied with and committed to the manufacturer?

Enhancement Strategies

One strategy manufacturers can use to adjust to the changing market landscape and coordinate dealer behavior is to integrate by outright ownership of downstream intermediaries or through franchising. This strategy is fairly common among manufacturers of consumer goods such as clothing (Gap Inc., www.gapinc.com, for example) or foods and beverages (McDonalds' Corp., www.mcdonalds.com, for example). Coca-Cola (www.coca-cola.com) also relies on control through ownership, having acquired many of the independent bottlers and distributors that were the critical link to creating value.

A second strategy available to a manufacturer is to leverage its market power to affect dealer behavior. Procter and Gamble's (P&G) relationships with its retailers are a prime example of power. Because of its market power (based on brand equity, among other things), P&G (www.pg.com) does not pay slotting allowances, a rare exception in consumer products. It drastically has changed the manner in which trade promotions are allocated. Power affords it a high degree of control in relationships with channel intermediaries. Similarly, Anheuser-Busch (www.anheuser-busch.com) is using a variety of incentives to get distributors to focus more exclusively on its products. Under its somewhat controversial "100 percent share of mind" program, Anheuser-Busch rates distributors according to how much they concentrate on pushing its products. It then ties these ratings to discounts, marketing assistance, and favorable credits with the goal of pushing wholesalers to carry Anheuser-Busch products exclusively. Miller Brewing (www.millerbrewing.com) has recently introduced its Fair Share Standards which require wholesalers to spend a specific share of their time and money marketing Miller brands. By using leverage with channel members, both Anheuser-Busch and Miller are seeking improved market positions by limiting other competitors' access to the market through their distribution systems.

The use of integration and power-based channel strategies are also evident in the revolution that is taking place around the distribution of automobiles. In fact, auto retailing has changed more in the last three years than the last half century. A combination of changing consumer attitudes toward shopping, the rapid emergence of public dealer groups such as AutoNation (http://corp.autonation.com), and the explosion of Internet services for car shopping are changing how consumers buy and sell cars. Faced with new players offering nicer stores and less hassle, auto makers are scrambling to keep their dealer base from becoming obsolete.

The automotive retailing revolution gives manufacturers a unique opportunity to change the way they do business with their dealers and customers. In the most radical step taken by an American auto maker, General Motors Corp. (www.gm.com) is launching its own superstore car dealerships. In 1997, it initiated an integration strategy by buying all 12 GM dealers in Southern California's San Fernando Valley. GM plans to consolidate these dealerships by bulldozing most of the existing stores and replacing them with a handful of megastores. The idea is to pare costly overhead and inventories, while offering consumers a wider selection and better service. GM plans to pick one dealer-partner who would invest in and run all the dealerships as a single retailing group. In a less sweeping experiment, Ford (www.ford.com) recently outlined its plan to purchase the eight existing Ford, Lincoln-Mercury, and Jaguar dealerships in Tulsa, Oklahoma, and combine them into four new dealerships jointly owned by Ford and the dealers.

Many auto manufacturers have plans to consolidate and upgrade their U.S. dealership systems. Manufacturers' attempts to manage their dealers have long been stymied by state franchise laws that limit their ability to end a franchise or make changes without the consent of all the dealers. To win over reluctant dealers, GM dangles cash in the form of either a buyout or loans and stipends to rebuild in a new locale. Ford's Lincoln-Mercury (www.lincolnvehicles.com and www.mercuryvehicles.com) is allocating its hot Navigator sports utility vehicle only to those dealers that follow its recommended training and stocking requirements. Mercedes Benz (www.mercedes.com) is offering the new M-class Mercedes to dealers that conform to the new exclusive showroom requirements. Ford's recently acquired Volvo (www.volvocars.com) withheld the new S80 model from dealers unless they furnished their dealerships with Volvo-approved Scandinavian furniture. Offering cash or allocating hot products is a form of reward power. The auto makers are using reward power to achieve substantial influence over dealers' decisions.

[pc-5]Adapted by the authors from Jakki J. Mohr, Robert J. Fisher, and John R. Nevin. "Communicating for Better Channel Relationships," *Marketing Management* (Summer 1999), pp. 38–45. Reprinted by permission of the American Marketing Association.

Collaborative Communication

But, what about the many manufacturers that can't afford outright ownership or franchising? What about those that don't have the power to dictate dealer activities? When levels of integration and control are low, dealers are free to act with a high degree of autonomy. Because each party is free to make its own decisions with little or no constraint, low levels of integration and control may be associated with freewheeling decisions, which may or may not be synergistic and mutually reinforcing. For example, some distributors or retail dealers may sell a manufacturer's products to unauthorized retailers or gray markets in order to increase their sales and profits. Paul Mitchell (www.paulmitchell.com) hair care products are marketed under a salon-only customer restriction policy. Recently, however, Paul Mitchell products have been gray marketed and are showing up on the shelves of some mass retailers at discounted prices. This situation can create tremendous conflict for the manufacturer. Not only can it harm the reputation of the manufacturer's products, it also can cause consumers to believe that their hair care dealers and salons are charging excessive prices for products. In situations such as these, manufacturers may lack sufficient market clout to influence the decisions of channel intermediaries, and outright ownership of the channel would not be feasible. What tools can manufacturers use to manage channel relationships when integration or power is lacking?

We conducted a study, examining the possibility of using communication to manage channel relationships in order to enhance outcomes. See Table 1. In particular, we wondered whether collaborative communication, defined here as intensive communication designed to signal collaborative intents to dealers, would help manufacturers enhance channel outcomes. Collaborative communication includes four important components:

- Higher frequency of interaction across all possible types of communication (including face-to-face interaction, telephone calls, E-mail, and so forth).
- More two-way communication, an ongoing dialogue shared between manufacturer and dealer.
- Reliance on set policies and procedures regarding communication (what we called communication formality).
- The use of influence tactics that emphasize common goals, such as discussions to improve dealer operations, simple requests, and recommendations based on improving dealer profitability, rather than more explicit forms of influence.

Reliance on these four communication components allows a manufacturer to communicate collaboratively with its dealers.

Importantly, no single component alone can capture the collaborative essence of communication. Say a dealer filed a lawsuit against a manufacturer. The communication characterizing such a lawsuit would be both formal and frequent; however, it likely would be lacking a two-way dialogue and noncoercive nature. The point is that collaborative communication is comprised of at least the four components mentioned here; the presence of even two of the four components may not alone signal collaborative intents.

In the study, we examined the effect of collaborative communication on different channel outcomes, including channel member commitment to and satisfaction with the manufacturer and degree of coordination of dealer activities with the manufacturer's programs, under various levels of integration and control. We chose these outcomes because dealer satisfaction and commitment are vital to the success of a particular manufacturer's brand. In addition, improved coordination between manufacturer and dealer can deliver benefits to all members of the channel and is a precursor to improved financial outcomes. It is possible for manufacturers to "buy" their retailers' support, but without the corresponding favorable attitudes, such support may be given begrudgingly rather than willingly. In today's business environment, where dealers have choices about which products they carry and how much support they get, measures that tap into the dealer's sense of a partnering relationship with the manufacturer (satisfaction, commitment, and coordination) are vitally important.

Tools to Enhance Outcomes

Table 2 shows that both collaborative communication and manufacturer control have positive effects on the dealer's commitment, satisfaction, and perceived coordination with the manufacturer. In addition, moving from independent relationships to franchise relationships is positively associated with dealer satisfaction, while moving from independent to outright ownership has a positive impact on satisfaction and coordination. Thus, all of these tools—collaborative communication, manufacturer control, and integration—can play a role in enhancing channel outcomes.

Clearly, manufacturers improve channel member perceptions when they proactively manage their communications with dealers. Our research suggests that they should interact frequently using a variety of communication methods. In addition, manufacturers should structure communication so that it occurs regularly in a fairly planned manner. This is not to say that informal communication is not desirable—it only means that for industries where change is rapid and products are complex, some type of formal communication is important.

TABLE 1   Study on Channel Relationships

About the Study

The personal computer industry was used as the setting for the study because it uses a wide variety of channels to distribute personal computers and related products, including independent channels, franchise channels, and company- or manufacturer-owned channels.

Respondents initially were contacted by telephone (prior to the mailing of a questionnaire). During the pre-screening, the owner or manager was asked to participate in the mail survey and one randomly identified manufacturer was chosen to serve as the referent for that dealer's responses. A total of 557 surveys were mailed and 140 surveys were returned for a response rate of 25 percent. Fifteen surveys were eliminated from analysis due to incomplete or inconsistent responses. Thus, the final sample size was 125. The mean number of employees was 22.3; the mean monthly sales volume was $970,000.

The variables in the study were assessed for adequate reliability and validity prior to data analysis. Results are presented in Tables 2 and 3.

Variables in the Study

Integration. Three types of manufacturer/retailer relationships were used:

- <u>Conventional/independent relationships.</u> Parties in conventional or independent channel relationships. In this study, 70 dealers fell into this category.
- <u>Franchise relationships.</u> Parties under franchise contracts relying on contractual agreements. Franchisees make royalty payments to the franchisor in exchange for business assistance (advertising, national image and reputation, training, and so forth). In this study, 31 dealers were in this category.
- <u>Ownership.</u> Either individual store outlets owned by a channel intermediary (in the case of some ComputerLand stores that are company-owned and operated) or by computer manufacturers (in the case of Radio Shack). In this study, 18 dealers were owned by a channel intermediary, while 5 were owned by a computer manufacturer.

Control. The dealer's perceptions of the degree to which the manufacturer controlled aspects of the dealer's decisions and operations. If a manufacturer exerts control successfully over a dealer, the dealer has less opportunity to implement its own policies and procedures.

Collaborative communication. The extent to which communication is frequent, formal, noncoercive, and initiated by both the manufacturer and retailer.

Satisfaction. The dealer's evaluation of various characteristics of the relationship, including interactions with the manufacturer's sales force, cooperative advertising, promotional support, and off-invoice promotional allowances.

Commitment. The dealer's desire to maintain a relationship with the specific manufacturer.

Coordination. The extent to which the dealer perceives that its activities are smoothly synchronized with the manufacturer's for effective planning and implementation.

TABLE 2   Effects on Commitment, Satisfaction, and Coordination[a]

| Variables | Outcomes | | |
	Commitment	Satisfaction	Coordination
Collaborative communication	Positive	Positive	Positive
Manufacturer control	Positive	Positive	Positive
Franchise structure	No effect	Positive [b]	No effect
Company-owned structure	No effect	Positive [c]	Positive

[a]We controlled for the effects of relationship length, dealer size, and conflict in all of our analyses.
[b]Read as: Franchise retailers were more satisfied than independent retailers.
[c]Read as: Company-owned retailers were more satisfied than independent retailers.

Manufacturers should seek a dialogue with the dealers, not only concerning dealer operations and strategies, but also with respect to feedback on the manufacturer's operations and strategies. This give-and-take means open-mindedness and a nondefensive attitude. Good listening is essential for both parties. Collaborative communication has a great effect arising from enhanced information sharing, in which strategies and operations are modified and improved, as well as a symbolic impact. Collaborative communication signals the importance of the relationship and the respect that parties have for each other.

Table 2 also shows that manufacturer control has a positive impact on commitment, satisfaction, and coordination. Manufacturers can use power in a nurturing fashion to help dealers improve their business performance. Rather than viewing manufacturer control as an infringement on their autonomy, given the nature of our study's context (in which products were complex and subject to rapid changes), dealers likely relied on manufacturers for information regarding product capabilities, performance, limitations, and so forth. Therefore, to the extent that power is not used in an exploitative fashion, manufacturers can see a positive relationship between their use of power and dealer satisfaction and commitment.

As the level of integration rose from independent to franchise, dealers reported more satisfaction. Further, as integration changed from independent to company-owned, dealers reported higher satisfaction and coordination. The change from independent to either level of integration did not affect commitment.

Unlike integration and control, collaborative communication can be flexible, relatively inexpensive (compared to the fixed costs of integration), and implemented on short notice. Its versatility makes it an attractive way to gain dealer cooperation. At the same time, collaborative communication can be costly and may not be appropriate across all trading relationships. A critical issue is whether the gains from collaborative communication are greater under high or low levels of integration and control. Should manufacturers with the ability and desire to rely on integration and control also use collaborative communication to cement channel relationships and gain compliance from dealers? Can manufacturers that are not able to rely on integration and control use collaborative communication in a similar fashion?

To answer these questions, interactions between collaborative communication and the various levels of integration and between collaborative communication and manufacturer control must be examined.

When It Works Best

Our study found that the positive effects of collaborative communication on outcomes are stronger when:

- Ownership and franchising are not used (i.e., the relationship between the manufacturer and dealer is between two completely independent parties or exhibits low integration).
- When the manufacturer lacks power over the dealer (low control).

More specifically, as indicated in Table 3, the positive effect of collaborative communication on commitment, satisfaction, and coordination is very strong when manufacturer control is low. The positive effect of collaborative communication on two of the three outcomes—satisfaction and coordination—is strong when channel members are independent from (not integrated in some fashion with) manufacturers.

TABLE 3   Is the Effect Stronger Under Different Levels of Integration and Control?

Level of Integration and Control	Effect of Collaborative Communication on		
	Commitment	Satisfaction	Coordination
Low integration (dealer integration)	No effect	Strong effect [a]	Strong effect
High integration (dealer dependence)	No effect	Weak effect	Weak effect
Low manufacturer control	Strong effect	Strong effect	Strong effect
High manufacturer control	Weak effect	Weak effect	Weak effect

[a]Read as: The effect of collaborative communication on satisfaction is strong under low integration.

By fostering shared values, mutual support, and aligning interests, collaborative communication may make the independent, autonomous dealer feel like more of a partner with the manufacturer. Collaborative communication may be used to solicit dealers' views on channel matters, incorporating their concerns and suggestions into decisions. Such involvement may give the dealer added incentive to work on behalf of the manufacturer's product. By creating a situation in which dealers find themselves feeling valued and appreciated, they may become more satisfied and committed to that manufacturer.

When dealers have more decision autonomy (low integration or low control), collaborative communication has the potential to have a great effect on outcomes. This collaborative approach assists the manufacturer, in a fairly unobtrusive manner, in bringing the dealers "on board" and helping them work in concert with the manufacturer. Such collaborative communication may be both unexpected and welcomed by dealers in relationships with low-control manufacturers; and, because dealers have not yielded to manufacturers due to integration or control, the effect of collaborative communication under low integration or low control strongly enhances commitment, satisfaction, and coordination.

While collaborative communication does have a positive effect when integration and control are high, the effect is not nearly as strong as when integration and control are low. When manufacturer control is high and more integrated relationships exist, dealers relinquish a degree of autonomy and surrender decision making to another party in the channel, adopting the decisions, policies, and procedures of the other firm. Dealers yield to manufacturers' wishes, acceding to demands and requests. Collaborative communication may be used then to maintain a positive relationship and make dealers feel like an integral part of a team. Since dealer latitude in decision making is already restricted, collaborative communication has less opportunity to affect dealer outcomes than in low-integration/low-control situations.

How to Manage Relationships

To what extent should manufacturers and dealers rely on collaborative communication? Our findings suggest that it has strong positive effects. Yet, it is also important to acknowledge that dealers that are satisfied, committed, and coordinated with manufacturers are likely to engage in more collaborative communication. It becomes a chicken-and-egg question: Which comes first, collaborative communication or positive outcomes? Collaborative communication may be just one step between more cooperative trading arrangements and improved channel outcomes. In some contexts,

collaborative communication may not be worth the costs and efforts, and attempts to bring dealers on board may be unprofitable. While collaborative communication may not be a panacea for all channel woes, it is clearly an important tool.

Highly collaborative trading arrangements and partnering behaviors have the potential to enhance channel outcomes. Trading arrangements with cooperative attitudes and processes to guide and administer channel relationships can create an atmosphere of mutual support and respect; such arrangements also may be characterized by collaborative communication and, consequently, may display enhanced channel outcomes. Collaborative communication can create voluntary compliance between partners.

These findings can be useful to manufacturers who lack the ability or desire to use ownership, franchising, or power to manage dealer relationships. Collaborative communication, with its frequent, two-way, formalized, and cooperative interactions, can deliver positive benefits in channel relationships. Rather than relying on power and ownership, it lets independent, autonomous dealers participate in the relationship in a valued manner, which aids in securing their satisfaction, commitment, and coordination. In light of the challenges in today's markets, collaborative communication appears to be a useful option for manufacturers and dealers in their channel strategies. We believe the findings apply to other industries with consolidation at the manufacturer and retail levels, fairly high uncertainty regarding products and markets (requiring frequent and formal communications), and a variety of channels to distribute products.

Questions

1. What are the implications of the material in this case from the perspective of the value chain and the value delivery chain?
2. Evaluate the enhancement strategies available to manufacturers.
3. What logistics decisions must General Motors make if it sells cars over the Internet?
4. Comment on the methodology of the study described in Table 1. How would you improve it?
5. Discuss the findings presented in Tables 2 and 3.
6. Are there any disadvantages with collaborative communication? Explain your answer.
7. What could a wholesaler learn from this case?
8. What could a retailer learn from this case?

Promotion Planning

Part 6 covers the third major element of the marketing mix, promotion.

17 Integrated Marketing Communications

Here, we broadly discuss promotion planning, which involves all communication used to inform, persuade, and/or remind people about an organization's or individual's goods, services, image, ideas, community involvement, or impact on society. We describe the basic types of promotion and the stages in a channel of communication. Next, we present the steps in developing an overall promotion plan. We conclude the chapter with global promotion considerations, and the legal environment and criticisms of promotion.

18 Advertising and Public Relations

In this chapter, we examine two of the four types of promotion: advertising and public relations. We define advertising as paid, nonpersonal communication by an identified sponsor, and public relations as any form of image-directed communication by an identified sponsor or the independent media. We detail the scope of advertising and public relations and their attributes, and describe the role of publicity. We discuss the development of advertising and public relations plans in depth.

19 Personal Selling and Sales Promotion

Here, we focus on the two other key elements of a promotion mix: personal selling and sales promotion. We define personal selling as oral communication with one or more prospective buyers by paid representatives for the purpose of making sales, and sales promotion as the paid marketing communication activities (other than advertising, publicity, or personal selling) that stimulate consumer purchases and dealer effectiveness. We describe the scope, characteristics, and stages in planning for both personal selling and sales promotion.

After reading Part 6, you should understand element 12 of the strategic marketing plan outlined in Table 3-2 (pages 72–75).

17

Integrated Marketing Communications

Chapter Objectives

1 To define promotion planning, show its importance, and demonstrate the value of integrated marketing communications

2 To describe the general characteristics of advertising, public relations, personal selling, and sales promotion

3 To explain the channel of communication and how it functions

4 To examine the components of a promotion plan

5 To discuss global promotion considerations, and the legal environment and criticisms and defenses of promotion

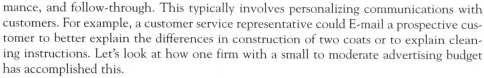

A firm that wants to build and sustain customer loyalty online needs to create a fantastic customer experience. In their book *Brand Leadership*, David Aaker and Erich Joachimsthaler describe the core elements of Virgin's brand (www.virgin.com). They are its essence (iconoclasm), its core identity (service quality, innovation, fun and entertainment, and value for the money), its extended identity (underdog personality), and its relationship with customers (fun companions).

One way of developing and reinforcing a branded customer experience is by focusing on the personal touch, performance, and follow-through. This typically involves personalizing communications with customers. For example, a customer service representative could E-mail a prospective customer to better explain the differences in construction of two coats or to explain cleaning instructions. Let's look at how one firm with a small to moderate advertising budget has accomplished this.

Ireland's Kennys Bookshop & Art Galleries (www.kennys.ie) is well-known for its knowledge of Irish history, culture, and art. To increase its sales abroad, the company started a book club that sends members three to four books based on their interests every three months or so. Kenny found that if the firm calls prospects after they have registered on the Web site, 85 percent of them can be converted into members of a book club. Although the overseas calls can be costly, Kennys has determined that the profits on the first shipment cover the costs of the long-distance phone calls.

Other experts sum it up thusly: "Even if you're on a tight budget, don't neglect the basics. Focus on performance and follow through. And, if your branded customer experience includes the personal touch, make sure you're offering truly personalized service from your Web site. Don't worry about expensive personalization engines; put a caring person on the phone, or have them actually compose E-mails, or engage in online chats with confused customers. Then, leverage that good service with a referral-generating engine. And watch your profits roll in!"[1]

In this chapter, we will study many dimensions of promotion planning, including integrated marketing communications, enhancing a customer's shopping experience, and the use of personal and nonpersonal media.

17-1 OVERVIEW

Promotion is any communication used to inform, persuade, and/or remind people about an organization's or individual's goods, services, image, ideas, community involvement, or impact on society. *Promotion planning* is systematic decision making relating to all aspects of an organization's or individual's communications efforts.

> **Promotion planning** *focuses on a total* **promotion** *effort—informing, persuading, and reminding.*

[1]Patricia B. Seybold, "High-Touch, Low-Budget Marketing," *Business 2.0* (July 11, 2000), pp. 96, 98.

Communication occurs through brand names, packaging, company marquees and displays, personal selling, customer service, trade shows, sweepstakes, and messages in mass media (such as newspapers, television, radio, direct mail, billboards, magazines, and transit). It can be company sponsored or controlled by independent media. Messages may emphasize information, persuasion, fear, sociability, product performance, humor, and/or comparisons with competitors.

In this chapter, the context of integrated promotion planning is provided. Included are discussions on promotion's importance, integrated marketing communications, promotion types, the channel of communication, promotion planning, global considerations, the legal environment, and general criticisms and defenses of promotion. Chapter 18 covers advertising and public relations. Chapter 19 deals with personal selling and sales promotion.

17-2 THE IMPORTANCE OF PROMOTION

Promotion is a key element of the marketing mix. For new products, people must be informed about items and their features before they can develop favorable attitudes toward them. For products with some consumer awareness, the focus is on persuasion: converting knowledge to liking. For very popular products, the focus is on reminding: reinforcing existing consumer beliefs.

The people and organizations at whom a firm's promotional efforts are aimed may fall into various categories: consumers, stockholders, consumer advocates, government, channel members, employees, competitors, and the public. Communication often goes on between a firm and each group, not just with consumers. Communication with each may differ because each has distinct goals, knowledge, and needs.

Word-of-mouth communication *occurs as people state opinions to others.*

Within an audience category (such as consumers), a firm needs to identify and appeal to opinion leaders—those who influence others' decisions. It also should understand ***word-of-mouth communication,*** the process by which people express opinions and product-related experiences to one another. Unless there is sustained, positive word-of-mouth communication, it is hard to succeed. With such communication, a firm's popularity can readily grow:

> There are hundreds of occasions when people ask others—friends, relatives, business associates—for a recommendation for a doctor, a plumber, a hotel, a restaurant, or a movie. If we trust the person making the recommendation, we often act upon the referral. And some lucky business gets one more customer without having to spend a nickel on advertising or promotion. Word of mouth is the only method of promotion that is of the consumer, by the consumer, and for the consumer. Every business owner dreams of having loyal, satisfied customers who brag about his or her business to others. Not only are they repeat purchasers, but they become walking billboards for the company. Best of all, it's one of the lowest-cost forms of promotion there is. Keeping in touch with satisfied customers and encouraging them to talk up your business costs relatively little.[2]

These three Web sites offer advice on how to stimulate positive word-of-mouth communication among consumers: "How to Harness Word of Mouth" (www.mnav.com/womtitlepage.htm), "How to Promote Your Business by Word of Mouth" (www.smalltownmarketing.com/promoteword.html), and "Essentials of Word of Mouth Marketing" (http://allaboutnewsletters.com/onsite/busnarcs/03womktg.htm).

A company's promotion plan usually stresses individual goods and services, with the intent of moving people from awareness to purchase. Yet, the firm may also convey its overall image (industry innovator), views on ideas (nuclear energy), community service (funding a new hospital), or impact on society (the size of its work force).

A good promotion plan complements the product, distribution, and price aspects of marketing, and it is properly designed. For example, Allen Edmonds (www.allenedmonds.com)—a maker of quality shoes—distributes products at finer stores and sets

[2]Robert Grede, "Word of Mouth," www.tsbj.com/editorial/03051501.htm (May 1, 2001).

premium prices. It advertises in such magazines as GQ and *Fortune*, and expects retailers to do first-rate personal selling. Ads are in color and refer to product features, not prices.

Good promotion plans are feasible even if companies have limited resources. For instance:

> Chase Rosade, the owner of Rosade Bonsai Studio, in New Hope, Pennsylvania, has been in business for nearly 30 years, in a market that can only be described as niche. Bonsai trees are those dwarfed, ornamentally shaped trees and shrubs that are grown in small shallow pots or trays. Their branches are cut, and then wrapped in wire to train them to grow in a particular way. One wrinkle in Rosade's marketing strategy—people have to come to his studio to buy them. Which is a problem for two reasons: The studio is on an unmarked road outside of New Hope. And it is open only three days a week. Yet, he draws hundreds of people to his studio each year by holding up a powerful magnet: Rosade offers a series of classes and workshops. When people come to his classes, they buy supplies. When people buy supplies, they sign up for a class. It's an essential synergy. "We wouldn't survive, one without the other," he says. Rosade put it all in motion by giving free lectures at his local school district, "And some one said 'hey can you teach a class'?" He thought it would be fun, so he gave it a shot. "And it just mushroomed." Today, he gives nine classes and workshops each month, and limits enrollment to eight students. He gets the word out by advertising in bonsai publications and at his Web site (www.rosadebonsai.com). The best tool to let people know about his studio and classes is the Philadelphia Flower show, the world's largest indoor flower show (www.philaflowershow.com).[3]

Promotion's importance is also evident from the expenditures and jobs in this area. The world's 10 largest advertising agencies have overall annual billings of $115 billion and gross incomes approaching $15 billion. The International Advertising Association (www.iaaglobal.org) has 5,000 members from 90 nations. In the United States alone, each year, auto makers spend $15 billion and retailers spend $14 billion; 16 million people work in sales; 250 billion coupons are given out; and there are several thousand trade shows.[4]

17-3 AN INTEGRATED APPROACH TO PROMOTION PLANNING

When a well-coordinated promotion plan is developed and applied, a firm uses ***integrated marketing communications (IMC).*** As defined by the American Association of Advertising Agencies (www.aaaa.org), IMC "recognizes the value of a comprehensive plan that evaluates the strategic roles of a variety of communication disciplines—advertising, public relations, personal selling, and sales promotion—and combines them to provide clarity, consistency, and maximum communication impact."[5] For example, Frito-Lay (www.frito.com) has a sales force that visits every store stocking its products, advertises in newspapers and magazines and on TV, and distributes cents-off coupons. Hitachi (www.hitachi.com) has a large technical sales force, advertises in business and trade publications, and sends representatives to trade shows. Table 17-1 shows the value of integrated marketing communications.

A superior IMC plan properly addresses these points:

- *It is synergistic*, taking into account the multiple ways to reach potential consumers at different points during their decision process.

- *There is tactical consistency*, whereby various promotion tools complement each other and communicate the same basic themes.

Integrated marketing communications (IMC) *evaluates the strategic roles of various communication disciplines and combines them for clarity, consistency, and impact.*

IMC efforts should be synergistic, tactically consistent, interactive, positive influences, and so forth.

---

[3]Alison Wellner, "The Beauty of Branching Out," www.chamberbiz.com/bizcenter (January 3, 2001).

[4]"Agency Report," *Advertising Age* (April 23, 2001); "Domestic Spending by Category and Medium," *Advertising Age* (September 25, 2000); U.S. Department of Labor, Bureau of Labor Statistics; and "2001 Annual Report on the Promotion Industry," *Promo Magazine's SourceBook '01.*

[5]Adapted by the authors from Janet Smith, "Integrated Marketing," *Marketing Tools* (November-December 1995), p. 64.

TABLE 17-1	**Through an integrated marketing communications strategy, a firm can**
The Value of Integrated Marketing Communications	Coordinate all of its promotional activities. Establish and maintain a consistent image for the company and its goods and services. Communicate the features of goods and services. Create awareness for new goods and services. Keep existing goods and services popular. Reposition the images or uses of faltering goods and services. Generate enthusiasm from channel members. Note where goods and services can be purchased. Persuade consumers to trade up from one product to a more expensive one. Alert consumers to sales. Justify (rationalize) the prices of goods and services. Answer consumer questions. Close transactions. Provide service for consumers after transactions are completed. Reinforce consumer loyalty. Place the company and its goods and services in a favorable light, relative to competitors. Encourage cross-marketing, whereby each element of the promotion mix reinforces the other (such as including a Web address on shopping bags, in the store, on the sales receipt, and in ads).

- *There is interactivity with consumers*, so that messages may be better tailored to specific market segments.

- *Every company message positively influences the target audience*, so that each contact builds on the contacts before it.

- *The company's basic promotion themes and differential advantages are clearly understood by all employees who interface with the targeted audience*, thereby avoiding the negative impact of misinformed employees passing on the wrong information to potential customers.

- *Advertising, public relations, sales, and sales promotion personnel cooperate with one another*, and view each other as partners rather than as adversaries.

- *Detailed data bases are maintained*, so that promotion efforts can be regularly reviewed.[6]

Nike (www.nike.com), a leading IMC practitioner, has won a number of awards for its promotion efforts. In 2000, Nike received the Best Integrated Campaign award from *Adweek*. Here is why:

> What makes a good integrated marketing campaign? Analysts say it's consistency: "The look and feel must be the same offline and online." Nike's 'Whatever' campaign not only was consistent, it was groundbreaking. The ads, which ran both online and on TV in 2000, dropped the viewer into an immediate situation: "You're racing Marion Jones. The fastest woman in the world. Look out for the glass door. (CRASH!) What do you do? Continued at

[6]Adapted by the authors from Kim Bartel Sheehan and Caitlin Doherty, "Re-Weaving the Web: Integrating Print and Online Communications," *Journal of Interactive Marketing*, Vol. 15 (Spring 2001), pp. 47–59; Anders Gronstedt, *The Customer Century: Lessons from World-Class Companies in Integrated Marketing and Communications* (London: Routledge, 2000); and Michael Render, "IMC Gets Better with Inflow Marketing," *Marketing News* (September 11, 2000), p. 23.

MARKETING *and the Web*

Using E-Mail as Part of an Integrated Marketing Communications Strategy

As Barnes&Noble.com's (www.barnes&noble.com) director of online marketing, Roe Johnson, says: "Experimentation" and "testing" have been key parts of the firm's E-mail marketing efforts. The company has used different themes, such as "pass this message along to a friend" offers, as well as cross-selling (by suggesting related titles and other books by the same author) and personalized messages.

Johnson feels that E-mail messages, which provide shipping and order confirmation represent the perfect opportunity for cross-selling since customers have their credit cards in hand to verify account numbers. She also believes that this is a particularly good time to offer customers a premium or to build a relationship by acknowledging their customer status.

To generate interest, Barnes&Noble.com makes more than 100 "B&N Insider" newsletters available to customers. Each of these newsletters contains content on specific subjects. Customers that "opt-in" for a newsletter subscription also receive special offers and announcements related to their particular interest areas. In addition, the firm produces co-branded newsletters with affiliate partners. Subscribers to these newsletters can decide whether or not they wish to receive special offers from partner companies.

Johnson offers two suggestions for firms developing E-mail communications programs: (1) It is important for them to respond quickly and properly to E-mail requests. A fast response can help rectify a customer service problem. (2) Firms must determine the frequency of E-mail communications with customers. They should ask customers what offers they wish to receive and how often they want to receive them. This gets around the problems of some customers feeling that they are being inundated with offers while others feel that a firm has not been responsive enough.

Develop an E-mail marketing campaign for a store selling point-and-shoot cameras to novices.

Source: Based on material in "Barnes&noble.com: An E-Mail Marketing Case Study." Direct Marketing (July 2000), pp. 40–41.

---

whatever.nike.com." When viewers visited the site, prompted by the tagline, they could choose the ad's ending. The ads not only got a lot of attention, they also worked. Sales went up: The shoe, the Air Cross Trainer II, "immediately shot to No. 1 in Nike sales" after the ads debuted, outselling the second most-popular shoe by a 10-to-1 margin. In the words of Internet marketing publication *ChannelSeven.com's* Seth Fineberg, the campaign "did what it set out to do. Nike increased sales and created yet another branding experience people would not soon forget—at least, in the advertising world." Nike's marketing director said that "Traditionally, a 30- or 60-second TV ad is an experience with the brand that you did not necessarily choose. But with campaigns like 'Whatever,' you can demand the experience by going to this active experiential site and it becomes a 10-minute interaction with the brand."[7] [*Authors' note: whatever.nike.com is no longer an active site.*]

Figures 17-1 and 17-2 highlight the integrated marketing communications approaches of Micro Warehouse (www.microwarehouse.com) and Hard Rock Cafe (www.hardrock.com), respectively.

[7]Janis Mara, "Nike: Best Integrated Campaign," *Adweek* (June 5, 2000), pp. IQ44–IQ47.

FIGURE 17-1
IMC and Micro Warehouse

As the company says, "Our expertise in data-base management allows us to target our customers and prospective customers with pinpoint accuracy."

Source: Reprinted with permission.

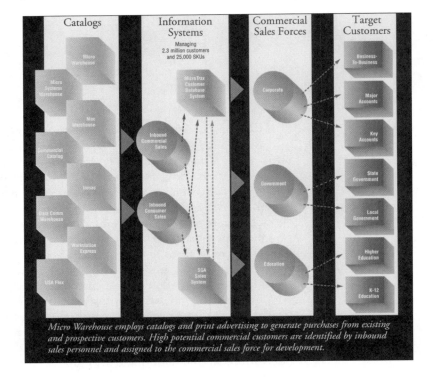

Micro Warehouse employs catalogs and print advertising to generate purchases from existing and prospective customers. High potential commercial customers are identified by inbound sales personnel and assigned to the commercial sales force for development.

FIGURE 17-2
IMC and Hard Rock Cafe

Everything that the Hard Rock Cafe does, such as the design of the store interior shown here, presents an integrated message to consumers. As the firms says at its Web site (www.hardrock.com), "Around the world, we have come to epitomize the timeless energy, originality, and unifying spirit that have helped shape rock music over the last 50 years. Every Hard Rock Cafe offers a unique experience, from specific memorabilia that pays tribute to legendary and new musicians rooted in each area to authentic, collectible merchandise that reflects the spirit of the city."

Source: Reprinted by permission of Retail Planning Associates. Photography by Michael Houghton/STUDIOHIO.

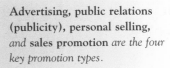
Advertising, public relations (publicity), personal selling, *and* sales promotion *are the four key promotion types.*

17-4 TYPES OF PROMOTION

In their communications programs, organizations use one or more of four basic types of promotion:

- *Advertising* is paid, nonpersonal communication regarding goods, services, organizations, people, places, and ideas that is transmitted through various media by business firms, government and other nonprofit organizations, and individuals who are identified in the advertising message as the sponsor. The message is generally controlled by the sponsor.

TABLE 17-2 Characteristics of Promotional Types

Factor	Advertising	Publicity Form of Public Relations[a]	Personal Selling	Sales Promotion
Audience	Mass	Mass	Small (one-to-one)	Varies
Message	Uniform	Uniform	Specific	Varies
Cost	Low per viewer or reader	None for media space and time; can be some costs for media releases and publicity materials	High per customer	Moderate per customer
Sponsor	Company	No formal sponsor (media are not paid)	Company	Company
Flexibility	Low	Low	High	Moderate
Control over content and placement	High	None (controlled by media)	High	High
Credibility	Moderate	High	Moderate	Moderate
Major goal	To appeal to a mass audience at a reasonable cost, and create awareness and favorable attitudes	To reach a mass audience with an independently reported message	To deal with individual consumers, to resolve questions, to close sales	To stimulate short-run sales, to increase impulse purchases
Example	Television ad for a Sony CD player for use in cars	Magazine article describing the unique features of a Sony CD player for use in cars	Retail sales personnel explaining how a Sony CD player for cars works	A Sony CD player for cars exhibited at trade shows

[a]Please note: When public relations embodies advertising (an image-related message), personal selling (a salesperson describing his or her firm's public service efforts to college students), and/or sales promotion (distributing special discount coupons to low-income consumers), it takes on the characteristics of those promotional types. However, the goal would be more image-related than sales-related.

- *Public relations* includes any communication to foster a favorable image for goods, services, organizations, people, places, and ideas among their publics—such as consumers, investors, government, channel members, employees, and the general public. It may be nonpersonal or personal, paid or nonpaid, and sponsor controlled or not controlled. *Publicity* is the form of public relations that entails nonpersonal communication passed on via various media but not paid for by an identified sponsor. Wording and placement of publicity messages are generally media controlled.

- *Personal selling* involves oral communication with one or more prospective buyers by paid representatives for the purpose of making sales.

- *Sales promotion* involves paid marketing communication activities (other than advertising, publicity, or personal selling) that are intended to stimulate consumer purchases and dealer effectiveness. Included are trade shows, premiums, incentives, giveaways, demonstrations, and various other efforts not in the ordinary promotion routine.[8]

The general characteristics of each type of promotion are shown in Table 17-2. As discussed later in the chapter, many firms in some way combine them into an integrated promotional blend. This lets firms reach their entire target market, present both persuasive and believable messages, have personal contact with customers, sponsor special events, and balance the promotional budget.

[8]Adapted by the authors from Peter D. Bennett (Editor), *Dictionary of Marketing Terms*, Second Edition (Chicago: American Marketing Association, 1995), pp. 6, 206, 231, 232, and 253.

FIGURE 17-3

A Channel of Communication

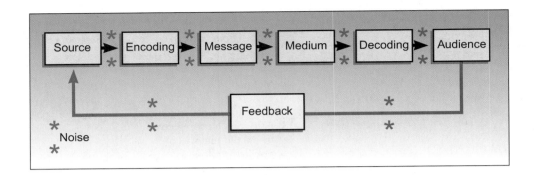

17-5 THE CHANNEL OF COMMUNICATION

A message is sent to an audience via a **channel of communication.**

To develop a proper promotion mix and interact effectively with a target audience, the **channel of communication (communication process)** shown in Figure 17-3 must be understood. Through such a channel, a source develops a message, transmits it to an audience via some medium, and gets feedback from the audience. The components of a communication channel are discussed next.

17-5a The Source

A **source** *presents a message.*

The **source** of communication is usually a company, an independent institution, or an opinion leader seeking to present a message to an audience. A firm communicates through a(n) spokesperson, celebrity, actor playing a role, representative consumer, and/or salesperson.

A company spokesperson is typically a long-time employee who represents the firm in communications. The spokesperson has an aura of sincerity, commitment, and expertise. Sometimes, the spokesperson is a top executive, like Wendy's (www.wendys.com) Dave Thomas or Ronco's (www.ronco.com) Ron Popeil. Other times, front-line workers are used, such as a Verizon (www.verizon.com) customer service representative or a Sheraton (www.starwood.com/sheraton) hotel chef. In general, this source has been quite effective.

A celebrity is used when the goal is to gain the audience's attention and improve product awareness.[9] Problems can arise if the celebrity is perceived as insincere or unknowledgeable. Popular celebrities include George Foreman for Meineke Discount Muffler Shops (www.meineke.com) and the George Foreman Grilling Machine (www.salton-maxim.com/salton/grill/georgeforeman.asp), Sela Ward for Sprint (www. sprint.com), and Snoopy and other *Peanuts* characters for Metropolitan Life Insurance.

Many ads have actors playing roles rather than celebrity spokespeople. In these commercials, the emphasis is on presenting a message about a good, service, or idea rather than on the consumer recognizing a celebrity. The hope is that the consumer will learn more about product attributes.

A representative consumer is one who likes a product and recommends it in an ad. The person is shown with his or her name and hometown. The intent is to present a real consumer in an actual situation. A hidden camera or blind taste test is often used with this source. Today, viewers are more skeptical about how "representative" the endorser is.

Finally, a firm may use a salesperson to communicate with consumers. Many salespeople are knowledgeable, assertive, and persuasive. However, consumers may doubt their objectivity and tactics. Auto salespeople rate particularly low in consumer surveys.

An independent institution is not controlled by the firms on which it reports. It presents information in a professional, nonpaid (by the firms) manner. Consumers Union (www.consumer.org), the publisher of *Consumer Reports* (www.consumerreports.org), and the local newspaper restaurant critic are examples of independent sources. They have

[9]See Betsy Cummings, "Star Power," *Sales & Marketing Management* (April 2001), pp. 52–59.

great credibility for readers because they discuss both good and bad points, but some segments of the population may not be exposed to these sources. The information presented may differ from that contained in a firm's commercials or sales-force presentations.

An opinion leader has face-to-face contact with and influences potential consumers. Because he or she deals on a personal level, an opinion leader often has strong persuasive impact and believability; and can offer social acceptance for followers. Firms often address initial messages to opinion leaders, who then provide word-of-mouth to others. Many marketers believe opinion leaders not only influence, but also are influenced by, others (opinion receivers); even opinion leaders need approval for their choices.

In assessing a source, these questions are critical: Is he/she believable? Is he/she convincing? Does he/she present an image consistent with the firm? Do consumers value the message of the source? Is he/she seen as knowledgeable? Does the source complement the product he/she communicates about, or does the source overwhelm it? Do significant parts of the market dislike the source?

17-5b Encoding

Encoding is the process whereby a thought or idea is translated into a message by the source. Preliminary decisions are made as to message content, such as the use of symbolism and wording. It is vital that the thought or idea be translated exactly as the source intends. A firm wanting to stress its product's prestige would include the product's status, exclusive ownership, and special features in a message. It would not stress a low price, availability in discount stores, or the millions of people who have already purchased.

*In **encoding**, a source translates a thought into a message.*

17-5c The Message

A *message* is a combination of words and symbols transmitted to an audience. It depends on whether a firm's goal is to inform, persuade, or remind. Almost all messages include some information on the firm's name, the product name, the desired image, differential advantages, and product attributes. A firm would also give information on availability and price at some point in the consumer's decision process. With integrated marketing communications, consistency in messages is important. As highlighted in Figure 17-4, Wal-Mart (www.walmart.com) recognizes this well.

*A **message** combines words and symbols.*

Most communication involves one-sided messages, in which only the benefits of a good, service, or idea are cited. Few firms use two-sided messages, in which both benefits and limitations are noted. Companies are not anxious to point out their shortcomings, although consumer perceptions of honesty may be improved via two-sided messages. Figure 17-5 shows an effective one-sided message from Ricoh Corporation (www.ricohcorp.com), a leading provider of digital office equipment.

Many messages use symbolism and try to relate safety, social acceptance, or sexual appeal to a purchase. In symbolic messages, a firm stresses psychological benefits rather than tangible product performance. Clothing ads may offer acceptance by peers; toothpaste may brighten teeth and make a person more sexually attractive. One type of symbolism, the use of fear appeals (such as anti-drug ads), has had mixed results. Although people respond to moderate fear appeals, strong messages may not be as well received.

Humor is sometimes used to gain audience attention and retain it. About.com (http://humor.about.com/cs/advertisinghumor) has several popular examples and related materials. Yet, a firm needs to be careful to get across the intended message when using

Our goal is to give you the same quality of service online that you'd get in our stores. We're here for you, so ask us anything you need to know!

Matt, Customer Service

FIGURE 17-4

The Consistent Message of Wal-Mart

Source: Reprinted by permission.

FIGURE 17-5

A Focused Message from Ricoh

Source: Reprinted by permission of Ricoh Corporation. Ad agency: Gigante Vaz & Partners Advertising.

humor—which should not make fun of the company, its goods, or its services; and humor should not dominate a message so the brand name or product attributes go unnoticed. Since humor has cultural underpinnings, successful ads in the home country may not work well in another nation:

> Advertising costs are high, and consumer attention spans are low. It's a scary combination that has every business owner searching for advertising's Holy Grail: the ad that's not only memorable but also has a measurable impact on the bottom line. The trend over the past few years has been toward wacky image ads seemingly unrelated to the products they're touting. A sign of the times, those ads emerged during the freewheeling late 1990s, when companies could put outrageous images and words onto a page or screen and still see unlimited cash flow in their pockets. Other companies have opted for the traditional approach, running "educational" ads using text rather than images, or featuring customer testimonials. What will work for *your* business? The good news is, probably any of these strategies will work—*if* you know how to use them.[10]

Comparative messages *position a firm versus competitors.*

Comparative messages implicitly or explicitly contrast a firm's offerings with those of competitors. Implicit comparisons use an indirect brand X or leading brand approach ("Our industrial glues are more effective than other leading brands"). Explicit comparisons use a direct approach (such as PepsiCo's promoting the "Pepsi Challenge" taste tests in which Pepsi beats Coke). Comparative messages are used in some TV and radio commercials, print ads, and other media; and salespeople often compare their products' attributes with those of competitors. In using comparative messages, a firm must be careful not to turn off consumers, place too much emphasis on a competitor's brand, or lose sight of its own differential advantages to promote.[11] Look at the Rayovac (www.rayovac.com) ad in Figure 17-6.

A message must be presented in a desirable, exclusive, and believable way. The good, service, or idea must be perceived as something worth buying or accepting. It also must be seen as unique to the seller—that is, it cannot be gotten elsewhere. Finally, the message must make believable claims.

Massed *or* **distributed promotion** *and the* **wearout rate** *must be carefully planned.*

Message timing must also be carefully planned. First, during what times of the year should a firm advertise, seek publicity, add salespeople, or run promotions? In **massed promotion,** communication efforts are concentrated in peak periods, like holidays. In **distributed promotion,** communication efforts are spread throughout the year. Figure 17-7 compares massed and distributed promotion.

[10]Chris Penttila, "Ad It Up," *Entrepreneur* (May 2001), pp. 66–71.

[11]See Stuart Elliott, "Take That! Campbell Responds to Progressive Ads," *New York Times* (March 7, 2001), p. C6.

FIGURE 17-6
Comparative Advertising from Rayovac
Source: Reprinted by permission.

Second, the **wearout rate**—the time it takes for a message to lose its effectiveness—must be determined. Some messages wear out quickly; others last for years. Wearout depends on the frequency of communications, message quality, the number of different messages used by a firm, and other factors. Ford has done such a good job with its "Quality is Job 1" message that it is still popular after many years.

17-5d The Medium

The **medium** is the personal or nonpersonal means used to send a message. Personal media are company salespeople and other representatives, as well as opinion leaders. Nonpersonal (mass) media include newspapers, television, radio, direct mail, billboards, magazines, and transit.

*A **medium** is a personal or nonpersonal channel for a message.*

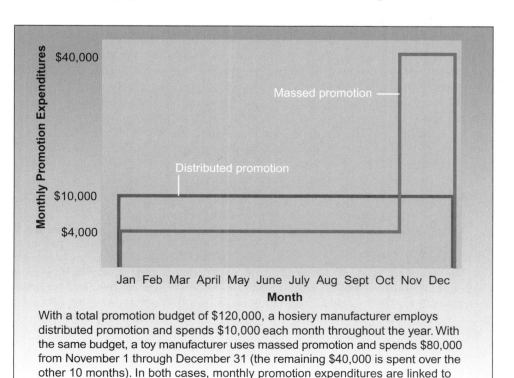

FIGURE 17-7
Massed Versus Distributed Promotion

With a total promotion budget of $120,000, a hosiery manufacturer employs distributed promotion and spends $10,000 each month throughout the year. With the same budget, a toy manufacturer uses massed promotion and spends $80,000 from November 1 through December 31 (the remaining $40,000 is spent over the other 10 months). In both cases, monthly promotion expenditures are linked to monthly sales.

Personal media offer one-to-one audience contact. They are flexible, can adapt messages to individual needs, and can answer questions. They appeal to a small audience and are best with a concentrated market. Nonpersonal media have a large audience and low per-customer costs. They not as flexible and dynamic as one-to-one contacts. They work best with a dispersed target market.

In deciding between personal and nonpersonal media, a firm should consider both total and per-unit costs, product complexity, audience attributes, and communication goals. The two kinds of media go well together since nonpersonal media generate consumer interest and personal media help close sales.

17-5e Decoding

*In **decoding,** the audience translates the message sent by the source.*

Decoding is the process by which a message sent by a source is interpreted by an audience. The interpretation is based on the audience's background and on message clarity and complexity. For example, a housewife and a working woman might have different interpretations of a message on the value of child-care centers. Usually, as symbolism and complexity increase, clarity decreases. CNA's (www.cna.com) "Any business insurer knows the importance of risk. How many know the importance of a pencil?" is not as understandable a message as "When you belong to the National Geographic Society (www.nationalgeographic.com), you don't just read about adventures. You help make them happen." As noted earlier, it is essential that a message be decoded in the manner intended by the source (encoding = decoding). Is an ad too provocative or merely attention grabbing? Is a serious message buried in the imagery or quite clear to the targeted audience?

Subliminal advertising *aims at a consumer's subconscious.*

Subliminal advertising is a highly controversial kind of promotion because it does not enable the audience to consciously decode a message. Visual or verbal messages are presented so quickly that people do not see, hear, or remember them. Yet, the assumption is that they will buy products due to subconscious impulses stimulated by the messages. The overwhelming evidence shows that subliminal ads cannot get people to buy things they do not want. In addition, because these ads are often misinterpreted, clearly perceived ads are much more effective. In the United States, state laws and self-regulation by business associations (such as the National Association of Broadcasters, www.nab.org) have all but eliminated subliminal ads.

17-5f The Audience

*The **audience** is usually the target market; but it can also be others.*

An ***audience*** is the object of a source's message. In most marketing situations, it is the target market. However, a source may also want to communicate an idea, build an image, or give information to stockholders, independent media, the public, government officials, and others.

The way a communication channel is used by a firm depends on the size and dispersion of the audience, demographic and life-style audience traits, and the availability of appropriate media. Thus, because the communication process should be keyed to the audience, AIDS prevention groups have had a tough time getting their message across to teens and young adults:

> Past AIDS-related public service announcements have defined the problem as one of HIV/AIDS awareness, the assumption being that once young people are aware of AIDS, they will be motivated to practice APBs (AIDS preventive behaviors). However, this definition is outdated. It is now evident that AIDS awareness has been accomplished among teens and young adults. They are already aware that sexual intercourse and IV drug use represent the major modes of AIDS transmission. The challenge facing communicators is how to convert AIDS awareness into APBs. Although there is some need to keep generic AIDS messages before the public, rudimentary information/awareness-based appeals are of little use to a market that knows the elementary facts or when there is little evidence that basic knowledge leads to adoption of APBs.[12]

[12]Kristina D. Frankenberger and Ajay S. Sukhdial, "Segmenting Teens for AIDS Preventive Behaviors with Implications for Marketing Communications," *Journal of Public Policy & Marketing*, Vol. 13 (Spring 1994), p. 134.

To make matters still tougher for marketers, a global consumer survey found that people are rather down on promotion messages:

- 72 percent believe marketers exaggerate health benefits.
- 70 percent do not believe marketers respect consumers' intelligence.
- 70 percent believe marketers brainwash children.
- 62 percent do not believe marketers give accurate information.
- 55 percent do not believe marketers sponsor worthwhile events.
- 40 percent do not believe ads are creative and entertaining.[13]

17-5g Feedback

Feedback is the response an audience has to a message. It may be a purchase, an attitude change, or a nonpurchase. A firm must realize that each response is possible and devise a way to monitor them.

The most desirable feedback occurs if a consumer buys a good or service (or accepts an idea) after communication with or from a firm. The message is effective enough to stimulate a transaction. A second type of feedback occurs if a firm finds promotion elicits a favorable attitude toward it or its offerings. For new goods or services, positive attitudes must often be formed before purchases (awareness→favorable attitude→purchase). For existing products, people may have bought another brand just before receiving a message or be temporarily out of funds; generating their favorable attitudes may lead to future purchases.

The least desirable feedback is if the audience neither makes a purchase nor develops a favorable attitude. This may happen for one of several reasons: There is no recall of the message. There is contentment with another brand. The message is not believed. No differential advantage is perceived.

> **Feedback** *consists of purchase, attitude, or nonpurchase responses to a message.*

17-5h Noise

Noise is interference at any point along a channel of communication. Because of it, messages are sometimes encoded or decoded incorrectly or weak audience responses are made. Examples of noise are

- A phone call interrupting a marketing manager while he or she is developing a promotional theme.
- A salesperson misidentifying a product and giving incorrect information.
- An impatient customer interrupting a sales presentation.
- A broken page link at a Web site.
- A conversation between two consumers during a TV commercial.
- A direct-mail ad being opened by the wrong person.
- A consumer seeing a sale on a competitor's item while waiting in line at a checkout counter.

> **Noise** *may interfere with the communication process at any stage.*

17-6 PROMOTION PLANNING

After a firm gains an understanding of the communication process, it is ready to develop an overall promotion plan. Such a plan consists of three parts: objectives, budgeting, and the promotion mix.

---

[13]Roper Starch, "The World's View of Marketers," *Advertising Age* (January 15, 1996), p. 1–10. For a recent study on American attitudes toward promotion, see Abhilasha Metha, "Advertising Attitudes and Advertising Effectiveness," *Journal of Advertising Research*, Vol. 40 (May-June 2000), pp. 67–72.

17-6a Objectives

Promotion objectives can be divided into two main categories: stimulating demand and enhancing company image.

The **hierarchy-of-effects model**
outlines demand goals.

In setting demand goals, the **hierarchy-of-effects model** should be used. It outlines the sequential short-term, intermediate, and long-term promotion goals for a firm to pursue—and works in conjunction with the consumer's decision process that was discussed in Chapter 8:

1. *Provide information*—Obtain consumer product recognition, then gain consumer knowledge of product attributes.

2. *Develop positive attitudes and feelings*—Obtain favorable attitudes, then gain preference for the company's brand(s) over those of competitors.

3. *Stimulate purchases and repeat purchases*—Obtain strong consumer preference, gain purchase of good or service, encourage continued purchases (brand loyalty).

Primary demand *is for a product category;* **selective demand** *is for a brand.*

By using this model, a firm can go from informing to persuading and then to reminding consumers about its offerings. When a good or service is little known, **primary demand** should be sought. This is consumer demand for a *product category*. Later, with preference the goal, **selective demand** should be sought. This is consumer demand for a *particular brand*. Sometimes, organizations may try to sustain or revitalize interest in mature products and revert to a primary demand orientation. Thus, the Florida Citrus Growers association (www.floridajuice.com) sponsors ads to generate primary demand for oranges. On the other hand, sales promotions tend to focus on selective demand.

Institutional advertising *is involved with image goals.*

With image-related promotion goals, a firm engages in public relations—via suitable advertising, publicity, personal selling, and/or sales promotion (as noted in Table 17-2). **Institutional advertising** is used when the advertising goal is to enhance company image—and not to sell specific goods or services. More than one-half of the leading advertisers in the United States run such ads.

17-6b Budgeting

There are five basic methods to set a total promotion budget: all-you-can-afford, incremental, competitive parity, percentage-of-sales, and objective-and-task. The choice depends on the requirements of the individual firm. Budgets typically range from 1 to 5 percent of sales for industrial-products firms to up to 20 to 30 percent of sales for consumer-products firms.

Budgeting methods are **all-you-can-afford, incremental, competitive parity, percentage-of-sales,** *and* **objective-and-task.**

In the **all-you-can-afford method,** a firm first allots funds for other elements of marketing; any remaining marketing funds then go to the promotion budget. It is the weakest technique and is used most often by small, production-oriented firms. It gives little importance to promotion, spending is not linked to goals, and there is a risk of having no promotion budget if finances are low.

With the **incremental method,** a company bases its new promotion budget on the previous one. A percentage is added to or subtracted from this year's budget to determine next year's. The technique is also used by small firms. It has these advantages: a reference point, a budget based on a firm's feelings about past performance and future trends, and easy calculations. Key disadvantages do exist: budget size is rarely tied to goals, "gut feelings" are overemphasized, and it is hard to evaluate success or failure.

In the **competitive parity method,** a firm's promotion budget is raised or lowered according to competitors' actions. It is useful to both large and small firms. The benefits are that it is keyed to a reference point, market-oriented, and conservative. The shortcomings are that it is a follower and not a leadership approach, it is difficult to get competitors' promotion data, and there is an assumption of a similarity between the firm and its competitors (as to years in business, goods or services, image, prices, and so on). However, firms usually have basic differences from competitors.

With the *percentage-of-sales method,* a firm ties its promotion budget to sales revenue. In the first year, a promotion-to-sales ratio is set. During succeeding years, the ratio of promotion to sales dollars is constant. The benefits are the use of sales as a base, the adaptability, and the link of revenues and promotion. However, there is no relation to promotion goals; promotion is a sales follower, not a sales leader; and promotion cuts occur in poor sales periods (when increases could help). The technique yields too large a budget in high sales periods and too small a budget in low sales periods.

Under the *objective-and-task method,* a firm sets promotion goals, determines the activities needed to satisfy them, and then establishes the proper budget. It is the best method. The advantages are that goals are clearly stated, spending is related to goal-oriented tasks, adaptability is offered, and it is rather easy to evaluate performance. The major weakness is the complexity of setting goals and specific tasks, especially for small firms. Most large companies use some form of objective-and-task technique.

During promotional budgeting, a firm should keep the concept of marginal return in mind. The **marginal return** is the amount of sales each increment of promotion spending will generate. When a product is new, the marginal return tends to be high because the market is expanding. When a product is established, the marginal return tends to be lower because each additional increment of promotion has less of an impact on sales (due to a saturated target market).

The **marginal return** *refers to the sales generated through incremental promotional spending.*

17-6c The Promotion Mix

After establishing a total promotion budget, a company must determine its *promotion mix.* This is the firm's overall and specific communication program, including its involvement with advertising, public relations (publicity), personal selling, and/or sales promotion. Seldom does a company use just one type of promotion—such as a mail-order firm relying on ads, a hospital on publicity, or a flea-market vendor on selling. Typically, a promotion mix is used. These two Web sites have good online resources regarding the promotion mix: Idea Site for Business (www.ideasiteforbusiness.com/ideas.htm) and MarketitRight.com (www.marketitright.com).

A **promotion mix** *somehow combines advertising, public relations, personal selling, and/or sales promotion.*

Within an integrated marketing communications program, each type of promotion has a distinct function and complements the other types. Ads appeal to big audiences and create awareness; without them, selling is more difficult, time consuming, and costly. Publicity provides credible information to a wide audience, but content and timing cannot be controlled. Selling has one-to-one contact, flexibility, and the ability to close sales; without it, the interest caused by ads might be wasted. Sales promotion spurs short-run sales and supplements ads and selling.

The selection of a promotion mix depends on company attributes, the product life cycle, media access, and channel members. A small firm is limited in the kinds of ads it can afford or use efficiently; it may have to stress personal selling and a few sales promotions. A large firm covering a sizable geographic area could combine many ads, personal selling, and frequent sales promotions. As products move through the life cycle, promotion emphasis goes from information to persuasion to reinforcement; different media and messages are needed at each stage. Some media may not be accessible (no cigarette ads on TV) or require lengthy lead time (Yellow Pages). Channel members may demand special promotions, sales support, and/or cooperative advertising allowances.

It is the job of a firm's marketing director (or vice-president) to set up a promotion budget and a promotion mix, as well as to allocate resources to each aspect of promotion. In large firms, there may be separate managers for advertising, public relations, personal selling, and sales promotion. They report to, and have their efforts coordinated by, the marketing director.

Figure 17-8 contrasts promotion mixes in which advertising and personal selling would dominate.

FIGURE 17-8
Contrasting Promotion Mixes

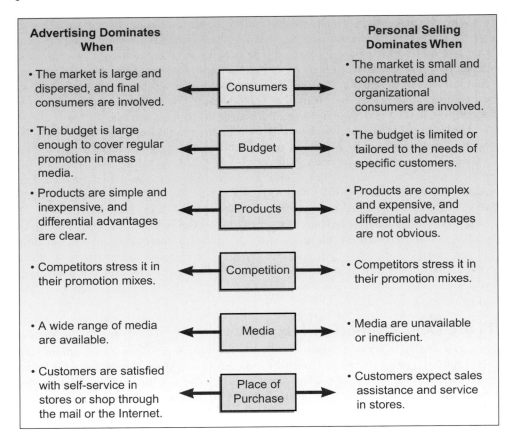

17-7 GLOBAL PROMOTION CONSIDERATIONS

International promotion decisions should not be made until each market is carefully studied.

While preparing a promotion strategy for foreign nations, the channel of communication, promotion goals, budgeting, and the promotion mix should be carefully reviewed as they pertain to each market.

With regard to the channel of communication, a firm should recognize that

- Source recognition and credibility vary by nation or region. As celebrities, Elizabeth Taylor, Sean Connery, and Sophia Loren have high recognition rates in both the United States and Japan. Sarah Michelle Gellar and Tim Green are not well known in Japan, despite their U.S. popularity.

- Encoding messages can be quite challenging, particularly if the messages must be translated into another language.

- Because the effects of message symbolism depend on the nation or region, care must be taken if fear, humorous, and/or sexual messages are used. Themes have to correspond to local customs. Thus, French print ads are more apt to have emotional, humorous, and sexual themes than U.S. ones.

- In some locales, few residents have TVs, a limited number of newspapers and magazines are printed, and programs (channels) limit or do not accept ads.

- Ensuring that messages are decoded properly can be demanding: When Procter & Gamble (www.pg.com) first entered Eastern European, the firm "blanketed Polish TV and mailed samples to promote its Wash & Go shampoo. Poles found the dubbed ad culturally out of touch: It showed a woman popping out of a swimming pool and into a shower. 'We don't have swimming pools, and most of us don't have showers. We have baths,' sniffed the president of a Warsaw research group."[14]

[14]Gail E. Schares, "Colgate-Palmolive Is Really Cleaning Up in Poland," *Business Week* (March 15, 1993), p. 56.

GLOBAL *Marketing in Action*

Promotion in India: New Strategies Come into Focus

Many marketing analysts believe that promotion is just "coming of age" in India as a strategic business tool. There are currently about 200 promotion agencies in India that specialize in regional marketing, and most national advertising agencies are adding promotion services.

Traditional streetwide events, sports sponsorships, and school-based campaigns are popular. PepsiCo India (www.agroindia.org/agroindia/aicmember/pepsico/default.htm) and Hindustan Lever (www.hll.com) recently tied for the Gold award in the All India Promo Awards. Pepsi's campaign used an under-the-cap sweepstakes with a grand prize of a trip to a World Cup cricket game; other prize winners received televisions and athletic gear. To complement this theme, multipacks of PepsiCo products included trading cards of top cricket players. Purchasers of single units of beverages could collect points and receive T-shirts and other items.

Lever received its share of the award for its launch of Sunsilk shampoo. In a variation of a "free sample" offer, Lever offered free shampoos in hair salons in its "Take the First Step with Us" campaign. The program resulted in 18,143 free shampoos being given out in 65 salons in five cities. Lever arranged for the salons to give the free shampoos in exchange for getting a list of potential new clients.

The use of school-based programs has also increased in India. These programs typically include small games, diaries, or essays. As the senior manager of an Indian advertising agency says, "Those go in their backpacks, then moms see them when they check their children's schoolwork."

Firms are now beginning to engage in online promotions, because more than 30 million Indians will have Internet access as of 2004. Most of their access will be through cable television or computer kiosks that are similar to long-distance phone services located in each town.

How should a PepsiCo campaign differ between the United States and India?

Source: Based on material in Betsy Spethmann, "A Passage for India," *Promo* (October 2000), p. 121.

- Making assumptions about audience traits in foreign markets without adequate research may lead to wrong assumptions: "An *average* U.S. farmer uses a $100,000 combine while an *average* Chinese farmer uses an ox-pulled hand plow. Yet, niche marketing, along with the media ability to reach just those customers who need specific products, lets a John Deere economically reach the 30,000 U.S. farmers and the 2,000 Chinese cooperatives who can afford and who need a $100,000 combine."[15]

- Global techniques for measuring promotion effectiveness are emerging, particularly on the Web.

In terms of promotion goals, budgeting, and the promotion mix, these points should be considered:

- For nations where a firm and its brands are unknown, there must be a series of promotion goals as people are taken through the hierarchy-of-effects model. For nations

[15]Tom Duncan, "Standardized Global Marketing Communication Campaigns Are Possible, They're Just Hard to Do" in Robert P. Leone and V. Kumar (Editors), *1992 AMA Educators' Proceedings* (Chicago: American Marketing Association, 1992), p. 355.

TABLE 17-3	Selected U.S. Regulations Affecting Promotion

Factor	Legal Environment
Access to media	Cigarettes and liquor have restricted access. Legal, medical, and other professions have been given the right to advertise.
Deception	It is illegal to use messages that would mislead reasonable consumers and potentially harm them.
Bait-and-switch	It is illegal to lure a customer with an ad for a low-priced item and then, once the customer talks to a salesperson, to use a strong sales pitch intended to switch the shopper to a more expensive item.
Door-to-door selling	Many locales restrict door-to-door sales practices. A cooling-off period allows a person to cancel an in-home sale up to three days after an agreement is reached.
Promotional allowances	Such allowances must be available to channel members in a fair and equitable manner.
Comparative advertisements	Claims must be substantiated. The Federal Trade Commission favors naming competitors in ads (not citing a competitor as brand X).
Testimonials or endorsements	A celebrity or expert endorser must actually use a product if he or she makes such a claim.

in which a product category is new, primary demand must be created before selective demand is gained. To show goodwill, image ads may be even more important in foreign than in domestic markets.

- The promotion budgets in foreign countries must be keyed to the size of the markets and the activities required to succeed there. The objective-and-task method is highly recommended in setting international promotion budgets.

- Due to cultural, socioeconomic, infrastructure, and other differences, promotion mixes must be consistent with the nations served. In Western Europe, Germans listen to the most radio; the Dutch and British watch the most TV. When Procter & Gamble mailed free samples (a sales promotion) of Wash & Go shampoo to homes in Poland, thieves broke into mailboxes to get the samples—which they resold. As a Procter & Gamble manager said, "The tools we were using were new to that area."[16]

There are several Web sites, such as Ad Age Global (www.adageinternational.com) and the University of Texas' Advertising World (http://advertising.utexas.edu/world/International.html), to help marketers better understand global promotion.

17-8 THE LEGAL ENVIRONMENT OF PROMOTION

Full disclosure, substantiation, cease-and-desist orders, corrective advertising, and fines are major governmental limits on promotion activities.

Federal, state, and local governmental bodies—in the United States and other nations around the globe—have laws and rules regarding promotion practices. These regulations range from banning billboards in some locales to requiring celebrity endorsers to use products if they say they do. The U.S. agencies most involved with promotion are the Federal Trade Commission (www.ftc.gov) and the Federal Communications Commission (www.fcc.gov). Table 17-3 shows selected U.S. regulations.

---

[16]"Data Watch," *Advertising Age* (October 26, 1992), p. I-10; and E. S. Browning, "Eastern Europe Poses Obstacles for Ads," *Wall Street Journal* (July 30, 1992), p. B6.

ETHICAL *Issues in Marketing*

The Creativity of Big Tobacco

After signing the November 1998 master settlement agreement (MSA) limiting marketing activity by cigarette marketers, the tobacco industry revised its marketing plans to stay within the agreement. Nonetheless, cigarette firms still spend a lot of money on advertising. The Federal Trade Commission says that the five largest cigarette manufacturers spend billions of dollars per year on ads and promotions.

Many manufacturers have shifted the focus of their advertising to include corporate responsibility messages that are presented via image-oriented ads, as well as ads that encourage young people not to smoke. Examples include Philip Morris Companies' television ads explaining the MSA provisions, Winston-Salem's "Right Decisions, Right Now" campaign that distributes antismoking materials to middle-school teachers, and Brown & Williamson's financial support of the "We Card" program aimed at verifying the age of cigarette purchasers. All of the cigarette companies also fund the American Legacy Foundation (www.americanlegacy.org), a nonprofit, antismoking organization.

However, the cigarette manufacturers take a different view with regard to marketing to adults who have already chosen to smoke. To appeal to this group, almost all cigarette manufacturers provide samples (as many as four packs at a time) at urban bars. Company reps are careful to check the age of each recipient, as well as to only approach consumers who are smoking. These sampling programs are conducted in metropolitan areas. R. J. Reynolds' Salem brand sets up a Green Room promotional area at local bars and often sponsors a local band. Brown & Williamson's Lucky Strike brand seeks out smokers in downtown areas, and provides them with coffee and free packs of Lucky Strike.

As marketing manager for Lucky Strike, defend the current promotion program on ethical grounds. How would you respond to consumer advocates who oppose any promotion of tobacco products?

Source: Based on material in Steve Jarvis, "They're Not Quitting: Big Tobacco Gets Creative—Within Limits," *Marketing News* (November 20, 2000), pp. 1, 9; and Bernard Stamler, "Advertising: Tobacco Companies Look for New Ways to Get the Message Out," *New York Times on the Web* (May 2, 2001).

There are five major enforcement tools to protect consumers and competing firms from undesirable practices: full disclosure, substantiation, cease-and-desist orders, corrective advertising, and fines.

Full disclosure requires that all data necessary for a consumer to make a safe and informed decision be provided in a promotion message. That is why Alka-Seltzer (www.alkaseltzer.com) must mention that its regular version contains aspirin, and diet products must note how many calories they contain. In this way, consumers can assess the overall benefits and risks of a purchase. Promotion is considered to be deceptive only if claims mislead a "reasonable" person and lead to "injury" (physical, financial, or other).

Substantiation requires a firm to be able to prove all the claims it makes in promotion messages. This means thorough testing and evidence of performance are needed before making claims. If a tire maker says a brand will last for 70,000 miles, it must be able to verify this with test results. In early 2001, the Food and Drug Administration (www.fda.gov) asked Ocean Spray (www.oceanspray.com) to "stop making unapproved health claims about its juices on the company Web site. Taking aim at assertions by Ocean Spray that its juices 'may help the body fight cancer' or 'may help lower cholesterol,' the FDA concluded that the firm promoted its drinks as if they were medications, going 'beyond the scope of the types of claims that are permitted on foods.'" Ocean Spray voluntarily complied with the FDA request.[17]

Under a *cease-and-desist order,* a firm must stop a promotion practice that is deemed deceptive and modify a message accordingly. The firm is often not forced to admit guilt or pay fines, as long as it obeys an order to stop running a particular message. Sometimes, the legal system can be harsher. A U.S. federal judge recently ordered H&R Block (www.hrblock.com) to "stop using the phrase 'rapid refund' and other terms deliberately intended to disguise expensive loans that Block arranges for people anticipating income tax refunds. The judge found that Block had engaged in false advertising and went to great lengths to conceal the reality that rather than receiving refunds, clients were getting high-interest loans to obtain their money a few days sooner than the Treasury would have sent it at no charge. On some loans, the annual percentage rate was more than 500 percent. Block 'strongly disagrees with the judge's finding of maliciousness'." When the lawsuit was filed, a Block spokesman called it ridiculous."[18]

Corrective advertising requires a firm to run new ads to correct the false impressions left by previous ones. For example, "the FTC ruled that Novartis (www.novartis.com) had advertised Doan's pills as more effective against back pain than rivals—without substantiation. The FTC ordered corrective ads with the statement 'Although Doan's is an effective pain reliever, there is no evidence that Doan's is more effective than other pain relievers for back pain.' It was to be put on packaging for a year, and in ads, until $8 million had been spent on the campaign. The firm has complied with the packaging order, but a Novartis spokeswoman said no Doan's ads are running, partially because of the decision."[19]

The last major remedy is fines, which are dollar penalties for deceptive promotion. A company may have to pay a sum to the government or consumers, as with Rose Creek Health Products and Staff of Life. The FTC filed a complaint in federal court accusing the firms "of making blatantly false and unsubstantiated health claims." As a result, "the companies, without admitting or denying guilt, agreed to pay $375,000 to consumers. As part of the settlement, the FTC prohibited the parties from making any unsupported claims for vitamin O—for instance, that it could help the body absorb more oxygen through a liquid. 'Only fish can do that,' said a lawyer in the agency's division of advertising practices."[20]

Besides government rules, the media have their own voluntary standards for promotion practices. The National Association of Broadcasters (www.nab.org) monitors TV and radio ads. General industry groups, such as the Better Business Bureau (www.bbb.org), the American Association of Advertising Agencies (www.aaaa.org), and the International Advertising Association (www.iaaglobal.org), also participate in the self-regulation of promotion.

---

[17]Gregg Winter, "FDA Action Could Change Food Marketing on the Web," *New York Times* (February 14, 2001), p. C11.

[18]David Cay Johnston, "Block Is Ordered to Stop Advertising 'Rapid Refunds' of Taxes," *New York Times* (February 28, 2001), p. C1.

[19]Ira Teinowitz, "Doan's Decision Sets Precedent for Corrective Ads," *Advertising Age* (September 4, 2000), p. 57.

[20]Sana Siwolop, "Back Pain? Arthritis? Step Right Up to the Mouse," *New York Times on the Web* (January 7, 2001).

FIGURE 17-9

A Strong Defense of Promotion by the American Association of Advertising Agencies

Source: Reprinted by permission.

17-9 CRITICISMS AND DEFENSES OF PROMOTION

For many years, industry trade groups have campaigned to improve the overall image of promotion. This is illustrated in Figure 17-9. As the general director of the International Advertising Association (www.iaaglobal.org) once remarked, "There's been enough talk about the bad—the clutter, the obtrusiveness, the stuffed mailboxes. It's time that people know about the good."[21]

Nonetheless, promotion is the most heavily criticized area of marketing. Here are a number of criticisms and the defenses of marketers to them:

Promotion controversies center on materialism, honesty, prices, symbolism, and consumer expectations.

Detractors Feel That Promotion	*Marketing Professionals Answer That Promotion*
Creates an obsession with material possessions.	Responds to consumer desires for material possessions. In affluent societies, these items are plentiful and paid for with discretionary earnings.
Is basically dishonest.	Is basically honest. The great majority of companies abide by all laws and set strict self-regulations. A few dishonest firms give a bad name to all.
Raises the prices of goods and services.	Holds down prices. By increasing consumer demand, promotion enables firms to use mass production and mass distribution and reduce per-unit costs. Employment is higher if demand is stimulated.
Overemphasizes symbolism and status.	Differentiates goods and services by symbolic and status appeals. Consumers desire distinctiveness and product benefits.
Causes excessively high expectations.	Keeps expectations high; it thereby sustains consumer motivation and worker productivity in order to satisfy expectations.

[21]Cyndee Miller, "The Marketing of Advertising," *Marketing News* (December 7, 1992), p. 2.

WEB SITES YOU CAN USE

There are many specialized service firms that work with their clients to develop and enact integrated marketing communications strategies. These service firms help clients develop goals, coordinate promotion efforts, and devise the best mix of promotion tools. The following integrated marketing communications service firms have attractive Web sites that highlight their capabilities and successes:

Carbonhouse (www.carbonhouse.com)

Godbe Communications (www.godbe.com)

Hale Integrated Marketing Communications (www.haleinc.com)

Harpell/Martins & Company (www.harpell.com)

Pacifico Integrated Marketing Communications (www.pacifico.com)

SSD&W Integrated Marketing Communications (www.ssdw.com)

SUMMARY

1. *To define promotion planning, show its importance, and demonstrate the value of integrated marketing communications* Promotion involves any communication that informs, persuades, and/or reminds people about an organization's or individual's goods, services, ideas, community involvement, or impact on society. Promotion planning systematically relates to all communication.

Promotion efforts are needed for both new and existing products. The audience may be consumers, stockholders, consumer advocacy groups, government, channel members, employees, competitors, and the public. With word-of-mouth communication, people express opinions and product-related experiences to one another. A firm may communicate its image, views on ideas, community involvement, or impact on society—as well as persuade people to buy. Good promotion enhances the other elements of the marketing mix. Promotion is a major activity around the world.

With well-coordinated promotion plans, a firm is applying integrated marketing communications. This means the strategic roles of a variety of communication disciplines are evaluated and combined for clarity, consistency, and maximum communication impact. A good plan properly addresses these points: It is synergistic. There is tactical consistency. There is interactivity with consumers. Every company message positively influences the target audience. The company's basic promotion themes and differential advantages are clearly understood by all employees who interface with the targeted audience. Promotion personnel cooperate with one another. Data bases are maintained.

2. *To describe the general characteristics of advertising, public relations, personal selling, and sales promotion* Advertising is paid, nonpersonal communication transmitted through various media by organizations and individuals who are in some way identified as the sponsor. Public relations includes any communication (paid or nonpaid, nonpersonal or personal, sponsored by a firm or reported by an independent medium) designed to foster a favorable image. Publicity is the nonpaid, nonpersonal, nonsponsored form of public relations. Personal selling involves oral communication with one or more prospective buyers by paid representatives for the purpose of making sales. Sales promotion involves paid marketing activities to stimulate consumer purchases and dealers.

3. *To explain the channel of communication and how it functions* A source sends a message to its audience via a channel of communication. A channel consists of a source, encoding, the message, the medium, decoding, the audience, feedback, and noise.

A source is a company, an independent institution, or an opinion leader that seeks to present a message to an audience. Encoding is the process by which a thought or an idea is translated into a message by the source. A message is a combination of words and symbols transmitted to the audience. A medium is a personal or nonpersonal channel used to convey a message. Decoding is the process by which a message sent by a source is translated by the audience. The audience is the object of a source's message. Feedback is the response the audience makes to a message: purchase, attitude change, or nonpurchase. Noise is interference at any stage.

4. *To examine the components of a promotion plan* Goals may be demand- or image-oriented. Demand goals should correspond to the hierarchy-of-effects model, moving a consumer from awareness to purchase. Primary demand is total demand for a product category; selective demand refers to interest in a particular brand. Institutional advertising is used to enhance company image.

Five ways to set a promotion budget are all-you-can-afford (the weakest method), incremental, competitive parity, percentage-of-sales, and objective-and-task (the best method). Marginal return should be considered when budgeting.

A promotion mix is the overall and specific communication program of a firm, including its use of advertising, public relations (publicity), personal selling, and/or sales promotion. Many factors need to be considered in developing a promotion mix.

5. *To discuss global promotion considerations, and the legal environment and criticisms and defenses of promotion* In devising an international promotion plan, the channel of communication, promotion goals, budgeting, and promotion mix should be studied for and applied to each market.

There are many laws and rules affecting promotion. The major ways to guard against undesirable promotion are full disclosure, substantiation, cease-and-desist orders, corrective ads, and fines. Critics are strong in their complaints about promotions. Marketers are equally firm in their defenses.

KEY TERMS

promotion (p. 511)
promotion planning (p. 511)
word-of-mouth communication (p. 512)
integrated marketing communications
    (IMC) (p. 513)
advertising (p. 516)
public relations (p. 517)
publicity (p. 517)
personal selling (p. 517)
sales promotion (p. 517)
channel of communication (communication
    process) (p. 518)
source (p. 518)
encoding (p. 519)

message (p. 519)
comparative messages (p. 520)
massed promotion (p. 520)
distributed promotion (p. 520)
wearout rate (p. 521)
medium (p. 521)
decoding (p. 522)
subliminal advertising (p. 522)
audience (p. 522)
feedback (p. 523)
noise (p. 523)
hierarchy-of-effects model (p. 524)
primary demand (p. 524)

selective demand (p. 524)
institutional advertising (p. 524)
all-you-can-afford method (p. 524)
incremental method (p. 524)
competitive parity method (p. 524)
percentage-of-sales method (p. 525)
objective-and-task method (p. 525)
marginal return (p. 525)
promotion mix (p. 525)
full disclosure (p. 529)
substantiation (p. 530)
cease-and-desist order (p. 530)
corrective advertising (p. 530)

REVIEW QUESTIONS

1. Why is integrated marketing communications so important?
2. Distinguish among advertising, public relations, personal selling, and sales promotion.
3. What is a two-sided message? Why do few companies use such messages?
4. What should be the relationship between encoding and decoding messages? Why?

5. A consumer listens to a sales presentation but does not make a purchase. Has the presentation failed? Explain your answer.
6. Explain the hierarchy-of-effects model. How is it related to demand objectives?
7. Describe each of the methods of promotional budgeting.
8. When should personal selling dominate the promotion mix?

DISCUSSION QUESTIONS

1. What are the advantages and disadvantages of changing messages (themes) frequently?
2. Present a promotion campaign to increase APBs (AIDS preventive behaviors) among teens.
3. As the marketing manager for a small U.S.-based French book publisher that is entering the African market for the first time, devise a promotion budget relying on the objective-and-task method.

4. Develop a promotion mix for
  a. A global toy.
  b. A small janitorial service.
  c. A four-person CPA practice.
  d. A medium-sized printer manufacturer.

WEB EXERCISE

Visit the reSources Web site (http://resources.harpell.com) of Harpell/Martins & Company. Discuss what general IMC principles you can glean from the information at this site.

18

Advertising and Public Relations

When Chanel (www.chanel.com) introduced its Allure perfume in 1996, it featured professional models in its ads. Two years later, as Chanel introduced its Allure line for men, it decided to change the strategy and use "real men" in ads. According to Laurie Palma, Chanel's vice-president for fragrance marketing, "We thought it would be more appealing and interesting to men to use real guys." Chanel chose "guys that men could either look up to, who were inspirational or whom they could relate to on some level." The concept worked so well that Chanel decided to use the "real people" concept for its women's brands.

The intent of the current ads is to focus on people who have interesting lives, as well as strong personalities. Palma says, "Yes, all these people are physically appealing and physically wonderful looking." To add an element of mystery, Chanel's men's and women's fragrance ads both feature people who are identified in the ad by their profession, hobbies, and where they live, but not by their name. For example, the Allure Homme ads carry the headline "Real men. Real Allure" and feature a New York City writer, a Beverly Hills plastic surgeon, and a French sailor who has sailed solo around the world. Likewise, Allure's female products carry the similar headline "Every women has her own special allure." They feature such personalities as a French magazine editor and a Somalian women's rights activist.

These advertisements are aimed at consumers 25 to 49 years old. The print ads are in black-and-white, except for the Allure bottle, which is in four-color. The similarity in men's and women's ads is by design so that they will be a common image for both product versions.

The 30-second television commercials share some of the design elements of the print ads. Therefore, the ads are in black and white, and feature men and women who are enjoying themselves at work. In one TV ad, an architect states, "It smells great," while a sculptor says that "I feel sexy." The spot closes with an announcer stating that "Allure is irresistible. Allure from Chanel."[1]

In this chapter, we will study both the advertising and public relations aspects of promotion, including the use of creative strategies in the development of advertisements.

18-1 OVERVIEW

This chapter covers two promotion forms: advertising and public relations. As defined in Chapter 17, *advertising* is paid, nonpersonal communication regarding goods, services, organizations, people, places, and ideas; it may be used by businesses, government and other nonprofit organizations, and individuals. Its distinguishing features are that a sponsor pays for its message, a set format is sent to an entire audience via mass media, the sponsor's name is clearly presented, and the sponsor controls the message.

Advertising and public relations are two of the major forms of promotion.

[1]Courtney Kane, "Scents," *New York Times on the Web* (December 21, 2000).

TABLE 18-1   **Advertising Expenditures by Medium: United States Versus Japan and Germany**

In the United States[a]		In Japan[a]		In Germany[a]	
Media	*Percent of Total Expenditures*	*Media*	*Percent of Total Expenditures*	*Media*	*Percent of Total Expenditures*
Television	23.9	Television	45.1	Newspapers	45.1
Newspapers	21.2	Newspapers	26.8	Magazines	24.0
Direct mail	19.1	Outdoor	13.2	Television	23.2
Radio	7.9	Magazines	9.9	Radio	3.6
Yellow Pages	5.8	Radio	5.0	Outdoor	3.2
Magazines	5.1	Total	100.0	Cinema	0.9
Business publications	2.0			Total	100.0
Internet	2.3				
Outdoor	0.8				
Miscellaneous	11.9				
Total	100.0				

[a]The media designations in the three areas differ because the sources for the data are different.

Sources: Compiled by the authors from data reported in "2000 Marketing Factbook," *Marketing News* (July 3, 2000); and "Rankings: Top Global Ad Markets," www.adageglobal.com (May 17, 2001).

In contrast, *public relations* involves communication that fosters a favorable image for goods, services, organizations, people, places, and ideas among their various publics. Its unique features are that it is more image- than sales-oriented; it embodies image-oriented advertising, personal selling, and sales promotion; and it often seeks favorable publicity for a firm. As an aspect of public relations, publicity entails nonpersonal communication that is transmitted via mass media but not paid for by an identified sponsor. The media usually control the wording and placement of publicity messages.

The distinctions between advertising and publicity are in part revealed by this statement: "Advertising is paid for, publicity is prayed for." The scope and importance, characteristics, and planning considerations for both advertising and public relations are examined in Chapter 18. InfoTech Marketing has an excellent Web site with resources related to advertising (www.smsource.com/advertis.htm) and public relations (www. smsource.com/publicrelations.htm). Note: These sites require a free registration.

18-2 THE SCOPE AND IMPORTANCE OF ADVERTISING

In 2000, about $500 billion was spent on advertising around the world—one-half in the United States and the rest elsewhere.[2] Table 18-1 shows expenditures by medium for the three countries with the highest ad spending: United States, Japan, and Germany. In all of these countries, newspapers and TV are among the top media. But in Japan and Germany, these media account for a great proportion of ad spending, much more than in the United States, partly due to the level of U.S. media choice. Direct mail is a key U.S. medium, where Internet advertising has grown from virtually zero five years ago to become a growing presence.

[2]Universal McCann, "Worldwide Ad Spending," *Advertising Age* (January 1, 2001), p. 10.

Advertising as a percent of sales varies by industry and firm, and company advertising as a percent of sales is low. During 2000, expenditures were less than 2.5 percent of sales in 41 percent of U.S. industries; 2.5 to 4.9 percent of sales in 32 percent of U.S. industries; and at least 5.0 percent of sales in 27 percent of U.S. industries.[3] Among the leading advertisers, such as Procter & Gamble, the percentages often far exceed industry averages. Table 18-2 shows ad expenditures by selected industry category, while Table 18-3 indicates the highest-spending advertisers in the world.

An advertising emphasis is most likely if products are standardized, have easily communicated features, appeal to a large market, have low prices, are marketed via independent resellers, and/or are new. Leading brands often get large ad budgets to hold their positions. At Charles Schwab (www.schwab.com), the discount stock broker, ads stress two themes: low prices and quality service. It has an in-house ad agency and runs ads on traditional and cable TV, as well as the Internet. By advertising, it has raised awareness and introduced new products.

Consider this: "The term 'niche' typically has been used to describe consumer market segments. But now it's about putting advertising in any place possible, from coffee cups and fruit bowls to sidewalks. It's about ferreting out opportunities to become part of a consumer's day-to-day activities. Bag Media (www.bagmedia.com), a British company with U.S. headquarters in Port Chester, New York, sells space on paper bags to advertisers who want to drive urban workers to their Web sites. The company figured that if a consumer picks up coffee and a bag of doughnuts on the way to work, odds are that bag will be seen quite a few times before it's trashed. So an ad on that bag would get quite a few impressions."[4]

The following general observations can be made as to the usefulness of advertising:

- When there are low-involvement purchases, consumer behavior may be easier to change than attitudes.
- One ad can have a strong effect on brand awareness.
- By advertising, it is easier to raise people's opinions about a little-known item than a well-known one.
- Effectiveness often rises over long-term campaigns.

The vast majority of U.S. firms spend less than 5 percent of sales on advertising. Ads are most important for standardized products aimed at large markets.

TABLE 18-2   Advertising in Selected U.S. Industries, 2000

Industry	Advertising as Percent of Sales	Industry	Advertising as Percent of Sales
Leather products	17.5	Department stores	4.3
Dolls and stuffed toys	15.2	Household appliances	2.3
Watches and clocks	15.2	Motion picture theaters	2.0
Perfume and cosmetics	12.8	Computer and office equipment	1.5
Soaps and detergents	12.5	Auto dealers	1.3
Cutlery, hand tools, general hardware	12.0	Air courier services	1.2
Books	11.0	Accident and health insurance	1.0
Food products	11.0	Management services	0.8
Household furniture	9.7	Drugstores	0.4

Source: Derived from Schonfeld & Associates, "2000 Advertising-to-Sales Ratios for the 200 Largest Ad Spending Industries," *Advertising Age* (July 24, 2000), p. 44.

[3]Computed by the authors from Schonfeld & Associates, "2000 Advertising-to-Sales Ratios for the 200 Largest Ad Spending Industries," *Advertising Age* (July 24, 2000), p. 44.
[4]Jennifer Gilbert, "Cheap Tricks," *Business 2.0* (February 6, 2001), pp. 60, 62.

TABLE 18-3 The Leading Advertisers in the World (1999 data)

In the United States	Outside the United States	Worldwide
General Motors	Unilever	Procter & Gamble
Procter & Gamble	Procter & Gamble	General Motors
Philip Morris	Nestlé	Unilever
Pfizer	Coca-Cola	Philip Morris
AT&T	Ford	Ford
DaimlerChrysler	General Motors	DaimlerChrysler
Ford	L'Oreal	Pfizer
Sears	Volkswagen	Nestlé
PepsiCo	Toyota	Coca-Cola
Verizon	PSA Peugeot Citroën	Toyota

Sources: Estimated by the authors based on data in various issues of *Advertising Age.*

18-3 THE CHARACTERISTICS OF ADVERTISING

Advertising attracts an audience, has low per-customer costs, offers varied media, is surrounded by information, and aids selling.

On the positive side, advertising reaches a large, geographically dispersed market; and, for print media, circulation is supplemented by the passing of a copy from one reader to another. Costs per viewer or listener are low. A single TV ad may cost $360,000 to air and reach 30 million people—a cost of $0.012 per person (for media time). A broad range of media is available: from national (global) TV to local newspapers. Thus, a firm's goals and resources may be matched with the most appropriate medium.

A sponsor can control message content, graphics, timing, and size or length, as well as the audience targeted. A uniform message is sent to the whole audience. With print media, people can study and restudy messages. Editorial content (a news story or segment of a broadcast show) often borders an ad. This can raise readership or viewing/listening, enhance an image, and create the proper mood. A firm may even seek specialized media or sections of media (like a sports section for a men's clothing ad).

Ads ease the way for personal selling by creating audience awareness and liking for brands. They also enable self-service wholesalers and retailers to operate, and they sustain an industry—mail order. With a pulling strategy, advertising enables a firm to show its resellers that consumer demand exists.

Advertising is inflexible and can be wasteful, costly, and limit information and feedback.

On the negative side, since messages are standardized, they are rather inflexible and not responsive to questions. This makes it hard to satisfy the needs of a diverse audience. And since many media appeal to broad audiences, a large portion of viewers or readers may be wasted for a sponsor. A single-unit health spa might find that only one-fifth of a newspaper's readers live in its shopping area.

Advertising sometimes requires high total expenditures, although costs per viewer or reader are low. This may keep smaller firms from using some media. In the example earlier in this section, it was said that a TV ad might cost only $0.012 per viewer. Yet, media time alone for that ad would be $360,000—for one ad, placed once. Also, because high costs lead to brief messages, most ads do not provide much information. TV commercials are very short, averaging 30 seconds or less; few are as long as one minute. Further, because ads are impersonal, feedback is harder to get and it may not be immediately available.

Mass media are used by many people who do not view or listen to ads. They watch TV, read print media, and so on, but ignore ads and discard direct mail. Of concern to television advertisers is "zapping," whereby a viewer uses a remote-control device to switch programs when an ad comes on.

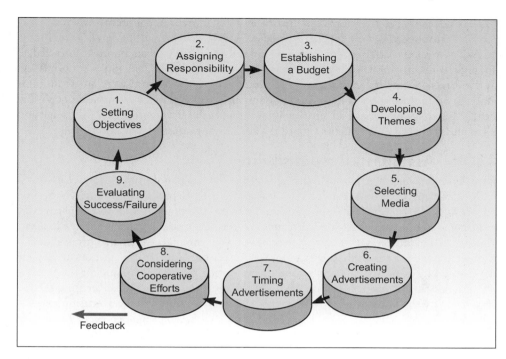

FIGURE 18-1
Developing an Advertising Plan

18-4 DEVELOPING AN ADVERTISING PLAN

An advertising plan consists of the nine steps shown in Figure 18-1. These steps are now highlighted.

18-4a Setting Objectives

Advertising goals can be divided into demand and image types, with image-oriented ads being part of a public relations effort. Table 18-4 cites several goals. Usually, a number of them are pursued.

Type of Objective	Illustrations
Demand-Oriented	
Information	To create target market awareness for a new brand
	To acquaint consumers with new business or store hours
	To reduce the time salespeople take to answer basic questions
Persuasion	To gain brand preference
	To increase store traffic
	To achieve brand loyalty
Reminding (retention)	To stabilize sales
	To maintain brand loyalty
	To sustain brand recognition and image
Image-Oriented	
Industry	To develop and maintain a favorable industry image
	To generate primary demand
Company	To develop and maintain a favorable company image
	To generate selective demand

TABLE 18-4

Illustrations of Specific Advertising Objectives

As an example, the Canadian Institute of Chartered Accountants (www.cica.ca) recently introduced a new image-oriented campaign to portray chartered accountants (CAs) as strategic advisers for complex tasks that require broad business knowledge, strategic thinking, expertise with numbers, and a global view: "The aim is to show CAs as the drivers of success, in all kinds of organizations, in a wide array of roles. It's an integral part of the theme of our new strategic communications plan for the profession: Visible Leadership. National image advertising is our most visible communications initiative and its focus is to show CAs contributing to the success of leading organizations."[5]

18-4b Assigning Responsibility

In assigning advertising responsibility, a firm can rely on its internal personnel involved with marketing functions, use an in-house advertising department, or hire an outside advertising agency. Although many firms use internal personnel or in-house departments, most companies involved with advertising on a regular or sizable basis hire outside agencies (some in addition to their own personnel or departments). Diversified firms may hire a different agency for each product line. A firm's decision to use an outside agency depends on its own expertise and resources and on the role of advertising for the firm.

*An **advertising agency** may work with a firm to develop its ad plan, conduct research, or provide other services.*

An ***advertising agency*** is an organization that provides a variety of advertising-related services to client firms. It often works with clients in devising their advertising plans—including themes, media choice, copywriting, and other tasks. A large agency may also offer market research, product planning, consumer research, public relations, and more. The largest U.S.-based ad agencies are Omnicom Group (www.omnicomgroup.com), Interpublic Group (www.interpublic.com), Bcom3 Group (www.bcom3.com), and Grey Global Group (www.grey.com).

18-4c Establishing a Budget

After figuring its overall spending by the all-you-can-afford, incremental, competitive parity, percentage-of-sales, or objective-and-task method, a firm sets a detailed ad budget—to specify the funds for each type of advertising (such as product and institutional messages) and each medium (such as newspapers and radio). Because demand-oriented ads generate revenues, firms should be cautious about reducing these budgets. A better campaign, not a lower budget, may be the answer if goals are not reached.

These points should be addressed: What do various alternatives cost for time or space (a 30-second TV spot versus a full-page magazine ad)? How many placements are needed to be effective (if it takes four telecasts of a single ad to make an impact, a budget must allow four placements)? How have media prices risen recently? How should a firm react during an industry sales slump? What channel members are assigned which promotion tasks? Do channel members require contributions toward advertising? What does it cost to produce an ad? How should a budget be allocated for domestic versus foreign ads? Consider that the cost of producing one 30-second national TV commercial in the United States is now $350,000 (not including the cost for airtime).[6]

According to a survey of international advertising executives, 28 percent of firms allow personnel in each pan-geographic region to determine their needs and petition headquarters for a budget; 28 percent let each individual market have its own advertising strategy and budget; and 20 percent control budgeting decisions from their world headquarters. Airlines are most apt to use the pan-geographic approach. Consumer products and high-tech firms are most apt to have individual market budgeting.[7]

---

[5]"Your CA: Your Competitive Advantage," CA *Magazine* (October 2000), pp. 48–49.

[6]"AAAA's TV Commercial Production Survey Shows Largest Cost Increase in 13 Years," *American Association of Advertising Agencies' News Release* (November 16, 2000).

[7]Jan Jaben, "Ad Decision Makers Favor Regional Angle," *Advertising Age* (May 15, 1995), pp. I–3, I–16.

MARKETING *and the Web*

What's Ahead for Online Advertising

Although marketing research firm Jupiter Communications (www.jup.com) predicted that advertising expenditures on the Web would increase from $3.5 billion in 1999 to $5.4 billion in year 2000, other observers were much less optimistic in their growth estimates. McCann-Erickson WorldGroup (www.mccann.com), for example, anticipated that online ad spending would only reach $3.9 billion in 2000. That is only 1.7 percent of total ad spending via all media. DoubleClick (www.doubleclick.com), the giant online advertising firm that places ads for 1,300 Web companies, reported slow growth in 2000.

Jack Kerry, president of an online consulting firm says, "Everybody needs to realize that the full potential of the Internet is still a real long time away. Until Web companies tailor their offerings to the needs of advertisers, like television, newspapers, and magazines do, the Internet will see slow growth."

Kerry, as well as traditional advertisers, have a number of suggestions that could speed up the adoption process for Internet-based advertising. Here are three of them: (1) Online advertising agencies must better learn what types of online ads work best for traditional bricks-and-mortar firms. (2) Since banner ads have not worked that well, successful marketing on the Web should resemble direct marketing. Kerry comments that, "You have to give buyers a reason to go from one site to another. That is most often fulfilled by giving out useful information or services." (3) Internet advertising needs some consistent ways to evaluate its impact. While television advertising can be judged by a Nielsen rating, there is no comparable system to measure Internet advertising. Kerry reports that traditional marketers won't do anything big on the Net until they know they can truly measure their results.

As marketing director of DoubleClick, present a marketing strategy to increase Internet advertising by traditional bricks-and-mortar retailers.

Source: Based on material in Andy Cohen, "Why Online Advertising Is Failing," *Sales & Marketing Management* (November 2000), p. 13.

18-4d Developing Themes

A firm next develops *advertising themes,* the overall appeals for its campaign. A good or service appeal centers on the item and its attributes. A consumer appeal describes a product in terms of consumer benefits rather than its features. An institutional appeal deals with a firm's image. Table 18-5 presents a full range of advertising themes from which a firm may select. Figures 18-2 and 18-3 show thematic ads from Aiwa (www.aiwa.com) and Jaguar (www.jaguar.com).

Basic **advertising themes** *are product, consumer, and/or institutional appeals.*

18-4e Selecting Media

There are many media available, as noted in Table 18-6. In selecting them, costs, reach, waste, message permanence, persuasive impact, narrowcasting, frequency, clutter, lead time, and media innovations should be reviewed.

Advertising media costs are outlays for media time or space. They are related to ad length or size, and media attributes. First, the total costs to place an ad in a medium are computed—such as, $30,000 for a full-page color magazine ad. Second, per-reader or per-viewer costs are derived (stated in cost per thousand). If a $30,000 ad goes in a magazine with a 500,000 circulation, the cost per thousand is $60.

Advertising media costs *include total and per-person costs.*

TABLE 18·5   **Advertising Themes**

Theme	Example
Good or Service Related	
Dominant features described	Whirlpool washers emphasize dependability and durability.
Competitive advantages cited	Aiwa stresses the superior quality of its portable stereos.
Price used as dominant feature	Private-label beauty products advertise low prices.
News or information domination	New-model laser printers point out enhancements in color and fonts.
Size of market detailed	Hertz emphasizes its leading position in car rentals.
Primary demand sought	Grapes are advertised.
Consumer Related	
Good or service uses explained	Pillsbury ads have cake recipes.
Cost benefits of good or service shown	Owens-Corning states how consumers reduce heating bills with Fiberglas insulation.
Emphasis on how good or service helps consumer	The Regent Beverly Wilshire hotel says that its customer service is so good that it gives clients complete peace of mind.
Threatening situation	The American Heart Association points out the risks of smoking.
Incentives given to encourage purchases	An ad mentions $1 off a purchase as an introductory offer for a new brand of coffee.
Institutional Related	
Favorable image sought	ExxonMobil explains how it is searching for new energy sources.
Growth, profits, and potential described to attract investors	Companies regularly take out full-page ads in business sections of major newspapers.

FIGURE 18-2
Aiwa: Citing Competitive Advantages

Source: Reprinted by permission.

IF IT'S NOT AIWA QUALITY, IT'S NOT QUITE RIGHT.

aiwa
Turn Me On™

FIGURE 18-3

Jaguar: Showing How a Product Benefits the Consumer

Source: Reprinted by permission of Ford.

TABLE 18-6 Advertising Media

Medium	Market Coverage	Best Uses	Selected Advantages	Selected Disadvantages
Commercial television	Regional, national, or international	Regional manufacturers and large retailers; national, large manufacturers and largest retailers	Reach, low cost per viewer, persuasive impact, creative options, flexible, high frequency, surrounded by programs	High minimum total costs, general audience, lead time for popular shows, short messages, limited availability
Cable television	Local, regional, national, or international	Local, regional, and national manufacturers and retailers	More precise audience and more creative than commercial television	Not all consumers hooked up; ads not yet fully accepted on programs
Daily newspaper	Entire metropolitan area; local editions used sometimes	Medium and large firms	Short lead time, concentrated market, flexible, high frequency, passalongs, surrounded by content	General audience, heavy ad competition, limited color, limited creativity
Weekly newspaper	One community	Local firms	Same as daily	Heavy ad competition, very limited color, limited creativity, small market

continues

TABLE 18-6   Advertising Media (*continued*)

Medium	Market Coverage	Best Uses	Selected Advantages	Selected Disadvantages
Direct mail	Advertiser selects market	New products, book clubs, financial services, catalog sales	Precise audience, flexible, personal approach, less clutter from other messages	High throwaway rate, receipt by wrong person, low credibility
Radio	Entire metropolitan area	Local or regional firms	Low costs, selective market, high frequency, immediacy of messages, surrounded by content	No visual impact, commercial clutter, channel switching, consumer distractions
Telephone directories	Entire metropolitan area (with local supplements)	All types of retailers, professionals, service companies	Low costs, permanence of messages, repetition, coverage of market, specialized listings, action-oriented messages	Clutter of ads, limited creativity, very long lead time, low appeal to passive consumers
Magazines	Local, national, or international (with regional issues)	Local service retailers and mail-order firms; major manufacturers and retailers	Color, creative options, affluent audience, permanence of messages, passalongs, flexible, surrounded by content	Long lead time, poor frequency (if monthly), ad clutter, geographically dispersed audience
Business publications	National, regional, or international	Corporate advertising, industrial firms	Selective market, high readability, surrounded by content, message permanence, passalongs	Restricted product applications, may not be read by proper decision maker, not final-consumer oriented
Internet	Local, national, or international	All types and sizes of firms	Low costs, huge potential audience, vast geographic coverage, amount of information conveyed, interactivity	Clutter of ads, viewed as a novelty by some, goals unclear (advertising vs. entertainment and education), no set rate structure
Outdoor	Entire metropolitan area or one location	Brand-name products, nearby retailers, reminder ads	Large size, color, creative options, repetition, less clutter, message permanence	Legal restrictions, consumer distractions, general audience, inflexible, limited content, lead time
Transit	Urban community with a transit system	Firms located along transit route	Concentrated market, message permanence, repetition, action-oriented messages, color, creative options	Clutter of ads, consumer distractions, geographically limited audience
Flyers	Single neighborhood	Local firms	Low costs, market coverage, little waste, flexible	High throwaway rate, poor image

Reach refers to the number of viewers, readers, or listeners in a medium's audience. For TV and radio, it is the total number of people who watch or listen to an ad. For print media, it has two aspects: *circulation* and *passalong rate*. Circulation is the number of copies sold or distributed to people. The passalong rate is the number of times each copy is read by another reader. For instance, each copy of *Newsweek* is read by several people. The magazine passalong rate is much higher than that for daily papers.

Waste is the part of a medium's audience not in a firm's target market. Because media appeal to mass audiences, it can be a big factor. This can be shown by continuing the magazine example noted in media costs. If the magazine is a special-interest one for amateur photographers, a film producer would know that 450,000 readers might be interested in new fast-speed film; 50,000 have no interest. The latter is the wasted audience. The real cost is $66.67 ($30,000/450,000 × 1,000 = $66.67) per-thousand circulation. The firm also knows a general-interest magazine runs ads for film, sells one million copies, and prices a full-page ad at $40,000—$40 per thousand. The firm expects only 200,000 people to be interested in photography. So, the real cost is $200 ($40,000/200,000 × 1,000 = $200) per thousand. See Figure 18-4.

Message permanence refers to the number of exposures one ad generates (repetition) and how long it remains available to the audience. Outdoor ads, transit ads, and phone directories yield many exposures per message; and many magazines are retained by consumers for long periods. On the other hand, radio and TV ads last only 5 to 60 seconds and are over.

Persuasive impact is the ability of a medium to stimulate consumers. Television often has the highest persuasive impact because it is able to combine audio, video, color, and animation. Magazines also have high persuasive impact. Many newspapers are improving their technology so as to feature color ads and increase their persuasive impact.

Narrowcasting, which presents advertising messages to rather limited and well-defined audiences, is a way to reduce the audience waste with mass media. It may be done via direct mail, local cable TV, specialty magazines, the Internet, and other targeted media. In narrowcasting, a firm gets less waste in return for a smaller reach. Now that the majority of U.S. homes get cable TV programs, this medium has great potential for local

Reach *includes circulation and passalongs.*

Waste *is the audience segment not in the target market.*

Message permanence *refers to exposures per ad.*

Persuasive impact *is highest for TV.*

In **narrowcasting,** *advertisers seek to reduce waste.*

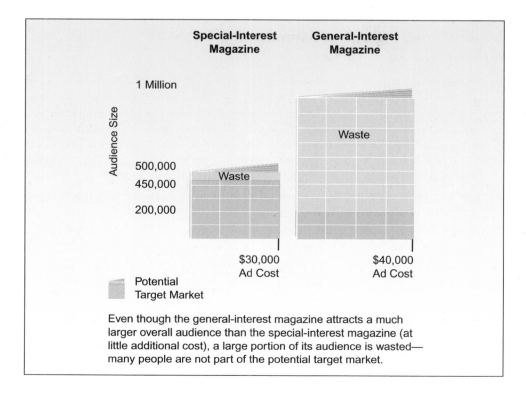

Even though the general-interest magazine attracts a much larger overall audience than the special-interest magazine (at little additional cost), a large portion of its audience is wasted—many people are not part of the potential target market.

FIGURE 18-4
Waste in Advertising

narrowcasting. As one observer recently noted about narrowcasting: "It's well known that targeting is the name of the game in advertising, although a lot of companies forget that rule. You may be able to buy national media at half the cost per thousand impressions; but if you're only reaching a sliver of your target market, and only reaching them once, you're better off buying locally."[8]

Frequency *is highest for daily media.*

Frequency refers to how often a medium can be used. It is greatest for the Internet, newspapers, radio, and TV. Different ads may appear daily and a strategy may be easily changed. Phone directories, outdoor ads, and magazines have the poorest frequency. A Yellow Pages ad can be placed only once per year.

Clutter *occurs when there are many ads.*

Clutter involves the number of ads found in a single program, issue, and so forth, of a medium. It is low when few ads are presented, such as Hallmark placing only scattered commercials on the TV specials for which it is the exclusive sponsor. It is high when there are many ads, such as the large number of supermarket ads in a newspaper's Wednesday issue. Overall, magazines have the highest clutter. And TV is criticized for allowing too much clutter, particularly for assigning more time per hour to commercials and for letting firms show very brief messages (e.g., 15 seconds or shorter). About one-third of all television ads are 15-second spots.

Lead time *is needed for placing an ad.*

Lead time is the period required by a medium for placing an ad. It is shortest for newspapers and longest for magazines and phone directories. Popular TV shows may also require a lengthy lead time since the number of ads they can carry is limited. Because a firm must place ads well in advance, with a long lead time, it risks improper themes in a changing environment.

There have been many recent media innovations. These include online computer services such as America Online (www.aol.com) and other services that let people "surf the Web"; regional editions and special one-sponsor issues ("advertorials") to revitalize magazines; specialized Yellow Pages; TV ads in supermarkets, movie theaters, and aircraft; more radio stations handling ads in stereo; better quality in outdoor signs; and full-length advertising programs ("infomercials").[9]

According to Forrester Research, in 1960, the typical U.S. consumer had access to 4 TV channels, 18 local radio stations, and 4,500 magazine titles. As of 2004, the typical U.S. consumer will have access to 44 local radio stations, 200 TV channels, 2,400 Internet radio stations, 18,000 magazine titles, and 20 million Internet sites.[10]

18-4f Creating Advertisements

In creating ads, there are four fundamental decisions:

Ad creation involves content, scheduling, media placement, and variations.

1. *Determine message content and devise ads.* Each ad needs a headline or opening to create interest, and copy that presents the message. Content decisions also involve the use of color and illustrations, ad size or length, the source, the use of symbolism, and the adaptations needed for foreign markets. The role of these factors depends on a firm's goals and resources. Figure 18-5 shows a humorous ad for Purina Dog Chow (www.dogchow.com), while Figure 18-6 shows a high-gloss ad for the Olympus Stylus Epic camera (www.olympusamerica.com).

2. *Outline a promotion schedule.* This should allow for all copy and artwork and be based on the lead time needed for the chosen media.

3. *Specify each ad's location in a broadcast program or print medium.* As costs have risen, more firms have become concerned about ad placement.

4. *Choose how many variations of a basic message to use.* This depends on the frequency of presentations and the ad quality.

---

[8]Joe Ashbook Nickell, "Ads in the 'Hood," *Business 2.0* (December 12, 2000), p. 146.

[9]See Evantheia Shibstead, "Ab Rockers, Ginsu Knives, E320s," *Business 2.0* (May 29, 2001), pp. 46–49.

[10]Forrester Research, "Media Overload," *Business 2.0* (October 24, 2000), p. 126.

FIGURE 18-5
Subtle Humor and Purina Dog Chow
Source: Reprinted by permission.

FIGURE 18-6
A Stylish Ad from Olympus
Source: Reprinted by permission.

18-4g Timing Advertisements

Timing refers to how often an ad is shown and when to advertise during the year.

There are two major decisions about the timing of ads: how often an ad is shown and when to advertise during the year. First, a firm must balance audience awareness and knowledge versus irritation if it places an ad several times in a very short period. McDonald's (www.mcdonalds.com) runs ads often, but changes them repeatedly. Second, a firm must choose whether to advertise over the year or in certain periods. *Distributed ads* hold brand recognition and increase sales in nonpeak periods. They are used by most manufacturers and general-merchandise retailers. *Massed ads* are used in peak times to foster short-run consumer interest; they ignore nonpeak periods. Specialty manufacturers and retailers use this method.

Other timing considerations include when to advertise new products, when to stop advertising existing products, how to coordinate advertising and other promotional tools, when to change basic themes, and how to space messages during the hierarchy-of-effects process.

18-4h Considering Cooperative Efforts

*In **cooperative advertising,** costs are shared by multiple parties.*

To stimulate advertising by channel members and/or to hold down its own ad budget, a firm should consider cooperative efforts. With **cooperative advertising,** two or more firms share some advertising costs. In *vertical cooperative advertising*, firms at different stages in a distribution channel (such as a manufacturer and a wholesaler) share costs. In *horizontal cooperative advertising*, two or more independent firms at the same stage in a distribution channel share costs (such as retailers in a mall).

Good agreements state the share of costs paid by each party, the functions and responsibilities of each party, the advertisements to be covered, and the basis for termination. They also benefit each participant.

Each year, $15 to $20 billion in vertical-cooperative advertising support is made available by manufacturers in the United States. Yet, distribution intermediaries actually use only two-thirds of this amount. The nonuse by so many resellers is due to their perceptions of manufacturer inflexibility with messages and media, the costs of cooperative advertising to the resellers, restrictive provisions (such as high minimum purchases to be eligible), and the emphasis on manufacturer names in ads. To remedy this, more manufacturers are now flexible as to the messages and media they support, pay a larger share of advertising costs, have eased restrictive provisions, and feature reseller names more prominently in ads.

18-4i Evaluating Success or Failure

The assessment of advertising depends on how well it helps to reach promotion goals. Gaining awareness and expanding sales are distinct goals; success or failure in reaching them must be measured differently. Advertising can also be quite difficult to isolate as the one factor leading to a certain image or sales level.

Here are various examples dealing with the evaluation of advertising's success or failure:

- The typical U.S. consumer is bombarded with hundreds of advertising messages each day. According to a major research study, two-thirds of people believe a nationally advertised brand creates the perception that it is of better quality than brands that are not heavily advertised, and in choosing among two unfamiliar brands, two-thirds of people will select the one advertised most.[11]

- In a survey asking TV viewers to name both a particularly irritating, disliked ad and an ad they enjoyed watching, 15 percent more respondents cited an ad that they liked than one that they disliked, and twice as many respondents could describe the ad they liked than the ad they disliked.[12]

- A study for the Association of National Advertisers (www.ana.net) indicated that advertising is a reliable way to boost sales but is less consistent in raising market share and profits.[13]

---

[11]"Advertising Makes the Difference," *Advertising Age* (January 15, 1996), p. 30.

[12]Gerald Stone, Donna Besser, and Loran E. Lewis, "Recall, Liking, and Creativity in TV Commercials: A New Approach," *Journal of Advertising Research*, Vol. 40 (May-June 2000), pp. 7–18.

[13]Gary Levin, "Ads Show Power to Help Sales," *Advertising Age* (December 13, 1993), p. 28.

ETHICAL Issues in Marketing

Should There Be a "Cocktail Hour" on Television?

The U.S. liquor industry had a self-imposed ban on radio and television advertising from the repeal of Prohibition in the 1930s until 1996, when the industry quietly dropped the ban. As a result, annual liquor advertising on radio and television has increased from virtually nothing to $20 million. Although this amount is less than one-tenth of the $255 million the liquor industry spends on print media, some brands have begun large TV campaigns. As a spokesperson for the Distilled Spirits Council of the United States (www.discus.health.org) puts it, "We [the hard liquor industry] vie for market share with beer and wine and yet we're being discriminated against. All forms of beverage alcohol should be judged by the same criteria. There's no such thing as soft and hard alcohol—alcohol is alcohol."

Joe Tripoli, the chief marketing officer at the Seagram Spirits and Wine Group (www.seagram.com) says, "TV is the quickest way to build a brand." He believes that it should be possible to advertise on TV and reach an audience that is overwhelmingly adult. Thus, the existence of programs and whole networks that are tailored to adults explains why the industry has been able to drop its ban on broadcast media.

Because national television networks and most cable networks still ban liquor advertising, the media buyers for the industry often bypass the networks and purchase advertising time directly from local station affiliates or cable system operators. As a result, more than 100 local television station affiliates in close to 90 markets now accept Seagram's liquor ads. Many local radio stations have also been willing to accept liquor advertising.

As an executive with a television station, develop a policy for accepting or rejecting hard-liquor advertising.

Source: Based on material in Patricia Winters Lauro, "Advertising: Cocktail Hour Returns to TV," *New York Times on the Web* (December 7, 2000).

- A survey of regular magazine readers found that 40 percent feel too many products do not perform as well as ads claim, 37 percent think advertising is more manipulative than informative, and 37 percent believe much of advertising is way too annoying.[14]

- Around the world, the EFFIE Awards (www.effie.org) are presented annually for outstanding ad efforts: "Winning an EFFIE is about meeting a challenge and succeeding. What makes a winning entry? Campaigns need to successfully combine all the disciplines that enter into a successful marketing program: planning, market research, media, creative, and account management. They must demonstrate a partnership between agency and client in the creation, management, and building of a brand. Twenty years ago, the EFFIE awards program crossed the border from the United States and introduced itself to the ad community in Germany. Other nations soon followed suit in recognizing its importance and prestige and the need to salute effective ads in their own markets. There are currently 18 national EFFIE programs. In addition, there is the EURO EFFIE competition for campaigns that have proven to be effective in at least three European countries."[15]

[14]Abhilasha Mehta, "Advertising Attitudes and Advertising Effectiveness," *Journal of Advertising Research*, Vol. 40 (May-June 2000), p. 69.

[15]"The EFFIE Awards: The Award for Effective Advertising," www.effie.org/what.htm (May 19, 2001).

18-5 THE SCOPE AND IMPORTANCE OF PUBLIC RELATIONS

Public relations efforts can have a major impact.

Each firm would like to foster the best possible relations with its publics and to receive favorable publicity about its offerings or the firm itself, such as "Amica Insurance (www.amica.com) is considered one of the top insurance firms by this magazine." Sometimes, as with restaurant or theater reviews, publicity can greatly increase sales or virtually put a firm out of business.

In the United States, thousands of firms and hundreds of trade associations have their own public relations departments, and there are 1,800 public relations agencies. The leading U.S. organization in the field is the Public Relations Society of America (www.prsa.org), which has almost 20,000 members around the globe. The International Public Relations Association (www.ipra.org) has 1,000 members from 80 nations; nevertheless, the role of public relations varies greatly by nation:

> Globalization of business has created the need for international public relations practitioners to identify, study, and understand the world view, mindsets, and habits of their global publics in order to effectively communicate. Some of the approaches used in contrasting cultural values that may be helpful to the international PR practitioners are: (1) individualism versus collectivism, (2) high-context and low-context communication styles, (3) degree of media independence and cultural impact on media content and channels, and (4) orientation to time. To be successful abroad, international PR practitioners have to recognize that the strong belief in rugged individualism is essentially an American trait which many other societies may not necessarily welcome.[16]

The competition to gain media attention for publicity is intense. In the United States, there are rather few national television networks and only 87 magazines and newspapers with circulations of one million or more. However, there are many opportunities for publicity—with 4,800 AM radio stations, 5,700 FM radio stations, 1,570 conventional television stations, 10,500 newspapers, and 11,000 periodicals around the United States. In addition, there are 11,000 cable television systems and millions of Web sites.[17]

Some firms have poor policies to deal with their publics and the media, and do not have a sustained public relations approach. Table 18-7 shows public relations-related situations and how a firm could deal with them. Since unfavorable publicity can happen to any firm, a successful one will have a plan to handle it. A firm may foster media fairness by being candid and communicating promptly; media may be used to explain complex issues; and preconceived ideas may be dispelled by cooperating with reporters.

Public relations encompasses image-directed ads, selling, and sales promotion—as well as publicity.

The interrelationship of public relations and other promotion forms must be understood. If advertising, personal selling, and sales promotion are image-oriented, public relations is involved. If they are demand-oriented, it is not. Figure 18-7 shows the interface between public relations and other promotion tools. Figures 18-8 and 18-9 show two effective institutional ads.

For organizations of all sizes and types,

> Public relations is a necessary part of the marketing mix. This is as true for the two-person SOHO (small office/home office) operation as it is for the multinational corporation. Lack of a big budget for PR is no excuse: Public relations has been called the last free thing in America, and that's very nearly true. It's possible to run a whole PR campaign with a pen, a fax machine, and a little brainpower. A lot of PR has to do with timing. The real name of the game in public relations is contacts—the editors, reporters, and other media people you need to get your story out.[18]

---

[16]Augustine Ihator, "Understanding the Cultural Patterns of the World—An Imperative in Implementing Strategic International PR Programs," *Public Relations Quarterly*, Vol. 45 (Winter 2000), pp. 38–44.

[17]*Statistical Abstract of the United States 2000* (Washington, D.C.: U.S. Department of Commerce, 2000), various pages.

[18]Gene Koprowski, "Extra: Smart Companies Use Public Relations Tactics to Get Good Ink," *Marketing Tools* (October 1995), p. 48.

TABLE 18-7   **Public Relations-Related Situations and How a Firm Could Respond to Them**

Situation	Poor Response	Good Response
Fire breaks out in a company plant	Requests for information by media are ignored.	Company spokesperson explains the fire's causes and the precautions to avoid it, and answers questions.
New product introduced	Advertising is used without publicity.	Pre-introduction news releases, product samples, and testimonials are used.
News story about product defects	Media requests for information are ignored, blanket denials are issued, and there is hostility to reporters.	Company spokesperson says tests are being done, describes the procedure for handling defects, and takes questions.
Competitor introduces new product	A demand-oriented advertising campaign is stepped up.	Extensive news releases, statistics, and spokespeople are made available to media to present firm's competitive features.
High profits reported	Profits are justified and positive effects on the economy are cited.	Profits are explained, comparative data are provided, and profit uses are noted: research and community development.
Overall view of public relations	There is an infrequent need for public relations; crisis fighting is used when bad reports are circulated.	There is an ongoing need for public relations, strong planning, and plans to counter bad reports.

18-6 THE CHARACTERISTICS OF PUBLIC RELATIONS

Public relations offers several benefits. Since it is image-oriented, good feelings toward a firm by its external publics can be fostered. In addition, employee morale (pride) is enhanced if the firm is community and civic minded.

When publicity is involved, there are no costs for message time or space. A prime-time television ad may cost $300,000 to $750,000 or more per minute of media time; a five-minute report on a network newscast does not cost anything for media time. Yet,

Public relations engenders good feelings; publicity has no time costs, a large audience, high credibility, and attentiveness.

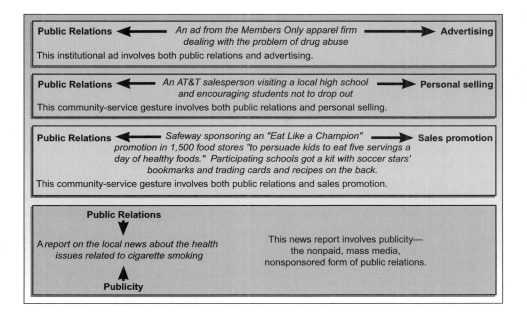

FIGURE 18-7
The Relationship Between Public Relations and the Other Elements of the Promotion Mix

Public Relations ← An ad from the Members Only apparel firm dealing with the problem of drug abuse → Advertising
This institutional ad involves both public relations and advertising.

Public Relations ← An AT&T salesperson visiting a local high school and encouraging students not to drop out → Personal selling
This community-service gesture involves both public relations and personal selling.

Public Relations ← Safeway sponsoring an "Eat Like a Champion" promotion in 1,500 food stores "to persuade kids to eat five servings a day of healthy foods." Participating schools got a kit with soccer stars' bookmarks and trading cards and recipes on the back. → Sales promotion
This community-service gesture involves both public relations and sales promotion.

Public Relations
A report on the local news about the health issues related to cigarette smoking
This news report involves publicity— the nonpaid, mass media, nonsponsored form of public relations.
Publicity

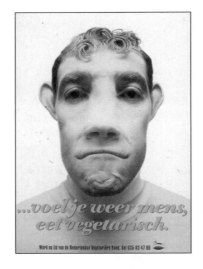

there are costs for news releases, a public relations department, and so on. As with advertising, publicity reaches a mass audience. In a short time, new products or company policies are well known.

Message believability is higher with publicity since stories are in independent media. A newspaper's movie review is more credible than an ad in the same paper—the reader links independence with objectivity. Similarly, people may pay more attention to news than to ads. *Women's Wear Daily* (www.wwd.com) has both fashion reports and ads; people read the stories, but flip through ads. There are a dozen or more ads in a half-hour TV show and hundreds in a typical magazine; feature stories are fewer and thus stand out.

Public relations also has limitations, compared to other promotion forms. Some firms question the value of image-oriented communications and are disinterested in activities not directly tied to sales and profits. They may give the poor responses that were indicated in Table 18-7.

With publicity, a firm has less control over messages and their timing, placement, and coverage by the media. It may issue detailed press releases and find only parts cited in the media; and media may be more critical than a firm would like. Media tend to find disasters, scandals, and product recalls more newsworthy than press releases. This shows how intense bad publicity can be:

Public relations may be downplayed by some firms; publicity cannot be controlled or timed accurately by a company.

> Business manager Rick Mancini characterizes his school district's contract with Coca-Cola as nothing but a win-win situation. In exchange for agreeing to sell only Coke products through 2009 in school cafeterias and school functions, the district will get free teacher and student supplies and at least $15,000 a year in school vending machine commissions. Not to mention a new $60,000 concession stand for the district's football stadium. "It was an excellent deal for the district. If we didn't get the money from Coke, we'd have to get it from tax dollars." But recent negative publicity about the role of soft-drink companies in schools might make such lucrative deals obsolete. A Boston Children's Hospital study reported that just one soft drink a day gives children a 60 percent greater chance of becoming obese, regardless of what kind of food they eat or how much they exercise. Some school nutrition experts have urged the government to restrict the sale of soft drinks and snacks in schools to keep youngsters from filling up on junk food and skipping cafeteria meals. The U.S. Department of Agriculture, which administers the federal school lunch program, recently asked Congress for legal authority to regulate the foods and beverages that can be sold in schools.[19]

A firm may want publicity during certain periods, such as when a new product is introduced or a new store opened, but the media may not provide coverage until much later. Similarly, the media determine a story's placement; it may follow a crime or sports report. Finally, the media choose whether to cover a story at all and the amount of coverage for it. A firm-sponsored jobs program might go unreported or get three-sentence coverage in a local paper.

Publicity may be hard to plan in advance since newsworthy events occur quickly and unexpectedly. Thus, short-run and long-run public relations plans should differ in approach. Publicity must complement advertising and not be a substitute. The assets of each (credibility and low costs for publicity, control and coverage for ads) are needed for a good communications program.

To optimize their public relations efforts, at many companies

- Public relations personnel have regular access to senior executives.
- The publicity value of annual reports is recognized.
- Public relations messages are professionally prepared (with the same care as used in writing ad copy) and continuously given to media.
- Internal personnel and media personnel interaction is fostered.
- Public-service events are planned to obtain maximum media coverage.
- Part of the promotion budget goes to publicity-generating tasks.
- There is a better understanding of the kinds of stories the media are apt to cover and how to present stories to the media.[20]

[19]Gretchen McKay, "Negative Publicity Threatens School Funding Deals with Soft Drink Companies," *Knight-Ridder/Tribune Business News* (April 8, 2001), p. ITEM01098044.

[20]See Robert L. Dilenschneider, "Getting Your Message Across While Under Attack," *Public Relations Quarterly*, Vol. 45 (Summer 2000), pp. 9–11; William C. Adams, "Responding to the Media During a Crisis: It's What You Say and When You Say It," *Public Relations Quarterly*, Vol. 45 (Spring 2000), pp. 26–28; Meg Major, "Before It Hits the Fan," *Supermarket Business* (February 15, 2001), p. 65; and Betsy Spethmann, "Making an Impression," *Promo* (November 2000), pp. 81–84.

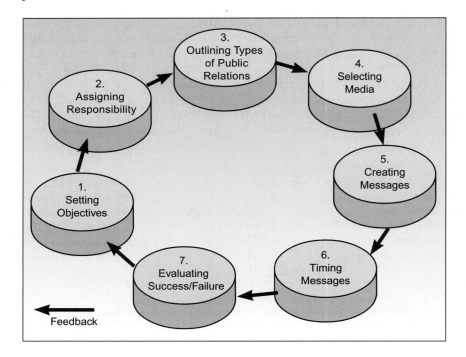

18-7 DEVELOPING A PUBLIC RELATIONS PLAN

Developing a public relations plan is much like devising an advertising plan. It involves the steps shown in Figure 18-10 and described next.

18-7a Setting Objectives

Public relations goals are image-oriented (firm and/or industry). The choice guides the entire public relations plan. These are some goals that could be set:

- To gain placement for news releases and appearances for company spokespersons with a variety of media.
- To have the media report on the accomplishments of the company.
- To have the company's viewpoint presented when controversy arises.
- To coordinate publicity with advertising.
- To gain more media coverage than competitors.
- To sustain favorable publicity as long as possible.
- To reach out to community groups.
- To have publics view the firm and its industry favorably.

In setting goals, this truism should be kept in mind: "PR involves both *performance* and *recognition*. It is possible to boast excellent performance without being properly recognized, but it is not possible to earn recognition that is not based on solid performance. Woe to the firm that tries to get the R (recognition) without the P (performance)."[21]

18-7b Assigning Responsibility

A firm can use an in-house department, hire an outside ad agency, or hire a specialist.

A firm has three options in assigning public relations responsibility: it may use its existing marketing personnel, an in-house public relations department, or an in-house publicity department; it may have an outside advertising agency handle public relations; or it

[21]Nat B. Read, "Sears PR Debacle Shows How Not to Handle a Crisis," *Wall Street Journal* (January 11, 1993), p. A16.

may hire a specialized public relations firm. Internal personnel or an in-house department ensure more control and secrecy. An outside firm often has better contacts and expertise. Each approach is popular, and they may be combined.

Procter & Gamble (www.pg.com) has an in-house publicity department and several outside public relations agencies. In contrast, some smaller firms rely on the services of specialists, which may charge annual fees of $25,000 to $50,000. Computer software, like Press Submitter (www.sharpspider.com/press) and Automated Press Releases (www.automatedpr.com), also let small firms easily arrange media contacts. Public Relations Online (www.public-relations-online.net) has a wealth of information on the industry and service providers.

GLOBAL *Marketing in Action*

U.S. Public Relations Blunders Overseas

The U.S. government's failure to include an Egyptian official as a partner in the team investigating the crash of an EgyptAir plane just after takeoff from New York is an example of insensitivity to foreign cultures. Although this public relations failure was the fault of the U.S. government, American companies have also been offenders.

Recent examples of improper attention to cultural sensitivity by U.S. firms involved Coca-Cola, Monsanto, McDonald's, Burger King, and Cargill. Coca-Cola conducted an overly aggressive acquisition campaign to buy up foreign soft-drink brands; Monsanto tried to promote genetically altered foods to Europeans who are very concerned about food safety; McDonald's and Burger King both unknowingly became involved in Middle East politics; and Cargill was incorrectly perceived by millions of small farmers as attempting to dominate the world's food supply.

It is not unusual to hear of American companies being characterized as "exploitative, swaggering, or imprudent." And the expressions "Bully" and "Ugly American" have been used. Some foreign critics are concerned that the American culture may come to dominate foreign cultures. Canada, for example, recently convened a summit of 129 nations to discuss strategies to filter out American movies and television to "protect local cultures." In no instance was the criticism caused by the inappropriateness of an American firm's objectives.

One way of avoiding potential cultures pitfalls is for American executives to realize that respect for foreign traditions and cultures deserves more serious attention in every company. Thus, patience and corporate diplomacy are necessary virtues that should hopefully avoid cultural errors.

What steps can a firm could take to avoid cultural insensitivities in its public relations efforts?

Source: Based on material in John F. Budd Jr., "Still the Ugly American," *Across the Board* (February 2000), p. 9.

18-7c Outlining the Types of Public Relations to Be Used

In this step, a firm first chooses the mix of institutional advertising, image-oriented personal selling, image-oriented sales promotion, and publicity to incorporate into an overall promotion plan. Next, public relations efforts must be coordinated with the demand-oriented promotion activities of the firm.

Finally, the general *publicity types* must be understood and envisioned. Each can play a role in an integrated public relations program:

Publicity types *include news, features, releases, background material, and emergency information.*

- *News publicity* deals with global, national, regional, or local events. Planned releases can be prepared and regularly given out by a firm.
- *Business feature articles* are detailed stories about its products that are given to business media.
- *Service feature articles* are lighter stories focusing on personal care, household items, and similar topics that are sent to newspapers, TV stations, magazines, and Internet sites.
- *Finance releases*, such as quarterly earnings, are stories aimed at the business sections of newspapers, TV news shows, magazines, and other media.
- *Product releases* deal with new products and product improvements; they aim at all media forms.
- *Pictorial releases* are illustrations or pictures sent to the media.
- *Video news releases* are videotaped segments supplied to the media.
- *Background editorial material* is extra information (like the biography of the chief executive of a firm) given to media writers and editors; it enhances standard releases and provides filler for stories.
- *Emergency publicity* consists of special spontaneous news releases keyed to unexpected events.[22]

18-7d Selecting the Media for Public Relations Efforts to Appear

For institutional ads, personal selling, and sales promotion, traditional nonpersonal and/or personal media would be used. For publicity, a firm would typically focus on newspapers, television, magazines, radio, business publications, and the Internet. Due to the infrequent nature of many magazines and some business publications, publicity-seeking efforts may be aimed at daily or weekly media.

Public relations executives rank newspapers and business publications the highest. The *Wall Street Journal* (www.wsj.com), *New York Times* (www.nytimes.com), and *USA Today* (www.usatoday.com) are preferred newspapers. *Business Week* (www.businessweek.com), *Fortune* (www.fortune.com), and *Forbes* (www.forbes.com) are preferred business publications. *Time* (www.time.com), *Newsweek* (www.newsweek-int.com), and *U.S. News & World Report* (www.usnews.com) are preferred general news magazines.

18-7e Creating Messages

Creating public relations messages entails the same factors as other promotion forms—content, variations, and a production schedule. Messages can be sent in one or a combination of forms, such as news conferences, media releases, phone calls or personal

---

[22]Adapted by the authors from Gordon C. Bruner II, "Public Relations," www.siu.edu/departments/coba/mktg/courses/mktg363/PR/sld009.htm (1998).

contacts, media kits (a group of materials on a story), special events (Macy's Thanksgiving Parade—www.nyctourist.com/macys_menu.htm), or videos.

Because it is essential that the media find a firm's publicity messages to be useful, these points need to be kept in mind:

1. Messages should be newsworthy.
2. Reporter deadlines should be respected.
3. Appropriate company representatives should be accessible to reporters.
4. "Mind-fogging" jargon should be avoided.
5. The phrase "no comment" should not be used.
6. Attribution rules (making the source and the content of a story "on" or "off" the record) should be set in advance.
7. A reporter should not be asked to kill a story.
8. Releases should be both easy to read, view, or hear and to use.
9. There should be no hesitancy to volunteer a "bad" story (it will probably get out anyway).
10. Attention should be paid to the needs of each type of medium.[23]

18-7f Timing Messages

Public relations efforts should precede new-product introductions and generate excitement for them. For emergencies, media releases and spokespeople should be immediately available. For ongoing public relations, messages should be properly spaced through the year. As already noted, a firm may find it hard to anticipate media coverage for both unexpected and planned publicity since the media control timing.

18-7g Evaluating Success or Failure

There are several straightforward ways to rate a public relations campaign:

- With institutional ads, image-oriented personal selling, and image-oriented sales promotion, a firm can conduct simple surveys to see how well these communications are received and their impact on its image.

- With publicity, a firm can count the stories about it, analyze coverage length and placement, review desired with actual timing of stories, evaluate audience reactions, and/or compute the cost of comparable advertising.

- Firms such as Wal-Mart now track the *quality*, as well as the quantity of media coverage. Wal-Mart classifies items as news stories, letters to the editor, editorials, or opinion articles.

- Through the Internet, companies can track media coverage rather simply. For example, 1st Headlines (www.1stheadlines.com) can do a key-word search for stories appearing in media around the world.

[23]Christel K. Beard and H. J. Dalton, Jr., "The Power of Positive Press," *Sales & Marketing Management* (January 1991), pp. 37–43. See also Daniel P. Dern, "News That's Fit to Print," *Marketing Tools* (October 1995), pp. 52–53.

 *WEB SITES YOU CAN USE*

> There are numerous Web sites that provide access to current and past advertisements. Many offer real-time video commercials. Here is a cross-section of sites where you can view or read ads [Please note: TV ads are best viewed through a high-speed connection. The download time may be lengthy with a telephone modem]:

AdCritic.com (www.adcritic.com)—TV commercials

Adeater (www.adeater.com)—Click on "Cinema library" to access thousands of TV commercials from around the world

Adflip (www.adflip.com)—Print ads

AdReview (www.adreview.com)—TV commercials

Advertising Council (www.adcouncil.org/fr_camp.html)—Multimedia public service announcements (PSAs)

USA TV Ads (www.usatvads.com)—TV commercials

SUMMARY

1. *To examine the scope, importance, and characteristics of advertising* Advertising is paid, nonpersonal communication sent through various media by identified sponsors. Worldwide ad spending is $500 billion annually, one-half in the United States, via such media as TV, newspapers, direct mail, radio, Yellow Pages, magazines, business publications, the Internet, and outdoor (billboards). In the United States, advertising is under 5.0 percent of sales in three-quarters of industries.

Ads are most apt with standardized products and when features are easy to communicate, the market is large, prices are low, resellers are used in distribution, and/or products are new. In general, behavior is easier to change than attitudes; one ad can have an impact; ads do well with little-known products; and effectiveness rises during extended campaigns.

Among advertising's advantages are its appeal to a geographically dispersed audience, low per-customer costs, the availability of a broad variety of media, the firm's control over all aspects of a message, the surrounding editorial content, and how it complements personal selling. Disadvantages include message inflexibility, some viewers or readers not in the target audience, high media costs, limited information provided, difficulty in getting audience feedback, and low audience involvement.

2. *To study the elements in an advertising plan* An advertising plan has nine steps: setting goals—demand and image types; assigning duties—internal and/or external; setting a budget; developing themes—good/service, consumer, and institutional; selecting media—based on costs, reach, waste, message permanence, persuasive impact, narrowcasting, frequency, clutter, lead time, and media innovations; creating ads—including content, placement, and variations; timing ads; considering cooperative efforts—both vertical and horizontal; and evaluating success or failure.

3. *To examine the scope, importance, and characteristics of public relations* Public relations includes any communication that fosters a favorable image among a firm's various publics. It is more image- than sales-oriented; embodies image-oriented ads, personal selling, and sales promotion; and seeks favorable publicity—the nonpersonal communication sent via various media but not paid for by identified sponsors. There are thousands of companies with their own public relations departments and many specialized public relations firms. Companies try to get positive publicity and to avoid negative publicity. Competition is intense for placing publicity releases. Some firms have ineffective policies to deal with independent media or develop a sustained publicity campaign.

Among its advantages are the image orientation, the positive effects on employee morale, and—for publicity—the lack of costs for message time, the high credibility, and audience attentiveness. The disadvantages of public relations—compared with other promotion forms—include the lack of interest by some firms in image-oriented communications and the lesser control of publicity placements by the firm, the media interest in negative events, and the difficulty of planning publicity in advance.

4. *To study the elements in a public relations plan* A public relations plan has seven steps: setting goals—company and/or industry; assigning duties—internally and/or externally; outlining types of public relations—the mix of image-oriented promotion forms and the categories of publicity (news publicity, business and service feature articles, finance releases, product and pictorial releases, video news releases, background editorial releases, and emergency publicity); choosing media; creating messages; timing messages; and weighing success or failure.

KEY TERMS

advertising agency (p. 540)
advertising themes (p. 541)
advertising media costs (p. 541)
reach (p. 545)
waste (p. 545)

message permanence (p. 545)
persuasive impact (p. 545)
narrowcasting (p. 545)
frequency (p. 546)

clutter (p. 546)
lead time (p. 546)
cooperative advertising (p. 548)
publicity types (p. 556)

REVIEW QUESTIONS

1. Explain the statement "Advertising is paid for, publicity is prayed for."
2. List five objectives of advertising and give an example of how each may be accomplished.
3. A small firm has an overall annual budget of $30,000 for advertising. What specific decisions must it make in allocating the budget?

4. Differentiate among these advertising concepts: reach, narrowcasting, waste, clutter, and frequency.
5. What are the pros and cons of cooperative advertising?
6. Describe the role of public relations in many foreign countries.
7. According to public relations executives, which are the two most preferred media for receiving publicity?
8. State three ways for a firm to evaluate the success or failure of its public relations efforts.

DISCUSSION QUESTIONS

1. Devise an advertising plan for generating primary demand for American-made radios.
2. A motel chain knows a full-page ad in a general-interest magazine would cost $75,000; the magazine's total audience is 2.5 million—800,000 of whom are part of the chain's target market. A full-page ad in a travel magazine would cost $30,000; its total audience is 375,000—300,000 of whom are part of the chain's target market. Which magazine should be selected? Why?

3. Present and evaluate current examples of companies using institutional advertising, image-oriented personal selling, image-oriented sales promotion, and publicity.
4. How would you obtain publicity for a small company that has developed a "talking" computer—one that gives instructions on how to set up the computer, how to use various software, and how to diagnose and correct computer errors?

WEB EXERCISE

Go to the Web site of *Advertising Age* (www.adage.com), and visit the "Ad Age Dataplace." Discuss five interesting facts that you obtain from the Web site and state their implications for marketers.

19

Personal Selling and Sales Promotion

Chapter Objectives

1 To examine the scope, importance, and characteristics of personal selling

2 To study the elements in a personal selling plan

3 To examine the scope, importance, and characteristics of sales promotion

4 To study the elements in a sales promotion plan

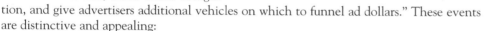

V H1 (www.vh1.com), the cable music TV channel founded in 1985 as an offshoot of MTV (www.mtv.com), now reaches 75 million "active, music-loving cable subscribers aged 18 to 49 with (primarily) mainstream pop-music programming. And like sister network MTV, it reaches those viewers by going beyond music videos." A large part of VH1's success is due to its heavy use of special events (sales promotion) in its marketing efforts.

As *Promo* magazine recently reported, "Events are now cornerstones of VH1's regular broadcast rotation, used to attract and retain viewers, build brand recognition, and give advertisers additional vehicles on which to funnel ad dollars." These events are distinctive and appealing:

- The celebrity-filled *Fairway to Heaven* golf tourney.
- The similarly celebrity-packed *VH1 Backyard Bar-B-Q*.
- The *Divas Live* series.
- The *VH1/Vogue Fashion Awards*.

VH1 group vice-president of marketing Mark McIntire notes, "The world of music is always changing, And we understand the importance of music in a marketing message."

How popular are VH1's special events? Here's what *Promo* says: "BMW USA used its sponsorship with the *VH1/Vogue Fashion Awards* to launch its high-priced Z8 model in the New York City area. *Divas Live* sponsor Maybelline rolled out a *Diva Hits* cosmetics line, and commissioned some 25,000 point-of-purchase displays to support it. Boston Beer Company's Samuel Adams brand linked to the summer *Rock Across America* program with a "Grill and Groove" sweepstakes that served winners cold beer and a Stone Temple Pilots concert (Webcast supported). Kia activated its *Fairway to Heaven* sponsorship with a dealership sweepstakes on the West Coast."[1]

Next, we will study the personal selling and sales promotion aspects of promotion and see how these tools can be used effectively.

19-1 OVERVIEW

This chapter looks at the other major promotion forms: personal selling and sales promotion. As defined in Chapter 17, *personal selling* involves oral communication with one or more prospective buyers by paid representatives for the purpose of making sales. It relies on personal contact, unlike advertising and publicity. Its goals are similar to other promotion forms: informing, persuading, and/or reminding.

Sales promotion involves paid marketing communication activities (other than advertising, publicity, or personal selling) that stimulate consumers and dealers. Among the

Personal selling is one-on-one with buyers. Sales promotion includes paid supplemental efforts.

[1]"Behind the Music," *Promo* (December 2000), pp. 86–87.

kinds of promotion classed as sales promotion are coupons, trade shows, contests and sweepstakes, and point-of-purchase displays.

The scope and importance, characteristics, and planning considerations for both personal selling and sales promotion are examined in Chapter 19.

19-2 THE SCOPE AND IMPORTANCE OF PERSONAL SELLING

In the United States, 16 million people work in the sales positions defined by the Department of Labor (www.dol.gov); millions more in other nations are also employed in sales jobs. Professional salespeople generate new customers, ascertain needs, interact with consumers, emphasize knowledge and persuasion, and offer service. They include stockbrokers, insurance agents, manufacturer sales representatives, and real-estate brokers. Top ones can earn more than $100,000 per year. Clerical salespeople answer simple queries, retrieve stock from inventory, recommend the best brand in a category, and complete orders by receiving payments and packing products. They include retail, wholesale, and manufacturer sales clerks.

From a marketing perspective, personal selling really goes far beyond the people in identified sales positions because every contact between a company representative and a customer entails some personal interaction. Lawyers, hairdressers, and cashiers are not defined as salespeople. Yet, they have lots of customer contact. Both ConAgra (www.conagra.com) and Home Depot (www.homedepot.com) know the value of customer contact. See Figures 19-1 and 19-2.

In various situations, a strong personal-selling emphasis may be needed. Large-volume customers require special attention. Geographically concentrated consumers may be more efficiently served by a sales force than via ads in mass media. Custom-made, expensive, and complex goods or services require in-depth consumer information, demonstrations, and follow-up calls. Tangential sales services—like gift wrapping and delivery—may be requested. If ads are not informative enough, questions can be resolved only by personal selling. New products may need personal selling to gain reseller acceptance. Foreign-market entry may be best handled by personal contacts with prospective resellers and/or consumers. Finally, many organizational customers expect a lot of personal contact.

Selling is stressed when orders are large, consumers are concentrated, items are expensive, and service is required.

FIGURE 19-1
Personal Selling Throughout the Channel

ConAgra recognizes that it has two customers: the stores that purchase its food products and the final consumers who buy them. To enhance its relationship marketing efforts, the firm has increased its in-store sales force. This is part of an overall program to provide greater ordering and display support for resellers, as well as to encourage more frequent communication with store personnel.

Source: Reprinted by permission.

FIGURE 19-2
Personal Selling and the Final Consumer

One of the major reasons why Home Depot has become the dominant home improvement chain is the strength of its sales staff. At Home Depot, sales associates "take great pride in providing the very best in customer service. Our stores offer a variety of services, including free design and decorating consultations, truck and tool rental, home delivery, free potting, and many services to accommodate our customers' home improvement needs. To ensure complete satisfaction, Home Depot offers our No Hassle Return Policy on every item in our stores. And our free in-store clinics help homeowners develop their do-it-yourself skills."

Source: Reprinted by permission.

Generally, a decision to stress personal selling depends on such factors as costs, audience size and needs, and a desire for flexibility.

Selling costs are often greater than advertising costs. Auto parts firms, office and equipment firms, and appliance makers all spend far more on selling than on ads. Fuller Brush (www.fullerbrush.com) sales commissions range up to 50 percent of sales. The average cost of a single business-to-business field sales call is several hundred dollars; and it may take several visits to make a sale.

A number of strategies have been devised to keep selling costs down and improve the efficiency of the sales force, as these examples show:

- Many firms are more effectively routing salespeople to minimize travel time and expenses. Some firms are bypassing smaller customers in their personal selling efforts and specifying minimum order sizes for personalized service. This means opportunities for sellers willing to serve small accounts.

- With **telemarketing,** telephone communications are used to sell or solicit business or to set up an appointment for a salesperson to sell or solicit business. Salespeople can talk to several consumers per hour, centralize operations and lower expenses, screen prospects, process orders and arrange shipments, provide customer service, assist the field sales staff, speed communications, and increase repeat business. A lot of companies rely on telephone personnel to contact customers; outside sales personnel (who actually call on customers) are then more involved with customer service and technical assistance. A broad range of small and large firms use some form of telemarketing. The American Teleservices Association (www.ataconnect.org) is dedicated exclusively to telemarketing issues.

- Computerization is improving efficiency by providing salespeople detailed and speedy data, making ordering easier, coordinating orders by various salespeople, and identifying the best prospects and their desires (such as preferred brands)—based on prior purchases. Many salespeople use their laptop computers to communicate with the home office to get the latest product data, learn about inventory status, and so on. Firms are also using the Internet to train salespeople. In nearly every issue, *Sales & Marketing Management* (www.salesandmarketing.com) reports on computerization and selling.

- A lot of firms now view computerized customer data bases as among their most valuable sales resources. These data bases enable the firms to focus efforts better, make sure key accounts are regularly serviced, and use direct mailings to complement telephone calls and salesperson visits.

High selling costs have led to a concern for efficiency. In **telemarketing,** *phone calls initiate sales or set up sales appointments.*

19-3 THE CHARACTERISTICS OF PERSONAL SELLING

*Selling uses a **buyer-seller dyad** and is flexible and efficient, closes sales, and provides feedback.*

On the positive side, personal selling provides individual attention for each consumer and passes on a lot of information. There is a dynamic interplay between buyer and seller. This lets a firm use a ***buyer-seller dyad,*** the two-way flow of communication between both parties. See Figure 19-3. That is not possible with advertising. Thus, personal selling can be flexible and adapted to specific consumer needs. For example, a real-estate broker can use one sales presentation with a first-time buyer and another with a person who has already bought a home. A salesperson can also apply as much persuasion as needed and balance it against the need for information. Furthermore, through the buyer-seller dyad, a *relationship selling* approach is possible, whereby customer bonds may be developed. Consider this example: "Andy Jacobson sells insurance. And people don't avoid him. Successful as an insurance salesperson, then as a sales manager, now the owner of his own firm, Meridian Benefits Group, Andy still calls what he does business, but he's reluctant to call it selling. 'I just build relationships. The rest takes care of itself.'"[2]

Personal selling targets a more defined and concentrated audience, which means less waste than with ads. In addition, people who enter a store or who are contacted by a salesperson are more apt to buy than those watching a TV ad. Since ads stimulate interest, those who make it to the personal selling stage are often in the target market. When unsolicited, direct selling has the most waste in personal selling.

Selling clinches sales and is usually conducted during the purchase stage of the consumer's decision process, taking place after information search and exposure to ads. It holds repeat customers and those already convinced by advertising—and resolves any concerns of undecided consumers by answering questions about price, warranty, and other factors. It settles service issues, like delivery and installation. Feedback is immediate and clear-cut: Consumers may be asked their feelings about product features or they may complain; and salespeople may unearth a marketing program's strengths and weaknesses.

Selling has a limited audience, high costs per customer, and a poor image.

On the negative side, selling is ineffective for generating awareness because salespeople can handle only a limited number of consumers. A retail furniture salesperson may be able to talk to fewer than 20 people per day if the average length of a customer contact is 15 minutes to a half hour. Sales personnel who call on customers can handle even fewer accounts, due to travel. In addition, many consumers drawn by advertising may want self-service. This is discouraged by some aggressive salespeople.

FIGURE 19-3
The Buyer-Seller Dyad

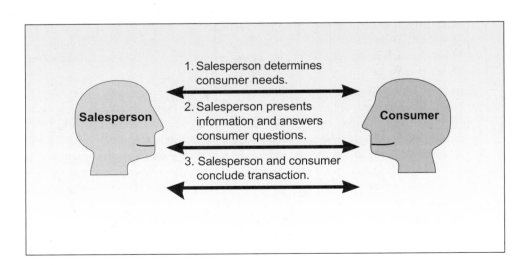

[2]Jeffrey Gitomer, "Don't Think of It as Selling. It's Relationship Building," *Washington Business Journal* (December 1, 2000), p. 49.

Personal selling costs per customer can be very high due to the one-on-one nature of selling. An in-store furniture salesperson who talks to 20 customers daily might cost a firm $7 per presentation ($140/day compensation divided by 20), an amount much higher than an ad's cost per-customer contact. For outside salespeople, hotel stays, meals, and transportation can amount to $200 or more daily per salesperson, and compensation must be added to these costs.[3]

Finally, personal selling, especially among final consumers, has a poor image. It is criticized for a lack of honesty and pressure tactics:

> The public's consistent interpretation of the term *salesperson* has provided fodder for many dramatic works, anecdotes, and jokes that reflect the widely held negative stereotype of salespeople. As a result, people may avoid them deliberately. The consumer practice of visiting car dealerships after business hours personifies a common reaction to salespeople. This practice may be due to beliefs that consumers can evaluate alternative cars better in the absence of the "dreaded" salesperson. Sometimes, salespeople may even inhibit, rather than facilitate, mutually satisfying exchanges.[4]

The situation can be improved by better sales-force training and the use of consumer-oriented rather than seller-oriented practices. Industry organizations such as the Direct Selling Association (www.dsa.org), Manufacturers' Agents National Association (www.manaonline.org), and National Association of Sales Professionals (www.nasp.com) are also striving to improve the image of personal selling.

19-4 DEVELOPING A PERSONAL SELLING PLAN

A personal selling plan can be divided into the seven steps shown in Figure 19-4 and highlighted here.

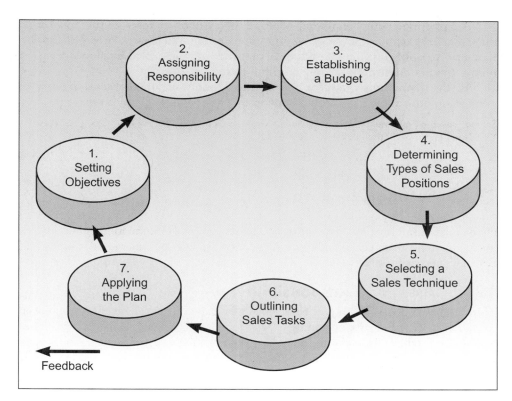

FIGURE 19-4

Developing a Personal Selling Plan

---

[3]"Costs on the Road," *Sales & Marketing Management* (April 2001), p. 11.

[4]Barry J. Babin, James S. Boles, and William R. Darden, "Salesperson Stereotypes, Consumer Emotions, and Their Impact on Information Processing," *Journal of the Academy of Marketing Science*, Vol. 23 (Spring 1995), p. 94. See also Mary Susan Kennedy, Linda K. Ferrell, and Debbie Thorne LeClair, "Consumers' Trust of Salesperson and Manufacturer: An Empirical Study," *Journal of Business Research*, Vol. 51 (January 2001), pp. 73–86.

ETHICAL *Issues in Marketing*

The Controversy Behind Free Drug Samples

A small, but growing, number of health care administrators at hospitals and clinics are either banning free samples of branded prescription drugs or limiting the number of samples their physicians may accept from pharmaceutical sales representatives. Even some hospitals which cater to uninsured patients are limiting the dispensing of samples. The administrators believe that since pharmaceutical firms typically give out samples of their most costly drugs (and rarely give out low-cost generics), sampling programs encourage physicians to prescribe higher-cost drugs even when a generic is just as effective.

Some hospitals and clinics have also decided to limit samples because of safety concerns. Unlike with prescriptions, where there is a record of a consumer's purchase of a medication, samples pass from doctors to patients with no paper trail. Thus, there is no way of determining who had access to a drug that is later recalled or found to be unsafe for patients with various conditions.

Annually, pharmaceutical companies give U.S. physicians more than $7.5 billion worth of samples, valued at their retail price. (The actual cost of the free samples to the companies is generally between 20 and 30 percent of the retail value.) This is a growth of 10 percent over the value of samples given out just a couple of years ago. In comparison, pharmaceutical companies spend $2 billion in yearly advertising.

The pharmaceutical companies defend their use of samples on the basis of their role in educating physicians about new drugs. Industry spokespeople say that free samples also enable patients and their physicians to evaluate drugs before the patients spend money on a full dosage.

As the marketing manager for a major pharmaceutical manufacturer, present an ethical plan for drug sampling by pharmaceutical sales reps.

Source: Based on material in Melody Petersen, "Growing Opposition to Free Drug Samples," *New York Times on the Web,* (November 15, 2000).

19-4a Setting Objectives

Selling goals can be demand- and/or image-oriented. When image-oriented, they involve public relations. Although many firms have some interest in information, reminder, and image goals, the major goal usually is persuasion: converting consumer interest into a sale. Examples appear in Table 19-1.

19-4b Assigning Responsibility

A manager must oversee selling functions.

The personal selling function may be assigned to a marketing or sales manager who oversees all areas of selling, from planning to sales force management. A small or specialized firm is likely to have its marketing manager oversee selling or use one general sales manager. A large or diversified firm may have multiple sales managers—assigned by product line, customer type, and/or region.

These are the basic responsibilities of a sales manager:

- To understand the firm's goals, strategies, market position, and basic marketing plan and to convey them to the sales force.
- To determine and outline a sales philosophy, sales force characteristics, selling tasks, a sales organization, and methods of customer contact.

TABLE 19-1   Specific Personal Selling Objectives

Type of Objective	Illustrations
Demand-Oriented	
Information	To fully explain all attributes of goods and services To answer any questions To probe for any further questions
Persuasion	To distinguish attributes of goods or services from those of competitors To maximize the number of purchases relative to the presentations made To convert undecided consumers into buyers To sell complementary items—e.g., a telephoto lens with a camera To placate dissatisfied customers
Reminding	To ensure delivery, installation, etc. To follow-up after a good or service has been purchased To follow-up when a repurchase is near To reassure previous customers as they make a new purchase
Image-Oriented	
Industry and company	To have a good appearance for all personnel having customer contact To follow acceptable (ethical) sales practices To be respected by customers, employees, and other publics

- To prepare and update sales forecasts.
- To allocate selling resources based on sales forecasts and customer needs.
- To select, train, assign, compensate, and supervise sales personnel.
- To synchronize selling tasks with advertising, product planning, distribution, marketing research, production, and other activities.
- To assess sales performance by salesperson, product, product line, customer, customer group, and geographic area.
- To continuously monitor competitors' actions.
- To make sure the sales force acts in an ethical manner.
- To convey the image sought by the company.

19-4c Establishing a Budget

A *sales-expense budget* allots selling costs among salespeople, products, customers, and geographic areas for a given period. It is usually tied to a sales forecast and relates selling tasks to sales goals. It should be somewhat flexible in case expected sales are not reached or are exceeded.

These items should be covered in a budget: sales forecast, overhead (manager's compensation, office costs), sales force compensation, sales expenses (travel, lodging, meals, entertainment), sales meetings, selling aids (including computer equipment), and sales management (employee selection and training) costs. Table 19-2 shows a budget for a small maker of business machinery.

The budget will be larger if customers are geographically dispersed and a lot of travel is required. Complex products need costly, time-consuming sales presentations and result in fewer calls per salesperson. An expanding sales force needs expenditures for recruiting and training salespeople.

*A **sales-expense budget** assigns spending for a specific time*

TABLE 19-2

A Sales-Expense Budget for a Small Manufacturer Specializing in Business Machinery, 2001

Item	Estimated Annual Costs (Revenues)
Sales Forecast	$1,950,000
Overhead (1 sales manager, 1 office)	$100,000
Sales force compensation (2 salespeople)	90,000
Sales expenses	40,000
Sales meetings	5,000
Selling aids	15,000
Sales management costs	10,000
Total personal selling budget	$260,000
Personal selling costs as a percentage of sales forecast	13.3

19-4d Determining the Type(s) of Sales Positions

Salespeople can be broadly classed as order takers, order getters, or support personnel. Some firms employ one type of salesperson; others, a combination.

An **order taker** handles routine orders and sells items that are pre-sold.

An ***order taker*** processes routine orders and reorders. This person is involved more with clerical than creative selling, typically for pre-sold goods or services. He or she arranges displays, restocks items, answers simple questions, writes up orders, and completes transactions. He or she may work in a warehouse (manufacturer clerk) or store (retail clerk) or call on customers (a field salesperson). An order taker has these advantages for a firm: compensation is rather low, little training is required, both selling and nonselling tasks are performed, and a sales force can be expanded or contracted quickly. Yet, an order taker is an improper choice for goods and services that need creative selling or extensive information for customers. Personnel turnover is high. Enthusiasm may be limited due to the low salary and routine tasks.

An **order getter** obtains leads, provides information, persuades customers, and closes sales.

An ***order getter*** generates customer leads, provides information, persuades customers, and closes sales. He or she is the creative salesperson used for high-priced, complex, and/or new products. There is less emphasis on clerical work. The person may be inside (jewelry store salesperson) or outside (Xerox, www.xerox.com, salesperson). He or she is expert and enthusiastic, expands sales, and can convince undecided customers to buy or decided customers to add peripheral items—such as carpeting and appliances along with a newly built house. Yet, for many people, the order getter has a high-pressure image. He or she may also need expensive training. Such nonsales tasks as writing reports may be avoided because they take away from a seller's time with customers and are seldom rewarded. Compensation can be very high for salespersons who are effective order getters. Figure 19-5 contrasts order takers and order getters.

Missionary salespersons, sales engineers, and **service salespersons** are support personnel.

Support personnel supplement a sales force. A ***missionary salesperson*** gives out information on new goods or services. He or she does not close sales but describes items' attributes, answers questions, and leaves written matter. This paves the way for later sales and is commonly used with prescription drugs. A ***sales engineer*** accompanies an order getter if a very technical or complex item is involved. He or she discusses specifications and long-range uses, while the order getter makes customer contacts and closes sales. A ***service salesperson*** ordinarily deals with customers after sales. Delivery, installation, and other follow-up tasks are done.

19-4e Selecting a Sales Technique

The **canned sales presentation** is memorized and nonadaptive.

Two basic selling techniques are the canned sales presentation and the need-satisfaction approach. The ***canned sales presentation*** is a memorized, repetitive presentation given to all customers interested in a given item. It does not adapt to customer needs or traits but

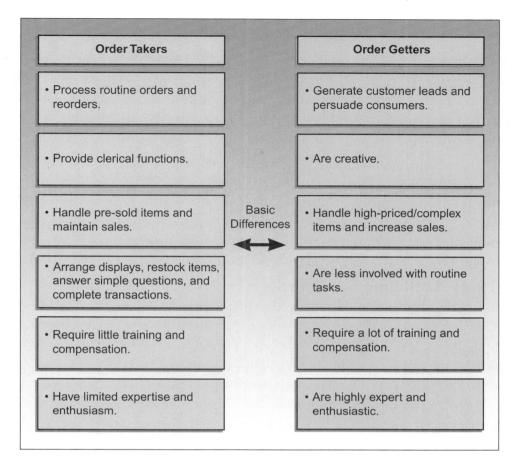

FIGURE 19-5
**Contrasting Order Takers
and Order Getters**

presumes that a general presentation will appeal to everyone. While criticized for its inflexibility and a nonmarketing orientation, it does have value for companies that employ inexperienced salespeople and have little time or interest in training them in creative selling techniques. With this approach, salespeople have a consistent sales presentation and a structured order of topics to discuss; and basic customer questions-and-answers can be scripted.

The *need-satisfaction approach* is a high-level selling method based on the principle that each customer has different attributes and wants, and therefore the sales presentation should be adapted to the individual consumer. With this technique, a salesperson first asks the consumer: What type of product are you looking for? Have you ever purchased this product before? What price range are you considering? Then the sales presentation is more responsive to the particular person, and a new shopper is treated differently from an experienced one. The need-satisfaction approach is more popular and customer-oriented; yet, it requires better training and skilled sales personnel. This approach includes

The **need-satisfaction approach** *adapts to individual consumers.*

- Using the buyer-seller dyad to generate two-way respect.
- Listening well.
- Making presentations based on a good grasp of the facts.
- Spending time on pre-sales research ("homework").
- Being punctual for appointments (and willing to leave when the allotted time is over).
- Allowing the customer to talk.
- Offering "solutions," not goods and services.
- Showing competence.
- Acknowledging if a question cannot be answered, but getting back to the customer immediately with the correct answer.

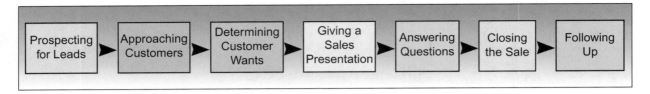

| Prospecting for Leads | Approaching Customers | Determining Customer Wants | Giving a Sales Presentation | Answering Questions | Closing the Sale | Following Up |

FIGURE 19-6
The Selling Process

The **selling process** *consists of seven steps.*

Prospecting *creates customer leads.*

The pre-approach and greeting are the two parts of **approaching customers.**

The **sales presentation** *converts an uncertain consumer.*

The **closing** *clinches a sale.*

- Not wasting a prospect's time.
- Providing superior service after the sale.[5]

The canned sales presentation works best with inexpensive, routine items that are heavily advertised and relatively pre-sold. The need-satisfaction approach works best with more expensive, more complex items that have moderate advertising and require substantial additional information for consumers.

19-4f Outlining Sales Tasks

The tasks to be performed by the personal sales force need to be outlined. The **selling process** consists of prospecting for leads, approaching customers, determining consumer wants, giving a sales presentation, answering questions, closing the sale, and following up. See Figure 19-6.

Outside selling requires a procedure, known as **prospecting,** to generate a list of customer leads. Blind prospecting uses phone directories, the Internet, and other general listings of potential customers; with it, a small percentage of those contacted will be interested in a firm's offering. Lead prospecting depends on past customers and others for referrals; thus, a greater percentage of people will be interested because of the referral from someone they know. Inside selling does not involve prospecting because customers have already been drawn to a store or office through ads or prior purchase experience.

Approaching customers is a two-stage procedure: pre-approach and greeting. During pre-approach, a salesperson tries to get information about the customer from the firm's data base, census materials, and/or other secondary data—as well as from referrals. The salesperson is then better equipped to interact with that customer. Inside retail salespeople may be unable to use a pre-approach; they often know nothing about a consumer until he or she enters the store. During the greeting, a salesperson begins a conversation. The intention is to put the customer at ease and build rapport.

The next step is to ascertain customer wants by asking the person a variety of questions regarding past experience with the product category, price, product features, intended uses, and the kinds of information still needed.

The **sales presentation** includes a verbal description of a product, its benefits, options and models, price, associated services like delivery and warranty, and a demonstration (if needed). A canned sales presentation or need-satisfaction method may be used. The purpose of a sales presentation is to convert an undecided consumer into a purchaser.

After a presentation, the salesperson usually answers consumer questions. They are of two kinds: the first request more information; the second raise objections that must be settled before a sale is made.

Once any questions have been answered, a salesperson is ready for **closing the sale.** This means getting a person to agree to a purchase. The salesperson must be sure no major questions remain before trying to close a sale; and the salesperson must not argue with a consumer.

[5]Adapted by the authors from James E. Lukaszewski and Paul Ridgeway, "To Put Your Best Foot Forward, Start by Taking These 21 Simple Steps," *Sales & Marketing Management* (June 1990), pp. 84–86. See also John R. Graham, "Myths That Menace Selling Success," *American Salesman* (March 2001), pp. 11–16; and Bernard L. Rosenbaum, "Seven Emerging Sales Competencies," *Business Horizons*, Vol. 44 (January-February 2001), pp. 33–36.

For a large purchase, the salesperson should follow-up after a sale to be sure the customer is pleased. The person is then better satisfied, referrals are obtained, and repurchases are more likely. "Relationship selling is not about getting an order; it is about convincing customers that you will be there after an order, no matter what. Relationships are based on doing what is right, not doing what you can get way with."[6]

Besides the tasks in the selling process, a firm must clearly enumerate the nonselling tasks it wants sales personnel to perform. Among the nonselling tasks that may be assigned are setting up displays, writing up information sheets, marking prices on products, checking competitors' strategies, doing test marketing analysis and consumer surveys, and training new employees.

19-4g Applying the Plan

Sales management—planning, implementing, and controlling the personal sales function—should be used in applying a personal selling plan. It covers employee selection, training, territory allocation, compensation, and supervision.

In selecting salespeople, a combination of personal attributes should be assessed: mental (intelligence, ability to plan), physical (appearance, speaking ability), experiential (education, sales/business background), environmental (group memberships, social influences), personality (ambition, enthusiasm, tact, resourcefulness, stability), and willingness to be trained and to follow instructions.[7] What makes a superior sales force?

> To turn a good sales force into a great one, companies must ensure they're attracting and retaining quality talent—those special salespeople who are motivated simply by making a customer successful. These are the people who will do whatever is necessary to make a customer relationship profitable for both sides. They're creative in how they use internal and external resources, and they always make sure that their customers are satisfied before they go home at night. Companies have to invest in these people, and do whatever they can to retain them. Richard Justice, senior vice-president of worldwide sales for Cisco Systems (www.cisco.com), has the type of customer-focused attitude that Cisco looks for in its sales employees. "If I'm in a board meeting and a customer calls, then I'll excuse myself to talk with them." Cisco employs a rigorous interview process to ensure that it identifies the right people to hire. Job candidates go through five to 10 face-to-face interviews and managers are held responsible for their hires, because some of their compensation is tied to those new reps' performance. Cisco looks for people who "see a ringing phone as an opportunity," says Justice, and the firm gets a large percentage of new hires through the Internet.[8]

The traits of potential salespeople must be compatible with the customers with whom they will interact and the requirements of the good or service being sold. The buyer-seller dyad operates better when there are some similarities in salesperson and customer characteristics. And certain product categories require much different education, technical training, and sales activities than others (such as jewelry versus computer sales).[9]

Once these factors are studied, the firm would develop a formal procedure that specifies the personal attributes sought, sources of employees (such as colleges and employment agencies), and methods for selection (such as interviews and testing). It would be based on the firm's overall selling plan.

Salesperson training may take one or a combination of forms. A formal program uses a trainer, a classroom setting, lectures, and printed materials. It may also include role playing (in which trainees act out parts) and case analysis. Field trips take trainees out on actual calls so they can observe skilled salespeople. On-the-job training places trainees in their own selling situations under the close supervision of a trainer or senior salesperson.

Sales management *tasks range from employee selection to supervision.*

[6]Michael Collins, "Breaking into the Big Leagues," *Marketing Tools* (January-February 1996), p. 28.

[7]Adapted by the authors from William J. Stanton, Rosann L. Spiro, and Richard H. Buskirk, *Management of a Sales Force*, Tenth Edition (New York: Irwin McGraw-Hill, 1998).

[8]Andy Cohen, "The Traits of Great Sales Forces," *Sales & Marketing Management* (October 2000), pp. 69–70.

[9]See J. David Lichtenthal and Thomas Tellesfsen, "Toward a Theory of Business Buyer-Seller Similarity," *Journal of Personal Selling & Sales Management*, Vol. 21 (Winter 2001), pp. 1–14.

Training often covers a range of topics; it should teach selling skills and include information on the firm and its offerings, the industry, and employee duties. For example, "Home Depot (www.homedepot.com), provides 50 hours of training to new employees, while Restoration Hardware (www.restorationhardware.com) and Stew Leonard's (www.stewleonards.com) provide 40 hours. The Container Store (www.containerstore.com) offers a whopping 235 hours. The Container Store views training not merely as an investment in its staff but also as a way to maintain its standards. Just days after the White Plains store opened, and after its staff of 70 had completed weeks of training, the company flew in Charles Lyon, one of 12 'super' sales trainers, to help employees polish their skills."[10] Besides initial training, continuous training or retraining of sales personnel may teach new techniques, explain new products, or improve performance.

> A **sales territory** *contains the area, customers, and/or products assigned to a salesperson.*

Territory size and salesperson allocation are decided next. A **sales territory** consists of the geographic area, customers, and/or product lines assigned to a salesperson. If territories are assigned by customer type or product category, two or more salespeople may cover the same area. Territory size depends on customer locations, order size, travel time and expenses, the time per sales call, the yearly visits for each account, and the number of hours per year each salesperson has for selling tasks. The mix of established versus new customer accounts must also be considered. Allocating salespeople to specific territories depends on their ability, the buyer-seller dyad, the mix of selling and nonselling tasks (such as one salesperson training new employees), and seniority. Proper territory size and allocation provide adequate coverage of customers, minimize overlap, recognize geographic boundaries, minimize travel expenses, encourage solicitation of new accounts, provide enough sales potential for good salespeople to be well rewarded, and are fair to everyone. Sales territory software, such as that marketed by Territory Mapper (www.territorymapper.com) and AlignStar (www.alignstar.com), can facilitate planning.

> *Sales compensation may be* **straight salary, straight commission,** *or a* **combination** *of the two.*

Salespeople are compensated by straight salary, straight commission, or a combination of salary and commission or bonus. With a **straight salary plan,** a salesperson is paid a flat amount per time period. Earnings are not tied to sales. The advantages are that both selling and nonselling tasks can be specified and controlled, salespeople have security, and expenses are known in advance. The disadvantages are the low incentive to increase sales, expenses not being tied to productivity, and the continuing costs even if there are low sales. Order takers are usually paid straight salaries.

With a **straight commission plan,** a salesperson's earnings are directly related to sales, profits, customer satisfaction, or some other type of performance. The commission rate is often keyed to a quota, which is a productivity standard. The advantages of this plan are the use of motivated salespeople, no fixed sales compensation costs, and expenses being tied to productivity. The disadvantages are the firm's lack of control over nonselling tasks, the instability of a firm's expenses, and salesperson risks due to variable pay. Insurance, real-estate, and direct-selling order getters often earn straight commissions. A real-estate salesperson might receive a 3 percent commission of $5,250 for selling a $175,000 house.

To gain the advantages of both salary- and commission-oriented methods, many firms use elements of each in a **combination sales compensation plan.** This balances control, flexibility, and employee incentives; and some award bonuses for superior individual or firm performance. All types of order getters work on a combination basis. Two-thirds of U.S. firms compensate sales personnel by some form of combination plan, one-fifth use a straight-salary plan, and the rest use straight commissions. Smaller firms are more apt to use a straight-salary plan and less apt to use a combination plan.

Supervision encompasses four aspects of sales management:

> *Supervision involves motivation, performance measures, nonselling tasks, and modifying behavior.*

- *Sales personnel must be motivated.* Their motivation depends on such factors as the clarity of the job (what tasks must be performed), the salesperson's desire to achieve, the variety of tasks performed, the incentives for undertaking each task, the style of the sales manager, flexibility, and recognition.

---

[10]Scotty Dupree, "Creating a Better Sales Force," *New York Times* (November 12, 2000), p. C8.

- *Performance must be measured.* To do this, achievements must be gauged against such goals as sales and calls per day. The analysis should take into account territory size, travel time, and experience. Salesperson failure is often related to poor listening skills, the failure to concentrate on priorities, a lack of effort, the inability to determine customer needs, a lack of planning for presentations, promising too much, and inadequate knowledge.

- *The sales manager must ensure that all nonselling tasks are completed,* even if sales personnel are not rewarded for them.

- *Some action may be needed to modify behavior* if performance does not meet expectations.

In sales management, these key factors should also be taken into account: the evolving role of women in selling and the special nature of selling in foreign markets.

With regard to women in personal selling, there has been a dramatic increase in the proportion of sales personnel and sales managers who are female. According to the U.S. Bureau of Labor Statistics (www.bls.gov), women now comprise 50 percent of the total sales force in the United States and 41 percent of sales supervisors (up from 25 percent twenty years ago). And as a recent study found, female sales managers may be quite different from their male counterparts:

> Mixed-gender sales teams reported that female sales managers use significantly higher levels of behavior control. Sales teams led by females display significantly higher levels of job involvement, job satisfaction (with supervision, fellow workers, and customers), as well as lower levels of role ambiguity, job anxiety, and burnout. Female sales managers' teams also display superior work outcomes in higher levels of organizational commitment, and a lower propensity to leave. A tentative yet provocative conclusion here is that in a sales force which shows few gender-related differences between salespeople, female sales managers pursue control strategies of a more behavior-based orientation than do male sales managers, and consequently their sales teams evidence more desirable attitudes, lower stress characteristics, and more positive work outcomes. In a symbolic sense, the finding suggests that first line female sales managers do not imitate the behavior of male managers Instead, they exercise latitude through behavior-based control activities.[11]

There are more women in sales than ever before, and international markets require special decisions.

When firms go international, sales managers must recognize that sales personnel have to deal with vastly differing cultures: "It's more than just teaching sellers to say hello and goodbye in a foreign language. It also involves training." When the marketing director of one U.S. Web integration software firm visited Munich, lunch with the German client "was more a discussion of wiener schnitzel than Web integration software. For three hours, the marketing director and a colleague met with two of the client's executives who wanted to know the Americans' favorite beer, travel spots, and food. Although business was never discussed, 'The lunch was such a cultivation of our partnership.'" It was also the only way to secure a sale. In general, "American salespeople often try to rush the sale abroad. Instead, managers should train them to spend days or weeks getting to know clients."[12] In particular, the attributes of salespeople; salesperson training, compensation, and supervision; the dynamics of the buyer-seller dyad; and the selling process may need to be tailored to distinct foreign markets.

19-5 THE SCOPE AND IMPORTANCE OF SALES PROMOTION

Due to intense competition in their industries, numerous firms are aggressively seeking every marketing edge possible. Thus, sales promotion activities worldwide are at their highest level. In the United States alone, spending exceeds $225 billion a year, including

Sales promotion efforts are now quite extensive.

---

[11]Nigel F. Piercy, David W. Cravens, and Nikala Lane, "Sales Manager Behavior Control Strategy and Its Consequences: The Impact of Gender Differences," *Journal of Personal Selling & Sales Management*, Vol. 21 (Winter 2001), pp.39–49.

[12]Betsy Cummings, "Selling Around the World," *Sales & Marketing Management* (May 2001), p. 70.

some sales promotion activities (such as direct mail and promotion-oriented ads) that may also be viewed as advertising.

The extent of sales promotion activities can be shown via the following:

- About 250 billion coupons are distributed annually in the United States. Most American households use coupons, half on a regular basis. Yet, people redeem only 2 percent of distributed coupons.[13]

- Business-to-business firms spend one-eighth of their marketing budgets on trade shows and exhibits. Fifty percent of industrial trade show attendees report signing a purchase order due to a trade show visit.[14] The TSNN.com Web site (www. tsnn.com) contains data on 15,000 trade shows worldwide.

- According to International Events Group (www.sponsorship.com), firms spend $10 billion annually in North America to sponsor special events—two-thirds on sports-related events. The leading sponsors are Anheuser-Busch (www.anheuser-busch.com), Philip Morris (www.philipmorris.com), General Motors (www.gm.com), Coca-Cola (www.coca-cola.com), and PepsiCo (www.pepsico.com).[15]

- Safeway (www.safeway.com), the California-based supermarket chain, has 1.5 million members in its frequent-shopper program. Customers are rewarded with special discounts and Safeway is able to build customer loyalty. See Figure 19-7.

- $17 billion is spent on point-of-purchase displays in U.S. stores each year.[16] These displays stimulate impulse purchases and provide information. Besides traditional cardboard, metal, and plastic displays, more stores are now using digital electronic signs and video displays.

FIGURE 19-7
The Safeway Club Card: Benefiting Customers and the Retailer

Source: Reprinted by permission.

[13]"The 2001 Annual Report on the Promotion Industry," *Promo* (May 2001), special supplement, p. S14.

[14]Cyndee Miller, "Marketing Industry Report: Who's Spending What on Biz-to-Biz Marketing," *Marketing News* (January 1, 1996), p. 1; and John F. Tanner, Jr. and Lawrence B. Chonko, "Trade Show Objectives," *Industrial Marketing Management*, Vol. 24 (August 1995), pp. 257–264.

[15]"The 2001 Annual Report on the Promotion Industry," p. S17.

[16]"The 2001 Annual Report on the Promotion Industry," p. S10.

- Because toothpaste use is low in rural India (with 720 million people), Colgate-Palmolive (www.colgate.com) hires "video vans" to regularly visit local villages. The vans show an infomercial on the value of toothpaste, free samples are given out, and brushing demonstrations are provided.[17]

Several factors account for sales promotion's strength as a marketing tool. As noted earlier, firms look for any competitive edge they can get, and this often involves some kind of sales promotion. The various forms of sales promotions are more acceptable to firms and consumers than in the past. Quick returns are possible, and numerous firms want to improve short-run profits. Today, more shoppers seek promotions before buying, and resellers put pressure on manufacturers for promotions. In economic slowdowns, more shoppers look for value-oriented sales promotions. Due to rising costs, advertising and personal selling have become more expensive relative to sales promotion. Technology advances make aspects of sales promotion, like coupon redemption, easier to administer.

GLOBAL *Marketing in Action*

Loyalty Programs Welcomed in South America

As more U.S.-based companies decide to enter South America, their use of loyalty marketing programs has greatly increased there. Even though South American airlines have used frequent-flyer marketing programs since the 1980s, the newer programs have introduced rewards at the retail level. For example, Pao de Acucar (www.paodeacucar.com.br), one of Brazil's largest supermarket chains, has launched a loyalty program in which consumers give personal information in exchange for a free gift and a membership card. Customers can earn coupons based on their buying habits. During the first six months of this program, 800,000 consumers signed up. The director of international business for Frequency Marketing, a promotion-based agency, says this response was "probably five or 10 times" that for a similar program in the United States.

An important step in developing an international loyalty program for a U.S.-based firm is to gain an alliance with a local company. Michael Briggs, the country manager for Carlson Marketing Group—Chile agrees. According to Briggs, "The learning curve would have been a nightmare if we had come down here and tried to get into these markets without having a local partner. Business is done based on relationships and contacts, and there's no way we could have penetrated that."

A common error relates to how the award structure is set up in a foreign country. Briggs states, "Awards such as dream trips don't have as much relevance in the region as they do in the United States. Talk to someone about a trip to Tahiti, and you may lose them. But talk about supermarket coupons for groceries and a TV or stereo, then you've got more attention."

As global promotions manager for a car rental firm, describe a loyalty program for the Brazilian market.

Source: Based on material in Paula Lyon Abdruss, "Running for the Border," *Marketing News* (December 4, 2000), p. 19.

[17]Miriam Jordan, "In Rural India, Video Vans Sell Toothpaste and Shampoo," *Wall Street Journal* (January 10, 1996), pp. B1, B5.

19-6 THE CHARACTERISTICS OF SALES PROMOTION

Sales promotion lures customers, maintains loyalty, creates excitement, is often keyed to patronage, and appeals to channel members.

Sales promotion has many advantages. It helps attract customer traffic and keep brand or company loyalty: New-product samples and trial offers draw customers. A manufacturer can retain brand loyalty by giving gifts to regular customers and coupons for its brands. A reseller can retain loyal customers by having incentives for frequent shoppers and using store coupons.

Rapid results can be gained. Some promotions provide consumer value and are kept by them (such as calendars, matchbooks, T-shirts, pens, and posters with the firm's name); they provide a reminder function. Impulse purchases can be stimulated via in-store displays. For example, an attractive supermarket display for batteries can dramatically raise sales. In addition, a good display may lead a shopper to a bigger purchase than originally intended.

Excitement is created via certain short-run promotions involving gifts, contests, or sweepstakes; and high-value items or high layoffs encourage consumers to participate. Contests offer the further benefit of customer involvement (through the completion of some skill-oriented activity). Many promotions are keyed to customer patronage—with the awarding of coupons, frequent-shopper gifts, and referral gifts directly related to purchases. In these cases, promotions can be a fixed percentage of sales and their costs not incurred until transactions are completed. And resellers may be stimulated if support is provided in the form of displays, manufacturer coupons, manufacturer rebates, and trade allowances.

Sales promotion may hurt image, cause consumers to wait for special offers, and shift the focus from the product.

Sales promotion also has limitations. A firm's image may be lessened if it always runs promotions. People may view discounts as representing a decline in product quality and believe a firm could not sell its offerings without them. Profit margins are often lower for a firm if sales promotion is used. When coupons, rebates, or other special deals are employed frequently, people may not buy when products are offered at regular prices; they will stock up each time there is a promotion. Some consumers may even interpret a regular price as an increase for items that are heavily promoted.

Some promotions shift the marketing focus away from the product itself to secondary factors. People may be lured by calendars and sweepstakes instead of product quality and features. In the short run, this generates consumer enthusiasm. In the long run, it may adversely affect a brand's image and sales because a product-related advantage has not been communicated. Sales promotion can enhance—not replace—advertising, personal selling, and public relations.

19-7 DEVELOPING A SALES PROMOTION PLAN

A sales promotion plan consists of the steps shown in Figure 19-8 and explained next.

19-7a Setting Objectives

Goals are usually demand-oriented. They may be related to channel members and to consumers.

Objectives associated with channel-member sales promotions include gaining distribution, receiving adequate shelf space, increasing dealer enthusiasm, raising sales, and getting cooperation in sales promotion expenditures. Objectives pertaining to consumer sales promotions include boosting brand awareness, increasing product trials, hiking average purchases, encouraging repurchases, obtaining impulse sales, emphasizing novelty, and supplementing other promotional tools.

19-7b Assigning Responsibility

Sales promotion duties are often shared by advertising and sales managers, with each directing the promotions in his or her area. Thus, an advertising manager would work on coupons, customer contests, calendars, and other mass promotions. A sales manager would work on trade shows, cooperative promotions, special events, demonstrations, and other efforts involving individualized attention directed at channel members or consumers.

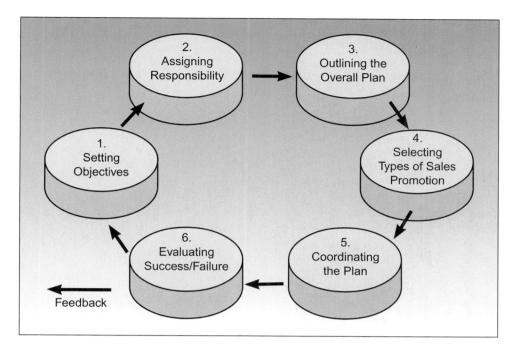

FIGURE 19-8

Developing a Sales Promotion Plan

Some companies have their own sales-promotion departments or hire outside promotion firms, like PromoWorks (www.promoworkspromotions.com). Outside sales-promotion firms often operate in specific areas—such as coupons, contests, or gifts—and generally can develop a sales promotion campaign at less expense than the user company could. These firms offer expertise, swift service, flexibility, and, when requested, distribution.

19-7c Outlining the Overall Plan

Next, a sales promotion plan should be outlined and include a budget, an orientation, conditions, media, duration and timing, and cooperative efforts. In setting a sales promotion budget, it is important to include all costs. The average face value of a grocery coupon is 75 cents; supermarkets get a handling fee for each coupon they redeem; and there are costs for printing, mailing, and advertising coupons.

Sales promotion orientation refers to its focus—channel members or consumers—and its theme. Promotions for channel members should raise their product knowledge, provide sales support, offer rewards for selling a promoted product, and seek better cooperation and efficiency. Promotions for consumers should induce impulse and larger-volume sales, sustain brand-name recognition, and gain participation. A promotion theme refers to its underlying channel member or consumer message—such as a special sale, new-product introduction, holiday celebration, or customer recruitment. See Figure 19-9.

Sales promotion conditions are requirements channel members or consumers must meet to be eligible for a specific sales promotion. These may include minimum purchases, performance provisions, and/or minimum age. A channel member may have to stock a certain amount of merchandise to receive a free display case from a manufacturer. A consumer may have to send in proofs of purchase for a refund or gift. In some cases, strict time limits are set as to the closing dates for participation in a promotion.

The media are the vehicles through which sales promotions reach channel members or consumers. They include direct mail, newspapers, magazines, television, the personal sales force, trade shows, and group meetings.

A promotion's duration may be short or long, depending on its goals. Coupons usually have quick closing dates since they are used to increase store traffic. Frequent-shopper points often can be redeemed for at least one year; the goal is to maintain loyalty. As noted earlier, if promotions are lengthy or offered often, consumers may come to expect

Sales promotion orientation *may be toward channel members or final consumers.*

Sales promotion conditions *are eligibility requirements.*

FIGURE 19-9

The Dual Orientation of Sales Promotion

Microsoft provides in-store displays as marketing support for its resellers. These displays make it easy for shoppers to browse through Microsoft software products.

Source: Reprinted by permission of Retail Planning Associates. Photography by Michael Houghton/STUDIOHIO.

them as part of a purchase. Some promotions are seasonal, and for these timing is crucial. They must be tied to such events as fall school openings or model changes.

Finally, the use of shared promotions should be decided. With cooperative efforts, each party pays some costs and gets benefits. Promotions can be sponsored by trade associations, manufacturers and/or service firms, wholesalers, and retailers. For example, since 1996, McDonald's (www.mcdonalds.com) has had a strong relationship with Walt Disney Co. (www.disney.com), to capitalize on the latter's strength with animated films:

> As McDonald's chief executive recently noted, "We have made enormous amounts of progress. We have moved way beyond doing only movie promotions with Happy Meal toys." In addition to developing joint marketing efforts and opening foodservice venues on Disney properties, the chief executive explained that the partnership extends to such arenas as creating in-store entertainment for children, as well as helping with operational upgrades.[18]

19-7d Selecting the Types of Sales Promotion

There is a wide range of sales promotion tools available. The attributes of promotion tools oriented to channel members are shown in Table 19-3. The attributes of promotion tools oriented to consumers are noted in Table 19-4. Examples for each tool are also provided in these tables. The selection of sales promotions should be based on such factors as company image, company goals, costs, participation requirements, and the enthusiasm of channel members or customers.

19-7e Coordinating the Plan

It is essential that sales promotion activities be well coordinated with other elements of the promotion mix. In particular:

Advertising and sales promotion should be integrated.

- Advertising and sales promotion plans should be integrated.
- The sales force should be notified of all promotions well in advance and trained to implement them.

[18]Amy Zuber, "McD-Disney Marketing Alliances Grow with Burger Invasion Concept's Debut," *Nation's Restaurant News* (January 22, 2001), pp. 4–6.

TABLE 19-3 **Selected Types of Sales Promotion Directed at Channel Members**

Type	Characteristics	Illustration
Trade shows or meetings	One or a group of manufacturers invites channel members to attend sessions where products are displayed and explained.	The annual National Hardware Show attracts more than 3,000 exhibitors and tens of thousands of attendees.
Training	The manufacturer provides training for personnel of channel members.	Compaq trains retail salespeople in how to operate and use its computers.
Trade allowances or special offers	Channel members are given discounts or rebates for performing specified functions or purchasing during certain time periods.	A local distributor receives a discount for running its own promotion for GE light bulbs.
Point-of-purchase displays	The manufacturer or wholesaler gives channel members fully equipped displays for its products and sets them up.	Coca-Cola provides refrigerators with its name on them to retailers carrying minimum quantities of Coca-Cola products.
Push money	Channel members' salespeople are given bonuses for pushing the brand of a certain manufacturer. Channel members may not like this if their salespeople shift loyalty to the manufacturer.	A salesperson in an office-equipment store is paid an extra $50 for every desk of a particular brand that is sold.
Sales contests	Prizes or bonuses are distributed if certain performance levels are met.	A wholesaler receives $2,500 for selling 1,000 microchips in a month.
Free merchandise	Discounts or allowances are provided in the form of merchandise.	A retailer gets one case of ballpoint pens free for every 10 cases purchased.
Demonstration models	Free items are given to channel members for demonstration purposes.	A hospital-bed manufacturer offers demonstrator models to its distributors.
Gifts	Channel members are given gifts for carrying items or performing functions.	During one three-month period, a book publisher gives computerized cash registers to bookstores that agree to purchase a specified quantity of its books.
Cooperative promotions	Two or more channel members share the costs of a promotion.	A manufacturer and retailer each pay part of the costs for T-shirts with the manufacturer's and retailer's names embossed.

- For special events, such as the appearance of a major celebrity, publicity should be generated.
- Sales promotions should be consistent with channel members' activities.

19-7f Evaluating Success or Failure

The success or failure of many sales promotions is straightforward to measure since promotions may be closely linked to performance or sales. By analyzing before-and-after data, the impact of these promotions is clear. Trade show effectiveness can be gauged by counting the number of leads generated, examining sales from those leads and the cost per lead, getting customer feedback about a show from the sales force, and determining the amount of literature given out at a show. Companies can verify changes in sales as a result of dealer-training programs. Firms using coupons can review sales and compare redemption rates with industry averages. Surveys of channel members and consumers can indicate satisfaction with promotions, suggestions for improvements, and the effect of promotions on image.

The success or failure of some sales promotions is simple to measure.

Type	Characteristics	Illustration
Coupons	Manufacturers or channel members advertise special discounts for customers who redeem coupons.	P&G mails consumers a 50-cents-off coupon for Sure deodorant, which can be redeemed at any supermarket.
Refunds or rebates	Consumers submit proof-of-purchases (usually to the manufacturer) and receive an extra discount.	First Alert provides rebates to consumers submitting proofs of purchase for its fire alarms.
Samples	Free merchandise or services are given to consumers, generally for new items.	America Online offers a free one-month trial of services.
Contests or sweepstakes	Consumers compete for prizes by answering questions (contests) or filling out forms for random drawings of prizes (sweepstakes).	Publishers Clearing House sponsors annual sweepstakes and awards cash and other prizes.
Bonus packs or multipacks	Consumers receive discounts for purchasing in quantity.	An office-supply store runs a "buy one, get one free" sale on desk lamps.
Shows or exhibits	Many firms co-sponsor exhibitions for consumers.	The Auto Show is annually scheduled for the public in New York.
Point-of-purchase displays	In-store displays remind customers and generate impulse purchases.	*TV Guide* sales in supermarkets are high because displays are placed at checkout counters.
Special events	Firms sponsor the Olympics, fashion shows, and other activities.	Visa USA is a worldwide sponsor of the Olympics.
Product placements	Branded goods and services are depicted in movies and TV shows.	Nike sneakers appear in movies.
Gifts	Consumers get gifts for making a purchase or opening a new account.	Savings banks offer a range of gifts for consumers opening new accounts or expanding existing ones.
Frequent-shopper gifts	Consumers get gifts or special discounts, based on cumulative purchases. Points are amassed and exchanged for gifts or money.	Airline travelers can accumulate mileage and receive free trips or gifts when enough miles have been earned.
Referral gifts	Existing customers are given gifts for referring their friends to the company.	Tupperware awards gifts to the woman hosting a Tupperware party in her home.
Demonstrations	Goods or services are shown in action.	Different models of Apple computers are demonstrated in a free lesson.

Some sales promotions—such as event sponsorships and T-shirt giveaways—are more difficult to evaluate. Objectives are less definitive.

Here are three examples relating to the effectiveness of sales promotion:

- About one-quarter of supermarket shoppers say they use their frequent-shopper cards "pretty much every time they shop."[19]

[19]Food Marketing Institute, "Here's My Card," *American Demographics* (February 2000), p. 37.

MARKETING *and the Web*

Reviving Green Stamps Through Greenpoints. com

S&H Greenpoints (www.greenpoints.com) is the new rewards program of Sperry & Hutchinson, a firm that started in 1896 with its Green Stamp program. Consumers received stamps for purchases, accrued the stamps, and redeemed them for gifts. But S&H now faces extensive competition from online and offline loyalty programs. The Incentive Federation (www. incentivecentral.org) estimates that firms give away $4.2 billion annually in consumer premiums.

By early 1999, when a group of investors acquired S&H, only a few retailers were offering Green Stamp. Yet, research conducted by S&H found that one-half of adults aged 30 and older knew the S&H brand and talked fondly about their Green Stamp experiences. In awareness studies, S&H outscored the rewards programs of firms such as American Airlines and Netincentives. Focus groups with consumers also found that shoppers want simple loyalty programs with rewards for their daily activities.

S&H recently signed deals with more than 100 E-merchants that will give out Greenpoints. And the Greenpoints program is being used by regional grocery store chains (such as New York's Foodtown and Michigan's J&J Food Centers) to develop co-branded frequent-shopper programs. Members earn 10 Greenpoints for each dollar spent. These points can be redeemed for more than 1,000 items, including jewelry, sports equipment, and electronics. Within one year of enacting its Greenpoints program, J&J had attracted 6,000 customers (roughly 45 percent of J&J's total customer base). And its Greenpoints members are responsible for 70 percent of J&J's total sales. What is also particularly attractive about Greenpoints are the demographic data that S&H collects about members and shares with its merchants.

As a supermarket chain's marketing vice-president, evaluate the pros and cons of Greenpoints versus your own loyalty program.

Source: Based on material in Jennifer Lach, "Redeeming Qualities," *American Demographics* (May 2000), pp. 36–38.

- Colgate-Palmolive (www.colgate.com) doubled its Vietnamese sales three months after launching an aggressive sales promotion effort. The program, called "Realizing Your Dream," comprised three lucky drawings with awards such as an apartment in Phu My Hung, 30 flat-screen TVs, and 1,500 consolation prizes. [20]

- In many places, coupons hold little appeal. As an Egyptian shopper said, "When I lived in the States, we used coupons all the time, but here I never felt the shop would really apply the discount. If more people offered coupons and were trustworthy, I would use them." Added a Canadian shopper, "Why buy peanut butter with 50 cents off, when you can get no-name peanut butter more cheaply?"[21]

[20]"Colgate-Palmolive Doubles Sales in Promotion Program," *Saigon Times Daily* (September 4, 2000), p. SGTD12662971.

[21]Jan Jaben, "Shoppers Tell Marketers to Save Breath on Offers," *Advertising Age* (January 15, 1996), p. I–2.

WEB SITES YOU CAN USE

: Looking for a bargain? Try one of these sales promotion Web sites:

Catalina Marketing Corporation
(www.catmktg.com)

ContestListings.com (contestlistings.com)

Cool Savings (www.coolsavings.com)

Coupons1 (www.coupon1.com)

e-centives (www.e-centives.com)

eDirect.com (www.edirect.com)

FreeClutter.com (www.freeclutter.com)

Hot Coupons (www.hotcoupons.com)

Insta$avings (www.instasavings.com)

MilePoint.com (www.milepoint.com)

MyCoupons (www.mycoupons.com)

MyPoints (www.mypoints.com)

StartSampling (www.startsampling.com)

Suzi Coupon (www.suzicoupon.com)

Val-Pak (www.valpak.com)

ValuPage (www.valupage.com)

SUMMARY

1. *To examine the scope, importance, and characteristics of personal selling* Personal selling involves oral communication with one or more prospective buyers by paid representatives for the purpose of making sales. About 16 million people work in U.S. selling jobs; millions more work in sales jobs outside the United States. Yet, these numbers understate the value of personal selling because every contact between a company employee and a customer involves some degree of selling.

Selling is emphasized with high-volume clients, geographically concentrated customers, expensive/complex products, customers wanting sales services, and entries into foreign markets. Selling also resolves questions and addresses other issues. Selling costs are higher than advertising costs at many firms. Thus, efficiency is important.

Selling fosters a buyer-seller dyad (a two-way communication flow), offers flexibility and adaptability, adds to relationships with customers, results in less audience waste, clinches sales, and provides immediate feedback. Yet, personal selling can handle only a limited number of customers, is rather ineffective for creating consumer awareness, has high costs per customer, and has a poor image for some consumers.

2. *To study the elements in a personal selling plan* A selling plan has seven steps: setting goals—demand- and/or image-related; assigning oversight—to one manager or to several managers; setting a budget; choosing the type(s) of sales positions—order takers, order getters, and/or support salespeople; selecting a sales technique—the canned sales presentation or the need-satisfaction approach; outlining tasks—including each of the relevant steps in the selling

process and nonselling tasks; and applying the plan—which centers on sales management.

3. *To examine the scope, importance, and characteristics of sales promotion* Sales promotion encompasses paid marketing communication activities (other than advertising, publicity, or personal selling) that stimulate consumer purchases and dealer effectiveness. In the United States, sales promotion expenditures exceed $225 billion annually.

The growth of sales promotion is due to firms looking for a competitive edge, the greater acceptance of sales promotion tools by both firms and consumers, quick returns, the pressure by consumers and channel members for promotions, the popularity during economic downturns, the high costs of other promotional forms, and technological advances.

A sales promotion helps attract customer traffic and loyalty, provides value and may be retained by people, increases impulse purchases, creates excitement, is keyed to patronage, and improves reseller cooperation. Yet, it may hurt a firm's image, encourage consumers to wait for promotions before making purchases, and shift the focus away from product attributes. Sales promotion cannot replace other forms of promotion.

4. *To study the elements in a sales promotion plan* A promotion plan has six steps: setting goals—ordinarily demand-oriented; assigning responsibility—to advertising and sales managers, company departments, and/or outside specialists; outlining the overall plan—including orientation, conditions, and other factors; selecting the types of sales promotion; coordinating the plan with the other elements of the promotion mix; and evaluating success or failure.

KEY TERMS

telemarketing (p. 563)
buyer-seller dyad (p. 564)
sales-expense budget (p. 567)
order taker (p. 568)
order getter (p. 568)
missionary salesperson (p. 568)
sales engineer (p. 568)
service salesperson (p. 568)

canned sales presentation (p. 568)
need-satisfaction approach (p. 569)
selling process (p. 570)
prospecting (p. 570)
approaching customers (p. 570)
sales presentation (p. 570)
closing the sale (p. 570)

sales management (p. 571)
sales territory (p. 572)
straight salary plan (p. 572)
straight commission plan (p. 572)
combination sales compensation plan (p. 572)
sales promotion orientation (p. 577)
sales promotion conditions (p. 577)

REVIEW QUESTIONS

1. Under what circumstances should personal selling be emphasized? Why?
2. Draw and explain the buyer-seller dyad.
3. Distinguish among order-taker, order-getter, and support sales personnel.
4. When is a canned sales presentation appropriate? When is it inappropriate?

5. Outline the steps in the selling process.
6. Why is sales promotion growing as a marketing tool?
7. What are the limitations associated with sales promotion?
8. Differentiate between sales promotion orientation and conditions.

DISCUSSION QUESTIONS

1. Comment on this statement: "Although its role may differ, telemarketing may be successfully used during the selling process for any type of good or service."
2. How would you handle these objections raised at the end of a sales presentation for a new air conditioner?
   a. "I saw the price of the same item at a competing store for 10 percent less than what you are asking."
   b. "Your warranty period is much too short."

   c. "None of the alternatives you showed me is satisfactory."
3. List several sales promotion techniques that would be appropriate for a university. List several that would be appropriate for a high school soccer team. Explain the differences in your two lists.
4. How could a sales promotion be *too* successful?

WEB EXERCISE

Visit the "Online Exclusives" section of the *Sales & Marketing Management* Web site (www.salesandmarketing.com) and read the material on "Best Sales Forces." Cite five valuable sales tips that you can offer based on the information at the Web site.

PART 6 SHORT CASES

Case 1

At Soapworks, Marketing to One Customer at a Time[c6-1]

Amilya Antonetti began developing hypoallergenic cleaning products after learning that her son's health problems were being further aggravated by the chemicals found in traditional laundry detergents. She persuaded a retired soap buyer to put her in touch with detergent formulators and set up California-based Soapworks (www.soapworks.com) with loans secured by the Small Business Administration.

Breaking into the $4.7 billion laundry detergent market in 1994 was far from easy. Antonetti constantly heard comments from grocery store buyers such as "Have you ever heard of Tide?" or "None of our customers would be interested in your products." Today, grocery store buyers have stopped laughing. Soapworks is distributed in 3,000 stores located from coast to coast, and the firm had sales of $10 million in 2000. As Antonetti says, "There was clearly a niche that was not being served."

Marketing analysts believe the real secret to Soapworks' success is the customer loyalty due to what the product stands for, as much as the product's formulation. It's also a story of how a small firm has been able to use a low advertising budget to expand its market reach. As the author of the book *Home Safe Home* observed, "[Soapworks'] customers are buying into the concept and the message of the company as much as they are buying the product."

Soapworks' initial ads were placed with KFAX, a local, family-oriented radio station. Antonetti bought airtime for about $2,500 for the first three months and $4,000 for the six months thereafter, and reached KFAX's 250,000 weekly listeners. Instead of having the station announcer present Soapworks' advertising message, Antonetti insisted that she do it herself. And to appeal to listeners, she presented herself in the dual roles of mom and chief executive officer. To further increase her visibility, Antonetti also agreed to appear as a frequent guest on the station's "Life Line" program. The media attention was reported favorably in other media including the *San Jose Mercury News* and *Time*.

Currently, Soapworks' annual budget for advertising is under $60,000, far less than the cost of one 30-second prime-time TV ad. This amount is also tiny when compared with Clorox's quarterly ad expenditures of $100 million or more. So, instead of using mass promotions, Antonetti seeks to win "one customer at a time." She knows that her advertising "can't compete against Procter & Gamble and Clorox when they are right after *Sesame Street* and right before *Mister Rogers*. I had to find a different way to let people know who I am."

As an important component in her communication strategy, Antonetti seeks to form a personal bond with current and prospective customers. She personally accepts the 75 or so calls from customers that she receives daily, and hands out 100,000 samples per year in children's hospital wards and women's shelters. The connection to customers is so strong that when a supermarket chain pulled Soapworks' products, the chain's management was confronted with a series of customer complaints. Soon thereafter, the chain decided to restock the brand.

One chronic problem for Soapworks is that new distribution channels such as drugstores typically require special promotions, like "buy one-get-one free," that are costly for the firm. A second problem is Soapworks' lack of cash to cope with its growth. For example, funding is needed for a new plant that would reduce its production costs as well as supply needed products.

Questions

1. Assess Soapworks' initial promotional plan from the perspective of integrated marketing communications.
2. How should Soapworks' promotional plan change as the firm matures?
3. Describe the pros and cons of Antonetti as company spokesperson.
4. Develop specific promotional objectives for Soapworks for the next two years.

[c6-1]The data in the case are drawn from D. M. Osborne, "Taking on Procter & Gamble," *Inc.* (October 2000), pp. 67–71.

Case 2

How Can Web Sites Be Tasteful Enough to Attract Advertisers? [c6-2]

Although some Web sites that feature short films, animations, and other types of programming have secured advertising sponsorships, many advertisers are holding back support for this form of Web-based content. Marketing analysts report that image-conscious advertisers are quite concerned about being associated with Web content that may be viewed as tasteless by some consumers. The interactive creative director at a major advertising agency sums up the situation succinctly: "A tremendous amount of the content is of a bizarre nature. A lot of our advertisers don't want to sponsor that kind of program."

For example, Coca-Cola is "very sensitive about where its trademark is used," says the account director at its main advertising agency for interactive media planning and buying in North America. "Coke is a lightning rod for people to call into the consumer hotline and say, 'How can you associate yourself with this kind of content?'" Adds the director of E-business strategy at Nissan North America, "If it is edgy and out there, then the upside pales in comparison to the overall risks of the content. I'm not going to make that decision."

Due to the extent of the concern that advertisers have with the content of entertainment Web sites (such as film, music, and theater sites), these sites currently generate just 4 percent of all online advertising revenues, according to a recent study prepared for the Internet Advertising Bureau. In contrast, search engines such as Yahoo! receive 36 percent of online ad revenues. The remaining online ad revenues go to sites devoted to technology, business information, news, and classified advertising.

Industry analysts state that a major concern among online advertisers is that some online entertainment sites frequently push the boundaries of taste. Thus, Pfizer, the marketer of Viagra, is careful to avoid placing its brand near any "content that glamorizes negative social behaviors." These include anything that "features a gratuitous amount of violence, sex, nudity, or profanity."

Nonetheless, some advertisers seeking a college student audience have accepted online content that would be normally be rejected by advertisers seeking a mass-market audience. One online company that features animations such as "The Tardz" and "Booty Call" states that these sites appeal to entertainment, liquor, and apparel marketers. As the chairman and chief executive of Alltrue Networks notes, "We have to create content that has credibility to a young, marketing-savvy audience." One of the online company's short Web films showed a cow defecating and a pigeon vomiting. "I don't think Procter & Gamble is ever going to be an Alltrue sponsor," he adds.

Some sites are so controversial that they attract little advertising revenue. Even though "Lil' Pimp," a Web animation about a nine-year-old street hustler, has won an award from a dot.com publication, as well as a growing audience, it generates little advertising revenue. Subway, the fast-food chain, was the major sponsor in 2001. Asked about advertising revenues, the chairman and chief executive officer of the site's developer remarked, "We're working on it."

It is expected that many Web-based entertainment sites will not last long due to their small audiences and the fact that they are shunned by larger advertisers. As an executive at McCann-Erickson, a major advertising agency, puts it, "It's hard enough to get advertising to support regular programming that delivers big numbers."

Questions

1. How can a marketer coordinate Web-based advertising into an integrated marketing communications program?
2. Under what circumstances should an advertiser place advertising in Web sites with questionable taste?
3. What is the role of a Web entertainment site sponsorship in the hierarchy-of-effects model?
4. As the operator of a Web entertainment site, how would you attract more sponsors without giving up your artistic freedom of expression?

[c6-2] The data in the case are drawn from Anna Wilde Mathews, "Advertisers Find Many Web Sites Too Tasteless," *New York Times* (October 12, 2000), pp. B1, B14.

Case 3

Personal Selling in the Promotion Mix: Reacting to E-Commerce[c6-3]

No one knows for sure how deeply new business-to-business (b-to-b) trading communities will affect the role of industrial salespeople, but many marketing experts feel that their impact will be profound. While there is little fear that the traditional salesperson will disappear "with the click of a mouse," many sales executives think the sales force may spend more time on new products and on local buying opportunities.

Among the recently formed b-to-b trading communities is the WorldWide Retail Exchange (www.worldwideretailexchange.org). Its members include many of the world's largest retailers: Royal Ahold, Albertson's, Auchan, Casino, Kmart, Target, Tesco, Safeway, CVS, Marks & Spencer, and Kingfisher. As of mid-2001, this exchange was representing more than 100,000 suppliers, partners, and distributors in selling to 30,000 stores with sales revenues that total over $300 million. Trade associations such as the Grocery Manufacturers of America, the Food Marketing Institute, and Food Distributors International are also in the process of forming b-to-b exchanges. Wal-Mart also announced that it is extending its exchange that is currently private to the entire grocery business.

These exchanges offer their retailer members access to market information, opportunities for relationship marketing, entrée to bidding prospects, and connectivity to the computer systems of suppliers. Bill James, a vice-president for the Grocery Manufacturers of America feels that exchanges will result in additional information and an improved dialogue between suppliers and their customers. Janet Suleski, an industry analyst for AMR Research, says, "As retail trading exchanges begin to enhance functionality and broaden their reach, retailers will gain benefits such as lower transaction costs, faster time to market, and real-time access to market opportunities." According to Richard Alt, the president of Internet Commerce Systems, the exchanges will enable grocery stores to secure promotional and descriptive data for new products online; online ordering will also be provided. These services will allow retailers to receive new products in their stores in as little as seven days.

Let's look at the impact these exchanges are already having on the personal selling function in the grocery business. One expert states that, although the exchanges will redistribute sales personnel, they will not necessarily reduce the number of salespeople. For example, one food broker might have had 10 salespeople in the field: 7 traditional salespeople and 3 merchandisers. Now, the broker might have 13 salespeople, of whom 10 are merchandisers. Since its changeover, Hy-Vee, a wholesaler that is a member of the Internet Commerce Systems Group, gets fewer calls at its headquarters and at stores.

With the decrease in the number of sales calls, other aspects of a salesperson's job may increase. According to Pete Cowles, senior vice-president of sales for Authentic Specialty Foods, a maker of Mexican foods sold under the La Victoria and Embassa brands, "You can put attachments on E-mail and provide spreadsheets, pie charts, and depth charts. But any major presentation of a new item is face-to-face where the supplier goes to the kitchen and cooks and serves the product." Even Hy-Vee continues to hold one-on-one meetings with individual manufacturers in an effort to take better care of its customers and increase sales.

Questions

1. What should be the industrial salesperson's role in an environment of b-to-b trading exchanges?
2. What should be the activities of order takers versus order getters in the new world of online exchanges?
3. How can a wholesaler apply the buyer-seller dyad in dealing with retailers that participate in online exchanges?
4. How can salespeople be motivated in this marketplace?

[c6-3]The data in the case are drawn from Len Lewis, "E-Business: The Next Killer App," *Progressive Grocer* (May 2000), pp. 125–130; and Steve Weinstein, "Trade Relations: Death of a Salesman?" *Progressive Grocer* (June 2000), pp. 33–38.

Case 4

Dunkin' Donuts in Thailand: Selling with Promotions[c6-4]

The brand marketing director for Dunkin' Donuts (www. dunkindonuts.com) says that, "In most international markets, Dunkin' Donuts is a meeting place. It's not like the U.S., where you get in and out fast. Overseas, you go in, you sit down, you meet your friends, you relax." And in contrast to the United States, where its business is generally booming in the morning, Dunkin' Donuts shops in Thailand and other countries are busier during afternoon and evening hours, much like cafés. Dunkin' Donuts is often used by teenagers and young adults as a place to socialize. Young Thais view Dunkin' Donuts as a "trendy type of brand."

Dunkin' Donuts now operates about 130 shops in Thailand. These units serve more than 300,000 customers each week. Because Thais view the royal family as a symbol of national identity, Dunkin' Donuts recently scheduled its "Longest Love Message to Moms" promotion to coincide with the birthday of Thailand's queen mother (which is also Thailand's national Mother's Day). The campaign was especially meaningful to Thais since they are very family oriented and tend to live with their parents for a long time—possibly their whole lives.

For the five-week duration of the promotion, all Thais were invited to visit any Dunkin' Donuts outlet and write a note to their mothers on a special vinyl banner. A purchase was not required to participate in the promotion. The campaign had two objectives: (1) to increase Dunkin' Donuts market share in Thailand by 2 percent and (2) to increase brand loyalty among the store's target customer group of teenagers and young adults aged 15 to 25.

Dunkin' Donuts launched the promotion by inviting popular young Thai actors to sign a banner at its flagship store in Bangkok. Posters were then displayed in each store and company employees distributed 100,000 leaflets inviting customers to participate in the campaign. During the campaign, the chain also offered a "Millennium Moms" box of five donuts. Customers could complete an entry form on the box that made them eligible to win cash, as well as other prizes (with a total retail value of $16,000). In keeping with the Thai tradition for being societally-conscious, the grand prize winner and his/her mother also would serve as hosts for a company-sponsored lunch for underprivileged children.

Public relations was effectively used throughout the campaign. Thailand's prime minister signed a banner. And 2,000 banners, containing more than 5,000 love messages, were sewn together to form a mile-long banner. The banner was carried by hundreds of store employees in a national parade honoring the queen mother's birthday.

In total, Dunkin' Donuts spent $14,000 on packaging, public relations, banners, and prizes. The company computed that it sold over 200,000 "Millennium Moms" boxes of donuts, which resulted in $373,000 of additional donut sales. Since the campaign was featured on every major TV channel in Thailand, it secured the equivalent of $207,000 in advertising value. Furthermore, an analysis by A.C. Nielsen showed that during the campaign, the company's market share in the donut category increased from 67 percent to 71 percent.

Questions

1. What are the pros and cons of Dunkin' Donuts' decision not to require a purchase to participate in its banner promotion?
2. How was this campaign an effective example of integrated marketing communications?
3. What other measures of success for the Thai sales promotion described in this case are appropriate for Dunkin' Donuts to assess?
4. What other sales promotions should Dunkin' Donuts consider using in Thailand? Why?

[c6-4]The data in the case are drawn from Paula Lyon Andruss, "Thais Sweet on Mom, 'Love' Campaign," *Marketing News* (September 11, 2000), pp. 6–7.

PART 6 COMPREHENSIVE CASE

Communications and Sports Marketing[pc-6]

Introduction

So you've locked out your players and are no longer playing your league's games. Now what?

What's that? You say you've been caught bribing international officials to bring a sports event to your city? How are you going to explain this to the athletes, your governing bodies, your sponsors, and the media?

Tell me again—your star running back just retired abruptly, less than one month before the start of the season? So what do you do with your printed marketing materials built around that player?

Sound familiar? It should. That's because in the high-visibility world of sports marketing, the script is rarely known and the outcomes are frequently unpredictable. It's why "recovery marketing" should be required learning for most senior executives and marketing managers in the sports business community. For sports marketers, the concept of recovery entails returning a disaffected customer to satisfaction after a service breakdown—one that's often unexpected and unscripted.

While this case focuses on sports, it would be difficult to find any organization or sector that doesn't periodically face uncontrollable and potentially calamitous service breakdowns. Marketing managers would be well served to develop recovery plans that anticipate "worst-case" or "what-if" circumstances. In many areas of marketing, the topic of recovery marketing is limited to the hotel industry in which a hurricane destroys a popular tourist destination or, unfortunately, an airline suffers a fatal crash. For other marketers, it might be made familiar by an unforeseen consumer action such as the Tylenol tampering during the 1980s or interest in Nike's labor contracts in the 1990s. The marketing department can even create the need for recovery strategies, such as when Coca-Cola Co. decided to modify the taste of its then 99-year-old product (Coke Classic), and created New Coke. Or when Volvo shot a TV ad touting its safety features but got caught rigging cars with special support systems during the ad's production.

Common among these instances was that the activity was unexpected and largely unpredictable, and in most cases, the history of the product's marketing was unblemished or unnoticed by the community at large. In the situations faced by Coke and Volvo, the product marketers were in control of their destinies.

Unfortunately, that's usually not the case in the sports world. In fact, it's only a matter of time before an unexpected "bombshell" is dropped on sports marketers' laps. In the United States, sports is a crucial business industry—one that involves many unscripted moments. With the right strategies and tools, marketers can get through these moments, whether by creating a checklist, using a marketing approach that retains and possibly gains customers, creating an action plan, or offering guarantees and incentives.

[pc-6]Adapted by the authors from Rick Burton and Dennis Howard, "Recovery Strategies for Sports Marketers," *Marketing Management* (Spring 2000), pp. 42–49. Reprinted by permission of the American Marketing Association.

Unexpected Bombshells

There are too many examples of those unexpected bombshells to list, but a selection of the sports headlines from the last few years alone provides context:

- "Will Conviction Send SLOC [Salt Lake City Olympics Committee] Sponsors Scattering for Cover?"
- "Fans Love This Game But Don't Miss It"
- "Sprewell Chokes Coach"
- "Galloway Threatens to Sit Out Entire Season"
- "NBA May Be Forced to Cancel Season"

In the last headline, the situation involved the National Basketball Association's (NBA) 1998 decision to lock out its players and suspend play until an agreement was reached with the NBA's Player Association (NBAPA). This was the second time in less than five years that a major professional sports league decided it was better to "take its product off the shelf" than to resolve matters privately.

Unlike the NBA lockout which occurred at the beginning of the season, the August 1994 baseball strike effectively ended a particularly exciting baseball season so completely that the World Series was not held for the first time when a regular season had been played. By some accounts, due to the lingering effects of that strike (and five other strikes or lockouts since 1972), major league attendance in 1999 was down 12 percent from pre-strike (1994) levels.

While the NBA ultimately was able to secure a strict salary cap plus a rookie salary scale, and resume its games, albeit three months late, league officials were deeply concerned about how fans would react to a squabble among extremely wealthy players and even wealthier owners. As one NBA executive remarked, "There was a lot of residual damage. It's like any other consumer product business—it can take years and years to come back. We tried to learn from other sports about how to recover."

In some ways, the same situation has existed in Salt Lake City. Stung by global allegations that a bribing scandal had taken place, the once-pure Olympic movement was tarnished by fallout that seems less about athlete greed and more about influence, power, and "perks."

For Dick Schultz, executive director of the United States Olympic Committee (USOC), the Salt Lake City bid scandal created a firestorm of opinions from official Olympic sponsors. One particularly vocal critic was David D'Alessandro, president of John Hancock Mutual Life Insurance, who indicated his company had conducted three research surveys finding that 20 percent of the people interviewed had "lost faith in not only the Olympics, but in the companies that sponsor the Olympics."

While Olympic officials vociferously challenged John Hancock's findings, the issue remained highly visible in the mainstream press. Additionally, the scandal emerged just at a point when the Salt Lake Organizing Committee (SLOC) and USOC needed to conclude their $1.34 billion in fundraising to underwrite the cost of staging the Salt Lake Olympic games. "Hopefully, [these investigations] didn't refuel it," said Schultz in August 1999, as court decisions were handed down. This is kind of a new twist on old news. You don't want to do something [wrong] that stirs people up again."

In the case of sports, doing something wrong is why sports marketers dealing with professional sports franchises wipe their hands nervously whenever they talk about building an integrated marketing plan. How can you confidently integrate marketing strategies when you can't control the most visible tactical elements (team performance, star players, coaches, or owner)? There are numerous uncontrollable factors, and many, when exposed in a negative light, are highly volatile as lead stories on the evening news. Still, sports executives must market their team or league after learning a star player has spent the afternoon practice strangling the head coach or after reading that the ego-focused owner has told a reporter he is moving the franchise to North Carolina if the city (and its taxpayers) doesn't build him a new stadium.

Team (or league) marketers may not fully control the product, pricing, or packaging, but they still must observe the laws of disciplined thinking, strategic positioning, fiscal responsibility, risk management, and bottom-line accountability.

In the case of Coca-Cola, risk was less on the soda giant's mind, after the disastrous introduction of New Coke, than the "scientific approach" that allowed Coke executives "to look at data dispassionately" and "get on with trying the next experiment." According to Sergio Zyman, Coke's former senior vice-president of marketing, "Being able to stand up and say, 'That was a mistake and I want to correct it' is more important and powerful than saying, 'I was right the first time and now I'm going to justify it.'" Zyman wrote in a recent book, *The End of Marketing As We Know It,* that "under the old rules, we would have been so committed to proving we were right [about New Coke] that we would not have been able to admit even the possibility that we had a real problem—or opportunity—on our hands." Naturally in hindsight, it's possible to bravely assert that the big cola machine was able to create new rules. What is more interesting, though, is the open admission that a problem actually existed.

Obviously, it's not a simple case of words or semantics. Marketing of any kind requires attention to detail, situation analysis, clear objective setting, viable strategies, and exciting tactics. What makes sports marketing different from traditional consumer marketing is the comfort level the marketer develops with handling the unknown. While a marketer at Coke, General Motors, or McDonald's is intimately familiar with the product and may be brought up through a rigid system of conservative marketing dic-

tums, the touchstone in corporate America remains that the organization controls the product.

Not so in sports marketing. Here, the players or participants control the action and frequently go in strange new directions on a moment's notice. Bernard Mullin, Stephen Hardy, and William Sutton defined sport marketing as "consist[ing] of all activities designed to meet the needs and wants of sport consumers through exchange processes." Sport marketing has developed two major thrusts: marketing sport products directly to the consumers of sport, and marketing other consumer and industrial products through the use of sports promotions." They add that the term "sports consumers" covers a variety of involvement forms including "playing, officiating, watching, listening, reading, and collecting."

By some accounts, sports marketing might be viewed as no different than toy marketing or consumer services marketing in general. What makes sports marketing notable is its size, visibility and variability, and the passions it engenders. Also the age and maturity of certain leagues or sports, the saturation of the sports marketplace, and the substitutability of entertainment options set it apart.

Recently, the *Sports Business Journal* ran advertising that suggested the size of the U.S. sports industry exceeded $320 billion in revenues. This would make activities involving sport (or physical participation), one of the largest industries in America. Naturally, experts have difficulty agreeing on what exactly constitutes the sports industry, but according to the advertisement, the categories covered included: sport product manufacturing, stadium construction, media delivery of sport, travel to sporting events, sponsorship, the staging of sports events, licensing of sport teams/products, and sports medicine.

Sports marketing involves unscripted moments, delivered by uncontrollable individuals. Sometimes, outcomes are negative, and marketers wake up in the morning and realize they have a fire burning. Maybe a player got arrested. Maybe an ad using an unpredictable sports personality such as former basketball player Dennis Rodman inflamed the public. Maybe players just went on strike. Maybe a participant (or spectator) was killed during the race. Maybe the hero missed hitting the winning basket and went ballistic with the media. Maybe the league or event's TV ratings are down 40 percent over the previous year.

What to Do?

Like many forms of marketing, a simple checklist can be constructed to ensure that marketers or senior executives think logically and functionally. Because time is key in a negative situation, crisis leadership is quite important. Here are some questions that can help shape many sports marketing situations:

- What's the essence of the problem?
- How are our core consumer and fringe consumer bases likely to react?
- What contingency planning steps have been designed?

- Does our contingency planning address this "hot" issue?
- Has public relations staff/agency/counsel been notified and briefed on an initial statement?
- Which senior executives should be involved with the creation of solutions?
- Are we overreacting? (Is it bad or really bad?)
- Do we anticipate a long-term or short-term negative media reaction?
- Are we prepared to be honest and truthful (or will we run and hide until we develop an acceptable "spin")?
- Are our frontline executives comfortable with negative attention?

On the surface, the approach seems to accentuate the negative, and in some ways, it must. This is because sports tend to be a high-profile activity or occupation, and consumer and media sophistication is notable. Many average fans know how much money a player or coach makes. They know won-loss records, shooting percentages, batting averages, and championship trophies delivered. They have a vague (but often false) sense, from ads and game broadcasts/interviews, of what a player or coach is like. They believe that they have seen most sports situations before.

Media are fully aware that any negative or questionable development is "news," that the right unforeseen activity can and will sell newspapers and draw listeners or viewers. Unlike traditional consumer products, which may only be covered in trade publications, sports are covered daily in most traditional media such as newspapers, television, and radio. Thus, in many cases, editors or beat reporters, already familiar with the team and players will be able to ask detailed and comprehensive questions immediately. To wit, the media will not need a "brush-up" period to cover the story. And just as the media can serve as a positive marketing arm, they also can become a negative marketing influence.

Despite this volatility, sports marketers can thrive and survive if they know what to do.

Lemonade Out of Lemons

Many dissatisfied clients can be retained if the right actions are taken. In fact, effective recovery efforts can result in higher customer satisfaction. Recovery has important implications for almost all businesses. But for professional sport franchises, most working on modest profit margins of just 3 percent, the economics of customer retention take on a more critical monetary significance. Continuing to put fannies into seats is an absolute necessity for those sports properties most dependent on game revenues.

The National Hockey League (NHL) receives 60 percent of its total revenues from ticket sales. When you add in the average income from concessions, parking, and other attendance-related activities, the typical NHL team depends on live attendance for almost three-fourths of gross revenues. While other leagues may not be as dependent on gate-related income, live attendance revenue is still crucial to the NBA (41 percent), Major League Baseball (MLB) (39 percent), and the National Football League (NFL) (29 percent). A disruption to that fan revenue can be felt immediately.

The crucial economics of recovery marketing to sport franchises becomes even more evident when the prominence of repeat attendance is taken into account. Mullin and his associates have shown the potency of the "80-20 principle" for sports teams. In their analysis of season attendance at Pittsburgh Pirates baseball games, they found that 80 percent of the increase in ticket sales from one season to another was produced by 20 percent of the existing attendees buying more tickets. This indicates that teams must rely on core customers, season ticket holders, for the lion's share of gate receipts. The defection of just 10 percent of key customers could have a devastating effect on a team's bottom line.

For an NBA team with 10,000 full season ticket holders, the failure of 1,000 current fans to renew could conceivably result in 41,000 fewer seats sold over the 41-game home schedule. With league averages of $42 per ticket and per-capita expenditures of $8.25 for concessions and parking, 10 percent fewer ticket renewals could cost an NBA team more than $2 million in lost revenues.

An Action Plan

Adapting service marketing expert Ron Zemke's process for handling disappointed customers, we suggest five simple recovery procedures that should make a big difference in overcoming fan disaffection: (1) Apologize to the consumers experiencing the service failure. (2) Make it personal. (3) Offer a value-added solution to the problem. (4) Atone for the inconvenience by offering risk-reducing incentives (such as a satisfaction guarantee) and/or rewards for repurchase (such as attractive gifts). (5) Follow up.

Consider how the NBA applied these steps to effectively recover from the potentially devastating 1998-1999 season-shortened lockout. The league orchestrated a systematic campaign to overcome widespread fan disaffection. Key elements of the campaign included the crucial role players assumed in reaching out to fans through a much-publicized Valentine's Day card promotion accenting the personal touch so important to successful recovery marketing.

The league's proactive approach to recovering fan loyalty appeared to have some positive impact. Contrary to industry experts' doom-and-gloom predictions that suggested an attendance drop of as much as 20 percent by the end of the season, the decline was a mere 2.2 percent; and almost 88 percent of all available seats were sold at NBA arenas.

Many NBA teams supplemented the league's recovery efforts at the local level. The Portland Trail Blazers mounted a personal contact campaign in which 300 staff members from ticket clerks to Head Coach Mike Dunleavy began calling every one of the team's 16,500 season ticket holders the day the lockout ended. The 3-day calling campaign relayed a simple message to core customers, "We're Back in Business and We Need You!" Season ticket holders were personally extended the NBA's offer of free admission to a team scrimmage or preseason game. Both options sold out immediately. According to the director of ticket sales for the Trail Blazers, the personal contact campaign and gift incentives "contributed significantly to achieving season ticket renewals that far exceeded our expectations."

Incentives Work!

Management specialist Alice Kendrick has found that offering added-value gifts significantly enhances customer retention and loyalty. While her research did not focus specifically on service failures, Kendrick's work suggests that gift promotions may be particularly relevant in recovery situations because they serve as tangible atonement for the service breakdown.

Kendrick discovered that providing unsolicited gifts engendered substantial goodwill among existing customers, leading to greater purchase activity. Her findings may provide a partial explanation, at least, for why the Trail Blazers' ticket renewal goals were realized so quickly. In the team's telemarketing campaign, in addition to conveying the NBA's offer of free admission to games and scrimmages, the Trail Blazers extended coupons for free food and beverages to each fan. While the "treats-are-on-us gesture was modest in nature, it obviously meant a lot to our season ticket holders."

Service Guarantees

Appropriately designed unconditional guarantees have proven to be highly effective in a number of service contexts. Interestingly, there is only limited evidence of their use by professional sports teams. The NBA's New Jersey Nets provide an example of one team that successfully initiated a satisfaction guarantee program. The Nets extended the guarantee offer to new corporate season ticket buyers promising that if the season tickets didn't help ticket holders increase their companies' sales, the Nets would refund the cost of the tickets ($8,500) plus interest.

According to the Nets' vice-president for ticket operations, "Everybody we issued that money-back guarantee to, renewed—the program helped the team generate $250,000 in new season ticket business."

Recent research suggests that a promise of complete satisfaction or a full refund would be most effective in attempting to win back consumer confidence. From a recovery standpoint, the extension of a guarantee not only appeases the client for the existing service breach but, at the same time, offers protection against any potential future service failure. An appropriately designed and executed guarantee program should convey several messages crucial to effective recovery:

- A genuine willingness on the part of the company to redress the consumer's problem.

- The service provider's commitment to quality and customer service.
- The virtual elimination of any (re)purchase risk by consumers.

Conclusion

It would be naive to imagine that the sports world would ever change so dramatically that unforeseen events will stop occurring. The beauty of sport, be it participatory or spectator-driven, is that every performance allows for the possibility of the unknown. That means, however, that marketers involved with sports must be fully prepared for sudden, unscripted activities or outcomes.

Greed, dishonesty, anger, failure to perform, and other human frailties can be logically projected to occur at different times in the course of a season or career. This is not to suggest that all athletes, agents, managers, or executives are morally or emotionally corrupted. It is rather to suggest that all humans are capable of actions that under certain microscopes (media review, fan speculation, and so on) bring about a potential uproar. Managers in sports business are wise to think about recovery strategies in advance and allow themselves the benefit of some pre-planning. In the world of sports, the Boy Scout motto of "Be prepared" is particularly relevant.

Questions

1. What are the implications of this case for a firm taking an integrated marketing communications perspective?
2. Comment on this statement: "While this case focuses on sports, it would be difficult to find any organization or sector that doesn't periodically face uncontrollable and potentially calamitous service breakdowns."
3. What are the potential rewards and risks for companies that hire athletes as celebrity spokespersons?
4. Present three specific promotion goals for firms that suffer negative publicity.
5. In presenting its position to the public after negative publicity occurs, what media should a firm utilize? Explain your answer.
6. Evaluate the public relations efforts described in the case.
7. Comment on the personal selling efforts described in the case.
8. Is it a good idea to use sales promotion to address negative publicity? Why or why not?

Price Planning

Part 7 covers pricing, the fourth and final element of the marketing mix.

20 Considerations in Price Planning

In this chapter, we study the role of price, its importance in transactions, and its interrelationship with other marketing variables. We contrast price-based and nonprice-based approaches. We also look at each of the factors affecting price decisions in depth: consumers, costs, government, channel members, and competition.

21 Developing and Applying a Pricing Strategy

Here, we explain how to construct and enact a pricing strategy. First, we distinguish among sales, profit, and status quo objectives. Next, we discuss the role of a broad price policy. Then, we introduce three approaches to pricing (cost-, demand-, and competition-based) and show how they may be applied. We also explain why cost-, demand-, and competition-based pricing methods should be integrated. We examine a number of pricing tactics, such as customary and odd pricing. We conclude the chapter by noting methods for adjusting prices.

After reading Part 7, you should understand element 13 of the strategic marketing plan outlined in Table 3-2 (pages 72–75).

20

Considerations in Price Planning

1 To define the terms price and price planning

2 To demonstrate the importance of price and study its relationship with other marketing variables

3 To differentiate between price-based and nonprice-based approaches

4 To examine the factors affecting pricing decisions

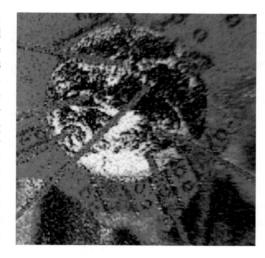

Saks Inc. (www.saksincorporated.com) plans to bring its high-end fashion oriented stores to the Middle East, Mexico, and Asia. The firm's image has been built on selling cutting-edge fashions from such designers as Dolce & Gabbana, Prada, Gucci, and other luxury labels. The foreign markets being pursued by Saks are characterized by their fast growth in luxury goods sales and by significant numbers of consumers who shop at Saks when visiting the United States. As Saks' vice-president for international business development says, "Developing markets are important for us because they are underserved."

Saks' first foreign store will be in Riyadh, Saudi Arabia. It will be a joint venture with Saudi Prince Alwaleed Bin Talal, who owns about 2 percent of Saks' stock. The prince believes "There is growing demand in the Saudi market for upscale fashion and superb customer service." He will pay a licensing fee to Saks for the use of its name. The company intends to send store personnel, including buyers and store managers, to plan and run the store—for additional compensation.

Most of the new 57,000-square-foot store, which will be located in the Kingdom Centre in Riyadh, will feature women's merchandise. Because the store will conform to Islamic standards, men will not be allowed on floors where women's clothing is sold.

What makes this joint venture so unusual is that with the exception of Tiffany (www.tiffany.com), few luxury-goods retailers have international ventures. Bloomingdale's (www.bloomingdales.com), Neiman Marcus (www.neimanmarcus.com), and Nordstrom (www.nordstrom.com) are strictly based in the United States. In contrast, international expansion has been widespread by such mass merchandisers as Wal-Mart (www.walmart.com), which operates well over 1,000 stores outside the United States. What makes Saks different, reports one marketing analyst, is that "The Saks brand has more worldwide recognition." Saks's chief executive adds, "Saks Fifth Avenue is clearly a global brand and opportunities for international growth I believe are outstanding."[1]

In this chapter, we will learn more about price-based and nonprice-based approaches to marketing strategy, and the role of consumers in setting a price strategy. We will also examine other factors that affect pricing decisions: costs, government, channel members, and competition.

20-1 OVERVIEW

A **price** represents the value of a good or service for both the seller and the buyer. **Price planning** is systematic decision making by an organization regarding all aspects of pricing.

The value of a good or service can involve both tangible and intangible factors. An example of a tangible factor is the cost saving a soda distributor obtains from buying a new bottling machine; an example of an intangible factor is a consumer's pride in the

> Through **price planning**, each **price** places a value on a good or service

[1]Devon Spurgein, "Saks Plans Store in Saudi Arabia in an Expansion," *Wall Street Journal* (November 8, 2000), pp. B1, B4.

ownership of a Porsche (www.porsche.com) rather than another brand of car. For an exchange to take place, both the buyer and seller must feel that the price of a good or service provides an equitable ("fair") value. To the buyer, the payment of a price reduces the purchasing power available for other items. To the seller, the receipt of a price is a source of revenue and a key determinant of sales and profit levels.

Many words are substitutes for the term *price*, including admission fee, membership fee, rate, tuition, service charge, donation, rent, salary, interest, retainer, and assessment. No matter what it is called, a price refers to all the terms of purchase: monetary and non-monetary charges, discounts, handling and shipping fees, credit charges and other forms of interest, and late-payment penalties. A nonmonetary exchange would be a department store awarding a gift to a person who gets a friend to shop at that store or an airline offering tickets as payment for advertising space and time. Monetary and nonmonetary exchanges may be combined. This is common with autos, where the buyer gives the seller money plus a trade-in. That combination leads to a lower monetary price.

From a broader perspective, price is the mechanism for allocating goods and services among potential buyers and for ensuring competition among sellers in an open marketplace. If demand exceeds supply, prices are usually bid up by consumers. If supply exceeds demand, prices are usually reduced by sellers. See Figure 20-1.

In this chapter, the importance of price and its relationship to other marketing variables, price-based and nonprice-based approaches, and the factors affecting price decisions are studied. Chapter 21 deals with devising and enacting a price strategy, and applying techniques for setting prices.

FIGURE 20-1

The Role of Price in Balancing Supply and Demand

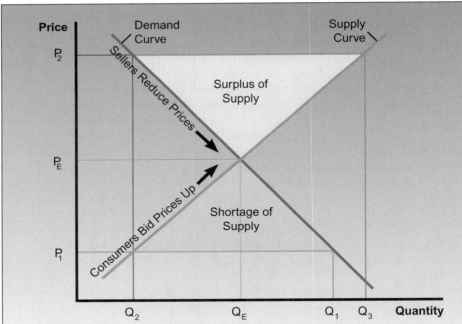

At equilibrium ($P_E Q_E$), the quantity demanded equals the supply.

At price, P_1, consumers demand Q_1 of an item. However, at this price, suppliers will make available only Q_2. There is a shortage of supply of $Q_1 Q_2$. The price is bid up as consumers seek to buy greater quantities than offered at P_1.

At price P_2, suppliers will make available Q_3 of any product of an item. However, at this price, consumers demand only Q_2. There is a surplus of supply of $Q_3 - Q_2$. The price is reduced by sellers in order to attract greater demand by consumers.

20-2 THE IMPORTANCE OF PRICE AND ITS RELATIONSHIP TO OTHER MARKETING VARIABLES

The importance of price decisions has risen considerably over the last 30 years. First, because price in a monetary or nonmonetary form is a component of the exchange process, it appears in every marketing transaction. More firms now realize the impact of price on image, sales, and profits. Second, deregulation in several industries has led to more price competition among firms. Third, to increase their profit levels, many firms have become more cost-conscious and more focused on operating as efficiently as possible. Fourth, the growth of the global economy has led to greater interest in currency valuations and exchange rates. Many firms adapt their marketing strategies to reflect international currency fluctuations. Fifth, the rapid pace of technological advances has caused intense price competition for such products as PCs, CD players, and VCRs. Sixth, service-based firms are placing more emphasis on how they set prices. Seventh, in slow economies, it is hard for firms to raise prices.

The stature of price decisions has risen because more firms recognize their far-reaching impact.

Many marketers share this view:

> Managing prices in today's competitive markets is not an easy task for companies. The fluctuations in prices and the quick reactions by competitors to any price moves by large firms has made it difficult to establish consistent long-term pricing policies. This short-term approach has increased competition, precipitated numerous price wars, and reduced margins. Nowhere is this unstable environment more prevalent than in the high-technology economy enjoyed by the United States. Here, numerous firms race to develop the best technology-driven products and price them high to recover their research and development costs; and often, in less than five years, are faced with the situation of having to lower them (prices) because of intense competition. The inability to hold prices constant for a sustainable period has made it difficult for marketing managers to use the unique benefit aspects of their products for long periods to maintain and increase market shares. Instead, price becomes the dominant competitive weapon.[2]

Inasmuch as a price places a value on the overall marketing mix offered to consumers (such as product features, product image, store location, and customer service), pricing decisions must be made in conjunction with product, distribution, and promotion plans. For instance, Parfums de Coeur (www.parfumsdecoeur.com) makes imitations of expensive perfumes from Chanel (www.chanel.com), Estée Lauder (www.esteelauder.com), and Giorgio (www.giorgiobeverlyhills.com) and sells them for one-third to one-fifth the price of those perfumes. It uses similar ingredients but saves on packaging, advertising, and personal selling costs. It distributes via such mass merchants as Wal-Mart and online.

These are some basic ways in which pricing is related to other marketing and company variables:

- Prices ordinarily vary over the life of a product category, from high prices to gain status-conscious innovators to lower prices to lure the mass market.

- Customer service is affected since low prices are often associated with less customer service.

- From a distribution perspective, the prices charged to resellers must adequately compensate them for their functions, yet be low enough to be competitive with other brands at the wholesale or retail level.

- There may be conflict in a distribution channel if a manufacturer tries to control or suggest prices.

- Product lines with different features—and different prices—can attract different market segments.

---

[2]Michael F. Smith, Indrajit Sinha, Richard Lancioni, and Howard Forman, "Role of Market Turbulence in Shaping Pricing Strategy," *Industrial Marketing Management*, Vol. 28 (November 1999), p. 637.

- A sales force may need some flexibility in negotiating prices and terms, particularly with large business accounts.

- The roles of marketing and finance personnel must be coordinated. Marketers often begin with the prices that people are willing to pay and work backward to ascertain acceptable company costs. Finance people typically start with costs and add desired profits to set prices.

- As costs change, decisions must be made as to whether to pass these changes on to consumers, absorb them, or modify product features.

Pricing internationally can be quite complicated.

When firms market products internationally, they must consider the following: "Offering prices in a foreign currency to the target market and failing to offer appropriate payment options can hurt a campaign. Local payment preferences are too important to be ignored. When setting pricing and payment strategies for an international campaign, consider (1) Currency. In what currency will prices be set? (2) Options. What payment methods will you offer? (3) Clearance. How will you clear and collect payments? Whatever your distribution channel, make payment a convenient exercise for your customers."[3] The complexity of pricing in foreign markets is often due to the divergent company goals in different markets, the varying attributes of each market, and other factors. Furthermore, the ability to set prices in foreign markets may be affected by varying government rules, competition, anti-dumping laws, operating costs, the rate of inflation, the standard of living, and so on.

20-3 PRICE-BASED AND NONPRICE-BASED APPROACHES

*A **price-based approach** occurs when sellers stress low prices; a **nonprice-based approach** emphasizes factors other than price.*

With a ***price-based approach,*** sellers influence consumer demand primarily through changes in price levels. With a ***nonprice-based approach,*** sellers downplay price as a factor in consumer demand by creating a distinctive good or service via promotion, packaging, delivery, customer service, availability, and other marketing factors. The more unique a product offering is perceived by consumers, the greater a firm's freedom to set prices above competitors'. See Figure 20-2.

FIGURE 20-2

Price-Based and Nonprice-Based Approaches

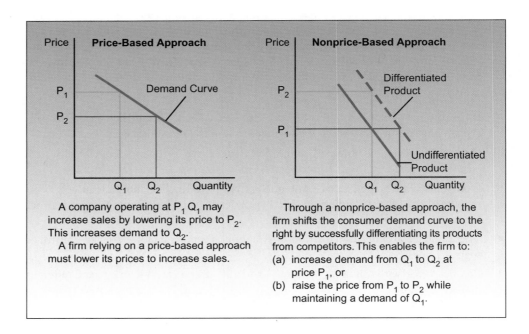

A company operating at P₁Q₁ may increase sales by lowering its price to P₂. This increases demand to Q₂.

A firm relying on a price-based approach must lower its prices to increase sales.

Through a nonprice-based approach, the firm shifts the consumer demand curve to the right by successfully differentiating its products from competitors. This enables the firm to:
(a) increase demand from Q₁ to Q₂ at price P₁, or
(b) raise the price from P₁ to P₂ while maintaining a demand of Q₁.

[3]Renee Frappier, "Hit Close to Home," *Target Marketing* (July 2000), p. 48. See also John Quelch and Gordon Swartz, "Prepare Your Company for Global Pricing," *Sloan Management Review,* Vol. 42 (Fall 2000), pp. 61–70.

FIGURE 20-3
Kmart's Price-Oriented Web Strategy
Source: Reprinted by permission.

In a price-based approach, sellers move along a demand curve by raising or lowering prices. This is a flexible marketing technique because prices can be adjusted quickly and easily to reflect demand, cost, or competitive factors. Yet, of all the controllable marketing variables, price is the easiest for a competitor to copy. This may result in "me-too" strategies or even in price wars. Furthermore, the government may monitor anti-competitive aspects of price-based strategies.

In a nonprice-based approach, sellers shift demand curves by stressing the distinctive attributes of products. This lets firms increase unit sales at a given price or sell their original supply at a higher price. The risk with this strategy is that people may not perceive a seller's product as better than a competitor's. People would then buy the lower-priced item believed to be similar to the higher-priced one.

These are examples of price- and nonprice-oriented strategies:

- Kmart (www.kmartcorp.com/corp) is one of the "big three" discount retailing chains in the United States, along with Wal-Mart (www.walmart.com) and Target (www.target.com). Its BlueLight.com (www.bluelight.com) shows the aggressive pricing approach taken by the firm. See Figure 20-3.

- Since being introduced nearly 20 years ago, hundreds of millions of low-price Swatch watches (www.swatch.com) have been sold around the world. They are fashionable, yet have fewer working parts than costlier models. To learn more about the Swatch story, visit its Web site. Click on "Information," "About Swatch," and "Student Guide."

- The Lincoln division (www.lincolnvehicles.com) of Ford has overtaken the Cadillac division (www.cadillac.com) of General Motors as the best-selling American luxury car brand. Its ads reflect the successful positioning strategy of Lincoln. See Figure 20-4.

FIGURE 20-4
Lincoln's Nonprice-Oriented Luxury Car Strategy
Source: Reprinted by permission.

● Lenox makes fine china and crystal, which are elegant and expensive. Ads rarely mention price, but focus on product quality and design. As its Lenox Collections (www.lenoxcollections.com) Web site notes, "The tradition began in 1889. A young artist-potter named Walter Scott Lenox founded a company dedicated to the daring proposition that an American firm could create the finest china, collectibles, and art pieces in the world. He possessed a zeal for perfection that he applied to the relentless pursuit of his artistic goals. Today, in every work of art created by Lenox Collections, the traditions begun by Walter Scott Lenox are carried forward."

20-4 FACTORS AFFECTING PRICING DECISIONS

Before a firm develops a pricing strategy (which is described in Chapter 21), it should analyze the outside factors affecting decisions. Like distribution planning, pricing depends heavily on elements external to the firm. This contrasts with product and promotion decisions, which are more controlled by a firm (except for publicity). Sometimes, outside elements greatly influence the ability to set prices; in other cases, they have little impact. Figure 20-5 outlines the major factors, which are discussed next.

20-4a Consumers

Company personnel involved with pricing decisions must understand the relationship between price and consumer purchases and perceptions. This relationship is explained by two economic principles—the law of demand and the price elasticity of demand—and by market segmentation.

The *law of demand* states that consumers usually purchase more units at a low price than at a high price. The *price elasticity of demand* indicates the sensitivity of buyers to price changes in terms of the quantities they will purchase.[4] Price elasticity represents the percentage change in the quantity demanded relative to a specific percentage change in the price charged. This formula shows the percentage change in demand for each 1 percent change in price:

*According to the **law of demand**, more is bought at low prices; **price elasticity** explains reactions to changes.*

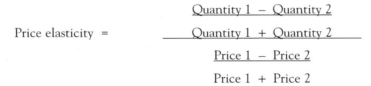

$$\text{Price elasticity} = \frac{\dfrac{\text{Quantity 1} - \text{Quantity 2}}{\text{Quantity 1} + \text{Quantity 2}}}{\dfrac{\text{Price 1} - \text{Price 2}}{\text{Price 1} + \text{Price 2}}}$$

Because the quantity demanded usually falls as price rises, elasticity is a negative number. However, for purposes of simplicity, elasticity calculations are usually expressed as positive numbers.

FIGURE 20-5
Factors Affecting Price Decisions

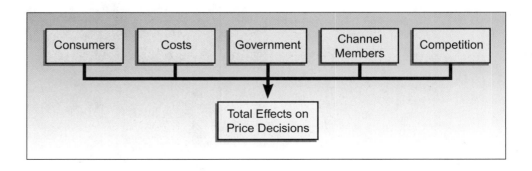

4For more detailed information, visit this Web site: "Microeconomics: Elasticity Overview" (www.mintercreek.com/micro/overview.html).

Elastic demand occurs if relatively small changes in price result in large changes in quantity demanded. Elasticity is more than 1. Total revenue goes up when prices are decreased and goes down when prices rise. *Inelastic demand* takes place if price changes have little impact on the quantity demanded. Elasticity is less than 1. Total revenue goes up when prices are raised and goes down when prices decline. *Unitary demand* exists if price changes are exactly offset by changes in the quantity demanded, so total sales revenue remains constant. Price elasticity is less than 1.

Demand elasticity is based mostly on two criteria: availability of substitutes and urgency of need. If people *believe* there are many similar goods or services from which to choose or have no urgency to buy, demand is elastic and greatly influenced by price changes: Price increases lead to purchases of substitutes or delayed purchases, and decreases expand sales as people are drawn from competitors or move up the date of their purchases. For some people, the airfare for a vacation is highly elastic. If prices go up, they may travel to a nearer location by car or postpone a trip.

If consumers believe a firm's offering is unique or there is an urgency to buy, demand is inelastic and little influenced by price changes: Neither price increases nor declines will have much impact on demand. In most locales, when heating oil prices go up or down, demand remains relatively constant because there is often no feasible substitute and homes and offices must be properly heated. Brand loyalty also generates inelastic demand; consumers then feel their brands are distinctive and do not accept substitutes. Finally, emergency conditions increase demand inelasticity. A truck driver with a flat tire would pay more for a replacement than one with time to shop around. Figure 20-6 illustrates elastic and inelastic demand.

Elasticity usually varies over a wide range of prices for the same good or service. At very high prices, even revenues for essential goods and services may fall (mass-transit ridership would drop a lot if fares rise from $1.50 to $3; driving would become a more reasonable substitute). At very low prices, demand cannot be stimulated further; saturation is reached and shoppers may begin to perceive quality as inferior.

Table 20-1 shows elasticity for an office-equipment repair business. There is a clear relationship between price and demand. At the lowest price, $60, daily demand is greatest: 10 service calls. At the highest price, $120, demand is least: 5 service calls. Demand is inelastic between $60 and $84; total service-call revenues rise as price increases. Demand is unitary between $84 and $96; total service-call revenues remain the same

> *Demand may be **elastic, inelastic,** or **unitary.** It depends on the availability of substitutes and urgency of need.*

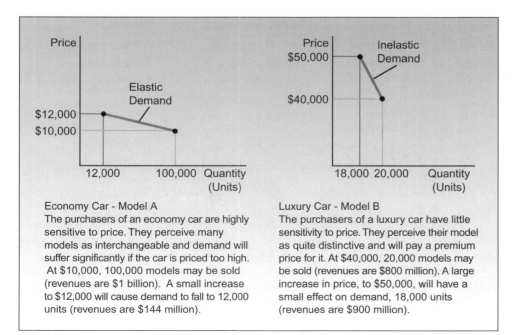

Economy Car - Model A
The purchasers of an economy car are highly sensitive to price. They perceive many models as interchangeable and demand will suffer significantly if the car is priced too high. At $10,000, 100,000 models may be sold (revenues are $1 billion). A small increase to $12,000 will cause demand to fall to 12,000 units (revenues are $144 million).

Luxury Car - Model B
The purchasers of a luxury car have little sensitivity to price. They perceive their model as quite distinctive and will pay a premium price for it. At $40,000, 20,000 models may be sold (revenues are $800 million). A large increase in price, to $50,000, will have a small effect on demand, 18,000 units (revenues are $900 million).

FIGURE 20-6

Demand Elasticity for Two Models of Automobiles

TABLE 20-1 Price Elasticity for Service Calls by an Office-Equipment Repair Business

Price of Service Call	Service Calls Demanded Per Day	Revenues from Service Calls	Price Elasticity of Demand[a]	Type of Demand
$ 60.00	10	$600.00		
			0.76	Inelastic
$ 72.00	9	$648.00		
			0.76	Inelastic
$ 84.00	8	$672.00		
			1.00	Unitary
$ 96.00	7	$672.00		
			1.31	Elastic
$108.00	6	$648.00		
			1.73	Elastic
$120.00	5	$600.00		

[a]Expressed as positive numbers.

($672). Demand is elastic between $96 and $120; total service-call revenues decline as the price rises within this range. Although a fee of either $84 or $96 yields the highest service-call revenues, $672, other criteria must be evaluated before selecting a price. The repair firm should consider costs per call; the number of servicepeople required at different levels; the overall revenues generated by each service call, including parts and added labor charges; travel time; the percentage of satisfied customers at different prices (expressed by repeat business); and the potential for referrals.

Consumers can be segmented in terms of their price orientation.

Price sensitivity varies by market segment because all people are not equally price-conscious. Consumers can be divided into such segments as these:

- *Price shoppers*—They are interested in the "best deal" for a product.
- *Brand-loyal customers*—They believe their current brands are better than others and will pay "fair" prices for those products.
- *Status seekers*—They buy prestigious brands and product categories and will pay whatever prices are set; higher prices signify greater status.
- *Service/features shoppers*—They place a great value on customer service and/or product features and will pay for them.
- *Convenience shoppers*—They value ease of shopping, nearby locations, long hours by sellers, and other approaches that make shopping simple; they will pay above-average prices.

A consumer's perception of a price level is the subjective price.

A firm must decide which segment or segments are represented by its target market and plan accordingly.

The consumer's (market segment's) perception of the price of a good or service as being high, fair, or low—its **subjective price**—may be more important than its actual price. Thus, a consumer may feel a low price represents a good buy or inferior quality—or a high price represents status or poor value, depending on his/her perception. Such factors as these affect a consumer's (market segment's) subjective price:

- *Purchase experience with a particular good or service*—"How much have I paid in the past?"
- *Purchase experience with other, rather similar goods or services*—"What's a fair price for an item in the same or adjacent product category that I bought before?"

MARKETING *and the Web*

Shopping Online Without a Credit Card

Cyber Dialogue (www.cyberdialogue.com), a marketing research firm that specializes in E-commerce, reports that 88 percent of Web-based transactions involve a credit card. Yet, even though credit cards are clearly the currency of choice for Web-based transactions, some marketing experts feel that E-commerce can benefit from additional payment alternatives.

Many of the 17 million teen and young adult shoppers who cruise online do not have access to credit. Cyber Dialogue found that while consumers ages 18 to 29 comprise one-quarter of cybershoppers who pay for Web transactions with a credit card, they represent 36 percent of shoppers who pay with cash or check. Cyber Dialogue also discovered that 54 percent of adults who browse online feel that it's easy for their credit card number to be stolen. This fear is a limiting factor to their online purchases.

Web sites such as Rocketcash (www.rocketcash.com) enable teens and young adults to purchase goods on the Web through online bank accounts. These accounts are generated by parents or other family members who mail in a check or charge their own credit card. Several systems have also been developed to improve security for Web sales. PayPal.com (www.paypal.com) and Billpoint (www.billpoint.com) let consumers pay for Web orders by deducting money from their credit card. Unlike a traditional credit card purchase, with PayPal or Billpoint, the online merchant receives payment directly from these firms without knowing the purchaser's credit card number. Lastly, American Express (www.americanexpress.com) offers a Private Payments service that generates a new credit card number for each purchase on the Web. This also eliminates concern for credit card security.

As a marketing manager for a Web retailer, explain the pros and cons of accepting payment through services such as RocketCash or PayPal.

Source: Based on material in Roger O. Crockett, "No Plastic? No Problem," *Business Week* (October 23, 2000), p. EB18.

- *Self-image*—"How much should a person like me pay for something like this?"
- *Social situation*—"How much do my friends expect me to pay for something like this?"
- *Context of the purchase*—"What should this cost in these circumstances?"[5]

KB Home (www.kbhome.com), formerly Kaufman Broad, is a leading U.S. housing developer that strives hard to offer prices perceived as fair by its target market: "We survey 300,000 home buyers each year to find out what they truly want and need in their homes. This means KB Home is ready to respond to the needs of today's young buyers, who expect more, but don't want to pay more."[6]

---

[5] G. Ray Funkhouser, "Using Consumer Expectations as an Input to Pricing Decisions," *Journal of Product & Brand Management*, Vol. 1 (Spring 1992), p. 48. See also Margaret C. Campbell, "Perceptions of Price Unfairness: Antecedents and Consequences," *Journal of Marketing Research*, Vol. 36 (May 1999), pp. 187–199; and Robert Slonim and Ellen Garbarino, "The Effect of Price History on Demand as Mediated by Perceived Price Expensiveness," *Journal of Business Research*, Vol. 45 (May 1999), pp. 1–14.

[6] "Company Information," www.kbhome.com/corporate/facts.jsp (June 1, 2001).

20-4b Costs

The costs of raw materials, supplies, labor, transportation, and other items are commonly beyond a firm's control. Yet, they have a great impact on prices. Since the early 1980s, overall U.S. cost increases have been rather low. While the 1980 inflation rate was 13.5 percent, the recent annual rate has been less than 4 percent. This means better cost control and more stable prices for most firms. Nonetheless, the costs of some goods and services have risen rapidly or fluctuated a lot in recent years. For example,

- In 2001, the price for regular unleaded gasoline reached more than $2.00 per gallon in such cities as San Francisco and Chicago—largely due to the higher costs of crude oil resulting from the OPEC (www.opec.com) trade group's decision to cut production.

- The U.S. minimum wage rose from $3.80 per hour in 1990 to $4.25 per hour in 1991, $4.75 in 1996, and $5.15 in 1997—a 35 percent increase. This affected fast-food retailers and others using semiskilled and unskilled labor. The minimum wage has not changed since 1997.

- The cost of prime-time TV ads have gone up dramatically. A 30-second ad on the 1996 Super Bowl telecast cost $1.3 million. In 2001, the cost was $2.1 million.

- Auto makers and PC makers have been affected by the rising cost of palladium, a precious metal used in catalytic converters and some laptop PCs. From late 1996 to early 2001, the price of palladium rose from $115 an ounce to $1,100 an ounce, before falling to $650 an ounce.

- Gold and silver prices have been very volatile. Gold went from $325 per ounce in mid-1999 to $250 per ounce in early 2001, before rebounding to $300 per ounce in mid-2001. High gold prices adversely affect dentists and jewelers. Silver went from $7 per ounce in 1998 to $4.50 an ounce in early 2001, before rebounding slightly. The decline had a positive impact on the photography industry, which uses silver as a film ingredient.

When costs rise, companies pass along increases, alter products, or delete some items.

During periods of rising costs, firms can react in one or more ways: They can leave products unchanged and pass along all of their cost increases to consumers, leave products unchanged and pass along part of their increases and absorb part of them, modify products to hold down costs and maintain prices (by reducing size, using lesser-quality materials, or offering fewer options), modify products to gain consumer support for higher prices (by increasing size, using better-quality materials, offering more options, or upgrading customer service), and/or abandon unprofitable products. For instance,

> In an effort to offset rising production costs, Frito-Lay (www.frito.com), the world's largest maker of salty snack foods, has begun putting fewer chips in bags of Fritos, Chee-tos, and other well-known brands, while keeping the price the same. A supermarket-size sack of Lay's potato chips has lost an ounce, or about 7.5 percent of its previous weight, but still costs $2.99. A 99-cent box of Cracker Jack has shed about 6.7 percent of its weight. And a $3.29 bag of Doritos has dropped almost 7 percent of its weight. Procter & Gamble (www.pg.com) has scaled back the number of disposable diapers in its Luvs and Pampers packages by an average of 13 percent, while cutting prices only 7 percent. Company officials say the change, which comes out to eight fewer diapers in a jumbo pack that previously had 56, leaves parents with just enough diapers to get through the week, while providing Procter a price increase for each diaper sold.[7]

Cost decreases have mostly positive benefits for marketing strategies.

If costs decline, firms can drop prices or raise margins, as these examples show: Using microchips has reduced PC costs by requiring less wiring and assembly time, improving durability, and enlarging information-processing capability. PC prices have gone down steadily, thus expanding the market. On the other hand, low sugar prices let candy makers increase package size (and profits) without raising prices.

---

[7]Greg Winter, "What Keeps a Bottom Line Healthy? Weight Loss," *New York Times* (January 2, 2001), p. A1.

GLOBAL *Marketing in Action*

The Euro: An Under-achieving New Currency

When the Euro was introduced in January 1, 1999, a single currency for 11 members of the European Community was seen as very advantageous. The Euro was touted by some economists as creating a more liquid market than the separate national currencies. It was also seen as facilitating trade across European Community members. Unfortunately, in its first twenty months, the Euro lost more than one-quarter of its value relative to the U.S. dollar. As an additional blow, 53.1 percent of Denmark's electorate voted not to join the Euro union.

To restore confidence in the Euro in the short run, the leaders of Europe's core countries (excluding Great Britain, which has never backed the concept of the Euro or participated in its use)—France, Germany, Italy, the Netherlands, and Spain— have to back the Euro with adequate reserves from their national treasuries and central banks. A more immediate move would be a coordinated buying of Euros on a large enough scale to build up its value relative to the U.S. dollar. The European Central Bank holds the equivalent of close to $40 billion in foreign currency reserves and its 11-member central banks hold an additional $222 billion in reserves. In the medium run, Europe must show its commitment to reducing taxes, deregulating labor markets, and facilitating the process for setting new businesses.

Also important is the need for the 11 EU countries who use the Euro to act in unison. Too often, members of the Eurocracy have publicly disagreed about policy issues. This has undermined public and investor confidence.

What are the consequences of a weak Euro in terms of European price-setting for a U.S. multinational firm?

Sources: Based on material in David Fairlamb, Jack Ewing, Heidi Dawley, Rich Miller, and John Rossant, "The Euro Mess," *Business Week* (October 2, 2000), pp. 140–146; and Roger Cohen, "Danish Voters Say No to Euro," *New York Times on the Web* (September 29, 2000).

Sometimes, low costs can actually have a negative long-run impact: "Ironically, cheap gasoline prices during the final years of the recent U.S. economic boom, which helped propel sales of fuel-gobbling SUVs, pushed refineries to the wall. To make matters worse, most distributors believed that OPEC would boost production. Betting that oil and gasoline would soon be cheaper, they neglected to build any significant reserves. Result: inventories of gasoline, home heating oil, and other refined products have been at a low ebb for nearly two years, leaving prices vulnerable to the slightest market upset. Now, consumers are dealing with it in a tough economic climate."[8]

20-4c Government

U.S. government (federal and/or state) actions related to pricing can be divided into the five major areas shown in Figure 20-7 and discussed next.

[8]Daniel Kadlec and Frank Gibney, Jr., "Power Struggle," *Time* (May 21, 2001), pp. 44–49.

FIGURE 20-7
Selected U.S. Government Actions Affecting Price Decisions

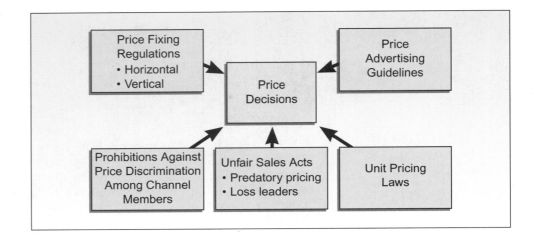

Price Fixing

Horizontal price fixing is illegal and results from agreements among companies at the same stage in a channel.

There are restrictions pertaining to horizontal and vertical price fixing. **Horizontal price fixing** results from agreements among manufacturers, among wholesalers, or among retailers to set prices at a given stage in a channel of distribution. Such agreements are illegal according to the federal Sherman Antitrust Act and the Federal Trade Commission Act, regardless of how "reasonable" prices are.

If there are violations, federal penalties may be severe: A firm can be fined up to $10 million, and individuals can be fined up to $350,000 each and imprisoned for up to 3 years. The Justice Department investigates and prosecutes price-fixing cases (www.usdoj.gov/atr/public/guidelines/guidelin.htm). In 1999, it achieved convictions resulting in fines amounting to $1.1 billion. Over the last few years, Hoffman-La Roche (of Switzerland), BASF (of Germany), Archer Daniels Midland (of the United States), and Eisai (of Japan) have each been fined more than $30 million for price-fixing activities.[9]

To avoid price-fixing charges, a firm must be careful not to

- Coordinate discounts, credit terms, or conditions of sale with competitors.
- Talk about price levels, markups, and costs at trade association meetings.
- Plan with competitors to issue new price lists on the same date.
- Plan with competitors to rotate low bids on contracts.
- Agree with competitors to limit production to keep high prices.
- Exchange information with competitors, even informally.

*Under **vertical price fixing**, manufacturers or wholesalers try to control resale prices. This practice is now limited.*

Vertical price fixing occurs when manufacturers or wholesalers seek to control the final selling prices of their goods or services. Until 1976, the Miller-Tydings Act allowed these firms to set and strictly enforce resale prices if they so desired. This practice was known as fair trade. It protected small resellers and maintained brand images by forcing all resellers within fair-trade states to charge the same price for affected products. The practice was criticized by consumer groups and many resellers and manufacturers as being noncompetitive, keeping prices too high, and rewarding reseller inefficiency. The Consumer Goods Pricing Act terminated all interstate use of fair trade or resale price maintenance. Today, resellers cannot be forced to adhere to manufacturer or wholesaler list prices. Most times, they are free to set their own prices.

Manufacturers or wholesalers may control final prices only by one of these methods:

- Manufacturer or wholesaler ownership of sales facilities.
- Consignment selling. The manufacturer or wholesaler owns items until they are sold and assumes costs normally associated with the reseller, such as advertising and selling.

[9]*U.S. Department of Justice Antitrust Division Annual Report 1999.*

- Careful screening of the channel members that sell goods or services. A supplier can bypass or drop distributors if they are not living up to the supplier's performance standards, as long as there is no collusion between the supplier and other distributors. (A firm must be careful not to threaten channel members that do not adhere to suggested prices.)

- Suggesting realistic selling prices.

- Pre-printing prices on products.

- Establishing customary prices (such as 50 cents for a newspaper) that are accepted by consumers.

Price Discrimination

The **Robinson-Patman Act** prohibits manufacturers and wholesalers from price discrimination in dealing with different channel-member purchasers of products with "like quality" if the effect of such discrimination is to injure competition. Covered by the act are prices, discounts, rebates, premiums, coupons, guarantees, delivery, warehousing, and credit rates. Terms and conditions of sale must be made available to all competing channel-member customers on a proportionately equal basis.

The Robinson-Patman Act was enacted in 1936 to protect small retailers from unfair price competition by large chains. It was feared that small firms would be driven out of business due to the superior bargaining power (and the resultant lower selling prices) of chains. This act requires that the price differences charged to competing resellers be limited to the supplier's cost savings in dealing with the different resellers. It remains a legal restraint on pricing.

There are exceptions to the Robinson-Patman Act. Price discrimination within a channel is allowed if each buyer purchases items with substantial physical differences, if noncompeting buyers are involved, if prices do not injure competition, if price differences are justified by costs, if market conditions change (such as production costs rising), or if the seller reduces prices in response to another supplier.

Discounts are permissible if a seller demonstrates that they are available to all competing resellers on a proportionate basis, sufficiently graduated so both small and large buyers can qualify, or cost-justified. For instance, a seller must prove that discounts for cumulative purchases (total volume during the year) or multistore purchases by chains are based on cost savings.

Although the Robinson-Patman Act is geared toward sellers, it has specific liabilities for purchasing firms under Section 2(F): "It shall be unlawful for any person engaged in commerce, in the course of such commerce, knowingly to induce or receive a discrimination in price which is prohibited in this section." Accordingly, resellers should try to get the lowest prices charged to any competitor in their class, but not bargain so hard that their discounts cannot be explained by one of the acceptable exceptions to the act.

*The **Robinson-Patman Act** prohibits price discrimination in selling to channel members.*

Minimum Prices

A number of states have enacted **unfair-sales acts (minimum price laws)** to prevent firms from selling products for less than their cost plus a fixed percentage that includes overhead and profit. About one-half of the states have unfair-sales acts covering all kinds of products and retail situations; two-thirds have laws involving specific products, such as bread, dairy items, and liquor. The acts are intended to protect small firms from predatory pricing by larger competitors and to limit the use of loss leaders by retailers.

With **predatory pricing,** large firms cut prices on products to below their cost in selected geographic areas so as to eliminate small, local competitors. At the federal level, predatory pricing is banned by the Sherman and Clayton Acts. Manufacturers, wholesalers, and retailers are all subject to these acts. However, predatory pricing is extremely difficult to prove.[10]

Unfair-sales acts *protect small firms from **predatory pricing** by large companies and restrict the use of **loss leaders**.*

[10]See Gunnar Niels, "Predatory Pricing Standards: Is There a Growing International Consensus?" *Antitrust Bulletin*, Vol. 45 (Fall 2000), pp. 787–809; and Dan Carney, "Predatory Pricing: Cleared for Takeoff," *Business Week* (May 14, 2001), p. 50.

Loss leaders, items priced below cost to attract customers to a seller—usually in a store setting—are also restricted by some state unfair-sales acts. Sellers use loss leaders, typically well-known and heavily advertised brands, to increase their overall sales. They assume customers drawn by loss leaders will also buy nonsale items. Because consumers benefit, loss-leader laws are rarely enforced.

Unit Pricing

With **unit pricing,** *consumers can compare prices for different-sized packages.*

The lack of uniformity in package sizes has led to unit-pricing legislation in several states.[11] *Unit pricing* lets consumers compare price per quantity for competing brands and for various sizes of the same brand.

Food stores are most affected by unit-pricing laws; they often must show price per unit of measure, as well as total price. For example, through unit pricing, a shopper could learn that a 12-ounce can of soda selling for 40 cents is priced at 3.3 cents per ounce, whereas a 67.6-ounce (2-liter) bottle of the same brand selling for $2.09 is priced at 3.1 cents per ounce. The larger size is cheaper than the smaller one.

Retailers' unit-pricing costs include computing per-unit prices, printing shelf labels, and maintaining computer records. The costs are affected by the number of stores in a chain, the sales per store, the number of items under unit pricing, and the frequency of price changes.

When unit-pricing laws were first enacted in the early 1970s, research found that people generally did not use the data and that low-income consumers (for whom the laws were most intended) were least apt to look at unit prices. Critics felt the laws were costly without providing benefits. More recent research has shown unit pricing to be effective and suggests that consumer learning and the subsequent behavioral changes take time. Upscale suburban residents are still more prone to use the data than others.

Price Advertising

FTC guidelines establish standards for price ads.

Price advertising guidelines have been set by the FTC (www.ftc.gov) and various trade associations, such as the Better Business Bureau (www.bbb.org). The FTC's guidelines specify standards of permissible conduct in several categories:

- A firm may not claim or imply that a price has been reduced from a former level unless the original price was offered to the public on a regular basis during a reasonable, recent period of time.

- A firm may not claim its price is lower than that of competitors or the manufacturer's list price without verifying, via price comparisons involving large quantities of merchandise, that an item's price at other companies in the same trading area is in fact higher.

- A suggested list price or a pre-marked price cannot be advertised as a reference point for a sale or a comparison with other products unless the advertised product has really been sold at that price.

- Bargain offers ("free," "buy one, get one free," and "half-price sale") are deemed deceptive if terms are not disclosed at the beginning of a sales presentation or in an ad, the stated regular price of an item is inflated to create an impression of savings, or the quality or quantity of a product is lessened without informing consumers. A firm cannot continuously advertise the same item as being on sale.

Under **bait-and-switch advertising,** *sellers illegally draw customers by deceptive pricing.*

- *Bait-and-switch advertising* is an illegal practice whereby customers are lured to a seller that advertises items at very low prices and then told the items are out of stock or of poor quality. Salespeople try to switch shoppers to more expensive substitutes, and there is no intent to sell advertised items. Signs of bait-and-switch are refusals to demonstrate sale items, the belittling of sale items, inadequate quantities of sale items on hand, refusals to take orders, demonstrations of defective items, and the use of compensation plans encouraging salespeople to use the tactic.

[11]See Ken Clark, "Sticker Shock," *Chain Store Age* (September 2000), pp. 88–92.

20-4d Channel Members

Generally, each channel member seeks a major role in setting prices so as to generate sales volume, obtain adequate profit margins, have a proper image, ensure repeat purchases, and meet specific goals.

A manufacturer can gain greater control over prices by using an exclusive distribution system or avoiding price-oriented resellers; pre-marking prices on products; owning sales outlets; offering products on consignment; providing adequate margins to resellers; and, most importantly, by having strong brands to which people are brand loyal and for which they will pay premium prices.

A wholesaler or retailer can gain better control over prices by stressing its importance as a customer to the supplier, linking resale support to the profit margins allowed by the supplier, refusing to carry unprofitable items, stocking competing items, having strong private brands so people are loyal to the seller and not the supplier, and purchasing outside traditional channels.

Wholesalers and retailers may engage in ***selling against the brand,*** whereby they stock well-known brands, place high prices on them, and then sell other brands for lower prices. This is done to increase sales of their private brands and is disliked by manufacturers since sales of their brands decline.

Sometimes, wholesalers and retailers go outside traditional distribution channels and buy ***gray market goods***—foreign-made products imported into countries such as the United States by distributors (suppliers) that are not authorized by the products' manufacturers. Personal stereos, VCRs, car stereos, watches, and cameras are just some of the items handled in this way. If wholesalers and retailers buy gray market goods, their purchase prices are less than they would be otherwise and they have greater control over their own selling prices. The result is often discounted prices for consumers, which may be upsetting to both manufacturers and their authorized dealers.[12]

To maximize channel-member cooperation regarding price decisions, these factors should be considered: channel-member profit margins, price guarantees, special deals, and the impact of price increases. Wholesalers and retailers require appropriate profit margins to cover their costs (such as shipping, storage, credit, and advertising) and earn reasonable profits. Thus, the prices that are charged to them must take these profit margins into account. An attempt to reduce traditional margins for channel members may lose their cooperation and perhaps find them unwilling to carry a product. Pricing through a distribution channel is discussed further in Chapter 21.

Channel members may seek price guarantees to maintain inventory values and profit. Such guarantees assure resellers that the prices they pay are the lowest available. Any discount given to competitors will also be given to the original purchasers. Guarantees are most frequently requested for new firms or new products that want to gain entry into an established channel.

Special deals—consisting of limited-time discounts and/or free products—are often used to stimulate reseller purchases. The deals may require channel members to share their savings with final consumers to increase the latter's demand. For example, soda bottlers normally give retailers large price discounts on new products to encourage them to make purchases and then offer low introductory prices to consumers.

The effects of price increases on channel members' behavior must also be assessed. When firms raise prices to resellers, these increases tend to be passed along to consumers. This practice is more difficult for items with customary prices, such as candy, where small cost rises may be absorbed by the resellers. In any event, cooperation depends on an equitable distribution of costs and profit within the channel.

To increase private brand sales, some channel members **sell against the brand.**

Gray market goods *bypass authorized channels.*

[12]See Jennifer Read, "The Strategy That Distributors Built: Making Money from the Hot Potato," *Electronic News* (February 19, 2001), p. 44; and Melody Petersen, "When Good Drugs Go Gray," *New York Times on the Web* (December 14, 2000).

The Winners and Losers in Gray Markets

With international gray marketing, goods are imported by unauthorized parties to the United States and other markets. Because gray market goods bypass a manufacturer's or importer's established distribution channel, gray marketers set up parallel channels to handle various functions. For example, Kodak film from Great Britain may be sold along side the familiar U.S.-packaged film in U.S. stores. The British film is purchased by independent importers and then shipped to the United States. Clever importers monitor price differentials on products such as film, cameras, and perfume, and then import goods only when the price difference for the products (including shipping) is high enough.

Gray marketers say that they are purchasing goods legally, and that they enable consumers to purchase goods at lower prices than through a manufacturer's traditional channels. They also assert that manufacturers and importers that criticize their practices do so to defend their high price strategies.

Those that question gray market activity say that these products may be stale, counterfeit, or defective. For example, even though Kodak's British film is produced to high standards, the gray market importer may not have properly stored it in shipment. And because nontraditional channels sell and then resell a product, the opportunity for counterfeit merchandise is high. Lastly, gray market retailers may offer poor quality service in that they have not received the same training as authorized retailers.

It is difficult to curb gray market activity. It is hard to differentiate between products being sold in the proper manner and those that involve gray marketing. Furthermore, educating consumers about the risks of buying gray market products may reduce a brand's positive reputation.

As the channel manager for a Japanese camera company, develop a strategy to curb current gray market activity for your products. Defend the strategy on ethical grounds.

Source: Based on material in Melvin Prince and Mark Davies, "Seeing Red Over International Gray Markets," *Business Horizons*, Vol. 43 (March-April 2000), pp. 71–75.

20-4e Competition

Another factor contributing to the degree of control a firm has over prices is the competitive environment within which it operates. See Figure 20-8.

A *market-controlled price environment* is characterized by a high level of competition, similar goods and services, and little control over prices by individual firms. Those trying to charge much more than the going price would attract few customers because demand for any single firm is weak enough that customers would switch to competitors. There would similarly be little gained by selling for less because competitors would match price cuts.

*A firm may face a **market-controlled**, **company-controlled**, or **government-controlled** price environment.*

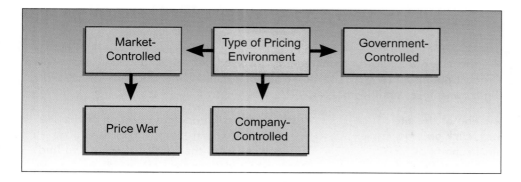

FIGURE 20-8
**The Competitive
Environment of Pricing**

A *company-controlled price environment* is characterized by moderate competition, well-differentiated goods and services, and strong control over prices by individual firms. Companies can succeed with above-average prices because people view their offerings as unique. Differentiation may be based on brand image, features, associated services, assortment, or other elements. Discounters also can carve out a niche in this environment by attracting consumers interested in low prices.

A *government-controlled price environment* is characterized by prices being set or strongly influenced by some level of government. Examples are public utilities, mass transit, insurance, and state universities. In each case, government bodies determine or affect prices after getting input from relevant firms, institutions, and/or trade associations, as well as other parties such as consumer groups.

Companies may have to adapt to a changing competitive environment in their industries. Firms in the transportation, telecommunications, and financial industries have seen their price environment shift from government- to market-controlled, although some strong firms in these industries have managed to develop a company-controlled price environment.

Because price strategies are rather easy and quick to copy, competitors' reactions are predictable if the firm initiating a price change does well. Thus, marketers must view price from both short- and long-run perspectives. Excessive price competition may lead to lengthy and costly *price wars,* in which various firms continually try to undercut each other's prices to draw customers. These wars often result in low profits or even losses for the participants and in some companies being forced out of business.

In recent years, there have been price wars among some car-rental firms, airlines, blank videocassette tape manufacturers, PC makers, semiconductor manufacturers, supermarkets, insurance companies, and others. Although price wars have been more common in the United States (due to fierce competition in some industries), they are now spreading overseas—particularly to Europe and, to a lesser extent, to Japan. The impact of price wars can be dramatic:

> The combination of a slowing economy, weaker demand, and bloated inventories has electronics makers whacking prices faster than a slasher in a teen flick. Indeed, price wars once limited to the mature PC industry have even spread to the recently red-hot markets for products such as hand-held computers and digital music players. Making things worse, many markets are now crowded with too many players. That means the industry's smallest and weakest are getting squeezed—and a wave of industry consolidations and bankruptcies is likely.[13]

Price wars *occur when competitors constantly lower prices.*

[13]Cliff Edwards, "Attention Shoppers: Enjoy the High-Tech Price War," *Business Week* (April 23, 2001), p. 46.

WEB SITES YOU CAN USE

As the chief U.S. government agency involved with pricing issues, the Federal Trade Commission's Web site has a lot of excellent information—beneficial for both consumers and businesses:

- At the *Consumer Protection* section of the site (www.ftc.gov/ftc/consumer.htm), click on "Advertising" to find such online reports as "FTC Consumer Alert! 'Free' and 'Low Cost' PC Offers. Go Figure," "FTC Business Alert! Long-Distance Deals," "FTC Consumer Alert! Taking the 'Bait' Out of Rebates," "Advertising Consumer Leases," and "Big Print. Little Print. What's the Deal?"

- At the *Antitrust/Competition* section of the site (www.ftc.gov/ftc/antitrust.htm), click on "Guidelines" from the "Antitrust Menu" to find "Antitrust Guidelines for Collaborations Among Competitors" and "Guides to Advertising and Promotional Allowances."

SUMMARY

1. *To define the terms price and price planning*   A price represents the value of a product for both the seller and the buyer. Price planning is systematic decision making relating to all aspects of pricing by a firm; it involves both tangible and intangible factors, purchase terms, and the nonmonetary exchange of goods and services. Exchange does not take place unless the buyer and seller agree that a price represents an equitable value. Price also balances supply and demand.

2. *To demonstrate the importance of price and study its relationship with other marketing variables*   During the last three decades, price decisions have become more important to business executives. This is due to price (monetary or nonmonetary) being part of every type of exchange, deregulation, cost increases, currency rates, technological advances, the greater emphasis by service companies, and periodic economic slowdowns.

Price decisions must be made in conjunction with other marketing-mix elements. And pricing is often related to the product life cycle, customer service levels, and other specific marketing and company variables. In addition, setting prices for foreign markets can be complex and influenced by country factors.

3. *To differentiate between price-based and nonprice-based approaches*   Under a price-based approach, sellers influence demand primarily via changes in price levels; they move consumers along a demand curve by raising or lowering prices. With a nonprice-based approach, sellers downplay price and emphasize such other marketing attributes as image, packaging, and features; they shift the demand curves of consumers by stressing product distinctiveness.

4. *To examine the factors affecting pricing decisions*   Several factors affect pricing decisions: consumers, costs, government, channel members, and competition. The law of demand states that consumers usually buy more units at a low price than at a high price. The price elasticity of demand explains the sensitivity of buyers to price changes in terms of the amounts they buy. Demand may be elastic, inelastic, or unitary; and it is impacted by the availability of substitutes and urgency of need. Consumers can be divided into segments based on their level of price sensitivity. Subjective price may be more important than actual price.

The costs of raw materials, supplies, labor, ads, transportation, and other items affect prices. Large increases often lead firms to raise prices, modify products, or abandon some offerings. Cost declines benefit marketing strategies by improving firms' ability to plan prices.

Government restrictions affect a broad variety of pricing areas. Price fixing, both horizontal and vertical, is subject to severe limitations. The Robinson-Patman Act bans most price discrimination to resellers that is not justified by costs. A number of states have unfair-sales acts (minimum price laws) to protect small firms against predatory pricing. Unit-pricing laws require specified retailers to post prices in terms of quantity. The FTC has a series of guidelines for price advertising.

Often, each channel member seeks a role in pricing. Manufacturers exert control via exclusive distribution, pre-ticketing, opening their own outlets, offering goods on consignment, providing adequate margins, and having strong brands. Resellers exert control by making large purchases, linking sales support to margins, refusing to carry items, stocking competing brands, developing private brands, and purchasing outside traditional channels. Reseller profit margins, price guarantees, special deals, and the ramifications of price increases all need to be considered.

A market-controlled price environment has a high level of competition, similar products, and little control over prices by individual firms. A company-controlled price environment has a moderate level of competition, well-differentiated products, and strong control over prices by individual firms. In a government-controlled price environment, the government sets or influences prices. Some competitive actions may result in price wars, in which firms try to undercut each other's prices.

KEY TERMS

price (p. 595)
price planning (p. 595)
price-based approach (p. 598)
nonprice-based approach (p. 598)
law of demand (p. 600)
price elasticity of demand (p. 600)
elastic demand (p. 601)
inelastic demand (p. 601)
unitary demand (p. 601)

subjective price (p. 602)
horizontal price fixing (p. 606)
vertical price fixing (p. 606)
Robinson-Patman Act (p. 607)
unfair-sales acts (minimum price laws)
  (p. 607)
predatory pricing (p. 607)
loss leaders (p. 608)
unit pricing (p. 608)

bait-and-switch advertising (p. 608)
selling against the brand (p. 609)
gray market goods (p. 609)
market-controlled price environment (p. 610)
company-controlled price environment
  (p. 611)
government-controlled price environment
  (p. 611)
price wars (p. 611)

REVIEW QUESTIONS

1. Explain the role of price in balancing supply and demand. Refer to Figure 20-1.
2. What is the risk with using a nonprice-oriented strategy?
3. Distinguish between elastic and inelastic demand. Why is it necessary for a firm to understand these differences?
4. At a price of $40, a firm could sell 1,000 units. At a price of $25, it could sell 1,250 units. Calculate the elasticity of demand and state what price the firm should charge—and why.

5. If costs rise rapidly, how could a company react?
6. Is horizontal price fixing always illegal? Explain your answer.
7. Does the buyer have any potential liability under the Robinson-Patman Act? Why or why not?
8. How can a firm turn a market-controlled price environment into a company-controlled one?

DISCUSSION QUESTIONS

1. How could a firm estimate price elasticity for a new product? A mature product?
2. When would you pass along a cost decrease to consumers? When would you not pass the decrease along?
3. You are the marketing vice-president of a telemarketing firm that sells chimney cleaning services at prices ranging from

$250 to $650 (depending on the size and condition of the chimney). What would you do to persuade consumers that you offer fair prices?
4. Present five examples of price advertising for a car dealer that would violate FTC guidelines.

WEB EXERCISE

Visit and evaluate one of these Web sites: Auction Hawk (www. auctionhawk.com), Overstock.com (www.overstock.com), or 999central.com (www.999central.com). Apply several of the pricing concepts discussed in this chapter when writing up the exercise.

21

Developing and Applying a Pricing Strategy

Chapter Objectives

1 To present an overall framework for developing and applying a pricing strategy

2 To analyze sales-based, profit-based, and status quo-based pricing objectives, and to describe the role of a broad price policy

3 To examine and apply the alternative approaches to a pricing strategy

4 To discuss several specific decisions that must be made in implementing a pricing strategy

5 To show the major ways that prices can be adjusted

T he Internet has been known as a place for free music, free news, free access to E-mail, and free shipping. Yet, today, many Web-based firms that once were part of the "free" frenzy blame many of their current difficulties on the free goods and services that they gave out in the hopes of building marketing share or long-term customers. The basic strategy was simple: They gave potential customers free items as a sample to get them to try their products. In some cases, free services were missing an important feature that could be received only by paying an additional fee.

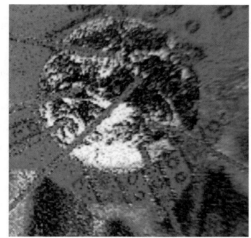

An example of the current trend is Juno's (www.juno.com) decision to restrict its free Internet provider service by making it more difficult for heavier users to stay continually connected to the Web. Consumers who pay full price for Juno would have unrestricted access. Other free Internet service providers such as AltaVista and 1stUp.com were forced to close due to lower than anticipated advertising revenues and higher costs.

According to some marketing analysts, investors are now interested in companies that have multiple revenue streams. As one analyst says, "I think it's clear the big river called Free is not going to tolerate a dam all of a sudden, but companies are going to have to develop all sorts of small tributaries that will eventually be as powerful." Thus, the latest shift for Web-based marketers is "P-to-P" or path to profitability. (Some analysts joke among themselves that "P-to-P" stands for "prepare to pray.")

Before it shut down, Webvan, the online grocery delivery service unsuccessfully introduced delivery fees of $4.95 on orders that were less than $75. Previously, all delivery fees were waived. Amazon.com (www.amazon.com) has raised the minimum purchase quantities that qualify for free shipping. And free goods or services are more typically linked to large purchases, such as a consumer's receiving free access to Microsoft Network with the purchase of a Dell personal computer.[1]

In this chapter, we will look at the overall process of developing and applying a pricing strategy—setting pricing objectives, the use of various pricing approaches, how a pricing strategy is implemented, and how prices can be adjusted.

21-1 OVERVIEW

As Figure 21-1 shows, a pricing strategy has five steps: objectives, broad policy, strategy, implementation, and adjustments. All of them are affected by the outside factors noted in this chapter. Like any planning activity, a pricing strategy begins with a clear statement of goals and ends with an adaptive or corrective mechanism. Pricing decisions are integrated with the firm's overall marketing program during the broad price-policy step. A

---

[1]Kara Swisher, "The Giveaway Is Going Away on Web Sites," *Wall Street Journal* (December 4, 2000), pp. B1, B6; and Saul Hansell, "Free Rides Now Passé on Information Highway," *New York Times on the Web* (May 1, 2001).

good introductory Web site for price planning is the Small Business Administration's (www.sba.gov/library/pubs.html) "Small Business Management Series" (click on the pricing module in the "Financial Management Series").

The development of a pricing strategy is not a one-time occurrence. It needs to be reviewed when a new product is introduced, an existing product is revised, the competitive environment changes, a product moves through its life cycle, a competitor initiates a price change, costs rise or fall, the firm's prices come under government scrutiny, and/or other events take place.

These are some indications a pricing strategy may be performing poorly:

- Prices are changed too frequently.
- Pricing policy is difficult to explain to consumers.
- Channel members complain that profit margins are inadequate.
- Price decisions are made without adequate marketing-research information.
- Too many different price options are available.
- Too much sales personnel time is spent in bargaining.
- Prices are inconsistent with the target market.
- A high percentage of goods is marked down or discounted late in the selling season to clear out surplus inventory.
- Too high a proportion of customers is price-sensitive and attracted by competitors' discounts. Demand is elastic.
- The firm has problems conforming with pricing legislation.

This chapter describes in detail the pricing framework outlined in Figure 21-1.

FIGURE 21-1

A Framework for Developing and Applying a Price Strategy

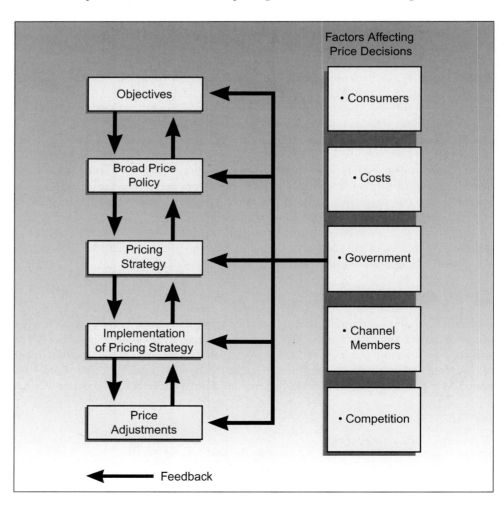

21-2 PRICING OBJECTIVES

A pricing strategy should be consistent with and reflect overall company goals. It is possible for different firms in the same industry to have dissimilar objectives and, therefore, distinct pricing strategies.

There are three general objectives from which a firm may select: sales-based, profit-based, and status quo-based. See Figure 21-2. With sales-based goals, a firm wants sales growth and/or to maximize market share. With profit-based goals, it wants to maximize profit, earn a satisfactory profit, optimize the return on investment, and/or secure an early recovery of cash. With status quo-based goals, it seeks to avoid unfavorable government actions, minimize the effects of competitor actions, maintain good channel relations, discourage the entry of competitors, reduce demands from suppliers, and/or stabilize prices.

A firm may pursue more than one pricing goal, such as increasing sales by 5 to 10 percent each year, achieving a 15 percent return on capital investments, and keeping prices near those of competitors. It may also set distinct short- and long-run goals. In the short run, it may seek high profit margins on new products; in the long run, these profit margins would drop to discourage potential competitors.

21-2a Sales-Based Objectives

A firm with **sales-based pricing objectives** is oriented toward high sales volume and/or expanding its share of sales relative to competitors. The company focuses on sales-based goals for any (or all) of three reasons: It sees market saturation or sales growth as a major step leading to market control and sustained profits. It wants to maximize unit sales and will trade low per-unit profits for larger total profits. It assumes greater sales will enable it to have lower per-unit costs.

To gain high sales volume, **penetration pricing** is often employed, whereby low prices are used to capture the mass market for a good or service. It is a proper approach if customers are highly sensitive to price, low prices discourage actual and potential competitors, there are economies of scale (per-unit production and distribution costs fall as sales rise), and a large consumer market exists. Penetration pricing also recognizes that a high price may leave a product vulnerable to competition.[2]

Penetration pricing is used by such companies as Compaq, Malt-O-Meal, and Kellwood. Compaq (www.compaq.com) now markets a $799 "entry level" PC whose price includes a monitor, a high-speed AMD processor, a 40-gigabyte hard drive, a CD-RW drive, an Internet video camera, and a lot more. Malt-O-Meal (www.malt-o-meal.com) makes no-frills cereals and sells many of them in bags rather than boxes. Its prices are far less than those of better-known brands. Cricket Lane is a division of the Kellwood Company (www.kwdco.com) that makes private-label apparel for such retailers as J.C. Penney and Target. It specializes in separates and coordinated sportswear for petite, misses, and women's sizes.

> **Sales-based pricing objectives** *seek high volume or market share.*

> **Penetration pricing** *aims at the mass market.*

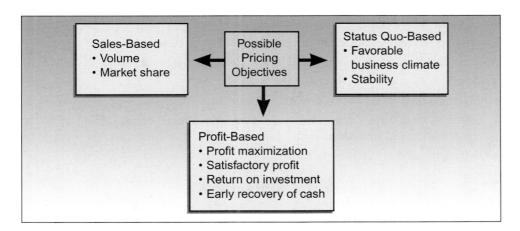

FIGURE 21-2
Pricing Objectives

2See Norm Brodsky, "The Right Price," *Inc.* (April 2001), pp. 25–26.

Penetration pricing may even tap markets not originally anticipated. For example, few people forecast that cordless phones would reach the sales attained during their peak. The market expanded rapidly after prices fell below $100. It grew again as new models were introduced for $50 and less.

21-2b Profit-Based Objectives

A firm having *profit-based pricing objectives* orients its strategy toward some type of profit goals. With profit-maximization goals, high dollar profits are sought. With satisfactory-profit goals, stability over time is desired; rather than maximum profits in a given year (which could cause a fall in nonpeak years), steady profits for many years are sought. With return-on-investment goals, profits are related to outlays; these goals are often sought by regulated utilities to justify rate increases. With early-recovery-of-cash goals, high initial profits are sought because firms are short of funds or uncertain about their future.

Profit may be expressed in per-unit or total terms. Per-unit profit equals the revenue a seller receives for one unit sold minus its costs. A product like custom-made furniture has a high unit profit. Total profit equals the revenue a seller receives for all items sold minus total costs. It is computed by multiplying per-unit profit times the number of units sold. A product like mass-marketed furniture has a low unit profit; success is based on the number of units sold (turnover). Products with high per-unit profits may have lower total profits than ones with low per-unit profits if the discount prices of the latter generate a much greater level of consumer demand. However, this depends on the elasticity of demand.

Skimming pricing uses high prices to attract the market segment more concerned with product quality, uniqueness, or status than price. It is proper if competition can be minimized (via patent protection, brand loyalty, raw material control, or high capital requirements), funds are needed for early cash recovery or further expansion, consumers are insensitive to price or willing to pay a high initial price, and unit costs remain equal or rise as sales increase (economies of scale are absent).

Skimming prices are used by such firms as Genentech, Canondale, and British Airways. Genentech (www.gene.com) makes Activase, a patented brand of TPA (tissue plasminogen activator), which quickly clears the blood clots associated with heart attacks and effectively treats certain strokes. It sells Activase for about $2,000 per dose. Cannondale's (www.cannondale.com) Jekyll 4000 SL mountain bicycle, voted the 2001 "Bike Of The Year" by France's *Velo Vert* magazine, retails for $5,000. The bicycle is full-suspension and disc-brake equipped. British Airways (www.britishairways.com) has over-hauled its first-class cabins to provide passengers with fully reclining seats ("When you're ready to settle down, your seat converts at the touch of a button into a 6'6" horizontal bed."), greater privacy, and more room. It targets those willing to pay $10,000 for a round-trip between London and New York.

Firms may first use skimming pricing and then penetration pricing, or they may market a premium brand and a value brand. There are many advantages to this:

- High prices are charged when competition is limited.
- High prices help cover development and introductory advertising costs.
- The first group of customers to buy a new product is usually less price-sensitive.
- High initial prices portray a high-quality image.
- Raising initial prices may be resisted by consumers; lowering them is viewed favorably.
- After the initial market segment is saturated, penetration pricing can appeal to the mass market and expand total sales volume.
- Multiple segments can be reached.

21-2c Status Quo-Based Objectives

Status quo-based pricing objectives are sought by a firm interested in continuing a favorable business climate for its operations or in stability. The pricing strategy is used to minimize the impact of such outside parties as government, competitors, and channel members—and to avoid sales declines.

Profit-based pricing objectives *range from maximization of profit to recovery of cash. Goals can be per unit or total.*

Skimming pricing *is aimed at the segment interested in quality or status.*

Status quo-based pricing objectives *seek good business conditions and stability.*

GLOBAL *Marketing in Action*

Is It Possible for Prices to Be Too Low?

Fierce competition in the United States can often result in low-price specials for consumers. However, this is not the case in Germany where the German Cartel Office, an antitrust agency, regulates minimum prices of staples (like milk, butter, flour, and cooking oil).

The German Cartel Office recently ordered Wal-Mart's (www.walmart.com) German unit and two German supermarket chains, Lidi and Aldi (www.aldi.com), to raise their prices on these staple items. The Cartel Office determined that these companies had used their market size and bargaining power to sell products below cost on a continuing basis. Even though consumers could benefit from these actions, competition would be hurt as small and medium-sized retailers could not match the low prices. Selling goods below their cost is allowed in Germany if limited to perishables and practiced occasionally; but these retailers regularly used below-cost sales on a variety of products.

The Cartel Office's actions have not been universally endorsed. As one German consumer said, "I have nothing against these prices if it makes foods cheaper for the consumer. Moreover, Wal-Mart and the two rivals have plenty of competitors that don't need regulators' protection." Some marketing analysts have also observed that while the German Cartel Office has blocked Wal-Mart from price-cutting in Germany, German-based Aldi is able to sell at reduced prices in its United States stores.

In contrast, the German Retail Trade Association, a trade group representing small and mid-sized retailers, views the Cartel Office's decision as a "hopeful signal for the end of the ruinous cutthroat competition" between Wal-Mart and two German supermarket chains.

As the Wal-Mart marketing manager in Germany, what would you do now?

Source: Based on material in Daniel Akst, "Why Pay More? Go Ask the Germans," *New York Times on the Web* (October 1, 2000); and Ernest Beck, "Stores Told to Lift Prices in Germany," *Wall Street Journal* (September 11, 2000). pp. A27, A30.

One should not infer that status quo goals require no effort. A firm must instruct salespeople not to offer different terms to competing channel members or else it may be accused of a Robinson-Patman Act violation. It may have to match competitors' price cuts to keep customers—while striving to avoid price wars. It may have to accept lower profit margins in the face of rising costs to hold channel cooperation. It may have to charge penetration prices to discourage competitors from marketing certain product lines.

21-3 BROAD PRICE POLICY

A *broad price policy* sets the overall direction (and tone) for a firm's pricing efforts and makes sure pricing decisions are coordinated with the firm's choices as to a target market, an image, and other marketing-mix factors. It incorporates short- and long-term pricing goals, as well the role of pricing. Pricing can play a passive role—with customer purchases based on superior service, convenience, and quality—or it can play an active role—with purchases based on discount prices. Thus, a high-income segment buying status brands at upscale stores would expect premium prices. A moderate-income segment buying private brands at flea markets would expect low prices.

*A **broad price policy** links prices with the target market, image, and other marketing elements.*

A firm outlines a broad price policy by integrating individual decisions. It then decides on the interrelationship of prices for items within a product line, how often discounts are used, how prices compare to competition, the frequency of price changes, and the method for setting new-product prices.

Utilizing an integrated broad price policy is not necessarily effortless:

> Pricing is highly complex, and many firms truncate the process and apply standard operating procedures, such as the cost-plus formula, to simplify the tasks involved. Unfortunately, these practices ignore too many relevant internal and external variables, and numerous pricing errors are made. Pricing is too important to forego deep analyses of relevant company and market influences. Decisions should be based on a comprehensive, systematic multistage process that examines and integrates the full range of forces that impact pricing effectiveness.[3]

21-4 PRICING STRATEGY

A pricing strategy may be cost-, demand-, and/or competition-based. When the three approaches are integrated, combination pricing is involved. See Figure 21-3. Next, each technique is explained and illustrations provided.

FIGURE 21-3

The Alternative Ways of Developing a Pricing Strategy

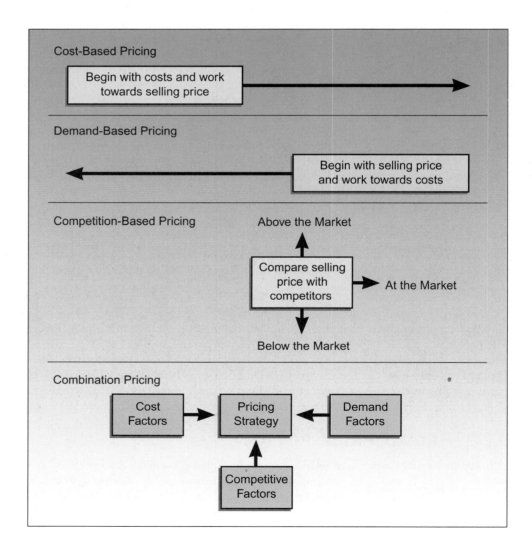

---

[3]David Shipley and David Jobber, "Integrative Pricing Via the Pricing Wheel," *Industrial Marketing Management*, Vol. 30 (April 2001), p. 301.

21-4a Cost-Based Pricing

In *cost-based pricing,* a firm sets prices by computing merchandise, service, and overhead costs and then adding an amount to cover its profit goal. Table 21-1 defines the key concepts in cost-based pricing and how they may be applied to big-screen television sets.

Cost-based prices are rather easy to derive because there is no need to estimate elasticity of demand or competitive reactions to price changes. There is also greater certainty about costs than demand or competitor responses to prices. Finally, cost-based pricing seeks reasonable profits since it is geared to covering all types of costs. It is often used by firms whose goals are stated in terms of profit or return on investment. A *price floor* is the lowest acceptable price a firm can charge and attain its profit goal.

When used by itself, cost-based pricing does have some significant limitations. It does not consider market conditions, the full effects of excess plant capacity, competitive prices, the product's phase in its life cycle, market share goals, consumers' ability to pay, and other factors.

> *Under* **cost-based pricing,** *expenses are computed, profit is projected, and a* **price floor** *set.*

TABLE 21-1	**Key Cost Concepts and How They May Be Applied to Big-Screen Television Sets**

Cost Concept	Definition	Examples[a]	Sources of Information	Method of Computation
Total fixed costs	Ongoing costs not related to volume. They are usually constant over a given range of output for a specified time.	Rent, salaries, electricity, real-estate taxes, plant, and equipment.	Accounting data, bills, cost estimates.	Addition of all fixed cost components.
Total variable costs	Costs that change with increases or decreases in output (volume).	Parts (such as tuners and speakers), hourly employees who assemble sets, and sales commissions.	Cost data from suppliers, estimates of labor productivity, sales estimates.	Addition of all variable cost components.
Total costs	Sum of total fixed and total variable costs.	See above.	See above.	Addition of all fixed and variable cost components.
Average fixed costs	Average fixed costs per unit.	See above under total fixed costs.	Total fixed costs and production estimates.	Total fixed costs/ Quantity produced in units.
Average variable costs	Average variable costs per unit.	See above under total variable costs.	Total variable costs and production estimates.	Total variable costs/ Quantity produced in units.
Average total costs	Sum of average fixed costs and average variable costs.	See above under total fixed and total variable costs.	Total costs and production estimates.	Average fixed costs + Average variable costs or Total costs/Quantity produced in units.
Marginal costs	Costs of making an additional unit.	See above under total fixed and total variable costs.	Accounting data, bills, cost estimates of labor and materials.	(Total costs of producing current quantity + one unit) − (Total costs of producing current quantity).

[a]Such marketing costs as advertising and distribution are often broken down into both fixed and variable components.

FIGURE 21-4

Cost-Based Pricing Techniques

Traditional Break-Even Analysis
• Determines sales quantity needed to break even at a given price

Cost-Plus Pricing
• Pre-determined profit added to costs

Price-Floor Pricing
• Determines lowest price at which to offer additional units for sale

Cost-Based Pricing Techniques

Markup Pricing
• Calculates percentage markup needed to cover selling costs and profit

Target Pricing
• Seeks specified rate of return at a standard volume of production

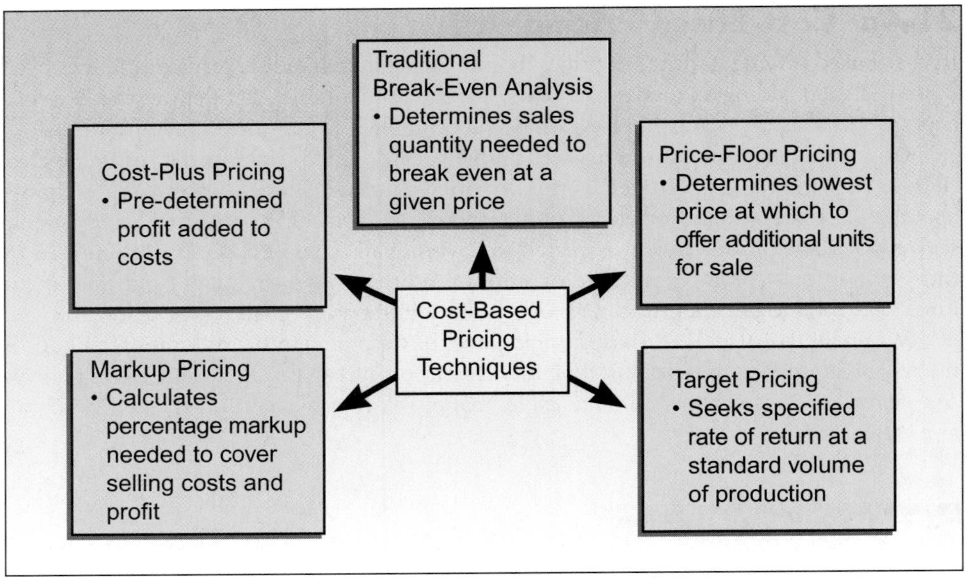

Sometimes, it is hard to figure how such overhead costs as rent, lighting, personnel, and other general expenses should be allocated. These costs are often assigned in terms of product sales or the personnel time associated with each item. If product A accounts for 10 percent of sales, it may be allotted 10 percent of overhead costs. If product B gets 20 percent of personnel time, it may be allotted 20 percent of overhead costs. Problems may arise since different ways of assigning costs may yield varying results: How are costs allotted if a product yields 10 percent of sales and needs 20 percent of personnel time?

In the following subsections, five cost-based pricing techniques are covered: cost-plus, markup, target, price-floor, and traditional break-even analysis. Figure 21-4 gives a synopsis of each technique. And at the end of these subsections, Table 21-2 contains numerical examples of them.

Cost-Plus Pricing

For *cost-plus pricing,* prices are set by adding a pre-determined profit to costs. It is the simplest form of cost-based pricing. Generally, the steps for computing cost-plus prices are to estimate the number of units to be produced, calculate fixed and variable costs, and add a desired profit to costs. The formula is

$$\text{Price} = \frac{\text{Total fixed costs} + \text{Total variable costs} + \text{Projected profit}}{\text{Units produced}}$$

This method is easy to compute; yet, it has shortcomings. Profit is not expressed in relation to sales but in relation to costs, and price is not tied to consumer demand. Adjustments for rising costs are poorly conceived, and there are no plans for using excess capacity. There is little incentive to improve efficiency to hold down costs, and marginal costs are rarely analyzed.

Cost-plus pricing is most effective when price fluctuations have little influence on sales and when a firm is able to control prices. For example, the prices of custom-made furniture, ships, heavy machinery, and extracted minerals typically depend on the costs incurred in producing these items; thus, companies set prices by computing costs and adding a reasonable profit. Cost-plus pricing often allows firms to get consumer orders, produce items, and then derive prices after total costs are known. This protects sellers.

Cost-plus pricing is the easiest form of pricing, based on units produced, total costs, and profit.

Markup Pricing

In *markup pricing,* a firm sets prices by computing the per-unit costs of producing (buying) goods and/or services and then determining the markup percentages needed to cover selling costs and profit. It is most commonly used by wholesalers and retailers, although it is employed by all types of organizations. The formula for markup pricing is[4]

$$\text{Price} = \frac{\text{Product cost}}{(100 - \text{Markup percent})/100}$$

There are several reasons why markups are commonly stated in terms of selling price instead of cost. One, since expenses, markdowns, and profits are computed as percentages of sales, when markups are also cited as percentages of sales, they aid in profit planning. Two, firms quote their selling prices and trade discounts to channel members as percentage reductions from final list prices. Three, competitive price data are more readily available than cost data. Four, profitability appears smaller if based on price rather than on cost. This may be useful to avoid criticism over high earnings.

Markup size depends on traditional profit margins, selling and operating expenses, suggested list prices, inventory turnover, competition, the extent to which products must be serviced, and the effort needed to complete transactions. Due to differences in selling costs among products, some firms use a *variable markup policy,* whereby separate categories of goods and services receive different percentage markups. Variable markups recognize that some items require greater personal selling, customer service, alterations, and end-of-season markdowns than others. For example, expensive cosmetics need more personal selling and customer service than paperback books, suits need greater custom alterations than shirts, and fashion items are marked down more than basic clothing late in the selling season.

Markup pricing, while having many of cost-plus pricing's limitations, is popular. It is fairly simple, especially for firms with uniform markups for several items. Channel members get fair profits. Price competition is less if firms have similar markups. Resellers can show their actual prices compared to suggested prices. Adjustments can be made as costs rise. Variable markups are responsive to selling cost differences among products or channel members.

Target Pricing

In *target pricing,* prices are set to provide a particular rate of return on investment for a standard volume of production—the level of production a firm anticipates achieving. For example, in the paper industry, the standard volume of production is usually set at around 90 to 92 percent of plant capacity. For target pricing to operate properly, a company must sell its entire standard volume at specified prices.

Target pricing is used by capital-intensive firms (like auto makers) and public utilities (like water companies). The prices charged by utilities are based on fair rates of return on invested assets and must be approved by regulatory commissions. Mathematically, a target price is computed as

$$\text{Price} = \frac{\text{Investment costs} \times \text{Target return on investment (\%)}}{\text{Standard volume}}$$
$$+ \text{ Average total costs (at standard volume)}$$

Target pricing has five major shortcomings. First, it is not useful for firms with low capital investments; it understates selling price. Second, because prices are not keyed to demand, the entire standard volume may not be sold at the target price. Third, production problems may hamper output and standard volume may not be attained. Fourth, price

Markup pricing *considers per-unit product costs and the markups required to cover selling costs and profits. Markups should be expressed in terms of price rather than cost.*

A **variable markup policy** *responds to differences in selling costs among products.*

Target pricing *enables a rate of return on investment to be earned for a standard volume of production.*

---

[4]Markup can be calculated by transposing the formula into

$$\text{Markup percentage} = \frac{\text{Price} - \text{Product cost}}{\text{Price}} \times 100$$

cuts to handle overstocked inventory are not planned under this approach. Fifth, if the standard volume is reduced due to unexpected poor sales performance, the price would be raised under a target-pricing calculation.

Price-Floor Pricing

A firm's usual goal is to set prices to cover the sum of average fixed costs, average variable costs, and profit per unit. But when a firm has excess (unused) capacity, it may use ***price-floor pricing*** to find the lowest price at which it is worthwhile to raise the amount of goods or services it makes available for sale. The general principle is that the sale of additional units can be used to increase profits or help pay for fixed costs (which exist whether or not these items are made), as long as marginal revenues are greater than marginal costs. Although a firm cannot survive in the long run unless its average total costs are covered by prices, it may improve performance through price-floor pricing. The formula is

$$\text{Price-floor price} = \text{Marginal revenue per unit} > \text{Marginal cost per unit}$$

Traditional Break-Even Analysis

Like target pricing, traditional break-even analysis looks at the relationship among costs, revenues, and profits. While target pricing yields the price that results in a specified return on investment, ***traditional break-even analysis*** finds the sales quantity in units or dollars that is needed for total revenues (price × units sold) to equal total costs (fixed and variable) at a given price. If sales exceed the break-even quantity, a firm earns a profit. If sales are less than the break-even quantity, it loses money. Traditional break-even analysis does not consider return on investment, but can be extended to take profit planning into account. It is used by all kinds of sellers.

The break-even point can be computed in terms of units or sales dollars:

$$\text{Break-even point (units)} = \frac{\text{Total fixed costs}}{\text{Price} - \text{Variable costs (per unit)}}$$

$$\text{Break-even point (sales dollars)} = \frac{\text{Total fixed costs}}{1 - \frac{\text{Variable costs (per unit)}}{\text{Price}}}$$

These formulas are derived from the equation: Price × Quantity = Total fixed costs + (Variable costs per unit × Quantity).

Break-even analysis can be adjusted to take into account the profit sought by a firm:

$$\text{Break-even point (units)} = \frac{\text{Total fixed costs} + \text{Projected profit}}{\text{Price} - \text{Variable costs (per unit)}}$$

$$\text{Break-even point (sales dollars)} = \frac{\text{Total fixed costs} + \text{Projected profit}}{1 - \frac{\text{Variable costs (per unit)}}{\text{Price}}}$$

There are limitations to traditional break-even analysis. First, as with all cost-based pricing, demand is not considered. The presumption is that wide variations in quantity can be sold at the same price; this is highly unlikely. Second, it is assumed that all costs can be divided into fixed and variable categories. Yet, some, like advertising, are difficult to define; advertising can be fixed or a percent of sales. Third, it is assumed that variable costs per unit are constant over a range of quantities, but purchase discounts or overtime wages may alter the costs. Fourth, it is assumed that fixed costs remain constant; but increases in production may lead to higher costs for new equipment, new full-time employees, and other items.

By including demand considerations, each of the cost-based techniques can be improved. Demand-based pricing techniques are discussed next.

TABLE 21-2   **Examples of Cost-Based Pricing Techniques**

Cost-Plus Pricing—A custom-sofa maker has total fixed costs of $50,000, variable costs of $500 per sofa, desires $10,000 in profits, and plans to produce 100 couches. What is the selling price per couch?

$$\text{Price} = \frac{\text{Total fixed costs } + \text{ Total variable costs } + \text{ Projected profit}}{\text{Units produced}} = \$1,100$$

Markup Pricing—A retailer pays $30 for telephones and wants a markup on selling price of 40 percent (30 percent for selling costs and 10 percent for profit). What is the final selling price?

$$\text{Price} = \frac{\text{Merchandise costs}}{(100 - \text{Markup percent})/100} = \$50$$

Target Pricing—A specialty auto maker has spent $160,000,000 for a new plant. It has a 25 percent target return on investment. Standard production volume for the year is 5,000 units. Average total costs, excluding the new plant, are $14,000 for each car (at a production level of 5,000 cars). What is the selling price to the firm's retail dealers?

$$\text{Price} = \frac{\text{Investment costs} \times \text{Target return on investment (\%)}}{\text{Standard volume}} + \text{Average total costs (at standard volume)} = \$22,000$$

Price-Floor Pricing—A big-screen TV manufacturer's plant capacity is 1,000 units. Its total fixed costs are $500,000 and variable costs are $375 per unit. At full production, average fixed costs are $500 per unit. The firm sets a price of $1,100 to retailers and gets orders for 800 TVs at that price. It must operate at 80 percent of capacity, unless it re-evaluates its pricing strategy. With price-floor pricing, it can sell the 200 additional sets to retailers. How?

The firm could let resellers buy one TV at $425 for every four they buy at $1,100. Then, it earns a profit of $90,000 [revenues of ($1,100 × 800) + ($425 × 200) less costs of ($875 × 1,000)]. If it just makes and sells 800 TVs at full price, it earns $80,000 [revenues of ($1,100 × 800) less variable costs of ($375 × 800) and fixed costs of ($500,000)]. The higher profits are due to marginal revenue > marginal cost.

Traditional Break-Even Analysis—A small candy maker has total fixed costs of $150,000 and variable costs per unit of $0.25. It sells to retailers for $0.40 per bar. What is the break-even point in units? In sales dollars?

$$\text{Break-even point (units)} = \frac{\text{Total fixed costs}}{\text{Price} - \text{Variable costs (per unit)}} = 1,000,000$$

$$\text{Break-even point (sales dollars)} = \frac{\text{Total fixed costs}}{1 - \frac{\text{Variable costs (per unit)}}{\text{Price}}} = \$400,000$$

21-4b Demand-Based Pricing

With **demand-based pricing,** a firm sets prices after studying consumer desires and ascertaining the range of prices acceptable to the target market. This approach is used by firms that believe price is a key factor in consumer decision making. These firms identify a **price ceiling,** which is the maximum amount consumers will pay for a given good or service. If the ceiling is exceeded, consumers will not make purchases. Its level depends on the elasticity of demand (availability of substitutes and urgency of need) and consumers' subjective price regarding the particular good or service.

Demand-based methods require consumer research as to the quantities that will be bought at various prices, sensitivity to price changes, the existence of market segments, and consumers' ability to pay. Demand estimates tend to be less precise than cost estimates. Also, firms that do inadequate cost analysis and rely on demand data may end up losing money if they make unrealistically low cost assumptions.

Under demand-based pricing, very competitive situations may lead to small markups and lower prices since people will buy substitutes; costs must be held down or prices will be too high—as might occur via cost-based pricing. For noncompetitive situations, firms can set large markups and high prices since demand is rather inelastic. There is less emphasis on costs when setting prices in these situations. With cost-based pricing, firms are more apt to set overly low prices in noncompetitive markets.

*Under **demand-based pricing,** consumers are researched and a **price ceiling** set.*

FIGURE 21-5
Demand-Based Pricing Techniques

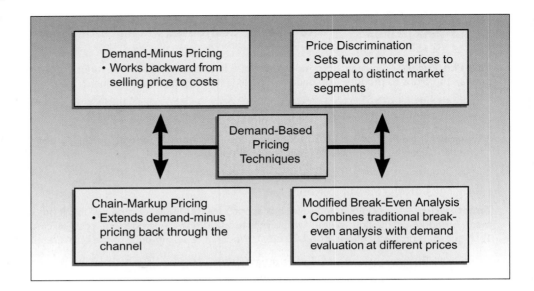

Four demand-based pricing techniques are reviewed next: demand-minus, chain-markup, modified break-even, and price discrimination. Figure 21-5 gives a synopsis of each technique. And at the end of these subsections, Table 21-3 contains numerical examples of them.

Demand-Minus Pricing

In **demand-minus (demand-backward) pricing,** *selling price, then markup, and finally maximum product costs are computed.*

Through **demand-minus (demand-backward) pricing,** a firm finds the proper selling price and works backward to compute costs. This approach stipulates that price decisions revolve around consumer demand rather than company operations. It is used by firms selling directly to consumers.

Demand-minus pricing has three steps: Selling price is determined via consumer surveys or other research. The required markup percentage is set based on selling expenses and desired profits. The maximum acceptable per-unit cost for making or buying a product is computed. This formula is used:

$$\text{Maximum product cost} = \text{Price} \times [(100 - \text{Markup percent})/100]$$

It shows that product cost is derived after selling price and markup are set.

The difficulty in demand-minus pricing is that research may be time-consuming or complex, especially if many items are involved. Also, new-product pricing research may be particularly inaccurate.

Chain-Markup Pricing

Chain-markup pricing *traces demand-minus calculations from channel members to suppliers.*

Chain-markup pricing extends demand-minus calculations all the way from resellers back to suppliers (manufacturers). With it, final selling price is determined, markups for each channel member are examined, and the maximum acceptable costs to each member are computed.

In a traditional consumer-goods channel, the markup chain is composed of

1. Maximum selling price = Final selling price ×
   to retailer   [(100 − Retailer's markup)/100]

2. Maximum selling price = Selling price to retailer ×
   to wholesaler   [(100 − Wholesaler's markup)/100]

3. Maximum product cost = Selling price to wholesaler ×
   to manufacturer   [(100 − Manufacturer's markup)/100]

By using chain-markup pricing, price decisions can be related to consumer demand and each reseller is able to see the effects of price changes on the total distribution channel. The interdependence of firms becomes more clear; they cannot set prices independently of one another.

Modified Break-Even Analysis

Modified break-even analysis combines traditional break-even analysis with an evaluation of demand at various levels of price. Traditional analysis focuses on the sales needed to break even at a given price. It does not indicate the likely level of demand at that price, examine how consumers respond to different levels of price, consider that the break-even point can vary greatly depending on the price the firm happens to select, or calculate the price that maximizes profits.

Modified analysis reveals the price-quantity mix that maximizes profits. It shows that profits do not inevitably rise as the quantity sold increases because lower prices may be needed to expand demand. It also verifies that a firm should examine various price levels and select the one with the greatest profits. Finally, it relates demand to price, rather than assuming that the same volume could be sold at any price.

Melding traditional break-even analysis with demand evaluation at various prices is **modified break-even analysis.**

Price Discrimination

With a *price discrimination* approach, a firm sets two or more distinct prices for a product so as to appeal to different final consumer or organizational consumer segments. Higher prices are offered to inelastic segments and lower prices to elastic ones. Price discrimination can be customer-based, product-based, time-based, or place-based.

In *customer-based price discrimination*, prices differ by customer category for the same good or service. Price differentials may relate to a consumer's ability to pay (doctors, lawyers, and accountants partially set prices in this manner), negotiating ability (the price of an office building is usually set by bargaining), or buying power (discounts are given for volume purchases).

Through *product-based price discrimination*, a firm markets a number of features, styles, qualities, brands, or sizes of a product and sets a different price for each product version. Price differentials are greater than cost differentials for the various versions. For example, a dishwasher may be priced at $400 in white and $450 in brown, although the brown color costs the manufacturer only $10 more. There is inelastic demand by customers desiring the special color, and product versions are priced accordingly.

Under *time-based price discrimination*, a firm varies prices by day versus evening (movie theater tickets), time of day (telephone and utility rates), or season (hotel rates). Consumers who insist on prime-time use pay higher prices than those who are willing to make their purchases during nonpeak times.

In *place-based price discrimination*, prices differ by seat location (sports events), floor location (office buildings), or geographic location (resort cities). The demand for locations near the field, elevators, or warm climates drives the prices of these locations up. General admission tickets, basement offices, and moderate-temperature resorts are priced lower to attract consumers to otherwise less desirable purchases.

Setting distinct prices to reach different market segments is **price discrimination.**

When a firm engages in price discrimination, it should use **yield management pricing**—whereby it determines the mix of price-quantity combinations that generates the highest level of revenues for a given time. A company wants to be sure that it gives itself every opportunity to sell as many goods and services at full price as possible, while also seeking to sell as many units as it can. It does not want to sell so many low-price items that it jeopardizes full-price sales. Thus, a 1,000-seat theater offering first-run plays must decide how many tickets to sell as orchestra (at $75 each) and how many to sell as general admission (at $35 each). If it tries to sell too many orchestra tickets, there may be empty seats. If it looks to sell too many general admission tickets, the theater may be full—but total revenues may be unsatisfactory. Yield management pricing is now much easier to undertake because of the availability of sophisticated computer software. It is

Yield management pricing *lets firms optimize price discrimination efforts.*

Hello, We Have a Cheaper Fare Online

The U.S. Transportation Department (www.dot.gov) recently warned airlines that they would face legal sanctions if they did not inform travelers who made reservations on the phone that less expensive fares might be available on the Internet. In testimony to Congress, the inspector general of the Transportation Department revealed that there could be a vast difference in fares for the same trip depending on where they were quoted. For example, a reservation agent might quote a $1,791 fare for a round trip between Newark and New Orleans on the phone, while this same trip might be $140 online. Currently, 6 percent of airline tickets are bought via the Web. This is expected to rise to 11 percent by 2003.

The airlines were informed that they could satisfy the new legal requirement through a recorded phone message stating that cheaper fares were sometimes available over the Web. The Transportation Department decided to not require airlines to divulge the price difference as this would increase costs and could deter airlines from offering lower Internet fares. It also ruled that the existence of low-cost Internet fares was not discriminatory since "access to the Internet is now available to virtually anyone."

The change in the regulation was based on a complaint by Donald Pevsner, an attorney and consumer advocate who argued that low-cost Internet fares unfairly discriminated against travelers who did not have Internet access. According to Pevsner, "To say that virtually everyone has access to the Internet is a gross exaggeration. Low-income people, who need the lower fares the most, are the ones who have the least access to the Internet."

As the pricing manager for an airline with an Internet site offering last-minute specials, how would you respond to the new legislation?

Source: Based on material in Laurence Zuckerman, "Airlines Ordered to Tell Callers Internet May Offer Cheaper Fares," *New York Times on the Web* (October 21, 2000).

especially popular with airlines and hotels, and widely used by Internet firms.[5] These Web sites are two good sources for further information on yield management pricing: Veritec Solutions (www.veritecsolutions.com), click on "Articles" at the tool bar, and ITech2000 (www.itech2000.com/yieldmanagement).

Before using price discrimination, a firm should address these questions: Are there distinct market segments? Do people talk to each other about prices? Can product versions be differentiated? Will some people choose low-priced models when they might buy high-priced models if those are the only ones sold? How do the marginal costs of adding product alternatives compare with marginal revenues? Will channel members stock all models? How hard is it to explain product differences to consumers? Under what conditions is price discrimination legal (so as to not violate the Robinson-Patman Act)?

[5]Michael Menduno, "Priced to Perfection," *Business 2.0* (March 6, 2001), pp. 40–41.

TABLE 21-3 **Examples of Demand-Based Pricing Techniques**

Demand-Minus Pricing—A hardware manufacturer has done consumer research and found that contractors are willing to spend $60.00 for its flagship electric drill. Selling expenses and profits are expected to be 35 percent of the selling price. What is the maximum the manufacturer can spend to develop and produce each drill?

Maximum = Price × [(100 – Markup per cent)/100] = $39.00
merchandise costs

Chain-Markup Pricing—A ladies' shoe maker knows women will pay $100.00 for a pair of its shoes. It sells via wholesalers and retailers. Each requires a markup of 30 percent; the manufacturer wants a 25 percent markup. (a) What is the maximum price that retailers and wholesalers will spend for a pair of shoes? (b) What is the maximum the manufacturer can spend to make each pair of shoes?

(a) Maximum selling price = Final selling price × [(100 – Retailer's markup)/100] = $70.00
   to retailer

   Maximum selling price = Selling price to retailer × [(100 – Wholesaler's markup)/100] = $49.00
   to wholesaler

(b) Maximum merchandise = Selling price to wholesaler × [(100 – Manufacturer's markup)/100] = $36.75
   costs to manufacturer

Modified Break-Even Analysis—An aspirin maker has total fixed costs of $2,000,000 and variable costs of $1.50 per bottle. Research shows the following demand schedule. At what price should the company sell its aspirin?

Selling Price	Quantity Demanded	Total Revenue	Total Cost	Total Profit (Loss)	
$3.00	2,000,000	$6,000,000	$5,000,000	$1,000,000	Maximum
2.50	3,200,000	8,000,000	6,800,000	1,200,000	←profit at
2.00	5,000,000	10,000,000	9,500,000	500,000	price of $2.50

Price Discrimination—A sports team knows people will pay different prices for tickets, based on location. It offers 10,000 tickets at $30 each, 25,000 at $20 each, and 20,000 at $12 each. What are profits if total costs per game are $750,000?

Profit = (Revenues from segment A + segment B + segment C) – Total costs = $290,000

21-4c Competition-Based Pricing

In *competition-based pricing,* a firm uses competitors' prices rather than demand or cost considerations as its primary pricing guideposts. The company may not respond to changes in demand or costs unless those changes also have an effect on competitors' prices. It can set prices below the market, at the market, or above the market, depending on its customers, image, marketing mix, consumer loyalty, and other factors. This approach is applied by firms contending with others selling similar items (or those perceived as similar).

Competition-based pricing *is setting prices relative to other firms.*

Competition-based pricing is popular. It is simple, not relying on demand curves, price elasticity, or costs per unit. The ongoing market price is assumed to be fair for both consumers and companies. Pricing at the market level does not disrupt competition and, therefore, does not lead to retaliations. However, it may lead to complacency, and different firms may not have the same demand and cost structures.

Two aspects of competition-based pricing are discussed in the following subsections: price leadership and competitive bidding.

Price Leadership

Price leadership exists in situations where one firm (or a few firms) is usually the first to announce price changes and others in the industry follow. The price leader's role is to set prices that reflect market conditions, without disrupting the marketplace—it must not turn off consumers with price increases perceived as too large or precipitate a price war with competitors by excessive price cuts.

Price leaders are generally firms that have significant market shares, well-established positions, respect from competitors, and the desire to initiate price changes. As an illustration, a frequent price leader in the newsprint industry has been Canada's Abitibi Consolidated (www.abicon.com). It is the world's largest newsprint maker, has the largest production capacity, and has the dominant market share. Because 60 percent of its revenues are in newsprint, the firm is committed to maintaining stable prices.

Over the last several years, the role of price leaders has been greatly reduced in many industries, including steel, chemical, glass container, and newsprint, as many smaller firms have sought to act more independently. Even Abitibi Consolidated has been affected by this trend. At various times, it has announced higher newsprint prices, but had to backtrack—after competitors decided not to go along.

Announcements of price changes by industry leaders must be communicated through the media. It is illegal for firms in the same industry or in competing ones to confer regarding their prices.

Competitive Bidding

Through *competitive bidding* (discussed in Chapter 9), two or more firms independently submit prices to a customer for a specific good, project, and/or service. Sealed bids may be requested by some government or organizational consumers; each seller then has one chance to make its best offer.

Various mathematical models have been applied to competitive bidding. All use the expected profit concept, which states that as the bid price increases the profit to a firm increases, but the probability of its winning a contract decreases. Although a firm's potential profit (loss) at a given bid amount can usually be estimated accurately, the probability of getting a contract (underbidding all other qualified competitors) can be hard to determine.

21-4d Combination Pricing

Although cost-, demand-, and competition-based pricing methods have been discussed separately, aspects of the three approaches should be integrated into a **combination pricing** approach. This is done often in practice. A cost-based approach sets a price floor and outlines the costs incurred in doing business. It establishes profit margins, target prices, and/or break-even quantities. A demand-based approach finds the prices consumers will pay and the ceiling prices for each channel member. It develops the price-quantity mix that maximizes profits and lets a firm reach different market segments (if it so desires). A competition-based approach examines the proper price level for the firm in relation to competitors.

Unless the approaches are integrated, critical issues may be overlooked. Table 21-4 shows a list of questions a firm should consider in setting prices.

21-5 IMPLEMENTING A PRICING STRATEGY

Implementing a pricing strategy involves a variety of separate—but related—specific decisions, besides the broader concepts just discussed. The decisions involve whether and how to use customary versus variable pricing, a one-price policy versus flexible pricing, odd pricing, the price-quality association, leader pricing, multiple-unit pricing, price lining, price bundling, geographic pricing, and purchase terms.

Cost-Based

What profit margin does a price level permit?

Do markups allow for differences in product investments, installation and servicing, and selling effort and merchandising skills?

Are there accurate and timely cost data by good, service, project, process, and/or store?

Are cost changes monitored and prices adjusted accordingly?

Are there specific profit or return-on-investment goals?

What is the price-floor price for each good, service, project, process, and/or store?

What are the break-even points for each good, service, project, process, and/or store?

Demand-Based

What type of demand does each good, service, project, process, and/or store face?

Have price elasticities been estimated for various price levels?

Are demand-minus, chain-markup, and modified break-even analyses utilized?

Has price discrimination been considered?

How loyal are customers?

Competition-Based

How do prices compare with those of competitors?

Is price leadership used in the industry? By whom?

How do competitors react to price changes?

How are competitive bids determined?

Is the long-run expected profit concept used in competitive bidding?

TABLE 21-4

Selected Issues to Consider When Combining Pricing Techniques

21-5a Customary Versus Variable Pricing

Customary pricing occurs when a firm sets prices and seeks to maintain them for an extended time. Prices are not changed during this period. Customary pricing is used for items like candy, gum, magazines, restaurant food, and mass transit. Rather than modify prices to reflect cost increases, firms may reduce package size, change ingredients, or have a more restrictive transfer policy among bus lines. The assumption is that consumers prefer one of these alternatives to a price hike.

Variable pricing lets a firm intentionally alter prices in response to cost fluctuations or differences in consumer demand. When costs change, prices are lowered or raised; the fluctuations are not absorbed and product quality is not modified to maintain customary prices. Through price discrimination, a firm can offer distinct prices to appeal to different market segments. Thus, the prices charged to diverse consumers are not based on costs, but on consumer price sensitivity. Many firms use some form of variable pricing.

It is possible to combine customary and variable pricing. For example, a magazine may be $3 per single copy and $24 per year's subscription ($2 an issue)—two customary prices are charged; and the consumer selects the offer he or she finds most attractive.

*With **customary pricing,** one price is maintained over an extended period. Under **variable pricing,** prices reflect costs or differences in demand.*

21-5b A One-Price Policy Versus Flexible Pricing

A *one-price policy* lets a firm charge the same price to all customers seeking to purchase a good or service under similar conditions. Prices may differ according to the quantity bought, time of purchase, and services obtained (such as delivery and installation), but all consumers are given the opportunity to pay the same price for the same combinations of

*All buying the same product pay the same price under a **one-price policy.** Different customers may pay different prices with **flexible pricing.***

goods and services. This builds consumer confidence, is easy to administer, eliminates bargaining, and permits self-service and catalog sales. Today, throughout the United States, one-price policies are the rule for most retailers. In industrial marketing, a firm with a one-price policy would not allow sales personnel to deviate from a published price list.

With *flexible pricing,* a firm sets prices based on the consumer's ability to negotiate or on the buying power of a large customer. People who are knowledgeable or are good bargainers pay less than those who are not knowledgeable or are weaker bargainers. Jewelry stores, car dealers, real-estate brokers, and many industrial marketers tend to use flexible pricing. Commissions may be keyed to profitability to encourage salespeople to solicit higher prices. Flexible prices to resellers are subject to Robinson-Patman limits. Flexible pricing is more likely outside the United States, where "haggling" may be culturally ingrained. To remedy consumer insecurities about bargaining, Web sites now have guides to educate people. The *Woman Motorist New Car Buying Guide* (www.womanmotorist. com/handbook/dealers.shtml) has a chapter on "Dealing with Dealers: Negotiating a New Car Purchase."

One result of flexible pricing is that some people gather information from full-service sellers, shop around for the best price, and then challenge discount sellers to "beat the lowest price." This practice is detrimental to full-service firms and lets discounters hold down selling costs (and encourage bargaining).

MARKETING *and the Web*

Bargaining for a Vacation with an Internet Auction

Travel auction sites such as Bid4Vacations (www.bid4vacations.com), All Cruise Auction (www.allcruiseauction.com), and Egghead (www.auctions. egghead.com) resemble auctions on Ebay, Yahoo!, and Amazon, except that instead of bidding for general merchandise, consumers bid for cruises, air fares, and resort vacations. Like the general merchandise sites, these sites offer "bid tracking" capabilities that keep bidders up-to-date on the status of bids and E-mail notices of new opportunities based upon a traveler's specific preferences. The bid prices for travel auctions can start as low as $1, but the real bidding activity typically begins a few hours before the bidding closes. At that time, bidders anxiously watch a particular auction and adjust their offers based on activity by others.

The travel auction sites usually get their inventory from wholesale consolidators that purchase blocks of hotel rooms and seats for resale as travel packages. These consolidators then sell any of their unsold seats or rooms to auction sites, which resell this stock for their own accounts. The consolidators often arrange with the auction site to sell their unsold inventory on a fee basis.

To encourage bidding, the sites generally list the "retail price" for the seats and rooms up for bid, along with the current bid prices. The bid prices are generally significantly lower than the retail price due to the presence of "no cancellation" clauses or limited travel itineraries. Some of the sites do not bundle air and hotel offers together. Thus, consumers have to bid separately for each and run the risk of having to pay high air fares or having flights that do not match the dates of room availability.

As vice-president of marketing for a cruise line with unsold rooms, would you utilize a travel auction site? Explain your answer.

Source: Based on material in Bob Tedeschi, "Cyberscout: Bidding for a Trip Online," *New York Times on the Web* (October 7, 2000).

FIGURE 21-6
Odd Pricing: A Worldwide Pricing Tool

Odd pricing is used by firms around the globe, such as Mexico-based Gigante (www.gigante.com), a chain of food superstores.

Source: Reprinted by permission of PricewaterhouseCoopers.

21-5c Odd Pricing

Odd pricing is used when selling prices are set at levels below even dollar values, such as 49 cents, $4.95, and $199. It has proven popular for several reasons: People like getting change. Because the cashier must make change, employers ensure that sales are recorded and money is placed in the cash register. Consumers gain the impression that a firm thinks carefully about prices and sets them as low as possible. They may also believe odd prices represent price reductions; a price of $8.95 may be viewed as a discount from $10. See Figure 21-6.

Odd prices one or two cents below the next even price (29 cents, $2.98) are common up to $4 or $5. Beyond that point and up to $50 or so, five-cent reductions from the highest even price ($19.95, $49.95) are more usual. For expensive items, odd endings are in dollars ($499, $5,995).

Odd prices may help consumers stay within their price limits and still buy the best items available. A shopper willing to spend "less than $30" for a tie will be attracted to a $29.95 tie and might be as likely to buy it as a $24 tie since it is within the defined price range. The sales tax in 45 states (www.salestaxinstitute.com/sales_tax_rates.html) has the effect of raising odd prices into higher dollar levels and may reduce the impact of odd pricing as a selling tool.

> **Odd prices** *are those set below even-dollar values.*

21-5d The Price-Quality Association

According to the *price-quality association,* consumers may believe high prices represent high quality and low prices represent low quality. This association tends to be most valid when quality is difficult to judge on bases other than price, buyers perceive large differences in quality among brands, buyers have little experience or confidence in assessing quality (as with a new product), high prices exclude the mass market, brand names are unknown, or brand names require certain price levels to sustain their images.[6]

If brand names are well-known and/or people are confident of their ability to compare brands on nonprice factors, the price-quality association may be less valid. Consumers may then be more interested in the perceived value they receive for their money—and not necessarily believe a higher price represents better quality. It is essential that prices properly reflect both the quality and the image of the firm.

> *The* **price-quality association** *deals with perceptions.* **Prestige pricing** *indicates that consumers may not buy when a price is too low.*

[6]See Merrie Brucks, Valarie A. Zeithaml, and Gillian Naylor, "Price and Brand Name as Indicators of Quality Dimensions for Consumer Durables," *Journal of the Academy of Marketing Science*, Vol. 28 (Summer 2000), pp. 359–374.

FIGURE 21-7
Demand for Designer Jeans Under Prestige Pricing

Price
$90
$60
$40

Consumers'
Price Ceiling

Range of
Acceptable
Prices

Consumers'
Price Floor

Q₁ Q₃ Q₂   Quantity (Units)

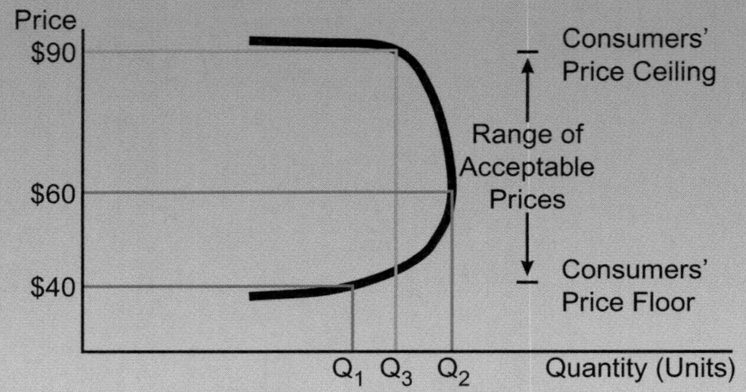

At a price under $40, consumers believe designer jeans are labeled incorrectly, an old style, seconds, or otherwise of poor quality. Demand is negligible.

At $40, consumer demand is Q_1. A small group of discount-oriented consumers will buy the jeans. This is the minimum price they will pay for a good pair of designer jeans.

As the price goes from $40 to $60, demand rises continuously as more consumers perceive the jeans as a high-quality, status product. At $60, sales peak at Q_2.

As the price goes from $60 to $90, consumer demand drops gradually to Q_3. During this range, some consumers begin to see the jeans as too expensive. But, many will buy the jeans until they reach $90, their ceiling price.

At a price over $90, consumers believe designer jeans are too expensive. Demand is negligible.

With *prestige pricing*, a theory drawn from the price-quality association, it is assumed that consumers will not buy goods or services at prices they consider to be too low. Most people set price floors and will not buy at prices below those floors—they feel quality and status would be inferior at extremely low prices. Most people also set ceilings as to the prices they consider acceptable for particular goods or services. Above those ceilings, items are seen as too expensive. For each good or service, a firm should set prices in the target market's acceptable range between the floor and ceiling. See Figure 21-7.

21-5e Leader Pricing

Leader pricing *is used to attract customers to low prices.*

With *leader pricing,* a firm advertises and sells key items in its product assortment at less than usual profit margins. The wholesaler's or retailer's goal is to increase customer traffic. The manufacturer's goal is to gain greater consumer interest in its overall product line. In both cases, it is hoped that consumers will buy regularly priced products in addition to the specially priced items that attract them.

Leader pricing is most used with well-known, high-turnover, frequently bought products. For example, in some drugstores, one of the best-selling items in terms of dollar sales is Kodak film. To stimulate customer traffic into these stores, film may be priced very low; in some cases, it is sold at close to cost. Film is a good item for leader pricing because consumers are able to detect low prices and they are attracted into a store by a discount on the item, which regularly sells for several dollars.

There are two kinds of leader pricing: loss leaders and prices higher than cost but lower than regular prices. As stated in Chapter 20, the use of loss leaders is regulated or illegal in a number of states.

21-5f Multiple-Unit Pricing

With **multiple-unit pricing,** *quantity discounts are intended to result in higher sales volume.*

Multiple-unit pricing is a practice whereby a firm offers discounts to consumers to encourage them to buy in quantity, so as to increase overall sales volume. By offering items at two for 89 cents or six for $139, a firm attempts to sell more units than would be sold at 50 cents or $25 each.

There are four major benefits from multiple-unit pricing: Customers may increase their immediate purchases if they feel they get a bargain. They may boost long-term consumption if they make larger purchases, as occurs with soda. Competitors' customers may be attracted by the discounts. A firm may be able to clear out slow-moving and end-of-season merchandise, as KB Toys does through its Kbwholesale.com Web site (www.kbwholesale.com), which sells closeout items in bulk.

Multiple-unit pricing will not be successful if consumers merely shift their purchases and do not hike their consumption. For example, multiple-unit pricing for Heinz ketchup may not result in consumers using more ketchup with their meals. Thus, it would not raise total dollar sales; consumers would simply buy ketchup less frequently because it can be stored.

21-5g Price Lining

Price lining involves selling products at a range of prices, with each representing a distinct level of quality (or features). Instead of setting one price for a single version of a good or service, a firm sells two or more versions (with different levels of quality or features) at different prices. Price lining involves two decisions: prescribing the price range (floor and ceiling) and setting specific price points in that range.

A price range may be low, intermediate, or high. For example, inexpensive radios may be priced from $8 to $20, moderately priced radios from $25 to $50, and expensive radios from $75 to $120. After the range is chosen, a limited number of price points is set. The price points must be distinct and not too close together. Inexpensive radios could be priced at $8, $12, and $20. They would not be priced at $8, $9, $10, $11, $12, $13, $14, $15, $16, $17, $18, $19, and $20. This would confuse consumers and be inefficient for the firm.

When price lining, a firm must consider these factors: Price points must be spaced far enough apart so customers perceive differences among product versions—otherwise, consumers might view the price floor as the price they should pay and believe there is no difference among models. Price points should be spaced farther apart at higher prices because consumer demand becomes more inelastic. Relationships among price points must be kept when costs rise, so clear differences are retained. If radio costs rise 25 percent, prices should be set at $10, $15, and $25 (up from $8, $12, and $20).

Price lining offers benefits for both sellers and consumers. Sellers can offer a product assortment, attract market segments, trade up shoppers within a price range, control inventory by price point, reduce competition by having versions over a price range, and increase overall sales volume. Consumers are given an assortment from which to choose, confusion is lessened, comparisons may be made, and quality options are available within a given price range.

Price lining can also have constraints: Consumers may feel price gaps are too large—a $25 handbag may be too low, while the next price point of $100 may be too high. Rising costs may squeeze individual prices and make it hard for a firm to keep the proper relationships in its line. Markdowns or special sales may disrupt the balance in a price line, unless all items in the line are proportionately reduced in price.

Price lining *sets a range of selling prices and price points within that range.*

21-5h Price Bundling

Some form of price bundling can be used in a strategy. With **bundled pricing,** a firm sells a basic product, options, and customer service for one total price. An industrial-equipment manufacturer may have a single price for a drill press, its delivery, its installation, and a service contract. Individual items, such as the drill press, would not be sold separately. With **unbundled pricing,** a firm breaks down prices by individual components and allows the consumer to decide what to purchase. A discount appliance store may have separate prices for a refrigerator, its delivery, its installation, and a service contract.

Many companies choose to offer consumers both pricing options and allow a slight discount for bundled pricing. See Figure 21-8.

A firm can use **bundled** *or* **unbundled pricing.**

FIGURE 21-8
Price Bundling for a Bookcase

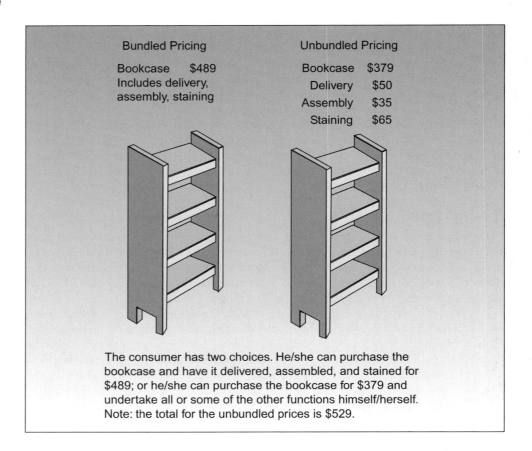

The consumer has two choices. He/she can purchase the bookcase and have it delivered, assembled, and stained for $489; or he/she can purchase the bookcase for $379 and undertake all or some of the other functions himself/herself. Note: the total for the unbundled prices is $529.

21-5i Geographic Pricing

Geographic pricing outlines responsibility for transportation charges. Many times, it is not negotiated but depends on the traditional practices in the industry in which the firm operates; and all companies in the industry normally conform to the same geographic pricing format. Geographic pricing often involves industrial marketing situations.

These are the most common methods of geographic pricing:

- *FOB mill (factory) pricing*—The buyer picks a transportation form and pays all freight charges, the seller pays the costs of loading the goods (hence, "free on board"), and the delivered price to the buyer depends on freight charges.
- *Uniform delivered pricing*—All buyers pay the same delivered price for the same quantity of goods, regardless of their location; the seller pays for shipping.
- *Zone pricing*—It provides for a uniform delivered price to all buyers within a geographic zone; through a multiple-zone system, delivered prices vary by zone.
- *Base-point pricing*—Firms in an industry establish basing points from which the costs of shipping are computed; the delivered price to a buyer reflects the cost of transporting goods from the basing point nearest to the buyer, regardless of the actual site of supply.

21-5j Purchase Terms

Purchase terms are the provisions of price agreements. They include discounts, the timing of payments, and credit arrangements.

Discounts are the reductions from final selling prices available to resellers and consumers for doing certain functions, paying cash, buying large amounts, buying in off-seasons, or enhancing promotions. A wholesaler may buy goods at 40 percent off a man-

Geographic pricing *alternatives are FOB mill (factory), uniform delivered, zone, and base-point pricing.*

Purchase terms *outline pricing provisions.*

ufacturer's suggested final selling price. This covers its expenses, profit, and the discount to the retailer. The retailer could buy for 25 percent off list (the wholesaler keeping 15 percent for its costs and profit). Discounts must be proportionately available to all competing channel members, to avoid violating the Robinson-Patman Act.

Payment timing must be specified in a purchase agreement. Final consumers may pay immediately or after delivery. In credit transactions, payments are not made until bills are received; they may be made over time. Organizational consumers are also quite interested in the timing of payments and negotiate for the best terms: For example, terms of net 30 mean products do not have to be paid for until 30 days after receipt. They must then be paid for in full. Terms of 2/10, net 30 mean a buyer receives a 2 percent discount if the full bill is paid within 10 days after merchandise receipt. The buyer must pay the face value of a bill within 30 days after the receipt of products. Various time terms are available.

When marketing internationally, sellers must sometimes be prepared to wait an extended period to receive payments. It takes U.S. firms up to 100 days or more—from invoice to payment—to get paid by organizational consumers in Iran, Kenya, Argentina, Brazil, Greece, Italy, and elsewhere.

A firm that allows credit purchases may use open accounts or revolving accounts. With an *open credit account*, the buyer receives a monthly bill for the goods and services bought during the preceding month. The account must be paid in full each month. With a *revolving credit account*, the buyer agrees to make minimum monthly payments during an extended period of time and pays interest on outstanding balances. Today, various types of firms (from Xerox to many colleges) offer some form of credit plan. Auto makers provide their own cut-rate financing programs to stimulate sales and leasing.

Open and revolving credit accounts are possible.

21-6   PRICE ADJUSTMENTS

After a price strategy is enacted, it often requires continuous fine-tuning to reflect changes in costs, competitive conditions, and demand. **Price adjustment tactics** include alterations in list prices, escalator clauses and surcharges, added markups, markdowns, and rebates.

List prices are the regularly quoted prices provided to customers. They may be pre-printed on price tags, in catalogs, and in dealer purchase orders. Modifications in list prices are necessary if there are sustained changes in labor costs, raw material costs, and market segments, and as a product moves through its life cycle. When these events are long-term in nature, they enable customary prices to be revised, new catalogs to be printed, and adjustments to be completed in an orderly fashion.

Costs or economic conditions may sometimes be so volatile that revised list prices cannot be printed or distributed efficiently. Escalator clauses or surcharges can then be used. Both allow prices to be adjusted quickly. With *escalator clauses,* a firm is contractually allowed to raise the prices of items to reflect higher costs in those items' essential ingredients without changing printed list prices. It may even be able to set prices at the time of delivery. *Surcharges* are across-the-board published price increases that supplement list prices. These may be used with catalogs because of their simplicity; an insert is distributed with the catalog. American Airlines (www.aa.com) recently began to impose a $10 fee on some of its paper tickets to encourage travelers to use electronic ticketing (which cuts distribution costs).[7]

When list prices are not involved, *additional markups* can be used to raise regular selling prices if demand is unexpectedly high or costs are rising. There is a risk to this. For example, supermarkets get bad publicity for relabeling low-cost existing items at higher prices so they match those of newer merchandise purchased at higher costs.

Markdowns are reductions from items' original selling prices. All types of sellers use them to meet the lower prices of competitors, counteract overstocking of merchandise, clear out shopworn merchandise, deplete assortments of odds and ends, and lift customer traffic.

List prices, escalator clauses, surcharges, additional markups, markdowns, and **rebates** *are key* **price adjustment tactics.**

[7]Jane L. Levere, "American Puts $10 Fee on Paper Tickets," *New York Times on the Web* (April 10, 2001).

Although manufacturers regularly give discounts to resellers, they may periodically offer cash *rebates* to customers to stimulate the purchase of an item or a group of items. Rebates are flexible, do not alter basic prices, involve direct communication between consumers and manufacturers (since rebates are usually sent to consumers by manufacturers), and do not affect reseller profits (as regular reductions do). Price cuts by individual resellers may not generate the same kind of consumer enthusiasm. Rebate popularity can be traced to its usage by the auto industry to help cut down on inventory surpluses. Rebates are regularly offered by Canon (www.canon.com), Fedders (www.fedders.com), Gillette (www.gillette.com), and a number of others. The major disadvantage is that so many firms have used rebates that their impact may be lessened.

Whenever adjustments are needed, channel members should cooperatively agree on their individual roles. Price hikes or cuts should not be unilateral.

WEB SITES YOU CAN USE

The Business Owner's Toolkit Web site (www.toolkit.cch.com/text/P03_5200.asp) offers a tremendous amount of information on price planning. Look at its "Pricing Your Product" section at the site. The Center for Business Planning Resource Web site (www.businessplans.org/plan.asp) is also quite useful. On the "Sections" tool bar at the left of the screen, scroll down to "Marketing & Sales." Then click on "Pricing" to access a wide range of resources. For a change of pace, take a look at the Price.com (www.price.com) and PriceScan.com (www.pricescan.com) comparison shopping Web sites.

SUMMARY

1. *To present an overall framework for developing and applying a pricing strategy* A pricing strategy has five stages: objectives, broad policy, strategy, implementation, and adjustments. The stages are affected by outside factors and must be integrated with a firm's marketing mix.

2. *To analyze sales-based, profit-based, and status quo-based pricing objectives, and to describe the role of a broad price policy* Sales goals center on volume and/or market share. In penetration pricing, low prices capture a mass market. Profit goals focus on profit maximization, satisfactory profits, optimum return on investment, and/or early cash recovery. In skimming pricing, a firm seeks the segment less concerned with price than quality or status. Status quo goals seek to minimize the impact of outside parties and ensure stability. Two or more pricing objectives may be combined.

A broad price policy sets the overall direction for a firm's pricing efforts. Through it, a firm decides if it is price- or nonprice-oriented.

3. *To examine and apply the alternative approaches to a pricing strategy* A price strategy may be cost-based, demand-based, competition-based, or a combination of these.

With cost-based pricing, merchandise, service, and overhead costs are computed and then an amount to cover profit is added. Cost-plus pricing adds costs and a desired profit to set prices. In

markup pricing, prices are set by calculating the per-unit costs of producing (buying) goods and/or services and then finding the markup percentages to cover selling costs and profit; a variable markup policy has different markups for distinct products. In target pricing, prices provide a rate of return on investment for a standard volume of production. When a firm has excess capacity, it may use price-floor pricing, in which prices are above variable costs rather than total costs. Traditional break-even analysis determines the sales quantity at which total costs equal total revenues for a chosen price.

With demand-based pricing, prices are set after doing consumer research and learning the range of acceptable prices to the target market. In demand-minus pricing, a firm finds the proper selling price and works backward to set costs. Chain-markup pricing extends demand-minus calculations from resellers back to suppliers (manufacturers). Modified break-even analysis combines traditional break-even analysis with an evaluation of demand at various prices. With price discrimination, a firm sets two or more distinct prices for a product so as to appeal to different market segments.

In competition-based pricing, competition is the main guidepost. Prices may be below, at, or above the market. A firm would see whether it has the ability to be a price leader or price follower. In competitive bidding, two or more firms submit prices in response to precise customer requests.

These three approaches should be integrated via combination pricing, so that a firm includes all necessary factors in its pricing strategy. Otherwise, critical decisions are likely to be overlooked.

4. *To discuss several specific decisions that must be made in implementing a pricing strategy* Enacting a price strategy involves several specific decisions. Customary pricing is used when a firm sets prices for an extended time. In variable pricing, prices coincide with cost or consumer demand fluctuations.

In a one-price policy, all those buying under similar conditions pay the same price. Flexible pricing lets a firm vary prices based on shopper negotiations or the buying power of a large customer.

With odd pricing, amounts are set below even-dollar values. The price-quality theory suggests people may feel there is a relation between price and quality. Prestige pricing assumes people do not buy products at prices that are considered too low. They set price floors, as well as price ceilings.

Under leader pricing, key items are sold at less than their usual amounts to increase consumer traffic. Multiple-unit pricing is a practice which offers discounts to consumers for buying in quantity.

Price lining involves the sale of products at a range of prices, with each embodying a distinct level of quality (or features). In bundled pricing, a firm offers a product, options, and customer service for a total price; unbundled pricing breaks down prices by individual components.

Geographic pricing outlines the responsibility for transportation. Purchase terms are the provisions of price agreements, including discounts, timing of payments, and credit.

5. *To show the major ways that prices can be adjusted* Once a pricing strategy is enacted, it often needs fine-tuning to reflect cost, competition, and demand changes. Prices can be adjusted by altering list prices, using escalator clauses and surcharges, marking prices up or down, and offering rebates.

KEY TERMS

sales-based pricing objectives (p. 617)
penetration pricing (p. 617)
profit-based pricing objectives (p. 618)
skimming pricing (p. 618)
status quo-based pricing objectives (p. 618)
broad price policy (p. 619)
cost-based pricing (p. 621)
price floor (p. 621)
cost-plus pricing (p. 622)
markup pricing (p. 623)
variable markup policy (p. 623)
target pricing (p. 623)
price-floor pricing (p. 624)
traditional break-even analysis (p. 624)

demand-based pricing (p. 625)
price ceiling (p. 625)
demand-minus (demand-backward) pricing (p. 626)
chain-markup pricing (p. 626)
modified break-even analysis (p. 627)
price discrimination (p. 627)
yield management pricing (p. 627)
competition-based pricing (p. 629)
price leadership (p. 630)
combination pricing (p. 630)
customary pricing (p. 631)
variable pricing (p. 631)
one-price policy (p. 631)

flexible pricing (p. 632)
odd pricing (p. 633)
price-quality association (p. 633)
prestige pricing (p. 634)
leader pricing (p. 634)
multiple-unit pricing (p. 634)
price lining (p. 635)
bundled pricing (p. 635)
unbundled pricing (p. 635)
geographic pricing (p. 636)
purchase terms (p. 636)
price adjustment tactics (p. 637)
rebates (p. 638)

REVIEW QUESTIONS

1. When should a firm pursue penetration pricing? Skimming pricing?

2. Why are markups usually computed on the basis of selling price?

3. A firm requires a 14 percent return on an $800,000 investment in order to produce a new electric garage-door opener. If the standard volume is 50,000 units, fixed costs are $550,000, and variable costs are $48 per unit, what is the target price?

4. A company making office desks has total fixed costs of $2.5 million per year and variable costs of $450 per desk. It sells the desks to retailers for $800 apiece. Compute the traditional break-even point in both units and dollars.

5. Discuss chain-markup pricing from the perspective of a retailer.

6. Contrast customary pricing and variable pricing. How may the two techniques be combined?

7. Under what circumstances is the price-quality association most valid? Least valid?

8. How does price lining benefit manufacturers? Retailers? Consumers?

DISCUSSION QUESTIONS

1. A movie theater has weekly fixed costs (land, building, and equipment) of $4,500. Variable weekly costs (movie rental, electricity, ushers, etc.) are $2,000. From a price-floor pricing perspective, how much revenue must a movie generate during a slow week for it to be worthwhile to open the theater? Explain your answer.

2. A retailer determines that customers are willing to spend $22.95 on a new John Grisham (author of *The Client* and other best-sellers in the legal arena) novel. The publisher charges the retailer $15.50 for each copy. The retailer wants a 30 percent markup. Comment on this situation.

3. a. A wholesaler of small industrial tools has fixed costs of $350,000, variable costs of $20 per tool, and faces this demand schedule from its hardware-store customers:

Price	Quantity Demanded
$26	100,000
$29	85,000
$32	65,000
$36	40,000

   At what price is profit maximized?

   b. If the firm noted in Question 3a decides to sell 40,000 small tools at $36 and 45,000 of these tools at $29, what will its profit be? What are the risks of this approach?

4. A wholesaler of plumbing supplies recently added a new line of kitchen sinks and priced them at $129 each (to plumbers). The manufacturer has just announced a 10 percent price increase on the sinks—due to higher materials and labor costs. Yet, for this wholesaler, the initial response of plumbers to the sinks has been sluggish. Also, some competing wholesalers are selling the sinks for $109—$30 under the manufacturer's new suggested list price. What should the wholesaler do next?

WEB EXERCISE

Visit the "Where to Find Pricing & Strategy Software" section of the Professional Pricing Society's Web site (www.pricing-advisor.com/res_soft.htm). Click on any two software links that appear and discuss what you learn from exploring them.

PART 7 SHORT CASES
Case 1

Supermarkets: Learning Not to Price by the Seat of the Pants[c7-1]

Many industry observers agree that the supermarket industry is now becoming more scientific in its pricing decisions. This is a result of the increasingly competitive pricing environment, caused by the existence of power retailers and increased merger and acquisition activity. Let's look at these recent developments and how small grocery chains are responding to them via innovative pricing strategies.

According to John Hauptman, a director of Willard Bishop Consulting (www.bishop-consulting.com), retailers are now facing an unprecedented amount of competitive pricing, fueled by power retailers like Wal-Mart (www.walmart.com). In response, the president of IGA Foodliners, an operator of four Festival stores, reduced margins on health-and-beauty care items to make them more competitive. When the margins were reduced from 25 percent to 16 percent, sales increased between 12 to 15 percent.

As the result of two mergers, Albertson's (www.albertsons.com) purchase of American Stores (which already owned Lucky Stores) and Kroger's (www.kroger.com) acquisition of Fred Meyer (which owned Ralphs and the former Hughes stores), the competitive power of these chains has increased. Bill MacAloney, president of MacAloney grocery stores in Latino areas of Southern California, says that the majors are trying to reduce their costs, primarily to reduce their huge debts. "Since the acquisition, Albertson's has been very aggressive in pricing." Joe Pagano, president of Pagano's IGA in Bayonne, New Jersey, agrees that competition has also become more fierce in his marketplace. To compete, Pagano uses the "personal touch" as well as having competitive prices. "With all the mergers, guess who stays around? The independent, if the store is clean and customers are treated well."

More small retailers are also beginning to strengthen their product offerings in major categories to make them more competitive against warehouse clubs, supercenters, and limited assortment stores. For many retailers, this means increasing their offerings of private labels and larger sizes.

Hauptman suggests that retailers re-examine their key item lists as part of their overall pricing strategy: "Historically, supermarkets have had a key item list with about 200 items that they price most aggressively. But those are generally heavy on soft drinks, and other DSD [direct store delivery] items. Now, progressive grocers are studying their key items. They are looking at the top one or two items in each category across the store, and sharpening prices on top sellers. This enhances their price reputation."

Retailers must pay even more attention to their costs. Bill Lancaster, vice-president of corporate sales for Associated Wholesale Grocers (www.awginc.com) says that "Wal-Mart has a 16 percent blended margin on food, and an overall store margin of 21 percent." For smaller firms to compete with this margin, they need to reduce the number of slow-selling items: "If they get their costs down, they can stay close to Wal-Mart on prices. But they can't do it unless they make adjustments in their inventory."

Loyalty programs also have had a significant affect on pricing. Instead of offering the same prices to all customers, Dorothy Lane Markets, a two-store operation in Dayton, Ohio, has reduced its prices only to loyal customers. This avoids "cherry picking" by customers who only buy specials. As the firm's president notes, "We're taking care of the customers who take care of us." The next stage of loyalty programs is to send special price offers to the best customers who are also price sensitive.

Questions

1. How can a local supermarket chain successfully develop a nonprice-based approach?
2. Has the Web increased or decreased price competition? Explain your answer.
3. What are the pros and cons of a grocery store's using a key item list as the basis of its pricing strategy?
4. What are the pros and cons of charging different prices to store-loyal customers based on their price sensitivity?

[c7-1]The data in the case are drawn from Steve Weinstein, "The Price is Righter," *Progressive Grocer* (May 2000), pp. 89–94.

Case 2

Swiss Watches: High Prices with Obsolete Technology[c7-2]

Even though a quartz watch with great accuracy can be made anywhere in the world, almost all high-priced mechanical watches are produced in Switzerland. Annual sales of these watches, which have an average wholesale price of $1,000, have risen by 80 percent in the United States since 1996 to $377 million (at wholesale). Interestingly, even the costliest of these spring-wound timekeeping mechanisms is only accurate to within 8 seconds per day. A $20 Timex (www.timex.com) quartz watch that does not require winding is more accurate!

The robust economy of recent years has been credited for much of the growth of the Swiss watch industry. However, some industry observers believe that Swiss watches took on their mystique when quartz technology rendered these watches technologically obsolete. Recall that obsolescence made fountain pens into status symbols. Another factor that accounts for the success of luxury watches is the perception of scarcity. For example, when Rolex (www.rolex.com) placed its Daytona model back on the market after not selling any for a three-year period, consumers were so attracted to it that a six-year waiting list quickly developed. Finally, while many men eschew necklaces, bracelets, and fancy rings, a $15,000 watch is socially acceptable to them.

Some industry analysts feel that the sales data on the luxury market actually understates real demand. Henry Edelman, president of Patek Phillipe (www.patek.com) in the United States says, "We could have sold 20 percent to 25 percent more watches in each of the last few years if we could have produced them. You walk through our workshops and you see people over 50 and people under 35 and no one in between. The Swiss felt there was no future in it. All of a sudden it became a career again." Patek's newest model is a nonautomatic mechanism that has a 240-hour power reserve. This model will keep time for over a week after a thorough winding. Patek is making only 3,000 of these watches, priced at $27,500 and up.

Although there are many famous brands of luxury watches, perhaps the best-known is Rolex, which sells an estimated 650,000 watches a year at a retail value of around $1.4 billion. Unlike other manufacturers that are constantly developing new dies for their current models, Rolex has far lower costs since it has changed as little as possible in its watch movements. As Walter Fischer, Rolex's chief executive in the United States says, "Our Submariner is a diver's watch—what is it you want to change?"

Let's look at the economics of watch making. According to industry sources, a steel case with a sapphire crystal can be purchased from a supplier for somewhere between $40 to $250, and a watch's movement typically costs between $10 to $2,000. The manufacturer doubles its manufacturing costs to compute the wholesale price. Retailers, in turn, double their wholesale cost to arrive at a retail price to the consumer. Thus, a watch that costs about $1,000 to manufacture has a retail sales price of $4,000 to $5,000.

A significant nonproduction-related cost for all luxury watchmakers is marketing-related expenditures. Omega (www.omega.ch), for example, spends $10 million on advertising each year. Tag Heuer (www.tagheuer.com) often bids against competitors to have its watches displayed in feature films (at a cost of $2 to $3 million per film). Omega is often featured in James Bond films.

Questions

1. What should be the role of costs in price-setting for luxury watches?
2. What role do channel members have in price-setting in the luxury watch business? Should they ever run special sales for luxury watches?
3. How can luxury watch makers employ price discrimination?
4. Discuss how luxury watch makers use chain-markup pricing.

[c7-2]The data in the case are drawn from Joshua Levine, "Time Is Money," *Forbes* (September 18, 2000), pp. 178–182.

Case 3

The Sotheby's Price-Fixing Fiasco[c7-3]

In settling a major horizontal class-action price-fixing case against Sotheby's (www.sothebys.com) and Christie's International (www.christies.com), brought by 100,000 U.S. buyers and sellers of art, Judge Lewis Kaplan gave preliminary approval to a $512 million civil settlement. In addition, Sotheby's former chief executive officer, Diana D. Brooks, pled guilty to conspiring to violate antitrust laws and agreed to testify against her boss, A. Alfred Taubman, Sotheby's ex-chairman of the board. Taubman has also been the target of a criminal investigation. Together, Sotheby's and Christie's control more than 90 percent of the $4 billion auction business.

The civil settlement is considered to be unusually high. Attorneys with experience in such cases say it is about 1.8 times the estimated damages of $286 million. According to these attorneys, settlements in antitrust cases are usually for less than actual damages. If this case had gone to trial, the plaintiffs could have legally sought treble damages.

Some industry experts view the settlement as ironic, since the rival auction houses, which secretly colluded to fix their commissions, only managed to escape disaster by banding together. In most antitrust cases, the conspirators generally agree to cooperate so that the plaintiffs lawyers would be unable to play one side against the other. In this instance, however, the contempt between the two auction houses was so great that they refused to talk, which may have enabled the class-action plaintiffs' lawyer to settle with one firm for a small sum, and then have that firm provide evidence against the rival auction house. Eventually, both firms agreed to split the costs.

This is the essence of the price-fixing case against Sotheby's and Christie's: According to published sources, in 1995, Diana Brooks made a presentation to the Sotheby's board of directors whereby she proposed changing the commission structure from a flat fee to a sliding scale. Sellers would pay a 10 percent commission on a $10,000 item, but just 2 percent on a $5 million sale. Brooks also recommended that Sotheby's refuse to negotiate its commission scale, as it had done in the past with important sellers and buyers or with clients getting a lower commission offer from rival Christie's. One Sotheby's director remembers Brooks saying, "We'll hold fast, with no discounts—what we want is profits. We'll compete on service, not on price. If we lose consignments, we lose them. Let Christie's buy market share, but it would be crazy for them to undercut us and beat their brains out."

Clearly, what the board of Sotheby's did not know was that Diana Brooks had already met with Christopher Davidge, the chief executive officer at Christie's. Davidge agreed to set identical fees to those at Sotheby's and also to refuse to accept lower commissions. Thus, price competition between the two rivals was eliminated and sellers could no longer pit one auction house against the other as a means of obtaining lower commissions.

What is not clear is whether Taubman, as chairman of Sotheby's board, told Brooks to meet with Christie's management. While Brooks insists that he did, Taubman maintains his innocence. There is some documentation, however, that the antitrust conspiracy may have begun with a 1993 conversation between Taubman and Sir Anthony Tennant, who was Christie's chairman at that time.

Questions

1. Differentiate between vertical and horizontal price fixing, and apply your answer to this case.
2. What is the pricing environment in a horizontal price-fixing scenario: market-, company-, or government-controlled? Explain your answer.
3. Comment on this aspect of the settlement: Should Sotheby's be allowed to distribute $50 million in coupons that would reduce a buyer's or seller's commission on a future auction? Why or why not?
4. What should Sotheby's and Christie's do to avoid getting themselves into this situation in the future?

[c7-3]The data in the case are drawn from Shawn Tully, "Sotheby's: A House Divided," *Fortune* (December 18, 2000), pp. 264–275; and Kathryn Kranhold, "Big Settlement Between Auction Houses, Buyers and Sellers of Art is Approved," *Wall Street Journal* (November 15, 2000), p. B8.

Case 4

Amazon.com Discovers Dynamic Pricing[c7-4]

During one recent two-week period, Amazon.com (www.amazon.com) both apologized and issued refunds to appease customers angered by its policy of charging different prices for the same goods. This strategy of setting prices based on shopper demographics or buying habits is called "dynamic pricing."

Amazon.com denies that its price discrimination policy was based on demographic data (such as a shopper's address) or shopping behavior (such as what items and how frequently a shopper buys from Amazon.com). According to Jeff Bezos, Amazon.com's founder, "We've never tested and we never will test prices based on customer demographics." An Amazon.com spokesperson stated that the different prices were part of a test to determine the price sensitivity of consumers.

Marketing analysts note that, while a retailer can charge different prices for the same item in different stores (based on the costs of doing business or customer price sensitivity), the Internet enables retailers to charge different prices on a transaction basis. For example, a Web-based retailer could quote a low price to encourage a new shopper. In contrast, a loyal shopper could be charged a higher price for the same good. Some experts believe that Amazon.com's detailed records on the buying habits of 23 million customers make it easy to use dynamic pricing on a massive scale.

As one Internet consultant states, "Dynamic pricing is the new reality, and it's going to be used by more and more retailers. In the future, what you pay will be determined by where you live and who you are. It's unfair, but that doesn't mean it's not going to happen." On the other hand, an electronic commerce analyst at J.P. Morgan does not think that dynamic pricing will become more widespread: "With popular sites like Amazon, you really can't get much past the consumers anymore. They're out there trading notes all the time, looking for the best deals."

This is the situation that caused the problem for Amazon.com: After some customers who purchased DVD movies began comparing notes on online discussion boards, the news media discovered the firm's use of dynamic pricing. One shopper recalled that he ordered a DVD copy of "Titus" for $24.49. The following week, he discovered that the price was raised to $26.24. As an experiment, he removed the cookies linking his last purchases to Amazon.com. A price of $22.74 then appeared. The consumer was upset to know that regular Amazon buyers were charged higher prices. Said another consumer angered by this practice, "This is a very strange business model, to charge customers more when they buy more or come back to the site more. I have no problem for first-time customers as marketing enticements, but I thought the idea was to attract customers first and then work hard to keep them. This is definitely not going to earn customer loyalty."

Amazon.com refunded an average of $3 to the 6,986 customers affected by this practice. Yet, while the firm stated that it had no immediate plans for more dynamic price testing, it would not rule out using this practice in the future. An Amazon.com spokesperson did state that customers involved in any tests would get a refund if they paid more than others for the same item as a result of a test.

Questions

1. What are the pros and cons of dynamic pricing from the perspective of Amazon.com?
2. How could Amazon.com use dynamic pricing to determine consumers' price sensitivity?
3. Is it unethical to charge new customers lower prices as a form of inducement to try an E-tailer? Explain your answer.
4. Is it unethical to charge loyal shoppers a higher price due to their continued patronage? Explain your answer.

[c7-4] The data in the case are drawn from David Streitfeld, "On the Web, Price Tags Blur," *Washington Post* (September 27, 2000), p. A1; and "Pricing Errors Hurting Amazon.com," *New York Times on the Web* (September 28, 2000).

PART 7 COMPREHENSIVE CASE

Value Measures in the Executive Suite[pc-7]

Introduction

In general, senior executives have a voracious appetite for information. They want to know the facts and they want to act on them. When asked questions about the financial or operational characteristics of their firms, senior executives typically can pull out a report and point to the relevant statistic. Yet, when the same executive is asked about market performance, he or she often lapses into generalities and suggests we speak with "Ace Jones, vice-president of marketing, who has done market studies." In many cases, top executives are out of touch with their markets and customers:

- The top management of a major industrial-manufacturing firm had invested more than $40 million in a new product and was excited about the prospect of the increased growth and profitability that would accrue from a successful launch. Market studies, however, revealed the primary drivers of purchase behavior in the product category were service quality and parts distribution, areas in which the firm was well behind the competition.
- Over several years, a high-tech firm in a rapidly growing market had doubled revenues, tripled profits, and doubled return on assets. The business unit general manager was quite pleased with the performance. He was not aware, however, that the unit's share had declined by 45 percent, it was losing customers, and perceived offering quality had fallen behind the competition.

In both cases, an information system that delivered market-based performance information to the senior manager in a regular and timely manner would have changed the strategic direction of the firm. Top management should expect the same rigor in performance measurement from sales and marketing that they currently expect from finance and operations. Sure, market information is a little harder to gather and interpret, but that shouldn't let sales and marketing, not to mention top management themselves, off the hook. Given the continuing growth in importance of market-based success factors, the increasing portion of overall budgets allocated to marketing-related activities, and the growing need for more timely decision making, improving market-based performance measures should be a priority.

Beginning with Profitability

Make no mistake about it. The senior management mandate is profitability. Every project, program, or initiative within a business ultimately is intended to improve the profit potential of the business. Profitability is the best measure of value created in the marketplace, value created for the channel, value created for employees, and value created for shareholders.

For our purposes, the real question is not whether to chase profitability, but rather how to calculate it. For accounting purposes, most business systems are set up to calculate revenues and costs by product, factory overhead, and business expenses. Yet, a firm's customers are its most important asset and, except for Internet startups, its only significant source of cash flow. The goal of the marketing strategy is to attract, satisfy, and retain target customers in a way that grows profits.

When looking at market-based value measures, the appropriate accounting unit is not products, but customers. Groups of customers with common needs form markets (or segments). The profitability of a business is a sum of the profitability of the markets in which the business competes, minus unallocable operating and overhead expenses. Table 1 contrasts customer-based with product-based accounting.

The term "net marketing contribution" (NMC) represents the profitability of the firm, at the market level, that is driven by the market strategy. The NMC of a market is a measure of the revenues derived from that group of customers, less direct expenses associated with marketing to and servicing them. NMC specifically excludes overhead and operating expenses that are fixed indirect or allocated expenses with little relation to performance in individual markets, for example, corporate overhead. The profitability of a business unit, then, is the profitability (NMC) of individual markets, less operating and overhead expenses. Table 2 shows NMC equations for market-level and business-level profitability.

The concept of net marketing contribution is important not only because it directly links customers to profitability, but also because it can be a powerful lever for the development of a more market-oriented enterprise. The benefits of the NMC approach are that it

- Gets the attention of top management because of the focus on profitability.
- Integrates internal and external sources of information into a coherent whole.
- Is easily intelligible because it is couched in the language of business.
- Is not dependent on complicated and expensive marketing research.
- Can be targeted to measure the strategic focal areas of the business.
- Can be used in variance analysis of planned versus actual.
- Can be assembled in a timely manner for decision support.

[pc-7]Adapted by the authors from Timothy Matanovich, "Value Measures in the Executive Suite," *Marketing Management* (Spring 2000), pp. 34–40. Reprinted by permission of the American Marketing Association.

TABLE 1 Customer-Based Versus Product-Based Accounting

Product-Based		Market-Based	
Market demand	22,000	Market demand (customers)	3,500
Market share	8%	Market share (customers)	8%
Unit volume	1,760	Customer volume	280
Price per unit	$12,000	Revenue per customer	$75,429
Variable cost per unit	$8,000	Variable cost per unit	$50,286
Margin per unit	$4,000	Margin per unit	$25,143
Total revenue	$264,000,000	Total revenue	$264,000,000
Total variable costs	$176,000,000	Total variable costs	$176,000,000
Total contribution	$88,000,000	Total contribution	$88,000,000
Marketing expenses	$33,100,000	Marketing expenses	$33,100,000
Net marketing contribution	$54,900,000	Net marketing contribution	$54,900,000
Operating expenses	$30,000,000	Operating expenses	$30,000,000
Overhead expenses	$9,000,000	Overhead expenses	$9,000,000
Net profit	**$15,900,000**	**Net profit**	**$15,900,000**

TABLE 2 NMC Defined

- Net Profit$_{Bus}$ = NMC$_{Mkts}$ – Opg Exps – Ohd Exps
- NMC$_{Mkt}$ = (# existing customers – lost + new)
  × (rev/cust – var exp/cust) – mktg exp

  - NMC$_{Mkts}$ = Net Marketing Contribution

    ➤Measure of revenues minus direct expenses associated with individual markets in which the firm competes

  - Operating Expenses; Overhead Expenses

    ➤Fixed indirect or allocated expenses that have little relation to performance in individual markets, e.g., corporate overhead

Linking Strategy to Profitability

The NMC approach can be used to evaluate virtually any market strategy decision, from decisions on market entry or withdrawal to measuring marketing productivity. Figure 1 shows the fit between generic market strategies and the NMC approach.

This technique is a framework in which we can build a powerful system for measuring how well the firm creates value for customers, as well as how well it leverages that value to create profitability for the enterprise. It's simple for the firm to create value for customers and profitability for itself. It can

- Gain new customers.
- Retain the customers it has.
- Sell more stuff to customers it already has.
- Lower its costs of servicing customers.
- Lower its costs of marketing to customers.
- Use some combination of these options.

Gaining and Retaining Customers

The first component of the NMC equation concerns itself with growing the number of customers. Because of our focus on value, we're taking the number of existing customers at the end of the last period, subtracting customers lost through the year, and add-

ing new customers gained. In the interest of making the direct link between customers and profitability, it's vital that the firm distinguish and measure customer retention and new customer acquisition separately. This is because the profit impact of customer-retention strategies is markedly different from the profit impact of new customer acquisition.

In general, the first priority of a business should be to retain existing customers. These customers are the most profitable because they're apt to buy more items from the firm, and be less price sensitive, easier to service, and less costly to market. Further, because the cost of acquiring new customers is high, poor retention results in a higher cost of marketing. The impact of customer retention on profitability can be striking. A widely publicized study of MBNA America Bank over a period of years showed that a 5 percent improvement in customer retention resulted in a 16-fold increase in profitability. With that kind of profit impact, customer retention should be measured well and monitored in the executive suite.

Customer retention, however, is an end-result lagging indicator. It is an end result of strategy success in the marketplace over some prior period. Improved retention may be the result of a customer-service initiative instituted months before. Therefore, shouldn't top executives know the barn door is open before the horses begin to run out?

At one large firm, senior managers track their performance against critical-to-quality (CTQ) measures. At another, they

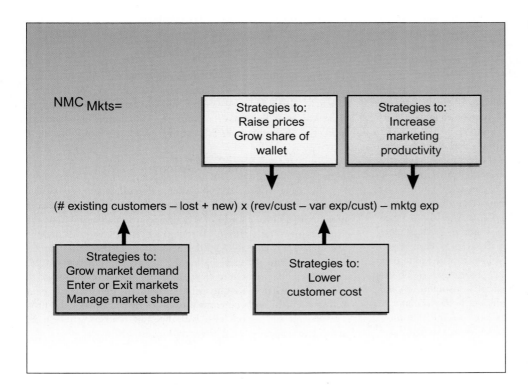

FIGURE 1
The Fit Between Strategy and Profits

employ value mapping; and at yet another, they attribute success to choice modeling. In each case, the firms have learned to model the value they create in the marketplace, relative to that of the competition, on attributes of importance to customers. These firms have developed leading indicators as a way to understand the value they create for existing customers as well as to attract new customers. ABB Ltd. electronics company grew to 40 percent market share from a 5 percent position in the power-transformer market against entrenched competitors such as General Electric and Westinghouse Electric by staying focused on the offering attributes that created the most value for customers. An IBM business unit that focuses on customer satisfaction found that a 1 percent change in satisfaction corresponds to a change in revenue of $250 million over five years.

There is no single, leading indicator of customer value that works best in all situations or fits within every budget. Every firm, however, should measure the value it creates for customers relative to the competition. Firms should choose a measure that they're committed to using regularly and that demonstrates over time that it tracks with customer retention.

Growing Customer Margins

Most markets are ultimately limited; there are a finite number of customers the firm can call on to sell. The second component of the NMC equation is about customer margin, or profitability per customer. At this point, we're interested in the basket of goods that people buy, how much they will pay for them, and our costs in delivering the goods and services to them. We want to maximize margin per customer.

"Share of wallet" is a useful term for thinking about the basket of goods that customers purchase. Share of wallet for any given customer is the firm's share of the customer's total expenditures in a product category. If a trucking firm purchases 50 trucks per year and it bought 10 of them from us, then our share of wallet is 20 percent, assuming all the trucks were priced similarly.

Share-of-wallet analysis can be time- and information-intensive. As a result, firms have employed the technique prudently, focusing on a defined set of customers. For example, firms may look at their top 20 customers and ask: What can we do to deliver greater value and increase sales to this group? Senior managers in most firms are very interested in the needs of their top 20 customers. The answer to this question often is used to drive product development and to measure the potential payback. From a top management perspective, the share-of-wallet measure is a nice refinement of the more broadly used market-share measure. Share-of-wallet analysis permits a more intimate look at competition and the nature of competitive advantage within a customer account.

Another driver of customer margins, and possibly the most powerful, is price. No other element of a marketing mix can have a more rapid or dramatic impact on profits than improved price management. Price is the most powerful profit lever in the business. For the big company, a 1 percent price increase means a 12 percent increase in profitability if volume remains the same. In most firms, however, price is not well managed. An audit of pricing practices at 11 large firms revealed that this generally is true:

- Firms are internally focused rather than market-focused in their price-related information gathering and performance measurement.
- Managers generally work hard to make good pricing decisions, but they're not employing the information, tools, and techniques to work smart.
- Top management gives lip service to better price management, but does not have management systems in place to make it happen.

If this sampling indicates the behavior of many firms—and we believe it does—then many firms are missing the boat on building value, higher prices, and greater profitability.

Value maps and price bands are useful tools in measuring price performance. Both tools help explain how customers view the value of competing offerings and how prices compare. Both are easy to use and interpret, and data are rather easy to gather. Once price and value are fully understood, opportunities often emerge for improving price performance through better price management. With the substantial impact of offering price on margins and the profitability of the enterprise, a price-performance measure should be part of the top executive's briefing book.

Marketing Productivity

The third component of the NMC equation deals with marketing expenses, such as advertising, customer service, and market research, which don't vary with volume in the short run. Tracking these expenses by market permits the calculation of return-on-marketing investment (ROMI) at the market level, as follows:

$$\text{ROMI} = \frac{\text{NMC}}{\text{Marketing Expenditures}}$$

ROMI is an essential calculation. After all, what's the purpose of marketing expenditures if they are not an investment that creates profitability? Further, if ROMI is not calculated, marketing is viewed as an expense rather than an investment. An adverse economic wind blows, top management decides to cut expenses, and marketing is the first to go, exacerbating the already bad situation. ROMI permits top management to view marketing as an investment and to see the payback from that investment. Thus, the investment in marketing is salient and comparable to other investments of the firm. The playing field is more level. ROMI permits marketing to be more appreciated as an essential driver of the business.

Some of our colleagues might argue that this is too simplistic an approach to truly measure the marketing investment. After all, the payback of an investment in marketing might not be seen in the current year, might not affect profitability directly, or might be extremely difficult to measure. For all its limitations, it's still the right place to start. Do this first, then build a better measurement infrastructure.

Leading the Leading Indicators

Except for the measures of relative offering or customer value, most of the value metrics described are lagging indicators. In essence, we're passengers in a vehicle in which the driver is looking out the back window most of the time. Are there other indicators of value that top management can rely on to set a strategic direction? Two proven measures merit consideration: employee value and market orientation.

A host of sources have documented the close relationship between employee satisfaction and customer satisfaction. In most cases, the two measures travel in tandem: Improve employee satisfaction, and customer satisfaction rises. In the previous discussion, however, we didn't used the term "customer satisfaction," but used "customer value." The distinction is important. Customers might be satisfied with our services, but they might choose to do business with a competitor because the value they receive from the competitor is higher. The better metric, thus, is customer value.

Similarly the employee-satisfaction measure is limited. We care whether employees value the relationship with the firm. If they value the relationship, then they must be satisfied. In an era in which knowledge workers are becoming more important to business success, the role of an employee value measure is also growing. The measure of employee value becomes a leading indicator of customer value.

Another measure proven over the last decade is market orientation. Research instruments have been developed that measure how well the firm focuses on customers, considers competitive threats, and works to achieve objectives. Firms that are more market-oriented grow more rapidly, are more profitable, are more successful with new products, and demonstrate greater customer satisfaction and employee loyalty.

A Note on E-Business

Today, we'd be negligent to not address the impact of E-business on value measurement. In this environment, the NMC profitability model remains a valid overall model for viewing market-based performance. Competing on the Web, however, has implications for value measurement, such as:

- Understanding that the foundation of customer value is even more imperative.

- Customer value must be assessed in a broader competitive context.
- Timeliness is next to Godliness.

Competition on the Web is like the weather in Chicago. You don't like what you see today? Just wait until tomorrow. The tactics and technologies of the Web are changing so fast they are literally impossible to keep up with for most mortals. The underpinnings of value, however, are changing much more slowly. To keep a constant heading in this sea of change, it's imperative to focus on the drivers of customer value.

In the world of E-business, startups often pursue goals of market share growth and strategic control; profitability is less important. This is a radical departure from the traditional view of prudent business and financial management. Startups have succeeded in gobbling chunks of share and more traditional players are stymied. In an ROI view of the world, these plays make little sense. Traditional players need to find new approaches for evaluating the risk and return of E-business plays.

One E-business firm we know manages to offer development with a 90-day rule. If we have an idea for building the business, then within 90 days, we must determine if that idea is worth three-quarters of a million dollars in profit or not, and make a go, no-go decision.

Questions

1. Comment on this statement: "The real question is not whether to chase profitability, but rather how to calculate it." Refer to Table 1 in your answer.
2. Why is net marketing contribution (NMC) an important concept for company executives to grasp? Refer to Table 2 in your answer.
3. Discuss how *each* strategy highlighted in Figure 1 relates to net marketing contribution.
4. Relate the notion of "share of wallet" to these two concepts: price elasticity of demand and subjective price.
5. Explain this formula: ROMI = NMC/Marketing Expenditures. How could a company actually calculate ROMI (return on marketing investment)?
6. Do you agree or disagree with the conclusions stated in this case regarding pricing and E-business? Why?
7. Apply the points noted in this case to a discount start-up airline.
8. Apply the points noted in this case to a mature pet food manufacturer.

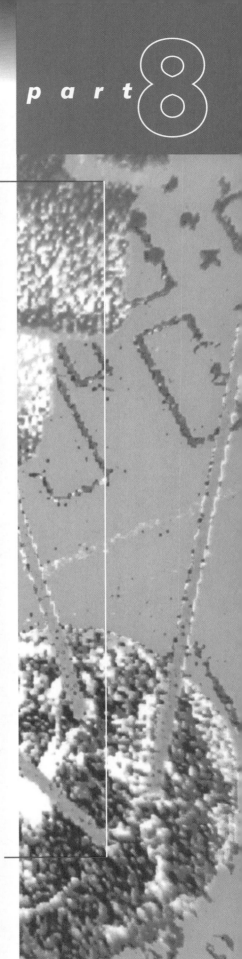

Marketing Management

In Part 8, we tie together the concepts introduced in Chapters 1 through 21 and discuss planning for the future.

22 Pulling It All Together: Integrating and Analyzing the Marketing Plan

We first note the value of developing and analyzing integrated marketing plans. Next, we examine the elements in a well-integrated marketing plan: clear organizational mission, long-term competitive advantages, precisely defined target market, compatible subplans, coordination among SBUs, coordination of the marketing mix, and stability over time. Then, we study five types of marketing plan analysis: benchmarking, customer satisfaction research, marketing cost analysis, sales analysis, and the marketing audit. These are important tools for evaluating the success or failure of marketing plans. We conclude with a look at why and how firms should anticipate and plan for the future.

After reading Part 8, you should understand elements 14 and 15 of the strategic marketing plan outlined in Table 3-2 (pages 72–75).

Pulling It All Together: Integrating and Analyzing the Marketing Plan

1 To show the value of an integrated marketing plan

2 To discuss the elements of a well-integrated marketing plan

3 To present five types of marketing plan analysis: benchmarking, customer satisfaction research, marketing cost analysis, sales analysis, and the marketing audit

4 To see the merit of anticipating and planning for the future

Becoming a larger firm relative to competitors can be beneficial. In a study by the Windermere Associates consulting firm (http://www. strategystreet.com), the market share leader was found to beat the industry's average return on assets in the 300 industries analyzed. For example, Amgen (www.amgen.com), the leader in the biological products industry, has a return on assets that places it into the top 10 percent of all firms studied. In comparison, most firms in that industry have poor returns on assets. Other high-performing firms that are market share leaders include Deere (www.deere.com) for farm products and Walgreen Company (www.walgreens.com) for drugstores.

However, 41 percent of the 300 industries have leaders whose return on assets is below average for their industry. These include A.C. Nielsen (www.acnielsen.com) for marketing research, Moore (www.moore.com) for business forms, and Occidental (www.oxy.com) for alkalies and chlorine. Based on these findings, the impact of market share on profitability may be less important than once thought.

The Windermere study also found that relative size provides even less benefit in highly competitive industries, as well as in industries where return on assets is traditionally low. In fact, in the one-quarter of the 300 industries with the lowest return on assets, the industry market share leader had a lower return on assets than the average share leader in all 300 industries.

Because economies of scale may not always exist, how can a firm increase its return on investment? It must identify the best customers, focus the products and cost structure on them, and apply economies of scale to the volume in this market. A firm should limit its customer base by getting rid of those who "ask for too much" and "offer to pay too little." Some customers consistently pay low prices—when demand conditions are poor and excellent. Furthermore, a firm needs to develop, market, and support products that core customers (not its bad customers) desire. Lastly, a firm needs a disciplined approach to managing its costs. It cannot be assumed that costs will fall automatically because volume expands.

In this chapter, we will study how a firm can integrate and analyze its marketing plan by assessing the target market, as well as by undertaking marketing cost analysis. We will also see the value of developing and implementing a clear, forward-looking, cohesive, and adaptable strategy.[1]

22-1 OVERVIEW

Chapters 1 and 2 introduced basic marketing concepts and described the marketing environment. Chapters 3 and 4 presented the strategic planning process as it applies to marketing and the role of marketing information systems and marketing research. Chapters 5

---

[1]Donald V. Potter, "Scale Matters," *Across the Board* (July 2000), p. 36.

to 7 broadened our scope to include the societal, ethical, and consumer implications of marketing; global marketing efforts; and marketing applications of the Internet. Chapters 8 to 21 centered on specific aspects of marketing: describing and selecting target markets, and the marketing mix (product, distribution, promotion, and price planning).

This chapter ties things together, and describes how a marketing plan can be integrated and assessed. It builds on the strategic planning discussion in Chapter 3—particularly, the total quality approach (whereby a firm strives to fully satisfy customers in an effective and efficient way). With an integrated effort, individual marketing components are synchronized and everyone is "on the same page." When an organization wants to appraise performance, capitalize on strengths, minimize weaknesses, and plan for the future, marketing analysis (including benchmarking and customer satisfaction) is necessary. The overall process is shown in Figure 22-1.

This is the challenge, as one expert sees it:

Do you know where your marketing plan is? In a world where competitors observe and rapidly imitate each other's advancements in product development, pricing, packaging, and distribution, internal and external communication is more important than ever as a way of differentiating your business from those of competitors. At its most basic level, a marketing plan defines a business niche, summarizes objectives, and presents strategies for getting from point A to point B. But roadmaps need constant updating to reflect the addition of new routes. Because technology, international relations, and the competitive landscape are constantly changing, the concept of a static marketing plan has to be reassessed. Two of today's buzzwords are "interactive" and "integrated." A successful marketing plan has to be both. "Interactive" means your marketing plan should be a conversation between your business and your customers. It's your chance to tell customers about your business and to listen and act on their responses.

FIGURE 22-1

Integrating and Assessing Strategic Marketing Plans

Source: Clark Crouch, "A New Simplified Model for Planning," http://crouchnet.com/planning.html (May 5, 2001). Reprinted by permission.

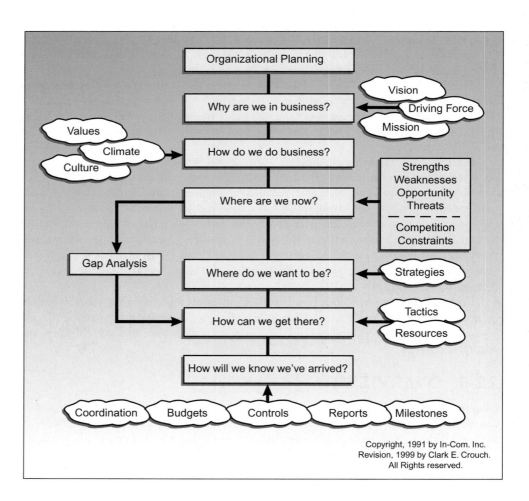

"Integrated" means the message in your marketing is consistently reinforced by every department within your company. Marketing is as much a function of the finance and manufacturing areas as it is the advertising and public relations areas.[2]

Here is what four diverse companies are doing to optimize their marketing strategies:

- Green Hills Farms (www.greenhills.com) is an independent supermarket in Syracuse, New York. *Inc.* calls it "the best little grocery store in America." It is renowned for its customer loyalty program. The company tries out all sales promotions on its employees before offering them to customers (to see what works best), intensely monitors its customer data base, and exchanges ideas with noncompeting supermarkets that are leaders in the field.[3]

- Swiss-based pharmaceutical giant Novartis (www.novartis.com) has brought in 80 veteran executives from outside the company to strengthen its senior marketing team. It is building global brands for the first time, supported by a coordinated worldwide sales effort; spending $1.2 billion to launch five new drugs; and increasing its marketing research efforts.[4]

- Southwest Airlines (www.southwest.com) is the most admired U.S. airline. It adheres to three basic rules: (1) Be prepared for every plausible occurrence in a changing marketplace (such as a merger of two rivals or rising fuel prices). (2) Act more quickly than competitors to seize opportunities. (3) Listen to both customers and employees. They often have good ideas to improve the business.[5]

- Market-leading Microsoft (www.microsoft.com), despite its legal battles with the U.S. Justice Department, still has an aggressive, four-stage approach to marketing: "(1) Start with an existing monopoly. Microsoft controls desktop computing. When it ships its Windows XP in October 2001, the product will be included with most personal computers sold. (2) Bundle a new service into your monopoly product. When consumers access the Web from Windows XP, they will be asked to join Passport, a service that packages their name, address, and credit-card numbers into a digital wallet. With Passport, they don't have to type in their vital data each time they go to a Web site. (3) Extend into a new market. By turning most PC users into Passport users, Microsoft hopes to build a large base of consumers using the service. That makes it attractive for more Web-site operators to adopt Passport for authenticating customer data. (4) Cash in. Once a large number of consumers and Web sites are using Passport, the company could be in a position to charge transaction fees for services based on Passport—such as alerts when a traveler's airplane flight is late."[6]

22-2 INTEGRATING THE MARKETING PLAN

When a marketing plan is properly integrated, all of its various parts are unified, consistent, and coordinated; and a total quality approach can be followed. Although this appears to be a simple task, it is important to recall that a firm may have long-run, moderate-length, and short-run plans; the different strategic business units in an organization may require separate marketing plans; and each aspect of the marketing mix requires planning. For example:

From a total quality perspective, the many parts of a marketing plan should be unified, consistent, and coordinated.

- An overall plan would be poorly integrated if short-run profits are earned at the expense of moderate- or long-term profits. This could occur if marketing research or new-product planning expenditures are reduced to raise profits temporarily. A firm

[2]Shelly Reese, "The Very Model of a Modern Marketing Plan," *Marketing Tools* (January/February 1996), pp. 56–59.

[3]Susan Greco, "The Best Little Grocery Store in America," *Inc.* (June 2001), pp. 54–61.

[4]Kerry Capell, "Novartis' Marketing Doctor," *Business Week* (March 5, 2001), p. 56.

[5]Katrina Brooker, "The Chairman of the Board Looks Back," *Fortune* (May 28, 2001), pp. 63–76.

[6]"How Microsoft Stays Two Steps Ahead of the Courts," *Business Week* (June 4, 2001), p. 84.

could also encounter difficulties if plans are changed too frequently, leading to a blurred image for consumers and a lack of focus for executives.

● Resources need to be allocated among SBUs so that funds are given to those with high potential. The target markets, product images, price levels, and so on, of each SBU must be distinctive, yet not in conflict with one another. Physical distribution efforts and channel member arrangements need to be timed so the system and its role in a total quality program are not strained by two or more SBUs making costly demands simultaneously.

● Although a promotion plan primarily deals with one strategic element, it must also be integrated with product, distribution, and pricing plans. It must reflect the proper image for a firm's products, encourage channel cooperation, and show that products are worth the prices set.

A well-integrated marketing plan incorporates the elements shown in Figure 22-2. These elements are explained next.

GLOBAL *Marketing in Action*

Paying the Price for Growing Too Fast in Global Markets

McDonald's strategy is to double the number of restaurants in Brazil between 2000 and 2003. According to Ronaldo Marques, McDonald's marketing director in Brazil, even though Brazil is McDonald's eighth largest market, "We're still only in a quarter of all cities that have more than 50,000 people."

The high anticipated growth is not welcomed by many of McDonald's franchisees which feel that their original territories have become increasingly saturated. For example, John Rowell, an American who now owns two Brazilian McDonald's franchises, had only one competing McDonald's franchise that bordered his original unit in 1994; there are now 15 competing McDonald's units nearby. Rowell says that, "With every new store that opened, I lost more sales." Another problem for franchisees is the high cost for interest and imported products (such as ketchup) due to Brazil's 1999 currency devaluation.

Marques defends the chain's expansion plan on the grounds that McDonald's seeks to pre-empt competitors by taking the best available locations and to lock in potential investors to McDonald's. He believes that John Rowell and other franchisees have been spoiled by quick profits as a result of the boom times in Brazil during the mid 1990s. In 1998, McDonald's also came to Rowell's aid by agreeing to lower the rent on a restaurant location for a period of six months.

Some marketing experts also feel McDonald's growth goal conflicts with the goals of franchisees in another way. McDonald's receives income from franchisees based on total retail sales in a territory, not franchise profitability. Thus, a saturated area is more profitable to McDonald's, but less profitable to the franchisees located there.

As a marketing specialist for McDonald's, prepare a short report on the pros and cons of its fast-growth strategy in Brazil.

Source: Based on material in Miriam Jordan, "McDonald's Strikes Sparks with Fast Growth in Brazil," *Wall Street Journal* (October 4, 2000), p. A23.

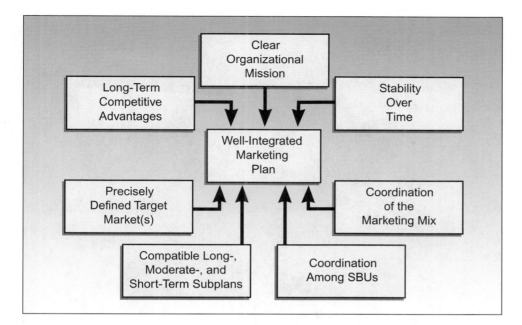

FIGURE 22-2
Elements Leading to a Well-Integrated Marketing Plan

22-2a Clear Organizational Mission

A clear organizational mission outlines a firm's commitment to a type of business and a place in the market. It directs total quality efforts. The mission is involved whenever a firm seeks new customer groups or abandons existing ones, adds or deletes product lines, acquires other firms or sells part of its own business, does different marketing functions, and/or shifts technological focus (as noted in Chapter 3). Both top management and marketing personnel must be committed to a mission for it to be achieved; and the mission must be communicated to customers, company employees, suppliers, and distribution intermediaries. For example, fast-growing Kohl's Department Store (www.kohls.com), depicted in Figure 22-3, has a marketing-oriented organizational mission based on a total quality approach:

> You, our customer, are what makes us who we are. Our number-one priority is to make your shopping experience the best it can be. Kohl's is a family-focused, value-oriented, specialty department store offering moderately priced, national-brand apparel, shoes, accessories, and home products. You may best know Kohl's for our selection of national brands; we carry the biggest names from apparel leaders such as Nike and Levi's to home goods leaders such as Pfaltzgraff and KitchenAid. However, just as important as our brand assortment, are the Kohl's Associates. At Corporate, our Associates plan and execute the strategies that build, merchandise, and run our stores. Our Distribution Centers serve up to 100 stores each, ensuring merchandise gets to the correct destination, on time. At the storefront, our Associates are trained to deliver a satisfying, hassle-free shopping experience for every customer. As a customer-focused organization, we seek to earn and maintain your loyalty every day. We not only carry the best merchandise and practice a "yes, we can" customer service motto, but we offer the best savings opportunities, too. You only have to look at our weekly savings to know that Kohl's is committed to offering quality merchandise at a fair price.[7]

Many experts think a firm should reappraise its mission if that company has values which do not fit a changing environment, its industry undergoes rapid changes, its performance is average or worse, it changes size (from small to large or large to small), or opportunities unrelated to its original mission arise. To learn more about devising superior organizational missions, visit the About.com Web site (www.about.com) and type "mission statement" in the "Find It Now" box.

The organizational mission should be clear and directive.

[7]"Who We Are," www.kohls.com/about_kohls/about_kohls_who_we_are.htm (May 29, 2001).

The Distinctive Mission of Kohl's

As Kohl's Web site (www.kohls.com) notes, "If you've ever shopped a Kohl's Department Store, you'll quickly recognize our focus on family, value, and national brands. Our stores feature a merchandise mix of apparel, shoes, and accessories for women, men, and children, and home products from small electronics to luggage. Combining convenience and selection in a single location strategically positions us as the ideal shopping experience: great prices found in a traditional department-store setting. Take our online tour to learn more about our departments, the merchandise we carry, and the general layout of a Kohl's Store."

Source: Reprinted by permission of PricewaterhouseCoopers.

Competitive advantages should center on company, product, and marketing attributes with long-range distinctiveness.

22-2b Long-Term Competitive Advantages

Long-term competitive advantages are company, product, and marketing attributes whose distinctiveness and appeal to consumers can be maintained over an extended period of time. A firm must capitalize on the attributes that are most important to consumers and prepare competitive advantages accordingly. For advantages to be sustainable, consumers must perceive a consistent positive difference in key attributes between the company's offerings and those of competitors; that difference must be linked to a capability gap that competitors will have difficulty in closing (due to patents, superior marketing skills, customer loyalty, and other factors); and the company's offerings must appeal to an enduring consumer need. This is highlighted in Figure 22-4 for Lean Cuisine (www.leancusine.com), whose very name signifies its long-term advantage. While concentrating on its competitive advantages, a company should not lose sight of the importance of customer service and its role in a total quality program.

As Michael Treacy and Fred Wiersema said in their best-selling *The Discipline of Market Leaders:*

> Today's market leaders understand the battle. They know they must redefine value by raising customer expectations in the one component of value they choose to highlight. Casio (www.casio.com), for instance, sets new affordability levels for familiar products such as calculators; Hertz (www.hertz.com) makes car rental nearly as convenient as taking a cab; Lands' End (www.landsend.com) shows individuals that they're not just a number; and Home Depot (www.homedepot.com) proves that old-fashioned, knowledgeable advice hasn't gone the way of trading stamps. But wait a minute. These firms don't shine in every way. Wal-Mart (www.walmart.com) doesn't peddle haute couture; Lands' End doesn't sell clothing for the lowest possible cost; and Starbucks (www.starbucks.com) doesn't slide a cup of java under your nose any faster or more conveniently than anyone else. Yet, they are all thriving because they shine in a way their customers care most about. They have honed at least one component of value to a level of excellence that puts all competitors to shame. No firm can succeed today by trying to be all things to all people. It must instead find the unique value that it alone can deliver to a chosen market.[8]

---

[8]Michael Treacy and Fred Wiersema, *The Discipline of Market Leaders* (Reading, Mass.: Addison-Wesley, 1995).

FIGURE 22-4
Lean Cuisine: Do Something Good for Yourself
Source: Reprinted by permission of Nestlé USA, Inc.

Because smaller firms often cannot compete on the basis of low prices, they tend to concentrate on other competitive advantages, such as

- Targeting underserved market niches, including foreign ones.
- Having unique offerings by specializing. Firms can be innovative, process customized orders, or otherwise adapt products for particular customers.
- Emphasizing product quality and reliability to reduce customers' price sensitivity.
- Working harder to attain shopper loyalty. Hands-on customer service is particularly effective.
- Emphasizing relationship marketing, whereby relationships with both suppliers and customers are viewed as important.

When implementing a marketing strategy, a firm should note that its competitive advantages may not apply in all situations. For instance, an advantage can lose its value when transferred to another nation, because it is not relevant in a different context or because it can easily be countered by local competitors.

22-2c Precisely Defined Target Market(s)

By precisely defining its target market(s), a firm identifies the specific consumers to be addressed in its marketing plans. This guides current marketing efforts and future direction. When a firm engages in concentrated marketing or differentiated marketing (multiple segmentation), it is essential that each segment be understood. For example, TCF Bank (www.tcfbank.com) has more than 300 bank offices in Minnesota, Illinois, Wisconsin, Michigan, and Colorado. While most of its loans are for residential real estate, TCF also engages in commercial real-estate, business, and consumer loans. The firm offers other services via real estate, mortgage, and insurance subsidiaries. Unlike many competitors, it does not aim at upscale consumers. Its marketing strategy is rather unique: "TCF's primary focus is lower- and middle-income customers and small to

The target market(s) should be identified precisely.

medium-sized businesses in our markets. TCF emphasizes convenience in banking; we're open 12 hours a day, seven days a week, and holidays. We provide customers with targeted, innovative products through multiple banking channels, including traditional and supermarket branches, ATMs, debit cards, and online and phone banking."[9]

A firm's target market approach may have to be fine-tuned due to changing demographics and lifestyles—or declining sales. Consider the men's toiletries market:

> This market is a tricky one. For years, men's toiletries were hailed as a hot niche, even as male consumers failed to respond. "Growth in men's toiletries has been slower than expected," says John Gilmore, a consultant with Datamonitor (www.datamonitor.com). "People have been talking about the men's market for 25 years." Traditionally, men have spent very little time at the toiletries fixture in stores and purchasing authority is often delegated to their partner. "The rise of single-person households, working women, divorce rates, and marrying later in life have created a strong trend toward individualism, with men increasing their role in purchasing decisions. Skincare has traditionally been perceived as a feminine product, but brands such as Nivea for Men (www.niveaformen.com) are helping to overcome traditional barriers to growth," according to a Datamonitor report. And while men's toiletry products are most frequently line extensions of brands originally targeted to women, there's increasing attention to the athletic and crossover markets.[10]

In this context, a total quality approach is especially crucial in attracting and retaining consumers. This is aided through the use of data-base marketing.

22-2d Compatible Long-, Moderate-, and Short-Term Subplans

Long-, moderate-, and short-term subplans must be compatible.

The long-, moderate-, and short-term marketing subplans of a firm need to be compatible with one another. Long-term plans are the most general and set a broad framework for moderate-term plans. Short-term plans are the most specific, but they need to be derived from both moderate- and long-term plans. Unfortunately, adequate plans and subplans are not always set—or are not communicated to employees.

One important trend among many companies is the shrinking time frame of marketing plans:

> Because customer priorities are constantly changing, a marketing plan should change with them. For years, conventional wisdom was "prepare a five-year marketing plan and review it every year." But change happens a lot faster than it did 20 or even 10 years ago. For that reason, some consultants recommend that firms prepare three-year plans and review them quarterly. Frequent reviews let companies identify potential problems and opportunities before the competition does. "Preventative maintenance for a firm is as important as putting oil in a car," one consultant says. "You don't wait a whole year to do it. You can't change history, but you can anticipate what's going to happen."[11]

22-2e Coordination Among SBUs

SBUs should be coordinated.

Coordination among an organization's SBUs is enhanced when the functions, strategies, and resources allocated to each are described in long-, moderate-, and short-term plans. For larger firms, SBU coordination can be challenging. For instance, Arcadia Group (www.principles.co.uk/promostores/principles/franchise) is the second-largest apparel retailer in Great Britain, with more than 2,600 stores. It operates a number of store divisions (SBUs), such as Burton Menswear for men, Dorothy Perkins for women, Principles for women, and many more. The company also owns Zoom (www.zoom.co.uk), an E-commerce Web site and Internet service provider, and Arcadia Group is growing internationally. To position its SBUs properly, each division targets distinct segments. Thus, Burton

---

[9]"TCF Bank Profile," www.tcfbank.com/ab_profi.htm (May 17, 2001); and "Philosophy," www.tcfbank.com/ab_philo.htm (May 17, 2001).

[10]Alice Naude, "Men's Toiletries in a New Age," *Chemical Market Reporter* (May 8, 2000) pp. FR20–FR21.

[11]Reese, "The Very Model of a Modern Marketing Plan," pp. 60–61.

FIGURE 22-5
Arcadia's Principles Division
Principles is the contemporary clothing division of the Arcadia Group. The division is well positioned within Arcadia: "Your search is now over if you want to find the latest contemporary looks, beautifully designed to suit your lifestyle."

Source: Reprinted by permission of PricewaterhouseCoopers.

Menswear and Dorothy Perkins sell "affordable, mainstream clothing for men and women, respectively, while Principles is known for its distinctive smart clothing for men and women." The firm has 2.7 million active credit-card customers. The Principles division is featured in Figure 22-5.

The coordination of SBUs by large multinational firms can be particularly complex. For example, until recently, ABB (Asea Brown Boveri, www.abb.com), had 175 global managers at its Swiss headquarters. They oversaw 200,000 employees and more than 1,000 companies operating in 140 countries around the globe. In 2001, it made some major changes:

> Traditionally, corporations in our business have been organized around technology or geography—sometimes both. For large global companies, this leads to many units serving customers in parallel with different goods and services. Quite simply, we've decided to break that mold. As an industry first, we are fully organizing around customers and channels to market, building our whole company from the customers' perspective and working our way in. To meet demand and anticipate customer needs, we've structured ABB along seven customer divisions. Four divisions—Utilities, Process Industries, Manufacturing and Consumer Industries, and Oil, Gas and Petrochemicals—provide end users with faster and easier access to the full range of ABB's products, services, and solutions. Two divisions—Power Technology Products and Automation Technology Products—are responsible for all generic products in ABB. They also serve external channel partners, such as wholesalers, distributors, original equipment manufacturers (OEMs), and system integrators. The Financial Services division serves internal and external customers with a full range of financing solutions.[12]

22-2f Coordination of the Marketing Mix

The components of the marketing mix (product, distribution, promotion, and price) need to be coordinated and consistent with a firm's organizational mission. As an example, JetBlue (www.jetblue.com) is a discount airline that had its first flight in February 2000. Unlike other start-up airlines, JetBlue has been very successful. After only six months, the firm was earning a profit—a feat rarely achieved in the passenger service business. When it began, JetBlue operated only one route between New York City and Buffalo, New York. By summer 2001, it was serving 14 destinations from its East Coast hub at New York's JFK

The marketing mix within each SBU has to be coordinated.

---

[12]*ABB Group Annual Report 2000.*

airport and adding a second hub at Long Beach Airport in California. As of 2003, it expects to serve 14 cities from the California hub. The key to JetBlue's success is an outstanding marketing mix that adheres to a total quality philosophy:

● Product—To maximize productivity and standardize maintenance, JetBlue uses just one type of plane, the Airbus A320, and flies its fleet up to 14 hours per day. In contrast to other discount airlines with their no-frills approach, JetBlue flies new planes with leather seats and free onboard television. Yet, it does not offer meals. According to one survey, JetBlue is already considered a customer service "role model" for discount airlines and "trying to be the U.S. version of Virgin Airlines."

● Distribution—JetBlue flies to many underserved destinations, such as Buffalo, Rochester, and Syracuse, New York; Burlington, Vermont; Fort Myers and West Palm Beach, Florida; and Oakland, California. This keeps costs down (because airport fees are less). There is also less marketplace competition. Since its new planes are relatively quiet, JetBlue gained access to the Long Beach Airport that had been denied to others.

● Promotion—Although its advertising expenditures are modest, JetBlue runs regular ads in print media and always emphasizes its low prices in the ads. The airline has generated a huge amount of free publicity because of its unique approach, with full-length articles appearing in *USA Today*, *Wall Street Journal*, *Fortune*, and elsewhere.

● Price—JetBlue offers consistently low airfares and special companion rates. Consider this recent excerpt from the firm's Web site: "JetBlue 'Get-It-Together' fares offer great value for parties of two or more when traveling between JFK, Burlington, Buffalo, Rochester, Syracuse, New Orleans and ALL Florida destinations including Ft. Lauderdale, Orlando, Tampa, West Palm Beach, and Ft. Myers. Just book online at www.jetblue.com or through 1-800-JETBLUE to receive our lowest available 'Get-It-Together' fares. One-way fares between JFK and Burlington, Buffalo, Rochester and Syracuse range from $49 to $85, while fares between JFK and Ft. Lauderdale, Orlando, Tampa, West Palm Beach, and Ft. Myers range from $84 to $144. Fares between JFK and New Orleans range from $89 to $169. Fares between Burlington, Buffalo, Rochester, Syracuse and Ft. Lauderdale, Orlando, Tampa, West Palm Beach, and Ft. Myers range from $104 to $164. Fares between New Orleans and Buffalo, Rochester, and Syracuse range from $109 to $199."[13]

22-2g Stability Over Time

The stability of the basic plan should be maintained over time.

A marketing plan must have a certain degree of stability over time to be implemented and evaluated properly. This does not mean it should be inflexible and thus unable to adjust to a dynamic environment. Rather, it means a broad marketing plan, consistent with the firm's mission and total quality approach, should guide long-term efforts and be fine-tuned regularly; the basic plan should remain in effect for a number of years. Short-run marketing plans can be much more flexible, as long as they conform to long-term goals and the organizational mission. Thus, low prices might be part of a long-term marketing plan. However, in any particular year, prices might have to be raised in response to environmental forces.

An example of a firm striving to maintain a stable—but flexible—approach is U.S.-based Illinois Tool Works (ITW). It began in 1912 as a maker of machine tools. Today, ITW (www.itw.com) is a multinational company with more than 500 decentralized operating units. It engineers and manufactures value-added fasteners, components, assemblies,

---

[13]JetBlue Web site, www.jetblue.com (June 6, 2001); Eryn Brown, "A Smokeless Herb," *Fortune* (May 28, 2001), pp. 78–79; David Field, "JetBlue Earns Its Wings," *USA Today* (February 12, 2001), p. B4; Keith Naughton, "Try Lounging in Leather," *Newsweek* (April 23, 2001), p. 40; Randy Kennedy, "The Skies Are Blue and the Chips Are, Too," *New York Times on the Web* 2001; and "JetBlue Decides to Add Long Beach, Calif., as Second 'Focus City,'" *Wall Street Journal* (May 24, 2001), p. A10.

and systems for customers around the world. ITW businesses are small and focused. After about 90 years, ITW's mission is still true to its heritage. The firm has major facilities in dozens of countries. Due to its global presence, "ITW" is now used more than the full name. Every year since 1987, ITW has been ranked first or second in its industry (metal products) in *Fortune's* annual list of the most admired corporations in the United States.

In keeping with its strong total-quality orientation, the firm adheres to these principles:

ITW strives to improve our customers' competitive positions by increasing productivity and quality while reducing manufacturing and assembly costs. ITW achieves this goal through decentralized operations in 40 countries. These units respond to customer needs by establishing production facilities in proximity to the markets served and creating close working relationships with our customers. ITW's many businesses are focused on serving their customers' and industries' diverse requirements. Despite the variety of markets served, the underlying goals that drive all ITW businesses are common: to create value and improve operating efficiencies for every customer.[14]

22-3 ANALYZING THE MARKETING PLAN

Marketing plan analysis involves comparing actual performance with planned or expected performance for a specified period of time. If actual performance is unsatisfactory, corrective action may be needed. Also, plans must sometimes be revised because of the impact of uncontrollable variables.

Five of the techniques used to analyze marketing plans are discussed in the following sections: benchmarking, customer satisfaction research, marketing cost analysis, sales analysis, and the marketing audit. Although our discussion of these tools is limited to their utility in evaluating marketing plans, they may also be employed when developing and modifying these plans.

Marketing plan analysis *compares actual and targeted achievements.*

22-3a Benchmarking

For a firm to properly assess the effectiveness of its marketing plans, it must set performance standards. That is, it must specify what exactly is meant by "success." One way to do this is to utilize **benchmarking,** whereby a firm sets its own marketing performance standards based on prior actions by the firm itself, the prowess of direct competitors, the competence of the best companies in its industry, and/or the approaches of innovative companies in other industries anywhere around the world. As a Hewlett-Packard (www.hp.com) E-commerce development manager recently remarked: "We have an aggressive schedule of participation in benchmarking activities to obtain best-practice information and leading-edge ideas. By sharing practices and ideas with other companies, both inside and out of our industry, we find that we can build real momentum for benchmarking."[15] Among the growing number of firms—besides Hewlett-Packard—now using benchmarking are AT&T (www.att.com), DuPont (www.dupont.com), Ford (www.ford.com), IBM (www.ibm.com), Kodak (www.kodak.com), Marriott (www.marriott.com), Metropolitan Life (www.metlife.com), Motorola (www.motorola.com), and Walt Disney (www.disney.com). According to one worldwide study of 475 senior executives at leading firms, 77 percent of their companies regularly engage in benchmarking.[16]

In **benchmarking,** *a firm sets specific points of comparison so performance can be measured.*

Benchmarking may be divided into two main categories:

Process benchmarking is often most appropriate, as it has to do with the more easily measurable aspects of a company's operation. Each firm has critical business processes that, if improved, accrue significant competitive advantages. Flexibility in the use of human and other resources, rapid new-product introduction, reduced defects, faster delivery time, and lower

---

[14]*Illinois Tool Works Inc. 2000 Annual Report.*

[15]"Turn Benchmarking into a Strategic Procurement Tool," *Supplier Selection & Management Report* (January 2001), p. 7.

[16]Darrell Rigby, "Management Tools and Techniques: A Survey," *California Management Review,* Vol. 43 (Winter 2001), pp. 139–160.

distribution costs (through better inventory management and scheduling) can all contribute in either developing or sustaining a strong competitive advantage. *Strategic benchmarking* is more difficult, because each firm must cope with a different unique set of internal and external conditions, as identified by a SWOT (strengths, weaknesses, threats, opportunities) analysis. Benchmarking at the strategic level is further complicated by the firm's need to change strategic posture at different times, based on its level of maturity and the specific circumstances relevant to its market, available technologies, etc.[17]

A good benchmarking process comprises these eight steps:

1. *Determine what to benchmark:* Decide which processes or issues are most important or most need improvement.

2. *Build "buy in" and plan the project:* Management and employees must "buy in" to benchmarking. Careful planning results in a well-organized project that is completed on budget and on time.

3. *Understand existing operations ("as is"):* If the firm's current practices are not understood properly, it is almost impossible to assess them in a benchmarking review.

4. *Research others' practices and potential partners ("should be"):* To make worthwhile comparisons with peers, a company must be aware of other perspectives and approaches. External research "helps refine what a company knows about its own processes and encourages out-of-the-box thinking in the pursuit of creative insights." It also helps to find the best benchmarking partners.

5. *Identify best practices:* The firm should carefully look at its own practices that work well, and the best practices of others (especially industry leaders).

6. *Pinpoint improvement areas:* When best practices are identified, they should be compared with the practices currently being used by the firm. Performance gaps must be identified and traced to root causes.

7. *Conclude and communicate:* Integrated, thoughtful conclusions must be drawn and then communicated to all involved parties in the company.

8. *Create an action plan for the future:* Benchmarking reviews lead to the insights necessary to improve performance. To be effective, the reviews must be converted into action plans for change.[18]

> *There are three rungs in the benchmarking ladder: novice, journeyman, and master.*

When formulating a program, a company needs to consider the experience it has with benchmarking and act accordingly.[19] A *novice* firm should try to emulate direct competitors, not world-class companies. It should rely on customers for new-product ideas and choose suppliers mostly on price and reliability. There should be a focus on cost reduction, with a "don't develop it, buy it" thrust. The firm should look for processes to add value, simplify those processes, and be faster responding to the marketplace.

A *journeyman* firm should encourage workers to find ways to do their jobs better and simplify operations. It should emulate market leaders and selected world-class companies. Consumer input, formal marketing research, and internal ideas should be used in generating new products. The firm should select good-quality suppliers, and then look at their prices. The firm should refine practices to improve value added per employee, time to market, and customer satisfaction.

A *master* firm should rely on self-managed, multiskilled teams that emphasize horizontal processes (like product development and logistics). It should measure its product development, distribution, and customer service against the world's best. Consumer input,

---

[17]Kostas N. Dervitsiotis, "Benchmarking and Business Paradigm Shifts," *Total Quality Management* (July 2000), pp. S642–S643.

[18]Adapted by the authors from Susan J. Leandri, "Improving Financial Performance Through Benchmarking and Best Practices," *CPA Journal* (January 2001), pp. 44–48.

[19]Otis Port, John Carey, Kevin Kelly, and Stephanie Anderson Forest, "Quality: Small and Midsize Companies Seize the Challenge—Not a Moment Too Soon," *Business Week* (November 30, 1992), pp. 66–72.

benchmarking, and internal research and development should be used in generating new products. The firm should select suppliers that are technologically advanced and offer superior quality. Compensation for executives should be linked to teamwork and quality. The firm should continue refining its practices to improve the value added per employee, the time to market, and customer satisfaction.

Two especially useful benchmarks are the Malcolm Baldridge National Quality Award (www.quality.nist.gov) and *Fortune's* corporate reputations surveys (www.fortune.com). A firm does not have to actually participate in either of these competitions to benefit from the benchmarks. Any organization can internally assess itself and compare its results with others.

The Baldridge Award rates U.S. firms in these seven areas: leadership, strategic planning, customer and market focus, information and analysis (such as competitive comparisons and benchmarks), human resource focus, process management, and business results. Of the maximum 1,000 points a company can score, 210 are for customer and market focus and customer-focused results. *Fortune's* corporate reputations surveys (one for U.S. firms and one for global firms, including American companies) rate companies in these eight areas: quality of management; quality of goods and services; innovativeness; long-term investment value; financial soundness; the ability to attract, develop, and keep talented people; responsibility to the community and the environment; and wise use of corporate resources. The global survey also asks about global business acumen. Companies are rated within their own industry.

These three Web sites offer further insights into benchmarking: Benchmark Index (www.benchmarkindex.com), Benchmarking Network (www.well.com/user/benchmar), and Best Practices (www.benchmarkingreports.com).

22-3b Customer Satisfaction Research

As defined in Chapter 1, *customer satisfaction* is the degree to which there is a match between a customer's expectations of a good or service and the actual performance of that good or service, including customer service. Today, due to the intensely competitive global marketplace, it is more important than ever that companies regularly—and properly—measure the level of customer satisfaction:

> Customer satisfaction is undoubtedly one of the top strategic issues in the new decade. It has been a major topic of discussion in American boardrooms since the 1980s, yet the exact formula for creating an effective customer satisfaction program is still murky. Given that customer satisfaction is positively related to loyalty, which in turn leads to increased profitability, market share, and growth, the importance of developing an effective program is critical. A major problem with most customer satisfaction programs is that they begin with an attempt by the marketing research department to send customers an "off-the-shelf" survey, or one from another company, to probe their attitudes about customer service. Although this seems to be an easy and inexpensive method, the results are generally less than satisfactory. Each firm should take the initiative to develop its own measurement program based on its needs and the needs of its customers. Only then will survey results be useful to management and lead to future improvements.[20]

The largest ongoing research project on customer satisfaction is the American Customer Satisfaction Index (ACSI), a joint effort by the University of Michigan, the American Society for Quality Control (www.asq.org), and CFI Group (www.cfigroup.com). To compute ACSI (www.bus.umich.edu/research/nqrc/acsi.html), 50,000 consumers are surveyed annually regarding 200 companies and government agencies in 34 different industries: "The ACSI model is a set of equations that link customer expectations, perceived quality, and perceived value to customer satisfaction. ACSI is

Research is needed to gauge customer satisfaction. ACSI is a broad project that does so.

[20]Earl Naumann, Donald W. Jackson Jr., and Mark S. Rosenbaum, "How to Implement a Customer Satisfaction Program," *Business Horizons*, Vol. 44 (January-February 2001), p. 37.

linked, in turn, to its consequences in terms of customer complaints and customer loyalty (measured by price tolerance and customer retention). For most companies, repeat customers are major contributors to profit. Thus, customer retention (estimated as repurchase probability) is a major indicator of financial performance. By translating that estimate into dollar amounts, the ACSI can calculate the net present value of a firm's customer base as an asset over time." With a maximum score of 100, these were the 2000 ratings for several organizations: Heinz (www.heinz.com), 90; Maytag (www.maytag.com), 87; Coca Cola Company (www.cocacola.com), 86; Amazon.com (www.amazon.com), 84; Nike (www.nike.com), 78; Compaq (www.compaq.com), 71; Sprint (www.sprint.com), 70; Kmart (www.bluelight.com), 67; United Airlines (www.ual.com), 62; McDonald's (www.mcdonalds.com), 59; AOL (www.aol.com), 56; and Internal Revenue Service (www.irs.gov), 51. The average score for all companies was 73.[21]

Any firm can measure customer satisfaction. Here is an eight-step approach as to how it can do so:

1. "Institute a process to tap management, employees, outside consultants, and industry sources for input on the dimensions critical to customer satisfaction. Environmental scanning of trade publications and competitors and a regular program of internal focus groups can accomplish this."

2. "Use this feedback to develop an ongoing program of customer focus groups and personal interviews to identify critical customer satisfaction dimensions."

3. "Work with a professional staff to develop telephone and/or mail survey instruments to reliably and validly incorporate identified dimensions."

4. "Regardless of whether the people developing the survey are internal or external, make sure they understand the theoretical basis of the instruments and are familiar with standard procedures for developing and testing reliable, valid items. Keep in mind that customer satisfaction survey results that simply describe what was found provide no guidance for developing an action plan to improve satisfaction."

5. "Regularly do surveys and re-evaluate their reliability and validity."

6. "From these data, develop a customer satisfaction metric that not only relates the level of satisfaction of your customers, but also analyzes the importance of the various dimensions of that satisfaction."

7. "Use the dimensional information to develop an action plan for improving each dimension and communicating these improvements to customers. Remember: Delivery of customer satisfaction is not a reality if the customer does not notice it."

8. "Tie the performance evaluation and compensation of each employee involved in the action plan to its accomplishment. This will ensure that the customers' goals match employees' goals. Remember: What gets measured gets rewarded, and what gets rewarded gets done."[22]

The Entrepreneurial Edge has an excellent online discussion and examples of customer satisfaction measurement. Go to the Web site (www.lowe.org), click on "Customers" from the left menu box, and then click on "Customer Satisfaction."

---

[21]"ACSI Methodology," www.bus.umich.edu/research/nqrc/method.html (June 1, 2001); and "American Customer Satisfaction Index Scores by Industry Sector 1994–2000," www.bus.umich.edu/research/nqrc/ind.html (June 1, 2001).

[22]John T. Mentzer, Carol C. Bienstock, and Kenneth B. Kahn, "Benchmarking Satisfaction," *Marketing Management* (Summer 1995), pp. 41–46. See also Subhash Sharma, Ronald W. Niedrich, and Greg Dobbins, "A Framework for Monitoring Customer Satisfaction: An Empircial Illustration," *Industrial Marketing Management*, Vol. 28 (May 1999); pp. 231–243; and David M. Szymanski and David H. Henard, "Customer Satisfaction: A Meta-Analysis of the Empirical Evidence," *Journal of the Academy of Marketing Science*, Vol. 29 (Winter 2001), pp. 16–35.

MARKETING *and the Web*

Testing for Web Site Usability

Due to their worry about undetected problems that could reduce sales on the Web, many E-tailers are now seeking input from Web-testing firms before making their sites live. Two popular evaluation projects are from Forrester.

A study by Forrester (www.forrester.com) and User Interface Engineering (www.uie.com) found that many Web sites are difficult to use by typical consumers. And this is a real customer turn-off. The firms also found that flaws existed on each of the 30 sites tested. This finding was based on the experiences of a sample of consumers who were each given $50 to buy products online. Among the problems that shoppers encountered were the inability to locate products, to secure the information needed to make a decision, and to complete a transaction. In one instance, a firm asked for a purchaser's credit card number before the order was totaled. "Who gives someone a blank check?", Forrester's research director asked when observing this practice. Other sites had unreadable text that was either too small or that blended in with the background color. As the director says, "if you can't find it, you can't buy it."

Unlike Forrester, NetRaker (www.netraker.com) automatically polls Web users with popup windows. It recently released a study comparing shopping experiences on Amazon.com, America Online, and Yahoo! Shopping in terms of content, navigation, and overall design. The study, based on 259 responses from Web users, found that while AOL's site loaded the fastest, it ranked last in performance. Yahoo! Shopping was ranked best, closely followed by Amazon.com. AOL was ranked a distant third.

As a Web designer for L.L. Bean (www.llbean.com), what are the pros and cons of using a Web-site evaluation company?

*Source: Based on material in Patricia Riedman, "Latest Hot Trend Tests Usability of Web Sites," *Advertising Age* (October 2, 2000), pp. 48, 56.*

22-3c Marketing Cost Analysis

Marketing cost analysis is used to evaluate the cost efficiency of various marketing factors, such as different total quality configurations, product lines, order sizes, distribution methods, sales territories, channel members, salespersons, advertising media, and customer types. Even if a firm is very profitable, it is unlikely that all its products, distribution methods, and so on are equally cost efficient (or profitable).

> *Cost efficiency is measured in* **marketing cost analysis.**

With marketing cost analysis, a firm can determine which factors (classifications) are the most efficient and which are the least efficient, and make appropriate adjustments. It can also generate information that may be needed to substantiate price compliance with the Robinson-Patman Act. At Amazon.com, the online retailing giant that has never turned a profit, "the watchwords have changed from the buoyant 'get big fast' to the pedestrian 'march to profitability.' And instead of designing zippy new features for its Web site and plotting new industries to conquer, its employees are turning to the tedious work of ordinary companies: cutting costs and raising revenue."[23]

[23]Saul Hansell, "A Front-Row Seat as Amazon Gets Serious," *New York Times* (May 20, 2001), p. C1.

TABLE 22-1 **Examples of Marketing Cost Analysis**

Marketing Factor	Strategy/Tactics Studied	Problem/Opportunity Discovered	Action Applied
Customer type	What are the relative costs of selling X-rays to dentists, doctors, and hospitals?	Per-unit costs of hospital sales are lowest (as are prices); per-unit costs of dentist and doctor sales are highest (as are prices).	Current efforts are maintained. Each customer is serviced.
Product	Should a manufacturer accept a retailer's proposal that the firm make 700,000 private-label sneakers?	Substantial excess capacity exists; the private label would require no additional fixed costs.	A contract is signed. Different features for private and manufacturer labels are planned.
Distribution	Should a men's suit maker sell directly to consumers, as well as through normal channels?	Start-up and personal selling costs would be high. Additional sales would be minimal.	Direct sales are not undertaken.
Order size	What is the minimum order size a hardware manufacturer should accept?	Orders below $30 do not have positive profit margins; they are too costly to process.	Small orders are discouraged through surcharges and minimum order size.
Advertising media	Which is more effective, TV or magazine advertising?	TV ads cost $0.05 for every potential customer reached; magazine ads cost $0.07.	TV ads are increased.
Personal selling	What are the costs of making a sale?	15 percent of sales covers compensation and selling expenses, 2 percent above the industry average.	Sales personnel are encouraged to phone customers before visiting them, to confirm appointments.

For this type of analysis to work properly, a firm needs to obtain and to use continuous and accurate cost data. Table 22-1 presents several examples of marketing cost analysis.

Marketing cost analysis consists of three steps: studying natural account expenses, reclassifying natural accounts into functional ones, and allocating functional accounts by marketing classification.

Studying Natural Account Expenses

Natural accounts *are reported as salaries, rent, insurance, and other expenses.*

The first step is to determine the level of expenses for all **natural accounts,** which report costs by the names of the expenses and not by their purposes. Such expense categories include salaries, rent, advertising, supplies, insurance, and interest. These are the names most often entered in accounting records. Table 22-2 shows a natural-account expense classification.

Reclassifying Natural Accounts into Functional Accounts

Functional accounts *denote the purpose or activity of expenditures.*

Natural accounts are then reclassified into **functional accounts,** which indicate the purposes or activities for which expenditures have been made. Included as functional expenses are marketing administration, personal selling, advertising, transportation, warehousing, marketing research, and general administration. Table 22-3 reclassifies the natural accounts of Table 22-2 into functional accounts.

Net sales (after returns and discounts)	$1,000,000	
Less: Costs of goods sold	450,000	
Gross profit		$550,000
Less: Operating expenses (natural account expenses)		
Salaries and fringe benefits	220,000	
Rent	40,000	
Advertising	30,000	
Supplies	6,100	
Insurance	2,500	
Interest expense	1,400	
Total operating expenses		300,000
Net profit before taxes		$250,000

TABLE 22-2

A Natural-Account Expense Classification

Once functional accounts are set, cost analysis is clearer. For instance, if salaries and fringe benefits increase by $25,000 over the prior year, natural account analysis cannot allocate the rise to a functional area. Functional account analysis can pinpoint the areas of marketing having higher personnel costs.

Allocating Functional Accounts by Marketing Classification

The third step assigns functional costs by product, distribution method, customer, or other marketing classification. Each classification is reported as a profit center. Table 22-4 shows how costs can be allocated to different products, using the data in Tables 22-2 and 22-3. From Table 22-4, it is clear that product A has the highest sales and total profit. Product C has the greatest profit as a percent of sales.

In assigning functional costs, these points should be kept in mind. One, assigning some costs—such as marketing administration—to different products, customers, or other classifications is often somewhat arbitrary. Two, the elimination of a poorly performing classification would lead to overhead costs—such as general administration—being allotted among the remaining product or customer categories. This may actually lead to lower overall total profit. A firm should distinguish between the separable expenses directly associated with a given classification category that can be eliminated if a category is dropped and the common expenses shared by various categories that cannot be eliminated if one is dropped.

Functional costs are assigned with each marketing classification becoming a profit center.

TABLE 22-3   **Reclassifying Natural Accounts into Functional Accounts**

		Functional Accounts						
Natural Accounts	**Total**	**Marketing Administration**	**Personal Selling**	**Advertising**	**Transportation**	**Warehousing**	**Marketing Research**	**General Administration**
Salaries and fringe benefits	$220,000	$30,000	$50,000	$15,000	$10,000	$20,000	$30,000	$65,000
Rent	40,000	3,000	7,000	3,000	2,000	10,000	5,000	10,000
Advertising	30,000			30,000				
Supplies	6,100	500	1,000	500			1,100	3,000
Insurance	2,500		1,000			1,200		300
Interest expense	1,400							1,400
Total	$300,000	$33,500	$59,000	$48,500	$12,000	$31,200	$36,100	$79,700

TABLE 22-4   **Allocating Functional Expenses by Product**

	Total	Product A	Product B	Product C
Net sales	$1,000,000	$500,000	$300,000	$200,000
Less: Cost of goods sold	450,000	250,000	120,000	80,000
Gross profit	$550,000	$250,000	$180,000	$120,000
Less: Operating expenses (functional account expenses)				
Marketing administration	33,500	16,000	10,000	7,500
Personal selling	59,000	30,000	17,100	11,900
Advertising	48,500	20,000	18,000	10,500
Transportation	12,000	5,000	5,000	2,000
Warehousing	31,200	20,000	7,000	4,200
Marketing research	36,100	18,000	11,000	7,100
General administration	79,700	40,000	23,000	16,700
Total operating expenses	300,000	149,000	91,100	59,900
Net profit before taxes	$250,000	$101,000	$ 88,900	$ 60,100
Profit as percent of sales	25.0	20.2	29.6	30.1

A firm must differentiate between order-generating and order-processing costs (as described in Chapter 3) before making any strategic changes suggested by marketing cost analysis:

> After a period of cost-cutting, the downside of downsizing can take its toll: Decimated sales staffs turn in lousy numbers. "Survivor syndrome" takes hold, and overburdened staffers just go through the motions of working. New-product ideas languish. Risk-taking dwindles because the culture of cost-cutting emphasizes the certainties of cutting costs over the uncertainties—and expense—of trying something new."[24]

In making cost cuts, a company must be especially sure to judge the effects of those cuts on the total quality of its goods and services.

22-3d Sales Analysis

Sales analysis is the detailed study of sales data to appraise the appropriateness and effectiveness of a marketing strategy. Without it, a poor response to the total value chain offered by a firm may not be seen early enough, the strength of certain market segments and territories may be overlooked, sales effort may be poorly matched with market potential, trends may be missed, or support for sales personnel may not be forthcoming. Sales analysis enables plans to be set in terms of revenues by product, product line, salesperson, region, customer type, time period, price line, method of sale, and so on. It also compares actual sales against planned sales. More firms engage in sales analysis than in marketing cost analysis.

The main source of sales analysis data is the sales invoice, which may be written, typed, or computer generated. An invoice may contain such data as the customer's name and address, the quantity ordered, the price paid, purchase terms, all the different items

Sales analysis *looks at sales data to assess the effectiveness of a marketing strategy.*

[24]Bernard Wysocki, Jr., "Some Companies Cut Costs Too Far, Suffer 'Corporate Anorexia,'" *Wall Street Journal* (July 5, 1995), p. A1.

bought at the same time, the order date, shipping arrangements, and the salesperson. Summary data are generated by adding invoices. Computerized marking, cash register, and inventory systems speed data recording and improves their accuracy.

In conducting sales analysis, proper control units must be selected. **Control units** are the sales categories for which data are gathered, such as boys', men's, girls', and women's clothing. Although a marketing executive can broaden a control system by adding sales categories together, wide categories cannot be broken down into components. Thus, a narrow sales category is preferable to one that is too wide. It is also helpful to select control units consistent with other company, trade association, and government data. A stable classification system is necessary to compare data from different time periods.

Control units *are an essential aspect of sales analysis.*

A key concept when undertaking sales analysis is that summary data, such as overall sales or market share, are usually insufficient to diagnose a firm's areas of strength and weakness. More intensive investigation is needed. Two techniques that offer in-depth probing are the 80-20 principle and sales exception reporting.

According to the **80-20 principle,** in many organizations, a large proportion of total sales (profit) is likely to come from a small proportion of customers, products, or territories. Thus, to function as efficiently as possible, firms need to determine sales and profit by customer, product, or territory. Marketing efforts can then be allocated accordingly. Firms err if they do not isolate and categorize data. Through faulty reasoning, they would place equal effort into each sale instead of concentrating on key accounts. These errors are due to a related concept, the **iceberg principle,** which states that superficial data are insufficient to make sound evaluations.

The **80-20 principle** *notes that a large share of sales (profits) often comes from few customers, products, or territories. Analysis errors may be due to the* **iceberg principle.**

This is the way that Illinois Tool Works (www.itw.com) is applying the 80-20 principle:

> Today, after nearly 20 years of expansion and refinement, ITW has assembled a comprehensive 80/20 body of knowledge which is vital to our success. It's part of the annual review and planning process each of our business units undertakes. This process is really about simplifying and focusing on the key parts of each business. Simplicity focuses action, while complexity often blurs what is important. Complexity creates overhead, while simplicity removes it. In the process of simplification, we view all areas of the business on an 80/20 basis. This includes finding ways to simplify our product lines, customer and supply base, business processes, and systems. In the end, 80/20 improves quality, productivity, delivery, innovation, market penetration, and ultimately, customer satisfaction. As a result, virtually all aspects of financial performance are improved.[25]

Analysis can be further enhanced by **sales exception reporting,** which highlights situations where goals are not met or opportunities are present. A slow-selling item report cites products whose sales are below forecasts. It could suggest such corrective actions as price reductions, promotions, and sales incentives to increase sales. A fast-selling item report cites items whose sales exceed forecasts. It points out opportunities, as well as items that need more inventory to prevent stockouts. Finally, sales exception reporting lets a firm evaluate the validity of forecasts and make the proper modifications in them. Figure 22-6 presents examples of the 80-20 principle, the iceberg principle, and sales exception reporting.

Sales exception reporting *centers on unmet goals or special opportunities.*

Organizations also may use sales analysis to identify and monitor consumer buying patterns by answering such questions as these:

- *Who purchases?* Organizational versus final consumer, geographic region, end use, purchase history, customer size, customer demographics
- *What is purchased?* Product line, price, brand, country of origin, package size, options purchased
- *Where are purchases made?* Place of customer contact, purchase location, warehouse location

---

[25]*Illinois Tool Works Inc. 2000 Annual Report.*

FIGURE 22-6
Sales Analysis Concepts

80-20 Principle					Iceberg Principle
	Annual Sales		Marketing Expenditures		Only the tip of the iceberg is seen with superficial analysis (aggregate data).
	$	%	$	%	
Product A	1,000,000	50.0	200,000	44.4	
Product B	750,000	37.5	150,000	33.3	
Product C	250,000	12.5	100,000	22.2	
Total	$2,000,000	100.0	$450,000	100.0*	

*Rounding error

Although a company gets only 12.5 percent of total sales from Product C, it spends 22.2 percent of its marketing budget on that product.

Sales Exception Reporting

SALES REPORT		
	Expected Sales	Actual Sales
Product 1	$50,000	$100,000
Product 2	$50,000	$50,000
Product 3	$75,000	$75,000
Product 4	$75,000	$50,000

A review of the sales report indicates that Product 1 has done much better than expected, while Product 4 has done much worse.

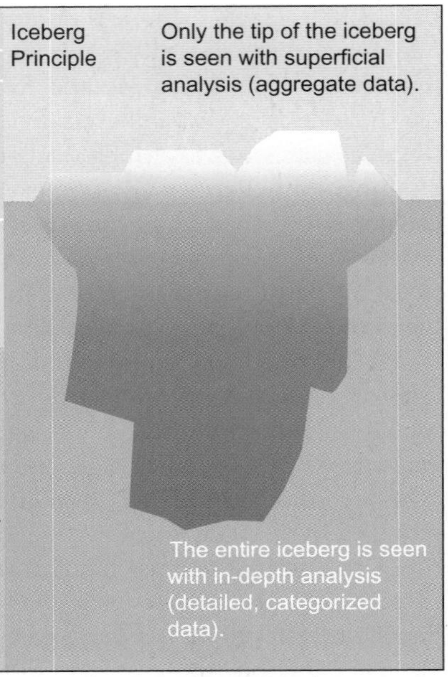

The entire iceberg is seen with in-depth analysis (detailed, categorized data).

- *How are items purchased?* Form of payment, billing terms, delivery form, packaging technique
- *When are purchases heaviest and lightest?* Season, day of week, time of day
- *How much is purchased?* Unit sales volume, dollar sales volume, profit margin
- *What types of promotion get the best sales results?* Advertising, personal selling, sales promotion
- *What prices are paid?* List prices versus discounted prices

22-3e The Marketing Audit

A **marketing audit** examines a firm in a systematic, critical, and unbiased manner.

A ***marketing audit*** is a systematic, critical, impartial review and appraisal of the basic goals and policies of the marketing function, and of the organization, methods, procedures, and personnel employed to implement the policies and achieve the goals. The purpose of a marketing audit is to determine (1) how well a firm's marketing efforts are being conducted and (2) how they can be improved. Audits should be conducted on a regular basis.[26]

The marketing audit process involves the six steps shown in Figure 22-7:

1. A marketing audit may be conducted by company specialists, by company division or department managers, or by outside specialists. Expertise, access to information, costs, and potential biases are some of the factors to be considered when choosing audit personnel.

2. An audit may be undertaken at the end of a calendar year, at the end of a firm's annual reporting year, or when conducting a physical inventory. An audit should be performed at least annually, although some firms prefer more frequent analysis. It should be completed during the same time period each year to allow comparisons. In some cases, unannounced audits are useful to keep employees alert and to ensure spontaneous answers.

[26]See Douglas Brownlie, "Benchmarking Your Marketing Process," *Long Range Planning*, Vol. 32 (Number 1, 1999), pp. 88–95. Also, the classic marketing audit article by Philip Kotler, William T. Gregor, and William H. Rodgers III is online at www.hamiltonco.com/features/hampub/SMR.html.

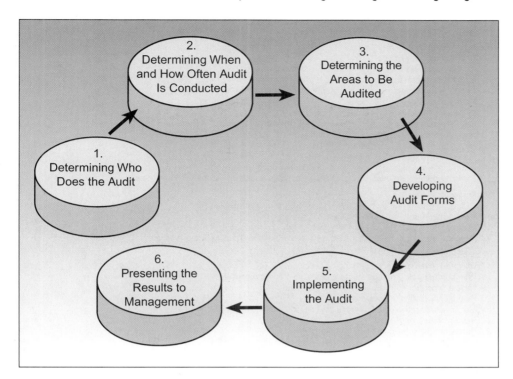

FIGURE 22-7
The Marketing Audit Process

3. A ***horizontal audit*** (a marketing-mix audit) studies the overall marketing performance of a firm with particular emphasis on the interrelationship of variables and their relative importance. A ***vertical audit*** (a functional audit) is an in-depth analysis of one aspect of a firm's marketing strategy, such as product planning. The two audits should be used in conjunction with one another because a horizontal audit often reveals areas needing further study.

4. Audit forms list the topics to be examined and the exact information required to evaluate each topic. Forms usually resemble questionnaires, and they are completed by the auditor. Examples of audit forms are contained in Figures 22-8 and 22-9.

5. When implementing an audit, decisions need to be made as to its duration, whether employees are to be aware of the audit, whether the audit is performed while a firm is open or closed for business, and how the final report is to be prepared.

6. The last step is to present findings and recommendations to management. However, the auditing process is complete only after suitable responses are taken by management. It is the responsibility of management, not the auditor, to determine these responses.

Despite the merits, many firms still do not use formal marketing audits. Three factors mostly account for this. One, success or failure is difficult to establish in marketing. A firm may have poor performance despite the best planning if environmental factors intervene; and good results may be based on a firm's being at the right place at the right time. Two, if marketing audits are done by company personnel, they may not be detailed enough to be considered audits. Three, the pressures of other activities often mean that only a small part of a marketing strategy is audited or that audits are done infrequently.

A **horizontal audit** *studies overall marketing performance; a* **vertical audit** *analyzes one aspect of marketing.*

FIGURE 22-8

A Horizontal Marketing Audit Form

Does Your Department, Division, or Firm...	Answer Yes or No to Each Question
Planning, Organization, and Control	
1. Have specific objectives?	_____
2. Devise objectives to meet changing conditions?	_____
3. Study customer needs, attitudes, and behavior?	_____
4. Organize marketing efforts in a systematic way?	_____
5. Have a market planning process?	_____
6. Engage in comprehensive sales forecasting?	_____
7. Integrate buyer behavior research in market planning?	_____
8. Have strategy and tactics within the market plan?	_____
9. Have clearly stated contingency plans?	_____
10. Monitor environmental changes?	_____
11. Incorporate social responsiblity as a criterion for decision making?	_____
12. Control activities via marketing cost analysis, sales analysis, and the marketing audit?	_____
Marketing Research	
13. Utilize marketing research for planning, as well as problem solving?	_____
14. Have a marketing information system?	_____
15. Give enough support to market research?	_____
16. Have adequate communication between marketing research and line executives?	_____
Products	
17. Utilize a systematic product-planning process?	_____
18. Plan product policy relative to the product life-cycle concept?	_____
19. Have a procedure for developing new products?	_____
20. Periodically review all products?	_____
21. Monitor competitive developments in product planning?	_____
22. Revise mature products?	_____
23. Phase out weak products?	_____
Distribution	
24. Motivate channel members?	_____
25. Have sufficent market coverage?	_____
26. Periodically evaluate channel members?	_____
27. Evaluate alternative shipping arrangements?	_____
28. Study warehouse and facility locations?	_____
29. Compute economic order quantities?	_____
30. Modify channel decisions as conditions warrant?	_____
Promotion	
31. Have an overall promotion plan?	_____
32. Balance promotion components within the plan?	_____
33. Measure the effectiveness of advertising?	_____
34. Seek out favorable publicity?	_____
35. Have a procedure for recruiting and retaining sales personnel?	_____
36. Analyze the sales-force organization periodically?	_____
37. Moderate the use of sales promotions?	_____
Prices	
38. Have a pricing strategy that is in compliance with government regulations?	_____
39. Have a pricing strategy that satisfies channel members?	_____
40. Estimate demand and cost factors before setting prices?	_____
41. Plan for competitive developments?	_____
42. Set prices that are consistent with image?	_____
43. Seek to maximize total profits?	_____

22-4 ANTICIPATING AND PLANNING FOR THE FUTURE

The future promises to be complex for firms everywhere as they try to anticipate trends and plan their long-run marketing strategies. On the positive side, there should be greater consumer affluence in many countries, advances in technological capabilities, expanded worldwide markets, further industry deregulation, and other opportunities. On the negative side, there will probably be greater competition among firms based in different countries, relatively moderate growth in U.S. and European markets, some resource instability, and an uncertain worldwide economy among the potential problems.

Long-range plans must take into account both the external variables facing a firm and its capacity for change. Specifically, what variables will affect the firm? What trends are forecast for them? Is the firm able to respond to these trends because it has the necessary

Planning efforts for the future must consider external factors and company abilities.

Total Quality
Health Check-up Questionnaire

After filling out questionnaire, return to: _____

The purpose of this questionnaire is to provide a means for companies to conduct a study of their employees, to determine the degree of involvement and commitment to the principles and practices of Total Quality Management.

The questionnaire is based on the criteria embodied in the Baldridge Quality Award categories (Being employed by many companies as an integrated management system and to conform to requirements in attaining the award).

INDIVIDUAL INSTRUCTIONS

Identify your position title and company department in the spaces below, then respond to each of the following ten statements, indicating your personal opinion as to the degree of compliance with the criteria in company operations. When completed, return to the individual identified at the top of the sheet for tabulation and reporting of results.

Your Position: _____   Department: _____

QUALITY HEALTH CRITERIA (Circle numbers at right to indicate agreement)	HOW ARE WE DOING? Not true → Very true
1. External customer expectations define the quality of our goods and services.	0 1 2 3 4 5
2. Cross-functional and inter-departmental cooperation are encouraged and supported.	0 1 2 3 4 5
3. There is active leadership for quality improvement at all levels of management.	0 1 2 3 4 5
4. Employees have the authority to act on goods and service quality problems.	0 1 2 3 4 5
5. A team approach is used to solve quality problems and to meet customer expectations.	0 1 2 3 4 5
6. Measurements of internal and external customer expectations are well understood.	0 1 2 3 4 5
7. Employees are brought into decisions that affect the quality of their work.	0 1 2 3 4 5
8. There is major emphasis on the prevention and solving of quality problems.	0 1 2 3 4 5
9. Individuals and teams are given recognition for contributions to quality improvement.	0 1 2 3 4 5
10. Systems are in place to assess and respond to changing customer expectations.	0 1 2 3 4 5

FIGURE 22-9

A Total-Quality Vertical-Audit Form

Source: Dick Berry, "How Healthy Is Your Company?" *Marketing News* (February 15, 1993), p. 2. Reprinted by permission of the American Marketing Association.

resources and lead time? For example, the manufacturers that have recognized the retailing trend toward self-service have successfully redesigned their packaging to provide more information for shoppers.

A firm that does not anticipate and respond to future trends has a good possibility of falling into Levitt's marketing myopia trap and losing ground to more farsighted competitors:

> Competition has never been hotter. Yet complacency still exists, particularly in stable or slow-growing businesses. It's no surprise then that one-time luminaries suddenly find themselves out of touch with the marketplace, their products no longer relevant to changing consumer needs, their sales falling, and shareholder value dwindling. Desperate times call for desperate remedies, and many declining businesses stake their future on a bold new product that they hope will transform their fortunes. Some savior products succeed, others fail. And there are distinct lessons to be drawn from troubled firms that have adopted this strategy in recent years.

When the bottom fell out of the jeans market five years ago, Levi-Strauss (www.levi.com) was hit hard. After 11 consecutive years of rising global sales, which peaked in 1996, sales plummeted in 1998 by 23 percent in Great Britain alone. In 1999, profits fell dramatically, and during the 1990s, market share fell from more than 30 percent. Levi-Strauss was forced to rethink its strategy. "We were complacent," admits Rachel Johnson, marketing director for northern Europe. "The traditional 401s were still a huge seller, but we rode too long on that glory. We suddenly started to lose customers, particularly the 15- to 19-year-olds, who had switched to cargo and combat pants. Levi's weren't cool or sexy any more. We needed to get youth back into the brand." In February 2000, it launched a new product line aimed at the youth market called Levi's Engineered Jeans (LEJs). With their trademark twisted seams, LEJs look different and fit better. The launch was backed by a massive ad campaign around the theme of "the twisted original." "LEJs have been massively successful," says Johnson. "We have sold far more than we ever expected to, and we've got the youth market back. Our share of the 11- to 24-year-old market has grown, and people see Levi's as being cool, sexy, and interesting again, and older consumers have started buying Levi's again."

Sega (www.sega.com) on the other hand has failed to recapture its core market. A pioneer in computer games, Sega recently decided to stop producing the Dreamcast console on which it staked its future. The company spent a fortune on developing and launching the console, which was technologically impressive, but failed to produce an adequate supply of games—thus committing the cardinal sin of forgetting the end user. Sega sold only 5.9 million of its forecast ten million Dreamcast consoles, and the competition—Sony's PlayStation 2, Microsoft's imminent debut with Xbox, and the growth of online games—has proved too fierce.[27]

To prepare for the future, organizations can engage in the following:

- *Company vision planning*—This articulates the firm's future mission.
- *Scenario planning*—This identifies the range of events that may occur in the future.
- *Contingency planning*—This prepares alternative strategies, each keyed to a specific scenario.
- *Competitive positioning*—This outlines where a firm will be positioned versus competitors.
- *Competitive benchmarking*—This keeps a firm focused on how well it is doing versus competitors.
- *Ongoing marketing research*—This entails consumer and other relevant research.[28]

As we look ahead, it is clear that the role of marketing will take on greater importance at many companies. For instance, with the use of advanced computer data bases, market segmentation efforts will be even more focused and responsive than ever before.

At forward-looking firms, the best uses of marketing are yet to come:

Consumers and business customers—empowered by the Net, equipped with 24-hour access—are disrupting standard practices. Companies must change pricing structures, distribution channels, and the way they design and deliver goods and services. This can't be ignored. The savviest companies jump at the chance to meet those demands head-on by inviting customers to participate in design and R&D and turning customers into working assets. National Semiconductor (www.national.com) brings in engineers to create scenarios for designing and testing prototypes to save themselves time. Cisco Systems (www.cisco.com) customers can make last-minute changes to orders, even as products are being manufactured. Hewlett-Packard (www.hp.com) uses satisfaction surveys at all points of customer contact. Surrendering to the network-driven customer is a long-term winning proposition. Why? Because firms built on a customer-caring culture win the hearts and minds of employees, too.[29]

---

[27]Jane Simms, "When Brands Bounce Back," *Marketing* (February 15, 2001), pp. 26–27.

[28]Adapted by the authors from Bernard Taylor, "The New Strategic Leadership: Driving Change, Getting Results," *Long Range Planning*, Vol. 28 (Number 5, 1995), pp. 71–81.

[29]Edward Robinson, "Capitalize Your Customers," *Business 2.0* (March 20, 2001), p. 98.

ETHICAL *Issues in Marketing*

Can a New Napster Business Model Succeed?

Until recently, Napster (www.napster.com) allowed its users to download free music files onto their own computers and to make those files available to some 60 million other registered Napster users. To access songs on the network, a user would type the song's title on Napster's search engine, which would then return a list of the available files.

In response to a major, highly publicized copyright infringement lawsuit brought by the five largest music labels, on March 6, 2001, a federal judge ordered Napster to stop exchanging copyrighted music on its Internet site. This ruling requires the record companies to (1) show proof that they own the copyright to their music, and (2) show evidence that these songs are traded on Napster's site.

Napster is financed in part by a $50 million loan from German media giant Bertelsmann (www.bertelsmann.com). Bertlesmann initially planned to use Napster's technology to form a subscription service that would give consumers access to legitimate copies of music. Hank Barry, Napster's chief executive officer, made an agreement with Bertelsmann's BMG, even though it was one of the five companies in the lawsuit. The other companies have argued that Napster's offer of $1 billion in royalties is much too low. Bertelsmann is also considering selling music through its CDNow (www.cdnow.com) subsidiary to Napster users. It faces the dual challenge of attracting Napster's users (who are used to not paying for music) and getting the cooperation of the other music labels.

Develop a marketing plan for a new Napster subscription service. Defend the plan on ethical grounds.

Sources: Matt Richtel, "Napster to Start Blocking Access to Protected Music Files," *New York Times* (March 3, 2001), pp. C1–C2; Matt Richtel and David D. Kirkpatrick, "Napster to Charge Fee for Music Rights," *New York Times on the Web* (November 1, 2000); and Matt Richtel, "Judge Orders Napster to Police Trading," *New York Times* (March 7, 2001), pp. C1, C7.

WEB SITES YOU CAN USE

Here are several good Web sites related to the integration and assessment of marketing strategies:

Business Owner's Toolkit—*Business Tools*
(www.toolkit.cch.com/tools/tools.asp)

InfoTech Marketing—*Strategy*
(www.infotechmarketing.net/strategy.htm)

Maritz Loyalty Marketing—*Why Loyalty Marketing*
(www.loyalty.maritz.com/whylm.asp)

Marketing Process Company—*Marketing Planning*
(www.themarketingprocessco.com/mp_exmar.htm)

The Marketing Audit (www.marketingaudit.com)

U.S. Business Reporter
(www.activemedia-guide.com)

ZweigWhite—*Strategic Business Planning*
(www.zweigwhite.com/home/sbp)

SUMMARY

1. *To show the value of an integrated marketing plan* Integrated planning builds upon a firm's strategic planning efforts and its use of a total quality approach. In this way, everyone is "on the same page." An integrated marketing plan is one in which all of its various parts are unified, consistent, and coordinated.

2. *To discuss the elements of a well-integrated marketing plan* There are several major elements in an integrated marketing plan. A clear organizational mission outlines a firm's commitment to a type of business and a place in the market. Long-term competitive advantages are company, product, and marketing attributes—whose distinctiveness and appeal to consumers can be maintained over an extended period of time. A precisely defined target market enables a firm to identify the specific consumers it addresses in a marketing plan. Long-, moderate-, and short-term marketing subplans need to be compatible with one another. Coordination among SBUs is enhanced when the functions, strategies, and resources of each are described and monitored by top management. Marketing mix components need to be coordinated within each SBU. The plan must have a certain degree of stability over time.

3. *To present five types of marketing plan analysis: benchmarking, customer satisfaction research, marketing cost analysis, sales analysis, and the marketing audit* Marketing plan analysis compares a firm's actual performance with its planned or expected performance for a specified period of time. If actual performance is unsatisfactory, corrective action may be needed. Plans may have to be revised because of the impact of uncontrollable variables.

Through benchmarking, a company can set its own marketing performance standards by studying the best firms in its industry, innovative firms in any industry, direct competitors, and/or itself. There are process benchmarks and strategic benchmarks. In general, firms progress through three stages as they engage in benchmarking: novice, journeyman, and master. The Malcolm Baldrige National Quality Award and *Fortune's* corporate reputations surveys are good benchmarking tools.

In customer satisfaction research, a firm determines the degree to which customer expectations regarding a good or service are

actually satisfied. The largest research project in this area is the American Customer Satisfaction Index (ACSI), which rates thousands of goods and services. In 2000, the average ACSI score for all companies was 73 (out of 100).

Marketing cost analysis evaluates the efficiency of various marketing factors, such as different total quality configurations, product lines, order sizes, distribution methods, sales territories, channel members, salespersons, advertising media, and customer types. Continuous and accurate cost data are needed. Marketing cost analysis involves studying natural account expenses, reclassifying natural accounts into functional accounts, and allocating accounts by marketing classification.

Sales analysis is the detailed study of sales data to appraise the appropriateness and effectiveness of a marketing strategy. It enables plans to be set in terms of revenues by product, product line, salesperson, region, customer type, time period, price line, or method of sale. It also monitors actual sales against planned sales. More firms use sales analysis than marketing cost analysis. The main source of sales data is the sales invoice; control units must be specified. Sales analysis should take the 80-20 principle, the iceberg principle, and sales exception reporting into account.

The marketing audit is a systematic, critical, impartial review and appraisal of a firm's marketing objectives, strategy, implementation, and organization. It has six steps: determining who does the audit, establishing when and how often the audit is conducted, deciding what the audit covers, developing audit forms, implementing the audit, and presenting the results. A horizontal audit studies the overall marketing performance of a firm. A vertical audit is an in-depth analysis of one aspect of marketing strategy.

4. *To see the merit of anticipating and planning for the future* Long-range plans must take into account both the external variables facing a firm and its capacity for change. A firm that does not anticipate and respond to future trends has a good chance of falling into Levitt's marketing myopia trap—which should be avoided.

KEY TERMS

marketing plan analysis (p. 663)
benchmarking (p. 663)
marketing cost analysis (p. 667)
natural accounts (p. 668)
functional accounts (p. 668)

sales analysis (p. 670)
control units (p. 671)
80-20 principle (p. 671)
iceberg principle (p. 671)

sales exception reporting (p. 671)
marketing audit (p. 672)
horizontal audit (p. 673)
vertical audit (p. 673)

REVIEW QUESTIONS

1. Explain Figure 22-1, which deals with a well-integrated marketing plan.
2. Why might competitive advantages not travel well internationally?
3. What is benchmarking? How should a *novice* firm use it differently from a *master* firm?
4. Explain the American Customer Satisfaction Index (www.bus.umich.edu/research/nqrc/acsi.html).
5. Why is functional account cost analysis more useful than natural account analysis?
6. Distinguish between marketing cost analysis and sales analysis.
7. Differentiate between a vertical and a horizontal marketing audit.
8. What are some of the positive and negative trends firms are likely to face over the coming decade?

DISCUSSION QUESTIONS

1. Do you think your college or university is applying an integrated marketing approach? Why or why not? What marketing recommendations would you make for your school?
2. Develop a customer satisfaction survey for a local restaurant. Discuss the kinds of information you are seeking.
3. Develop a vertical marketing audit form for Microsoft to appraise its relationship with the retailers that carry its products.
4. As the marketing vice-president for a small candy manufacturer, how would you prepare for the future? What key trends do you foresee over the next decade? How would you address them?

WEB EXERCISE

Explore the iSixSigma Web site on benchmarking (www.isixsigma.com/me/benchmarking). Visit at least three of the sites that are described there, and discuss what you learn from these sites. How is this information useful to marketers?

PART 8 SHORT CASES
Case 1

Roche Diagnostics: Linking Customer Satisfaction and Profits[c8-1]

Roche Diagnostics Systems (www.roche.com/diagnostics) is the U.S. affiliate of Swiss-based Roche Group (www.roche.com) that specializes in instruments and testing equipment used by medical staff for diagnostic purposes and by pharmaceutical firms for product testing. In 1991, after Carlo Medici was appointed president of Roche Diagnostics, he sought to refocus the company to "achieve leadership and profitability through customer satisfaction." As part of this initiative, he created a new position, head of global service quality and satisfaction. This case describes Roche Diagnostics' process for developing a measure of customer satisfaction, its efforts at increasing customer satisfaction scores, and the link between customer satisfaction and profitability.

Roche Diagnostics' initial efforts in customer satisfaction research were focused on devising a suitable measure. It used focus groups with customers and with all company personnel having direct customer contact (such as on-site technical specialists and customer service representatives). The goal of these focus groups was to better understand the critical interactions between Roche Diagnostic personnel and customers. These interactions are frequently referred to as "moments of truth" since they represent implicit promises to customers.

The first customer satisfaction questionnaire used a five-point scale with respondents choosing among very satisfied, satisfied, somewhat satisfied, dissatisfied, and very dissatisfied to designate their degree of satisfaction. The survey was completed by 508 customers, with 36 percent being "very satisfied" and 15 percent being "somewhat" to "very dissatisfied." When asked about their future buying plans, 39 percent said they would "definitely buy again, " and 57 percent said they would "definitely recommend" the company's products.

Roche Diagnostics then participated in an industrywide audit of global health-care manufacturers conducted by a leading consulting firm. The audit analyzed Roche Diagnostic's ranking on such specific aspects of customer service as speed of arrival of engineers, hotline response speed, and the "first time fix rate." The firm selected about 70 of these measures for review and assigned respon-

sibility to a specific manager for improving Roche Diagnostics' performance on each benchmarked measure.

In 1994, the firm transferred the data analysis to another consulting firm, which improved the questionnaire several ways. In one key change, it implemented "key driver analysis" to identify those practices that were most important to consumers. For example, the consulting firm found that Roche Diagnostics needed to better focus on toll-free telephone support since consumers rated this as important and the firm's customer satisfaction scores on this dimension were relatively low. After examining its telephone support, Roche Diagnostics realized that customers requesting product information were always transferred to a message mailbox and often transferred between departments. Instead, consumers wanted live access to a single person for assistance.

As a result of this initiative, the firm created a single group of service representatives who were cross-trained to provide ordering assistance. Medical technical support personnel were also grouped into product teams so that a customer would not have to wait for a return call. Lastly, Roche Diagnostics ended its use of the automated voice response system during normal business hours. Due to these efforts, there was a significant increase in the number of customers who were "very satisfied" with Roche Diagnostic's telephone support, as well as its overall performance.

Roche Diagnostics has gone from a low-growth division to the fastest-growing competitor within its industry and in the Roche worldwide healthcare group.

Questions

1. Analyze Roche Diagnostic's approach for improving customer satisfaction.
2. What are the pros and cons of benchmarking specific performance measures?
3. Why would a linkage between customer satisfaction and profitability be expected?
4. Develop a 10-item vertical marketing audit on customer satisfaction for Roche Diagnostics.

[c8-1]The data in the case are drawn from Timothy L. Keiningham, Melinda K. M. Goddard, Terry G. Vavra, and Andrew J. Iaci, "Customer Delight and the Bottom Line," *Marketing Management* (Fall 1999), pp. 57–63.

Case 2

Benchmarking Return on Innovation[c8-2]

Because most corporate executives are more comfortable with managing costs than creating innovative products, "the low-hanging fruit" has already been picked—whereby easily-obtained cost savings have been achieved at many companies. This case presents a measure of "return on innovation management" that better enables executives to manage the risks inherent with truly innovative products.

There are numerous examples of firms that have successfully managed their investments in innovation:

- S.C. Johnson (www.scjohnson.com) has generated millions of dollars in sales and profits from such new products as Glade Candle Scents, Glade Spin Fresh, Windex No Drip, and Windex Outdoor.
- Gillette's Mach 3 razor (www.mach3.com) is considered one of its best product innovations. Today, an estimated 40 percent of Gillette's sales can be traced to products that have been introduced within the past five years.
- An ongoing study of more than 200 firms found that those with successful innovation programs were more likely to have growth rates of 20 percent or more than firms that did not.

One recent research project found that the top five barriers to innovation are a lack of measures relating to innovation, the lack of a cohesive new-product development strategy, insufficient human resources, poor communication, and a risk-averse corporate culture. Although this case deals with the first barrier, proper measurement helps with all of the other barriers.

According to the project author, the first step in managing innovation is to develop consistent standards to measure all aspects of the investment in innovation. There are two types of metrics that firms need to consider: innovation performance metrics that measure growth, and innovation program metrics that measure program management and control. Examples of *innovation performance metrics* include return on innovation investment, cumulative profits from new products, the new-product success rate (the "hit rate"), the new-product survival rate (the number of new products remaining in the market for a given time period), and cumulative new-product revenues and growth impact (revenues from new products over 3 to 5 years). Examples of *innovation program metrics* include process pipeline flow (the number of new products in each stage of product development), innovation revenues per employee (annual revenues from commercialized new products divided by the number of full-time equivalent employees), and speed to market (the time from idea generation to launch).

The preceding metrics are important benchmarks to measure intermediate as well as final objectives relating to innovation management: "They provide the answer to the question 'Are we there yet?' They also provide the road map, the signposts, and the goal." Although there are no specific prescriptions as to which data a firm should use, the best measures relate to a firm's overall strategy, are used within the industry (to provide benchmarks), and are readily available.

In any firm, the innovation effort should be seen as a three-legged stool which requires dedication to purpose, process, and people. Purpose provides a direction for the firm's innovation efforts, defines the functions that a product serves in supporting the firm's goals, and identifies the number of new products required and their revenues and profits. Through a process, the firm generates a formalized new-product development process, including means of screening out poor candidates. People are the human resources that effectively implement innovation programs. They may be organized on the basis of teams or through product champions.

Questions

1. Describe the benefits from developing specific performance standards for innovation management.
2. What are the potential difficulties associated with the following performance metrics: cumulative profits, success rate, and new product survival rate?
3. Beyond those stated in the case, present five additional performance or program metrics that relate to the management of mature products.
4. Develop a vertical marketing audit for a firm's new-product planning activity.

[c8-2]The data in the case are drawn from Thomas D. Kuczmarski, "Measuring Your Return on Innovation," *Marketing Management* (Spring 2000), pp. 25–32.

Case 3

Nestlé: How to Keep the Magic Going[c8-3]

Peter Brabeck, Nestlé's (www.nestle.com) chief executive officer, is seen by many investors as a determined executive who is ready, willing, and able to keep Nestlé's profits growing. Since 1997, when he assumed his position as head of one of the world's largest food companies, Brabeck has reorganized his executive team, created a strong brand management structure with six worldwide brands (such as Nescafé, Nestlé, Perrier, and Buitoni), and invested $1 billion to prepare Nestlé for the Internet.

Nestlé is far from an easy company to effectively manage. It operates in 70 countries, and has 8,000 products (ranging from Nestlé chocolate to Stouffer's prepared foods to Poland Spring water). In addition, the firm owns Alcon, an eye-care firm and more than 25 percent of L'Oréal, the cosmetics company. Some of its products, like water and pharmaceuticals, have had healthy annual growth rates of over 7 percent, but others, like chocolate and dairy products, have had slow growth.

Brabeck's goal is to achieve a 4 percent "real internal growth rate;" this standard removes the effect of price increases, acquisitions, and exchange rate fluctuations. According to Brabeck, "If we wanted to be a leader—and we call ourselves the leading food and beverage company in the world—then we had to introduce a rate of internal change that was faster than the rate of external change." To achieve this growth, Brabeck is using a four-part strategy comprised of (1) operational efficiency, (2) innovation and renovation, (3) the sale of products "whenever, wherever, and however," and (4) improved communication with customers.

At first, Brabeck focused the firm's energies on improving efficiency by reducing operational costs: "These were things you can feel and you can touch." Some critics feel that Brabeck has not been aggressive enough in negotiating with Western Europe's trade unions. They typically cite data showing that Nestlé's work force has been stable since 1977. Brabeck, on the other hand, argues that improved efficiency has reduced costs by 1.1 percent of sales. Additional savings will be made after all of Nestlé's operations, from purchasing through distribution, are better automated and integrated.

Through successful management of innovation, Nestlé staff is now encouraged to apply innovations to multiple products. For example, LC1, a bacterium that aids digestion and guards against infection, was initially developed for yogurt. Now, Nestlé will add that ingredient to other products.

By selling products "whenever, wherever, and however," the firm's brand equity will be used to expand sales of related products, as well as from new distribution channels. As an example, the firm's Nescafé coffee will be available in different dispensers, in Nescafé-branded cafés, and even on planes.

Lastly, Brabeck wants to build targeted communities of customers with special food-related interests. Nespresso (www.nespresso.com) is Nestlé's club for consumers who "treasure quality coffee as part of the simple moments of everyday life." Members are eligible to purchase special coffee machines that use Nespresso premium filter coffee. In addition, the firm's Club Buitoni (named after its Italian pasta brand) boasts 400,000 members and is aimed at people who admire Italian culture. There is a Web site (www.buitoni.com) where visitors can view Italian recipes. As Brabeck notes, "we have been able to launch [Buitoni] products without television advertising, based upon a fine targeting of people who really have an interest in the Italian lifestyle."

Questions

1. Evaluate Nestlé's overall strategy.
2. How can Nestlé effectively coordinate its diverse SBUs?
3. How can Nestlé effectively utilize benchmarking?
4. What are the pros and cons of Nestlé's using an internal growth rate measure versus a traditional sales growth percentage?

[c8-3] The data in the case are drawn from Richard Tomlinson, "Can Nestlé Be the Very Best?" *Fortune* (November 13, 2000), pp. 353–360.

Case 4

Can Xerox Be Fixed? [c8-4]

Over the past twenty years, Xerox (www.xerox.com) has had its share of problems. In the 1980s, the company was overwhelmed by Japanese competitors that, through cost efficiencies, were able to sell copiers at retail for what it cost Xerox to make them. Xerox ultimately was able to cut its costs, refocus on core customers, and improve its quality. But, in a repetition of the same saga, during the early 1990s, Xerox fell behind both Hewlett-Packard (www.hp.com) and Kodak (www.kodak.com) in digital-imaging technology. Once again, Xerox regained its competitive footing. Now, the firm is in deep trouble again. Xerox posted a loss of $198 million in the last 3 months of 2000, its largest loss in 10 years.

As stated in a *Business Week* report, Xerox is struggling like "dozens of other corporations around the world, to make the transition from selling high-tech boxes to selling high-tech solutions and services. It finds itself losing market share to Japanese rivals in its old business, yet is unable to find a profitable place in the Net-centric digital world. For some time, Xerox has clearly needed a new vision."

Xerox's latest plan is to reduce manufacturing expenses, trim overhead costs, and lessen operations in developing markets. In an effort to raise cash, Xerox has been negotiating to sell its operations in China and a European paper business. It recently sold one-half of its 50 percent ownership in the Fuji Xerox joint venture to Fuji for $1.3 billion. The company hopes to generate a total of $2 billion and as much as $4 billion from the sale of its assets.

There are also rumors that Xerox's Palo Alto Research Center (PARC)—where many important computer technologies, such as the mouse, the graphical user interface, the Ethernet card, and the laser printer, were invented—is up for sale at the right price. Ironically, PARC has become a symbol of missed opportunities for Xerox. For example, competitors like Hewlett-Packard are more technologically savvy in delivering print-on-demand products than Xerox. Some analysts feel that Xerox will not sell PARC, but will seek partners to develop the technologies developed there.

Rick Thoman, who was promoted to chief executive officer in 1999, began a massive reorganization at Xerox. Rather than concentrate on copiers, which are now viewed as low-profit items, Thoman refocused Xerox's organizational mission on super-fast and color copiers, as well as document management services. Unfortunately, Thoman was fired 13 months after being appointed. His successor is Anne Mulcahy, an executive with 24 years of experience at Xerox.

Some insiders and outside analysts are weary of Xerox's strategy of selling off assets. According to one senior Xerox sales executive, "I hear about asset sales, about refinancing. But I don't hear anyone saying convincingly, 'Here is our future.' What I see is a retreat back to the comfort zone of the way things used to be before Rick Thoman." And others are critical of Xerox's having too many insiders on its board. The board, for example, promoted its former chief executive officer, Paul Allaire to chairman after appointing Rick Thoman. Thus, Thoman never really had a free hand to make changes.

Questions

1. What factors account for Xerox's continuing problems?
2. How can Xerox better integrate its marketing plan?
3. How can Xerox better anticipate and plan for the future?
4. Comment on this statement: "I hear about asset sales, about refinancing, but I don't hear anyone saying convincingly, 'Here is our future.'"

[c8-4] The data in the case are drawn from Anthony Bianco and Pamela L. Moore, "Downfall: The Inside Story of the Management Fiasco at Xerox," *Business Week* (March 5, 2001), pp. 82–92; Claudia H. Deutsch, "Xerox to Sell Half of Its Stake in Fuju Xerox for $1.3 Billion," *New York Times* (March 7, 2001), p. C6; and Jeremy Kahn, "The Paper Jam from Hell," *Fortune* (November 13, 2000), pp. 141, 146.

PART 8 COMPREHENSIVE CASE

Creating Long-Term Marketing Health[pc-8]

Introduction

When financial results are not up to standard, marketing generally is viewed as a prescription drug to be taken in larger doses to help cure lackluster performance. The advice is to increase advertising and sales promotion, cut prices, expand distribution, and add more products aimed at smaller target markets. Dispensed in strong dosages, the medicine seldom works. Moreover, the marketers who have prescribed it have become more suspect. They've fostered the view that marketing is a "quick fix" to a firm's poor results, rather than convincing chief executive officers (CEOs) of marketing's long-term strategic role.

Marketing is viewed as a short-term fix because the metrics used are calibrated to measure short-term organizational outcomes or results. Like a thermometer measuring body temperature on a real-time basis, marketing is evaluated on daily, weekly, or monthly sales, market share, and profit margin. Economist John Maynard Keynes said, "We may plan for the long run but we eat in the short run." CEOs and chief marketing officers (CMOs) have jointly embraced marketing's central role in helping the organization eat in the short run. We feast on short-term gains of marketing expenditures today; however, if we don't do things that invest in marketing's long-term contribution to the firm today, we won't eat tomorrow.

Marketing Health

A marketing organization is healthy when it can build and maintain exchange relationships with both customers and suppliers under conditions of competitive, technological, and economic turbulence. These unstable environments create stress for the organization, making it difficult to survive and prosper. During such times, it won't work to take more drugs because the weakened or faltering firm must have a reservoir of good health to survive and recover.

There are 10 indicators of marketing health that can be divided into three areas: potential, people, and performance. CMOs wanting to guide their organization's health must focus them on markets with long-term potential; recruit and retain people with the necessary knowledge, skills, and experience; and develop performance metrics that foster a long-term orientation.

Potential

Organizations with good long-term marketing health focus on future market potential. One such firm is Procter & Gamble Co. (www.pg.com), which continually focuses on both high-potential geographic and product markets. More than a quarter century ago, it began to put a high priority on global expansion, and by 1993,

international business represented more than half of total annual sales. Today, P&G employs more than 100,000 people in 140 nations. Although the firm had focused on North America and Western Europe, it now commits to obtaining more growth from emerging markets. Product innovation aimed at developing new brands and improving existing brands is a constant priority and essential to a strategy to double business over the next decade. This doesn't prevent P&G from pursuing acquisitions in attractive and high-potential markets, such as acquiring Tambrands and its market-leading tampon brand, Tampax.

Metric No. 1: Percent of sales from products introduced in the last three years; and percent of sales from markets (geographic or product) entered in the last three years. All products and markets have life cycles; they are born, and then they grow, mature, decline, and decay. Companies that don't recognize this continue to live off past product and market successes. Importantly, they're not staying fit by innovating and creating tomorrow's breadwinners. Consequently, once sales and profits begin to stagnate or decline, it's too late to recover. Drugs and marketing quick fixes won't work.

It is suggested that the CMO and CEO (possibly in conjunction with the chief financial officer) set specific goals for Metric No. 1. No matter whether the goal is 10 percent or 50 percent or for three or five years, it will communicate and send a clear signal throughout the organization that new product and market development are critical to future success. Because financial markets favor sales largely derived from new products, if a company succeeds in achieving its goals regarding this metric, it also will find that the financial markets will respond with increased firm valuation (see Metrics No. 7 and No. 8). This is because firm valuation is a function of expected future cash flows.

Metric No. 2: Percent growth projected over the next three years in size of target market(s). Another indicator of potential is in the growth of the firm's target market(s). The huge attention today on the over-65 age group stems from its projected growth and its specialized needs for many goods and services. As a former director of the U.S. Census Bureau said, "When firms fail to focus their marketing efforts toward the future, they may discover their markets do not have much of a future." If a firm focuses substantial marketing resources on yesterday's growth markets, then it's misallocating its marketing resources.

Metric No. 3: Percent of sales over the last three years from new-wave marketing channels. Perhaps one of the most significant opportunity sources occurs in distribution channels. These channels respond to changes in how people would like to buy or source goods and services. Although with the growth of E-commerce, we tend to view this as a recent phenomenon; it's not new. Department stores, supermarkets, category killers, membership stores, supercenters,

[pc-8]Adapted by the authors from Robert F. Lusch, "Creating Long-Term Marketing Health," *Marketing Management* (Spring 2000), pp. 18–22. Reprinted by permission of the American Marketing Association.

and a host of other retail innovations dramatically changed the competitive landscape and the winners and losers in numerous industries.

People

Potential alone is not sufficient. One also needs the "right" people in the marketing organization. Today, the "people" element of marketing is seen most clearly in successful high-tech firms. It takes more than technology to have economically viable, highly demanded products. It takes high-performance marketing personnel who direct the firm toward transforming state-of-the-art technology into user-friendly products. It's not surprising that increasingly, venture capitalists in the high-tech sector first ask, "Who is your CMO?" Better yet is when the CEO, and not only the CMO, signals this emphasis on marketing.

Metric No. 4: Percent of time the CEO spends on strategic marketing. Former Microsoft (www.microsoft.com) CEO Bill Gates characterizes this orientation. After 25 years as CEO, he removed himself in January 2000 from this position to devote more time to product development. Gates, who remains as chairman of the board, clearly is signaling the critical importance of product development in the firm's strategic marketing efforts. He has been the principal visionary for the company's focus on great software that helps people work, communicate, play, and learn. As the chief marketing visionary, he has directed Microsoft in pivotal strategic directions and with the authority to get things done quickly. He's the stimulus behind such products as Windows, Internet Explorer, Microsoft Office, and WebTV. Additionally, Gates foresaw the potential of interactive media and moved the firm aggressively in this strategic direction with such products as Expedia travel service, CarPoint automotive service, Hotmail, MSN Investor, MSN Gaming Zone, and Microsoft HomeAdvisor real-estate service. Gates believes strongly in research and development. As a result of his understanding and appreciation of marketing, R&D is focused on making products easier to use so customers don't have to learn as many commands. As a true marketer, Gates believes in spending on technical support for customers and constantly seeks feedback from them and partners. He thinks that "every dollar we spend on technology, product development, marketing, and support is focused on delighting our customers." Now, as the firm's chief product development visionary, Gates spends 75 percent of his time in software development.

The one person needed most is not the CMO. It is the CEO, who must become a quasi or covert member of the marketing organization. Yes, you want the CEO paying attention and looking into strategic (not operational) marketing issues. CMOs won't like this, but it's critical to long-term marketing health.

Look to the first three metrics in the "potential" category, and you'll see the types of things for the CEO to think and strategize about. The CEO must see that new products, new markets, rapid-growth target market(s), and new-wave distribution channels are critical to success. Also, the CEO needs to think about the exter-

nal environments of the firm and how they can be shaped by its marketing efforts.

Metric No. 5: Percent of senior marketing executives whose work is central to their lives. We live in a world where work is becoming less central. As economies mature and the quality of life increases, more time is spent on leisure and luxuries. Often, consumption becomes more central than work. The reality is that for the vast majority of workers or employees, firms will need to live with this. However, for the CMO and his or her direct reports, the work of marketing must be central to their lives. As is occurring in the many new E-commerce and high-tech firms, employees will need to work, eat, and sleep marketing. This also will become necessary for old-line industrial companies, however, because the competitive pressures and economic and technological turbulence will require having an environmental signal corps spot and respond to changes. The work cannot be delegated to staff and consultants. The CMOs and their direct reports must read the environmental signals and separate the signal from the noise.

Metric No. 6: Percent of unsuccessful sales calls, unsuccessful new products, unsuccessful new advertising programs, or unsuccessful marketing initiatives. Playing for safety is dangerous. The surest way for a firm to falter and have declining health is not to take risks. Associated with taking risks is failure. But when we don't take risks, we never learn. If we succeed, we learn; if we fail, we learn. How does a company know if it is taking sufficient risk? That is almost impossible to answer. If a company has no failures, however, then it's surely not taking sufficient risk. Failure in marketing needs to be evaluated at all levels in the marketing organization. Salespeople need to fail, product managers need to fail, advertising managers need to fail, and so on.

If a company always fails in its initiatives, it eventually will declare bankruptcy; however, if a firm never fails, it won't learn and will decline. But what percent of sales calls, new products, or new ad programs should be unsuccessful? We cannot offer an answer. What we can say is that a certain level of failure should not be punished, but encouraged. It's important to debrief salespeople, product managers, advertising managers, and others on their failures. Knowing why a new product failed or a new ad campaign failed can provide insights into how to develop better products or ad programs the next time.

Performance

Wal-Mart Stores (www.walmart.com) has focused on its long-term marketing health by driving operating expenses as a percent of sales down to 16 percent. This compares extremely favorably to competitors such as Kmart (www.bluelight.com). This has allowed more aggressive value pricing, which has further enhanced sales performance and allowed the firm to operate well above its break-even sales level.

Much of Wal-Mart's success can be attributed to its placing a high priority on meeting customer expectations. Customers shopping at Wal-Mart are looking for great values, and Wal-Mart consistently delivers. Wal-Mart has accomplished this by primarily focusing on driving costs out of its supply or value chain. Consequently, it has focused on the long-neglected transportation, logistics, warehousing, and communications activities in the value chain. Through cross-docking, automatic inventory replenishment, electronic data interchange, and satellite communication, the company has been able to increase inventory turnover. By linking together distribution centers, suppliers, and retail stores, it has been able to develop a system in which orders can be executed in a few hours. At the same time, its state-of the-art sales forecasting system, which can be adjusted to local conditions, has enabled the company to modify its merchandise mix to changing customer needs and further enhance inventory turnover while increasing sales per square foot. The firm clearly recognizes, however, that some of the best communications are face-to-face. Therefore, regional managers fly weekly from Wal-Mart's headquarters in Bentonville, Arkansas, to visit stores, and store managers often are flown to Bentonville to participate in merchandising and training meetings.

Metric No. 7: Price-earnings multiple relative to the top competitor. Traditional performance measures include profitability measures such as return on sales, return on assets, or return on equity. Undoubtedly, these popular measures aren't to be ignored; however, they tend to characterize past performance as opposed to potential future performance. Consequently, the metrics suggested are intended to be more forward looking in nature.

Companies have market values. These market values are a multiplicative function of price per share times the price-to-earnings ratio, times the total number of shares outstanding. In this equation, the price-to-earnings ratio best represents the consensus of financial and market analysts, as well as individual and institutional investors, of the firm's future earnings. Within the same industry, if one firm such as Wal-Mart is selling at a substantially higher price-earnings ratio than its competitors, the consensus is that it has more potential. And potential almost always relates to the ability to sell more and more products and services to more and more customers in the future, while maintaining appropriate cost controls.

Metric No. 8: Share of total market valuation today versus five years ago. Examining market valuation over time is insightful. Rather than looking at how a firm's market share changes over time, we suggest examining how a firm's share of the total market valuation in the industry has changed over time. This is an important metric because a firm's profit and market share may continue to be acceptable, but it may be missing substantial opportunity. When a firm in an industry is seizing opportunities, it's reflected in its market valuation. The key is not market valuation in isolation, but the share of total industry valuation.

Metric No. 9: Break-even sales as a percent of current sales. In a world of increased competitive, economic, and technological turbulence, all firms face increased uncertainty. Even the best planning and executive leadership cannot make the organization immune to surprises requiring substantial resources. Given this reality, it's disquieting to CEOs, and should be disquieting to CMOs, that most profitable firms actually operate very close to the break-even point. This is because most firms have very high fixed costs, and reaching and exceeding break-even is a continuous challenge. Thus, CEOs have been asking all functional areas to look at outsourcing so that fixed costs become variable costs and at how each area can contribute to the reduction of costs in the value chain. The net effect is to lower break-even points and make it economically feasible to profitably operate under more diverse economic conditions.

Many firms have break-even sales as a percent of current sales of more than 90 to 92 percent. This suggests that an 8 to 10 percent drop in sales will result in a profitable firm becoming unprofitable. Yet, it isn't unusual for a major competitive assault, technological breakthrough, or economic downturn to cause an 8 to 10 percent decline in sales. Consequently, firms need to reorganize and restructure operations with a goal of achieving break-even sales at 80 percent or less of current sales.

Metric No. 10: Percent of customers over the last year who had an unsatisfactory service experience. There isn't a firm today for which customer service should not be a high priority. Even previously protected and highly government-regulated industries face increased competitive pressures. Coupled with this are a multitude of aggressive competitive strategies directed at taking customers away from other firms. Companies understand well that the most transient customer is one who receives inferior service.

Customers avoid firms that provide poor service. In addition, they tell others of their bad service experiences. In short, poor or good service today is an excellent predictor of future failure or success.

Twenty-First Century Marketing

As the CMO considers the long-term health of the marketing function, it's important to have a sense of the broader issues facing managers in the twenty-first century. This understanding will assist the marketing manager in properly representing and arguing for marketing's role in the firm, and importantly, marketing's contribution to the organization's long-term health.

For most of the twentieth century, managers focused on balance-sheet assets or resources. They concentrated on physical facilities and working capital, and financially engineered the leverage of the firm. Control systems were designed to protect assets on the balance sheet. However, when we see many firms selling for multiples of their book value, it becomes clear that the majority of assets of these high-performance marketing firms are nonbalance sheet in nature. Today, managers increasingly recognize that the firms' value and future are more tied to managing and controlling nonbalance or off-balance sheet resources, and to managing such things as core competencies, human resources, intellectual property, brand equity, and a host of other resources within the firm but not on the balance sheet. They also recognize that resources are anything that can be drawn on for support and can include internal resources and external resources. Key external resources are channel relations, government relations, and the general area of public relations. Organizations that excel at total resource management (balance sheet and off-balance sheet management) will score well on performance Metrics No. 7 (price-earnings multiple relative to the top competitor) and No. 8 (share of total market valuation today versus five years ago).

Managers in the twentieth century were taught to be outcome-oriented, and managerial reward systems reinforced this behavior. In the twenty-first century, attention is shifting to the management of processes, not outcomes. Total quality management (TQM) and other management process-oriented systems have shown that managing processes properly leads to appropriate outcomes. Increasingly, everyone in the value chain is viewed as a customer of the next link, and this philosophy is being applied both within and between organizations. If each person does his or her job right and manages the process, the outcome will take care of itself. But a note of caution: It's not only important to "do things right," it's also important to "do the right things." Doing the right things relates to focusing marketing efforts on the areas of highest potential. This suggests that monitoring Metric No. 1 (percent of sales from products introduced in the last three years; and percent of sales from markets entered in the last three years), Metric No. 2 (percent of growth in size of target markets) projected over the next three years), and Metric No. 3 (percent of sales from new-wave marketing channels over the last three years) is paramount.

During the twentieth century, managers largely focused on managing internal resources in response to what was perceived as an uncontrollable external environment. Now, leading-edge firms take a more proactive approach to the external environment by setting industry standards by technological innovation, protecting the physical environment through ecologically responsive production and marketing, shaping the economy through partnerships with local and state governments, shaping the social environment through human resource practices, and shaping government policies through aggressive lobbying efforts. Companies that believe they can influence their external environment will be more apt to pursue the higher risk strategies used in doing so. Consequently, Metric No. 6 (percent of unsuccessful sales calls, unsuccessful new products, unsuccessful new advertising programs, or unsuccessful marketing initiatives) should be closely monitored. Such bold strategies will demand full attention of the CEO, and this points up the key importance of following Metric No. 4 (percent of time a CEO spends on strategic marketing).

Marketing Is an Investment

CEOs and senior executives throughout the organization will continue to view marketing as a short-term fix to the firm's financial challenges and woes. They view marketing as an expense, not an asset. This should be disquieting to marketers; and they must take it upon themselves to alter this predominant view of marketing. As illustrated by Procter & Gamble, Microsoft, and Wal-Mart, marketing can be more than a short-term fix; it can be an instrumental part of, and investment in, the firm's long-term future.

Marketing is much more than an operating expense. CMOs must take a leadership role in promoting the long-term marketing health of their organization. To do this, CMOs will need good communication and political skills. Marketers will need to learn more about finance and accounting so they can communicate with CEOs in a language they understand. Specifically, communicating both the short- and long-term profit and cash flow impact of marketing programs will be crucial. Increasingly, marketing is managing business processes in the entire value chain and playing a pivotal role in managing the external environment. By doing so, it creates off-balance sheet resources and is itself a major off-balance sheet resource. Marketing is an investment and not an expense, and marketers must champion this message.

Questions

1. Comment on this statement: "When financial results are not up to standard, marketing generally is viewed as a prescription drug to be taken in larger doses to help cure lackluster performance."
2. Of the 10 marketing metrics described in the case, which do you consider to be the most important? Why?
3. If you were to add an 11th metric, what would it be? Explain your answer.
4. How could a firm use the metrics described in the case in benchmarking its marketing strategy? Refer to specific metrics in your answer.
5. Relate these statements to the 80-20 principle and the iceberg principle: "Failure in marketing needs to be evaluated at all levels in the marketing organization. Salespeople need to fail, product managers need to fail, advertising managers need to fail, and so on."
6. Present a 7-item horizontal marketing audit form for a discount store chain that competes with Wal-Mart.
7. Present a 7-item vertical marketing audit form related to customer service.
8. Do you agree that marketing should be viewed as an investment rather than as an expense? Explain your answer.

Appendix A

Careers in Marketing

Career opportunities in marketing are extensive and diversified. Many marketing positions give a lot of responsibility to people early in their careers. For example, within six months to one year of being hired, assistant retail buyers are usually given budget authority for purchases involving hundreds of thousands of dollars. Beginning salespeople typically start to call on accounts within several weeks of being hired. Marketing research personnel actually develop preliminary questionnaires, determine sampling procedures, and interpret study results within a short time after their initial employment. A marketing career is excellent preparation for a path to top management positions in all types of organizations.

Marketing positions are often highly visible. These include salespeople, sales managers, retail buyers, brand managers, industrial traffic managers, credit managers, and advertising and public relations personnel. For instance, a bank manager of deposits development at Canadian Imperial Bank (www.cibc.com), one of North America's largest banks, develops localized marketing strategies within bank branches. Such a manager trains branch personnel in identifying market opportunities, using bank data bases, seeking prospects, telemarketing, and writing marketing letters. In general, the visibility of marketing positions allows effective persons to be recognized, promoted, and well compensated.

Marketing offers career opportunities for people with varying educational backgrounds. An associate's or a bachelor's degree is generally required for most management training positions in retailing, inventory management, sales, public relations, and advertising. A master of business administration degree is increasingly necessary for marketing research, marketing consulting, brand management, middle and senior management, and industrial sales positions. Marketing consultants, marketing research directors, and marketing professors frequently have earned Ph.D. degrees in marketing or related subjects.

A marketing background can also train a person to operate his or her own business. Among the entrepreneurial opportunities available are careers as retail store owners, manufacturers' agents, wholesalers, insurance and real-estate brokers, marketing consultants, marketing researchers, and free-lance advertising illustrators or copywriters.

Table 1 contains a detailed listing of job titles in marketing. Jobs in marketing are growing at a much more rapid rate than those in other occupational categories—and this is expected to continue. For example, today, there are about 28 million people who work in U.S. retailing and wholesaling activities, representing more than one-fifth of all civilian employees 16 years old and older. And according to U.S. Bureau of Labor Statistics (www.bls.gov) projections, employment in marketing, advertising, sales, and public relations occupations will increase much faster than average between now and the year 2010.

TABLE 1   Selected Job Titles in Marketing

Job Title	Description
Account executive	Liaison between an ad agency and its clients. This person is employed by the agency to study clients' promotion goals and create promotion programs (including messages, layout, media, and timing).
Advertising copywriter	Creator of headlines and content for ads.
Advertising layout person	Producer of illustrations or one who uses other artists' materials to form ads.
Advertising manager	Director of a firm's ad program. He or she determines media, copy, budget size, ad frequency, and the choice of an ad agency.
Advertising production manager	Person who arranges to have an ad filmed (for TV), recorded (for radio), or printed (for newspaper, magazine, etc.).
Advertising research director	Person who researches markets, evaluates alternative ads, assesses media, and tests reactions.
Agent (broker)	Wholesaler who works for a commission or fee.
Catalog manager	Person who determines target market, products, copy, displays, and pricing for sales catalogs.
Commercial artist	Creator of ads for TV, print media, and product packaging. This artist selects photos and drawings, and determines the layout and type of print used in newspaper and magazine ads. Sample scenes of TV commercials are sketched for clients.

continues

TABLE 1  Selected Job Titles in Marketing *(continued)*

Job Title	Description
Consumer affairs specialist (customer relations specialist)	Firm's contact with consumers. The person handles consumer complaints and attempts to have the firm's policies reflect customer needs. Community programs, such as lectures on product safety, are devised.
Credit manager	Supervisor of the firm's credit process, including eligibility for credit, terms, late payments, consumer complaints, and control.
Customer service	Person responsible for order status inquiries, expediting deliveries, representative field sales support, and returns and claims processing.
Direct-to-home (or office) salesperson	Person who sells goods and services to consumers by personal contact at the consumer's home or office.
Display worker	Person who designs and sets up retail store displays.
Exporter	Individual who arranges for foreign sales and distribution, mostly for domestic firms having a small presence internationally.
Fashion designer	Designer of such apparel as beachwear, hats, dresses, scarves, and shoes.
Franchisee	Person who leases or buys a business with many outlets and a popular name. A franchisee often has one outlet and engages in cooperative planning and ads. The franchisor sets operating rules for all.
Franchisor	Person who develops a company name and reputation and then leases or sells parts of a firm to independent businesspeople. The franchisor oversees the firm, sets policy, and often trains franchisees.
Freight forwarder	Wholesaler who consolidates small shipments from many companies.
Industrial designer	Person who enhances the appearance and function of machine-made products.
Industrial traffic manager	Arranger of transportation to and from firms and customers for raw materials, fabricated parts, finished goods, and equipment.
International marketer	Person who works abroad or in the international department of a domestic firm and is involved with some aspect of marketing. Positions are available in all areas of marketing.
Inventory manager	Person who controls the level and allocation of merchandise throughout the year. This manager evaluates and balances inventory amounts against the costs of holding merchandise.
Life insurance agent (broker)	Person who advises clients on the policy types available relative to their needs. Policies offer insurance and/or retirement income.
Manufacturers' representative (agent)	Salesperson representing several, often small, manufacturers that cannot afford a sales force. The person often sells to wholesalers and retailers.
Marketing manager (vice-president)	Executive who plans, directs, and controls all of a firm's marketing functions. He or she overseas marketing decisions and personnel.
Marketing research project supervisor	Person who develops the research methodology, evaluates the accuracy of different sample sizes, and analyzes data.
Media analyst	Person who evaluates the characteristics and costs of available media. He or she examines audience size and traits, legal restrictions, types of messages used, and other factors. The effectiveness of company messages is also measured.

continues

TABLE 1   **Selected Job Titles in Marketing (continued)**

Job Title	Description
Media director (space or time buyer)	Person who determines the day, time (for radio and TV), media, location, and size of ads. The goal is to reach the largest desirable audience efficiently. This person negotiates contracts for ad space or air time.
Missionary salesperson	Support salesperson who provides information about new and existing products.
Order-fulfillment manager	Supervisor responsible for shipping merchandise. He or she verifies orders, checks availability of goods, oversees packing, and requests delivery.
Packaging specialist	Person responsible for package design, durability, safety, appeal, size, and cost. This specialist must be familiar with all key laws.
Political consultant	Person who advises political candidates on media relations, opinion polling, fund raising, and overall campaign strategy.
Pricing economist	Specialist who studies sources of supply, consumer demand, government restrictions, competition, and costs and then offers short-run and long-run pricing recommendations.
Product manager (brand manager)	Person who supervises the marketing of a product or brand category. In some firms, there are product (brand) managers for existing items and new-product (brand) managers for new items. For a one-brand or one-product firm, this manager is really the marketing manager.
Property and casualty insurance agent (broker)	Person who evaluates client risks from such perils as fire, burglary, and accidents; assesses coverage needs; and sells policies to indemnify losses.
Public relations director	Manages firm's efforts to keep the public aware of its societal accomplishments and to minimize negative reactions to its policies and activities. He or she constantly measures public attitudes and seeks to keep a favorable public opinion of a firm.
Purchasing agent	Buyer for a manufacturer, wholesaler, or retailer. He or she purchases the items necessary for operating the firm and usually buys in bulk, seeks reliable suppliers, and sets precise specifications.
Real-estate agent (broker)	Liaison who brings together a buyer and a seller, lessor and lessee, or landlord and tenant. This salesperson receives a commission.
Retail buyer	Person responsible for purchasing items for resale. The buyer normally concentrates on a product area and develops a plan for proper styles, assortments, sizes, and quantities.
Retail department manager	Supervisor of one retail department, often at a branch store. This is often the first job a college graduate gets after initial training.
Retail merchandise manager	Supervisor of several buyers. He or she sets the retailer's direction in terms of styles, product lines, image, pricing, and other factors and allocates budgets among buyers.
Retail salesperson	Salesperson for a firm that sells to final consumers.

continues

TABLE 1   **Selected Job Titles in Marketing (continued)**

Job Title	Description
Retail store manager	Supervisor of day-to-day operations of a store. All in-store personnel report to this manager.
Sales engineer	Support salesperson involved with technical goods or services.
Sales manager	Sales force supervisor who is responsible for recruitment, selection, training, motivation, evaluation, compensation, and control.
Salesperson	Company representative who interacts with consumers. He or she may require limited or extensive skills, deal with final or organizational customers, work from an office or go out in the field, and be a career salesperson or progress in management.
Sales promotion director	Person involved with supplementary promotional activities, such as frequent-shopper programs, coupons, contests, and free samples.
Securities salesperson (commodities broker)	Salesperson involved with buying and selling stocks, bonds, government securities, mutual funds, and other financial transactions.
Traffic manager	Supervisor of the purchase and use of alternative transportation methods. This manager routes shipments and monitors performance.
Warehouser	Person responsible for storage and movement of goods within a firm's warehouse facilities. He or she keeps inventory records and makes sure older items are shipped before newer ones (rotating stock).
Wholesale salesperson	Salesperson representing a wholesaler to retailers and other firms.

The strong demand for marketing personnel is based on several factors. More service firms, nonprofit institutions, political candidates, and others are applying marketing principles. The deregulation of several industries (such as banking, communication, and transportation) has encouraged firms in these industries to increase their marketing efforts. Although production can be mechanized and automated, many marketing activities require personal contact. The rise in foreign competition, the attraction of many international markets, and the maturity of several market segments in the United States are causing more U.S. firms to expand and upgrade their marketing programs.

Such new technologies as electronic checkouts, marketing-based computer software, and data-base marketing techniques are creating marketing opportunities for firms. The changes in U.S. and foreign societies (such as blurring gender roles, recreational activities, and the rise in single-person households) need to be monitored through marketing research and marketing information systems, and adapted to via careful marketing planning.

Figure 1 shows four potential marketing career paths. They are general and intended to give you a perspective about "moving up the ladder." Individual firms have their own versions of these career paths. Specialized opportunities also exist in each area shown (such as sales training, support sales, and final consumer versus organizational consumer sales in the sales area); and these are not revealed in Figure 1.

Starting salaries for marketing personnel range from $15,000 to $30,000 for those with an associate's degree, $25,000 to $45,000 for those with a bachelor's degree, and $45,000 to $85,000+ for those with a master of business administration degree. On average, in 2001, those with a bachelor's degree who majored in marketing had beginning salaries of $35,000 and those with an MBA and a nontechnical bachelor's degree had beginning salaries of $55,000. MBAs with a technical bachelor's degree averaged more than $65,000. In addition to salary, some marketing positions (especially in sales) provide a company car, bonus, and/or expense account that are not common to other professions.

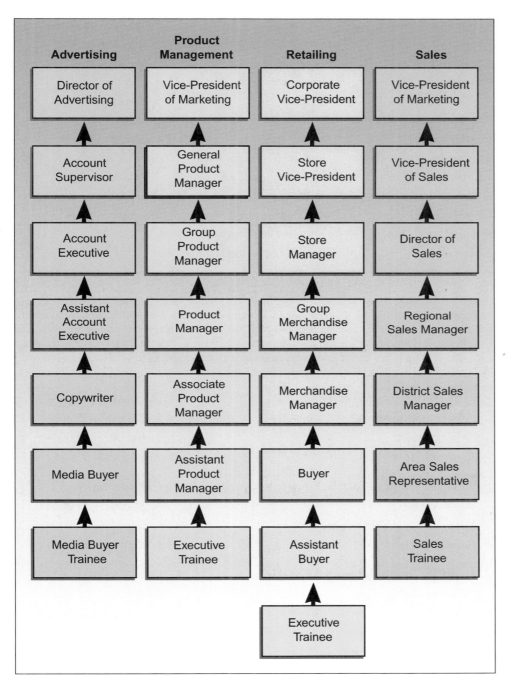

FIGURE 1
Selected Marketing Career Paths

TABLE 2

Selected Employers of Marketing Personnel

Advertising agencies	Franchisors	Public relations firms
Agents and brokers	Fund-raising organizations	Raw material extractors
Common carriers	Government	Real-estate firms
Computer service bureaus	Health-care firms	Retailers
Consulting firms	Industrial firms	Self-employed
Credit bureaus	International firms	Service firms
Delivery firms	Manufacturers	Shopping centers
Direct marketing businesses	Marketing research firms	Sports teams
Educational institutions	Marketing specialists	Transportation firms
Entertainment firms	Media	Warehousers
Exporting companies	Multinational firms	Wholesalers
Financial institutions	Nonprofit institutions	
Franchisees	Product-testing laboratories	

Worldwide, and especially in the United States, marketing executives often are chosen as the chief executive officers (CEOs) of major industrial and nonindustrial corporations. They each typically earn at least several hundred thousand dollars per year plus bonuses.

Table 2 shows the types of firms that employ people in marketing positions. Table 3 presents salary ranges for a number of marketing positions (with a focus on entry level, middle management, and top management jobs). Table 4 gives the Web site addresses of several sources with useful information relating to marketing careers.

TABLE 3

Annual Compensation for Personnel in Selected Marketing Positions (Including Bonus)

Advertising Positions	Compensation
Assistant media planner	$ 22,000–$ 35,000+
Chief copywriter	$ 40,000–$ 80,000+
Creative director	$ 60,000–$100,000+

Marketing Research Positions	Compensation
Junior analyst	$ 22,000–$ 35,000+
Senior analyst/project director	$ 40,000–$ 75,000+
Research director	$ 80,000–$120,000+

Product Management Positions	Compensation
Senior marketing analyst	$ 30,000–$ 50,000+
Product manager	$ 55,000–$100,000+
Group product manager	$ 75,000–$150,000+

Public Relations Positions	Compensation
Account executive	$ 25,000–$45,000+
Account supervisor	$ 50,000–$80,000+

Retailing Positions	Compensation
Assistant buyer	$ 25,000–$ 35,000+
Buyer	$ 40,000–$ 85,000+
General merchandise manager	$ 75,000–$200,000+

continues

Sales Positions	Compensation
Sales trainee	$ 25,000–$ 40,000+
Real-estate agent (broker)	$ 30,000–$100,000+
Regional sales manager	$ 70,000–$125,000+

Miscellaneous Marketing Positions	Compensation
Customer service representative	$ 22,000–$ 35,000+
Customer service supervisor	$ 35,000–$ 60,000+
Distribution general manager	$ 40,000–$ 90,000+
Sales promotion director	$ 50,000–$ 85,000+
International general sales executive	$ 60,000–$ 90,000+

Top Marketing Positions	Compensation
Branch office manager—advertising agency	$ 60,000–$200,000+
Senior public relations executive	$ 75,000–$150,000+
Senior sales executive	$ 75,000–$150,000+
President—distributor	$ 75,000–$200,000+
Executive vice-president—advertising agency	$ 80,000–$200,000+
Vice-president of sales	$100,000–$275,000+
Vice-president of marketing	$100,000–$500,000+
President—advertising agency	$125,000–$500,000+

TABLE 3

Annual Compensation for Personnel in Selected Marketing Positions (Including Bonus) *(continued)*

Source: Compiled by the authors from various publications.

Source	Web Address
Abbott, Langer & Associates Salary Survey	www.abbott-langer.com/amasumm.html
American Marketing Association	www.marketingpower.com
Career Magazine	www.careermag.com
Careers in Marketing	www.careers-in-marketing.com
DSN'S Careers in Retailing	www.careersinretailing.com
HotJobs.com's Marketing Channel	www.hotjobs.com/htdocs/channels/marketing
InfoTech's Marketing Careers Center	http://www.smsource.com/careers.htm
KnowThis.com	www.knowthis.com/careers/careersmkt.htm
MarketingJobs.com	www.marketingjobs.com
Monster Sales	http://sales.monster.com
NationJob's Marketing and Sales Job Page	www.nationjob.com/marketing
Occupational Outlook Handbook	http://stats.bls.gov/ocohome.htm
Peterson's JobsDirect.com	http://petersons.jobdirect.com

TABLE 4

Selected Online Sources of Marketing Career Information

Appendix B

Marketing Mathematics

To design, implement, and review marketing programs properly, it is necessary to understand basic business mathematics from a marketing perspective. Accordingly, this appendix describes and illustrates the types of business mathematics with which marketers should be most familiar: the profit-and-loss statement, marketing performance ratios, pricing, and determining an optimal marketing mix.

The crucial role of marketing mathematics can be seen via the following:

- By utilizing marketing mathematics well, a firm can evaluate monthly, quarterly, and annual reports; and study performance on a product, market, SBU, division, or overall company basis.
- Marketing plans for all types of channel members (manufacturers, wholesalers, and retailers) and all time periods (short term through long term) should be based on marketing mathematics.
- Both small and large, goods and services, and profit and nonprofit organizations need to rely on marketing mathematics in making decisions.
- Marketing mathematics provide a systematic basis for establishing standards of performance, reviewing that performance, and focusing attention on opportunities and problem areas.
- By understanding marketing mathematics, better marketing mix decisions can be made.
- By grasping marketing mathematics, decision making with regard to entering or withdrawing from a market, budgeting expenditures, and the deployment of marketing personnel can be aided.

THE PROFIT-AND-LOSS STATEMENT

The *profit-and-loss (income) statement* presents a summary of the revenues and costs for an organization over a specific period of time. Such a statement is generally developed on a monthly, quarterly, and yearly basis. The profit-and-loss statement enables a firm to examine overall and specific revenues and costs over similar time periods (for example, July 1, 2000 to June 30, 2001 versus July 1, 1999 to June 30, 2000), and to analyze its profitability. Monthly and quarterly statements enable a firm to monitor progress toward goals and revise performance estimates.

The profit-and-loss statement consists of these major components:

- *Gross sales*—The total revenues generated by a firm's goods and services.
- *Net sales*—The revenues received by a firm after subtracting returns and discounts (such as trade, quantity, cash, and special promotional allowances).

- *Cost of goods sold*—The cost of merchandise sold by a manufacturer, wholesaler, or retailer.
- *Gross margin (profit)*—The difference between net sales and the cost of goods sold; consists of operating expenses plus net profit.
- *Operating expenses*—The cost of running a business, including marketing.
- *Net profit before taxes*—The profit earned after all costs have been deducted.

When examining a profit-and-loss statement, it is important to recognize a key difference between manufacturers and wholesalers or retailers. For manufacturers, the cost of goods sold involves the cost of producing products (raw materials, labor, and overhead). For wholesalers or retailers, the cost of goods sold involves the cost of merchandise purchased for resale (purchase price plus freight charges).

Table 1 shows the fiscal 2001 annual profit-and-loss statement (in dollars) for a manufacturer, the General Toy Company. From this table, these observations can be made:

- Total company sales for fiscal year 2001 were $1,000,000. However, the firm gave refunds worth $20,000 for returned merchandise and allowances. Discounts of $50,000 were also provided. This left the firm with actual (net) sales of $930,000.
- As a manufacturer, General Toy computed its cost of goods sold by adding the cost value of the beginning inventory on hand (items left in stock from the previous period) and the merchandise manufactured during the time period (costs included raw materials, labor, and overhead), and then subtracting the cost value of the inventory remaining at the end of the period. For General Toy, this was $450,000 ($100,000 + $400,000 − $50,000).
- The gross margin was $480,000, calculated by subtracting the cost of goods sold from net sales. This sum was used for operating expenses, with the remainder accounting for net profit.
- Operating expenses involve all costs not considered in the cost of goods sold. Operating expenses for General Toy included sales force compensation, advertising, delivery, administration, rent, office supplies, and miscellaneous costs, a total of $370,000. Of this amount, $225,000 was directly allocated for marketing costs (sales force, advertising, delivery).
- General Toy's net profit before taxes was $110,000, computed by deducting operating expenses from gross margin. This amount would be used to cover federal and state taxes as well as company profits.

TABLE 1    General Toy Company, Profit-and-Loss Statement for the Fiscal Year July 1, 2000 through June 30, 2001 (in Dollars)

Gross sales			$1,000,000
Less: Returns and allowances		$ 20,000	
Discounts		50,000	
Total sales deductions			70,000
Net sales			$ 930,000
Less cost of goods sold:			
Beginning inventory (at cost)		$100,000	
New merchandise (at cost)ᵃ		400,000	
Merchandise available for sale		$500,000	
Ending inventory (at cost)		50,000	
Total cost of goods sold			450,000
Gross margin			$ 480,000
Less operating expenses:			
Marketing expenses			
Sales force compensation	$125,000		
Advertising	75,000		
Delivery	25,000		
Total marketing expenses		$225,000	
General expenses			
Administration	$ 75,000		
Rent	30,000		
Office supplies	20,000		
Miscellaneous	20,000		
Total general expenses		145,000	
Total operating expenses			370,000
Net profit before taxes			$ 110,000

ᵃFor a manufacturer, new-merchandise costs refer to the raw materials, labor, and overhead costs incurred in the production of items for resale. For a wholesaler or retailer, new-merchandise costs refer to the purchase costs of items (including freight) bought for resale.

PERFORMANCE RATIOS

Performance ratios are used to measure the actual performance of a firm against company goals or industry standards. Comparative data can be obtained from trade associations, Dun & Bradstreet (www.dnb.com), Risk Management Association (www.rmahq.org), and other sources. Among the most valuable performance ratios for marketing analysis are the following:

$$(1) \text{ Sales efficiency ratio} = \frac{\text{Net sales}}{\text{Gross sales}}$$
(percentage)

The *sales efficiency ratio (percentage)* compares net sales against gross sales. The highest level of efficiency is 1.00; in that case, there would be no returns, allowances, or discounts. General Toy had a sales efficiency ratio of 93 percent ($930,000/$1,000,000) in fiscal

2001. This is a very good ratio; anything greater would mean General Toy was too conservative in making sales.

$$(2) \text{ Cost-of-goods-sold ratio} = \frac{\text{Cost of goods sold}}{\text{Net sales}}$$
(percentage)

The *cost-of-goods-sold ratio (percentage)* indicates the portion of net sales used to manufacture or purchase the goods sold. When the ratio is high, a firm has little revenue left to use for operating expenses and net profit. This could mean costs are too high or selling price is too low. In fiscal 2001, General Toy had a cost-of-goods-sold ratio of 48.4 percent ($450,000/$930,000), a satisfactory figure.

$$(3) \text{ Gross margin ratio} = \frac{\text{Gross margin}}{\text{Net sales}}$$
(percentage)

The *gross margin ratio (percentage)* shows the proportion of net sales allotted to operating expenses and net profit. If the ratio is high, a firm has substantial revenue left for these items. During fiscal 2001, General Toy had a gross margin ratio of 51.6 percent ($480,000/$930,000), a satisfactory figure.

(4) Operating expense ratio = $\frac{\text{Operating expenses}}{\text{Net sales}}$
      (percentage)

The *operating expense ratio (percentage)* expresses these expenses in terms of net sales. When the ratio is high, a firm is spending a large amount on marketing and other operating costs. General Toy had an operating expense ratio of 39.8 percent in fiscal 2001 ($370,000/$930,000), meaning that almost 40 cents of every sales dollar went for operations, a moderate amount.

(5) Net profit ratio = $\frac{\text{Net profit before taxes}}{\text{Net sales}}$
      (percentage)

The *net profit ratio (percentage)* indicates the portion of each sales dollar going for profits (after deducting all costs). The net profit ratio varies a lot by industry. For example, in the supermarket industry, net profits are about 2 percent of net sales; in the industrial chemical industry, net profits are about 5 percent of net sales. The fiscal 2001 net profit for General Toy was 11.8 percent of net sales ($110,000/$930,000), well above the industry average.

(6) Stock turnover = $\frac{\text{Net sales (in units)}}{\text{Average inventory (in units)}}$
      ratio

or

$\frac{\text{Net sales (in sales dollars)}}{\text{Average inventory (in sales dollars)}}$

or

$\frac{\text{Cost of goods sold}}{\text{Average inventory (at cost)}}$

The *stock turnover ratio* shows the number of times during a specified period, usually one year, that average inventory on hand is sold. It can be calculated in units or dollars (in selling price or at cost). In the case of General Toy, the fiscal 2001 stock turnover ratio can be calculated on a cost basis. The cost of goods sold during fiscal 2001 was $450,000. Average inventory at cost =

(Beginning inventory at cost + Ending inventory at cost)/2 = ($100,000 + $50,000)/2 = $75,000. The stock turnover ratio was ($450,000/75,000) = 6. This compared favorably with the industry average, which meant General Toy sold its goods more quickly than competitors.

(7) Return on investment = $\frac{\text{Net sales}}{\text{Investment}} \times \frac{\text{Net profit before taxes}}{\text{Net sales}}$

= $\frac{\text{Net profit before taxes}}{\text{Investment}}$

The *return on investment (ROI)* compares profitability with the investment necessary to manufacture or distribute merchandise. For a manufacturer, this investment includes land, plant, equipment, and inventory costs. For a wholesaler or retailer, it involves inventory, the costs of land, the outlet and its fixtures, and equipment. To determine General Toy's return on investment, total investment costs are culled from its *balance sheet,* which lists the assets and liabilities of a firm at a particular time.

There are two components to the return on investment measure—investment turnover ratio and net profit ratio (percentage):

Investment turnover ratio = $\frac{\text{Net sales}}{\text{Investment}}$

Net profit ratio   = $\frac{\text{Net profit before taxes}}{\text{Net sales}}$
(percentage)

The investment turnover ratio computes the sales per dollar of investment. The General Toy management calculated that an overall investment of $550,000 was needed to yield fiscal 2001 net sales of $930,000. Thus, its investment turnover ratio was 1.7 times ($930,000/$550,000). Because General Toy's net profit ratio was 11.8 percent ($110,000/$930,000), the firm's return on investment equaled 20.1 percent (1.7 × .118). This figure was above the industry norm.

Table 2 shows a percentage profit-and-loss statement for the General Toy Company, using the same period as in Table 1. All figures in the table are computed on the basis of net sales equaling 100 percent. This table allows a firm to quickly observe such performance measures as the cost-of-goods-sold percentage, operating expense percentage, and net profit percentage.

TABLE 2		
General Toy Company, Profit-and-Loss Statement for the Fiscal Year July 1, 2000 Through June 30, 2001 (in Percent, with Net Sales = 100.0)		
Net sales		100.0
Less cost of goods sold		48.4
Gross margin		51.6
Less operating expenses:		
Marketing expenses	24.2	
General expenses	15.6	
Total operating expenses		39.8
Net profit before taxes		11.8

PRICING

The material here complements Chapters 20 and 21. Five specific aspects of pricing are examined: price elasticity, fixed versus variable costs, markups, markdowns, and profit planning using markups and markdowns.

Price Elasticity

As defined in Chapter 20, ***price elasticity*** refers to the buyer sensitivity to price changes in terms of the quantities they will purchase.

Elasticity is based on the availability of substitutes and the urgency of need. It is expressed as the percentage change in quantity demanded divided by the percentage change in price:

$$\text{Price elasticity} = \frac{\dfrac{\text{Quantity 1} - \text{Quantity 2}}{\text{Quantity 1} + \text{Quantity 2}}}{\dfrac{\text{Price 1} - \text{Price 2}}{\text{Price 1} + \text{Price 2}}}$$

For purposes of simplicity, elasticity is often shown as a positive number (as it will be in this section).

Table 3 shows a demand schedule for women's blouses at several different prices. When selling price is reduced by a small percentage, from \$40 to \$35, the percentage change in quantity demanded rises materially, from 120 to 150 units. Maxine's Blouses

then gains a strong competitive advantage. Demand is highly elastic (price sensitive). As price is reduced, total revenues go up:

$$\text{Price elasticity} = \frac{\dfrac{120 - 150}{120 + 150}}{\dfrac{\$40 - \$35}{\$40 + \$35}} = 1.7 \text{ (expressed as a positive number)}$$

At a price of \$25, the market becomes more saturated—the percentage change in price, from \$25 to \$20, is directly offset by the percentage change in quantity demanded, from 240 to 300 units:

$$\text{Price elasticity} = \frac{\dfrac{240 - 300}{240 + 300}}{\dfrac{\$25 - \$20}{\$25 + \$20}} = 1.0 \text{ (expressed as a positive number)}$$

Total revenues remain the same at a price of \$25 or \$20. This is unitary demand, whereby total revenues stay constant as price changes.

At a price of \$20, the market becomes extremely saturated, and further price reductions have little impact on demand. A large percentage change in price, from \$20 to \$15, results in a small percentage change in quantity demanded, from 300 to 350 units. Maxine's is able to sell relatively few additional blouses. Demand is inelastic (insensitive to price changes):

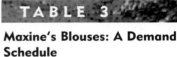

TABLE 3

Maxine's Blouses: A Demand Schedule

Selling Price	Quantity Demanded	Elasticity[a]	Total Revenue[b]
\$40	120		\$4,800
		1.7	
35	150		5,250
		1.5	
30	190		5,700
		1.3	
25	240		6,000 ← Maximum total revenue
		1.0	
20	300		6,000 ←
		0.5	
15	350		5,250
		0.3	
10	390		3,900

[a]Expressed as positive numbers.
[b]Total revenue = Selling price × Quantity demanded.

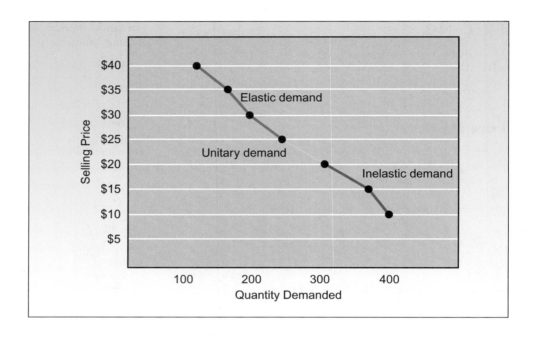

FIGURE 1

Maxine's Blouses, Demand Elasticity

$$\text{Price elasticity} = \frac{\frac{300-350}{300+350}}{\frac{\$20-\$15}{\$20+\$15}} = 0.5 \text{ (expressed as a positive number)}$$

Total revenue falls as demand goes from elastic to inelastic; at this point, price cuts are not effective.

Total revenue is maximized at the price levels where price and demand changes directly offset each other (in this example, $25 and $20). How does a firm choose between those prices? It depends on the marketing philosophy. At a price of $25, profit will probably be higher because the firm needs to produce and sell fewer products, thus reducing costs. At a price of $20, more units are sold; this may increase the customer base for other products the firm offers and thereby raise overall company sales and profits.

Figure 1 graphically depicts demand elasticity for Maxine's Blouses. This figure indicates that a demand curve is not necessarily straight and that a single demand schedule has elastic, unitary, and inelastic ranges.

It is important to remember that elasticity refers to percentage changes, not to absolute changes. A demand shift from 120 to 150 units involves a greater percentage change than one from 300 to 350 units. In addition, each product or brand faces a distinct demand schedule. Milk and magazines have dissimilar schedules, despite similar price ranges, due to different availability of substitutes and urgency of need.

Fixed Versus Variable Costs

In making pricing decisions, it is essential to distinguish between fixed and variable costs. **Fixed costs** are ongoing costs that are unrelated to production or sales volume; they are generally constant for a given range of output for a specific period. In the short run, fixed costs cannot usually be changed. Examples are rent, full-time employee salaries, physical plant, equipment, real-estate taxes, and insurance.

Variable costs are directly related to production or sales volume. As volume increases, total variable costs increase; as volume declines, total variable costs decline. Per-unit variable costs often remain constant over a given range of volume (e.g., total sales commissions go up as sales rise, while sales commissions as a percent of sales remain constant). Examples are raw materials, sales commissions, parts, salaries of hourly employees, and product advertising.

Figure 2 shows how fixed, variable, and total costs vary with production or sales for Eleanor's Cosmetics, a leased-department operator selling popular-priced cosmetics in a department store. Total fixed costs are $10,000. Variable costs are $5.00 per unit. Figure 2A depicts total costs: as volume rises, total fixed costs are constant at $10,000, while total variable costs and total costs go up by $5.00 per unit. At 1,000 units, total fixed costs are $10,000, total variable costs are $5,000, and total costs are $15,000. At 5,000 units, total fixed costs are $10,000, total variable costs are $25,000, and total costs are $35,000.

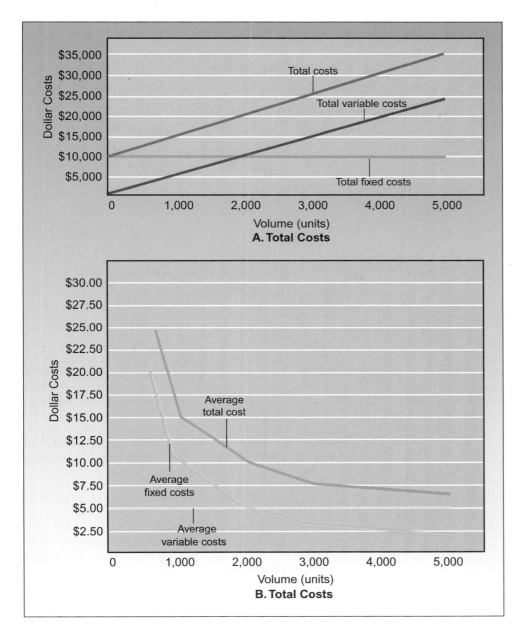

FIGURE 2
Fixed and Variable Costs for Eleanor's Cosmetics

Figure 2B depicts average costs: as volume increases, average fixed costs and average total costs decline (because fixed costs are spread over more units), while average variable costs remain the same. At 1,000 units, average fixed costs are $10.00 ($10,000/1,000 units), average variable costs are $5.00, and average total costs are $15.00. At 5,000 units, average fixed costs are $2.00 ($10,000/5,000 units), average variable costs are $5.00, and average total costs are $7.00.

By knowing the relationship between fixed and variable costs, firms are better able to set prices. They recognize that average total costs usually decline as sales volume expands, which allows them to set skimming prices when volume is low and penetration prices when volume is high. They also realize that losses can be reduced with selling prices that are lower than average total costs—as long as prices are above average variable costs, transactions will contribute toward the payment of fixed costs. Finally, the break-even point can be shown on a total-cost curve graph. See Figure 3.

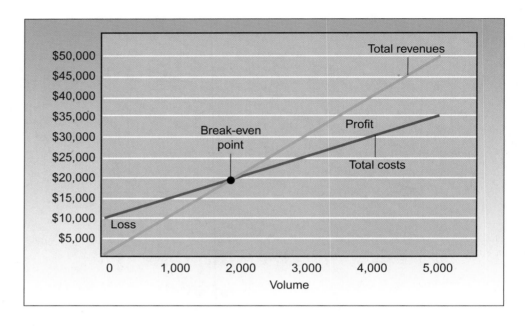

FIGURE 3
Break-Even Analysis for Eleanor's Cosmetics

With a selling price of $10.00 per unit, Eleanor's Cosmetics loses money unless 2,000 units could be sold. At that amount, the firm breaks even. For all sales volumes above 2,000 units, the company earns a profit of $5.00 per unit, an amount equal to the difference between selling price and average variable costs (fixed costs are assumed to be "paid off" when sales reach 2,000 units). A sales volume of 5,000 units returns a profit of $15,000 (total revenues of $50,000 – total costs of $35,000).

Markups

A *markup* is the difference between merchandise cost and selling price for each channel member. Markup is usually expressed as a percentage:

Markup percentage = $\dfrac{\text{Selling price} - \text{Merchandise cost}}{\text{Selling price}}$
(on selling price)

Markup percentage = $\dfrac{\text{Selling price} - \text{Merchandise cost}}{\text{Merchandise cost}}$
(at cost)

Table 4 shows markup percentages on selling price and at cost for an item selling for $10.00 under varying costs. Because firms often consider a markup percentage as the equivalent of the gross margin percentage discussed earlier in this appendix, they use the markup percentage on selling price in their planning. As with gross margins, firms use their markups to cover operating expenses and net profit.

Channel members need to understand the discounts given to them by vendors (suppliers). Besides the markups they receive for providing regular marketing functions, they may also obtain quan-

tity, cash, seasonal, and/or promotional discounts. Transportation costs are added to the price; they are not discounted.

Table 5 shows the computation of a purchase price by a TV retailer, based on a functional markup of 40 percent and individual discounts of 10 (quantity), 2 (cash), 5 (seasonal), and 5 (promotional) percent. The discounts do not total 62 percent off final selling price. They total 52.2 percent because the discounts are computed upon successive balances. For example, the 10 percent quantity discount is computed on $165, which is the purchase price after deducting the functional markup allowed by the vendor.

Markdowns

A key price adjustment made by most firms is a *markdown*, which is a reduction in the original selling price of an item so as to sell it. Markdowns are due to slow sales, model changes, and other factors.

Markdown percentages can be computed in either of two ways:

Markdown percentage = $\dfrac{\text{Original selling price} - \text{Reduced selling price}}{\text{Original selling price}}$
(off-original price)

Markdown percentage = $\dfrac{\text{Original selling price} - \text{Reduced selling price}}{\text{Reduced selling price}}$
(off-sale price)

The off-original markdown percentage for an item that initially sold for $20 and has been marked down to $15 is ($20–$15)/ $20=25. The off-sale markdown percentage is ($20–$15)/$15=33. The off-original percentage is more accurate for price planning, but the off-sale percentage shows a larger price reduction to consumers and may generate increased interest.

Selling Price	Merchandise Cost	Markup (% on Selling Price)	Markup (% at Cost)
$10.00	$9.00	10	11
10.00	8.00	20	25
10.00	7.00	30	43
10.00	6.00	40	67
10.00	5.00	50	100
10.00	4.00	60	150
10.00	3.00	70	233
10.00	2.00	80	400
10.00	1.00	90	900

TABLE 4

Markups on Selling Price and at Cost

Formulas to convert markup percentages:

$$\text{Markup percentage (on selling price)} = \frac{\text{Markup percentage (at cost)}}{100\% + \text{Markup percentage (at cost)}}$$

$$\text{Markup percentage (at cost)} = \frac{\text{Markup percentage (on selling price)}}{100\% - \text{Markup percentage (on selling price)}}$$

Discounts Offered by Manufacturer (in %)

Functional	40
Quantity	10
Cash	2
Seasonal	5
Promotional	5

TABLE 5

A TV Retailer's Final Purchase Price, After Deducting All Discounts— Model 123

Suggested Final Selling Price	$275.00
Shipping Charges	$15.30

Computation of Purchase Price Paid by Retailer

List price	$275.00
Less functional markup ($275.00 × 0.40)	110.00
Balance	$165.00
Less quantity discount ($165.00 × 0.10)	16.50
Balance	$148.50
Less cash discount ($148.50 × 0.02)	2.97
Balance	$145.53
Less seasonal discount ($145.53 × 0.05)	7.28
Balance	$138.25
Less promotional discount ($138.25 × 0.05)	6.91
Balance after all discounts	$131.34
Plus shipping charges	15.30
Price to channel member	$146.64

Total of Discounts	$143.66
Total Discount % ($143.66/$275)	52.2

TABLE 6 Determining an Optimal Marketing Mix for a Company with a $3 Million Annual Marketing Budget

Alternative Marketing Mix	Selling Price	Unit Sales	Sales Revenue	Total Product Costs[a]	Advertising Costs	Personal Selling Costs	Distribution Costs	Total Costs	Profit
Mass marketing	$11.00	2,507,000	$27,577,000	$22,563,000	$1,400,000	$ 300,000	$1,300,000	$25,563,000	$2,014,000
Selective marketing	29.00	432,000	12,528,000	7,776,000	900,000	1,200,000	900,000	10,766,000	1,762,000
Exclusive marketing	43.00	302,000	12,986,000	9,966,000	600,000	1,850,000	550,000	12,966,000	20,000

[a]Mass marketing = $9.00 per unit for labor, materials, and other production costs; selective marketing = $18.00 per unit for labor, materials, and other production costs; and exclusive marketing = $33.00 per unit for labor, materials, and other production costs.

Profit Planning Using Markups and Markdowns

Although lower markups (higher markdowns) generally result in higher unit sales and higher markups (lower markdowns) generally result in lower unit sales, it is essential that a firm determine the effect of a change in selling price on its profitability. The impact of a price adjustment on total gross profit (also known as gross margin) can be determined through the use of this formula:

Unit sales required to earn the same total gross profit with a price adjustment = $\dfrac{\text{Original markup (\%)}}{\text{Original markup (\%)} +/- \text{Price change (\%)}} \times$ Expected unit sales at original price

If a wholesaler pays $7 to buy one unit of an item and decides to reduce that item's selling price by 10 percent—from an original price of $10 to $9—its markup on selling price drops from 30 percent ($3/$10) to 22.2 percent ($2/$9). Because the wholesaler originally planned to sell 1,000 units at $10, it must now sell 1,500 units at $9 to keep the same gross profitability (30/20 × 1,000). Conversely, if it decides to raise its price by 10 percent—to $11—its new markup on selling price is 36.4 percent ($4/$11), and it must sell only 750 units to keep the original gross profit level (30/40 × 1,000).

DETERMINING AN OPTIMAL MARKETING MIX

When devising, enacting, and assessing a marketing plan, a firm should consider alternative marketing mixes and find the most effective one. Because many marketing costs (such as packaging, distribution, advertising, and personal selling) can be both order generating and variable, marketers need to estimate and compare sales for various combinations at various levels of costs. Table 6 shows how a firm could set prices and allot its $3 million annual marketing budget among product, distribution, advertising, and personal selling—so as to maximize profit. In this situation, the firm would choose a mass marketing mix resulting in a low price, a lower-quality product, extensive distribution, and an emphasis on advertising.

The concepts of opportunity costs and sales response curves provide valuable information in determining an optimal marketing mix. *Opportunity costs* measure the foregone revenues (profit) from not using the optimal marketing mix. For example, it may be possible for a firm to sell an additional 10,000 units in a selective marketing strategy by raising advertising expenditures by $100,000 and reducing distribution expenditures by $100,000. A firm that is unaware of this option would have opportunity costs—in terms of profit—of $110,000:

Opportunity costs = (Foregone unit sales × Selling price) – (Added costs)

= (10,000 × $29.00) – (10,000 × $18.00)

= $110,000

At its optimal marketing strategy, a firm's opportunity costs equal zero.

Sales response curves show the expected relationships between sales revenue and functional marketing efforts. These curves are estimated on the basis of executives' judgment, surveys, industry data, and/or experiments (whereby marketing mix factors are systematically varied in a controlled way).

Figure 4 shows sales response curves for a firm examining four aspects of its marketing effort: depth of product line, number of outlets carrying products, advertising expenditures, and price level. For each of these factors, the expected impact of a strategy change on sales is shown; it is clear that different actions will result in different sales responses.

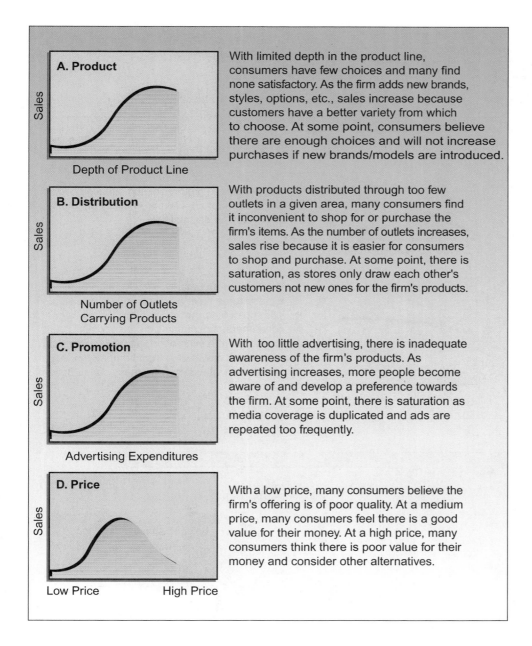

A. Product

Sales

Depth of Product Line

With limited depth in the product line, consumers have few choices and many find none satisfactory. As the firm adds new brands, styles, options, etc., sales increase because customers have a better variety from which to choose. At some point, consumers believe there are enough choices and will not increase purchases if new brands/models are introduced.

B. Distribution

Sales

Number of Outlets
Carrying Products

With products distributed through too few outlets in a given area, many consumers find it inconvenient to shop for or purchase the firm's items. As the number of outlets increases, sales rise because it is easier for consumers to shop and purchase. At some point, there is saturation, as stores only draw each other's customers not new ones for the firm's products.

C. Promotion

Sales

Advertising Expenditures

With too little advertising, there is inadequate awareness of the firm's products. As advertising increases, more people become aware of and develop a preference towards the firm. At some point, there is saturation as media coverage is duplicated and ads are repeated too frequently.

D. Price

Sales

Low Price   High Price

With a low price, many consumers believe the firm's offering is of poor quality. At a medium price, many consumers feel there is a good value for their money. At a high price, many consumers think there is poor value for their money and consider other alternatives.

FIGURE 4

Selected Sales Response Curves for Marketing Mix Functions

When using sales response curves, these points should be kept in mind:

- Sales responsiveness may vary by product and by market segment. For example, marketing expenditures have a much greater influence on new products/growing markets than on mature products/mature markets. See Figure 5.
- The range of efficient marketing efforts must be determined. At low levels, marketing activities may be insufficient to generate consumer interest. At high levels, these activities may be redundant and appeal to a saturated market. The range of marketing efforts having the greatest impact on sales is the appropriate one. See Figure 6.

- Sales response curves are related to the combination of marketing mix factors employed by a firm. To determine its overall sales response curve, a company would combine all the individual curves shown in Figure 4 (or use all the data in Table 6).
- Sales response curves examine revenue fluctuations. Before making marketing decisions, profit response curves should also be studied.
- Sales response curves should be projected under different conditions, such as good economy/poor economy or heavy competition/light competition.

FIGURE 5
Sales Response Curves and Product/Market Maturity

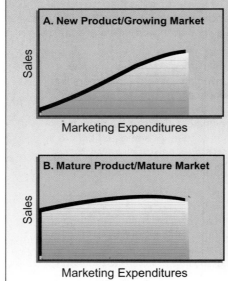

A. New Product/Growing Market

Sales / Marketing Expenditures

Due to product/market newness, marketing expenditures have a large impact on sales. By adding product features, increasing distribution and promotion, and offering special credit terms or special introductory prices, sales will rise dramatically.

B. Mature Product/Mature Market

Sales / Marketing Expenditures

When a product/market is mature, marketing expenditures have a limited impact on sales. With no or little marketing effort, brand-loyal consumers continue to purchase. With extensive marketing effort, a small number of consumers may switch from competitors, buy earlier than intended, or increase consumption.

FIGURE 6
Optimal Marketing Expenditures

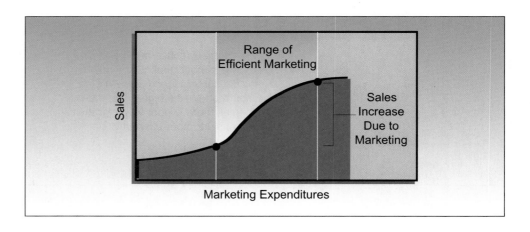

Questions

1. What information can a firm obtain from a profit-and-loss statement (in dollars)?

2. Develop a profit-and-loss statement for The Flying Carpet, a retail store, based on the following:

Beginning inventory (at cost)	$ 750,000
New merchandise (at cost)	800,000
Ending inventory (at cost)	600,000
Gross sales	2,000,000
Returns and allowances	200,000
Marketing expenses	400,000
General expenses	350,000

3. Using the profit-and-loss statement from Question 2, calculate:
   a. Return on investment. (Assume that investment equals $500,000 plus average inventory.)
   b. Stock turnover ratio.
   c. Net profit ratio (percentage).
   d. Operating expense ratio (percentage).
   e. Gross margin ratio (percentage).
   f. Cost-of-goods-sold ratio (percentage).
   g. Sales efficiency ratio (percentage).

4. How would The Flying Carpet Company determine whether its performance ratios are satisfactory?

5. a. What is the impact on return on investment if a firm increases its investment turnover from three times to four times?
   b. List five ways for a firm to increase its investment turnover.

6. A wholesaler estimates that it can sell 10,000 CD changers at $100 each or 6,500 at $115 each. The CD changers cost the wholesaler $60 each.
   a. Calculate the price elasticity between the $100 and $115 price levels.
   b. What factors should determine the price to be set?

7. A full-service car wash has done research on its customers' sensitivity to price. These are the results:

Price	Number of Car Washes Demanded in Market Area per Year
$5.25	80,000
5.75	70,000
6.25	60,000
6.75	25,000
7.25	15,000
7.75	10,000

   a. Calculate price elasticity for all price levels.
   b. At what price is total revenue maximized?
   c. What price should be set? Why?
   d. What other information, not given in this question, is important in setting price?

e. Which expenses for a car wash are fixed? Which expenses are variable?

8. The car wash in Question 7 can accommodate up to 40,000 cars per year with fixed costs of $90,000. Above 40,000 cars, fixed costs rise to $110,000. Variable costs are $2.50 per car wash.
   a. Compute average fixed costs, average variable costs, and average total costs for the car wash at each price.
   b. At what price is profit maximized?
   c. Why might the car wash set a price that does not maximize profit?

9. A tire manufacturer has fixed costs of $1,000,000 and variable costs of $57.00 per tire.
   a. Calculate total costs for volumes of 10,000, 25,000, and 50,000 tires.
   b. Calculate average total, fixed, and variable costs for the same volumes.
   c. At a volume of 25,000 tires, would the firm make a profit or loss with a wholesale selling price of $68.00? What is the total profit or loss?

10. A supermarket retailer sells medium-sized shaving cream containers for $1.49; they are purchased for $0.92. Large-sized containers sell for $2.09; they are purchased for $1.45.
    a. For each size container, determine the markup percentage on selling price and at cost.
    b. Why would the retailer use a different markup percentage for medium containers from that for large containers?
    c. If a shaving cream manufacturer offers the supermarket a 25 percent markup on selling price for medium-sized containers, as well as a cash discount of 2 percent and a quantity discount of 5 percent, what is the purchase price to the supermarket? What is the overall discount? There are no transportation costs.

11. A wholesaler requires a 50 percent markup on selling price for profit projections to be met. The merchandise costs $47.00.
    a. What must the selling price be for the wholesaler to meet its markup goal?
    b. What would be the minimum selling price if the wholesaler has a markup goal of 40 percent on selling price?

12. Convert the following markups from selling price to cost:
    a. 40 percent markup on selling price.
    b. 50 percent markup on selling price.
    c. 70 percent markup on selling price.

13. Convert the following markups from cost to selling price:
    a. 100 percent markup at cost.
    b. 140 percent markup at cost.
    c. 150 percent markup at cost.

14. An auto parts distributor is offered the following discounts: functional markup, 45 percent; quantity discount, 5 percent; cash discount, 2 percent; and seasonal discount, 3 percent. If the suggested final selling price of the total order is $1,000 and shipping charges are $50.00, compute the total order cost to the firm.

15. A glove manufacturer originally sold suede gloves for $49 per pair. An end-of-season sale has reduced the price of these gloves to $32.
    a. Compute the off-original and off-sale markdown percentages.
    b. Why is there a difference in these calculations?

16. a. A firm expects to sell 1,000 advanced PC systems yearly at a price of $1,400 per system (including color monitor, CD-RW drive, hard drive, 1.7 gigobite processor chip, printer, keyboard, and graphics board). At the $1,400 price, the company's markup is 15 percent. How many units would the firm need to sell to earn the same gross profit at a selling price of $1,600 as it would at a selling price of $1,400?
    b. How many units must the firm sell to earn the same gross profit at a selling price of $1,300 as it would at a selling price of $1,400?

17. A manufacturer estimates the following relationship between marketing expenses and sales:

Marketing Expenses	Unit Sales
$100,000	200,000
200,000	250,000
300,000	300,000
400,000	325,000
500,000	370,000

If a product has a gross profit of $4 per unit and general operating expenses are constant at $100,000, at what marketing expenditure level is profit maximized?

18. Calculate the opportunity costs associated with each marketing expenditure level in Question 17.

19. a. Why do most sales response curves have "S" shapes?
    b. Under what conditions would sales response curves have different shapes?
    c. Draw sales response curves based on the information in Table 6.

Appendix C

Computer-Based Marketing Exercises

An accompanying computer program enables you to engage in marketing decision making under simulated conditions and to apply many of the concepts studied during your principles of marketing course. The exercises described in this appendix are designed to reinforce text material; to have you manipulate controllable marketing factors and see their impact on costs, sales, and profits; to have you better understand the impact of uncontrollable factors; and to have you gain experience using a computer to assess marketing opportunities and solve marketing problems. All 18 exercises are designed to be handed in for class assignments or for your own use. They are balanced in terms of subject and level.

Please note: A separate, more-detailed computer exercise, entitled *StratMktPlan*, covers the basic elements of a strategic marketing plan. It is tied to all eight parts in *Marketing*. An overview of this exercise is presented at the end of Chapter 3 ("Developing and Enacting Strategic Marketing Plans"). The *StratMktPlan* software is available on the online Resources page for this book. The Resources page may be accessed by clicking the online Resources link in your Backpack.

HOW TO USE THE COMPUTER-BASED EXERCISE PROGRAM

Program Downloading and Operation Using a Computer with a Hard Drive

This section explains how to install and operate your copy of *Computer-Based Marketing Exercises*; and how to permanently place your name, class, and section on your copy (so that assignments may be submitted with your name printed on them).

To run Computer-Based Marketing Exercises, you must first download the compressed installation program from the online Resources page for this book. The Resources page may be accessed by clicking the online Resources link in your Backpack. Save this program in a folder on your hard drive. It is recommended that you save this program in a folder labeled as TEMP. If you do not have this folder, make one with this title. (Since this program is compressed and then extracted, it cannot be run from a traditional 3-1/2 inch disk.)

Complete the following steps to extract the installation program and install the exercise program on your hard drive.
1. From your Windows Desktop, choose Start and then Run.
2. Click the Browse button and locate the CBME Unzip.exe file that you downloaded from the Atomic Dog online Resources page. Select the file and click the Open button.
3. From the Run dialog, click the OK button.
4. From the WinZip Self-Extractor dialog, click the Unzip button. Close the dialog box when the installation is complete.
5. From your Windows Desktop, choose Start and then Run.
6. Click the Browse button and locate the Setup.exe file that was extracted in Step 4. (The default location for the Setup.exe file is C:\Temp\CBME.) Select the file and click the Open button.
7. From the Run dialog, click the OK button.
8. Follow the screen prompts to install the *Computer-Based Marketing Exercises* program.

You are now ready to run *Computer-Based Marketing Exercises* from your hard drive. If you are still in the Windows environment, open the Marketing Exercise application by choosing Start, Programs, and then Marketing Exercises from your desktop. If you have exited your computer and then return at another time, initialize the Windows environment. Then, simply adhere to the instructions just cited.

The first time you run *Computer-Based Marketing Exercises*, you should enter your name, class, and section to identify your responses. Enter this information by choosing the Reset name button. Once you enter this information, it will appear on each computer screen and printout—and become a permanent part of your exercise program. It will not have to be repeated. The program will do the rest and guide you to the main menu.

The Main Menu

When running *Computer-Based Marketing Exercises*, all exercises can be accessed from the MAIN MENU. Use the mouse to select an exercise. You can also choose an exercise by repeatedly hitting the tab key until the desired exercise is highlighted and then pressing the Enter key. Selecting Exit will enable you to quit the program.

The menu is arranged in the order the topics appear in the text; see the following table.

MAIN MENU

How to Operate Each Exercise

At the bottom of each exercise screen, there are a number of commands. They include the Exit button [E] to quit the program, the Menu button [M] to return to the main menu, the Next button [N] to proceed to the following screen, the Back button [B] to return to the prior screen, the Objectives button [O] to go to the Objectives section, the Questions button [Q] to go to the first page of the questions, the Print Screen button [P], and the Analysis button [A]. All commands can be executed by either clicking your mouse (or trackball) or by holding down the [Alt] key and then pressing the respective letter key.

How to Print from the Exercise Program

While using the exercise program, you may print any screen for your own reference or for the submission of a class assignment. Simply turn on the printer connected to the computer you are using. Then, click the Print Screen button located at the bottom of each exercise screen (or hold down the [Alt] key and then press the [P] key). The screen appearing on your computer monitor will automatically be printed—including your name, class, and section.

THE EXERCISES

In the following sections, the basic premise of each exercise is described.

Exercise 1: Marketing Orientation

As the owner of a local florist, a table allows you to enter your degree of agreement to 10 questions (on a five-point scale ranging from strongly agree to strongly disagree). Questions relate to such areas as the importance of various markets, planning for seasonality, the impact of the Web, forecasting sales and profits, assessing customer needs, understanding competitors' strategies, and selling flowers with a limited shelf life. The exercise is keyed to "The Marketing Concept" in Chapter 1, pages 10–12 in the printed text.

Exercise 2: Boston Consulting Group Matrix

As a marketing executive for Packard Athletic Shoe Company, a table allows you to enter revised values for the relative market shares and industry growth rates for any or all of Packard's product categories (SBUs). The products are then displayed in a Boston Consulting Group matrix. The exercise is keyed to "The Boston Consulting Group Matrix" in Chapter 3, pages 65–66 in the printed text.

Exercise 3: Questionnaire Analysis

In this exercise, you are a market researcher who is requested to collect data for a consumer survey on boom boxes (portable self-contained stereos with multiple speakers). The exercise screens explain how blank copies of the survey may be printed, as well as how the survey may be administered at the computer. The exercise is keyed to "Data Analysis" in Chapter 4, page 107 in the printed text.

Exercise 4: Ethics in Action

As a marketing executive for an industrial-goods manufacturer, a table allows you to enter your degree of agreement to 10 questions (on a five-point scale ranging from strongly agree to strongly disagree). These questions present a variety of ethical situations relating to salespersons, marketing managers, buyers, retailers, and importers. The exercise is keyed to "Ethics" in Chapter 5, pages 134–136 in the printed text.

Exercise 5: Standardizing Marketing Plans

By answering a series of questions, you—as an international marketing consultant—are able to make decisions regarding the level of standardization for five factors: a product's brand name, its design, its manufacturing process, its advertising, and its pricing. You can vary each factor from pure standardized (global) to glocal to nonstandardized. This exercise is keyed to "Standardizing Plans" in Chapter 6, pages 172–173 in the printed text.

Exercise 6: Vendor Analysis

As the purchasing director for a firm, you are to assign weights to eight important vendor attributes: delivery speed, delivery reliability, product quality, quality of final customer support, quality of intermediate customer support, purchase terms, pricing, and availability of styles and colors in all sizes. The exercise is keyed to "Differences from Final Consumers Due to Nature of Purchases" in Chapter 9, pages 260–261 in the printed text.

Exercise 7: Segmentation Analysis

A table allows you, the vice-president of marketing for a medium-sized local company, to allocate a $3-million annual marketing budget between final and organizational market segments. By varying the budget, unit sales, sales revenues, manufacturing costs, total costs, and profit are affected. Different levels of marketing expenditures are required to be successful in each market segment. The exercise is keyed to "Targeting the Market" in Chapter 10, page 296 in the printed text.

Exercise 8: Product Positioning

A product positioning map lets you—acting as an outside consultant—evaluate Hewlett Packard's (HP's) personal computer positioning relative to other major brands (Dell, Compaq, Gateway, IBM, and NEC). By rating HP's updated image on the basis of a series of statements, a revised product-positioning map for HP and five other brands is generated and displayed. In addition, the computer program calculates revised market shares for HP and the other brands, leading to an adjusted market-share table. The exercise is keyed to "Product Positioning" in Chapter 11, pages 333–337 in the printed text.

Exercise 9: Services Strategy

By making a number of marketing decisions, you—as a manager of a hotel chain—are able to develop an overall services strategy. You are seeking to increase your hotel's occupancy rate and profits by offering free breakfasts, exercise facilities, and the use of a print shop. Each of these strategies can be offered at four different levels; cost data are provided for each level. By varying the level of each strategy, total revenues, costs, operating profit, and the hotel's occupancy rate are affected. You can revise your overall strategy by re-entering a new strategy. This exercise is keyed to "Special Considerations in Marketing of Services" in Chapter 12, pages 364–369 in the printed text.

Exercise 10: Product Screening Checklist

A new-product screening checklist lets you—acting as an outside consultant who specializes in new-product concepts—weight the importance of various general, marketing, and production characteristics; and then rate a new product idea in terms of each of these characteristics. The computer program then computes separate indexes for general, marketing, and production factors—as well as an overall evaluation index. The exercise is keyed to "Product Screening" in Chapter 13, pages 396–397 in the printed text.

Exercise 11: Economic Order Quantity

As the purchasing manager for a firm, you can determine its economic order quantity under various assumptions by answering questions about expected annual demand for a product, its unit cost at wholesale, order-processing costs, and inventory-holding costs (as a percentage of a unit's wholesale cost). The computer program uses the EOQ formula, and a screen graphically displays the results. The exercise is keyed to "How Much to Reorder" in Chapter 14, pages 451–452 in the printed text.

Exercise 12: Wholesaler Cost Analysis

As a consultant for a manufacturer, you have been retained to review that firm's selection of manufacturer wholesaling versus merchant wholesaling. The total costs of each wholesaling alternative differ on the basis of sales. The exercise is keyed to "Manufacturer/Service Provider Wholesaling" in Chapter 15, page 464 in the printed text.

Exercise 13: Advertising Budget

As advertising director for Sunshine Cruise Lines, a leading cruise ship operator, one of your tasks is to allocate the firm's ad budget among various magazines via a computerized-spreadsheet table. The exercise is keyed to "Establishing a Budget" in Chapter 18, page 540 in the printed text.

Exercise 14: Salesperson Deployment

As a regional sales manager, one of your more important responsibilities is to determine the required number of salespeople in your territory. Your firm has four types of industrial accounts ("A", "B", "C", and "D"). "A" accounts are key customers, "B" accounts have high potential but only moderate sales, "C" accounts are smaller firms with lower sales potential, and "D" are the smallest accounts. The exercise is keyed to "Establishing a Budget" in Chapter 19, pages 567–568 in the printed text.

Exercise 15: Price Elasticity

As the owner-operator of an auto repair firm specializing in quick oil changes, you are concerned about what price to charge for an oil change. First, you answer a series of questions about the price range to be considered and the expected average amount of consumer demand (which may be expressed in fractions) at various prices. The computer program then calculates elasticity of demand for the various price intervals and graphically displays it. The exercise is keyed to "Consumers" in Chapter 20, pages 600–602 in the printed text.

Exercise 16: Key Cost Concepts

As a pricing consultant for Ultimate Audiovision, you answer questions about the fixed and variable costs of making the home-entertainment system at various production levels. Ultimate Audiovision contains a state-of-the-art 55-inch rear projection TV, a hi-fi stereo VCR, a DVD player, a 500-watt digital receiver, and a six-speaker home theater stereo package. The exercise is keyed to "Cost-Based Pricing" in Chapter 21, page 621 in the printed text.

Exercise 17: Performance Ratios

As a General Toy Company executive vice-president, you are quite interested in using performance ratios to measure your company's relative success or failure across several criteria. The pre-set data in this exercise (those programmed into the exercise) are drawn from Appendix B in the text. By entering new data onto a profit-and-loss screen, you can see the impact of changes in General Toy's sales efficiency, cost of goods sold, gross margin, operating expenses, net profit, stock turnover, and return on investment on the company's related performance ratios. For example, what would happen to ROI if General Toy's assets rise by 5 percent? The exercise is keyed to "Performance Ratios" in Appendix B, pages A-9–A-10 in the printed text.

Exercise 18: Optimal Marketing Mix

A table allows you—the marketing director for a small industrial manufacturer—to make decisions regarding your firm's $3 million annual marketing budget. You have the ability to make decisions regarding the expenditures for advertising, personal selling, and distribution and to set the price for your product for each of three strategy alternatives: mass marketing, selective marketing, and exclusive marketing. Thus, you are involved with two distinct areas of decision making: (1) For each strategy alternative (mass marketing, selective marketing, and exclusive marketing), what is the best marketing mix? (2) Which strategy alternative should your firm pursue? Once you enter decisions, the computer program automatically calculates and displays unit sales, revenues, total product costs, total costs, and profit. The results will differ substantially for the three alternative strategies. The exercise is keyed to "Determining an Optimal Marketing Mix" in Appendix B, pages A-16–A-18 in the printed text.

Appendix D

Glossary

A

Absolute Product Failure Occurs if a firm is unable to regain its production and marketing costs. The firm incurs a financial loss.

Accelerator Principle States that final consumer demand affects many layers of organizational consumers.

Adaptation A firm's responses to the surrounding environment, while continuing to capitalize on differential advantages, including looking for new opportunities and responding to threats.

Adoption Process The mental and behavioral procedure an individual consumer goes through when learning about and purchasing a new product. It consists of five stages: knowledge, persuasion, decision, implementation, and confirmation.

Advertising Paid, nonpersonal communication regarding goods, services, organizations, people, places, and ideas that is transmitted through various media by business firms, government and other nonprofit organizations, and individuals who are identified in the advertising message as sponsors.

Advertising Agency An organization that provides a variety of advertising-related services to client firms. It often works with clients in devising their advertising plans—including themes, media choice, copywriting, and other tasks.

Advertising Media Costs Outlays for media time or space. They are related to ad length or size, as well as media attributes.

Advertising Themes The overall appeals for a campaign. Themes can be good or service, consumer, or institutional.

Agents Wholesalers that do not take title to products. They work for commissions or fees as payment for their services and are comprised of manufacturers'/service providers' agents, selling agents, and commission (factor) merchants.

All-You-Can-Afford Method A promotional budget method in which a firm first allots funds for every element of marketing except promotion; remaining marketing funds go to the promotion budget.

Approaching Customers The stage in the selling process that consists of the pre-approach and greeting.

Atmosphere (Atmospherics) The sum total of the physical attributes of a retailer, whether in a store or a nonstore format, that are used to develop an image and draw customers.

Attitudes (Opinions) An individual's positive, neutral, or negative feelings about goods, services, firms, people, issues, and/or institutions.

Audience The object of a source's message in a channel of communication.

B

Backward Invention An international product-planning strategy in which a firm appeals to developing and less-developed nations by making products less complex than those sold in its domestic market.

Bait-and-Switch Advertising An illegal practice whereby customers are lured to a seller that advertises items at very low prices and then told the items are out of stock or of poor quality. There is no intent to sell advertised items.

Balanced Product Portfolio A strategy by which a firm maintains a combination of new, growing, and mature products.

Barter Era Earliest use of the exchange process. With barter, people trade one resource for another.

Battle of the Brands Manufacturer, private, and generic brands each striving to gain a greater share of the consumer's dollar, control over marketing strategy, consumer loyalty, product distinctiveness, maximum shelf space and locations, and a large share of profits.

Benchmarking A procedure used by a firm to set its marketing performance standards based on prior actions by the firm itself, the prowess of direct competitors, the competence of the best companies in its industry, and/or the approaches of innovative companies in other industries anywhere around the world.

Benefit Segmentation A procedure for grouping consumers into segments on the basis of the different benefits sought from a product.

Blanket Branding See *Family Branding*.

Boston Consulting Group Matrix Lets a firm classify each strategic business unit (SBU) in terms of market share relative to major competitors and annual industry growth. The matrix identifies four types of SBUs: star, cash cow, question mark, and dog, and offers strategies for them.

Brand A name, term, design, symbol, or any other feature that identifies the goods and services of one seller from those of other sellers.

Brand Equity A branding concept that recognizes the worth of brands. It reflects the amount of additional income expected from a branded product over and above what might be expected from an identical, but unbranded product.

Brand Extension A strategy by which an established brand name is applied to new products.

Brand Loyalty The consistent repurchase of and preference toward a particular brand. With it, people can reduce time, thought, and risk.

Brand Manager System See *Product Manager System*.

Brand Mark A symbol, design, or distinctive coloring or lettering that cannot be spoken.

Brand Name A word, letter (number), group of words, or letters (numbers) that can be spoken.

Bricks-and-Clicks Firms Companies that operate in both a traditional setting and on the Internet.

Bricks-and-Mortar Firms Traditional companies that have not gotten involved with the Internet.

Broad Price Policy Sets the overall direction (and tone) for a firm's pricing efforts and makes sure pricing decisions are coordinated with the choices as to a target market, an image, and other marketing-mix factors. It incorporates short- and long-term pricing goals, and the role of pricing.

Brokers Temporary wholesalers, paid by a commission or fee, who introduce buyers and sellers and help complete transactions.

Bundled Pricing An offering of a basic product, options, and customer service for one total price.

Business Analysis The stage in the new-product planning process which involves the detailed review, projection, and evaluation of such factors as consumer demand, production costs, marketing costs, break-even points, competition, capital investments, and profitability for each new proposed product.

Buyer-Seller Dyad A two-way flow of communication between buyer and seller.

C

Canned Sales Presentation   A memorized, repetitive presentation given to all customers interested in a given item. It does not adapt to customer needs or traits but presumes a general presentation will appeal to everyone.

Cash-and-Carry Wholesaling   A limited-service merchant wholesaler format in which people from small businesses drive to wholesalers, order products, and take them back to a store or business. No credit, delivery, merchandise, and promotional assistance are provided.

Category Killer   An especially large specialty store that features an enormous selection in its product category and relatively low prices.

Cause-Related Marketing   A somewhat controversial practice in which profit-oriented firms contribute specific amounts to given nonprofit organizations for each consumer purchase of certain goods and services during a special promotion.

Cease-and-Desist Order   A consumer-protection legal concept which requires a firm to discontinue a promotion practice that is deemed deceptive and modify a message accordingly.

Chain-Markup Pricing   A form of demand-based pricing in which final selling price is determined, markups for each channel member are examined, and maximum acceptable costs to each member are computed. It extends demand-minus calculations from resellers back to suppliers (manufacturers).

Chain-Ratio Method   A method of sales forecasting in which a firm starts with general market data and then computes a series of more specific information. These combined data yield a sales forecast.

Channel Functions   The functions completed by some member of a channel: marketing research, buying, promotion, customer services, product planning, pricing, and distribution.

Channel Members   Those organizations or people participating in the distribution process. They may be manufacturers, service providers, wholesalers, retailers, and/or consumers.

Channel of Communication (Communication Process)   The mechanism by which a source develops a message, transmits it to an audience via some medium, and gets feedback from the audience.

Channel of Distribution   Composed of all the organizations or people in the distribution process.

Class-Action Suit   A legal action on behalf of many affected consumers.

Class Consciousness   The extent to which a person seeks social status.

Clicks-Only Firms   Companies that do business just online. They do not have traditional facilities.

Clients   The constituency for which a nonprofit organization offers membership, elected officials, locations, ideas, goods, and services.

Closing the Sale   The stage in the selling process that means getting a person to agree to a purchase. The salesperson must be sure no major questions remain before trying to close a sale.

Clustered Demand   A demand pattern in which consumer needs and desires for a good or service category can be classified into two or more clusters (segments), each with distinct purchase criteria.

Clutter   Involves the number of ads found in a single program, issue, and so forth of a medium.

Co-Branding   A strategy in which two or more brand names are used with the same product to gain from the brand images of each.

Cognitive Dissonance   Doubt that a correct purchase decision has been made. To overcome dissonance, a firm must realize that the consumer decision process does not end with a purchase.

Combination Pricing   A pricing approach whereby aspects of cost-, demand-, and competition-based pricing methods are integrated.

Combination Sales Compensation Plan   A format that uses elements of both salary and commission methods. Such plans balance company control, flexibility, and employee incentives.

Combination Store   Unites food/grocery and general merchandise sales in one facility, with general merchandise providing 25 to 40 percent or more of sales.

Commercial Data Bases   Contain information on population traits, the business environment, economic forecasts, industry and companies' performance, and other items.

Commercialization   The final stage in the new-product planning process in which the firm introduces a product to its full target market. This corresponds to the introductory stage of the product life cycle.

Commercial Stock Brokers   Licensed sales representatives who advise business clients, take orders, and then acquire stocks and/or bonds for the clients. They may aid the firms selling the stocks or bonds, represent either buyers or sellers, and offer some credit.

Commission (Factor) Merchants   Agents that receive goods on consignment, accumulate them from local markets, and arrange for their sale in a central location.

Common Carriers   Companies that must transport the goods of any company (or individual) interested in their services; they cannot refuse any shipments unless their rules are broken. They provide service on a fixed and publicized schedule between designated points. A fee schedule is published.

Communication Process   See *Channel of Communication*.

Company-Controlled Price Environment   Characterized by moderate competition, well-differentiated goods and services, and strong control over prices by individual firms.

Comparative Advantage   A concept in international marketing which states that each country has distinct strengths and weaknesses based on its natural resources, climate, technology, labor costs, and other factors. Nations can benefit by exporting the goods and services with which they have relative advantages and importing the ones with which they have relative disadvantages.

Comparative Messages   Implicitly or explicitly contrast a firm's offerings with those of competitors.

Competition-Based Pricing   A pricing strategy approach whereby a firm uses competitors' prices rather than demand or cost considerations as its primary pricing guideposts. A firm can set prices below the market, at the market, or above the market.

Competitive Bidding   A situation in which two or more sellers submit independent price quotes for specific goods and/or services to a buyer, which chooses the best offer.

Competitive Parity Method   A method by which a firm's promotion budget is raised or lowered according to competitors' actions.

Concentrated Marketing   Exists when a company targets one well-defined market segment with one tailored marketing strategy.

Concept Testing   The stage in the new-product planning process that presents the consumer with a proposed product and measures attitudes and intentions at an early stage of the process.

Conclusive Research The structured collection and analysis of data about a specific issue or problem.

Conflict Resolution A procedure in organizational buying for resolving disagreements in joint decision making. The methods of resolution are problem solving, persuasion, bargaining, and politicking.

Consumer Bill of Rights A statement by President Kennedy saying that all consumers have four basic rights: to information, to safety, to choice in product selection, and to be heard.

Consumer Demand Refers to the attributes and needs of final consumers, industrial consumers, wholesalers and retailers, government institutions, international markets, and nonprofit institutions.

Consumer Demographics Objective and quantifiable population characteristics. They are rather easy to identify, collect, measure, and analyze—and show diversity around the globe.

Consumerism Encompasses the wide range of activities of government, business, and independent organizations designed to protect people from practices that infringe upon their rights as consumers.

Consumer Products Goods and services destined for the final consumer for personal, family, or household use.

Consumer's Brand Decision Process Consists of nonrecognition, recognition, preference (or dislike), and insistence (or aversion) stages that consumers pass through.

Containerization A coordinated transportation practice in which goods are placed in sturdy containers that can be loaded on trains, trucks, ships, or planes. The containers are mobile warehouses.

Continuous Monitoring Used to regularly study a firm's external and internal environment.

Contract Carriers Provide transportation services to shippers, based on individual agreements. Contract carriers do not have to maintain set routes or schedules and may negotiate rates.

Control Units The sales categories for which data are gathered, such as boys', men's, girls', and women's clothing.

Controllable Factors Decision elements internally directed by an organization and its marketers. Some of these factors are directed by top management; others are directed by marketers.

Convenience Store A retail store that is usually well situated and food-oriented, with long hours and a limited number of items. Consumers use a convenience store for fill-in merchandise, often at off-hours.

Conventional Supermarket A departmentalized food store with minimum annual sales of $2 million that emphasizes a wide range of food and related products.

Cooperative Advertising Allows two or more firms to share some advertising costs. It can be vertical or horizontal.

Core Services The basic services that firms provide to their customers to be competitive.

Corporate Culture The shared values, norms, and practices communicated to and followed by those working for a firm.

Corporate Symbols A firm's name (and/or divisional names), logos, and trade characters. They are significant parts of an overall company image.

Corrective Advertising A consumer-protection legal concept which requires a firm to run new ads to correct the false impressions left by previous ones.

Cost-Based Pricing A pricing strategy approach whereby a firm sets prices by computing merchandise, service, and overhead costs and then adding an amount to cover its profit goal.

Cost of Living The total amount consumers annually pay for goods and services.

Cost-Plus Pricing A form of cost-based pricing in which prices are set by adding a pre-determined profit to costs. It is the simplest form of cost-based pricing.

Culture Consists of a group of people sharing a distinctive heritage.

Customary Pricing Occurs when a firm sets prices and seeks to maintain them for an extended time.

Customer Satisfaction The degree to which there is a match between a customer's expectations of a good or service and the actual performance of that good or service, including customer service.

Customer Service Involves the identifiable, but rather intangible, activities undertaken by a seller in conjunction with the basic goods and/or services it offers.

D

Data Analysis The coding, tabulation, and analysis of marketing research data.

Data-Base Marketing A computerized technique that compiles, sorts, and stores relevant information about customers and potential customers; uses that information to highlight opportunities and prioritize market segments; and enables the firm to profitably tailor marketing efforts for specific customers or customer groups

Data Mining An in-depth, computerized search of available information to find profitable marketing opportunities that may otherwise be hidden.

Data Warehousing Involves retaining all types of relevant company records (sales, costs, personnel performance, etc.), and information collected by continuous monitoring and marketing research.

Decline Stage of the Product Life Cycle The period during which industry sales decline and many firms exit the market since customers are fewer and as a group they have less money to spend.

Decoding The process in a channel of communication by which a message sent by a source is interpreted by an audience.

Dealer Brands See *Private Brands*.

Demand-Backward Pricing See *Demand-Minus Pricing*.

Demand-Based Pricing A pricing strategy approach whereby a firm sets prices after studying consumer desires and ascertaining the range of prices acceptable to the target market.

Demand-Minus (Demand-Backward) Pricing A form of demand-based pricing whereby a firm finds the proper selling price and works backward to compute costs.

Demand Patterns Indicate the uniformity or diversity of consumer needs and desires for particular categories of goods and services.

Derived Demand Occurs for organizational consumers because the quantity of the items they buy is often based on anticipated demand by their subsequent customers for specific goods and services.

Desk Jobbers See *Drop Shippers*.

Developing Countries Have a rising education level and technology, but a per-capita Gross Domestic Product of about $3,000 to $8,000.

Differential Advantages The unique features in a firm's marketing program that cause consumers to patronize that firm and not its competitors.

Differentiated Marketing (Multiple Segmentation)   Exists when a company targets two or more well-defined market segments with a marketing strategy tailored to each segment.

Diffused Demand   A demand pattern in which consumer needs and desires for a good or service category are so diverse that clear clusters (segments) cannot be identified.

Diffusion Process   Describes the manner in which different members of the target market often accept and purchase a product. It spans the time from product introduction through market saturation.

Diminishing Returns   May occur in a firm with high sales penetration if the firm seeks to convert remaining nonconsumers because the costs of attracting them may outweigh revenues.

Direct Channel of Distribution   Involves the movement of goods and services from producer to consumers without the use of independent intermediaries.

Direct Marketing   Occurs when a consumer is first exposed to a good or service by a nonpersonal medium (direct mail, TV, radio, magazine, newspaper, PC, etc.) and orders by mail, phone, or PC.

Direct Ownership   A form of international marketing company organization in which a firm owns production, marketing, and other facilities in one or more foreign nations without any partners. The firm has full control over its international operations in those nations.

Direct Selling   A nonstore retail operation which involves both personal contact with consumers in their homes (and other nonstore locations) and phone solicitations initiated by the retailer.

Discretionary Income   What a person, household, or family has available to spend on luxuries after necessities are purchased.

Disposable Income   A person's, household's, or family's total after-tax income to be used for spending and/or savings.

Distributed Promotion   Communication efforts spread throughout the year.

Distribution Intermediaries   Wholesalers, retailers, and marketing specialists (such as transportation firms) that are facilitators (links) between manufacturers/service providers and consumers.

Distribution Planning   Systematic decision making about the physical movement of goods and services from producer to consumer, and the related transfer of ownership (or rental) of them. It encompasses such diverse functions as transportation, inventory management, and customer transactions.

Domestic Firm   Restricts its efforts to the home market.

Domestic Marketing   Encompasses a firm's efforts in its home country.

Donors   The constituency from which a nonprofit organization receives resources.

Drop Shippers (Desk Jobbers)   Limited-service merchant wholesalers that buy goods from manufacturers or suppliers and arrange for their shipment to retailers or industrial users. They have legal ownership, but do not take physical possession of products and have no storage facilities.

Dual Channel of Distribution (Multichannel Distribution)   A strategy whereby a firm appeals to different market segments or diversifies business by selling through two or more separate channels.

Dumping   Selling a product in a foreign country at a price much lower than that prevailing in the exporter's home market, below the cost of production, or both.

Durable Goods   Physical products that are used over an extended period of time.

E

E-commerce   Revenue-generating Internet transactions.

Economic Community   Promotes free trade among its member nations—but not necessarily with nonmember nations.

Economic Order Quantity (EOQ)   The order volume corresponding to the lowest sum of order-processing and inventory-holding costs.

EDI   See *Electronic Data Interchange*.

80-20 Principle   States that in many organizations, a large proportion of total sales (profit) is likely to come from a small proportion of customers, products, or territories.

Elastic Demand   Occurs if relatively small price changes result in large changes in quantity demanded.

Electronic Data Interchange (EDI)   Allows suppliers and their manufacturers/service providers, wholesalers, and/or retailers to exchange data via computer linkups.

E-marketing   Any marketing activity that is conducted through the Internet, from customer analysis to marketing-mix components.

Embargo   A form of trade restriction which disallows entry of specified products into a country.

Empowering Employees   When companies give their workers broad leeway to satisfy customer requests. Employees are encouraged and rewarded for showing initiative and imagination.

Encoding   The process in a channel of communication whereby a thought or idea is translated into a message by the source.

End-Use Analysis   The process by which a seller determines the proportion of its sales made to organizational consumers in different industries.

EOQ   See *Economic Order Quantity*.

Ethical Behavior   Based on honest and proper conduct.

Ethnicity/Race   Should be studied from a demographics perspective to determine the existence of diversity among and within nations in terms of language and country of origin or race.

European Union (EU)   Also known as the Common Market. Rules call for no trade restrictions among members; uniform tariffs with nonmembers; common product standards; and a free flow of people and capital.

Evaluation of Alternatives   The stage in the final consumer's decision process in which criteria for a decision are set and alternatives ranked.

Exchange   The process by which consumers and publics give money, a promise to pay, or support for the offering of a firm, institution, person, place, or idea.

Exclusive Distribution   A policy in which a firm severely limits the number of resellers utilized in a geographic area, perhaps having only one or two within a specific shopping district.

Exempt Carriers   Transporters that are excused from legal regulations and must only comply with safety rules. Exempt carriers are specified by law.

Experiment   A type of research in which one or more factors are manipulated under controlled conditions. Experiments are able to show cause and effect.

Exploratory Research   Used when a researcher is uncertain about the precise topic to be investigated, or wants to informally study an issue.

Exporting   A form of international marketing company organization in which a firm reaches international markets by selling products made in its home country directly through its own sales force or indirectly via foreign merchants or agents. An exporting structure requires minimal investment in foreign facilities.

Exporting Firm   One that is just embarking on sales expansion beyond its home borders.

Extended Consumer Decision Making   Occurs when a person fully uses the decision process. Much effort is spent on information search and evaluation of alternatives for expensive, complex items with which a person has little or no experience.

F

Factor Merchants   See *Commission Merchants*.

Family   Two or more persons residing together who are related by blood, marriage, or adoption.

Family (Blanket) Branding   A strategy in which one name is used for two or more individual products. It can be applied to both manufacturer and private brands, and to both domestic and international (global) brands.

Family Life Cycle   Describes how a family evolves through various stages from bachelorhood to solitary retirement. At each stage, needs, experience, income, family composition, and the use of joint decision making change.

Feedback (Channel of Communication)   The response an audience has to a message.

Feedback (Uncontrollable Environment)   Information about the uncontrollable environment, the organization's performance, and how well the marketing plan is received.

Final Consumers   Buy goods and services for personal, family, or household use.

Final Consumer's Decision Process   The way in which people gather and assess information and choose among alternative goods, services, organizations, people, places, and ideas. It has six stages: stimulus, problem awareness, information search, evaluation of alternatives, purchase, and post-purchase behavior. Demographic, social, and psychological factors affect this process.

Flexible Pricing   Allows a firm to set prices based on the consumer's ability to negotiate or on the buying power of a large customer.

Food-Based Superstore   A diversified supermarket that sells a broad range of food and nonfood items.

Food Brokers   Introduce buyers and sellers of food and related general-merchandise items to one another and bring them together to complete a sale.

Forward Invention   An international product-planning strategy in which a company develops new products for its international markets.

Franchise Wholesaling   A full-service merchant wholesaler format whereby independent retailers affiliate with an existing wholesaler to use a standardized storefront design, business format, name, and purchase system.

Freight Forwarding   A transportation service in which specialized firms (freight forwarders) collect small shipments (usually less than 500 pounds each) from several companies. They pick up merchandise at each shipper's place of business and arrange for delivery at buyers' doors.

Frequency   How often a medium can be used.

Full Disclosure   A consumer-protection legal concept which requires that all data necessary for a consumer to make a safe and informed decision be provided in a promotion message.

Full-Line Discount Store   A department store with lower prices, a broad product assortment, a lower-rent location, more emphasis on self-service, brand-name merchandise, wide aisles, shopping carts, and more goods displayed on the selling floor.

Full-Line Wholesalers   See *General-Merchandise Wholesalers*.

Full-Service Merchant Wholesalers   Perform a full range of distribution tasks. They provide trade credit, store and deliver products, offer merchandising and promotion assistance, have a personal sales force, offer research and planning support, pass along information to suppliers and customers, and give installation and repair services.

Functional Accounts   Occur when natural account expenses are reclassified by function to indicate the purposes or activities for which expenditures have been made. Included as functional expenses are marketing administration, personal selling, advertising, transportation, warehousing, marketing research, and general administration.

G

GDP   See *Gross Domestic Product*.

General Electric Business Screen   Categorizes strategic business units and products in terms of industry attractiveness and company business strengths.

General-Merchandise (Full-Line) Wholesalers   Full-service merchant wholesalers that carry a wide product assortment—nearly all the items needed by their customers.

Generic Brands   Emphasize names of the products themselves and not manufacturer or reseller names.

Geographic Demographics   Basic identifiable characteristics of towns, cities, states, regions, and countries.

Geographic Pricing   Outlines responsibility for transportation charges. The most common methods of geographic pricing are FOB (free on board) mill pricing, uniform delivered pricing, zone pricing, and base-point pricing.

Global Firm   One in which, because domestic sales are low, there is reliance on foreign transactions.

Global Marketing   An advanced form of international marketing in which a firm addresses global customers, markets, and competition.

Global Marketing Approach   See *Standardized Marketing Approach*.

Glocal Marketing Approach   An international marketing strategy in which combining standardized and nonstandardized efforts lets a firm attain production efficiencies, have a consistent image, have some home-office control, and still be sensitive and responsive to local needs.

Goods Marketing   Entails the sale of physical products.

Goods/Services Continuum   Categorizes products along a scale from pure goods to pure services.

Government   Consumes goods and services in performing its duties and responsibilities. There are 1 federal, 50 state, and 88,000 local governmental units.

Government-Controlled Price Environment   Characterized by prices being set or strongly influenced by some level of government.

Gray Market Goods   Foreign-made products imported into countries such as the United States by distributors (suppliers) that are not authorized by the products' manufacturers.

Green Marketing A form of socioecological marketing whereby the goods and services sold, and the marketing practices involved in their sale, take into account environmental ramifications for society.

Gross Domestic Product (GDP) The total annual value of goods and services produced in a country less net foreign investment.

Growth Stage of the Product Life Cycle The period during which industry sales increase rapidly as a few more firms enter a highly profitable market that has substantial potential.

H

Heavy Half See *Heavy-Usage Segment*.

Heavy-Usage Segment (Heavy Half) A consumer group that accounts for a large proportion of a good's or service's sales relative to the size of the market.

Hidden Service Sector Encompasses the delivery, installation, maintenance, training, repair, and other services provided by firms that emphasize goods sales.

Hierarchy-of-Effects Model Outlines the sequential short-term, intermediate, and long-term promotion goals for a firm to pursue—and works in conjunction with the consumer's decision process.

Homogeneous Demand A demand pattern in which consumers have rather uniform needs and desires for a good or service category.

Horizontal Audit Studies the overall marketing performance of a firm with particular emphasis on the interrelationship of variables and their relative importance. It is also called a marketing-mix audit.

Horizontal Price Fixing Results from agreements among manufacturers, among wholesalers, or among retailers to set prices at a given stage in a channel of distribution. Such agreements are illegal according to the federal Sherman Antitrust Act and the Federal Trade Commission Act, regardless of how "reasonable" prices are.

Household A person or group of persons, whether related or unrelated, occupying a housing unit.

Household Life Cycle Incorporates the life stages of both family and nonfamily households.

Hypermarket The European term for a *Supercenter*.

I

Iceberg Principle States that superficial data are insufficient to make sound marketing evaluations.

Idea Generation The stage in the new-product planning process which involves the continuous, systematic search for product opportunities. It involves new-idea sources and ways to generate ideas.

Ideal Points The combinations of attributes that people would most like products to have.

IMC See *Integrated Marketing Communications*.

Importance of a Purchase Related to the degree of decision making, level of perceived risk, and amount of money to be spent/invested. The level of importance of a purchase affects the time and effort a person spends shopping for a product—and the money allotted.

Incremental Method A promotional budget method in which a firm bases a new budget on the previous one. A percentage is added to or subtracted from this year's budget to determine next year's.

Independent Media Communication vehicles not controlled by a firm; yet, they influence government, consumer, and publics' perceptions of that firm's products and overall image.

Independent Retailer Operates only one outlet and offers personal service, a convenient location, and close customer contact.

Indirect Channel of Distribution Involves the movement of goods and services from producer to independent intermediaries to consumers.

Individual (Multiple) Branding Separate brands used for different items or product lines sold by a firm.

Industrialization of Services Improves service efficiency and variability by using hard, soft, and hybrid technologies.

Industrialized Countries Have high literacy, modern technology, and per-capita income of several thousand dollars.

Industrial Marketing Occurs when firms deal with organizational consumers.

Industrial Products Goods and services purchased for use in the production of other goods or services, in the operation of a business, or for resale to other consumers.

Inelastic Demand Takes place if price changes have little impact on the quantity demanded.

Information Search The stage in the final consumer's decision process that requires listing the alternatives that will solve the problem at hand and determining the characteristics of them. Information search may be either internal or external.

Innovativeness The willingness to try a new good or service that others perceive as risky.

Inseparability of Services Means a service provider and his or her services may be inseparable. Customer contact is often considered an integral part of the service experience.

Institutional Advertising Used when the advertising goal is to enhance company image—and not to sell specific goods or services.

Intangibility of Services Means that services often cannot be displayed, transported, stored, packaged, or inspected before buying.

Integrated Marketing Communications (IMC) Recognizes the value of a comprehensive plan that evaluates the strategic roles of a variety of communication disciplines—advertising, public relations, personal selling, and sales promotion—and combines them to provide clarity, consistency, and maximum communication impact.

Intensive Distribution A policy in which a firm uses a large number of resellers in order to have wide market coverage, channel acceptance, and high total sales and profits.

International Firm Goes beyond just exporting existing products by making modifications in those items for foreign markets or introducing new products there.

International Marketing Involves marketing goods and services outside a firm's home country, whether in one or several markets.

Internet A global electronic superhighway of computer networks—a network of networks in which users at one computer can get information from another computer (and sometimes talk directly to users at other computers).

Introduction Stage of the Product Life Cycle   The period during which only one or two firms have entered the market, and competition is limited. Initial customers are innovators.

Inventory Management   Involved with providing a continuous flow of goods and matching the quantity of goods kept in inventory as closely as possible with customer demand.

Isolated Store   A freestanding retail outlet located on a highway or street.

Issue (Problem) Definition   A statement of the topic to be looked into via marketing research. It directs the research process to collect and analyze appropriate data for the purpose of decision making.

Item Price Removal   A practice whereby prices are marked only on store shelves or aisle signs and not on individual items.

J

JIT Inventory System   See *Just-in-Time Inventory System*.

Joint Decision Making   The process whereby two or more people have input into purchases.

Joint Venture (Strategic Alliance)   A form of international marketing company organization in which a firm agrees to combine some aspect of its manufacturing or marketing efforts with those of a foreign company so as to share expertise, costs, and/or connections with important persons.

Jury of Executive (Expert) Opinion   A method of sales forecasting by which the management of a firm or other well-informed persons meet, discuss the future, and set sales estimates based on the group's experience and interaction.

Just-in-Time (JIT) Inventory System   A procedure by which a purchasing firm reduces the amount of inventory it keeps on hand by ordering more often and in lower quantity.

L

Law of Demand   States that consumers usually purchase more units at a low price than at a high price.

Leader Pricing   A firm's advertising and selling key items in its product assortment at less than their usual profit margins. For a wholesaler or retailer, the goal is to increase customer traffic. For a manufacturer, the goal is to gain greater consumer interest in its overall product line.

Lead Time   The period required by a medium for placing an ad.

Leased Department   A section of a retail store rented to an outside party. The lessee operates a department—under the store's rules—and pays a percentage of sales as rent.

Less-Developed Countries   Have low literacy, limited technology, and per-capita Gross Domestic Product below $2,000 (sometimes less than $1,000).

Licensing Agreement   A situation in which a company pays a fee to use a name or logo whose trademark rights are held by another firm.

Life-Style   Represents the way in which a person lives and spends time and money. It is based on the social and psychological factors that have been internalized by that person, as well as his or her demographic background.

Limited Consumer Decision Making   Occurs when a person uses every step in the purchase process but does not spend a great deal of time on some of them. The person has previously bought a given good or service, but makes fresh decisions when it comes under current purchase consideration.

Limited-Line Wholesalers   See *Specialty-Merchandise Wholesalers*.

Limited-Service Merchant Wholesalers   Buy and take title to products, but do not perform all the functions of full-service merchant wholesalers. They may not provide credit, merchandising assistance, or marketing research data.

Line of Business   Refers to the general goods/service category, functions, geographic coverage, type of ownership, and specific business of a firm.

Local Content Laws   Require foreign firms to set up local plants and use locally made components. The goal of these laws is to protect the economies and domestic employment of the nations involved.

Logistics (Physical Distribution)   Encompasses the broad range of activities concerned with efficiently delivering raw materials, parts, semifinished items, and finished products to designated places, at designated times, and in proper condition.

Loss Leaders   Items priced below cost to attract customers to a seller—usually in a store setting.

Low-Involvement Purchasing   Occurs when a consumer minimizes the time and effort expended in both making decisions about and shopping for those goods and services he or she views as unimportant.

M

Macroenvironment   Encompasses the broad demographic, societal, economic, political, technological, and other forces that an organization faces.

Mail-Order Wholesalers   Limited-service merchant wholesalers that use catalogs, instead of a personal sales force, to promote products and communicate with customers.

Major Innovations   Items not previously sold by any firm.

Majority Fallacy   Concept stating that firms may fail when they go after the largest market segment because competition is intense. A potentially profitable segment may be one ignored by other firms.

Manufacturer Brands   Use the names of their makers and generate the vast majority of U.S. revenues for most product categories. The marketing goal for manufacturer brands is to attract and retain loyal consumers, and for their makers to direct the marketing effort for the brands.

Manufacturers   Produce products for resale to other consumers.

Manufacturer/Service Provider Wholesaling   Occurs when a producer does all wholesaling functions itself. It may be carried out via sales offices and/or branch offices.

Manufacturers'/Service Providers' Agents   Agents who work for several manufacturers/service providers and carry noncompetitive, complementary products in exclusive territories. A manufacturer/service provider may use many agents.

Marginal Return   The amount of sales each increment of promotion spending will generate.

Market   Consists of all the people and/or organizations who desire (or potentially desire) a good or service, have sufficient resources to make purchases, and are willing and able to buy.

Market Buildup Method   A method of sales forecasting in which a firm gathers data from small, separate market segments and aggregates them.

Market-Controlled Price Environment   Characterized by a high level of competition, similar goods and services, and little control over prices by individual firms.

Marketing   The anticipation, management, and satisfaction of demand through the exchange process.

Marketing Audit   A systematic, critical, impartial review and appraisal of the basic goals and policies of the marketing function, and of the organization, methods, procedures, and personnel employed to implement the policies and achieve the goals.

Marketing Company Era   Recognition of the central role of marketing. The marketing department is the equal of others in the company. Company efforts are well integrated and regularly reviewed.

Marketing Concept   A consumer-oriented, market-driven, value-based, integrated, goal-oriented philosophy for a firm, institution, or person.

Marketing Cost Analysis   Used to evaluate the cost efficiency of various marketing factors, such as different total quality configurations, product lines, order sizes, distribution methods, sales territories, channel members, salespersons, advertising media, and customer types.

Marketing Department Era   Stage during which the marketing department shares in company decisions but remains in a subordinate position to the production, engineering, and sales departments.

Marketing Environment   Consists of controllable factors, uncontrollable factors, the organization's level of success or failure in reaching its objectives, feedback, and adaptation.

Marketing Functions   Include environmental analysis and marketing research, broadening the scope of marketing, consumer analysis, product planning, distribution planning, promotion planning, price planning, and marketing management.

Marketing Information System (MIS)   A set of procedures and methods designed to generate, analyze, disseminate, and store anticipated marketing decision information on a regular, continuous basis.

Marketing Intelligence Network   The part of a marketing information system that consists of continuous monitoring, marketing research, and data warehousing.

Marketing Manager System   A product management organizational format under which a company executive is responsible for overseeing a wide range of marketing functions and for coordinating with other departments that perform marketing-related activities.

Marketing Mix   The specific combination of marketing elements used to achieve objectives and satisfy the target market. It encompasses decisions regarding four major variables: product, distribution, promotion, and price.

Marketing Myopia   A shortsighted, narrow-minded view of marketing and its environment.

Marketing Organization   The structural arrangement that directs marketing functions. It outlines authority, responsibility, and tasks to be done.

Marketing Performers   The organizations or individuals that undertake one or more marketing functions. They include manufacturers and service providers, wholesalers, retailers, marketing specialists, and organizational and final consumers.

Marketing Plan Analysis   Involves comparing actual performance with planned or expected performance for a specified period of time.

Marketing Research   Involves systematically gathering, recording, and analyzing information about specific issues related to the marketing of goods, services, organizations, people, places, and ideas.

Marketing Research Process   Consists of a series of activities: defining the issue or problem to be studied; examining secondary data; generating primary data, if necessary; analyzing information; making recommendations; and implementing findings.

Marketing Strategy   Outlines the way in which the marketing mix is used to attract and satisfy the target market(s) and achieve an organization's goals.

Market Segmentation   Involves subdividing a market into clear subsets of customers that act in the same way or that have comparable needs.

Markup Pricing   A form of cost-based pricing in which a firm sets prices by computing the per-unit costs of producing (buying) goods and/or services and then determining the markup percentages needed to cover selling costs and profit.

Mass Customization   A process by which mass-market goods and services are individualized to satisfy a specific customer need, at a reasonable price.

Massed Promotion   Communication efforts that are concentrated in peak periods, like holidays.

Mass Marketing   See *Undifferentiated Marketing*.

Maturity Stage of the Product Life Cycle   The period during which industry sales stabilize as the market becomes saturated and many firms enter to capitalize on the still sizable demand. Companies seek to maintain a differential advantage.

Medium   The personal or nonpersonal means in a channel of communication used to send a message.

Membership Warehouse Club   A retailing format in which final consumers and businesses pay small yearly dues to shop in a huge, austere warehouse. Consumers buy items at deep discounts.

Merchant Wholesalers   Buy, take title, and take possession of products for further resale. Merchant wholesalers may be full or limited service.

Message   A combination of words and symbols sent to an audience via a channel of communication.

Message Permanence   Refers to the number of exposures one ad generates (repetition) and how long it remains available to the audience.

Microenvironment   Encompasses the forces close to an organization that have a direct impact on its ability to serve customers, including distribution intermediaries, competitors, consumer markets, and the capabilities of the organization itself.

Minimum Price Laws   See *Unfair-Sales Acts*.

Minor Innovations   Items not previously marketed by a firm that have been marketed by others.

MIS   See *Marketing Information System*.

Missionary Salesperson   A type of sales support person who gives out information on new goods or services. He or she does not close sales, but describes items' attributes, answers questions, and leaves written matter.

Mixed-Brand Strategy   Occurs when a combination of manufacturer and private brands (and maybe generic brands) are sold by manufacturers, wholesalers, and retailers.

Modifications   Alterations in or extensions of a firm's existing products. They include new models, styles, colors, features, and brands.

Modified Break-Even Analysis A form of demand-based pricing that combines traditional break-even analysis with an evaluation of demand at various levels of price. It reveals the price-quantity mix that maximizes profits.

Modified-Rebuy Purchase Process A moderate amount of decision making undertaken in the purchase of medium-priced products that an organizational consumer has bought infrequently before.

Monitoring Results Involves comparing the actual performance of a firm, business unit, or product against planned performance for a specified period.

Monopolistic Competition A situation in which there are several firms in an industry, each trying to offer a unique marketing mix—based on price or nonprice factors.

Monopoly A situation in which just one firm sells a given good or service and has a lot of control over its marketing plan.

Motivation Involves the positive or negative needs, goals, and desires that impel a person to or away from certain actions, objects, or conditions.

Motives The reasons for behavior.

Multichannel Distribution See *Dual Channel of Distribution*.

Multinational Firm One in which headquarters are in the home nation, but the domestic market often accounts for less than 50 percent of sales and profits. The firm operates in dozens of nations or more.

Multiple Branding See *Individual Branding*.

Multiple-Buying Responsibility Two or more employees formally participating in complex or expensive purchase decisions.

Multiple Segmentation See *Differentiated Marketing*.

Multiple-Unit Pricing A practice whereby a firm offers discounts to consumers to encourage them to buy in quantity, so as to increase overall sales volume.

N

NAFTA See *North American Free Trade Agreement*.

NAICS See *North American Industry Classification System*.

Narrowcasting Presenting advertising messages to rather limited and well-defined audiences. It is a way to reduce the audience waste with mass media.

Nationalism Refers to a country's efforts to become self-reliant and raise its stature in the eyes of the world community. At times, a high degree of nationalism may lead to tight restrictions on foreign firms to foster the development of domestic industry at their expense.

Natural Accounts Costs which are reported by the names of the expenses and not by their purposes. Such expense categories include salaries, rent, advertising, supplies, insurance, and interest.

Need-Satisfaction Approach A high-level selling method based on the principle that each customer has different attributes and wants; thus the sales presentation should adapt to the individual consumer.

Negotiation A situation in which a buyer uses bargaining ability and order size to get sellers' best possible prices.

New Product A modification of an existing product or an innovation the consumer sees as meaningful.

New-Product Manager System A product management organizational format which has product managers to supervise existing products and new-product managers to develop new ones. Once a product is introduced, it is given to the product manager.

New-Product Planning Process Involves a series of steps from idea generation to commercialization. The firm generates ideas, evaluates them, weeds out poor ones, obtains consumer feedback, develops the product, tests it, and brings it to market.

New-Task Purchase Process A large amount of decision making undertaken in the purchase of an expensive product an organizational consumer has not bought before.

Noise Interference at any point along a channel of communication.

Nondurable Goods Physical products made from materials other than metals, hard plastics, and wood; are rather quickly consumed or worn out; or become dated, unfashionable, or otherwise unpopular.

Nongoods Services Involve personal service on the part of the seller. They do not involve goods.

Nonprice-Based Approach A pricing strategy in which sellers downplay price as a factor in consumer demand by creating a distinctive good or service via promotion, packaging, delivery, customer service, availability, and other marketing factors.

Nonprofit Institutions Act in the public interest or to foster a cause and do not seek financial profits.

Nonprofit Marketing Conducted by organizations and individuals that operate in the public interest or that foster a cause and do not seek financial profits. It may involve organizations, people, places, and ideas, as well as goods and services.

Nonstandardized Marketing Approach An international marketing strategy in which a firm sees each nation or region as distinct, and requiring its own marketing plan.

Nonstore Retailing Occurs when a firm uses a strategy mix that is not store-based to reach consumers and complete transactions.

North American Free Trade Agreement (NAFTA) An agreement that created an economic community linking the United States, Canada, and Mexico. It will remove tariffs and trade restrictions among the three countries over the next several years.

North American Industry Classification System (NAICS) A coding system that may be used to derive information about most organizational consumers. The NAICS is the official classification system for the United States, Canada, and Mexico. It uses 20 industry categories.

O

Objective-and-Task Method A promotional budget method in which a firm sets promotion goals, determines the activities needed to satisfy them, and then establishes the proper budget.

Observation A research method whereby present behavior or the results of past behavior are observed and noted. People are not questioned and cooperation is unnecessary.

Odd Pricing Used when selling prices are set below even dollar values, such as 49 cents and $199.

Oligopoly A situation in which a few firms—usually large ones—account for most industry sales and would like to engage in nonprice competition.

One-Price Policy Lets a firm charge the same price to all customers seeking to purchase a good or service under similar conditions.

Opinion Leaders   People to whom other consumers turn for advice and information via face-to-face communication. They normally have an impact over a narrow product range.

Opinions   See *Attitudes*.

Opt-In (Permission-Based) E-mail   A Web-based promotion tool whereby Internet users agree to receive targeted E-mail from a firm.

Order Getter   A type of salesperson who generates customer leads, provides information, persuades customers, and closes sales.

Order Taker   A type of salesperson who processes routine orders and reorders. The order taker typically handles goods and services that are pre-sold.

Organizational Consumers   Buy goods and services for further production, usage in operating the organization, or resale to other consumers.

Organizational Consumer's Decision Process   Consists of expectations, the buying process, conflict resolution, and situational factors.

Organizational Mission   A long-term commitment to a type of business and a place in the market. It can be expressed in terms of the customer group(s) served, the goods and services offered, the functions performed, and/or the technologies utilized.

Outsourcing   When one company provides services for another company that could also be or usually have been done in-house by the client firm.

Owned-Goods Services   Involve alterations or maintenance/repairs of goods owned by consumers.

P

Package   A container used to protect, promote, transport, and/or identify a product.

Packaging Functions   Containment and protection, usage, communication, segmentation, channel cooperation, and new-product planning.

Patent   Grants an inventor of a useful product or process exclusive selling rights for a fixed period.

Penetration Pricing   Uses low prices to capture the mass market for a good or service.

Perceived Risk   The level of uncertainty a consumer believes exists as to the outcome of a purchase decision; this belief may or may not be correct. Perceived risk can be divided into six major types: functional, physical, financial, social, psychological, and time.

Percentage-of-Sales Method   A promotional budget method in which a firm ties its promotion budget to sales revenue.

Peripheral Services   Supplementary (extra) services that firms provide to customers.

Perishability of Services   Means that many services cannot be stored for future sale. A service firm must try to manage consumer usage so there is consistent demand over various times.

Permission-Based E-mail   See *Opt-In E-mail*.

Personal Demographics   Basic identifiable characteristics of individual final consumers and organizational consumers and groups of final consumers and organizational consumers.

Personal Selling   Involves oral communication with one or more prospective buyers by paid representatives for the purpose of making sales.

Personality   The sum total of a person's enduring internal psychological traits making the person unique.

Persuasive Impact   The ability of a medium to stimulate consumers.

Physical Distribution   See *Logistics*.

Planned Obsolescence   A marketing practice that capitalizes on short-run material wearout, style changes, and functional product changes.

Planned Shopping Center   A retail location that consists of centrally owned or managed facilities. It is planned and operated as an entity, ringed by parking, and based on balanced tenancy. The three types of planned center are regional, community, and neighborhood.

Porter Generic Strategy Model   Identifies two key marketing planning concepts and the options available for each: competitive scope (broad or narrow target) and competitive advantage (lower cost or differentiation).

Post-Purchase Behavior   The stage in the final consumer's decision process when further purchases and/or re-evaluation of the purchase are undertaken.

Predatory Pricing   An illegal practice in which large firms cut prices on products to below their cost in selected geographic areas so as to eliminate small, local competitors.

Prestige Pricing   Assumes consumers will not buy goods or services at prices they consider too low.

Price   Represents the value of a good or service for both the seller and the buyer.

Price Adjustment Tactics   Alterations in list prices, escalator clauses and surcharges, added markups, markdowns, and rebates.

Price-Based Approach   A pricing strategy in which sellers influence consumer demand primarily through changes in price levels.

Price Ceiling   The maximum amount customers will pay for a given good or service.

Price Discrimination   A form of demand-based pricing in which a firm sets two or more distinct prices for a product so as to appeal to different final consumer or organizational consumer segments. Price discrimination can be customer-, product-, time-, or place-based.

Price Elasticity of Demand   Indicates the sensitivity of buyers to price changes in terms of the quantities they will purchase. It is computed by dividing the percentage change in quantity demanded by the percentage change in price charged.

Price Floor   The lowest acceptable price a firm can charge and attain its profit goal.

Price-Floor Pricing   A form of cost-based pricing whereby a firm determines the lowest price at which it is worthwhile to increase the amount of goods or services it makes available for sale.

Price Leadership   A form of competition-based pricing in which one firm (or a few firms) is usually the first to announce price changes and others in the industry follow.

Price Lining   Involves selling products at a range of prices, with each representing a distinct level of quality (or features).

Price Planning   Systematic decision making by an organization regarding all aspects of pricing.

Price-Quality Association   A concept stating that consumers may believe high prices represent high quality and low prices represent low quality.

Price Wars   Situations in which firms continually try to undercut each other's prices to draw customers.

Primary Data   Consist of information gathered to address a specific issue or problem at hand.

Primary Demand   Consumer demand for a product category.

Private (Dealer) Brands   Use names designated by their resellers, usually wholesalers or retailers, and account for sizable U.S. revenues in many product categories. Resellers have more exclusive rights for these brands, and are more responsible for distribution and larger purchases.

Private Carriers   Shippers with their own transportation facilities.

Problem Awareness   The stage in the final consumer's decision process during which a consumer recognizes that the good, service, organization, person, place, or idea under consideration may solve a problem of shortage or unfulfilled desire.

Problem Definition   See *Issue Definition*.

Process-Related Ethical Issues   Involve the unethical use of marketing strategies or tactics.

Product   A bundle of attributes capable of exchange or use, usually a mix of tangible and intangible forms. It may be an idea, a physical entity, or a service, or any combination of the three.

Product Adaptation   A product planning strategy in which domestic products are modified to meet foreign language needs, taste preferences, climates, electrical requirements, laws, and other factors.

Product Development Stage of New-Product Planning   Converts an idea for a new product into a tangible form and identifies a basic marketing strategy.

Product Differentiation   Occurs when a product offering is perceived by the consumer to differ from its competition on any physical or non-physical product characteristic, including price.

Production Era   Devotion to physical distribution of products due to high demand and low competition. Consumer research, product modifications, and adapting to consumer needs are not needed.

Product Item   A specific model, brand, or size of a product that a company sells.

Product Life Cycle   A concept that attempts to describe a product's sales, competitors, profits, customers, and marketing emphasis from its beginning until it is removed from the market. It is divided into introduction, growth, maturity, and decline stages.

Product Line   A group of closely related product items.

Product (Brand) Manager System   A product management organizational format under which there is a level of middle managers, each of whom is responsible for planning, coordinating, and monitoring the performance of a single product (brand) or a small group of products (brands). The managers handle both new and existing products and are involved with all the marketing activities related to their product or group of products.

Product/Market Opportunity Matrix   Identifies four alternative marketing strategies to maintain and/or increase sales of business units and products: market penetration, market development, product development, and diversification.

Product Mix   All the different product lines a firm offers. It can be described in terms of its width, depth, and consistency.

Product Planning   Systematic decision making relating to all aspects of the development and management of a firm's products, including branding and packaging.

Product Planning Committee   A product management organizational format with high-level executives from various functional areas in a firm, such as marketing, production, engineering, finance, and R&D. It does product approval, evaluation, and development on a part-time basis.

Product Positioning   Enables a firm to map each of its products in terms of consumer perceptions and desires, competition, other company products, and environmental changes.

Product Recall   The primary enforcement tool of the Consumer Product Safety Commission, whereby the commission asks or orders firms to recall and modify (or discontinue) unsafe products.

Product-Related Ethical Issues   Involve the ethical appropriateness of marketing certain products.

Product Screening   The stage in the new-product planning process when poor, unsuitable, or otherwise unattractive ideas are weeded out from further consideration.

Profit-Based Pricing Objectives   Those that orient a firm's pricing strategy toward some type of profit goals: profit maximization, satisfactory profit, return on investment, and/or early recovery of cash.

Promotion   Any communication used to inform, persuade, and/or remind people about an organization's or individual's goods, services, image, ideas, community involvement, or impact on society.

Promotion Mix   A firm's overall and specific communication program, including its involvement with advertising, public relations (publicity), personal selling, and/or sales promotion.

Promotion Planning   Systematic decision making relating to all aspects of an organization's or individual's communications efforts.

Prospecting   The stage in the selling process which generates a list of customer leads. It is common with outside selling, and can be blind or lead in orientation.

Publicity   The form of public relations that entails nonpersonal communication passed on via various media but not paid for by an identified sponsor.

Publicity Types   News publicity, business feature articles, service feature articles, finance releases, product releases, pictorial releases, video news releases, background editorial material, and emergency publicity.

Public Relations   Includes any communication to foster a favorable image for goods, services, organizations, people, places, and ideas among various publics—such as consumers, investors, government, channel members, employees, and the general public.

Publics' Demand   The attributes and needs of employees, unions, stockholders, the general public, government agencies, consumer groups, and other internal and external forces that affect a company.

Pulling Strategy   Occurs when a firm first stimulates consumer demand and then gains dealer support.

Purchase Act   The stage in the final consumer's decision process in which there is an exchange of money, a promise to pay, or support in return for ownership of a specific good, the performance of a specific service, and so on.

Purchase Terms   The provisions of price agreements.

Pure Competition   A situation in which many firms sell virtually identical goods or services and they are unable to create differential advantages.

Pushing Strategy   Occurs when various firms in a distribution channel cooperate in marketing a product.

Q

Quick Response (QR) Inventory System   A cooperative effort between retailers and suppliers to reduce retail inventory while providing a merchandise supply that more closely addresses the actual buying patterns of consumers.

R

Rack Jobbers   Full-service merchant wholesalers that furnish the racks or shelves on which products are displayed. They own the products on the racks, selling them on a consignment basis.

Reach   Refers to the number of viewers, readers, or listeners in a medium's audience. For TV and radio, it is the total number of people who watch or listen to an ad. For print media, it has two aspects: circulation and passalong rate.

Real Income   The amount of income earned in a year adjusted by the rate of inflation.

Rebates   A form of price adjustment in which cash refunds are given directly from the manufacturer to the customer to stimulate the purchase of an item or a group of items.

Reciprocity   A procedure by which organizational consumers select suppliers that agree to purchase goods and services, as well as sell them.

Reference Group   A group that influences a person's thoughts or actions.

Relationship Marketing   Exists when marketing activities are performed with the conscious intention of developing and managing long-term, trusting relationships with customers.

Relative Product Failure   Occurs if a firm makes a profit on an item but that product does not reach profit goals and/or adversely affects a firm's image.

Rented-Goods Services   Involves the leasing of goods for a specified period of time.

Reorder Point   Sets an inventory level at which new orders must be placed. It depends on order lead time, the usage rate, and safety stock.

Research Design   Outlines the procedures for collecting and analyzing data. It includes decisions relating to the person collecting data, data to be collected, group of people or objects studied, data-collection techniques employed, study costs, method of data collection, length of study period and time, and location of data collection.

Retail Chain   Involves common ownership of multiple outlets.

Retail Franchising   A contractual agreement between a franchisor (a manufacturer, wholesaler, or service sponsor) and a retail franchisee, which allows the latter to run a certain form of business under an established name and according to specific rules.

Retail Store Strategy Mix   An integrated combination of hours, location, assortment, service, advertising, prices, and other factors retailers employ.

Retailing   Encompasses those business activities involved with the sale of goods and services to the final consumer for personal, family, or household use. It is the final stage in a channel of distribution.

Robinson-Patman Act   Prohibits manufacturers and wholesalers from price discrimination in dealing with different channel-member purchasers of products with "like quality" if the effect of such discrimination is to injure competition.

Routine Consumer Decision Making   Occurs when a person buys out of habit and skips steps in the decision process. In this category are items with which a person has much experience.

S

Sales Analysis   The detailed study of sales data for the purpose of appraising the appropriateness and effectiveness of a marketing strategy.

Sales-Based Pricing Objectives   Goals that orient a company's pricing strategy toward high sales volume and/or expanding the firm's share of sales relative to competitors.

Sales Engineer   A type of sales support person who accompanies an order getter if a very technical or complex item is being sold. He or she discusses specifications and long-range uses.

Sales Era   Involves hiring a sales force and sometimes advertising to sell inventory, after production is maximized. The goal is to make consumer desires fit the features of the products offered.

Sales Exception Reporting   Highlights situations where sales goals are not met or sales opportunities are present.

Sales-Expense Budget   Allots selling costs among salespeople, products, customers, and geographic areas for a given period.

Sales Forecast   Outlines expected company sales for a specific good or service to a specific consumer group over a specific period of time under a specific marketing program.

Sales Management   Planning, implementing, and controlling the personal sales function. It covers employee selection, training, territory allocation, compensation, and supervision.

Sales Penetration   The degree to which a firm is meeting its sales potential: Sales penetration = Actual sales/Sales potential

Sales Presentation   The stage in the selling process that includes a verbal description of a product, its benefits, options and models, price, associated services like delivery and warranty, and a demonstration (if needed).

Sales Promotion   Involves paid marketing communication activities (other than advertising, publicity, or personal selling) that are intended to stimulate consumer purchases and dealer effectiveness. Included are trade shows, premiums, incentives, giveaways, demonstrations, and various other efforts not in the ordinary promotion routine.

Sales Promotion Conditions   Requirements channel members or consumers must meet to be eligible for a specific sales promotion.

Sales Promotion Orientation   Refers to its focus—channel members or consumers—and its theme.

Sales Territory   The geographic area, customers, and/or product lines assigned to a salesperson.

Sampling   The analysis of selected people or objects in a designated population, rather than all of them.

SBU   See *Strategic Business Unit*.

Scientific Method   A research philosophy incorporating objectivity, accuracy, and thoroughness.

Scrambled Merchandising   Occurs if a retailer adds goods and services that are unrelated to each other and the firm's original business.

Secondary Data   Consist of information not collected for the issue or problem at hand but for some other purpose. The two sources of secondary data are internal and external.

Selective Demand   Consumer demand for a particular brand.

Selective Distribution   A policy in which a firm employs a moderate number of resellers.

Self-Fulfilling Prophecy   A situation in which a firm predicts falling sales and then ensures this by reducing or removing marketing support.

Selling Against the Brand   A practice used by wholesalers and retailers, whereby they stock well-known brands, place high prices on them, and then sell other brands for lower prices.

Selling Agents   Responsible for marketing the entire output of a manufacturer/service provider under a contractual agreement. They perform all wholesale tasks except taking title to products.

Selling Process   Consists of prospecting for leads, approaching customers, determining consumer wants, giving a sales presentation, answering questions, closing the sale, and following up.

Semantic Differential   A survey technique using rating scales of bipolar (opposite) adjectives. An overall company or product profile is then devised.

Service Blueprint   A visual portrayal of the service process by a firm. It is a detailed map or flowchart.

Service Gap   The difference between customer expectations and actual service performance.

Service Marketing   The rental of goods, servicing goods owned by consumers, and personal services.

Service Salesperson   A type of sales support person who ordinarily deals with customers after sales. Delivery, installation, and other follow-up tasks are done.

Simulation   A computer-based method to test the potential effects of various marketing factors via a software program rather than real-world applications.

Single-Source Data Collection   Allows research firms to track the activities of individual consumer households from the programs they watch on TV to the products they purchase at stores.

Situational Factors   Those that can interrupt the organizational consumer's decision process and the selection of a supplier or brand. They include strikes, machine breakdowns, etc.

Situation Analysis   Identifies an organization's internal strengths and weaknesses and external opportunities and threats. It seeks to answer: Where is a firm now? In what direction is it headed?

Skimming Pricing   Uses high prices to attract the market segment more concerned with product quality, uniqueness, or status than price.

Social Class   A status hierarchy by which groups and individuals are classified on the basis of esteem and prestige. Social classes are based on income, occupation, education, and type of dwelling.

Social Marketing   The use of marketing to increase the acceptability of social ideas.

Social Performance   How one carries out his/her roles as a worker, family member, citizen, and friend.

Social Responsibility   A concern for the consequences of a person's or firm's acts as they might affect the interests of others. Corporate social responsibility balances a company's short-term profit needs with long-term societal needs.

Social Styles Model   A classification system for segmenting organizational consumers in terms of a broad range of demographic and life-style factors. The model divides the personnel representing those consumers into life-style categories.

Socioecological View of Marketing   Considers all the stages in a product's life span in developing, selling, purchasing, using, and disposing of that product. It incorporates the interests of everyone affected by a good's or service's use.

Sorting Process   The distribution activities of accumulation, allocation, sorting, and assorting. Through this process, intermediaries can resolve the differences in the goals of manufacturers and consumers.

Source   A company, an independent institution, or an opinion leader seeking to present a message to an audience. It is part of the channel of communication.

Spam   Unsolicited and unwanted E-mail.

Specialty-Merchandise (Limited-Line) Wholesalers   Full-service merchant wholesalers that concentrate on a rather narrow product range and have an extensive selection in that range.

Specialty Store   A retailer that concentrates on one product line.

Standardized (Global) Marketing Approach   A marketing strategy in which a firm uses a common marketing plan for all nations in which it operates—because it assumes worldwide markets are more homogeneous due to better communications, more open borders, free-market economies, etc.

Standard of Living   Refers to the average quantity and quality of goods and services that are owned and consumed in a given nation.

Status Quo-Based Pricing Objectives   Sought by a firm interested in continuing a favorable business climate for its operations or in stability.

Stimulus   A cue (social, commercial, or noncommercial) or a drive (physical) meant to motivate a person to act.

Stock Turnover   The number of times during a stated period (usually one year) that average inventory on hand is sold. Stock turnover is calculated in units or dollars (in selling price or at cost).

Straight Commission Plan   A sales compensation plan in which a salesperson's earnings are directly related to sales, profits, customer satisfaction, or some other type of performance.

Straight Extension   An international product-planning strategy in which a firm makes and markets the same products for domestic and foreign sales.

Straight-Rebuy Purchase Process   Routine reordering by organizational consumers for the purchase of inexpensive items bought regularly.

Straight Salary Plan   A sales compensation plan in which a salesperson is paid a flat amount per period.

Strategic Alliance   See *Joint Venture.*

Strategic Business Plan   Describes the overall direction an organization will pursue within its chosen environment and guides the allocation of resources and effort. It integrates the perspectives of functional departments and operating units.

Strategic Business Unit (SBU)   A self-contained division, product line, or product department in an organization with a specific market focus and a manager with complete responsibility for integrating all functions into a strategy.

Strategic Marketing Plan   Outlines the marketing actions to undertake, why they are needed, who carries them out, when and where they will be completed, and how they will be coordinated.

Strategic Planning Process   Consists of seven interrelated steps: defining organizational mission, establishing strategic business units, setting marketing objectives, performing situation analysis, developing marketing strategy, implementing tactics, and monitoring results.

Subjective Price   A consumer's perception of the price of a good or service as being high, fair, or low.

Subliminal Advertising   A highly controversial kind of promotion because it does not enable the audience to consciously decode a message.

Substantiation   A consumer-protection legal concept which requires a firm to be able to prove all the claims it makes in promotion messages. This means thorough testing and evidence of performance are needed before making claims.

Supercenter (Hypermarket)   A combination store that integrates an economy supermarket with a discount department store, with at least 40 percent of sales from nonfood items.

Survey   Gathers information by communicating with respondents in person, by phone, or by mail.

Systems Selling   A combination of goods and services provided to a buyer by one vendor. This gives the buyer one firm with which to negotiate, as well as consistency among various parts and components.

T

Tactical Plan   Specifies the short-run actions (tactics) that a firm undertakes in implementing a given market strategy.

Target Market   The particular group(s) of customers a firm proposes to serve, or whose needs it proposes to satisfy, with a particular marketing program.

Target Market Strategy   Comprises three general phases: analyzing consumer demand, targeting the market, and developing the marketing strategy.

Target Pricing   A form of cost-based pricing in which prices are set to provide a particular rate of return on investment for a standard volume of production—the level of production a firm anticipates achieving.

Tariff   The most common form of trade restriction, in which a tax is placed on imported products by a foreign government.

Technology   Refers to developing and using machinery, products, and processes.

Telemarketing   An efficient way of operating, whereby telephone communications are used to sell or solicit business or to set up an appointment for a salesperson to sell or solicit business.

Test Marketing   The stage in the new-product planning process which involves placing a fully developed new product (a good or service) in one or more selected areas and observing its actual performance under a proposed marketing plan.

Time Expenditures   The activities in which a person participates and the time allocated to them.

Total-Cost Approach   Determines the distribution service level with the lowest total costs—including freight (shipping), warehousing, and lost business. An ideal system seeks a balance between low expenditures on distribution and high opportunities for sales.

Total Delivered Product   The bundle of tangible and intangible product attributes that are actually provided to consumers through a value chain and its related value delivery chain.

Total Quality   A process- and output-related philosophy, whereby a firm strives to fully satisfy customers effectively and efficiently. It requires a customer focus; top management commitment; an emphasis on continuous improvement; and support from employees, suppliers, and intermediaries.

Trade Character   A brand mark that is personified.

Trade Deficit   The amount by which the value of imports exceeds the value of exports for a country.

Trademark   A brand name, brand mark, or trade character or combination thereof with legal protection.

Trade Quota   A restriction that sets limits on the amounts of products imported into a country.

Trade Surplus   The amount by which the value of exports exceeds the value of imports for a country.

Traditional Break-Even Analysis   Finds the sales quantity in units or dollars that is needed for total revenues to equal total costs at a given price.

Traditional Department Store   A department store that has a great assortment of goods and services, provides many customer services, is a fashion leader, and often serves as an anchor store in a shopping district or shopping center.

Transportation Forms   The modes for shipping products, parts, raw materials, and so forth. These include railroads, motor carriers, waterways, pipelines, and airways.

Truck/Wagon Wholesalers   Limited-service merchant wholesalers that generally have a regular sales route, offer items from a truck or wagon, and deliver goods when they are sold.

U

Unbundled Pricing   Breaks down prices by individual components and allows the consumer to decide what to purchase.

Uncontrollable Factors   The external elements affecting an organization's performance that cannot be fully directed by that organization and its marketers. These include consumers, competition, suppliers and distributors, government, the economy, technology, and independent media.

Undifferentiated Marketing (Mass Marketing)   Exists when a company targets the whole market with a single basic marketing strategy intended to have mass appeal.

Unfair-Sales Acts (Minimum Price Laws)   Legislation in a number of states that prevents firms from selling products for less than their cost plus a fixed percentage that includes overhead and profit.

Unitary Demand   Exists if price changes are exactly offset by changes in the quantity demanded, so total sales revenue remains constant.

Unit Pricing   Lets consumers compare price per quantity for competing brands and for various sizes of the same brand. With it, prices are shown per unit of measure, as well as by total price.

Universal Product Code (UPC)   A series of thick and thin vertical lines used to pre-mark items. Price and inventory data are represented by the lines, but are not readable by employees and customers.

Unplanned Business District   A retail location form that exists where multiple stores are located close to one another without prior planning as to the number and composition of stores. The unplanned sites are central business district, secondary business district, neighborhood business district, and string.

UPC   See *Universal Product Code*.

V

VALS (Values and Life-Styles) Program   A classification system for segmenting consumers via a broad range of demographic and life-style factors. It divides final consumers into life-style categories.

Value Analysis   A comparison of the costs and benefits of alternative materials, components, designs, or processes so as to reduce the cost/benefit ratio of purchases.

Value Chain   Represents the series of business activities that are performed to design, produce, market, deliver, and service a product for customers.

Value Delivery Chain   Encompasses all of the parties who engage in value chain activities.

Values and Life-Styles Program   See *VALS Program*.

Variability in Service Quality   Differing service performance from one purchase occasion to another. Variations may be due to the service firm's difficulty in problem diagnosis (for repairs), customer inability to verbalize service needs, and the lack of standardization and mass production.

Variable Markup Policy   Cost-based markup pricing whereby separate categories of goods and services receive different percentage markups. Variable markups recognize that some items require greater personal selling, customer service, alterations, and end-of-season markdowns than others.

Variable Pricing   Allows a firm to intentionally alter prices in response to cost fluctuations or differences in consumer demand.

Vending Machine   A nonstore retail operation which uses coin- or card-operated machinery to dispense goods or services. It eliminates the need for salespeople, allows 24-hour sales, and can be placed outside rather than inside a store.

Vendor Analysis   An assessment of the strengths and weaknesses of current or new suppliers in terms of quality, customer service, reliability, and price.

Venture Team   A product management organizational format in which a small, independent department with a broad range of specialists is involved with a specific new product's entire development process. Team members work on a full-time basis and act in a relatively autonomous manner.

Vertical Audit   An in-depth analysis of one aspect of a firm's marketing strategy. It is also known as a functional audit.

Vertical Price Fixing   When manufacturers or wholesalers seek to control the final selling prices of their goods or services.

W

Warehousing   Involves the physical facilities used to store, identify, and sort goods in expectation of their sale and transfer within a distribution channel.

Warranty   An assurance to consumers that a product meets certain standards.

Waste   The part of a medium's audience not in a firm's target market.

Wearout Rate   The time it takes for a message to lose its effectiveness.

Wheel of Retailing   Describes how low-end (discount) strategies can evolve into high-end (full service, high price) strategies and thus provide opportunities for new firms to enter as discounters.

Wholesale Cooperatives   Full-service merchant wholesalers owned by member firms to economize functions and provide broad support. There are producer-owned and retailer-owned cooperatives.

Wholesalers   Buy or handle merchandise and its subsequent resale to organizational users, retailers, and other wholesalers.

Wholesaling   Includes buying and/or handling goods and services, and their subsequent resale to organizational users, retailers, and/or other wholesalers—but not the sale of significant volume to final consumers.

Word-of-Mouth Communication   The process by which people express opinions and product-related experiences to one another.

World Trade Organization (WTO)   An organization whose mission is to open up international markets even further and promote a cooperative atmosphere around the globe.

World Wide Web (WWW)   Comprises all of the resources and users on the Internet using the Hypertext Transfer Protocol (HTTP). It is a way of accessing the Internet, whereby people work with easy-to-use Web addresses and pages. Users see words, colorful charts, pictures, and video, and hear audio.

WTO   See *World Trade Organization*.

WWW   See *World Wide Web*.

Y

Yield Management Pricing   A form of demand-based pricing whereby a firm determines the mix of price-quantity combinations that generates the highest level of revenues for a given period.

Company Index

Name Index

Schiffman, Leon G., 224, 233, 234, 239, 325
Schlossberg, Howard, 148
Schnaars, Steven P., 305
Schneider, Ivan, 493
Schultz, Dick, 588, 589
Seckinger, Beverly, 348
Seckler, Valerie, 203
Sethi, Rajesh, 429
Seybold, Patricia B., 511
Shacklett, Mary, 91
Shah, Dharmesh, 62
Shapiro, Benson P., 36
Sharma, Subhash, 666
Shaw, Robert, 91
Sheehan, Kim Bartel, 514
Shemwell, Donald J., Jr., 366
Sherman, Elaine, 325
Sheth, Jagdish N., 158, 275, 276, 277
Shibstead, Evantheia, 546
Shipley, David, 9, 620
Shooshtari, Nadar H., 156
Sibberson, Diana, 295
Siekman, Philip, 155, 449
Simmons, Bill, 75, 76, 78
Simmons, Deb, 75, 76
Simms, Jane, 676
Sinclair, Chuck, 11
Sinha, Indrajit, 597
Sirgy, M. Joseph, 126
Sisodia, Rajendra S., 89
Sivadas, Eugene, 234
Siwolop, Sana, 530
Skov, Richard B., 305
Sloan, Pat, 405
Slonim, Robert, 603
Smith, Craig S., 145
Smith, Geri, 414
Smith, Janet, 513
Smith, Jeff, 413

Smith, Michael F., 597
Smith, Stephen A., 449
Snetsinger, Douglas W., 365
Snoj, Boris, 9
Sofres, Taylor Nelson, 199
Solomon, Robert C., 140
Sparks, John R., 96
Spethmann, Betsy, 95, 390, 527, 553
Spiro, Rosann L., 571
Spurgein, Devon, 595
Stamler, Bernard, 529
Stanton, William J., 571
Starobin, Paul, 234
Stellin, Susan, 113, 203
Stern, Aimee L., 429
Stock, James R., 445
Stolberg, Sheryl Gay, 210
Stone, Gerald, 548
Stone, Merlin, 91
Strang, William A., 135
Streitfeld, David, 644
Sukhdial, Ajay S., 522
Suleski, Janet, 586
Sullivan, Gary L., 293
Sutton, William, 589
Swartz, Gordon, 598
Swisher, Kara, 615
Szymanski, David M., 14, 396, 666

Talal, Alwaleed Bin, 595
Tam, Pui-Wing, 105
Tanner, John F., Jr., 275, 574
Tatgle, Mark, 54
Tauber, Edward M., 345
Taylor, Bernard, 676
Taylor, David, 139
Taylor, Elizabeth, 526
Taylor, Raymond E., 295
Tedeschi, Bob, 202, 203, 632

Teinowitz, Ira, 530
Tellesfsen, Thomas, 571
Thoman, Rick, 683
Thomas, Dave, 518
Thompson, Stephanie, 331
Thurow, Roger, 131
Tillett, L. Scott, 379
Tomlinson, Richard, 682
Traynor, Ian, 224
Treacy, Michael, 658
Tripoli, Joe, 549
Troy, Lisa C., 396
Tsui, Bonnie, 231
Tully, Shawn, 256, 273
Turcsik, Richard, 315, 450
Tzokas, Nikolaos X., 407

Ulwick, Tony, 394
Underhill, Paco, 477
Unger, Tom, 13
Upbin, Bruce, 502
Urbanski, Al, 223

Vaaler, Johan, 405
Van den Bulte, Christophe, 36
Van Story, Beth, 15
Varadarajan, P. Rajan, 396
Vavra, Terry G., 116, 680
Vitell, Scott J., 139

Wachner, Linda, 437
Wahl, Gregory, 12
Wahl, Jack, 12
Walters, Bruce A., 170
Wang, Zhengyuan, 249
Wansink, Brian, 293
Ward, Sela, 518
Waterschoot, Walter van, 36
Webb, Dave, 9
Webb, Jim, 426
Weber, Alan, 91

Weber, Joseph, 408
Webster, Cynthia, 9
Webster, Frederick E., Jr., 9, 10
Weil, David, 449
Weiner, Rebecca S., 380
Weinstein, Steve, 641
Weintraub, Arlene, 415
Welch, David, 169
Wellner, Alison Stein, 234, 513
Wheatley, Jonathan, 414
White, Joseph, 334, 409
Wiersema, Fred, 658
Wildstrom, Stephen H., 205
Wilkins, Keat, 86
Williams, Theresa, 14, 494
Williams, Venus, 177
Wilson, Marianne, 480
Wilson, Ray W., 369
Winter, Greg, 145, 232, 259, 530, 604
Wise, Richard, 257
Woellert, Lorraine, 169
Wong, Alfred, 429
Wyner, Gordon A., 112
Wysocki, Bernard, Jr., 670

Yadav, Manjit S., 369
Yankelovich, Daniel, 138
Yoo, Boonghee, 36

Zachary, G. Pascal, 393
Zagat, Tim and Nina, 213
Zeithaml, Valarie A., 366, 369, 633
Zemke, Ron, 501
Zimmerman, Ann, 423, 471
Zipkin, Amy, 137
Zuber, Amy, 94, 578
Zuckerman, Laurence, 628
Zyman, Sergio, 589

Subject Index

Asterisk (*) indicates the term is defined in the glossary.